HALSBURY'S
Laws of England

FIFTH EDITION
2009

Volume 72

This is volume 72 of the Fifth Edition of Halsbury's Laws of England, containing the first part of the title MATRIMONIAL AND CIVIL PARTNERSHIP LAW.

This title replaces the Fourth Edition title MATRIMONIAL LAW, contained in volume 29(3) (Reissue). That volume has been completely replaced and may now be archived.

For a full list of volumes comprised in a current set of Halsbury's Laws of England please see overleaf.

Fifth Edition volumes:

1 (2008), 2 (2008), 7 (2008), 48 (2008), 49 (2008), 50 (2008), 54 (2008), 65 (2008), 67 (2008), 68 (2008), 72 (2009), 73 (2009), 79 (2008), 93 (2008), 94 (2008)

Fourth Edition volumes (bold figures represent reissues):

1(1) (2001 Reissue), 1(2) (2007 Reissue), 2(2), 2(3), 3(1) (2005 Reissue), 3(2) (2002 Reissue), 4(1) (2002 Reissue), 4(2) (2002 Reissue), 4(3), 5(1) (2004 Reissue), 5(2) (2001 Reissue), 5(3) (2008 Reissue), 5(4) (2008 Reissue), 6 (2003 Reissue), 7(1) (2004 Reissue), 7(2) (2004 Reissue), 7(3) (2004 Reissue), 7(4) (2004 Reissue), 8(1) (2003 Reissue), 8(2), 8(3), 9(1), 9(2) (2006 Reissue), 10, 11(1) (2006 Reissue), 11(2) (2006 Reissue), 11(3) (2006 Reissue), 11(4) (2006 Reissue), 12(1), 12(2) (2007 Reissue), 12(3) (2007 Reissue), 13 (2007 Reissue), 14, 15(1) (2006 Reissue), 15(2) (2006 Reissue), 15(3) (2007 Reissue), 15(4) (2007 Reissue), 16(1A), 16(1B), 16(2), 17(1), 17(2), 18(2), 19(1) (2007 Reissue), 19(2) (2007 Reissue), 19(3) (2007 Reissue), 20(1), 20(2), 21 (2004 Reissue), 22 (2006 Reissue), 23(1), 23(2), 24, 25 (2003 Reissue), 26 (2004 Reissue), 27(1) (2006 Reissue), 27(2) (2006 Reissue), 27(3) (2006 Reissue), 28, 29(1), 29(2), 30(1), 30(2), 31 (2003 Reissue), 32 (2005 Reissue), 33, 34, 35, 36(1) (2007 Reissue), 36(2), 37, 38 (2006 Reissue), 39(1A), 39(1B), 39(2), 40(1) (2007 Reissue), 40(2) (2007 Reissue), 40(3) (2007 Reissue), 41 (2005 Reissue), 42, 43(2), 44(1), 44(2), 45(1) (2005 Reissue), 45(2), 46(1), 46(2), 46(3), 47 (2001 Reissue), 48 (2007 Reissue), 49(1) (2005 Reissue), 49(2) (2004 Reissue), 49(3) (2004 Reissue), 50 (2005 Reissue), 51, 52

Fourth and Fifth Edition volumes:

2008 Consolidated Index (A–E), 2008 Consolidated Index (F–O), 2008 Consolidated Index (P–Z), 2009 Consolidated Table of Statutes, 2009 Consolidated Table of Statutory Instruments, etc, 2009 Consolidated Table of Cases (A–L), 2009 Consolidated Table of Cases (M–Z, ECJ Cases)

March 2009

HALSBURY'S
Laws of England

FIFTH EDITION

LORD MACKAY OF CLASHFERN
Lord High Chancellor of Great Britain
1987–97

Volume 72

2009

 LexisNexis®

Members of the LexisNexis Group worldwide

United Kingdom	LexisNexis, a Division of Reed Elsevier (UK) Ltd, Halsbury House, 35 Chancery Lane, LONDON, WC2A 1EL, and London House, 20–22 East London Street, EDINBURGH, EH7 4BQ
Australia	LexisNexis Butterworths, Chatswood, New South Wales
Austria	LexisNexis Verlag ARD Orac GmbH & Co KG, Vienna
Benelux	LexisNexis Benelux, Amsterdam
Canada	LexisNexis Canada, Markham, Ontario
China	LexisNexis China, Beijing and Shanghai
France	LexisNexis SA, Paris
Germany	LexisNexis Deutschland GmbH Munster
Hong Kong	LexisNexis Hong Kong, Hong Kong
India	LexisNexis India, New Delhi
Italy	Giuffrè Editore, Milan
Japan	LexisNexis Japan, Tokyo
Malaysia	Malayan Law Journal Sdn Bhd, Kuala Lumpur
New Zealand	LexisNexis NZ Ltd, Wellington
Poland	Wydawnictwo Prawnicze LexisNexis Sp, Warsaw
Singapore	LexisNexis Singapore, Singapore
South Africa	LexisNexis Butterworths, Durban
USA	LexisNexis, Dayton, Ohio

FIRST EDITION	*Published in 31 volumes between 1907 and 1917*
SECOND EDITION	*Published in 37 volumes between 1931 and 1942*
THIRD EDITION	*Published in 43 volumes between 1952 and 1964*
FOURTH EDITION	*Published in 56 volumes between 1973 and 1987, with reissues between 1988 and 2009*
FIFTH EDITION	*Commenced in 2008*

A CIP Catalogue record for this book is available from the British Library.

ISBN 13 (complete set, standard binding): 9780406047762

ISBN 13: 9781405737272

ISBN 978-1-4057-3727-2

9 781405 737272

Typeset by Letterpart Ltd, Reigate, Surrey
Printed in the UK by CPI William Clowes Beccles NR34 7TL
Visit LexisNexis at www.lexisnexis.co.uk

Editor in Chief

THE RIGHT HONOURABLE

LORD MACKAY OF CLASHFERN
LORD HIGH CHANCELLOR OF GREAT BRITAIN

1987–97

Editors of this Volume

SIMON CADDE, LLB

DANIEL WRIGHT, LLB

Sub-editors

GAVIN DILLOW, MA

CLAIRE RAMSBOTTOM, LLB, MSC

Indexer

ALEXANDRA CORRIN, LLB,
of Gray's Inn, Barrister

Managing Editor

CLARE BLANCHARD, BA

Publisher

SIMON HETHERINGTON, LLB

MATRIMONIAL AND CIVIL PARTNERSHIP LAW

Consultant Editor

DAVID JOSIAH-LAKE, LLB,

a Solicitor of the Supreme Court;
Partner, Josiah-Lake Gardiner LLP;
Member of the Law Society's Family Law Accreditation Scheme

The law stated in this volume is in general that in force on 1 February 2009, although subsequent changes have been included wherever possible.

Any future updating material will be found in the Current Service and annual Cumulative Supplement to Halsbury's Laws of England.

TABLE OF CONTENTS

PAGE

How to use Halsbury's Laws of England 11

References and Abbreviations.. 13

Table of Statutes 19

Table of Statutory Instruments 33

Table of Practice Directions.. 41

Table of European Community Legislation 43

Table of Cases 45

Volume 72

MATRIMONIAL AND CIVIL PARTNERSHIP LAW

Table of Contents 1

1. Fundamental Principles... 11

2. Forms and Ceremonies... 45

3. Registration and Approval of Premises 147

4. Legal Incidents of Marriage and Civil Partnership........................... 163

5. Property Rights in the Family Home.. 207

6. Matrimonial and Civil Partnership Causes...................................... 243

7. Financial Relief.. 320

Index... 395

Volume 73

Table of Contents 1

7. Financial Relief *continued* 11

8. Injunctive Relief.. 156

9. Jurisdiction and Procedure 167

Index... 393

HOW TO USE HALSBURY'S LAWS OF ENGLAND

Volumes

Each text volume of Halsbury's Laws of England contains the law on the titles contained in it as at a date stated at the front of the volume (the operative date).

Information contained in Halsbury's Laws of England may be accessed in several ways.

First, by using the tables of contents.

Each volume contains both a general Table of Contents, and a specific Table of Contents for each title contained in it. From these tables you will be directed to the relevant part of the work.

Readers should note that the current arrangement of titles can be found in the Current Service.

Secondly, by using tables of statutes, statutory instruments, cases or other materials.

If you know the name of the Act, statutory instrument or case with which your research is concerned, you should consult the Consolidated Tables of statutes, cases and so on (published as separate volumes) which will direct you to the relevant volume and paragraph. The Consolidated Tables will indicate if the volume referred to is a Fifth Edition volume.

(Each individual text volume also includes tables of those materials used as authority in that volume.)

Thirdly, by using the indexes.

If you are uncertain of the general subject area of your research, you should go to the Consolidated Index (published as separate volumes) for reference to the relevant volume(s) and paragraph(s). The Consolidated Index will indicate if the volume referred to is a Fifth Edition volume.

(Each individual text volume also includes an index to the material contained therein.)

Updating publications

The text volumes of Halsbury's Laws should be used in conjunction with the annual Cumulative Supplement and the monthly Noter-Up.

The annual Cumulative Supplement

The Supplement gives details of all changes between the operative date of the text volume and the operative date of the Supplement. It is arranged in the same volume, title and paragraph order as the text volumes. Developments affecting particular points of law are noted to the relevant paragraph(s) of the text volumes. As from the commencement of the Fifth Edition, the Supplement will clearly distinguish between Fourth and Fifth Edition titles.

For narrative treatment of material noted in the Cumulative Supplement, go to the Annual Abridgment volume for the relevant year.

The Noter-Up

The Noter-Up is contained in the Current Service Noter-Up booklet, issued monthly and noting changes since the publication of the annual Cumulative Supplement. Also arranged in the same volume, title and paragraph order as the text volumes, the Noter-Up follows the style of the Cumulative Supplement. As from the commencement of the Fifth Edition, the Noter-Up will clearly distinguish between Fourth and Fifth Edition titles.

For narrative treatment of material noted in the Noter-Up, go to the relevant Monthly Review.

REFERENCES AND ABBREVIATIONS

ACT	Australian Capital Territory
A-G	Attorney General
Admin	Administrative Court
Admlty	Admiralty Court
Adv-Gen	Advocate General
affd	affirmed
affg	affirming
Alta	Alberta
App	Appendix
art	article
Aust	Australia
B	Baron
BC	British Columbia
C	Command Paper (of a series published before 1900)
c	chapter number of an Act
CA	Court of Appeal
CAC	Central Arbitration Committee
CA in Ch	Court of Appeal in Chancery
CB	Chief Baron
CCA	Court of Criminal Appeal
CCR	County Court Rules 1981 (SI 1981/1687) as subsequently amended
CCR	Court for Crown Cases Reserved
C-MAC	Courts-Martial Appeal Court
CO	Crown Office
COD	Crown Office Digest
CPR	Civil Procedure Rules 1998 (SI 1998/3132) as subsequently amended (see the Civil Court Practice)
Can	Canada
Cd	Command Paper (of the series published 1900–18)
Cf	compare
Ch	Chancery Division
ch	chapter
cl	clause

Cm	Command Paper (of the series published 1986 to date)
Cmd	Command Paper (of the series published 1919–56)
Cmnd	Command Paper (of the series published 1956–86)
Comm	Commercial Court
Comr	Commissioner
Court Forms (2nd Edn)	Atkin's Encyclopaedia of Court Forms in Civil Proceedings, 2nd Edn. See note 2 post.
Court Funds Rules 1987	Court Funds Rules 1987 (SI 1987/821) as subsequently amended
DC...	Divisional Court
DPP	Director of Public Prosecutions
EAT	Employment Appeal Tribunal
EC	European Community
ECJ..	Court of Justice of the European Community
EComHR.................................	European Commission of Human Rights
ECSC......................................	European Coal and Steel Community
ECtHR Rules of Court...........	Rules of Court of the European Court of Human Rights
EEC.......................................	European Economic Community
EFTA......................................	European Free Trade Association
EWCA Civ	Official neutral citation for judgments of the Court of Appeal (Civil Division)
EWCA Crim..........................	Official neutral citation for judgments of the Court of Appeal (Criminal Division)
EWHC....................................	Official neutral citation for judgments of the High Court
Edn..	Edition
Euratom	European Atomic Energy Community
Ex Ch.....................................	Court of Exchequer Chamber
ex p.......................................	ex parte
Fam	Family Division
Fed	Federal
Forms & Precedents (5th Edn)......................................	Encyclopaedia of Forms and Precedents other than Court Forms, 5th Edn. See note 2 post.
GLC	Greater London Council
HC	High Court
HC	House of Commons
HK	Hong Kong
HL...	House of Lords
IAT..	Immigration Appeal Tribunal
ILM	International Legal Materials

INLR	Immigration and Nationality Law Reports
IRC	Inland Revenue Commissioners
Ind	India
Int Rels	International Relations
Ir	Ireland
J	Justice
JA	Judge of Appeal
Kan	Kansas
LA	Lord Advocate
LC	Lord Chancellor
LCC	London County Council
LCJ	Lord Chief Justice
LJ	Lord Justice of Appeal
LoN	League of Nations
MR	Master of the Rolls
Man	Manitoba
n	note
NB	New Brunswick
NI	Northern Ireland
NS	Nova Scotia
NSW	New South Wales
NY	New York
NZ	New Zealand
OHIM	Office for Harmonisation in the Internal Market
OJ	The Official Journal of the European Community published by the Office for Official Publications of the European Community
Ont	Ontario
P	President
PC	Judicial Committee of the Privy Council
PEI	Prince Edward Island
Pat	Patents Court
q	question
QB	Queen's Bench Division
QBD	Queen's Bench Division of the High Court
Qld	Queensland
Que	Quebec
r	rule
RDC	Rural District Council
RPC	Restrictive Practices Court
RSC	Rules of the Supreme Court 1965 (SI 1965/1776) as subsequently amended

reg	regulation
Res	Resolution
revsd	reversed
Rly	Railway
s	section
SA	South Africa
S Aust	South Australia
SC	Supreme Court
SI	Statutory Instruments published by authority
SR & O	Statutory Rules and Orders published by authority
SR & O Rev 1904	Revised Edition comprising all Public and General Statutory Rules and Orders in force on 31 December 1903
SR & O Rev 1948	Revised Edition comprising all Public and General Statutory Rules and Orders and Statutory Instruments in force on 31 December 1948
SRNI	Statutory Rules of Northern Ireland
STI	Simon's Tax Intelligence (1973–1995); Simon's Weekly Tax Intelligence (1996-current)
Sask	Saskatchewan
Sch	Schedule
Sess	Session
Sing	Singapore
TCC	Technology and Construction Court
TS	Treaty Series
Tanz	Tanzania
Tas	Tasmania
UDC	Urban District Council
UKHL	Official neutral citation for judgments of the House of Lords
UKPC	Official neutral citation for judgments of the Privy Council
UN	United Nations
V-C	Vice-Chancellor
Vict	Victoria
W Aust	Western Australia
Zimb	Zimbabwe

NOTE 1. A general list of the abbreviations of law reports and other sources used in this work can be found at the beginning of the Consolidated Table of Cases.

NOTE 2. Where references are made to other publications, the volume number precedes and the page number follows the name of the publication; eg the reference '12 Forms & Precedents (5th Edn) 44' refers to volume 12 of the Encyclopaedia of Forms and Precedents, page 44.

NOTE 3. An English statute is cited by short title or, where there is no short title, by regnal year and chapter number together with the name by which it is commonly known or a description of its subject matter and date. In the case of a foreign statute, the mode of citation generally follows the style of citation in use in the country concerned with the addition, where necessary, of the name of the country in parentheses.

NOTE 4. A statutory instrument is cited by short title, if any, followed by the year and number, or, if unnumbered, the date.

TABLE OF STATUTES

PARA

A

Administration of Justice Act 1970
s 11 (a) 642
(b)(i) 642
Sch 8 para 1 642
2, 2A 642
3 642
8–11 642
13, 13A 642
14, 15 642
Administration of Justice Act 1982
s 2 (a) 221
Air Force Act 1955
s 185 694
Army Act 1955
s 185 694
Asylum and Immigration (Treatment of
Claimants, etc) Act 2004
s 19 (1) 176–177
(2)(a)–(d) 177
(3)(a)–(c) 176
(4)(a)–(d) 176
20 (1) 87
(2)(a) 90
(b) 22
Attachment of Earnings Act 1971
s 1 (1) 628
(2)(a) 628
(3)(a) 628
2 (a), (b) 628
(e) 628
3 (1)(a) 628
(c), (d) 628
(4)(a) 628, 631
6 (1)(a), (b) 629
(2), (3) 629
(5)(a), (b) 632
(6)(a), (b) 632
(7)(a)–(c) 629
(8) 629
7 (1) 629
(2) 634
8 (1) 631
(3) 631, 635
9 (1), (2) 634
(4), (5) 634
10 (1)–(4) 633
11 (1)(a)–(d) 635
(2), (3) 635
13 (2)(a), (b) 629
24 (1)–(3) 630
25 (2) 628
(3) 632
Sch 1 para 1–4 628
9–11 628
13–16 628

PARA

C

Charging Orders Act 1979
s 1 (1)–(4) 636
(5) 638
2 (1)–(3) 637
3 (1) 636
(4) 636
(5) 639
(7) 637
6 (2) 636
(3) 637
Children Act 1989
s 8 (4)(b), (ba) 885
(e), (ea) 885
(g) 885
Church of England Marriage
Measure 2008
s 1 68
(1) 59
(3)(a)–(e) 59
(4)–(6) 59
(7) 72
(8) 59
(a) 68
(9) 59
(11) 59
(12)(a)–(c) 59
(13) 59
City of London (Guild Churches)
Act 1952
s 22 (1), (2) 66
Civil Evidence Act 1995
s 6 (3) 831
Civil Partnership Act 2004
s 1 (1) 2
(3)–(5) 2
2 (1)–(6) 56
3 (1)(a), (b) 2
(c) 4, 32, 41
(d) 4, 35, 38–39
(2) 38–39
4 (4), (5) 46
5 (1)–(4) 56
6 (1)–(3) 56
(3A)–(3C) 56
6A 190
7 (1) 56, 133
8 (1) 133
(3) 133, 140
(4) 133
(5) 133, 140
(6) 133
(7) 133, 140
9 (1)–(3) 134
10 (1) 136
(2)(a) 136

PARA

Civil Partnership Act 2004—*continued*

s 10 (2)(c) 136
 (3) 136
 11 136
 12 (1)–(3) 136
 13 (1) 138
 (2)(b) 138
 (3) 138
 14 (1) 138
 (3)–(5) 138
 15 (1), (2) 138
 16 (4) 138
 17 (1)–(3) 139
 (4)(a) 139
 18 (1) 174
 (2) 169
 (3)(a), (b) 174
 (c)(i), (ii) 174
 (4) 174
 (5) 169, 174
 19 (1) 175
 (2) 170
 (3)(a), (b) 175
 (c)(i), (ii) 175
 (4)(a), (b) 175
 (5) 175
 (6)(a), (b) 175
 (7) 170
 21 (1) 140
 22 (1)–(3) 141
 23 140
 24 (1)–(3) 143
 25 (2) 143
 (3)(a), (b) 143
 (4) 143
 (6)(a), (b) 143
 (7) 143
 26 (1) 143
 (2)(a), (b) 143
 (3) 143
 27 (1), (2) 144
 28 47
 (a) 133
 29 (1)–(3) 139
 30 (2) 133
 (4) 133
 37 (1)(a) 346
 (b) 320, 346
 (c) 415
 (2) 863
 (3) 320
 (4) 346
 38 (1)–(4) 863
 39 (1), (2) 852
 (3), (4) 853
 (5)(a) 852
 (b), (c) 853
 40 (1) 877
 (2) 864
 (3) 864, 877
 (4) 864
 41 (1), (2) 757

PARA

Civil Partnership Act 2004—*continued*

s 42 (1)–(3) 414
 43 859
 44 (1) 346
 (2) 348
 (3) 347
 (4) 348, 863
 (5)(a) 347, 359
 (b) 347, 407
 (c) 347, 410
 (d) 347, 363
 (6), (7) 413
 45 (1), (2) 361
 (3), (4) 408
 (5) 347, 368, 389
 (6), (7) 365
 (8) 347
 46 (1)(a)–(d) 758
 (2), (3) 758
 (4) 366
 (5)(a), (b) 366
 47 (1) 411
 (2)(a)–(c) 411
 (3)(a), (b) 411
 (4) 411
 (5) 460
 48 (1) 409
 (2)–(5) 873
 49 (a)–(c) 327
 50 (1)(a) 331
 (b) 332
 (c) 333
 (d), (e) 334
 (2) 332
 51 (1), (2) 321
 (3), (4) 323
 (5) 321
 (6) 321, 334
 52 (1), (2) 26
 53 (1)–(5) 5
 54 (1)–(11) 324
 55 (1) 415
 (2) 416
 56 (1) 346
 (2), (3) 348
 (4) 346, 361
 57 209
 58 (1) 421
 (2) 422
 59 (1)–(6) 1004
 60 (1)–(3) 1002
 61 (1), (2) 1001
 (3) 1004
 (4), (5) 1003
 62 347
 63 (1)–(3) 884
 64 (1)(a), (b) 760
 (2), (3) 760
 65 283
 66 (1) 224
 (2) 224, 226
 (3) 224

PARA

Civil Partnership Act 2004—*continued*

s 67 (1)–(6)	228
68	224, 228
69 (1)–(3)	211
70	274, 276
73 (1)–(4)	16
74 (1)–(4)	230
(5)	253
80 (1)(a)–(d)	185
(2)	185
(3)(a), (b)	185
84	26
(1)	212
(3), (4)	212
210 (1)	145
(2)(a)–(d)	145
(3), (4)	145
211 (1)	153
(2)(a)(i)–(iii)	153
(b), (c)	153
(3)	153
(5)(a)	153
212 (1), (2)	19
213 (1), (2)	19
214	19
215 (1)–(5)	19
216 (1)–(5)	19
217 (1), (2)	19
218	19
219, 220	750
221 (1)(a), (b)	750
(c)(i)–(iii)	750
(2)(a)	750
(b)(i), (ii)	750
(c)(i), (ii)	750
(3)	750
222 (a)–(c)	750
223	840
224	1000
239 (1)–(3)	160
240 (1)–(3)	152
242	153
246 (1), (2)	129
Sch 1 para 1 (1), (2)	38
2 (1), (2)	39
3	38–39
5 (1)(a), (b)	135
(2)–(5)	135
6 (1), (2)	135
7 (1)	135
8	138
2 para 1, 2	46
3 (1)–(4)	47
4	47
5	133
6 (1), (2)	137, 142
(3)(a)–(c)	137, 142
(4)–(6)	137, 142
7–9	138
11	140
12 (a), (b)	142
13 (1)–(3)	140

PARA

Civil Partnership Act 2004—*continued*

Sch 2 para 14	143
15 (1)	48
5 para 1 (1)	458, 467, 476, 492
(2)–(4)	492
2 (1)	450
(a)	458
(b)	467
(c)	476
(d)–(f)	492
(2)	458, 467, 476
3 (1)	477
(2)	492
(3)	476, 492
(4)	476–477
(5)–(7)	479, 492, 569
4	459, 468, 481
5	492
6 (1)	499, 506, 510, 518
7	498
(1)(a)	499, 518
(b)	506, 518
(c)	510, 518
(d)	510
(2)	510, 518
(3)	499, 510, 518
8	502, 507
9	499, 518
10 (1), (2)	520
11 (1)–(4)	520
12 (1), (2)	521
13	520
14 (1)–(3)	520
15 (1)	524
(2)	523
16 (1)–(3)	523
(4), (5)	485
17	527
18 (1)–(3)	524
19	597
(1)–(3)	525
19A (1)	524
(2)	523
19B	523
19C	527
19D	524
19E	525
19F	523
20	589
21 (1)	590
(2)(a)	590
(b), (c)	590, 597
(d)	590
(e)	590, 597
(f)–(h)	590
22 (1)	597–598, 703
(2)	597
(3)	598, 703
23 (1)–(3)	592
(4)	458, 467
24 (1)	590, 597
(2)	590

PARA

Civil Partnership Act 2004—*continued*

Sch 5 para 24 (3) 485
25 (2)–(8) 485
26 (1)–(7) 486
27, 28 487
29 (1)–(3) 485
30 (1) 590, 597
(2) 590
31, 32 .... 485, 567
33 .... 485–486, 567
34 .... 485, 567
34A, 34B 526
35–37 .... 485, 567
38 456
39 (1), (2) 542
(3) 545
(4) 543
40 545
41 (1), (2) 543
42 543
43 (1), (2) 589–590
(4) 590
44 (1), (2) 597–598
(3)(a) 597
(b) 598
(4) 597
45 543
46 (1), (2) 902
(3) 916
47 (1) 460, 469, 546
(2) 460
(a) 546
(3) 469
(a) 546
(4) 460, 469
(5) 469
(6) 460, 469, 546
48 452
49 (1)(a) 492
(b) 518
(c) 543
(2)(a), (b) 495, 546
(3)(a), (b) 495, 546
(4) 495, 546
(5)(a), (b) 492, 495, 518,
543, 546
(6) 496, 550
(7)(a), (b) 495, 546
(8)(a), (b) 495, 546
(9)–(11) 495, 546
50 (1)(a)–(j) 567
(2) 567
(3) 515, 567
51, 52 567
53 (1)–(3) 569
54 (1)–(6) 569
55 (1) 570
(2)–(5) 571
56 515
57 (1) 529
(2)–(4) 567
58 (1) 569

PARA

Civil Partnership Act 2004—*continued*

Sch 5 para 59 (1)–(6) 568
60 (1)–(6) 474, 550
61 567
62 (1)–(5) 570
63 (1)–(4) 679
64 (1)–(8) 573
65 (1)–(7) 574
(8)–(10) 575
66 (1)–(3) 713
67 (1)–(3) 696
68 697
69 (1) 700
(2)(a), (b) 702
(4) 703
(5) 700
(6) 700, 704
70 (1) 700
(2) 703
71 (1)–(5) 704
73 (1)–(6) 701
74 (1) 587–588
(2) 588
(3)–(6) 587
75 (1), (2) 586
(3) 587
(4)(a) 587–588
(b) 587
76 (1)(a) 473, 504, 548
(2) 473, 504, 548
(3) 473, 504
77 .... 505, 509
78 455
79 (1)–(7) 528
79A 528
80 (1) 450
(a) 458, 543
(b) 467, 543
(c) 476, 543
(3) 346
(4), (5) 452
6 para 1 (1), (2) 553
2 (1)–(4) 553
3 553
(1), (2) 576
4 589
5 (1) 590
(2)(a), (b) 590, 597
(c)–(e) 590
(f) 590, 597
(g) 590
6 (1) 597–598
(2) 597
(3) 598
7 (1)–(3) 594
8 565
9 (1)–(3) 554
10 (1), (2) 554
11 (1), (2) 555
12 555
13 (1), (2) 555
14 554

PARA

Civil Partnership Act 2004—*continued*
Sch 6 para 15 (1)–(4) 556
         16 (1), (2) 556
         17 556
         18 (1), (2) 556
         19 .... 589–590, 597–598
         20 (1)–(5) 563
         21 (1)(a) 563
            (2) 563
         22 (1), (2) 563
         23 (1), (2) 563
         24 (1)–(3) 564
         25 (1), (2) 563
         26 (1), (2) 560
         27 (1) 557
            (2)(a), (b) 561
            (3)(a), (b) 561
            (4) 561
            (5)(a), (b) 557, 561
            (6) 562
            (7)(a), (b) 561
            (8)(a), (b) 561
            (9)–(11) 561
         28 (1) 560
            (2) 557, 561–562
            (3) 560–561
         29 (1)–(6) 658
         31 (1)–(4) 577
         32 578
         33 (1)–(3) 578
         34 (1)–(3) 579
         35 580
         36 (1)–(4) 580
         37 (1), (2) 580
         38 (1), (2) 580
         39 580
            (a), (b) 576–577
         40 (1)–(3) 583
         41 582
         42 576
         43 657
         44 (1)–(7) 584
            (8)–(10) 585
         45 .... 553, 555–556
         46 (a) 566
            (b) 900–901
            (c) 898
         47 (1), (2) 735
         48 553
    7 para 1 (1)–(3) 530
            (4) 477
         2 (1) 530
            (2)(a) 530
            (3) 530
         3 (1), (2) 530
         4 (1)–(4) 938
         5 (2)–(5) 536
         6 939–940
         7 (1)–(5) 939
         8 (1)–(3) 940
         9 (1)–(5) 531
         10 (1)–(9) 532

PARA

Civil Partnership Act 2004—*continued*
Sch 7 para 11 (1)–(7) 533
         12 (1)–(3) 535
            (5) 535
         13 .... 310, 530
         14 (1)–(5) 537
         15 (1) 587–588
            (2) 588
            (3), (4) 587
            (5) 587–588
            (6)–(8) 587
            (9) 586
         16 (1) 587–588
            (2) 587
            (3) 587–588
            (4) 586
         17 (1)–(5) 588
         18 (1) 586
            (2) 586, 588
         19 346
         20 19
         21 129
      23 para 1 (2), (3) 178
         2 (1)(a), (b) 178
            (2) 178
         3 179
         4 (1)(a)–(d) 179
            (2) 179
         5 178
         6 (1), (2) 178
         7 (2)(a) 133
            (b) 26
      27 para 17 37
County Courts Act 1984
    s 58 (1) 837
Courts Act 2003
    s 75 (1)–(4) 1005
Courts and Legal Services Act 1990
    s 9 (1)–(5) 749
Criminal Justice Act 1925
    s 47 208

D

Domestic Proceedings and Magistrates'
    Courts Act 1978
    s 1 553
      2 (1)–(3) 553
      3 (2)(a), (b) 590, 597
         (c)–(h) 590
         (3) 597
         (4) 598
      4 (1), (2) 560
      5 (1) 557
         (2) 561
         (3)(a)(i), (ii) 557
            (b)(i), (ii) 561
         (5)(a) 561
         (6)(a), (b) 561
         (7), (8) 561
      6 (1), (2) 554
         (3) 555
         (4) 554

PARA

Domestic Proceedings and Magistrates' Courts Act 1978—*continued*

s 6 (5) 555
(6) 560
(7) 557, 561
(8) 560–561
(9) 555
7 556
(2)–(4) 556
(5) 590, 597–598
(6) 560
(7) 557, 561
8 .... 553, 555–556
19 (1) 563
(3), (3A) 563
(5), (6) 564
(7)–(9) 563
20ZA (1)–(10) 580
20 (1), (2) 576–577
(3) 576
(5) 576
(7), (8) 577
(9) 578
(9A)–(9C) 578
(11) 579
(12) 580
(a), (b) 576–577
20A (1)–(3) 583
22 582
23 (2) 576
25 (1)–(4) 658
26 (1), (2) 594
27 565
28 (1) 566
(3) 566
29 (1) 900
(2) 900–901
(3) 901
(5) 901
30 (1) 735
(5) 735
31 (1), (2) 898
32 (1)–(5) 657
35 (1)–(5) 584
(7), (8) 585
88 (2) 658
(3) 560

Domicile and Matrimonial Proceedings Act 1973

s 1 (1), (2) 214
5 (1)(a), (b) 750
(1A) 750
(2)(a), (b) 750
(3)(a), (b) 750
(4)(a), (b) 750
(5) 750
(6)(b) 841–843
Sch 1 para 1, 2 840
3 (1) 842
(2) 841
(5) 842
4 (1), (2) 840

PARA

Domicile and Matrimonial Proceedings Act 1973—*continued*

Sch 1 para 5 840
7 840
8 (2) 841
9 (1)–(3) 842
(4) 840
10 (1), (2) 843
11 (1), (2) 844
(3), (3A) 844
(4) 844
(4A), (4B) 844
(5) 844

E

Ecclesiastical Licences Act 1533

s 9 76
11, 12 76

F

Family Law Act 1986

s 55 1000
(1) 421
(2) 1000
(3) 422, 1000
58 (1)–(6) 1004
59 (1)–(3) 1002
60 (1), (2) 1001
(3) 1004
(4) 1003

Family Law Act 1996

s 22 (1)–(3) 414
30 (1)–(9) 285
31 (1), (2) 286
(9), (10) 286
33 (1) 292
(2), (2A) 292
(3)(a) 293
(4), (5) 293
(6), (7) 295, 307
(8) 293
(9), (10) 292
34 (1), (2) 296
35 (1), (2) 297
(3)–(5) 298
(6)–(8) 300
(9)–(13) 297
36 (1), (2) 301
(4)–(5) 302
(6)–(8) 304
(9)–(13) 301
37 (1), (1A) 305
(2) 305
(3) 306
(4) 307
(5) 305
38 (1), (2) 305
(3) 306
(4), (5) 307
(6) 305
39 (1)–(4) 289
40 (1) 294, 299, 303

PARA

Family Law Act 1996—*continued*

s 40 (2) 295, 300, 304
   (3) 294, 299, 303
   42 (1) 716
      (2)–(4) 717
      (4ZA) 717
      (4A) 295
      (4B) 718
      (5) 718
      (6), (7) 716
      (8) 717
   43 (1), (2) 289, 717
   44 (1) 292, 717
      (2) 292
      (3) 292, 717
      (4) 292
   45 (1)–(3) 290, 719
      (4) 290
      (5) 290, 719
   46 (1), (2) 291, 720
      (3), (3A) 291, 720
      (4), (5) 291, 720
   47 (2)–(5) 988
      (6), (7) 990
      (8)–(10) 991
      (11) 993
      (12) 990–991
   48 (1)–(3) 994
   49 (1) 309
      (3) 309
   50 (1) 998
      (2)(a) 998–999
   51 (1), (2) 999
   54 (1)–(5) 285
   55 (1) 285, 287
      (2), (3) 287
   56 (1)–(5) 287
   57 (2)–(10) 958
      (12) 958
   58 961
   59 (1)–(3) 960
   60 (1)–(5) 963
   61 (1)–(4) 308, 721
      (5)–(7) 958
   62 (1) 292
      (2) 290
      (3)–(6) 292
      (7)(a), (b) 292
   63 (4) 285
   63A (1) 723
      (2), (3) 726
      (4), (5) 723
      (6) 723–724
      (7) 723
   63B (1)–(3) 728
   63C (1)(a) 724
       (b) 725
       (2)–(5) 724
       (6) 725
       (7) 722, 724
   63D (1)–(4) 727, 730
   63E (1)–(5) 729

PARA

Family Law Act 1996—*continued*

s 63F 728
   63G (1)–(5) 730
       (6), (7) 989
   63H (1)–(7) 989
   63I (1)–(3) 990
   63J (1)–(4) 991
   63K (1) 990–991
       (2), (3) 993
       (4), (5) 990–991
   63L (1)–(3) 994
   63M (1) 723, 958
       (2), (3) 958
   63N (1)–(4) 958
   63O 961
   63P (1)–(3) 958
   63Q (1)–(3) 723
   63R (1), (2) 723
   64 (1), (2) 743
Sch 5 993
    7 para 1 310
         2 (1), (2) 310
         3, 4 310
         5 311
         6 312
            (a)–(h) 311
         7 (1), (2) 312
            (3), (3A) 312
            (4), (5) 312
         8 (1)–(3) 313
         9 (1)–(3) 313
        10 (1)–(5) 314
        11 (1), (2) 315
        12 315
        13 (1)–(3) 310
        14 (1) 311
           (2) 310
        15 310

Family Law Reform Act 1969

s 2 (3) 90
   19 (1) 274
      (3) 274

Foreign Marriage Act 1892

s 1 (2) 28
   2 120
   3 (1) 120
   4 (1), (2) 121
      (4) 121
      (6) 121
   5 (1), (2) 123
      (3), (4) 122
   6 (a), (b) 120
   7 124
   8 (1), (2) 125
   9 (1) 125
      (2)–(5) 126
   10 (1), (2) 126
   11 (1)–(4) 119
      (5) 126
   13 (1) 28, 126
      (2) 28
   16 (1) 126

PARA

Foreign Marriage Act 1892—*continued*
s 16 (2) 125
17 126
19 122
20 120
23 119

I

Immigration and Asylum Act 1999
s 24 (1)(a) 11
(b) 90
(2) 102, 105, 111, 166, 173
(3) 90, 102, 105, 111, 166, 173
(4), (5) 11
24A (3)–(5) 11
53 (g) 102, 105, 111

Inheritance (Provision for Family and
Dependants) Act 1975
s 14 (1), (2) 540
14A (1)–(3) 540
15 (1)–(4) 882
15ZA (1)–(5) 882
15A (1)–(3) 534
15B (1)–(4) 534
16 (1)–(3) 572
17 (1)–(3) 701
18 (1) 541
(a) 474, 550
(b) 701
(2), (3) 474, 541, 550, 701
18A (1) 541
(a) 474, 550
(b) 701
(2), (3) 474, 541, 550, 701
25 (4), (4A) 534
(5), (5A) 534

L

Law Reform (Husband and Wife)
Act 1962
s 1 (1), (2) 211
3 (3) 211

Law Reform (Married Women and
Tortfeasors) Act 1935
s 1 205
(a) 204
(b), (c) 204, 206
(d) 204, 210
2 (1) 204
3 204
4 (2)(a), (b) 204
(c) 204, 206, 210
(d) 232

Law Reform (Miscellaneous Provisions)
Act 1970
s 1 (1), (2) 16
2 (1), (2) 230
3 (1), (2) 253
5 (a) 221
(c) 221

PARA

M

Magistrates' Courts Act 1980
s 59 (3)(a), (b) 580, 669–670
(c)–(cc) 580, 669–670
(d) 580, 669–670
(4) 669–670
60 (5)–(10) 670
(11)(a) 670

Maintenance Enforcement Act 1991
s 1 (1) 645
(2) 644
(3) 645
(4) 645
(a) 646
(5)–(7) 646
(8) 644
(9) 646
(a), (b) 644
(10) 644
12 (2) 644

Maintenance Orders Act 1958
s 1 (1), (1A) 664
(2) 664
(2A)(a) 664
(4) 664
2 (1) 666
(2) 667
(3) 671
(3A), (3B) 671
(4)(a) 948
(c) 948
(5) 667
(6) 672
(6ZA) 668
(6ZB)(a) 672
(b) 668
(6ZC) 668, 672
(6A) 666, 671
(7) 667
2A (1)–(5) 673
3 (1), (2) 665
(2A), (2B) 665
(3) 665
(3A) 668
(4) 665
4 (1), (2) 669
(2A)–(2C) 669
(4), (5) 669
(5A), (5B) 670
(6) 669
(6A), (6B) 669
(7) 669
4A 674
5 (1)–(3) 675
(4), (4A) 675
(5)–(7) 675

Marriage Act 1939
s 2 (1) 114
(3) 114

Marriage Act 1949
s 1 (1) 36

PARA

Marriage Act 1949—*continued*

s 1 (2), (3) 37
2 .... 41, 57
3 95
  (1) 46
    proviso (a), (b) 47
  (1A)(a)–(h) 46
  (1B) 46
  (2) 46
  (3), (4) 52
  (5) 48
  (6) 46–47
4 .... 82, 106
5 (a)–(d) 57–58
5A (a) 58
5B (1), (2) 58
6 (1), (2) 65
  (3) 59, 65
  (4) 66
7 (1), (2) 69
  (3), (4) 75
8 68
9 (1), (2) 70
10 (1), (2) 67
11 (1)–(4) 72
12 (1) 59
  (2) 71
13 73
14 (1), (2) 74
15 (1)(a), (b) 59
  (2) 59
16 (1)(a)–(c) 77
  (2) 78
  (2A), (2B) 78
  (3) 79
  (4) 77
17 .... 54, 80
18 (1)(a)–(c) 61
  (2), (3) 61
19 61
20 (1)–(8) 62
21 (1), (2) 63
22 83
23 59–60
24 (1), (2) 21, 59
25 (a)–(d) 328
26 80
  (1) 54
    (a) 54
    (b), (bb) 54
    (c), (d) 54
    (dd) 54, 171
    (e) 54
27 (1) 87
  (3) 87
  (4) 92
  (5) 88
  (6) 92
  (7) 172
27A (1), (2) 172
  (3)(a), (b) 173
  (4) 173

PARA

Marriage Act 1949—*continued*

s 27A (5), (6) 172
  (7) 169, 173
27B (1)–(6) 93
28 (1) 90
  (2) 90
28A (1)(b) 91
  (2), (3) 91
29 (1)–(5) 96
31 (1) 94
  (2), (3) 97
  (4) 82, 94, 97
  (4A) 94
  (5) 99
  (5A)–(5G) 94
31A (1)–(3) 97
33 (1)–(3) 82, 101
  (4) 101
34 100
35 (1)(a)–(d) 100
  (2) 100
  (2A), (2B) 100
  (3) 80, 100
  (4) 100
  (5) 87
37 (1) 112
38 (1)–(4) 113
39 (1)–(3) 131
39A (5) 101
40 (1) 97
41 (1), (2) 186
  (3)–(6) 187
  (7) 186
42 (1) 188
  (3) 188
  (5) 188
43 (1)–(3) 107
44 (1) 104
    proviso 104
  (2) 106
  (3), (3A) 105
  (4) 106
45 (1), (2) 102
45A (1)–(5) 173
46 (1)–(3) 57
46A (1)–(3) 190
46B (1) 111
  (2) 190
  (3), (4) 111
47 (1) 115
  (2)(b) 115
  (3), (4) 115
48 (1)(a)–(e) 22
  (2) 22
49 (a), (b) 329–330
  (d) 330
  (e), (ee) 330
  (f), (g) 330
  (gg) 111, 330
  (h) 330
50 (1)(a), (b) 98
  (c), (cc) 98

PARA

Marriage Act 1949—*continued*

s 50 (1)(d)–(f) 98
    (3) 98
51 (1), (1A) 98
    (2) 98
52 105
53 (a)–(c) 84
    (d), (e) 108
54 84
    (1) 85
55 (1)–(5) 84
56 84
57 (1) 85
59 86
60 (1) 86
61 (1)–(5) 84
62 (1) 86
    (2)(a), (b) 86
63 (1) 86, 116, 118
68 (1)–(3) 129
    (6) 129
69 (1)(a), (b) 129
    (3) 129
    (4), (5) 130
70 (1)–(3) 129
71 (a)–(c) 23
72 (1), (2) 66
    (3) 21–22
    (4) 21, 66
73 (1) 64
    (2), (3) 64, 189
74 (b) 87
75 (1)(a) 82, 180
    (b) 52, 65, 180
    (c), (d) 180
    (2)(a), (aa) 180
    (b), (bb) 180
    (c), (cc) 180
    (d) 180
    (e) 82, 180
    (3) 180
    (4) 52, 65, 82, 180
    (5) 180
76 (1) 84, 86, 181
    (2) 85, 181
    (3), (4) 181
    (5) 84, 181
    (6) 181
77 182
78 (1) 21, 37
    (2) 53
    (4) 170
    (5) 54, 171
79 (6) 58
    (7) 40
    (9) 40
    (10) 81
Sch 1 para 1(1), (2) 36
    2 37
    4 Pt II 59
    6 61–62

PARA

Marriage Act 1983

s 1 (1) 171
    (2) 169
    (4) 170
    (5), (6) 171

Marriage (Enabling) Act 1960

s 1 (1)–(3) 37

Marriage of British Subjects (Facilities) Act 1915

s 1 (1) 114
    (a) 114
    (b) 17
2 114

Marriage (Registrar General's Licence) Act 1970

s 1 (1) 161
    (2) 161–164, 167
2 (1)–(3) 162
3 (a)–(d) 163
4 163
5 164
6 163
7 165
8 (1), (2) 165
9 166
10 (1)(a), (b) 166
    (2), (3) 166
11 (1) 167
    (2) 57, 167
12 22
13 (a) 329
    (c)–(e) 329
14 (a)–(c) 168
16 (1)(a)–(e) 183
    (2)–(4) 183
17 (2) 162, 166
18 (2) 162
19 .... 76, 161
20 (2) 165–166

Marriage (Wales and Monmouthshire) Act 1962

s 1 (2) 21

Marriage with Foreigners Act 1906

s 1 (1) 128
    (3), (4) 128
2 (1)–(3) 128
3, 4 128
Schedule para 1 128
    2 (a)–(c) 128
    3–5 128
    6 (a)–(c) 128

Marriages Validity (Provisional Orders) Act 1924

s 1 15

Married Women (Restraint upon Anticipation) Act 1949

s 1 (1), (2) 204

Married Women's Property Act 1882

s 11 .... 274, 276
17 224
24 224

	PARA
Married Women's Property Act 1964	
s 1	245
Matrimonial and Family Proceedings Act 1984	
s 3 (1)	589
7 (5)	589
12 (1)–(3)	530
13 (1)–(3)	938
14 (1)–(3)	536
15 (2)	939
16 (1), (2)	940
17 (1), (2)	531
18 (1), (2)	532
(3), (3A)	532
(4)–(7)	532
19 (1)	535
(3)	535
20 (1)–(3)	533
21 (1)–(5)	537
22	310, 530
23 (1)	586
(2)(a)	588
(b)	587
(3)	587
(4)	587–588
(5), (6)	587
(7)(a)	587–588
(b)	587
(8), (9)	586
24 (1)–(3)	588
27	939
(3)(a)	588
32	737
33 (1)–(6)	732
34 (1)–(4)	733
35	732
36 (1), (2)	732
36A (1)–(8)	732
(10)	732
36B (1)–(3)	733
36C	732
36D (1), (2)	732
37	744
38 (1)	745
(2)(a)–(c)	745
(3), (3A)	745
(4), (5)	745
39 (1), (2)	746
40 (1)–(3)	1005
(3ZA)–(3ZC)	1005
(3A)	1005
(4)	1005
40A (1)–(4)	1005
(6)	1005
40B (1)–(3)	1005
Matrimonial Causes Act 1965	
s 8 (2)(a), (b)	81
Matrimonial Causes Act 1973	
s 1 (1)	346
(2)(a)	347, 350
(b)	347, 359
(c)	347, 363

	PARA
Matrimonial Causes Act 1973—*continued*	
s 1 (2)(d)	347, 407
(e)	347, 410
(3)	348
(4)	348, 863
(5)	863
2 (1), (2)	351
(3)	361
(4)	347, 368, 389
(5)	365, 413
(6)	347
(7)	408
3 (1), (2)	757
4 (1), (2)	758
(3)	366
(4)(a), (b)	366
(5)	366
5 (1)	411
(2)(a), (b)	411
(3)	411
(4)	562
6 (1), (2)	414
(7)	562
7	859
(7)	562
8 (1)(a)	852
(b)	853
(2)	853
(3)(a)	852
(b), (c)	853
9 (1)	864, 877
(2)	864
10 (1)	409
(2)–(4)	873
10A (1)–(8)	874
11 (a)–(d)	326
12 (a)	335
(b)	342
(c)	331
(d)	332
(e)	343
(f)	333
(g), (h)	334
13 (1)	321
(2), (2A)	321
(3)	321, 334
(4), (5)	323
14 (1)–(3)	324
15	852–853, 863
16	320
17 (1)	346, 361
(2)	348
(3)	348, 414, 859
18 (1)	219
(2)	209
19 (1)	415
(3)	416
(4)	852–853, 863
(6)	415
20	347
21 (1)	450
(a)	458, 492, 543

PARA

Matrimonial Causes Act 1973—*continued*
s 21 (1)(b) 467, 492, 543
      (c) 476, 492, 543
   (2) 498
21A (1) 523
   (2)(a), (b) 523
21B, 21C 523
22 456
23 (1)(a) 458
      (b) 467
      (c) 476
      (d)–(f) 492
   (2) 492
   (3)(a) 477
      (b) 492
      (c) 476, 492
   (4) 492
   (5) 459, 468, 481
   (6) 479, 492, 569
24 (1)(a) 499, 518
      (b) 506, 518
      (c) 510, 518
      (d) 510
   (2) 510, 518
   (3) 502, 507
24A (1), (2) 520
   (3), (4) 521
   (5), (6) 520
24B (1) 524
   (2) 525
   (3)–(5) 524
24C 525
24D 527
24E(1) 524
   (2) 525
   (3)–(10) 524
24F 525
24G 527
25 (1) 589
   (2)(a)–(c) 590, 597
      (d) 590
      (e) 590, 597
      (f) 590
   (3) 597
   (4) 598, 703
25A (1), (2) 592
   (3) 458, 467
25B (1)(a) 590, 597
      (b) 590
   (3)–(7) 485
   (7A)–(7C) 485
25C (1)–(4) 486
25D (1) 487
   (2), (2A) 487
   (3), (4) 485
25E (1)(a) 590, 597
      (b) 590
   (2)–(5) 485, 567
   (6) 485–486, 567
   (7)–(10) 485, 567
25F, 25G 526
26 (1) 902

PARA

Matrimonial Causes Act 1973—*continued*
s 26 (2) 916
27 (1), (2) 542
   (3) 589–590
   (3A) 589, 597–598
   (3B) 590, 597
   (5) 545
   (6) 543
   (6A) 570
   (6B) 571
   (7) 543
28 (1)(a) 460, 546
      (b) 469
   (1A) 460, 469
   (2) 460, 469, 546
   (3) 452
29 (1) 492, 518, 543
   (2) 495, 546
   (3)(a), (b) 492, 495, 518, 543, 546
   (4) 496, 550
   (5)(a) 546
      (b) 495, 546
   (6)(a), (b) 495, 546
   (7), (8) 495, 546
30 (a) 473, 504, 548
      (b) 473, 504
31 (1) 515, 567
   (2)(a)–(c) 567
      (d), (dd) 567
      (e) 515, 567
      (f), (g) 567
   (2A), (2B) 567
   (3) 515, 567
   (4) 515, 570
   (4A) 529
   (4B), (4C) 567
   (5) 569
   (6) 474, 550
   (7) 568
   (7A), (7B) 569
   (7D)–(7H) 569
   (8), (9) 474, 550
   (10) 567
   (11)–(13) 570
   (15) 567
32 (1)–(3) 679
33 (1)–(6) 573
33A (1)–(3) 713
34 (1) 697
   (2) 696
35 (1) 700
   (2) 700
      (a), (b) 702
      (i), (ii) 703
   (3) 700, 703
   (4), (5) 704
36 (1), (2) 701
   (4), (5) 701
37 (1) 586–588
   (2)(a) 588
      (b), (c) 587
   (3), (4) 587

PARA

Matrimonial Causes Act 1973—*continued*
s 37 (5)(a) 587–588
      (b) 587
      (6), (7) 586
   38 (1)–(5) 574
      (6), (7) 575
   39 .... 505, 509
   40 455
   40A (1)–(7) 528
   40B 528
   41 (1)–(3) 884
   47 (1)–(4) 9
   48 (1) 355
      (2) 336
   49 (1)–(5) 760
   52 (2)(b) 456
      (3), (3A) 452
   Sch 1 para 8 371
          11 (1)(a)–(e) 345
             (2) 345
             (3)(a)–(c) 345
             (3A) 345
             (4) 320
          12 325
          17 (1)–(4) 457
          18 457
Matrimonial Causes (Property and
   Maintenance) Act 1958
s 7 (1)–(6) 228
   (7) 226
Matrimonial Proceedings and Property
   Act 1970
s 37 283
   39 .... 224, 228

N

Naval Discipline Act 1957
s 102 694

P

Pastoral Measure 1983
s 29 (2) 59
Sch 3 para 14 (2) 59
           (3) 62

PARA

Pastoral Measure 1983—*continued*
   Sch 3 para 14 (4), (5) 59–60
Perjury Act 1911
s 3 (1) 184
   (a) 77, 184
   (b) 184
   (c) 78, 184
   (d) 184
      (ii) 93
   (2) 184
Private International Law (Miscellaneous
   Provisions) Act 1995
s 5 (1), (2) 9
Provisional Order (Marriages) Act 1905
s 1 (1), (2) 15

S

Sharing of Church Buildings Act 1969
s 6 (1) 108
   (2) 59
   Sch 1 para 7 108
Supreme Court Act 1981
s 18 (1)(d) 883
      (fa) 883
   38 (1) 641
   39 (1), (2) 641
   61 (1) 731
      (3) 731
   151 (1) 731
   Sch 1 para 3 (a) 731
             (c)–(e) 731
             (f)(i) 731
             (g) 731
             (i)–(k) 731

T

Tribunals, Courts and Enforcement
   Act 2007
s 62 (4)(a), (b) 651
      (c) 656

W

Welfare Reform and Pensions Act 1999
s 85 (3) 524

TABLE OF STATUTORY INSTRUMENTS

PARA

C

Civil Courts Order 1983, SI 1983/713
Sch 3 732
Civil Partnership Act 2004
(Commencement No 2)
Order 2005, SI 2005/3175 530
Civil Partnership (Armed Forces)
Order 2005, SI 2005/3188
art 2–4 153
6 (1) 154
(2)(a)–(g) 154
(3), (4) 154
(5)(a), (b) 154
7 (1)–(3) 153
8 (1) 155
(2)(a)–(c) 155
10 (1) 156
(2)(a), (b) 156
(3), (4) 156
11 (1)–(4) 159
12 (1)–(4) 158
14 (1)–(6) 160
Civil Partnership (Jurisdiction and
Recognition of Judgments)
Regulations 2005, SI 2005/3334
reg 4 751
12 839
Civil Partnership (Registration Abroad
and Certificates) Order 2005,
SI 2005/2761
art 1 (2) 29, 154
5 (1), (2) 146
(3)(a)–(f) 146
(4)–(6) 146
6 (1)–(3) 147
7 (1)–(5) 149
8 (1), (2) 148
9 (1), (2) 146
10 (1)–(3) 150
(4)(a) 150
(b)(i)–(v) 150
(c)(i), (ii) 150
(d)(i) 150
(5), (6) 150
12 151
17 (1)–(5) 152
Civil Partnership (Registration
Provisions) Regulations 2005, Si
2005/3176 .... 133, 135, 143
reg 7 (1) 136
(3)–(6) 136
8 136
Form 6 174
(w) 174

PARA

Civil Partnership (Treatment of Overseas
Relationships) Order 2005,
SI 2005/3042
art 3 (1) 757
(2) 283
Consular Fees Order 2008,
SI 2008/676 120
County Courts (Interest on Judgment
Debts) Order 1991, SI 1991/1184
art 6 (1), (2) 950
Courts Act 2003 (Commencement No 11
and Transitional Provision)
Order 2005, SI 2005/2744
art 2 (2)(a) 1005

D

Dissolution etc (Pension Protection Fund)
Regulations 2006, SI 2006/1934 485,
567
Dissolution etc (Pensions)
Regulations 2005, SI 2005/2920
reg 3 (1)(a) 488
(2) 488
4 (1)–(5) 487
5 (1)–(3) 489
6 (1)–(5) 490
7 (1)–(5) 491
8 .... 487, 489–492
9 (1) 525
(3) 525
Divorce etc (Pension Protection Fund)
Regulations 2006, SI 2006/1932 485,
567
Divorce etc (Pensions) Regulations 2000,
SI 2000/1123
reg 3 (1)(a) 488
(2) 488
4 (1)–(5) 487
5 (1)–(3) 489
6 (1)–(5) 490
7 (1)–(5) 491
8 .... 487, 489–491
9 (1), (2) 525

F

Family Law Act 1996 (Part IV)
(Allocation of Proceedings)
Order 1997, SI 1997/1896
art 2 959
3 960
4 (1)–(3) 962
5 (1), (2) 309, 722
6 964
7 965
8 (1)–(3) 966
9 967
10 968

PARA

Family Law Act 1996 (Part IV) (Allocation of
  Proceedings) Order 1997,
  SI 1997/1896—*continued*
art 11 969
  12 970
  13 971
  14 972
  15 990–991
  16 (1) 959
    (2) 968
  17 959
  18 .... 962, 964

Family Proceedings (Civil Partnership:
  Staying of Proceedings) Rules 2005,
  SI 2005/2921
r 1 (2)(a), (b) 840
  2 840
  3 (1), (2) 841
  4 (1)–(4) 842
    (5)–(7) 840
  5 (1)–(3) 843
  6 (3)(a)–(d) 844
    (4) 844
  7 (1)–(5) 844
  8 (5) 844
    (7), (8) 844
  9 (1), (2) 844
  10 841–844

Family Proceedings Courts (Matrimonial
  Proceedings etc) Rules 1991,
  SI 1991/1991
r 3 (1)–(3) 894
  3A (1)–(7) 977
    (8), (9) 964
    (10)–(12) 977
  4 (1)–(3) 1029
    (4), (5) 895
  5 894
  6 (1)–(7) 895
  7 (1)–(5) 1031
  8 (1)–(4) 896
  9 (1)–(3) 1028
  10 (1)–(3) 1032
  11 1034
  12 (1)–(3) 896
    (4)–(8) 899
  12A (1)–(7) 978
  12B 979
  13 (1), (2) 1041
  14 1033
  15 (1)–(3) 1035
  16 (1) 576
  17 555
  18 (1), (1A) 556
    (2) 556
  19 (1) 576
    (2) 583
  19A (1) 576
    (2) 583
  20 (1) 988
    (1A), (1B) 978, 988
    (2) 309, 722

PARA

Family Proceedings Courts (Matrimonial
  Proceedings etc) Rules 1991,
  SI 1991/1991—*continued*
r 20 (3) 991
  (4) 992
  (5) 996
  (6)–(10) 996–997
  (11), (12) 996
  (13) 996–997
  (15) 996
  (16) 996–997
  (17) 996
  (18) 992
  (19) 999
  (20) 996
  (21) 996–997
  (22) 992
  21 (1)–(3) 995
    (4) 993
    (a) 995
  22 (1) 576
    (2)–(6) 581
  23 (2) 898
  24 1030
  25 735
Sch 1 556
  Form 1–7 894
    9, 9A 894
    FL401 977
    FL403 979
    FL404 996
    FL404a 978
    FL406 988
    FL407, FL408 991
    FL410, FL411 .... 993, 995
    FL412 993
    FL413, FL414 999
    FL418–FL421 996–997
    FL422 997

Family Proceedings Fees Order 2008,
  SI 2008/1054 1036
art 2 717
Sch 1 Fee 1.2 755
    1.3 .... 289, 717
    1.4 .... 755, 770
    1.5 779
    3.3 944
    4.1 866
    4.2 814
    4.4 .... 916, 924
    5.1 737
    6.1 878
    7.1, 7.2 863
    10.1 776
    11.4 (a), (b) 944
    11.5 945
    11.6 947
    11.7 943
    13.1 947
    13.4 945

PARA

Family Proceedings (Miscellaneous Amendments) Rules 1999, SI 1999/1012
r 3 (1) 755, 1005

Family Proceedings Rules 1991, SI 1991/1247
r 1.2 (1) 732, 737, 747, 761
  (2) 755
  (6)–(8) 732
1.3 (1), (2) 1005
1.4 (1), (2) 755
1.5 (1)–(6) 1007
2.1 (1)–(3) 786
2.2 (1) 321, 755, 799
  (2) 767, 799
  (3) 799
2.3 756
  (1), (2) 826
2.4 (1), (2) 763
2.5 766
  (1) 867
  (2) 868
  (3) 867–868
2.6 (1) 714, 755, 919
  (2) 767, 919
  (3) 414, 767, 919
  (4) 755, 919
  (4A) 755
  (5) 768
  (6) 768, 798
2.6A (1)–(6) 767
2.6B 767
2.7 (1)–(5) 761, 926
  (6) 926
  (7)–(12) 927
  (13) 934
  (16), (17) 935
  (18)(a) 926–927, 935
    (ab) 927, 935
    (c) 926
    (d) 927
2.8 755
2.9 (1)–(4) 776
  (5) 408, 776
  (6) 776
  (6A), (6B) 776
  (7), (8) 776
  (9) 777
  (10) 776
  (11) 778
2.9A 776
2.11 (1) 770
  (2)(a), (b) 770
  (3)–(8) 770
2.12 (1)–(4) 779
2.12A (1), (1A) 779
  (2)–(6) 779
2.12B 779
2.13 (1)–(3) 797
2.14 775
2.15 (1)–(6) 780
2.16 (1), (2) 783

PARA

Family Proceedings Rules 1991, SI 1991/1247—continued
r 2.17 797–798
2.18 774
2.19 (1), (2) 787
  (3) 787, 789
2.21 (1)–(3) 800
2.22 (1)–(5) 803
  (6) 804
  (7), (8) 803–804
  (9) 803
  (10) 805
2.23 (1) 806
  (2), (3) 807
  (4)–(6) 808
2.24 (1), (2) 814
  (3), (3A) 361, 814
  (4)–(7) 814
2.25 (1) 818
  (2)–(6) 816
  (7) 818
  (8) 819
2.26 (1), (2) 816
2.27 (1) 841
  (2) 842
  (3), (4) 817
  (5) 843
2.27A (1)–(5) 839
2.27AA (1) 841
  (2) 842
  (3)–(5) 817
  (6) 843
2.28 (1), (2) 825
  (3)–(5) 837
2.29 838
2.32 (1) 823
  (2) 821
  (3), (3A) 821
  (4), (4A) 821
  (5) 822
  (6) 821
2.33 824
2.34 (1), (2) 813
2.35 820
2.36 (1)–(5) 815
2.37 (1)–(3) 1038
2.38 (1), (2) 767
2.39 (1), (2) 884
  (3)(a) 884
  (4), (5) 884
2.41 851
2.42 (1), (2) 739
  (3) 739, 874
  (4) 739
  (5) 739, 874
  (6)–(10) 739
2.43 (1), (2) 1011
2.44 (1)–(4) 870
2.45 (1) 873
  (4) 873
  (5), (5A) 873
  (6), (6A) 873

PARA

Family Proceedings Rules 1991,
SI 1991/1247—*continued*

r 2.45A (1)–(3) 874
2.45B (1)–(4) 874
2.46 (1)–(6) 875
2.47 (1)–(7) 876
2.48 (1)–(3) 869
2.49 (1), (2) 866
2.51 (1)–(4) 878
2.51A (1)–(4) 878
2.51B (1) 902
2.51D (1)–(6) 903
2.52 920
2.53 (1)–(3) 916
2.54 (1), (2) 493
2.57 (1)–(3) 510
2.59 (2)–(6) 918
2.61 714
2.61A (1)–(5) 924
2.61B (1)–(7) 925
(9) 925
2.61C 932
2.61D (1)–(5) 928
2.61E (1) 929
(2)–(9) 930
2.61F (1), (2) 1039
2.62 (2) 931
(4), (4A) 931
(7)–(9) 931
2.64 (1)–(3) 933
2.65 936
2.66 (1), (2) 937
(3), (3A) 937
(4) 937
2.67 (1)–(3) 461
2.68 588
2.69E (1), (2) 921
2.69F (1)–(6) 923
2.70A 935
2.71 (1)–(6) 1037
3.1 (1) 886, 995
(2) 886–887
(3) 887, 995
(4) 888, 993
(5) 890, 995
(6) 890
(a) 993, 995
(7)–(9) 890
(10) 886
3.2 706
(1)–(5) 48
3.3 706
(1)–(3) 981
3.4 706
3.5 706
3.6 (1)–(8) 955
(10) 956
(11), (12) 955
3.7 (1), (1A) 955
(3), (4) 955
3.8 (2) 974
(4)–(8) 974

PARA

Family Proceedings Rules 1991,
SI 1991/1247—*continued*

r 3.8 (9) 964
(11)–(14) 974
3.9 (1)–(6) 975
(8) 309, 722
3.9A (1) 988–989
(1A), (1B) 975, 984
(2) 309, 722
(3) 991
(3A), (3B) 991
(4)–(6) 992
(7) 992, 994
(8) 992
(9) 990
(10) 992
3.11 (1)–(5) 1010
3.12 (1)–(5) 1001
3.12A (1)–(6) 1001
3.16 (1)–(3) 1001
(4)–(8) 1003
3.17 (1), (1A) 938
(2), (3) 938
3.18 (1), (2) 941
(3) 535, 941
(4)–(9) 941
3.19 588
3.20A (1)–(5) 48
3.25 (1) 980
3.26 (1)–(3) 980
3.27 (1)–(3) 724
3.28 (1)–(4) 980
3.29 (1) 973
3.31 (1)–(5) 983
3.32 (1)–(8) 982
3.33 (1)–(7) 984
(4)–(8) 985
3.34 (1)–(4) 724
3.35 (1) 989, 992, 994
(2) 989
(3), (4) 984
(6) 991
(7), (8) 992
(9) 994
(11) 992
3.36 (1) 993
(4) 993
7.1 (1) 623
(2) 651
(4) 943
(3A) 988
7.3 (1), (2) 952
7.4 (1), (2) 945
(3), (3A) 945
(4)–(6) 945
(7B), (7C) 945
(8)–(11) 945
7.22 .... 667, 948
7.23 (1)–(4) 667
7.24 667
7.25 948
7.26 (1), (2) 948

PARA

Family Proceedings Rules 1991,
    SI 1991/1247—*continued*
r 7.28 669
    7.29 (1)–(5) 675
    8.1 (1)–(7) 737
    8.1A (1)–(3) 986
        (4) 999
        (5) 986
        (6) 974
    8.1B (1), (2) 987
        (3) 980, 985
    8.2 (1)–(9) 900
    8.3 731
    9.1 765
    9.2 (3), (4) 1019
    9.3 (1), (2) 1019
    9.4 (1), (1A) 759
        (2) 759
    10.1 1018
        (1), (1A) 747
        (2) 747, 1013
        (2A) 747
        (3)–(6) 747
    10.2 (1) 1013, 1017
        (2) 1017
        (3) 1013, 1017
    10.3 (1)–(3) 1018
    10.4 1020
    10.5 (1)–(3) 1021
    10.6 (1)–(5) 1022
    10.7 1008
    10.8 (1)–(3) 779
    10.9 1006
    10.10 747
    10.11 (1) 748
        (2)(a), (b) 748
        (3) 748
    10.12, 10.13 837
    10.14 (1) 27, 835
        (1A) 27
        (2), (3) 27, 835
    10.14A 831
    10.15 (1)–(7) 1014
    10.16 (1), (2) 863
    10.17 (1)–(4) 1023
    10.18 855
    10.19 1012
    10.21 (1), (1A) 1009
        (2) 1009
    10.21B 334
    10.26 (1)–(3) 1024
        (4) 1025
        (5) 1026
        (6) 1025
        (7)–(9) 1026
        (10)–(13) 1025
        (16) 1025
        (18) 1025–1027
        (19)–(22) 1027
    10.27 (1)–(5) 1037
Appendix 1 Form M3 .... 414, 767
            M4 767

PARA

Family Proceedings Rules 1991,
    SI 1991/1247—*continued*
Appendix 1 Form M5, M5A 768, 798
            M6, M6A 408, 768,
                                776, 798
        M7 para (a)–(e) 361
        M8 866
        M9, M9A 878
        M10, M10A 878
        M16 .... 945, 949
        M19 886
        M20 .... 706, 889
        M21, M22 706
        M23 955
        M23A 706, 888
        M24 1019
        M25 938
        M26 941
        M29, M29A 1001,
                                1004
        M33 667
        C8 1009
        FL401 .... 974, 977
        FL402 977
        FL402A 980
        FL403 .... 309, 722
        FL403A 985
        FL404A 978
        FL404B 984
        FL405 .... 975, 978
        FL406 .... 978, 988
        FL406A 989
        FL407, FL407A 991
        FL408 991
        FL409 990–991
        FL410, FL411 ... 993, 995
        FL411A 980
        FL412 993
        FL415 ...... 974, 977, 980
        FL416 .... 974, 977
        FL417 .... 964, 973
        FL430 724
        FL431 981
    1A Form A ... 493, 916, 924, 926–
                                927
            B 873, 926
            E ... 918, 923, 925, 927–
                                928
            F 919
            G 925, 928
            H 1039
            I 461
            P 928
            P1, P2 934
    2 para 1 756
            2 759
            3 762
            4 (a) 764
            (b), (c) 765
    4 para 2 (1) 533
            (2) 530, 533
            (3) 530

PARA

Family Proceedings Rules 1991,
SI 1991/1247—*continued*
Appendix 4 para 2 (4) 530, 533
3 (1) 941
(2) 938, 941
(3) 938
(a)–(c) 941
(4) 938, 941
(5) 938
4 (1) 706
(2) 890
(3) 706
(4)–(7) 890
5 (1)(a) 886
(b) 535
(2)–(4) 535, 886
6 (1), (2) 889
(4)–(6) 889
7 (1)(a) 891
(b) 708
(c) 956
(d) 976
(2) 942
(3) ... 708, 891, 956, 976
(4) 588, 708–709,
891–892, 942, 956–
957, 976
(5) 708, 891, 942,
956, 976
(6) ... 891, 942, 956, 976
8 (1)(a) 891
(b) 708
(c) 956
(2)–(4) 708, 891, 956
9 (1)(a) 892
(b) 709
(c) 957
(2) 588
(4) 942
(5) 709, 892, 957
(6), (7) 588, 709, 892,
942, 957
(8)–(10) ... 709, 892, 957
(11) 588, 709, 957
Foreign Marriage Order 1970,
SI 1970/1539
art 3 (1), (2) 122
4 (1) 120
(2) 124
5 125
6 (1) 126

I

Immigration (Procedure for Formation of
Civil Partnerships) Regulation 2005,
SI 2005/2917
reg 3, 4 178
5 (2) 179
Sch 1 178
Immigration (Procedure for Marriage)
Regulations 2005, SI 2005/15
reg 3 177

PARA

Immigration (Procedure for Marriage)
Regulations 2005, SI 2005/15—*continued*
reg 5 (1) 179
7, 8 176
Sch 1 177
2 .... 176, 179

M

Magistrates' Courts (Guardianship of
Minors) Rules 1974, SI 1974/706
r 5 (1), (2) 48
Magistrates' Courts (Increase of Lump
Sums) Order 1988, SI 1988/1069
art 2 553
Magistrates' Courts (Maintenance
Orders Act 1958) Rules 1959,
SI 1959/3
r 1 948
Marriage (Authorised Persons)
Regulations 1952, SI 1952/1869
reg 4 (1), (2) 107
5 107
6, 7 108
8 (1)–(5) 109
9 (1), (2) 98
11–26 108
Schedule 107
Marriages and Civil Partnerships
(Approved Premises)
Regulations 2005, SI 2005/3168
reg 3 191
4 192
5 193
6 194
7 195
8 196
9 197
10 198
11 199
12 200
13 201
15 202
Sch 1 193
2 194
Matrimonial and Family Proceedings
Act 1984 (Commencement No 2)
Order 1985, SI 1985/1316 530

R

Registration of Births, Deaths and
Marriages (Fees) Order 2002,
SI 2002/3076
art 2 98
3 116
Schedule 86, 94, 98, 103, 108, 116
Registration of Civil Partnerships (Fees)
(No 2) Order 2005, SI 2005/3167
Schedule 152
Registration of Civil Partnerships (Fees)
Order 2005, SI 2005/1996
Schedule 133

PARA

Registration of Marriages
  Regulations 1986, SI 1986/1442
  reg 6 (2), (3) 93
    6A (1)–(5) 94
  Sch 1 Form 1 87
        1A–1C 87
        6 172
        7 173
        8 93
        8A 94
        9 97
        12 99
        13 103
Registration of Marriages (Welsh
  Language) Regulations 1999,
  SI 1999/1621
  reg 7 (1) 94, 103, 108
  Sch 1 Form 1 87
        1A–1C 87
        4 173
        5 93
        6 97
        8 99
        8A 94

PARA

Registration of Marriages (Welsh Language)
  Regulations 1999,
  SI 1999/1621—*continued*
  Sch 1 Form 9 .... 103, 108
Reporting of Suspicious Civil
  Partnerships Regulations 2005,
  SI 2005/3174 11
Reporting of Suspicious Marriages and
  Registration of Marriages
  (Miscellaneous Amendments)
  Regulations 2000, SI 2000/3164 11
  reg 4 (3) 94

V

Visiting Forces and International
  Headquarters (Application of Law)
  Order 1999, SI 1999/1736
  art 12 (2) 129
  Sch 6 129

W

Welfare Reform and Pensions Act 1999
  (Commencement No 5)
  Order 2000, SI 2000/1116
  art 2 (e) 524

TABLE OF PRACTICE DIRECTIONS

PARA

Practice Direction [1945] WN 234 793
Practice Direction (Justices' clerks) [1954] 1 All ER 230, [1954] 1 WLR 213 897
Practice Direction (divorce: decree absolute application to expedite: practice)
    [1964] 3 All ER 775, [1964] 1 WLR 1473 864
Practice Direction [1965] 1 All ER 905, [1965] 1 WLR 600 512
Practice Direction (divorce: ancillary relief: application for monetary provision)
    [1966] 2 All ER 638, [1966] 1 WLR 1007 800
Practice Direction (divorce: expert evidence) [1967] 3 All ER 208, [1967] 1 WLR 1240 827
Practice Direction (divorce: form of petition) [1968] 2 All ER 88, [1968] 1 WLR 782 756
Practice Direction (divorce: adultery: proof) [1969] 2 All ER 873, [1969] 1 WLR 1192 358–
    359, 763
Practice Direction (husband and wife: property practice) [1971] 1 All ER 895,
    [1971] 1 WLR 260 904
Practice Direction (nullity: medical inspection: defended cases) [1971] 2 All ER 1310,
    [1971] 1 WLR 1193 803
Practice Direction (leave to issue execution) [1972] 1 All ER 576, sub nom Practice
    Direction (possession order: issue of execution) [1972] 1 WLR 240 947
Practice Direction [1972] 2 All ER 623, sub nom Practice Direction (petition: personal
    service) [1972] 1 WLR 775 776
Practice Direction (order approving terms of agreement) [1972] 3 All ER 704, sub nom
    Practice Direction (decrees and orders: agreed terms) [1972] 1 WLR 1313 860
Practice Direction (divorce petition: omission of petitioner's address) [1975] 2 All ER 384,
    [1975] 1 WLR 787 756
Practice Direction [1975] 3 All ER 432, [1975] 1 WLR 1325 777–778
Practice Direction (divorce: solicitor acting for petitioner) [1977] 1 All ER 844,
    [1977] 1 WLR 319 768
Practice Direction (divorce: decree absolute application to expedite) [1977] 2 All ER 714,
    [1977] 1 WLR 759 864
Practice Direction [1979] 1 All ER 112, [1979] 1 WLR 2 814
Practice Direction (divorce: petitioner's address for service) [1979] 2 All ER 45,
    [1979] 1 WLR 533 765
Practice Direction (minor: registration of maintenance orders) [1980] 1 All ER 1007, sub
    nom Practice Direction (maintenance: registration of orders) [1980] 1 WLR 354 666
Practice Direction (disclosure of addresses by government departments) [1989] 1 All ER
    765, sub nom Practice Direction (disclosure of address: 1989) [1989] 1 WLR 219 777
Practice Direction (family business: transfer between High Court and county court)
    [1992] 3 All ER 151, sub nom Practice Direction (Family Division: distribution of
    business) [1992] 1 WLR 586 .... 737, 744, 953
Practice Direction (Mareva Injunctions and Anton Piller Orders: forms) [1997] 1 All ER
    288, [1996] 1 WLR 1552 661
Practice Direction (domestic violence: injunction: arrest) [1998] 2 All ER 927,
    [1998] 1 WLR 476 988
Practice Direction (family proceedings: allocation to judiciary directions 1999) [1999] 2 FLR
    799 749
Practice Direction (attached powers of arrest) [2000] 1 All ER 544, sub nom Practice
    Direction (arresting officer: attending) [2000] 1 WLR 83 990
Practice Direction (family proceedings: court bundles) [2000] 2 All ER 287, [2000] 1 WLR
    737, [2000] 1 FLR 536 931
Practice Direction (family proceeding: ancillary relief) [2000] 3 All ER 379, sub nom
    Practice Direction (ancillary relief: procedure) [2000] 1 WLR 1480 .... 903, 905–915, 928–
    929, 932
Practice Direction [2000] 4 All ER 288, [2000] 2 FLR 429, sub nom Practice Direction
    (family proceedings: human rights) [2000] 1 WLR 1782 744
Practice Direction (family proceedings: committal) [2001] 2 All ER 704, [2001] 1 WLR
    1253 .... 945, 988
Practice Direction (Magistrates' courts: contempt) (2001) Times, 11 June 998

PARA
Practice Direction (family proceedings: allocation to judiciary: amendment: directions 2002)
[2002] 2 FLR 692 749
Practice Direction (ancillary relief: costs) [2006] 1 WLR 634 1037
Practice Direction (family proceedings: court bundles) [2006] 1 WLR 2843 1016
Practice Direction (family proceedings: allocation to judiciary: amendment No 1: directions
2006) [2006] 1 FLR 1147 749
Practice Direction (family proceedings: allocation to judiciary: amendment No 2: directions
2006) [2006] 1 FLR 1150 749
Practice Direction (family proceedings: allocation to judiciary: amendment: directions 2007)
[2007] 1 FLR 459 749
Practice Direction (family proceedings: allocation to judiciary: amendment: directions 2008)
[2008] All ER (D) 135 (Oct) 749
Practice Note (No 3) (matrimonial causes rules) [1957] 1 All ER 860, sub note Practice
Direction (ancillary relief) [1957] 1 WLR 555 769
Practice Note [1978] 2 All ER 919, sub nom Practice Direction [1978] 1 WLR 925 .... 290, 719
Practice Note (ancillary relief orders: conveyancing for mentally incapacitated adults)
[2006] 1 FLR 480 498

TABLE OF EUROPEAN COMMUNITY LEGISLATION

PARA

EC Council Regulation 2201/2003 (OJ L338, 23.12.2003, p 1)
art 1.1 (a) 751
1.2 751
2.3 751
3.1 751
4 753
5, 6 751
7.1, 7.2 751
16 (1) 839
17 754
18.1–18.3 754
19 (1) 839
(3) 839
20.1 751
66 (a), (b) 751

TABLE OF CASES

PARA

A

A (child of the family), Re [1998] 1 FCR 458, [1998] 1 FLR 347, [1998] Fam Law
14, CA 477
A (children) (contact: expert evidence), Re [2001] 1 FLR 723, [2001] 16 LS Gaz R 32,
[2001] NLJR 224, Times, 27 February 827
A v A (sued by B) (1887) 19 LR Ir 403, CA 341
A v A [1995] 2 FCR 137, [1995] 1 FLR 345, [1995] Fam Law 242 .... 601, 621
A v A (costs: appeal) [1996] 1 FCR 186, [1996] 1 FLR 14, [1996] Fam Law 79 601
A v A (financial provision) [1998] 3 FCR 421, [1998] 2 FLR 180, [1998] Fam Law
393 .... 483, 606, 618
A v A (forum conveniens) [1999] 3 FCR 376, [1999] 1 FLR 1, [1998] Fam Law 735 841
A v A (Maintenance pending suit: provision for legal costs) [2001] 1 WLR 605,
[2001] 1 FCR 226, [2001] Fam Law 96, [2000] All ER (D) 1627 456
A v A. See NA v MA
A v A [2007] EWHC 99 (Fam), [2007] 2 FLR 467, [2007] Fam Law 791 451
A v B (1868) LR 1 P & D 559, 17 WR 14, sub nom Anon 32 JP 743, sub nom P v S 37
LJP & M 80 .... 322, 345
A v B (financial relief: agreements) [2005] EWHC 314 (Fam), [2005] 2 FLR 730, sub
nom A v B (ancillary relief: property division) (2005) Times, 23 March, [2005] All
ER (D) 212 (May) 596
A (falsely called B) v B. See N-r (falsely called M-e) v M-e
A v J (nullity proceedings) [1989] 1 FLR 110, [1989] Fam Law 63 342
A v M (1884) 10 PD 178, 54 LJP 31, 33 WR 232 514
A v M (otherwise A). See Aldridge v Aldridge (otherwise Morton)
A and M Records Inc v Darakdjian [1975] 3 All ER 983, [1975] 1 WLR 1610, 119 Sol
Jo 644 636
A-M v A-M (divorce: jurisdiction: validity of marriage) [2001] 2 FLR 6,
[2001] Fam Law 495, [2001] All ER (D) 288 (Feb) 7, 326
Abbey National plc v Moss [1994] 2 FCR 587, [1994] 1 FLR 307, [1994] Fam Law
255, 26 HLR 249, CA 639
Abdy, Re, Rabbeth v Donaldson [1895] 1 Ch 455, 64 LJ Ch 465, 12 R 163, 43 WR
323, 39 Sol Jo 283, 72 LT 178, 11 TLR 245, CA 447
Abdy v Abdy (1896) 12 TLR 524 847
Abecasis v Brandon [1947] LJR 325, sub nom Abercasis v Brandon 176 LT 60, CA 643
Abell v Abell (1965) 109 Sol Jo 873n 833
Abercrombie v Abercrombie [1943] 2 All ER 465, 41 LGR 274, 107 JP 200, 87 Sol Jo
424, 169 LT 340, DC 378, 400, 403–405
Abraham v Abraham and Harding (1919) 63 Sol Jo 411, 120 LT 672, 35 TLR 371 876
Abson v Abson [1952] P 55, [1952] 1 All ER 370, 116 JP 92, 96 Sol Jo 134, [1952] 1
TLR 379 .... 349, 566
Adam's Policy Trusts, Re (1883) 23 Ch D 525, 52 LJ Ch 642, 31 WR 810, 48 LT 727 275
Adams v Adams [1941] 1 KB 536, [1941] 1 All ER 334, 110 LJKB 241, 85 Sol Jo 153,
165 LT 15, 57 TLR 329, CA 442, 514
Adams v Adams (A-G intervening) [1971] P 188, [1970] 3 All ER 572, [1970] 3 WLR
934, 114 Sol Jo 605 852
Adamson v Adamson (1907) 23 TLR 434 .... 372, 430, 699
Addison v Gandassequi (1812) 4 Taunt 574 259
Aggas v Aggas [1971] 2 All ER 1497, [1971] 1 WLR 1409, 135 JP 484, 115 Sol Jo
346 896
Aggs v Nicholson (1856) 1 H & N 165, 25 LJ Ex 348, 4 WR 776, 28 LTOS 66 257
Aguilar v Aguilar, Lousada (1820) 5 Madd 414, 56 ER 953 239
Ainslie v Ainslie (1927) 39 CLR 381, [1927] ALR 301, 27 SRNSW 524, NSW SC 366
Alderman v Alderman and Dunn [1958] 1 All ER 391, [1958] 1 WLR 177, 102 Sol Jo
126 354
Aldridge v Aldridge (otherwise Morton) (1888) 13 PD 210, 37 WR 240, 59 LT 896, sub
nom A v M (otherwise A) 58 LJP 8 .... 427, 431, 444

PARA

Aldridge v Aldridge and Ashton (1964) 108 Sol Jo 898 771
Alexander v Alexander and Amos (1860) Sea & Sm 153, 29 LJPM & A 56, 6 Jur NS
  56, 2 Sw & Tr 95, 8 WR 452 353
Alexander v Rayson [1936] 1 KB 169, [1935] All ER Rep 185, 105 LJKB 148, 80 Sol Jo
  15, 154 LT 205, 52 TLR 131, CA 851
Alexandre v Alexandre (1870) LR 2 P & D 164, 39 LJP & M 84, 18 WR 1087, 23 LT
  268 877
Alhadeff v Alhadeff [1951] WN 367, 95 Sol Jo 547, DC 739
Ali Ebrahim v Ali Ebrahim (Queen's Proctor intervening). See Ebrahim v Ali (otherwise
  Ebrahim) (Queen's Proctor intervening)
Allan, Re, Allan v Midland Bank Executor and Trustee Co Ltd [1954] Ch 295,
  [1954] 1 All ER 646, [1954] 2 WLR 512, 98 Sol Jo 193, CA 375
Allardyce v Allardyce 1954 SC 419 321
Allen v Allen [1951] 1 All ER 724, 115 JP 229, CA 393
Allen v Allen (1 February 1951, unreported), CA 352
Allen v Allen [1974] 3 All ER 385, [1974] 1 WLR 1171, 4 Fam Law 194, 118 Sol Jo
  613, CA 654
Allen v Allen [1986] 2 FLR 265, [1986] Fam Law 268, CA 602
Allen v Allen and Bell [1894] P 248, [1891–94] All ER Rep 540, 63 LJP 120, 6 R 597,
  42 WR 459, 38 Sol Jo 456, 70 LT 783, 10 TLR 456, CA 353
Allen v Papworth (1731) 1 Ves Sen 163 236
Allen v Snyder [1977] 2 NSWLR 685, NSW CA 279
Alli v Alli [1965] 3 All ER 480, 130 JP 6, 109 Sol Jo 629 .... 213, 370
Allied Arab Bank Ltd v Hajjar [1988] QB 787, [1987] 3 All ER 739, [1988] 2 WLR
  942, 132 Sol Jo 659, [1988] 15 LS Gaz R 37 661
Allied Irish Bank v Ashford Hotels Ltd [1997] 3 All ER 309, [1998] BCC 440, CA 648
Allison v Allison [1927] P 308, [1927] All ER Rep 671, 96 LJP 181, 71 Sol Jo 682, 137
  LT 823, 43 TLR 823 .... 472, 547
Allsopp's Marriage Settlement Trusts, Re, Public Trustee v Cherry [1959] Ch 81,
  [1958] 2 All ER 393, [1958] 3 WLR 78, 102 Sol Jo 489 513
Alonso v Alonso (1974) 4 Fam Law 164, 118 Sol Jo 660, CA 316
Alton v Alton (1920) 64 Sol Jo 308 776
Amadasun v Amadasun [1992] 1 FLR 585, [1992] Fam Law 235 756
Ames' Settlement, Re, Dinwiddy v Ames [1946] Ch 217, [1946] 1 All ER 689, 115 LJ
  Ch 344, 90 Sol Jo 188, 175 LT 222, 62 TLR 300 514
Amey v Amey [1992] 1 FCR 289, [1992] 2 FLR 89 .... 625–626, 686
Anderson v Anderson (1972) 117 Sol Jo 33 350
Anderson v Dawson (1808) 15 Ves 532 232
Anderson v Sanderson (1817) 2 Stark 204, Holt NP 591 .... 261, 270
Andrewes v Uthwatt (1886) 2 TLR 895 6
Andrews v Andrews [1974] 3 All ER 643 .... 360, 782
Andrews v Ross (1888) 14 PD 15, 58 LJP 14, 37 WR 239, 59 LT 900 .... 321, 344
Angel v Angel [1946] 2 All ER 635, 44 LGR 408, 111 JP 14, 91 Sol Jo 13, 176 LT 90,
  62 TLR 755, DC 368
Angier v Angier (1718) 2 Eq Cas Abr 150, Gilb Ch 152, Prec Ch 496, 25 ER 107 447
Anglesey (Marquis), Re, Countess De Galve v Gardner [1903] 2 Ch 727, 72 LJ Ch 782,
  52 WR 124, 89 LT 584, 19 TLR 719 648
Annesley v Annesley (1913) 47 ILT 38 845
Anon (1843). See Reibey, ex p
Anon (validity of marriage) (1953) Times, 17 October 416
Anon (1853). See N-r (falsely called M-e) v M-e
Anon (1857) Dea & Sw 295, 5 WR 750, 164 ER 581 .... 321, 795
Anon (1868). See A v B
Ansah v Ansah [1977] Fam 138, [1977] 2 All ER 638, [1977] 2 WLR 760, 121 Sol Jo
  118, CA 290, 719
Ansdell v Ansdell (1880) 5 PD 138, 49 LJP 57, 28 WR 832 .... 848, 863
Anstis, Re, Chetwynd v Morgan (1886) 31 Ch D 596, 34 WR 483, 54 LT 742, 2 TLR
  335, CA 234
Anstis, Re, Morgan v Chetwynd (1886) 31 Ch D 596, 34 WR 483, 54 LT 742, 2 TLR
  335, CA 234
Anthony v Anthony (1919) 35 TLR 559 833
Appleton v Appleton [1965] 1 All ER 44, [1965] 1 WLR 25, 108 Sol Jo 919, CA 283

PARA

Appleyard v Appleyard and Smith (1875) LR 3 P & D 257 777
Apt v Apt [1947] P 127, [1947] 1 All ER 620, 176 LT 359, 63 TLR 223; on appeal
    [1948] P 83, [1947] 2 All ER 677, [1948] LJR 539, 177 LT 620, 63 TLR
    618, CA 852
Apted and Bliss [1930] P 246, [1930] All ER Rep Ext 845, 99 LJP 73, 74 Sol Jo
    338, 143 LT 353, 46 TLR 456 852
Arab Monetary Fund v Hashim [1989] 3 All ER 466, [1989] 1 WLR 565, 133 Sol Jo
    749, [1989] 26 LS Gaz R 35 661
Araghchinchi v Araghchinchi [1997] 3 FCR 567, [1997] 2 FLR 142, CA 662
Archard v Coulsting (1843) 6 Man & G 75, 134 ER 815, sub nom Orchard v Coulsting
    6 Scott NR 843, 1 LTOS 230 445
Archer v Archer [1999] 2 FCR 158, [1999] 1 FLR 327, [1998] 46 LS Gaz R 34, CA 411
Arding v Arding [1954] 2 All ER 671n, [1954] 1 WLR 944, 98 Sol Jo 439 .... 369, 849
Argar v Holdsworth (1758) 2 Lee 515, 161 ER 424 .... 57, 81
Argyll (Duchess of) v Duke of Argyll [1967] Ch 302, [1965] 1 All ER 611,
    [1965] 2 WLR 790 223
Arkwright v Arkwright (1895) 73 LT 287 515
Armstrong v Armstrong (1974) 4 Fam Law 156, 118 Sol Jo 579, CA 621
Arnold v Earle (1758) 2 Lee 529 41
Ash v Ash [1972] Fam 135, [1972] 1 All ER 582, [1972] 2 WLR 347, 115 Sol Jo 911 ... 347, 360
Ashley v Ashley [1968] P 582, [1965] 3 All ER 554, [1965] 3 WLR 1194, 130 JP 1, 110
    Sol Jo 13 602
Ashley v Blackman [1988] Fam 85, [1988] 3 WLR 222, [1988] FCR 699, [1988] 2 FLR
    278, [1988] Fam Law 430, 132 Sol Jo 897, [1988] 38 LS Gaz R 52 .... 602, 617
Astro Exito Navegacion SA v Southland Enterprise Co Ltd (No 2) (Chase Manhattan
    Bank NA intervening), The Messiniaki Tolmi [1983] 2 AC 787, [1983] 2 All ER
    725, [1983] 3 WLR 130, [1983] Com LR 217, 127 Sol Jo 461,
    [1983] LS Gaz R 3083, HL 641
Astrope v Astrope (1859) 29 LJP & M 27 386
Atkins v Curwood (1837) 7 C & P 756 .... 264, 269, 273
Atkinson v Atkinson (1825) 2 Add 468 833
Atkinson v Atkinson [1988] Fam 93, [1987] 3 All ER 849, [1988] 2 WLR 204,
    [1988] FCR 356, [1988] 2 FLR 353, [1988] Fam Law 392, 132 Sol Jo 158,
    [1988] 8 LS Gaz R 35, [1987] NLJ Rep 847, CA 463, 593, 621
Atkinson v Atkinson (No 2) [1996] 1 FLR 51, CA 593
Atkinson v Castan (1991) Times, 17 April, [1991] CA Transcript 332, CA 625
Atkinson v Littlewood (1874) LR 18 Eq 595, [1874–80] All ER Rep 203, 31 LT 225 ..... 436, 440
Atkyns v Pearce (1857) 2 CBNS 763, 26 LJCP 252, 3 Jur NS 1180, 140 ER 616, 29
    LTOS 212 262
Attar v Attar (No 2) [1985] FLR 653, [1985] Fam Law 252 .... 614, 616, 618
A-G v Observer Ltd [1990] 1 AC 109, [1988] 3 WLR 776, [1988] LRC (Const) 938,
    [1988] NLJR 296, sub nom A-G v Guardian Newspapers Ltd (No 2)
    [1988] 3 All ER 545, HL 223
A-G v Parnther (1792) 3 Bro CC 441 45
A-G v Times Newspapers Ltd [1990] 1 AC 109, [1988] 3 WLR 776, [1988] LRC
    (Const) 938, [1988] NLJR 296, sub nom A-G v Guardian Newspapers Ltd (No 2)
    [1988] 3 All ER 545, HL 223
A-G for Alberta v Cook [1926] AC 444, [1926] All ER Rep 525, 95 LJPC 102, 134 LT
    717, 42 TLR 317, PC 214
Attwood (otherwise Pomeroy) v Attwood [1903] P 7, 71 LJP 129, 87 LT 750, 18 TLR
    833 514
Austin v Austin (1871) 41 LJP & M 8, 20 WR 128, 25 LT 856 769
Austin v Austin (1961) 105 Sol Jo 950 851
Austin-Fell v Austin-Fell [1990] Fam 172, [1990] 2 All ER 455, [1990] 3 WLR 33,
    [1990] FCR 743, [1989] 2 FLR 497, [1989] Fam Law 437, [1989] NLJR 1113 638
Aylesford (Countess) v Great Western Rly Co [1892] 2 QB 626, 57 JP 70, 41 WR 42,
    36 Sol Jo 714, 8 TLR 786, DC 210

B

B v B (1891) 27 LR Ir 587 34
B (otherwise H) v B [1901] P 39, 70 LJP 4 .... 338, 340
B v B (1935). See DB v WB

PARA

B v B [1955] P 42, [1954] 3 WLR 237, 98 Sol Jo 474, sub nom D v D [1954] 2 All ER
   598 .... 335, 340
B (otherwise S) v B [1958] 2 All ER 76, [1958] 1 WLR 619, 102 Sol Jo 421 336
B (V) v B (J) [1966] 3 All ER 768, sub nom Boyd v Boyd [1967] 1 WLR 122, 110 Sol
   Jo 771, CA 702
B (MAL) v B (NE) [1968] 1 WLR 1109, 112 Sol Jo 520 699
B (GC) v B (BA) [1970] 1 All ER 913, 113 Sol Jo 468, sub nom Brister v Brister
   [1970] 1 WLR 664 430
B v B (1975) 119 Sol Jo 610, (1975) Times, 15 May, CA 565
B v B [1978] Fam 181, [1979] 1 All ER 801, [1978] 3 WLR 624, 122 Sol Jo 643 800
B v B (financial provision) (1982) 3 FLR 298, 12 Fam Law 92, CA 450, 464, 498, 549, 617
B v B [1988] 2 FLR 490, [1988] Fam Law 435 621
B v B (financial provision) [1989] FCR 146, [1989] 1 FLR 119, [1989] Fam Law 105,
   [1989] NLJR 186 .... 609, 613
B v B [1990] FCR 105, [1990] 1 FLR 20, [1989] Fam Law 432 .... 483, 604
B v B [1994] 1 FCR 885, [1994] 1 FLR 219 593
B v B (consent order: variation) (1995). See SB v PB (financial provision)
B v B (injunction: restraint on leaving jurisdiction) [1997] 3 All ER 258, [1998] 1 WLR
   329, [1997] 2 FLR 148 663
B v B (financial provision for child) [1998] 1 FCR 49, [1998] 1 FLR 373,
   [1998] Fam Law 131, CA 493
B v B (occupation order) [1999] 2 FCR 251, [1999] 1 FLR 715, [1999] Fam Law 208,
   31 HLR 1059, CA 289
B v B (financial provision: welfare of the child and conduct) [2002] 1 FLR 555 612
B v B [2007] EWHC 2472 (Fam), [2008] 1 FLR 1279, [2007] Fam Law 1125, [2007]
   All ER (D) 404 (Oct) 568
B v B [2008] EWCA Civ 284, [2008] 2 FLR 1627, [2008] All ER (D) 282 (Mar) 607, 614
B v B (No 2) [1995] 2 FCR 827, [1995] 1 FLR 913, [1995] Fam Law 408 931
B v C [1995] 2 FCR 678, [1995] 1 FLR 467, [1995] Fam Law 243 679
B v L (falsely called B) (1869) LR 1 P & D 639, 38 LJP & M 35, 20 LT 280 810
B v United Kingdom (Application 36536/02) [2005] 3 FCR 353, [2006] 1 FLR 35,
   (2005) Times, 5 October, 19 BHRC 430, [2005] All ER (D) 63 (Sep), ECtHR 58
B-J (a child) (non-molestation order: power of arrest), Re [2001] Fam 415,
   [2001] 1 All ER 235, [2001] 2 WLR 1660, [2000] 2 FCR 599, [2000] 2 FLR 443,
   [2000] Fam Law 807, [2000] All ER (D) 874, CA 716
B-n v B-n (1854) 1 Ecc & Ad 248, 23 LTOS 99, 164 ER 144, sub nom B-n v M-e
   (falsely calling herself B-n) 2 Rob Eccl 580, PC 321, 339
Babanaft International Co SA v Bassatne [1990] Ch 13, [1989] 1 All ER 433,
   [1989] 2 WLR 232, [1988] 2 Lloyd's Rep 435, 133 Sol Jo 46,
   [1989] 4 LS Gaz R 43, [1988] NLJR 203, CA 661
Backhouse v Backhouse [1978] 1 All ER 1158, [1978] 1 WLR 243, 121 Sol Jo 710 430
Bacon v Bacon [1947] P 151, [1947] 2 All ER 327, [1948] LJR 530, 63 TLR 509 511
Bacon v Bacon and Bacon (1859) Sea & Sm 68, 29 LJPM & A 61, 2 Sw & Tr 53, 164
   ER 911 849
Bagnall v Carlton (1877) 6 Ch D 130, 47 LJ Ch 51, 26 WR 71, 36 LT 730 636
Bagot v Bagot (1890) 62 LT 612 760
Bagot v Oughton (1717) 1 P Wms 347, 24 ER 420 .... 239, 242
Bainbridge v Bainbridge [1962] 2 All ER 267, [1962] 1 WLR 495, 106 Sol Jo 246 755
Baindail (otherwise Lawson) v Baindail [1946] P 122, [1946] 1 All ER 342, 115 LJP 65,
   90 Sol Jo 151, 174 LT 320, 62 TLR 263, CA 33
Baker v Baker (1863) 32 LJPM & A 145, 3 Sw & Tr 213, 11 WR 502, 164 ER 1255, 9
   LT 117 831
Baker v Baker [1952] 2 All ER 248, 116 JP 447, [1952] 2 TLR 228, CA 368
Baker v Baker [1954] P 33, [1953] 2 All ER 1199, [1953] 3 WLR 857, 117 JP 556, 97
   Sol Jo 798, DC 393
Baker v Baker [1996] 1 FCR 567, [1995] 2 FLR 829, [1996] Fam Law 80, CA 595, 599
Baker v Baker (No 2) [1997] 2 FCR 249, [1997] 1 FLR 148, [1997] Fam Law
   163, CA 567
Baker v Pritchett (formerly Baker) and Pritchett (1963) 108 Sol Jo 37 .... 863, 879
Balcombe v Balcombe [1908] P 176, 77 LJP 81, 99 LT 308 .... 368, 374, 439, 699
Baldwin v Baldwin (1919) Times, 30 and 31 July 332

PARA

Balfour v Balfour [1919] 2 KB 571, [1918–19] All ER Rep 860, 88 LJKB 1054, 63 Sol
    Jo 661, 121 LT 346, 35 TLR 609, CA 206
Balfour v Carpenter (falsely called Balfour) (1810) 1 Phillim 204, 161 ER 961 76
Balfour v Carpenter (falsely called Balfour) (1811) 1 Phillim 221, 161 ER 966 49
Balloqui v Balloqui [1963] 3 All ER 989, [1964] 1 WLR 82, 107 Sol Jo 889, CA 879, 883
Balraj v Balraj (1980) 11 Fam Law 110, CA 411
Banik v Banik [1973] 3 All ER 45, [1973] 1 WLR 860, 117 Sol Jo 507, CA 411
Banik v Banik (No 2) (1973) 117 Sol Jo 874 411
Banister and Wife v Thompson [1908] P 362, 24 TLR 841, sub nom R v Dibdin,
    ex p Thompson 101 LT 106 81
Bank of Baroda v Dhillon [1998] 1 FCR 489, [1998] 1 FLR 524, [1998] Fam Law 138,
    30 HLR 845, CA 639
Bank of Montreal v Stuart [1911] AC 120, 80 LJPC 75, 103 LT 641, 27 TLR 117, PC 249
Banks v Banks [1952] P 249, [1952] 2 All ER 232, 96 Sol Jo 428, CA 787, 792
Banks v Banks [1999] 1 FLR 726, [1999] Fam Law 209, Cty Ct 290
Bannister v Bannister and Davis (1860) Sea & Sm 143, 29 LJPM & A 53 769
Banyard v Banyard [1984] FLR 643, CA 476
Barber v Barber [1993] 1 FCR 65, [1993] 1 FLR 476, [1992] Fam Law 436, CA 617
Barber v Pigden [1937] 1 KB 664, [1937] 1 All ER 115, 106 LJKB 858, 81 Sol Jo 78,
    156 LT 245, 53 TLR 246, CA 204
Barclays Bank plc v Hendricks [1996] 1 FCR 710, [1996] 1 FLR 258, [1996] Fam Law
    148, [1996] BPIR 17 ....: 639
Barder v Caluori [1988] AC 20, [1987] 2 All ER 440, [1987] 2 WLR 1350,
    [1987] 2 FLR 480, [1988] Fam Law 18, 131 Sol Jo 776, [1987] LS Gaz R 2046,
    [1987] NLJ Rep 497, HL 684–685, 861
Barefoot v Clarke [1949] 2 KB 97, [1949] 1 All ER 1039, 93 Sol Jo 372, 65 TLR
    325, CA 643
Barker v Barker [1950] 1 All ER 812, 94 Sol Jo 285, CA 400
Barker v Barker [1952] P 184, [1952] 1 All ER 1128, 96 Sol Jo 358, [1952] 1 TLR
    1479, CA 471–472, 494, 547
Barlow v Bateman (1730) 3 P Wms 64, [1558–1774] All ER Rep 310, 24 ER 971; revsd
    (1735) 2 Bro Parl Cas 272, [1558–1774] All ER Rep 310, 24 ER 971, 1 ER
    939, HL 69
Barnard v Barnard [1965] 1 All ER 1050n, [1965] 2 WLR 56n 400
Barnes v Barnes [1972] 3 All ER 872, [1972] 1 WLR 1381, 116 Sol Jo 801, CA 602
Barnes v Barnes and Beaumont (1868) LR 1 P & D 572, 38 LJP & M 10, 17 WR 75,
    19 LT 526 738
Barnes v Barnes and Grimwade (1867) LR 1 P & D 505, 37 LJP & M 4, 16 WR 281,
    17 LT 268 875
Barnett v Barnett [1955] P 21, [1954] 3 All ER 689, [1955] 2 WLR 229, 99 Sol Jo 79 ... 368, 371,
    399
Barnett v Hassett [1982] 1 All ER 80, [1981] 1 WLR 1385, 125 Sol Jo 376 285
Barrett v Barrett [1948] P 277, 46 LGR 251, [1948] LJR 1174, 92 Sol Jo 283, CA 402
Barrett v Barrett [1988] FCR 707, [1988] 2 FLR 516, [1988] Fam Law 475, CA 592, 600
Barrett v Barrett and Vaughan (1913) 30 TLR 63 877
Barron v Barron [1963] 1 All ER 215, [1963] 1 WLR 57 370
Bartholomew v Bartholomew [1952] 2 All ER 1035, 117 JP 35, [1952] 2 TLR
    934, CA 393–394
Bartlett v Bartlett (1918) 34 TLR 518 .... 473, 504, 548
Bartlett v Bartlett (1963) 107 Sol Jo 912 755
Bartlett (falsely called Rice) v Rice (1894) 72 LT 122 43
Bartram v Bartram [1950] P 1, [1949] 2 All ER 270, 47 LGR 692, 113 JP 422, [1949]
    LJR 1679, 93 Sol Jo 552, 65 TLR 492, CA 403
Basham, Re [1987] 1 All ER 405, [1986] 1 WLR 1498, [1987] 2 FLR 264,
    [1987] Fam Law 310, 130 Sol Jo 986, [1987] LS Gaz R 112 278
Basing v Basing (1864) 33 LJPM & A 150, 10 Jur NS 806, 3 Sw & Tr 516, 164 ER
    1375, 10 LT 756 .... 372, 397, 400
Bastable v Bastable and Sanders [1968] 3 All ER 701, [1968] 1 WLR 1684, 112 Sol Jo
    542, CA 352
Batchelor v Batchelor [1983] 3 All ER 618, [1983] 1 WLR 1328, [1984] FLR 188,
    [1984] Fam Law 116, 127 Sol Jo 509 868

PARA

Bateman v Bateman (otherwise Harrison) (1898) 78 LT 472, [1895–9] All ER Rep Ext
1692 .... 344, 453
Bateman v Countess of Ross (1813) 1 Dow 235, 3 ER 684, HL 447, 449
Bater v Bater (otherwise Lowe) [1906] P 209, 75 LJP 60, 50 Sol Jo 389, 94 LT 835, 22
TLR 408, CA 880
Bater v Bater [1951] P 35, [1950] 2 All ER 458, 48 LGR 466, 114 JP 416, 94 Sol Jo
533, 66 (pt 2) TLR 589, CA 346, 349, 352
Bates v Bates (1964) Times, 8 December, CA 738, 879, 883
Batey, Re, ex p Neal (1880) 14 Ch D 579, 28 WR 875, 43 LT 264, CA 446
Baxter v Baxter [1947] 1 All ER 387, [1947] LJR 785, 91 Sol Jo 220, 176 LT 368, 63
TLR 169, CA; affd [1948] AC 274, [1947] 2 All ER 886, [1948] LJR 479, 92 Sol
Jo 25, 64 TLR 8, HL 335, 339, 342, 346, 852
Bayer AG v Winter [1986] 1 All ER 733, [1986] 1 WLR 497, [1986] FSR 323, 130 Sol
Jo 246, [1986] LS Gaz R 974, [1986] NLJ Rep 187, CA 663
Baynham v Baynham [1969] 1 All ER 305, [1968] 1 WLR 1890, 112 Sol Jo 839, 209
Estates Gazette 379, CA 451, 904
Baynon v Batley (1832) 8 Bing 256, 1 LJCP 75, 1 Moo & S 339, 131 ER 400 438
Bayspoole v Collins (1871) 6 Ch App 228, 35 JP 517, 40 LJ Ch 289, 19 WR 363, 25
LT 282 711
Beach v Beach [1995] 2 FCR 526, [1995] 2 FLR 160, [1995] Fam Law 545 621
Beal v Beal (Reade cited) [1953] 2 All ER 1228n, [1953] 1 WLR 1365, 97 Sol Jo 781 851
Beale v Bragg [1902] 1 IR 99 641
Beales v Beales [1972] Fam 210, [1972] 2 All ER 667, [1972] 2 WLR 972, 116 Sol Jo
196 408
Beamish v Beamish (1861) 9 HL Cas 274, 8 Jur NS 770, 11 ER 735, 5 LT 97 .... 80, 83
Beatty v Beatty [1924] 1 KB 807, [1924] All ER Rep 314, 93 LJKB 750, 131 LT
226, CA 465, 677
Beauchamp v Beauchamp and Watt (1904) 20 TLR 273, CA 511
Beauclerk v Beauclerk [1895] P 220, 64 LJP 102, 11 R 654, 43 WR 655, 11 TLR 379 699
Beck v Beck (1916) 50 ILT 135 249
Bedson v Bedson [1965] 2 QB 666, [1965] 3 All ER 307, [1965] 3 WLR 891, 109 Sol
Jo 776, 195 Estates Gazette 437, CA 225–226, 511
Beeken v Beeken [1948] P 302, 92 Sol Jo 498, CA 362, 364, 368, 386
Beer v Beer (1906) 54 WR 564, 94 LT 704, 22 TLR 338, 367 369
Beer v Beer (Neilson cited) [1948] P 10, [1947] 2 All ER 711, 46 LGR 47, 112 JP 50,
[1948] LJR 743, 92 Sol Jo 12, 63 TLR 606 369
Beevor v Beevor [1945] 2 All ER 200, 44 LGR 268, 109 JP 241, 89 Sol Jo 393 .... 379, 385
Beigan v Beigan [1956] P 313, [1956] 2 All ER 630, [1956] 3 WLR 281, 100 Sol Jo
470, CA 367–369, 399
Bekhor (A J) & Co Ltd v Bilton [1981] QB 923, [1981] 2 All ER 565, [1981] 2 WLR
601, [1981] 1 Lloyd's Rep 491, [1981] Com LR 50, 125 Sol Jo 203, CA 661
Bell v Drummond (1791) Peake 45 69
Bell v Graham (1859) 24 JP 20, 13 Moo PCC 242, 8 WR 98, 1 LT 221 .... 42, 344
Bell's Estate, Re (1882) 11 LR Ir 512 711
Bellinger v Bellinger [2000] 3 FCR 733, [2001] 1 FLR 389, [2001] Fam Law 107, 58
BMLR 52, [2000] All ER (D) 1639; affd [2001] EWCA Civ 1140, [2002] Fam 150,
[2002] 1 All ER 311, [2002] 2 WLR 411, [2001] 3 FCR 1, [2001] 2 FLR 1048,
[2001] Fam Law 807, 65 BMLR 1, [2001] 31 LS Gaz R 30, (2001) Times,
15 August, 145 Sol Jo LB 207, [2001] All ER (D) 214 (Jul); affd sub nom Bellinger
v Bellinger (Lord Chancellor intervening) [2003] UKHL 21, [2003] 2 AC 467,
[2003] 2 All ER 593, [2003] 2 WLR 1174, [2003] 2 FCR 1, [2003] 1 FLR 1043,
72 BMLR 147, [2003] NLJR 594, (2003) Times, 11 April, 147 Sol Jo LB 472, 14
BHRC 127, [2004] 1 LRC 42, [2003] All ER (D) 178 (Apr) 1, 326
Bennett v Bennett (by her guardian) [1939] P 274, [1939] 2 All ER 387, 108 LJP 119,
83 Sol Jo 441, 161 LT 96, 55 TLR 622 389
Bennett v Bennett [1952] 1 KB 249, [1952] 1 All ER 413, [1952] 1 TLR 400, CA 428, 698
Bennett v Bennett (1961) 105 Sol Jo 885, CA 10, 344, 416
Bennett v Bennett [1969] 1 All ER 539, [1969] 1 WLR 430, 113 Sol Jo 284 .... 332, 345
Bentley v Griffin (1814) 5 Taunt 356, 128 ER 727 .... 205, 258–259, 273
Benton v Benton [1958] P 12, [1957] 3 All ER 544, [1957] 3 WLR 801, 101 Sol Jo
884, CA 349
Benyon v Benyon and O'Callaghan (1876) 1 PD 447, 45 LJP 93, 24 WR 950 442

PARA

Benyon v Benyon and O'Callaghan (1890) 15 PD 29; on appeal (1890) 15 PD 54, 59
LJP 39, 62 LT 381, CA 515
Bergin v Bergin [1983] 1 All ER 905, [1983] 1 WLR 279, 4 FLR 344, 12 Fam Law 212,
147 JP 118, 126 Sol Jo 624 .... 360, 553
Berkovits v Grinberg (A-G intervening) [1995] Fam 142, [1995] 2 All ER 681,
[1995] 2 WLR 553, [1996] 1 FCR 587, [1995] 1 FLR 477, [1995] Fam Law 296 .... 24, 376,
530
Bernard v Bernard (Sutton cited) [1958] 3 All ER 475, [1958] 1 WLR 1275, 102 Sol Jo
937 734
Bernard v Josephs [1982] Ch 391, [1982] 3 All ER 162, [1982] 2 WLR 1052, 4 FLR
178, 126 Sol Jo 361, CA 278–279, 282, 284
Bernard v Minshull (1859) John 276, 28 LJ Ch 649, 5 Jur NS 931, 70 ER 427 .... 232, 236
Bernstein v O'Neill [1989] FCR 79, [1989] 2 FLR 1, [1989] Fam Law 275 .... 655, 679
Berry v Berry [1929] 2 KB 316, [1929] All ER Rep 281, 98 LJKB 748, 141 LT 461, 45
TLR 524 427
Berzins (otherwise Lilje) v Berzins [1956] CLY 2817 7
Besant v Wood (1879) 12 Ch D 605, [1874–80] All ER Rep 822, 23 Sol Jo 443, 40 LT
445 .... 346, 423, 434, 439, 443–444
Bessela v Stern (1877) 2 CPD 265, 42 JP 197, 46 LJCP 467, 25 WR 561, 37 LT
88, CA 16
Best v Best (1823) 1 Add 411 .... 349, 354, 794
Besterman, Re, Besterman v Grusin [1984] Ch 458, [1984] 2 All ER 656, [1984] 3 WLR
280, [1984] FLR 503, [1984] Fam Law 203, 128 Sol Jo 515, CA 606
Bethell, Re, Bethell v Hildyard (1888) 38 Ch D 220, [1886–90] All ER Rep 614, 57 LJ
Ch 487, 36 WR 503, 58 LT 674, 4 TLR 319 1
Bevan (falsely called M'Mahon) v M'Mahon (1861) 30 LJPM & A 61, 7 Jur NS 218, 2
Sw & Tr 230, 164 ER 983, 3 LT 820 76
Bevan v Bevan [1955] 2 QB 227, [1955] 2 All ER 206, [1955] 2 WLR 948, 99 Sol Jo
306 .... 423, 699
Bevan v Bevan [1955] 3 All ER 332, [1955] 1 WLR 1142, 119 JP 576, 99 Sol Jo 782 ... 369, 396,
399
Bevan v McMahon and Bevan (falsely called McMahon) (1859) 23 JP 472, 28 LJP & M
127, 5 Jur NS 686, 2 Sw & Tr 58, 8 WR 453, 164 ER 913, 2 LT 255 .... 322, 861
Bhatia v Immigration Appeal Tribunal. See R v Immigration Appeal Tribunal,
ex p Bhatia
Bidie, Re, Bidie v General Accident Fire and Life Assurance Corpn Ltd [1948] Ch 697,
[1948] 1 All ER 885, 46 LGR 313, 112 JP 257, [1948] LJR 1219, 92 Sol Jo 310,
64 TLR 309; on appeal [1949] Ch 121, [1948] 2 All ER 995, 47 LGR 465, 113 JP
22, [1949] LJR 386, 92 Sol Jo 705, 65 TLR 25, CA 685
Biffin v Bignell (1862) 7 H & N 877, 31 LJ Ex 189, 8 Jur NS 647, 10 WR 322, 6 LT
248 430
Biggs v Biggs and Wheatley [1977] Fam 1, [1977] 1 All ER 20, [1976] 2 WLR 942, 120
Sol Jo 403 .... 351, 863, 866, 875–876
Billington v Billington [1974] Fam 24, [1974] 1 All ER 546, [1974] 2 WLR 53, 138 JP
228, 118 Sol Jo 66 .... 602, 632
Bindon's (Viscountess) Case (1586) Moore KB 213 246
Birch v Birch [1992] 2 FCR 545, [1992] 1 FLR 564, [1992] Fam Law 290, CA 360
Bird v Jones (1828) 3 Man & Ry KB 121, sub nom Burge v Jones 7 LJOS 59 267
Bishop, Re, National Provincial Bank Ltd v Bishop [1965] Ch 450, [1965] 1 All ER 249,
[1965] 2 WLR 188, 109 Sol Jo 107 245
Bishop v Bishop [1897] P 138, 66 LJP 69, 76, 45 WR 567, 41 Sol Jo 559, 76 LT 409,
13 TLR 366, CA 444
Bishop v Bishop [1901] P 325, 70 LJP 93, 85 LT 173, 17 TLR 616 791
Black v Black (May intervening) [1960] 1 All ER 251, [1960] 1 WLR 182, 104 Sol Jo
190 825
Blacker v Blacker [1960] P 146, [1960] 2 All ER 291, [1960] 2 WLR 800, 104 Sol Jo
368, CA 793
Blackledge v Blackledge [1913] P 9, 77 JP 427, 82 LJP 13, 23 Cox CC 230, 57 Sol Jo
159, 107 LT 720, 29 TLR 120, DC 736
Blackmore and Thorp v Brider (1816) 1 Hag Con 393n, 2 Phillim 359, 161 ER 593 35
Blades v Free (1829) 9 B & C 167, 7 LJOS 211, 4 Man & Ry KB 282, 109 ER 63 262–263
Bland v Bland (1875) LR 3 P & D 233, 44 LJP & M 14, 23 WR 419, 32 LT 404 776

PARA

Blezard v Blezard and Mul (1978) 1 FLR 253, 9 Fam Law 249, CA 621
Blood v Blood [1902] P 78, 65 JP 823, 71 LJP 40, 50 WR 138, 86 LT 121, 18 TLR 73;
    affd [1902] P 190, 71 LJP 97, 50 WR 547, 46 Sol Jo 499, 86 LT 641, 18 TLR
    588, CA 511, 513
Bluff v Bluff (otherwise Kelly) [1946] 2 All ER 63, 90 Sol Jo 557, 175 LT 112 .... 849, 875–876
Blum v Blum (1963) 107 Sol Jo 512, CA 353
Blunt v Park Lane Hotel Ltd [1942] 2 KB 253, [1942] 2 All ER 187, 111 LJKB 706,
    167 LT 359, 58 TLR 356, CA 349
Blyth v Blyth and Pugh [1966] AC 643, [1966] 1 All ER 524, [1966] 2 WLR 634, 110
    Sol Jo 148, HL 352, 369
Board v Checkland [1987] 2 FLR 257, [1987] Fam Law 236, CA 459, 468, 481, 502, 507
Boddy v Boddy and Grover (1858) 28 LJP & M 16 787
Boddy v Boddy and Grover (1860) 30 LJPM & A 23 .... 349, 353
Bodman v Bodman (otherwise Perry) (1913) 57 Sol Jo 359, 108 LT 383, 29 TLR 348 21
Boger v Boger [1908] P 300, 77 LJP 151, 52 Sol Jo 552, 99 LT 881, 24 TLR 744 760
Bohnel v Bohnel (No 2) [1963] 2 All ER 325, [1964] 1 WLR 179, 107 Sol Jo 236 734
Bolsom v Bolsom (1982) 4 FLR 21, 12 Fam Law 143, CA 476, 501
Bon v Smith (1596) Cro Eliz 532 69
Bond v Taylor (1861) 2 John & H 473, 31 LJ Ch 784, 8 Jur NS 1090, 10 WR 169, 70
    ER 1144, 5 LT 445 236
Bonsor v Bonsor [1897] P 77, 66 LJP 35, 45 WR 304, 76 LT 168, 13 TLR 184 599
Boreham v Boreham (1866) LR 1 P & D 77, 35 LJP & M 49, 14 WR 317 771
Borham v Borham and Brown (1870) LR 2 P & D 193, 40 LJP & M 6, 19 WR 215,
    sub nom Boreham v Boreham and Brown 23 LT 600 769
Bosley v Bosley [1958] 2 All ER 167, [1958] 1 WLR 645, 102 Sol Jo 437, CA 362, 371, 373,
    436
Bostock v Bostock [1950] P 154, [1950] 1 All ER 25, 48 LGR 423, 114 JP 59, 66((pt
    1) TLR 339 833
Boston v Boston [1904] 1 KB 124, 73 LJKB 17, 52 WR 65, 48 Sol Jo 32, 89 LT 468, 20
    TLR 23, CA 206
Bosvile v Bosvile and Craven (1888) 13 PD 76, 57 LJP 62, 36 WR 912, 58 LT 640 513
Bosworthick v Bosworthick [1927] P 64, [1926] All ER Rep 198, 95 LJP 171, 70 Sol Jo
    857, 136 LT 211, 42 TLR 719, CA 511, 517
Bourne v Bourne [1913] P 164, 82 LJP 117, 108 LT 1039, 29 TLR 657 438
Bourne v Colodense Ltd [1985] ICR 291, [1985] IRLR 339, 129 Sol Jo 153,
    [1985] LS Gaz R 923, CA 647–648
Bowen v Bowen [1958] 1 All ER 770, [1958] 1 WLR 508, 122 JP 202, 102 Sol Jo
    308 566
Bowen v Bowen and Evans (1864) 33 LJPM & A 129, 3 Sw & Tr 530, 13 WR 109,
    164 ER 1381 876
Bower v Smith (1871) LR 11 Eq 279, 40 LJ Ch 194, 19 WR 399, 24 LT 118 236
Bowes v Shand (1877) 2 App Cas 455, [1874–80] All ER Rep 174, 46 LJQB 561, 3 Asp
    MLC 461, 25 WR 730, 36 LT 857, HL 205
Bown v Bown and Weston [1949] P 91, [1948] 2 All ER 778, [1948] LJR 1912, 64 TLR
    516 511
Bowron v Bowron [1925] P 187, [1925] All ER Rep 148, 23 LGR 223, 89 JP 43, 94
    LJP 33, 27 Cox CC 769, 69 Sol Jo 325, 132 LT 773, 41 TLR 245, CA 369, 391, 400
Bowzer v Ricketts (falsely calling herself Bowzer) (1795) 1 Hag Con 213, 161 ER 529 ..... 10, 344
Boyd v Boyd [1955] P 126n, [1938] 4 All ER 181, 37 LGR 50, 102 JP 525, 108 LJP 25,
    82 Sol Jo 912, 159 LT 522, 55 TLR 3 394
Boyd v Boyd. See B (V) v B (J)
Boylan v Boylan [1988] FCR 689, [1988] 1 FLR 282, [1988] Fam Law 62 .... 599, 614
Bozzelli's Settlement, Re, Husey-Hunt v Bozzelli [1902] 1 Ch 751, 71 LJ Ch 505, 50 WR
    447, 46 Sol Jo 318, 86 LT 445, 18 TLR 365 35
Bradley v Bradley (1882) 7 PD 237, 51 LJP 87, 31 WR 200, 47 LT 355 .... 473, 548
Bradley v Bradley [1973] 3 All ER 750, [1973] 1 WLR 1291, 117 Sol Jo 632, CA 360–361
Bradley v Bradley and Queen's Proctor (intervening) [1986] 1 FLR 128, [1986] Fam Law
    25 876
Bradshaw, Re, Blandy v Willis [1938] 4 All ER 143, 82 Sol Jo 909 6
Bradshaw v Bradshaw [1956] P 274n, [1955] 3 WLR 965n, 99 Sol Jo 890 .... 344, 416
Bradshaw v Bradshaw [1897] P 24, [1895–9] All ER Rep 1155, 61 JP 8, 66 LJP 31, 45
    WR 142, 75 LT 391, 13 TLR 82 .... 362, 378, 412

PARA

Bragg v Bragg [1925] P 20, [1924] All ER Rep 45, 94 LJP 11, 27 Cox CC 729, 69 Sol
Jo 73, 132 LT 346, 41 TLR 8 566
Brailey v Brailey [1922] P 15, [1921] All ER Rep Ext 875, 91 LJP 65, 126 LT 277, 38
TLR 28, 66 Sol Jo (WR) 13, CA 432, 435, 860
Bramwell, Re, Campbell v Tobin [1988] 2 FLR 263, [1988] Fam Law 391 684–685
Branford v Branford (1879) 4 PD 72, 48 LJP 40, 27 WR 691, 40 LT 659 .... 346, 349, 833
Brannan v Brannan [1973] Fam 120, [1973] 1 All ER 38, [1973] 2 WLR 7, 116 Sol Jo
968 542
Brassford v Patel [2007] BPIR 1049, [2007] All ER (D) 256 (Feb) 279, 282
Brassington v Brassington [1962] P 276, [1961] 3 All ER 988n, [1961] 3 WLR 1411,
105 Sol Jo 910, CA 738
Breadalbane Case, Campbell v Campbell (1867) LR 1 Sc & Div 182, 39 Sc Jur 576,
5 M 115, HL 6
Brealy (falsely called Reed) v Reed (1841) 2 Curt 833, 163 ER 601, 1 Notes of Cases
121 69
Bremner (a bankrupt), Re [1999] 1 FLR 912, [1999] Fam Law 293, [1999] BPIR 185 639
Brewer v Brewer [1962] P 69, [1961] 3 All ER 957, [1961] 3 WLR 1208, 105 Sol Jo
948, CA 398–399
Brickell v Brickell [1974] Fam 31, [1973] 3 All ER 508, [1973] 3 WLR 602, 4 Fam Law
116, 117 Sol Jo 727, CA 411
Bridgman v Bridgman and Puckrin (1869) 20 LT 87 845
Briggs v Morgan (1820) 2 Hag Con 324, 3 Phillim 325 340
Bright v Bright [1954] P 270, [1953] 2 All ER 939, [1953] 3 WLR 659, 117 JP 529, 97
Sol Jo 729 734
Brink's Mat Ltd v Elcombe [1988] 3 All ER 188, [1988] 1 WLR 1350, CA 661–662
Brinkley v Brinkley [1965] P 75, [1963] 1 All ER 493, [1963] 2 WLR 822, 127 JP 197,
107 Sol Jo 77 .... 358, 897
Briscoe v Briscoe [1968] P 501, [1966] 1 All ER 465, [1966] 2 WLR 205, 130 JP 124,
109 Sol Jo 996 849
Brister v Brister. See B (GC) v B (BA)
Bristol and West Building Society v Henning [1985] 2 All ER 606, [1985] 1 WLR 778,
50 P & CR 237, 17 HLR 432, 129 Sol Jo 363, [1985] LS Gaz R 1788, [1985] NLJ
Rep 508, CA 284
Bristol Corpn v Ross [1973] Ch 447, [1973] 3 All ER 393, [1973] 3 WLR 71, 117 Sol
Jo 448, 227 Estates Gazette 985, CA 947
Brocas v Brocas (1861) 30 LJPM & A 172, 2 Sw & Tr 383, 164 ER 1044, 5 LT 137 .... 755, 858,
861
Brodie v Brodie [1917] P 271, [1916–17] All ER Rep 237, 86 LJP 140, 62 Sol Jo 71,
117 LT 542, 33 TLR 525 .... 375, 424
Bromberg v Bromberg and Gross [1962] 3 All ER 289, [1962] 1 WLR 1143, 106 Sol Jo
592 872
Bromfield v Bromfield (1871) 41 LJP & M 17, 26 LT 264 771
Brook v Brook (1861) 9 HL Cas 193, [1861–73] All ER Rep 493, 7 Jur NS 422, 25 JP
259, 9 WR 461, 4 LT 93, 11 ER 703, HL 35
Brooks v Brooks [1996] AC 375, [1995] 3 All ER 257, [1995] 3 WLR 141,
[1995] 3 FCR 214, [1995] 2 FLR 13, [1995] Fam Law 545,
[1995] 31 LS Gaz R 34, [1995] NLJR 995, 139 Sol Jo LB 165, HL 510–511, 710
Broome v Broome (Edmundson cited) [1955] P 190, [1955] 1 All ER 201,
[1955] 2 WLR 401, 99 Sol Jo 114 833
Brown, Re, Ingall v Brown [1904] 1 Ch 120, 73 LJ Ch 130, 52 WR 173, 90 LT 220 50
Brown v Brown (1828) 1 Hag Ecc 523 .... 336–337, 340, 345
Brown v Brown (1868) LR 7 Eq 185, 38 LJ Ch 153, 17 WR 98, 19 LT 594 429
Brown v Brown [1937] P 7, [1936] 2 All ER 1616, 105 LJP 103, 80 Sol Jo 817, 155 LT
418, 53 TLR 9 511
Brown (otherwise Nuttall) v Brown [1955] CLY 870, (1955) Times, 15 February 342
Brown v Brown [1959] P 86, [1959] 2 All ER 266, [1959] 2 WLR 776, 103 Sol Jo
414, CA 511
Brown v Brown (1972) 117 Sol Jo 87, DC 590
Brown v Brown (1981) 3 FLR 161, 11 Fam Law 247, 126 Sol Jo 15, CA 610
Brown v Brown and Shelton (1874) LR 3 P & D 202, 43 LJP & M 47, 31 LT 272 860
Brown v Jones (1744) 1 Atk 188 711
Browne v Browne [1989] 1 FLR 291, [1989] Fam Law 147, CA 464, 549, 599

PARA

Browne (formerly Pritchard) v Pritchard [1975] 3 All ER 721, [1975] 1 WLR 1366, 119
  Sol Jo 679, CA 316, 451, 601
Browne's Policy, Re, Browne v Browne [1903] 1 Ch 188, [1900–3] All ER Rep Ext
  1245, 72 LJ Ch 85, 51 WR 364, 87 LT 588, 19 TLR 98 275
Browning v Reane (1812) 2 Phillim 69, [1803–13] All ER Rep 265, 161 ER 1080 .... 42, 45
Bruce v Burke (1825) 2 Add 471, 162 ER 367 .... 10, 344
Brydges v Brydges and Wood [1909] P 187, 78 LJP 97, 100 LT 744, 25 TLR 505, CA ... 685, 879
Brykiert v Jones (1981) 2 FLR 373, 125 Sol Jo 323, CA 278
Buchler v Buchler [1947] P 25, [1947] 1 All ER 319, 45 LGR 442, 111 JP 179, [1947]
  LJR 820, 91 Sol Jo 99, 176 LT 341, 63 TLR 100, CA 346, 362, 368–369, 387–388, 391–
  395
Buckeridge v Buckeridge (1962) 106 Sol Jo 471 802
Buckland v Buckland [1968] P 296, [1967] 2 All ER 300, [1967] 2 WLR 1506, 109 Sol
  Jo 212, 111 Sol Jo 456 .... 43, 345
Buckley v Buckley (1912) 57 Sol Jo 9, 107 LT 590 1022
Buckley v Crawford [1893] 1 QB 105, 57 JP 89, 62 LJQB 87, 5 R 125, 41 WR 239, 37
  Sol Jo 67, 67 LT 681, 9 TLR 85, DC 624, 643, 933
Buckmaster v Buckmaster (1869) LR 1 P & D 713, 38 LJP & M 73, 17 WR 1114, 21
  LT 231 362
Bucknell v Bucknell [1969] 2 All ER 998, [1969] 1 WLR 1204, 113 Sol Jo 586 650
Buffery v Buffery [1988] FCR 465, [1988] 2 FLR 365, [1988] Fam Law 436, CA 346–347, 360
Bull v Bull [1953] P 224, [1953] 2 All ER 601, [1953] 3 WLR 326, 117 JP 415, 97 Sol
  Jo 489, CA 368
Bull v Bull (Queen's Proctor showing cause) [1968] P 618, [1965] 1 All ER 1057,
  [1965] 3 WLR 1048, 109 Sol Jo 50 877
Bull v Vardy (1791) 1 Ves 270 238
Bullock v Bullock [1960] 2 All ER 307, [1960] 1 WLR 975, 104 Sol Jo 685 .... 321, 344, 416
Burdett v Horne (1911) 28 TLR 83, CA 204
Burge v Jones. See Bird v Jones
Burgess v Burgess [1997] 1 FCR 89, [1996] 2 FLR 34, [1996] Fam Law 465, CA 662
Burke v Burke [1974] 2 All ER 944, [1974] 1 WLR 1063, 118 Sol Jo 98, CA 225–226
Burne v Robinson (1844) 7 I Eq R 188 946
Burnet v Mann (1748) 1 Ves Sen 156, 27 ER 953 233
Burnett v Burnett [1936] P 1, [1935] All ER Rep 490, 105 LJP 1, 79 Sol Jo 642, 153 LT
  318, 51 TLR 574 511
Burns v Burns [1984] Ch 317, [1984] 1 All ER 244, [1984] 2 WLR 582, [1984] FLR
  216, [1984] Fam Law 24, 128 Sol Jo 173, [1984] LS Gaz R 893, CA 279, 281–282, 284
Burrell v Burrell (1863) 32 LJPM & A 136 787
Burridge v Burridge [1983] Fam 9, [1982] 3 All ER 80, [1982] 3 WLR 552, 4 FLR 170,
  12 Fam Law 152, 126 Sol Jo 276 553
Burroughes v Abbott [1922] 1 Ch 86, [1921] All ER Rep 709, 91 LJ Ch 157, 66 Sol Jo
  141, 126 LT 354, 38 TLR 167 .... 473, 548
Burrow v Burrow [1999] 2 FCR 549, [1999] 1 FLR 508, [1999] Fam Law 83 622
Burton v Burton (1969) 113 Sol Jo 852, DC 387, 393–394
Burton v Burton [1986] 2 FLR 419, [1986] Fam Law 330 .... 476, 520, 601
Burton v Pierpoint (1722) 2 P Wms 78 246
Burvill v Burvill (1974) 4 Fam Law 121, 118 Sol Jo 205 411
Bush v Bush [1939] P 142, [1938] 4 All ER 598, 108 LJP 46, 83 Sol Jo 16, 55 TLR
  194 364
Bushell v Bushell (1803) 1 Sch & Lef 90 232
Butchart v Butchart and Hill [1901] AC 266, 70 LJP 29, 84 LT 209, HL 738
Butcher v Vale (1891) 8 TLR 93 430
Butland v Butland (1913) 29 TLR 729 384
Butler, Re, Joyce v Brew [1918] 1 IR 394 40
Butler v Butler (1885) 16 QBD 374, 55 LJQB 55, 34 WR 132, 54 LT 591, 2 TLR
  132, CA 206
Butler v Butler [1894] P 25, 63 LJP 1, 1 R 535, 42 WR 49, 38 Sol Jo 24, 69 LT 545, 10
  TLR 26, CA 871
Butler v Butler [1917] P 244, 86 LJP 135, 61 Sol Jo 631, 117 LT 542, 33 TLR
  494, DC 343
Butler v Butler [1961] P 33, [1961] 1 All ER 810, [1961] 2 WLR 397, 40 ATC 19,
  [1961] TR 19, 105 Sol Jo 178, CA 643

PARA

Butler v Butler (Queen's Proctor intervening) [1990] FCR 336, [1990] 1 FLR 114,
  [1990] Fam Law 21, [1989] 22 LS Gaz R 34 757
Butler v Butler [1997] 2 All ER 822, [1998] 1 WLR 1208, [1997] 2 FCR 300,
  [1997] 2 FLR 311, [1997] Fam Law 603, [1997] 12 LS Gaz R 22, [1997] NLJR
  525, 141 Sol Jo LB 57, CA 842
Butterfield v Heath (1852) 15 Beav 408, 22 LJ Ch 270, 20 LTOS 242 711
Butterworth v Butterworth [1998] 1 FCR 159, [1997] 2 FLR 336, CA 360
Button v Button [1968] 1 All ER 1064, [1968] 1 WLR 457, 19 P & CR 257, 112 Sol Jo
  112, 205 Estates Gazette 883, CA 283, 451

C

C v C (otherwise H) (1911) 27 TLR 421 340
C (otherwise H) v C [1921] P 399, [1921] All ER Rep 268, 90 LJP 345, 125 LT 768, 37
  TLR 759 .... 340–341, 832
C v C [1942] NZLR 356 44
C v C [1946] 1 All ER 562 833
C v C (1962) 106 Sol Jo 959 .... 343, 345
C v C (1965) 109 Sol Jo 473 883
C v C [1973] 3 All ER 770, [1973] 1 WLR 568, 117 Sol Jo 322 .... 354, 800
C v C [1989] FCR 558, [1989] 1 FLR 11 608
C v C (ancillary relief: structured settlement) [1996] 1 FCR 283, sub nom C v C
  (financial provision: personal damages) [1995] 2 FLR 171 .... 601, 617
C v C (financial provision: short marriage) [1997] 3 FCR 360, [1997] 2 FLR 26,
  [1997] Fam Law 472, CA 616
C v C (non-molestation order: jurisdiction) [1998] Fam 70, [1998] 2 WLR 599,
  [1998] 1 FCR 11, [1998] 1 FLR 554, [1998] Fam Law 254,
  [1997] 47 LS Gaz R 30, 141 Sol Jo LB 236 716
C v C (Divorce: Stay of English Proceedings) [2001] 1 FLR 624 842
C v C (ancillary relief: nuptial settlement) [2004] EWCA Civ 1030, [2005] Fam 250,
  [2005] 2 WLR 241, sub nom Charalambous v Charalambous [2004] 2 FCR 721,
  [2004] 2 FLR 1093, (2004) Times, 7 September, [2004] All ER (D) 582 (Jul), ... 510–511,
                                                                                        518
C v C and M (1910) 55 Sol Jo 141, 27 TLR 161 792
C v F (disabled child: maintenance orders) [1999] 1 FCR 39, [1998] 2 FLR 1,
  [1998] Fam Law 389, CA 492, 495, 518, 543, 546, 558, 561, 571, 583
C v S [1988] QB 135, [1987] 1 All ER 1230, [1987] 2 WLR 1108, [1987] 2 FLR 505,
  [1987] Fam Law 269, 131 Sol Jo 624, [1987] LS Gaz R 1410, CA 211
C v S (maintenance order: enforcement) [1997] 3 FCR 423, [1997] 1 FLR 298 .... 655, 679
CL v CFW [1928] P 223, 97 LJP 138 455
Cackett (otherwise Trice) v Cackett [1950] P 253, [1950] 1 All ER 677, 94 Sol Jo 256,
  66 (pt 1) TLR 723 335
Cahill v Cahill (1883) 8 App Cas 420, 31 WR 861, 49 LT 605, HL 428
Cairns v Cairns [1940] NI 183 369
Calder v Calder (1975) 6 Fam Law 242, CA 601
Calder v Dobell (1871) LR 6 CP 486, 40 LJCP 224, 19 WR 978, 25 LT 129, Ex Ch 259
Calderbank v Calderbank [1976] Fam 93, [1975] 3 All ER 333, [1975] 3 WLR 586,
  [1976] Fam Law 93, 119 Sol Jo 490, CA 450, 498, 610
Callaghan v Hanson-Fox [1992] Fam 1, [1991] 3 WLR 464, [1991] FCR 989,
  [1991] 2 FLR 519, [1991] Fam Law 477, 135 Sol Jo LB 77, sub nom Callaghan v
  Andrew-Hanson [1992] 1 All ER 56 .... 864, 880
Callot v Nash (1923) 39 TLR 292 .... 259, 264, 266
Calvert v Flower (1836) 7 C & P 386 802
Camm v Camm (1982) 4 FLR 577, 13 Fam Law 112, CA 596
Campbell v Campbell [1922] P 187, 91 LJP 126, 127 LT 29, 38 TLR 320 .... 456, 466, 552
Campbell v Campbell [1998] 2 FCR 123, [1997] 2 FLR 609, [1997] Fam Law
  539, CA 613, 737
Campbell v Corley (1856) 4 WR 675, 28 LTOS 109, PC 102
Campion v Cotton (1810) 17 Ves 263, [1803–13] All ER Rep 580, 34 ER 102 283
Canham v Howard (1887) 3 TLR 458, DC 264
Cann v Cann (1967) 111 Sol Jo 810 379
Cannon v Hartley [1949] Ch 213, [1949] 1 All ER 50, [1949] LJR 370, 92 Sol Jo 719,
  65 TLR 63 445

PARA

Cannon v Smalley (otherwise Cannon) (1885) 10 PD 80, 1 TLR 338 45
Capua (Prince) v Count De Ludolf (1836) 30 LJPM & A 71n 76
Caras v Caras [1955] 1 All ER 624n, [1955] 1 WLR 254, 99 Sol Jo 186 542
Cardross's Settlement, Re (1878) 7 Ch D 728, [1874–80] All ER Rep Ext 1695, 47 LJ
    Ch 327, 26 WR 389, 38 LT 778 234
Carew-Hunt v Carew-Hunt (1972) Times, 28 June 360
Cargill v Cargill (1858) 27 LJP & M 69, 4 Jur NS 764, 1 Sw & Tr 235, 6 WR 870, 164
    ER 708, 31 LTOS 332 400
Carr v Carr [1974] Fam 65, [1974] 3 All ER 366, [1974] 3 WLR 449, 118 Sol Jo 580 700
Carr v Carr [1974] 1 All ER 1193, [1974] 1 WLR 1534, 118 Sol Jo 831, CA 350
Carson v Carson [1983] 1 All ER 478, [1983] 1 WLR 285, 2 FLR 352, 125 Sol Jo
    513, CA 476, 499
Carter v Carter (King's Proctor intervening) [1910] P 4, 79 LJP 12, 54 Sol Jo 102, 101
    LT 812, 26 TLR 84; affd sub nom King's Proctor v Carter [1910] P 151,
    [1908–10] All ER Rep 104, 79 LJP 37, 54 Sol Jo 405, 102 LT 259, 26 TLR
    303, CA 853
Carter v Carter (1919) 64 Sol Jo 148, 36 TLR 121 776
Carter v Hind (1853) 2 WR 27, 22 LTOS 116 711
Carter-Fea v Carter-Fea [1987] Fam Law 131, CA 360
Cartledge v Cartledge (1862) 31 LJPM & A 135, 8 Jur NS 493, 4 Sw & Tr 249, 164
    ER 1511 771
Case v Case (1860) 29 LJPM & A 127, 2 Sw & Tr 65, 8 WR 532, 164 ER 916, 2 LT
    391 802
Casey v Casey [1952] 1 All ER 453, 116 JP 111 .... 400, 403–404
Cathcart, Re [1893] 1 Ch 466, 62 LJ Ch 320, 2 R 268, 41 WR 277, 37 Sol Jo 114, 68
    LT 358, 9 TLR 134, CA 641
Catherwood v Caslon (1844) 13 LJ Ex 334, 8 Jur 1076, 13 M & W 261, 153 ER 108 80
Catterall v Sweetman (1845) 1 Rob Eccl 304, 9 Jur 951, 4 Notes of Cases 222, sub nom
    Catterall v Catterall 6 LTOS 19 82
Cavell v Prince (1866) LR 1 Exch 246, 4 H & C 368, 35 LJ Ex 162, 12 Jur NS 475, 14
    WR 968, 15 LT 83 322
Central London Property Trust Ltd v High Trees House Ltd [1947] KB 130,
    [1956] 1 All ER 256n, [1947] LJR 77, 175 LT 332, 62 TLR 557 698
Chadwick v Chadwick (1964) Times, 24 October 395
Chadwick v Chadwick [1985] FLR 606, [1985] Fam Law 96, CA 316, 617
Chalmers v Chalmers (1892) 1 R 504, [1891–4] All ER Rep 461, 68 LT 28 .... 511, 516
Chalmers v Chalmers [1930] P 154, [1930] All ER Rep Ext 862, 99 LJP 60, 74 Sol Jo
    216, 142 LT 654, 46 TLR 269 .... 353, 357, 876–877
Chalmers v Johns [1999] 2 FCR 110, [1999] 1 FLR 392, [1999] Fam Law 16, CA 289
Chamberlain v Chamberlain [1974] 1 All ER 33, [1973] 1 WLR 1557, 4 Fam Law 46,
    117 Sol Jo 893, CA 316, 492, 518
Chambers v Chambers (1810) 1 Hag Con 439 353
Chambers v Chambers (1979) 1 FLR 10, 10 Fam Law 22, 123 Sol Jo 689 595
Chandler v Chandler (1858) 28 LJP & M 6, 27 LJP & M 35 777
Chaplin v Chaplin [1949] P 72, [1948] 2 All ER 408, [1948] LJR 1839, 92 Sol Jo 540,
    64 TLR 524, CA 345
Chaplin & Co Ltd v Brammall [1908] 1 KB 233, [1904–7] All ER Rep Ext 1124, 77
    LJKB 366, 97 LT 860, CA 249
Chaplin's Petition, Re (1867) LR 1 P & D 328, 36 LJP & M 49, 16 LT 154 512
Chapman v Chapman [1972] 3 All ER 1089, [1972] 1 WLR 1544, 116 Sol Jo
    843, CA 410
Chapman v Chapman and Buist [1910] P 271, 79 LJP 115, 54 Sol Jo 721, 103 LT 430,
    26 TLR 634 742
Chapman v Chapman and Thomas [1938] P 93, [1938] 1 All ER 635, 107 LJP 30, 82
    Sol Jo 216, 158 LT 424, 54 TLR 462 769
Chapman v Guest (1887) 3 TLR 438 436
Chappell v Chappell [1938] 4 All ER 814, 82 Sol Jo 1051 865
Charalambous v Charalambous. See C v C (ancillary relief: nuptial settlement)
Chard v Chard (otherwise Northcott) [1956] P 259, [1955] 3 All ER 721,
    [1955] 3 WLR 954, 99 Sol Jo 890 .... 7, 10, 344, 416
Charlesworth v Holt (1873) LR 9 Exch 38, [1861–73] All ER Rep 266, 43 LJ Ex 25, 22
    WR 94, 29 LT 647, Exch Ct 442

PARA

Charleton, Re, Bracey v Sherwin [1911] WN 54, 55 Sol Jo 330 222
Charman v Charman [2005] EWCA Civ 1606, [2006] 1 WLR 1053, [2006] 2 FLR 422,
    [2006] Fam Law 516, [2005] All ER (D) 298 (Dec) 599
Charman v Charman [2007] EWCA Civ 503, [2007] 2 FCR 217, [2007] 1 FLR 1246,
    [2007] Fam Law 682, [2007] NLJR 814, 151 Sol Jo LB 710, [2007] All ER (D)
    425 (May) 591
Charter v Charter (1901) 65 JP 246, [1900–3] All ER Rep Ext 1524, 84 LT 272, 17
    TLR 327 .... 362, 391, 393, 400
Chaterjee v Chaterjee [1976] Fam 199, [1976] 1 All ER 719, [1976] 2 WLR 397, 120
    Sol Jo 165, CA 917
Chebaro v Chebaro [1987] Fam 127, [1987] 1 All ER 999, [1987] 2 WLR 1090,
    [1987] 2 FLR 456, [1987] Fam Law 380, 130 Sol Jo 442, [1987] LS Gaz R 741,
    [1987] NLJ Rep 170, CA 530
Chechi v Bashier [1999] 2 FCR 241, [1999] 2 FLR 489, [1999] Fam Law 528, 143 Sol
    Jo LB 113, [1999] All ER (D) 263, CA 716
Cheetham v Cheetham [1954] 2 All ER 535n, [1954] 1 WLR 990, 98 Sol Jo 455, CA 770, 796
Cheni (otherwise Rodriguez) v Cheni [1965] P 85, [1962] 3 All ER 873, [1963] 2 WLR
    17 .... 1, 33, 35
Chesworth v Chesworth (1973) 4 Fam Law 22, 118 Sol Jo 183, DC 553
Chetti v Chetti [1909] P 67, [1908–10] All ER Rep 49, sub nom Venugopal Chetti v
    Venugopal Chetti 78 LJP 23, 53 Sol Jo 163, 99 LT 885, 25 TLR 146 33
Chettle v Chettle (1821) 3 Phillim 507, 161 ER 1399 353
Chetwynd v Allen [1899] 1 Ch 353, 68 LJ Ch 160, 47 WR 200, 43 Sol Jo 140, 80 LT
    110 252
Chichester v Chichester [1936] P 129, [1936] 1 All ER 271, 105 LJP 38, 80 Sol Jo 207,
    154 LT 375, 52 TLR 265 .... 471, 494
Chichester v Mure (falsely called Chichester) (1863) 32 LJPM & A 146, 9 Jur NS 779, 2
    New Rep 493, 3 Sw & Tr 223, 11 WR 990, 164 ER 1259, 8 LT 676 .... 34, 344
Chief Adjudication Officer v Bath [2000] 1 FCR 419, [2000] 1 FLR 8, [2000] Fam Law
    91, [1999] All ER (D) 1149, CA 6, 7
Childs, Re, ex p New (1874) 9 Ch App 508, 43 LJ Bcy 89, 30 LT 447 207
Chilton v Chilton [1952] P 196, [1952] 1 All ER 1322, 116 JP 313, 96 Sol Jo 378,
    [1952] 1 TLR 1316, DC 393
Chipchase v Chipchase [1939] P 391, [1939] 3 All ER 895, 108 LJP 154, 83 Sol Jo 798,
    55 TLR 1067 .... 69, 328, 416
Chipchase v Chipchase (otherwise Leetch, otherwise Matthews) [1942] P 37,
    [1941] 2 All ER 560, 110 LJP 65, 85 Sol Jo 323, 165 LT 333, 57 TLR 606 .... 69, 328
Chisholm's Settlement, Re, Re Hemphill's Settlement, Hemphill v Hemphill
    [1901] 2 Ch 82, 70 LJ Ch 533, CA 237
Cholmely v Cholmely (1688) 2 Vern 82 246
Choppy v Bibi (otherwise Choppy) [1967] AC 158, [1966] 1 All ER 203, [1966] 2 WLR
    711, 109 Sol Jo 1010, PC 322
Chorley v Chorley [2005] EWCA Civ 68, [2005] 1 WLR 1469, [2005] 2 FLR 38,
    [2005] Fam Law 276, (2005) Times, 18 January, [2005] All ER (D) 34 (Jan) 839
Chorlton v Chorlton [1952] P 169, [1952] 1 All ER 611, 116 JP 166, [1952] 1 TLR
    807 349
Christian v Christian (1897) 67 LJP 18, 78 LT 86 847
Christopher (Hove) Ltd v Williams [1936] 3 All ER 68, 80 Sol Jo 853, CA 259
Chudley v Chudley (1893) 17 Cox CC 697, 69 LT 617, 10 TLR 63, CA 372, 378
Church v Church (1933) 31 LGR 185, 97 JP 91, 29 Cox CC 592, 148 LT 432, 49 TLR
    206 897
Church v Church [1952] P 313, [1952] 2 All ER 441, 96 Sol Jo 514, [1952] 2 TLR
    557 369
Church v Church (1983) 13 Fam Law 254 211
Churchill v Churchill (1980) 11 Fam Law 179, CA 595
Churchman v Churchman [1945] P 44, [1945] 2 All ER 190, 114 LJP 17, 89 Sol Jo 508,
    173 LT 108, 61 TLR 464, CA 349, 352
Churner v Churner (1912) 106 LT 769, 28 TLR 318 364
Ciocci v Ciocci (1854) 1 Ecc & Ad 121, 18 Jur 194 354
Clapham v Clapham and Guest (1868) 17 LT 584 875
Clarges v Albemarle (1691) Nels 174, 2 Vern 245 246

PARA

Clark, Re, ex p Schulze [1898] 2 QB 330, 67 LJQB 759, 5 Mans 201, 46 WR 678, 42
Sol Jo 573, 78 LT 735, 14 TLR 462, CA 207
Clark v Chief Land Registrar [1993] Ch 294, [1993] 2 All ER 936, [1993] 2 WLR 141,
65 P & CR 186, [1993] 2 FLR 500, [1993] Fam Law 579, [1992] 44 LS Gaz R 35;
affd [1994] Ch 370, [1994] 4 All ER 96, [1994] 3 WLR 593, [1995] 1 FLR 212,
[1995] Fam Law 132, [1994] 24 LS Gaz R 47, 138 Sol Jo LB 123, CA 637
Clark v Clark (1885) 10 PD 188, 49 JP 516, 54 LJP 57, 33 WR 405, 52 LT 234, CA 433, 444
Clark v Clark [1953] 1 All ER 704n, [1953] 1 WLR 490, 97 Sol Jo 172 802
Clark v Clark (1954) Times, 3 June, CA 349
Clark v Clark (by her guardian) [1956] 1 All ER 823, [1956] 1 WLR 345, 100 Sol Jo
264 .... 362, 381, 389
Clark v Clark [1989] FCR 101, [1989] 1 FLR 174, [1989] Fam Law 111, [1988] NLJR
101 649
Clark v Clark [1995] 2 FLR 487n, [1996] Fam Law 17, CA 883
Clark v Clark (No 2) [1939] P 257, [1939] 2 All ER 392, 108 LJP 117, 83 Sol Jo 381 ... 372, 374
Clark v Clark (No 2) [1990] FCR 753, [1991] 1 FLR 179, [1991] NLJR 206 649
Clarke v Clarke. See Ford v Stier
Clarke (otherwise Talbott) v Clarke [1943] 2 All ER 540, 112 LJP 41, 87 Sol Jo 8, 168
LT 62 .... 321, 340
Clarke v Clarke (1961) 105 Sol Jo 386 756
Clarke v Clarke [2004] EWCA Civ 1185, [2004] 3 FCR 161, [2004] All ER (D) 56
(Jul) 720
Clarke v Clarke and Lindsay [1911] P 186, 80 LJP 135, 55 Sol Jo 535, 105 LT 1, CA 516
Clarkson v Clarkson (1930) 143 LT 775, 46 TLR 623 349
Claughton v Charalamabous [1999] 1 FLR 740, [1999] Fam Law 205, [1998] BPIR
558 639
Claxton v Claxton (1981) 3 FLR 415, 12 Fam Law 62, 147 JP 94 599
Claxton v Claxton [1959] P 33, [1959] 1 All ER 386, [1959] 2 WLR 236, 123 JP 145,
103 Sol Jo 132 .... 740, 897
Clayton v Clayton and Sharman [1932] P 45, 101 LJP 23, 76 Sol Jo 96, 146 LT 327, 48
TLR 191 852
Cleary v Cleary [1974] 1 All ER 498, 117 Sol Jo 834, sub nom Cleary v Cleary and
Hutton [1974] 1 WLR 73, CA 350
Cleaver v Cleaver (1884) 9 App Cas 631, HL 883
Cleaver v Mutual Reserve Fund Life Association [1892] 1 QB 147, [1891–4] All ER Rep
335, 56 JP 180, 61 LJQB 128, 40 WR 230, 36 Sol Jo 106, 66 LT 220, 8 TLR
139, CA 275
Clements v Clements and Thomas (1864) 33 LJPM & A 74, 3 Sw & Tr 394, 13 WR
110, 164 ER 1327, 10 LT 352 876
Clifford v Clifford [1948] P 187, [1948] 1 All ER 394, [1948] LJR 969, 92 Sol Jo 166,
64 TLR 209, CA 321
Clifford v Clifford [1961] 3 All ER 231, [1961] 1 WLR 1274, 105 Sol Jo 709 828
Clifford v Clifford (1963) 107 Sol Jo 515 851
Clifford v Clifford [1985] FLR 732, CA 777
Clifford v Laton (1827) 3 C & P 15, Mood & M 101 .... 264, 267
Clifton (otherwise Packe) v Clifton [1936] P 182, [1936] 2 All ER 886, 105 LJP 87, 80
Sol Jo 555, 155 LT 205, 52 TLR 616 453
Clinton v Clinton (1866) LR 1 P & D 215, 14 WR 545, 14 LT 257 599
Clinton v Hooper (1791) 1 Hov Supp 65, 1 Ves 173, 3 Bro CC 201, 29 ER 490 239
Clough v Lambert (1839) 10 Sim 174, 3 Jur 672, 59 ER 579 .... 427, 436
Clowes v Jones (falsely calling herself Clowes) (1842) 3 Curt 185, 7 Jur 908, 163 ER
697, 2 Notes of Cases 1, 77 76
Clutton v Clutton [1991] 1 All ER 340, [1991] 1 WLR 359, [1991] FCR 265,
[1991] 1 FLR 242, [1991] Fam Law 304, [1990] NLJR 1682, CA 316, 610, 612
Co v Co (ancilliary relief: pre-marriage cohabitation) [2004] EWHC 287 (Fam),
[2004] 1 FLR 1095, [2004] Fam Law 406 616
Coates v Coates [1898] 1 IR 258, 32 ILT 7 440
Cobb v Cobb [1955] 2 All ER 696, [1955] 1 WLR 731, 99 Sol Jo 453, CA 225–226
Cochrane, Re (1840) 8 Dowl 630, 4 Jur 534 219
Cochrane v Cochrane (otherwise Millamootz) (1930) Times, 7 June 45
Cockburn v Cockburn [1957] 3 All ER 260, [1957] 1 WLR 1020, 101 Sol Jo 798, CA ... 602, 945

PARA

Cocksedge v Cocksedge (1844) 14 Sim 244, 13 LJ Ch 384, 8 Jur 659, 65 RR 574, 60
ER 351, 3 LTOS 374 375
Codrington v Codrington and Anderson (1864) 33 LJPM & A 62, 3 Sw & Tr 368, 164
ER 1317, 10 LT 139 772
Coffey v Coffey [1898] P 169, 67 LJP 86, 78 LT 796 .... 349, 358
Cohen v Cohen (1876) 24 WR 283, 34 LT 33 784
Cohen v Cohen [1939] 2 All ER 39n, CA; affd [1940] AC 631, [1940] 2 All ER 331,
109 LJP 53, 84 Sol Jo 270, 163 LT 183, 56 TLR 597, HL 362, 364
Cohen v Cohen [1940] AC 631, [1940] 2 All ER 331, 109 LJP 53, 84 Sol Jo 270, 163
LT 183, 56 TLR 597, HL 369, 396, 406
Cohen v Sellar [1926] 1 KB 536, [1926] All ER Rep 312, 95 LJKB 629, 70 Sol Jo 505,
135 LT 21, 42 TLR 409 16
Cole v Cottingham (1837) 8 C & P 75 16
Coleman v Coleman [1973] Fam 10, [1972] 3 All ER 886, [1972] 3 WLR 681, 116 Sol
Jo 746 476
Coleman v Coleman and Simpson [1920] P 71, 89 LJP 107, 122 LT 804, 36 TLR 255 685
Coles v Coles [1957] P 68, [1956] 3 All ER 542, [1956] 3 WLR 861, 100 Sol Jo 842 .... 466, 552,
649
Collett v Collett [1968] P 482, [1967] 2 All ER 426, [1967] 3 WLR 280, 111 Sol Jo
294 .... 7, 127
Collier, Re [1930] 2 Ch 37, [1930] All ER Rep 447, 99 LJ Ch 241, [1929] B & CR 173,
143 LT 329 275
Collins v Bishop (1878) 48 LJ Ch 31 6
Collins v Collins (1961) 3 FLR 17 412
Collins v Collins [1972] 2 All ER 658, [1972] 1 WLR 689, 116 Sol Jo 296, CA 779
Collins v Collins (1973) 4 Fam Law 133, CA 285
Colston v Gardner. See Coulston v Gardiner
Combe v Combe [1951] 2 KB 215, [1951] 1 All ER 767, 95 Sol Jo 317, [1951] 1 TLR
811, CA 698
Compagnie Financière et Commerciale du Pacifique v Peruvian Guano Co (1882) 11
QBD 55, 52 LJQB 181, 31 WR 395, 48 LT 22, CA 799
Connelly v Lawson (1876) 34 LT 903 264
Conradi v Conradi, Worrall and Way (1868) LR 1 P & D 514, 37 LJP & M 55, 16 WR
1023, 18 LT 659 .... 349, 357–358
Conran v Conran [1998] 1 FCR 144, [1997] 2 FLR 615, [1997] Fam Law 724 ...... 603, 618–619
Constantinidi v Constantinidi and Lance [1904] P 306, 73 LJP 91, 48 Sol Jo 571, 91 LT
273, 20 TLR 573, CA 516
Conway v Rimmer [1968] AC 910, [1968] 1 All ER 874, [1968] 2 WLR 998, 112 Sol
Jo 191, HL 833
Cook, Re, ex p Vernall (1892) 10 Morr 8, DC 263, 266
Cook v Cook [1962] P 181, [1962] 2 All ER 262, [1962] 2 WLR 963, 106 Sol Jo 38;
affd [1962] P 235, [1962] 2 All ER 811, [1962] 3 WLR 441, 106 Sol Jo 668, CA 511
Cooke v Head [1972] 2 All ER 38, [1972] 1 WLR 518, 116 Sol Jo 298, CA 224, 284
Cooke (J) & Sons Ltd v Binding [1961] 2 QB 200, [1961] 2 All ER 693, [1961] 3 WLR
1, 105 Sol Jo 442, CA 945
Cooper v Cooper [1964] 3 All ER 167n, [1964] 1 WLR 1323, 108 Sol Jo 524 755
Cooper v Cooper (No 2) [1955] P 168, [1954] 3 All ER 358, [1954] 3 WLR 923, 118
JP 549, 98 Sol Jo 853 734–736
Cooper v Cooper and Ford [1932] P 75, 101 LJP 28, 76 Sol Jo 249, 147 LT 16, 48 TLR
275 442
Cooper v Crane [1891] P 369, 61 LJP 35, 40 WR 127 42–43
Cooper v Kaur [2001] 1 FCR 12, [2000] All ER (D) 1331, CA 601
Cope v Barber (1872) LR 7 CP 393, 36 JP 439, 41 LJMC 137, 20 WR 885, 26 LT
891 80
Cope v Burt (falsely calling herself Cope) (1809) 1 Hag Con 434, 161 ER 608; affd
(1811) 1 Phillim 224 .... 69, 76
Copham (otherwise Dobbin) v Copham [1959] CLY 1030, (1959) Times, 15 January 321
Copps v Follon (1794) 1 Phillim 145n, 161 ER 943 69
Corbets Case (1482) 7 Co Rep 44a, 2 Bl Com 497 41
Corbett v Corbett [1957] 1 All ER 621, [1957] 1 WLR 486, 101 Sol Jo 267 376
Corbett v Corbett (otherwise Ashley) (1969) 113 Sol Jo 982 833

PARA

Corbett v Corbett (otherwise Ashley) [1971] P 83, [1970] 2 All ER 33, [1970] 2 WLR
   1306, 114 Sol Jo 131 .... 1, 321, 336–337, 340, 344, 453
Corke v Corke and Cook (or Cooke) [1958] P 93, [1958] 1 All ER 224, [1958] 2 WLR
   110, 102 Sol Jo 68, CA 353–354
Cornick v Cornick (No 3) [2001] 2 FLR 1240 568
Cornish v Cornish (1890) 15 PD 131, 59 LJP 84, 62 LT 667 760
Corpataux v Corpataux and Staub (1875) 23 WR 456 771
Cossey v United Kingdom (Application 10843/84) (1990) 13 EHRR 622, [1993] 2 FCR
   97, [1991] 2 FLR 492, [1991] Fam Law 362, ECtHR 1
Costard v Winder (1600) Cro Eliz 775, 78 ER 1005 80
Cotter v Layer (1731) 2 P Wms 623 238
Cotterell v Cotterell [1998] 3 FCR 199, CA 360
Coulston v Gardiner (1681) 3 Swan 279n, sub nom Colston v Gardner 2 Cas in
   Ch 43 650
Court v Court [1982] Fam 105, [1982] 2 All ER 531, [1982] 3 WLR 199, 3 FLR 334,
   12 Fam Law 116, 126 Sol Jo 412 866
Courtney v Courtney [1923] 2 IR 31, 57 ILT 42 .... 423, 427, 431
Cousins v Sun Life Assurance Society [1933] Ch 126, [1932] All ER Rep 404, 102 LJ
   Ch 114, 148 LT 101, 49 TLR 12, CA 274–275
Covell v Sweetland [1968] 2 All ER 1016, [1968] 1 WLR 1466, 112 Sol Jo 821 442
Cowan v Cowan [2001] EWCA Civ 679, [2002] Fam 97, [2001] 3 WLR 684,
   [2001] 2 FCR 331, [2001] 2 FLR 192, [2001] Fam Law 498, [2001] All ER (D)
   173 (May) 419, 450, 498, 589, 591, 607
Cowcher v Cowcher [1972] 1 All ER 943, [1972] 1 WLR 425, 116 Sol Jo 142 279–280
Cowen v Cowen [1946] P 36, [1945] 2 All ER 197, 114 LJP 57, 173 LT 176, 61 TLR
   525, CA 335
Cowley (Earl) v Countess of Cowley [1900] P 118; on appeal [1900] P 305, 69 LJP 121,
   49 WR 19, 83 LT 218, 16 TLR 563, CA; affd [1901] AC 450, 70 LJP 83, 50 WR
   81, 85 LT 254, 17 TLR 725, HL 215
Cowper v Taylor (1848) 16 Sim 314 650
Cox v Cox (1883) 70 LT 200, [1891–4] All ER Rep 674, CA 790
Cox v Cox (1889) 61 LT 698 777
Cox v Cox [1958] 1 All ER 569, [1958] 1 WLR 340, 122 JP 173, 102 Sol Jo 217 .... 353, 381,
   393
Crabb v Crabb (1868) LR 1 P & D 601, [1861–73] All ER Rep 291, 37 LJP & M 42,
   16 WR 650, 18 LT 153 .... 368, 374, 429–430, 699
Crabtree v Crabtree [1953] 2 All ER 56, [1953] 1 WLR 708, 117 JP 334, 97 Sol Jo
   371, CA 371, 373, 436
Craig v Kanssen [1943] KB 256, [1943] 1 All ER 108, 112 LJKB 228, 87 Sol Jo 48, 168
   LT 38, CA 879, 883
Craven v Craven and Johnson (1957) 107 Sol Jo 505, CA 854
Crawford v Crawford and Dilke (1886) 11 PD 150, 34 WR 677, 55 LT 305, 2 TLR
   768, CA 354, 875, 877
Cresswell v Cosins (1815) 2 Phillim 281, 161 ER 1145 .... 42, 49
Cresswell v Eaton [1991] 1 All ER 484, [1991] 1 WLR 1113 492
Crewe v Crewe [1984] Fam Law 213, CA 610
Crittenden v Crittenden [1991] FCR 70, [1990] 2 FLR 361, [1990] Fam Law 432, CA ... 520, 609
Crocker v Crocker [1921] P 25, [1920] All ER Rep 134, 90 LJP 136, 65 Sol Jo 153, 124
   LT 493, 37 TLR 137, CA 425
Crone v O'Dell (1824) 2 Mol 355 649
Crosby's Trusts, Re, Smith v Metherell (1919) 147 LT Jo 66 40
Croshaw v Lyndhurst Ship Co [1897] 2 Ch 154, 66 LJ Ch 576, 45 WR 570, 41 Sol Jo
   508, 76 LT 553 648
Crosland v Crosland [1947] P 12, [1946] 2 All ER 91, 90 Sol Jo 530, 175 LT 117, 62
   TLR 413 876
Crossfield v Shurmur (1883) 24 Ch D 597, 53 LJ Ch 87, 31 WR 884, 49 LT 156 711
Crossley v Crossley [2007] EWCA Civ 1491, [2008] 1 FCR 323, [2008] 1 FLR 1467,
   [2008] Fam Law 395, [2007] All ER (D) 396 (Dec) 596, 712
Crouch v Crouch [1912] 1 KB 378, 81 LJKB 275, 56 Sol Jo 188, 106 LT 77, 28 TLR
   155, DC 438
Crouch v Waller (1859) 4 De G & J 302, 7 WR 523, 45 ER 117, 33 LTOS 215 ..... 436, 439, 441
Crowden v Crowden (1906) 23 TLR 143 875

PARA

Crown Prosecution Service v Richards [2006] EWCA Civ 849, [2006] 2 FCR 452,
    [2006] 2 FLR 1220, [2006] Fam Law 731, (2006) Times, 10 July, 150 Sol Jo LB
    888, [2006] All ER (D) 312 (Jun) 500
Crowther v Crowther [1951] AC 723, [1951] 1 All ER 1131, 95 Sol Jo 450, [1951] 1
    TLR 1149, HL 368–369, 385–387, 389, 396
Crozier v Crozier [1994] Fam 114, [1994] 2 All ER 362, [1994] 2 WLR 444,
    [1994] 1 FCR 781, [1994] 1 FLR 126, [1994] Fam Law 245 .... 492, 518
Crystall v Crystall [1963] 2 All ER 330, [1963] 1 WLR 574, 107 Sol Jo 415, CA 227
Cudlipp v Cudlipp (1858) 27 LJP & M 64, 1 Sw & Tr 229, 164 ER 705, 31 LTOS
    318 400
Culley v Charman (1881) 7 QBD 89, 45 JP 768, 50 LJMC 111, 29 WR 803, 45 LT
    28, DC 216
Culling v Culling [1896] P 116, 65 LJP 59, 74 LT 252, 12 TLR 210 .... 57, 80
Cumbers v Cumbers [1975] 1 All ER 1, [1974] 1 WLR 1331, 118 Sol Jo 598, CA 873
Cummins, Re, Cummins v Thompson [1972] Ch 62, [1971] 3 All ER 782,
    [1971] 3 WLR 580, 115 Sol Jo 567, CA 224, 278
Cummins v Hall and Cummins [1933] IR 419 710
Cuno v Cuno. See Mansfield (falsely called Cuno) v Cuno
Currie v Nind (1836) 1 My & Cr 17, 5 LJ Ch 169 711
Curtin v Curtin [1952] 2 QB 552, [1952] 1 All ER 1348, 116 JP 361, 96 Sol Jo 361,
    [1952] 1 TLR 1394 368
Curtis v Curtis (1858) 27 LJP & M 73, 1 Sw & Tr 192, 164 ER 688, 31 LTOS 272;
    affd (1859) 28 LJP & M 55, 4 Sw & Tr 234 850
Curtis v Curtis (1868) 38 LJP & M 9, 19 LT 610 845
Curtis v Curtis (1905) 21 TLR 676 354
Curtis v Curtis [1969] 2 All ER 207, [1969] 1 WLR 422, 113 Sol Jo 242, CA 484, 552
Curtis v Williamson (1874) LR 10 QB 57, 44 LJQB 27, 23 WR 236, 31 LT 678 259
Customs and Excise Comrs v A [2002] EWCA Civ 1039, [2003] Fam 55,
    [2003] 2 All ER 736, [2003] 2 WLR 210, [2002] 3 FCR 481, [2003] 1 FLR 164,
    [2003] Fam Law 85, [2002] 37 LS Gaz R 36, (2002) Times, 25 July, [2002] All ER
    (D) 312 (Jul) 500
Cuzner (formerly Underdown) v Underdown [1974] 2 All ER 351, [1974] 1 WLR 641,
    117 Sol Jo 465, CA 621
Czepek v Czepek [1962] 3 All ER 990 386

D

D (minors), Re [1993] Fam 231, [1993] 2 All ER 693, [1993] 2 WLR 721,
    [1993] 1 FCR 877, [1993] 1 FLR 932, [1993] Fam Law 410, [1993] NLJR
    438, CA 929
D v D (1911) 55 Sol Jo 331 801
D v D (1954). See B v B (1955)
D v D (1974) 5 Fam Law 61, 118 Sol Jo 715 702
D v D [1979] Fam 70, [1979] 3 All ER 337, [1979] 3 WLR 185, 9 Fam Law 182, 123
    Sol Jo 473 321
D v D [1995] 3 FCR 183, [1995] 2 FLR 497, [1995] Fam Law 670 931
D v D (financial provision: lump sum order) [2001] 1 FCR 561, [2001] 1 FLR 633,
    [2000] All ER (D) 1848 478
D (J) v D (S). See D'Este v D'Este
D v P (forum conveniens) [1998] 3 FCR 403, [1998] 2 FLR 25, [1998] Fam Law 458 846
D v W [1984] Fam Law 152 .... 595, 917
DB v WB [1935] P 80, [1935] All ER Rep 428, sub nom B v B 33 LGR 182, 99 JP 162,
    104 LJP 25, 30 Cox CC 204, 79 Sol Jo 216, 152 LT 419 .... 213, 370
DE v AG (falsely calling herself DE) (1845) 1 Rob Eccl 279, 163 ER 1039 .... 335, 339–340
Dackham v Dackham [1987] 2 FLR 358, [1987] Fam Law 345, CA 866
Daglish v Daglish [1936] P 49, [1935] All ER Rep 903, 105 LJP 19, 80 Sol Jo 129, 154
    LT 246, 52 TLR 171 771
Dailey v Dailey (otherwise Smith) [1947] 1 All ER 847, 63 TLR 356; on appeal
    [1947] 2 All ER 269n, CA 453
Dallas v Dallas (1874) 43 LJP & M 87, 31 LT 271 402
Dalrymple v Dalrymple (1811) 2 Hag Con 54; on appeal (1814) 2 Hag Con 137n 1, 10, 42,
                                                             344

PARA

Dancer v Dancer [1949] P 147, [1948] 2 All ER 731, [1949] LJR 138, 92 Sol Jo 528, 64
TLR 505 .... 69, 328
Danchevsky v Danchevsky [1975] Fam 17, [1974] 3 All ER 934, [1974] 3 WLR 709,
118 Sol Jo 701, CA 641, 654
Daniel v Bowles (1826) 2 C & P 553 16
Darlington v Pulteney (1775) 1 Cowp 260, [1775–1802] All ER Rep 353, 98 ER 1075 232
Dart v Dart [1997] 1 FCR 21, [1996] 2 FLR 286, [1996] Fam Law 607, CA 450, 456, 591,
603–606, 608, 619
Darvill v Darvill (1973) 117 Sol Jo 223 407
Daubney v Daubney [1976] Fam 267, [1976] 2 All ER 453, [1976] 2 WLR 959, 120 Sol
Jo 330, CA 601
Davenport, Re, Turner v King [1895] 1 Ch 361, 64 LJ Ch 252, 13 R 167, 43 WR 217,
71 LT 875 237
Davidson v Davidson (1856) Dea & Sw 132, 2 Jur NS 547, 4 WR 590, 27 LTOS 176 353
Davidson v Davidson [1953] 1 All ER 611, [1953] 1 WLR 387, 117 JP 152, 97 Sol Jo
156 213
Davies v Davies [1956] P 212, [1955] 3 All ER 588, [1955] 3 WLR 840, 99 Sol Jo
834 771
Davies v Davies [1957] P 357, [1957] 2 All ER 444, [1957] 3 WLR 34, 121 JP 369, 101
Sol Jo 482 565
Davies v Davies [1986] 1 FLR 497, [1986] Fam Law 138, CA 478, 601
Davies v Davies and M'Carthy (1868) 37 LJP & M 17 513
Davies v Elmslie [1938] 1 KB 337, [1937] 4 All ER 471, 107 LJKB 113, 81 Sol Jo 1000,
158 LT 362, 54 TLR 170, CA 219
Davies' Policy Trusts, Re [1892] 1 Ch 90, 61 LJ Ch 650, 66 LT 104 275
Davis v Artingstall (1880) 49 LJ Ch 609, 29 WR 137, 42 LT 507 251
Davis v Black (1841) 1 QB 900, 10 LJQB 338, 1 Gal & Dav 432, 6 Jur 55 81
Davis v Clarke (1844) 6 QB 16, 13 LJQB 305, 8 Jur 688, 3 LTOS 159 257
Davis v Davis (1920) 124 LT 795, 37 TLR 109 368
Davis v Davis [1950] P 125, [1950] 1 All ER 40, 48 LGR 199, 114 JP 56, 94 Sol Jo
81, CA 346, 352, 354
Davis v Davis (1966) Times, 17 March 771
Davis v Johnson [1979] AC 264, [1978] 1 All ER 841, [1978] 2 WLR 182, 121 Sol Jo
815, CA; affd [1979] AC 264, [1978] 1 All ER 1132, [1978] 2 WLR 553, 122 Sol
Jo 178, HL 716
Davis v Vale [1971] 2 All ER 1021, [1971] 1 WLR 1022, 115 Sol Jo 347, CA 283
Davy v Garrett (1878) 7 Ch D 473, sub nom Davy Bros Ltd v Garrett 47 LJ Ch 218, 26
WR 225, 38 LT 77, CA 877
Dawson v Dawson and Reilly (1907) 23 TLR 716 776
Day v Day [1957] P 202, [1957] 1 All ER 848, [1957] 2 WLR 683, 101 Sol Jo 321 ...... 362, 380,
852
Day v Day [1980] Fam 29, [1979] 2 All ER 187, [1979] 2 WLR 681, 9 Fam Law 54,
123 Sol Jo 251, CA 348, 815
Day v Day [1988] FCR 470, [1988] 1 FLR 278, [1988] Fam Law 209 616
Deacock v Deacock [1958] P 230, [1958] 2 All ER 633, [1958] 3 WLR 191, 102 Sol Jo
526, CA 415, 417, 454
Dean v Dean [1978] Fam 161, [1978] 3 All ER 758, [1978] 3 WLR 288, 122 Sol Jo
211 626
D'Angibau, Re, Andrews v Andrews (1880) 15 Ch D 228, [1874–80] All ER Rep 1184,
49 LJ Ch 756, 28 WR 930, 43 LT 135, CA 234, 236
Debenham v Mellon (1880) 6 App Cas 24, [1874–80] All ER Rep Ext 1397, 45 JP 252,
50 LJQB 155, 29 WR 141, 43 LT 673, HL 256, 264–266, 270
Debenham's Ltd v Perkins (1925) 133 LT 252, [1925] All ER Rep 234 259
Debtor (No 24 of 1971), Re, ex p Marley v Trustee of property of debtor
[1976] 2 All ER 1010, [1976] 1 WLR 952, 120 Sol Jo 553 244
Debtor (No 68/SD/97), a, Re [1998] 4 All ER 779 692
Debtor, Re, ex p Trustee v Solomon. See Solomon (a bankrupt), Re, ex p Trustee of
Property of Bankrupt v Solomon
Debtor, a, Re, JP v Debtor [1999] 2 FCR 637, [1999] 1 FLR 926, [1999] Fam Law 293,
[1999] 2 BCLC 571, [1999] BPIR 206 689

PARA

De Dampierre v De Dampierre [1988] AC 92, [1987] 2 All ER 1, [1987] 2 WLR 1006,
   [1987] 2 FLR 300, [1987] Fam Law 418, 131 Sol Jo 471, [1987] LS Gaz R 1493,
   [1987] NLJ Rep 341, HL 842
D'Este v D'Este [1973] Fam 55, [1973] 2 WLR 183, 116 Sol Jo 969, sub nom D (J) v
   D (S) [1973] 1 All ER 349 .... 538, 684
De Greuchy v Wills (1879) 4 CPD 362, 43 JP 818, 48 LJQB 726, 28 WR 169, 41 LT
   345 204
Delahunty v Delahunty (Nobes cited) [1961] 1 All ER 923, [1961] 1 WLR 515, 105 Sol
   Jo 211 .... 761, 861
Delaney v Delaney [1991] FCR 161, [1990] 2 FLR 457, [1991] Fam Law 22, CA 602, 610
de Lasala v de Lasala [1980] AC 546, [1979] 2 All ER 1146, [1979] 3 WLR 390, 123
   Sol Jo 301, PC 476
De Laubenque v De Laubenque [1899] P 42, [1895–9] All ER Rep 478, 68 LJP 20, 79
   LT 708 362
Demetriou v Demetriou [1950] P 261, [1950] 2 All ER 49, 94 Sol Jo 383, CA 755
De Niceville v De Niceville (1868) 37 LJP & M 43 776
Dennis v Dennis [1955] P 153, [1955] 2 All ER 51, [1955] 2 WLR 817, 99 Sol Jo
   259, CA 349
Dennis v Dennis (Queen's Proctor intervening) [2000] Fam 163, [2000] 3 WLR 1443,
   [2000] 2 FCR 108, [2000] 2 FLR 231, [2005] Fam Law 605 .... 865, 878
Dennys v Sargeant (1834) 5 C & P 419 264
Densham (a bankrupt), Re, ex p trustee of bankrupt v Densham [1975] 3 All ER 726,
   [1975] 1 WLR 1519, 119 Sol Jo 774 279–280
Dent v Dent (1865) 34 LJPM & A 118, 4 Sw & Tr 105, 164 ER 1455, 13 LT 252 771
De Pret-Roose v De Pret-Roose (1934) 78 Sol Jo 914 430
Derby & Co Ltd v Weldon [1990] Ch 48, [1989] 1 All ER 469, [1989] 2 WLR 276,
   [1989] 1 Lloyd's Rep 122, 133 Sol Jo 83, [1989] 6 LS Gaz R 43, [1988] NLJR
   236, CA 661
Derby & Co Ltd v Weldon (Nos 3 and 4) [1990] Ch 65, [1989] 2 WLR 412, 133 Sol Jo
   83, sub nom Derby & Co Ltd v Weldon (No 2) [1989] 1 All ER 1002, CA 661
De Reneville (otherwise Sheridan) v De Reneville [1948] P 100, [1948] 1 All ER 56,
   [1948] LJR 1761, 92 Sol Jo 83, 64 TLR 82, CA 34, 320, 322, 514
De Ricci v De Ricci [1891] P 378, 61 LJP 17 .... 473, 504, 548, 641, 860
Dering v Dering and Blakeley (1868) LR 1 P & D 531, 37 LJP & M 52, 16 WR 1176,
   19 LT 48 .... 538, 876
Desmarest v Desmarest (1861) 31 LJPM & A 34 855
De Thoren v A-G (1876) 1 App Cas 686, 3 R 28, HL 6
Dewe v Dewe [1928] P 113, [1928] All ER Rep 492, 26 LGR 191, 92 JP 32, 97 LJP 65,
   72 Sol Jo 69, 138 LT 552, 44 TLR 274 446
Dewhirst, Re, Flower v Dewhirst [1948] Ch 198, [1948] 1 All ER 147, [1948] LJR 912,
   92 Sol Jo 84, 64 TLR 74 514
De Wilton, Re, De Wilton v Montefiore [1900] 2 Ch 481, 69 LJ Ch 717, 48 WR 645,
   44 Sol Jo 626, 83 LT 70, 16 TLR 507 .... 35, 118
Dharamshi v Dharamshi [2001] 1 FCR 492, [2001] 1 FLR 736, [2001] Fam Law 98,
   [2000] All ER (D) 2121, CA 450, 498, 591, 603, 607
Dickens v Pattison [1985] FLR 610, [1985] Fam Law 163, sub nom R v Camberwell
   Green Justices, ex p Pattison and Dickens 149 JP 271, 129 Sol Jo 31 679
Dickenson, Re, ex p Hall (1810) 1 Rose 30, 1 Ves & B 112 711
Dicker v Dicker (otherwise Parris) (1959) Times, 10 November 321
Dickinson v Dickinson (1889) 62 LT 330 393
Dickinson v Jones Alexander & Co [1993] 2 FLR 521, [1990] Fam Law 137, 6 PN 205,
   [1989] NLJR 1525 609
Diddear (falsely called Fawcit otherwise Savill) v Faucit (1821) 3 Phillim 580, 161 ER
   1421 .... 21, 69
Dillon v Dillon (1842) 3 Curt 86, 6 Jur 422, 1 Notes of Cases 415 349
Dinch v Dinch [1987] 1 All ER 818, [1987] 1 WLR 252, [1987] 2 FLR 162,
   [1987] Fam Law 267, 131 Sol Jo 296, [1987] LS Gaz R 1142, HL 476, 499, 609, 715,
                                                                                                                      933
Dinizulu v A-G and Registrar-General [1958] 3 All ER 555, [1958] 1 WLR 1252, 102
   Sol Jo 879 89
Dipple v Dipple [1942] P 65, [1942] 1 All ER 234, 111 LJP 18, 86 Sol Jo 70, 166 LT
   120, 58 TLR 141 .... 474, 538, 550, 684

PARA

Disher v Disher [1965] P 31, [1963] 3 All ER 933, [1964] 2 WLR 21, 108 Sol Jo 37 897
Dixon, Re, Heynes v Dixon [1900] 2 Ch 561, [1900–3] All ER Rep Ext 1618, 69 LJ
    Ch 609, 48 WR 665, 44 Sol Jo 515, 83 LT 129, CA 206, 251
Dixon v Dixon (1878) 9 Ch D 587, 27 WR 282 251
Dixon v Dixon [1953] P 103, [1953] 1 All ER 910, [1953] 2 WLR 748, 97 Sol Jo 249 ... 395, 734
Dixon v Rowe (1876) 35 LT 548 650
Dobbyn v Corneck (1812) 2 Phillim 102 69
Dodd v Dodd [1906] P 189, 70 JP 163, 75 LJP 49, 54 WR 541, 50 Sol Jo 528, 94 LT
    709, 22 TLR 484 406
Doe d Blomfield v Eyre (1848) 5 CB 713, 18 LJCP 284, 10 LTOS 525, Ex Ch 232
Doe d Fleming v Fleming (1827) 4 Bing 266, 5 LJOS 169, 12 Moore CP 500, 130 ER
    769 6
Doe d Egremont (Earl) v Grazebrook (1843) 4 QB 406, 12 LJQB 221, 3 Gal & Dav
    334, 7 Jur 530, 114 ER 951 .... 6, 76
Doe d Barnes v Rowe (1838) 4 Bing NC 737, 1 Arn 279, 6 Scott 525 711
Doherty v Doherty [1976] Fam 71, [1975] 2 All ER 635, [1975] 3 WLR 1, 119 Sol Jo
    423, CA 451–452
Donnelly v Donnelly (1886) 31 Sol Jo 45 211
Dormer (otherwise Ward) v Ward [1900] P 130, [1900–03] All ER Rep 363, 82 69 LJP
    65, 48 WR 524, LT 469, 16 TLR 220, CA; revsd [1901] P 20, [1900–3] All ER
    Rep 363, 83 69 LJP 144, 49 WR 149, LT 556, 17 TLR 12, CA 511, 514
Dormer (falsely called Williams) v Williams (1838) 2 JP 809, 1 Curt 870, 163 ER 301 328
Dorney-Kingdom v Dorney-Kingdom [2000] 3 FCR 20, [2000] 2 FLR 855, CA 497, 551
Dorrell v Dorrell [1972] 3 All ER 343, [1972] 1 WLR 1087, 116 Sol Jo 617 411
Douglas v Douglas [1951] P 85, [1950] 2 All ER 748, 94 Sol Jo 487, 66 (pt 2) TLR
    531, CA 349, 353
Douglas v Douglas and Trevor (1897) 78 LT 88 512
Dove v Dove [1963] P 321, [1963] 2 All ER 10, [1963] 2 WLR 774, 107 Sol Jo
    213, CA 771, 865
Dowell v Dowell [1952] 2 All ER 141, [1952] WN 296, 116 JP 350, 96 Sol Jo
    362, DC 542
Dowling v Dowling [1898] P 228, 68 LJP 8, 47 WR 272 .... 438, 699
Downes v Timperon (1828) 4 Russ 334, 38 ER 831 232
Downing v Downing [1976] Fam 288, [1976] 3 All ER 474, [1976] 3 WLR 335, 120
    Sol Jo 540 .... 492–493, 495, 518, 543, 546, 558, 561, 571, 583
Drake v Whipp [1996] 2 FCR 296, [1996] 1 FLR 826, [1996] Fam Law 472, 28 HLR
    531, CA 282
Draper's Conveyance, Re, Nihan v Porter [1969] 1 Ch 486, [1967] 3 All ER 853,
    [1968] 2 WLR 166, 19 P & CR 71, 111 Sol Jo 867 227
Draskovic v Draskovic (1980) 11 Fam Law 87, 125 Sol Jo 306 492
Dredge v Dredge (otherwise Harrison) [1947] 1 All ER 29, 63 TLR 113 .... 321, 852
Drew v Drew (1888) 13 PD 97, [1886–90] All ER Rep 664, 57 LJP 64, 36 WR 927, 58
    LT 923 386
Drew v Nunn (1879) 4 QBD 661, [1874–80] All ER Rep 1144, 43 JP 541, 48 LJQB
    591, 27 WR 810, 40 LT 671, CA 262, 271
Drexel v Drexel [1916] 1 Ch 251, 85 LJ Ch 235, 114 LT 350, 32 TLR 208 443
Drinkwater v Drinkwater [1984] FLR 627, [1984] Fam Law 245, CA 316, 612, 616
Drummond v Drummond (1861) 30 LJPM & A 177, 7 Jur NS 762, 2 Sw & Tr 269,
    164 ER 998, 4 LT 416 771
Drummond v Drummond (1868) 37 LJ Ch 811, 17 WR 6, 18 LT 896 239
Dryden v Dryden [1973] Fam 217, [1973] 3 All ER 526, [1973] 3 WLR 524, 117 Sol Jo
    393 .... 866, 873, 879, 883
Du Boulay v Du Boulay (1869) LR 2 PC 430, 6 Moo PCCNS 31, 38 LJPC 35, 17 WR
    594, 22 LT 228 215
Ducarrey v Gill (1830) 4 C & P 121, Mood & M 450 257
Duckworth, Re (1889) 5 TLR 608 .... 368, 400–401
Duffield v Scott (1789) 3 Term Rep 374, [1775–1802] All ER Rep 621, 100 ER 628 435
Du Moulin v Druitt (1860) 13 ICLR 212, 13 Ir Jur 76 80
Dunbar (otherwise White) v Dunbar [1909] P 90, [1908–10] All ER Rep 76, 78 LJP 35,
    100 LT 380, 25 TLR 230 453
Duncan, Re, Garfield v Fay [1968] P 306, [1968] 2 All ER 395, [1968] 2 WLR 1479,
    112 Sol Jo 254 833

PARA

Dunn v Dunn [1949] P 98, [1948] 2 All ER 822, 46 LGR 531, 112 JP 436, [1949] LJR
87, 92 Sol Jo 633, 64 TLR 570, CA 369, 384
Dunn v Dunn [1967] P 217, [1965] 1 All ER 1043, [1965] 2 WLR 947, 109 Sol Jo
289 .... 397, 400
Dunn v Dunn's Trustees 1930 SC 131 344
Duplany v Duplany [1892] P 53, 61 LJP 49, 66 LT 267, 8 TLR 169 771
Durand v Durand (1789) 2 Cox Eq Cas 207, 30 ER 96 439
Durham v Durham (1885) 10 PD 80, 1 TLR 338 .... 42, 45
Durrant v Holdsworth (1886) 2 TLR 763 269
Duxbury v Duxbury [1992] Fam 62n, [1990] 2 All ER 77, [1991] 3 WLR 639n,
[1987] 1 FLR 7, [1987] Fam Law 13, CA 483, 593
Dysart Peerage Case (1881) 6 App Cas 489, HL 42, 344

E

E v C (child maintenance) [1996] 1 FCR 612, [1996] 1 FLR 472, [1996] Fam Law
205 .... 492, 602
E v E (otherwise C). See Edwards v Edwards
E v E (otherwise T) (1902) 50 WR 607, 46 Sol Jo 586, 87 LT 149, 18 TLR 643 .... 338, 340, 511
E v E (otherwise T) [1903] P 88, 72 LJP 44, 88 LT 570 515
E v E (1907) 23 TLR 364 789
E v E [1989] FCR 591, [1990] 2 FLR 233, [1990] Fam Law 297 618
E v G (lump sum order: bankruptcy) [1997] 1 FCR 261, [1996] 2 FLR 171,
[1996] Fam Law 534 689
E– v T– (falsely called E) (1863) 33 LJPM & A 37, 3 Sw & Tr 312, 12 WR 444, sub
nom Ewens v Tytherleigh (falsely called Ewens) 9 Jur NS 1301, 9 LT 424 321
Eadie v IRC [1924] 2 KB 198, [1924] All ER Rep 760, 9 TC 1, 93 LJKB 914, 68 Sol Jo
667, 131 LT 350, 40 TLR 553 412
Earnshaw v Earnshaw [1939] 2 All ER 698, 83 Sol Jo 496, CA 368
Eaves, Re, Eaves v Eaves [1940] Ch 109, [1939] 4 All ER 260, 109 LJ Ch 97, 83 Sol Jo
942, 162 LT 8, 56 TLR 110, CA 514
Eaves v Eaves [1939] P 361, [1939] 2 All ER 789, 109 LJP 27, 83 Sol Jo 549, 161 LT
119, 55 TLR 706 699
Ebrahim v Ali (otherwise Ebrahim) (Queen's Proctor intervening) [1983] 3 All ER 615,
sub nom Ali Ebrahim v Ali Ebrahim (Queen's Proctor intervening) [1983] 1 WLR
1336, [1984] FLR 95, [1984] Fam Law 20, 127 Sol Jo 732 .... 776, 853, 883
Edgar v Edgar [1980] 3 All ER 887, [1980] 1 WLR 1410, 2 FLR 19, 124 Sol Jo
809, CA 596, 626
Edgcome, Re, ex p Edgcome [1902] 2 KB 403, [1900–3] All ER Rep 862, 71 LJKB 722,
9 Mans 227, 50 WR 678, 46 Sol Jo 649, 87 LT 108, 18 TLR 734, CA 643
Edmonds v Edmonds [1965] 1 All ER 379n, [1965] 1 WLR 58, 108 Sol Jo 1047 630
Edwards, Re, Owen v Edwards [1885] WN 74 641
Edwards v Edwards (1893) 62 LJP 33 397
Edwards v Edwards (otherwise Cowtan) [1934] P 84, sub nom E v E (otherwise C) 103
LJP 37, 78 Sol Jo 137, 151 LT 36, 50 TLR 235 453
Edwards v Edwards [1948] P 268, [1948] 1 All ER 157, 46 LGR 93, 112 JP 109, [1948]
LJR 670, 92 Sol Jo 98, 64 TLR 61 .... 362, 368, 394–395, 397
Edwards v Edwards [1950] P 8, [1949] 2 All ER 145, 47 LGR 541, 113 JP 383, [1949]
LJR 1335, 93 Sol Jo 450, 65 TLR 419, CA 381, 393
Edwards v Edwards [1951] P 228, [1951] 1 All ER 63, 94 Sol Jo 823, [1951] 1 TLR
600 .... 739, 865, 883
Edwards v Edwards (Moore intervening) (Jamieson and Brierly cited) (1965) 109 Sol Jo
175 393
Edwards v Edwards and Wilson [1897] P 316, 67 LJP 1, 77 LT 406, 13 TLR 592 760
Edwards v Edwards and Wilson (1899) Times, 17, 20 June 831, 863
Edwards v Towels (1843) 12 LJCP 239, 5 Man & G 624, 6 Scott NR 641, 134 ER
709 267
Ehlers v Ehlers (1915) 113 LT 1215 .... 425, 438
Eldred v Eldred (1840) 2 Curt 376, 163 ER 445 794
Ellard v Warren (1681) 3 Rep Ch 87 650
Ellaytt v Ellaytt, Taylor and Halse. See Ellyatt v Ellyatt, Taylor and Halse
Elliott v Gurr (1812) 2 Phillim 16, [1803–13] All ER Rep 698, 161 ER 1064 .... 41, 322
Elliott v Totnes Union (1892) 57 JP 151, 9 TLR 35 6

PARA

Ellis v Bowman (1851) 17 LTOS 10 45
Ellis v Ellis (1883) 8 PD 188, [1881–5] All ER Rep Ext 1510, 52 LJP 99, 31 WR 942,
    49 LT 223, CA 879
Ellis v Ellis (1929) 93 JP 175 736
Ellis v Ellis and Wilby [1962] 1 All ER 797, [1962] 1 WLR 450, 106 Sol Jo 152, CA 830
Ellyatt v Ellyatt, Taylor and Halse (1864) 33 LJPM & A 137, 10 Jur NS 1035, 11 LT
    44, sub nom Elyett v Elyett, Taylor and Halse 4 New Rep 159, sub nom Ellaytt v
    Ellaytt, Taylor and Halse 3 Sw & Tr 503, 164 ER 1370 738
Elsley v Elsley, Beacham and Bagshaw (1863) 32 LJPM & A 145 777
Elwes v Elwes (1794) 1 Hag Con 269 353
Elworthy v Bird (1825) 2 Sim & St 372, 3 LJOS 190, 57 ER 388 426
Elyett v Elyett, Taylor and Halse. See Ellyatt v Ellyatt, Taylor and Halse
Emanuel v Emanuel [1946] P 115, [1945] 2 All ER 494, 114 LJP 60, 173 LT 118, 61
    TLR 538 369
Emerson v Blonden (1794) 1 Esp 141 261
Emery v Emery (1963) Times, 10 October 771
Emmett v Norton (1838) 8 C & P 506 264
Empringham v Short (1844) 3 Hare 461, 13 LJ Ch 300, 8 Jur 856 650
Engelbach's Estate, Re, Tibbetts v Engelbach [1924] 2 Ch 348, [1923] All ER Rep 93,
    93 LJ Ch 616, 68 Sol Jo 208, 130 LT 401 274
England v England [1953] P 16, [1952] 2 All ER 784, 116 JP 584, 96 Sol Jo 730,
    [1952] 2 TLR 705 352–353
England v England (1979) 10 Fam Law 86, CA 872
Equitable Life Assurance Society of US Policy and Mitchell, Re (1911) 27 TLR 213 274–275
Equity and Law Home Loans Ltd v Prestidge [1992] 1 All ER 909, [1992] 1 WLR 137,
    63 P & CR 403, [1992] 1 FCR 353, [1992] 1 FLR 485, [1992] Fam Law 288, 24
    HLR 76, [1992] 2 LS Gaz R 31, CA 284
Essex v Atkins (1808) 14 Ves 542, 33 ER 629 249
Essex's (Countess) Case (1613) 2 State Tr 785, 2 Dyer 179an, 1 Hargrave's State Tr
    307 341
Etherington v Parrot (1703) 2 Ld Raym 1006, 1 Salk 118, Holt KB 102, 90 ER 955 265
Evans v Carrington (1860) 25 JP 195, 2 De GF & J 481, 30 LJ Ch 364, 7 Jur NS 197,
    45 ER 707, 4 LT 65 429
Evans v Edmonds (1853) 13 CB 777, 22 LJCP 211, 17 Jur 883, 93 RR 732, 1 WR 412,
    138 ER 1407, 1 CLR 653, 21 LTOS 155 429
Evans v Evans [1948] 1 KB 175, [1947] 2 All ER 656, 45 LGR 666, 112 JP 23, [1948]
    LJR 276, 91 Sol Jo 664, 63 TLR 638, DC 347, 368
Evans v Evans [1989] FCR 133, [1989] 1 FLR 351, [1989] Fam Law 193, CA 621
Evans v Evans [1990] 2 All ER 147, [1990] 1 WLR 575n, [1990] FCR 498,
    [1990] 1 FLR 319, [1990] Fam Law 215, 134 Sol Jo 785, [1990] 12 LS Gaz R 40,
    [1990] NLJR 291 609
Evans v Evans and Blyth [1904] P 274, 378, [1904–7] All ER Rep 110, 73 LJP 87, 91
    LT 356, 20 TLR 516 512
Evans v Evans and Robinson (1858) 27 LJP & M 57, 1 Sw & Tr 173, 6 WR 640, 31
    LTOS 170, 164 ER 680 357–358
Evans v Evans and Robinson (1859) 23 JP 407, 28 LJP & M 136, 5 Jur NS 606, 1 Sw
    & Tr 328, 7 WR 181, 164 ER 751, 32 LTOS 244 349
Evans v Wills (1876) 1 CPD 229, 40 JP 552, 45 LJQB 420, 24 WR 883, 34 LT 679,
    CPD 643
Evelyn v Templar (1787) 2 Bro CC 148 711
Evered v Evered and Graham (1874) 43 LJP & M 86, 22 WR 845, 31 LT 101 513
Everitt v Everitt [1948] 2 All ER 545, 92 Sol Jo 586, 65 TLR 121, CA 879, 883
Everitt v Everitt [1949] P 374, [1949] 1 All ER 908, 47 LGR 377, 113 JP 279, 93 Sol Jo
    286, CA 368, 377, 397, 400
Eves v Eves [1975] 3 All ER 768, [1975] 1 WLR 1338, 119 Sol Jo 394, CA 279, 284
Ewart v Ewart [1959] P 23, [1958] 3 All ER 561, [1958] 3 WLR 680, 123 JP 63, 102
    Sol Jo 861 424
Ewens v Tytherleigh (falsely called Ewens). See E– v T– (falsely called E)
Ewing v Wheatley (1814) 2 Hag Con 175, 161 ER 706 .... 76–77, 349
Eyre-Williams, Re, Williams v Williams [1923] 2 Ch 533, [1923] All ER Rep Ext 748,
    92 LJ Ch 582, 67 Sol Jo 500, 129 LT 218 206
Ezekiel v Orakpo [1997] 1 WLR 340, CA 636, 680

PARA

F

F v F [1968] P 506, [1968] 1 All ER 242, [1968] 2 WLR 190, 112 Sol Jo 214 352
F v F (1983) 4 FLR 382, 13 Fam Law 16 456
F v F (ancillary relief: substantial assets) [1996] 2 FCR 397, [1995] 2 FLR 45,
    [1995] Fam Law 546 .... 483, 604, 614, 712, 931
F v F (Duxbury calculation: rate of return). See FN v FN (financial provision)
F v F (otherwise P). See F v P (otherwise F)
F v P (falsely called F) (1896) 75 LT 192 340
F v P (otherwise F) (1911) 27 TLR 429, sub nom F v F (otherwise P) 55 Sol Jo 482 340
FN v FN (financial provision) [1996] 3 FCR 56, sub nom F v F (Duxbury calculation:
    rate of return) [1996] 1 FLR 833, [1996] Fam Law 467 .... 601, 604, 613
Failes v Failes [1906] P 326, 75 LJP 95, 95 LT 547, 22 TLR 687 406
Fairman v Fairman [1949] P 341, [1949] 1 All ER 938, 47 LGR 455, 113 JP 275,
    [1949] LJR 1073, 93 Sol Jo 321, 65 TLR 320 .... 349, 352, 354
Faremouth v Watson (1811) 1 Phillim 355 322
Farmer v Farmer (1884) 9 PD 245, 53 LJP 113, 33 WR 169 .... 372, 400
Farnham v Farnham (1925) 133 LT 320, 41 TLR 543 353
Farquharson v Farquharson (1971) 115 Sol Jo 444, CA 226
Farrow, Re [1987] 1 FLR 205, [1987] Fam Law 14 476
Farrow v Farrow (1955) Times, 14 December, CA 883
Fassbender v Fassbender [1938] 3 All ER 389, 107 LJP 123, 82 Sol Jo 626, 54 TLR
    1006 362
Fatima, Re [1986] AC 527, [1986] 2 WLR 693, 130 Sol Jo 315, [1986] LS Gaz R 1720,
    [1986] NLJ Rep 372, sub nom Fatima v Secretary of State for the Home
    Department [1986] 2 All ER 32, sub nom R v Secretary of State for the Home
    Department, ex p Ghulam Fatima [1986] 2 FLR 294, [1986] Fam Law 2070, HL 530
Faulkner v Faulkner [1941] 2 All ER 748, 110 LJP 70, 85 Sol Jo 370, 165 LT 381, 57
    TLR 628 .... 364, 781
Fearon v Earl of Aylesford (1884) 14 QBD 792, [1881–5] All ER Rep 778, 49 JP 596,
    54 LJQB 33, 33 WR 331, 52 LT 954, 1 TLR 68, CA 432, 434, 438–439
Fellowes v Stewart (1814) 2 Phillim 238 69
Felton v Callis [1969] 1 QB 200, [1968] 3 All ER 673, [1968] 3 WLR 951, 112 Sol Jo
    672 663
Fendall (otherwise Goldsmid) v Goldsmid (1877) 2 PD 263, 46 LJP 70 .... 34, 69, 215
Fender v St John-Mildmay [1938] AC 1, 81 Sol Jo 549, 53 TLR 885, sub nom Fender v
    Mildmay [1937] 3 All ER 402, 106 LJKB 641, 157 LT 340, HL 16, 417, 879
Fengl v Fengl [1914] P 274, 84 LJP 29, 59 Sol Jo 42, 112 LT 173, 31 TLR 45, DC 362, 371,
    427, 699
Fenton v Livingstone (1859) 5 Jur NS 1183, [1843–60] All ER Rep 236, 23 JP 579, 7
    WR 671, 33 LTOS 335, 3 Macq 497, HL 35
Ferne, ex p (1801) 5 Ves 832 45
Fick and Fick Ltd v Assimakis [1958] 3 All ER 182, [1958] 1 WLR 1006, 102 Sol Jo
    632, CA 205, 258, 263
Field's Marriage Annulling Bill (1848) 2 HL Cas 48, 9 ER 1010 43
Fielding v Fielding [1978] 1 All ER 267, [1977] 1 WLR 1146n, 121 Sol Jo 729, CA 224, 231,
    278
Filmer v Lynn (1835) 1 Har & W 59, 4 Nev & MKB 559 .... 269, 271
Finch v Finch (Hayes intervening) [1960] 2 All ER 52, [1960] 1 WLR 429, 104 Sol Jo
    331 .... 782, 788, 831
Findlay v Findlay [1947] P 122, [1947] 2 All ER 71, [1947] LJR 1338, 91 Sol Jo 397,
    63 TLR 391, CA 852
Finegan v Finegan (otherwise McHardy) (1917) 33 TLR 173 340
Finney v Finney (1868) LR 1 P & D 483, [1861–73] All ER Rep 365, 37 LJP & M 43,
    18 LT 489 734
Firminger v Firminger and Ollard (1869) 17 WR 335 796
Fishburn v Fishburn [1955] P 29, [1955] 1 All ER 230, [1955] 2 WLR 236, 119 JP 86,
    99 Sol Jo 80 .... 368, 394, 399
Fisher v Fisher [1960] P 36, [1959] 3 All ER 131, [1959] 3 WLR 471, 103 Sol Jo
    581, CA 734, 736
Fisher v Fisher [1989] FCR 309, [1989] 1 FLR 423, [1989] Fam Law 269, CA 600

PARA

Fisher v Owen (1878) 8 Ch D 645, 42 JP 758, 47 LJ Ch 681, 26 WR 581, 38 LT
577, CA 790
Fisk v Fisk (1920) 122 LT 803, 36 TLR 248 384
Fitzgerald v Chapman (1875) 1 Ch D 563, 45 LJ Ch 23, 24 WR 130, 33 LT 587 510
Fitzgerald v Fitzgerald (1862) 32 LJPM & A 12, 11 WR 85 349
Fitzgerald v Fitzgerald (1869) LR 1 P & D 694, 38 LJP & M 14, 17 WR 264, 19 LT
575 362
Fitzgerald v Fitzgerald (1874) LR 3 P & D 136, 43 LJP & M 13, 22 WR 267, 31 LT
270 863
Fitzpatrick v Sterling Housing Association Ltd [2001] 1 AC 27, [1999] 4 All ER 705,
[1999] 3 WLR 1113, 79 P & CR D4, [2000] 1 FCR 21, [1999] 2 FLR 1027,
[2000] 1 FLR 271, [2000] Fam Law 14, 32 HLR 178, [1999] NPC 127,
[1999] 43 LS Gaz R 34, [1999] EGCS 125, 7 BHRC 200, [2000] 3 LRC
294, HL 284
Flavell v Flavell [1997] 1 FCR 332, [1997] 1 FLR 353, CA 568, 592, 615
Fleet Mortgage and Investment Co Ltd v Lower Maisonette 46 Eaton Place Ltd
[1972] 2 All ER 737, [1972] 1 WLR 765, 116 Sol Jo 434 947
Fleetwood's Policy, Re [1926] Ch 48, [1925] All ER Rep 262, 95 LJ Ch 195, 135 LT
374 274–275
Flegg v Prentis [1892] 2 Ch 428, [1891–4] All ER Rep 1272, 61 LJ Ch 705, 67 LT
107 648
Fleming v Fleming [1942] 2 All ER 337, 86 Sol Jo 332, 167 LT 191, DC 397
Fletcher v Fletcher (1788) 2 Cox Eq Cas 99, 3 Bro CC 619n, 30 ER 46 443
Fletcher v Fletcher [1945] 1 All ER 582, 114 LJP 26, 173 LT 128, 61 TLR 354 ..... 379, 384, 393
Flower v Flower (1873) LR 3 P & D 132, [1861–73] All ER Rep Ext 104642 LJP & M
45, 21 WR 776, 29 LT 253, ... 346
Flower v Flower [1893] P 290, 63 LJP 28, 1 R 534, 42 WR 204 875
Fluister v Fluister and Hutton [1897] P 22, 66 LJP 33, 41 Sol Jo 126, CA 738
Foley v Foley [1981] Fam 160, [1981] 2 All ER 857, [1981] 3 WLR 284, 2 FLR 215,
125 Sol Jo 442, CA 616
Ford v Stier [1896] P 1, 11 R 668, sub nom Clarke v Clarke 65 LJP 13, sub nom Clark
(falsely called Stier) v Stier 73 LT 632 44
Ford v Stuart (1852) 15 Beav 493, 21 LJ Ch 514 711
Formosa v Formosa. See Gray (otherwise Formosa) v Formosa
Forristall v Lawson (1876) 34 LT 903 264
Forster v Forster (1910) 54 Sol Jo 403 .... 213, 370
Forster (otherwise Street) v Forster (1923) 39 TLR 658 44
Forster v Forster and Berridge (1863) 32 LJPM & A 206, 3 Sw & Tr 151, 164 ER
1231, 9 LT 148 876
Forster v Forster and Nanni (1912) 29 TLR 22 875
Forsyth v Forsyth [1891] P 363, 61 LJP 13, 65 LT 556 500
Forte v Forte (1966) 110 Sol Jo 52 .... 370, 802
Foster v Bates (1843) 1 Dow & L 400, 13 LJ Ex 88, 7 Jur 1093, 12 M & W 226, 2
LTOS 150 262
Foster v Foster [1954] P 67, [1953] 2 All ER 518, [1953] 3 WLR 623, 117 JP 377, 97
Sol Jo 608 735–736
Foster v Foster [2003] EWCA Civ 565, [2005] 3 FCR 26, [2003] 2 FLR 299,
[2003] Fam Law 562, [2003] 26 LS Gaz R 37, (2003) Times, 2 May, [2003] All ER
(D) 302 (Apr) 618
Foster and Lister, Re (1877) 6 Ch D 87, 46 LJ Ch 480, 25 WR 553, 36 LT 582 711
Fournier v Fournier [1999] 2 FCR 20, [1998] 2 FLR 990, [1998] Fam Law 662, CA 483
Fowke v Fowke [1938] Ch 774, [1938] 2 All ER 638, 107 LJ Ch 350, 82 Sol Jo 415,
159 LT 8, 54 TLR 801 .... 322, 442
Fowler v Fowler (1979) 2 FLR 141, 10 Fam Law 119 679
Fox v Bearblock (1881) 17 Ch D 429, 45 JP 648, 50 LJ Ch 489, 29 WR 661, 44 LT
508 6
Frampton v Framtpon (1841) 4 Beav 287, 5 Jur 980, 49 ER 349 449
France v France [1969] P 46, [1969] 2 All ER 870, [1969] 2 WLR 1141, 113 Sol Jo
266, CA 404
Frankland v Nicholson (1805) 3 M & S 259n, 105 ER 607 69
Fraser v Fraser [1969] 3 All ER 654, [1969] 1 WLR 1787, 113 Sol Jo 624 .... 371–372, 397

PARA

Freeman v Swatridge and Swatridge [1984] FLR 762, [1984] Fam Law 215, 148 JP
  619, CA 492
Freestone v Butcher (1840) 9 C & P 643 .... 205, 258–259, 263–266
French v Howie [1906] 2 KB 674, 75 LJKB 980, 95 LT 274, CA 205, 259
French-Brewster v French-Brewster (1889) 62 LT 609 .... 368–369, 402
Fribance v Fribance [1957] 1 All ER 357, [1957] 1 WLR 384, 101 Sol Jo 188, CA 206, 225
Frisbee v Frisbee (1983) 14 Fam Law 19 .... 592, 600
Froud v Froud (1920) 26 Cox CC 605, [1920] All ER Rep 478, 123 LT 176, 36 TLR
  505 736
Frowd v Frowd [1904] P 177, [1904–7] All ER Rep 104, 68 JP 436, 73 LJP 60, 90 LT
  175, DC 362
Fuggle v Bland (1883) 11 QBD 711, DC 648
Fuller (otherwise Penfold) v Fuller [1973] 2 All ER 650, [1973] 1 WLR 730, 117 Sol Jo
  224, CA 347
Furneaux v Furneaux (1973) 118 Sol Jo 204 703
Furniss v Furniss (1982) 3 FLR 46, 12 Fam Law 30, CA 591, 602
Fussell v Dowding (1872) LR 14 Eq 421, 41 LJ Ch 716, 20 WR 881, 27 LT 406 236
Fust v Bowerman (1790) 2 Add 402, 2 Hag Con 171, 161 ER 705 332

G

G (children) (care proceedings: wasted costs), Re [2000] Fam 104, [1999] 4 All ER 371,
  [2000] 2 WLR 1007, [2000] Fam Law 24, sub nom Re G, S and H (care
  proceedings: wasted costs) [1999] 3 FCR 303, sub nom Re G, S and M (wasted
  costs) [2000] 1 FLR 52 931
G v G (1871) LR 2 P & D 287, [1861–73] All ER Rep Ext 1360, 40 LJP & M 83, 20
  WR 103, 25 LT 510 .... 336–337, 340, 345
G v G (falsely called K) (1908) 25 TLR 328, CA 338, 341
G v G [1912] P 173, 81 LJP 90, 106 LT 647, 28 TLR 481 .... 341, 863
G v G [1924] AC 349, [1924] All ER Rep Ext 900, 93 LJPC 163, 68 Sol Jo 417, 61
  SLR 445, 131 LT 70, 40 TLR 322, 1924 SC (HL) 42, 1924 SLT 248, HL 340
G v G [1930] P 72, 94 JP 79, 142 LT 311, 46 TLR 69, sub nom G-M v G-AD 99 LJP
  14, 74 Sol Jo 59 382
G v G (otherwise H) [1961] P 87, [1960] 3 All ER 56, [1960] 3 WLR 648, 104 Sol Jo
  826 .... 321, 340
G v G [1964] P 133, [1964] 1 All ER 129, [1964] 2 WLR 250 .... 380, 382, 385, 389
G v G [1974] 1 WWR 79, Man SC 342
G v G [1990] FCR 572, [1990] 1 All ER 395, [1990] Fam Law 254, CA 290, 719, 975
G v G (occupation order) [2000] 3 FCR 53, [2000] 2 FLR 36, CA 289, 295, 307
G v G (maintenance pending suit: legal costs) [2002] EWHC 306 (Fam), [2002] 3 FCR
  339, [2003] 2 FLR 71, [2003] Fam Law 393, [2002] All ER (D) 306 (Feb) 456
G v G (financial provision: equal division) [2002] EWHC 1339 (Fam), [2002] 2 FLR
  1143, [2003] Fam Law 14 607
G v M (1885) 10 App Cas 171, [1881–5] All ER Rep 397, 12 R 36, 22 SLR 461, 53 LT
  398, 1 TLR 326, HL 321
G-s (falsely called T-e) v T-e (1854) 1 Ecc & Ad 389, 164 ER 224 340
GW v RW [2003] EWHC 611 (Fam), [2003] 2 FCR 289, [2003] 2 FLR 108,
  [2003] Fam Law 386, [2003] All ER (D) 40 (May) 616
Gadd v Gadd [1985] 1 All ER 58, [1984] 1 WLR 1435, [1985] FLR 220,
  [1985] Fam Law 57, 128 Sol Jo 799, CA 842
Gain v Gain [1962] 1 All ER 63, [1961] 1 WLR 1469, 105 Sol Jo 970 833
Gaisberg v Storr [1950] 1 KB 107, [1949] 2 All ER 411, 93 Sol Jo 600, 65 TLR
  485, CA 698
Gallacher v Gallacher (Queen's Proctor showing cause) (1964) 108 Sol Jo 523 417
Gallagher v Gallagher [1965] 2 All ER 967, [1965] 1 WLR 1110, 109 Sol Jo 513, CA ... 362, 368,
  372
Galler v Galler [1954] P 252, [1954] 1 All ER 536, [1954] 2 WLR 395, 118 JP 216, 98
  Sol Jo 176, CA 346, 352, 354
Galloway v Galloway (1914) 30 TLR 531 430
Gandolfo v Gandolfo [1981] QB 359, [1980] 1 All ER 833, [1980] 2 WLR 680, 10 Fam
  Law 152, 124 Sol Jo 239, CA 624, 933
Gandy v Gandy (1882) 7 PD 168, [1881–5] All ER Rep 376, 51 LJP 41, 30 WR 673, 46
  LT 607, CA 346, 444

PARA

Gandy v Gandy (1885) 30 Ch D 57, [1881–5] All ER Rep 376, 54 LJ Ch 1154, 33 WR
803, 53 LT 306, 1 TLR 520, CA 441, 445, 711
Garcia v Garcia (1888) 13 PD 216, 52 JP 584, 57 LJP 101, 59 LT 524, 4 TLR 702 397
Garcia v Garcia [1992] Fam 83, [1991] 3 All ER 451, [1992] 2 WLR 347, [1991] FCR
927, [1992] 1 FLR 256, [1992] Fam Law 103, CA 873
Gardiner (otherwise Phillips) v Gardiner (1920) 36 TLR 294 453
Garner v Garner (1920) 36 TLR 196 833
Garner v Garner [1992] 1 FCR 529, [1992] 1 FLR 573, [1992] Fam Law 331, CA 568
Garratt v Garratt and Garratt [1922] P 230, [1922] All ER Rep 728, 91 LJP 207, 127
LT 559, 38 TLR 620 515
Garrow v Garrow (1966) 110 Sol Jo 850 376
Garven v Garven [1962] 3 All ER 241, [1963] 1 WLR 38, 106 Sol Jo 411 787
Gaskell v Gaskell (1963) 108 Sol Jo 37 .... 397, 400
Gaskill v Gaskill [1921] P 425, [1921] All ER Rep 365, 90 LJP 339, 126 LT 115, 37
TLR 977, 38 TLR 1 852
Gatehouse v Gatehouse (1867) LR 1 P & D 331, 36 LJP & M 121, 16 LT 34 .... 368, 372, 390
Gay v Sheeran [1999] 3 All ER 795, [2000] 1 WLR 673, [1999] 2 FCR 705,
[1999] 2 FLR 519, [1999] Fam Law 619, 31 HLR 1126,
[1999] 30 LS Gaz R 29, CA 301, 310, 312
Gaynor v Gaynor [1901] IR 217 211
Gee v Gee (1972) 116 Sol Jo 219, CA 225, 904
Gee v Smart (1857) 8 E & B 313, 26 LJQB 305, 3 Jur NS 1056, 5 WR 761, 120 ER
116, 29 LTOS 278 .... 239, 241
Geering v Geering and Mockford (1921) 38 TLR 109 .... 851, 862
Germany v Germany [1938] P 202, [1938] 3 All ER 64, 107 LJP 124, 82 Sol Jo 456,
159 LT 487, 54 TLR 799 403
Gerrard v Gerrard [1958] CLY 498, (1958) Times, 18 November 368, 396
Gethin v Gethin (1862) 31 LJPM & A 57, 2 Sw & Tr 560, 10 WR 266, 164 ER 1114,
5 LT 721 738
Getty v Getty [1907] P 334, [1904–7] All ER Rep 741, 76 LJP 158, 98 LT 60 354
Ghoth v Ghoth [1992] 2 All ER 920, [1993] 1 FCR 177, [1992] 2 FLR 300,
[1992] Fam Law 531, [1992] NLJR 673, CA 661
Gibbs v Harding (1870) 5 Ch App 336, 39 LJ Ch 374, 18 WR 361 431–432
Gibson v Gibson (1859) 23 JP 535, 29 LJP & M 25 402
Gibson v Gibson [1956] CLY 2599, (1956) Times, 18 July, CA 399
Gibson or Scoullar or Archibald v Archibald [1989] 1 All ER 257, [1989] 1 WLR 123,
133 Sol Jo 219, 1989 SC (HL) 1, 1989 SLT 199, HL 478
Gilbert v Gilbert and Abdon (Adams intervening) [1958] P 131, [1957] 3 All ER 604,
[1958] 2 WLR 8, 102 Sol Jo 15 851
Gilbert v Gilbert and Brooks [1948] P 314, [1948] 2 All ER 64, [1948] LJR 1310, 92
Sol Jo 424, 64 TLR 319, CA 776
Giles v Grover (1832) 9 Bing 128, [1824–34] All ER Rep 547, 6 Bli NS 277, 1 Cl & Fin
72, 2 Moo & S 197, 131 ER 563, HL 651
Gill v Gill (1889) 37 WR 623, 60 LT 712 760
Gillespie, Re, ex p Knapman v Gillespie (1913) 20 Mans 311 711
Gillett v Gillett [1952] 1 All ER 1399, CA 769
Gillett v Holt [2001] Ch 210, [2000] 2 All ER 289, [2000] 3 WLR 815, [2000] 1 FCR
705, [2000] FLR 266, [2000] Fam Law 714, [2000] 12 LS Gaz R 40, CA 278
Gilling, Re, Procter v Watkins (1905) 74 LJ Ch 335, 53 WR 427, 49 Sol Jo 401, 92 LT
533 .... 436, 442
Gillman v Gillman (1946) 44 LGR 105, 110 JP 177, 90 Sol Jo 105, 174 LT 272 .... 206, 430
Gillon v Gillon (1961) Times, 4 July 376
Ginesi v Ginesi [1948] P 179, [1948] 1 All ER 373, 46 LGR 124, 112 JP 194, [1948]
LJR 892, 92 Sol Jo 140, 64 TLR 167, CA 349, 352
Ginn v Ginn (1869) 20 LT 87 855
Gipps v Gipps and Hume (1861) 11 HL Cas 1, [1861–73] All ER Rep 138, 33 LJPM &
A 161, 10 Jur NS 641, 4 New Rep 303, 12 WR 937, 10 LT 735, 11 ER
1230, HL 349
Gipps v Gipps and Hume (1863) 32 LJPM & A 179, 2 New Rep 135, 11 WR 1063 863
Gipps v Hume (1861) 26 JP 196, 2 John & H 517, 31 LJ Ch 37, 7 Jur NS 1301, 10
WR 38, 70 ER 1163, 5 LT 307 860

PARA

Gissing v Gissing [1971] AC 886, [1970] 2 All ER 780, [1970] 3 WLR 255, 21 P & CR
    702, 114 Sol Jo 550, 216 Estates Gazette 1257, HL 278–280, 282
Gladitz, Re, Guaranty Executor and Trustee Co Ltd v Gladitz [1937] Ch 588,
    [1937] 3 All ER 173, 106 LJ Ch 254, 81 Sol Jo 527, 157 LT 163, 53 TLR 857 274
Gladstone v Gladstone (1875) LR 3 P & D 260, 44 LJP & M 46, 23 WR 519, 32 LT
    404 875–876
Gladstone v Gladstone (1876) 1 PD 442, 45 LJP 82, 24 WR 739, 35 LT 380 515
Glaister-Carlisle v Glaister-Carlisle (1968) 112 Sol Jo 215, CA 227
Glasspoole v Young (1829) 9 B & C 696, 7 LJOS KB 305, 4 Man & Ry KB 533 652
Gleig v Gleig (1906) 22 TLR 716 699
Glenister v Glenister [1945] P 30, [1945] 1 All ER 513, 43 LGR 250, 109 JP 194, 114
    LJP 69, 172 LT 250 .... 369, 381, 393
Glennie v Glennie and Bowles (1862) 32 LJPM & A 17, 8 Jur NS 1158, 11 WR 28 850
Gliksten v Gliksten and Deane (1917) 116 LT 543, [1916–17] All ER Rep Ext 1313, 33
    TLR 203 352
Goff v Goff [1934] P 107, 103 LJP 57, 78 Sol Jo 299, 151 LT 36, 50 TLR 318 .... 500, 1022
Gojkovic v Gojkovic [1992] Fam 40, [1990] 2 All ER 84, [1991] 3 WLR 621,
    [1990] FCR 119, [1990] 1 FLR 140, [1990] Fam Law 100, CA 483, 604, 618
Gold v Gold (1908) 52 Sol Jo 715 855
Goldsmid v Bromer (1798) 1 Hag Con 324, 161 ER 568 118
Goldsmith v Goldsmith [1965] P 188n, [1964] 3 All ER 321, [1964] 3 WLR
    953n, CA 877
Goldstone v Goldstone (1922) 127 LT 32, 38 TLR 403 .... 7, 24
Goldstone v Tovey (1839) 6 Bing N C 98, 3 Jur 1175, 8 Scott 394, 133 ER 38 257
Gollins v Gollins [1964] AC 644, [1963] 2 All ER 966, [1963] 3 WLR 176, 107 Sol Jo
    532, HL 387–388, 391–392
Gomme v Franklin (1859) 1 F & F 465 263
Gompertz v Kensit (1872) LR 13 Eq 369, 36 JP 548, 41 LJ Ch 382, 20 WR 313, 26 LT
    95 328
Gooch v Gooch (1851) 15 Jur 1166, 17 LTOS 274 252
Gooch v Gooch [1893] P 99, 62 LJP 73, 1 R 516, 41 WR 655, 68 LT 462, 9 TLR
    303 425
Goodall v Jolly [1984] FLR 143, [1984] Fam Law 23, 147 JP 513 .... 565, 590, 597, 669
Goode v Goode and Hamson (1861) 30 LJPM & A 105, 7 Jur NS 317, 2 Sw & Tr 253,
    4 LT 122, 9 WR 552, 164 ER 992 349
Goodinson v Goodinson [1954] 2 QB 118, [1954] 2 All ER 255, [1954] 2 WLR 1121,
    98 Sol Jo 369, CA 698
Goodman v Gallant [1986] Fam 106, [1986] 1 All ER 311, [1986] 2 WLR 236, 52 P &
    CR 180, [1986] 1 FLR 513, [1986] Fam Law 159, 129 Sol Jo 891, CA 278
Goodman v Goodman (1859) 28 LJ Ch 745, 5 Jur NS 902, 33 LTOS 70 6
Goodrich v Goodrich [1971] 2 All ER 1340, [1971] 1 WLR 1142, 115 Sol Jo 303 350
Goodright d Humphreys v Moses (1775) 2 Wm Bl 1019 711
Goodyear v Part (1897) 13 TLR 395 266
Gordon v Douce [1983] 2 All ER 228, [1983] 1 WLR 563, 4 FLR 508, 13 Fam Law
    149, 127 Sol Jo 324, CA 282
Gordon (otherwise Greene) v Gordon [1948] NI 174 42
Gorman (a bankrupt), Re, ex p Trustee of the Bankrupt v Bankrupt [1990] 1 All ER
    717, [1990] 1 WLR 616, [1990] 2 FLR 284, [1990] Fam Law 430,
    [1990] 19 LS Gaz R 41, DC 278–279, 282, 284
Gorman v Gorman [1964] 3 All ER 739, [1964] 1 WLR 1440, 108 Sol Jo 878, CA 702
Gort (Viscount) v Viscountess Gort (1925) Times, 13 June 742
Goshawk v Goshawk (1965) 109 Sol Jo 290 349
Goslin v Clark (1862) 12 CBNS 681, 31 LJCP 330, 9 Jur NS 520, 142 ER 1310, 6 LT
    824 .... 436, 442
Gould v Gould (1963) 107 Sol Jo 831 353
Gould v Gould [1970] 1 QB 275, [1969] 3 All ER 728, [1969] 3 WLR 490, 113 Sol Jo
    508, CA 206
Govier v Hancock (1796) 2 C & P 25n, 6 Term Rep 603, 101 ER 726 216
Gower v Gower [1950] 1 All ER 804, 48 LGR 227, 114 JP 221, 94 Sol Jo 193, 66
    (pt 1) TL 717, CA 346, 349, 352
Graeff v Graeff (1928) 27 LGR 6, 93 JP 48 371
Graham v Graham [1993] 1 FCR 339, [1992] 2 FLR 406, CA 628, 636, 642–643

PARA

Graham v Londonderry (1746) 3 Atk 393, 26 ER 1026 246
Grainger v Grainger [1954] 2 All ER 665, [1954] 1 WLR 1270, 118 JP 432, 98 Sol Jo
   700 566
Grant v Budd (1874) 22 WR 544, 30 LT 319 442
Grant v Callaghan (1956) 107 L Jo 105 239
Grant v Edwards [1986] Ch 638, [1986] 2 All ER 426, [1986] 3 WLR 114,
   [1987] 1 FLR 87, [1986] Fam Law 300, 130 Sol Jo 408, [1986] LS Gaz R 1996,
   [1986] NLJ Rep 439, CA 278, 280–281
Grant (falsely called Giannetti) v Giannetti [1913] P 137, 82 LJP 111, 57 Sol Jo 774,
   108 LT 1037, 29 TLR 654 321
Grant v Grant (1839) 2 Curt 16 353
Grant v Grant and Bowles and Pattison (1862) 31 LJPM & A 174, 2 Sw & Tr 522, 6
   LT 660, 164 ER 1099 .... 349, 861
Granz's Question, Re, Granz v Granz (1968) 112 Sol Jo 439 227
Graves v Graves (1842) 3 Curt 235, 7 Jur 181 349
Graves v Graves (1864) 33 LJPM & A 66, 10 Jur NS 546, 3 Sw & Tr 350, 12 WR
   1016, 164 ER 1310, 10 LT 273 .... 349, 362, 391, 397
Graves v Graves (1893) 28 LJNC 558, 1 R 485, 69 LT 420 860
Graves v Graves (1973) 4 Fam Law 124, 117 Sol Jo 679 592
Gray v Dowman (1858) 27 LJ Ch 702, 6 WR 571, 31 LTOS 279 .... 239–240, 242
Gray (otherwise Formosa) v Formosa [1963] P 259, [1962] 3 WLR 1246, sub nom
   Formosa v Formosa [1962] 3 All ER 419, 106 Sol Jo 629, CA 33
Gray v Gray (1861) 30 LJPM & A 119, 7 Jur NS 472, 2 Sw & Tr 263, 4 LT 218; on
   appeal (1861) 7 Jur NS 783, 2 Sw & Tr 266, 4 LT 478, 164 ER 997 875
Gray v Gray [1976] Fam 324, [1976] 3 All ER 225, [1976] 3 WLR 181, 120 Sol Jo
   300 216
Greatorex v Greatorex (1864) 34 LJPM & A 9, 4 New Rep 122 769
Greaves v Greaves (1872) LR 2 P & D 423, 41 LJP & M 66, 20 WR 802, 26 LT 745 328
Green (a bankrupt), Re, ex p Official Receiver v Cutting [1979] 1 All ER 832,
   [1979] 1 WLR 1211, 122 Sol Jo 572 .... 631, 689
Green, Re, Green v Meinall [1911] 2 Ch 275, 80 LJ Ch 623, 55 Sol Jo 552, 105 LT
   360, 27 TLR 490 40
Green, Re, Noyes v Pitkin (1909) 25 TLR 222 6
Green v Dalton (1822) 1 Add 289 69
Green v Green (1840) 5 Hare 400n 211
Green v Green (1869) 21 LT 401 790
Green v Green [1946] P 112, [1946] 1 All ER 308, 174 LT 237, 62 TLR 180 .... 364, 366
Green v Green (Barclays Bank, third party) [1981] 1 All ER 97, [1981] 1 WLR 391 587
Green v Green [1993] 1 FLR 326, [1993] Fam Law 119 609
Green v Knight [1895] 2 Ch 148, 64 LJ Ch 546, 12 R 252, 43 WR 465, 39 Sol Jo 448,
   72 LT 574, CA 711
Green v Paterson (1886) 32 Ch D 95, 56 LJ Ch 181, 34 WR 724, 54 LT 738, CA 711
Greene v Greene [1916] P 188, [1916–17] All ER Rep Ext 1366, 85 LJP 224, 60 Sol Jo
   620, 115 LT 127, 32 TLR 520 369
Greenfield v Greenfield [1955] CLY 875, (1955) Times, 24 May, CA 738, 851, 862
Greenstreet (falsely called Cumyns) v Cumyns (1812) 2 Hag Con 332, 2 Phillim 10 345
Gregory v Parker (1808) 1 Camp 394 261
Gregory v Tavernor (1833) 6 C & P 280, 2 Nev & MMC 175 802
Grenfell v Grenfell [1978] Fam 128, [1978] 1 All ER 561, [1977] 3 WLR 738, 121 Sol
   Jo 355; affd [1978] Fam 128, [1978] 1 All ER 561, [1977] 3 WLR 738, 121 Sol Jo
   814, CA 347, 410–411
Greville-Bell v Greville-Bell and Primo de Rivera [1958] CLY 934, (1958) Times,
   21 November 353
Griffiths v Dawson & Co [1993] 2 FCR 515, [1993] 2 FLR 315, [1993] Fam Law
   476 873
Griffiths v Fleming [1909] 1 KB 805, [1908–10] All ER Rep 760, 78 LJKB 567, 53 Sol
   Jo 340, 100 LT 765, 25 TLR 377, CA 274
Griffiths v Griffiths (1912) 56 Sol Jo 364, 106 LT 646, 28 TLR 281 .... 771, 876
Griffiths v Griffiths [1973] 3 All ER 1155, [1973] 1 WLR 1454, 4 Fam Law 114; on
   appeal [1974] 1 All ER 932, [1974] 1 WLR 1350, 5 Fam Law 59, 118 Sol Jo
   810, CA 283, 450, 498, 904
Griffiths v Griffiths (1976) unreported 865

PARA

Griffiths v Griffiths [1984] Fam 70, [1984] 2 All ER 626, [1984] 3 WLR 165,
[1984] FLR 662, 128 Sol Jo 299, [1984] LS Gaz R 1051, CA 492

Griffiths' Policy, Re [1903] 1 Ch 739, [1900–3] All ER Rep Ext 1101, 72 LJ Ch 330, 88
LT 547 275

Grigson v Grigson [1974] 1 All ER 478, [1974] 1 WLR 228, 118 Sol Jo 116, CA 873

Grimes (otherwise Edwards) v Grimes [1948] P 323, [1948] 2 All ER 147, [1948] LJR
1471, 92 Sol Jo 325, 64 TLR 330 335

Gsell v Gsell [1971] 1 All ER 559n, [1971] 1 WLR 225n, 135 JP 163, 115 Sol Jo 144 669

Guest v Shipley (falsely calling herself Guest) (1820) 2 Hag Con 321, 161 ER 757 .... 321, 349

Guise v Small (1793) 1 Anst 277 232

Gulbenkian v Gulbenkian [1927] P 237, 96 LJP 53, 71 Sol Jo 311, 136 LT 800, 43 TLR
26 511

Gullan v Gullan (otherwise Goodwin) [1913] P 160, 82 LJP 118, 109 LT 411 453

Gunner v Gunner and Stirling [1949] P 77, [1948] 2 All ER 771, [1948] LJR 1904, 64
TLR 513 .... 275, 511

Gurasz v Gurasz [1970] P 11, [1969] 3 All ER 822, [1969] 3 WLR 482, 113 Sol Jo 565,
211 Estates Gazette 727, CA 226

Guth v Guth (1792) 3 Bro CC 614, 29 ER 729 443

H

H (minors) (sexual abuse: standard of proof), Re [1996] AC 563, [1996] 1 All ER 1,
[1996] 2 WLR 8, [1996] 1 FCR 509, [1996] 1 FLR 80, [1996] Fam Law 74, 140
Sol Jo LB 24, HL 587

H (a child) (occupation order: power of arrest), Re [2001] 1 FCR 370, [2001] 1 FLR
641, [2000] All ER (D) 2067, CA 988

H– (falsely called C–) v C– (1859) 1 Sw & Tr 605, 29 LJP & M 29, 1 LT 489, sub nom
Hall (falsely called Castleden) v Castleden Sea & Sm 29; on appeal sub nom
Castleden v Castleden (1861) 9 HL Cas 186, 8 Jur NS 1, 11 ER 701, 5 LT 164,
sub nom H (falsely called C) v C 31 LJPM & A 103 321

H v H (otherwise N) (1929) 98 LJP 155, 45 TLR 618 863

H v H [1954] P 258, [1953] 2 All ER 1229, [1953] 3 WLR 849, 97 Sol Jo 782 ... 42–43, 344–345

H v H (31 March 1954, unreported), CA 337, 345

H v H [1962] P 244, [1962] 3 WLR 105, 106 Sol Jo 328, sub nom Holman v Holman
[1962] 2 All ER 477, CA 787

H v H (1981) 2 FLR 303, 11 Fam Law 209, 125 Sol Jo 529 931

H v H (minor) [1990] Fam 86, [1989] 3 WLR 933, [1989] FCR 356, 134 Sol Jo 21,
[1989] NLJR 864, sub nom H v H and C [1989] 3 All ER 740, sub nom Re H (a
minor) [1989] 2 FLR 313, [1989] Fam Law 388, CA 352

H v H [1993] 2 FCR 357, [1993] 2 FLR 35, [1993] Fam Law 406 601

H v H (financial provision) (1993). See Horsman v Horsman

H v H (clean break: non-disclosure: costs) [1994] 2 FLR 309, sub nom H v H (financial
provision: lump sum) [1994] Fam Law 15 614

H v H [1994] 2 FCR 1031, [1994] 2 FLR 801 .... 601, 621

H v H (financial relief: conduct) [1999] 1 FCR 225, [1998] 1 FLR 971, [1998] Fam Law
395 621

H v H (rescission of decree nisi: pension sharing provision) [2002] EWHC 767 (Fam),
[2002] 2 FLR 116, [2002] All ER (D) 285 (May) 524

H v H (lump sum: interest payable) [2005] EWHC 1513 (Fam), [2006] 1 FLR 327, sub
nom Harold v Harold [2005] Fam Law 848 .... 479, 492, 569

H v H (financial relief: attempted murder as conduct) [2005] EWHC 2911 (Fam),
[2006] 1 FLR 990, [2006] Fam Law 264 601

H v M. See Hammond v Mitchell

H v O. See Hager v Osborne

H v P (falsely called H) (1873) LR 3 P & D 126 340

H–J v H–J (financial provision: equality) [2002] 1 FLR 415 607

Hackney v Hackney (1973) 117 Sol Jo 224 846

Hackney London Borough Council v White (1995) 28 HLR 219, CA 947

Hackshaw v Hackshaw [1999] 3 FCR 451, [1999] 2 FLR 876 669

Hadkinson v Hadkinson [1952] P 285, [1952] 2 All ER 567, [1952] 2 TLR 416, CA 567

Hager v Osborne [1992] Fam 94, [1992] 2 All ER 494, [1992] 2 WLR 610, sub nom H
v O [1992] 1 FCR 125, [1992] 1 FLR 282, [1992] Fam Law 105, 135 Sol Jo LB
76 736

PARA

Hale v Tanner [2000] 1 WLR 2377, [2000] 3 FCR 62, [2000] 2 FLR 879,
[2000] Fam Law 876, CA 988
Halfen (otherwise Boddington) v Boddington (1881) 6 PD 13, sub nom Halpen
(otherwise Boddington) v Boddington 50 LJP 61, 29 WR 444, 44 LT 252 341
Halifax Building Society v Brown [1995] 3 FCR 110, [1996] 1 FLR 103,
[1996] Fam Law 85, 27 HLR 511, CA 280
Hall (falsely called Castleden) v Castleden Sea & Sm 29. See H– (falsely called C–) v C–
Hall v Hall (1908) 24 TLR 756 44
Hall v Hall [1911] 1 Ch 487, 80 LJ Ch 340, 104 LT 529 240
Hall v Hall [1960] 1 All ER 91, [1960] 1 WLR 52, 104 Sol Jo 52 372
Hall v Hall [1962] 3 All ER 518, [1962] 1 WLR 1246, 106 Sol Jo 650, CA 387–388, 393
Hall v Hall (1981) 3 FLR 379, CA 282
Hall v Hall [1984] FLR 631, [1984] Fam Law 54, CA 621
Hall v Hall and Richardson (1879) 48 LJP 57, [1874–80] All ER Rep 642, 27 WR 664,
40 LT 357, 796
Hall v King (1988) 55 P & CR 307, [1988] 1 FLR 376, [1988] Fam Law 88, 19 HLR
440, 131 Sol Jo 1186, [1987] 2 EGLR 121, [1987] LS Gaz R 2273, [1987] NLJ
Rep 616, 283 Estates Gazette 1400, CA 285
Hall (Arthur J S) & Co (a firm) v Simons [2002] 1 AC 615, [2000] 3 All ER 673,
[2000] 3 WLR 543, [2000] 2 FCR 673, [2000] 2 FLR 545, [2000] Fam Law 806,
[2001] 3 LRC 117, [2000] BLR 407, 144 Sol Jo LB 238, [2000] 32 LS Gaz R 38,
[2000] NLJR 1147, [2000] EGCS 99, [2000] All ER (D) 1027, HL 715
Hallam v Hallam (1903) 20 TLR 34 776
Hallam v Hallam (1930) 75 Sol Jo 157, 47 TLR 207 353
Halpen (otherwise Boddington) v Boddington. See Halfen (otherwise Boddington) v
Boddington
Halpern v Halpern [1951] P 204, [1951] 1 All ER 315, 95 Sol Jo 123, [1951] 1 TLR
461 511
Hamer v Tilsley (1859) John 486, 29 LJ Ch 32, 5 Jur NS 1344, 8 WR 20, 70 ER 513, 1
LT 54 283
Hamerton v Hamerton (1828) 2 Hag Ecc 8; on appeal (1829) 2 Hag Ecc 618 353
Hamilton v Brogden [1891] WN 14, 35 Sol Jo 206 648
Hamilton v Hector (1872) LR 13 Eq 511, 36 JP 676 428
Hamlin v Hamlin [1986] Fam 11, [1985] 2 All ER 1037, [1985] 3 WLR 629,
[1986] 1 FLR 61, [1985] Fam Law 323, 129 Sol Jo 700, CA 227, 500, 601
Hammersmith and Fulham London Borough Council v Hill (1994) 92 LGR 665, 27
HLR 368, [1994] 2 EGLR 51, [1994] 22 LS Gaz R 35, [1994] 35 EG 124, CA 654
Hammond v Mitchell [1992] 2 All ER 109, [1991] 1 WLR 1127, sub nom H v M
[1991] FCR 938, [1992] 1 FLR 229, [1991] Fam Law 473 .... 278, 280, 284
Hampson v Hampson [1908] P 355, 77 LJP 148, 52 Sol Jo 729, 99 LT 882, 24 TLR
868 .... 756, 879
Hanbury v Hanbury [1892] P 222, 61 LJP 115; affd (1892) 8 TLR 559, CA 349, 385
Hancock v Hancock and Smith (1867) LR 1 P & D 334, 36 LJP & M 86 855
Hancock v Peaty (1867) LR 1 P & D 335, 36 LJP & M 57, 15 WR 719, 16 LT 182 45
Hanson v Hanson (1954) Times, 10 March, CA 368, 393
Haque v Haque [1977] 3 All ER 667, [1977] 1 WLR 888, 121 Sol Jo 171 .... 360, 782
Harb v King Fahd Bin Abdul Aziz (Secretary of State for Constitutional Affairs
intervening) [2005] EWCA Civ 1324, [2006] 1 WLR 578, [2006] 1 FLR 825,
[2006] Fam Law 96, (2005) Times, 21 November, [2005] All ER (D) 110 (Nov) 861
Hardie v Hardie (1901) 17 TLR 190 699
Hardy v Hardy (1981) 2 FLR 321, 11 Fam Law 153, 125 Sol Jo 463, CA 478, 595, 614
Hardy's Trust, Re, Sutherst v Sutherst (1970) 114 Sol Jo 864, (1970) Times,
23 October 226
Harford v Morris (1776) 2 Hag Con 423, 161 ER 792 43
Hargood (formerly Jenkins) v Jenkins [1978] Fam 148, [1978] 2 WLR 969, sub nom
Jenkins v Hargood (formerly Jenkins) [1978] 3 All ER 1001, 122 Sol Jo 296 452
Hargrave v Newton (formerly Hargrave) [1971] 3 All ER 866, [1971] 1 WLR 1611, 115
Sol Jo 809, CA 279
Hargreaves v Hargreaves [1926] P 42, [1926] All ER Rep 195, 95 LJP 31, 134 LT 543,
42 TLR 252 511
Harman v Glencross [1986] Fam 81, [1986] 1 All ER 545, [1986] 2 WLR 637,
[1986] 2 FLR 241, [1986] Fam Law 215, 130 Sol Jo 224, CA 638

PARA
Harman v Richards (1852) 10 Hare 81, 22 LJ Ch 1066, 90 RR 297 711
Harnett v Harnett [1973] Fam 156, [1973] 2 All ER 593, [1973] 3 WLR 1, 117 Sol Jo
    447; affd [1974] 1 All ER 764, [1974] 1 WLR 219, 118 Sol Jo 34, CA 283, 316, 621
Harold v Harold. See H v H (lump sum: interest payable)
Harper (a bankrupt), Re, Harper v O'Reilly [1998] 3 FCR 475, [1997] 2 FLR 816,
    [1998] Fam Law 18, [1997] BPIR 656 .... 520, 676
Harries v Harries and Gregory (1901) 86 LT 262, 18 TLR 219 876
Harriman v Harriman [1909] P 123, [1908–10] All ER Rep 85, 73 JP 193, 78 LJP 62,
    53 Sol Jo 265, 100 LT 557, 25 TLR 291, CA 357–358, 362, 369, 371, 391, 406, 734,
                                                                                        830, 852
Harris v Beauchamp Bros [1894] 1 QB 801, 63 LJQB 480, 9 R 653, 42 WR 451, 70 LT
    636, CA 647
Harris v Harris [1931] P 10, 28 LGR 641, 95 JP 1, 99 LJP 149, 29 Cox CC 189, 74 Sol
    Jo 755, 144 LT 159, 47 TLR 15 833
Harris v Harris [1986] 1 FLR 12, [1986] Fam Law 16, CA 975
Harris v Harris [2001] 1 FCR 68, [2000] All ER (D) 2229, CA 569
Harris v Harris and Woodden (1872) 41 LJP & M 61, 21 WR 80, 27 LT 428 425
Harris (formerly Manahan) v Manahan [1996] 4 All ER 454, [1997] 2 FCR 607,
    [1997] 1 FLR 205, CA 715
Harrison v Grady (1861) 12 Jur NS 140, [1861–73] All ER Rep 663, 14 WR 139, 13
    LT 369 263–264
Harrison v Hall (1832) 1 Mood & R 185 273
Harrison v Harrison (1888) 13 PD 180, [1886–90] All ER Rep Ext 1460, 58 LJP 28, 36
    WR 748, 60 LT 39, 4 TLR 646, CA 475, 552
Harrison v Harrison (1910) 54 Sol Jo 619 .... 368, 378
Harrison v Harrison. See Sparrow (falsely called Harrison) v Harrison
Harrison v Southampton Corpn (1853) 4 De GM & G 137, 22 LJ Ch 722, 1 Eq Rep
    299, 18 Jur 1, 1 WR 422, 43 ER 459, 21 LTOS 294 50
Harrod v Harrod (1854) 1 K & J 4, 18 Jur 853, 2 WR 612, 69 ER 344, 23 LTOS
    243 .... 1, 3, 42, 45, 83
Harrop v Harrop [1920] 3 KB 386, 90 LJKB 101, 64 Sol Jo 586, 123 LT 580, 36 TLR
    635 .... 465, 677
Harry v Harry (1919) Times, 4, 5 April 353
Hart v Hart (1881) 18 Ch D 670, [1881–5] All ER Rep Ext 1745, 50 LJ Ch 697, 30
    WR 8, 45 LT 13 .... 431–432, 438, 443, 860
Harthan v Harthan [1949] P 115, [1948] 2 All ER 639, [1949] LJR 115, 92 Sol Jo
    586, CA 322, 341–342
Hartley v Hartley and Fleming (1919) 35 TLR 298 357–358
Hartnell v Hartnell [1951] WN 555, DC 364
Hartopp v Hartopp and Earl of Cowley (1902) 71 LJP 78, 87 LT 188, CA 787
Harvey v Harvey [1956] P 102, [1955] 3 All ER 772, [1955] 3 WLR 946, 99 Sol Jo
    886, CA 371, 395–396, 398
Harvey v Harvey [1982] Fam 83, [1982] 1 All ER 693, [1982] 2 WLR 283, 3 FLR 141,
    12 Fam Law 83, 126 Sol Jo 15, CA 316, 612
Harvey v Johnston (1848) 6 CB 295, 6 Dow & L 120, 17 LJCP 298, 12 Jur 981, 136
    ER 1265, 11 LTOS 244, 245 16
Harvey v Norton (1840) 4 Jur 42 259
Harwood v Harwood [1992] 1 FCR 1, [1991] 2 FLR 274, [1991] Fam Law 418, CA 451, 500,
                                                                                        601
Hastings (Lady), Re, Hallett v Hastings (1887) 35 Ch D 94, 52 JP 100, 56 LJ Ch 631,
    35 WR 584, 57 LT 126, 3 TLR 499, CA 206
Hastings (Lord) v Douglas (1634) Cro Car 343, [1558–1774] All ER Rep 576, W Jo
    332, 79 ER 901 246
Hastings and Thanet Building Society v Goddard [1970] 3 All ER 954, [1970] 1 WLR
    1544, 22 P & CR 295, 114 Sol Jo 807, CA 285
Haswell v Haswell and Gilbert (1881) 51 LJP 15, 30 WR 231 76
Haswell v Haswell and Sanderson (1859) 23 JP 825, Sea & Sm 32, 29 LJP & M 21, 1
    Sw & Tr 502, 8 WR 76, 1 LT 69, 164 ER 832 .... 362, 381
Hathaway v Hathaway [1970] 2 All ER 701, [1970] 1 WLR 1156n, 114 Sol Jo 433 354
Hatwell v Hatwell (1963) 107 Sol Jo 394, CA 883
Haviland v Haviland (1863) 32 LJPM & A 65, 11 WR 373 362

PARA

Haviland v Haviland (1863) 32 LJPM & A 67, 9 Jur NS 208, 1 New Rep 377, 3 Sw &
Tr 114, 11 WR 550, 164 ER 1216, 7 LT 757 393

Hawes, Re, Re Burchell, Burchell v Hawes (1892) 62 LJ Ch 463, 3 R 133, 41 WR 173,
67 LT 756 251

Hawke v Corri (1820) 2 Hag Con 280, 161 ER 743 80

Hawkins, Re, ex p Hawkins [1894] 1 QB 25, 1 Mans 6, 10 R 29, 42 WR 202, 69 LT
769 .... 466, 552

Haydon v Haydon and Cooke (1860) 30 LJPM & A 112 862

Hayes (falsely called Watts) v Watts (1819) 3 Phillim 43 .... 10, 344

Haynes, Re, Haynes v Carter (1906) 94 LT 431 6

Hayward v Hayward (1858) 1 Sw & Tr 81, 6 WR 638, 164 ER 638, 31 LTOS 24 390

Hayward v Hayward (otherwise Prestwood) [1961] P 152, [1961] 1 All ER 236,
[1961] 2 WLR 993, 105 Sol Jo 570 321

Hayward v Hayward (1969) 119 NLJ 554, (1969) Times, 4 June, CA 863

Hazell v Hazell [1972] 1 All ER 923, [1972] 1 WLR 301, 116 Sol Jo 142, CA 279

Heanan v Heanan (1963) 107 Sol Jo 702 .... 879, 883

Hearle v Greenbank (1749) 3 Atk 695, [1558–1774] All ER Rep 190, 1 Ves Sen 298, 26
ER 1200 234

Hearn v Hearn and Jarvis [1953] 1 All ER 797n, 117 JP 200n 830

Heath v Chilton (1844) 13 LJ Ex 225, 12 M & W 632, 2 LTOS 424 273

Heath v Heath [1950] P 193, [1950] 1 All ER 877, 94 Sol Jo 319, 66 (pt 1) TLR
1093, CA 776

Heaven v Heaven (King's Proctor showing cause) (Parr intervening) (1933) Times,
24 March 877

Hedderwick, Re, Morton (or Morten) v Brinsley [1933] Ch 669, [1933] All ER Rep 73,
102 LJ Ch 193, 149 LT 188, 49 TLR 381 685

Hedderwick v Hedderwick (1930) 74 Sol Jo 863 853

Hedges v Hedges [1990] FCR 952, [1991] 1 FLR 196, [1991] Fam Law 267, CA 616

Heffer v Heffer (1812) 3 M & S 265n 69

Hemain v Hemain [1988] 2 FLR 388, [1988] Fam Law 432, CA 847

Henderson, Re, ex p Shaw [1884] WN 60, CA 651

Henley v Henley (Bligh cited) [1955] P 202, [1955] 1 All ER 590n, [1955] 2 WLR 851,
119 JP 215n, 99 Sol Jo 260 833

Henley v Henley and Davies (1954) Times, 12 November 863

Henty v Henty (1875) 33 LT 263 372

Hepburn v Hepburn [1989] FCR 618, [1989] 1 FLR 373, [1989] Fam Law 271, CA 463

Hepworth v Hepworth (1860) 30 LJPM & A 215, 6 Jur NS 831 .... 787, 792

Hepworth v Hepworth (1861) 31 LJPM & A 18, 2 Sw & Tr 414, 10 WR 195, 164 ER
1057, 5 LT 365 845

Herod v Herod [1939] P 11, [1938] 3 All ER 722, 108 LJP 27, 82 Sol Jo 665, 159 LT
530, 54 TLR 1134 .... 362, 369, 381, 391, 393–394

Heseltine v Heseltine [1971] 1 All ER 952, [1971] 1 WLR 342, 135 JP 214, 114 Sol Jo
972, CA 245, 251

Hewett v Hewett and Dupin (1929) 73 Sol Jo 402 .... 756, 879

Hewison v Negus (1853) 16 Beav 594, 22 LJ Ch 655, 1 Eq Rep 230, 17 Jur 445, 1 WR
262, 51 ER 909; affd (1853) 16 Beav 600n, 22 LJ Ch 657, 17 Jur 567, 21 LTOS
203, 51 ER 912n 206, 711

Hewitson v Hewitson [1995] Fam 100, [1995] 1 All ER 472, [1995] 2 WLR 287,
[1995] 2 FCR 588, [1995] 1 FLR 241, [1995] Fam Law 129,
[1994] 41 LS Gaz R 41, [1994] NLJR 1478, 138 Sol Jo LB 211, CA 530, 938

Hewitt v Hewitt [1948] P 150, [1948] 1 All ER 242, [1948] LJR 843, 92 Sol Jo 96, 64
TLR 121, CA 849–850

Hewitt v Hewitt [1952] 2 QB 627, [1952] 2 All ER 250, 116 JP 434, 96 Sol Jo 428,
[1952] 2 TLR 1 368

Higgins v King's Proctor [1910] P 151, [1908–10] All ER Rep 104, 79 LJP 37, 54 Sol Jo
405, 102 LT 259, 26 TLR 303, CA 853

Hill v Hill (1861) 31 LJPM & A 193, 7 Jur NS 1206, 2 Sw & Tr 407, 10 WR 194, 164
ER 1054, 5 LT 363 738

Hill v Hill [1954] P 291, [1954] 1 All ER 491, [1954] 2 WLR 473, 118 JP 163, 98 Sol
Jo 180 734

Hill v Hill [1959] 1 All ER 281, [1959] 1 WLR 127, 103 Sol Jo 111, PC 6–7, 17, 42

Hills v Hills and Easton (1915) 31 TLR 541 776

PARA

Hills v Webber (1901) 17 TLR 513, CA 647
Hind v Hind [1969] 1 All ER 1083, [1969] 1 WLR 480, 133 JP 293, 113 Sol Jo
    284, DC 393
Hinde v Hinde [1953] 1 All ER 171, [1953] 1 WLR 175, 97 Sol Jo 47, CA 538, 684
Hindley v Hindley [1957] 2 All ER 653, [1957] 1 WLR 898, 101 Sol Jo 593 .... 511, 517
Hinton v Hudson (1677) Freem KB 248, 89 ER 178 .... 269, 271
Hipkin v Hipkin [1962] 2 All ER 155, [1962] 1 WLR 491, 106 Sol Jo 246 650
Hirani v Hirani (1982) 4 FLR 232, CA 12
Hobbs v Hobbs [1920] P 40, 89 LJP 64, 80, 122 LT 464, 36 TLR 121, 187 776
Hobbs v Hull (1788) 1 Cox Eq Cas 445, 29 ER 1242 431
Hobby v Hobby [1954] 2 All ER 395, [1954] 1 WLR 1020, 118 JP 331, 98 Sol Jo
    474 897
Hoddinott v Hoddinott [1949] 2 KB 406, 93 Sol Jo 296, 65 TLR 266, CA 206
Hodgkins v Hodgkins [1950] P 183, [1950] 1 All ER 619, 66 (pt 1) TLR 1011, CA 341, 832
Hodgkins v Hodgkins [1965] 3 All ER 164, [1965] 1 WLR 1448, 109 Sol Jo 899, CA 769
Hodgkinson v Wilkie (1795) 1 Hag Con 262, 161 ER 546 .... 46, 49–50
Hodgson v Trapp [1988] 1 FLR 69, [1988] Fam Law 60; on appeal [1989] AC 807,
    [1988] 3 All ER 870, [1988] 3 WLR 1281, [1989] 2 LS Gaz R 36, HL 221
Hodgson v Williamson (1880) 15 Ch D 87, 29 WR 944, 42 LT 676 205
Holborn v Holborn [1947] 1 All ER 32, 45 LGR 90, 111 JP 36, 176 LT 57, 63 TLR
    87, DC 393, 397
Holden v Holden and Pearson (1910) 54 Sol Jo 328, 102 LT 398, 26 TLR 307 862
Holdowanski v Holdowanska (otherwise Bialoszewska) and Price [1956] 3 All ER 457,
    [1956] 3 WLR 935, 100 Sol Jo 875 6
Holland v Holland [1961] 1 All ER 226, [1961] 1 WLR 194, 105 Sol Jo 107, CA 734
Hollens v Hollens (1971) 115 Sol Jo 327 412
Hollington v F Hewthorn & Co Ltd [1943] KB 587, [1943] 2 All ER 35, 112 LJKB 463,
    87 Sol Jo 247, 169 LT 21, 59 TLR 321, CA 358
Holman v Holman. See H v H (1962)
Holmes v Holmes [1989] Fam 47, [1989] 3 All ER 786, [1989] 3 WLR 302,
    [1990] FCR 157, [1989] 2 FLR 364, [1989] Fam Law 470, CA 938, 940
Holmes v Millage [1893] 1 QB 551, 57 JP 551, 62 LJQB 380, 4 R 332, 41 WR 354, 37
    Sol Jo 338, 68 LT 205, 9 TLR 331, CA 648
Holmes v Simmons (falsely called Holmes) (1868) LR 1 P & D 523, 37 LJP & M 58, 16
    WR 1024, 18 LT 770 .... 69, 89, 328
Holroyd v Holroyd (1920) 36 TLR 479 .... 372, 430, 699
Holt v Brien (1821) 4 B & Ald 252, 106 ER 930 .... 266, 270, 273
Holzer v Holzer (Morley intervening) [1964] 3 All ER 989, [1964] 1 WLR 1478, 108
    Sol Jo 640 851
Home, Re, ex p Home (1885) 54 LT 301 206
Hood Barrs v Cathcart [1895] 2 Ch 411, 64 LJ Ch 461, 13 R 489, 43 WR 586, 39 Sol
    Jo 428, 72 LT 583 641
Hook v Hook (1858) 27 LJP & M 61, 1 Sw & Tr 183, 6 WR 868, 31 LTOS 269 760
Hook v Hook and Brown [1917] P 56, 86 LJP 41, 61 Sol Jo 284, 116 LT 383, 33 TLR
    181 877
Hooper v Hooper (1861) 30 LJPM & A 49, 3 Sw & Tr 251, 164 ER 1270 860
Hooper (otherwise Harrison) v Hooper [1959] 2 All ER 575, [1959] 1 WLR 1021, 103
    Sol Jo 546 328
Hope v Hope and Erdody (1874) LR 3 P & D 226, 44 LJP & M 31, 23 WR 110, 31 LT
    592 513
Hope v Hope and Johnson (1924) 130 LT 761, 40 TLR 282 875
Hopes v Hopes [1949] P 227, [1948] 2 All ER 920, 46 LGR 538, 113 JP 10, [1949]
    LJR 104, 92 Sol Jo 660, 64 TLR 623, CA 362, 368
Horlock v Wiggins (1888) 39 Ch D 142, [1886–90] All ER Rep 1125, 58 LJ Ch 46, 59
    LT 710, CA 440
Horn v Noel (1807) 1 Camp 61 .... 24, 118
Hornal v Neuberger Products Ltd [1957] 1 QB 247, [1956] 3 All ER 970,
    [1956] 3 WLR 1034, 100 Sol Jo 915, CA 346
Hornbuckle v Hornbury (1871) 2 Stark 177 273
Horner v Horner [1982] Fam 90, [1982] 2 All ER 495, [1982] 2 WLR 914, 4 FLR 50,
    12 Fam Law 144, 126 Sol Jo 243, CA 716
Horrell v Horrell (1882) 46 JP 295, DC 206

PARA

Horseman v Abbey (1819) 1 Jac & W 381, 37 ER 420 233
Horsman v Horsman [1993] 2 FCR 357, sub nom H v H (financial provision)
  [1993] 2 FLR 35 .... 606, 625, 679, 933
Horton v Horton [1947] 2 All ER 871, [1948] LJR 396, 92 Sol Jo 95, 64 TLR
  62, HL 342
Horton v Horton [1960] 1 All ER 503, [1960] 1 WLR 987, 124 JP 206, 104 Sol Jo
  684, DC 851
Horton v Horton (No 2) [1961] 1 QB 215, [1960] 3 All ER 649, [1960] 3 WLR 914,
  104 Sol Jo 955, CA 431
Hosegood v Hosegood (1950) 48 LGR 253, 66 (pt 1) TLR 735, CA 367, 384, 391, 393–394
Hounslow London Borough v Peake [1974] 1 All ER 688, [1974] 1 WLR 26, 71 LGR
  109, [1973] RA 468, 138 JP 210, 117 Sol Jo 911, DC 216
Howard v Howard (1897) 77 LT 140 860
Howard v Howard [1945] P 1, [1945] 1 All ER 91, 114 LJP 11, 172 LT 38, 61 TLR
  189, CA 464, 549, 599
Howard v Howard [1965] P 65, [1962] 2 All ER 539, [1962] 3 WLR 413, 106 Sol Jo
  690 404
Howard v Jones [1989] Fam Law 231, CA 281
Howard-Williams v Howard-Williams [1944] P 85, 113 LJP 71, 171 LT 278, 60 TLR
  52 769
Howarth v Howarth (1884) 9 PD 218, 51 LT 872, CA 876–877
Howarth v Howarth (1886) 11 PD 68, 95, 50 JP 376, 55 LJP 49, 34 WR 633, 55 LT
  303, 2 TLR 705, CA 473, 504, 548, 641
Howell v Hanforth (1775) 2 Wm Bl 1016, 96 ER 597 436
Hubbard (otherwise Rogers) v Hubbard [1901] P 157, [1900–3] All ER Rep 342, 70 LJP
  34, 84 LT 441, CA 511
Hubbock v Hubbock [1948] 2 All ER 412, CA 787
Hudson v Carmichael (1854) Kay 613, 23 LJ Ch 893, 2 Eq Rep 1077, 18 Jur 851, 2
  WR 503, 69 ER 260, 23 LTOS 168 239–240
Hudson v Hudson [1948] P 292, [1948] 1 All ER 773, [1948] LJR 907, 64 TLR 258 734–735,
                                                                                      830
Hudson v Hudson [1965] 2 All ER 82, [1965] 1 WLR 567, 129 JP 288, 109 Sol Jo
  174 897
Hudston v Hudston (otherwise Newbigging) (1922) 39 TLR 108 340
Hughes v Hughes (1966) 110 Sol Jo 349, (1966) Times, 29 April, CA 379
Hughes v Wells (1852) 9 Hare 749, 16 Jur 927, 89 RR 651, 68 ER 717, 20 LTOS
  136 .... 238, 249
Hulbert v Hulbert [1957] P 174, [1957] 2 All ER 226, [1957] 2 WLR 808, 101 Sol Jo
  338, CA 800
Hulbert and Crowe v Cathcart [1894] 1 QB 244, 63 LJQB 121, 70 LT 558, DC; on
  appeal [1896] AC 470, 65 LJQB 644, 75 LT 302, 12 TLR 379, HL 649, 946
Hulme v Chitty (1846) 9 Beav 437, 10 Jur 323, 50 ER 411, 7 LTOS 278 437
Hulme v Tenant (1778) Dick 560, 1 Bro CC 16 204
Hulse v Hulse (1910) 103 LT 804, CA 431
Hulse v Hulse and Tavernor (1871) LR 2 P & D 259, [1861–73] All ER Rep Ext 1316,
  40 LJP & M 51, 19 WR 880, 24 LT 847 .... 875–876, 879
Hulse v Hulse and Tavernor (1871) LR 2 P & D 357, 41 LJP & M 19, 20 WR 447, 25
  LT 764 876
Hulton v Hulton [1917] 1 KB 813, 86 LJKB 633, 61 Sol Jo 268, 116 LT 551, 33 TLR
  197, CA 429
Humphrey v Williams (falsely calling herself Humphrey) (1860) 29 LJPM & A 62, 6 Jur
  NS 151 795
Hunt v De Blaquiere (1829) 5 Bing 550, 7 LJOS 198, 3 Moo & P 108, 130 ER 1174 .... 264, 271
Hunt v Hunt (1856) Dea & Sw 121, 2 Jur NS 239, 4 WR 356 .... 353, 794
Hunt v Hunt (1862) 26 JP 243, 4 De GF & J 221, 31 LJ Ch 161, 8 Jur NS 85, 10 WR
  215, 45 ER 1168, 5 LT 778 423
Hunt v Hunt [1897] 2 QB 547, 67 LJQB 18, 77 LT 421, 14 TLR 53, CA 434
Hunt v Hunt (1908) 25 TLR 132 206
Hunter v Edney (otherwise Hunter) (1881) 10 PD 80 45
Hunter v Hunter [1905] P 217, 74 LJP 157, 53 WR 666, 93 LT 451, 21 TLR 602 877
Hunter v Hunter (1961) 105 Sol Jo 990 393

PARA

Hunter v Hunter and Waddington [1962] P 1, [1961] 2 All ER 121, [1961] 2 WLR 691,
　105 Sol Jo 283 .... 511, 641
Huntingford v Hobbs [1993] 1 FCR 45, [1993] 1 FLR 736, [1992] Fam Law 437, 24
　HLR 652, [1992] NPC 39, [1992] EGCS 38, CA 279
Huntington (Earl) v Countess of Huntington (1702) 2 Eq Cas Abr 672, 2 Bro Parl Cas
　1, 2 Vern 437, 23 ER 881, HL 239
Hurlstone v Hurlstone [1956] 1 All ER 804, [1956] 1 WLR 286, 100 Sol Jo 224, CA 883
Hussain v Hussain [1983] Fam 26, [1982] 3 All ER 369, [1982] 3 WLR 679, 4 FLR
　339, 126 Sol Jo 624, CA 326
Hussein (otherwise Blitz) v Hussein [1938] P 159, [1938] 2 All ER 344, 107 LJP 105, 82
　Sol Jo 336, 54 TLR 632 43
Hussey v Hussey (1913) 109 LT 192, 29 TLR 673 374
Hutchinson v Hutchinson [1947] 2 All ER 792, 92 Sol Jo 55, 63 TLR 645 227
Hutchinson v Hutchinson [1963] 1 All ER 1, [1963] 1 WLR 280, 106 Sol Jo 836 .... 379, 402
Hutton v Mansell (1705) 6 Mod Rep 172, 3 Salk 16, 64, Holt KB 458, 87 ER 928 16
Huxford v Huxford [1972] 1 All ER 330, [1972] 1 WLR 210, 115 Sol Jo 831 779
Huxtable v Huxtable (1899) 68 LJP 83 .... 372, 378
Hyde v Hyde (1888) 13 PD 166, 57 LJP 89, 36 WR 708, 59 LT 529, 4 TLR 586, CA 651
Hyde v Hyde [1948] P 198, [1948] 1 All ER 362, [1948] LJR 641, 92 Sol Jo 98, 64
　TLR 105 .... 474–475, 550, 552, 684–685
Hyde v Hyde and Woodmansee (1866) LR 1 P & D 130, [1861–73] All ER Rep 175, 35
　LJP & M 57, 12 Jur NS 414, 14 WR 517, 14 LT 188 .... 1, 9
Hyde v Price (1797) 3 Ves 437, 30 ER 1093 436
Hyman v Hyman [1929] AC 601, [1929] All ER Rep 245, 27 LGR 379, 93 JP 209, 98
　LJP 81, 73 Sol Jo 317, 141 LT 329, 45 TLR 444, HL 698, 712
Hyman v Hyman and Goldman [1904] P 403, 78 LJP 106, 91 LT 361, 20 TLR 696 879

I

I v I (otherwise J). See Intract v Intract (otherwise Jacobs)
Ibbetson v Ibbetson [1984] FLR 545, [1984] Fam Law 309 621
Iddenden (otherwise Brians) v Iddenden [1958] 3 All ER 241, [1958] 1 WLR 1041, 102
　Sol Jo 759 345
Ideal Bedding Co Ltd v Holland [1907] 2 Ch 157, 76 LJ Ch 441, 14 Mans 113, 96 LT
　774, 23 TLR 467 647
Igra v Igra [1951] P 404, 95 Sol Jo 563, [1951] 2 TLR 670 33
Indyka v Indyka [1969] 1 AC 33, [1967] 2 All ER 689, [1967] 3 WLR 510, 111 Sol Jo
　456, HL 214
Inglis v Inglis and Baxter [1968] P 639, [1967] 2 All ER 71, [1967] 2 WLR 488, 109 Sol
　Jo 273, 291 851
Ingram v Ingram [1956] P 390, [1956] 1 All ER 785, [1956] 2 WLR 782, 100 Sol Jo
　227 .... 358, 362, 371, 386, 394
Ingram v Little (1883) Cab & El 186 261
Intract v Intract (otherwise Jacobs) [1933] P 190, [1933] All ER Rep 890, 77 Sol Jo 404,
　149 LT 334, sub nom I v I (otherwise J) 102 LJP 65, 49 TLR 456 .... 338, 803, 810
Inverclyde (otherwise Tripp) v Inverclyde [1931] P 29, 29 LGR 353, 95 JP 73, 100 LJP
　16, 144 LT 212, 47 TLR 140 322
Ioakimidis' Policy Trusts, Re, Ioakimidis v Hartcup [1925] Ch 403, [1925] All ER Rep
　164, 95 LJ Ch 24, 69 Sol Jo 662, 133 LT 796, 41 TLR 486 274
Irvin v Irvin [1968] 1 All ER 271, [1968] 1 WLR 464, 111 Sol Jo 982, DC 397, 553
Ives v Ives [1968] P 375, [1967] 3 All ER 79, [1968] 2 WLR 807, 111 Sol Jo 518 404
Ivett v Ivett (1930) 28 LGR 479, 94 JP 237, 29 Cox CC 172, 143 LT 680 344
Ivory, Re, Chippendale v Ivory (1886) 2 TLR 468 6

J

J v J [1947] P 158, [1947] 2 All ER 43, [1947] LJR 1468, 91 Sol Jo 325, 177 LT 157,
　63 TLR 435, CA 335, 339
J v J. See J–PC v J–AF
J v J (ancillary relief: periodical payments) [2004] EWHC 53 (Fam), [2004] 1 FCR 709,
　[2004] Fam Law 408, [2004] All ER (D) 141 (Mar) 458
J v S–T (formerly J) (transsexual: ancillary relief). See S–T (formerly J) v J
J v V (disclosure: offshore corporations) [2003] EWHC 3110 (Fam), [2004] 1 FLR 1042,
　[2004] Fam Law 398 601

PARA

J–PC v J–AF [1955] P 215, [1955] 3 WLR 72, 48 R & IT 644, [1955] TR 193, 99 Sol
   Jo 399, sub nom J v J [1955] 2 All ER 617, CA 429, 599
Jackson (otherwise Macfarlane) v Jackson [1908] P 308, 77 LJP 147, 52 Sol Jo 535, 24
   TLR 674 45
Jackson v Jackson [1924] P 19, [1923] All ER Rep Ext 776, 93 LJP 1, 27 Cox CC 536,
   130 LT 188, 40 TLR 45 .... 362, 368, 379
Jackson v Jackson (1932) 30 LGR 106, [1932] All ER Rep 553, 96 JP 97, 29 Cox CC
   433, 76 Sol Jo 129, 146 LT 406, 48 TLR 206 .... 384, 402
Jackson v Jackson (otherwise Prudom) [1939] P 172, [1939] 1 All ER 471, 108 LJP 83,
   83 Sol Jo 260, 160 LT 365, 55 TLR 412 .... 333, 345
Jackson v Jackson [1970] 3 All ER 854, [1971] 1 WLR 59, 114 Sol Jo 846, 216 Estates
   Gazette 1404; affd [1971] 3 All ER 774, [1971] 1 WLR 1539, 115 Sol Jo
   723, CA 226, 229
Jackson v Jackson [1973] Fam 99, [1973] 2 All ER 395, [1973] 2 WLR 735, 117 Sol Jo
   145 452
Jackson v Jackson [1994] 2 FCR 393, [1993] 2 FLR 848, [1993] Fam Law 675, CA 411
Jacobs v Davis [1917] 2 KB 532, [1916–17] All ER Rep 374, 86 LJKB 1497, 117 LT
   569, 33 TLR 488 .... 16, 253
Jacobs v Jacobs [1943] P 7, [1942] 2 All ER 471, 111 LJP 98, 167 LT 386, 59 TLR
   13, CA 511
Jago v Jago and Graham (1862) 32 LJPM & A 10, 8 Jur NS 1081, 1 New Rep 35, 3 Sw
   & Tr 103, 11 WR 86, 7 LT 645, 164 ER 1211 738
James, Re, Hole v Bethune [1910] 1 Ch 157, 79 LJ Ch 45, 101 LT 625 234
James v James [1948] 1 All ER 214, 46 LGR 156, 112 JP 156, 92 Sol Jo 126 735
James v James [1964] P 303, [1963] 2 All ER 465, [1963] 3 WLR 331, 127 JP 352, 107
   Sol Jo 116 .... 466, 552, 655
Jamieson v Jamieson [1952] AC 525, [1952] 1 All ER 875, 116 JP 226, [1952] 1 TLR
   833, 1952 SC (HL) 44, 1952 SLT 257, HL 394
Janion v Janion [1929] P 237n, 98 LJP 111n, 141 LT 226n, 45 TLR 381n 511
Jansen v Jansen [1965] P 478, [1965] 3 All ER 363, [1965] 3 WLR 875, 109 Sol Jo
   612, CA 225
Jayne v Jayne and Prothero (1869) 18 WR 53, 21 LT 401 769
Jeanes v Wilkins (1749) 1 Ves Sen 195 652
Jee v Thurlow (1824) 2 B & C 547, 2 LJOS 81, 4 Dow & Ry KB 11, 107 ER 487 .... 431, 438
Jefferson v Jefferson [1956] P 136, [1956] 1 All ER 31, [1955] 3 WLR 1001, 35 ATC
   320, 49 R & IT 335, [1955] TR 321, 99 Sol Jo 911, CA 643
Jeffrey v Jeffrey [1951] P 32, [1950] 2 All ER 449, 94 Sol Jo 458, 66 (pt 2) TLR 294 771
Jeffreys v Jeffreys (1912) 28 TLR 504 760
Jenion, Re, Jenion v Wynne [1952] Ch 454, [1952] 1 All ER 1228, 96 Sol Jo 360,
   [1952] 2 TLR 17, CA 355
Jenkins v Barrett (1827) 1 Hag Ecc 12 57
Jenkins v Hargood (formerly Jenkins). See Hargood (formerly Jenkins) v Jenkins
Jenkinson v Bullock (1891) 8 TLR 61 264
Jenkinson v Jenkinson (1963) Times, 15 March, CA 738
Jenner v Hill (1858) 1 F & F 269 273
Jenson v Jenson (1898) 78 LT 764 777
Jervoise v Jervoise (1853) 17 Beav 566, 23 LJ Ch 703, 2 WR 91 246
Jetley v Hill (1884) Cab & El 239 269
Jewsbury v Newbold (1857) 26 LJ Ex 247, 29 LTOS 128 .... 205, 258–259, 264
Jinkings v Jinkings (1867) LR 1 P & D 330, 36 LJP & M 48, 15 LT 512 760
Jinks v Jinks [1936] 3 All ER 1051, 81 Sol Jo 97, CA 643
Jodla v Jodla (otherwise Czarnomska) [1960] 1 All ER 625, [1960] 1 WLR 236, 104 Sol
   Jo 233 342
Jodrell v Jodrell (1845) 9 Beav 45, 15 LJ Ch 17, 9 Jur 1022, 73 RR 274, 50 ER 259, 6
   LTOS 186 431
John's Assignment Trusts, Re, Niven v Niven [1970] 2 All ER 210n, [1970] 1 WLR 955,
   114 Sol Jo 396 225
Johnson v Brown 1823 2 Sh (Ct of Sess) 495 345
Johnson v Johnson [1950] P 23, [1949] 2 All ER 247, 93 Sol Jo 551, CA 511
Johnson v Johnson (1981) 12 Fam Law 116 411
Johnson v Walton [1990] FCR 568, [1990] 1 FLR 350, [1990] Fam Law 260, CA 716

PARA

Johnston v Sumner (1858) 3 H & N 261, 27 LJ Ex 341, 4 Jur NS 462, 6 WR 574, 31 LTOS 166, 157 ER 469 .... 216, 267

Jolliffe v Jolliffe [1965] P 6, [1963] 3 All ER 295, [1964] 2 WLR 13, 107 Sol Jo 78, DC 897

Jolly v Jolly and Fryer (1919) 63 Sol Jo 777 353

Jolly v Rees (1864) 28 JP 534, 15 CBNS 628, 33 LJCP 177, 10 Jur NS 319, 3 New Rep 473, 12 WR 473, 143 ER 931, 10 LT 298 .... 263, 265

Jones v Challenger [1961] 1 QB 176, [1960] 1 All ER 785, [1960] 2 WLR 695, 104 Sol Jo 328, 175 Estates Gazette 695, CA 229

Jones v Cuthbertson (1873) LR 8 QB 504, 42 LJQB 221, 21 WR 919, 28 LT 673, Ex Ch 240

Jones v Jones [1896] P 165, 65 LJP 101, 75 LT 190, 12 TLR 416 760

Jones v Jones [1924] P 203, 22 LGR 697, 93 LJP 94, 132 LT 63, 40 TLR 794 736

Jones v Jones (1941) 39 LGR 266, 105 JP 353, 85 Sol Jo 308, 165 LT 398, DC 897

Jones v Jones [1952] WN 375, 96 Sol Jo 513, [1952] 2 TLR 225, CA 368, 391, 393

Jones v Jones [1959] P 38, [1958] 3 All ER 410, [1958] 3 WLR 635, 123 JP 16, 102 Sol Jo 846 542

Jones v Jones [1971] 3 All ER 1201, 115 Sol Jo 869, CA 480

Jones v Jones [1972] 3 All ER 289, [1972] 1 WLR 1269, 116 Sol Jo 745 .... 451, 513

Jones v Jones [1976] Fam 8, [1975] 2 All ER 12, [1975] 2 WLR 606, 119 Sol Jo 235, CA 601, 621

Jones v Jones [1997] Fam 59, [1997] 2 WLR 373, [1997] 1 FCR 1, [1997] 1 FLR 27, [1997] Fam Law 164, 29 HLR 561, CA 500, 601

Jones v Jones (No 2) [1958] CLY 1091, (1958) Times, 4 November 876

Jones v Jones, Queen's Proctor intervening [1984] FLR 835, [1985] Fam Law 52 .... 853, 877

Jones v Maynard [1951] Ch 572, [1951] 1 All ER 802, 95 Sol Jo 269, [1951] 1 TLR 700 245

Jones v Newtown and Llanidloes Guardians [1920] 3 KB 381, 18 LGR 481, 84 JP 237, 89 LJKB 1161, 124 LT 23, 36 TLR 758 .... 216, 389

Jones v Padavatton [1969] 2 All ER 616, [1969] 1 WLR 328, 112 Sol Jo 965, CA 206

Jones v Waite (1842) 9 Cl & Fin 101, 6 Jur 653, 4 Man & G 1104, 5 Scott NR 951, 8 ER 353, HL 423, 427

Jones' Settlement, Re, Stunt v Jones [1915] 1 Ch 373, 84 LJ Ch 406, 59 Sol Jo 364, 112 LT 1067 277

Jordan v Jordan [1939] P 239, [1939] 2 All ER 29, 108 LJP 104, 83 Sol Jo 300, 160 LT 368, 55 TLR 540 364

Joseph (otherwise King) v Joseph [1909] P 217, 78 LJP 51, 53 Sol Jo 400, 100 LT 864, 25 TLR 439 227

Joseph v Joseph [1915] P 122, 78 JP 520, 84 LJP 104, 112 LT 170, DC 213, 370

Joseph v Joseph [1939] P 385, 83 Sol Jo 716, 55 TLR 951 397–398

Joseph v Joseph [1953] 2 All ER 710, [1953] 1 WLR 1182, 97 Sol Jo 586, CA 375–376

Joseph v Joseph and Burnhill (1897) 76 LT 236 845

Joss v Joss [1943] P 18, [1943] 1 All ER 102, 112 LJP 19, 86 Sol Jo 385, 167 LT 419, 59 TLR 6 511

Joyce v Hutton (1860) 11 I Ch R 123; on appeal (1861) 12 I Ch R 71, Ir CA 711

Joyce v Joyce [1966] P 84, [1966] 1 All ER 905, [1966] 2 WLR 660, 110 Sol Jo 229, CA 877

Judd v Judd [1907] P 241, 76 LJP 120, 51 Sol Jo 500, 98 LT 59, 23 TLR 538 370

Judd v Minster of Pensions and National Insurance [1966] 2 QB 580, [1965] 3 All ER 642, [1966] 2 WLR 218, 109 Sol Jo 815 352

Judgment Debtor (No 23 of 1934), Re [1935] WN 128, [1934–1935] B & CR 197, 79 Sol Jo 625, 51 TLR 524 643

Judkins v Judkins [1897] P 138, 66 LJP 69, 76, 45 WR 567, 41 Sol Jo 559, 76 LT 409, 13 TLR 366, CA 444

Julian v Julian (1972) 116 Sol Jo 763 411

Jump v Jump (1883) 8 PD 159, 52 LJP 71, 31 WR 956 .... 441, 511

K

K v K. See Kokosinski v Kokosinski

K v K (otherwise R) [1910] P 140, 79 LJP 33 453

K v K [1961] 1 All ER 130, [1961] 1 WLR 802; revsd [1961] 2 All ER 266, [1961] 1 WLR 802, 105 Sol Jo 231, CA 702

PARA

K v K (1982) 4 FLR 31, 12 Fam Law 143, CA 587
K v K (financial provision: conduct) [1990] FCR 372, [1990] 2 FLR 225,
[1990] Fam Law 19 .... 601, 617, 621
K v K (financial provision) [1996] 3 FCR 158, sub nom K v K (financial relief: widow's
pension) [1997] 1 FLR 35 411
Kaczmarz v Kaczmarz [1967] 1 All ER 416, [1967] 1 WLR 317, 110 Sol Jo 831 389
Kafton v Kafton [1948] 1 All ER 435, 92 Sol Jo 154, CA 369
Kalinowska v Kalinowski (Balentine intervening) (1964) 108 Sol Jo 260 6
Kalsi v Kalsi [1992] 2 FCR 1, [1992] 1 FLR 511, [1992] Fam Law 333, CA 285
Kara v Kara and Holman [1948] P 287, [1948] 2 All ER 16, [1948] LJR 1741, 92 Sol
Jo 349, 64 TLR 329, CA 734–735, 830
Kashich v Kashich [1951] WN 557, 116 JP 6, DC 391, 897
Kaslefsky v Kaslefsky [1951] P 38, [1950] 2 All ER 398, 48 LGR 520, 114 JP 404, 94
Sol Jo 519, 66 (pt 2) TLR 616, CA 393–394
Kassim (otherwise Widmann) v Kassim (otherwise Hassim) (Carl and Dickson cited)
[1962] P 224, [1962] 3 All ER 426, [1962] 3 WLR 865, 106 Sol Jo 453, 632 ..... 10, 44, 344
Katz v Katz [1972] 3 All ER 219, [1972] 1 WLR 955, 116 Sol Jo 546 360
Kaur v Singh [1972] 1 All ER 292, [1972] 1 WLR 105, 115 Sol Jo 967, CA 342
Kay (otherwise Gunson) v Kay (1934) 78 Sol Jo 899, 152 LT 264, 51 TLR 152 340
Kaye v Kaye (1902) 50 WR 499, 86 LT 638, CA 513
Kaye v Kaye [1965] P 100, [1964] 1 All ER 620, [1964] 2 WLR 672, 128 JP 193, 108
Sol Jo 56 897
Kaye (formerly Kazlowski) v Kazlowska (1953) Times, 1 April 377, 386
Keane v Keane (1873) LR 3 P & D 52, 42 LJP & M 12, 21 WR 248, 27 LT 768 847
Keech v Keech (1868) LR 1 P & D 641, 38 LJP & M 7, 19 LT 462 .... 372, 383
Keeley v Keeley [1952] WN 496, [1952] 2 TLR 756, CA 385, 389
Keighley, Maxsted & Co v Durant [1901] AC 240, [1900–3] All ER Rep 40, 70 LJKB
662, 45 Sol Jo 536, 84 LT 777, 17 TLR 527, HL 273
Kelly (otherwise Hyams) v Kelly (1932) 76 Sol Jo 832, 148 LT 143, 49 TLR 99 44
Kelly v Kelly and Brown [1961] P 94, [1960] 3 All ER 232, [1960] 3 WLR 822, 104 Sol
Jo 685–686
Kelner v Kelner [1939] P 411, [1939] 3 All ER 957, 108 LJP 138, 83 Sol Jo 832, 55
TLR 1058 227
Kemmis v Kemmis (Welland intervening) [1988] 1 WLR 1307, [1988] 2 FLR 223,
[1989] 3 LS Gaz R 43, CA 587
Kemp v Kemp [1961] 2 All ER 764, [1961] 1 WLR 1030, 105 Sol Jo 725 393
Kemp-Welch v Kemp-Welch and Crymes [1912] P 82, [1911–13] All ER Rep Ext 1252,
81 LJP 25, 106 LT 643, 28 TLR 185 880
Kendall v Kendall [1952] 2 All ER 1038n, 117 JP 8 736
Kenn's Case (1606) 7 Co Rep 42b, Jenk 289, sub nom Robertson v Lady Stallage Cro
Jac 186 41
Kennedy v Kennedy [1907] P 49, 76 LJP 34, 96 LT 476, 23 TLR 139 .... 439, 699
Kenney v Kenney (1925) 133 LT 400, 41 TLR 571 736
Kenward v Kenward [1951] P 124, [1950] 2 All ER 297, 94 Sol Jo 383, 66 (pt 2) TLR
157, CA 1, 44, 384
Kenward v Kenward. See Way v Way
Kerr v Kerr [1897] 2 QB 439, [1895–9] All ER Rep 865, 66 LJQB 828, 4 Mans 207, 46
WR 46, 41 Sol Jo 679, 77 LT 29, 13 TLR 534 .... 466, 552
Kershaw v Kershaw [1966] P 13, [1964] 3 All ER 635, [1964] 3 WLR 1143, 128 JP
589, 108 Sol Jo 640 .... 602, 614
Keyes v Keyes and Gray [1921] P 204, 90 LJP 242, 65 Sol Jo 435, 124 LT 797, 37 TLR
499 852
Khan v Khan [1980] 1 All ER 497, [1980] 1 WLR 355, 11 Fam Law 19, 124 Sol Jo
239 .... 553, 600
Kiely v Kiely [1988] 1 FLR 248, [1988] Fam Law 51, CA 492, 518
King v King [1942] P 1, [1941] 2 All ER 103, 111 LJP 90, 167 LT 241, 57 TLR 52 384
King v Read and Slack [1999] 1 FLR 425, [1999] Fam Law 90, CA 737
King's Proctor v Carter. See Carter v Carter (King's Proctor intervening)
Kingsnorth Trust Ltd v Bell [1986] 1 All ER 423, [1986] 1 WLR 119, [1985] FLR 948,
[1985] Fam Law 225, 17 HLR 352, 130 Sol Jo 88, [1985] LS Gaz R 1329, CA 249
Kingston v Kingston (Gilder cited) [1958] P 122, [1958] 1 All ER 397, [1958] 2 WLR
310, 102 Sol Jo 123, CA 883

PARA

Kinnane v Kinnane [1954] P 41, [1953] 2 All ER 1144, [1953] 3 WLR 782, 117 JP 552,
97 Sol Jo 764 .... 362, 369, 371
Kinnoul (Earl) v Money (1767) 3 Swan 202, 1 Ves 186, 36 ER 830 239
Kinzler v Kinzler [1985] Fam Law 26, CA 285
Kirby and Watson's Marriage, Re (1977) 3 Fam LR 11, 318 10
Kirk v Eustace [1937] AC 491, [1937] 2 All ER 715, 106 LJKB 617, 81 Sol Jo 376, 157
LT 171, 53 TLR 748, HL 436
Kirk v Kirk [1947] 2 All ER 118, 45 LGR 537, 111 JP 435, 91 Sol Jo 356, 177 LT 151,
63 TLR 422 566
Kisala v Kisala (1973) 3 Fam Law 90, 117 Sol Jo 664 .... 348, 360
Klucinski v Klucinski [1953] 1 All ER 683, [1953] 1 WLR 522, 117 JP 187, 97 Sol Jo
192 599
Knapp v Knapp (1880) 6 PD 10, [1874–80] All ER Rep 684, 49 LJP 69, 29 WR 80, 43
LT 38 400
Knapp's Settlement, Re, Cowan v Knapp [1952] 1 All ER 458n, 96 Sol Jo 150, [1952] 1
TLR 467 710
Knibb v Knibb [1987] 2 FLR 396, [1987] Fam Law 346, 131 Sol Jo 692,
[1987] LS Gaz R 1058, CA 316
Knight v Gordon (1931) 76 Sol Jo 68 264
Knight's Question, Re [1959] Ch 381, [1958] 1 All ER 812, [1958] 2 WLR 685, 102 Sol
Jo 291 227
Knox v Bushell (1857) 3 CBNS 334, 140 ER 769, 30 LTOS 153 263
Koch v Koch [1899] P 221, 68 LJP 90, 81 LT 61 391
Kochanski v Kochanska [1958] P 147, [1957] 3 All ER 142, [1957] 3 WLR 619, 101
Sol Jo 763 6
Kokosinski v Kokosinski [1980] Fam 72, [1980] 1 All ER 1106, [1980] 3 WLR 55, 1
FLR 205, 124 Sol Jo 16, sub nom K v K 10 Fam Law 91 616
Korda, Re (1957) Times, 23 November; affd (1958) Times, 19 July, CA 436
Korel v Korel (1921) Times, 28 May 43
Kowalczuk v Kowalczuk [1973] 2 All ER 1042, [1973] 1 WLR 930, 117 Sol Jo
372, CA 281, 904
Krenge v Krenge [1999] 1 FLR 969, [1999] Fam Law 304 842
Kunski v Kunski (1898) 68 LJP 18 .... 439, 699
Kunski v Kunski and Josephs (1907) 23 TLR 615 .... 346, 438
Kunstler v Kunstler [1969] 3 All ER 673, [1969] 1 WLR 1506, 113 Sol Jo 656 760
Kynaston v Hickson and Brown (1919) Times, 6 November 876

L

L (an infant), Re [1968] P 119, [1967] 2 All ER 1110, [1967] 3 WLR 1149, 111 Sol Jo
717, CA; affd [1968] P 119, [1968] 1 All ER 20, [1968] 3 WLR 1645, 111 Sol Jo
908, CA 338, 810
L (otherwise B) v B [1895] P 274, 64 LJP 121, 11 R 673 321
L v L (falsely called W) (1882) 7 PD 16, sub nom L v W (falsely called L) 51 LJP 23, 30
WR 444, 47 LT 132 .... 337, 340
L v L (otherwise M) (1908) 53 Sol Jo 32, 25 TLR 43 849
L v L (1949). See REL (otherwise R) v EL
L v L [1954] NZLR 386 321
L v L [1962] P 101, [1961] 3 All ER 834, [1961] 3 WLR 1182, 105 Sol Jo 930, CA 567
L v L (1992). See Lauerman v Lauerman (Practice Note)
L v L (financial provision: lump sum) [1994] 1 FCR 134, [1993] Fam Law 471 621
L v L (lump sum: interest) [1995] 1 FCR 60, [1994] 2 FLR 324, [1994] Fam Law 620 ... 479, 492,
569, 680
L v L (payment of school fees) [1997] 3 FCR 520, [1997] 2 FLR 252, CA 636, 642–643
L v L (financial provision: contributions) [2002] 2 FCR 413, [2002] 1 FLR 642,
[2002] Fam Law 11, [2001] All ER (D) 40 (Nov); revsd sub nom Lambert v
Lambert [2002] EWCA Civ 1685, [2003] Fam 103, [2003] 4 All ER 342,
[2003] 2 WLR 631, [2002] 3 FCR 673, [2003] 1 FLR 139, [2003] Fam Law 16,
[2002] NLJR 1751, (2002) Times, 27 November, [2002] All ER (D) 208 (Nov) 607
L v L and B (1963) 107 Sol Jo 872 851
L– v L– (otherwise D–) (1922) 66 Sol Jo 613, 38 TLR 697 339
L v W (falsely called L). See L v L (falsely called W)
Lacey v Lacey [1919] WN 304 699

PARA

Lacey v Lacey (1931) 29 LGR 566, 95 JP 179, 75 Sol Jo 572, 146 LT 48, 47 TLR
577 .... 402, 427
Lacey v Lacey (1858) 28 LJP & M 24 777
Laing v Laing [2005] EWHC 3152 (Fam), [2007] 2 FLR 199, [2007] Fam Law 580 567
Laing v Walker (1891) 64 LT 527 246
Lake v Lake [1955] P 336, [1955] 2 All ER 538, [1955] 3 WLR 145, 99 Sol Jo
432, CA 830, 863
Lake v Lake [2006] EWCA Civ 1250, [2007] 1 FLR 427, (2006) Times, 16 August,
[2006] All ER (D) 297 (Jul) 311
Lal Chand Marwari v Mahant Ramrup Gir (1925) 42 TLR 159, PC 344
Lamagni v Lamagni [1996] 1 FCR 408, [1995] 2 FLR 452, [1995] Fam Law 607, CA 938, 940
Lambart v Lambart (1907) 51 Sol Jo 345 877
Lambert v Lambert (1767) 2 Bro Parl Cas 18, 1 ER 764, HL 430
Lambert v Lambert. See L v L (financial provision: contributions)
Lancaster v Evors (1847) 10 Beav 266, 16 LJ Ch 308, 50 ER 585 239
Lance v Lance and Gardiner (or Gardner) [1958] P 134n, [1958] 1 All ER 388n,
[1958] 2 WLR 316n, 102 Sol Jo 126 851
Land v Land [1949] P 405, [1949] 2 All ER 218, 47 LGR 566, 113 JP 403, [1949] LJR
1579, 93 Sol Jo 540, 65 TLR 452 736
Lane, Re, Lane v Lane [1986] 1 FLR 283, [1986] Fam Law 74 685–686
Lane v Goodwin (1843) 4 QB 361, 12 LJQB 157, 3 Gal & Dav 610, 7 Jur 372, 114 ER
935 76
Lane v Ironmonger (1844) 1 New Pract Cas 105, 14 LJ Ex 35, 13 M & W 368, 153 ER
152, 4 LTOS 117 .... 264–265, 273
Lane v Lane [1951] P 284, [1951] 1 TLR 1125; affd [1952] P 34, [1952] 1 All ER 223n,
116 JP 72n, [1952] 1 TLR 250, CA 362, 369, 393–395
Lane v Sterne (1862) 3 Giff 629, 9 Jur NS 320, 10 WR 555 647
Lang v Lang 1921 SC 44, 1920 2 SLT 353, 58 SLR 38, Ct of Sess 43
Lang v Lang (1953) Times, 7 July, CA 397
Lang v Lang [1955] AC 402, [1954] 3 All ER 571, [1954] 3 WLR 762, 119 JP 368, 98
Sol Jo 803, PC 368–387, 391, 394
Langley v Langley [1994] 2 FCR 294, [1994] 1 FLR 383, [1994] Fam Law 564, CA 659
Langley's Settlement Trusts, Re, Lloyds Bank Ltd v Langley [1962] Ch 541,
[1961] 3 All ER 803, [1961] 3 WLR 1169, 105 Sol Jo 866, CA 33
Langstone v Hayes [1946] KB 109, [1946] 1 All ER 114, 115 LJKB 225, 175 LT 353,
62 TLR 74, CA 436
Langworthy v Langworthy and Storey (1964) 108 Sol Jo 621 872
Lanitis v Lanitis [1970] 1 All ER 466, [1970] 1 WLR 503, 134 JP 188, 114 Sol Jo
188 897
Lapington v Lapington (1888) 14 PD 21, [1886–90] All ER Rep 1117, 52 JP 727, 58
LJP 26, 37 WR 384, 59 LT 608 769
Larkman v Lindsell [1989] Fam Law 229, CA 654
Latham v Latham and Gethin (1861) 30 LJPM & A 163, 2 Sw & Tr 299, 9 WR 680,
164 ER 1011 876
Lauderdale Peerage (1885) 10 App Cas 692, HL 6, 7
Lauerman v Lauerman (Practice Note) [1992] 1 WLR 734, [1992] 2 FCR 497, sub nom
L v L [1992] 2 FLR 145, [1992] Fam Law 339 737
Laurie v Raglan Building Co Ltd [1942] 1 KB 152, [1941] 3 All ER 332, 111 LJKB 292,
86 Sol Jo 69, 166 LT 63, CA 851
Lautour v Queen's Proctor (1864) 10 HL Cas 685, 33 LJPM & A 89, 10 Jur NS 325,
12 WR 611, 11 ER 1193, 10 LT 198 876
Law v Harragin (1917) 61 Sol Jo 546, 33 TLR 381 430
Lawlor v Lawlor [1995] 1 FCR 412, [1995] 1 FLR 269, [1995] Fam Law 241, CA 779
Lawrence v Lawrence (1862) 31 LJPM & A 145, 8 Jur NS 972, 2 Sw & Tr 575, 164
ER 1120, 6 LT 550 386
Lawrance v Lawrance [1950] P 84, 48 LGR 62, 93 Sol Jo 792, 66 (pt 1) TLR 9 ..... 379, 391, 393
Lawrence v Lawrence (2 June 1954, unreported) 343
Lawry v Lawry [1967] 2 All ER 1131, [1967] 1 WLR 789, 111 Sol Jo 353, CA 863
Lawson v Lawson [1955] 1 All ER 341, [1955] 1 WLR 200, 119 JP 279, 99 Sol Jo
167, CA 213, 354, 370, 408
Laxton v Laxton (1861) 30 LJPM & A 208 879

PARA

Laxton v Laxton and Hitchcock [1962] 2 All ER 364, [1962] 1 WLR 729, 106 Sol Jo
    513 1038
Layton v Martin [1986] 2 FLR 227, [1986] Fam Law 212 281
Lazarewicz (otherwise Fadanelli) v Lazarewicz [1962] P 171, [1962] 2 All ER 5,
    [1962] 2 WLR 933, 106 Sol Jo 38 6
Lea Bridge District Gas Co v Malvern [1917] 1 KB 803, 15 LGR 412, 81 JP 141, 86
    LJKB 553, 116 LT 311 .... 205, 258
Leadbeater v Leadbeater [1985] FLR 789, [1985] Fam Law 280 .... 601, 616
Leake (formerly Bruzzi) v Bruzzi [1974] 2 All ER 1196, [1974] 1 WLR 1528, 118 Sol Jo
    831, CA 279
Le Brocq v Le Brocq [1964] 3 All ER 464, [1964] 1 WLR 1085, 108 Sol Jo 501, CA 368
Lee v Lau [1967] P 14, [1964] 2 All ER 248, [1964] 3 WLR 750, 108 Sol Jo 239 .... 349, 852
Lee v Lee (1872) LR 2 P & D 409, 41 LJP & M 85, 27 LT 324 738
Lee v Lee [1952] 2 QB 489n, [1952] 1 All ER 1299, [1952] 1 TLR 968, CA 226
Lee v Lee (1973) 117 Sol Jo 616 411
Lee Shires v Lee Shires (1910) 54 Sol Jo 874 362
Leeds v Leeds (1886) 57 LT 373 514
Leeser (otherwise May) v Leeser (otherwise Bohrer) [1955] CLY 408, (1955) Times,
    5 February 376
Leete v Leete (1862) 31 LJPM & A 121, 2 Sw & Tr 568, 164 ER 1118, 6 LT 507 787
Le Foe v Le Foe and Woolwich plc [2002] 1 FCR 107, [2001] 2 FLR 970,
    [2001] Fam Law 739, [2001] All ER (D) 325 (Jun) 587
Legey v O'Brien (1834) Milw 325 45
Legrove v Legrove [1995] 1 FCR 102, [1994] 2 FLR 119, [1994] Fam Law 563, CA 693
Leicester City Council v Aldwinckle (1991) 24 HLR 40, CA 947
Le Marchant v Le Marchant [1977] 3 All ER 610, [1977] 1 WLR 559, 7 Fam Law 241,
    121 Sol Jo 334, CA 411
Lempriere v Lempriere and Roebel (1868) LR 1 P & D 569, 37 LJP & M 78, 16 WR
    1192, 19 LT 50 771
Leng v Leng [1946] 2 All ER 590, 44 LGR 411, 110 JP 385, 90 Sol Jo 630, 175 LT
    517, 62 TLR 722, DC 390, 393, 397
Lennon v News Group Newspapers Ltd and Twist [1978] FSR 573, CA 223
Lepre v Lepre [1965] P 52, [1963] 2 All ER 49, [1963] 2 WLR 735, 106 Sol Jo 1035 ..... 33, 368,
                                                                                            378
Le Roy-Lewis v Le Roy-Lewis [1955] P 1, [1954] 3 All ER 57, [1954] 3 WLR 549, 118
    JP 444, 98 Sol Jo 718 542
Leslie, Re, Leslie v French (1883) 23 Ch D 552, [1881–5] All ER Rep 274, 48 52 LJ
    Ch 762, 31 WR 561, LT 564 277
Lesser (otherwise May) v Lesser (otherwise Bohrer) (1955) Times, 5 February 852
Le Sueur v Le Sueur (1877) 2 PD 79, 25 WR 402, 36 LT 276, CA 852
Lett v Lett (1907) 51 Sol Jo 532, 23 TLR 569 364
Levermore v Levermore [1980] 1 All ER 1, [1979] 1 WLR 1277, 1 FLR 375, 10 Fam
    Law 87, 123 Sol Jo 689 647
Levy v Legal Services Commission [2001] 1 All ER 895, [2001] 1 FCR 178,
    [2001] Fam Law 92, [2000] BPIR 1065, [2000] All ER (D) 1775, CA 687, 689, 692
Levy v Levy (1904) 21 TLR 157 406
Lewis (falsely called Hayward) v Hayward (1866) 35 LJP & M 105, HL 34, 340
Lewis v Lewis (1860) 29 LJPM & A 123 771
Lewis v Lewis (1861) 30 LJPM & A 199, 7 Jur NS 831, 2 Sw & Tr 394, 164 ER 1048,
    4 LT 772 .... 856, 876
Lewis v Lewis [1956] P 205n, [1955] 3 All ER 598, [1955] 3 WLR 862n, 120 JP 21, 99
    Sol Jo 873 395
Lewis v Lewis [1958] P 193, [1958] 1 All ER 859, [1958] 2 WLR 747, 102 Sol Jo
    306, CA 349, 828
Lewis v Lewis [1977] 3 All ER 992, [1977] 1 WLR 409, 121 Sol Jo 271, CA 568
Lewis v Nangle (1752) Amb 150, 1 Cox Eq Cas 240, 2 Ves Sen 431, 29 ER 1146 239–240
Liff v Liff (otherwise Rigby) [1948] WN 128 345
Lilford (Lord) v Glynn [1979] 1 All ER 441, [1979] 1 WLR 78, 9 Fam Law 81, 122 Sol
    Jo 433, CA 518, 702
Lilley v Lilley [1960] P 158, [1959] 3 All ER 283, [1959] 3 WLR 306, 123 JP 525, 103
    Sol Jo 657, CA 216–217, 382, 385–386, 389, 542

PARA

Lindo v Belisario (1795) 1 Hag Con 216, [1775–1802] All ER Rep 293, 161 ER 531;
 affd (1796) 1 Hag Con App 7 [1775–1802] All ER Rep 293n 24, 118
Lindus v Bradwell (1848) 5 CB 583, 17 LJCP 121, 12 Jur 230, 136 ER 1007, 10 LTOS
 393 .... 257, 273
Lindwall v Lindwall [1967] 1 All ER 470, [1967] 1 WLR 143, 110 Sol Jo 849, CA 851, 886
Ling v Ling and Croker (1858) 27 LJP & M 58, 1 Sw & Tr 180, 6 WR 674, 164 ER
 683, 31 LTOS 186 358
Linton v Linton (1885) 15 QBD 239, [1881–5] All ER Rep 867, 54 LJQB 529, sub nom
 Linton, Re, ex p Linton 49 JP 597, 2 Morr 179, 33 WR 714, 52 LT 782, CA 466, 552,
 649
Lister v Lister [1922] P 227, 91 LJP 180, 127 LT 493, 38 TLR 609 438
Littlewood v Littlewood [1943] P 11, [1942] 2 All ER 515, 112 LJP 17, 86 Sol Jo 341,
 167 LT 388, 59 TLR 29 368
Livesey (formerly Jenkins) v Jenkins [1985] AC 424, [1985] 1 All ER 106,
 [1985] 2 WLR 47, [1985] FLR 813, [1985] Fam Law 310, 129 Sol Jo 17, [1985]
 NLJ Rep 55, HL 593, 715, 933
Livingstone-Stallard v Livingstone-Stallard [1974] Fam 47, [1974] 2 All ER 766,
 [1974] 3 WLR 302, 4 Fam Law 150, 118 Sol Jo 462 .... 346, 360, 553
Lloyd-Davies v Lloyd-Davies [1947] P 53, [1947] 1 All ER 161, [1947] LJR 279, 91 Sol
 Jo 160, 176 LT 158, 63 TLR 80, CA 883
Lloyds Bank Ltd, Re, Bomze and Lederman v Bomze [1931] 1 Ch 289, [1930] All ER
 Rep 479, 100 LJ Ch 45, 144 LT 276, 47 TLR 38 249
Lloyds Bank plc v Byrne [1993] 2 FCR 41, [1993] 1 FLR 369, [1993] Fam Law 183, 23
 HLR 472, CA 639
Lloyds Bank plc v Carrick [1996] 4 All ER 630, 73 P & CR 314, [1996] 2 FCR 771,
 [1996] 2 FLR 600, [1997] Fam Law 94, [1996] 14 LS Gaz R 30, [1996] NLJR
 405, 140 Sol Jo LB 101, CA 280
Lloyds Bank plc v Rosset [1991] 1 AC 107, [1990] 1 All ER 1111, [1990] 2 WLR 867,
 60 P & CR 311, [1990] 2 FLR 155, [1990] Fam Law 395, 22 HLR 349,
 [1990] 16 LS Gaz R 41, [1990] NLJR 478, HL 278, 280–281
Lloyds Bowmaker Ltd v Britannia Arrow Holdings plc (Lavens, third party)
 [1988] 3 All ER 178, [1988] 1 WLR 1337, [1989] 1 LS Gaz R 40, [1987] NLJ Rep
 344, CA 661–662
Lodge v Lodge (1890) 15 PD 159, 59 LJP 84, 63 LT 467 400
Logan v Birkett (1833) 1 My & K 220, 2 LJ Ch 52, 39 ER 664 431
Lomas v Parle [2003] EWCA Civ 1804, [2004] 1 All ER 1173, [2004] 1 WLR 1642,
 [2004] 1 FCR 97, [2004] 1 FLR 812, (2004) Times, 13 January, [2003] All ER (D)
 328 (Dec) 716
Lombardi v Lombardi [1973] 3 All ER 625, [1973] 1 WLR 1276, 4 Fam Law 80, 117
 Sol Jo 775, CA 595, 599
London and Birmingham Rly Co v Grand Junction Canal Co (1835) 1 Ry & Can Cas
 224 .... 624, 649
LCC v Henry Boot & Sons Ltd [1959] 3 All ER 636, [1959] 1 WLR 1069, 59 LGR
 357, 103 Sol Jo 918, HL 630
Long v Long and Johnson (1890) 15 PD 218, 60 LJP 27 349
Long of Wraxall (Lord) v Lady Long of Wraxall [1940] 4 All ER 230, 110 LJP 17, 84
 Sol Jo 491, 57 TLR 165, CA 371, 373, 436
Looker v Looker [1918] P 132, 87 LJP 72, 62 Sol Jo 405, 118 LT 654, 34 TLR 27 374
Loraine v Loraine and Murphy [1912] P 222, 82 LJP 29, 56 Sol Jo 687, 107 LT 363, 28
 TLR 534, CA 511
Lord v Hall (1849) 2 Car & Kir 698, 8 CB 627, 19 LJCP 47, 137 ER 653, 14 LTOS
 253 257
Lort-Williams v Lort-Williams [1951] P 395, [1951] 2 All ER 241, 95 Sol Jo 529,
 [1951] 2 TLR 200, CA 511
Loseby v Newman [1996] 1 FCR 647, [1995] 2 FLR 754, [1996] Fam Law 24, CA 290, 719
Loveden v Loveden (1810) 2 Hag Con 1, [1803–13] All ER Rep 339, 161 ER 648 353
Lovell, Re, Sparks v Southall [1920] 1 Ch 122, 88 LJ Ch 540, 64 Sol Jo 35, 122 LT 26,
 35 TLR 715 222
Lowe v Fox (1885) 15 QBD 667, 50 JP 244, 54 LJQB 561, 34 WR 144, 53 LT
 886, CA; on appeal (1887) 12 App Cas 206, 51 JP 468, 56 LJQB 480, 36 WR 25,
 56 LT 406, HL 206
Lowe v Lowe (1855) Dea & Sw 130, 4 WR 92 734

PARA

Lowry v Lowry [1952] P 252, [1952] 2 All ER 61, 116 JP 343, 96 Sol Jo 379, [1952] 1
  TLR 1508 403–404
Lowsley v Forbes (t/a LE Design Services) [1999] 1 AC 329, [1998] 3 All ER 897,
  [1998] 3 WLR 501, [1998] 2 Lloyd's Rep 577, [1998] NLJR 1268, 142 Sol Jo LB
  247, [1998] All ER (D) 382, HL 678, 680, 683
Lucas v Harris (1886) 18 QBD 127, 51 JP 261, 56 LJQB 15, 35 WR 112, 55 LT 658, 3
  TLR 106, CA 650
Lucas v Lucas (1738) 1 Atk 270, West temp Hard 456 246
Lulham, Re, Brinton v Lulham (1885) 33 WR 788, 53 LT 9, CA 251
Lurie v Lurie [1938] 3 All ER 156, 107 LJ Ch 289, 82 Sol Jo 476, 159 LT 249, 54 TLR
  889 424
Lutwyche v Lutwyche and Cox (1859) 28 LJP & M 56, 5 Jur NS 76 856
Lyle v Ellwood (1874) LR 19 Eq 98, 44 LJ Ch 164, 23 WR 157 6
Lyle v Lyle (1972) 3 Fam Law 41, 117 Sol Jo 70 860
Lynch, Re, Lynch v Lynch (1879) 4 LR Ir 210, Ir CA 711

M

M (falsely called B) v B (1864) 33 LJPM & A 203, 3 Sw & Tr 550, 164 ER 1389, 10
  LT 847, sub nom Marriott (falsely called Burgess) v Burgess 10 Jur NS 885 321
M v B (1874) LR 3 P & D 200, 43 LJP & M 42, 22 WR 556, 30 LT 910 863
M v B (ancillary proceedings: lump sum) [1998] 1 FCR 213, [1998] 1 FLR 53,
  [1998] Fam Law 75, CA 601, 610, 613
M (otherwise D) v D (1885) 10 PD 75, 54 LJP 68, 33 WR 657 321
M (otherwise D) v D (1885) 10 PD 175, 34 WR 48 849
M (falsely called H) v H (1864) 33 LJPM & A 159, 3 Sw & Tr 517, 13 WR 108, 10 LT
  787, sub nom Marshall (falsely called Hamilton) v Hamilton 10 Jur NS 853 337
M v M (otherwise H) (1906) 22 TLR 719 321
M v M [1928] P 123, [1928] All ER Rep 589, 97 LJP 101, 72 Sol Jo 155, 138 LT 648,
  44 TLR 299 456
M v M (otherwise B) [1957] P 139, [1956] 3 All ER 769, [1956] 3 WLR 975, 100 Sol
  Jo 876 .... 336, 340
M v M (1981) 3 FLR 83, 11 Fam Law 118 621
M v M (enforcement: judgment summons) [1993] Fam Law 469, Cty Ct 624, 636, 642, 686
M v M (property adjustment: impaired life expectancy) [1994] 2 FCR 174,
  [1993] 2 FLR 723, [1993] Fam Law 521, CA 617
M v M [1994] 2 FCR 448, [1994] 1 FLR 399 .... 938, 940
M v M (financial provision: party incurring excessive costs) [1995] 3 FCR 321 621
M v M (prenuptial agreement) [2002] 1 FLR 654 712
M v M (maintenance pending suit) [2002] EWHC 317 (Fam), [2002] 2 FLR 123 599
M v M [2006] 2 FCR 555, [2006] 2 FLR 1253, [2006] All ER (D) 58 (Jun) 621, 931
M v W (non-molestation order: duration) [2000] 1 FLR 107, [2000] Fam Law 13 716
MB v KB [2007] EWHC 789 (Fam), [2007] 2 FLR 586, sub nom B v B [2007] Fam Law
  660, [2007] Fam Law 801, [2007] All ER (D) 144 (Mar) 568
MD and TD (minors) (time estimates), Re [1994] 2 FCR 94, [1994] 2 FLR 336,
  [1994] Fam Law 488 931
MH v MH (1981) 3 FLR 429 593
MT v MT [1991] FCR 649, [1992] 1 FLR 362, [1992] Fam Law 99 .... 478, 595, 601
M'Adam v Walker (1813) 1 Dow 148, HL 42, 344
Macalpine v Macalpine [1958] P 35, [1957] 3 All ER 134, [1957] 3 WLR 698, 101 Sol
  Jo 816 33
Macan v Macan (1900) 70 LJQB 90, 45 Sol Jo 120, 17 TLR 131 448
Macartney, Re, Macfarlane v Macartney [1921] 1 Ch 522, 90 LJ Ch 314, 65 Sol Jo 435,
  124 LT 658 .... 465, 677
Macaskill v Macaskill 1939 SC 187, 1939 SLT 139, 1939 SN 5, Ct of Sess 369
McCarthy v Hastings [1933] NI 100, CA 6, 7
McCartney v Mills McCartney [2008] EWHC 401 (Fam), [2008] 1 FCR 707,
  [2008] 1 FLR 1508, [2008] Fam Law 507, [2008] All ER (D) 269 (Mar) 603, 607, 614
McConnell v McConnell (1980) 10 Fam Law 214, CA 291, 720
MacDarmaid v A-G [1950] P 218, [1950] 1 All ER 497, 94 Sol Jo 211, 66 (pt 1) TLR
  543 416
Macdonald v Macdonald (1859) 4 Sw & Tr 242, 164 ER 1508 .... 362, 371, 373
McDowell v McDowell (1957) 169 Estates Gazette 264, CA 226

PARA

Macey v Macey (1981) 3 FLR 7, 11 Fam Law 248 .... 590, 602
McFarlane v McFarlane [1972] NI 59, CA 279
McFarlane v McFarlane [2006] UKHL 24, [2006] 2 AC 618, [2006] 3 All ER 1,
    [2006] 2 WLR 1283, [2006] 2 FCR 213, [2006] 1 FLR 1186, [2006] Fam Law
    629, [2006] NLJR 916, (2006) Times, 25 May, 150 Sol Jo LB 704, [2006] All ER
    (D) 343 (May) 591
McG (formerly R) v R [1972] 1 All ER 362, sub nom McGill v Robson [1972] 1 WLR
    237, 116 Sol Jo 37 408
M'George v Egan (1839) 5 Bing NC 196, 1 Arn 462, 3 Jur 266, 7 Scott 112, 132 ER
    1080 269
McGill v Robson. See McG (formerly R) v R
McGladdery v McGladdery [2000] 1 FCR 315, [1999] 2 FLR 1102, [2000] Fam Law
    160, [1999] 32 LS Gaz R 32, [2000] BPIR 1078, CA 587
McGowan v McGowan [1948] 2 All ER 1032, 47 LGR 118, 113 JP 27, [1949] LJR
    197, 92 Sol Jo 647, 64 TLR 634 .... 384, 402
McGregor v McGregor (1888) 21 QBD 424, 52 JP 772, 57 LJQB 591, 37 WR 45, 58
    LT 227, 4 TLR 760, CA 426–427, 431
McHardy and Sons (a firm) v Warren [1994] 2 FLR 338, [1994] Fam Law 567, CA 280
Macintosh v Pogose. See Mackintosh v Pogose
Mackenzie v Mackenzie [1895] AC 384, HL 369
McKenzie v McKenzie [1971] P 33, [1970] 3 All ER 1034, [1970] 3 WLR 472, 114 Sol
    Jo 667, CA 850, 897
McKerrell, Re, McKerrell v Gowans [1912] 2 Ch 648, 82 LJ Ch 22, 107 LT 404 277
McKinley v McKinley [1960] 1 All ER 476, [1960] 1 WLR 120, 124 JP 171, 104 Sol Jo
    168 833
Mackintosh v Pogose [1895] 1 Ch 505, 2 Mans 27, 13 R 254, 43 WR 247, 39 Sol Jo
    218, 72 LT 251, sub nom Macintosh v Pogose 64 LJ Ch 274 207
McLarnon v McLarnon (1968) 112 Sol Jo 419 43
MacLean v MacLean [1951] 1 All ER 967, CA 511
McLean v McLean, Queen's Proctor intervening [1984] FLR 835, [1985] Fam Law 52 .... 853, 877
MacLennan v MacLennan (or Shortland) 1958 SC 105, 1958 SLT 12, Ct of Sess 349
McLeod v McLeod [1963] CLY 1676, 113 L Jo 420 211
M'Loughlin's Estate, Re (1878) 1 LR Ir 421, Ir CA 6
MacLulich v MacLulich [1920] P 439, 89 LJP 242, 124 LT 66, CA 788
Maclurcan v Maclurcan (1897) 42 Sol Jo 32, 77 LT 474, CA 475, 552
McMillan v McMillan 1961 SLT 429 393
Macnaghten v Paterson [1907] AC 483, 76 LJPC 94, 97 LT 442, 25 TLR 727, PC 436
Maconochie v Maconochie [1916] P 326, 86 LJP 10, 61 Sol Jo 57, 115 LT 790, 33 TLR
    50 861
McPhail v Persons (names unknown) [1973] Ch 447, [1973] 3 All ER 393,
    [1973] 3 WLR 71, 117 Sol Jo 448, 227 Estates Gazette 985, CA 947
McPherson v McPherson [1936] AC 177, [1935] All ER Rep 105, 105 LJPC 41, 80 Sol
    Jo 91, 154 LT 221, 52 TLR 166, PC 879–880, 883
McQuiban v McQuiban [1913] P 208, 83 LJP 19, 109 LT 412, 29 TLR 766 ... 446, 466, 552, 699
McTaggart v McTaggart [1949] P 94, [1948] 2 All ER 754, 46 LGR 527, [1949] LJR
    82, 92 Sol Jo 617, 64 TLR 558, CA 833
Mahadervan v Mahadervan [1964] P 233, [1962] 3 All ER 1108, [1963] 2 WLR 271,
    106 Sol Jo 533 .... 6–7, 17, 21, 42
Maher v Maher [1951] P 342, [1951] 2 All ER 37, 95 Sol Jo 468, [1951] 1 TLR 1163 33
Mahoney v M'Carthy [1892] P 21, 61 LJP 41, 8 TLR 97 .... 368, 372
Main v Main (1949) 78 CLR 636, Aus HC 412
Mainwaring v Leslie (1826) 2 C & P 507, Mood & M 18 267
Major v Major (9, 10 March 1959, unreported) 833
Malo v Malo (1786) 32 LJPM & A 67n, 2 Sw & Tr 657n, 164 ER 1153, 7 LT 437n 599
Manchanda v Manchanda [1996] 1 FCR 733, [1995] 2 FLR 590, [1995] Fam Law 603,
    [1995] 23 LS Gaz R 32, CA 863, 883
Manchester Corpn v Connolly [1970] Ch 420, [1970] 1 All ER 961, [1970] 2 WLR 746,
    68 LGR 379, 21 P & CR 154, 114 Sol Jo 108, 213 Estates Gazette 1277, CA 654
Mann v Mann [1922] P 238, [1922] All ER Rep 777, 91 LJP 204, 126 LT 222, 66 Sol
    Jo (WR) 7 699
Manners, Re, Public Trustee v Manners [1949] Ch 613, [1949] 2 All ER 201, [1949]
    LJR 1574, CA 440

PARA

Manners v Manners and Fortescue [1936] P 117, [1936] 1 All ER 41, 105 LJP 26, 80 Sol Jo 187, 154 LT 271, 52 TLR 244 739

Manning v Manning [1950] 1 All ER 602, 94 Sol Jo 238, CA 353

Manser v Manser (King's Proctor showing cause) [1940] P 224, [1940] 4 All ER 238, 110 LJP 7, 84 Sol Jo 647, 165 LT 9, 57 TLR 45 .... 417, 877

Mansey v Mansey [1940] P 139, [1940] 2 All ER 424, 109 LJP 83, 84 Sol Jo 370, 163 LT 157, 56 TLR 676 384

Mansfield (falsely called Cuno) v Cuno (1873) 42 LJP & M 65, 29 LT 316, sub nom Cuno v Cuno LR 2 Sc & Div 300, HL 321, 832

Marczuk v Marczuk [1956] P 217, [1955] 3 All ER 758, [1956] 2 WLR 1, 120 JP 64, 100 Sol Jo 15; revsd [1956] P 217, [1956] 1 All ER 657, [1956] 2 WLR 849, 120 JP 75, 100 Sol Jo 263, CA 352, 404

Mareva Cia Naviera SA v International Bulkcarriers SA, The Mareva [1980] 1 All ER 213n, [1975] 2 Lloyd's Rep 509, 119 Sol Jo 660, CA 661

Marjoram v Marjoram [1955] 2 All ER 1, [1955] 1 WLR 520, 119 JP 291, 99 Sol Jo 320 .... 213, 370, 393–394, 897

Marlborough (Lily, Duchess) v Duke of Marlborough [1901] 1 Ch 165, 70 LJ Ch 244, 49 WR 275, 45 Sol Jo 116, 83 LT 578, 17 TLR 137, CA 375

Marriage of C and D (falsely called C), Re (1979) 35 FLR 340, 5 Fam LR 636 .... 1, 44

Marriott (falsely called Burgess) v Burgess. See M (falsely called B) v B

Marsden v Marsden [1972] Fam 280, [1972] 2 All ER 1162, [1972] 3 WLR 136, 116 Sol Jo 415 860

Marsh v Marsh [1945] AC 271, 114 LJPC 89, 62 TLR 20, PC 876, 879

Marsh v Marsh [1993] 2 All ER 794, [1993] 1 WLR 744, [1993] 1 FLR 467, [1993] Fam Law 346, [1993] NLJR 364, CA 737

Marsh v Von Sternberg [1986] 1 FLR 526, [1986] Fam Law 160 282

Marshall (falsely called Hamilton) v Hamilton. See M (falsely called H) v H

Marshall v Marshall (1879) 5 PD 19, 48 LJP 49, 27 WR 399, 39 LT 640 .... 375, 431, 444

Marshall v Marshall (1909) 25 TLR 716 879

Martin v Martin (1898) 78 LT 568 400–401

Martin v Martin (1919) P 283, [1918–19] All ER Rep 1116, 88 LJP 163, 63 Sol Jo 641, 121 LT 337, 35 TLR 602, CA 599

Martin v Martin [1976] Fam 335, [1976] 3 All ER 625, [1976] 3 WLR 580, 6 Fam Law 246, 120 Sol Jo 503, CA 621

Martin v Martin [1978] Fam 12, [1977] 3 All ER 762, [1977] 3 WLR 101, 121 Sol Jo 335, CA 316

Marya v Marya [1996] 1 FCR 153, [1995] 2 FLR 911, [1996] Fam Law 17, CA 883

Masich v Masich (1977) 7 Fam Law 245, 121 Sol Jo 645, CA 290, 719

Mason v Mason [1972] Fam 302, [1972] 3 All ER 315, [1972] 3 WLR 405, 116 Sol Jo 485 408

Mason v Mason (1980) 11 Fam Law 143, CA 360, 379

Massey v Massey [1949] WN 422 698

Masson Templier & Co v De Fries [1909] 2 KB 831, 79 LJKB 24, 53 Sol Jo 744, 101 LT 476, 25 TLR 784, sub nom Masson Templier [1908–10] All ER Rep 944, CA 246

Masters v Masters (1864) 34 LJPM & A 7, 4 New Rep 200 876

Mather v Ney (1807) 3 M & S 265n 69

Mather v Rhodes (1934) 78 Sol Jo 414 222

Mathias v Mathias [1972] Fam 287, [1972] 3 All ER 1, [1972] 3 WLR 201, 116 Sol Jo 394, CA 411, 592, 600

Matthews v Matthews (1860) 29 LJPM & A 118, 6 Jur NS 659, 3 Sw & Tr 161, 8 WR 591, 164 ER 1235, 2 LT 472 346

Maudslay v Maudslay (1877) 2 PD 256, 47 LJP 26, 38 LT 323 513

Mawford v Mawford (1866) 14 WR 516 349

Mawson v Mawson [1994] 2 FCR 852, [1994] 2 FLR 985, [1995] Fam Law 9 616

Maxted v Maxted (1961) Times, 26 January 417

Maxwell v Keun [1928] 1 KB 645, [1927] All ER Rep 335, 97 LJKB 305, 72 Sol Jo 48, 138 LT 310, 44 TLR 100, CA 897

May v May [1929] 2 KB 386, [1929] All ER Rep 484, 98 LJKB 770, 141 LT 629, CA 442

Mayes v Mayes [1971] 2 All ER 397, [1971] 1 WLR 679, 135 JP 487, 115 Sol Jo 111 897

Mayhew v Mayhew (1812) 2 Phillim 11, 3 M & S 266n, 161 ER 1062 69

Mehta (otherwise Kohn) v Mehta [1945] 2 All ER 690, 174 LT 63 .... 44, 344

PARA

Meier v Meier [1948] P 89, [1948] 1 All ER 161, [1948] LJR 436, 92 Sol Jo 54, 64
TLR 39, CA 883
Melvill v Melvill and Woodward [1930] P 99; revsd [1930] P 159, [1930] All ER Rep
79, 99 LJP 65, 74 Sol Jo 233, 143 LT 206, 46 TLR 327, CA 511
Mercantile Credit Co Ltd v Ellis [1987] CLY 2917, (1987) Times, 1 April, CA 636
Meredith v Footner (1843) 12 LJ Ex 183, 11 M & W 202, 152 ER 775 270
Merker v Merker [1963] P 283, [1962] 3 All ER 928, [1962] 3 WLR 1389, 106 Sol Jo
881 ...... 6, 119
Merritt v Merritt [1970] 2 All ER 760, [1970] 1 WLR 1211, 114 Sol Jo 455, 214
Estates Gazette 1355, CA 206
Mesher v Mesher and Hall (1973) [1980] 1 All ER 126n, CA 316
Messiniaki Tolmi, The. See Astro Exito Navegacion SA v Southland Enterprise Co Ltd
(No 2) (Chase Manhattan Bank NA intervening), The Messiniaki Tolmi
Metcalfe v Shaw (1811) 3 Camp 22 ...... 205, 259, 264
Meters Ltd v Metropolitan Gas Meters Ltd (1907) 51 Sol Jo 499 649
Mette v Mette (1859) 28 LJP & M 117, 1 Sw & Tr 416, 7 WR 543, 33 LTOS 139 35
Meyer v Meyer (Hodge cited) [1959] 2 All ER 633n, [1959] 1 WLR 957, 103 Sol Jo
835 851
Meyrick's Settlement, Re, Meyrick v Meyrick [1921] 1 Ch 311, 90 LJ Ch 152, 65 Sol Jo
155, 124 LT 531 423–424
Mezger v Mezger [1937] P 19, [1936] 3 All ER 130, 34 LGR 608, 100 JP 475, 106 LJP
1, 30 Cox CC 467, 80 Sol Jo 916, 155 LT 491, 53 TLR 18 566
Michael v Michael [1986] 2 FLR 389, [1986] Fam Law 334, 130 Sol Jo 713,
[1986] LS Gaz R 2488, CA 601
Micklethwait v Micklethwait (1859) 4 CBNS 790, 862, 29 LJCP 75, 5 Jur NS 437, 7
WR 451, Ex Ch 511
Middlebrook v Middlebrook [1965] P 262, [1965] 1 All ER 404, [1965] 2 WLR 360,
108 Sol Jo 900 853
Middleton v Crofts (1736) 2 Atk 650, 2 Barn KB 351, Cunn 55, 114, Kel W 148, Ridg
temp H 109, 2 Stra 1056, Lee temp Hard 57, 326, 26 ER 788 ...... 57, 59
Midgeley (falsely called Wood) v Wood (1859) Sea & Sm 70, 30 LJPM & A 57, 4 Sw &
Tr 267, 164 ER 1518 328
Midland Bank plc v Cooke [1995] 4 All ER 562, [1996] 1 FCR 442, [1995] 2 FLR 915,
[1995] Fam Law 675, 27 HLR 733, [1995] 30 LS Gaz R 34, [1995] NLJR 1543,
139 Sol Jo LB 194, CA 282
Midland Bank plc v Dobson and Dobson [1986] 1 FLR 171, [1986] Fam Law 55, 75,
[1985] NLJ Rep 751, CA 281
Midland Bank plc v Pike [1988] 2 All ER 434 639
Midland Bank Trust Co Ltd v Green (No 3) [1982] Ch 529, [1981] 3 All ER 744,
[1982] 2 WLR 1, 125 Sol Jo 554, CA 204
Miell v English (1866) 15 LT 249 204
Mighell v Sultan of Johore [1894] 1 QB 149, [1891–4] All ER Rep 1019, 58 JP 244, 63
LJQB 593, 9 R 447, 70 LT 64, 10 TLR 115, CA 742
Miles v Chilton (falsely calling herself Miles) (1849) 1 Rob Eccl 684, 6 Notes of Cases
636, 163 ER 1178 ...... 42, 321, 344
Miles v Miles (1896) Times, 20 March 761
Miles v Miles [1979] 1 All ER 865, [1979] 1 WLR 371, 9 Fam Law 53, 123 Sol Jo
232, CA 630
Militante v Ogunwomoju [1993] 2 FCR 355, [1994] Fam Law 17 44
Millard v Harvey (1864) 34 Beav 237, 10 Jur NS 1167, 13 WR 125, 55 ER 626, 11 LT
360 273
Miller v Huddlestone (1882) 22 Ch D 233, [1881–5] All ER Rep 894, 52 LJ Ch 208, 31
WR 138, 47 LT 570 650
Miller (formerly Kozubowski) v Kozubowski, Hekner (cited as Hepner), Denester (cited
as Dennister) and Niekrasz cited [1956] 1 All ER 177n, [1956] 1 WLR 93, 100 Sol
Jo 56 863
Miller v Miller [2006] UKHL 24, [2006] 2 AC 618, [2006] 3 All ER 1, [2006] 2 WLR
1283, [2006] 2 FCR 213, [2006] 1 FLR 1186, [2006] Fam Law 629, [2006] NLJR
916, (2006) Times, 25 May, 150 Sol Jo LB 704, [2006] All ER (D) 343 (May) 591
Miller v Miller and Hicks (1862) 31 LJPM & A 73, 2 Sw & Tr 427, 164 ER 1062, 5 LT
850 738

PARA

Miller v Minister of Pensions [1947] 2 All ER 372, [1948] LJR 203, 91 Sol Jo 484, 177
    LT 536, 63 TLR 474 352
Millet v Rowse (1802) 7 Ves 419, 32 ER 169 77
Millichamp v Millichamp (1931) 29 LGR 671, [1931] All ER Rep 477, 95 JP 207, 29
    Cox CC 391, 75 Sol Jo 814, 146 LT 96 .... 216, 384, 402
Milne v Milne (1981) 2 FLR 286, 125 Sol Jo 375, CA 458, 476, 601
Milne v Milne (1865) 34 LJPM & A 143, 4 Sw & Tr 183, 164 ER 1487 776
Milnes v Busk (1794) 2 Ves 488, 30 ER 738 249
Minton v Minton [1979] AC 593, [1979] 1 All ER 79, [1979] 2 WLR 31, 122 Sol Jo
    843, HL 476, 567, 592
Mir v Mir [1992] Fam 79, [1992] 1 All ER 765, [1992] 2 WLR 225, [1992] 1 FLR 624,
    [1992] Fam Law 378, [1992] 4 LS Gaz R 33, 136 Sol Jo LB 10 641
Miss Gray Ltd v Earl of Cathcart (1922) 38 TLR 562 263–266
Mitchell v Mitchell [1984] FLR 387, [1984] Fam Law 176, 127 Sol Jo 858,
    [1984] LS Gaz R 117, CA 600, 612
Mitchell v Mitchell [1984] Fam 1, [1983] 3 All ER 621, [1983] 3 WLR 666, [1984] FLR
    50, [1984] Fam Law 150, 127 Sol Jo 617, [1983] LS Gaz R 2210, CA 815
Mitchell v Torrington Union (1897) 61 JP 598, 76 LT 724, DC 216
Mogridge v Mogridge (1965) 109 Sol Jo 814, CA 341
Mole v Mole [1951] P 21, [1950] 2 All ER 328, 48 LGR 439, 94 Sol Jo 518, 66 (pt 2)
    TLR 129, CA 833
Monro's Settlement, Re, Monro v Hill [1933] Ch 82, [1932] All ER Rep 934, 102 LJ
    Ch 89, 148 LT 279 513
Montague v Benedict (1825) 3 B & C 631, 107 ER 867, sub nom Montague v Espinasse
    1 C & P 502, sub nom Montague v — 3 LJOS 94, sub nom Montague v Baron 5
    Dow & Ry KB 532 .... 264, 273
Moor v Moor. See More v More
Moore, Re, Trafford v Maconochie (1888) 39 Ch D 116, [1886–90] All ER Rep 187, 52
    JP 596, 57 LJ Ch 936, 37 WR 83, 59 LT 681, 4 TLR 591, CA 219, 222
Moore v Moore [2004] EWCA Civ 1243, [2004] 3 FCR 461, [2005] 1 FLR 666,
    [2005] Fam Law 112, [2004] All ER (D) 231 (Oct) 285, 292
Moore v Napier (formerly Moore) [1953] 2 All ER 1401, 118 JP 22 566
Moorish v Moorish [1984] Fam Law 26, CA 609, 621
Moosa v Moosa (1983) 4 FLR 131, 12 Fam Law 181, CA 815
Mordant, Re, Mordant v Halls [1997] 2 FCR 378, [1996] 1 FLR 334, [1996] Fam Law
    211, [1995] BCC 209, [1996] BPIR 302 587
Mordaunt v Moncreiffe (1874) LR 2 Sc & Div 374, [1874–80] All ER Rep 288, 39 JP
    4, 43 LJP & M 49, 23 WR 12, 30 LT 649, HL 346
More v More (1741) 2 Atk 157, 26 ER 499, sub nom Moor v Moor Barn Ch 404 83
Morel Bros & Co Ltd v Earl of Westmoreland [1904] AC 11, [1900–3] All ER Rep 397,
    73 LJKB 93, 52 WR 353, 89 LT 702, 20 TLR 38, HL 256, 259, 266, 270
Morgan v Chetwynd (1865) 4 F & F 451 264–266
Morgan v Hart [1914] 2 KB 183, 83 LJKB 782, 110 LT 611, 30 TLR 286, CA 647
Morgan v Morgan [1949] WN 250, 93 Sol Jo 450, CA 335, 342, 863
Morgan v Morgan (otherwise Ransom) [1959] P 92, [1959] 1 All ER 539,
    [1959] 2 WLR 487, 103 Sol Jo 313 .... 42, 341–342
Morgan v Morgan (1973) 117 Sol Jo 223, Times, 24 February 360, 365
Morgan v Morgan [1977] Fam 122, [1977] 2 All ER 515, [1977] 2 WLR 712, 121 Sol
    Jo 157 931
Morgan v Morgan and Kirby [1923] P 1, 92 LJP 8, 128 LT 252, 39 TLR 47 516
Morgans v Launchbury [1973] AC 127, [1972] 2 All ER 606, [1972] 2 WLR 1217,
    [1972] RTR 406, [1972] 1 Lloyd's Rep 483, 116 Sol Jo 396, HL 204
Morison v Morison (1745) 2 Hag Con 169 at 170 332
Morley v Morley (1972) 117 Sol Jo 69 347
Morris v Howes (1845) 4 Hare 599; on appeal (1846) 16 LJ Ch 121, 10 Jur 955, 8
    LTOS 229 233
Morris v Morris (1977) 7 Fam Law 244, CA 478, 601
Morss v Morss [1972] Fam 264, [1972] 1 All ER 1121, [1972] 2 WLR 908, 116 Sol Jo
    143, CA 227

PARA

Mortgage Corpn v Shaire [2001] Ch 743, [2001] 4 All ER 364, [2001] 3 WLR 639, 80
    P & CR 280, [2000] 2 FCR 222, [2000] 1 FLR 973, [2000] Fam Law 402,
    [2000] 3 EGLR 131, [2000] 11 LS Gaz R 37, [2000] EGCS 35, [2000] BPIR 483,
    [2000] All ER (D) 254 639
Mortimer v Mortimer-Griffin [1986] 2 FLR 315, [1986] Fam Law 305, CA 612
Morton v Fenn (1783) 3 Doug KB 211, 99 ER 618 16
Morton v Morton, Daly and McNaught [1937] P 151, [1937] 2 All ER 470, 106 LJP
    100, 81 Sol Jo 359, 157 LT 46, 53 TLR 659 349
Mosey v Mosey and Barker [1956] P 26, [1955] 2 All ER 391, [1955] 2 WLR 1118, 99
    Sol Jo 371 .... 474–475, 550, 552, 684–685
Moss v Moss [1897] P 263, 66 LJP 154, 45 WR 635, 77 LT 220, 13 TLR 459 ... 42–44, 321, 344
Mossop v Mossop [1989] Fam 77, [1988] 2 All ER 202, [1988] 2 WLR 1255,
    [1988] 2 FLR 173, [1988] Fam Law 334, 132 Sol Jo 1033, [1988] NLJR 86, CA 230, 284
Mouncer v Mouncer [1972] 1 All ER 289, [1972] 1 WLR 321, 116 Sol Jo 78 .... 347, 368, 412
Mountney v Treharne [2002] EWCA Civ 1174, [2003] Ch 135, [2002] 3 WLR 1760,
    [2002] 3 FCR 97, [2002] 2 FLR 930, [2002] Fam Law 809,
    [2002] 39 LS Gaz R 38, [2002] 39 LS Gaz R 38, (2002) Times, 9 September,
    [2002] BPIR 1126, [2002] All ER (D) 35 (Aug) 499, 505
Moynihan v Moynihan (Nos 1 and 2) [1997] 2 FCR 105, [1997] 1 FLR 59,
    [1997] Fam Law 88 .... 852–853, 880
Mubarak v Mubarak. See Murbarak v Murbarak
Mubarak v Mubarak [2004] EWHC 1158 (Fam), [2004] 2 FLR 932, [2005] Fam Law
    355 567
Mubarak v Mubarik [2007] EWHC 220 (Fam), [2007] All ER (D) 28 (Nov) 586–587
Mudge v Mudge and Honeysett (Goodwin cited) [1950] P 173, [1950] 1 All ER 607, 94
    Sol Jo 195, 66 (pt 1) TLR 631 353
Mullard v Mullard (1981) 3 FLR 330, 12 Fam Law 63, 126 Sol Jo 98, CA 476, 601, 612–613
Mummery v Mummery [1942] P 107, [1942] 1 All ER 553, 111 LJP 58, 86 Sol Jo 120,
    166 LT 343, 58 TLR 203 403–404
Munks v Munks [1985] FLR 576, [1985] Fam Law 131, 129 Sol Jo 65, CA ... 459, 468, 481, 502,
                                                                        507, 715
Munro v De Chemant (1815) 4 Camp 215 .... 263, 271
Munt v Munt (1862) 31 LJPM & A 134, 2 Sw & Tr 661, 164 ER 1155, 7 LT 438 650
Murbarak v Murbarak [2001] 1 FCR 193, sub nom Mubarak v Mubarak [2001] 1 FLR
    698, [2001] Fam Law 178, CA 945
Murray v Murray (1961) Times, 22 November 384
Muscato v Muscato (1967) 111 Sol Jo 332 863
Muspratt v Muspratt (1861) 31 LJPM & A 28 761
Mustafa v Mustafa [1975] 3 All ER 355, [1975] 1 WLR 1277, 119 Sol Jo 642 347
Musurus Bey v Gadban [1894] 2 QB 352, [1891–4] All ER Rep 761, 38 63 LJQB 621,
    9 R 519, 42 WR 545, Sol Jo 511, 71 LT 51, 10 TLR 493, CA 742
Myatt v Myatt and Parker [1962] 2 All ER 247, [1962] 1 WLR 570, 106 Sol Jo 246 851
Mycock v Mycock (1870) LR 2 P & D 98, 39 LJP & M 56, 18 WR 1144, 23 LT 238 771

N

N v N (1928) 138 LT 693, [1928] All ER Rep 462, 44 TLR 324, 72 Sol Jo 156 599
N v N [1957] P 385, [1957] 1 All ER 536, [1957] 2 WLR 477, 101 Sol Jo 230 778
N v N (C (by her guardian) intervening) (1963) 107 Sol Jo 1025 349
N v N (consent order: variation) [1994] 2 FCR 275, [1993] 2 FLR 868,
    [1993] Fam Law 676, CA 600
N v N (overseas divorce: financial relief) [1997] 1 FCR 573, [1997] Fam Law 396, sub
    nom (foreign divorce: financial relief) [1997] 1 FLR 900 .... 530, 938
N v N (divorce: ante-nuptial agreement) [1999] 2 FCR 583, [1999] 2 FLR 745,
    [1999] Fam Law 691, [1999] 31 LS Gaz R 39, [1999] NLJR 1074, [1999] All ER
    (D) 732 .... 409, 625, 712, 863
N v N (financial provision: sale of company) [2001] 2 FLR 69 .... 591, 607
N v N and L [1957] P 333, [1957] 1 All ER 914, [1957] 2 WLR 796, 101 Sol Jo 340 785
NA v MA [2006] EWHC 2900 (Fam), [2007] 1 FLR 1760, [2007] Fam Law 295, sub
    nom A v A [2007] All ER (D) 41 (Jan) 591
N-r (falsely called M-e) v M-e (1853) 2 Rob Eccl 625, sub nom A (falsely called B) v B 1
    Ecc & Ad 12, sub nom Anon 17 Jur 628 340–341

PARA

NS v MI [2006] EWHC 1646 (Fam), [2007] 2 FCR 748, [2007] 1 FLR 444,
[2006] Fam Law 839, [2006] All ER (D) 48 (Jul) 43

Nachimson v Nachimson [1930] P 217, [1930] All ER Rep 114, 28 LGR 617, 94 JP
211, 99 LJP 104, 74 Sol Jo 370, 143 LT 254, 46 TLR 444, CA 1

Napier v Napier [1915] P 65, 84 LJP 77, 59 Sol Jo 287, 31 TLR 179; affd [1915] P
184, 84 LJP 177, 59 Sol Jo 560, 113 LT 764, 31 TLR 472, CA 336, 340

Nash (otherwise Lister) v Nash [1940] P 60, [1940] 1 All ER 206, 109 LJP 60, 84 Sol Jo
153, 164 LT 48, 56 TLR 274 321

Nash v Nash [1968] P 597, [1967] 1 All ER 535, [1967] 2 WLR 1009, 110 Sol Jo
869 739

Nast v Nast and Walker [1972] Fam 142, [1972] 1 All ER 1171, [1972] 2 WLR 901,
116 Sol Jo 159, CA 354, 799–800

Nathan v Woolf (1899) 15 TLR 250 .... 115, 117

National Assistance Board v Parkes [1955] 2 QB 506, [1955] 3 All ER 1, [1955] 3 WLR
347, 99 Sol Jo 540, CA 216–217

National Assistance Board v Prisk [1954] 1 All ER 400, [1954] 1 WLR 443, 118 JP 194,
98 Sol Jo 147, DC 217

National Assistance Board v Wilkinson [1952] 2 QB 648, [1952] 2 All ER 255, 40 LGR
454, 116 JP 428, 96 Sol Jo 414, [1952] 2 TLR 11, DC 216–217

National Provincial Bank Ltd v Ainsworth [1965] AC 1175, [1965] 2 All ER 472,
[1965] 3 WLR 1, 109 Sol Jo 415, HL 225

National Westminster Bank Ltd v Stockman [1981] 1 All ER 800, [1981] 1 WLR 67,
124 Sol Jo 810 637

National Westminster Bank plc v Powney [1991] Ch 339, [1990] 2 All ER 416,
[1990] 2 WLR 1084, 60 P & CR 420, 134 Sol Jo 285, CA 678

Naylor v Naylor [1962] P 253, [1961] 2 All ER 129, [1961] 2 WLR 751, 125 JP 358,
105 Sol Jo 235 368

Neal v Neal (1971) 115 Sol Jo 772, DC 897

Nedby v Nedby (1852) 5 De G & Sm 377, 21 LJ Ch 446, 64 ER 1161, 19 LTOS 294 236

Neesom v Clarkson (1845) 4 Hare 97, 9 Jur 822, 67 ER 576 283

Negus v Forster (1882) 30 WR 671, 46 LT 675, CA 436

Neil v Ryan [1999] 1 FCR 241, [1998] 2 FLR 1068, [1998] Fam Law 728, (1998)
Times, 1 September, CA 737

Nelson v Nelson (1964) 108 Sol Jo 381 .... 876–877, 879, 883

Nelson v Nelson and Slinger [1958] 2 All ER 744, [1958] 1 WLR 894, 102 Sol Jo
599, CA 769

Nepean (otherwise Lee Warner) v Nepean [1925] P 97, [1925] All ER Rep 166, 94 LJP
42, 133 LT 287, 41 TLR 366 .... 511, 514

Neuman v Neuman (otherwise Greenberg) (1926) Times, 15 October 44

Nevill v Nevill (1893) 69 LT 463 .... 513, 516

New Monckton Collieries v Keeling [1911] AC 648, [1911–13] All ER Rep Ext 1586,
80 LJKB 1205, 4 BWCC 332, 55 Sol Jo 687, 105 LT 337, 27 TLR 551, HL 216

Newbould v A-G [1931] P 75, [1931] All ER Rep 377, 100 LJP 54, 75 Sol Jo 174, 144
LT 728, 47 TLR 297 34

Newlon Housing Trust v Alsulaimen [1999] 1 AC 313, [1998] 4 All ER 1,
[1998] 3 WLR 451, [1998] 3 FCR 183, [1998] 2 FLR 690, [1998] Fam Law 589,
30 HLR 1132, [1998] NLJR 1303, 142 Sol Jo LB 247, [1998] All ER (D)
383, HL 500, 601

Newman v Newman [1971] P 43, [1970] 3 All ER 529, [1970] 3 WLR 1014, 114 Sol Jo
846 884

Newman v Newman, Queen's Proctor intervening [1984] FLR 835, [1985] Fam Law
52 .... 853, 877

Newmarch v Newmarch [1978] Fam 79, [1978] 1 All ER 1, [1977] 3 WLR 832, 7 Fam
Law 143, 121 Sol Jo 253 216

Newte v Newte and Keen [1933] P 117, 102 LJP 44, 77 Sol Jo 235, 148 LT 572, 49
TLR 314 515

Newton v Newton (1966) 110 Sol Jo 72, CA 879, 883

Newton v Newton [1989] FCR 521, [1990] 1 FLR 33, [1990] Fam Law 25, CA 599

Niboyet v Niboyet (1878) 4 PD 1, [1874–80] All ER Rep Ext 1628, 48 LJP 1, 27 WR
203, 39 LT 486, CA 203

Nicholas v Nicholas [1984] FLR 285, [1984] Fam Law 118, CA 609, 614

PARA

Nicholson, Re, Nicholson v Perks [1974] 2 All ER 386, [1974] 1 WLR 476, 118 Sol Jo
133 283
Nicholson v Squire (1809) 16 Ves 259, 33 ER 983 .... 21, 68
Nicol v Nicol (1886) 31 Ch D 524, [1886–90] All ER Rep 297, 50 JP 468, 55 LJ
Ch 437, 34 WR 283, 54 LT 470, 2 TLR 280, CA 436, 699
Nicolson v Nicolson and Fairley (1892) 1 R 498, 68 LT 28 825
Niedersachen, The. See Ninemia Maritime Corpn v Trave Schiffahrtsgesellschaft mbH
& Co KG, The Niedersachen
Nikitenko v Leboeuf Lambe Greene & Macrae (a firm) (1999) Times, 26 January 659
Ninemia Maritime Corpn v Trave Schiffahrtsgesellschaft mbH & Co KG, The
Niedersachen [1984] 1 All ER 398, [1983] 1 WLR 1412, [1983] 2 Lloyd's Rep
600, [1983] Com LR 234, 127 Sol Jo 824; affd [1984] 1 All ER 398,
[1983] 1 WLR 1412, [1983] 2 Lloyd's Rep 600, [1984] LS Gaz R 198, CA 661
Nixon v Fox (formerly Nixon) [1978] Fam 173, [1978] 3 All ER 995, [1978] 3 WLR
565, 122 Sol Jo 280 452
Noble v Noble and Godman (1869) LR 1 P & D 691, 38 LJP & M 52, 20 LT 1016 ...... 344, 879
Noel v Noel (1885) 10 PD 179, 54 LJP 73, 33 WR 552 513
Norfolk's (Duke) Case (1692) 12 State Tr 927 349
Norman v Mathews (1916) 85 LJKB 857, 114 LT 1043, 32 TLR 303, [1916] WN 78;
affd (1916) 32 TLR 369, [1916–17] All ER Rep 696, CA 96
Norman v Norman [1908] P 6, 77 LJP 8, 98 LT 61, 24 TLR 37 425
Norman v Norman (1939) unreported 374
Norman v Norman [1983] 1 All ER 486, [1983] 1 WLR 295, 4 FLR 446, 13 Fam Law
17, 126 Sol Jo 707, [1983] LS Gaz R 30 .... 476, 499
Norman v Villars (1877) 2 Ex D 359, 42 JP 292, 46 LJQB 579, 25 WR 780, 36 LT
788, CA 879
North v North [2007] EWCA Civ 760, [2007] 2 FCR 601, [2008] 1 FLR 158,
[2008] Fam Law 508, (2007) Times, 17 August, [2007] All ER (D) 386 (Jul) 568
Northover v Northover (1910) 26 TLR 224 790
Northrop v Northrop [1968] P 74, [1967] 2 All ER 961, [1967] 3 WLR 907, 111 Sol Jo
476, CA 216–217
Norton v Fazan (1798) 1 Bos & P 226, 126 ER 873 272
Norton v Norton [1945] P 56, [1945] 2 All ER 122, 114 LJP 54, 89 Sol Jo 487, 173 LT
320, 61 TLR 451 793
Norton v Seton (falsely called Norton) (1819) 3 Phillim 147 341
Notley v Notley (otherwise Roberts) (1960) Times, 4 November 321
Nott v Nott (1866) LR 1 P & D 251, 36 LJP & M 10, 15 LT 299 .... 371, 373
Nottingham Guardians v Tomkinson (1879) 4 CPD 343, 43 JP 735, 48 LJMC 171, 28
WR 151, CPD 358
Nouvion v Freeman (1889) 15 App Cas 1, 59 LJ Ch 337, 38 WR 581, 62 LT 189, HL 677
Nowell v Nowell (1953) Times, 25 February, CA 400
Noyes v Pollock (1886) 32 Ch D 53, 55 LJ Ch 513, 34 WR 383, 54 LT 473, CA 239
Nugent-Head v Jacob (Inspector of Taxes) [1948] AC 321, [1948] 1 All ER 414, 30 TC
83, [1948] TR 23, [1948] LJR 759, 92 Sol Jo 193, 64 TLR 127, L(TC) 444, HL 412
Nunneley v Nunneley and Marrian (1890) 15 PD 186, 39 WR 190, 63 LT 113 500
Nurcombe v Nurcombe [1985] 1 All ER 65, [1985] 1 WLR 370, [1984] BCLC 557, 128
Sol Jo 766, CA 476
Nutley v Nutley [1970] 1 All ER 410, [1970] 1 WLR 217, 114 Sol Jo 72, CA 362, 368
Nuttall v Nuttall (1862) 31 LJPM & A 164 777
Nuttall v Nuttall and Twyman (1964) 108 Sol Jo 605 833
Nwogbe v Nwogbe [2000] 3 FCR 345, [2000] 2 FLR 744, CA 294, 299, 303

O

O v O (jurisdiction: jewish divorce) [2000] 2 FLR 147, [2000] Fam Law 532 865
O'Brien v O'Brien (1959) Times, 16 July 371
O'D v O'D [1976] Fam 83, [1975] 3 WLR 308, 119 Sol Jo 560, sub nom O'Donnell v
O'Donnell [1975] 2 All ER 993, CA 499, 601, 603, 609
Offord v Offord (1981) 3 FLR 309, 11 Fam Law 208 456
Ogden v Ogden [1969] 3 All ER 1055, [1969] 1 WLR 1425, 113 Sol Jo 585, CA 397
Ohochuku v Ohochuku [1960] 1 All ER 253, [1960] 1 WLR 183, 104 Sol Jo 190 879
Oldroyd v Oldroyd [1896] P 175, [1895–9] All ER Rep 372, 65 LJP 113, 75 LT 281, 12
TLR 442 369

PARA

Oleszko (formerly Pietrucha) v Pietrucha (1963) Times 22 March 6
Oliver v Lowther (1880) 28 WR 381, 42 LT 47 648
O'Mahoney v O'Mahoney [1959] P 1, [1959] 1 All ER 163, [1959] 2 WLR 22, 103 Sol
    Jo 35 643
O'Malley v Blease (1869) 17 WR 952, 20 LT 899 .... 436, 447
Omielan v Omielan [1996] 3 FCR 329, [1996] 2 FLR 306, [1996] Fam Law 608, CA 316
O'Neill v O'Neill [1975] 3 All ER 289, [1975] 1 WLR 1118, 5 Fam Law 159, 119 Sol
    Jo 405, CA 346, 360, 553
O'Neill v O'Neill [1993] 2 FCR 297, CA 606
Onobrauche v Onobrauche (1978) 8 Fam Law 107, 122 Sol Jo 210 349
Onslow, Re, Plowden v Gayford (1888) 39 Ch D 622, 57 LJ Ch 940, 36 WR 883, 59
    LT 308 237
Onslow v Onslow, Jones and Campbell (1889) 60 LT 680 .... 755, 845
Oppenheim v Oppenheim and Ricotti (1884) 9 PD 60, 53 LJP 48, 32 WR 723 513
Orchard v Coulsting. See Archard v Coulsting
Orme v Holloway (falsely calling herself Orme) (1847) 5 Notes of Cases 267 69
Orme v Orme (1824) 2 Add 382 379
O'Rourke v Darbishire [1920] AC 581, [1920] All ER Rep 1, 89 LJ Ch 162, 64 Sol Jo
    322, 123 LT 68, 36 TLR 350, HL 799
Orton v Orton (1958) unreported, noted at (1959) 109 L Jo 50 705
Osborn v Osborn (otherwise Ivil) (1926) 70 Sol Jo 388 863
Osborne v Osborne (1961) 105 Sol Jo 650 389
Ostick v Ostick [1917] P 20, 86 LJP 6, 61 Sol Jo 100, 115 LT 789, 33 TLR 28 849
Otobo v Otobo [2002] EWCA Civ 949, [2002] 3 FCR 123, [2003] 1 FLR 192,
    [2003] Fam Law 12, [2002] All ER (D) 27 (Jul) 842
Ousey v Ousey and Atkinson (1874) LR 3 P & D 223, [1874–80] All ER Rep 635, 43
    LJP & M 35, 22 WR 556, 30 LT 911 349
Ousey v Ousey and Atkinson (1875) 1 PD 56, 4[1874–80] All ER Rep 637, 5 LJP 33,
    24 WR 436, 33 LT 789 876
Outram v Hyde (1875) 24 WR 268 252
Owen v Owen (1831) 4 Hag Ecc 261 352
Oxley v Hiscock [2004] EWCA Civ 546, [2005] Fam 211, [2004] 3 All ER 703,
    [2004] 3 WLR 715, [2004] 2 P & CR D35, [2004] 2 FCR 295, [2004] 2 FLR 295,
    [2004] Fam Law 569, [2004] 21 LS Gaz R 35, [2004] 20 EG 166 (CS), (2004)
    Times, 14 July, 148 Sol Jo LB 571, [2004] All ER (D) 48 (May) 279, 284

P

P (a minor), Re [1994] Fam Law 131, Cty Ct 717
P v L (falsely called P) (1873) 3 PD 73n 340
P v P (otherwise G) (1909) 25 TLR 638 340
P (LE) v P (JM) [1971] P 318, [1971] 3 WLR 57, 115 Sol Jo 405, sub nom P (JM) v P
    (LE) [1971] 2 All ER 728 492
P v P [1978] 3 All ER 70, [1978] 1 WLR 483, 122 Sol Jo 230, CA 450, 498, 591, 609, 618
P v P [1989]. See Priestley v Priestley
P v P [1994] 1 FCR 293, [1994] 2 FLR 381, [1994] Fam Law 498 599
P v P [1995] 1 FCR 47, [1994] 2 FLR 400, [1994] Fam Law 565, CA 320
P v P (inherited property) [2004] EWHC 1364 (Fam), [2006] 2 FCR 579, [2005] 1 FLR
    576, sub nom V, Re (financial relief: family farm) [2005] Fam Law 101 591
P v P (financial relief: illiquid assets) [2004] EWHC 2277 (Fam), [2005] 1 FLR 548,
    [2005] Fam Law 207 591
P v P and T (1910) 54 Sol Jo 683, 26 TLR 607 .... 845, 856
P v S (1868) 37 LJP & M 80, sub nom A v B LR 1 P & D 559, 17 WR 14, sub nom
    Anon 32 JP 743 42
P v S: C-13/94 [1996] ECR I-2143, [1996] All ER (EC) 397, [1996] 2 CMLR 247,
    [1996] ICR 795, [1996] IRLR 347, sub nom P v S (sex discrimination): C-13/94
    [1997] 2 FCR 180, [1996] 2 FLR 347, [1996] Fam Law 609, ECJ 1
P and G (transsexuals), Re. See R v Registrar General, ex p P and G
Pace (formerly Doe) v Doe [1977] Fam 18, [1977] 1 All ER 176, [1976] 3 WLR 865,
    120 Sol Jo 818 703
Page v Page (1981) 2 FLR 198, CA 591, 603, 605, 618–619
Paget v Paget [1898] 1 Ch 470, [1895–9] All ER Rep 1150, 67 LJ Ch 266, 46 WR 472,
    42 Sol Jo 378, 78 LT 306, 14 TLR 315, CA 239

PARA

Pais v Pais [1971] P 119, [1970] 3 All ER 491, [1970] 3 WLR 830, 114 Sol Jo 720 833
Pakenham v Pakenham [1937] 3 All ER 549, 81 Sol Jo 652 852
Palethorp v Furnish (1783) 2 Esp 511n 261
Palmer v Maclear and M'Grath (1858) 1 Sw & Tr 149 802
Palmer v Palmer (1859) 23 JP 535, 29 LJP & M 26, 1 Sw & Tr 551, 164 ER 855, 2 LT
　　88 357–358
Palmer v Palmer [1923] P 180, [1923] All ER Rep 604, 92 LJP 129, 67 Sol Jo 748, 129
　　LT 665, 39 TLR 609, CA 699
Palmer v Palmer, Re Thomasson's Petition [1921] P 378, 90 LJP 361, 65 Sol Jo 736, 125
　　LT 864, 37 TLR 867 1022
Pandiani v Pandiani (1963) 107 Sol Jo 832 366
Pannell, Re, ex p Bates (1879) 11 Ch D 914, 48 LJ Bcy 113, 27 WR 927, 41 LT
　　263, CA 446
Paolantonio v Paolantonio [1950] 2 All ER 404, 94 Sol Jo 519, 66 (pt 2) TLR
　　235, CA 778
Papadopoulos v Papadopoulos [1930] P 55, [1929] All ER Rep 310, 28 LGR 73, 94 JP
　　39, 99 LJP 1, 142 LT 237 33
Papadopoulos v Papadopoulos [1936] P 108, [1935] All ER Rep 311, 105 LJP 21, 80
　　Sol Jo 56, 154 LT 242, 52 TLR 190 375–376
Paquin Ltd v Beauclerk [1906] AC 148, [1904–7] All ER Rep 729, 75 LJKB 395, 54
　　WR 521, 50 Sol Jo 358, 94 LT 350, 22 TLR 395, HL 205, 258, 263
Paquine v Snary [1909] 1 KB 688, 78 LJKB 361, 100 LT 220, 25 TLR 212, CA 456
Pardy v Pardy [1939] P 288, [1939] 3 All ER 779, 108 LJP 145, 83 Sol Jo 714, 161 LT
　　210, 55 TLR 1037, CA 362, 368, 371–372, 374, 699
Parghi v Parghi (1973) 4 Fam Law 82, 117 Sol Jo 582 411
Park, Re, ex p Koster (1885) 14 QBD 597, 54 LJQB 389, 2 Morr 35, 33 WR 606, 52
　　LT 946, CA 643
Park's Estate, Re, Park v Park [1954] P 89, [1953] 2 All ER 408, [1953] 3 WLR 307, 97
　　Sol Jo 491; affd [1954] P 112, [1953] 2 All ER 1411, [1953] 3 WLR 1012, 97 Sol
　　Jo 830, CA 42
Parker v Brooke (1804) 9 Ves 583, 32 ER 729 251
Parker v Carter (1845) 4 Hare 400 711
Parker v Harvey (1726) 4 Bro Parl Cas 604 246
Parker v Parker (1757) 2 Lee 382 45
Parker v Parker [1972] Fam 116, [1972] 1 All ER 410, [1972] 2 WLR 21, 115 Sol Jo
　　949 411
Parker's Policies, Re [1906] 1 Ch 526, 75 LJ Ch 297, 54 WR 329, 50 Sol Jo 272, 94 LT
　　477, 22 TLR 259 275
Parkes v Parkes [1971] 3 All ER 870, [1971] 1 WLR 1481, 115 Sol Jo 507, CA 411
Parkin, Re, Hill v Schwarz [1892] 3 Ch 510, 62 LJ Ch 55, 3 R 9, 41 WR 120, 36 Sol Jo
　　647, 67 LT 77 237
Parkinson v Parkinson (1869) LR 2 P & D 27, 39 LJP & M 21, 21 LT 597 771
Parkinson v Parkinson [1939] P 346, [1939] 3 All ER 108, 83 Sol Jo 642, 161 LT 251,
　　55 TLR 860 .... 344, 416
Parkinson v Parkinson (1959) Times, 14 April 362, 397, 436
Parnell v Parnell (1814) 2 Hag Con 169, 2 Phillim 158, 161 ER 704 332
Parojcic (otherwise Ivetic) v Parojcic [1959] 1 All ER 1, [1958] 1 WLR 1280, 102 Sol Jo
　　938 .... 43, 345
Parra v Parra [2002] EWHC 877 (Fam), [2002] 3 FCR 513, [2002] All ER (D) 394
　　(May); revsd [2002] EWCA Civ 1886, [2003] 1 FCR 97, [2003] 1 FLR 942,
　　[2003] Fam Law 314, [2002] All ER (D) 362 (Dec) 600
Parrington v Parrington [1951] 2 All ER 916, [1951] 2 TLR 918 .... 510–511, 517
Parry v Aluminium Corpn Ltd [1940] WN 44, 84 Sol Jo 252, 162 LT 236, 56 TLR
　　318, CA 851
Parsons v Parsons [1907] P 331, 76 LJP 159, 23 TLR 749 771
Parsons v Parsons [1975] 3 All ER 344, [1975] 1 WLR 1272, 5 Fam Law 187, 119 Sol
　　Jo 590 410
Parteriche v Powlet (1742) 2 Atk 383, 26 ER 632 239
Partington v Partington and Atkinson [1925] P 34, 94 LJP 49, 69 Sol Jo 294, 132 LT
　　495, 41 TLR 174 358
Partridge v Partridge (1957) Times, 13 December 393
Paspati v Paspati [1914] P 110, 83 LJP 56, 58 Sol Jo 400, 110 LT 751, 30 TLR 390 ...... 332, 801

PARA

Passee v Passee [1988] 1 FLR 263, [1988] Fam Law 132, CA 282

Patching v Patching [1958] CLY 990, (1958) Times, 25 April 393

Patel v Patel (1977) 8 Fam Law 215, 121 Sol Jo 408 411

Paton v British Pregnancy Advisory Service Trustees [1979] QB 276, [1978] 2 All ER
    987, [1978] 3 WLR 687, 142 JP 497, 122 Sol Jo 744 .... 211, 219

Patrick v Patrick (1810) 3 Phillim 496 349

Patrickson v Patrickson (1865) LR 1 P & D 86, 35 LJP & M 48, 12 Jur NS 30, 14 WR
    212, 13 LT 567 6

Paul v Paul and Farquhar (1870) LR 2 P & D 93, sub nom St Paul v St Paul and
    Farquhar 39 LJP & M 50, 18 WR 1007, 23 LT 196 .... 511, 516

Pavlou (a bankrupt), Re [1993] 3 All ER 955, [1993] 1 WLR 1046, [1993] 2 FLR 751,
    [1993] Fam Law 629, [1993] 11 LS Gaz R 43 282

Payne v Harrison [1961] 2 QB 403, [1961] 2 All ER 873, [1961] 3 WLR 309, 105 Sol
    Jo 528, CA 851

Payne v Payne, Rodway and Eddels (1888) 60 LT 238 760

Pazpena de Vire v Pazpena de Vire [2000] 1 FLR 460, [2001] Fam Law 95, [2000] All
    ER (D) 2101 6

Peabody Donation Fund Governors v Hay (1986) 19 HLR 145, CA 654

Peacock v Monk (1751) 2 Ves Sen 190, 28 ER 123 232

Peacock v Peacock [1984] 1 All ER 1069, [1984] 1 WLR 532, [1984] FLR 263,
    [1984] Fam Law 112, 148 JP 444, 128 Sol Jo 116, 134 NLJ 126 .... 450, 456

Pearce v Johns (1897) 41 Sol Jo 661, CA 648

Pearce v Pearce [1960] 3 All ER 21, [1960] 1 WLR 855, 104 Sol Jo 624, CA 371

Pearce v Pearce (1979) 1 FLR 261, 10 Fam Law 209, CA 595

Pearce v Pearce [2003] EWCA Civ 1054, [2004] 1 WLR 68, [2003] 3 FCR 178,
    [2003] 2 FLR 1144, [2003] Fam Law 723, [2003] 36 LS Gaz R 39, (2003) Times,
    1 September, [2003] All ER (D) 467 (Jul) 569

Pearce v Pearce and French (1861) 30 LJPM & A 182 513

Pearson v Pearson [1948] WN 225, [1948] LJR 1435, 92 Sol Jo 336, 64 TLR
    445, CA 362

Pearson v Pearson (1955) Times, 13 July, CA 738, 851, 862

Peckover v Peckover and Jolly (1858) 1 Sw & Tr 219, 164 ER 700, 31 LTOS 269 777

Peek v Peek [1948] P 46, [1947] 2 All ER 578, [1948] LJR 833, 64 TLR 56; affd [1948]
    P 46, [1948] 2 All ER 297, 92 Sol Jo 454, 64 TLR 429, 66 (pt 2) TLR 503, CA 739

Peel v Drummond (1932) Times, 9, 10 December; on appeal (1933) Times,
    8 March, CA 860

Peete, Re, Peete v Crompton [1952] 2 All ER 599, [1952] WN 406, 96 Sol Jo 561,
    [1952] 2 TLR 383 .... 7, 42, 344

Pelling v Bruce-Williams [2004] EWCA Civ 845, [2004] Fam 155, [2004] 3 All ER 875,
    [2004] 3 WLR 1178, [2004] 3 FCR 108, [2004] 2 FLR 823, [2004] Fam Law 784,
    [2004] All ER (D) 15 (Jul) 1013

Penn v Dunn [1970] 2 QB 686, [1970] 2 All ER 858, [1970] 3 WLR 321, 21 P & CR
    898, 114 Sol Jo 532, 215 Estates Gazette 578, CA 285

Penrose v Penrose [1994] 2 FCR 1167, [1994] 2 FLR 621, [1994] Fam Law 618, CA 567

Pepper v Pepper [1960] 1 All ER 529, [1960] 1 WLR 131, 124 JP 184, 104 Sol Jo
    190 .... 630, 632

Perks v Perks [1946] P 1, [1945] 2 All ER 580, 110 JP 94, 115 LJP 7, 89 Sol Jo 577,
    173 LT 349, 62 TLR 26, CA 565

Perrin v Perrin (1822) 1 Add 1 349

Perry v Perry [1952] P 203, [1952] 1 All ER 1076, 116 JP 258, 96 Sol Jo 358, [1952] 1
    TLR 1633, CA 362, 364, 368–369, 378–379, 397–398, 403–405

Perry v Perry [1963] 3 All ER 766, [1964] 1 WLR 91, 107 Sol Jo 739 .... 369, 385, 389–390

Perryman v Dinham (1641) 1 Rep Ch 152 649

Peters v Peters and Willett (1861) 3 Sw & Tr 264 760

Peters' Executors v IRC [1941] 2 All ER 620, 24 TC 45, CA 373, 427

Pettit v Pettit [1963] P 177, [1962] 3 All ER 37, [1962] 3 WLR 919, 106 Sol Jo
    507, CA 341

Pettitt v Pettitt [1970] AC 777, [1969] 2 All ER 385, [1969] 2 WLR 966, 20 P & CR
    991, 113 Sol Jo 344, 211 Estates Gazette 829, HL ... 206, 224–225, 229, 278, 280, 282–283

Petty v Anderson (1825) 3 Bing 170, 2 C & P 38, 3 LJOS 223, 10 Moore CP 577, 130
    ER 479 270

PARA

Petty v Petty [1943] P 101, [1943] 2 All ER 511, 112 LJP 97, 87 Sol Jo 283, 169 LT
224, 59 TLR 385 739
Pew v Pew (1851) unreported 393
Phair v Phair (1963) 107 Sol Jo 554, CA 371
Pheasant v Pheasant [1972] Fam 202, [1972] 1 All ER 587, [1972] 2 WLR 353, 116 Sol
Jo 120 .... 347, 350, 360
Philipps v Philipps (1878) 4 QBD 127, [1874–80] All ER Rep Ext 1684, 48 LJQB 135,
27 WR 436, 39 LT 556, CA 787, 877
Philipson v Philipson (1933) 148 LT 455, 49 TLR 235 .... 473, 548
Phillips, Re, Re Howard, Charter v Ferguson [1919] 1 Ch 128, 88 LJ Ch 27, 63 Sol Jo
116, 120 LT 213, 35 TLR 98 35
Phillips v Pearce [1996] 2 FCR 237, [1996] 2 FLR 230, [1996] Fam Law 603 492
Phillips v Phillips [1917] P 90, 86 LJP 57, 61 Sol Jo 370, 116 LT 544, 33 TLR 226 699
Phillipson v Hayter (1870) LR 6 CP 38, 40 LJCP 14, 19 WR 130, 23 LT 556 264
Pickett v Pickett (otherwise Moss) [1951] P 267, [1951] 1 All ER 614, 95 Sol Jo 270,
[1951] 1 TLR 585 .... 764, 795, 849
Pierce v Pierce (1892) 66 LT 861 875
Piers v Piers (1849) 2 HL Cas 331, [1843–60] All ER Rep 159, 13 Jur 569, 9 ER 1118,
13 LTOS 41, HL 6–7, 76, 83
Piglowska v Piglowski [1999] 3 All ER 632, [1999] 1 WLR 1360, [1999] 2 FCR 481,
[1999] 2 FLR 763, [1999] Fam Law 617, HL 610, 737
Pike v Cave (1893) 62 LJ Ch 937, 68 LT 650 210
Pike v Pike [1954] P 81n, [1953] 1 All ER 232, [1953] 3 WLR 634n, CA 391–393
Pilcher v Pilcher [1955] P 318, [1955] 2 All ER 644, [1955] 3 WLR 231, 119 JP 458, 99
Sol Jo 473 .... 566, 1022
Pilcher v Pilcher (No 2) [1956] 1 All ER 463, [1956] 1 WLR 298, 120 JP 127, 100 Sol
Jo 227, DC 679
Piller (Anton) KG v Manufacturing Processes Ltd [1976] Ch 55, [1976] 1 All ER 779,
[1976] 2 WLR 162, [1976] FSR 129, [1976] RPC 719, 120 Sol Jo 63, CA 662
Pinede's Settlement, Re (1879) 12 Ch D 667, [1874–80] All ER Rep Ext 1530, 48 LJ
Ch 741, 28 WR 178, 41 LT 579 235
Pink v Lawrence (1977) 36 P & CR 98, CA 278–279
Pinnick v Pinnick [1957] 1 All ER 873, [1957] 1 WLR 644, 121 JP 256, 101 Sol Jo
375 362
Pinochet Ugarte, Re. See R v Bow Street Metropolitan Stipendiary Magistrate,
ex p Pinochet Ugarte
Piper v Piper [1902] P 198, [1900–3] All ER Rep Ext 1226, 71 LJP 100, 87 LT 150 ...... 372, 699
Piper v Piper (1978) 8 Fam Law 243, CA 658
Pitt v Pitt (1823) Turn & R 180, 37 ER 1065 .... 242, 252
Pittortou (a bankrupt), Re, ex p Trustee of the Property of the Bankrupt v Bankrupt
[1985] 1 All ER 285, [1985] 1 WLR 58, 129 Sol Jo 47, [1985] LS Gaz R 680 .... 239, 244
Pizey v Pizey and Stephenson [1961] P 101, [1961] 2 All ER 658, [1961] 3 WLR 183,
105 Sol Jo 491, CA 368, 371, 393, 396, 404
Pizzala v Pizzala (1896) 68 LJP 91n, 12 TLR 451 393–394
Platt v Platt (1976) 6 Fam Law 107, 120 Sol Jo 199, CA 689
Plumer v Plumer and Bygrave (1859) Sea & Sm 147, 29 LJPM & A 63, 4 Sw & Tr 257,
164 ER 1514 773
Plummer v Plummer [1917] P 163, [1916–17] All ER Rep 591, 86 LJP 145, 61 Sol Jo
558, 117 LT 321, 33 TLR 417, CA 89
Pocock v Lee (1707) 2 Vern 604, 23 ER 995 239
Polhill v Walter (1832) 3 B & Ad 114, [1824–34] All ER Rep 161, 1 LJKB 92, 110 ER
43 257
Pollack v Pollack, Deane and M'Namara (1863) 34 LJPM & A 49 875
Pollard, Re, ex p Pollard [1903] 2 KB 41, 72 LJKB 509, 10 Mans 152, 51 WR 483, 47
Sol Jo 492, 88 LT 652, CA 649
Pollard (falsely called Wybourn) v Wybourn (1828) 1 Hag Ecc 725 340
Pollard v Pollard and Hemming (1864) 3 Sw & Tr 613, 164 ER 1413, 11 LT 749 802
Polly Peck International plc v Nadir (No 2) [1992] 4 All ER 769, [1992] 2 Lloyd's Rep
238, [1992] NLJR 671, CA 661
Ponsonby v Ponsonby (1884) 9 PD 58; affd (1881) 9 PD 122, [1881–5] All ER Rep
1118, 53 LJP 112, 32 WR 746, 51 LT 174, CA 511, 513
Pool v Pool [1951] P 470, [1951] 2 All ER 563, 95 Sol Jo 480, [1951] 2 TLR 662 833

PARA

Poole's Settlements' Trusts, Re, Poole v Poole [1959] 2 All ER 340, [1959] 1 WLR 651,
  103 Sol Jo 432 513
Poon v Poon [1994] 2 FCR 777, [1994] 2 FLR 857 609
Pope, Re, ex p Dicksee [1908] 2 KB 169, 77 LJKB 767, 15 Mans 201, 52 Sol Jo 458, 98
  LT 775, 24 TLR 556, CA 431
Porter v Porter [1969] 3 All ER 640, [1969] 1 WLR 1155, 113 Sol Jo 163, CA 922
Porter v Porter [1971] P 282, [1971] 2 All ER 1037, [1971] 3 WLR 73, 115 Sol Jo
  485 922
Portsmouth (Countess) v Earl of Portsmouth (1828) 1 Hag Ecc 355, [1824–34] All ER
  Rep 673, 162 ER 611 45
Potter v Potter (1975) 5 Fam Law 161, CA 342
Potter v Potter [1982] 3 All ER 321, [1982] 1 WLR 1255, 4 FLR 331, 12 Fam Law
  208, 126 Sol Jo 480, CA 591, 609
Potts v Potts and Bateman (1862) 32 LJPM & A 32, 11 WR 192 855
Pouget v Tomkins (1812) 2 Hag Con 142 68–69
Pounds v Pounds [1994] 4 All ER 777, [1994] 1 WLR 1535, [1994] 2 FCR 1055,
  [1994] 1 FLR 775, [1994] Fam Law 436, [1994] NLJR 459, CA 459, 468, 481, 502, 507,
                                                                              596, 715
Powell v Powell [1922] P 278, [1922] All ER Rep 235, 92 LJP 6, 128 LT 26, 38 TLR
  844 368
Powell v Powell (1957) Times, 22 February, CA 382–383
Powell's Trusts, Re (1869) 39 LJ Ch 188, 18 WR 228 235
Pownall v Anderson (1856) 2 Jur NS 857, 4 WR 407 711
Powys v Powys [1971] P 340, [1971] 3 All ER 116, [1971] 3 WLR 154, 115 Sol Jo
  347 .... 480, 569
Prager v Prager and Goodison (1913) 108 LT 734, 29 TLR 556 24
Pratt v Inman (1889) 43 Ch D 175, [1886–90] All ER Rep 1030, 59 LJ Ch 274, 38 WR
  200, 61 LT 760, 6 TLR 91 649
Pratt v Pratt (1927) 28 Cox CC 413, [1927] All ER Rep 234, , 96 LJP 12371 Sol Jo
  433, 137 LT 491, 43 TLR 523, [1927] WN 140 736
Pratt v Pratt [1939] AC 417, [1939] 3 All ER 437, 108 LJP 97, 83 Sol Jo 730, 161 LT
  49, 55 TLR 910, HL 368–369, 396, 400–401
Pratt v Pratt [1962] 106 Sol Jo 876, CA 391, 393
Pratt v Pratt [1966] 3 All ER 272, [1966] 1 WLR 1568, 110 Sol Jo 686, DC 739
Prescott (formerly Fellowes) v Fellowes [1958] P 260, [1958] 1 All ER 824,
  [1958] 2 WLR 679, 102 Sol Jo 271, CA; revsd [1958] P 260, [1958] 3 All ER 55,
  [1958] 3 WLR 288, 102 Sol Jo 581, CA 510–511
Prescott v Prescott [1906] 1 IR 155 275
Prest v Prest [1950] P 63, [1949] 2 All ER 790, 48 LGR 307, 114 JP 1, 65 TLR 729 566
Preston (otherwise Putynski) v Preston (otherwise Putynska) (otherwise Basinska) [1963]
  P 141, [1962] 3 All ER 1057, [1962] 3 WLR 1401, 106 Sol Jo 882; affd [1963] P
  411, [1963] 2 All ER 405, [1963] 2 WLR 1435, 107 Sol Jo 491, CA 6
Preston v Preston [1982] Fam 17, [1982] 1 All ER 41, [1981] 3 WLR 619, 2 FLR 331,
  12 Fam Law 57, 125 Sol Jo 496, CA 483, 591, 603, 605, 608, 614, 619, 680
Preston v Preston and Alcock (No 2) (1963) 107 Sol Jo 157 851
Preston-Jones v Preston-Jones [1951] AC 391, [1951] 1 All ER 124, 49 LGR 417, 95 Sol
  Jo 13, [1951] 1 TLR 8, HL 346, 352, 355
Pretty v Pretty [1911] P 83, [1908–10] All ER Rep Ext 985, 80 LJP 19, 104 LT 79, 27
  TLR 169 877
Price v Price [1951] 1 All ER 877, 115 JP 273,; on appeal [1951] P 413,
  [1951] 2 All ER 580n, 115 JP 468n, 95 Sol Jo 560, CA 393, 397, 400–401
Price v Price [1968] 3 All ER 543, [1968] 1 WLR 1735, 112 Sol Jo 881; revsd
  [1970] 2 All ER 497, [1970] 1 WLR 993, 114 Sol Jo 454, CA 367–368
Pride v Bubb (1871) 7 Ch App 64, 41 LJ Ch 105, 20 WR 220, 25 LT 890 232
Priest v Priest (1978) 1 FLR 189, 9 Fam Law 252, CA 601, 933
Priestley v Lamb (1801) 6 Ves 421, 31 ER 1124 .... 65, 68
Priestley v Priestley [1989] FCR 657, sub nom P v P [1989] 2 FLR 241,
  [1989] Fam Law 313 .... 609, 614
Primavera v Primavera [1992] 1 FCR 78, [1992] 1 FLR 16, [1991] Fam Law 471, CA 590
Prince v Prince [1951] P 71, [1950] 2 All ER 375, 94 Sol Jo 533, 66 (pt 2) TLR
  493, CA 739

PARA

Prinsep v Prinsep [1929] P 225, 98 LJP 105, 73 Sol Jo 429, 141 LT 220, 45 TLR 376;
varied [1930] P 35, [1929] All ER Rep 436, 99 LJP 35, 142 LT 172, 46 TLR
29, CA 511
Prior v Prior and Strong (1929) 73 Sol Jo 441 349
Prole v Soady (1868) 3 Ch App 220, 32 JP 279, 37 LJ Ch 246, 16 WR 445 879
Prowse v Spurway and Bowley (1877) 46 LJP 49, 26 WR 116 89
Prynne, Re (1885) 53 LT 465 210
Pryor v Pryor and Shelford (1887) 12 PD 165, 56 LJP 77, 35 WR 349, 57 LT 533 512–513
Pugh v Pugh (1920) 37 TLR 105 699
Pugh v Pugh [1951] P 482, [1951] 2 All ER 680, 95 Sol Jo 468, [1951] 2 TLR 806 41
Pulford v Pulford [1923] P 18, [1922] All ER Rep 121, 92 LJP 14, 67 Sol Jo 170, 128
LT 256, 39 TLR 35 .... 362, 372, 385, 390–391
Purba v Purba [2000] 1 FCR 652, [2000] 1 FLR 444, [2000] Fam Law 86, CA 679
Purse v Purse [1981] Fam 143, [1981] 2 All ER 465, [1981] 2 WLR 759, 11 Fam Law
144, 125 Sol Jo 115, CA 454, 778, 861, 881
Pursey v Pursey [1959] CLY 1027, (1959) Times, 9 April 368, 396

Q

Q v Q (ancillary relief: periodical payments) [2005] EWHC 402 (Fam), [2005] 2 FLR
640, [2005] Fam Law 539, [2005] All ER (D) 335 (Apr) 590, 592, 597
Q v V (1960) Times, 12 May 321
Quartermaine v Quartermaine and Glenister [1911] P 180, 80 LJP 89, 55 Sol Jo 522,
105 LT 80, 27 TLR 458 876
Quicke v Quicke (1861) 31 LJPM & A 28, 2 Sw & Tr 419, 10 WR 448, 5 LT 690 760
Quoraishi v Quoraishi [1985] FLR 780, [1985] Fam Law 308, CA 380
Qureshi v Qureshi [1972] Fam 173, [1971] 1 All ER 325, [1971] 2 WLR 518, 114 Sol
Jo 908 .... 33, 852

R

R v Algar [1954] 1 QB 279, [1953] 2 All ER 1381, [1953] 3 WLR 1007, 37 Cr App
Rep 200, 118 JP 56, 97 Sol Jo 833, CCA 320
R v Althausen (1893) 17 Cox CC 630 .... 24, 118
R v Bham [1966] 1 QB 159, [1965] 3 All ER 124, [1965] 3 WLR 696, 49 Cr App Rep
355, 109 Sol Jo 573, CCA 53
R v Billingshurst Inhabitants (1814) 3 M & S 250, 105 ER 603 69
R v Birmingham County Court Judge [1902] 2 KB 283, [1900–3] All ER Rep 685, 71
LJKB 881, 51 WR 75, 87 LT 296, 18 TLR 698, DC 643
R v Birmingham Inhabitants (1828) 8 B & C 29, 6 LJOSMC 67, 2 Man & Ry KB 230,
108 ER 954 .... 46, 51, 328
R v Birmingham Justices, ex p Bennett [1983] 1 WLR 114, 147 JP 279, 127 Sol Jo 35 656
R v Bow County Court, ex p Pelling [1999] 4 All ER 751, [1999] 1 WLR 1807,
[1999] 3 FCR 97, [1999] 2 FLR 1126, [1999] Fam Law 698,
[1999] 32 LS Gaz R 33, [1999] NLJR 1369, CA 850
R v Bow Street Metropolitan Stipendiary Magistrate, ex p Pinochet Ugarte (No 2)
[2000] 1 AC 119, [1999] 1 All ER 577, [1999] 2 WLR 272, 6 BHRC 1,
[1999] 1 LRC 1, sub nom Pinochet Ugarte, Re [1999] NLJR 88, [1999] All ER (D)
18, HL 737
R v Brentwood Superintendent Registrar of Marriages, ex p Arias [1968] 2 QB 956,
[1968] 3 All ER 279, [1968] 3 WLR 531, 112 Sol Jo 672 96
R v Brighton Inhabitants (1861) 1 B & S 447, [1861–73] All ER Rep 471, 30 LJMC
197, 25 JP 630, 9 WR 831, 5 LT 56, 121 ER 782 35
R v Brighton Magistrates' Court, ex p Budd [1986] 1 FLR 426, [1986] Fam Law 134 .... 554, 736
R v Bristol Justices, ex p Hodge [1997] QB 974, [1996] 4 All ER 924, [1997] 2 WLR
756, [1997] 1 FCR 412, [1997] Fam Law 89, sub nom R v Bristol Magistrates'
Court, ex p Hodge [1997] 1 FLR 88 741
R v Burton-upon-Trent Inhabitants (1815) 3 M & S 537, 105 ER 712 .... 69, 76
R v Camberwell Green Justices. See Dickens v Pattison
R v Cambridge County Court, ex p Ireland [1985] FLR 102, [1985] Fam Law 23 .... 458, 467
R v Cardiff Magistrates, ex p Czech [1999] 1 FCR 721, [1999] 1 FLR 95,
[1998] Fam Law 658 .... 655–656, 679
R v Chadwick (1847) 11 QB 173, 11 JP 839, 17 LJMC 33, 2 Cox CC 381, Cripps'
Church Cas 32, 12 Jur 174, 116 ER 441, 10 LTOS 155 35

PARA

R v Chester Justices, ex p Holland [1984] FLR 725, [1984] Fam Law 184, 148 JP 257,
128 Sol Jo 245 .... 554, 736
R v Clarke [1949] 2 All ER 448, 33 Cr App Rep 216 219
R v Creamer [1919] 1 KB 564, [1918–19] All ER Rep 222, 14 Cr App Rep 19, 83 JP
120, 88 LJKB 594, 26 Cox CC 393, 120 LT 575, 35 TLR 281, CCA 267, 412
R v Cresswell (1876) 1 QBD 446, 40 JP 536, 45 LJMC 77, 13 Cox CC 126, 24 WR
281, 33 LT 760, CCR 61
R v Davidson etc, Durham Justices (1889) 5 TLR 199 .... 368, 397, 400
R v Dibdin, ex p Thompson. See Banister and Wife v Thompson
R v Ellis (1888) 16 Cox CC 469 80
R v Flintan (1830) 1 B & Ad 227, [1824–34] All ER Rep 685, 9 LJOS 33, 109 ER
771 216
R v Gordon (1803) Russ & Ry 48 41
R v Hammer [1923] 2 KB 786, 17 Cr App Rep 142, 87 JP 194, 92 LJKB 1045, 27 Cox
CC 458, 68 Sol Jo 120, 129 LT 479, 39 TLR 670, CCA 24, 118
R v Hammersmith Superintendent Registrar of Marriages, ex p Mir-Anwaruddin [1917]
1 KB 634, [1916–17] All ER Rep 464, 15 LGR 83, 81 JP 49, 86 LJKB 210, 61 Sol
Jo 130, 115 LT 882, 33 TLR 78, CA 33, 96
R v High Peak Magistrates' Court, ex p B [1995] 3 FCR 237, [1995] 1 FLR 568,
[1995] Fam Law 295 741
R v Hind (1813) Russ & Ry 253, CCR 21
R v Holley [1963] 1 All ER 106, [1963] 1 WLR 199, 47 Cr App Rep 13, 127 JP 71,
107 Sol Jo 116, CCA 208
R v Immigration Appeal Tribunal, ex p Bhatia [1985] Imm AR 39; affd sub nom Bhatia
v Immigration Appeal Tribunal [1985] Imm AR 50, CA 42
R v Jackson [1891] 1 QB 671, [1891–4] All ER Rep 61, 55 JP 246, 60 LJQB 346, 39
WR 407, 64 LT 679, 7 TLR 382, CA 219
R v James (1850) 14 JP 339, 3 Car & Kir 167, 2 Den 1, T & M 300, 19 LJMC 179, 1
Cox CC 217, 14 Jur 940, 15 LTOS 262, CCR 57, 81, 83
R v Lamb (1934) 30 Cox CC 91, [1934] All ER Rep 540, 24 Cr App Rep 145, 78 Sol
Jo 279, 150 LT 519, 50 TLR 310, CCA 89
R v Lancashire Justices, ex p Tyrer [1925] 1 KB 200, [1924] All ER Rep 304, 23 LGR
32, 89 JP 17, 94 LJKB 331, 27 Cox CC 711, 69 Sol Jo 194, 132 LT 382, 41 TLR
103, DC 655
R v Leggatt (1852) 18 QB 781, 16 JP 472, 118 ER 295, 19 LTOS 201, sub nom Ex p
Sandilands 21 LJQB 342, 17 Jur 317 219
R v Leresche [1891] 2 QB 418, [1891–4] All ER Rep 181, 56 JP 37, 60 LJMC 153, 17
Cox CC 384, 40 WR 2, 65 LT 602, 7 TLR 685, CA 362, 368
R v Manwaring (1856) 20 JP 804, Dears & B 132, 5 WR 119, sub nom R v
Mainwaring 26 LJMC 10, 7 Cox CC 192, 2 Jur NS 1236, 28 LTOS 189, CCR 7
R v Mead (1758) 1 Burr 542, 2 Keny 279, 96 ER 1182 443
R v Millis (1844) 10 Cl & Fin 534, 8 Jur 717, 8 ER 844, 1 LTOS 502, HL 44, 80
R v Nasillski (1897) 61 JP 520 24
R v Nottingham County Court, ex p Byers [1985] 1 All ER 735, [1985] 1 WLR 403,
[1985] FLR 695, 128 Sol Jo 873 815
R (otherwise K) v R (1907) 24 TLR 65 340
R v R (otherwise F) [1952] 1 All ER 1194, 96 Sol Jo 362, [1952] 1 TLR 1201 .... 335, 339
R v R (by her guardian) (1965) 109 Sol Jo 154 825
R v R [1988] FCR 307, [1988] 1 FLR 89, CA 492
R v R [1992] 1 AC 599, [1991] 3 WLR 767, 94 Cr App Rep 216, [1992] 1 FLR 217,
[1992] Fam Law 108, 155 JP 989, [1992] Crim LR 207, 135 Sol Jo LB 181, sub
nom R v R (Rape: marital exemption) [1991] 4 All ER 481, HL 220
R v R (financial provision: reasonable needs) [1994] 2 FLR 1044, [1995] Fam Law 15 614
R v R [1995] 1 FCR 745, [1994] 2 FLR 1036, [1995] Fam Law 69 .... 776, 842
R v Rea (1872) LR 1 CCR 365, 36 JP 422, 41 LJMC 92, 12 Cox CC 190, 20 WR 632,
26 LT 484 328
R v Registrar General, ex p P and G [1996] 2 FCR 588, sub nom P and G
(transsexuals), Re [1996] 2 FLR 90, [1996] Fam Law 469 1
R v Reid [1973] QB 299, [1972] 2 All ER 1350, [1972] 3 WLR 395, 56 Cr App Rep
703, 136 JP 624, 116 Sol Jo 565, CA 219
R v Robson (1990) 92 Cr App Rep 1, 12 Cr App Rep (S) 387, 134 Sol Jo 1122, CA 281
R v Rudd (1948) 32 Cr App Rep 138, 92 Sol Jo 206, 64 TLR 240, CCA 354

PARA

R v Rushmoor Borough Council, ex p Barrett [1989] QB 60, [1988] 2 All ER 268,
[1988] 2 WLR 1271, 86 LGR 481, [1988] 2 FLR 252, [1988] Fam Law 335, 20
HLR 366, 132 Sol Jo 821, CA 520
R v St Faith's, Newton Inhabitants (1823) 2 Dow & Ry MC 34, 3 Dow & Ry KB 348 69
R v St Giles in the Fields Inhabitants (1847) 11 QB 173, 11 JP 839, 17 LJMC 33, 2 Cox
CC 381, Cripps' Church Cas 34, 12 Jur 174, 116 ER 441, 10 LTOS 155 35
R v Secretary of State for Social Services, ex p Ward. See Ward v Secretary of State for
Social Services
R v Secretary of State for the Home Department, ex p Ghulam Fatima. See Fatima, Re
R v Slough Justices, ex p Lindsay [1997] 2 FCR 636, [1997] 1 FLR 695,
[1997] Fam Law 322, 140 Sol Jo LB 239 656
R v Smith (1865) 4 F & F 1099 89
R v Steane [1947] KB 997, [1947] 1 All ER 813, 45 LGR 484, 32 Cr App Rep 61, 111
JP 337, [1947] LJR 969, 91 Sol Jo 279, 177 LT 122, 63 TLR 403, CCA 394
R v Tibshelf Inhabitants (1830) 1 B & Ad 190, 8 LJOS 120, 109 ER 758 69
R v Winton (1792) 5 Term Rep 89, [1775–1802] All ER Rep 551, 101 ER 51 443
R v Wroxton Inhabitants (1833) 4 B & Ad 640, 2 LJMC 64, 1 Nev & MMC 479, 1
Nev & MKB 712, 110 ER 597 328
R (on the application of the Crown Prosecution Service) v Registrar General of Births,
Deaths and Marriages [2002] EWCA Civ 1661, [2003] QB 1222, [2003] 1 All ER
540, [2003] 2 WLR 504, [2003] 1 FCR 110, [2003] 03 LS Gaz R 33, (2002)
Times, 14 November, [2002] All ER (D) 110 (Nov) 97, 172
REL (otherwise R) v EL [1949] P 211, sub nom L v L [1949] 1 All ER 141, [1949] LJR
275, 93 Sol Jo 42, 65 TLR 88 .... 321, 340
RP v RP [2006] EWHC 3409 (Fam), [2008] 2 FCR 613, [2007] 1 FLR 2105,
[2007] Fam Law 581, [2007] All ER (D) 294 (Mar) 591
Radziej (otherwise Sierkowska) v Radziej [1967] 1 All ER 944, [1967] 1 WLR 659, 111
Sol Jo 153; affd [1968] 3 All ER 624, [1968] 1 WLR 1928, 112 Sol Jo 822, CA 227, 511
Ram v Ram [2004] EWCA Civ 1684, [2004] 3 FCR 673, [2005] 2 FLR 75,
[2005] Fam Law 348, 148 Sol Jo LB 1371, [2004] All ER (D) 272 (Nov) 520
Rampal v Rampal [2001] 2 FCR 543, [2000] 2 FLR 763 739
Rampal v Rampal (No 2) [2001] EWCA Civ 989, [2002] Fam 85, [2001] 3 WLR 795,
[2001] 2 FCR 552, [2001] 2 FLR 1179, [2001] Fam Law 731,
[2001] 29 LS Gaz R 37, [2001] NLJR 1006, (2001) Times, 24 July, 145 Sol Jo LB
165, [2001] All ER (D) 295 (Jun) 453
Ramsay v Ramsay (otherwise Beer) (1913) 108 LT 382 453
Ramsden v Hylton (1751) 2 Ves Sen 304, [1558–1774] All ER Rep 439, 28 ER 196 711
Ramsden v Ramsden [1954] 2 All ER 623, [1954] 1 WLR 1105, 118 JP 430, 98 Sol Jo
559, ... 897
Ramsey v Ramsey [1956] 2 All ER 165, [1956] 1 WLR 542, 100 Sol Jo 361 800
Randle v Gould (1857) 8 E & B 457, 27 LJQB 57, 4 Jur NS 304, 6 WR 108, 120 ER
170, 30 LTOS 198 .... 436, 699
Ranson v Ranson [1988] 1 WLR 183, [1988] 1 FLR 292, [1988] Fam Law 128, 132 Sol
Jo 90, [1988] 3 LS Gaz R 35, CA 601
Rantanen v Rantanen (Queen's Proctor showing cause) (1963) 107 Sol Jo 873 877
Raspin v Raspin [1953] P 230, [1953] 2 All ER 349n, [1953] 3 WLR 343, 97 Sol Jo
509, ... 353
Ratcliffe v Ratcliffe [1962] 3 All ER 993, [1962] 1 WLR 1455, 106 Sol Jo 900, CA 702
Rawlings v Rawlings [1964] P 398, [1964] 2 All ER 804, [1964] 3 WLR 294, 108 Sol
Jo 424, CA 225
Ray v Sherwood and Ray (1835) 1 Curt 193, [1835–42] All ER Rep 631, 12 ER 848;
affd sub nom Sherwood v Ray (1837) 1 Moo PCC 353, [1835–42] All ER Rep
631, PC 21, 322
Rayment v Rayment and Stuart [1910] P 271, 79 LJP 115, 54 Sol Jo 721, 103 LT 430,
26 TLR 634 742
Razelos v Razelos [1969] 3 All ER 929, 114 Sol Jo 167, sub nom Razelos v Razelos
(No 2) [1970] 1 WLR 392 .... 227, 229, 500, 601
Read v Legard (1851) 20 LJ Ex 309, 6 Exch 636, 15 Jur 494, 155 ER 698, 17 LTOS
145 216
Read v Teakle. See Reid v Teakle
Reder v Reder [1948] WN 238, 92 Sol Jo 469, CA 756, 879

PARA

Redfern v Redfern [1891] P 139, [1886–90] All ER Rep 524, 55 JP 37, 60 LJP 9, 39
  WR 212, 64 LT 68, 7 TLR 157, CA 801
Redpath v Redpath and Milligan [1950] 1 All ER 600, 48 LGR 334, 114 JP 199, 94 Sol
  Jo 193, CA 349, 352
Reece v Reece (1924) 132 LT 349, 41 TLR 24 1022
Reed v Moore (1832) 5 C & P 200 267
Rees v United Kingdom (Application 9532/81) (1986) 9 EHRR 56, [1993] 2 FCR 49,
  [1987] 2 FLR 111, [1987] Fam Law 157, ECtHR 1
Reeves v Reeves (1813) 2 Phillim 125, 161 ER 1097 349
Regan v Regan [1977] 1 All ER 428, [1977] 1 WLR 84, 75 LGR 257, 7 Fam Law 17,
  121 Sol Jo 84 601
Reibey, ex p (1843) 12 LJ Ch 436, 7 Jur 589, sub nom Anon 1 LTOS 383 .... 46, 50
Reid v Aull (1914) 32 OLR 68, Ont HC 345
Reid v Shergold (1805) 10 Ves 370, [1803–13] All ER Rep 363, 32 ER 888 232
Reid v Teakle (1853) 13 CB 627, 22 LJCP 161, 17 Jur 841, 138 ER 1346, sub nom
  Read v Teakle 1 CLR 200 265
Reiss v Woolf [1952] 2 QB 557, [1952] 2 All ER 112, [1952] 1 TLR 1606, CA 787
Reiterbund v Reiterbund [1975] Fam 99, [1975] 1 All ER 280, [1975] 2 WLR 375, 118
  Sol Jo 831, CA 411
Remmington v Broadwood (1902) 18 TLR 270, CA 266
Renaux v Teakle (1853) 22 LJ Ex 241, 17 Jur 351, 1 WR 312, 1 CLR 61, sub nom
  Reneaux v Teakle 8 Exch 680, 155 ER 1525 266
Rennick v Rennick [1978] 1 All ER 817, [1977] 1 WLR 1455, 121 Sol Jo 792, CA 975
Republic of Haiti v Duvalier [1990] 1 QB 202, [1989] 1 All ER 456, [1989] 2 WLR
  261, [1989] 1 Lloyd's Rep 111, [1989] 2 LS Gaz R 38, [1988] NLJR 234, CA 661
Restall (otherwise Love) v Restall (1929) 73 Sol Jo 385, 45 TLR 518 35
Reynolds (otherwise Wilkins) v Reynolds. See W (falsely called R) v R
Rice, Re, ex p Rice (1864) 10 LT 103 .... 466, 552
Richards v Dove [1974] 1 All ER 888 .... 224, 284
Richards v Richards [1972] 3 All ER 695, [1972] 1 WLR 1073, 116 Sol Jo 599 360
Richards v Richards and Flockton (1940) 111 LJP 20n, 58 TLR 142n 686
Richards v Richards [2006] EWCA Civ 849, [2006] 2 FCR 452, [2006] 2 FLR 1220,
  [2006] Fam Law 731, (2006) Times, 10 July, 150 Sol Jo LB 888, [2006] All ER (D)
  312 (Jun) 500
Richardson, Re, Weston v Richardson (1882) 47 LT 514 274
Richardson v Richardson (1978) 9 Fam Law 86, CA 601
Richardson v Richardson [1993] 4 All ER 673, [1994] 1 WLR 186, [1994] 1 FCR 53,
  [1994] 1 FLR 286 .... 492, 495, 518, 543, 546, 558, 561, 571, 583, 592
Richardson v Richardson (No 2) [1994] 2 FCR 826, [1994] 2 FLR 1051,
  [1995] Fam Law 14; affd [1997] 2 FCR 453, [1996] 2 FLR 617, [1997] Fam Law
  14, CA 592
Riches v Riches and Clinch (1918) 63 Sol Jo 230, 35 TLR 141 354
Richman v Richman [1950] WN 233, 94 Sol Jo 371, 66 (pt 2) TLR 44 226
Riding v Riding [1958] P 88, [1958] 1 All ER 65, [1958] 2 WLR 64, 102 Sol Jo
  53, CA 643, 945
Ridley v Ridley [1953] P 150, [1953] 1 All ER 798, [1953] 2 WLR 681, 97 Sol Jo
  231 542
Ridout v Earl of Plymouth (1740) 2 Atk 104 246
Riley v Riley [1987] FCR 65, [1988] 1 FLR 273, [1988] Fam Law 167, 151 JP 650 579
Rippingall v Rippingall and Lockhart (1882) 48 LT 126 863
Risbourg v Bruckner (1858) 3 CBNS 812, 27 LJCP 90, 6 WR 215, 30 LTOS 258 273
Risch v McFee (1990) 61 P & CR 42, [1991] FCR 168, [1991] 1 FLR 105,
  [1991] Fam Law 176, [1990] 29 LS Gaz R 33, CA 282
Robb v Watson [1910] 1 IR 243 274–275
Roberts, Re, Roberts v Roberts [1978] 3 All ER 225, [1978] 1 WLR 653, 122 Sol Jo
  264, CA 209, 320, 331–332
Roberts v Roberts [1986] 2 All ER 483, [1986] 1 WLR 437, [1986] 2 FLR 152, 130 Sol
  Jo 315, [1986] LS Gaz R 1554 601
Roberts v Savill. See Savile v Roberts

PARA

Roberts Petroleum Ltd v Bernard Kenny Ltd [1983] 2 AC 192, [1982] 1 All ER 685,
  [1982] 1 WLR 301, 126 Sol Jo 81, CA; revsd [1983] 2 AC 192, [1983] 1 All ER
  564, [1983] 2 WLR 305, [1983] Com LR 564, [1983] BCLC 28, 127 Sol Jo
  138, HL 638
Robertson v Lady Stallage. See Kenn's Case
Robertson v Robertson [1954] 3 All ER 413n, [1954] 1 WLR 1537, 98 Sol Jo 887 .... 764, 793
Robin v Robin (1983) 4 FLR 632, 13 Fam Law 147, CA 452, 530, 920
Robinson, Re (1884) 27 Ch D 160, 53 LJ Ch 986, 33 WR 17, 51 LT 737, CA 456, 466, 552
Robinson v Bailey [1942] Ch 268, [1942] 1 All ER 498, 111 LJ Ch 161, 86 Sol Jo 105,
  166 LT 216 636
Robinson v Grant (1811) 18 Ves 289, 34 ER 327 21
Robinson v Murray [2005] EWCA Civ 935, [2005] 3 FCR 504, [2006] 1 FLR 365,
  [2005] Fam Law 859, (2005) Times, 19 August, [2005] All ER (D) 129 (Jul) 716
Robinson v Nahon (1808) 1 Camp 245 263
Robinson v Robinson [1919] P 352, 88 LJP 126, 63 Sol Jo 705, 122 LT 222, 35 TLR
  637 406
Robinson v Robinson (by his guardian) [1965] P 192, [1964] 3 All ER 232,
  [1964] 3 WLR 935, 108 Sol Jo 505 345
Robinson v Robinson (1973) (1981) 2 FLR 1, CA 599
Robinson v Robinson [1983] Fam 42, [1983] 1 All ER 391, [1983] 2 WLR 146, 4 FLR
  521, 13 Fam Law 48, 147 JP 33, 126 Sol Jo 745, [1983] LS Gaz R 99, CA 590
Robinson v Robinson and Lane (1859) 29 LJPM & A 178, 5 Jur NS 392, 1 Sw & Tr
  362, 31 LTOS 268, 33 LTOS 96 .... 353–354, 370, 850–851
Robinson v Smith [1915] 1 KB 711, 84 LJKB 783, 59 Sol Jo 269, 112 LT 929, 31 TLR
  191, CA 16
Roblin v Roblin (1881) 28 Gr 439 345
Robotham v Robotham (1858) 27 LJP & M 33, 4 Jur NS 148, sub nom Rowbotham v
  Rowbotham 1 Sw & Tr 73, 6 WR 328, 164 ER 635, 30 LTOS 326 777
Roche v Roche [1905] P 142, 74 LJP 50, 92 LT 668, 21 TLR 332 877
Roche v Roche (1981) 11 Fam Law 243, CA 660
Rodewald v Rodewald [1977] Fam 192, [1977] 2 All ER 609, [1977] 2 WLR 191, 75
  LGR 280, 121 Sol Jo 70, CA 478, 599, 601
Roe v Roe [1916] P 163, [1916–17] All ER Rep Ext 1438, 85 LJP 141, 60 Sol Jo 495,
  114 LT 1184, 32 TLR 490 .... 374, 439, 699
Roe v Roe [1956] 3 All ER 478, [1956] 1 WLR 1380, 100 Sol Jo 820 393
Rogers (otherwise Briscoe, falsely called Halmshaw) v Halmshaw (1864) 3 Sw & Tr
  509 .... 34, 344
Rogers v Rogers [1894] P 161, 63 LJP 97, 6 R 650, 70 LT 699 877
Rogers v Rogers (1894) 6 R 589 863
Rogers v Rogers (1960) Times, 22 November, CA 883
Rogers v Rogers (1961) Times, 23 February, CA 883
Rogers v Rogers [1974] 2 All ER 361, [1974] 1 WLR 709, 118 Sol Jo 364, CA 779
Rogers' Question, Re [1948] 1 All ER 328, CA 227
Roker International Properties Inc v Couvaras [2001] 1 FCR 320, [2000] 2 FLR 976,
  [2001] Fam Law 20 941
Romilly v Romilly [1964] P 22, [1963] 3 All ER 607, [1963] 3 WLR 732, 106 Sol Jo
  1034 649
Rooker v Rooker and Newton (1863) 33 LJPM & A 42, 9 Jur NS 1329, 3 Sw & Tr
  526, 12 WR 807, 164 ER 1379 .... 6, 836
Rose v Laskington Ltd [1990] 1 QB 562, [1989] 3 All ER 306, [1989] 3 WLR 873,
  [1989] NLJR 973, DC 649
Rose v Rose (1881) 8 PD 98, [1881–5] All ER Rep 194, 52 LJP 25, 31 WR 573, 48 LT
  378, CA 425, 438
Rose v Rose (1970) 115 Sol Jo 12, CA 779, 922
Rose v Rose [2002] EWCA Civ 208, [2002] 1 FCR 639, [2002] 1 FLR 978, (2002)
  Times, 12 March, [2002] All ER (D) 269 (Feb) 929
Rosenberg v Rosenberg (1954) Times, 16 July 375, 425
Ross v Ellison (or Ross) [1930] AC 1, 96 LJPC 163, 141 LT 666, HL 353
Ross v Pearson [1976] 1 All ER 790, [1976] 1 WLR 224, 140 JP 282, 119 Sol Jo
  864, DC 655, 679
Rothery v Rothery (1966) 116 NLJ 669, (1966) Times, 30 March, ... 391, 393–395
Round v Round (1869) 20 LT 87 855

PARA
Rous v Jackson (1885) 29 Ch D 521, 54 LJ Ch 732, 33 WR 773, 52 LT 733 235
Rowbotham v Rowbotham. See Robotham v Robotham
Rowell v Rowell [1900] 1 QB 9, [1895–9] All ER Rep 249, 69 LJQB 55, 81 LT 429, 16
    TLR 10, CA 403–405, 436, 449, 699
Rowell v Rowell (1903) 47 Sol Jo 726, 89 LT 288, 19 TLR 657, CA 441
Rowley v Rowley (1864) 33 LJPM & A 54, 10 Jur NS 253, 3 Sw & Tr 338, 12 WR
    809, 9 LT 846; on appeal (1865) 34 LJPM & A 97, 11 Jur NS 532, 4 Sw & Tr
    137, 164 ER 1468, 12 LT 505; affd (1866) LR 1 Sc & Div 63, 35 LJP & M
    110, HL 425, 438, 442, 860
Ruddock v Marsh (1857) 1 H & N 601, 5 WR 359, 156 ER 1342, 28 LTOS 290 .... 264, 270
Ruding v Smith (1821) 2 Hag Con 371, [1814–23] All ER Rep 472, 1 State Tr NS 1054,
    161 ER 774 118
Rudman v Rudman and Lee (Queen's Proctor showing cause) [1964] 2 All ER 102,
    [1964] 1 WLR 598, 108 Sol Jo 180 .... 875, 877
Ruffles v Alston (1875) LR 19 Eq 539, 44 LJ Ch 308, 23 WR 465, 32 LT 236 436
Rukat v Rukat [1975] Fam 63, [1975] 1 All ER 343, [1975] 2 WLR 201, 4 Fam Law
    81, 119 Sol Jo 30, CA 411
Rumsey v Sterne (1967) 111 Sol Jo 113 6
Rush v Rush, Bailey and Pimenta [1920] P 242, 89 LJP 129, 64 Sol Jo 323, 122 LT 792,
    36 TLR 302, CA 742
Russ (otherwise Geffers) v Russ (Russ otherwise de Waele intervening) [1964] P 315,
    [1962] 3 All ER 193, [1962] 3 WLR 930, 106 Sol Jo 508, CA 33
Russell v A-G [1949] P 391, [1949] LJR 1247, 93 Sol Jo 406, 65 TLR 369 .... 7, 42
Russell v Russell [1895] P 315, 64 LJP 105, 44 WR 213, 39 Sol Jo 722, 73 LT 295, 11
    TLR 579, CA; on appeal [1897] AC 395, [1895–9] All ER Rep 1, 61 JP 756, 771,
    66 LJP 122, 41 Sol Jo 660, 77 LT 249, 13 TLR 516, HL 381
Russell v Russell (1922) Times, 22 July 353
Russell v Russell [1935] P 39, [1934] All ER Rep 569, 104 LJP 10, 78 Sol Jo 930, 152
    LT 283, 51 TLR 173 734
Russell v Russell (1972) Times, 20 April 863
Russell v Russell [1986] 1 FLR 465, [1986] Fam Law 156, 129 Sol Jo 684,
    [1985] LS Gaz R 3084, [1985] NLJ Rep 829, CA 679
Russell v Russell [1999] 2 FCR 137, [1998] 1 FLR 936, [1998] Fam Law 313, [1998]
    BPIR 259 .... 687, 692
Russell v Russell and Mayer (1923) 129 LT 151, 39 TLR 287; on appeal [1924] P 1, 67
    Sol Jo 789, 39 TLR 696, CA; revsd [1924] AC 687, 93 LJP 97, 68 Sol Jo 682, 131
    LT 482, 40 TLR 713, HL 353
Rust v Rust [1996] CLY 2884 612
Rutherford v Rutherford [1922] P 144, 91 LJP 129, 66 Sol Jo 283, 126 LT 740, 38 TLR
    353, CA; affd sub nom Rutherford v Richardson [1923] AC 1, [1922] All ER Rep
    13, 92 LJP 1, 67 Sol Jo 78, 128 LT 399, 39 TLR 42, HL 349, 353–354, 734, 771, 851–
    852
Rutter, Re, Donaldson v Rutter [1907] 2 Ch 592, 77 LJ Ch 34, 97 LT 883, 24 TLR
    12 89
Rutter v Rutter (No 2) [1921] P 421, 90 LJP 366, 126 LT 120, 37 TLR 967 876
Ryan v Sams (1848) 12 QB 460, 17 LJQB 271, 12 Jur 745, 116 ER 940, 11 LTOS
    221 .... 263, 271
Ryberg v Ryberg and Smith (1863) 32 LJPM & A 112, 11 WR 502 831
Ryder v Ryder (1861) 30 LJPM & A 164 .... 755, 856, 858
Rye v Rye [2002] EWHC 956 (Fam), [2002] 2 FLR 981, [2002] All ER (D) 249
    (May) 463, 471, 482, 494, 522, 524, 526
Rysak v Rysak and Bugajaski [1967] P 179, [1966] 2 All ER 1036, [1966] 3 WLR 455,
    110 Sol Jo 485 .... 686, 1040

S

S v A (otherwise S) (1878) 3 PD 72, 47 LJP 75, 39 LT 127 340
S v B (falsely called S) (1905) 21 TLR 219 .... 321, 338, 810
S (falsely called E) v E (1863) 9 Jur NS 698, 3 Sw & Tr 240, sub nom Stagg (falsely
    called Edgecombe) v Edgecombe 32 LJPM & A 153, 2 New Rep 429, 12 WR 19, 8
    LT 643 .... 337, 340
S v F. See Shaw v Fitzgerald
S v F (occupation order) [2000] 3 FCR 365, [2000] 1 FLR 255 .... 292, 300, 304

PARA

S (otherwise G) v S [1907] P 224, 76 LJP 118, 51 Sol Jo 430, 23 TLR 460 .... 764, 849
S v S (otherwise C) [1956] P 1, [1954] 3 All ER 736, [1955] 2 WLR 246, 99 Sol Jo
    80 .... 335–337, 342, 345, 852, 863
S v S (O otherwise P intervening, B cited) [1962] P 133, [1961] 3 All ER 133,
    [1961] 3 WLR 742, 105 Sol Jo 532 349
S v S (otherwise W) [1963] P 162, [1962] 2 All ER 816, [1962] 3 WLR 396, 106 Sol Jo
    429, CA; on appeal [1962] 3 WLR 651, HL 336–337
S (otherwise P) v S [1970] P 208, [1970] 2 All ER 251, [1970] 3 WLR 40, 114 Sol Jo
    189 .... 349, 764, 795, 849
S v S [1972] AC 24, [1970] 3 All ER 107, [1970] 3 WLR 366, 114 Sol Jo 635, HL 355
S v S [1977] Fam 127, [1977] 1 All ER 56, [1976] 3 WLR 775, 120 Sol Jo 780, CA 610, 616
S v S (1980) 10 Fam Law 240, (1980) Times, 10 May; affd [1980] CA Transcript
    664, CA 619
S v S (financial provision) [1989] FCR 582, [1990] 2 FLR 252, [1990] Fam Law
    333, CA 595
S v S [1994] 2 FCR 1225, [1994] 2 FLR 228, [1994] Fam Law 438 617
S v S (matrimonial proceedings: appropriate forum) [1997] 1 WLR 1200, [1997] 3 FCR
    272, [1997] 15 LS Gaz R 27, 141 Sol Jo LB 92 .... 712, 842
S v S (financial provision: departing from equality) [2001] 3 FCR 316, [2001] 2 FLR
    246 .... 591, 607
S v S (Rescission of decree nisi: pension sharing provision) [2002] 1 FCR 193,
    [2002] 1 FLR 457, [2002] Fam Law 171, [2001] All ER (D) 379 (Dec) 524
S v S (ancillary relief: appeal against consent order) [2002] EWHC 223 (Fam),
    [2003] Fam 1, [2002] 1 FLR 992, [2002] 15 LS Gaz R 34, [2002] NLJR 398,
    [2002] All ER (D) 58 (Mar) 568
S v S (ancillary relief after lengthy separation) [2006] EWHC 2339 (Fam), [2007] 2 FCR
    762, [2007] 1 FLR 2120, [2007] Fam Law 482, [2006] All ER (D) 118 (Oct) 590, 619
S v S (divorce: distribution of assets) [2006] EWHC 2793 (Fam), [2007] 1 FLR 1496,
    (2007) Times, 15 January, [2006] All ER (D) 137 (Nov) 619
S v S [2008] EWHC 2038 (Fam), [2008] Fam Law 1182, 152 Sol Jo (no 35) 28, [2008]
    All ER (D) 16 (Sep) 596
S v S (otherwise W) (No 2). See SY v SY (otherwise W)
S v S and W (1966) 110 Sol Jo 686 863
S's Marriage, Re (1980) 42 FLR 94, 5 Fam LR 831 43
SB v PB (financial provision) [1995] 2 FCR 62, sub nom B v B (consent order: variation)
    [1995] 1 FLR 9, [1995] Fam Law 70 592
SRJ v DWJ (financial provision) [1999] 3 FCR 153, [1999] 2 FLR 176, [1999] Fam Law
    448, CA 589
S–T (formerly J) v J [1998] Fam 103, sub nom ST v J (transsexual: void marriage)
    [1998] 1 All ER 431, [1997] 3 WLR 1287, sub nom J v S–T (formerly J)
    (transsexual: ancillary relief) [1997] 1 FCR 349, [1997] 1 FLR 402, CA 453
SY v SY (otherwise W) [1963] P 37, [1962] 3 WLR 526, sub nom S v S (otherwise W)
    (No 2) [1962] 3 All ER 55, 106 Sol Jo 467, CA 340
Sabbagh v Sabbagh [1985] FLR 29, [1985] Fam Law 187 458
Sabine v Legge (1921) 152 LT Jo 364 265
Sackville-West v A-G [1910] P 143, 79 LJP 34, 26 TLR 33 6
Safford's Settlement, Re, Davies v Burgess [1915] 2 Ch 211, [1914–15] All ER Rep 939,
    84 LJ Ch 766, 59 Sol Jo 666, 113 LT 723, 31 TLR 529 233
Sage v Sage [1947] P 71, [1947] 1 All ER 492, [1948] LJR 124, 176 LT 420, 63 TLR 760
St George's, Albemarle Street Petition, Re (1890) Trist 134 62
St Paul v St Paul and Farquhar (1869) LR 1 P & D 739, 38 LJP & M 57, 17 WR 1111,
    21 LT 108 853
St Paul v St Paul and Farquhar. See Paul v Paul and Farquhar
Sakkas v Sakkas [1987] Fam Law 414 .... 316, 617
Salvesen (or von Lorang) v Austrian Property Administrator [1927] AC 641,
    [1927] All ER Rep 78, 96 LJPC 105, 137 LT 571, 43 TLR 609, HL 320
Sampson v Sampson (1962) 106 Sol Jo 489, CA 738
Samson v Samson [1960] 1 All ER 653, [1960] 1 WLR 190, 104 Sol Jo 208, CA 227, 247
Sanders v Rodway (1852) 16 Beav 207, 22 LJ Ch 230, 16 Jur 1005, 1 WR 11, 51 ER
    757, 20 LTOS 122 444
Sanders v Sanders [1911] P 101, 80 LJP 44, 55 Sol Jo 312, 104 LT 231, CA 847

PARA

Sanders (otherwise Saunders) v Sanders (otherwise Saunders) [1952] 2 All ER 767, 116
     JP 564, 96 Sol Jo 804 735
Sanderson v Sanderson, Stephens and Hiscox (1871) 41 LJP & M 24, 20 WR 261, 25
     LT 857 790
Sandford v Sandford [1986] 1 FLR 412, [1986] Fam Law 104, CA 499
Sandler v Sandler [1934] P 149, [1934] All ER Rep 213, 103 LJP 88, 78 Sol Jo 383, 151
     LT 313, 50 TLR 397, CA 769
Santos v Santos [1972] Fam 247, [1972] 2 All ER 246, [1972] 2 WLR 889, 116 Sol Jo
     196, CA 267, 347, 365, 368, 389–390, 412–413, 658
Santos v Santos. See Smith v Smith
Sapsford v Sapsford and Furtado [1954] P 394, [1954] 2 All ER 373, [1954] 3 WLR 34,
     98 Sol Jo 392 .... 349, 353
Sartoris' Estate, Re, Sartoris v Sartoris [1892] 1 Ch 11, 60 LJ Ch 634, 64 LT 730, CA;
     on appeal [1892] 1 Ch 11, [1891–4] All ER Rep 193, 61 LJ Ch 1, 40 WR 82, 36
     Sol Jo 41, 65 LT 544, 8 TLR 51, CA 647
Sastry Velaider Aronegary v Sembecutty Vaigalie (1881) 6 App Cas 364,
     [1881–5] All ER Rep Ext 1804, 50 LJPC 28, 44 LT 895, PC 6, 7
Saunders v Saunders [1897] P 89, [1895–9] All ER Rep Ext 1796, 66 LJP 57, 45 WR
     583, 41 Sol Jo 404, 76 LT 330, 13 TLR 328, CA 760
Saunders v Saunders [1965] P 499, [1965] 1 All ER 838, [1965] 2 WLR 32, 108 Sol Jo
     605 393
Saunderson v Griffiths (1826) 5 B & C 909, 4 LJOS 318, 8 Dow & Ry KB 643, 198 ER
     338 273
Savage v Dunningham [1974] Ch 181, [1973] 3 All ER 429, [1973] 3 WLR 471, 26 P
     & CR 177, 117 Sol Jo 697, 228 Estates Gazette 923 279
Savage v Norton [1908] 1 Ch 290, 77 LJ Ch 198, 98 LT 382 641
Savage v Savage [1982] Fam 100, [1982] 3 All ER 49, [1982] 3 WLR 418, 4 FLR 126,
     12 Fam Law 180, 126 Sol Jo 537 866
Savary v Savary (1898) 43 Sol Jo 170, 79 LT 607, CA 511
Savile v Roberts (1698) 1 Ld Raym 374, [1558–1774] All ER Rep 456, 12 Mod Rep
     208, 5 Mod Rep 394, 3 Salk 16, 1 Salk 13, Holt KB 150, 193, Carth 416, sub
     nom Roberts v Savill, 5 Mod Rep 405, Holt KB 8, 91 ER 1147 16
Savill v Goodall [1994] 1 FCR 325, [1993] 1 FLR 755, [1993] Fam Law 289, CA 280
Scharrer v Scharrer (1909) Times, 7 July, CA 769, 858
Scheeres v Scheeres [1999] 2 FCR 476, [1999] 1 FLR 241, [1999] Fam Law 18, CA 478, 591
Schenck v Schenck (1908) 52 Sol Jo 551, 24 TLR 739 .... 685, 861
Schira v Schira and Sampajo (1868) LR 1 P & D 466 794
Schlesinger v Schlesinger (Nystrom and Swanson intervening) (Hall cited)
     [1959] 1 All ER 155, [1959] 1 WLR 92, 103 Sol Jo 74, CA 734, 860, 863
Schneider v Schneider (1968) 112 Sol Jo 600, CA 879, 883
Scholefield v Lockwood (1863) 4 De GJ & Sm 22, 33 LJ Ch 106, 9 Jur NS 1258, 3
     New Rep 177, 12 WR 114, 46 ER 832, 9 LT 400 243
Schreiber v Dinkel (1884) 54 LJ Ch 241 711
Schuller v Schuller [1990] FCR 626, [1990] 2 FLR 193, [1990] Fam Law 299, CA 500, 595,
     618
Schumacher, Re (1907) 23 TLR 336 687
Scotcher v Scotcher [1947] P 1, 44 LGR 351, 110 JP 342, [1948] LJR 147, 90 Sol Jo
     490, 175 LT 441, 62 TLR 517 379
Scott v A-G (1886) 11 PD 128, 50 JP 824, 55 LJP 57, 56 LT 924 33
Scott v Scott (1863) 33 LJPM & A 1, 9 Jur NS 1251, 3 Sw & Tr 319, 12 WR 216, 164
     ER 1298, 9 LT 454 738
Scott v Scott [1951] P 193, [1950] 2 All ER 1154, 94 Sol Jo 762, 66 (pt 2) TLR
     1077, CA 517
Scott v Scott [1951] P 245, [1951] 1 All ER 216 542
Scott v Scott [1952] 2 All ER 890, 96 Sol Jo 853, [1952] 2 TLR 786 684
Scott v Scott (otherwise Fone) [1959] P 103n, [1959] 1 All ER 531, [1959] 2 WLR
     497n, 103 Sol Jo 313 .... 321, 342, 375
Scott (falsely called Sebright) v Sebright (1886) 12 PD 21, [1886–90] All ER Rep 363,
     56 LJP 11, 35 WR 258, 57 LT 421, 3 TLR 79 42–43
Scutt v Scutt (1950) 48 LGR 368, [1950] WN 286, 94 Sol Jo 422 897
Sealey (otherwise Callan) v Callan [1953] P 135, [1953] 1 All ER 942, [1953] 2 WLR
     910, 97 Sol Jo 301 847

PARA

Searle v Price (falsely called Searle) (1816) 2 Hag Con 187, 161 ER 710 836
Sears Tooth (a firm) v Payne Hicks Beach [1998] 1 FCR 231, [1997] 2 FLR 116,
    [1997] Fam Law 392, [1997] 05 LS Gaz R 32, 141 Sol Jo LB 37 .... 466, 484, 552
Seaton v Benedict (1828) 5 Bing 28, 2 Moo & P 66, 130 ER 969, sub nom Seaton v
    Espinasse 6 LJOS 208 266
Seaton v Seaton [1986] 2 FLR 398, [1986] Fam Law 267, 130 Sol Jo 242, CA 617
Seeling v Crawley (1700) 1 Eq Cas Abr 67, 2 Vern 386, 3 Bro CC 618, 23 ER 847 443
Senat v Senat [1965] P 172, [1965] 2 All ER 505, [1965] 2 WLR 981 .... 354, 802, 832
Sergeson v Sealey (1742) 2 Atk 412, 9 Mod Rep 370 238
Serio v Serio (1983) 4 FLR 756, 13 Fam Law 255, CA 352
Seymore v Tresilian (1737) 3 Atk 358 246
Seymour v Kingscote (1922) 38 TLR 586 266
Seyton, Re, Seyton v Satterthwaite (1887) 34 Ch D 511, 56 LJ Ch 775, 35 WR 373, 56
    LT 479, 3 TLR 377 275
Shallow v Shallow [1979] Fam 1, [1978] 2 All ER 483, [1978] 2 WLR 583, 121 Sol Jo
    830, CA 602
Sharma v Sharma and Davis [1959] 3 All ER 321, [1959] 1 WLR 1035, 103 Sol Jo
    897, CA 849
Sharpe (otherwise Morgan) v Sharpe [1909] P 20, 78 LJP 21, 99 LT 884, 25 TLR 131 ... 453, 514
Shaw, Re, Shaw v Jones (1906) 94 LT 93 206
Shaw v Fitzgerald [1992] 1 FCR 162, [1992] 1 FLR 357, sub nom S v F
    [1992] Fam Law 107, 135 Sol Jo 127 .... 224, 284
Shaw v Shaw [1939] P 269, [1939] 2 All ER 381, 108 LJP 135, 83 Sol Jo 420, 161 LT
    63, 55 TLR 609 362
Shaw v Shaw [1979] Fam 62, [1979] 3 All ER 1, [1979] 3 WLR 24, 9 Fam Law 187,
    123 Sol Jo 142 742
Shaw v Shaw [2002] EWCA Civ 1298, [2002] 3 FCR 298, [2002] 2 FLR 1204, [2002]
    All ER (D) 505 (Jul) 593
Shearn v Shearn [1931] P 1, [1930] All ER Rep 310, 100 LJP 41, 74 Sol Jo 536, 143 LT
    772, 46 TLR 652 .... 467, 471, 494, 689
Shears v Shears (1972) 117 Sol Jo 33 360
Sheffield v Sheffield and Paice (1881) 29 WR 523 863
Sheffield and Horsham v United Kingdom (Applications 22985/93 and 23390/94))
    (1998) 27 EHRR 163, [1998] 3 FCR 141, [1998] 2 FLR 928, [1998] Fam Law
    731, 5 BHRC 83, ECtHR 1
Sheldon v Sheldon (1865) 34 LJPM & A 80, 4 Sw & Tr 75, 13 WR 507, 164 ER
    1444 875
Sheldon v Sheldon [1966] P 62, [1966] 2 All ER 257, [1966] 2 WLR 993, 110 Sol Jo
    269, CA 379
Shelton v Shelton and Campbell (1869) 38 LJP & M 34, 17 WR 401, 20 LT 232 863
Shemshadfard v Shemshadfard [1981] 1 All ER 726, 10 Fam Law 189 842
Shephard, Re, Atkins v Shephard (1889) 43 Ch D 131, 59 LJ Ch 83, 38 WR 133, 62 LT
    337, 6 TLR 55, CA 647
Shephard, Re, George v Thyer [1904] 1 Ch 456, [1904–7] All ER Rep 186, 73 LJ
    Ch 401, 90 LT 249 .... 6, 7
Shepherd, Re, ex p Shepherd (1879) 10 Ch D 573, 48 LJ Bcy 35, 27 WR 310, 39 LT
    652, CA 260
Sheppard v Sheppard [1905] P 185, [1904–7] All ER Rep Ext 1395, 74 LJP 102, 53 WR
    608, 93 LT 443, 21 TLR 526 268
Sherdley v Sherdley [1988] AC 213, [1987] 2 All ER 54, [1987] 2 WLR 1071,
    [1987] STC 217, [1987] FCR 149, [1987] 2 FLR 242, [1987] Fam Law 385, 151
    JP 715, 131 Sol Jo 504, [1987] LS Gaz R 1492, [1987] NLJ Rep 363, HL 450
Sherry v Sherry [1991] 1 FLR 307, [1991] Fam Law 180, CA 587, 659
Sherwood v Ray. See Ray v Sherwood and Ray
Shilston v Shilston (1945) 174 LT 105 368
Shinh v Shinh [1977] 1 All ER 97, 6 Fam Law 245 282
Shipman v Shipman [1991] FCR 628, [1991] 1 FLR 250, [1991] Fam Law 145 .... 609, 660
Shipp v Shipp [1988] 1 FLR 345, [1988] Fam Law 168, CA 975
Shoolbred v Baker (1867) 16 LT 359 264–265
Short v Short [1960] 3 All ER 6, [1960] 1 WLR 833, 104 Sol Jo 602, CA 225–226
Shurmur v Sedgwick (1883) 24 Ch D 597, 53 LJ Ch 87, 31 WR 884, 49 LT 156 711
Sibley v Sibley (1979) 2 FLR 121, 10 Fam Law 49 599

PARA

Sichel v Lambert (1864) 15 CBNS 781, 33 LJCP 137, 10 Jur NS 616, 3 New Rep 385,
  12 WR 312, 143 ER 992, 9 LT 687 7
Sickert v Sickert [1899] P 278, [1895–9] All ER Rep 279, 68 LJP 114, 48 WR 268, 81
  LT 495, 15 TLR 506 .... 362, 368, 381, 391, 394
Sievwright v Sievwright [1956] 3 All ER 616, [1956] 1 WLR 1452, 100 Sol Jo 842 511
Sifton v Sifton [1939] P 221, [1939] 1 All ER 109, 108 LJP 131, 83 Sol Jo 97, 55 TLR
  339 369
Silver (otherwise Kraft) v Silver [1955] 2 All ER 614, [1955] 1 WLR 728, 99 Sol Jo
  438 .... 43, 345
Silver v Silver (1870) 21 LT 734 784
Silver v Silver (1962) 106 Sol Jo 1012 376
Simister v Simister [1987] 1 All ER 233, [1986] 1 WLR 1463, [1987] 1 FLR 189,
  [1987] Fam Law 50, 151 JP 17, 130 Sol Jo 682, [1986] LS Gaz R 3001 450
Simms v Moore [1970] 2 QB 327, [1970] 3 All ER 1, [1970] 2 WLR 1099, 54 Cr App
  Rep 347, 134 JP 573, 114 Sol Jo 416, DC 897
Simons v Simons [1939] 1 KB 490, [1938] 4 All ER 436, 108 LJKB 177, 82 Sol Jo 933,
  159 LT 576, 55 TLR 120 465
Simpson v Simpson [1951] P 320, [1951] 1 All ER 955, 115 JP 286, [1951] 1 TLR
  1019 .... 352, 367, 391, 393–394
Sinclair v Fell [1913] 1 Ch 155, 82 LJ Ch 105, 57 Sol Jo 145, 108 LT 152, 29 TLR
  103 879
Singh v Kaur (1981) 11 Fam Law 152, CA 12
Singh v Singh [1971] P 226, [1971] 2 All ER 828, [1971] 2 WLR 963, 115 Sol Jo
  205, CA 42–43, 345
Singh v Singh 2005 SLT 749, OH 43
Six Arlington Street Investments Ltd v Persons Unknown [1987] 1 All ER 474,
  [1987] 1 WLR 188, 131 Sol Jo 224, [1987] LS Gaz R 339 947
Skeats v Skeats and White (1865) 35 LJP & M 47 863
Skipp v Kelly (1926) 42 TLR 258, PC 16
Skone v Skone [1971] 2 All ER 582, [1971] 1 WLR 812, 115 Sol Jo 424, HL 799
Skottowe v Williams (1861) 3 De GF & J 535, 7 Jur NS 665, 4 LT 719 239
Skull v Skull [1954] P 458, [1954] 1 All ER 1030, [1954] 2 WLR 1049, 98 Sol Jo 355 735
Slade, Re, Slade v Hulme (1881) 18 Ch D 653, 50 LJ Ch 729, 30 WR 28, 45 LT 276 650
Slater v Parker (1908) 52 Sol Jo 498, 24 TLR 621, DC 266
Slater v Slater [1952] 1 All ER 1343n, [1952] 1 TLR 1314 782
Slater v Slater [1953] P 235, [1953] 1 All ER 246, [1953] 2 WLR 170, 97 Sol Jo
  46, CA 321
Slater v Slater (1982) 3 FLR 364, 12 Fam Law 153, CA 599, 602
Slater v Slater and Bolderson (1900) 69 LJP 48 857
Slawson v Slawson [1942] 2 All ER 527, 86 Sol Jo 254, 167 LT 260 402
Slaytor v Slaytor and Jackson [1897] P 85, 66 LJP 97, 77 LT 141, 13 TLR 244 761
Slon v Slon [1969] P 122, [1969] 1 All ER 759, [1969] 2 WLR 375, 113 Sol Jo
  53, CA 379
Small v Small and Furber (1923) 67 Sol Jo 277 328
Smallman v Smallman [1972] Fam 25, [1971] 3 All ER 717, [1971] 3 WLR 588, 115
  Sol Jo 527, CA 859
Smallpiece v Dawes (1835) 7 C & P 40 270
Smillie v Smillie (1981) 11 Fam Law 147, CA 876
Smith v Huson (falsely called Smith) (1811) 1 Phillim 287; on appeal (1811) 1 Phillim
  306, 161 ER 993 .... 46, 49
Smith v Smith (1859) 28 LJP & M 27, 1 Sw & Tr 359, 7 WR 382, 164 ER 765, 32
  LTOS 394 .... 362, 771
Smith v Smith (1888) 58 LT 639 372
Smith v Smith [1905] P 249, 74 LJP 113, 54 WR 220, 93 LT 457 406
Smith v Smith [1915] P 288, 85 LJP 16, 60 Sol Jo 25, 113 LT 1166, 32 TLR 43 .... 374, 439, 699
Smith v Smith [1923] P 191, [1923] All ER Rep 362, 92 LJP 132, 67 Sol Jo 749, 130
  LT 8, 39 TLR 632, CA 456
Smith v Smith [1940] P 49, [1939] 4 All ER 533, 109 LJP 100, 84 Sol Jo 117, 162 LT
  333, 56 TLR 97 .... 347, 368
Smith v Smith [1945] 1 All ER 584, 114 LJP 30, 173 LT 8, 61 TLR 331 .... 511, 516
Smith v Smith [1948] P 77, [1947] 2 All ER 741, [1948] LJR 378, 91 Sol Jo 691, 63
  TLR 587, CA 333, 345

PARA

Smith v Smith [1957] 2 All ER 397, [1957] 1 WLR 802, 121 JP 391, 101 Sol Jo 483 ..... 354, 897
Smith v Smith [1970] 1 All ER 244, [1970] 1 WLR 155, 113 Sol Jo 920, 213 Estates
    Gazette 755, CA 513
Smith v Smith (by her guardian) (1973) 4 Fam Law 24, 118 Sol Jo 184 389
Smith v Smith (1973) Times, 15 December 360
Smith v Smith (1976) 6 Fam Law 245, CA 601
Smith v Smith (1982) 4 FLR 154, CA 478
Smith v Smith [1990] FCR 790, [1990] 1 FLR 438, [1990] Fam Law 300 .... 866, 872
Smith v Smith (Smith intervening) [1992] Fam 69, [1991] 2 All ER 306, [1991] 3 WLR
    646, [1991] FCR 791, [1991] 2 FLR 432, [1991] Fam Law 412, CA 617–618
Smith v Smith [2000] 3 FCR 374, CA 596
Smith v Smith and Armstrong (1919) 64 Sol Jo 226 776
Smith v Smith and Liddard (1859) 23 JP 809, Sea & Sm 1, 29 LJPM & A 62, 5 Jur NS
    1318 787
Smith v Smith and Rutherford [1920] P 206, 89 LJP 175, 123 LT 174, 36 TLR 480 845
Smith's Estate, Re (or Re Smith), Bilham v Smith [1937] Ch 636, [1937] 3 All ER 472,
    106 LJ Ch 377, 81 Sol Jo 611, 157 LT 511, 53 TLR 910 275
Smout v Ilbery (1842) 12 LJ Ex 357, 10 M & W 1, 152 ER 357 256
Smyth v Smyth [1956] P 427, [1956] 2 All ER 476, [1956] 3 WLR 210, 120 JP 307,
    100 Sol Jo 437 565
Smythe v Smythe (1887) 18 QBD 544, 56 LJQB 217, 35 WR 346, 56 LT 197, 3 TLR
    357 860
Snowdon v Snowdon [1928] P 113, 97 LTP 65, 138 LT 552, 92 JP 32, 44 TLR 274, 72
    Sol Jo 69, 26 LGR 191 446
Socket v Wray (1794) 2 Atk 68n, 4 Bro CC 483, 26 ER 440 232
Soinco SACI v Novokuznetsk Aluminium Plant [1998] QB 406, [1997] 3 All ER 523,
    [1998] 2 WLR 334, [1997] 2 Lloyd's Rep 330; affd [1998] 2 Lloyd's Rep
    337, CA 647–648
Solomon (a bankrupt), Re, ex p Trustee of Property of Bankrupt v Solomon
    [1967] Ch 573, [1967] 2 WLR 172, 110 Sol Jo 978, sub nom Re Debtor,
    ex p Trustee v Solomon [1966] 3 All ER 255 .... 225, 466, 552
Soni v Soni [1984] FLR 294, [1984] Fam Law 268 .... 592, 615
Sopwith v Sopwith (1859) Sea & Sm 118, 4 Sw & Tr 243 353
Sopwith v Sopwith (1861) 30 LJPM & A 131, 7 Jur NS 554, 2 Sw & Tr 160, 164 ER
    954, 4 LT 256 357–358
Sorrell v Sorrell [2005] EWHC 1717 (Fam), [2006] 1 FLR 497, [2005] All ER (D) 104
    (Oct) 607
Sotherden v Sotherden [1940] P 73, [1940] 1 All ER 252, 109 LJP 13, 84 Sol Jo 77, 162
    LT 150, 56 TLR 298, CA 372, 390
Soulsbury v Soulsbury [2007] EWCA Civ 969, [2008] Fam 1, [2008] 2 WLR 834,
    [2007] 3 FCR 811, [2008] 1 FLR 90, (2007) Times, 14 November, [2007] All ER
    (D) 132 (Oct) 859
Southern v Southern (1890) 62 LT 668 856
Southwell v Bowditch (1876) 1 CPD 374, 45 LJQB 630, 24 WR 838, 35 LT 196, CA 205
Sowa v Sowa [1961] P 70, [1961] 1 All ER 687, [1961] 2 WLR 313, 125 JP 289, 105
    Sol Jo 154, CA 1
Spalenkova v Spalenkova [1954] P 141, [1953] 2 All ER 880, [1953] 3 WLR 681, 97
    Sol Jo 729 778
Spark's Trusts, Re, Spark v Massey [1904] 1 Ch 451, 73 LJ Ch 259, 52 WR 426, 90 LT
    54; on appeal [1904] 2 Ch 121, CA 436–437
Sparrow (falsely called Harrison) v Harrison (1841) 3 Curt 16; affd sub nom Harrison v
    Harrison (1842) 4 Moo PCC 96, 6 Jur 899, 13 ER 238, 1 Notes of Cases 294,
    PC 338, 810
Spawforth v Spawforth [1946] P 131, [1946] 1 All ER 379, 115 LJP 38, 174 LT 260, 62
    TLR 262 769
Speller (otherwise Spearman) v Speller (1952) Times, 25 November 345
Spellman v Spellman [1961] 2 All ER 498, [1961] 1 WLR 921, 105 Sol Jo 405, CA 206, 227
Spence v Spence [1939] 1 All ER 52, 83 Sol Jo 156, 55 TLR 316 ... 362, 367–369, 371, 391, 393–
    394
Spendley v Spendley and Goard [1920] P 40, 89 LJP 64, 80, 122 LT 464, 36 TLR 121,
    187 776
Spicer v Spicer [1954] 3 All ER 208, [1954] 1 WLR 1051, 98 Sol Jo 493 851

PARA

Spier's Estate, Re, Spier and Spier v Bengon (otherwise Spier) and Mason [1947] WN 46,
   203 LT Jo 88 42
Spill v Spill [1972] 3 All ER 9, [1972] 1 WLR 793, 116 Sol Jo 434, CA 779
Spiro v Lintern [1973] 3 All ER 319, [1973] 1 WLR 1002, 117 Sol Jo 584, CA 269
Spittle v Lavender (1821) 2 Brod & Bing 452, 5 Moore CP 270, 23 RR 508 273
Spivack v Spivack (1930) 29 Cox CC 91, [1930] All ER Rep 133, 28 LGR 188, [1930]
   WN 46, 94 JP 91, 99 LJP 52, 74 Sol Jo 155, 142 LT 492, 46 TLR 243 .... 7, 24
Spizewski v Spizewski and Krywanski [1970] 1 All ER 794n, [1970] 1 WLR 522, 114
   Sol Jo 107, 213 Estates Gazette 1536, CA 513
Spring v Spring and Jiggins [1947] 1 All ER 886 354
Springette v Defoe (1992) 65 P & CR 1, [1992] 2 FCR 561, [1992] 2 FLR 388,
   [1992] Fam Law 489, 24 HLR 552, [1992] NPC 34, CA 280, 282
Springfield, Re, Davies v Springfield (1922) 66 Sol Jo 268, 38 TLR 263 40
Spurgeon v Spurgeon (1930) 46 TLR 396 .... 344, 416
Squire v Squire [1949] P 51, [1948] 2 All ER 51, 46 LGR 289, 112 JP 319, [1948] LJR
   1345, 92 Sol Jo 323, 64 TLR 371, CA 393–394
Squires v Squires [1959] 2 All ER 85, [1959] 1 WLR 483, 103 Sol Jo 328 853
Stack v Dowden [2007] UKHL 17, [2007] 2 AC 432, [2007] 2 All ER 929,
   [2008] 2 P & CR 56, [2007] 2 FCR 280, [2007] 1 FLR 1858, [2007] Fam Law
   593, [2007] NLJR 634, (2007) Times, 26 April, 151 Sol Jo LB 575,
   [2007] 2 P & CR D28, [2007] All ER (D) 208 (Apr) 231, 279, 284
Stagg (falsely called Edgecombe) v Edgecombe. See S (falsely called E) v E
Stamford Spalding and Boston Banking Co v Ball (1862) 4 De GF & J 310, 31 LJ
   Ch 143, 8 Jur NS 420, 10 WR 196, 45 ER 1203, 5 LT 594 239
Standen v Standen (1791) Peake 45 69
Standley v Stewkesbury [1998] 3 FCR 564, [1998] 2 FLR 610, [1998] Fam Law
   397, CA 625–626
Stanes v Stanes (1877) 3 PD 42, 47 LJP 19, 26 WR 238, 39 LT 46 860
Stanga v Stanga [1954] P 10, [1954] 2 All ER 16, [1953] 3 WLR 609, 97 Sol Jo 607 876
Stanhope v Baldwin (1822) 1 Add 93, 162 ER 33 69
Stanhope v Stanhope (1886) 11 PD 103, 50 JP 276, 55 LJP 36, 34 WR 446, 54 LT 906,
   2 TLR 447, CA 349, 417, 456, 685, 861, 879
Starkowski v A-G [1954] AC 155, [1953] 2 All ER 1272, [1953] 3 WLR 942, 97 Sol Jo
   810, HL 14
Statham v Statham and Gaekwar of Baroda [1912] P 92, [1911–13] All ER Rep 320, 81
   LJP 33, 105 LT 991, 28 TLR 180 742
Stayte v Farquharson (1826) 3 Add 282 69
Stephens v Green [1895] 2 Ch 148, 64 LJ Ch 546, 12 R 252, 43 WR 465, 39 Sol Jo
   448, 72 LT 574, CA 711
Stephens v Olive (1786) 2 Bro CC 90, 29 ER 51 431
Stephenson v Hardy. See Stevenson v Hardie
Stephenson v Strutt (1872) 20 WR 745, 26 LT 690 879
Sterbini v Sterbini (1870) 39 LJP & M 82, 22 LT 552 860
Sternberg v Sternberg [1963] 3 All ER 319, [1963] 1 WLR 1036, 127 JP 523, 107 Sol Jo
   515 566
Stevens v Stevens (1929) 27 LGR 362, 93 JP 120 368
Stevens v Stevens [1965] P 147, [1965] 1 All ER 1003, [1965] 2 WLR 736, 109 Sol Jo
   211, CA 879, 883
Stevens v Stevens [1979] 1 WLR 885, 123 Sol Jo 488 360
Stevens v Stevens and Field (1889) 61 LT 844 852
Stevenson v Hardie (1773) 2 Wm Bl 872, 96 ER 513, sub nom Stephenson v Hardy 3
   Wils 388 .... 256, 273
Stevenson v Stevenson [1911] P 191, 80 LJP 137, 105 LT 183, 27 TLR 547, CA 369
Stewart v Stewart [1948] 1 KB 507, [1947] 2 All ER 813, [1948] LJR 799, 92 Sol Jo
   111, 64 TLR 115, CA 227
Stickland v Stickland (1876) 25 WR 114, 35 LT 767 .... 368, 372
Stileman v Ashdown (1742) 2 Atk 477, [1558–1774] All ER Rep 318, 26 ER 688; affd
   (1743) 2 Atk 608, Amb 13 711
Stoate v Stoate (1861) 30 LJPM & A 102, 2 Sw & Tr 223, 3 LT 756 358
Stoate v Stoate (1861) 30 LJPM & A 173, 2 Sw & Tr 384, 164 ER 1045, 5 LT 138 876
Stockford v Stockford (1981) 3 FLR 58, 12 Fam Law 30, 126 Sol Jo 64, CA 591, 602
Stokes v Anderson [1991] FCR 539, [1991] 1 FLR 391, [1991] Fam Law 310, CA 278, 282

PARA

Stokes v Stokes [1911] P 195, 75 JP 502, 80 LJP 142, 55 Sol Jo 690, 105 LT 416, 27
TLR 553, DC 736
Stone v Stone [1949] P 165, [1949] LJR 639, 92 Sol Jo 633, 64 TLR 542, CA 370
Stone v Stone and Osborne [1917] P 125, 86 LJP 101, 61 Sol Jo 461, 117 LT 156, 33
TLR 319 346
Stopher v National Assistance Board [1955] 1 QB 486, [1955] 1 All ER 700,
[1955] 2 WLR 622, 119 JP 272, 99 Sol Jo 221 216–217
Storey v Storey [1961] P 63, [1960] 3 All ER 279, [1960] 3 WLR 653, 124 JP 485, 104
Sol Jo 825, CA 851, 897
Storey v Storey [1965] 1 All ER 1052n, 106 Sol Jo 429, CA 397, 400
Storey v Storey and Laycock (1954) Times, 3 March, CA 352–353
Strefford v Strefford (1966) 110 Sol Jo 568, CA 879, 883
Stringfellow v Stringfellow [1976] 2 All ER 539, [1976] 1 WLR 645, 120 Sol Jo
183, CA 360
Stroud v Stroud [1963] 3 All ER 539, [1963] 1 WLR 1080, 107 Sol Jo 273 802
Stuart v Stuart (1862) 32 LJPM & A 110, 3 Sw & Tr 219, 11 WR 463, 164 ER 1258, 8
LT 703 856
Stuart v Stuart and Holden [1930] P 77, 99 LJP 17, 74 Sol Jo 58, 142 LT 359, 46 TLR
132 876
Studholme v Studholme and Cullum (1876) 25 WR 165 875
Stumpel v Stumpel and Zepfel (1900) 70 LJP 6, 17 TLR 17 .... 777, 1022
Stupple v Royal Insurance Co Ltd [1971] 1 QB 50, [1970] 3 All ER 230, [1970] 3 WLR
217, [1970] 2 Lloyd's Rep 127, 114 Sol Jo 551, CA 358
Style v Style and Keiller [1954] P 209, [1954] 2 All ER 836, [1955] 3 WLR 613, 97 Sol
Jo 609; revsd [1954] P 209, [1954] 1 All ER 442, [1954] 2 WLR 306, 98 Sol Jo
126, CA 511
Styles v Styles and Jackson (1890) 62 LT 613 349
Sugden v Sugden [1957] P 120, [1957] 1 All ER 300, [1957] 2 WLR 210, 121 JP 121,
101 Sol Jo 109, CA 538, 684–685
Sullivan v Sullivan (falsely called Oldacre) (1818) 2 Hag Con 238, 161 ER 728; affd sub
nom Sullivan v Oldacre (falsely called Sullivan) (1819) 3 Phillim 45,
[1814–23] All ER Rep 693, 161 ER 1253 .... 42–44, 69, 345
Sullivan v Sullivan (1824) 2 Add 299, 162 ER 303 349
Sullivan v Sullivan [1970] 2 All ER 168, [1970] 1 WLR 1008, 114 Sol Jo 264, CA 391
Summers v Ball (1841) 10 LJ Ex 368, 8 M & W 596, 151 ER 1177 435
Sussex Peerage Case (1844) 11 Cl & Fin 85, [1843–60] All ER Rep 55, 3 LTOS 277, 6
State Tr NS 79, 8 Jur 793, 8 ER 1034, HL 119
Suter v Suter and Jones [1987] Fam 111, [1987] 2 All ER 336, [1987] 3 WLR 9,
[1987] FCR 52, [1987] 2 FLR 232, [1987] Fam Law 239, 151 JP 593, 131 Sol Jo
471, [1987] LS Gaz R 1142, CA 463, 532, 589, 592–593, 600, 614
Sutocki v Sutocka (1963) 107 Sol Jo 373, CA 216
Suttill v Graham [1977] 3 All ER 1117, [1977] 1 WLR 819, 7 Fam Law 211, 121 Sol Jo
408, CA 282
Sutton, Re, Boscawen v Wyndham [1921] 1 Ch 257, 90 LJ Ch 71, 65 Sol Jo 155, 124
LT 526 234
Sutton v Sutton and Peacock (1863) 32 LJPM & A 156 861
Swan and Edgar Ltd v Mathieson (1910) 27 TLR 153, [1908–10] All ER Rep 523, 103
LT 832, DC 263, 271
Sweet v Sweet [1895] 1 QB 12, 59 JP 373, 64 LJQB 108, 15 R 146, 43 WR 303, 71 LT
672, DC 427, 434, 438
Swettenham v Swettenham [1939] 3 All ER 989, 83 Sol Jo 455, 55 TLR 801, CA 455
Swift v Kelly (1835) 3 Knapp 257, PC 42
Syed v Syed (1980) 1 FLR 129 285
Symmons v Symmons [1993] 2 FCR 247, [1993] 1 FLR 317, [1993] Fam Law 135 ...... 624, 628,
636, 642, 686, 933
Symons v Symons and Pike (1862) 31 LJPM & A 84, 2 Sw & Tr 435, 10 WR 449, 164
ER 1065, 6 LT 163 855
Synge v Synge [1900] P 180, [1900–3] All ER Rep 452, 64 JP 454, 69 LJP 106, 83 LT
224, 16 TLR 388; affd [1901] P 317, [1900–3] All ER Rep 452, 70 LJP 97, 85 LT
83, 17 TLR 718, CA 381, 402
Szajna v Szajna (1954) Times, 19 June 377, 386

PARA

Szechter (otherwise Karsov) v Szechter [1971] P 286, [1970] 3 All ER 905,
[1971] 2 WLR 170, 114 Sol Jo 588 .... 42–43, 345

T

T (falsely called D) v D (1866) LR 1 P & D 127, 12 Jur NS 673, 14 LT 227, sub nom
Tavernor (falsely called Ditchfield) v Ditchfield 35 LJP & M 51, 12 Jur NS 344 321
T v M (falsely called T) (1865) LR 1 P & D 31, 35 LJP & M 10, 13 LT 644 .... 337–338, 810
T v S [1994] 1 FCR 743, [1994] 2 FLR 883, [1995] Fam Law 11 ... 492, 495, 518, 543, 546, 558,
561, 571, 583
T v T (otherwise T) (1908) 24 TLR 580 876
T v T (otherwise J) (1931) 146 LT 18, 47 TLR 629 .... 321, 340
T v T [1990] FCR 169, [1989] Fam Law 438, sub nom Re T [1990] 1 FLR 1 .... 316, 456
T v T [1992] 1 FCR 329, [1992] 1 FLR 43, [1992] Fam Law 194 841
T v T [1995] 1 FCR 478, [1995] 2 FLR 660, [1995] Fam Law 671 842
T v T (financial relief: pensions) [1998] 2 FCR 364, [1998] 1 FLR 1072,
[1998] Fam Law 398 .... 450, 622
TL v ML (ancillary relief: claim against assets of extended family) [2005] EWHC 2860
(Fam), [2006] 1 FCR 465, [2006] 1 FLR 1263, [2006] Fam Law 183 601
Taczanowska (otherwise Roth) v Taczanowski [1957] P 301, [1957] 2 All ER 563,
[1957] 3 WLR 141, 101 Sol Jo 534, CA 6, 7
Talbot (otherwise Poyntz) v Talbot (otherwise Talbot) (1967) 111 Sol Jo 213 344
Talbot v Talbot (1971) 115 Sol Jo 870 411
Talbrys v Talbrys (28 May 1959, unreported), CA 854
Tallack v Tallack and Broekema [1927] P 211, [1927] All ER Rep 676, 96 LJKB 117, 71
Sol Jo 521, 137 LT 487, 43 TLR 467 500
Taplin, Re, Watson v Tate [1937] 3 All ER 105, 81 Sol Jo 526 6
Tarr v Tarr [1973] AC 254, [1972] 2 All ER 295, [1972] 2 WLR 1068, 136 JP 484, 116
Sol Jo 353, HL 226
Tasker v Tasker [1895] P 1, 64 LJP 36, 11 R 619, 43 WR 255, 71 LT 779, 11 TLR
51 .... 225, 227, 246
Tate v Austin (1714) 1 P Wms 264, 2 Vern 689, 24 ER 382 239
Tavernor (falsely called Ditchfield) v Ditchfield. See T (falsely called D) v D
Taylor v Brittan (1823) 1 C & P 16n 259
Taylor v Dickens [1998] 3 FCR 455, [1998] 1 FLR 806, [1998] Fam Law 191 278
Taylor v Eckersley (1876) 2 Ch D 302, 45 LJ Ch 527, 2 Char Pr Cas 84, 24 WR 450,
34 LT 637, CA 648
Taylor v Green (1837) 8 C & P 316 204
Taylor (formerly Kraupl) v National Assistance Board [1956] P 470, [1956] 2 All ER
455, [1956] 3 WLR 290, 100 Sol Jo 473; revsd [1957] P 101, [1957] 1 All ER 183,
[1957] 2 WLR 189, 101 Sol Jo 110, CA; affd [1958] AC 532, [1957] 3 All ER
703, [1958] 2 WLR 11, 102 Sol Jo 14, HL 456
Taylor v Taylor (1907) 51 Sol Jo 515, 23 TLR 566, 71 JP Jo 244 406
Taylor v Taylor (1926) 161 LT Jo 236 515
Taylor v Taylor [1967] P 25, [1965] 1 All ER 872, [1965] 2 WLR 779 7
Taylor v Taylor [1968] 1 All ER 843, [1968] 1 WLR 378, 19 P & CR 193, 112 Sol Jo
111, CA 225
Taylor v Taylor (Taylor intervening, Holmes cited) [1970] 2 All ER 609, [1970] 1 WLR
1148, 114 Sol Jo 415, CA 358
Taylor, Re, Taylor v Taylor [1961] 1 All ER 55, [1961] 1 WLR 9, 105 Sol Jo 37, CA 6
Teall v Teall [1938] P 250, [1938] 3 All ER 349, 36 LGR 574, 102 JP 428, 107 LJP
118, 82 Sol Jo 682, 54 TLR 960 .... 364, 391, 393
Teasdale v Braithwaite (1876) 4 Ch D 85; affd (1877) 5 Ch D 630, 46 LJ Ch 725, 25
WR 546, 36 LT 601, CA 711
Tebbutt v Haynes [1981] 2 All ER 238, 131 NLJ 241, CA 500, 601
Templeton v Tyree (1872) LR 2 P & D 420, 41 LJP & M 86, 21 WR 81, 27 LT 429 .... 43, 328
Tennant's Application, Re [1956] 2 All ER 753, [1956] 1 WLR 874, 100 Sol Jo
509, CA 466, 552
Tennent v Welch (1888) 37 Ch D 622, 57 LJ Ch 481, 36 WR 389, 58 LT 368 249
Thaha v Thaha [1987] 2 FLR 142, [1987] Fam Law 234, [1987] NLJ Rep 904 663
Theodoropoulas v Theodoropoulas [1964] P 311, [1963] 2 All ER 772, [1963] 3 WLR
354, 107 Sol Jo 632 833
Thomas v Everard (1861) 6 H & N 448, 30 LJ Ex 214, 158 ER 184 434

PARA

Thomas v Fuller-Brown [1988] 1 FLR 237, [1988] Fam Law 53, CA 281

Thomas v Thomas (1855) 2 K & J 79, 25 LJ Ch 159, 1 Jur NS 1160, 4 WR 135, 69 ER
701 243

Thomas v Thomas (1923) 27 Cox CC 462, 129 LT 575, 39 TLR 520; on appeal [1924]
P 194, [1924] All ER Rep 48, 22 LGR 653, 93 LJP 61, 68 Sol Jo 339, 130 LT 716,
40 TLR 250, CA 362, 364, 378, 381, 391, 397, 400, 403

Thomas v Thomas [1946] 1 All ER 170, 44 LGR 99, 110 JP 203, 115 LJP 75, 90 Sol Jo
152, 62 TLR 166 .... 368, 398

Thomas v Thomas [1948] 2 KB 294, [1948] 2 All ER 98, 46 LGR 396, 112 JP 345,
[1948] LJR 1943, 92 Sol Jo 393, 64 TLR 377 368

Thomas v Thomas [1961] 1 All ER 19, [1961] 1 WLR 1, 125 JP 95, 105 Sol Jo 17 897

Thomas v Thomas (1972) 117 Sol Jo 88, CA 860

Thomas v Thomas [1996] 2 FCR 544, [1995] 2 FLR 668, [1995] Fam Law 672, CA 464, 549,
599, 601, 609

Thompson, Re, Langham v Thompson (1904) 91 LT 680, [1904–7] All ER Rep 474 6

Thompson v Dibdin [1912] AC 533, 81 LJKB 918, 56 Sol Jo 647, 107 LT 66, 28 TLR
490, HL 81

Thompson v Thompson (1858) 27 LJP & M 65, 4 Jur NS 717, 1 Sw & Tr 231, 6 WR
867, 164 ER 706, 31 LTOS 302 .... 362, 372

Thompson v Thompson [1916] P 165, 85 LJP 159, 60 Sol Jo 512, 114 LT 1211, 32
TLR 507 438

Thompson (otherwise Hulton) v Thompson [1938] P 162, [1938] 2 All ER 727, 54 TLR
723; affd [1939] P 1, [1938] 4 All ER 1, 107 LJP 150, 82 Sol Jo 853, 159 LT 467,
55 TLR 10, CA 349, 353, 853

Thompson v Thompson [1956] P 414, [1956] 1 All ER 603, [1956] 2 WLR 814, 100
Sol Jo 247 .... 7, 415–416

Thompson v Thompson [1957] P 19, [1957] 1 All ER 161, [1957] 2 WLR 138, 101 Sol
Jo 87, CA 734, 787

Thompson v Thompson (1961) 105 Sol Jo 108, [1961] CLY 2847, CA 807

Thompson v Thompson [1976] Fam 25, [1975] 2 All ER 208, [1975] 2 WLR 868, 73
LGR 488, 30 P & CR 91, 119 Sol Jo 255, CA 601

Thompson v Thompson [1986] Fam 38, [1985] 2 All ER 243, [1985] 3 WLR 17,
[1985] FLR 863, [1985] Fam Law 195, 129 Sol Jo 284, [1985] NLJ Rep
155, CA 316

Thomson v Thomson and Rodschinka [1896] P 263, 65 LJP 80, 45 WR 134, 40 Sol Jo
583, 74 LT 801, 12 TLR 464, CA 684

Thornton v Thornton (1886) 11 PD 176, [1886–90] All ER Rep 311, 55 LJP 40, 34 WR
509, 54 LT 774, CA 847

Thurlow v Thurlow [1976] Fam 32, [1975] 2 All ER 979, [1975] 3 WLR 161, 119 Sol
Jo 406 .... 360, 389–390

Thurston v Thurston (1910) 26 TLR 388 403

Thynne (Marchioness of Bath) v Thynne (Marquess of Bath) [1955] P 272,
[1955] 2 All ER 377, [1955] 3 WLR 108, 99 Sol Jo 437; revsd [1955] P 272,
[1955] 3 All ER 129, [1955] 3 WLR 465, 99 Sol Jo 580, CA 756, 852, 879

Thyssen-Bornemisza v Thyssen-Bornemisza [1986] Fam 1, [1985] 1 All ER 328,
[1985] 2 WLR 715, [1985] FLR 670, [1985] Fam Law 160, 129 Sol Jo 65,
[1984] LS Gaz R 3590, CA 840, 842

Thyssen-Bornemisza v Thyssen-Bornemisza (No 2) [1985] FLR 1069, [1985] Fam Law
283, CA 608

Tickle v Tickle [1968] 2 All ER 154, [1968] 1 WLR 937, 112 Sol Jo 397 .... 385, 389

Tickler v Tickler [1943] 1 All ER 57, CA 397

Tickner v Tickner [1924] P 118, [1924] All ER Rep Ext 894, 22 LGR 692, 93 LJP 39,
131 LT 159, 40 TLR 367 852

Tidswell, Re, ex p Tidswell (1887) 56 LJQB 548, 4 Morr 219, 35 WR 669, 57 LT 416,
3 TLR 688 207

Tilley v Tilley [1949] P 240, [1948] 2 All ER 1113, [1949] LJR 929, 65 TLR 211, CA ... 349, 370

Tilley v Tilley (1979) 10 Fam Law 89, CA 567

Timmins v Timmins [1953] 2 All ER 187, [1953] 1 WLR 757, 97 Sol Jo 419, CA 393

Timoney v Timoney [1926] NI 75 362

Tindall v Tindall [1953] P 63, [1953] 1 All ER 139, [1953] 2 WLR 158, 97 Sol Jo
47, CA 321

Tinsdale v Tinsdale (1983) 4 FLR 641, 13 Fam Law 148, CA 593

PARA

Tollemache v Tollemache (1858) 28 LJP & M 2 761
Tollet v Tollet (1728) 2 Eq Cas Abr 663, 2 P Wms 489 238
Tomkin v Tomkin (1858) 27 LJP & M 54, 1 Sw & Tr 182, 31 LTOS 186 760
Tomkins v Tomkins (1872) 20 WR 497 875
Tomkins v Tomkins [1948] P 170, [1948] 1 All ER 237, [1948] LJR 1028, 92 Sol Jo
    111, 64 TLR 106, CA 442
Tomlinson v Tomlinson [1980] 1 All ER 593, [1980] 1 WLR 322, 10 Fam Law 88, 124
    Sol Jo 47 897
Tongue v Tongue (1836) 1 Moo PCC 90, PC 69
Tooth v Barrow (1854) 1 Ecc & Ad 371, 164 ER 214 69
Topley v Topley (1967) 111 Sol Jo 497, DC 216
Topper v Topper (1869) 38 LJP & M 36, 20 LT 279 769
Torok v Torok [1973] 3 All ER 101, [1973] 1 WLR 1066, 117 Sol Jo 484 863
Townend v Toker (1866) 1 Ch App 446, [1861–73] All ER Rep Ext 2221, 35 LJ
    Ch 608, 12 Jur NS 477, 14 WR 806, 14 LT 531 711
Townsend v Townsend (1873) LR 3 P & D 129, [1861–73] All ER Rep 367, 42 LJP &
    M 71, 21 WR 934, 29 LT 254 .... 362, 386
Townshend (Lord) v Windham (1750) 2 Ves Sen 1, [1558–1774] All ER Rep 428, 28 ER
    1 246
Travers v Sen (1917) 33 TLR 202, DC 267
Tree v Quin (1812) 2 Phillim 14, 3 M & S 266 .... 21, 69
Treharne v Treharne (1966) 111 Sol Jo 34, DC 216
Tress v Tress (1887) 12 PD 128, 51 JP 504, 56 LJP 93, 35 WR 672, 57 LT 501 699
Trestain v Trestain [1950] P 198, [1950] 1 All ER 618n, 94 Sol Jo 162, 66 (pt 1) TLR
    621, CA 922
Trevalion v Anderton (1897) 66 LJQB 489, 76 LT 642, 13 TLR 401, CA 436
Trevor v Trevor (1965) 109 Sol Jo 574, CA 397, 400
Trew v Trew (otherwise Lineham) (1953) Times, 13 February 344
Troward v Troward (1884) 32 WR 864 856
Trubner v Trubner and Cristiani (1889) 15 PD 24, 54 JP 167, 59 LJP 56, 38 WR 464,
    62 LT 186 .... 777, 1022
Trueman, Re, ex p Trueman (1872) 42 LJ Bcy 1, 21 WR 105 243
Tuck v Nicholls [1989] FCR 300, [1989] 1 FLR 283, [1989] Fam Law 103, CA 975
Tuckness v Alexander (1863) 2 Drew & Sm 614, 32 LJ Ch 794, 9 Jur NS 1026, 2 New
    Rep 480, 11 WR 938, 2 ER 752, 8 LT 821 77
Tudzinski v Tudzinska (otherwise Rusin) (1960) Times, 9 November 342
Tuff, Re, ex p Nottingham (1887) 19 QBD 88, [1886–90] All ER Rep Ext 1819, 56
    LJQB 440, 4 Morr 116, 35 WR 567, 56 LT 573 207
Tulk v Tulk [1907] VLR 64 .... 362, 412
Tulley v Tulley [1967] P 285, [1967] 1 All ER 639, [1967] 2 WLR 840, 111 Sol Jo
    233 .... 774, 793
Tumath v Tumath [1970] P 78, [1970] 1 All ER 111, [1970] 2 WLR 169, 113 Sol Jo
    960, CA 922
Tupper v Tupper and Terrell (1890) 62 LT 665 513
Turnbull & Co v Duval [1902] AC 429, [1900–3] All ER Rep Ext 1229, 71 LJPC 84,
    87 LT 154, 18 TLR 521, PC 249
Turner v Meyers (1808) 1 Hag Con 414, [1803–13] All ER Rep 134, 161 ER 600 .... 45, 332, 344
Turner v Thompson (1888) 13 PD 37, [1886–90] All ER Rep 576, 52 JP 151, 36 WR
    702, 58 LT 387, 4 TLR 243 345
Turner v Turner [1916] P 324, 86 LJP 13, 61 Sol Jo 58, 115 LT 790, 33 TLR 33 777
Turner v Turner [1962] P 283, [1961] 3 All ER 944, [1961] 3 WLR 1269, 105 Sol Jo
    910, CA 830
Turpin v Turpin [1965] 1 All ER 1051n, [1965] 2 WLR 956n, CA 400
Tursi v Tursi [1958] P 54, [1957] 2 All ER 828, [1957] 3 WLR 573, 101 Sol Jo 680 ..... 366, 376,
    406
Turton v Turton [1988] Ch 542, [1987] 2 All ER 641, [1987] 3 WLR 622, 55 P & CR
    88, [1988] 1 FLR 23, [1987] Fam Law 383, 131 Sol Jo 540,
    [1987] LS Gaz R 1492, CA 278, 282
Tweney v Tweney [1946] P 180, [1946] 1 All ER 564, 115 LJP 60, 174 LT 335, 62 TLR
    266 .... 7, 344, 416
Twiname v Twiname [1992] 1 FCR 185, [1992] 1 FLR 29, [1991] Fam Law 520, CA 595, 917
Twisleton v Twisleton and Kelly (1872) LR 2 P & D 339, 20 WR 448, 26 LT 265 856

PARA
Tyndale v Tyndale (1958) unreported 353
Tyrrell v Painton [1895] 1 QB 202, 64 LJP 33, 11 R 589, 43 WR 163, 39 Sol Jo 79, 71
   LT 687, CA 647–648
Tyrrell v Tyrrell (1928) 28 Cox CC 485, [1928] All ER Rep 422, 26 LGR 188, 92 JP
   45, 138 LT 624 736

U
U (falsely called J) v J (1867) LR 1 P & D 460, 37 LJP & M 7, 16 WR 518 .... 340, 832
Underwood v Underwood and Haigh [1939] 3 All ER 1001, 83 Sol Jo 748, 55 TLR
   1048, ... 853
Ungurian v Lesnoff [1990] Ch 206, [1989] 3 WLR 840, [1990] FCR 719, [1990] 2 FLR
   299, [1990] Fam Law 93 280
Upton and Wells Case (1589) 1 Leon 145 947
Ussher v Ussher [1912] 2 IR 445, 46 ILT 109 42

V
V, Re (financial relief: family farm). See P v P (inherited property)
VB v JP [2008] EWHC 112 (Fam), [2008] 2 FCR 682, [2008] 1 FLR 742, [2008] All ER
   (D) 230 (Jan) 568, 591
Valier v Valier (otherwise Davis) (1925) 69 Sol Jo 746, 133 LT 830 44
Van den Boogaard v Laumen: C-220/95 [1997] QB 759, [1997] ECR I-1147, [1997] All
   ER (EC) 517, [1997] 3 WLR 284, [1997] 3 FCR 493, [1997] 2 FLR 399,
   [1997] Fam Law 599, ECJ 712
Vane's (Lord) Case (1744) 13 East 171n, 2 Stra 1202, 104 ER 334 443
Vansittart v Vansittart (1858) 22 JP 704, 2 De G & J 249, 27 LJ Ch 289, 4 Jur NS 519,
   119 RR 109, 6 WR 386, 44 ER 984, 31 LTOS 4 .... 423, 428, 431
Vasey v Vasey [1985] FLR 596, [1985] Fam Law 158, 149 JP 219, 129 Sol Jo 17,
   [1984] LS Gaz R 3500, CA 590, 621
Vaughan v Vaughan [1953] 1 QB 762, [1953] 1 All ER 209, [1953] 1 WLR 236, 97 Sol
   Jo 65, CA 226
Venugopal Chetti v Venugopal Chetti. Chetti v Chetti
Vervaeke v Smith (Messina and A-G intervening) [1983] 1 AC 145, [1982] 2 All ER
   144, [1982] 2 WLR 855, 126 Sol Jo 293, HL 42, 44, 321
Vicary v Vicary [1993] 1 FCR 533, [1992] 2 FLR 271, [1992] Fam Law 428, CA ... 483, 604–605
Vickers v Vickers 1996 SLT (Notes) 69 271
Vickery v Vickery (otherwise Cox) (1920) 65 Sol Jo 343, 37 TLR 332 340
Victor v Victor [1912] 1 KB 247, [1911–13] All ER Rep 959, 81 LJKB 354, 19 Mans
   53, 56 Sol Jo 204, 105 LT 887, 28 TLR 131, CA 446, 466, 552
Vida v Vida (1961) 105 Sol Jo 913 41
Vineall v Veness (1865) 4 F & F 344 16
Viney v Viney [1951] P 457, [1951] 2 All ER 204, 115 JP 397, 95 Sol Jo 516, [1951] 2
   TLR 705 403–404
Volkers v Volkers (Wingate cited) [1935] P 33, 104 LJP 4, 78 Sol Jo 785, 152 LT 95, 51
   TLR 87 .... 796, 855
Volp v Volp (14 October 1940, unreported) 400
Von Eckhardstein v Von Eckhardstein (1907) 23 TLR 539; on appeal (1907) 23 TLR
   593, CA 847
Vye v Vye [1969] 2 All ER 29, [1969] 1 WLR 588, 112 Sol Jo 763 .... 851, 897

W
W, Re (1975) 119 Sol Jo 439, (1975) Times, 22 April 480
W v H (falsely called W) (1861) 30 LJPM & A 73, 7 Jur NS 315, 2 Sw & Tr 240, 9
   WR 619, 164 ER 987, 4 LT 89 .... 337–338, 340
W v Official Solicitor (or W) [1972] AC 24, [1970] 3 All ER 107, [1970] 3 WLR 366,
   114 Sol Jo 635, HL 355
W (falsely called R) v R (1876) 1 PD 405, sub nom Reynolds (otherwise Wilkins) v
   Reynolds 45 LJP 89, 25 WR 25 321
W v S (otherwise W) [1905] P 231, 93 LT 456, sub nom W v W 74 LJP 112 .... 338, 810
W v W (otherwise L) [1912] P 78, 81 LJP 29 .... 338, 340, 810
W (otherwise B) v W (1944). See Wise (otherwise Blakeley) v Wise
W v W [1951] 2 TLR 1135 227
W v W [1952] P 152, [1952] 1 All ER 858, [1952] 1 TLR 879, CA 321
W v W (1953). See Watson v Watson

PARA
W v W [1961] P 113, [1961] 2 All ER 56, [1961] 2 WLR 878, 105 Sol Jo 403, CA 685
W v W (1965) 109 Sol Jo 920 .... 333, 345
W (otherwise K) v W [1967] 3 All ER 178n, [1967] 1 WLR 1554, 111 Sol Jo 926 335
W v W (disclosure by third party) (1981) 2 FLR 291, 11 Fam Law 247 931
W v W (child of the family) [1984] FLR 796, CA 342
W v W [1989] FCR 721, [1989] 1 FLR 22, [1989] Fam Law 19 .... 938, 940
W v W (financial provision) [1996] 3 FCR 641, [1995] 2 FLR 259, [1995] Fam Law
    548 604
W v W (financial provision) [1997] 2 FCR 126, sub nom W v W (periodical payments:
    pensions) [1996] 2 FLR 470[1996] Fam Law 537 617
W v W (financial relief: appropriate forum) [1997] 2 FCR 659, [1997] 1 FLR 257 842
W v W (decree absolute) [1998] 2 FCR 304, 142 Sol Jo LB 148, sub nom Wickler v
    Wickler [1998] 2 FLR 326, [1998] Fam Law 457 876
W v W (Physical Inter-sex) [2001] Fam 111, [2001] 2 WLR 674, [2000] 3 FCR 748,
    [2001] 1 FLR 324, [2001] Fam Law 104, 58 BMLR 15, [2000] All ER (D) 1440 1
W v W (No 2) [1954] P 486, [1954] 2 All ER 829, [1954] 3 WLR 381, 118 JP 467, 98
    Sol Jo 557, CA 364, 369, 396–397, 400
W v W (No 2) [1962] P 49, [1961] 2 All ER 626, [1961] 3 WLR 473, 105 Sol Jo 649 394
W– (MJ) v W— (HRW) [1936] P 187, [1936] 2 All ER 1112, 105 LJP 97, 80 Sol Jo
    656, 155 LT 319, 52 TLR 639 876
WY v AY 1946 SC 27 337
Wachtel v Wachtel [1973] Fam 72, [1973] 1 All ER 113, [1973] 2 WLR 84, 116 Sol Jo
    762, CA; varied [1973] Fam 72, [1973] 1 All ER 829, [1973] 2 WLR 366, 117 Sol
    Jo 124, CA 360, 590–591, 593, 618, 621
Waddell v Waddell and Craig [1892] P 226, 61 LJP 110, 67 LT 389 1040
Wadham v Wadham [1938] 1 All ER 206, 82 Sol Jo 115 513
Wagstaff v Wagstaff [1992] 1 All ER 275, [1992] 1 WLR 320, [1992] 1 FCR 305,
    [1992] 1 FLR 333, [1992] Fam Law 111, [1992] 16 LS Gaz R 31, 135 Sol Jo LB
    213, CA 601
Waithman v Wakefield (1807) 1 Camp 120 .... 264, 273
Wakefield v Mackay (1807) 1 Hag Con 394, 1 Phillim 134n, 161 ER 593 .... 44, 69
Wakeford v Wakeford [1953] 2 All ER 827, [1953] 1 WLR 1222, 117 JP 455, 97 Sol Jo
    609 .... 464, 549
Wales v Wadham [1977] 2 All ER 125, [1977] 1 WLR 199, 7 Fam Law 19, 121 Sol Jo
    154 429
Wales v Wales [1900] P 63, 69 LJP 34 .... 349, 353
Walker v Hall [1984] FLR 126, [1984] Fam Law 21, 127 Sol Jo 550,
    [1983] LS Gaz R 2139, CA 282
Walker v Walker (1862) 31 LJPM & A 117 851
Walker v Walker (1912) 57 Sol Jo 175, 107 LT 655 789
Walker v Walker [1952] 2 All ER 138, 116 JP 346, [1952] 1 TLR 1094, CA 368
Walker v Walker [1967] 1 All ER 412, [1967] 1 WLR 327, 110 Sol Jo 789 897
Walker v Walker (1982) 4 FLR 44, 12 Fam Law 122, CA 600
Walker v Walker [1983] Fam 68, [1983] 2 All ER 909, [1983] 3 WLR 421, 4 FLR 779,
    13 Fam Law 181, 127 Sol Jo 442, CA 693
Walker v Walker [1987] 1 FLR 31, [1987] Fam Law 50, CA 815
Walker v Walker and Walker [1937] P 206, [1937] 3 All ER 523, 106 LJP 103, 81 Sol
    Jo 613, 157 LT 122, 53 TLR 902 876
Wall v Wall (1930) 28 LGR 477, 94 JP 200 736
Wall v Wall [1950] P 112, [1949] 2 All ER 927, 93 Sol Jo 804, 65 TLR 731 454
Wallace v Wallace 1952 SC 197, 1952 SLT 165, Ct of Sess 369
Waller v Waller (1910) 26 TLR 223 699
Wallis v Biddick (1873) 22 WR 76 .... 267, 269, 271
Walls (J) Ltd v Legge [1923] 2 KB 240, 92 LJKB 717, 129 LT 129, CA 648
Walpole v Walpole and Chamberlain [1901] P 86, 70 LJP 23, 84 LT 63, 17 TLR 143 .... 685, 761,
    861
Walrond v Walrond (1858) 22 JP 754, John 18, 28 LJ Ch 97, 4 Jur NS 1099, 7 WR 33,
    70 ER 322, 32 LTOS 122 .... 427–428, 431
Walsh v Corcoran (1982) 4 FLR 59, 12 Fam Law 147, CA 601
Walsh v Walsh (1919) 122 LT 463 374
Walter v Aldridge (1884) 1 TLR 138, DC 264
Walter v Walter [1921] P 302, 90 LJP 372, 65 Sol Jo 607, 125 LT 575, 37 TLR 673 ..... 362, 371

PARA
Walter v Walter [1949] LJR 1718, 93 Sol Jo 695, 65 TLR 680 .... 367, 384
Walters v Walters [1992] 2 FCR 499, [1992] 2 FLR 337 737
Wanbon v Wanbon [1946] 2 All ER 366 368
Warburton v Warburton (1965) 109 Sol Jo 290, CA 369, 371
Ward v Secretary of State for Social Services [1990] FCR 361, sub nom R v Secretary of
    State for Social Services, ex p Ward [1990] 1 FLR 119, [1990] Fam Law 58, 133
    Sol Jo 1133 320
Ward v Shakeshaft (1860) 1 Drew & Sm 269, 8 WR 335, 2 LT 203 636
Ward v Ward [1956] CLY 2816, (1956) Times, 10 February, CA 7, 416
Ward v Ward (1858) 27 LJP & M 63, 1 Sw & Tr 185, 6 WR 867, 164 ER 685, 31
    LTOS 238 .... 362, 851
Warden v Warden [1982] Fam 10, [1981] 3 All ER 193, [1981] 3 WLR 435, 125 Sol Jo
    530, CA 700
Ware v Ware [1942] P 49, [1942] 1 All ER 50, 111 LJP 17, 86 Sol Jo 8, 166 LT 168, 58
    TLR 109 400–401
Warr v Warr [1975] Fam 25, [1975] 1 All ER 85, [1975] 2 WLR 62, 5 Fam Law 18,
    118 Sol Jo 715 .... 364, 407, 410
Warren v Warren [1962] 3 All ER 1031, [1962] 1 WLR 1310, 106 Sol Jo 532 734
Warter v Warter (1890) 15 PD 152, [1886–90] All ER Rep Ext 1223, 54 JP 631, 59 LJP
    87, 63 LT 250, 6 TLR 391 33
Warter v Yorke (1815) 19 Ves 451, 34 ER 584 68
Warwick v Warwick (1901) 45 Sol Jo 639, 85 LT 173, 17 TLR 632 857
Warwick v Warwick and Giovanni (1907) Times, 25 July 354
Wassell v Leggatt [1896] 1 Ch 554, 65 LJ Ch 240, 44 WR 298, 40 Sol Jo 276, 74 LT
    99, 12 TLR 208 251
Wasteneys v Wasteneys [1900] AC 446, 69 LJPC 83, PC 429, 438
Waterman v Waterman [1989] FCR 267, [1989] 1 FLR 380, [1989] Fam Law
    227, CA 600, 616
Waters v Waters [1956] P 344, [1956] 1 All ER 432, [1956] 2 WLR 661, 120 JP 105,
    100 Sol Jo 172 .... 394, 897
Waters v Waters and Gentel (1875) 33 LT 579 349
Watkins, Re, Watkins v Watkins [1953] 2 All ER 1113, [1953] 1 WLR 1323, 97 Sol Jo
    762 .... 7, 344, 416
Watkins v Watkins [1896] P 222, [1895–9] All ER Rep Ext 2014, 65 LJP 75, 44 WR
    677, 74 LT 636, 12 TLR 456, CA 456, 466, 552
Watson v Threlkeld (1798) 2 Esp 637 263
Watson v Watson [1954] P 48, [1953] 3 WLR 708, 97 Sol Jo 746, sub nom W v W
    [1953] 2 All ER 1013 355
Watson-Parker v Watson-Parker (1967) Times, 2 March 6
Watt (or Thomas) v Thomas [1947] AC 484, [1947] 1 All ER 582, [1947] LJR 515, 176
    LT 498, 63 TLR 314, 1947 SC 45, HL 352
Watts (otherwise Carey) v Watts (1922) 38 TLR 430 126
Watts v Watts (1968) 112 Sol Jo 964 345
Way v Way [1950] P 71, [1949] 2 All ER 959, 94 Sol Jo 50, 65 TLR 707; revsd sub
    nom Kenward v Kenward [1951] P 124, [1950] 2 All ER 297, 94 Sol Jo 383, 66
    (pt 2) TLR 157, CA 342
Weatherley v Weatherley (1854) 1 Ecc & Ad 193, 18 Jur 882, 164 ER 112, 24 LTOS
    35 349
Weatherley v Weatherley [1946] 2 All ER 1, 44 LGR 295, 110 JP 255, 90 Sol Jo 296,
    174 LT 346, 62 TLR 362, CA; affd [1947] AC 628, [1947] 1 All ER 563, 45 LGR
    217, 111 JP 220, [1947] LJR 869, 176 LT 434, 63 TLR 209, HL ... 346, 362, 368, 379, 391,
                                                                                      852
Webb v Stenton (1883) 11 QBD 518, [1881–5] All ER Rep 312, 55 LJQB 584, 49 LT
    432, CA 648
Webb v Webb (1828) 1 Hag Ecc 349, 162 ER 609 769
Webber v Webber (1982) 12 Fam Law 179, CA 609
Webster v Webster (1853) 4 De GM & G 437, 22 LJ Ch 837, 1 WR 509, 43 ER 577 447
Webster v Webster (by her guardian) [1967] 3 All ER 560n, [1968] 1 WLR 372n, 111
    Sol Jo 618, 112 Sol Jo 273 825
Webster v Webster and Mitford (1862) 32 LJPM & A 29, 9 Jur NS 182, 1 New Rep
    109, 3 Sw & Tr 106, 11 WR 86, 164 ER 1212, 7 LT 646 513
Wechsler v Wechsler (1954) Times, 18 June 876–877

                                                                                               PARA
Weddell v Weddell (1961) 105 Sol Jo 153, CA 397–398
Weekes v Weekes and Marshall (1905) 21 TLR 227 860
Wehmeyer v Wehmeyer [2001] 2 FLR 84 .... 687, 689
Weighman v Weighman [1947] 2 All ER 852, 64 TLR 40, CA 778
Welch v Welch (1916) 85 LJP 188, 115 LT 1, CA 698
Weld v Chamberliane (1683) 2 Show 300 83
Welde (alias Aston) v Welde (1731) 2 Lee 580 337
Welfare v Welfare (1977) 8 Fam Law 55, 121 Sol Jo 743 360
Wellesley v Wellesley (1839) 10 Sim 256, 59 ER 612; on appeal (1839) 4 My & Cr 561,
    9 LJ Ch 21, 4 Jur 2 431
Wells v Cottam (falsely called Wells) (1863) 33 LJPM & A 41, 10 Jur NS 444, 3 Sw &
    Tr 364, 12 WR 672, 164 ER 1316, 10 LT 138 322
Wells v Wells [1954] 3 All ER 491, [1954] 1 WLR 1390, 98 Sol Jo 804, CA 400
West v West [1978] Fam 1, [1977] 2 All ER 705, [1977] 2 WLR 933, 121 Sol Jo
    253, CA 590
West v Wheeler (1849) 2 Car & Kir 714 273
Westcott v Westcott [1908] P 250, 77 LJP 102, 99 LT 310, 24 TLR 425 853
Westhead v Riley (1883) 25 Ch D 413, 53 LJ Ch 1153, 32 WR 273, 49 LT 776 648
Westmeath (Marquis) v Marchioness of Westmeath (1831) 1 Dow & Cl 519, sub nom
    Westmeath (Marquis) v Marquis of Salisbury 5 Bli NS 339, 35 RR 54, 5 ER
    349, HL 447
Weston, Re, Davies v Tagart [1900] 2 Ch 164, 69 LJ Ch 555, 48 WR 467, 82 LT 591 .... 431, 433
Wevill v Wevill (1962) 106 Sol Jo 155 367
Wharam v Routledge (1805) 5 Esp 235 802
Wheatley v Wheatley [1950] 1 KB 39, [1949] 2 All ER 428, 47 LGR 712, 113 JP 459,
    93 Sol Jo 588, 65 TLR 602 368
Wheatley v Wheatley [1999] 2 FLR 205, [1999] Fam Law 375, [1999] BPIR 431 692
Wheeler-Cherry v Wheeler-Cherry [1939] 2 All ER 603, 83 Sol Jo 496, CA 787
Whiston v Whiston [1995] Fam 198, [1998] 1 All ER 423, [1995] 3 WLR 405,
    [1995] 2 FCR 496, [1995] 2 FLR 268, [1995] Fam Law 549, CA 453
Whitbread v Smith (1854) 3 De GM & G 727, 23 LJ Ch 611, 2 Eq Rep 377, 18 Jur
    475, 98 RR 285, 2 WR 177, 23 LTOS 2 711
White (otherwise Berry) v White [1948] P 330, [1948] 2 All ER 151, [1948] LJR 1476,
    92 Sol Jo 325, 64 TLR 332 335
White v White [2001] 1 AC 596, [2001] 1 All ER 1, [2000] 3 WLR 1571, [2000] 3 FCR
    555, [2000] 2 FLR 981, [2001] Fam Law 12, [2000] 43 LS Gaz R 38,
    [2000] NLJR 1716, 144 Sol Jo LB 266, HL 419, 450, 483, 498–500, 568, 589, 591, 601,
                                                                    603–605, 607–609, 611, 615, 618–620
White v White and Jerome (1890) 62 LT 663 354
Whitehead v Harrison (1730) 2 Eq Cas Abr 712, 1 Barn KB 431 650
Whitehead v Whitehead (otherwise Vasbor) [1963] P 117, [1962] 3 All ER 800,
    [1962] 3 WLR 884, 106 Sol Jo 612, CA 778, 883
Whitfield, Re, Hill v Mathie [1911] 1 Ch 310, 80 LJ Ch 263, 55 Sol Jo 237, 103 LT
    878, 27 TLR 203 40
Whitfield v Whitfield [1986] 1 FLR 99, [1985] Fam Law 329, CA 599
Whiting v Whiting [1988] 2 All ER 275, [1988] 1 WLR 565, [1988] FCR 569,
    [1988] 2 FLR 189, [1988] Fam Law 429, 132 Sol Jo 658, [1988] NLJR 39, CA 882
Whitlock v Whitlock [1990] FCR 129, [1989] 1 FLR 208, [1989] Fam Law 104,
    [1988] NLJR 303, CA 975
Whittingham v Whittingham [1979] Fam 9, [1978] 3 All ER 805, [1978] 2 WLR 936,
    36 P & CR 164, 8 Fam Law 171, 122 Sol Jo 247; affd [1979] Fam 9,
    [1978] 3 All ER 805, [1978] 2 WLR 936, 36 P & CR 164, 8 Fam Law 171, 122
    Sol Jo 247, CA 676
Whittingstall v Whittingstall [1989] FCR 759, [1990] 2 FLR 368, [1990] Fam Law
    401 897
Whitton v Devizes Magistrates' Court [1985] Fam Law 125, 150 JP 330 579
Whitton v Whitton [1901] P 348, [1900–3] All ER Rep 141, 71 LJP 10, 85 LT 646 513
Whybrow v Whybrow (1953) Times, 16 June 358
Whytte (or Whyte) v Ticehurst [1986] Fam 64, [1986] 2 All ER 158, [1986] 2 WLR
    700, [1986] 2 FLR 83, [1986] Fam Law 192, 130 Sol Jo 185,
    [1986] LS Gaz R 875 685

PARA

Wicken v Wicken [1999] Fam 224, [1999] 2 WLR 1166, [1999] 1 FCR 109,
  [1999] 1 FLR 293, [1999] Fam Law 16 .... 6, 10, 326
Wickens v Wickens [1952] 2 All ER 98, 96 Sol Jo 426, [1952] 1 TLR 1473, CA 389
Wickham v Wickham (1880) 6 PD 11, 49 LJP 70, 43 LT 445 344
Wickler v Wickler. See W v W (decree absolute) (1998)
Wicks v Wicks [1999] Fam 65, [1998] 1 All ER 977, [1998] 3 WLR 277, [1998] 1 FCR
  465, [1998] 1 FLR 470, [1998] Fam Law 311, [1998] 05 LS Gaz R 29, 142 Sol Jo
  LB 76, CA 476, 501
Wiggins v Wiggins (otherwise Brooks) and Ingram [1958] 2 All ER 555, [1958] 1 WLR
  1013, 102 Sol Jo 656 320
Wigglesworth v Wigglesworth, Bennett and Smith (1911) 27 TLR 463 861
Wigley v Treasury Solicitor [1902] P 233, 71 LJP 115, 87 LT 745 6
Wigney v Wigney (1882) 7 PD 228, 51 LJP 84, 31 WR 140, 47 LT 129 516
Wilbraham v Snow (1670) 2 Keb 588, 1 Lev 282, 1 Sid 438, 1 Vent 52, 2 Wms Saund
  47, sub nom Willbraham v Snow 1 Mod Rep 30 651
Wilcox v Tait [2006] EWCA Civ 1867, [2007] 3 FCR 611, [2007] 2 FLR 871,
  [2007] Fam Law 988, [2007] Fam Law 667, [2007] BPIR 262, [2007] All ER (D)
  167 (Mar) 282
Wiles v Cooper (1846) 9 Beav 294, 15 LJ Ch 129, 50 ER 357 283
Wilkes v Wilkes [1943] P 41, [1943] 1 All ER 433, 112 LJP 33, 87 Sol Jo 49, 168 LT
  111, 59 TLR 199 368
Wilkins v Wilkins [1896] P 108, 65 LJP 55, 44 WR 305, 40 Sol Jo 274, 74 LT 62, 12
  TLR 212, CA 321, 453, 738
Wilkins v Wilkins [1969] 2 All ER 463, [1969] 1 WLR 922, 113 Sol Jo 226 429–430
Wilkinson v Payne (1791) 4 Term Rep 468, 100 ER 1123 .... 6, 42
Wilkinson v Wilkinson (1871) LR 12 Eq 604, 40 LJ Ch 242, 19 WR 558, 24 LT 314 .... 219, 222
Williams v Lindley [2005] EWCA Civ 103, [2005] 1 FCR 269, [2005] 2 FLR 710,
  [2005] Fam Law 541, (2005) Times, 23 March, [2005] All ER (D) 158 (Feb) 568
Williams v Skottowe (1861) 3 De GF & J 535, 7 Jur NS 665, 4 LT 719 239
Williams v Williams (1864) 33 LJPM & A 172, 10 Jur NS 870, 3 Sw & Tr 547, 164 ER
  1388, 10 LT 846 .... 362, 378
Williams v Williams (1866) LR 1 P & D 178, 35 LJP & M 85, 14 WR 1022, 14 LT
  770 346
Williams v Williams [1904] P 145, 68 JP 188, 73 LJP 31, 90 LT 174, 20 TLR
  213, DC 553
Williams v Williams [1921] P 131, 90 LJP 97, 65 Sol Jo 156, 124 LT 768, 37 TLR
  131 699
Williams v Williams (1928) 27 LGR 4, 93 JP 32 213
Williams v Williams (1932) 29 Cox CC 499, [1932] All ER Rep 907, 30 LGR 362, 96
  JP 267, 76 Sol Jo 461, 147 LT 219 .... 213, 370
Williams v Williams [1938] 4 All ER 445 386
Williams v Williams (by his guardian) [1939] P 365, [1939] 3 All ER 825, 108 LJP 140,
  83 Sol Jo 700, 161 LT 202, 55 TLR 1040, CA 368–369, 389, 396
Williams v Williams [1943] 2 All ER 746, 113 LJP 18, 88 Sol Jo 25, 169 LT 375, CA ... 362, 369,
                                                                                          381
Williams v Williams [1957] 1 All ER 305, [1957] 1 WLR 148, 121 JP 93, 101 Sol Jo
  108, CA 431, 698
Williams v Williams (1962) 106 Sol Jo 858 897
Williams v Williams [1971] P 271, [1971] 2 All ER 764, [1971] 3 WLR 92, 115 Sol Jo
  304 569
Williams v Williams [1976] Ch 278, [1977] 1 All ER 28, [1976] 3 WLR 494, 120 Sol Jo
  434, CA 904
Williams v Williams and Harris [1966] P 97, [1966] 2 All ER 614, [1966] 2 WLR 1248,
  110 Sol Jo 287, CA 877
Williams' Settlement, Re, Greenwell v Humphries [1929] 2 Ch 361, [1929] All ER Rep
  632, 98 LJ Ch 358, 73 Sol Jo 384, 141 LT 579, 45 TLR 541, CA 375, 511
Williamson v Williamson (1882) 7 PD 76, 51 LJP 54, 30 WR 616, 46 LT 920 386
Willis v Barron [1902] AC 271, [1900–3] All ER Rep 876, 71 LJ Ch 609, 86 LT 806, 18
  TLR 602, HL 249
Willis v Cooper (1900) 44 Sol Jo 698 648
Willis v Willis [1928] P 10, 96 LJP 177, 137 LT 621, 43 TLR 657, CA 860

PARA

Willoughby Osborne v Holyoake (1882) 22 Ch D 238, 31 WR 236, 48 LT 152, sub
    nom Re Willoughby-Osborne, Willoughby-Osborne v Holyoake 52 LJ Ch 331 235
Wills v Luff (1888) 38 Ch D 197, 57 LJ Ch 563, 36 WR 571 647
Wills v Wills [1984] FLR 672, [1984] Fam Law 309 .... 590, 597
Willson v Smyth (1831) 1 B & Ad 801, 109 ER 984, sub nom Wilson v Smyth 9 LJOS
    155 267
Wilson v Barker (1833) 4 B & Ad 614, 1 Nev & MKB 409 273
Wilson v Bowie (1823) 1 C & P 8 802
Wilson v Brockley (1810) 1 Phillim 132, 161 ER 937 69
Wilson v Carnley [1908] 1 KB 729, [1908–10] All ER Rep 120, 77 LJKB 594, 52 Sol Jo
    239, 98 LT 265, 24 TLR 277, CA 16
Wilson v Glossop (1886) 20 QBD 354, [1886–90] All ER Rep 1058, 52 JP 246, 57
    LJQB 161, 36 WR 296, 58 LT 707, 4 TLR 239, CA 267
Wilson v Mushett (1832) 3 B & Ad 743, 1 LJKB 250, 110 ER 271 .... 436, 447
Wilson v Smyth. See Willson v Smyth
Wilson v Webster [1998] 2 FCR 575, [1998] 1 FLR 1097, [1998] Fam Law 391,
    [1998] 16 LS Gaz R 23, CA 737
Wilson v Wilson (1848) 1 HL Cas 538, 12 Jur 467, 73 RR 158, 1 White & Tud LC
    604, 9 ER 870; on appeal (1854) 5 HL Cas 40, 23 LJ Ch 697, HL 423, 428, 430–431,
                                                                    443
Wilson v Wilson (1854) 5 HL Cas 40, 23 LJ Ch 697, 10 ER 811, 23 LTOS 134, HL 423, 432
Wilson v Wilson [1958] 3 All ER 195, [1958] 1 WLR 1090, 102 Sol Jo 794 851
Wilson v Wilson [1963] 2 All ER 447, [1963] 1 WLR 601, 107 Sol Jo 314, CA 225
Wilson v Wilson [1973] 2 All ER 17, [1973] 1 WLR 555, 117 Sol Jo 322, CA 873
Wilson v Wilson [1976] Fam 142, [1975] 3 All ER 464, [1975] 3 WLR 537, 119 Sol Jo
    658, CA 452, 769
Wilson v Wilson [1986] 2 FLR 104, [1986] Fam Law 212, CA 897
Wilson v Wilson and Howell (1871) LR 2 P & D 292, 40 LJP & M 58, 19 WR 1072,
    25 LT 206 847
Wiltshire v Fell [1960] 1 QB 181, [1959] 3 All ER 862, [1959] 3 WLR 984, 103 Sol Jo
    1028, CA 945
Wiltshire v Prince (1830) 3 Hag Ecc 332, 162 ER 1176 69
Wily v Wily [1918] P 1, 87 LJP 31, 62 Sol Jo 55, 117 LT 703, 34 TLR 33 .... 368, 401
Windeler v Whitehall [1990] FCR 268, [1990] 2 FLR 505, [1990] Fam Law 424 281
Wing v Taylor (falsely calling herself Wing) (1861) 30 LJPM & A 258,
    [1861–73] All ER Rep Ext 1637, 7 Jur NS 737, 2 Sw & Tr 278, 164 ER 1002, 4
    LT 583 .... 35, 83
Wingfield and Blew (Solicitors), Re [1904] 2 Ch 665, [1904–7] All ER Rep 667, 73 LJ
    Ch 797, 48 Sol Jo 700, 91 LT 783, CA 268
Winkle, Re [1894] 2 Ch 519, 63 LJ Ch 541, 7 R 255, 42 WR 513, 38 Sol Jo 455, 70 LT
    710, CA 652
Winkworth v Edward Baron Development Co Ltd [1987] 1 All ER 114, [1986] 1 WLR
    1512, 53 P & CR 378, [1987] 1 FLR 525, [1987] Fam Law 166, [1987] BCLC
    193, 3 BCC 4, 130 Sol Jo 954, [1987] LS Gaz R 340, HL 280
Winnan v Winnan [1949] P 174, [1948] 2 All ER 862, 47 LGR 10, [1949] LJR 345, 92
    Sol Jo 688, 65 TLR 22, CA 391, 393, 734–735
Winter v Winter [1942] P 151, [1942] 2 All ER 390, 111 LJP 95, 86 Sol Jo 323, 167 LT
    258, 58 TLR 365 .... 739, 830
Wise (otherwise Blakeley) v Wise [1944] P 56, 113 LJP 47, 88 Sol Jo 112, 170 LT 272,
    60 TLR 285, sub nom W (otherwise B) v W [1944] 1 All ER 446 787
Wiseman v Wiseman [1953] P 79, [1953] 1 All ER 601, [1953] 2 WLR 499, 97 Sol Jo
    147, CA 777, 879–880, 883
Witt v Witt and Klindworth (1862) 32 LJPM & A 179, 9 Jur NS 207, 3 Sw & Tr 143,
    11 WR 154, 8 LT 175 833
Wood, Re, ex p Naden (1874) 9 Ch App 670, 43 LJ Bcy 121, 22 WR 936, 30 LT 743 35
Wood v Rost [2007] EWHC 1511 (Fam), [2007] 2 FCR 728, [2007] All ER (D) 198
    (Jun) 596
Wood v Wood (1870) LR 10 Eq 220, 39 LJ Ch 790, 18 WR 819, 23 LT 295 .... 233, 236
Wood v Wood (1871) 19 WR 1049 211
Wood v Wood (1949) 47 LGR 391, [1949] WN 59, 93 Sol Jo 200 566
Wood v Wood [1957] P 254, [1957] 2 All ER 14, [1957] 2 WLR 826, 121 JP 302, 101
    Sol Jo 356, CA 566

PARA

Wood v Wood and Brereton (1919) Times, 16 December 876
Wood's Estate, Re, Davidson v Wood (1863) 27 JP 628, 1 De GJ & Sm 465, 32 LJ
    Ch 400, 9 Jur NS 589, 11 WR 791, 46 ER 185, 8 LT 476 266
Woodard v Woodard and Curd [1959] 1 All ER 641, [1959] 1 WLR 493, 103 Sol Jo
    352 353
Woodhead v Woodhead and Jones (1907) 23 TLR 334 876
Woodland v Woodland (otherwise Belin or Barton) [1928] P 169, [1928] All ER Rep
    690, 97 LJP 92, 72 Sol Jo 303, 139 LT 262, 44 TLR 495 321
Woodley v Woodley [1993] 1 FCR 701, [1992] 2 FLR 417, [1993] Fam Law 24, CA 643, 687
Woodley v Woodley (No 2) [1993] 4 All ER 1010, [1994] 1 WLR 1167, [1993] 2 FCR
    661, [1993] 2 FLR 477, [1993] Fam Law 471, [1993] NLJR 475n, CA ... 614, 642–643, 687,
                                                                                                                       689
Woodman v Woodman [1967] 1 All ER 410, [1967] 1 WLR 32, 110 Sol Jo 771 739
Woods v Woods (1840) 2 Curt 516, 163 ER 493 825
Woods v Woods (1982) 12 Fam Law 213, CA 609
Woodward v Woodward (1863) 3 De GJ & Sm 672, 9 Jur NS 882, 11 WR 1007, 46 ER
    797, 8 LT 749 .... 206, 251
Wookey v Wookey; Re S (a child) (injunction) [1991] Fam 121, [1991] 3 All ER 365,
    [1991] 3 WLR 135, [1991] FCR 811, [1991] 2 FLR 319, CA 717
Woolf v Woolf [1931] P 134, [1931] All ER Rep 196, 100 LJP 73, 145 LT 36, 47 TLR
    277, CA 349, 353
Woolfenden v Woolfenden [1948] P 27, [1947] 2 All ER 653, [1948] LJR 622, 92 Sol Jo
    56, 63 TLR 582 .... 863, 865, 879, 883
Woolgar, Re, Woolgar v Hopkins [1942] Ch 318, [1942] 1 All ER 583, 111 LJ Ch 209,
    86 Sol Jo 161, 167 LT 60, 58 TLR 252 685
Woolley v Woolley (by her guardian) [1968] P 29, [1966] 3 All ER 855, [1966] 3 WLR
    1117 345
Woolwich plc v Le Foe and Le Foe [2002] 1 FCR 107, [2001] 2 FLR 970,
    [2001] Fam Law 739, [2001] All ER (D) 325 (Jun) 587
Wormald v Neale and Wormald (falsely called Neale) (1868) 19 LT 93 328
Worrall v Jacob (1817) 3 Mer 256, 36 ER 98 431
Worsley v Worsley and Wignall (1869) LR 1 P & D 648, 38 LJP & M 43, 17 WR 743,
    20 LT 546 .... 442, 511
Wray v Wray and D'Almeida [1901] P 132, 70 LJP 32, 84 LT 64, 17 TLR 242 .... 777, 1022
Wren v Bradley (1848) 2 De G & Sm 49, 17 LJ Ch 172, 12 Jur 168, 10 LTOS 438 222
Wright v Elwood (1837) 1 Curt 662, 163 ER 231 328
Wright v Elwood (1935) 1 Curt 49 328
Wright v Wright (1964) Times, 19 June 771
Wright v Wright [1970] 3 All ER 209, [1970] 1 WLR 1219, 114 Sol Jo 619, CA 698
Wright v Wright [1976] Fam 114, [1976] 1 All ER 796, [1976] 2 WLR 269, 119 Sol Jo
    864 873
Wyatt v Henry (1817) 2 Hag Con 215, 161 ER 720 69
Wyler v Lyons [1963] P 274, [1963] 1 All ER 821, [1963] 2 WLR 610, 107 Sol Jo 37 500
Wynn v Davies and Weever (1835) 1 Curt 69, 163 ER 24 .... 65, 68
Wynne v Wynne [1898] P 18, 67 LJP 5, 46 WR 560 .... 378, 386
Wynne v Wynne and Jeffers [1980] 3 All ER 659, [1981] 1 WLR 69, sub nom W v W
    10 Fam Law 241, 124 Sol Jo 397, CA 931

X

X v X (Crown Prosecution Service intervening) [2005] EWHC 296 (Fam), [2005] 2 FLR
    487, [2005] Fam Law 543 621
X, Y and Z v United Kingdom (1997) 24 EHRR 143, [1997] 3 FCR 341, [1997] 2 FLR
    892, [1997] Fam Law 605, 39 BMLR 128, [1997] 17 LS Gaz R 25, [1997] EHRLR
    227, ECtHR 1
Xydhias v Xydhias [1999] 2 All ER 386, [1999] 1 FCR 289, [1999] 1 FLR 683,
    [1999] Fam Law 301, [1999] NLJR 52, CA 596, 626

Y

Y (children) (occupation order), Re [2000] 2 FCR 470, CA 289
Y– v Y– (1860) 1 Sw & Tr 598, 8 WR 273, 1 LT 414, 164 ER 877, sub nom Re
    Chaddock v Chaddock, ex p Verax 29 LJPM & A 55, 6 Jur NS 348 876

PARA

Yarrow v Yarrow [1892] P 92, [1891–4] All ER Rep 538, 61 LJP 69, 66 LT 383, 8 TLR
215 349
Yeatman v Yeatman (1868) LR 1 P & D 489, [1861–73] All ER Rep 293, 37 LJP & M
37, 16 WR 734, 18 LT 415 .... 369, 381, 393
Yeatman v Yeatman and Rummell (1870) 21 LT 733 346
Yonge v Furse (1856) 26 LJ Ch 117, sub nom Young v Furse 2 Jur NS 864, 27 LTOS
286; on appeal (1857) 26 LJ Ch 352 50
Yonge v Toynbee [1910] 1 KB 215, [1908–10] All ER Rep 204, 79 LJKB 208, 102 LT
57, 26 TLR 211, CA 256
Young v Lauretani [2007] EWHC 1244 (Ch), [2008] 1 FCR 669, [2007] 2 FLR 1211,
[2007] Fam Law 906, [2007] 2 P & CR D32, [2007] All ER (D) 389 (May) 282
Young v Schuler (1883) 11 QBD 651, 4[1881–5] All ER Rep Ext 1469, 9 LT 546, CA 205
Young v Young [1962] P 27, [1961] 3 All ER 695, [1961] 3 WLR 1109, 105 Sol Jo
665, CA 511
Young v Young [1964] P 152, [1962] 3 All ER 120, [1962] 3 WLR 946, 126 JP 406,
106 Sol Jo 453 .... 381, 393
Young v Young (1973) 117 Sol Jo 204 511
Young v Young [1984] FLR 375, [1984] Fam Law 271, CA 279
Yuill v Yuill [1945] P 15, [1945] 1 All ER 183, 114 LJP 1, 89 Sol Jo 106, 172 LT 114,
61 TLR 176, CA 851
Yukong Line Ltd of Korea v Rendsburg Investments Corpn of Liberia [1996] 2 Lloyd's
Rep 604, CA 661

Z

Z v Z [1992] 2 FCR 152, [1992] 2 FLR 291 938–940
Z Ltd v A-Z and AA-LL [1982] QB 558, [1982] 1 All ER 556, [1982] 2 WLR 288,
[1982] 1 Lloyd's Rep 240, 126 Sol Jo 100, CA 661
Zamet v Hyman [1961] 3 All ER 933, [1961] 1 WLR 1442, 105 Sol Jo 911, CA 230
Zandfarid v Bank of Credit and Commerce International SA (in liquidation)
[1996] 1 WLR 1420, [1997] 1 FCR 78, [1997] 1 FLR 274, [1996] BPIR 501 639

Decisions of the European Court of Justice are listed below numerically. These decisions
are also included in the preceding alphabetical list.

PARA

C-13/94: P v S [1996] ECR I-2143, [1996] All ER (EC) 397, [1996] 2 CMLR 247,
[1996] ICR 795, [1996] IRLR 347, sub nom P v S (sex discrimination): C-13/94
[1997] 2 FCR 180, [1996] 2 FLR 347, [1996] Fam Law 609, ECJ 1
C-220/95: Van den Boogaard v Laumen [1997] QB 759, [1997] ECR I-1147, [1997] All
ER (EC) 517, [1997] 3 WLR 284, [1997] 3 FCR 493, [1997] 2 FLR 399,
[1997] Fam Law 599, ECJ 712

MATRIMONIAL AND CIVIL PARTNERSHIP LAW

VOLUME 72

	PARA
1. FUNDAMENTAL PRINCIPLES	1
(1) Legality and Validity	1
(i) Marriage and Civil Partnership Generally	1
(ii) Foreign and Overseas Marriages and Civil Partnerships	17
(iii) Proof	21
(2) Capacity to Marry or Enter into Civil Partnership	31
(3) Prohibited Degrees of Relationship	35
(4) Consent	41
(i) Consent of Parties	41
(ii) Parental Consent	46
2. FORMS AND CEREMONIES	53
(1) Methods of Marriage and Civil Partnership	53
(2) Church of England Marriages	57
(i) Entitlement to be Married according to the Rites of the Church of England	57
(ii) Place for Banns and Marriage	59
(iii) Publication of Banns	65
(iv) Marriage Licences	76
(v) Solemnisation of Marriage in Church	80
(vi) Registration	84
(3) Marriage on the Authority of Superintendent Registrar's Certificates	87
(i) Notices and Declarations	87
(ii) Certification	95
(iii) Place and Manner of Solemnisation	102
A. Solemnisation at Superintendent Registrar's Office	102
B. Solemnisation in a Registered Building	104
C. Solemnisation on Approved Premises	111
(iv) Parties Resident outside England and Wales	112
(v) Quaker and Jewish Marriages	115

PARA

(4) Marriages Conducted Abroad 119

(5) Naval, Military and Air Force Marriages 129

(6) Civil Partnerships 132

    (i)   In general 132

    (ii)   The Standard Procedure 133

    (iii)   Special Procedure for Civil Partnerships of Seriously Ill
          Persons 140

    (iv)   Registration of Civil Partnerships Abroad 145

         A.   Registration Generally 145

         B.   Registration by Armed Forces Personnel 153

(7) Marriage of Seriously Ill Persons by Registrar General's Licence 161

(8) Housebound or Detained Persons 169

(9) Persons subject to Immigration Control 176

(10) Offences 180

3. REGISTRATION AND APPROVAL OF PREMISES 186

(1) Registration of Buildings for Marriages 186

(2) Approval of Premises for Marriages and Civil Partnerships 190

4. LEGAL INCIDENTS OF MARRIAGE AND CIVIL
PARTNERSHIP 203

(1) Status of Married Persons and Civil Partners 203

(2) Maintenance and Cohabitation 216

(3) Ownership of Property 224

    (i)   Resolution of Disputes 224

    (ii)   Property Rights in the Family Home 231

    (iii)   Powers of Appointment 232

    (iv)   Equity of Exoneration 239

    (v)   Minor Financial Matters 245

    (vi)   Gifts between Parties 248

    (vii) Property Rights after Spouse or Civil Partner's Death 254

(4) Authority to make Contracts 256

    (i)   Authority and Liability 256

    (ii)   Contract for Necessaries 263

    (iii)   Ratification and Holding Out 269

(5) Life Assurance Policies 274

PARA

5. PROPERTY RIGHTS IN THE FAMILY HOME 278

(1) Applicable Principles in Determination of Property Rights 278

(2) Home Rights 285

(3) Occupation Orders 289

    (i) Applications and Orders 289

    (ii) Circumstances and Conditions for Orders 292

        A. Applicant having Estate or Interest or Home Rights 292

        B. One Former Spouse or Civil Partner with no Existing
        Right to Occupy 297

        C. One Cohabitant or Former Cohabitant with no
        Existing Right to Occupy 301

        D. Neither Spouse, Civil Partner, Cohabitant or Former
        Cohabitant Entitled to Occupy 305

    (iii) Appeals 308

    (iv) Variation and Discharge 309

(4) Transfer of Tenancy Orders 310

(5) Mesher and Martin Orders 316

6. MATRIMONIAL AND CIVIL PARTNERSHIP CAUSES 317

(1) The Causes 317

(2) Nullity 319

    (i) Powers of Annulment 319

    (ii) Void Marriages and Civil Partnerships 326

    (iii) Voidable Marriages and Civil Partnerships 331

        A. Consent, Mental Disorder, Pregnancy and Gender
        Reassignment 331

        B. Failure to Consummate Marriage 335

        C. Venereal Disease 343

    (iv) Marriages Celebrated before 1 August 1971 344

(3) Divorce, Dissolution and Judicial and Legal Separation 346

    (i) Grounds 346

    (ii) Adultery 349

    (iii) Behaviour 359

    (iv) Desertion 362

        A. Fundamental Principles 362

        B. Desertion and Consensual Separation 371

        C. Desertion without Separation 377

PARA

  D. Separation with Just Cause 380

  E. Absence of Intention to Desert 386

  F. Constructive Desertion 391

  G. Termination of Desertion 396

(v) Separation 407

  A. Two Years' Living Apart and Consent to Divorce or
      Dissolution 407

  B. Five Years' Living Apart: No Consent to Divorce or
      Dissolution Required 410

  C. General Principles 412

(vi) Reconciliation 414

(4) Presumption of Death 415

(5) Related and Subsidiary Causes 418

(i) Division of Property 418

(ii) Financial Relief and Provision of Reasonable
      Maintenance 419

(iii) Declarations of Marital or Civil Partnership Status 421

(iv) Separation Agreements 423

  A. Form and Validity 423

  B. Construction and Operation 432

  C. Remedies for Breach 443

  D. Effect of Reconciliation 447

7. FINANCIAL RELIEF 450

(1) Financial Relief on Divorce, Dissolution, Nullity, Separation and
     Presumption of Death 450

(i) Financial Provision Orders 450

  A. Scope and Effect of Orders 450

  B. Periodical Payments 458

  C. Secured Periodical Payments 467

  D. Lump Sum Payments 476

  E. Pension Attachments 485

  F. Orders for the Benefit of Children 492

(ii) Property Adjustment Orders 498

  A. Scope and Effect of Orders 498

  B. Transfers of Property 499

  C. Settlements of Property 506

PARA

       D.   Variation of Settlements 510

            (A)   Powers of the Court 510

            (B)   Duration and Effect 515

       E.   Orders for the Benefit of Children 518

(iii)   Orders for Sale of Property 520

(iv)   Pension Sharing Orders and Pension Compensation
Sharing Orders 523

(v)   Financial Relief and Property Adjustment following
Overseas Divorce, Dissolution, Separation or Annulment 530

(vi)   Financial Relief following Death of Former Spouse or Civil
Partner 538

VOLUME 73

7.   FINANCIAL RELIEF 542

(2)   Financial Provision during Subsistence of Marriage or Civil
Partnership 542

    (i)   Powers of the High Court 542

    (ii)   Powers of Magistrates' Courts 553

(3)   Variation, Discharge and Suspension of Orders 567

    (i)   Orders of the High Court 567

    (ii)   Orders of Magistrates' Courts 576

(4)   Prevention of Attempts to Defeat Claims 586

(5)   Principles of Assessment 589

    (i)   Matters to which Court is to have Regard 589

    (ii)   Welfare of Children 597

    (iii)   Income, Earning Capacity and Resources 599

    (iv)   Needs, Obligations and Responsibilities 610

    (v)   Standard of Living 614

    (vi)   Age of Parties and Duration of Marriage or Civil
Partnership 615

    (vii)   Disability 617

    (viii)   Contributions 618

    (ix)   Conduct 621

    (x)   Loss of Benefit 622

(6)   Enforcement 623

    (i)   Enforcement Generally 623

PARA

    (ii)   Methods of Enforcement 627

           A.   Attachment of Earning Orders 627

           B.   Charging Orders 636

           C.   Third Party Debt Orders 640

           D.   Orders for the Execution of Documents 641

           E.   Judgment Summonses 642

           F.   Means of Payment Orders 644

           G.   Receivership and Sequestration 647

           H.   Execution against Goods 651

           I.   Orders for Possession of Land 654

           J.   Enforcement in Magistrates' Courts 655

    (iii)   Aids to Enforcement 659

           A.   Injunctions 659

           B.   Registration of Maintenance Orders 664

                (A)   Registration Generally 664

                (B)   Registration of High Court and County Court Orders in Magistrates' Courts 666

                (C)   Registration of Magistrates' Court Orders in the High Court 671

                (D)   Cancellation of Registration 675

           C.   Registration of Interests in Land 676

    (iv)   Reciprocal Enforcement 677

    (v)   Limitation of Actions 678

    (vi)   Interest 680

    (vii) Death of Party 684

    (viii) Bankruptcy of Party 687

    (ix)   Armed Forces Personnel 693

(7)   Settlements and Agreements 696

    (i)   Maintenance Agreements 696

           A.   Status and Validity 696

           B.   Alteration 700

           C.   Procedure 706

    (ii)   Settlements 710

    (iii) Ante-nuptial and Pre-registration Agreements 712

    (iv) Consent Orders 713

                                                              PARA
8.   INJUNCTIVE RELIEF 716

(1) Non-molestation Orders 716

(2) Forced Marriage Protection Orders 723

9.   JURISDICTION AND PROCEDURE 731

(1) Powers of Courts 731

     (i)   Jurisdiction in Family Business 731

     (ii)   Allocation, Distribution and Transfer of Business 744

(2) Matrimonial and Civil Partnership Causes 750

     (i)   Jurisdictional Matters 750

     (ii)   Institution of Proceedings by Petition 755

            A.   Form, Content and Filing of Petitions 755

            B.   Supplemental Petitions and Amendment of
                 Petitions 769

            C.   Service of Petitions 776

     (iii) Answers to Petitions 779

            A.   Notice of Intention to Defend 779

            B.   Consent to Grant of Decree or Civil Partnership
                 Order 786

            C.   Request for Particulars 787

            D.   Cross-petitions and Cross-prayers 793

            E.   Reply to Answer 797

     (iv)   Preparations and Arrangements for Trial 799

            A.   Discovery and Interrogatories 799

            B.   Medical Inspections 803

            C.   Setting Down of Causes and Directions 811

            D.   Mode of Trial 823

     (v)   Witnesses and Evidence 825

     (vi)   Stay of Proceedings 839

            A.   Stay of Proceedings pending Actions in Other
                 Jurisdictions 839

            B.   Stay of Proceedings for Procedural Reasons 845

     (vii) Disposal of Causes 848

            A.   Disposal by Trial 848

            B.   Disposal without Hearing or Trial 855

                 (A)   Dismissal for Want of Prosecution 855

                 (B)   Compromise 859

PARA

       (C)   Abatement and Striking Out 861

(viii)   Decrees and Orders 863

       A.   Decrees Nisi and Absolute, and Conditional and
           Final Orders 863

       B.   Orders relating to Children 884

(3)   Procedure in Applications for Financial Relief 886

   (i)   Financial Provisions during Subsistence of Marriage or
       Civil Partnership 886

       A.   Applications to the High Court and County Courts 886

       B.   Applications to Magistrates' Courts 894

   (ii)   Financial Relief on Divorce, Dissolution, Nullity,
       Separation and Presumption of Death 902

       A.   The Procedural Code 902

       B.   The Pre-application Protocol 905

       C.   Applications for Relief 916

       D.   Interlocutory Procedure 924

       E.   Hearing the Application and Making the Order 931

   (iii) Financial Relief following Overseas Divorce, Dissolution,
       Separation or Annulment 938

   (iv) Enforcement of Financial Orders 943

       A.   Methods of Enforcement 943

       B.   Interest and Arrears 949

       C.   Transfer of Proceedings 951

(4)   Orders concerning Matrimonial or Civil Partnership Property 955

(5)   Occupation Orders, Non-molestation Orders, Transfer of
   Tenancy Orders and Forced Marriage Protection Orders 958

   (i)   Powers of Courts 958

   (ii)   Commencement and Transfer of Proceedings 962

       A.   Occupation Orders and Non-molestation Orders 962

       B.   Forced Marriage Protection Orders 973

   (iii) Procedure on Application 974

       A.   Occupation Orders and Non-molestation Orders 974

         (A)   Procedure in High Court and County Courts 974

         (B)   Procedure in Magistrates' Courts 977

       B.   Forced Marriage Protection Orders 980

   (iv) Appeals 986

                                                                    PARA
     (v)   Enforcement and Arrest 988
(6) Declarations of Marital or Civil Partnership Status 1000
(7) Administrative Provisions 1005
     (i)   Rules of Court 1005
     (ii)   Administration in the High Court 1006
            A.   Administration 1006
            B.   Provisions as to Service 1017
            C.   Human Rights Applications 1024
     (iii) Administration in the Magistrates' Court 1028
     (iv)   Fees 1036
     (v)   Costs 1037

1. FUNDAMENTAL PRINCIPLES

(1) LEGALITY AND VALIDITY

(i) Marriage and Civil Partnership Generally

1. Marriage. Holy matrimony is the estate into which a man and a woman enter when they consent and contract to cohabit with each other and each other only[1]. The solemnisation of matrimony in church is on their part the attestation in the presence of God and of the Church of their consent and contract so to do, and on the Church's part its blessing on their union[2]. According to the doctrine of the Church of England marriage is in its nature a union permanent and life-long, for better for worse, till death them do part, of one man and one woman, to the exclusion of all others on either side, for the procreation and nurture of children, for the hallowing and right direction of the natural instincts and affections, and for the mutual society, help and comfort which the one ought to have of the other, both in prosperity and adversity[3].

It has been said that the only kind of marriage which English law recognises is one which is essentially the voluntary union for life of one man with one woman to the exclusion of all others[4]. If two persons of the same sex contrive to go through the formalities of a ceremony of marriage, the ceremony is not a marriage ceremony at all, but it has been held that the court in such circumstances is precluded from granting purely declaratory relief but must grant a nullity decree[5]. A marriage celebrated after 31 July 1971 is void where the parties are not respectively male and female[6].

To be recognised by English law a marriage must at its inception be for life[7] and must not be illusory[8].

English law does not acknowledge the concept of a trial or temporary marriage[9].

1   Book of Common Prayer, Form of Solemnization of Matrimony; *Harrod v Harrod* (1854) 1 K & J 4.
2   Book of Common Prayer, Form of Solemnization of Matrimony; *Harrod v Harrod* (1854) 1 K & J 4. As to the celebration of Church of England marriages see PARA 57 et seq.
3   Revised Canons Ecclesiastical, Canon B30 para 1. See also Canon B30 para 2, which states that the teaching of our Lord, affirmed by the Church of England, is expressed and maintained in the Form of Solemnization of Matrimony in the Book of Common Prayer. When application is made to a minister for a marriage in his church it is his duty to explain this doctrine to the parties: see Canon B30 para 3.
4   *Nachimson v Nachimson* [1930] P 217, CA; *Hyde v Hyde and Woodmansee* (1866) LR 1 P & D 130; *Re Bethell, Bethell v Hildyard* (1888) 38 ChD 220; *Sowa v Sowa* [1961] P 70, [1961] 1 All ER 687, CA.
5   *Corbett v Corbett (otherwise Ashley)* [1971] P 83, [1970] 2 All ER 33 (operated male transsexual); *Re Marriage of C and D (falsely called C)* (1979) 35 FLR 340, 5 Fam LR 636; and see Application 9532/81 *Rees v United Kingdom* [1993] 2 FCR 49, [1987] 2 FLR 111, ECtHR; *Cossey v United Kingdom* [1993] 2 FCR 97, [1991] 2 FLR 492, ECtHR (inability of a post-operative male to female transsexual to obtain a birth certificate or contract a valid marriage under English law with a man); *R v Registrar General, ex p P and G* [1996] 2 FCR 588, sub nom *Re P and G (transsexuals)* [1996] 2 FLR 90, DC (two men undergoing 'gender reassignment' surgery); Case C-13/94 *P v S* [1996] All ER (EC) 397, [1996] ECR I-2143, ECJ (sex discrimination); Application 21830/93 *X, Y and Z v United Kingdom* [1997] 3 FCR 341, [1997] 2 FLR 892, ECtHR (refusal to register a post-operative transsexual as the father of a child born to a partner by artificial insemination by donor); Applications 22885/93, 23390/94 *Sheffield and Horsham v United Kingdom* [1998] 3 FCR 141, [1998] 2 FLR 928, ECtHR (no positive obligation to recognise in law the applicants' post-operative gender); *Bellinger v Bellinger* [2000] 3 FCR 733; [2001] 1 FLR 389; affd sub nom *Bellinger v Bellinger*

(Lord Chancellor intervening) [2003] UKHL 21, [2003] 2 AC 467, [2003] 2 All ER 593 (sex of wife indeterminate at birth; wife registered as male at birth; wife undergoing sex-change operation before marriage; social, medical and legal developments since *Corbett v Corbett (otherwise Ashley)* reviewed); *W v W (physical inter-sex)* [2001] Fam 111, [2001] 2 WLR 674 (same). Provision is now made in relation to civil partnerships between same-sex couples: see the Civil Partnership Act 2004; and PARA 2.

6   See the Matrimonial Causes Act 1973 s 11(c); and PARA 326.

7   See *Nachimson v Nachimson* [1930] P 217, CA; *Cheni (otherwise Rodriguez) v Cheni* [1965] P 85, [1962] 3 All ER 873.

8   *Kenward v Kenward* [1951] P 124, [1950] 2 All ER 297, CA.

9   See *Dalrymple v Dalrymple* (1811) 2 Hag Con 54.

2.   Civil partnership. A civil partnership is a relationship between, and affording the same legal status and rights as a married couple to, two people of the same sex[1] which is formed when they register as civil partners of each other[2] or which they are treated[3] as having formed by virtue of having registered an overseas relationship[4]. Two people are not eligible to register as civil partners of each other if they are not of the same sex[5], or if either of them is already a civil partner or is lawfully married[6]. A civil partnership ends only on death, dissolution or annulment[7].

1   Ie 'civil partners': Civil Partnership Act 2004 s 1(1). The Interpretation Act 1978 Sch 1 (amended by the Civil Partnership Act 2004 Sch 27 para 59) defines 'civil partnership' as a civil partnership which exists under or by virtue of the Civil Partnership Act 2004, and provides that any reference to a 'civil partner' is to be read accordingly.

2   Ie in the United Kingdom under the Civil Partnership Act 2004, or outside the United Kingdom under the Civil Partnership (Registration Abroad and Certificates) Order 2005, SI 2005/2761, or the Civil Partnership (Armed Forces) Order 2005, SI 2005/3188: Civil Partnership Act 2004 s 1(1)(a). As to registration in England and Wales see the Civil Partnership Act 2004 Pt 2 (ss 2–84); and PARA 132 et seq. As to registration abroad see PARAS 145–152; and as to registration in the armed forces see PARAS 153–160.

3   Ie under the Civil Partnership Act 2004 Pt 5 Chapter 2 (ss 212–218) (see PARA 19).

4   Civil Partnership Act 2004 s 1(1)(b). References in the Civil Partnership Act 2004 to an 'overseas relationship' are to be read in accordance with Pt 5 Chapter 2: s 1(5). The Civil Partnership Act 2004 s 1(1) is subject to s 49 (void civil partnerships) and s 50 (voidable civil partnerships): see PARA 4; and PARA 331 et seq.

5   Civil Partnership Act 2004 s 3(1)(a). For special provisions relating to gender reassignment see PARA 334.

6   Civil Partnership Act 2004 s 3(1)(b).

7   Civil Partnership Act 2004 s 1(3). References to dissolution and annulment are to dissolution and annulment having effect under or recognised in accordance with the Civil Partnership Act 2004: s 1(4). As to dissolution, nullity and other proceedings see s 37 et seq; and PARA 346 et seq.

3.   Requisites of valid marriage and presumption of validity. The requisites of a valid marriage according to English law are:

(1)   that each of the parties should as regards age and mental and physical capacity be capable of contracting marriage[1];

(2)   that they should not by reason of kindred or affinity be prohibited from marrying one another[2];

(3)   that, except where a second or subsequent polygamous marriage has been entered into under a law that permits polygamy[3], there should not be a valid subsisting marriage or civil partnership of either of the parties with any other person[4];

(4)   that the parties, understanding the nature of the contract, should freely consent to marry one another[5]; and

(5)   that certain forms and ceremonies should be observed[6].

Persons who are deaf and dumb are competent to marry, showing their consent by signs, provided that they sufficiently understand the nature of the contract[7].

Absence of one of the requisites of a valid marriage results in the marriage being void or voidable, and, in the case of marriages celebrated after 31 July 1971, the only grounds on which they may be void or voidable are those laid down by statute[8].

1 See PARA 31 et seq.
2 See PARA 35 et seq.
3 As to polygamous marriages generally see PARA 9; and CONFLICT OF LAWS vol 8(3) (Reissue) PARA 234 et seq.
4 It is immaterial that there may be good faith and an honest belief in the death of the existing wife or husband, and that the circumstances may be such as would not sustain an indictment for bigamy. A marriage during the lifetime of an existing wife or husband must necessarily be void. As to absence of one of the spouses for seven years and the presumption thus raised see PARA 416; CRIMINAL LAW, EVIDENCE AND PROCEDURE vol 11(2) (2006 Reissue) PARAS 828, 831; EVIDENCE vol 17(1) (Reissue) PARAS 580, 581. As to the jurisdiction of the court to grant a decree of presumption of death and dissolution of marriage see PARA 750 et seq; and as to the marriage of divorced persons see PARA 34.
5 As to the consent of parents or guardians in the case of children see PARA 46 et seq. The absence of such consent does not affect the validity of the marriage: see PARA 51.
6 See PARA 53 et seq. As to sham marriages see PARA 11; and as to the effect and consequences of marriages being void see PARA 320.
7 *Harrod v Harrod* (1854) 1 K & J 4 (it is sufficient if they understand that they have agreed to cohabit together during their joint lives and not to cohabit with any other person).
8 As to the grounds on which marriages celebrated after 31 July 1971 may be void or voidable see PARA 344 et seq.

4. Requisites of a civil partnership. The requisites of a valid civil partnership according to English law are:
(1) that each of the parties should as regards age and mental and physical capacity be eligible to register as civil partners of each other[1];
(2) that they should not by reason of being within prohibited degrees of relationship be prohibited from registering as civil partners of one another[2];
(3) that either of them is not already a civil partner or lawfully married[3];
(4) that the parties, understanding the nature of the contract, should freely consent to register as civil partners[4]; and
(5) that certain forms and ceremonies should be observed[5].

Absence of one of the requisites of a valid civil partnership results in it being void or voidable as laid down by statute[6].

1 See the Civil Partnership Act 2004 ss 3(1)(c), 50(1)(a), (b); and PARAS 32, 33, 42.
2 See the Civil Partnership Act 2004 s 3(1)(d); and PARA 35.
3 See the Civil Partnership Act 2004 s 3(1)(b); and PARA 2.
4 See the Civil Partnership Act 2004 s 50(1)(a), (b); and PARAS 331, 332. As to the consent of parents or guardians see PARA 46 et seq. The absence of such consent does not affect the validity of the civil partnership: see PARA 51.
5 As to the forms and ceremonies to be observed in registering a civil partnership see PARA 53 et seq.
6 See the Civil Partnership Act 2004 ss 49, 50; and PARAS 327, 331–334.

5. Validation of civil partnership. The Lord Chancellor may, where two people have registered as civil partners of each other in England and Wales, by order[1] validate the civil partnership if it appears to him that the civil partnership is void[2] because at the time of registration both partners knew:
(1) that the due notice of proposed civil partnership[3] had not been given[4];

(2)   the civil partnership document[5] was not valid[6];

(3)   the place of registration[7] was a place other than that specified in the notice or notices, or was not an approved premises[8]; or

(4)   that a civil partnership registrar[9] was not present[10].

Such an order may include provisions for relieving a person from any liability for certain offences committed in relation to civil partnership schedules[11] and the recording of civil partnerships[12].

1   The draft of an order must be advertised in such manner as the Lord Chancellor thinks fit, not less than one month before the order is made: Civil Partnership Act 2004 s 53(3). The Lord Chancellor must also consider all objections to the order sent to him in writing during that month, and if it appears to him necessary, direct a local inquiry into the validity of any such objections: s 53(4). Such an order is subject to special parliamentary procedure: s 53(5). As to special parliamentary procedure see PARLIAMENT vol 34 (Reissue) PARA 912 et seq.
2   Ie under the Civil Partnership Act 2004 s 49(b) (see PARA 5).
3   As to notice of proposed civil partnership see the Civil Partnership Act 2004 s 8; and PARAS 133, 140.
4   See the Civil Partnership Act 2004 ss 49(b)(i), 53(1); and PARA 133.
5   As to civil partnership documents see the Civil Partnership Act 2004 s 7(1); and PARA 56.
6   See the Civil Partnership Act 2004 s 49(b)(ii), (iii); and PARA 327.
7   As to the place of registration see the Civil Partnership Act 2004 s 6; and PARA 56.
8   See the Civil Partnership Act 2004 s 49(b)(iv), (vi); and PARA 56.
9   As to the civil partnership registrar see the Civil Partnership Act 2004 s 29; and PARA 139 note 8.
10 See s 49(b)(v); and PARA 139.
11 Ie the offences under the Civil Partnership Act 2004 s 31(2), 32(2), 33(5) or (7). As to civil partnership schedules see the Civil Partnership Act 2004 s 14(1); and PARA 138.
12 Civil Partnership Act 2004 s 53(2).

6.   Presumption from cohabitation without ceremony. Where a man and woman have cohabited for such a length of time, and in such circumstances, as to have acquired the reputation of being man and wife, a lawful marriage between them will be presumed[1], even if there is no positive evidence of any marriage ceremony having taken place[2], particularly where the relevant facts have occurred outside the jurisdiction; and this presumption can be rebutted only by strong and weighty evidence to the contrary[3].

1   Cohabitation and reputation are not, however, sufficient proof of a first marriage in bigamy proceedings: see CRIMINAL LAW, EVIDENCE AND PROCEDURE vol 11(2) (2006 Reissue) PARA 832.
2   As to the presumption arising where a ceremony has taken place see PARA 21.
3   *Re Shephard, George v Thyer* [1904] 1 Ch 456; *Wilkinson v Payne* (1791) 4 Term Rep 468; *Doe d Fleming v Fleming* (1827) 4 Bing 266; *Doe d Earl of Egremont v Grazebrook* (1843) 4 QB 406; *Piers v Piers* (1849) 2 HL Cas 331 (followed in *Hill v Hill* [1959] 1 All ER 281, [1959] 1 WLR 127, PC); *Goodman v Goodman* (1859) 28 LJ Ch 745 (cohabitation of a Jew with a Christian woman for 28 years); *Rooker v Rooker and Newton* (1863) 33 LJPM & A 42 (cohabitation for five years in Virginia); *Patrickson v Patrickson* (1865) LR 1 P & D 86; *Breadalbane Case, Campbell v Campbell* (1867) LR 1 Sc & Div 182, HL (a connection, adulterous at first, may become matrimonial); *Lyle v Ellwood* (1874) LR 19 Eq 98; *Collins v Bishop* (1878) 48 LJ Ch 31; *De Thoren v A-G* (1876) 1 App Cas 686, HL (Scots doctrine of 'habit and repute'); *Re M'Loughlin's Estate* (1878) 1 LR Ir 421, Ir CA; *Sastry Velaider Aronegary v Sembecutty Vaigalie* (1881) 6 App Cas 364; *Fox v Bearblock* (1881) 17 ChD 429; *Re Ivory, Chippendale v Ivory* (1886) 2 TLR 468; *Andrewes v Uthwatt* (1886) 2 TLR 895; *Elliott v Totnes Union* (1892) 9 TLR 35; *Wigley v Treasury Solicitor* [1902] P 233; *Lauderdale Peerage* (1885) 10 App Cas 692, HL; *Re Haynes, Haynes v Carter* (1906) 94 LT 431 (cohabitation of man and woman, with two children, from 1878 to 1893); *Re Thompson, Langhan v Thompson* (1904) 91 LT 680 (cohabitation as man and wife from 1856 to 1866; five children; reputed by friends and neighbours to be married; separation in 1866; marriage in 1874 of the man, during lifetime of the woman, to another woman; presumption of marriage held to have been established); *Re Green, Noyes v Pitkin* (1909) 25 TLR 222 (foreign marriage); *Re Taplin, Watson v Tate* [1937] 3 All ER 105; *McCarthy v Hastings* [1933] NI 100, CA; *Re*

Bradshaw, Blandy v Willis [1938] 4 All ER 143 (presumption rebutted by certificate of later marriage between the parties); *Re Taylor, Taylor v Taylor* [1961] 1 All ER 55, [1961] 1 WLR 9, CA (evidence of cohabitation and acceptance as husband and wife by a small community for five years; no clear evidence to rebut presumption of marriage); *Rumsey v Sterne* (1967) 111 Sol Jo 113. Cf *Sackville-West v A-G* [1910] P 143 (declaration of validity refused); *Watson-Parker v Watson-Parker* (1967) Times, 2 March (Gretna Green ceremony held to be valid marriage); *Taczanowska (otherwise Roth) v Taczanowski* [1957] P 301, [1957] 2 All ER 563, CA, overruling *Holdowanski v Holdowanska (otherwise Bialoszewska) and Price* [1956] 3 All ER 457; followed in *Kochanski v Kochanska* [1958] P 147, [1957] 3 All ER 142 (marriage of Poles in what was held to be a displaced persons' camp which had been placed under the direction of the British Occupying Forces); *Merker v Merker* [1963] P 283, [1962] 3 All ER 928; *Preston (otherwise Putynski) v Preston (otherwise Putnyska) (otherwise Basinska)* [1963] P 141, [1962] 3 All ER 1057; affd [1963] P 411, [1963] 2 All ER 405, CA (courts should be reluctant to extend the instances where compliance with the lex loci was unnecessary to constitute a valid marriage); *Oleszko (formerly Pietrucha) v Pietrucha* (1963) Times, 22 March (marriage of inmates of displaced persons' camp, not members of a military force of an occupying power but part of a Polish community living separate from local population; parties held not to have subjected themselves to the local law); *Pazpena de Vire v Pazpena de Vire* [2001] 1 FLR 460, [2001] Fam Law 95 (husband claimed that he had forged marriage certificate; 35 years of cohabitation as husband and wife and public recognition as such); but see *Preston (otherwise Putynski) v Preston (otherwise Putnyska) (otherwise Basinska)*; and CONFLICT OF LAWS vol 8(3) (Reissue) PARAS 211, 213. Cf *Lazarewicz (otherwise Fadanelli) v Lazarewicz* [1962] P 171, [1962] 2 All ER 5 (parties deliberately submitted themselves to the local law when celebrating their marriage; husband was Polish, wife Italian; void by local law; common law not applicable; marriage null and void in England); and CONFLICT OF LAWS vol 8(3) (Reissue) PARA 208. See also *Mahadervan v Mahadervan* [1964] P 233, [1962] 3 All ER 1108, DC; *Kalinowska v Kalinowski (Balentine intervening)* (1964) 108 Sol Jo 260; *Wicken v Wicken* [1999] Fam 224, [1999] 2 WLR 1166; *Chief Adjudication Officer v Bath* [2000] 1 FCR 419, [2000] 1 FLR 8, CA.

7.   **Presumption from cohabitation after ceremony.**   Where there is evidence of a ceremony of marriage having been conducted, followed by the cohabitation of the parties, everything necessary for the validity of the marriage will be presumed, in the absence of decisive evidence to the contrary[1], even though it may be necessary to presume the granting of a special licence[2], or the death of a former spouse[3]. Where the formalities are challenged, there is an equally strong presumption that they have been properly observed[4]. While this presumption as to validity of marriage may be rebutted, the evidence in rebuttal must be firm and clear[5]. In most cases a certificate of marriage will be available, and this will usually suffice to prove the marriage[6]. The principle which emerges from the corpus of legislation regulating the formation of marriages in England and Wales, and from the reported cases arising from it, is that, if a ceremony of marriage has taken place which, as a ceremony, would be sufficient to constitute a valid marriage, the courts will hold the marriage valid unless constrained by express statutory provision to hold otherwise[7].

1   *Mahadervan v Mahadervan* [1964] P 233, [1962] 3 All ER 1108, DC. The presumption is not rendered inapplicable by cohabitation having also preceded the marriage: *Hill v Hill* [1959] 1 All ER 281, [1959] 1 WLR 127, PC. Where there has been a ceremony of marriage followed by cohabitation, the presumption of a valid marriage cannot be rebutted merely by showing that it could not be valid according to the lex loci celebrationis: *Re Shephard, George v Thyer* [1904] 1 Ch 456; *Goldstone v Smith (otherwise Goldstone)* (1922) 127 LT 32 (Jewish ceremony performed in Russia believed valid by others present; husband represented himself as married, person who performed ceremony presumed to have been an authorised person); *Spivack v Spivack* (1930) 99 LJP 52 (similar case); *McCarthy v Hastings* [1933] NI 100, HL (evidence of ceremony; cohabitation and reputation as man and wife); *Russell v A-G* [1949] P 391 (marriage at Roman Catholic church; it was alleged that 21 days had not elapsed between the date of notice of the marriage and the ceremony and that no registrar was present; validity of the marriage was to be presumed in the absence of decisive evidence to the contrary, even though it might be necessary to presume the grant of a special licence); *Taylor v Taylor* [1967] P 25,

[1965] 1 All ER 872; cf *Taczanowska (otherwise Roth) v Taczanowski* [1957] P 301, [1957] 2 All ER 563, CA. See also *Chief Adjudication Officer v Bath* [2000] 1 FCR 419, [2000] 1 FLR 8, CA (where a man and a woman went through a ceremony of marriage at a place of worship which, unbeknown to them, was not registered under the Marriage Act 1949 and thereafter lived together as man and wife for 37 years; valid marriage presumed; s 49 (see PARA 330) did not render the marriage void since the parties were not aware of non-compliance with formal requirements); *A-M v A-M (divorce: jurisdiction: validity of marriage)* [2001] 2 FLR 6 (polygamous Islamic marriage).

2   *Piers v Piers* (1849) 2 HL Cas 331 (marriage solemnised by a clergyman in a private house, as if by special licence; no such licence, record of it or registration of the marriage could be found; 30 years later the bishop testified his belief that he had not granted the licence; but it might have been granted by his predecessor, who died a year and a half before the marriage; the grant of a special licence was to be presumed), followed in *Hill v Hill* [1959] 1 All ER 281, [1959] 1 WLR 127, PC; *R v Manwaring* (1856) Dears & B 132 (due registration of dissenting chapel presumed); *Sichel v Lambert* (1864) 15 CBNS 781 (evidence of solemnisation in a Roman Catholic church, followed by cohabitation; it was to be presumed that the chapel was duly registered, and that a registrar of marriages was present). See also *Lauderdale Peerage* (1885) 10 App Cas 692, HL; *Sastry Velaider Aronegary v Sembecutty Vaigalie* (1881) 6 App Cas 364.

3   *Tweney v Tweney* [1946] P 180, [1946] 1 All ER 564 (wife previously married but husband deserted her and was never heard of again, although exhaustive inquiries were made; after a lapse of ten years wife married again and described herself as a widow; she then sought a decree of dissolution of the second marriage on the ground of desertion; it was held that the court had jurisdiction to dissolve the second marriage as, it having been in proper form and duly consummated, it was to be deemed to be a valid marriage unless the contrary be proved); but see *Re Peete, Peete v Crompton* [1952] 2 All ER 599 (where it was held that the court could not accept the marriage certificate as proof of a valid marriage where the wife had described herself as a widow on hearsay evidence alone as to the death of her first husband); cf *Re Watkins, Watkins v Watkins* [1953] 2 All ER 1113 (where the facts were similar, but the lapse of time between the husband's disappearance and the wife's remarriage was much longer; it was held that on the facts a jury would be entitled to infer the death of the husband before the remarriage, and that, in the absence of evidence to the contrary, the certificate of the remarriage should be accepted as proof of its validity). See also *Ward v Ward* [1956] CLY 2816, CA (where it was held that the disappearance of the husband for a period of over seven years before the wife's remarriage, notwithstanding efforts made to trace him, entitled the wife to assume that he had died before that ceremony, which was accordingly valid); *Chard v Chard (otherwise Northcott)* [1956] P 259, [1955] 3 All ER 721; *Thompson v Thompson* [1956] P 414, [1956] 1 All ER 603. In *Berzins (otherwise Lilje) v Berzins* [1956] CLY 2817, the petitioner had married in Latvia in 1940, and shortly afterwards her husband was arrested by the occupying forces. A year later all prisoners were released, but the husband could not be traced. In 1947 the petitioner remarried in England. In 1954 she received a letter from Latvia which indicated that the first husband might be alive, and in 1955 a letter which she swore was in his handwriting. On this evidence and having regard to *Chard v Chard (otherwise Northcott)* the second ceremony of marriage was annulled.

4   *Mahadervan v Mahadervan* [1964] P 233, [1962] 3 All ER 1108, DC.

5   *Mahadervan v Mahadervan* [1964] P 233, [1962] 3 All ER 1108, DC. See further PARA 6.

6   See PARA 25; and EVIDENCE vol 17(1) (Reissue) PARAS 843, 844.

7   *Collett v Collett* [1968] P 482, [1967] 2 All ER 426.

8.   Domicile of parties. If a marriage is celebrated in England or Wales between parties of full age[1] and capacity, with the forms and ceremonies required by English law, its validity in England is not affected by the fact that the law of the domicile of either of the parties, being a foreigner, is not complied with as regards the consent of the parents or the observance of any formalities required by that law[2]. It follows that a marriage may be valid in England and Wales and void by the law of the domicile of both or either of the parties[3].

Where satisfactory arrangements have been made with any foreign country for the issue, in the case of persons who are subject to the marriage law of that country and propose to marry British subjects in any part of the United Kingdom other than Scotland, of certificates that, after proper notices have been given, no impediment according to the law of that country has been shown to exist to the marriage, Her Majesty may by Order in Council make regulations requiring any person subject to the marriage law of that country who is to be married to a British subject in any part of the United Kingdom other than Scotland to give notice of the fact that he is subject to such law to the person by or in the presence of whom the marriage is to be solemnised, and forbidding any person to whom notice is so given to solemnise the marriage or to allow it to be solemnised until such a certificate is produced to him[4].

Any person knowingly acting in contravention of, or failing to comply with, any such regulation is guilty of an offence and liable to imprisonment for a term not exceeding one year or to a fine[5].

These provisions do not apply to marriages between two persons professing the Jewish religion solemnised according to the usages of the Jews in the presence of a secretary of a synagogue duly authorised to register such marriages[6], or of a deputy appointed by that secretary by writing under his hand, and approved by the president for the time being of the London Committee of Deputies of the British Jews by writing under his hand[7].

1   See PARA 41.
2   See CONFLICT OF LAWS vol 8(3) (Reissue) PARA 208 et seq. As to the effect of marriage on the
     nationality and status of women see BRITISH NATIONALITY, IMMIGRATION AND ASYLUM vol 4(2)
     (2002 Reissue) PARA 17 et seq.
3   See note 2.
4   See the Marriage with Foreigners Act 1906 s 2(1); and PARA 128. At the date at which this
     volume states the law no such order had been made. As to marriages abroad generally see PARA
     119 et seq.
5   See the Marriage with Foreigners Act 1906 s 2(2); and PARA 128.
6   Ie authorised by the Marriage Act 1949 s 53(c): see REGISTRATION CONCERNING THE
     INDIVIDUAL vol 39(2) (Reissue) PARA 558.
7   See the Marriage with Foreigners Act 1906 s 2(3); and PARA 128. As to the London Committee
     of Deputies of the British Jews see ECCLESIASTICAL LAW vol 14 PARA 1426.

9.   Polygamous marriages.   A marriage entered into outside England and Wales between parties neither of whom is already married is not void under English law on the ground that it is entered into under a law which permits polygamy[1] and that either party is domiciled in England and Wales[2]. A court in England and Wales is not precluded from granting matrimonial relief[3] or making a declaration concerning the validity of a marriage[4] by reason only that either party to the marriage is, or has during the subsistence of the marriage been, married to more than one person[5].

1   As to polygamous marriages see CONFLICT OF LAWS vol 8(3) (Reissue) PARA 234 et seq.
2   See the Private International Law (Miscellaneous Provisions) Act 1995 s 5(1); and CONFLICT OF
     LAWS vol 8(3) (Reissue) PARA 240. This does not affect the determination of the validity of a
     marriage by reference to the law of another country to the extent that it falls to be so determined
     in accordance with the rules of private international law: s 5(2).
3   For these purposes 'matrimonial relief' means: (1) any decree under the Matrimonial Causes
     Act 1973 Pt I (ss 1–20) (see PARA 319 et seq); (2) a financial provision order under s 27 (see
     PARA 542 et seq); (3) an order under s 35 (see PARA 700) altering a maintenance agreement; (4)
     an order under any provision of the Matrimonial Causes Act 1973 which confers a power
     exercisable in connection with, or in connection with proceedings for, such decree or order as is
     mentioned in heads (1)–(3); (5) an order under the Matrimonial and Family Proceedings
     Act 1984 Pt III (ss 12–27) (see PARA 530 et seq); (6) an order under the Domestic Proceedings
     and Magistrates' Courts Act 1978 Pt I (ss 1–35) (see PARA 553 et seq): Matrimonial Causes
     Act 1973 s 47(2) (amended by the Domestic Proceedings and Magistrates' Courts Act 1978
     Sch 2 para 39; the Matrimonial and Family Proceedings Act 1984 Sch 1).
4   For these purposes, 'declaration concerning the validity of a marriage' means any declaration
     under the Family Law Act 1986 Pt III (ss 55–62) (see PARA 1000 et seq) involving a

determination as to the validity of a marriage: Matrimonial Causes Act 1973 s 47(3) (substituted by the Family Law Act 1986 Sch 1 para 14).

5   Matrimonial Causes Act 1973 s 47(1) (amended by the Private International Law (Miscellaneous Provisions) Act 1995 s 8(2), Schedule para 2(3)(a)). The Matrimonial Causes Act 1973 s 47 (as originally enacted) abolished the rule in *Hyde v Hyde and Woodmansee* (1866) LR 1 P & D 130, under which a party to a polygamous marriage was not entitled to matrimonial relief or to a declaration as to the validity of marriage in the English courts.

Provision may be made by rules of court: (1) for requiring notice of proceedings brought by virtue of the Matrimonial Causes Act 1973 s 47 to be served on any additional spouse of a party to the marriage in question; and (2) for conferring on any such additional spouse the right to be heard in the proceedings, in such cases as may be specified in the rules: s 47(4) (substituted by the Private International Law (Miscellaneous Provisions) Act 1995 Schedule para 2(3)(b)). As to proceedings in respect of polygamous marriages see PARA 1010.

10.   Bigamous marriages.

10.   Bigamous marriages. Bigamy, that is to say having two living spouses, is forbidden by English law, both civil[1] and criminal[2]. A marriage will be declared null and void where one or both of the spouses was or were, at the time of the marriage the subject of the suit, party or parties to a prior valid and subsisting marriage to another person or persons, as the case may be[3].

1   See the Matrimonial Causes Act 1973 s 11(b); and PARA 326.
2   See CRIMINAL LAW, EVIDENCE AND PROCEDURE vol 11(2) (2006 Reissue) PARA 828 et seq.
3   *Dalrymple v Dalrymple* (1811) 2 Hag Con 54; *Chard v Chard* [1956] P 259, [1955] 3 All ER 721 (petitioner entitled to decree of nullity on the ground of his own bigamy); *Bennett v Bennett* (1961) 105 Sol Jo 885, CA (husband, then aged 40, disappeared in 1945; wife 'remarried' in 1950; it was held, on the balance of probabilities, that the first husband was alive in 1950, and so the second marriage was void for bigamy); *Kassim (otherwise Widmann) v Kassim (otherwise Hassim)* [1962] P 224, [1962] 3 All ER 426 (marriage in July 1945 by native ceremony in Southern Rhodesia; further ceremony in same month in accordance with the Southern Rhodesian Marriage Act; later the husband married another woman in South Africa, first by native custom, and secondly by Sunni law; in June 1952 the husband went through a ceremony of marriage with a third woman in Kensington in accordance with the rites of the Roman Catholic Church; on proof of the marriage of July 1945 under the Southern Rhodesia Marriage Act, and assuming that such marriage was polygamous and not monogamous, it was held that the marriage in June 1952 was bigamous and void: decree of nullity pronounced), applying *Hayes (falsely called Watts) v Watts* (1819) 3 Phillim 43; *Bowzer v Ricketts (falsely calling herself Bowzer)* (1795) 1 Hag Con 213; and *Bruce v Burke* (1825) 2 Add 471; cf *Re Kirby and Watson's Marriage* (1977) 3 Fam LR 11, 318 (no presumption that woman of 37 dead after eight years' absence). As to the standard of proof where an issue arises as to the authenticity and effect of a document purporting to dissolve an earlier marriage see *Wicken v Wicken* [1999] Fam 224, [1999] 2 WLR 1166.

11.   Sham marriages and civil partnerships.

11.   Sham marriages and civil partnerships. A marriage or civil partnership is a sham marriage or civil partnership if a least one of the parties to it is neither a British citizen[1] nor a national of another EEA state[2] and it is entered into for the purpose or effect of avoiding United Kingdom immigration law or the immigration rules[3].

If a superintendant registrar to whom notice of marriage has been given[4], a registration authority to whom a notice of proposed civil partnership has been given[5], or any other person who has attested a declaration accompanying such a notice[6], has reasonable grounds for suspecting that the marriage or civil partnership will be a sham marriage or civil partnership, the person concerned must report his suspicion to the Secretary of State without delay[7].

1   As to the meaning of 'British citizen' see BRITISH NATIONALITY, IMMIGRATION AND ASYLUM vol 4(2) (2002 Reissue) PARA 23 et seq.
2   'EEA state' means a state which is a contracting party to the Agreement on the European Economic Area (Oporto, 2 May 1992 (Cm 2073; OJ L1, 3.1.94, p 3)); adjusted by the Protocol (Brussels, 17 March 1993 (OJ L1, 3.1.94, p 572)), as it has effect for the time being: Immigration and Asylum Act 1999 s 167(1).

3   Immigration and Asylum Act 1999 ss 24(5), 24A(5) (s 24A added by the Civil Partnership Act 2004 Sch 27 para 162). 'Immigration rules' has the same meaning as in the Immigration Act 1971 (see BRITISH NATIONALITY, IMMIGRATION AND ASYLUM vol 4(2) (2002 Reissue) PARA 83): Immigration and Asylum Act 1999 s 167(2). Such a marriage or civil partnership is a sham marriage or civil partnership whether it is also void or not: Immigration and Asylum Act 1999 ss 24(5), 24A(5) (s 24A(5) as so added). As to void marriages and civil partnerships generally see PARA 326 et seq.

4   Ie under the Marriage Act 1949 s 27 (see PARA 87).

5   Ie under the Civil Partnership Act 2004 s 8 (see PARAS 133, 140).

6   Ie under the Marriage Act 1949 s 28(2) (see PARA 90) or the Civil Partnership Act 2004 s 8 (see PARAS 133, 140).

7   Immigration and Asylum Act 1999 ss 24(1)(a), (3), 24A(1)(a), (3) (s 24A as added: see note 3). Such regulations are to be made, in relation to England and Wales, by the Registrar General for England and Wales with the approval of the Chancellor of the Exchequer: ss 24(4), 24A(4) (s 24A(4) as so added; amended by SI 2008/678). Accordingly, in relation to marriages, a registration officer must: (1) report his suspicions to the Secretary of State by making a report in writing or other permanent form, giving the following information: (a) the name and surname of each party to the marriage; (b) the date of birth and/or age of each party to the marriage; (c) the condition of each party to the marriage; (d) the address (and district of residence) of each party to the marriage; (e) the nationality of each party to the marriage; (f) the date of marriage; (g) the place of marriage; (h) the time of marriage; (i) the nature of evidence produced in respect of name and age, condition and nationality of the parties to the marriage; (j) the reason for making the report; (k) the full name of the registration officer making the report; and (l) the date the report is made; and (2) forward that report to the address specified or, where the Secretary of State has notified the Registrar General of another address to be used in relation to any particular registration district, that address: Immigration and Asylum Act 1999 s 24(3); Reporting of Suspicious Marriages and Registration of Marriages (Miscellaneous Amendments) Regulations 2000, SI 2000/3164, reg 2, Sch 1 (amended by SI 2005/3177). In relation to civil partnerships, a registration officer must: (i) report his suspicions to the Secretary of State by making a report in writing or other permanent form giving the following information: (A) the name and surname of each of the civil partners; (B) the date of birth and/or age of each of the civil partners; (C) the sex of each of the civil partners; (D) the condition of each of the civil partners; (E) the address (and registration authority) of each of the civil partners; (F) the nationality of each of the civil partners; (G) the date of formation of the civil partnership; (H) the place of formation of the civil partnership; (I) the time of the civil partnership; (J) the nature of evidence produced in respect of name and age, condition and nationality of the of the civil partners; (K) the reason for making the report; (L) the full name of the registration officer making the report; (M) the name of the registration authority on whose behalf the report is being made; and (N) the date the report is made; and (ii) forward that report to the address specified or, where the Secretary of State has notified the Registrar General of another address to be used in relation to any particular registration district, that address: Immigration and Asylum Act 1999 s 24A(3) (as so added); Reporting of Suspicious Civil Partnerships Regulations 2005, SI 2005/3174, reg 2, Sch 1.

12.   Arranged and forced marriages. An arranged marriage is not invalid as such, although it would be otherwise if the marriage were in consequence of threats to life, limb or liberty or some equally serious threat[1]. A forced marriage is similarly not unlawful, but where threats or duress are proven may well be invalid owing to an absence of consent[2]. Provision has been made under civil law to protect persons who have been, or are at risk of being, forced into marriage by the making of forced marriage protection orders[3].

1   *Singh v Kaur* (1981) 11 Fam Law 152, CA; *Hirani v Hirani* (1982) 4 FLR 232, CA.

2   See PARA 51.

3   See the Family Law Act 1996 ss 63A–63S; and PARA 723 et seq.

13.   Royal weddings. Nothing in the Marriage Act 1949 or the Marriage Act 1983 affects any law or custom relating to the marriage of members of the royal family[1].

1   Marriage Act 1949 s 79(5); Marriage Act 1983 s 12(3). As to the monarch's consent to royal marriages see CROWN AND ROYAL FAMILY vol 12(1) (Reissue) PARA 36.

14. Statutes confirming invalid marriages. Numerous statutes, both public and private, have from time to time been passed legalising marriages which were invalid and confirming others of doubtful validity by reason of their having been solemnised in a church or chapel or other place not duly licensed or registered for the solemnisation of marriages, or without the presence of a duly ordained clergyman, or by reason of some other irregularity or informality[1].

1   The following are the more important Acts which contained provisions of general application in relation to England: 21 Geo 3 c 53 (1780–81) (repealed); the Marriages Confirmation Act 1804 (repealed); the Marriages Confirmation Act 1808 (repealed); 3 Geo 4 c 75 (1822) ss 2–7 (marriages solemnised without consent of parent or guardian) (repealed); 4 Geo 4 c 5 (1823) (licences granted by unauthorised persons) (repealed); the Marriages Confirmation Act 1825 (marriages in churches and chapels erected since 1753) (in part repealed); the Marriage Confirmation Act 1830 s 1 (repealed), s 3 and ss 4, 5 (repealed) (marriages during repair or rebuilding of church or chapel (cf the Marriage Act 1949 ss 18, 19; and PARA 61), marriages in certain newly-built parish churches, in churches or chapels duly consecrated but not authorised, and in chapels where consecration doubtful); the Church Building (Banns and Marriages) Act 1844 s 3 (marriages in certain district chapelries) (repealed); 10 & 11 Vict c 58 (1847) (Quakers' and Jews' marriages) (repealed); the Church Building Act 1851 s 25 (marriages at certain churches without authority before 1851) (repealed); the Places of Worship Registration Act 1855 s 13 (marriages in buildings registered but not certified) (repealed); 24 & 25 Vict c 16 (1861) s 4 (marriages in churches or chapels consecrated but not authorised) (repealed); the Greek Marriages Act 1884 (marriages of members of Greek Church in England) (repealed); the Marriages Validity Act 1886 (repealed); the Marriages Validity Act 1899 (repealed); the Marriages Validity Act 1939 (repealed) (banns published in Scotland or Ireland: see now the Marriage Act 1949 s 13; and PARA 73). In addition numerous other Acts have been passed relating eg to marriages in particular churches or chapels or to marriages in particular places abroad. As to foreign validating Acts cf *Starkowski v A-G* [1954] AC 155, [1953] 2 All ER 1272, HL.

15. Confirmation by order. In the case of marriages solemnised in England which appear to him to be invalid or of doubtful validity by reason of some lack of formality, the Lord Chancellor may make an order for the purpose of removing the invalidity or doubt[1]. The order may include such supplemental, incidental and consequential provisions, including provisions for relieving from liability ministers who may have solemnised the marriages to which the order relates, as appear to the Lord Chancellor to be necessary or expedient[2]. The draft of every such order must be advertised in such manner as the Lord Chancellor thinks fit, not less than one month before the order is made; and he must consider all objections to the order sent to him in writing during that month, and must, if it appears to him necessary, direct a local inquiry into the validity of any such objections[3]. The order is subject to special parliamentary procedure[4].

1   Provisional Order (Marriages) Act 1905 s 1(1) (amended by SI 1949/2393).
2   Marriages Validity (Provisional Orders) Act 1924 s 1 (amended by SI 1949/2393).
3   Provisional Order (Marriages) Act 1905 s 1(2). After the holding of an inquiry the Lord Chancellor must, if requested, give the reasons for his decision: see the Tribunals and Inquiries Act 1992 s 10(1); the Tribunals and Inquiries (Discretionary Inquiries) Order 1975, SI 1975/1379, Schedule para 5; and ADMINISTRATIVE LAW vol 1(1) (2001 Reissue) PARA 112.
4   Provisional Order (Marriages) Act 1905 s 1(3) (amended by SI 1949/2393). As to special parliamentary procedure see PARLIAMENT vol 34 (Reissue) PARA 912 et seq.

16. Agreements to marry or to form civil partnership not enforceable at law. An agreement between two persons to marry one another, or an agreement between two persons to register as civil partners of each other[1] or to enter into an overseas relationship[2] (a 'civil partnership agreement'[3]), does not have effect as a contract giving rise to legal rights, and no action lies in England and Wales for breach of such an agreement, whatever the law applicable to the agreement[4].

1   Ie in England and Wales under the Civil Partnership Act 2004 Pt II (ss 1–84), in Scotland under Pt 3 (ss 97–123), in Northern Ireland under Pt 4 (ss 137–209), or outside the United Kingdom under an Order in Council made under Pt 5 Chapter 1 (ss 210–211) (see PARAS 145, 153).

2   As to the meaning of 'overseas relationship' see PARA 19 note 1.

3   Civil Partnership Act 2004 s 73(3).

4   Law Reform (Miscellaneous Provisions) Act 1970 s 1(1); Civil Partnership Act 2004 s 73(1), (2). These provisions have effect in relation to agreements to marry and civil partnership agreements whenever entered into but do not affect any action concerning an agreement to marry commenced before 1 January 1971 (ie the date on which the Law Reform (Miscellaneous Provisions) Act 1970 s 1 was brought into force by virtue of s 7(3)) or any action concerning a civil partnership agreement commenced before 5 December 2005 (ie the date on which the Civil Partnership Act 2004 s 73 was brought into force by virtue of the Civil Partnership Act 2004 (Commencement No 2) Order 2005, SI 2005/3175): see the Law Reform (Miscellaneous Provisions) Act 1970 s 1(2) and the Civil Partnership Act 2004 s 73(4).

     For the former law as to the formation of a contract to marry see *Vineall v Veness* (1865) 4 F & F 344 (there must be mutual promises); *Skipp v Kelly* (1926) 42 TLR 258, PC; *Jacobs v Davis* [1917] 2 KB 532; *Cohen v Sellar* [1926] 1 KB 536 (inference of mutual promises from the conduct of the parties, such as the giving of an engagement ring); *Bessela v Stern* (1877) 2 CPD 265, CA; *Harvey v Johnston* (1848) 6 CB 295 (inference drawn from parties' behaviour); *Hutton v Mansell* (1705) 3 Salk 16; *Daniel v Bowles* (1826) 2 CP 553 (behaviour to indicate acceptance of marriage offer); *Cole v Cottingham* (1837) 8 C & P 75 (declaration of intent to third party is not a promise of marriage). As to considerations of public policy under the old law where an action for breach of promise lay see *Wilson v Carnley* [1908] 1 KB 729, CA (where a promise by a married man to marry the plaintiff after the death of his wife was held void); *Robinson v Smith* [1915] 1 KB 711, CA; cf *Fender v St John-Mildmay* [1938] AC 1, sub nom *Fender v Mildmay*[1937] 3 All ER 402, HL (where it was held that the principle did not apply in the case of a promise made after a decree nisi of divorce to marry after the decree had been made absolute). A promise of marriage made in consideration of the promisee permitting the promisor to have sexual intercourse with her was void: *Morton v Fenn* (1783) 3 Doug KB 211. As to the minimum age for marriage and civil partnership see PARA 41.

(ii) Foreign and Overseas Marriages and Civil Partnerships

17.   Marriages outside England and Wales. A marriage solemnised in the manner provided by the Foreign Marriage Act 1892 in any foreign country or place, by or before a marriage officer[1], between parties of whom at least one is a United Kingdom national, is as valid as if it had been solemnised in the United Kingdom with a due observance of all the forms required by law[2].

Where the local forms are inapplicable, or where there is insuperable difficulty in complying with them, a marriage is formally valid if celebrated in accordance with the English common law[3].

Special provisions apply to marriages in merchant ships[4]; marriages in countries under belligerent occupation[5]; and marriages by chaplains of Her Majesty's forces[6].

The forms and ceremonies required for marriages in British possessions overseas have been prescribed, in most cases, by local legislation[7].

Where a marriage is intended to be solemnised or contracted in a part of Her Majesty's dominions[8] outside the United Kingdom, or in a British protectorate[9], to which the Marriage of British Subjects (Facilities) Act 1915 has been applied[10], between a British subject resident in that part and a British subject resident in England, Wales, Scotland or Northern Ireland, a certificate for marriage may be issued in England or Wales by a superintendent registrar, or in Scotland or Northern Ireland by a registrar, in the like manner as if the marriage was to be solemnised or contracted under circumstances requiring the issue of such a certificate and as if both such British subjects were resident in England, Wales, Scotland or Northern Ireland[11].

1   As to marriage officers see the Foreign Marriage Act 1892 s 11; and PARA 119 et seq.

2   See the Foreign Marriage Act 1892 s 1(1); and PARA 119 et seq.
3   See CONFLICT OF LAWS vol 8(3) (Reissue) PARA 211.
4   See CONFLICT OF LAWS vol 8(3) (Reissue) PARA 212.
5   See CONFLICT OF LAWS vol 8(3) (Reissue) PARA 213.
6   See CONFLICT OF LAWS vol 8(3) (Reissue) PARA 214.
7   See eg *Hill v Hill* [1959] 1 All ER 281, [1959] 1 WLR 127, PC (Barbados); *Mahadervan v Mahadervan* [1964] P 233, [1962] 3 All ER 1108, DC (Sri Lanka). As to the validation of marriages contracted in a dependent British territory see the Colonial Marriages Act 1865 s 1; and CONFLICT OF LAWS vol 8(3) (Reissue) PARAS 208, 210.
8   As to the meaning of 'Her Majesty's dominions' see COMMONWEALTH vol 6 (2003 Reissue) PARA 703.
9   As to the extension of these provisions to protectorates see PARA 114.
10 As to the territories to which the Marriage of British Subjects (Facilities) Act 1915 has been applied see PARA 114.
11 Marriage of British Subjects (Facilities) Act 1915 s 1(1)(b).

18. Civil partnerships outside England and Wales. A civil partnership registered in the manner provided by the Civil Partnership Act 2004 in a specified country or territory, by or before a civil partnership officer[1], between parties of whom at least one is a United Kingdom national, is as valid as if it had been registered in the United Kingdom with a due observance of all the forms required by law[2].

Special provision is made for a civil partnership to be registered in a foreign country or place where one of the proposed civil partners is a member of a part of Her Majesty's forces and is employed in the country or territory[3].

1   'Civil partnership officer' means a British Consular officer: Civil Partnership (Registration Abroad and Certificates) Order 2005, SI 2005/2761. As to the procedure for civil partnerships abroad see PARA 145 et seq.
2   See the Civil Partnership Act 2004 s 210; the Civil Partnership (Registration Abroad and Certificates) Order 2005, SI 2005/2761; and PARAS 145–152.
3   See the Civil Partnership Act 2004 s 211; the Civil Partnership (Armed Forces) Order 2005, SI 2005/3188; and PARAS 153–160.

19. Overseas relationships treated as civil partnerships. Two people who have registered an overseas relationship[1] are to be treated as having formed a civil partnership if under the relevant law[2] they had the capacity to enter into the relationship and met all the necessary requirements[3]. However, they are not to be treated as having formed a civil partnership if:

(1)   they were not of the same sex under United Kingdom law[4] at the critical time[5];

(2)   at the critical time either party was under 16 or would have been within the prohibited degrees of relationship if they had been registered as civil partner in England and Wales[6]; or

(3)   it was manifestly contrary to public policy to recognise the capacity, under the relevant law, of one or both of them to enter into the relationship[7].

1   'Overseas relationship' means a relationship which is: (1) either a specified relationship or a relationship which meets the general conditions; and (2) is registered, whether before or after 18 November 2004 (ie the day that the Civil Partnership Act 2004 received the Royal Assent), with a responsible authority in a country or territory outside the United Kingdom, by two people: (a) who under the relevant law are of the same sex at the time when they do so; and (b) neither of whom is already a civil partner or lawfully married: s 212(1). 'Specified relationship' means certain relationships in the following countries or territories: Andorra, Australia, Belgium, Canada, Denmark, Finland, France, Germany, Iceland, Luxembourg, Netherlands, New Zealand, Norway, Spain, Sweden, and the United States of America: s 213(1), Sch 20 (Sch 20 amended by SI 2005/3129; SI 2005/3135). The Lord Privy Seal may by order add a

relationship, amend the description of a relationship, or omit a relationship from the list of specified relationships: Civil Partnership Act 2004 s 213(2) (amended by SI 2007/2914). The 'general conditions' are that: (i) the relationship may not be entered into if either of the parties is already a party to a relationship of that kind or lawfully married; (ii) the relationship is of indeterminate duration; and (iii) the effect of entering into it is that the parties are treated as a couple either generally or for specified purposes, or treated as married: Civil Partnership Act 2004 s 214. 'Relevant law' means the law of the country or territory where the relationship is registered, including its rules of private international law: s 212(2).

2 As to the relevant law see note 1.

3 Civil Partnership Act 2004 s 215(1). The time when they are to be treated as having formed the civil partnership is the time when the overseas relationship is registered, under the relevant law, as having been entered into: s 215(2). If the overseas relationship is registered under the relevant law as having been entered before that date, the time when they are to be treated as having formed a civil partnership is 5 December 2005 (ie the date on which s 215 was brought into force by SI 2005/3175): Civil Partnership Act 2004 s 215(3). However it will not be so treated, if before 5 December 2005, a dissolution or annulment of the overseas relationship was obtained outside the United Kingdom and the dissolution or annulment would be recognised if the overseas relationship had been treated as a civil partnership at the time of the dissolution or annulment, and s 215(1), (2) will have effect subject to s 215(5): s 215(4). The overseas relationship is not to be treated as having been a civil partnership for the purposes of any provisions except: (1) Schs 7 (see PARA 938 et seq), 11 and 17; (2) such provisions as are specified in an order under s 259; or (3) Chapter 3 so far as necessary under heads (1) and (2): s 215(5). The following provisions have been specified: (a) in the case in the case of a marriage celebrated on or after 5 December 2005, the Marriage Act 1949 s 28A (power to require evidence) (see PARA 91), and Sch 1 (kindred and affinity) (see PARA 35 et seq); (b) in the case of a notice of marriage given on or after 5 December 2005, the Marriage Act 1949 s 27 (notice of marriage) (see PARA 87); (c) the Inheritance (Provision for Family and Dependants) Act 1975 (see PARAS 538–541; and EXECUTORS AND ADMINISTRATORS); (d) the Fatal Accidents Act 1976 (see NEGLIGENCE vol 33 (Reissue) PARA 624 et seq); (e) in the case of a bankruptcy where the bankruptcy order was made on or after 5 December 2005: (i) the Insolvency Act 1986 s 283A (bankrupt's home ceasing to form part of estate) (see BANKRUPTCY AND INDIVIDUAL INSOLVENCY), s 313 (charge on bankrupt's home) (see BANKRUPTCY AND INDIVIDUAL INSOLVENCY vol 3(2) (2002 Reissue) PARA 401), s 313A (low value home: application for sale, possession or charge) (see BANKRUPTCY AND INDIVIDUAL INSOLVENCY), s 332 (saving for bankrupt's home) (see BANKRUPTCY AND INDIVIDUAL INSOLVENCY vol 3(2) (2002 Reissue) PARA 606), s 335A (rights under trusts of land) (see BANKRUPTCY AND INDIVIDUAL INSOLVENCY vol 3(2) (2002 Reissue) PARA 647), s 366 (inquiry into bankrupt's dealings and property) (see BANKRUPTCY AND INDIVIDUAL INSOLVENCY vol 3(2) (2002 Reissue) PARA 307); and (ii) the Insolvency Rules 1986, SI 1986/1925, rr 6.237, 6.237A, 6.237B, 6.237D (see BANKRUPTCY AND INDIVIDUAL INSOLVENCY vol 3(2) (2002 Reissue) PARA 401); (f) the Children Act 1989 Sch 1 (financial provision for children) (see CHILDREN AND YOUNG PERSONS); (g) the Family Law Act 1996 s 33 (occupation orders where application has estate or interest etc or has home rights) (see PARA 292), s 35 (one former spouse or former civil partner with no existing right to occupy) (see PARAS 297–298), s 37 (neither spouse nor civil partner entitled to occupy) (see PARAS 305–306), Sch 7 (transfer of tenancy); and (h) the Civil Partnership Act 2004 ss 9 (power to require evidence of name etc) (see PARA 134), s 65 (contribution by civil partner to property improvement) (see PARA 283), s 68 (applications under s 66 by former civil partners) (see PARA 224), Sch 1 (prohibited degrees of relationship: England and Wales) (see PARA 35 et seq): Civil Partnership (Treatment of Overseas Relationships) Order 2005, SI 2005/3042, art 2.

4 'United Kingdom law' means any enactment or rule of law applying in England and Wales, Scotland and Northern Ireland: Civil Partnership Act 2004 s 216(5).

5 Civil Partnership Act 2004 s 216(1). 'Critical time' means the time determined in accordance with s 215(2) or (3): s 216(5). If a full gender recognition certificate is issued under the Gender Recognition Act 2004 (see CONSTITUTIONAL LAW AND HUMAN RIGHTS) to a person who has registered an overseas relationship after the issue of the certificate, the relationship is no longer prevented from being treated as a civil partnership on the ground that, at the critical time, the parties were not of the same sex: Civil Partnership Act 2004 s 216(2). However, this does not apply to an overseas relationship if either of the parties has formed a subsequent civil partnership or lawful marriage: s 216(3). An 'overseas relationship' is within this provision if, at the critical time one of the parties, the first party, was regarded under the relevant law as having changed gender, but was not regarded under United Kingdom law as having done so, and the other party was, under United Kingdom law, of the gender to which the first party had changed under the relevant law: s 216(4).

6   See the Civil Partnership Act 2004 s 217(1), (2). As to the prohibited degrees see Sch 1 Pt I; and
    PARA 35.
7   See the Civil Partnership Act 2004 s 218.

20.   Recognition of divorces, dissolutions etc outside England and Wales.   The
validity of any divorce, dissolution, annulment or judicial or legal separation
granted or ordered by a court of civil jurisdiction in any part of the British
Islands[1] is to be recognised[2] throughout the United Kingdom[3], although no
divorce, dissolution or annulment obtained in any part of the United Kingdom is
to be regarded[4] as effective unless granted by a court of civil jurisdiction[5]. The
validity of a divorce, dissolution annulment or separation obtained in a country
outside the British Islands is to be recognised[6] in the United Kingdom if, and only
if, it is entitled to recognition by virtue of the relevant statutory provisions
governing the recognition of overseas divorces, dissolutions etc[7] or any other
enactment[8].

1   As to the meaning of 'British Islands' see STATUTES vol 44(1) (Reissue) PARA 1383.
2   Ie subject to the Family Law Act 1986 s 51; the Civil Partnership Act 2004 ss 236, 237(2); and
    the Civil Partnership (Supplementary Provisions relating to the Recognition of Overseas
    Dissolutions, Annulments or Legal Separations) (England and Wales and Northern Ireland)
    Regulations 2005, SI 2005/3104, reg 2(4), (5) (refusal of recognition): see CONFLICT OF LAWS
    vol 8(3) (Reissue) PARA 259.
3   See the Family Law Act 1986 s 44(2); the Civil Partnership Act 2004 s 233(2); and CONFLICT OF
    LAWS vol 8(3) (Reissue) PARA 253.
4   Ie, in the case of marriage, subject to the Family Law Act 1986 s 52(4), (5)(a) (for which there
    are no corresponding civil partnership provisions): see CONFLICT OF LAWS vol 8(3) (Reissue)
    PARA 253.
5   See the Family Law Act 1986 s 44(1); the Civil Partnership Act 2004 s 233(1); and CONFLICT OF
    LAWS vol 8(3) (Reissue) PARA 253.
6   Ie subject to the Family Law Act 1986 ss 45(2), 51, 52; the Civil Partnership Act 2004
    ss 233(3), (4), 234(2), (3), 236; and the Civil Partnership (Supplementary Provisions relating to
    the Recognition of Overseas Dissolutions, Annulments or Legal Separations) (England and
    Wales and Northern Ireland) Regulations 2005, SI 2005/3104, reg 2(4), (5) (see CONFLICT OF
    LAWS vol 8(3) (Reissue) PARAS 254, 259).
7   Ie by virtue of the Family Law Act 1986 s 46 and the Civil Partnership Act 2004 s 235 (see
    CONFLICT OF LAWS vol 8(3) (Reissue) PARAS 255, 256), the Family Law Act 1986 s 47 and the
    Civil Partnership (Supplementary Provisions relating to the Recognition of Overseas
    Dissolutions, Annulments or Legal Separations) (England and Wales and Northern Ireland)
    Regulations 2005, SI 2005/3104, regs 4, 5(1) (see CONFLICT OF LAWS vol 8(3) (Reissue) PARAS
    255, 256), the Family Law Act 1986 s 48 and the Civil Partnership (Supplementary Provisions
    relating to the Recognition of Overseas Dissolutions, Annulments or Legal Separations)
    (England and Wales and Northern Ireland) Regulations 2005, SI 2005/3104, reg 6(1)–(3) (see
    CONFLICT OF LAWS vol 8(3) (Reissue) PARA 255) and the Family Law Act 1986 s 49 and the
    Civil Partnership (Supplementary Provisions relating to the Recognition of Overseas
    Dissolutions, Annulments or Legal Separations) (England and Wales and Northern Ireland)
    Regulations 2005, SI 2005/3104, reg 2(1)–(6) (see CONFLICT OF LAWS vol 8(3) (Reissue) PARA
    257).
8   See the Family Law Act 1986 s 45(1); the Civil Partnership Act 2004 s 234(1); and CONFLICT OF
    LAWS vol 8(3) (Reissue) PARA 254. The Family Law Act 1986 s 45(1) does not apply to an
    overseas divorce, annulment or legal separation as regards which provision as to recognition is
    made by EC Council Regulation 2201/2003 (OJ L160, 23.12.2003, pp 9–11, 13) arts 21–27,
    41(1), 42(1) (see CONFLICT OF LAWS): see the Family Law Act 1986 s 45(2); and CONFLICT OF
    LAWS vol 8(3) (Reissue) PARA 254.

(iii)   Proof

21.   Marriage after banns or by common licence.   Where any marriage has
been solemnised:
    (1)   after the publication of banns of matrimony[1], it is not necessary, in

support of the marriage, to give any proof of the residence of the parties or either of them in any parish[2] or other ecclesiastical district[3] in which the banns were published[4];

(2) in the usual place of worship of the parties or one of them, it is not necessary, in support of the marriage, to give any proof of the actual enrolment of the parties or of one of them on the church electoral roll[5] of the area in which the parish church or authorised chapel in which the marriage was solemnised is situated[6]; and

(3) on the authority of a common licence[7], it is not necessary, in support of the marriage, to give any proof that the usual place of residence of one of the parties was for 15 days immediately before the grant of the licence in the parish or other ecclesiastical district in which the marriage was solemnised[8],

and nor is any evidence to be given to prove the contrary in any proceedings touching the validity of such a marriage[9].

1 As to banns see PARAS 58, 68.
2 As to the meaning of 'parish' see PARA 59 note 8.
3 For the purposes of the Marriage Act 1949, 'ecclesiastical district', in relation to a district other than a parish, means a district specified in a licence granted under the Marriage Act 1949 s 20 (see PARA 62), a chapelry or an extra-parochial place: s 78(1).
4 Marriage Act 1949 s 24(1). Where a marriage has been solemnised in accordance with the Church of England Marriage Measure 2008 s 1(1), (2) (see PARA 59), it will not be necessary in support of the marriage to give any proof that either party had a qualifying connection with the parish in which the marriage was solemnised and no evidence will be given to prove the contrary in any proceedings touching the validity of the marriage: s 4(2).
5 For these purposes, 'church electoral roll' means, in England, a church electoral roll provision for which is made in the Church Representation Rules contained in the Synodical Government Measure 1969 Sch 3 (Marriage Act 1949 s 72(4)), and, in Wales and Monmouthshire, an electoral roll of a parish kept in accordance with the constitution and regulations of the Church in Wales for the time being in force (Marriage (Wales and Monmouthshire) Act 1962 s 1(2)). As to church electoral rolls generally see ECCLESIASTICAL LAW vol 14 PARA 591 et seq.
6 Marriage Act 1949 s 72(3). Section 72 extends to Wales and Monmouthshire.
7 As to common licences see PARAS 58, 76 et seq.
8 Marriage Act 1949 s 24(2).
9 Marriage Act 1949 ss 24(1), (2), 72(3). See also *Bodman v Bodman (otherwise Perry)* (1913) 108 LT 383; *Nicholson v Squire* (1809) 16 Ves 259; *Robinson v Grant* (1811) 18 Ves 289; *Tree v Quin* (1812) 2 Phillim 14; *R v Hind* (1813) Russ & Ry 253, CCR; *Diddear (falsely called Fawcit, otherwise Savill) v Faucit* (1821) 3 Phillim 580; *Ray v Sherwood and Ray* (1836) 1 Curt 193; *Mahadervan v Mahadervan* [1964] P 233, [1962] 3 All ER 1108, DC.

22. Marriages under certificate of superintendent registrar or licence of Registrar General. Where a marriage has been solemnised on the authority of a certificate of a superintendent registrar[1], it is not necessary, in support of the marriage, to give any proof:

(1) that before the marriage either of the parties to the marriage resided, or resided for any period, in the registration district[2] stated in the notices of marriage to be that of his or her place of residence[3];

(2) that any person whose consent to the marriage was required[4] had given his consent[5];

(3) that the registered building[6] in which the marriage was solemnised had been certified as required by law as a place of religious worship[7];

(4) that that building was the usual place of worship of either of the parties to the marriage[8];

(5) that the facts stated in the declaration made[9] at the time of the notice of marriage were correct[10]; or

(6)   that the parties, or one of them, were enrolled in the church electoral roll[11],

and nor is any evidence to be given to prove the contrary in any proceedings touching the validity of the marriage[12]. Special provision is made in connection with marriages involving persons subject to immigration control[13].

These provisions also apply, with the appropriate modifications, to a marriage solemnised under the authority of the Registrar General's licence[14] as they apply to a marriage solemnised under the authority of a certificate of a superintendent registrar[15].

1   Ie under the provisions of the Marriage Act 1949 Pt III (ss 26–52): see PARA 54 et seq. 'Superintendent registrar' means a superintendent registrar of births, deaths and marriages: Marriage Act 1949 s 78(1).

2   As to the meaning of 'registration district' see PARA 87 note 4.

3   Marriage Act 1949 s 48(1)(a) (amended by the Immigration and Asylum Act 1999 Sch 14 paras 3, 26).

4   Ie by the Marriage Act 1949 s 3: see PARA 46.

5   Marriage Act 1949 s 48(1)(b).

6   As to the meaning of 'registered building' see PARA 54 note 3.

7   Marriage Act 1949 s 48(1)(c). A marriage solemnised in accordance with the provisions of Pt III in a registered building which has not been certified as required by law as a place of religious worship is as valid as if the building had been so certified: s 48(2).

8   Marriage Act 1949 s 48(1)(d).

9   Ie under the Marriage Act 1949 s 35(1): see PARA 100.

10   Marriage Act 1949 s 48(1)(e).

11   Marriage Act 1949 s 72(3). As to the circumstances in which enrolment is necessary see PARA 100 note 17. As to the meaning of 'church electoral roll' see PARA 21 note 5. As to the application of s 72(3) to Wales see PARA 21 note 6.

12   Marriage Act 1949 ss 48(1), 72(3).

13   In relation to the marriage of a person who is subject to immigration control, the Marriage Act 1949 s 48 has effect as if the list of matters in s 48(1)(a)–(e) (see the text and notes 1–10) included compliance with the Asylum and Immigration (Treatment of Claimants, etc) Act 2004 s 19 (see PARAS 176–177): s 20(2)(b).

14   As to marriages under the authority of the Registrar General's licence see PARA 161 et seq.

15   Marriage (Registrar General's Licence) Act 1970 s 12.

23. Marriages in naval, military and air force chapels. Where a marriage has been solemnised in a naval, military or air force chapel[1], it is not necessary, in support of the marriage, to give any proof:

(1)   that the chapel in which the marriage was solemnised was[2] duly certified, licensed or registered[3];

(2)   that either of the parties was a qualified person[4]; or

(3)   in the case of a marriage according to the rites of the Church of England, that the marriage was solemnised in the presence of a clergyman[5] duly appointed[6] for the purpose of registering marriages[7],

and no evidence is to be given to prove the contrary in any proceedings touching the validity of the marriage[8].

1   Ie under the Marriage Act 1949 Pt V (ss 68–71): see PARAS 129–130.

2   Ie in accordance with the Marriage Act 1949 Pt V.

3   Marriage Act 1949 s 71(a).

4   Marriage Act 1949 s 71(b). As to the meaning of 'qualified person' see PARA 129 note 1.

5   'Clergyman' means a clerk in holy orders of the Church of England: Marriage Act 1949 s 78(1).

6   See note 1. As to the appointment of a clergyman for this purpose see PARA 130.

7   Marriage Act 1949 s 71(c).

8   Marriage Act 1949 s 71.

24. Jewish marriages. Jewish marriages in England and Wales may be proved in the usual way by the production of the Registrar General's certificate[1]. The validity of a Jewish marriage celebrated in a foreign jurisdiction is a question of fact, to be ascertained by evidence[2], and it is not necessary in order to prove such a marriage to produce a written contract of marriage between the parties[3].

1   See PARA 25; and EVIDENCE vol 17(1) (Reissue) PARAS 843–844. As to the duty of the secretary of a synagogue to make quarterly returns of marriages to the superintendent registrar, and as to the duty of the superintendent registrar to make quarterly returns to the Registrar General, see the Marriage Act 1949 ss 57, 58; and REGISTRATION CONCERNING THE INDIVIDUAL vol 39(2) (Reissue) PARA 618. It was said in *Prager v Prager and Goodison* (1913) 29 TLR 556 that the secretary should sign the certificate as 'secretary and registrar', but this does not seem to be required by the statutory provisions. As to proof of marriage in matrimonial proceedings see PARA 825 et seq.
2   Such a marriage may be proved by the evidence of an expert in Jewish law, as in the case of foreign marriages: *Lindo v Belisario* (1795) 1 Hag Con 216. See generally EVIDENCE vol 17(1) (Reissue) PARA 551 et seq.
3   *R v Hammer* [1923] 2 KB 786, CCA (explaining *Horn v Noel* (1807) 1 Camp 61; and overruling *R v Althausen* (1893) 17 Cox CC 630 and *R v Nasillski* (1897) 61 JP 520). See also *Lindo v Belisario* (1795) 1 Hag Con 216; *Goldstone v Goldstone* (1922) 127 LT 32; *Spivack v Spivack* (1930) 46 TLR 243. For an example of the refusal of the Registrar General to grant a licence permitting a Jewish husband to remarry in England following delivery of a get to his wife in Israel see *Berkovits v Grinberg (A-G intervening)* [1995] Fam 142, [1995] 2 All ER 681.

25. Registers and certificates as evidence. Registers of marriages in England kept in pursuance of statutory requirements[1], and also certified copies of entries in such registers, are admissible as evidence of marriages, and of the particulars stated in them, without further or other proof, provided, in the case of certified copies from the General Register Office, that they purport to be sealed or stamped with the seal of that office[2], and in the case of other copies, that they purport to be signed and certified as true copies by the officer to whose custody the register is entrusted[3]. Certain non-parochial marriage registers and records and certified extracts from them are also admissible in evidence[4].

1   Ie in accordance with the provisions of the Marriage Act 1949 Pt IV (ss 53–67): see REGISTRATION CONCERNING THE INDIVIDUAL vol 39(2) (Reissue) PARA 558 et seq.
2   See the Marriage Act 1949 s 65(3); and REGISTRATION CONCERNING THE INDIVIDUAL vol 39(2) (Reissue) PARA 607.
3   See the Evidence Act 1851 s 14; and EVIDENCE vol 17(1) (Reissue) PARAS 821, 843–844. As to proof of marriage in matrimonial proceedings see PARA 825 et seq.
4   See EVIDENCE vol 17(1) (Reissue) PARA 848 et seq.

26. Proof of civil partnerships. Where two people have registered as civil partners of each other in England and Wales, it is not necessary in support of the civil partnership to give any proof:

(1)   that any person whose consent to the civil partnership was required[1] had given his consent[2]; or

(2)   that before the registration either of the civil partners resided, or resided for any period, in the area stated in the notices of proposed civil partnership[3] to be the area of that person's place of residence[4],

and no evidence is to be given to prove the contrary in any proceedings touching the validity of the civil partnership[5].

Where a civil partnership involves a person who is subject to immigration control, these provisions have effect as if the matters proof of which it is not necessary to give in support of the civil partnership include compliance with the statutory provisions governing the formation of civil partnerships by such persons[6].

Any preserved rule of law[7] and under which in any proceedings evidence of reputation or family tradition is admissible for the purpose of proving or disproving the existence of a marriage, is to be treated in an equivalent way for the purpose of proving or disproving the existence of a civil partnership[8].

1   Ie under the Civil Partnership Act 2004 s 4: see PARA 46.
2   Civil Partnership Act 2004 s 52(1)(a). This is subject to the civil partnership being void if forbidden under s 49(c) (see PARA 327): see s 52(2).
3   As to notices of proposed civil partnership see PARAS 133, 140.
4   Civil Partnership Act 2004 s 52(1)(aa) (added by SI 2005/2000).
5   Civil Partnership Act 2004 s 52(1).
6   Civil Partnership Act 2004 Sch 23 para 7(2)(b). For the relevant statutory provisions see Sch 23 Pt 2; and PARAS 178, 179.
7   Ie a rule of law preserved under the Civil Evidence Act 1995 s 7(3) (see EVIDENCE vol 17(1) (Reissue) PARA 702 et seq) or the Criminal Justice Act 2003 s 118(1) (see CRIMINAL LAW, EVIDENCE AND PROCEDURE vol 11(3) (2006 Reissue) PARA 1523 et seq).
8   Civil Partnership Act 2004 s 84(5).

27.   Proof in family proceedings of marriages or overseas relationships celebrated outside England and Wales.   The celebration of a marriage or the formation of an overseas relationship other than a marriage outside England and Wales and its validity under the law of the country where it was celebrated or formed may, in any family proceedings[1] in which the existence and validity of the marriage or relationship are not disputed, be proved by the evidence of one of the parties to it and the production of a document purporting to be a certificate or similar document issued under the law in force in that country evidencing its celebration or formation or a certified copy of an entry in a register of marriages or such relationships kept under the law in force in that country[2]. Where a document so produced is not in English, it must, unless otherwise directed, be accompanied by a translation certified by a notary public or authenticated by affidavit[3].

These provisions are not to be construed as precluding the proof of a marriage, or the existence of an overseas relationship which is not a marriage, in accordance with the Evidence (Foreign, Dominion and Colonial Documents) Act 1933[4] or in any other manner otherwise authorised[5].

1   As to the meaning of 'family proceedings' see PARA 737 note 2.
2   Family Proceedings Rules 1991, SI 1991/1247, r 10.14(1), (1A) (r 10.14(1A) added by SI 2005/2922).
3   Family Proceedings Rules 1991, SI 1991/1247, r 10.14(2) (amended by SI 2005/2922).
4   As to the Evidence (Foreign, Dominion and Colonial Documents) Act 1933 see EVIDENCE vol 17(1) (Reissue) PARAS 859–860.
5   Family Proceedings Rules 1991, SI 1991/1247, r 10.14(3) (amended by SI 2005/2922).

28.   Marriages under the Foreign Marriage Act 1892.   After a marriage has been solemnised abroad between parties of whom at least one is a United Kingdom national[1], by or before a marriage officer[2] under the Foreign Marriage Acts 1892[3], it is not necessary, in support of the marriage, to give any proof of the residence for the required time[4] of either of the parties previous to the marriage, or of the consent of any person whose consent was required by law; nor is any evidence to prove the contrary to be given in any legal proceedings touching the validity of the marriage[5].

Where a marriage purports to have been solemnised and registered under the Foreign Marriage Act 1892 in the official house of a British ambassador or consul, it is not necessary, in support of the marriage, to give any proof of the authority of the marriage officer by or before whom the marriage was solemnised and registered; nor is any evidence to prove his want of authority, whether by reason of his not being a duly authorised marriage officer or of any prohibitions or restrictions or otherwise, to be given in any legal proceeding touching the validity of the marriage[6].

1   For these purposes, 'United Kingdom national' means a person who is: (1) a British citizen, a British overseas territories citizen, a British Overseas citizen or a British National (Overseas); (2) a British subject under the British Nationality Act 1981; or (3) a British protected person: Foreign Marriage Act 1892 s 1(2). As to British citizens see BRITISH NATIONALITY, IMMIGRATION AND ASYLUM vol 4(2) (2002 Reissue) PARAS 8, 23–43. As to British overseas territories citizens and citizenship (formerly known as British dependent territories citizens and citizenship) see BRITISH NATIONALITY, IMMIGRATION AND ASYLUM vol 4(2) (2002 Reissue) PARAS 8, 44–57. As to British national (overseas) status see BRITISH NATIONALITY, IMMIGRATION AND ASYLUM vol 4(2) (2002 Reissue) PARAS 8, 63–65. As to British overseas citizens see BRITISH NATIONALITY, IMMIGRATION AND ASYLUM vol 4(2) (2002 Reissue) PARAS 8, 58–62. As to British subjects see BRITISH NATIONALITY, IMMIGRATION AND ASYLUM vol 4(2) (2002 Reissue) PARAS 9, 66–71. As to British protected persons see BRITISH NATIONALITY, IMMIGRATION AND ASYLUM vol 4(2) (2002 Reissue) PARAS 10, 72–76.

2   As to marriage officers see the Foreign Marriage Act 1892 s 11; and PARA 119 et seq.

3   As to such marriages generally see PARA 119 et seq; and as to evidence of such marriages see EVIDENCE vol 17(1) (Reissue) PARA 856.

4   As to the period of residence required see PARAS 120–127.

5   See the Foreign Marriage Act 1892 s 13(1); and PARAS 119–128.

6   See the Foreign Marriage Act 1892 s 13(2) (amended by the Foreign Marriage Act 1947 s 4(2)); and PARAS 119–128.

29.   Civil partnerships registered abroad. After two people, one of whom is a United Kingdom national[1], have registered as civil partners of each other by or before a civil partnership officer[2] it is not necessary to prove that they fulfilled any requirement of residence[3] that may have been on them, that any necessary consent was obtained[4], that the civil partnership officer had the authority to register the civil partners or that registration took place within the official house of the civil partnership officer[5], and no evidence to prove the contrary will be given in any legal proceeding touching the validity of the civil partnership[6].

No corresponding provision is made in relation to civil partnerships registered abroad by armed forces personnel[7].

1   'United Kingdom National' means a person who is, (1) a British citizen, a British overseas territories citizen, a British Overseas citizen or a British National (Overseas); (2) a British subject under the British Nationality Act 1981; or (3) a British protected person, within the meaning of the British Nationality Act 1981: Civil Partnership Act 2004 s 245(1). As to these categories of citizenship see PARA 28 note 1.

2   For these purposes 'civil partnership officer' means British Consular officer: Civil Partnership (Registration Abroad and Certificates) Order 2005, SI 2005/2761, art 1(2). As to such civil partnerships generally see PARAS 145–152.

3   As to requirements of residence see PARA 146.

4   As to necessary consent see the Civil Partnership (Registration Abroad and Certificates) Order 2005, SI 2005/2761, art 7; and PARAS 119–128, 149.

5   As to the civil partnership officer's authority see PARA 145.

6   See the Civil Partnership (Registration Abroad and Certificates) Order 2005, SI 2005/2761, art 12; and PARA 151.

7   As to the registration of civil partnerships involving armed forces personnel see PARAS 153–160.

30.   Colonial and foreign registers. In certain circumstances, and where certain conditions are fulfilled, colonial and foreign registers and certified and examined copies of entries in them are admissible in English courts to prove the facts stated in those registers[1].

1   See EVIDENCE vol 17(1) (Reissue) PARA 854 et seq. As to proof of marriages solemnised abroad involving members of Her Majesty's armed forces see EVIDENCE vol 17(1) (Reissue) PARA 857; and as to proof of foreign marriages in family proceedings see PARA 27.

(2) CAPACITY TO MARRY OR ENTER INTO CIVIL PARTNERSHIP

31.   Legal capacity generally.   Capacity[1] to marry or enter a civil partnership is governed by the law of each party's domicile and, subject to certain exceptions, a marriage or civil partnership is valid as regards capacity if each of the parties has under the law of his or her domicile, capacity to marry the other or enter into a civil partnership with the other[2].

Generally a marriage or civil partnership is invalid if it is or would be invalid:

(1)   under the law of either party's domicile on the ground that it is within that law's prohibited degrees of consanguinity, affinity, or relationship[3];

(2)   under the law of either party's domicile on the ground of the impediment of lack of age[4];

(3)   under the law of either party's domicile on the ground that he or she is party to a prior subsisting marriage or civil partnership[5];

(4)   under the law of the petitioner's domicile at the date of the marriage on the ground of either party's incapacity or wilful refusal to consummate a marriage[6].

The English court will not recognise an incapacity to marry imposed by a foreign law if to do so would be contrary to English public policy[7].

1   'Capacity' means legal capacity. As to the law governing the consent of the parties and their physical capacity see PARA 41 et seq.
2   See CONFLICT OF LAWS vol 8(3) (Reissue) PARA 227.
3   See CONFLICT OF LAWS vol 8(3) (Reissue) PARA 228; and PARA 35 et seq.
4   See CONFLICT OF LAWS vol 8(3) (Reissue) PARA 229; and PARAS 32, 41.
5   See CONFLICT OF LAWS vol 8(3) (Reissue) PARA 230.
6   See CONFLICT OF LAWS vol 8(3) (Reissue) PARA 233.
7   See CONFLICT OF LAWS vol 8(3) (Reissue) PARA 231.

32.   Minimum age.   A marriage solemnised between persons either of whom is under the age of 16 is void[1]. Similarly, two people are not eligible to register as civil partners of each other if either of them is under 16[2].

1   See PARA 41.
2   Civil Partnership Act 2004 s 3(1)(c).

33.   Disabilities.   The law of a party's domicile, which governs his or her capacity to marry or, where applicable, to enter into a civil partnership[1], must not offend against English public policy. Thus, English law does not recognise a disability to marry, imposed by foreign law, of a religious[2] or penal[3] character. Prohibitions against remarriage are sometimes penal, as may be discriminatory racial laws[4]. The court retains a residual discretion not to apply the law of the domicile where it is not proper to do so in the circumstances of the case[5].

1   See CONFLICT OF LAWS vol 8(3) (Reissue) PARA 227 et seq.
2   The marriage of monks and nuns in England would be regarded as legal, if valid in other respects, as in England the disabilities of the clergy were taken away by the Clergy Marriage Act 1548 (repealed) and the Clergy Marriage Act 1551 (repealed). See also *Chetti v Chetti* [1909] P 67 (a Hindu who marries an English woman in England does not carry with him a disability of a personal character imposed by the rules of his caste); *Lepre v Lepre* [1965] P 52, [1963] 2 All ER 49 (attempt by Maltese court to impose incapacity based on creed); following

Gray (otherwise Formosa) v Formosa [1963] P 259, subnom *Formosa v Formosa* [1962] 3 All ER 419, CA (to like effect); *R v Hammersmith Superintendent Registrar of Marriages, ex p Mir-Anwaruddin* [1917] 1 KB 634, CA (a Muslim can contract a valid monogamous marriage with an English woman, and such a marriage cannot be dissolved by any act of his under the law of his religion), distinguished in *Russ (otherwise Geffers) v Russ* [1964] P 315, [1962] 3 All ER 193, CA, and *Papadopoulos v Papadopoulos* [1930] P 55 (a member of the Greek church can contract a valid marriage in England although in a form not in accordance with the rules of that church). *Maher v Maher* [1951] P 342, [1951] 2 All ER 37 (Muslim divorce by declaration at court in Egypt not recognised in England), was disapproved in *Russ (otherwise Geffers) v Russ* (talak divorce declared in Egypt recognised). See also *Qureshi v Qureshi* [1972] Fam 173, [1971] 1 All ER 325.

3   See *Scott v A-G* (1886) 11 PD 128; *Warter v Warter* (1890) 15 PD 152; and CONFLICT OF LAWS vol 8(3) (Reissue) PARA 231.

4   See *Igra v Igra* [1951] P 404 (no notice of proceedings to respondent out of country, in time of war; not necessarily offensive to English notion of natural justice); c f *MacAlpine v MacAlpine* [1958] P 35, [1957] 3 All ER 134. The status of slavery will not be recognised in this country: *Baindail (otherwise Lawson) v Baindail* [1946] P 122, [1946] 1 All ER 342, CA.

5   *Russ (otherwise Geffers) v Russ* [1964] P 315, [1962] 3 All ER 193, CA; *Cheni (otherwise Rodriguez) v Cheni* [1965] P 85, [1962] 3 All ER 873; c f *Re Langley's Settlement Trusts, Lloyds Bank Ltd v Langley* [1962] Ch 541, [1961] 3 All ER 803, CA (status of 'incompetency' under Californian law not given effect to in regard to an English settlement). See also *Gray (otherwise Formosa) v Formosa* [1963] P 259, sub nom *Formosa v Formosa* [1962] 3 All ER 419, CA; and CONFLICT OF LAWS vol 8(3) (Reissue) PARA 231.

34.   Remarriage and entering into a new civil partnership. Where a decree of divorce[1] has been made absolute or a conditional order for the dissolution of a civil partnership has been made final[2], and the time for appealing from the decree nisi or conditional order has expired without an appeal having been brought[3], or an appeal has been brought but has been dismissed, either party to the marriage or civil partnership may marry again or enter into a civil partnership[4]. A decree nisi of nullity of marriage in respect of a voidable marriage, or a nullity order in respect of a voidable civil partnership, operates to annul the marriage or civil partnership only as respects any time after the decree has been made absolute or the order made final, and the marriage or civil partnership is, notwithstanding the decree or order, treated as if it had existed up to that time[5]. In certain cases marriages between persons related by affinity[6], and civil partnerships between persons within the prohibited degrees[7] are valid. There is nothing to prevent persons whose marriage or civil partnership has been dissolved from marrying, or re-forming a civil partnership with, one another again[8].

1   As to the effect of decree of divorce relating only to the later of two celebrations of a marriage which has been twice celebrated see PARAS 756, 879. Where the prohibition is only temporary, it will be recognised in England: see CONFLICT OF LAWS vol 8(3) (Reissue) PARA 260.

2   As to the conditional and final order for the dissolution of a civil partnership see PARA 863 et seq.

3   See PARA 883.

4   A ceremony gone through before these requirements are fulfilled is void: see *Chichester v Mure (falsely called Chichester)* (1863) 3 Sw & Tr 223; *Rogers (otherwise Briscoe, falsely called Halmshaw) v Halmshaw* (1864) 3 Sw & Tr 509.

5   See the Matrimonial Causes Act 1973 s 16; the Civil Partnership Act 2004 s 37(3); and PARA 320. The right to remarry or enter into a civil partnership after a decree or order of nullity in the case of a void marriage or civil partnership does not depend so much on any statute as on the effect of the decree or order which declares the marriage or civil partnership to have been and to be absolutely null and void to all intents and purposes in the law whatsoever: *Lewis (falsely called Hayward) v Hayward* (1866) 35 LJP & M 105, HL; *B (otherwise A) v B* (1891) 27 LR Ir 587; *Newbould v A-G* [1931] P 75. A decree or order is not strictly necessary in the case of a void marriage or civil partnership: see *De Reneville v De Reneville* [1948] P 100, [1948] 1 All ER 56, CA per Lord Greene MR. As to the preservation of the legitimacy of children of voidable marriages see PARA 325.

6 See PARA 37.
7 See PARA 39.
8 *Fendall (otherwise Goldsmid) v Goldsmid* (1877) 2 PD 263.

(3) PROHIBITED DEGREES OF RELATIONSHIP

35. Marriage and civil partnership within the prohibited degrees. A marriage solemnised, or a civil partnership celebrated, between persons within the prohibited degrees of relationship is prohibited and is, in general, void[1]. In reference to the prohibited degrees, relationship by the half-blood prohibits equally with relationship by the whole blood[2], and illegitimate equally with legitimate relationship[3]. It has been held that a sexual relationship without an actual and legal marriage does not constitute affinity[4]. The law of England with respect to the prohibited degrees of relationship affects all persons domiciled[5] in England or Wales, including Jews[6], Quakers[7] and Roman Catholics[8], wherever the solemnisation or celebration may take place[9]. If, however, the law of the domicile of each of the parties is complied with in this respect[10], the marriage or civil partnership will be recognised as valid, even if it is within the prohibited degrees according to English law[11].

1   See PARAS 36, 38 (absolute prohibitions) and PARAS 37, 39 (conditional prohibitions). The Civil Partnership Act 2004 s 3(1)(d) provides that two people are not eligible to register as civil partners of each other if they are within prohibited degrees of relationship. See also the Matrimonial Causes Act 1973 s 11(a)(i); PARA 326; and *Re Wood, ex p Naden* (1874) 9 Ch App 670.
    The prohibited degrees of relationship were formerly recognised in 28 Hen 8 c 7 (1536) s 7; the Ecclesiastical Licences Act 1536 s 2; the Marriage Act 1540; the Act of Supremacy 1558 s 3. The two former statutes, although repealed by 1 & 2 Phil & Mar c 8 (1554) ss 16, 17, may be referred to in order to explain the Marriage Act 1540, which was confirmed by the Act of Supremacy 1558 s 11: see *R v Chadwick* (1847) 11 QB 173; *Brook v Brook* (1861) 9 HL Cas 193; *Re Phillips, Re Howard, Charter v Ferguson* [1919] 1 Ch 128.
2   See the Marriage Act 1949 s 78(1); and PARA 36; *R v Brighton Inhabitants* (1861) 1 B & S 447 (marriage with daughter of half-sister of deceased wife); *Re Mette, Mette v Mette* (1859) 28 LJP & M 117 (half-sister of deceased wife).
3   *R v Brighton Inhabitants* (1861) 1 B & S 447; *Blackmore and Thorp v Brider* (1816) 2 Phillim 359; *R v Chadwick, R v St Giles-in-the-Fields Inhabitants* (1847) 11 QB 173 at 205, approved in *Brook v Brook* (1861) 9 HL Cas 193; *Restall (otherwise Love) v Restall* (1929) 45 TLR 518.
4   *Wing v Taylor (falsely calling herself Wing)* (1861) 30 LJPM & A 258.
5   As to domicile see CONFLICT OF LAWS vol 8(3) (Reissue) PARA 35 et seq.
6   See *Re De Wilton, De Wilton v Montefiore* [1900] 2 Ch 481 (where a Jewish man and his niece, both domiciled in England, went through a form of civil marriage and afterwards a marriage according to the usages of the Jews, at Wiesbaden, and also subsequently at Paris, and it was held that the marriage was void, although it would have been valid according to the local law and also according to Jewish law). The usages of the Jews permit marriages between a man and his deceased wife's sister or deceased wife's niece, or between a man and his niece or deceased nephew's wife. As to the solemnisation under superintendent registrar's certificate of marriages between persons professing the Jewish religion according to the usages of the Jews see PARA 118.
7   As to the solemnisation under superintendent registrar's certificate of marriages according to the usages of the Society of Friends see PARA 116.
8   *Peal v Peal* [1931] P 97 (marriage of nephew and aunt in India; special dispensation had been obtained; marriage nevertheless void).
9   *Re De Wilton, De Wilton v Montefiore* [1900] 2 Ch 481; *Brook v Brook* (1861) 9 HL Cas 193 (marriage with deceased wife's sister in Denmark); *Fenton v Livingstone* (1859) 3 Macq 497.
10 As to capacity to marry under the law of each party's ante-nuptial domicile see CONFLICT OF LAWS vol 8(3) (Reissue) PARA 227 et seq.
11 *Re Bozzelli's Settlement, Husey-Hunt v Bozzelli* [1902] 1 Ch 751; *Cheni (otherwise Rodriguez) v Cheni* [1965] P 85, [1962] 3 All ER 873. Cf the Marriage (Enabling) Act 1960 s 1(3) (marriages invalid under the law of domicile); and PARA 37.

36. Marriage absolutely prohibited. A person may not marry his adoptive child, adoptive parent, child, former adoptive child, former adoptive parent, grandparent, grandchild, parent, parent's sibling[1], sibling, or sibling's child[2].

A marriage solemnised between any such persons is void[3].

1 For these purposes, 'sibling' means a brother, sister, half-brother or half-sister (Marriage Act 1949 Sch 1 para 1(2) (Sch 1 para 1 substituted by the Civil Partnership Act 2004 Sch 27 para 17)); 'sister' and 'brother' include sister and brother of the half-blood (Marriage Act 1949 s 78(1)).
2 Marriage Act 1949 Sch 1 para 1(1) (as substituted: see note 1). See PARA 326.
3 Marriage Act 1949 s 1(1) (substituted by the Civil Partnership Act 2004 Sch 27 para 13).

37. Marriage conditionally prohibited. A person may not marry a child of a former civil partner, a child of a former spouse, a former civil partner of a grandparent, a former civil partner of a parent, a former spouse of a grandparent, a former spouse of a parent, a grandchild of a former civil partner, or a grandchild of a former spouse[1].

A marriage solemnised between any such persons is, in general, void[2].

However, any such marriage is not void by reason only of affinity if both the parties to the marriage have attained the age of 21 at the time of the marriage and the younger party has not at any time before attaining the age of 18 been a child of the family[3] in relation to the other party[4].

No marriage contracted, whether in or out of Great Britain, between a man and a woman who is the sister, aunt or niece of a former wife of his, whether living or not, or who was formerly the wife of his brother, uncle or nephew, whether living or not, is, by reason of that relationship, void or voidable under any enactment or rule of law applying to Great Britain as a marriage between persons within the prohibited degrees of affinity[5]; but a marriage is not so validated if either party to it is at the time of the marriage domiciled[6] in a country outside Great Britain and under the law of that country there cannot be a valid marriage between the parties[7].

1 Marriage Act 1949 Sch 1 para 2 (added by the Marriage (Prohibited Degrees of Relationship) Act 1986 Sch 1 para 8; substituted by the Civil Partnership Act 2004 Sch 27 para 17).
2 Marriage Act 1949 s 1(2) (amended by the Civil Partnership Act 2004 Sch 27 para 17).
3 For the purposes of the Marriage Act 1949, 'child of the family', in relation to any person, means a child who has lived in the same household as that person and been treated by that person as a child of his family: s 78(1) (amended by the Marriage (Prohibited Degrees of Relationship) Act 1986 Sch 1 para 7). For the purposes of the Marriage Act 1949, 'child' means a person under the age of 18: Marriage Act 1949 s 78(1) (amended by the Family Law Reform Act 1987 s 33(1), Sch 2 para 10(a)).
4 Marriage Act 1949 s 1(3) (added by the Marriage (Prohibited Degrees of Relationship) Act 1986 Sch 1 para 2).
5 Marriage (Enabling) Act 1960 s 1(1). In s 1(1) words of kinship apply equally to kin of the whole or of the half blood: s 1(2).
6 As to domicile see CONFLICT OF LAWS vol 8(3) (Reissue) PARA 35 et seq.
7 Marriage (Enabling) Act 1960 s 1(3).

38. Civil partnership absolutely prohibited. A person may not enter into a civil partnership with his adoptive child[1], adoptive parent, child, former adoptive child, former adoptive parent, grandparent, grandchild, parent, parent's sibling[2], sibling, or sibling's child[3].

1 For the purposes of the Civil Partnership Act 2004, 'child', except where used to express a relationship, means a person who is under 18: s 4(5).
2 For these purposes, 'sibling' means a brother, sister, half-brother or half-sister: Civil Partnership Act 2004 Sch 1 para 1(2).
3 Civil Partnership Act 2004 s 3(1)(d), Sch 1 para 1(1).

39.   Civil partnership conditionally prohibited.   A person may not enter into a civil partnership with a child[1] of a former civil partner, a child of a former spouse, a former civil partner of a grandparent, a former civil partner of a parent, a former spouse of a grandparent, a former spouse of a parent, a grandchild of a former civil partner or a grandchild of a former spouse unless both of them have reached 21 at the time when they register as civil partners of each other and the younger has not at any time before reaching 18 been a child of the family[2] in relation to the other[3].

A person may not enter into a civil partnership with the former civil partner or spouse of their child unless the child and the child's other parent are dead; may not enter into a civil partnership with the parent of a former civil partner unless the former civil partner, and the former civil partner's other parent are dead; and may not enter into a civil partnership with the parent of a former spouse unless the former spouse and the former spouse's other parent are dead; and in all cases unless both parties have reached 21 at the time when they register as civil partners of each other[4].

1   As to the meaning of 'child' see PARA 38 note 1.
2   'Child of the family' means, in relation to another person, a person who has lived in the same household as that other person and has been treated by that other person as a child of his family: Civil Partnership Act 2004 Sch 1 para 2(2).
3   Civil Partnership Act 2004 s 3(1)(d), (2), Sch 1 para 2(1).
4   Civil Partnership Act 2004 Sch 1 para 3.

40.   Saving of dignities and rights.   No right, title, estate or interest, whether in possession or expectancy, and whether vested or contingent, on the date when any of the Acts conferring exemptions from the prohibited degrees of affinity took effect[1], existing in, to or in respect of any dignity, title of honour or property, and nothing lawfully done or omitted, nor any claim by the Crown in respect of death duties due and payable, before that date is prejudicially affected, nor is any will deemed to have been revoked, by reason of any marriage contracted before that date having been rendered valid[2]; nor is the devolution or distribution of the real or personal estate of any intestate, not a party to the marriage, who on that date was, and until his death continues to be, a person of unsound mind so found by inquisition[3] thereby affected[4].

1   Certain marriages which would formerly have been void as being within prohibited degrees had been legalised before 1960 by earlier Acts: see the Deceased Wife's Sister's Marriage Act 1907 s 1 (which legalised as from 28 August 1907 a marriage, wherever contracted, between a man and his deceased wife's sister), as extended by the Deceased Brother's Widow's Marriage Act 1921 s 1 (which legalised as from 28 July 1921 a marriage, wherever contracted, between a man and his deceased brother's widow), and by the Marriage (Prohibited Degrees of Relationship) Act 1931 s 1 (which legalised as from 31 July 1931 a marriage, wherever contracted, between a man and his deceased wife's brother's daughter, deceased wife's sister's daughter, father's deceased brother's widow, mother's deceased brother's widow, deceased wife's father's sister, deceased wife's mother's sister, brother's deceased son's widow or sister's deceased son's widow). These enactments were repealed by the Marriage Act 1949 Sch 5 Pt I, without affecting the validity of any marriage solemnised before the repeal (see s 79(7)), and were replaced by Sch 1 Pt II (itself repealed and replaced by the Marriage (Enabling) Act 1960; the Marriage (Prohibited Degrees of Relationship) Act 1986 Sch 1 paras 2, 8; and the Civil Partnership Act 2004 Sch 27 para 17): see PARA 37.
2   Deceased Wife's Sister's Marriage Act 1907 s 2; Deceased Brother's Widow's Marriage Act 1921 s 1(4); Marriage (Prohibited Degrees of Relationship) Act 1931 s 1(3). Although those Acts were repealed by the Marriage Act 1949 (see note 1), their effect is preserved by s 79(9). A spes successionis of a person to a share of his brother's estate as next of kin, if he should die intestate, is not an 'interest in expectancy' for this purpose: *Re Green, Green v Meinall* [1911] 2 Ch 275; and see *Re Butler, Joyce v Brew* [1918] 1 IR 394. In *Re Whitfield, Hill v Mathie* [1911]

1 Ch 310, where the income of property was given in trust for a widow until her second marriage, and she married the husband of her deceased sister in 1904, it was held that the effect of the Deceased Wife's Sister's Marriage Act 1907 s 2 was that the income continued to be payable to her notwithstanding the marriage. See also *Re Springfield, Davies v Springfield* (1922) 38 TLR 263 (where the vested interest in remainder under a marriage settlement was held not to be affected by the legalising of the husband's second marriage with his deceased wife's sister); and *Re Crosby's Trusts, Smith v Metherell* (1919) 147 LT Jo 66.

3 Lunacy inquisitions were abolished by the Mental Health Act 1959 s 1 (repealed).

4 See the provisions cited in note 2.

(4) CONSENT

(i) Consent of Parties

41. Minimum age of consent. A marriage solemnised between, and a civil partnership registered by, persons either of whom is under the age of 16 is void[1]. The age of the parties to a marriage or a civil partnership is in English law a matter of capacity[2], and the statutory minimum age requirement applies to all persons domiciled in, or who marry persons domiciled in, the United Kingdom, no matter where the marriage was celebrated or the civil partnership formed[3]; but it is recognised that persons domiciled otherwise than in England and Wales may have a right to marry or enter into a relationship analogous to a civil partnership under the age of 16 by the law applicable to them[4].

Where a person who has attained the age of 16 but is not yet 18 wishes to marry or enter into a civil partnership, not being a widower or widow, certain prior consents are required[5].

1 Marriage Act 1949 s 2; Civil Partnership Act 2004 s 3(1)(c). See also the Matrimonial Causes Act 1973 s 11(a)(ii); the Civil Partnership Act 2004 s 49(a); and PARAS 32, 326, 327. Provision as to the minimum age for marriage was first contained in the Age of Marriage Act 1929 (repealed) which applied to marriages solemnised or contracted on or after 10 May 1929, the Act not being retrospective in its operation. Before that date the age at which a person could give consent and marry was 14 in the case of males and 12 in the case of females, and a marriage under the age of consent was not absolutely void, but only voidable by either party on the person under age reaching the age of consent: see Com Dig, Baron and Femme (B5); *Corbets Case* (1482) 7 Co Rep 44a, 2 Bl Com 497; *Kenn's Case* (1606) 7 Co Rep 42b; *Arnold v Earle* (1758) 2 Lee 529; *R v Gordon* (1803) Russ & Ry 48; *Elliott v Gurr* (1812) 2 Phillim 16 at 19. See also the Report of the Committee on the Age of Majority 1967 (Cmnd 3342) 20–22.

2 As to capacity see PARA 31 et seq.

3 See *Pugh v Pugh* [1951] P 482, [1951] 2 All ER 680 (where a marriage which took place in Austria between a man domiciled in England and a woman under 16 domiciled in Hungary, and which was valid under Hungarian and Austrian law, was held to be void under the Age of Marriage Act 1929 (repealed) (cited in note 1)); cf *Vida v Vida* (1961) 105 Sol Jo 913 (where both parties to the marriage were Hungarian nationals). See also CONFLICT OF LAWS vol 8(3) (Reissue) PARA 229.

4 See the Domicile and Matrimonial Proceedings Act 1973 s 3(1); and CONFLICT OF LAWS vol 8(3) (Reissue) PARAS 55, 229.

5 See the Marriage Act 1949 s 3; Civil Partnership Act 2004 s 4, Sch 2 Pt 1; and PARA 46.

42. Giving of valid consent. In order that a valid marriage or civil partnership be celebrated between the parties to it, it is essential that they should consent to marry one another or enter into the civil partnership[1]. A marriage or civil partnership is voidable where either party to the marriage or civil partnership did not validly consent to it, whether in consequence of duress[2], mistake[3], unsoundness of mind[4] or otherwise[5].

The test to be applied is whether the person in question was capable of understanding the nature of the contract into which he was entering, or whether his mental condition was such that he was incapable of understanding it; and that in order to ascertain the nature of the contract, that a person must be mentally capable of appreciating that it involves the responsibilities normally attaching to marriage or civil partnership[6]. There is a strong prima facie presumption that such consent has been given[7], as the contract is a simple one which does not require a high degree of intelligence to comprehend[8]. The burden of proof on a party attempting to impeach a marriage or civil partnership on the ground of want of consent is heavier than in the case of impeaching, for example, a commercial contract[9]. Consent may be absent because of mental reasons[10], because there has been abuse of or mistake as to the nature or effect of the ceremony, or because of mistake as to the person[11]. The mental reservations of one or both of the parties to a marriage or civil partnership do not affect its validity[12].

1   *Sullivan v Sullivan (falsely called Oldacre)* (1818) 2 Hag Con 238 (affd sub nom *Sullivan v Oldacre (falsely called Sullivan)* (1819) 3 Phillim 45); *Moss v Moss* [1897] P 263. See also *Browning v Reane* (1812) 2 Phillim 69; *P v S* (1868) 37 LJP & M 80; *Vervaeke v Smith (Messina v A-G intervening)* [1983] 1 AC 145, [1982] 2 All ER 144, HL; cf *R v Immigration Appeal Tribunal, ex p Bhatia* [1985] Imm AR 39. Although these decisions and the decisions cited in notes 6–12 pre-date the concept of civil partnerships and are concerned only with consent to marry, the Civil Partnership Act 2004 confers rights on civil partners which in all practicable respects are analogous to those enjoyed by married persons, and it is reasonable to infer that they must now apply in relation to civil partnerships. See further CONFLICT OF LAWS vol 8(3) (Reissue) PARA 232.
2   See PARA 43.
3   See PARA 44.
4   See PARA 45.
5   See the Matrimonial Causes Act 1973 s 12(c); the Civil Partnerships Act 2004 s 50(1)(a); and PARA 331.
6   See *Hill v Hill* [1959] 1 All ER 281, [1959] 1 WLR 127, PC, approving the formulation of the test laid down in *Re Park, Park v Park* [1954] P 112, [1953] 2 All ER 1411, CA. Deaf and dumb persons may show valid consent by signs, provided that they sufficiently understand the nature of the contract: *Harrod v Harrod* (1854) 1 K & J 4.
7   *Cooper v Crane* [1891] P 369.
8   *Durham v Durham* (1885) 10 PD 80; *Re Spier, Spier and Spier v Bengen (otherwise Spier) and Mason* [1947] WN 46; *Re Park, Park v Park* [1954] P 89, [1953] 2 All ER 408 (where the cases are reviewed); affd [1954] P 112, [1953] 2 All ER 1411, CA.
9   *Swift v Kelly* (1835) 3 Knapp 257, PC; *Scott (falsely called Sebright) v Sebright* (1886) 12 PD 21; cf *Re Spier, Spier and Spier v Bengen (otherwise Spier) and Mason* [1947] WN 46. The presumption is always that the marriage or civil partnership is valid: *Russell v A-G* [1949] P 391; *Wilkinson v Payne* (1791) 4 Term Rep 468; *Cresswell v Cosins* (1815) 2 Phillim 281; *Sullivan v Oldacre (falsely called Sullivan)* (1819) 3 Phillim 45; *Miles v Chilton (falsely called Miles)* (1849) 1 Rob Eccl 684; *Harrod v Harrod* (1854) 1 K & J 4. See also *Re Peete, Peete v Crompton* [1952] 2 All ER 599; *Mahadervan v Mahadervan* [1964] P 233, [1962] 3 All ER 1108, DC; *Singh v Singh* [1971] P 226, [1971] 2 All ER 828, CA; *H v H* [1954] P 258, [1953] 2 All ER 1229; *Szechter (otherwise Karsov) v Szechter* [1971] P 286, [1970] 3 All ER 905.
10 See PARAS 45, 332.
11 See PARA 44. If a marriage is otherwise valid, the fact that a stipulation for a perfect ecclesiastical marriage with two witnesses is not complied with is immaterial: *Ussher v Ussher* [1912] 2 IR 445; cf *Gordon (otherwise Greene) v Gordon* [1948] NI 174.
12 *Dalrymple v Dalrymple* (1811) 2 Hag Con 54; *Bell v Graham* (1859) 13 Moo PCC 242; cf *Dysart Peerage Case* (1881) 6 App Cas 489, HL; *M'Adam v Walker* (1813) 1 Dow 148, HL; *Morgan v Morgan (otherwise Ransom)* [1959] P 92, [1959] 1 All ER 539.

43.   Duress and intoxication. Fraudulent misrepresentation or concealment does not of itself affect the validity of a marriage or civil partnership to which the parties freely consented with a knowledge of the nature of the contract[1]. If, however, a person is induced to go through a ceremony of marriage or civil partnership by threats or duress[2], or in a state of intoxication[3], and without any real consent, it is invalid. In all such cases the test of validity is whether there was any real consent[4].

1   *Moss v Moss* [1897] P 263 (where the wife, who was pregnant by another man at the time of the marriage, deliberately deceived the husband as to her condition and previous conduct, but it was held that that was no ground for questioning the validity of the marriage); *Templeton v Tyree* (1872) LR 2 P & D 420; *Field's Marriage Annulling Bill* (1848) 2 HL Cas 48; *Sullivan v Sullivan (falsely called Oldacre)* (1818) 2 Hag Con 238; cf *Lang v Lang* 1921 SC 44, Ct of Sess. Although these decisions and the decisions cited in notes 2–4 pre-date the concept of civil partnerships and are concerned only with consent to marry, the Civil Partnership Act 2004 confers rights on civil partners which in all practicable respects are analogous to those enjoyed by married persons, and it is reasonable to infer that they must now apply in relation to civil partnerships.

2   *Bartlett (falsely called Rice) v Rice* (1894) 72 LT 122 (petitioner, a girl of 16, threatened with a pistol; marriage not consummated; nullity decreed); *Scott (falsely called Sebright)v Sebright* (1886) 12 PD 21 (petitioner, an heiress aged 22, threatened by respondent with bankruptcy and financial ruin; respondent told her marriage only way to avoid exposure; threat to shoot her; separation immediately after the ceremony; marriage not consummated; nullity decreed); *Harford v Morris* (1776) 2 Hag Con 423 (marriage of guardian with his ward, a girl of 12, declared void on the ground of abduction and duress); cf *Cooper v Crane* [1891] P 369 (where there was a threat by the respondent to shoot himself if the petitioner, his cousin, would not marry him, and the licence for the marriage was obtained by a false declaration, the parties separating immediately after the ceremony, and the marriage never being consummated, but it was held that the evidence was insufficient to rebut the presumption of consent from the petitioner having gone through the marriage ceremony and signed the register); and see *Korel v Korel* (1921) Times, 28 May; *Hussein (otherwise Blitz) v Hussein* [1938] P 159, [1938] 2 All ER 344; *Re S's Marriage* (1980) 42 FLR 94, 5 Fam LR 831 (mental oppression constituted duress). In *H v H* [1954] P 258, [1953] 2 All ER 1229, the wife, a Hungarian citizen, intended to marry the husband, a French citizen, but for the sole purpose of acquiring his nationality and being able to flee the country; the fear of danger was held to negative consent and the marriage was held invalid. Cf *Silver (otherwise Kraft) v Silver* [1955] 2 All ER 614, [1955] 1 WLR 728 (where in a similar case in the absence of duress the marriage was held to be valid). See also *Parojcic (otherwise Ivetic) v Parojcic* [1959] 1 All ER 1, [1958] 1 WLR 1280 (girl driven to go through ceremony by fear of father's threats; decree of nullity granted); *Buckland v Buckland (otherwise Camilleri)* [1968] P 296, [1967] 2 All ER 300 (threat of unjust charge of corrupting a minor); *McLarnon v McLarnon* (1968) 112 Sol Jo 419 (wife's parents forced the marriage after husband had lied that wife was pregnant); and *NS v MI* [2006] EWHC 1646 (Fam), [2007] 2 FCR 748, [2007] 1 FLR 444 (British citizen of Pakistani origin; forced into marriage when visiting Pakistan; parents refused to allow her to return to the United Kingdom, and threatened to kill themselves if she did not marry first cousin; decree of nullity granted). It has been held that in order for duress to vitiate an otherwise valid marriage, it must be proved that a party's will has been overborne by genuine and reasonably held fear caused by threat of immediate danger, for which that party is not responsible, to life, limb or liberty: *Szechter (otherwise Karsov) v Szechter* [1971] P 286, [1970] 3 All ER 905. Cf *Singh v Singh* [1971] P 226, [1971] 2 All ER 828, CA (no lack of consent where Sikh girl went through arranged marriage out of obedience to her parents and a proper sense of duty). See also *Singh v Singh* 2005 SLT 749, OH (threats of immediate danger to applicant's liberty caused her will to be overborne and vitiated her consent to marry).

3   *Sullivan v Sullivan (falsely called Oldacre)* (1818) 2 Hag Con 238.

4   See the cases cited in notes 2, 3.

44.   Mistake.   It is necessary for a valid marriage or civil partnership that the parties should consent to marry one another or enter into a civil partnership with one another[1]. If, therefore, there is a mistake as to the person with whom the contract is made, as where A goes through a ceremony of marriage with, or registers as the civil partner of, B, thinking he is marrying or entering into a civil partnership with C, or in the case of a marriage in masquerade, where one party has no knowledge as to who the other may be, the marriage or civil partnership is void[2]. The same is the case where there is a mistake on the part of one of the parties as to the nature of the ceremony, as where a person goes through a ceremony of marriage (or, conceivably, civil partnership) believing it to be merely a ceremony of betrothal[3], but it is otherwise if the mistake is only as to the effect of the ceremony[4]. No mistake as to the character or condition of the other party to the marriage or civil partnership will affect its validity[5].

1   See PARA 42.
2   *R v Millis* (1844) 10 Cl & Fin 534, HL; *Moss v Moss* [1897] P 263; cf *Forster (otherwise Street) v Forster* (1923) 39 TLR 658 (delusions as to own identity); *C v C* [1942] NZLR 356, NZ SC (mistake not as to identity); *Re Marriage of C and D (falsely called C)* (1979) 35 FLR 340, 5 Fam LR 636; and see *Militante v Ogunwomoju* [1993] 2 FCR 355, [1994] Fam Law 17 (woman married man using assumed name and who was deported as an illegal immigrant; on her petition the marriage declared null and void; respondent's fraud going to his identity said to have vitiated woman's consent to the marriage). Although these decisions and the decisions cited in notes 3–5 pre-date the concept of civil partnerships and are concerned only with consent to marry, the Civil Partnership Act 2004 confers rights on civil partners which in all practicable respects are analogous to those enjoyed by married persons, and it is reasonable to infer that they must now apply in relation to civil partnerships.
3   *Ford v Stier* [1896] P 1; *Hall v Hall* (1908) 24 TLR 756; *Valier v Valier (otherwise Davis)* (1925) 133 LT 830; *Kelly (otherwise Hyams) v Kelly* (1932) 49 TLR 99; *Neuman v Neuman (otherwise Greenberg)* (1926) Times, 15 October; *Mehta (otherwise Kohn) v Mehta* [1945] 2 All ER 690. It would seem that a marriage under such a mistake is voidable and may be ratified: see *Valier v Valier (otherwise Davis)* (1925) 133 LT 830; *Vervaeke v Smith (Messina and A-G intervening)* [1983] 1 AC 145, [1982] 2 All ER 144, HL.
4   *Kenward v Kenward* [1951] P 124, [1950] 2 All ER 297, CA (British subject marrying Russian wife in Russia; wife not permitted to leave Russia nor husband allowed to join wife in Russia); *Kassim (otherwise Widmann) v Kassim (otherwise Hassim)* [1962] P 224, [1962] 3 All ER 426 (mistaken belief that the marriage was polygamous).
5   *Wakefield v Mackay* (1807) 1 Hag Con 394. It has been held that even if a man is the victim of a plot to procure a marriage by him with a person in all respects unworthy, the validity of the marriage is not affected, provided that he consents: *Sullivan v Sullivan (falsely called Oldacre)* (1818) 2 Hag Con 238. As to the general presumption that consent has been given see PARA 42; and as to duress see PARA 43.

45.   Unsoundness of mind.   Want of consent may be founded on unsoundness of mind[1]. The burden of proving the existence of such a degree of unsoundness of mind at the time of a marriage or civil partnership as to invalidate it is in all cases on the person impugning its validity[2], everything being presumed in favour of the marriage or civil partnership[3]. If permanent unsoundness of mind is proved, however, the burden of showing that a marriage or civil partnership took place during a lucid interval lies on the person seeking to uphold its validity[4]. The validity of a marriage or civil partnership is decided by the party's capacity at the actual time of the union and not by his state of mind before or after[5]. The subsequent recovery of a person who was of unsound mind at the relevant time does not affect the question of validity[6].

1   See the Matrimonial Causes Act 1973 s 12(c); the Civil Partnership Act 2004 s 50(1)(a), (b); and PARAS 331, 332.
2   *Durham v Durham, Hunter v Edney (otherwise Hunter), Cannon v Smalley (otherwise Cannon)* (1885) 10 PD 80; *Parker v Parker* (1757) 2 Lee 382; *Browning v Reane* (1812) 2 Phillim 69. See also *A-G v Parnther* (1792) 3 Bro CC 441; *Cochrane v Cochrane (otherwise Millamootz)* (1930) Times, 7 June.
3   *Countess of Portsmouth v Earl of Portsmouth* (1828) 1 Hag Ecc 355; *Harrod v Harrod* (1854) 1 K & J 4. Cf PARA 3.
4   *Turner v Meyers* (1808) 1 Hag Con 414.
5   *Parker v Parker* (1757) 2 Lee 382; *Ex p Ferne* (1801) 5 Ves 832; *Ellis v Bowman* (1851) 17 LTOS 10; *Legey v O'Brien* (1834) Milw 325; *Hancock v Peaty* (1867) LR 1 P & D 335; cf *Jackson (otherwise Macfarlane) v Jackson* [1908] P 308.
6   *Turner v Meyers* (1808) 1 Hag Con 414.

(ii) Parental Consent

46.   Marriage or civil partnership involving person aged under 18. Where the marriage or civil partnership of a child[1], not being a widower, widow, or surviving civil partner, is intended to be solemnised on the authority of certificates issued by a superintendent registrar[2] or registered under the procedures for registering civil partners[3], the consent[4] of the following person or persons is required[5]:

(1)   subject to heads (2) to (8), any parent of the child who has parental responsibility[6] for him, and any guardian[7] of the child[8];

(2)   subject to heads (3) to (7) where a special guardianship order[9] is in force with respect to a child, each of the child's special guardians[10];

(3)   subject to head (5), where a care order[11] has effect with respect to the child, the local authority designated in the order, and each parent, guardian or special guardian[12];

(4)   subject to head (5), where a residence order[13] has effect with respect to the child, the persons with whom the child lives, or is to live, as a result of the order[14];

(5)   where an adoption agency[15] is authorised to place the child for adoption[16] that agency or, where a care order has effect with respect to the child, the local authority[17] designated in the order[18];

(6)   where a placement order[19] is in force with respect to the child, the appropriate local authority[20];

(7)   where a child has been placed for adoption with prospective adopters, the prospective adopters in addition to persons specified in head (5) or (6)[21];

(8)   where none of heads (2) to (7) applies but a residence order was in force with respect to the child immediately before he reached the age of 16, the persons with whom he lived, or was to live, as a result of the order[22].

Nothing in these provisions dispenses with the necessity of obtaining the consent of the High Court to the marriage or registration as a civil partner of a ward of court[23].

1   For these purposes, except where the context otherwise requires, 'child' means a person under the age of 18: Marriage Act 1949 s 78(1) (amended by the Family Law Reform Act 1987 Sch 2 para 10(a)); Civil Partnership Act 2004 s 4(5).

2   Ie under the Marriage Act 1949 Pt III (ss 26–52): see PARA 87 et seq. For these purposes, except where the context otherwise requires, 'superintendent registrar' means a superintendent registrar of births, deaths and marriages: s 78(1). As to the appointment and duties of superintendent registrars see REGISTRATION CONCERNING THE INDIVIDUAL vol 39(2) (Reissue) PARA 609 et seq.

3   As to the registration of civil partnerships see PARA 132 et seq.

4   Consent need not be express but may be implied (*Hodgkinson v Wilkie* (1975) 1 Hag Con 262; *Smith v Huson (falsely called Smith)* (1811) 1 Phillim 287) and may be expressly retracted (*Hodgkinson v Wilkie* at 265). It does not hold good if the person who gives it dies before the marriage is solemnised or the civil partnership is celebrated: *Ex p Reibey* (1843) 12 LJ Ch 436. A marriage solemnised or a civil partnership celebrated without the requisite consent is nevertheless valid: *R v Birmingham Inhabitants* (1828) 8 B & C 29.

5   Marriage Act 1949 s 3(1) (amended by the Children Act 1975 s 108(1)(a), Sch 3 para 7; the Family Law Reform Act 1987 Sch 2 para 9; the Children Act 1989 s 108(4), (7), Sch 12 para 5(1), Sch 15; the Immigration and Asylum Act 1999 s 169(1), (3), Sch 14 paras 3, 4(a), (b), Sch 16); Civil Partnership Act 2004 Sch 2 para 1. The Marriage Act 1949 s 3(1) applies to marriages intended to be solemnised on the authority of a common licence, with the substitution of references to the ecclesiastical authority by whom the licence was granted for references to the superintendent registrar and with the substitution of a reference to the Master of Faculties for the reference to the Registrar General: s 3(2) (amended by the Adoption and Children Act 2002

Sch 3 para 5). The Dean of the Arches and Auditor, as defined by the Ecclesiastical Jurisdiction Measure 1963 s 3(2)(a) (see ECCLESIASTICAL LAW vol 14 PARA 1286) is ex officio the Master of the Faculties: see the Ecclesiastical Jurisdiction Measure 1963 s 13(1); and ECCLESIASTICAL LAW vol 14 PARA 1286. As to common licences see PARAS 58, 76 et seq. For these purposes, except where the context otherwise requires, 'Registrar General' means the Registrar General of Births, Deaths and Marriages in England: Marriage Act 1949 s 78(1). As to the appointment and duties of the Registrar General of Births, Deaths and Marriages in England see REGISTRATION CONCERNING THE INDIVIDUAL vol 39(2) (Reissue) PARA 605 et seq.

6   For these purposes, 'parental responsibility' has the same meaning as in the Children Act 1989 (see CHILDREN AND YOUNG PERSONS vol 5(3) (2008 Reissue) PARA 134): Marriage Act 1949 s 3(1B) (added by Children Act 1989 Sch 12 para 5; and substituted by the Adoption and Children Act 2002 Sch 3 paras 1, 3); Civil Partnership Act 2004 Sch 2 para 2.

7   For these purposes, 'guardian of a child' has the same meaning as in the Children Act 1989 (see CHILDREN AND YOUNG PERSONS vol 5(3) (2008 Reissue) PARA 144): Marriage Act 1949 s 3(1B) (as added and substituted: see note 6); Civil Partnership Act 2004 Sch 2 para 2.

8   Marriage Act 1949 s 3(1A)(a) (s 3(1A) added by Children Act 1989 Sch 12 para 5; and substituted by the Adoption and Children Act 2002 Sch 3 para 3); Civil Partnership Act 2004 Sch 2 para 1.

9   For these purposes, 'special guardianship order' has the same meaning as in the Children Act 1989 (see CHILDREN AND YOUNG PERSONS vol 5(3) (2008 Reissue) PARA 151): Marriage Act 1949 s 3(1B) (as added: see note 6); Civil Partnership Act 2004 Sch 2 para 2.

10   Marriage Act 1949 s 3(1A)(b) (as added: see note 8); Civil Partnership Act 2004 Sch 2 para 1. For these purposes, 'special guardian' has the same meaning as in the Children Act 1989 (see CHILDREN AND YOUNG PERSONS vol 5(3) (2008 Reissue) PARA 151): Marriage Act 1949 s 3(1B) (as added: see note 6); Civil Partnership Act 2004 Sch 2 para 2.

11   For these purposes, 'care order' has the same meaning as in the Children Act 1989 (see CHILDREN AND YOUNG PERSONS vol 5(3) (2008 Reissue) PARA 271): Marriage Act 1949 s 3(1B) (as added: see note 6); Civil Partnership Act 2004 Sch 2 para 2.

12   Marriage Act 1949 s 3(1A)(c) (as added: see note 8); Civil Partnership Act 2004 Sch 2 para 1.

13   For these purposes, 'residence order' has the same meaning as in the Children Act 1989 (see CHILDREN AND YOUNG PERSONS vol 5(3) (2008 Reissue) PARA 271 note 4): Marriage Act 1949 s 3(1B) (as added: see note 6); Civil Partnership Act 2004 Sch 2 para 2.

14   Marriage Act 1949 s 3(1A)(d) (as added: see note 8); Civil Partnership Act 2004 Sch 2 para 1.

15   For these purposes, 'adoption agency' has the same meaning as in the Adoption and Children Act 2002 (see CHILDREN AND YOUNG PERSONS vol 5(3) (2008 Reissue) PARA 389): Marriage Act 1949 s 3(1B) (as added: see note 6); Civil Partnership Act 2004 Sch 2 para 2.

16   For these purposes, 'placed for adoption' has the same meaning as in the Adoption and Children Act 2002 (see CHILDREN AND YOUNG PERSONS vol 5(3) (2008 Reissue) PARA 331): Marriage Act 1949 s 3(1B) (as added: see note 6); Civil Partnership Act 2004 Sch 2 para 2.

17   For these purposes, 'local authority' has the same meaning as in the Adoption and Children Act 2002 (see CHILDREN AND YOUNG PERSONS vol 5(3) (2008 Reissue) PARA 331): Marriage Act 1949 s 3(1B) (as added: see note 6); and the Civil Partnership Act 2004 Sch 2 para 2.

18   Marriage Act 1949 s 3(1A)(e) (as added: see note 8); Civil Partnership Act 2004 Sch 2 para 1.

19   For these purposes, 'placement order' has the same meaning as in the Adoption and Children Act 2002 (see CHILDREN AND YOUNG PERSONS vol 5(3) (2008 Reissue) PARA 335): Marriage Act 1949 s 3(1B) (as added: see note 6); Civil Partnership Act 2004 Sch 2 para 2.

20   Marriage Act 1949 s 3(1A)(f) (as added: see note 8); and the Civil Partnership Act 2004 Sch 2 para 1. 'Appropriate local authority' means the local authority authorised by the placement order to place the child for adoption: Marriage Act 1949 s 3(1B) (as added: see note 6); Civil Partnership Act 2004 Sch 2 para 2.

21   Marriage Act 1949 s 3(1A)(g) (as added: see note 8); Civil Partnership Act 2004 Sch 2 para 1. The prospective adopters will be required to give their consent only in so far as their parental responsibility has not been restricted under the Adoption and Children Act 2002 s 25(4) (see CHILDREN AND YOUNG PERSONS vol 5(3) (2008 Reissue) PARA 334): Marriage Act 1949 s 3(1A)(g) (as so added); Civil Partnership Act 2004 Sch 2 para 1.

22   Marriage Act 1949 s 3(1A)(h) (as added: see note 8); Civil Partnership Act 2004 Sch 2 para 1.

23   Marriage Act 1949 s 3(6); Civil Partnership Act 2004 s 4(4). As to wards of court see CHILDREN AND YOUNG PERSONS vol 5(3) (2008 Reissue) PARA 218 et seq.

47.   Where consent is unobtainable or refused.   If the superintendent registrar[1] (in the case of marriage) or the registration authority[2] (in the case of civil partnership) is satisfied that the consent of any person whose consent is required to the marriage or entry into a civil partnership of a child[3], cannot be obtained by reason of absence or inaccessibility, or by reason of his being under any disability, the necessity for the consent of that person is to be dispensed with if there is any other person whose consent is also required[4]. If the consent of no other person is required, the Registrar General[5] may dispense with the necessity of obtaining any consent, or, on application being made[6], the court may consent to the marriage, or the civil partnership, and the consent of the court so given has the same effect as if it had been given by the person whose consent cannot be so obtained[7].

If any person whose consent for the marriage or civil partnership is required refuses his consent, then, on application being made, the court may consent to the marriage or to the registration of the civil partnership; and the consent so given has the same effect as if it had been given by the person whose consent is refused[8].

Nothing in these provisions dispenses with the necessity of obtaining the consent of the High Court to the marriage of a ward of court[9].

1   As to the meaning of 'superintendent registrar' see PARA 46 note 2.
2   'Registration authority' means, in relation to England, a county council, the council of any district comprised in an area for which there is no county council, a London borough council, the Common Council of the City of London or the Council of the Isles of Scilly, and in relation to Wales, a county council or a county borough council: Civil Partnership Act 2004 s 28. As to local government areas and authorities in England and Wales see LOCAL GOVERNMENT vol 29(1) (Reissue) PARA 23 et seq. As to the London boroughs and their councils see LONDON GOVERNMENT vol 29(2) (Reissue) PARAS 30, 35–39, 59 et seq. As to the Common Council of the City of London see LONDON GOVERNMENT vol 29(2) (Reissue) PARAS 51–55.
3   Ie by the Marriage Act 1949 s 3(1) or the Civil Partnership Act 2004 Sch 2 Pt 1: see PARA 46. As to the meaning of 'child' see PARA 37 note 3.
4   Marriage Act 1949 s 3(1) proviso (a); Civil Partnership Act 2004 Sch 2 para 3(1), (2).
5   As to the meaning of 'Registrar General' see PARA 46 note 5.
6   As to the court to which application may be made, and as to the procedure, see PARA 48.
7   Marriage Act 1949 s 3(1) proviso (a); Civil Partnership Act 2004 Sch 2 para 3(3), (4). As to the application of these provisions to marriages intended to be solemnised on the authority of a common licence see PARA 46 note 3.
8   Marriage Act 1949 s 3(1) proviso (b); Civil Partnership Act 2004 Sch 2 para 4.
9   Marriage Act 1949 s 3(6). As to wards of court see CHILDREN AND YOUNG PERSONS vol 5(3) (2008 Reissue) PARA 218 et seq.

48.   Application for consent of the court. Application for the consent of the court to the marriage or civil partnership of a child[1] may be made to the High Court[2], the county court of the district in which any applicant or respondent resides or a court of summary jurisdiction appointed for the commission area in which any applicant or respondent resides[3].

An application for the consent of the court to the marriage or civil partnership of a child must be dealt with in chambers unless the court otherwise directs[4]. The application must be heard and determined by a district judge[5]. An application may be brought without the intervention of the applicant's litigation friend, unless the court otherwise directs[6]. Where such an application follows a refusal to give consent to the marriage or to the registration of the child as a civil partner, every person who has refused consent must be made a defendant to the summons or a respondent to the application, as appropriate[7]. Unless the court orders otherwise, the application must be served not less than seven days before the date on which the application is to be heard[8].

An application for the consent of a magistrates' court to the marriage of, or the formation of a civil partnership by, a child may be made, either orally or in writing, to a justice of the peace[9]. On receiving such an application, the justice must, where the application was in consequence of a refusal to give consent to the marriage or civil partnership, give to any person whose consent is required and who has refused consent a notice of the application and of the date, time and place appointed for the hearing[10].

1   As to the circumstances in which the court may give consent see PARA 47. As to the meaning of 'child' see PARA 37 note 3.

2   Proceedings for obtaining the High Court's consent to the marriage of a child are assigned to the Family Division (see the Supreme Court Act 1981 s 61(1), (3), Sch 1 para 3(c); and PARA 731) and are, therefore, 'family proceedings' for the purposes of the Matrimonial and Family Proceedings Act 1984 Pt V (ss 32–42) (see PARA 749).

3   Marriage Act 1949 s 3(5) (amended by the Family Law Reform Act 1969 s 2(2); the Domestic Proceedings and Magistrates' Courts Act 1978 Sch 2 para 9; the Access to Justice Act 1999 s 106, Sch 15 Pt V; and the Courts Act 2003 Sch 8 para 85); Civil Partnership Act 2004 Sch 2 para 15(1).

4   Family Proceedings Rules 1991, SI 1991/1247, rr 3.20(1), 3.20A(1) (r 3.20A added by SI 2005/2922).

5   Family Proceedings Rules 1991, SI 1991/1247, rr 3.20(2), 3.20A(2) (r 3.20A as added: see note 4). As to district judges see COURTS vol 10 (Reissue) PARA 661.

6   Family Proceedings Rules 1991, SI 1991/1247, rr 3.20(3), 3.20A(3) (r 3.20A as added: see note 4).

7   Family Proceedings Rules 1991, SI 1991/1247, rr 3.20(4), 3.20A(4) (r 3.20A as added: see note 4).

8   Family Proceedings Rules 1991, SI 1991/1247, rr 3.20(5), 3.20A(5) (r 3.20A as added: see note 4).

9   Magistrates' Courts (Guardianship of Minors) Rules 1974, SI 1974/706, r 5(1) (amended by SI 1989/384; SI 2005/617).

10 Magistrates' Courts (Guardianship of Minors) Rules 1974, SI 1974/706, r 5(2) (r 5(2), (4) amended by SI 2005/2930). The Magistrates' Courts Rules 1981, SI 1981/552, r 99 (service of summons etc: see MAGISTRATES vol 29(2) (Reissue) PARA 690) applies in relation to the service of a notice so given as it applies in relation to the service of a summons issued on a person other than a corporation: Magistrates' Courts (Guardianship of Minors) Rules 1974, SI 1974/706, r 5(3). The provisions of the Magistrates' Courts Act 1980 Pt II (ss 51–74) (see MAGISTRATES) relating to the hearing of a complaint and of the Magistrates' Courts Rules 1981, SI 1981/552, r 14 (order of evidence and speeches: see MAGISTRATES vol 29(2) (Reissue) PARA 728) apply to the hearing of such an application as if it were made by way of complaint but as if for any reference therein to the complainant, the complaint and his defence there were substituted references to the applicant, the application, the respondent and his case respectively: Magistrates' Courts (Guardianship of Minors) Rules 1974, SI 1974/706, r 5(4) (as so amended).

49.   Evidence of consent.   Where, for the purpose of obtaining a certificate for marriage or for a civil partnership schedule, a person declares that the consent of any person or persons whose consent is required has been obtained, the superintendent registrar or registration authority may refuse to issue the certificate or schedule, unless satisfied by the production of written evidence that the consent of that person or of those persons has in fact been obtained[1].

If any person for the purpose of procuring a marriage or a civil partnership, or a notice, certificate or licence relating to a marriage or civil partnership, knowingly and wilfully makes or signs a false declaration, he is guilty of an offence[2].

1   See the Family Law Reform Act 1969 s 2(3); the Civil Partnership Act 2004 Sch 2 para 7; and PARAS 90, 138. As to forbidding the issue of a certificate or schedule see PARAS 95, 137. As to the persons whose consent is required see PARA 46. As to the meaning of 'child' see PARA 37 note 3. It is not necessary that the consent of any person whose consent is required to a marriage or civil partnership of a child should be given in any particular manner, and consent may be implied if that person has knowledge of the relevant relationship and does not expressly dissent:

Hodgkinson v Wilkie (1795) 1 Hag Con 262; *Smith v Huson (falsely called Smith)* (1811) 1 Phillim 287 at 306; *Cresswell v Cosins* (1815) 2 Phillim 281; cf *Balfour v Carpenter (falsely called Balfour)* (1811) 1 Phillim 221.

2 See PARAS 184–185.

50. Withdrawal of consent. Consent may be retracted at any time before the actual solemnisation or registration of the marriage or civil partnership[1], but once it is given it must not be capriciously withdrawn[2], and the clearest proof of subsequent dissent is necessary to displace it[3].

1 *Hodgkinson v Wilkie* (1795) 1 Hag Con 262. Although this decision and the decisions cited in notes 2, 3 pre-date the concept of civil partnerships and are concerned only with consent to marry, the Civil Partnership Act 2004 confers rights on civil partners which in all practicable respects are analogous to those enjoyed by married persons, and it is reasonable to infer that they must now apply in relation to civil partnerships.
2 *Re Brown, Ingall v Brown* [1904] 1 Ch 120.
3 *Hodgkinson v Wilkie* (1795) 1 Hag Con 262. The consent will be presumed until the contrary is proved: *Harrison v Southampton Corpn* (1853) 4 De GM & G 137. As to the position where the person who gives consent dies before a marriage is solemnised or a civil partnership is celebrated see *Ex p Reibey* (1843) 12 LJ Ch 436 (death of minor's father after consenting to his marriage; guardian unable to form opinion as to propriety of marriage; application to court for approval of marriage); cf *Yonge v Furse* (1856) 26 LJ Ch 117; on appeal 26 LJ Ch 352 (condition in will in restraint of legatee's marriage; legatee married after testator's death; testator alleged to have consented before his death to the marriage).

51. Effect of absence of consent. Where a marriage has been duly solemnised under superintendent registrar's certificate or two people have registered as civil partners of each other, it is not necessary in support of the marriage or civil partnership to give any proof that any person whose consent is required had given his consent, nor may any evidence be given to prove the contrary in any proceedings touching the validity of the marriage or civil partnership[1].

1 See the Marriage Act 1949 s 48(1)(b); the Civil Partnership Act 2004 s 52(1); and PARAS 22, 26. The marriage of a child without the requisite consent is not invalid, whether it is by banns or licence or superintendent registrar's certificate: *R v Birmingham Inhabitants* (1828) 8 B & C 29 (marriage by licence under the Marriage Act 1823 (repealed)). As to forbidding the issue of a certificate see PARA 95.

52. Declaration of dissent from marriage of child. Where the marriage of a child[1], not being a widower or widow, is intended to be solemnised after the publication of banns of matrimony[2], then, if any person whose consent to the marriage would have been required[3] in the case of a marriage intended to be solemnised otherwise than after the publication of the banns, openly and publicly declares or causes to be declared, in the church or chapel in which the banns are published, at the time of the publication, his dissent from the intended marriage, the publication of banns is void[4].

1 As to the meaning of 'child' see PARA 37 note 3.
2 As to banns of matrimony see PARA 58 et seq.
3 Ie under the Marriage Act 1949 s 3: see PARAS 46, 47.
4 Marriage Act 1949 s 3(3) (s 3(3), (4) amended by the Family Law Reform Act 1987 Sch 2 para 9). Affirmative consent to the marriage is not required in this case. A clergyman is not liable to ecclesiastical censure for solemnising the marriage of a child after the publication of banns without the consent of the parents or guardians of the child unless he had notice of the dissent of any person who is entitled to give notice of dissent under the Marriage Act 1949 s 3(3): s 3(4) (as so amended). If, however, a clergyman knowingly and wilfully solemnises the marriage without banns of marriage having been duly published (which would be the case if notice of dissent were given, the publication being void), except on the authority of a special or common licence or superintendent registrar's certificate, he is guilty of an offence and liable to

imprisonment for a term not exceeding 14 years (s 75(1)(b)) if a prosecution is commenced within three years from the commission of the offence (s 75(4)).

2. FORMS AND CEREMONIES

(1) METHODS OF MARRIAGE AND CIVIL PARTNERSHIP

53. Methods of lawful marriage. Every marriage should be by banns[1], licence[2] or superintendent registrar's certificates or naval officer's certificate[3], and, except in the case of a marriage according to the usages of the Society of Friends or between persons professing the Jewish religion according to the usages of the Jews[4] and of a marriage by special licence[5], should be solemnised:

(1) in a church or chapel of the Church of England[6] in which marriages may lawfully be solemnised[7];

(2) at a superintendent registrar's office[8];

(3) in a Non-conformist church or building duly registered for the solemnisation of marriages[9];

(4) in a naval, military or air force chapel[10];

(5) in an approved building[11]; or

(6) at the usual place of residence of a housebound or detained person[12].

Where, in the case of a marriage not to be solemnised according to the rites of the Church of England, one of the parties is seriously ill and cannot be moved to a place of solemnisation, the marriage may be solemnised by Registrar General's licence elsewhere than at a registered building or superintendent registrar's office[13].

1   As to banns see PARAS 58, 68.
2   As to licences see PARA 76 et seq.
3   As to marriage on the authority of superintendent registrar's certificates see PARA 87 et seq; as to marriage on the authority of a naval officer's certificate see PARA 129 et seq.
4   See PARAS 115–118.
5   See PARA 76.

6   Any reference in the Marriage Act 1949 to the Church of England is, unless the context otherwise requires, to be construed as including a reference to the Church in Wales: s 78(2). As to the Church in Wales generally see ECCLESIASTICAL LAW vol 14 PARA 322 et seq. The Marriage Act 1949 applies to the performing in England or Wales of a ceremony in a form known to, and recognised by, English law as capable of producing, when there performed, a valid marriage, namely one which will prima facie confer the status of husband and wife on the two persons: *R v Bham* [1966] 1 QB 159 at 169, [1965] 3 All ER 124 at 129, CCA. The Marriage Act 1949 ss 10, 19, 20(7) (banns: see PARAS 61, 62, 67) do not extend to Wales or Monmouthshire: s 80(3), Sch 6 (amended by the Marriage (Wales and Monmouthshire) Act 1962 s 1(1); the Marriage (Wales) Act 1986 s 1). The Marriage Act 1949 ss 6(4), 9, 11(2), 15(1)(b), 16(1)(b) (so far as it relates to marriages to be solemnised in the usual place of worship of one of the parties), 35(3) and 72, which originally did not extend to Wales or Monmouthshire (see s 80(3), Sch 6 (as originally enacted)) now extend to these areas: Marriage (Wales and Monmouthshire) Act 1962 s 1(1). Any parish which is treated for the purposes of the Welsh Church Act 1914 as being wholly within or wholly without Wales or Monmouthshire is to be so treated also for the purposes of the Marriage Act 1949 and the Marriage (Wales and Monmouthshire) Act 1962: s 2. As to the treatment of border parishes see CREMATION AND BURIAL vol 10 (Reissue) PARA 1012.
7   See PARAS 59, 82.
8   See PARA 102.
9   See PARA 186 et seq.
10   See PARA 129.
11   See PARAS 190–201.
12   See PARAS 171, 173.
13   See PARA 161 et seq.

54. Marriages on the authority of superintendent registrar's certificates. The following marriages may[1] be solemnised on the authority of two superintendent registrar's certificates[2]:

(1) a marriage in a registered building[3] according to such form and ceremony as the persons to be married see fit to adopt[4];

(2) a marriage in the office of a superintendent registrar[5];

(3) a marriage on approved premises[6];

(4) a marriage according to the usages of the Society of Friends (commonly called Quakers)[7];

(5) a marriage between two persons professing the Jewish religion according to the usages of the Jews[8];

(6) the marriage, other than a marriage in pursuance of head (4) or (5) above, of a person who is housebound[9] or is a detained person[10] at the place where he or she usually resides[11];

(7) a marriage according to the rites of the Church of England[12] in any church or chapel in which banns of matrimony may be published[13].

A marriage according to the rites of the Church of England may be solemnised on the authority of superintendent registrar's certificates[14] in any church or chapel in which banns of matrimony may be published or, in the case of persons who are housebound or are detained persons[15], the place specified in the notices of marriage and certificates as the place where the marriage is to be solemnised[16]; but a marriage is not to be so solemnised in any such church or chapel without the consent of the minister of the church or chapel or, wherever the marriage is solemnised, by any person other than a clergyman[17].

1   Ie subject to the provisions of the Marriage Act 1949 Pt III (ss 26–52): see PARA 87 et seq.

2   Marriage Act 1949 s 26(1) (amended by the Immigration and Asylum Act 1999 s 161(3)). As to the meaning of 'superintendent registrar' see PARA 22 note 1. The superintendent registrar may also issue certificates in certain circumstances for the purpose of marriages abroad of British nationals: see CONFLICT OF LAWS vol 8(3) (Reissue) PARA 226. As to offences in connection with solemnisation of marriages see PARA 180.

3   For the purposes of the Marriage Act 1949, 'registered building' means a building registered under the Marriage Act 1949 Pt III (see PARA 186 et seq): s 78(1).

4   Marriage Act 1949 s 26(1)(a).

5   Marriage Act 1949 s 26(1)(b). No religious service may be used: see PARA 102.

6   Marriage Act 1949 s 26(1)(bb) (added by the Marriage Act 1994 s 1(1)). For the purposes of the Marriage Act 1949, 'approved premises' means premises approved in accordance with regulations under s 46A (see PARAS 190–201) as premises on which marriages may be solemnised in pursuance of s 26(1)(bb): s 78(1) (amended by the Marriage Act 1994 Schedule paras 1, 8). As to marriages on approved premises see PARAS 190–201.

7   Marriage Act 1949 s 26(1)(c). As to marriages according to the usages of the Society of Friends see further PARAS 115–116.

8   Marriage Act 1949 s 26(1)(d). As to marriages between persons professing the Jewish religion according to the usages of the Jews see further PARAS 117–118.

9   As to the meaning of 'housebound' see PARA 169.

10 As to the meaning of 'detained person' see PARA 170.

11 Marriage Act 1949 s 26(1)(dd) (added by the Marriage Act 1983 Sch 1 para 4(a)). For these purposes, a person who is housebound or is a detained person is to be taken, if he or she would not otherwise be, to be resident and usually resident at the place where he or she is for the time being: Marriage Act 1949 s 78(5) (added by the Marriage Act 1983 Sch 1 para 21). As to marriages of persons who are housebound or detained persons see further PARAS 169–173.

12 As to the meaning of references to the Church of England see PARA 53 note 6.

13 Marriage Act 1949 s 26(1)(e) (amended by the Marriage Act 1983 Sch 1 para 4(a)). See the text and notes 14–17; and PARA 80. As to banns of matrimony see PARAS 58, 68.

14 Ie a certificate in force under the Marriage Act 1949 Pt III.

15 Ie in the case of a marriage in pursuance of the Marriage Act 1949 s 26(1)(dd): see text head (6).

16 Marriage Act 1949 s 17 (amended by the Marriage Act 1983 Sch 1 para 2(a); the Immigration and Asylum Act 1999 Sch 14 paras 3, 6).

17 Marriage Act 1949 s 17 proviso (amended by the Marriage Act 1983 Sch 1 para 2(b)). As to the meaning of 'clergyman' see PARA 23 note 5. See PARA 80 et seq.

55. Naval, military and air force marriages. Any chapel certified by the Admiralty[1] to be a naval chapel, or by the Secretary of State to be a military or airforce chapel may be licensed to authorise the publication of banns[2] and the solemnisation of marriages between parties of whom at least one is a qualified person[3]. The Admiralty, or any person authorised by it, in the case of a naval chapel, and the Secretary of State or any person authorised by him, in the case of any other licensed chapel, must appoint one or more clergymen[4] for the purpose of registering marriages solemnised in the chapel according to the rites of the Church of England[5]. Where one of the parties to a marriage intended to be solemnised in England on the authority of superintendent registrar's certificates[6] is an officer, seaman or marine on the books of one of Her Majesty's ships at sea, the officer, seaman or marine may give notice of his intention to the captain or other officer commanding the ship, together with the name and address of the other party to the marriage and such other information as may be necessary to enable the officer commanding to fill up a certificate[7].

1 As to the Admiralty see SHIPPING AND MARITIME LAW.
2 As to banns see PARAS 58, 68.
3 See PARA 129.
4 As to the meaning of 'clergyman' see PARA 23 note 5.
5 See PARA 130. As to such rites see PARA 57 et seq.
6 As to the meaning of 'superintendent registrar' see PARA 22 note 1.
7 See PARA 131.

56. Formation of civil partnership by registration. Two people may register as civil partners of each other under:
(1)   the standard procedure[1];
(2)   the procedure for housebound persons[2];
(3)   the procedure for detained persons[3]; and
(4)   the special procedure (which is for cases where a person is seriously ill and not expected to recover)[4].
Within these procedures, special provision is made for exceptional and unusual circumstances[5].

Two people are to be regarded as having registered as civil partners[6] of each other once each of them has signed the civil partnership document[7] at the invitation of, and in the presence of, a civil partnership registrar[8], and in the presence of each other and two witnesses[8]. No religious service is to be used while the civil partnership registrar is officiating at the signing of a civil partnership document[9].

The place at which two people may register as civil partners of each other must be in England or Wales, must not be in religious premises[10], and must be specified in the notices, or notice, of proposed civil partnership[11].

1 Civil Partnership Act 2004 s 5(1)(a). As to the standard procedure see PARA 133 et seq.
2 Civil Partnership Act 2004 s 5(1)(b). As to the procedure for housebound persons see PARAS 169, 171 et seq.
3 Civil Partnership Act 2004 s 5(1)(c). As to the procedure for detained persons see PARA 170 et seq.
4 Civil Partnership Act 2004 s 5(1)(d). As to the special procedure see PARA 140 et seq.
5 Civil Partnership Act 2004 s 5(1). The procedures under heads (1) to (3) are subject to s 20 (modified procedures for certain non-residents) and Sch 3 (former spouses one of whom has changed sex): s 5(2). The procedures under heads (1) to (4) are subject to Sch 1 Pt 2 (provisions applicable in connection with prohibited degrees of relationship) (see PARA 35) and Sch 2

Pts 2, 3 (provisions applicable where proposed civil partner is under 18) (see PARA 46): s 5(3). These provisions are also subject to s 249 and Sch 23 (immigration control and formation of civil partnerships) (see PARA 178): s 5(4).

6 As to the meaning of 'civil partner' see PARA 2 note 1.

7 'Civil partnership document' means, in relation to the special procedure, a Registrar General's licence, and, in relation to any other procedure, a civil partnership schedule: Civil Partnership Act 2004 ss 2(6), 7(1).

8 Civil Partnership Act 2004 s 2(1). After the civil partnership document has been signed it must also be signed, in the presence of the civil partners and each other, by each of the two witnesses, and the civil partnership registrar: s 2(3). After the witnesses and the civil partnership registrar have signed the civil partnership document, the relevant registration authority must ensure that the fact that the two people have registered as civil partners of each other, and any other information prescribed by the Civil Partnership (Registration Provisions) Regulations 2005, SI 2005/3176, is recorded in the register as soon as is practicable: Civil Partnership Act 2004 s 2(4). 'Relevant registration authority' means the registration authority in whose area the registration took place': s 2(7). Section 2(1) applies regardless of whether these provisions are followed: s 2(2).

9 Civil Partnership Act 2004 s 2(5).

10 'Religious premises' means premises which are used solely or mainly for religious purposes, or have been used and have not subsequently been used solely or mainly for other purposes: Civil Partnership Act 2004 s 6(2).

11 Civil Partnership Act 2004 s 6(1). In the case of registration under the standard procedure, the place must be on approved premises or in a register office: s 6(3), (3A) (s 6(3) substituted, and s 6(3A) added by SI 2005/2000). If it is in a register office provided under the Registration Service Act 1953 s 10, the place must be open to any person wishing to attend the registration: Civil Partnership Act 2004 s 6(3B), (3C) (added by SI 2005/2000).

(2) CHURCH OF ENGLAND MARRIAGES

(i) Entitlement to be Married according to the Rites of the Church of England

57. Conditions for church service. Persons legally qualified to intermarry[1] are in general entitled to be married according to the rites of the Church of England[2] in an authorised place[3] if one of them possesses the legal qualification of residence[4]. Marriage in England[5] according to the rites of the Church of England[6] can be solemnised after publication of banns[7], on the authority of a special or common licence[8], or on the authority of certificates issued by a superintendent registrar[9].

If the parties to a marriage solemnised in the presence of a superintendent registrar desire to add a Church of England service of solemnisation of matrimony they may present themselves, after giving notice to the clergyman[10] or minister, and he, on the production of their marriage certificate and on payment of the customary fee, if any, may, if he sees fit, use such form of service as may be approved by the General Synod[11] so long as he observes the canons and General Synod regulations for the time being in force[12].

1 Each party must be at least 16 years old (Marriage Act 1949 s 2), they must not be within the prohibited degrees of kindred and affinity (Sch 1 Pt I (substituted by the Civil Partnership Act 2004 Sch 27 para 17); PARA 35 et seq), and if either party (not being a widow or widower) is under 18 years of age the appropriate consent is normally required (see PARA 46). As to the validity of marriages see PARA 3.

2 *Argar v Holdsworth* (1758) 2 Lee 515; *R v James* (1850) 3 Car & Kir 167, CCR. Persons who are not members of the Church of England are entitled to be so married: *R v James* (1850) 3 Car & Kir 167, CCR. The question whether unbaptised persons can claim to be so married has never been decided (*Jenkins v Barrett* (1827) 1 Hag Ecc 12); it is thought that even where both parties were unbaptised such a claim could not lawfully be refused, at any rate in the case of marriage after publication of banns (as distinct from marriage by licence, which is always a matter of discretion: see PARA 76). It is clear that in the event of such a marriage being

    solemnised it will, if otherwise legal, be a valid marriage: *Jones v Robinson* (1815) 2 Phillim 285. As to customary fees relating to marriage see ECCLESIASTICAL LAW vol 14 PARA 1195.

3   As to authorised places see PARA 59.

4   For residential qualifications see PARAS 59, 76. As to the marriage rights of persons residing in a parish affected by a pastoral scheme see the Pastoral Measure 1983 Sch 3 para 14; and PARAS 59, 67. As to marriage in guild churches see the City of London (Guild Churches) Act 1952 s 22; and ECCLESIASTICAL LAW vol 14 PARA 606.

5   The law as to previous publication of banns or licence does not apply out of England: *Culling v Culling* [1896] P 116.

6   See PARA 53 note 6.

7   Marriage Act 1949 s 5(a). As to banns see PARA 59 et seq.

8   Marriage Act 1949 s 5(b), (c); *Middleton v Crofts* (1736) 2 Atk 650. As to licences see PARA 76 et seq.

9   Marriage Act 1949 s 5(d) (amended by the Immigration and Asylum Act 1999 Sch 14 paras 3, 5). See further PARA 161 et seq. As to the avoidance of marriages where the requirements in the text have to the parties' knowledge not been complied with see the Marriage Act 1949 s 25(b); and PARA 328.

10 As to the meaning of 'clergyman' see PARA 23 note 5.

11 Ie under the Revised Canons Ecclesiastical, Canon B2 (substituted by Amending Canon).

12 Revised Canons Ecclesiastical, Canon B36 para 1 (amended by Amending Canons Nos 1, 3); Marriage Act 1949 s 46(1) (amended by the Marriage Act 1983 s 1(7) Sch 1 para 12 (which is so worded as to extend to other religious denominations); Marriage (Registrar General's Licence) Act 1970 s 11(2)). There must be no banns, licence or certificate authorising a marriage in connection with this service (Canon B36 para 2), and no record of it must be entered in the marriage registers provided by the Registrar General (Canon B36 para 2; Marriage Act 1949 s 46(2)). The civil marriage is thus not superseded or invalidated by the service in church: s 46(2). No person who is not entitled to solemnise Church of England marriages may read or celebrate such a service: s 46(3).

58. Methods of authorising Church of England marriages. A marriage according to the rites of the Church of England[1] may be solemnised[2]:

  (1)   after the publication of banns of matrimony[3];

  (2)   on the authority of a special licence of marriage granted by the Archbishop of Canterbury or any other person by virtue of the Ecclesiastical Licences Act 1533 (a 'special licence')[4];

  (3)   on the authority of a licence of marriage, other than a special licence, granted by an ecclesiastical authority having power to grant such a licence (a 'common licence')[5]; or

  (4)   on the authority of certificates issued[6] by a superintendent registrar[7].

No clergyman[8] is obliged:

  (a)   to solemnise a marriage which, apart from statutory provision[9], would have been void by reason of the relationship of the persons to be married[10];

  (b)   to permit such a marriage to be solemnised in the church or chapel of which he is the minister[11]; or

  (c)   to solemnise the marriage of a person if the clergyman reasonably believes that the person's gender has become[12] the acquired gender[13].

Also, a clerk in Holy Orders of the Church in Wales is not obliged to permit the marriage of a person to be solemnised in the church or chapel of which the clerk is the minister if the clerk reasonably believes that the person's gender has become[14] the acquired gender[15].

Special provision is also made for the authorisation of Church of England marriages involving service personnel[16] or housebound or detained persons[17].

1   As to the meaning of references to the Church of England see PARA 53 note 6. As to the solemnisation of marriages in a guild church see the City of London (Guild Churches) Act 1952 s 22; and ECCLESIASTICAL LAW vol 14 PARA 606. The provisions of the Marriage Act 1949 s 5 relating to the publication of banns and the solemnisation of marriages according to the rites of

the Church of England apply to church buildings shared by the Church of England under a sharing agreement: see the Sharing of Church Buildings Act 1969 s 6(2)–(5); and ECCLESIASTICAL LAW vol 14 PARA 1412.

2 As to offences relating to the solemnisation of marriages see PARA 180.

3 Marriage Act 1949 s 5(a). Section 5(a) does not apply in relation to the solemnisation of any marriage mentioned in s 1(2) (see PARA 37): s 5 proviso (added by the Marriage (Prohibited Degrees of Relationship) Act 1986 Sch 1 para 3). As to the publication of banns see further PARA 65 et seq.

4 Marriage Act 1949 s 5(b). See further PARA 76. Nothing in the Marriage Act 1949 affects the right of the Archbishop of Canterbury or any other person by virtue of the Ecclesiastical Licences Act 1553 to grant special licences to marry at any convenient time or place, or affects the validity of any marriage solemnised on the authority of such a licence: Marriage Act 1949 s 79(6).

5 Marriage Act 1949 s 5(c). See further PARA 76.

6 Ie under the Marriage Act 1949 Pt III (ss 26–52): see PARA 87 et seq.

7 Marriage Act 1949 s 5(d) (amended by the Immigration and Asylum Act 1999 Sch 14 paras 3, 5).

8 As to the meaning of 'clergyman' see PARA 23 note 5.

9 Ie the Marriage (Prohibited Degrees of Relationship) Act 1986 and the Marriage Act 1949 (Remedial) Order 2007, SI 2007/438: Marriage Act 1949 s 5A(a) (s 5A added by the Marriage (Prohibited Degrees of Relationship) Act 1986 s 3; Marriage Act 1949 s 5A(a) amended by SI 2007/438). As to the Marriage (Prohibited Degrees of Relationship) Act 1986 see PARA 37. The Marriage Act 1949 (Remedial) Order 2007, SI 2007/438, repealed the Marriage Act 1949 s 1(4)–(8), Sch 1 Pt III, which provided that marriages between a man and the mother of his former wife or the former wife of his son, and marriages between a woman and the father of her former husband or the former husband of her daughter, were void, and was held in Application 36536/02 *B v United Kingdom* [2005] 3 FCR 353, [2006] 1 FLR 35, [2005] All ER (D) 63 (Sep) ECtHR, to be incompatible with the Convention for the Protection of Human Rights and Fundamental Freedoms (Rome, 4 November 1950; TS 71 (1953); Cmd 8969) art 12 (right to marry and found a family: see CONSTITUTIONAL LAW AND HUMAN RIGHTS vol 8(2) (Reissue) PARA 162).

10 Marriage Act 1949 s 5A(a) (as added and amended: see note 9).

11 Marriage Act 1949 s 5A(b) (as added: see note 9).

12 Ie under the Gender Recognition Act 2004: see CONSTITUTIONAL LAW AND HUMAN RIGHTS.

13 Marriage Act 1949 s 5B(1) (s 5B added by the Gender Recognition Act 2004 Sch 4 paras 1, 3).

14 See note 12.

15 Marriage Act 1949 s 5B(2) (as added: see note 13).

16 See PARA 55.

17 See PARA 169.

(ii) Place for Banns and Marriage

59. Places of solemnisation. Marriage after banns must normally be solemnised in the church or chapel[1] or, as the case may be, one of the churches or chapels in which banns have been published[2]. Where, however, after the completion of the publication of banns in any church, another church has become a church in which banns could be published in relation to the parties to the intended marriage[3], the marriage may be solemnised in that other church[4]. Departure from the general rule is authorised also in certain cases where two or more benefices[5] are held in plurality or where by virtue of a pastoral scheme there are two or more parishes or parish churches in the area of a single benefice[6].

Marriage by common licence[7] must be solemnised in the parish church of the parish[8], or an authorised chapel[9] of the ecclesiastical district[10] in which one of the persons to be married has had his or her usual place of residence for 15 days immediately before the grant of the licence[11] or in a parish church or authorised chapel which is the usual place of worship[12] of the parties or of one of them[13]. For the purpose of marriage by common licence a parish in which there is no parish church or chapel or none in which divine service is usually solemnised every Sunday and any extra-parochial place which has no authorised chapel are deemed to belong to any adjoining parish or chapelry[14]. Where, after the issue of a common licence for the solemnisation of the marriage in any church, another church has taken the place of that church as a church in which the marriage of the parties concerned ought to be solemnised in pursuance of a common licence[15], the marriage may be solemnised in that other church[16].

However, a person who intends to be married has the like, but no greater, right to have the marriage solemnised in a parish church[17] of a parish as he has to have the marriage solemnised in the parish church of the parish in which he resides or which is his usual place or worship, if he has one of the following 'qualifying connections'[18]:

(1) that he was baptised in that parish, unless the baptism took place in a combined rite which included baptism and confirmation, or is a person whose confirmation has been entered in the register book of confirmation for any church or chapel in that parish[19];

(2) that he has at any time had his usual place of residence in that parish for a period of not less than six months[20];

(3) he has at any time habitually attended public worship in that parish for a period of not less than six months[21];

(4) a parent[22] of that person has during the lifetime of that person had his usual place of residence in that parish for a period of not less than six months or habitually attended public worship in that parish for that period[23]; or

(5) a parent or grandparent of that person has been married in that parish[24].

Where a parish has ceased to exist as a result of a pastoral scheme[25] or otherwise, or the boundaries have been altered and a person can establish a qualifying connection with a place situated within such a parish, then if that place is situated within the parish in which the church where the marriage is to be solemnised, that person will be deemed to have a qualifying connection with that parish[26].

A person who has the right to have a marriage so solemnised will have the like right to have the banns of that marriage published in the parish church where the marriage is to be solemnised[27].

The fact that a church building is shared by the Church of England with another church is not in itself an impediment to the use of the building for the publication of banns and the solemnisation of marriages according to the rites of the Church of England[28].

1 Marriage in a private house or elsewhere than in a church or chapel, except under special licence, is an ecclesiastical offence: *Middleton v Crofts* (1736) 2 Atk 650. Any person who knowingly and wilfully solemnises a marriage according to the rites of the Church of England (other than a marriage by special licence or a marriage pursuant to the Marriage Act 1949 s 26(1)(dd) (marriage of housebound or detained persons: see PARA 171)) in any place other than a church or other building in which banns may be published is guilty of an offence and liable to imprisonment not exceeding 14 years if prosecuted within three years from the commission of the offence: Marriage Act 1949 s 75(1)(c), (4) (s 75(1)(c) amended by the Marriage Act 1983 Sch 1 para 20(a)). See PARA 57 note 1. As to marriages by special licence see PARA 76. As to offences relating to the solemnisation of marriages see PARA 180.

2 Marriage Act 1949 s 12(1). As to the place of publication of banns see PARA 65 et seq. Where a marriage has been solemnised after the publication of banns it is not necessary in support of the marriage to give any proof of the residence of the parties or either of them in any parish or district where banns were published and no evidence is to be given to prove the contrary in any proceedings touching the validity of the marriage: s 24(1).

3   Ie by virtue of, or of anything done under, the Pastoral Measure 1983; as to which see ECCLESIASTICAL LAW.
4   Pastoral Measure 1983 Sch 3 para 14(2).
5   As to benefices see ECCLESIASTICAL LAW vol 14 PARA 768.
6   Marriage Act 1949 s 23; Pastoral Measure 1983 Sch 3 para 14(4); see PARA 60. As to pastoral schemes see ECCLESIASTICAL LAW vol 14 PARA 856 et seq.
7   As to marriage by common licence see PARA 76.
8   'Parish' means an ecclesiastical parish, and includes a district constituted under the Church Building Act 1818 to 1884 (see ECCLESIASTICAL LAW vol 14 PARA 537), notwithstanding that the district has not become a new parish by virtue of the New Parishes Act 1856 s 14 (repealed), or the New Parishes Measure 1943 s 5 (repealed), being a district to which the Acts relating to the publication of banns and the solemnisation of marriages were applied by the Church Building Acts as if the district had been an ancient parish: Marriage Act 1949 s 78(1). As to the application of enactments relating to marriages to such districts see the Church Building Act 1822 s 18 (repealed); and cf generally ECCLESIASTICAL LAW vol 14 PARA 538 et seq. 'Parish church' must be construed in accordance with this definition of 'parish': Marriage Act 1949 s 78(1). A building designated as the parish centre of worship is deemed for the purposes of the Marriage Act 1949 to be the parish church (Pastoral Measure 1983 s 29(2); and see ECCLESIASTICAL LAW vol 14 PARA 539), but this is subject to the parties' right to have recourse at their option to the parish church of an adjoining parish (see the Pastoral Measure 1983 s 29(2) proviso (b); Marriage Act 1949 ss 6(3), 15(2)).
9   In relation to a chapelry, 'authorised chapel' means a chapel of the chapelry in which banns could lawfully be published immediately before the Marriage Act 1823 (repealed), or in which banns may be published and marriages may be solemnised by virtue of the Marriages Confirmation Act 1825 s 2 (which authorises the solemnisation of marriages in certain churches and chapels in which solemnisation was customary before the passing of that Act), or by virtue of an authorisation given under the Marriage Act 1823 s 3 (repealed): Marriage Act 1949 s 78(1). In relation to an extra-parochial place 'authorised chapel' means a church or chapel of that place in which banns may be published and marriages may be solemnised by virtue of the Marriage Confirmation Act 1825 s 2, or an authorisation given under the Marriage Act 1823 s 3 (repealed), or the Marriage Act 1949 s 21: s 78(1). In relation to a district specified in a licence granted under s 20 (see PARA 62) 'authorised chapel' means the chapel in which banns may be published and marriages may be solemnised by virtue of that licence: s 78(1).
10 As to the meaning of 'ecclesiastical district' see PARA 21 note 3.
11 Marriage Act 1949 s 15(1)(a). In relation to a licensed naval, military or air force chapel (as to which see PARA 129) s 15(1)(a) applies as if the chapel were the parish church of the parish in which the chapel is situated: Sch 4 Pt II. Where a marriage has been solemnised on the authority of a common licence it is not necessary in support of the marriage to give any proof that the requirements as to residence were complied with and no evidence is to be given to prove the contrary in any proceedings touching the validity of the marriage: s 24(2).
12 As to the meaning of 'usual place of worship' see PARA 66.
13 Marriage Act 1949 s 15(1)(b). Section 15(1)(b) does not apply in relation to licensed naval, military or air force chapels: see PARA 129 note 9.
14 Marriage Act 1949 s 15(2).
15 Ie by virtue of, or of anything done under, the Pastoral Measure 1983.
16 Pastoral Measure 1983 Sch 3 para 14(5).
17 For the purposes of the Church of England Marriage Measure 2008 'church' does not include a cathedral and 'parish' includes a conventional district: s 1(11), (12)(b).
18 Church of England Marriage Measure 2008 s 1(1). Where a church or other building licensed for public worship has been designated under the Pastoral Measure 1983 s 29(2) (see the text and note 8), as a parish centre of worship, these provisions apply to such a centre while the designation is in force, as they apply to a parish church: Church of England Marriage Measure 2008 s 1(2). A person who wishes to have his or her marriage solemnised in this way must provide such information, written or otherwise, as the minister of the parish in which the marriage is to be solemnised may require in order to satisfy himself that that person has a qualifying connection and: (1) the Marriage Act 1949 s 8 (see PARA 68) will apply as if the reference to clergyman were a reference to the minister; and (2) the minister will be under a duty, when considering whether any information provided to him is sufficient to satisfy himself that the person wishing to have the marriage solemnised has a qualifying connection, to have regard to any guidance issued under the Church of England Marriage Measure 2008 s 3: s 1(8). If the minister considers that it is necessary in order to satisfy himself that a person has a qualifying connection, he may require that person to supply or support any such information to be provided by means of a statutory declaration: s 1(9). The House of Bishops will from time to

time issue guidance as to the exercise of any functions by a minister under s 1(8), (9) or by the authority having power to grant a common licence under s 1(8) as applied by s 2 (as to which see PARA 41): s 3. 'Minister' means: (a) where a special cure of souls has been assigned to any priest for the area in which the church where the marriage is to be solemnised is situated, whether in a team ministry or otherwise, that priest; (b) where head (a) does not apply, the incumbent of the benefice in the area of which that church is situated; (c) where neither head (a) nor (b) applies, the priest-in-charge of that benefice; (d) where heads (a)–(c) do not apply, in the case of a team ministry, the vicar, if any, appointed by the bishop to act as rector under the Pastoral Measure 1983 s 20(14) (see ECCLESIASTICAL LAW) or, if there is no such vicar appointed, the vicar who has held office for the longest period in that ministry; or (e) where none of the above applies, the rural dean of the deanery in which that church is situated: Church of England Marriage Measure 2008 s 1(12)(a).

19 Church of England Marriage Measure 2008 s 1(3)(a). Any reference to baptism, confirmation, marriage or public worship is to be construed as a reference to baptism, confirmation, marriage or public worship, as the case may be, according to the rites of the Church of England: s 1(12)(c).

20 Church of England Marriage Measure 2008 s 1(3)(b).

21 Church of England Marriage Measure 2008 s 1(3)(c).

22 'Parent' includes an adoptive parent and any other person who has undertaken the care and upbringing of the person seeking to establish a qualifying connection and 'grandparent' is construed accordingly: Church of England Marriage Measure 2008 s 1(4).

23 Church of England Marriage Measure 2008 s 1(3)(d).

24 Church of England Marriage Measure 2008 s 1(3)(e).

25 As to pastoral schemes see ECCLESIASTICAL LAW vol 14 PARA 856 et seq.

26 Church of England Marriage Measure 2008 s 1(13). The place must be appropriately situated at the time when the notice under the Marriage Act 1949 s 8 (see PARA 68) is delivered: Church of England Marriage Measure 2008 s 1(13).

27 Church of England Marriage Measure 2008 s 1(5). This is in addition to the requirements of the Marriage Act 1949 s 6 (see PARA 65) for banns to be published in the parish church of the parish where the parties to the marriage reside or of each parish in which one of them resides: Church of England Marriage Measure 2008 s 1(6).

28 See the Sharing of Church Buildings Act 1969 s 6(2); and ECCLESIASTICAL LAW vol 14 PARA 330.

60.   Banns and marriages in cases of pastoral reorganisation. Where two or more benefices[1] are held in plurality[2] the bishop of the diocese or, during a vacancy in the see, the guardian of the spiritualities[3], may in writing direct where the banns of persons entitled to be married in any church of those benefices may be published and where marriages of those persons may be solemnised[4], but not so as to deprive a person of the right to be married in any church in which he would have been entitled to be married if no such directions had been given[5].

The same provision applies, subject to the necessary modifications, to a case where by virtue of anything done under the Pastoral Measure 1983 there are two or more parishes or parish churches in the area of a single benefice[6], and to a case where by virtue of a designation in a pastoral scheme a parish has more than one parish church, in which latter case marriages may be solemnised in any of the parish churches[7].

1 As to benefices see ECCLESIASTICAL LAW vol 14 PARA 768.

2 Ie under the Pastoral Reorganisation Measure 1949 (repealed and replaced: see now the Pastoral Measure 1983; and ECCLESIASTICAL LAW).

3 As to the guardian of the spiritualities see ECCLESIASTICAL LAW vol 14 PARA 489.

4 Marriage Act 1949 s 23. A person may be married in a church in which he would have been entitled to be married notwithstanding that the banns have by virtue of s 23 been published only in some other church: s 23 proviso (b).

5 Marriage Act 1949 s 23 proviso (a).

6 Pastoral Measure 1983 Sch 3 para 14(4).

7 Pastoral Measure 1983 Sch 3 para 14(5).

61.   Banns and marriages when church is being rebuilt or repaired.   Where any church or chapel in which banns[1] may be published and marriages solemnised is being rebuilt or repaired and on that account is not being used for divine service, banns may be published and marriages solemnised: (1) in any building licensed[2] by the bishop for the performance of divine service during the disuse of the church or chapel, being a building within the parish[3] or other ecclesiastical district[4] in which the disused church or chapel is situated[5]; (2) if no such building has been licensed, in any such consecrated chapel[6] within that parish or district as the bishop may in writing direct[7]; or (3) in the absence of a licensed building or direction as to a consecrated chapel, in a church or chapel of any adjoining parish or other ecclesiastical district in which banns may be published and marriages solemnised[8]. A marriage solemnised in accordance with these provisions is registered in the marriage register books kept by the incumbent of the disused church or chapel[9].

1   As to banns see PARAS 58, 68.
2   The place will be presumed to have been so licensed if divine service was several times performed there: *R v Cresswell* (1876) 1 QBD 446, CCR.
3   As to the meaning of 'parish' see PARA 59 note 8.
4   As to the meaning of 'ecclesiastical district' see PARA 21 note 3.
5   Marriage Act 1949 s 18(1)(a). This does not apply in relation to a licensed naval, military or air force chapel: see PARA 129 note 9. Where an order is in force under the Diocesan Reorganisation Committees Measure 1941 (repealed) deferring the church's restoration after war damage, banns of persons entitled to be married there may be solemnised in such other church, chapel or place of worship within the diocese as the bishop in writing directs: Marriage Act 1949 s 19 (which does not extend to Wales: Sch 6).
6   Any fees in respect of marriages in a consecrated chapel are to be applied as the bishop with the consent of the incumbent of the disused church or chapel may in writing direct: Marriage Act 1949 s 18(2).
7   Marriage Act 1949 s 18(1)(b). See also note 5.
8   Marriage Act 1949 s 18(1)(c). See also note 5.
9   Marriage Act 1949 s 18(3).

62.   Licensing of chapels for banns and marriages.   The bishop of the diocese in which a public chapel[1] is situated may, if he thinks it necessary to do so for the due accommodation and convenience of the inhabitants of any district[2] and if the incumbent of the church of the parish[3] in which the chapel is situated has signified his consent under his hand and seal[4], authorise by a licence under his hand and seal the publication of banns and solemnisation of marriages in that public chapel between parties both or either of whom reside or resides within a district[5] limited in the licence[6] or has a 'qualifying connection' with that district[7]. Any such licence may include such provisions as to the amount, appropriation or apportionment of dues and such other particulars as the bishop thinks fit[8].

The bishop may grant a licence without the consent of the incumbent of the parish church after two months' notice in writing given to the incumbent by the registrar of the diocese[9], in which case the incumbent may appeal within one month of the grant of the licence to the archbishop of the province who, after hearing the matter in a summary way, may make an order confirming, revoking or varying the licence[10].

Any licence or order may at any time be revoked by the bishop by writing under his hand and seal with the written consent of the archbishop of the province[11].

1   In this context 'public chapel' means any public chapel with or without a chapelry annexed to it, any chapel duly licensed for the celebration of divine service according to the rites and

ceremonies of the Church of England, or any chapel the minister of which is duly licensed to officiate there according to those rites and ceremonies: Marriage Act 1949 s 20(8).

2   Marriage Act 1949 s 20(1)(a); *Re St George's, Albemarle Street Petition* (1890) Trist 134 (licence to celebrate marriages).

3   As to the meaning of 'parish' see PARA 59 note 8.

4   Marriage Act 1949 s 20(1)(b) (amended by the Patronage (Benefices) Measure 1986 Sch 5).

5   The district specified in the licence may be taken out of more than one parish, in which case 'incumbent' for the purposes of the Marriage Act 1949 s 20, means the incumbent as the case may be of the church of every parish out of which the district is taken: s 20(7) (amended by the Patronage (Benefices) Measure 1986 Sch 5). This provision does not extend to Wales: Marriage Act 1949 Sch 6.

6   Marriage Act 1949 s 20(1). As to the exclusion of s 20 in relation to licensed naval, military and air force chapels see PARA 129 note 9. A notice 'that banns may be published and marriages may be solemnised in this chapel' must be placed in a conspicuous part of the interior of a chapel licensed under s 20: s 20(5).

7   The Church of England Measure 2008 s 1 (see PARA 59), which makes provision for the solemnisation of marriages including non-residents with a 'qualifying connection' to a parish, also applies to a parish church has been licensed under these provisions: s 1(10).

8   Marriage Act 1949 s 20(1).

9   Marriage Act 1949 s 20(2) (amended by the Patronage (Benefices) Measure 1986 Sch 5). An incumbent who refuses or withholds consent to the granting of the licence may deliver to the bishop under hand and seal a statement of reasons for so doing and the bishop is not to grant the licence until he has inquired into them: Marriage Act 1949 s 20(2) proviso. Instruments of consent of the incumbent, copies of notices by the registrar, and statements of reasons delivered by an incumbent under the bishop's adjudication thereon under hand and seal must be registered in the diocesan registry: s 20(6) (amended by the Patronage (Benefices) Measure 1986 Sch 5).

10 Marriage Act 1949 s 20(3) (amended by the Patronage (Benefices) Measure 1986 Sch 5). The order must be registered in the diocesan registry: Marriage Act 1949 s 20(6) (amended by the Patronage (Benefices) Measure 1986 Sch 5).

11 Marriage Act 1949 s 20(4). The revocation and consent must be registered in the diocesan registry (s 20(6)), and the registrar must notify the revocation in writing to the minister officiating in the chapel and give public notice of it by advertisement in some newspaper circulating in the county and in the London Gazette (s 20(4)). As to the disposal of the registers of marriages solemnised in a chapel under a licence after the licence is revoked see PARA 86. Where a declaration of redundancy is made in respect of a chapel of ease, any licence relating to that chapel granted under s 20 will be deemed to have been revoked: Pastoral Measure 1983 Sch 3 para 14(3).

63.   Banns and marriages in churches of extra-parochial places.   Where any extra-parochial place has belonging to it or within it any church or chapel of the Church of England, the bishop of the diocese in which the church or chapel is situated may, if he thinks fit, authorise in writing under his hand and seal the publication of banns and the solemnisation of marriages by banns or by licence in that church or chapel between parties both or either of whom reside or resides in that extra-parochial place[1].

1   Marriage Act 1949 s 21(1). Every authorisation must be registered in the diocesan registry of the diocese: s 21(2).

64.   List of chapels.   The registrar of every diocese must, within 15 days after 1 January in every year, send by post to the Registrar General for England and Wales[1] a list of all the chapels in the diocese in which marriages may lawfully be solemnised according to the rites of the Church of England (being chapels which belong to the Church of England or licensed naval, military and air force chapels[2]), distinguishing those which have a parish[3], chapelry or other ecclesiastical division annexed to them, those which are licensed by the bishop for limited districts[4], and those which are licensed under the enactments relating to naval, military and air force chapels[5]. The Registrar General must make out and cause to be printed a list of all such chapels and of all registered buildings[6] yearly[7] and send a copy to every registrar of marriages and superintendent registrar[8].

1	As to the meaning of 'Registrar General' see PARA 46 note 5.
2	As to the licensing of naval, military and air force chapels see PARA 129.
3	As to the meaning of 'parish' see PARA 59 note 8.
4	For the bishop's power to license a public chapel for the accommodation and convenience of the inhabitants of a district see PARA 62. The list sent to the Registrar General must state the district for which each chapel is licensed: Marriage Act 1949 s 73(1).
5	As to these enactments see PARA 129.
6	Ie buildings certified as places of religious worship and registered for the solemnisation of marriages under the Marriage Act 1949 s 41: see PARA 186.
7	Marriage Act 1949 s 73(2). The printed list must state the county and registration district within which each chapel or registered building is situated and the names and places of residence of the superintendent registrars, registrars and deputy registrars of each district: s 73(2).
8	Marriage Act 1949 s 73(3).

(iii) Publication of Banns

**65.	Publication of banns in parish of residence.** Banns of marriage between two persons must normally be published in the parish church of the parish[1] in which they reside[2] or, if they reside in different parishes, in the parish church of each parish[3], but if either of them resides in a chapelry or a district for which the bishop has licensed a chapel for the publication of banns and the solemnisation of marriages[4] the banns may be published in an authorised chapel[5] of that chapelry or district in which that person resides instead of in the parish church[6].

In relation to a person who resides in an extra-parochial place this provision has effect with the substitution for references to a parish of references to the extra-parochial place and with the substitution for references to the parish church of references to an authorised chapel of that place[7]. For the purpose of publishing banns a parish in which there is no parish church or chapel or none in which divine service is usually solemnised every Sunday is to be taken as belonging to any adjoining parish or chapelry[8].

1	As to the meanings of 'parish' and 'parish church' see PARA 59 note 8.
2	It is the minister's duty to inquire as to the residence of persons applying to be married by banns: *Priestly v Lamb* (1801) 6 Ves 421; *Wynn v Davies and Weaver* (1835) 1 Curt 69. Failure in this respect may constitute an ecclesiastical offence which is punishable in the ecclesiastical courts: *Wynn v Davies and Weaver*; see ECCLESIASTICAL LAW vol 14 PARA 1357. Any person who knowingly and wilfully solemnises a marriage according to the rites of the Church of England without the banns having been duly published, not being a marriage solemnised on the authority of a special licence, a common licence (see PARA 76) or superintendent registrar's certificate (see PARA 80) is guilty of an offence and liable to imprisonment not exceeding 14 years if prosecuted within three years after the commission of the offence: Marriage Act 1949 s 75(1)(b), (4) (s 75(1)(b) amended by the Immigration and Asylum Act 1999 Sch 14 para 30).
3	Marriage Act 1949 s 6(1). In relation to licensed naval, military and air force chapels (as to which see PARA 129) s 6(1) applies as if the chapel were the parish church of the parish where it is situated: Sch 4, Pt II. As to publication in Scotland, Northern Ireland or the Republic or Ireland or on board Her Majesty's ships see PARAS 73, 74.
4	See the Marriage Act 1949 s 20; and PARA 62.
5	As to the meaning of 'authorised chapel' see PARA 59 note 9.
6	Marriage Act 1949 s 6(1) proviso.
7	Marriage Act 1949 s 6(2).
8	Marriage Act 1949 s 6(3). In the case of an extra-parochial place having no authorised chapel similar provision is made: s 6(3).

**66.	Publication of banns in party's usual place of worship.** Banns may also be published in any parish church[1] or authorised chapel[2] which is the usual place of

worship of the parties to the intended marriage or one of them even though
neither of them is resident in the parish[3] or chapelry to which the church or
chapel belongs[4], but this publication is in addition to and not in substitution for
the publication required under the provisions relating to the publication of banns
in a person's parish of residence[5]. No person can claim[6] as his usual place of
worship any parish church or authorised chapel unless he is enrolled on the
church electoral roll[7] of the area in which that church or chapel is situated, but
where he is enrolled on the church electoral roll of an area in which he does not
reside, that enrolment is sufficient evidence that his usual place of worship is a
parish church or authorised chapel in that area[8].

1   As to the meaning of 'parish church' see PARA 59 note 8.
2   As to the meaning of 'authorised chapel' see PARA 59 note 9.
3   As to the meaning of 'parish' see PARA 59 note 8.
4   Marriage Act 1949 s 6(4). This provision does not apply in relation to a licensed naval, military
    or air force chapel: see PARA 129 note 9. Persons intending to be married have the like but no
    greater right of having their banns published and marriage solemnised by virtue of this provision
    and the other provisions of the Marriage Act 1949 (cited in note 6) in a parish church or
    authorised chapel which is the usual place of worship of one or both of them as they have in the
    parish church or public chapel of the parish or chapelry in which they or one of them resides:
    s 72(2). As to the meaning of 'authorised chapel' see PARA 57 note 9.
5   Marriage Act 1949 s 6(4) proviso. As to the publication of banns in a person's parish of
    residence see PARA 65.
6   Ie for the purpose of the Marriage Act 1949 ss 6(4), 15(1) (see PARA 59), 35(3) (see PARA 100
    note 18): see s 72(1).
7   As to the church electoral roll see ECCLESIASTICAL LAW vol 14 PARA 591 et seq.
8   Marriage Act 1949 s 72(1), (4). Proof of actual enrolment is not necessary to support the
    marriage, nor can any evidence be given to prove the contrary in any proceedings touching the
    validity of the marriage: s 72(3). Where a bishop has licensed a guild church in the City of
    London for the publication of banns of marriage and the solemnisation of marriages where one
    or both of the parties are on the church electoral roll, the church is for the purposes of the
    provisions referred to in note 6, deemed to be the usual place of worship of the person who is on
    the electoral roll: City of London (Guild Churches) Act 1952 s 22(1), (2).

67.   Completion of banns in another church.   Publication of banns which has
been duly commenced in any church may be completed either in that church or
in any other church which, by virtue of the Union of Benefices Measure 1923,
the New Parishes Measure 1943, or the Pastoral Measure 1983[1], has at the time
of the completion taken the place of the first-mentioned church for the purpose
of publication of banns either generally or in relation to the parties to the
intended marriage[2]. Where the building in which the publication has been
commenced ceases to be a parish church[3] or to be licensed for marriages by
virtue of a scheme made under the Reorganisation Areas Measure 1944,
publication may be completed in such other building being a parish church or a
building licensed for marriages as the bishop may direct to take the place of the
first-mentioned building for the purposes of publication of banns[4].

1   See the Pastoral Measure 1983 Sch 3 para 14(1).
2   Marriage Act 1949 s 10(1). This section does not apply to Wales: Marriage Act 1949 Sch 6.
3   As to the meaning of 'parish church' see PARA 59 note 6.
4   Marriage Act 1949 s 10(2). Relevant provisions of the Reorganisation Areas Measure 1944 have
    been repealed and replaced: see now the Pastoral Measure 1983; and ECCLESIASTICAL LAW.

68.   Notice of banns.   No clergyman (or where applicable, minister)[1] is obliged
to publish banns of matrimony unless the persons to be married, at least seven
days before the date on which they wish the banns to be published for the first
time, deliver or cause to be delivered to him a notice in writing, dated on the day

on which it is so delivered, stating the first name and surname[2] and the place of residence of each of them and the period during which each has resided at his or her place of residence[3].

1   These provisions apply in connection with the solemnisation by a minister of a person with a 'qualifying connection' under the Church of England Marriage Measure 2008 s 1 (see PARA 59): s 1(8)(a).

2   As to the names see PARA 69.

3   Marriage Act 1949 s 8. See also *Pouget v Tomkins* (1812) 2 Hag Con 142; *Warter v Yorke* (1815) 19 Ves 451. A clergyman or minister need not insist on this notice but if, not using due diligence, he marries persons neither of whom resides in the parish, he is liable at least to ecclesiastical censure and perhaps to other consequences: *Priestley v Lamb* (1801) 6 Ves 421; *Nicholson v Squire* (1809) 16 Ves 259; *Wynn v Davies and Weever* (1835) 1 Curt 69. In relation to a licensed naval, military or air force chapel (as to which see PARA 129) the notice must contain a statement that one at least of the persons to be married is a person qualified to be married in such a chapel and must specify the persons so qualified and the nature of the qualification (Marriage Act 1949 Sch 4 Pt II); similar provisions apply in connection with marriages involving persons with 'qualifying connection' (see PARA 59). As to the persons qualified see PARA 129 text and note 1.

69.   Mode of publication of banns.   Banns must be published in an audible manner and in the form of words prescribed by the rubric prefixed to the office of matrimony in the Book of Common Prayer[1] on three Sundays preceding the solemnisation of marriage during morning service or, if there is no morning service on a Sunday on which they are to be published, during evening service[2].

The form of the rubric and the enactment[3] contemplate mention of the true names of the persons[4] and of the parish or parishes in which they reside, but not of their descriptions; mention of these is therefore not essential, and a misdescription is immaterial[5]. The form need not be rigidly adhered to; it is sufficient that it should be followed in substance[6].

For the purpose of banns a person's true name is not necessarily the full and exact Christian name given in baptism and the original surname[7]. If a man has adopted a new first name in such a way as to supersede his original name, and so that it is known as his proper designation, it will be his true name for the purpose of banns[8]. Consequently there is due publication where the assumed name is one which has overridden the true name and is generally accredited[9], and banns are not unduly published where part of the first name is suppressed, not for the sake of concealment, but because the party has not been in the habit of using it[10].

If a person has acquired a name by repute, the use of the true name in the banns may be an act of concealment, and not a due publication[11]; so also is the use of a surname which the person has never borne, even if it was entered by mistake in the baptism register[12]. The use of the true name is, however, only wrong where another name has been so far obtained by repute as to obliterate it[13].

In general, where a wrong name has been used in the publication of banns the effect on the validity of the marriage will depend on whether the wrong name was given with the wilful intention of concealing a party's identity[14]. The publication will be undue or otherwise according as the addition or omission was for the purpose of fraud or concealment or was innocently made, in cases where a name is added to the true names[15] or is omitted from them[16]. The fact of the banns having been published in a wrong name is not sufficiently proved by a wrong name being entered in the record of banns[17], nor by the fact of the party having been married in a wrong name[18].

1   Marriage Act 1949 s 7(2). All the other rules prescribed by the rubric must, so far as they are
    consistent with Pt II (ss 5–25), be duly observed: s 7(2).
2   Marriage Act 1949 s 7(1); and see *Wynn v Davies and Weever* (1835) 1 Curt 69. Where a
    person's consent would have been required to the marriage of a minor if it had been intended to
    be solemnised otherwise than after publication of banns, he may declare his dissent at the time
    of publication: see PARA 46. As to the offence of solemnising a marriage without due publication
    of the banns see PARA 52 note 4. As to the fees for the publication of banns see ECCLESIASTICAL
    LAW vol 14 PARA 1195.
3   See note 2.
4   *Wakefield v Mackay* (1807) 1 Hag Con 394; *Cope v Burt* (1809) 1 Hag Con 434; *Pouget v
    Tomkins* (1812) 2 Hag Con 142; *Stayte v Farquharson* (1826) 3 Add 282; *Tongue v Tongue*
    (1836) 1 Moo PCC 90.
5   *Cope v Burt* (1809) 1 Hag Con 434; affd (1811) 1 Phillim 224; *Mayhew v Mayhew* (1812) 3 M
    & S 266; *Fendall (otherwise Goldsmid) v Goldsmid* (1877) 2 PD 263.
6   *Standen v Standen* (1791) Peake 45.
7   *Diddear (falsely called Faucit otherwise Savill) v Faucit* (1821) 3 Phillim 580.
8   *Wyatt v Henry* (1817) 2 Hag Con 215; see also *Mayhew v Mayhew* (1812) 3 M & S 266; *R v
    Burton-upon-Trent Inhabitants* (1815) 3 M & S 537.
9   *Dancer v Dancer* [1949] P 147, [1948] 2 All ER 731.
10 *Orme v Holloway (falsely calling herself Orme)* (1847) 5 Notes of Cases 267.
11 *Frankland v Nicholson* (1805) 3 M & S 259n; see also *Wilson v Brockley* (1810) 1 Phillim 132;
    R v Billingshurst Inhabitants (1814) 3 M & S 250; *R v St Faith's, Newton Inhabitants* (1823) 3
    Dow & Ry KB 348; *Orme v Holloway (falsely calling herself Orme)* (1847) 5 Notes of Cases
    267; *Tooth v Barrow* (1854) 1 Ecc & Ad 371.
12 *R v Tibshelf Inhabitants* (1830) 1 B & Ad 190.
13 *Fendall (otherwise Goldsmid) v Goldsmid* (1877) 2 PD 263. A person's liberty to change his
    surname was discussed by Sir Joseph Jekyll MR in *Barlow v Bateman* (1730) 3 P Wms 64, and
    by Sir William Scott in *Wakefield v Mackay* (1807) 1 Hag Con 394. In practice an illegitimate
    child usually bears his mother's surname: *Sullivan v Sullivan (falsely called Oldacre)* (1818) 2
    Hag Con 238. If, however, he has acquired a different name by repute, his banns should be
    published by that name, though they might be held valid if, from an innocent misapprehension
    of what is correct, the mother's name was used instead of that subsequently acquired: *Tooth v
    Barrow* (1854) 1 Ecc & Ad 371. The name conferred on a woman by marriage becomes her
    actual name unless obliterated by repute: *Bon v Smith* (1596) Cro Eliz 532; *Fendall (falsely
    called Goldsmid) v Goldsmid* (1877) 2 PD 263.
14 *Chipchase v Chipchase* [1939] P 391, [1939] 3 All ER 895; subsequent proceedings reported in
    [1942] P 37, [1941] 2 All ER 560. See, however, *Mather v Ney* (1807) 3 M & S 265n, where it
    was held that publication in a wrong name from mere thoughtless levity, without fraud or any
    necessity for concealment, was an undue publication. A slight error in the name has been held to
    be immaterial: *Dobbyn v Corneck* (1812) 2 Phillim 102.
15 *Heffer v Heffer* (1812) 3 M & S 265n (3); *Tree v Quin* (1812) 2 Phillim 14; *Sullivan v Sullivan
    (falsely called Oldacre)* (1818) 2 Hag Con 238; *Dobbyn v Corneck* (1812) 2 Phillim 102;
    Fellowes v Stewart (1815) 2 Phillim 238; *Green v Dalton* (1822) 1 Add 289.
16 *Pouget v Tomkins* (1812) 2 Hag Con 142; *Diddear (falsely called Faucit otherwise Savill) v
    Faucit* (1821) 3 Phillim 580; *Stanhope v Baldwin* (1822) 1 Add 93; *Wiltshire v Prince* (1830) 3
    Hag Ecc 332; *Brealy (falsely called Reed) v Reed* (1841) 2 Curt 833; *Orme v Holloway (falsely
    calling herself Orme)* (1847) 5 Notes of Cases 267. In *Holmes v Simmons (falsely called
    Holmes)* (1868) LR 1 P & D 523, Lord Penzance doubted whether a marriage would be
    invalidated by undue publication of banns if there was no one in existence who had a legal right
    to assent to or dissent from its solemnisation or if those who had such legal right assented to it;
    but see *Mather v Ney* (1807) 3 M & S 265n (3).
17 *Copps v Follon* (1794) 1 Phillim 145n (b).
18 *Heffer v Heffer* (1812) 3 M & S 265n.

70. Who may publish banns. Where on any Sunday in any church or other
building in which banns may be published a clergyman[1] does not officiate at the
service at which it is usual in that church or building to publish banns, the
publication may be made either: (1) by a clergyman at some other service at
which banns may be published[2]; or (2) by a layman during a public reading
authorised by the bishop of a portion or portions of Morning or Evening Prayer,
such public reading being at the hour when the service at which it is usual to

publish banns is commonly held or at such other hour as the bishop may authorise[3], and the incumbent or minister in charge of the church or building, or some other clergyman nominated in that behalf by the bishop, must have made or authorised to be made the requisite entry in the register book of banns of the church or building[4]. Except as above and in the case of a naval marriage where the banns are published at sea[5], no person other than a clergyman may publish banns of marriage[6].

1   As to the meaning of 'clergyman' see PARA 23 note 5.
2   Marriage Act 1949 s 9(2)(a). As to the issue of a certificate of publication see s 11(4); and PARA 72.

3   Marriage Act 1949 s 9(2)(b). Where a layman publishes banns by virtue of s 9 he must sign the register book of banns provided under s 7 (see PARA 75): s 9(3).

4   Marriage Act 1949 s 9(2) proviso.
5   See PARA 74.

6   Marriage Act 1949 s 9(1).

71.   Publication void after three months.   If a marriage is not solemnised within three months after the completion of the publication of the banns the publication is void and no clergymen may solemnise the marriage on the authority of those banns[1].

1   Marriage Act 1949 s 12(2). As to the avoidance of a marriage solemnised on the authority of a void publication of banns if the parties knew of the defect see s 25(c); and PARA 328.

72.   Certificate of banns.   Where persons who are to be married after banns do not reside in the same parish[1] or ecclesiastical district[2], a clergyman[3] must not solemnise a marriage in either the parish or district in which one resides without production of a certificate that the banns have been published in accordance with the statutory provisions in the other parish or district[4]. Where, because in any parish there is no parish church or chapel belonging to it or no church or chapel in which divine service is usually solemnised every Sunday, or because in any extra-parochial place there is no authorised chapel, banns have been published[5] in a parish or chapelry adjoining that parish or extra-parochial place, a certificate that banns have been published in that parish or chapelry is sufficient[6]. Any certificate required by the foregoing provisions must be signed by the incumbent or minister in charge of the building in which the banns were published or by a clergyman nominated by the bishop[7].

Where persons desire to be married in the usual place of worship of one of them although neither resides in the parish or chapelry to which that place of worship belongs[8], or where one of the parties to the intended marriage only has a 'qualifying connection' to the parish in question[9], a clergyman must not solemnise the marriage unless there is produced to him a certificate or certificates of due publication of banns in the parish or district or parishes or districts in which they reside[10].

1   As to the meaning of 'parish' see PARA 59 note 8.
2   As to the meaning of 'ecclesiastical district' see PARA 21 note 3.
3   As to the meaning of 'clergyman' see PARA 23 note 5.

4   Marriage Act 1949 s 11(1). As to certificates of publication in Scotland, Northern Ireland or the Republic of Ireland, or on board ship, see PARAS 73–74.
5   Ie by virtue of the Marriage Act 1949 s 6(3): see PARA 65.

6   Marriage Act 1949 s 11(3). The certificate has the same force and effect as a certificate that the banns have been published in a parish in which one of the parties resides: s 11(3).

7   Marriage Act 1949 s 11(4). This also applies to a marriage solemnised where one of the parties
    has a qualifying connection to the parish under the Church of England Marriage Measure 2008
    s 1(2) (see PARA 59): s 1(7). As to certificates of publication of banns outside England see PARA
    73.
8   As to banns in such a case see the Marriage Act 1949 s 6(4); and PARA 66.
9   Ie under the Church of England Marriage Measure 2008 s 1 (see PARA 59).
10 Marriage Act 1949 s 11(2). This also applies to a marriage solemnised where one of the parties
    has a qualifying connection to the parish under the Church of England Marriage Measure 2008
    s 1(2) (see PARA 59): s 1(7).

73.   Publication of banns outside England and Wales.   Where a marriage is
intended to be solemnised in England or Wales, after the publication of banns,
between parties of whom one is residing in England or Wales and the other is
residing in Scotland, Northern Ireland or the Republic of Ireland, and banns
have been published or proclaimed in any church of the parish or place in which
that other party is residing according to the law or custom there prevailing, a
certificate given in accordance with that law or custom that the banns have been
so published or proclaimed is, as respects that party, a sufficient certificate[1] and
the marriage is not void by reason only that the banns have not been published
in the manner required for publication of banns in England and Wales[2].

A certificate of the publication of banns issued in certain parts of Her
Majesty's dominions outside the United Kingdom has, for the purpose of an
intended marriage in the United Kingdom between a British subject resident in
England and a British subject resident in such a part of the dominions, the same
effect as a certificate for marriage issued by a superintendent registrar[3].

1   Ie for the purposes of the Marriage Act 1949 s 11: see PARA 72.
2   Marriage Act 1949 s 13; Wales and Berwick Act 1746 s 3. As to marriages intended to be
    solemnised on the authority of a superintendent registrar's certificate where one of the parties
    resides in Scotland or Northern Ireland, see the Marriage Act 1949 s 37 (see PARA 112) and s 38
    (see PARA 113).
3   See the Marriage of British Subjects (Facilities) Act 1915 s 1(1)(a); and PARA 114. As to the
    meaning of 'Her Majesty's dominions' see COMMONWEALTH vol 6 (2003 Reissue) PARA 703.

74.   Publication of banns on Her Majesty's ships.   Where a marriage is
intended to be solemnised in England or Wales, after the publication of banns,
between parties one of whom is residing in England or Wales and the other is an
officer, seaman or marine borne on the books of one of Her Majesty's ships at
sea, the banns may be published on three successive Sundays during morning
service on board the ship by the chaplain or, if there is no chaplain, by the
captain or other officer commanding the ship[1]. Where banns have been so
published the person who published them must, unless the banns have been
forbidden on any of the grounds on which banns may be forbidden, give a
certificate of publication[2], which is a sufficient certificate[3] as regards the party
who is an officer, seaman or marine[4].

1   Marriage Act 1949 s 14(1).
2   Marriage Act 1949 s 14(1).
3   Ie for the purposes of Marriage Act 1949 s 11: see PARA 72.
4   Marriage Act 1949 s 14(2). The certificate must be in such form as may be prescribed by the
    Admiralty: s 14(2). All provisions of the Marriage Act 1949 (including penal provisions) relating
    to the publication of banns and certificates of publication and all rules regarding the time and
    manner of publication (see s 7; and PARA 69) apply subject to such adaptations as may be made
    by Her Majesty by Order in Council: s 14(2). Orders in Council made under the corresponding
    provisions of the Naval Marriages Act 1908 (repealed) continue in force and have effect as if
    made under the Marriage Act 1949: s 79(2). For the provisions for the issue on board Her
    Majesty's ships of certificates for marriages to be solemnised in England on the authority of a

certificate of a superintendent registrar see the Marriage Act 1949 s 39; and PARA 131. As to marriages in naval, military and air force chapels see PARA 129 et seq.

75.   Register book.   The parochial church council[1] of a parish[2] must provide for every church and chapel in the parish in which marriages may be solemnised a register book of banns of durable materials and marked in the same manner as a register book of marriages[3]. All banns must be published from this book[4] and not from loose papers, and after each publication the entry in the book must be signed by the person publishing the banns or by some person under his direction[5].

1   In relation to an authorised chapel in an extra-parochial place, this must be construed as a reference to the chapel warden or other officer exercising analogous duties in the chapel or, if there is no such officer, such person as may be appointed by the bishop: Marriage Act 1949 s 7(4). As to the meaning of 'authorised chapel' see PARA 59 note 9. In relation to a licensed naval, army or air force chapel (as to which see PARA 129) a reference to the Admiralty in the case of a naval chapel, and a reference to a Secretary of State in the case of any other chapel, is to be substituted: Sch 4, Pt II.
2   As to the meaning of 'parish' see PARA 59 note 8.
3   Marriage Act 1949 s 7(3). As to the register book of marriages see the Marriage Act 1949 s 54; and PARA 84.
4   As to who may publish banns see PARA 70.
5   Marriage Act 1949 s 7(3).

(iv) Marriage Licences

76.   Common and special licences.   The powers of ecclesiastical authorities to grant licences dispensing with certain requirements in respect of the solemnisation of marriages have been preserved by modern legislation[1]. The archbishop of each province, the bishop of every diocese and all others who of ancient right have been accustomed to issue a common licence[2] may grant such a licence for the solemnisation of marriage without the publication of banns at a lawful time[3] and in lawful place[4] within the several areas of their jurisdiction; and the Archbishop of Canterbury may grant a common licence for the same throughout all England[5]. The Archbishop of Canterbury has the additional power of granting a special licence for the solemnisation of marriage without the publication of banns at any convenient time or place not only within the province of Canterbury but throughout all England[6].

The obtaining of such a licence is a matter of favour, and not of right[7]. The licence can only be used for the marriage of the parties for whose marriage it was intended to be obtained[8] but provided it sufficiently identifies them, their true names and addresses need not be stated in it[9].

A common licence may also be granted in respect of a marriage involving a person with a 'qualifying connection' to a parish[10].

1   See the Marriage Act 1949 s 5. See also the Ecclesiastical Licences Act 1533 ss 4–12; Ecclesiastical Jurisdiction Act 1847 s 5; Canons Ecclesiastical (1603) 101, 104 (repealed); 2 Burn's Ecclesiastical Law (4th Edn) 462e; *Balfour v Carpenter* (1810) 1 Phillim 204. The power to grant marriage licences is not affected by the Supreme Court Act 1981: see s 21.
2   The reference is, it seems, to ecclesiastical judges and their surrogates: cf the Marriage Act 1949 s 16(4); and PARA 77 note 1.
3   As to the hours during which marriages may be solemnised see PARA 82.
4   As to the places at which marriages may be solemnised see PARAS 59, 65 et seq.
5   Marriage Act 1949 s 5(c). During a vacancy in an archiepiscopal or episcopal see licences may be granted by the guardian of the spiritualities: see ECCLESIASTICAL LAW vol 14 PARAS 432, 441, 489.

6   Marriage Act 19490 ss 5(b), 79(6); *Doe d Earl of Egremont v Grazebrook* (1843) 4 QB 406.
    This power is not affected by the Marriage (Registrar General's Licence) Act 1970: s 19. As to
    the grant of special licences by commissioners see the Ecclesiastical Licences Act 1533 s 12, and
    note 7. As to the Bishop of Sodor and Man's power to grant special licences in the Isle of Man
    see *Piers v Piers* (1849) 2 HL Cas 331.

7   See *Prince Capua v Count De Ludolf* (1836) 30 LJPM & A 71n. If the Archbishop of
    Canterbury, however, or the guardian of the spiritualities of the archbishopric during a vacancy,
    refuses a licence without reasonable cause, an appeal lies to the Lord Chancellor who may, if it
    seems fit, enjoin the archbishop or guardian to grant it and, in the event of his refusal to do so,
    may commission two other bishops to grant it: Ecclesiastical Licences Act 1533 ss 11, 12. No
    appeal lies against the refusal of the Archbishop of York or any diocesan bishop to grant a
    common licence under the dispensing power reserved to them by s 9.

8   *Cope v Burt* (1809) 1 Hag Con 434; affd (1811) 1 Phillim 224; *Lane v Goodwin* (1843) 4 QB
    361. As to forgery of a marriage licence see the Forgery Act 1913 s 3(3)(i).

9   *Cope v Burt* (1809) 1 Hag Con 434; *Ewing v Wheatley* (1814) 2 Hag Con 175; *R v
    Burton-upon-Trent Inhabitants* (1815) 3 M & S 537; *Clowes v Jones* (1842) 3 Curt 185; *Lane
    v Goodwin* (1843) 4 QB 361; *Bevan (falsely called M'Mahon) v M'Mahon* (1861) 2 Sw & Tr
    230, where the licence was held good although, for the purposes of concealing the woman's
    identity from the surrogate, one of her names was suppressed and her residence was falsely
    stated; *Haswell v Haswell and Gilbert* (1881) 51 LJP 15, where two Christian names had been
    added in the licence to the man's true name. The licence is not vitiated by an immaterial
    alteration in it after it has been granted: *Ewing v Wheatley*.

10 Church of England Marriage Measure 2008 s 2(1). As to marriages involving persons with a
    'qualifying connection' see s 1; and PARA 59.

77.   Affidavit leading to grant of licence.   Before a common marriage licence is
granted, sworn declaration must be made by one of the parties before a
surrogate[1], or other person having authority to grant it, to the effect:

(1)   that the party believes that there is no impediment of kindred or alliance
      or any other lawful cause, nor any suit commenced in any court, to bar
      or hinder the solemnisation of the marriage in accordance with the
      licence[2];

(2)   that for 15 days immediately before the grant of the licence one of the
      parties has had his or her usual place of residence[3] in the parish[4] or
      other ecclesiastical district[5] in which the marriage is to be solemnised or
      that the parish church[6] or authorised chapel[7] in which the marriage is to
      be solemnised is the usual place of worship[8] of the parties or one of
      them[9];

(3)   where the marriage is being solemnised in a particular place by virtue of
      one of the parties having a 'qualifying connection'[10], that one or both of
      the persons involved has the qualifying connection, and the nature of
      that connection[11]; and

(4)   where one of the parties, not being a widower or widow, is a minor,
      either that the consent of the person or persons whose consent to the
      marriage is required by statute, has been obtained, or that the necessity
      of obtaining that consent has been dispensed with, or that the court has
      consented to the marriage[12], or that there is no person whose consent to
      the marriage is so required[13].

A common licence may not be granted for the solemnisation of a marriage
unless the person having authority to grant the licence is satisfied by the
production of evidence that both the persons to be married have attained the age
of 21[14]; and he has received a declaration in writing made by each of those
persons specifying their affinal relationship and declaring that the younger of
those persons has not at any time before attaining the age of 18 been a child of
the family in relation to the other[15].

A person who knowingly and wilfully makes a false declaration in order to obtain a marriage licence is guilty of an offence[16].

Where a marriage is solemnised by licence the responsibility as to whether one of the parties resides within the parish or district of the church or chapel in which it is proposed to be solemnised, and, it is submitted, whether a parish church or authorised chapel is the usual place of worship of the parties or one of them in instances in which the marriage is to be solemnised there[17], and whether the marriage law is in other respects observed, rests with the bishop by whose authority the licence is granted and not with the officiating minister, and if a licence is produced to a minister directing or authorising the marriage of two persons in his church or chapel he is required both by his canonical obedience and by the rights of the parties to solemnise the marriage according to the licence[18]. If from his knowledge of certain facts he takes the responsibility of refusing to solemnise the marriage in spite of the licence, he does so at his peril[19].

1   As to surrogates see ECCLESIASTICAL LAW vol 14 PARA 1275. Before a surrogate deputed by an ecclesiastical judge grants any licences he must take an oath before that judge, or a commissioner appointed under that judge's seal, faithfully to execute his office according to law to the best of his knowledge: Marriage Act 1949 s 16(4) (amended by the Statute Law (Repeals) Act 1975 Sch Pt VI).
2   Marriage Act 1949 s 16(1)(a).
3   As to residence see PARA 59.
4   As to the meaning of 'parish' see PARA 59 note 8.
5   As to the meaning of 'ecclesiastical district' see PARA 21 note 3.
6   As to the meaning of 'parish church' see PARA 59 note 8.
7   As to the meaning of 'authorised chapel' see PARA 59 note 9.
8   As to the usual place of worship see PARA 66.
9   Marriage Act 1949 s 16(1)(b).
10 Ie under the Church of England Marriage Measure 2008 s 1 (as to which see PARA 59).
11 Church of England Marriage Measure 2008 s 2(1).
12 As to consents see PARA 48.
13 Marriage Act 1949 s 16(1)(c). In relation to licensed naval, military and air force chapels, s 16 applies as if it required the oath to include a statement that at least one of the parties is a qualified person for the purpose of marriage in such a chapel and to specify the person so qualified and the nature of his qualification: Sch 4, Pt II. As to who is so qualified see PARA 129.
14 Marriage Act 1949 s 16(1A)(a) (s 16(1A) added by the Marriage (Prohibited Degrees of Relationship) Act 1996 Sch 1 para 4).
15 Marriage Act 1949 s 16(1A)(b) (as added: see note 14).
16 Perjury Act 1911 s 3(1)(a). The punishment on conviction of an offence under s 3(1) on indictment is imprisonment for a term not exceeding seven years or a fine or both, and on summary conviction a penalty not exceeding the prescribed sum: s 3(1). 'Prescribed sum' means £5,000 or such sum as is for the time being substituted in this definition by order under the Magistrates' Courts Act 1980 s 143(1): see s 32(9) (amended by the Criminal Justice Act 1991 s 17(2)); and CRIMINAL LAW, EVIDENCE AND PROCEDURE vol 11(4) (2006 Reissue) PARA 1675; MAGISTRATES vol 29(2) (Reissue) PARA 804.
17 See PARA 66.
18 *Tuckniss v Alexander* (1863) 32 LJ Ch 794.
19 *Tuckniss v Alexander* (1863) 32 LJ Ch 794. It may turn out that the bishop was misled in granting the licence: *Tuckniss v Alexander*. A clergyman who is aware that a statement in the licence as to the name or address of a party or otherwise is not in accordance with the facts is justified in hesitating before he solemnises the marriage (*Ewing v Wheatley* (1814) 2 Hag Con 175) and a clergyman who solemnised a marriage under a licence obtained by a false oath that the woman was of age, when she evidently appeared not to be so, was severely reprimanded in the Court of Chancery: *Millet v Rowse* (1802) 7 Ves 419.

78.   Caveat against grant of licence.   If any caveat is entered against the grant of a common licence, the caveat having been duly signed by or on behalf of the person by whom it is entered and stating his place of residence and the ground of objection on which the caveat is founded, no licence may be granted until the caveat or a copy thereof is transmitted to the ecclesiastical judge out of whose office the licence is to issue, and the judge has certified to the registrar of the diocese that he has examined into the matter of the caveat and is satisfied that it ought not to obstruct the grant of the licence, or until the caveat is withdrawn by the person who entered it[1].

A person who forbids the issue of a licence or certificate by falsely representing, knowing it to be false, that he is a person whose consent is required is guilty of an offence[2].

1   Marriage Act 1949 s 16(2). This is subject to the proviso that where a caveat in respect of a marriage which is void under s 1(2) (see PARA 37) on the ground that the persons to be married have not both attained the age of 21 or that one of those persons has at any time before attaining the age of 18 been a child of the family in relation to the other, then, notwithstanding that the caveat is withdrawn by the person who entered it, no licence will be issued unless the judge has certified that he has examined into that ground of objection and is satisfied that that ground ought not to obstruct the grant of the licence: s 16(2A) (s 16(2A), (2B) added by the Marriage (Prohibited Degrees of Relationship) Act 1986 Sch 1 para 4). In the case of such a marriage, one of the persons to be married may apply to the ecclesiastical judge out of whose office the licence is to issue for a declaration that, both those persons having attained the age of 21 and the younger of those persons not having at any time before attaining the age of 18 been a child of the family in relation to the other, there is no impediment of affinity to the solemnisation of the marriage; and where any such declaration is obtained the common licence may be granted notwithstanding that no declaration has been made under s 16(1A): s 16(2B) (as so added).

2   Perjury Act 1911 s 3(1)(c). As to the punishment see PARA 77 note 16.

79.   Period of validity of common licence. If the marriage does not take place within three calendar months after the grant of the common licence, the licence is void and no clergyman may solemnise the marriage on its authority[1].

1   Marriage Act 1949 s 16(3). As to the avoidance of a marriage solemnised when to the knowledge of the parties the licence has become void see s 25(c); and PARA 328.

(v) Solemnisation of Marriage in Church

80.   Who may solemnise marriage. Marriage according to the rites of the Church of England is properly solemnised by a priest[1], but may be solemnised by a deacon[2], and may be solemnised on the authority of a certificate of a superintendent registrar[3] in any church or chapel[4] in which banns of matrimony may be published[5]. A clergyman cannot solemnise his own marriage[6].

1   *R v Millis* (1844) 10 Cl & Fin 534, HL; *Catherwood v Caslon* (1844) 13 M & W 261; *Du Moulin v Druitt* (1860) 13 ICLR 212; *Beamish v Beamish* (1861) 9 HL Cas 274; *Culling v Culling* [1896] P 116. If persons knowingly and wilfully consent to or acquiesce in the solemnisation of their marriage by a person who is not in holy orders, the marriage is void (Marriage Act 1949 s 25), but it would be otherwise if he was believed to be in holy orders (*Costard v Winder* (1660) Cro Eliz 775; *Hawke v Corri* (1820) 2 Hag Con 280; *R v Millis*). A person who knowingly and wilfully solemnises a marriage according to the rites of the Church of England, falsely pretending to be in holy orders, is guilty of an offence and is liable to imprisonment for a term not exceeding five years if prosecuted within three years after the commission of the offence: Marriage Act 1949 s 75(1)(d), (4). See also *R v Ellis* (1888) 16 Cox CC 469. Where the General Synod has exercised its powers with regard to co-operation with other churches under the Church of England (Ecumenical Relations) Measure 1988 ss 1, 2 (see ECCLESIASTICAL LAW), no person may, unless he is a clerk in Holy Orders of the Church of England, solemnise a marriage according to the rites of the Church of England: s 3(b).

2   *R v Millis* (1844) 10 Cl & Fin 534, HL; *Cope v Barber* (1872) LR 7 CP 393. See also ECCLESIASTICAL LAW vol 14 PARA 664.

3   As to the meaning of 'superintendent registrar' see PARA 22 note 1.

4   A superintendent registrar may issue a certificate for the solemnisation of a marriage in any parish church or authorised chapel which is the usual place of worship of the persons to be

married or of one of them, notwithstanding that the church or chapel is not within a registration district in which either of those persons resides: Marriage Act 1949 s 35(3). For the exclusion of this provision in relation to naval, military and air force chapels see PARA 129 note 9. As to the meanings of 'parish church' and 'authorised chapel' see PARA 59 notes 8, 9; as to the meaning of 'usual place of worship' see PARA 66.

5   Marriage Act 1949 ss 17, 26. The consent of the minister of the church or chapel is requisite, and the marriage may not be celebrated by any person other than a clergyman: s 17 proviso. As to the application of this proviso in relation to a marriage in a licensed naval, military or air force chapel see PARA 129 note 9. As to the meaning of 'clergyman' see PARA 23 note 5. The certificate or, if notice has been given to more than one superintendent registrar, the certificates, must be delivered to the officiating clergyman (s 50(1)(f)), except in the case of a marriage in a licensed naval, military or air force chapel, when the certificate or certificates must be delivered to the appointed clergyman in whose presence the marriage is solemnised (Sch 4, Pt II; see PARA 129).

    As to the marriages that may be solemnised on the authority of superintendent registrar's certificates see PARA 54.

6   *Beamish v Beamish* (1861) 9 HL Cas 274, where it is explained that the clergyman whose presence is essential to the validity of the marriage must be a different person from the bridegroom.

81.   Minister's duty to solemnise marriage.   A minister who without just cause refuses to marry persons entitled to be married in his church or chapel commits an ecclesiastical offence for which he is punishable in the ecclesiastical courts[1].

No clergyman[2] is compelled to solemnise the marriage of any person whose former marriage has been dissolved on any ground and whose former husband or wife is still living[3], or to permit the marriage of such a person to be solemnised in the church or chapel of which he is the minister[4].

Formerly a clergyman was not liable to any suit, penalty or censure for refusing to publish banns of marriage or to solemnise marriages between a man and his deceased wife's sister, or his deceased brother's widow, or between persons and their nephews or nieces by marriage[5], although if he refused to solemnise such a marriage between persons who but for his refusal would be entitled to have it solemnised in his church or chapel he could allow it to be solemnised there by any other clergyman entitled to officiate in the diocese; and it appears that his rights in this respect are preserved[6].

1   *Argar v Holdsworth* (1758) 2 Lee 515. It is doubtful whether in case of refusal he is liable to an action for damages (*Davis v Black* (1841) 1 QB 900), or to be indicted for the refusal (*R v James* (1850) 3 Car & Kir 167, CCR). The offence of refusal is not committed unless a definite request for the marriage has been made to the minister by both parties and the parties have presented themselves to him to be married at a time when he was not engaged in some other duty (*Davis v Black*), and when he could legally have performed the service (*R v James*). See further ECCLESIASTICAL LAW vol 14 PARA 1357. As to the duty of marrying by licence see PARA 77.

2   As to the meaning of 'clergyman' see PARA 23 note 5.

3   Matrimonial Causes Act 1965 s 8(2)(a).

4   Matrimonial Causes Act 1965 s 8(2)(b).

5   See the Deceased Wife's Sister's Marriage Act 1907 s 1; the Deceased Brother's Widow's Marriage Act 1921 s 1; and the Marriage (Prohibited Degrees of Relationship) Act 1931 s 1 (all repealed). See *Thompson v Dibdin* [1912] AC 533, HL; *Banister v Thompson* [1908] P 362.

6   See the Marriage Act 1949 s 79(10), which provides that nothing in the Act is to enable any proceedings to be taken in an ecclesiastical court which could not have been taken if the Act had not been passed.

82.   Time of marriage.   A marriage according to the rites of the Church of England may not be solemnised on the authority of superintendent registrar's certificates within 15 days[1], or such period as may be determined by the Registrar General[2] or by a superintendent registrar[3] after the day on which notice was entered in the marriage notice book[4].

A marriage may be solemnised on the authority of certificates of a superintendent registrar at any time within the period which is the applicable period[5] in relation to that marriage[6]. If the marriage is not solemnised within the applicable period the notices of marriage and the certificates are void and no person may solemnise the marriage on the authority of those certificates[7].

Unless it is by special licence[8] a marriage according to the rites of the Church of England must conform to the general requirement concerning the hours for solemnisation of marriages: thus it must be solemnised between eight o'clock in the forenoon and six o'clock in the afternoon[9].

1 Marriage Act 1949 s 31(4A)(a) (added by the Immigration and Asylum Act 1999 s 160(5)).
2 As to the meaning of 'Registrar General' see PARA 46 note 5.
3 Marriage Act 1949 s 31(4A)(b) (added by the Immigration and Asylum Act 1999 s 160(5)). As to the meaning of 'superintendent registrar' see PARA 22 note 1.
4 Marriage Act 1949 s 31(4) (amended by the Immigration and Asylum Act 1999 s 160(4)(c)); see further PARA 94. As to the marriage notice book see the Marriage Act 1949 ss 27(4), 78(1); and PARA 92. A person who knowingly and wilfully solemnises a marriage in contravention of this provision is guilty of an offence and is liable to imprisonment for a term not exceeding five years if prosecuted within three years from the commission of the offence: s 75(2)(d), (4).
5 'Applicable period' means the period beginning with the day on which the notice of marriage was entered in the marriage notice book and ending: (1) in the case of a marriage which is to be solemnised in pursuance of s 26(1)(dd), 37 or 38, on the expiry of three months; and (2) in the case of any other marriage, on the expiry of 12 months: Marriage Act 1949 s 33(3). If the notices of marriage given by each person to be married are not given on the same date, the applicable period is to be calculated by reference to the earlier of the two dates: s 33(4).
6 Marriage Act 1949 s 33(1). A person who knowingly and wilfully solemnises a marriage after the expiration of the three months is guilty of an offence and is liable to imprisonment for a term not exceeding five years, if prosecuted within three years from the commission of the offence: s 75(2)(e), (4).
7 Marriage Act 1949 s 33(2). As to the avoidance of a marriage solemnised to the parties' knowledge on the authority of a certificate which has become void, or in a place not specified in the notice of marriage and certificate, see s 25(c), (d); and PARA 328.
8 As to the special licence of the Archbishop of Canterbury see ECCLESIASTICAL LAW vol 14 PARA 1023.
9 Marriage Act 1949 s 4. A person who knowingly and wilfully solemnises a marriage at any other time (not being a marriage by special licence or a Quaker or Jewish marriage) is guilty of an offence and liable to imprisonment for a term not exceeding 14 years if prosecuted within three years after the commission of the offence (Marriage Act 1949 s 75(1)(a), (4)), but a marriage so solemnised would not be void (see *Catterall v Sweetman* (1845) 1 Rob Eccl 304).

83. Conduct of marriage ceremony in church. The actual marriage should take place in the body of the church, in the presence of the congregation, and the minister and the parties should afterwards go up to the Lord's table, before which the parties should kneel for the conclusion of the office[1].

The essential parts of the ceremony have been held to be the reciprocal agreement of the parties to take each other for wedded wife and wedded husband till parted by death, the joining together of their hands, and the pronouncement by the clergyman that they are man and wife[2].

The marriage ceremony is sometimes performed between persons who are already married to one another[3].

A marriage solemnised according to the rites of the Church of England must be solemnised in the presence of at least two witnesses in addition to the officiating clergyman[4], but in spite of this direction a marriage in the presence of only one additional witness is not invalid[5].

1 Book of Common Prayer, rubrics in the Form of Solemnization of Matrimony; *R v James* (1850) 3 Car & Kir 167, CCR per Alderson B. Nevertheless a marriage in the vestry of the church is valid: *Wing v Taylor (falsely calling herself Wing)* (1861) 2 Sw & Tr 278. As to the validity of marriages generally see PARA 3.

2   *Harrod v Harrod* (1854) 1 K & J 4; *Beamish v Beamish* (1861) 9 HL Cas 274. Neither the use
    of the language of the marriage service, nor observance of the directions of the rubric respecting
    the opening address to the congregation, nor the adjuration to the parties as to confessing any
    lawful impediment to their union, nor the demand 'Who giveth this woman to be married to this
    man?', nor the putting of the ring on the bride's finger, nor the benediction, are absolutely
    essential to the validity of the marriage: *Weld v Chamberlaine* (1683) 2 Show 300; *Beamish v
    Beamish*. The giving away of the woman is not essential (*More v More* (1741) 2 Atk 157 per
    Lord Hardwicke LC); nor is the repetition by the parties of the words of the service essential
    (*Harrod v Harrod*). Therefore deaf and dumb persons can legally be married: *Harrod v Harrod*.
    For civil purposes the marriage is complete after the plighting of troth; what follows (the giving
    of the ring, joining of hands and publication by the minister of the marriage) is symbolical and
    declaratory of a marriage which has already taken place: *Beamish v Beamish* (1861) 9 HL Cas
    274.
3   *Piers v Piers* (1849) 2 HL Cas 331. As to the addition of the marriage service to a marriage
    contracted at a register office see PARA 57.
4   Marriage Act 1949 s 22. As to the meaning of 'clergyman' see PARA 23 note 5.
5   *Wing v Taylor (falsely calling herself Wing)* (1861) 2 Sw & Tr 278.

(vi) Registration

84. Duty to register marriages. A marriage celebrated according to the rites of
the Church of England must be registered by the clergyman by whom it is
solemnised[1] who, immediately after solemnising a marriage, must register in
duplicate in two of the marriage register books furnished by the Registrar
General for England and Wales[2] the particulars relating to the marriage in the
prescribed form[3]. Each entry must be signed by the clergyman, by the parties
married and by two witnesses[4].

1   Marriage Act 1949 s 53(a). In the case of a marriage according to the usages of the Society of
    Friends (Quakers) the marriage must be registered by the registering officer of that society
    appointed for the district (s 53(b)), and in the case of a Jewish marriage by the secretary of the
    synagogue of which the husband is a member (s 53(c)). As to the persons by whom marriages
    solemnised in registered buildings and register offices must be registered see s 53(d)–(f); and
    REGISTRATION CONCERNING THE INDIVIDUAL vol 39(2) (Reissue) PARA 558. For the exclusion
    of certain provisions relating to registration in relation to marriages according to Church of
    England rites in licensed naval, military and air force chapels see PARA 129 note 9, and PARA
    130 note 5.
2   As to the Registrar General see PARA 46 note 5.
3   Marriage Act 1949 ss 54, 55(1). For the form, see the Registration of Marriages
    Regulations 1986, SI 1986/1442, Sch 1 Form 13. As to the registration of marriages in guild
    churches see the City of London (Guild Churches) Act 1952 s 22(5); and ECCLESIASTICAL LAW
    vol 14 PARA 606. The clergyman may ask the parties to the marriage the particulars required to
    be entered in the marriage register book (Marriage Act 1949 s 56), and any person who
    knowingly and wilfully makes or causes to be made, for the purpose of being inserted in the
    register, any false statement as to any of the particulars required to be registered is guilty of an
    offence (Perjury Act 1911 s 3(1)(b)). As to offences in relation to the solemnisation of marriage
    see PARA 180.
        No penalties are incurred by the clergyman, however, if he discovers an error in the form or
    substance of the entry and within one calendar month after the discovery, in the presence of the
    parties married (or, in case of their death or absence, in the presence of the superintendent
    registrar and of two other credible witnesses, or in the presence of the churchwardens or chapel
    wardens of the church or chapel in which the marriage is solemnised), who attest the same,
    corrects the erroneous entry by entry in the margin, without any alteration of the original entry,
    and signs the marginal entry adding the date of the correction: Marriage Act 1949 s 61(1), (2),
    (5). In such case he must make the like marginal entry, attested in like manner, in the duplicate
    marriage register book (s 61(3)) and in the certified copy of the register book which he is
    required to make under s 57 or, if that copy has already been delivered, he must make and
    deliver to the superintendent registrar a separate certified copy of the original erroneous entry
    and of the marginal correction (s 61(4)).
        Where a marriage is solemnised according to the rites of the Church of England of a person
    who is housebound or is a detained person at the place where he or she usually resides (see

s 26(1)(dd); and PARA 171), the marriage must be registered in accordance with s 55 in the marriage register books of any church or chapel which is in the same parish or extra-parochial place as is the place where the marriage is solemnised or, if there is no such church or chapel, of any church or chapel in any adjoining parish: s 55(4) (s 55(4), (5) added by the Marriage Act 1983 Sch 1 para 17). Where such a clergyman is required to register a marriage in the marriage register books of a church or chapel of which he is not the incumbent, the incumbent may give the books into his custody at a convenient time before the marriage is solemnised and he must keep them safely and return them to the custody of the incumbent as soon as is reasonably practicable: Marriage Act 1949 s 55(5) (as so added). A clergyman who refuses or without reasonable cause omits to register a marriage solemnised by him is liable on summary conviction to a fine not exceeding level 3 on the standard scale: s 76(1). 'Standard scale' means the standard scale of maximum fines for summary offences as set out in the Criminal Justice Act 1982 s 37: see the Interpretation Act 1978 s 5, Sch 1 (definition added by the Criminal Justice Act 1988 s 170(1), Sch 15 para 58); and CRIMINAL LAW, EVIDENCE AND PROCEDURE vol 11(4) (2006 Reissue) PARA 1676; MAGISTRATES vol 29(2) (Reissue) PARA 804. At the date at which this volume states the law, the standard scale is as follows: level 1, £200; level 2, £500; level 3, £1,000; level 4, £2,500; level 5, £5,000: Criminal Justice Act 1982 s 37(2) (substituted by the Criminal Justice Act 1991 s 17(1)). As to the determination of the amount of the fine actually imposed, as distinct from the level on the standard scale which it may not exceed, see the Criminal Justice Act 2003 s 164; and CRIMINAL LAW, EVIDENCE AND PROCEDURE vol 11(4) (2006 Reissue) PARA 1678; MAGISTRATES vol 29(2) (Reissue) PARA 807. As to the superintendent registrar's power to prosecute see the Marriage Act 1949 s 76(5).

4   Marriage Act 1949 s 55(2). Every entry must be made in consecutive order from the beginning to the end of each book and the number of the entry in each duplicate marriage register book must be the same: s 55(3).

85.   Copies of register for superintendent registrar.   In the months of January, April, July and October the incumbent[1] of every church or chapel in which marriages may be solemnised according to the rites of the Church of England must make and deliver to the superintendent registrar, on forms supplied by the Registrar General, a true copy, certified under his hand, of all the entries of marriages in the register book kept by him during the period of three months ending with the last day of the month immediately before the month in which the copy is required to be made, or, if no marriage has been entered in it since the last certificate, he must certify the fact[2].

1   'Incumbent' means the rector, vicar or curate in charge of the church or chapel in question: Marriage Act 1949 s 54(1).
2   Marriage Act 1949 s 57(1). See further REGISTRATION CONCERNING THE INDIVIDUAL vol 39(2) (Reissue) PARA 618. The superintendent registrar must pay the incumbent £2 for every entry contained in a certified copy, and that sum must be reimbursed to the superintendent registrar in the case of a registration district in the City of London, the Inner Temple and the Middle Temple, by the Common Council of the City of London; and in any other case, by the council of the non-metropolitan county, metropolitan district or London borough in which his registration district is situated: s 57(4) (amended by the Local Government Act 1972 Sch 29 para 40; and SI 2002/3076; SI 2005/1997). Refusal to deliver any copy or certificate or failure to deliver a copy or certificate during any of the specified months renders the offender liable on summary conviction to a fine not exceeding level 1 on the standard scale: Marriage Act 1949 s 76(2) (amended by virtue of the Criminal Justice Act 1982 ss 38, 46). As to the superintendent registrar's power to prosecute see the Marriage Act 1949 s 76(5). As to the standard scale see PARA 84 note 3.
    Section 57 does not apply to licensed naval, military or air force chapels: see PARA 129 note 9.

86.   Register books.   The marriage register books must be kept safely by the incumbent[1] until filled[2]. When they are filled one copy must be delivered to the superintendent registrar, and the other is to remain in the custody of the incumbent and must be kept by him with the registers of baptism and burials of the parish or other ecclesiastical district in which the marriages registered in it have been solemnised[3].

Where any church or chapel ceases to be used for the solemnisation of marriages, whether by reason of demolition, revocation of a licence or otherwise, any marriage register books in the custody of the incumbent of that church or chapel must be delivered forthwith to the incumbent of the church which is, or becomes, the parish church of the parish in which the disused church or chapel is situated[4]. Unless the books in question are the only register books in use for the parish any such books as have not been filled must be forwarded to the Registrar General to be formally closed[5].

Every incumbent by whom a marriage register book is kept must at all reasonable hours allow searches to be made in any such book and on payment of the prescribed fee he must give a copy certified under his hand of any entry in such a book[6].

1　As to the meaning of 'incumbent' see PARA 85 note 1.
2　Marriage Act 1949 s 59. If he carelessly loses or injures a marriage register book or copy, or carelessly allows it to be injured while in his keeping, he is liable on summary conviction to a fine not exceeding level 3 on the standard scale: s 76(1). As to the superintendent registrar's power to prosecute see PARA 181. As to see CRIMINAL LAW, EVIDENCE AND PROCEDURE vol 11(1) (2006 Reissue) PARA 351. As to offences relating to altering a register see the Forgery and Counterfeiting Act 1981 s 5; and CRIMINAL LAW, EVIDENCE AND PROCEDURE vol 11(1) (2006 Reissue) PARA 351. The Marriage Act 1949 ss 59, 60 do not apply to licensed naval, military or air force chapels: see PARA 129 note 9.
3　Marriage Act 1949 s 60(1). As to the meaning of 'parish' see PARA 59 note 8; and as to the meaning of 'ecclesiastical district' see PARA 21 note 3. As to the care of register books see ECCLESIASTICAL LAW vol 14 PARA 1112 et seq.
4　Marriage Act 1949 s 62(1). When the incumbent of the parish church next delivers to the superintendent registrar a certified copy of the entries in the marriage register book of marriages solemnised in the parish church he must deliver also a copy of all entries made in the marriage register books of the disused church or chapel after the date of the last entry of which a certified copy has already been delivered to the superintendent registrar: s 62(2)(a).
5　Marriage Act 1949 s 62(2)(b).
6　Marriage Act 1949 s 63(1). The fee for a certified copy is £3.50 where application for a copy is made at the time of registering the marriage or is made to a registrar by whom the book containing the entry is kept, and £7 in any other case: s 63(1); Registration of Births, Deaths and Marriages (Fees) Order 2002, SI 2002/3076, Schedule. As to the fee for searching the register for the period before 1837 see ECCLESIASTICAL LAW vol 14 PARA 1198.

(3) MARRIAGE ON THE AUTHORITY OF THE SUPERINTENDENT REGISTRAR'S CERTIFICATES

(i) Notices and Declarations

87.　Giving and content of notice.　Where a marriage is intended to be solemnised on the authority of certificates of a superintendent registrar[1], notice of marriage in the prescribed form[2] must be given[3]:

(1)　if the persons to be married have resided in the same registration district[4] for the period of seven days immediately before the giving of the notice, by each of those persons to the superintendent registrar of that district[5]; or

(2)　if the persons to be married have not resided in the same registration district for such a period of seven days, by each of those persons to the superintendent registrar of the registration district in which he or she has resided for that period[6].

A notice of marriage must state the name and surname, occupation, place of residence[7] and nationality of each of the persons to be married, whether either of them has previously been married or formed a civil partnership, and if so how the marriage or civil partnership ended, and, in the case of a marriage intended to be solemnised at a person's residence[8], which residence is to be the place of solemnisation of the marriage and, in any other case, the church or other building or premises in or on which the marriage is to be solemnised[9]. The notice must state the period, not being less than seven days, during which each has resided in his or her place of residence[10]; but, if either of the persons to be married has resided in the place stated in the notice for more than one month, the notice may state that he or she has resided there for more than one month[11].

Where a marriage in a registration district in which neither party resides[12] is intended to be solemnised on the authority of certificates of a superintendent registrar, each notice of marriage given to the superintendent registrar and each certificate issued by the superintendent registrar must state, in addition to the description of the registered building[13] or, as the case may be, the parish church[14] or authorised chapel[15], in which the marriage is to be solemnised, that it is the usual place of worship of the persons to be married or of one of them and, in the latter case, must state the name of the person whose usual place of worship it is[16].

Additional provision is made as to the giving of notices where one or other of the parties to a marriage is subject to immigration control[17].

1   As to the meaning of 'superintendent registrar' see PARA 22 note 1.

2   The Registrar General may, with the approval of the Secretary of State, by statutory instrument make regulations prescribing any thing which by the Marriage Act 1949 is required to be prescribed: s 74(b) (amended by SI 2008/678). Except where the context otherwise requires, 'prescribed' means prescribed by regulations made under the Marriage Act 1949 s 74: s 78(1). In exercise of the power so conferred the Registration of Marriages Regulations 1986, SI 1986/1442, and the Registration of Marriages (Welsh Language) Regulations 1999, SI 1999/1621, were made. For the prescribed forms of notice see the Registration of Marriages Regulations 1986, SI 1986/1442, Sch 1, Form 1 (substituted by SI 2000/3164; amended by SI 2005/3177) (notice of marriage where both parties aged 18 or over); and the Registration of Marriages Regulations 1986, SI 1986/1442, Sch 1, Form 1A (added by SI 2000/3164; amended by SI 2005/3177) (notice of marriage where either or both parties under 18). For the corresponding forms in Welsh see the Registration of Marriages (Welsh Language) Regulations 1999, SI 1999/1621, Sch 1, Form 1 (substituted by SI 2000/3164; amended by SI 2005/3177) (notice of marriage where both parties aged 18 or over); and the Registration of Marriages (Welsh Language) Regulations 1999, SI 1999/1621, Sch 1, Form 1A (added by SI 2000/3164; amended by SI 2005/3177) (notice of marriage where either or both parties under 18). For the prescribed forms of notice where a party is subject to immigration control, see the Registration of Marriages Regulations 1986, SI 1986/1442, Sch 1 Forms 1B, 1C (added by SI 2005/155; amended by SI 2005/3177). For the corresponding forms in Welsh see Registration of Marriages (Welsh Language) Regulations 1999, SI 1999/1621, Sch 1 Forms 1B, 1C (added by SI 2005/155; amended by SI 2005/3177). As to persons subject to immigration control see PARA 176. As to the meaning of 'Registrar General' see PARA 46 note 5. For these purposes 'subject to immigration control' has the same meaning as in the Asylum and Immigration (Treatment of Claimants, etc) Act 2004 s 19(4) (see PARA 176 note 2): Registration of Marriages Regulations 1986, SI 1986/1442, reg 2(1) (amended by SI 2005/155).

3   Marriage Act 1949 s 27(1) (amended by the Immigration and Asylum Act 1999 ss 160(2)(a), 169(1), (3), Sch 14 paras 3, 8, Sch 16).

4   For these purposes, except where the context otherwise requires, 'registration district' means the district of a superintendent registrar: Marriage Act 1949 s 78(1). As to registration districts generally see REGISTRATION CONCERNING THE INDIVIDUAL vol 39(2) (Reissue) PARA 502.

5   Marriage Act 1949 s 27(1)(a) (amended by the Immigration and Asylum Act 1999 s 161(1)(a)).

6   Marriage Act 1949 s 27(1)(b) (amended by the Immigration and Asylum Act 1999 s 161(1)(b)). As to the procedure where one of the parties resides in Scotland or Northern Ireland see PARAS 112, 113 respectively.

7   It is not necessary in support of a marriage to give any proof that before the marriage either of the parties resided, or resided for any period, in the registration district stated in the notice of marriage to be that of his or her place of residence, nor may any evidence be given to prove the

contrary in any proceedings touching the validity of the marriage: see PARA 22. As to the acquisition of a residence qualification cf PARA 59.

8   Ie in pursuance of the Marriage Act 1949 s 26(1)(dd) (see PARA 54).

9   Marriage Act 1949 s 27(3) (amended by the Marriage Act 1983 Sch 1 para 5(a); the Marriage Act 1994 Schedule paras 1, 2; the Immigration and Asylum Act 1999 s 161(2); and the Civil Partnership Act 2004 Sch 27 para 14). In relation to marriages in naval, military or air force chapels otherwise than according to the rites of the Church of England, the Marriage Act 1949 s 27(3) applies as if it required the notice of marriage to include a statement that one at least of the persons to be married is a qualified person within the meaning of Pt V (ss 68–71: see PARA 129) and to specify the person so qualified and the nature of his qualification: s 70(1)(b), Sch 4 Pt IV.

10   Marriage Act 1949 s 27(3)(a) (amended by the Immigration and Asylum Act 1999 s 160(2)(c), Sch 16).

11   Marriage Act 1949 s 27(3) proviso.

12   Ie a certificate issued under the Marriage Act 1949 s 35(2) or s 35(3): see PARA 100.

13   As to the meaning of 'registered building' see PARA 54 note 3.

14   As to the meaning of 'parish church' see PARA 59 note 8.

15   As to the meaning of 'authorised chapel' see PARA 59 note 9.

16   Marriage Act 1949 s 35(5) (amended by the Immigration and Asylum Act 1999 Sch 14 paras 3, 17(5)). As to when a parish church or authorised chapel is deemed to be the usual place of worship of any person see PARA 100 note 17.

17   See the Asylum and Immigration (Treatment of Claimants, etc) Act 2004 s 20(1); and PARA 177.

88.   Notice requiring presence of registrar.   If the persons to be married wish to be married in the presence of a registrar[1] in a registered building[2] for which an authorised person[3] has been appointed[4], they must, at the time when notice of marriage is given to the superintendent registrar[5], give notice to him that they require a registrar to be present at the marriage[6].

1   For these purposes, except where the context otherwise requires, 'registrar' means a registrar of marriages: Marriage Act 1949 s 78(1). As to registrars of marriage see REGISTRATION CONCERNING THE INDIVIDUAL vol 39(2) (Reissue) PARA 611.

2   As to the meaning of 'registered building' see PARA 54 note 3.

3   As to the meaning of 'authorised person' see PARA 107.

4   As to the necessity for the presence of the registrar or other duly authorised person at a marriage in a registered building see PARAS 106–107.

5   As to the meaning of 'superintendent registrar' see PARA 22 note 1.

6   Marriage Act 1949 s 27(5).

89.   Effect of want of due notice and of misdescription.   If any persons knowingly and wilfully intermarry without having given due notice of marriage to the superintendent registrar[1], the marriage is void[2].

A misdescription in the notice of marriage of the name, age, condition or residence of both or either of the parties does not affect the validity of the marriage, even if both parties were aware of the irregularity[3], as the means resorted to by the legislature for protecting the public and the parties against such false notice are the imposition of penalties on those who sign a false notice or make a false declaration[4]. The fact that the marriage is void does not affect the duty to register all marriages solemnised[5]. The Registrar General has no power to strike out an entry altogether, or to make a note in the margin of an entry that the marriage was a void marriage[6].

1   As to the meaning of 'superintendent registrar' see PARA 22 note 1.

2   See the Marriage Act 1949 s 49(a); and PARA 330. As to the position where one of the parties is unaware of the irregularity see PARA 330. The marriage is similarly void if the parties knowingly and wilfully intermarry in any place other than the one specified in the notice (see s 49(e); and PARA 330); and any person who knowingly and wilfully solemnises a marriage in such a place is guilty of an offence (see s 75(2)(a), (4); and PARA 180).

3   *Re Rutter, Donaldson v Rutter* [1907] 2 Ch 592 (widow was liable to forfeit property on a remarriage; her surname, and the condition and residence of both parties, were misdescribed in

the notice of marriage; it was held that the irregularities did not affect the validity of the marriage); *Prowse v Spurway and Bowley* (1877) 46 LJP 49 (first Christian name of one party intentionally omitted, and false assertion that both parties were over 21); *Plummer v Plummer* [1917] P 163, CA; *R v Lamb* (1934) 50 TLR 310, CCA; and see *R v Smith* (1865) 4 F & F 1099. In this respect there is no analogy between a marriage by banns and a marriage under the superintendent registrar's certificates: *Holmes v Simmons (falsely called Holmes)* (1868) LR 1 P & D 523; *Plummer v Plummer*; and see PARA 69.

4 *Plummer v Plummer* [1917] P 163, CA; and see *R v Lamb* (1934) 50 TLR 310, CCA; and PARA 184.

5 *Dinizulu v A-G and Registrar-General* [1958] 3 All ER 555, [1958] 1 WLR 1252. As to the registration of marriages see PARA 108.

6 See note 5.

90. Declaration to accompany notice. No certificate for marriage is to be issued by a superintendent registrar[1] unless the notice of marriage is accompanied by a solemn declaration in writing by the party giving the notice[2]:

(1) that he or she believes that there is no impediment of kindred or alliance[3] or other lawful hindrance to the marriage[4];

(2) that the persons to be married have for the period of seven days immediately before the giving of the notice had their usual place of residence within the registration district[5] or registration districts in which notice is given[6];

(3) where one of the persons to be married is a child[7] and is not a widower or widow, that the consent of the person or persons whose consent to the marriage is required[8] has been obtained, that the necessity of obtaining any such consent has been dispensed with, that the court has consented to the marriage[9], or that there is no person whose consent to the marriage is so required[10].

The declaration must be in the body or at the foot of the notice of marriage and must be signed by the person by whom the notice is given, at the time it is given[11], in the presence of the superintendent registrar to whom it is given or his deputy, or in the presence of a registrar of births and deaths or of marriages for the registration district in which the person giving the notice, or his deputy, resides, and that official must attest the declaration by adding his name, description and place of residence[12]. If any person, other than a superintendent registrar, who has so attested a declaration accompanying a notice of marriage has reasonable grounds for suspecting that the marriage will be a sham marriage[13], he must report his suspicions to the Secretary of State without delay and in such form and manner as may be prescribed by regulations[14].

1 As to the meaning of 'superintendent registrar' see PARA 22 note 1.
2 Marriage Act 1949 s 28(1) (amended by the Immigration and Asylum Act 1999 Sch 16). A person who knowingly and wilfully makes a false declaration is guilty of an offence: see PARA 184.
3 As to the prohibited degrees of consanguinity and affinity see PARAS 35–37.
4 Marriage Act 1949 s 28(1)(a).
5 As to the meaning of 'registration district' see PARA 87 note 4.
6 Marriage Act 1949 s 28(1)(b) (substituted by the Immigration and Asylum Act 1999 Sch 14 paras 3, 11). In relation to the marriage of a person who is subject to immigration control, the Marriage Act 1949 s 28(1)(b) has effect as if it required a declaration that the notice of marriage is given in compliance with the Asylum and Immigration (Treatment of Claimants, etc) Act 2004 s 19(2) (see PARA 177) and the party subject to immigration control satisfies s 19(3)(a), (b) or (c) (see PARA 176): s 20(2)(a).
7 As to the meaning of 'child' see PARA 37 note 3.
8 Ie under the Marriage Act 1949 s 3: see PARA 46.
9 Ie where the minor is a ward of court (see PARA 46) or where the person whose consent is required refuses or is unable to give it (see PARAS 47–48).

10 Marriage Act 1949 s 28(1)(c) (amended by the Family Law Reform Act 1987 Sch 2 para 9). The Marriage Act 1949 s 28 also applies with modifications to certain marriages intended to be celebrated in Scotland: see PARA 112. As to the additional matters to be declared in the case of a marriage according to the usages of the Society of Friends see PARA 115.

Where, for the purpose of obtaining a certificate for marriage, a person declares that the consent of any person or persons whose consent to the marriage is required under s 3 (see PARA 46) has been obtained, the superintendent registrar may refuse to issue the certificate for marriage unless satisfied by the production of written evidence that the consent of that person or of those persons has in fact been obtained: Family Law Reform Act 1969 s 2(3) (amended by the Immigration and Asylum Act 1999 Sch 14 para 37, Sch 16).

11 Marriage Act 1949 s 28(1) (as amended: see note 2).

12 Marriage Act 1949 s 28(2).

13 As to the meaning of 'sham marriage' see PARA 11.

14 Immigration and Asylum Act 1999 s 24(1)(b), (3). As to the prescribed form and manner see PARA 11 note 7.

91. Superintendent registrar's power to require evidence. A superintendent registrar[1] to whom a notice of marriage is given[2], or any other person attesting a declaration accompanying such a notice[3], may require the person giving the notice to provide him with specified evidence[4]:

(1)   relating to that person[5]; or

(2)   if the superintendent registrar considers that the circumstances are exceptional, relating to each of the persons to be married[6].

Such a requirement may be imposed at any time on or after the giving of the notice of marriage but before the superintendent registrar issues[7] his certificate[8].

1   As to the meaning of 'superintendent registrar' see PARA 22 note 1.

2   Ie under the Marriage Act 1949 s 27: see PARA 87.

3   As to the declaration accompanying the notice of marriage see PARA 90.

4   For these purposes, 'specified evidence', in relation to a person, means such evidence of that person's: (1) name and surname; (2) age; (3) previous marriage or civil partnership and, if so, the ending of the marriage or civil partnership; and (4) nationality, as may be specified in guidance issued by the Registrar General: Marriage Act 1949 s 28A(3) (s 28A added by the Immigration and Asylum Act 1999 s 162(1); Marriage Act 1949 s 28A(3) substituted by the Civil Partnership Act 2004 Sch 27 para 15). As to the meaning of 'Registrar General' see PARA 46 note 5.

5   Marriage Act 1949 s 28A(1)(a) (as added: see note 4)

6   Marriage Act 1949 s 28A(1)(b) (as added: see note 4).

7   Ie under the Marriage Act 1949 s 31: see PARA 97.

8   Marriage Act 1949 s 28A(2) (as added: see note 4).

92. Entry in marriage notice book. The superintendent registrar[1] must file all notices of marriage and keep them with the records of his office, and he must[2] also forthwith enter the particulars given in every such notice, together with the date of the notice and the name of the person by whom the notice was given, in a book (the 'marriage notice book') furnished to him for that purpose by the Registrar General[3]; and the marriage notice book must be open for inspection free of charge at all reasonable hours[4]. The superintendent registrar is entitled to a fee of £30 for every such entry made in the marriage notice book[5].

1   As to the meaning of 'superintendent registrar' see PARA 22 note 1.

2   Ie subject to the Marriage Act 1949 s 27A (see PARA 172) and ss 27B, 27C (see PARA 93).

3   As to the meaning of 'Registrar General' see PARA 46 note 5.

4   Marriage Act 1949 ss 27(4), 78(1) (s 27(4) amended by the Marriage Act 1983 Sch 1 para 5(b)).

5   Marriage Act 1949 s 27(6) (amended by SI 2002/3076).

93. Notification where marriage is within the prohibited degrees. In relation to any marriage within the prohibited degrees of affinity[1], which is intended to be solemnised on the authority of certificates of a superintendent registrar[2]:

(1)　the superintendent registrar must not enter notice of the marriage in the marriage notice book[3] unless:

(a)　he is satisfied by the production of evidence that both the persons to be married have attained the age of 21[4]; and

(b)　he has received a declaration made in the prescribed form[5] by each of those persons, each declaration having been signed and attested in the prescribed manner[6], specifying their affinal relationship and declaring that the younger has not at any time before attaining the age of 18 been a child of the family[7] in relation to the other[8];

(2)　the fact that a superintendent registrar has received a declaration under head (1) above must be entered in the marriage notice book together with the particulars given in the notice of marriage and any such declaration must be filed and kept with the records of the office of the superintendent registrar or, where notice of marriage is required to be given to two superintendent registrars, of each of them[9]; and

(3)　where the superintendent registrar receives from some person other than the persons to be married a written statement signed by that person which alleges that the declaration made under head (1) above is false in a material particular, the superintendent registrar must not issue a certificate unless a declaration is obtained[10] from the High Court[11].

1　Ie any marriage mentioned in the Marriage Act 1949 s 1(2), Sch 1 Pt 2: see PARA 37.

2　Marriage Act 1949 s 27B(1) (s 27B added by the Marriage (Prohibited Degrees of Relationship) Act 1986 Sch 1 paras 1, 5; Marriage Act 1949 s 27B(1) amended by the Immigration and Asylum Act 1999 Sch 14 paras 3, 10(a)). The Marriage Act 1949 s 29 (see PARA 96) does not apply in relation to a marriage to which s 27B applies, except so far as a caveat against the issue of a certificate for the marriage is entered under s 29 on a ground other than the relationship of the persons to be married: s 27B(6) (as so added; amended by the Immigration and Asylum Act 1999 Sch 14 paras 3, 10(b), Sch 16). As to the meaning of 'superintendent registrar' see PARA 22 note 1.

3　As to the meaning of 'marriage notice book' see PARA 92.

4　Marriage Act 1949 s 27B(2)(a) (as added: see note 2).

5　For the prescribed form of declaration see the Registration of Marriages Regulations 1986, SI 1986/1442, Sch 1, Form 8 (substituted by SI 2005/3177); and for the corresponding form in Welsh see the Registration of Marriages (Welsh Language) Regulations 1999, SI 1999/1621, Sch 1, Form 5 (substituted by SI 2005/3177).

6　The declaration must be signed, in the space provided, by the person making it in the presence of the superintendent registrar who must then, in the space provided, sign the declaration as witness and add his description: Registration of Marriages Regulations 1986, SI 1986/1442, reg 6(2). The superintendent registrar so referred to is the superintendent registrar or, as the case may be, either of the two superintendent registrars to whom notice of the marriage is required to be given: reg 6(3).

7　As to the meaning of 'child of the family' see PARA 37 note 3.

8　Marriage Act 1949 s 27B(2)(b) (as added: see note 2).

9　Marriage Act 1949 s 27B(3) (as added: see note 2).

10　Either of the persons to be married may, whether or not any statement has been so received by the superintendent registrar, apply to the High Court for a declaration that, both those persons having attained the age of 21 and the younger of those persons not having at any time before attaining the age of 18 been a child of the family in relation to the other, there is no impediment of affinity to the solemnisation of the marriage; and, where such a declaration is obtained, the superintendent registrar may enter notice of the marriage in the marriage notice book and may issue a certificate, whether or not any declaration has been made under the Marriage Act 1949 s 27B(2): s 27B(5) (as added (see note 2); amended by the Immigration and Asylum Act 1999 Sch 14 paras 3, 10(c), Sch 16). Proceedings under the Marriage Act 1949 s 27B(5) are assigned to the Family Division (see the Supreme Court Act 1981 s 61(1), (3), Sch 1 para 3(c)); and are, therefore, 'family proceedings' for the purposes of the Matrimonial and Family Proceedings Act 1984 Pt V (ss 32–42: see PARA 732 et seq).

11 Marriage Act 1949 s 27B(4) (as added (see note 2); amended by the Immigration and Asylum
    Act 1999 Sch 14 paras 3, 10(b), Sch 16). A person who makes such a declaration which he
    knows to be false in material particular is guilty of an offence: Perjury Act 1911 s 3(1)(d)(ii)
    (added by the Marriage (Prohibited Degrees of Relationship) Act 1986 ss 1(8), 4). The
    punishment on conviction of an offence under s 3(1) on indictment is imprisonment for a term
    not exceeding seven years or a fine or both, and on summary conviction a penalty not exceeding
    the prescribed sum: s 3(1). As to the meaning of 'prescribed sum' see PARA 77 note 16.

94. Publication of notice. Where a marriage is intended to be solemnised on
the authority of certificates of a superintendent registrar[1], the superintendent
registrar to whom notice of marriage has been given must suspend or affix in a
conspicuous place in his office the notice of marriage, or an exact copy signed by
him of the relevant particulars as entered in the marriage notice book[2], for 15
successive days next after the day of entry of the notice in the marriage notice
book[3]. No marriage may be solemnised on the production of certificates of a
superintendent registrar until after the expiration of the waiting period in
relation to each notice of marriage[4].

For these purposes, 'waiting period', in relation to a notice of marriage,
means:

(1)   the period of 15 days; or
(2)   such shorter period as may be determined by the Registrar General[5] or
       by a superintendent registrar[6],

after the day on which the notice of marriage was entered in the marriage notice
book[7].

If, on an application made to the Registrar General, he is satisfied that there
are compelling reasons for reducing the 15-day period[8] because of the
exceptional circumstances of the case, he may reduce that period to such shorter
period as he considers appropriate[9]. Accordingly, where a marriage is intended to
be solemnised on the authority of certificates of a superintendent registrar, each
person has given notice of marriage and either of them has, or they each have, a
reason for applying for a reduction of the 15-day period, the following
provisions apply[10].

The applicant[11] must complete the prescribed form[12] and pass the completed
application[13], together with the fee[14], to the superintendent registrar of the
registration district[15] in which that person has given notice of marriage[16]. The
superintendent registrar must immediately forward the completed application
and fee to the Registrar General[17]. If, on receipt of a completed application, the
Registrar General requires further information, which may include documents,
before making his decision, he may request that the superintendent registrar who
forwarded the completed application obtain the information from the applicant
and forward it to him or request it from the applicant[18]. After the Registrar
General has considered the completed application and, where relevant, any
further information obtained, and he is satisfied that there are, or are not, as the
case may be, compelling reasons for reducing the 15-day period, he must notify
his decision both to the applicant and the superintendent registrar who
forwarded the completed application to him[19].

1   As to the meaning of 'superintendent registrar' see PARA 22 note 1.
2   As to the meaning of 'marriage notice book' see PARA 92.
3   Marriage Act 1949 s 31(1) (amended by the Immigration and Asylum Act 1999 s 160(4)(a),
    Sch 14 paras 3, 14(a), Sch 16).
4   Marriage Act 1949 s 31(4) (amended by the Immigration and Asylum Act 1999 s 160(4)(c),
    Sch 14 para 14(a), Sch 16).
5   Ie under the Marriage Act 1949 s 31(5A).

6　Ie under any provision of regulations made under the Marriage Act 1949 s 31(5D).
7　Marriage Act 1949 s 31(4A) (added by the Immigration and Asylum Act 1999 s 160(5)).
8　For these purposes, '15-day period' means the period of 15 days mentioned in the Marriage Act 1949 s 31(1) or s 31(2) (see PARA 97): s 31(5B) (added by the Immigration and Asylum Act 1999 s 160(6)).
9　Marriage Act 1949 s 31(5A) (added by the Immigration and Asylum Act 1999 s 160(6)). If the Registrar General reduces the 15-day period in a particular case, the reference to 15 days in the Marriage Act 1949 s 75(3)(a) (see PARA 180) is to be treated, in relation to that case, as a reference to the reduced period: s 31(5C) (added by the Immigration and Asylum Act 1999 s 160(6)).
　　The Registrar General may by regulations make provision with respect to the making, and granting, of applications under the Marriage Act 1949 s 31(5A): s 31(5D) (added by the Immigration and Asylum Act 1999 s 160(6)). The regulations: (1) may provide for the power conferred by the Marriage Act 1949 s 31(5A) to be exercised by a superintendent registrar on behalf of the Registrar General in cases falling within a category prescribed in the regulations; (2) may provide for the making of an appeal to the Registrar General against a decision taken by a superintendent registrar in accordance with regulations made by virtue of head (1); (3) may make different provision in relation to different cases; (4) require the approval of the Secretary of State: s 31(5E) (added by the Immigration and Asylum Act 1999 s 160(6); amended by SI 2008/678).
　　The Secretary of State may by order provide for a fee, of such an amount as may be specified in the order, to be payable on an application under the Marriage Act 1949 s 31(5A); and the order may make different provision in relation to different cases: s 31(5F), (5G) (added by the Immigration and Asylum Act 1999 s 160(6); amended by SI 2008/678).
　　In exercise of the powers so conferred the Registrar General, with the approval of the Secretary of State, has made the Reporting of Suspicious Marriages and Registration of Marriages (Miscellaneous Amendments) Regulations 2000, SI 2000/3164, reg 4(3).
10　Registration of Marriages Regulations 1986, SI 1986/1442, reg 6A(1) (added by SI 2000/3164).
11　For these purposes, 'applicant' means the person seeking a reduction in the 15-day period: Registration of Marriages Regulations 1986, SI 1986/1442, reg 6A(5) (added by SI 2000/3164).
12　For the prescribed form of application see the Registration of Marriages Regulations 1986, SI 1986/1442, reg 6A(2), Sch 1, Form 8A (added by SI 2000/3164); and for the corresponding form in Welsh see the Registration of Marriages (Welsh Language) Regulations 1999, SI 1999/1621, reg 7(1), Sch 1, Form 8A (added by SI 2000/3164).
13　For these purposes, 'completed application' means the completed application in the prescribed form together with any copy documents which support the reason given in that form for applying for a reduction of the 15-day period: Registration of Marriages Regulations 1986, SI 1986/1442, reg 6A(5) (as added: see note 11).
14　The fee so payable is £47: Registration of Births, Deaths and Marriages (Fees) Order 2002, SI 2002/3076, Schedule (amended by SI 2005/1997).
15　As to the meaning of 'registration district' see PARA 87 note 4.
16　Registration of Marriages Regulations 1986, SI 1986/1442, reg 6A(2) (added by SI 2000/3164).
17　Registration of Marriages Regulations 1986, SI 1986/1442, reg 6A(3) (added by SI 2000/3164).
18　Registration of Marriages Regulations 1986, SI 1986/1442, reg 6A(4) (added by SI 2000/3164).
19　Registration of Marriages Regulations 1986, SI 1986/1442, reg 6A(5) (added by SI 2000/3164).

(ii) Certification

95. Forbidding the issue of a certificate. Any person whose consent to a marriage intended to be solemnised on the authority of certificates of a superintendent registrar[1] is required[2] may forbid the issue of the certificate by writing, at any time before the issue of the certificate, the word 'forbidden' opposite to the entry of the notice of marriage in the marriage notice book[3], and by subscribing thereto his name and place of residence, and the capacity, in relation to either of the persons to be married, in which he forbids the issue of the certificate[4]. Where the issue of the certificate has been so forbidden, the notice of marriage and all proceedings on it are void[5]. Where, however, the court has consented to the marriage[6] and the consent of the court has the same effect as if it had been given by a person whose consent has been refused, that person is not so entitled to forbid the issue of a certificate for that marriage and the notice of marriage and the proceedings on it are accordingly not void[7].

1   As to the meaning of 'superintendent registrar' see PARA 22 note 1.
2   Ie required under the Marriage Act 1949 s 3: see PARA 46.
3   As to the meaning of 'marriage notice book' see PARA 92.
4   Marriage Act 1949 s 30 (amended by the Immigration and Asylum Act 1999 Sch 14 paras 3, 13). For observations of a general character as to the inquiries that ought to be made by a registrar on receiving notice of marriage in relation to persons appearing to be underage see *Norsworthy v Norsworthy* (1909) 26 TLR 9. To forbid the issue of a certificate for marriage by falsely representing oneself to be such a person is an offence: see PARAS 180, 184.
5   Marriage Act 1949 s 30 (as amended: see note 4).
6   Ie by virtue of the Marriage Act 1949 s 3(1) proviso (b): see PARA 47.
7   Marriage Act 1949 s 30 proviso.

96.   Caveat.   Any person may enter a caveat with the superintendent registrar[1] against the issue of a certificate for the marriage of any person named in the caveat[2]. If any caveat is so entered and has been signed by or on behalf of the person entering it and states his place of residence and the ground of objection on which the caveat is founded, no certificate is to be issued until the superintendent registrar has examined into the matter of the caveat and is satisfied that it ought not to obstruct the issue of the certificate, or until the caveat is withdrawn by the person who entered it[3]. If the superintendent registrar is doubtful whether to issue a certificate, he may refer the matter of the caveat to the Registrar General[4]; and, where a superintendent registrar refuses, by reason of the caveat, to issue the certificate, the party applying for it may appeal to the Registrar General, who must either confirm the refusal or direct that a certificate be issued[5].

Any person who enters a caveat against the issue of a certificate on grounds which the Registrar General declares to be frivolous[6] and such that they ought not to obstruct the issue of the certificate is liable for the costs of the proceedings before the Registrar General and for damages recoverable by the person against whose marriage the caveat was entered[7].

1   As to the meaning of 'superintendent registrar' see PARA 22 note 1.
2   Marriage Act 1949 s 29(1) (amended by the Immigration and Asylum Act 1999 Sch 14 paras 3, 12, Sch 16; SI 1968/1242). Cf the Marriage Act 1949 s 27B(6); and PARA 93.
3   Marriage Act 1949 s 29(2) (amended by the Immigration and Asylum Act 1999 Sch 14 paras 3, 12, Sch 16).
4   Marriage Act 1949 s 29(2) (as amended: see note 3). As to the meaning of 'Registrar General' see PARA 46 note 5.
5   Marriage Act 1949 s 29(3) (amended by the Immigration and Asylum Act 1999 Sch 14 paras 3, 12, Sch 16). There is also a remedy by way of mandatory order: see *R v Hammersmith Superintendent Registrar of Marriages, ex p Mir-Anwaruddin* [1917] 1 KB 634, CA; *R v Brentwood Superintendent Registrar of Marriages, ex p Arias* [1968] 2 QB 956, [1968] 3 All ER 279, DC.
6   It would seem that to be frivolous the grounds on which the caveat is entered must be such that no reasonable person could contend that there was any reason in law why the marriage should not take place: see *Norman v Mathews* (1916) 85 LJKB 857.
7   Marriage Act 1949 s 29(4) (amended by the Immigration and Asylum Act 1999 Sch 14 paras 3, 12, Sch 16). For the purpose of enabling any person to recover any such costs or damages, a copy of the Registrar General's declaration, purporting to be sealed with the seal of the General Register Office, is evidence that the Registrar General has declared the caveat to have been entered on frivolous grounds which ought not to obstruct the issue of the certificate: Marriage Act 1949 s 29(5) (amended by the Immigration and Asylum Act 1999 Sch 14 paras 3, 12, Sch 16).

97. Issue of certificate. At the expiration of the period of 15 successive days from the day on which the notice was entered in the marriage notice book[1], and on the request of the party giving the notice of marriage, the superintendent registrar[2] must issue a certificate in the prescribed form[3], unless:

(1)   the superintendent registrar is not satisfied that there is no lawful impediment to the issue of the certificate[4]; or

(2)   the issue of the certificate has been forbidden by any person authorised in that behalf[5].

If, relying on head (1), a superintendent registrar refuses to issue a certificate, the person applying for it may appeal to the Registrar General[6]; and, on such an appeal, the Registrar General must confirm the refusal or direct that a certificate be issued[7]. If, relying on head (1), a superintendent registrar refuses to issue a certificate as a result of a representation made to him and, on an appeal against the refusal, the Registrar General declares the representation to have been frivolous[8] and to be such that it ought not to obstruct the issue of a certificate, the person making the representation is liable for the costs of the proceedings before the Registrar General and for damages by the applicant for the certificate[9].

Every such certificate must set out the particulars contained in the notice of marriage, and the day on which the notice was entered in the marriage notice book, and must contain a statement that its issue has not been forbidden by anyone authorised to do so[10].

If any persons knowingly and wilfully intermarry without a certificate having been duly issued, in respect of each of the persons to be married, by the superintendent registrar to whom the notice of marriage was given, or in any place other than the one specified in the certificate, the marriage is void[11].

1   Ie the period referred to in the Marriage Act 1949 s 31(1): see PARA 94. As to the meaning of 'marriage notice book' see PARA 92.

2   As to the meaning of 'superintendent registrar' see PARA 22 note 1.

3   For the prescribed form of certificate see the Registration of Marriages Regulations 1986, SI 1986/1442, Sch 1, Form 9 (substituted by SI 1997/2204; amended by SI 2000/3164; SI 2005/3177); and for the corresponding form in Welsh see the Registration of Marriages (Welsh Language) Regulations 1999, SI 1999/1621, Sch 1, Form 6 (amended by SI 2000/3164; SI 2005/3177). The Registrar General must furnish every superintendent registrar with a sufficient number of forms of certificates for marriage: Marriage Act 1949 s 40(1). As to the meaning of 'Registrar General' see PARA 46 note 5. As to offences by superintendent registrars in relation to the issue of certificates without licence see s 75(3); PARA 181; and REGISTRATION CONCERNING THE INDIVIDUAL vol 39(2) (Reissue) PARA 535.

4   The entry of a caveat may furnish a ground for refusing to issue a certificate: see PARA 96.

5   Marriage Act 1949 s 31(2) (amended by the Immigration and Asylum Act 1999 ss 160(4)(b), 163(1)). As to the persons who may forbid the issue of a certificate see PARA 95. No marriage may be solemnised on the production of the certificates of a superintendent registrar until after the period of 15 days: see the Marriage Act 1949 s 31(4); and PARA 94. Any person who knowingly and wilfully solemnises a marriage under these provisions within that period is guilty of an offence: see PARA 180. See *R (on the application of the Crown Prosecution Service) v Registrar General of Births, Deaths and Marriages* [2002] EWCA Civ 1661, [2003] QB 1222, [2003] 1 All ER 450 (issue of a certificate relating to a marriage between prisoner awaiting trial and compellable witness not prevented on ground of public policy).

6   Marriage Act 1949 s 31A(1) (added by the Immigration and Asylum Act 1999 s 163(2)).

7   Marriage Act 1949 s 31A(2) (added by the Immigration and Asylum Act 1999 s 163(2)).

8   As to the meaning of 'frivolous' see PARA 96 note 6.

9   Marriage Act 1949 s 31A(3) (added by the Immigration and Asylum Act 1999 s 163(2)).

10   Marriage Act 1949 s 31(3).

11   See the Marriage Act 1949 s 49(b), (e); and PARA 330. Any person who knowingly and wilfully solemnises a marriage, other than a marriage by special licence or a Quaker or Jewish marriage, in any place other than the one specified in the certificate is guilty of an offence: see PARA 180.

98.   Delivery of certificate.   Where a marriage is intended to be solemnised on the authority of certificates of a superintendent registrar[1], the certificates must be delivered[2]:

(1)   if the marriage is to be solemnised in a registered building or at a person's residence in the presence of a registrar[3], to that registrar[4];

(2)   if the marriage is to be solemnised in a registered building[5] without the presence of the registrar, to the authorised person[6] in whose presence the marriage is to be solemnised[7];

(3)   if the marriage is to be solemnised in the office of a superintendent registrar[8], to the registrar in whose presence the marriage is to be solemnised[9];

(4)   if the marriage is to be solemnised on approved premises[10], to the registrar in whose presence the marriage is to be solemnised[11];

(5)   if the marriage is to be solemnised according to the usages of the Society of Friends[12], to the registering officer of that Society[13] for the place where the marriage is to be solemnised[14];

(6)   if the marriage is to be solemnised according to the usages of persons professing the Jewish religion[15], to the officer of a synagogue by whom the marriage is required[16] to be registered[17];

(7)   if the marriage is to be solemnised according to the rites of the Church of England, to the officiating clergyman[18].

For every marriage in his presence the registrar is entitled to receive a fee from the parties[19].

1   As to the meaning of 'superintendent registrar' see PARA 22 note 1.
2   Marriage Act 1949 s 50(1) (amended by the Immigration and Asylum Act 1999 Sch 14 paras 3, 28(a), Sch 16).
3   As to the meaning of 'registrar' see PARA 88 note 1.
4   Marriage Act 1949 s 50(1)(a) (amended by the Marriage Act 1983 Sch 1 para 14).
5   As to the meaning of 'registered building' see PARA 54 note 3.
6   As to the meaning of 'authorised person' see PARA 107.
7   Marriage Act 1949 s 50(1)(b). Before permitting the solemnisation of a marriage in his presence to begin, an authorised person must require the production of every document on the authority of which the marriage is to be solemnised, and must by scrutiny of the documents satisfy himself that the marriage may be lawfully solemnised in his presence on the authority of the documents: Marriage Act 1949 s 50(3) (amended by the Immigration and Asylum Act 1999 Sch 14 para 3, 28(c)); Marriage (Authorised Persons) Regulations 1952, SI 1952/1869, reg 9(1). The authorised person must make a note on every certificate delivered to him of the number of the entry in the marriage register books in which the marriage has been registered (see PARA 108) and must preserve every such certificate, in the fire-resisting receptacle required to be provided in the registered building (see PARA 109), until the end of the quarter, when it must be delivered to the superintendent registrar with the corresponding certified copy of the marriage entry (see PARA 108): reg 9(2) (amended by SI 2000/3164). The certificates must be produced with the marriage register books as and when required by the Registrar General: Marriage Act 1949 s 50(3) (amended by the Immigration and Asylum Act 1999 Sch 14 paras 3, 28(c)).
8   As to the meaning of 'superintendent registrar' see PARA 22 note 1.
9   Marriage Act 1949 s 50(1)(c). See also PARA 102.
10   As to the meaning of 'approved premises' see PARA 54 note 6.
11   Marriage Act 1949 s 50(1)(cc) (added by the Marriage Act 1994 Sch 1 paras 1, 4).
12   As to marriages according to the usages of the Society of Friends see PARA 116.
13   As to the meaning of 'registering officer of the Society of Friends' see REGISTRATION CONCERNING THE INDIVIDUAL vol 39(2) (Reissue) PARA 520.
14   Marriage Act 1949 s 50(1)(d).
15   As to marriages between persons professing the Jewish religion according to the usages of the Jews see PARA 118.
16   Ie under the Marriage Act 1949 Pt IV (ss 53–67): see REGISTRATION CONCERNING THE INDIVIDUAL.
17   Marriage Act 1949 s 50(1)(e).

18 Marriage Act 1949 s 50(1)(f).

19 Marriage Act 1949 s 51(1) (renumbered by the Marriage Act 1983 Sch 1 para 15). The registrar's fee under the Marriage Act 1949 s 51(1) is £40 for attending a marriage at a register office and £47 for attending at a registered building or at the place where a housebound or detained person usually resides: Registration of Births, Deaths and Marriages (Fees) Order 2002, SI 2002/3076, art 2, Schedule (amended by SI 2005/1997).

In the case of persons married on approved premises in pursuance of the Marriage Act 1949 s 26(1)(bb) (see PARA 54), s 51(1) does not apply but the superintendent registrar in whose presence the persons are married is entitled to receive from them a fee of an amount determined in accordance with regulations under s 46A (see PARA 190) by the local authority that approved the premises: s 51(1A) (added by the Marriage Act 1994 Schedule para 5).

A superintendent registrar is entitled to receive from persons married in his presence in pursuance of the Marriage Act 1949 s 26(1)(dd) (see PARA 54) the sum of £40: s 51(2) (added by the Marriage Act 1983 Sch 1 para 15; amended by SI 2002/3076).

99. Marriage without the presence of a registrar. Where a marriage is to be solemnised in a registered building[1] for which an authorised person[2] has been appointed, and no notice requiring a registrar[3] to be present at the marriage has been given[4] to the superintendent registrar[5], the superintendent registrar must, when issuing the certificate, give to the person by whom notice of marriage was given, printed instructions in the prescribed form[6] for the due solemnisation of the marriage[7].

1   As to the meaning of 'registered building' see PARA 54 note 3.
2   As to the meaning of 'authorised person' see PARA 107.
3   As to the meaning of 'registrar' see PARA 88 note 1.
4   Ie under the Marriage Act 1949 s 27(5): see PARA 88.
5   As to the meaning of 'superintendent registrar' see PARA 22 note 1.

6   For the prescribed form of instructions see the Registration of Marriages Regulations 1986, SI 1986/1442, Sch 1 Form 12 (substituted by SI 1997/2204; amended by SI 2000/3164); and for the corresponding form in Welsh see the Registration of Marriages (Welsh Language) Regulations 1999, SI 1999/1621, Sch 1 Form 8 (amended by SI 2000/3164).

7   Marriage Act 1949 s 31(5) (amended by the Immigration and Asylum Act 1999 s 169(1), Sch 14 paras 3, 14(b)).

100. Marriage in registration district in which neither party resides. In general, a superintendent registrar[1] must not issue a certificate for the solemnisation of a marriage elsewhere than within a registration district[2] in which one of the persons to be married has resided for seven days immediately before the giving of the notice of marriage[3].

A superintendent registrar may, however:

(1) issue a certificate for the solemnisation of a marriage in a registered building[4] which is not within a registration district in which either of the persons to be married resides, where the person giving the notice of marriage declares by indorsement on it in the prescribed form[5]:

(a) that the persons to be married desire the marriage to be solemnised according to a specified form, rite or ceremony, being a form, rite or ceremony of a body or denomination of Christians or other persons meeting for religious worship to which one of them professes to belong[6];

(b) that, to the best of his or her belief, there is not within the registration district in which one of them resides any registered building in which marriage is solemnised according to that form, rite or ceremony[7];

(c)   the registration district nearest to the residence of that person in which there is a registered building in which marriage may be solemnised[8]; and

(d)   the registered building in that district in which the marriage is intended to be solemnised[9],

and where any such certificate is issued in respect of each of the persons to be married, the marriage may be solemnised in the registered building stated in the notice[10];

(2)   issue a certificate for the solemnisation of a marriage in a registered building which is the usual place of worship of the persons to be married, or of one of them, notwithstanding that the building is not within a registration district in which either of those persons resides[11];

(3)   issue a certificate for the solemnisation of a marriage in the office of another superintendent registrar, notwithstanding that the office is not within a registration district in which either of the persons to be married resides[12];

(4)   issue a certificate for the solemnisation of a marriage on approved premises[13], notwithstanding that the premises are not within the registration district in which either of the persons to be married resides[14];

(5)   issue a certificate for the solemnisation of a marriage in any parish church[15] or authorised chapel[16] which is the usual place of worship[17] of the persons to be married or one of them, notwithstanding that the church or chapel is not within a registration district in which either of those persons resides[18]; and

(6)   issue a certificate for the solemnisation of a marriage according to the usages of the Society of Friends[19] or between persons professing the Jewish religion according to the usages of the Jews[20], notwithstanding that the building or place in which the marriage is to be solemnised is not within a registration district in which either of the persons to be married resides[21].

1   As to the meaning of 'superintendent registrar' see PARA 22 note 1.
2   As to the meaning of 'registration district' see PARA 87 note 4.
3   Marriage Act 1949 s 34 (substituted by the Immigration and Asylum Act 1999 Sch 14 paras 3, 16). As to the giving of notice of marriage see PARA 87.
4   As to the meaning of 'registered building' see PARA 54 note 3.
5   For the prescribed form of indorsement see the Registration of Marriages Regulations 1986, SI 1986/1442, Sch 1 Form 4 (amended by SI 2000/3164); and for the corresponding forms in Welsh see the Registration of Marriages (Welsh Language) Regulations 1999, SI 1999/1621, Sch 1 Form 3 (amended by SI 2000/3164).
6   Marriage Act 1949 s 35(1)(a) (substituted by the Marriage Act 1949 (Amendment) Act 1954 s 2).
7   Marriage Act 1949 s 35(1)(b).
8   Marriage Act 1949 s 35(1)(c).
9   Marriage Act 1949 s 35(1)(d).
10 Marriage Act 1949 s 35(1) (amended by the Immigration and Asylum Act 1999 Sch 14 paras 3, 17(1), (2), Sch 16). In such cases, the notice of marriage and the certificate must state that the building is the usual place of worship of one of the parties (see PARA 87), but it is not necessary to the validity of the marriage to give proof of that fact (see PARA 22).
11 Marriage Act 1949 s 35(2) (substituted by the Marriage Act 1949 (Amendment) Act 1954 s 2; amended by the Immigration and Asylum Act 1999 Sch 14 paras 3, 17(1), (3), Sch 16). See also note 10.
12 Marriage Act 1949 s 35(2A) (added by the Marriage Act 1994 s 2(1); amended by the Immigration and Asylum Act 1999 Sch 14 paras 3, 17(1), (4), Sch 16). See also note 10.
13 As to the meaning of 'approved premises' see PARA 54 note 6.

14 Marriage Act 1949 s 35(2B) (added by the Marriage Act 1994 s 2(1); amended by the Immigration and Asylum Act 1999 Sch 14 paras 3, 17(1), (4), Sch 16). See also note 10.
15 As to the meaning of 'parish church' see PARA 59 note 8.
16 As to the meaning of 'authorised chapel' see PARA 59 note 9.
17 No parish church or authorised chapel is deemed to be the usual place of worship of any person unless he is enrolled on the church electoral roll for that area: see the Marriage Act 1949 s 72(1); and PARA 66. As to proof of these matters see PARA 22.
18 Marriage Act 1949 s 35(3). In such cases, the notice of marriage and the certificate must state that the church or chapel is the usual place of worship of one of the parties (see PARA 87), but it is not necessary to the validity of the marriage to give proof of that fact (see PARA 22).
19 As to notice of marriage according to the usages of the Society of Friends see PARA 115.
20 As to notice of marriage between persons professing the Jewish religion according to the usages of the Jews see PARA 117.
21 Marriage Act 1949 s 35(4) (amended by the Immigration and Asylum Act 1999 Sch 14 paras 3, 17(1), (2), Sch 16).

101.   Time for solemnisation of marriage.   A marriage may be solemnised on the authority of certificates of a superintendent registrar[1] at any time within the period which is the applicable period in relation to that marriage[2]. If the marriage is not solemnised within the applicable period, the notice of marriage and the certificates are void and no person may solemnise the marriage on the authority of those certificates[3]. If any persons knowingly and wilfully intermarry on the authority of certificates which are so void, the marriage is itself void[4].

1 As to the meaning of 'superintendent registrar' see PARA 22 note 1.
2 Marriage Act 1949 s 33(1) (substituted by the Immigration and Asylum Act 1999 Sch 14 paras 3, 15). For these purposes the 'applicable period', in relation to a marriage, is the period beginning with the day on which the notice of marriage was entered in the marriage notice book and ending: (1) in the case of a marriage which is to be solemnised in pursuance of the Marriage Act 1949 s 26(1)(dd) (see PARA 54), s 37 (see PARA 112) or s 38 (see PARA 113), on the expiry of three months; and (2) in the case of any other marriage, on the expiry of 12 months: Marriage Act 1949 s 33(3) (added by SI 1997/986; substituted by the Immigration and Asylum Act 1999 Sch 14 paras 3, 15). Where a gender recognition certificate has been issued as a result of a final nullity order on the ground of an interim certificate being issued, and the former civil partners wish to marry, the applicable period is one month beginning with the day on which the notice of marriage was entered in the marriage notice book: Marriage Act 1949 s 39A(5) (added by SI 2005/3129). If the notices of marriage given by each person to be married are not given on the same date, the applicable period is to be calculated by reference to the earlier of the two dates: Marriage Act 1949 s 33(4) (added by the Immigration and Asylum Act 1999 Sch 14 paras 3, 15). As to the meaning of 'marriage notice book' see PARA 92.
3 Marriage Act 1949 s 33(2) (substituted by the Immigration and Asylum Act 1999 Sch 14 paras 3, 15). If a person does so solemnise a marriage, he is guilty of an offence: see PARA 180.
4 See the Marriage Act 1949 s 49(d); and PARA 330.

(iii) Place and Manner of Solemnisation

A. SOLEMNISATION AT SUPERINTENDENT REGISTRAR'S OFFICE

102.   Marriage at superintendent registrar's office.   Where a marriage is intended to be solemnised on the authority of certificates of a superintendent registrar[1], the persons to be married may state in the notices of marriage that they wish to be married in the office of the superintendent registrar or one of the superintendent registrars, as the case may be, to whom notice of marriage is given[2]. Where any such notices have been given and the certificates have been issued accordingly[3], the marriage may be solemnised in that office, with open doors[4], in the presence of the superintendent registrar and a registrar[5] of the registration district[6] of that superintendent registrar and of two witnesses[7]. The marriage must be solemnised within the applicable period[8], and between the hours of 8 am and 6 pm[9]. The persons to be married must make the declarations and use the form of words[10] used in the case of marriages in registered buildings[11]; but no religious service is to be used at any marriage solemnised in the office of a superintendent registrar[12].

If a marriage is solemnised in the presence of a registrar of marriages and before, during or immediately after solemnisation of the marriage the registrar has reasonable grounds for suspecting that the marriage will be, or is, a sham marriage[13], he must report his suspicion to the Secretary of State without delay and in such form and manner as may be prescribed by regulations[14].

1   As to the meaning of 'superintendent registrar' see PARA 22 note 1.

2   Marriage Act 1949 s 45(1) (amended by the Marriage Ceremony (Prescribed Words) Act 1996 s 1(2); and the Immigration and Asylum Act 1999 Sch 14 paras 3, 24(a)–(d)). As to the giving of notice of marriage see PARA 87 et seq.

3   As to the issue of a certificate see PARA 97.

4   A marriage will not be invalidated by reason of the doors of the register office being closed during its solemnisation, since there is no statutory provision declaring it void: see *Campbell v Corley* (1856) 28 LTOS 109, 4 WR 675, PC.

5   As to the meaning of 'registrar' see PARA 88 note 1.

6   As to the meaning of 'registration district' see PARA 87 note 4.

7   Marriage Act 1949 s 45(1) (as amended: see note 2). If any persons knowingly and wilfully intermarry in such an office in the absence of the superintendent registrar or of a registrar for the district, the marriage is void: see s 49(g); and PARA 330. Any person who knowingly and wilfully solemnises a marriage in such an office in the absence of a registrar for the district is guilty of an offence: see PARA 180.

8   See PARA 101.

9   See the Marriage Act 1949 s 4; and PARA 82.

10 Ie the declarations and form of words set out in the Marriage Act 1949 s 44(3) or s 44(3A) (see PARA 105). As to the use of the Welsh language see PARA 105 note 3.

11 Marriage Act 1949 s 45(1) (as amended: see note 2). As to the meaning of 'registered building' see PARA 54 note 3.

12 Marriage Act 1949 s 45(2). A religious ceremony may, however, follow a marriage before a superintendent registrar (see s 46; and PARA 57); but the religious ceremony may not be entered as a marriage in any marriage register book kept under the Marriage Act 1949 (see s 46(2); and PARA 57).

13 As to the meaning of 'sham marriage' see PARA 11.

14 Immigration and Asylum Act 1999 s 24(2), (3). As to the prescribed form and manner see PARA 11.

103.   Delivery of certificate to district registrar.   Where a marriage is solemnised in the office of a superintendent registrar[1], the certificate must be delivered to the registrar in whose presence the marriage is solemnised[2]; and it is his duty to register the marriage immediately after its solemnisation[3]. The registrar is entitled to receive a fee from the persons married in his presence[4]. Every registrar by whom a marriage register book is kept must allow searches to be made in it at all reasonable hours, and give a copy certified under his hand of any entry in the book, on payment of a fee[5].

1   As to the meaning of 'superintendent registrar' see PARA 22 note 1.

2   See the Marriage Act 1949 s 50(1)(c); and PARA 98.

3   See Marriage Act 1949 ss 53(f), 55(1); and REGISTRATION CONCERNING THE INDIVIDUAL vol 39(2) (Reissue) PARAS 558, 559. For the prescribed form of registration see the Registration of Marriages Regulations 1986, SI 1986/1442, Sch 1, Form 13 (amended by SI 2000/3164); and for the corresponding form in Welsh see the Registration of Marriages (Welsh Language) Regulations 1999, SI 1999/1621, reg 7(1), Sch 1, Form 9 (amended by SI 2000/3164).

4   See the Marriage Act 1949 s 51(1); and PARA 98.

5 See the Marriage Act 1949 s 63(1); and REGISTRATION CONCERNING THE INDIVIDUAL vol 39(2) (Reissue) PARA 524. The fee, when the application is made at the time of the register is £3.50, and in any other case is £7: Registration of Births, Deaths and Marriages (Fees) Order 2002, SI 2002/3076, Schedule.

B. SOLEMNISATION IN A REGISTERED BUILDING

104. When and how marriage may be solemnised. In general, where the notices of marriage and certificates issued by a superintendent registrar[1] state that a marriage between the persons named in them is intended to be solemnised in a registered building[2], the marriage may be solemnised in that building according to such form and ceremony as those persons may see fit to adopt[3]. The marriage may take place after the expiration of 15 days from the day of entry of notice of marriage[4] and within the applicable period[5]. No marriage may, however, be solemnised in any registered building without the consent of the minister or of one of the trustees, owners, deacons or managers of the building, or, in the case of a registered building of the Roman Catholic Church, without the consent of the officiating minister[6].

1 As to the meaning of 'superintendent registrar' see PARA 22 note 1.
2 As to the meaning of 'registered building' see PARA 54 note 3.
3 Marriage Act 1949 s 44(1) (amended by the Immigration and Asylum Act 1999 Sch 14 paras 3, 23). As to the form of marriage see further PARA 105; and as to the hours between which the marriage must be solemnised see PARA 101.
4 See PARA 97.
5 See PARA 101.
6 Marriage Act 1949 s 44(1) proviso. Such consent is not required in the case of a marriage in a naval, military or air force chapel: see PARA 129. As to the consent required in the case of a shared church building see ECCLESIASTICAL LAW vol 14 PARA 1412 note 4.

105. Forms and ceremonies. A marriage in a registered building[1] may be solemnised according to such forms and ceremonies as the parties think fit to adopt[2]; but in some part of the ceremony each of the persons contracting the marriage must make the following declaration: 'I do solemnly declare that I know not of any lawful impediment why I, AB, may not be joined in matrimony to CD', and each party must say to the other, 'I call upon these persons here present to witness that I, AB, do take thee, CD, to be my lawful wedded wife [or husband]'[3].

As an alternative to the declaration set out above the persons contracting the marriage may make the requisite declaration either by saying: 'I declare that I know of no legal reason why I [name] may not be joined in marriage to [name]', or by replying: 'I am' to the question put to them successively, 'Are you [name] free lawfully to marry [name]?'; and as an alternative to the words of contract set out above the persons to be married may say to each other: 'I [name] take you [or thee] [name] to be my wedded wife [or husband]'[4].

The declaration and form of contracting words must be spoken in the presence of the registrar[5] or authorised person[6] and of the witnesses[7].

If a marriage is solemnised in the presence of a registrar of marriages and before, during or immediately after solemnisation of the marriage the registrar has reasonable grounds for suspecting that the marriage will be, or is, a sham marriage[8], he must report his suspicion to the Secretary of State without delay and in such form and manner as may be prescribed by regulations[9].

1 As to the meaning of 'registered building' see PARA 54 note 3.
2 See PARA 104.

3   Marriage Act 1949 s 44(3) (amended by the Marriage Ceremony (Prescribed Words) Act 1996
     s 1(1)). In places where the Welsh language is commonly used, a true and exact translation into
     that language of the declarations and forms of words may be used, the authorised translation
     being furnished by the Registrar General to every registrar of marriages in Wales and in every
     place where the Welsh language is commonly used: Marriage Act 1949 s 52 (amended by the
     Marriage Ceremony (Prescribed Words) Act 1996 s 1(3)).
4   Marriage Act 1949 s 44(3A) (added by the Marriage Ceremony (Prescribed Words) Act 1996
     s 1(1)).
5   As to the meaning of 'registrar' see PARA 88 note 1.
6   As to the meaning of 'authorised person' see PARA 107.
7   Marriage Act 1949 s 44(3).
8   As to the meaning of 'sham marriage' see PARA 11.
9   Immigration and Asylum Act 1999 s 24(2), (3). As to the prescribed form and manner see PARA
     11.

106.   Presence of authorised person and other requirements.   In general, a
marriage in a registered building[1] must be solemnised with open doors between
the hours of 8 am and 6 pm, in the presence of two or more witnesses[2], and in
the presence of either:

(1)   a registrar[3] of the registration district[4] in which the registered building is
       situated[5]; or

(2)   an authorised person[6] whose name and address have been certified[7] by
       the trustees or governing body of that registered building or of some
       other registered building in the same registration district[8].

If any persons knowingly and wilfully intermarry on the authority of
superintendent registrar's certificates in a registered building, not being a
marriage in the presence of an authorised person, in the absence of a registrar,
the marriage is void[9]; and any person who knowingly and wilfully solemnises
such a marriage commits an offence[10]. A marriage may not be solemnised in a
registered building without the presence of a registrar until duplicate register
books have been supplied[11] by the Registrar General[12] to the authorised person
or to the trustees or governing body of the building[13].

1   As to the meaning of 'registered building' see PARA 54 note 3.
2   Marriage Act 1949 ss 4, 44(2).
3   As to the meaning of 'registrar' see PARA 88 note 1.
4   As to the meaning of 'registration district' see PARA 87 note 4.
5   Marriage Act 1949 s 44(2)(a). A marriage in a registered building for which an authorised
     person has been appointed will ordinarily take place in the presence of the authorised person,
     unless the parties request the presence of the registrar: see s 27(5); and PARA 88.
6   As to the meaning of 'authorised person' see PARA 107.
7   Ie certified in accordance with the Marriage Act 1949 s 43: see PARA 107.
8   Marriage Act 1949 s 44(2)(b).
9   See the Marriage Act 1949 s 49(f); and PARA 330.
10   See the Marriage Act 1949 s 75(2)(b); and PARA 180.
11   Ie under the Marriage Act 1949 Pt IV (ss 53–67): see REGISTRATION CONCERNING THE
     INDIVIDUAL vol 39(2) (Reissue) PARA 504.
12   As to the meaning of 'Registrar General' see PARA 46 note 5.
13   Marriage Act 1949 s 44(4).

107.   Appointment of authorised person.   For the purpose of enabling
marriages to be solemnised in a registered building[1] without the presence of a
registrar[2], the trustees or governing body[3] of that building may authorise a
person to be present at the solemnisation of marriages in that building; and,
where a person is so authorised in respect of any registered building, the trustees
or governing body of that building must certify the name and address of the
person so authorised (the 'authorised person') to the Registrar General[4] and to

the superintendent registrar[5] of the district in which the building is situated[6], within one day from the date when he is authorised[7].

No authorised person may act until his appointment has been certified[8]. The power to authorise a person to be present at the solemnisation of marriages is not exercisable before the expiration of one year from the date of registration of the building or, where the congregation on whose behalf the building is registered previously used for the purpose of public religious worship another building of which the registration has been cancelled not earlier than one month before that date of registration, one year from the date of registration of that other building[9].

Where an authorised person for a registered building ceases to be authorised to be present at the solemnisation of marriages in the building, the trustees or governing body[10] of the building must thereupon inform the Registrar General of the fact and must state whether they intend to certify, in place of that person, some other person to act as authorised person; and, where, when the vacancy occurs, there is no other authorised person for the building, the trustees or governing body must further inform the Registrar General what provision is being made for the solemnisation and registration of marriages in the building, and, if necessary, for the preparation and delivery of certain certified copies required to be delivered to the superintendent registrar[11], while there is no authorised person[12].

A person duly authorised to act for one registered building may officiate at any other registered building in the same registration district, but not at one in another registration district[13].

1   As to the meaning of 'registered building' see PARA 54 note 3.
2   As to the meaning of 'registrar' see PARA 88 note 1.
3   For these purposes, unless the context otherwise requires, 'trustees or governing body' includes, in relation to Roman Catholic registered buildings, a bishop or vicar-general of the diocese (Marriage Act 1949 s 78(1)), and means, in relation to a naval, military or air force chapel, the Admiralty or a Secretary of State, as the case may be, or any person authorised by it or him (s 70(1), Sch 4 Pt IV).
4   As to the meaning of 'Registrar General' see PARA 46 note 5.
5   As to the meaning of 'superintendent registrar' see PARA 22 note 1.
6   Marriage Act 1949 ss 43(1), (2), 78(1). Nothing in s 43 is to be taken to relate or have any reference to marriages solemnised according to the usages of the Society of Friends (see PARA 116) or of persons professing the Jewish religion (see PARA 118): s 43(3). As to authorised persons for shared church buildings see ECCLESIASTICAL LAW vol 14 PARA 1412 note 4.
    The Registrar General may, with the approval of the Chancellor of the Exchequer, by statutory instrument make regulations prescribing the duties of authorised persons under the Marriage Act 1949: s 74(a) (amended by the Registration Service Act 1953 s 23(2), Sch 2; SI 1996/273). In exercise of the power so conferred the Marriage (Authorised Persons) Regulations 1952, SI 1952/1869 (amended by SI 1971/1216; SI 1974/573; SI 1986/1444; SI 2000/3164; SI 2005/3177; SI 2007/2164) were made.
7   Marriage (Authorised Persons) Regulations 1952, SI 1952/1869, reg 4(1). The name and address of any such person must be certified in the prescribed form or in a form substantially to the like effect: reg 4(2). For the prescribed form of certification see reg 4(2), Schedule.
8   See the Marriage Act 1949 s 44(2)(b); and PARA 106.
9   Marriage Act 1949 s 43(1) proviso (added by the Marriage Acts Amendment Act 1958 s 1(2)). The Marriage Act 1949 s 43(1) proviso does not apply to naval, military and air force chapels (see PARA 129 note 8), or shared church buildings (see the Sharing of Church Buildings Act 1969 s 6(1), Sch 1 para 5; and ECCLESIASTICAL LAW vol 14 PARA 1412), and, if a sharing Church withdraws from the sharing of a registered church building, then, for the purpose of the application of the Marriage Act 1949 s 43(1) proviso to another building registered on behalf of the congregation of the withdrawing Church, the registration is deemed to have been cancelled at the time of the withdrawal (see the Sharing of Church Buildings Act 1969 Sch 1 para 5; and ECCLESIASTICAL LAW vol 14 PARA 1412).

10 For these purposes, 'trustees or governing body', in relation to Roman Catholic registered buildings, includes a bishop or vicar-general of the diocese and, in relation to chapels registered under the Marriage Act 1949 s 70 (see PARA 129), the Admiralty or any person authorised by it, in the case of a naval chapel registered under s 70, and a Secretary of State or any person authorised by him, in the case of any other chapel so registered: Marriage (Authorised Persons) Regulations 1952, SI 1952/1869, reg 2(1).

11 Ie under the Marriage Act 1949 s 57: see PARA 108; and REGISTRATION CONCERNING THE INDIVIDUAL vol 39(2) (Reissue) PARA 618.

12 Marriage (Authorised Persons) Regulations 1952, SI 1952/1869, reg 5.

13 See the Marriage Act 1949 s 44(2)(b); and PARA 106.

108.   Registration of marriage by authorised person.   A marriage solemnised in a registered building[1] or at a person's residence in the presence of a registrar[2] must be registered by that registrar[3]. A marriage solemnised in a registered building without the presence of a registrar must be registered by the authorised person[4] in whose presence the marriage is solemnised[5]. An authorised person must not register any marriage to which he is a party or witness[6]. Marriage register books and forms for making certified copies of entries must be furnished by the Registrar General to the authorised person appointed in respect of a registered building, or to the trustees or governing body[7]. Where a marriage is required to be registered by an authorised person, he must immediately after the solemnisation of the marriage register the particulars relating to it in duplicate in two marriage register books in a prescribed form[8]. The marriage must be registered in the registered building in the presence of the parties and two witnesses[9] and the entry signed by the authorised person and by the parties and two witnesses[10].

Provision is made for the correction of errors in entries in marriage register books[11].

Every authorised person must deliver quarterly to the superintendent registrar certified copies of all entries made in the marriage register book or a certificate on a form supplied by the Registrar General that no marriage has been registered[12].

1 As to the meaning of 'registered building' see PARA 54 note 3.

2 As to the meaning of 'registrar' see PARA 88 note 1.

3 Marriage Act 1949 s 53(d) (amended by the Marriage Act 1983 Sch 1 paras 1, 16). As to the registration of marriages by registrars see REGISTRATION CONCERNING THE INDIVIDUAL vol 39(2) (Reissue) PARAS 558–560. As to the registration of a person's residence see PARA 169 et seq.

4 As to the meaning of 'authorised person' see PARA 107.

5 Marriage Act 1949 s 53(e).

6 Marriage (Authorised Persons) Regulations 1952, SI 1952/1869, reg 6. A person who refuses or without reasonable cause omits to register a marriage which he is required to register is guilty of an offence: see PARA 181.

7 See the Marriage Act 1949 s 54; and REGISTRATION CONCERNING THE INDIVIDUAL vol 39(2) (Reissue) PARA 504. As to the meaning of 'trustees or governing body' see PARA 107 note 3. As to the inscribing of new register books by authorised persons see the Marriage (Authorised Persons) Regulations 1952, SI 1952/1869, reg 10 (amended by SI 1965/528; SI 1974/573). Where a church building is shared, the appointment of two or more authorised persons in respect of that building does not require any additional set or sets of duplicate marriage register books to be supplied: see the Sharing of Church Buildings Act 1969 s 6(1), Sch 1 para 7; and ECCLESIASTICAL LAW vol 14 PARA 1412. As to the registration of shared church buildings for the solemnisation of marriage generally see ECCLESIASTICAL LAW vol 14 PARA 1412.

8 See the Marriage Act 1949 s 55(1); and REGISTRATION CONCERNING THE INDIVIDUAL vol 39(2) (Reissue) PARA 559. For the prescribed form of particulars see the Registration of Marriages Regulations 1986, SI 1986/1442, Sch 1, Form 13 (amended by SI 2000/3164); and for the corresponding form in Welsh see the Registration of Marriages (Welsh Language) Regulations 1999, SI 1999/1621, reg 7(1), Sch 1, Form 9 (amended by SI 2000/3164). Entries

must be made in consecutive order from the beginning to the end of each book and the number of each entry must be the same in each duplicate marriage register book: Marriage Act 1949 s 55(3). For detailed instructions as to the making of entries see the Marriage (Authorised Persons) Regulations 1952, SI 1952/1869, reg 11 (cancelling of blank spaces), reg 13 (amended by SI 1965/528; SI 1974/573) (heading), the Marriage (Authorised Persons) Regulations 1952, SI 1952/1869, reg 14 (date of marriage), regs 15–21 (amended by SI 1986/1444; SI 2000/3164; SI 2007/2164) (names and surnames, ages, condition, ranks or professions and residence of parties; names and surnames and ranks or professions of parties' fathers). Entries must be in durable ink: Marriage (Authorised Persons) Regulations 1952, SI 1952/1869, reg 7. As to the power of an authorised person to ask for particulars from the parties see the Marriage Act 1949 s 56; and REGISTRATION CONCERNING THE INDIVIDUAL vol 39(2) (Reissue) PARA 560.

9 Marriage (Authorised Persons) Regulations 1952, SI 1952/1869, reg 12.

10 Marriage Act 1949 s 55(2). For the prescribed form of particulars of attestation see the Registration of Marriages Regulations 1986, SI 1986/1442, Sch 1, Form 13 (amended by SI 2000/3164); and for the corresponding form in Welsh see the Registration of Marriages (Welsh Language) Regulations 1999, SI 1999/1621, reg 7(1), Sch 1, Form 9 (amended by SI 2000/3164). As to the entering up of the form of attestation and the signing of the register see the Marriage (Authorised Persons) Regulations 1952, SI 1952/1869, reg 22 (amended by SI 2000/3164) and the Marriage (Authorised Persons) Regulations 1952, SI 1952/1869, reg 23. An entry is complete when the authorised person has signed it and appended to his signature his official description: reg 24.

11 See the Marriage Act 1949 s 61; and REGISTRATION CONCERNING THE INDIVIDUAL vol 39(2) (Reissue) PARA 519. As to the examination of entries by authorised persons, and as to the manner of correction by them of errors discovered before completion of the entry, see the Marriage (Authorised Persons) Regulations 1952, SI 1952/1869, regs 23(3), 25. An authorised person must not correct an error discovered after completion of the entry without first reporting to the Registrar General and must comply with any instructions which the Registrar General may give for the purpose of verifying the facts and ascertaining the parties or witnesses who will be available to witness a correction: reg 26.

12 See the Marriage Act 1949 s 57(1); and REGISTRATION CONCERNING THE INDIVIDUAL vol 39(2) (Reissue) PARA 618. The superintendent registrar must pay to the authorised person £2 for every entry in the certified copy: s 57(4) (amended by SI 2002/3076). The entries in certified copies must be in ink of durable quality: Marriage (Authorised Persons) Regulations 1952, SI 1952/1869, reg 7. A person who refuses to deliver a certified copy or certificate or fails to deliver any such copy or certificate during any month in which he is required to do so is guilty of an offence: see PARA 181.

109. Custody of marriage register books. Provision is made for the safe custody of marriage register books before they are filled, and of filled register books[1]. The marriage register books for a registered building must be kept in the custody of the authorised person for that building or, where there are two or more authorised persons, such one of them as is notified to the Registrar General by the trustees or governing body[2], or, in default of an authorised person, the trustees or governing body until another authorised person is appointed[3]. The marriage register books and certified copies must, when not actually in use, be kept locked up in a strong fire-resisting receptacle in the registered building or in some other place approved by the Registrar General[4].

If the Registrar General is not satisfied with respect to any building registered or proposed to be registered for the solemnisation of marriages that sufficient security exists for the due registration of marriages by an authorised person[5] and for the safe custody of the marriage register books, he may in his discretion attach to the continuance of the registration, or to the registration, of the building a condition that no marriage may be solemnised there without the presence of a registrar[6].

1 See the Marriage Act 1949 ss 59, 60; and REGISTRATION CONCERNING THE INDIVIDUAL vol 39(2) (Reissue) PARAS 520, 521.
2 As to the meaning of 'trustees or governing body' see PARA 107 note 3.
3 Marriage (Authorised Persons) Regulations 1952, SI 1952/1869, reg 8(1), (4).

4   Marriage (Authorised Persons) Regulations 1952, SI 1952/1869, reg 8(2). As to the meaning of
     'Registrar General' see PARA 46 note 5. As to the custody of the keys of the receptacle see
     reg 8(3). If the registration of the building is cancelled, or if the trustees or governing body
     decide that marriages are no longer to be solemnised without the presence of a registrar, or the
     Registrar General attaches a condition to that effect (see text to notes 5, 6), the books must be
     sent to the Registrar General in order that they may be closed and deposited in appropriate
     custody: reg 8(5). A person having the custody of a marriage register book or a certified copy
     who carelessly loses or injures the book or copy or allows it to be injured while in his keeping is
     guilty of an offence: see PARA 181.
5   Ie under the Marriage Act 1949 Pt IV (ss 53–67): see PARA 186 et seq; and REGISTRATION
     CONCERNING THE INDIVIDUAL. As to the meaning of 'authorised person' see PARA 107.
6   Marriage Act 1949 s 44(5). As to the meaning of 'registrar' see PARA 88 note 1.

110.   Searches in register books.   In the case of a registered building[1] for which
an authorised person[2] has been appointed, the person having custody of a
marriage register book[3] must at all reasonable hours allow searches to be made
in it, and must give a copy certified under his hand of any entry in that book, on
payment of a fee[4].

1   As to the meaning of 'registered building' see PARA 54.
2   As to the meaning of 'authorised person' see PARA 107.
3   As to the person having custody of a marriage register book see PARA 109.
4   See the Marriage Act 1949 s 63; and REGISTRATION CONCERNING THE INDIVIDUAL vol 39(2)
     (Reissue) PARA 524.

C. SOLEMNISATION ON APPROVED PREMISES

111.   Solemnisation of marriage on approved premises.   Any marriage on
approved premises[1] must be solemnised in the presence of two witnesses and the
superintendent registrar[2] and a registrar[3] of the registration district[4] in which the
premises are situated[5].

Each of the persons contracting such a marriage must make the prescribed
declaration and use the prescribed form of words[6] applicable in the case of
marriages in registered buildings[7].

No religious service is to be used at a marriage[8] on approved premises[9].

If a marriage is solemnised in the presence of a registrar of marriages and
before, during or immediately after solemnisation of the marriage the registrar
has reasonable grounds for suspecting that the marriage will be, or is, a sham
marriage[10], he must report his suspicion to the Secretary of State without delay
and in such form and manner as may be prescribed by regulations[11].

A marriage solemnised on approved premises[12] must be registered by the
registrar in whose presence the marriage is solemnised[13].

1   Ie in pursuance of the Marriage Act 1949 s 26(1)(bb) (see PARA 54). As to the meaning of
     'approved premises' see PARA 54 note 6.
2   As to the meaning of 'superintendent registrar' see PARA 22 note 1.
3   As to the meaning of 'registrar' see PARA 88 note 1.
4   As to the meaning of 'registration district' see PARA 87 note 4.
5   Marriage Act 1949 s 46B(1) (added by the Marriage Act 1994 s 1(2)).
6   Ie the declaration and form of words set out in the Marriage Act 1949 s 44(3) or s 44(3A): see
     PARA 105.
7   Marriage Act 1949 s 46B(3) (added by the Marriage Act 1994 s 1(2); amended by the Marriage
     (Prescribed Words) Act 1996 s 1(2)). As to the meaning of 'registered building' see PARA 54
     note 3.
8   See note 1.
9   Marriage Act 1949 s 46B(4) (added by the Marriage Act 1994 s 1(2)). If any persons knowingly
     and wilfully intermarry, in the case of a marriage on approved premises, in the absence of the

superintendent registrar of the registration district in which the premises are situated or in the absence of a registrar of that district, the marriage is void: see s 49(gg); and PARA 330.

10 As to the meaning of 'sham marriage' see PARA 11.

11 Immigration and Asylum Act 1999 s 24(2), (3). As to the prescribed form and manner see PARA 11.

12 Ie in pursuance of the Marriage Act 1949 s 26(1)(bb) (see PARA 54).

13 See Immigration and Asylum Act 1999 s 53(g) (added by the Marriage Act 1994 Schedule paras 1, 6); and REGISTRATION CONCERNING THE INDIVIDUAL vol 39(2) (Reissue) PARA 558.

(iv) Parties Resident outside England and Wales

112. One party resident in Scotland. Where a marriage is intended to be solemnised in England on the authority of certificates of a superintendent registrar[1] between parties of whom one is residing in Scotland and the other is residing in England, the following provisions have effect[2]:

(1)   the party residing in Scotland may give notice of the intended marriage in accordance with the appropriate provision applying in Scotland[3];

(2)   the party residing in England may[4] give notice of the intended marriage as if both parties were residing in different registration districts[5] in England[6];

(3)   a certificate as to capacity to marry issued in Scotland has the same force and effect in all respects as a certificate issued[7] by a superintendent registrar[8]; and

(4)   the notice given in Scotland is deemed[9] to have been entered in a marriage notice book[10] by a superintendent registrar in England on the day on which it was given[11].

1 As to the meaning of 'superintendent registrar' see PARA 22 note 1.

2 Marriage Act 1949 s 37(1) (amended by the Immigration and Asylum Act 1999 Sch 14 paras 3, 19).

3 Marriage Act 1949 s 37(1)(a) (substituted by the Marriage (Scotland) Act 1977 Sch 2 para 4(a)).

4 Ie subject to and in accordance with the provisions of the Marriage Act 1949 s 27 (see PARAS 87, 92), s 27A (see PARA 172) and s 28 (see PARA 90).

5 As to the meaning of 'registration district' see PARA 87 note 4.

6 Marriage Act 1949 s 37(1)(b) (amended by the Marriage Act 1983 Sch 1 para 8). The provisions of the Marriage Act 1949 Pt III (ss 26–52) (see PARA 54 et seq) relating to notices of marriage and the issue of certificates for marriage apply accordingly: s 37(1)(b).

7 Ie under the Marriage Act 1949 Pt III: see PARA 54 et seq.

8 Marriage Act 1949 s 37(1)(c) (substituted by the Marriage (Scotland) Act 1977 Sch 2 para 4(b)).

9 Ie for the purposes of the Marriage Act 1949 s 33: see PARA 101.

10 As to the meaning of 'marriage notice book' see PARA 92.

11 Marriage Act 1949 s 37(1)(d).

113. One party resident in Northern Ireland. Where a marriage is intended to be solemnised in England on the authority of certificates of a superintendent registrar[1] between parties of whom one is residing in Northern Ireland and the other is residing in England, the party residing in Northern Ireland may give notice of marriage, in the form used for that purpose in Northern Ireland or to the like effect, to the registrar of the district in Northern Ireland in which he or she has resided for not less than seven days immediately before the giving of the notice[2]. The notice must state the name and surname, marital status, occupation, age, place of residence and nationality of each of the persons to be married, and the period, not being less than seven days[3], during which each of them has resided in that place, and the place where the marriage is to be solemnised[4]. The notice must be dealt with, and a certificate issued, in the manner prescribed by the law of Northern Ireland[5]; but the registrar must not issue a certificate until the expiration of 15 days from the day on which the notice was entered in the marriage notice book[6].

The production to the person solemnising the marriage of a certificate so issued is as valid for authorising that person to solemnise the marriage as would be the production of a certificate for marriage of a superintendent registrar of a registration district[7] in England in the case of a person residing in that district[8].

1   As to the meaning of 'superintendent registrar' see PARA 22 note 1.
2   Marriage Act 1949 s 38(1) (amended by the Immigration and Asylum Act 1999 Sch 14 paras 3, 20(1), (2)).
3   If either of the persons to be married has resided in the place stated for more than one month, the notice may state that he or she has resided there for more than one month: Marriage Act 1949 s 38(2) proviso.
4   Marriage Act 1949 s 38(2) (amended by the Marriage Act 1938 Sch 1 para 9; the Immigration and Asylum Act 1999 Sch 14 paras 3, 20(1), (3)).
5   Marriage Act 1949 s 38(3).
6   Marriage Act 1949 s 38(3) proviso (amended by the Immigration and Asylum Act 1999 Sch 14 paras 3, 20(1), (4)).
7   As to the meaning of 'registration district' see PARA 87 note 4.
8   Marriage Act 1949 s 38(4).

114. One party resident in Her Majesty's dominions. Where a marriage is intended to be solemnised or contracted in the United Kingdom between a British subject[1] resident in England, Scotland or Northern Ireland and a British subject resident in any part of Her Majesty's dominions or protectorates[2] to which the Marriage of British Subjects (Facilities) Act 1915 has been applied[3], a certificate of the publication of banns or a certificate of notice of marriage issued in accordance with the law in force in that part of Her Majesty's dominions has in England the same effect as a certificate for marriage issued by a superintendent registrar[4].

Where Her Majesty is satisfied that the law in force in any part of Her Majesty's dominions outside the United Kingdom makes due provision:

(1)   for the publication of banns or for the giving of notice in respect of marriage between British subjects intended to be solemnised or contracted in the United Kingdom; and

(2)   for the recognition of certificates for marriages issued by superintendent registrars in England[5] as sufficient notice in respect of marriages to be solemnised in that part of Her Majesty's dominions,

Her Majesty may by Order in Council declare that the 1915 Act is to apply to that part of Her dominions[6]; but the condition in head (2) above may be waived where the dominion law does not require notice of marriage on the part of the person resident in the United Kingdom[7].

1   As to the meaning of 'British subject' see BRITISH NATIONALITY, IMMIGRATION AND ASYLUM vol 4(2) (2002 Reissue) PARA 9.
2   Her Majesty may by Order in Council extend the Marriage of British Subjects (Facilities) Act 1915 (see the test and notes 3–7) to protectorates and, on the making of any such Order, the Marriage of British Subjects (Facilities) Act 1915 has effect, subject to the provisions of the Order, as if the protectorate were part of Her Majesty's dominions: Marriage of British Subjects (Facilities) Act 1915 s 2. As to the meaning of 'Her Majesty's dominions' see COMMONWEALTH vol 6 (2003 Reissue) PARA 703.
3   The Marriage of British Subjects (Facilities) Act 1915 has been applied by Order in Council to: Bahamas (SR & O 1917/1242); Barbados (SR & O 1917/1242); Basutoland (SR & O 1917/1242); Bechuanaland (SR & O 1917/1243); Bermuda (SR & O 1917/210); British Honduras (SR & O 1917/210); Ceylon (now Sri Lanka) and its dependencies (SR & O 1918/249); Cyprus (SR & O 1925/1324); Dominica (SR & O 1916/555 (amended by

SR & O 1939/1896)); Fiji (SR & O 1918/1285); Gambia Colony (SR & O 1916/555); Gambia Protectorate (SR & O 1916/556); Gibraltar (SR & O 1917/1242); Gilbert and Ellice Islands Colony (SR & O 1917/747); Gold Coast Colony (SR & O 1916/555); Grenada (SR & O 1917/1242); Guernsey (SR & O 1927/1084); Hong Kong (SR & O 1916/555); Isle of Man (SR & O 1925/1032); Jamaica (SR & O 1917/747); Jersey (SR & O 1930/229); Kenya (SR & O 1916/556); Labuan (see Straits Settlements); Leeward Islands (SR & O 1916/555); Malacca (see Straits Settlements); Mauritius (SR & O 1916/555); New Zealand (SR & O 1920/2081); Newfoundland (SR & O 1,k 916/632); Nigeria Colony and Protectorate (SR & O 1920/826); Northern Rhodesia Protectorate (SR & O 1919/473); Nyasaland Protectorate (SR & O 1917/748); Pacific Protectorate (SR & O 1917/749); Penang (see Straits Settlements); St Lucia (SR & O 1916/862); St Vincent (SR & O 1916/555); Seychelles (SR & O 1916/862); Sierra Leone Colony (SR & O 1916/862); Sierra Leone Protectorate (SR & O 1916/822); Singapore (see Straits Settlements); Straits Settlements (Labuan, Malacca, Penang and Singapore) (SR & O 1916/555); Swaziland Protectorate (SR & O 1917/1243); Trinidad and Tobago (SR & O 1916/555); Uganda Protectorate (SR & O 1916/556); Victoria (SR & O 1916/632); Zanzibar Protectorate (SR & O 1917/748); and Zimbabwe (SR & O 1918/1066 (amended by SI 1980/701)). The above list is to be read in the light of the many constitutional changes and alterations in the names of territories: see COMMONWEALTH vol 6 (2003 Reissue) PARA 736 et seq.

4   Marriage of British Subjects (Facilities) Act 1915 s 1(1)(a). The superintendent registrar of the district in which the party in England is residing has power to accept notice of the marriage given by that party as if both parties were residing in different districts in England, and the normal statutory provisions (see PARA 54 et seq) apply: Marriage Act 1939 s 2(1), (3) (amended by the Marriage Act 1949 Sch 5 Pt I).

5   The Marriages of British Subjects (Facilities) Act 1915 may also be applied where that law makes due provision for the recognition of certificates for marriage issued by registrars and certificates of proclamation of banns in Scotland, and certificates for marriage issued by Northern Ireland: see the Marriage of British Subjects (Facilities) Act 1915 s 1.

6   Marriage of British Subjects (Facilities) Act 1915 s 1.

7   See the Marriage of British Subjects (Facilities) Amendment Act 1916 s 1.

(v) Quaker and Jewish Marriages

115. Notification of Quaker marriages. No person who is not a member of the Society of Friends (commonly called Quakers)[1] may be married according to the usages of that Society unless he or she is authorised to be so married under or in pursuance of a general rule of the Society in England[2].

A marriage solemnised according to the usages of the Society of Friends may be solemnised on the authority of a certificate issued, on due notice of marriage being given, by a superintendent registrar[3], notwithstanding that the building or place in which the marriage is to be solemnised is not within a registration district in which either of the persons to be married resides[4]. The provisions relating to notice of marriage, statement, declaration, forms and fees are the same as in other cases[5], but a marriage solemnised according to the usages of the Society of Friends is not valid unless either:

(1)   each person giving the notice of marriage declares, either verbally or, if so required, in writing, that each of the parties to the marriage is either a member of the Society of Friends or is in profession with or of the persuasion of that Society[6]; or

(2)   there is produced to the superintendent registrar, at the time when notice of marriage is given, a certificate purporting to be signed by a registering officer of the Society of Friends[7] in England to the effect that any party to the marriage who is not a member of the Society nor in profession with nor of the persuasion of that Society is authorised to be married according to the usages of the Society in pursuance of a general rule of the Society in England[8].

1   As to the status of the Society of Friends generally see ECCLESIASTICAL LAW vol 14 PARAS 1419, 1420.
2   Marriage Act 1949 s 47(1).
3   See the Marriage Act 1949 s 26(1)(c); and PARA 54. As to the meaning of 'superintendent registrar' see PARA 22 note 1.
4   See the Marriage Act 1949 s 35(4); and PARA 100.
5   Marriage Act 1949 s 47(2)(a) (amended by the Immigration and Asylum Act 1999 Sch 14 paras 3, 25).
6   See PARA 53 et seq. As to the effect of a marriage without due notice see PARA 89; and *Nathan v Woolf* (1899) 15 TLR 250 (Jewish marriage).
7   It seems that 'registering officer of the Society of Friends' means a person whom the recording clerk of the Society certifies in writing to the Registrar General to be a registering officer in England of the Society: see the Marriage Act 1949 s 67 (which is, however, only expressed to apply to Pt IV (ss 53–66)); and REGISTRATION CONCERNING THE INDIVIDUAL vol 39(2) (Reissue) PARA 520.
8   Marriage Act 1949 s 47(2)(b) (amended by the Immigration and Asylum Act 1999 Sch 14 paras 3, 25). Any such certificate is for all purposes conclusive evidence that any person to whom it relates is authorised to be married according to the usages of the Society of Friends; and the entry of the marriage in a marriage register book under the Marriage Act 1949 Pt IV (see REGISTRATION CONCERNING THE INDIVIDUAL) or a duly certified copy of it under Pt IV (see PARA 108) is conclusive evidence of the due production of the certificate: s 47(3). A copy of any general rule of the Society of Friends purporting to be signed by the recording clerk for the time being of the Society must be admitted as evidence of the general rule in all proceedings touching the validity of any marriage solemnised according to the usages of the Society of Friends: s 47(4). As to the time and manner of solemnisation of such a marriage see PARA 116.

116.   Solemnisation of Quaker marriages.

On production of the certificates of a superintendent registrar, a marriage may be solemnised according to the usages of the Society of Friends[1]. It is not necessary that either party be a member of the Society, but each must have been authorised to be so married under or in pursuance of a general rule of the Society[2]; nor is it necessary that the building in which the marriage is solemnised should be registered[3], nor that the building be situated within a district in which either of the parties resides[4]. The marriage may be solemnised at any hour[5]. The parties must, however, have capacity to marry[6], and the marriage must be solemnised within the applicable period[7].

The certificates must be delivered to the registering officer of the Society of Friends for the place where the marriage is solemnised[8], whose duty it is to satisfy himself that the marriage is solemnised according to the usages of the Society[9]. As soon as conveniently may be after its solemnisation, the marriage must be registered by the registering officer of the Society appointed for that district, in the prescribed form and manner[10].

Every registering officer of the Society of Friends by whom a marriage register book is kept[11] must allow searches to be made in it at all reasonable hours, and give a copy certified under his hand of any entry in the book, on payment of a fee[12].

Provision is made for the safe custody of marriage register books and filled marriage register books[13] and for the correction of errors in entries in such books[14].

Every registering officer must deliver quarterly to the superintendent registrar certified copies of all entries made in the marriage register book or a certificate on a form supplied by the Registrar General that no marriage has been registered[15].

1   See the Marriage Act 1949 s 26(1)(c); and PARA 54. As to the notice of marriage see PARA 115.
2   See the Marriage Act 1949 s 47(1); and PARA 115.
3   See the Marriage Act 1949 s 26(1)(c); and PARA 54.
4   See the Marriage Act 1949 s 35(4); and PARA 100.

5   See the Marriage Act 1949 s 75(1)(a); and PARA 180. It seems that witnesses are not required by
      law (see ss 26(1)(c), 44(3)), but witnesses are in fact required where a meeting for worship is
      held for the solemnisation of marriage according to the usages of the Society of Friends.
6   As to the minimum age for marriage see PARA 41; and as to the prohibited degrees of
      consanguinity and affinity see PARAS 35–37. See also PARA 118 note 5.
7   See PARA 101.
8   See the Marriage Act 1949 s 50(1)(d); and PARA 98.
9   See the Marriage Act 1949 s 55(1) proviso (b); and REGISTRATION CONCERNING THE
      INDIVIDUAL vol 39(2) (Reissue) PARA 559.
10   See the Marriage Act 1949 ss 53(b), 55(1); and REGISTRATION CONCERNING THE INDIVIDUAL
      vol 39(2) (Reissue) PARAS 558–559. For the prescribed form of registration see the Registration
      of Marriages Regulations 1986, SI 1986/1442, Sch 1, Form 13 (amended by SI 2000/3164); and
      for the corresponding form in Welsh see the Registration of Marriages (Welsh Language)
      Regulations 1999, SI 1999/1621, reg 7(1), Sch 1, Form 9 (amended by SI 2000/3164).
11   As to the provision of marriage register books by the Registrar General see the Marriage
      Act 1949 s 54; and REGISTRATION CONCERNING THE INDIVIDUAL vol 39(2) (Reissue) PARA 504.
12   Marriage Act 1949 s 63(1). The fee for a certified copy of an entry is £3.50 where application is
      made at the time of registering, and £7 in any other case: Registration of Births, Deaths and
      Marriages (Fees) Order 2002, SI 2002/3076, art 3, Schedule.
13   See the Marriage Act 1949 ss 59, 60; and REGISTRATION CONCERNING THE INDIVIDUAL
      vol 39(2) (Reissue) PARAS 520–521.
14   See the Marriage Act 1949 s 61; and REGISTRATION CONCERNING THE INDIVIDUAL vol 39(2)
      (Reissue) PARA 519.
15   See the Marriage Act 1949 s 57(1); and REGISTRATION CONCERNING THE INDIVIDUAL vol 39(2)
      (Reissue) PARA 618.

117.   Notification of Jewish marriages.   Marriages between two persons
professing the Jewish religion according to the usages of the Jews may be
solemnised on the authority of a certificate issued, on due notice of marriage
being given[1], by a superintendent registrar[2], notwithstanding that the building or
place in which the marriage is to be solemnised is not within the registration
district in which either of the persons to be married resides[3].

1   As to the notice of marriage and the statement, declaration, forms and fees, which are the same
      as in other cases, see PARA 22 et seq. As to the effect of a marriage without due notice see PARA
      89; and see *Nathan v Woolf* (1899) 15 TLR 250.
2   See the Marriage Act 1949 s 26(1)(d); and PARA 54. As to the meaning of 'superintendent
      registrar' see PARA 22 note 1.
3   See the Marriage Act 1949 s 35(4); and PARA 100. As to the time and manner of solemnisation
      of such a marriage see PARA 118.

118.   Solemnisation of Jewish marriages.   On production of the certificates of
a superintendent registrar, a marriage may be solemnised between two persons
professing the Jewish religion according to the usages of the Jews[1]. The building
in which the marriage is solemnised need not be registered[2], nor need it be
situated within a district in which either of the parties resides[3]; and the marriage
may be solemnised at any hour[4]. The parties must, however, have capacity to
marry[5], and the marriage must be solemnised within the applicable period[6].
   The certificates must be delivered to the officer of a synagogue by whom the
marriage is registered[7], whose duty it is to satisfy himself that the marriage is
solemnised according to the usages of the Jews[8]. Immediately after its
solemnisation, the marriage must be registered by the secretary of the synagogue
of which the husband is a member, in the prescribed form and manner[9].
   Every secretary of a synagogue by whom a marriage register book is kept[10]
must allow searches to be made in it at all reasonable hours and give a copy
certified under his hand of any entry in the book, on payment of a fee[11].
   Provision is made for the safe custody of marriage register books and filled
register books[12] and for the correction of errors in entries in such books[13].

Every secretary of a synagogue must deliver quarterly to the superintendent registrar certified copies of all entries made in the marriage register book or a certificate on a form supplied by the Registrar General that no marriage has been registered[14].

1 See the Marriage Act 1949 s 26(1)(d); and PARA 54. Cf *Ruding v Smith* (1821) 1 State Tr NS 1054. It appears that a written contract is necessary to constitute a valid marriage according to the usages of the Jews (see *R v Althausen* (1893) 17 Cox CC 630; *Horn v Noel* (1807) 1 Camp 61), but it is not necessary to produce the contract to prove the validity of the marriage (*R v Hammer* [1923] 2 KB 786, CCA). The marriage must be solemnised in the presence of witnesses who are not incompetent by reason of consanguinity to the parties: see *Goldsmid v Bromer* (1798) 1 Hag Con 324. A marriage purporting to be solemnised according to the usages of the Jews is void unless it complies with the Jewish law: *Goldsmid v Bromer*; *Lindo v Belisario* (1795) 1 Hag Con 216; affd (1796) 1 Hag Con App 7. As to notice of marriage in such cases see PARA 117.
2 See the Marriage Act 1949 s 26(1)(d); and PARA 54.
3 See the Marriage Act 1949 s 35(4); and PARA 100.
4 See the Marriage Act 1949 s 75(1)(a); and PARA 180.
5 As to the minimum age for marriage see PARA 41; and as to the prohibited degrees of consanguinity and affinity see PARAS 35–37. The various statutory exceptions in favour of Jews and Quakers relate only to questions of form and ceremony, and not to questions of capacity: *Re De Wilton, De Wilton v Montefiore* [1900] 2 Ch 481; and see PARA 35.
6 See PARA 101.
7 See the Marriage Act 1949 s 50(1)(e); and PARA 98.
8 See the Marriage Act 1949 s 55(1) proviso (b); and REGISTRATION CONCERNING THE INDIVIDUAL vol 39(2) (Reissue) PARA 559.
9 See the Marriage Act 1949 ss 53(b), 55(1); and REGISTRATION CONCERNING THE INDIVIDUAL vol 39(2) (Reissue) PARAS 558–559. For the prescribed form of registration see the Registration of Marriages Regulations 1986, SI 1986/1442, reg 10(1), Sch 1, Form 13 (amended by SI 2000/3164); and for the corresponding form in Welsh see the Registration of Marriages (Welsh Language) Regulations 1999, SI 1999/1621, reg 7(1), Sch 1, Form 9 (amended by SI 2000/3164). As to proof of Jewish marriages see PARA 24.
10 As to the provision of marriage register books by the Registrar General see the Marriage Act 1949 s 54; and REGISTRATION CONCERNING THE INDIVIDUAL vol 39(2) (Reissue) PARA 504.
11 Marriage Act 1949 s 63(1). The fee for a certified copy of an entry is £3.50 where application is made at the time of registering, and £7 in any other case: Registration of Births, Deaths and Marriages (Fees) Order 2002, SI 2002/3076, art 3, Schedule.
12 See the Marriage Act 1949 ss 59, 60; and REGISTRATION CONCERNING THE INDIVIDUAL vol 39(2) (Reissue) PARAS 520, 521.
13 See the Marriage Act 1949 s 61; and REGISTRATION CONCERNING THE INDIVIDUAL vol 39(2) (Reissue) PARA 519.
14 See the Marriage Act 1949 s 57(1); and REGISTRATION CONCERNING THE INDIVIDUAL vol 39(2) (Reissue) PARA 618.

(4) MARRIAGES CONDUCTED ABROAD

119. Marriages under the Foreign Marriage Act 1892. A marriage solemnised in the manner provided by the Foreign Marriage Act 1892[1] in any foreign country or place, by or before a marriage officer[2], between parties of whom at least one is a United Kingdom national[3], is as valid as if it had been solemnised in the United Kingdom with a due observance of all forms required by law[4], even though it may be invalid by the lex loci celebrationis[5].

1 The Foreign Marriage Act 1892 has been amended by the Foreign Marriage Act 1947 and by the Foreign Marriage (Amendment) Act 1988. See the Foreign Marriage Order 1970, SI 1970/1539 (amended by SI 1990/598). See also the Foreign Marriage (Armed Forces) Order 1964, SI 1964/1000 (amended by SI 1965/137; SI 1990/2592); and CONFLICT OF LAWS vol 8(3) (Reissue) PARA 214.

The Acts do not apply to marriages of members of the royal family: Foreign Marriage Act 1892 s 23. Such marriages, wherever they take place, are governed by the Royal Marriages Act 1772: see *Sussex Peerage Case* (1844) 11 Cl & Fin 85, HL; and CROWN AND ROYAL FAMILY vol 12(1) (Reissue) PARA 36.

By the Marriage of British Subjects (Facilities) Act 1915 and the Marriage of British Subjects (Facilities) Amendment Act 1916, provision is made for facilitating marriages between holders of British nationality resident in the United Kingdom and holders of British nationality resident in other parts of Her Majesty's dominions or in British protectorates: see PARAS 17, 114. As to the meaning of 'Her Majesty's dominions' see COMMONWEALTH vol 6 (2003 Reissue) PARA 703. Note that there are no longer any British protectorates: see COMMONWEALTH.

2   'Marriage officer' means a British ambassador (including a minister and a chargé d'affaires: Foreign Marriage Act 1892 s 24) residing in the country to whose government he is accredited, or any officer prescribed by marriage regulations as an officer for solemnising marriages in the official house of such an ambassador, or a British consul (ie a consul-general, consul, vice-consul, pro-consul and consular agent: s 24), governor, high commissioner, resident, consular or other officer, or any person appointed in pursuance of the marriage regulations to act in place of a high commissioner or resident, provided that he holds a marriage warrant signed by the Secretary of State, or any officer authorised by the marriage regulations to act as marriage officer without any marriage warrant: s 11(1), (2). As to the making of marriage regulations see s 21 (amended by the Foreign Marriage Act 1947 s 4; the Statute Law (Repeals) Act 1986; and the Foreign Marriage (Amendment Act) 1988 ss 1(3), 7(2), Schedule). No marriage regulations for this purpose were in force at the date at which this volume states the law, and accordingly a marriage warrant is in every case necessary.

If a marriage warrant refers to the office without designating the name of any particular person holding it, then, while the warrant is in force, the person for the time being holding or acting in that office is a marriage officer: Foreign Marriage Act 1892 s 11(3).

The Secretary of State may by warrant under his hand vary or revoke any marriage warrant previously issued under the Foreign Marriage Act 1892: s 11(4).

3   For these purposes, 'United Kingdom national' means a person who is:
   (1)   a British citizen, a British overseas territories citizen, a British overseas citizen or a British national (overseas) (Foreign Marriage Act 1892 ss 1(2)(a), 24 (s 1(2) added by the Foreign Marriage (Amendment) Act 1988 s 1(2); Foreign Marriage Act 1892 s 1(2)(a) amended by the British Overseas Territories Act 2002 s 2(3); and the Foreign Marriage Act 1892 s 24 amended by the Foreign Marriage (Amendment) Act 1988 s 1(4))); or
   (2)   a British subject under the British Nationality Act 1981 (Foreign Marriage Act 1892 s 1(2)(b)); or
   (3)   a British protected person within the meaning of the British Nationality Act 1981 (Foreign Marriage Act 1892 s 1(2)(c)).
As to categories of citizenship see BRITISH NATIONALITY, IMMIGRATION AND ASYLUM vol 4(2) (2002 Reissue) PARA 23 et seq.

4   Foreign Marriage Act 1892 s 1(1) (amended by the Foreign Marriage (Amendment) Act 1988 s 1). The marriage is thus formally valid, although not necessarily valid in other respects: Foreign Marriage Act 1892 s 23.

5   *Hay v Northcote* [1900] 2 Ch 262, where a marriage celebrated in accordance with the Consular Marriage Act 1849 (repealed and virtually re-enacted by the Foreign Marriage Act 1892) was held to be valid although it had been annulled by the court of the parties' domicile. The foreign nullity decree might now be recognised in the United Kingdom: see CONFLICT OF LAWS vol 8(3) (Reissue) PARA 254 et seq. See also *Merker v Merker* [1963] P 283, [1962] 3 All ER 928. As to the lex loci celebrationis see CONFLICT OF LAWS vol 8(3) (Reissue) PARA 208.

120.   Notice of intended marriage.   Where a marriage is intended to be solemnised under the Foreign Marriage Act 1892[1], one of the parties must sign a notice stating the name, surname, profession, condition and residence of each of the parties and whether each is or is not a minor, and give it to the marriage officer[2] within whose district[3] both parties have resided for not less than one week immediately preceding the notice, stating in the notice that they have so resided[4]. The marriage officer must file the notice in his registry, and, on payment of the proper fee[5], enter it in his book of notices, and keep a true copy of the notice posted up in some conspicuous place in his office[6] for 14 consecutive days before the marriage is solemnised[7]. If the marriage is not solemnised within three months of the date on which notice for it has been given to and entered by the marriage officer[8] the notice is void, and the marriage cannot be solemnised under it[9].

In special cases, where the Secretary of State is satisfied that for some good cause the requirements of the Act as to residence and notice cannot be complied with, and he is satisfied that the intended marriage is not clandestine and that adequate public notice has been given in the place or places where each of the parties resided not less than 15 days immediately preceding the giving of the notice, he may authorise the marriage officer to dispense with those requirements[10].

1   See PARA 119.

2   As to the meaning of 'marriage officer' see PARA 119 note 2.

3   Ie the area within which the duties of his office are exercisable, or any such lesser area as is assigned by the marriage warrant or any other warrant of a Secretary of State, or is fixed by the marriage regulations: Foreign Marriage Act 1892 s 11(1). As to marriage warrants see PARA 119 note 2. As to the making of marriage regulations see s 21 (amended by the Foreign Marriage Act 1947 s 4; the Statute Law (Repeals) Act 1986; and the Foreign Marriage (Amendment Act) 1988 ss 1(3), 7(2), Schedule). No marriage regulations for this purpose were in force at the date at which this volume states the law.

4   Foreign Marriage Act 1892 s 2. For a form of notice of marriage see the Foreign Marriage Order 1970, SI 1970/1539, Schedule Form 1.

5   The proper fee is such as is fixed under the Consular Fees Act 1980; and the fee so fixed as respects a consul is the fee which may be taken by any marriage officer. The provisions of the Consular Fees Act 1980 relating to the levying, application and remission of and accounting for fees are the same when the marriage officer taking the fee is not a consul: Foreign Marriage Act 1892 s 20 (amended by the Consular Fees Act 1980 s 1(5)). As to the levying, application and remission of, and accounting for, fees see the Consular Fees Act 1980 s 1(3); the Consular Fees Regulations 1981, SI 1981/476; the Consular Fees Order 2008, SI 2008/676; and FOREIGN RELATIONS LAW vol 18(2) (Reissue) PARA 610.

6   As to the office of a marriage officer see further PARA 125 note 5.

7   Foreign Marriage Act 1892 s 3(1). The book of notices and copy of the notice posted up must be open at all reasonable times, without fee, to the inspection of any person: s 3(2).

8   Foreign Marriage Act 1892 s 6(a). If, on a caveat being entered (see PARA 123), a statement has been transmitted to a Secretary of State, or if an appeal has been made to a Secretary of State (see PARA 122), the three months run from the date of the receipt from the Secretary of State of a decision directing the marriage to be solemnised: s 6(b).

9   Foreign Marriage Act 1892 s 6.

10 Foreign Marriage Order 1970, SI 1970/1539, art 4(1). As to the oath before marriage in such circumstances see PARA 124 note 5.

121.   Consents. The same consents are required, under the Foreign Marriage Act 1892[1], to a marriage of a party domiciled in England or in a country outside the United Kingdom as would be required in respect of that party to a marriage solemnised in England on the authority of a superintendent registrar's certificate[2]. The same consents are required, under the Act, to the marriage of a party domiciled in Northern Ireland as would be required in respect of that party to a marriage solemnised there[3].

Where by reason of the absence, inaccessibility or disability of a person whose consent is required that consent cannot be obtained, the requirement of obtaining the consent may be dispensed with by the Secretary of State or, in such cases as may be prescribed by marriage regulations[4], the Registrar General for England and Wales[5].

A person whose consent is required may forbid the marriage by an entry to this effect in the marriage officer's book of notices of marriage[6]. The effect of such an entry is to render the notice void, and the marriage cannot be solemnised under it[7].

1 See PARA 119.
2 Foreign Marriage Act 1892 s 4(1) (s 4 substituted by the Foreign Marriage (Amendment) Act 1988 s 2(1)). As to the consents required by English domestic law see PARA 41 et seq. The certificate referred to in the text is a certificate issued by a superintendent registrar under the Marriage Act 1949 Pt III (ss 26–52): see PARA 54 et seq.
3 Foreign Marriage Act 1892 s 4(2). Note, however, that consent may be dispensed with by order under Northern Ireland legislation, on application to a county court in Northern Ireland: see s 4(5).
4 As to the making of marriage regulations see Foreign Marriage Act 1892 s 21 (amended by the Foreign Marriage Act 1947 s 4; the Statute Law (Repeals) Act 1986; and the Foreign Marriage (Amendment Act) 1988 ss 1(3), 7(2), Schedule). No marriage regulations for this purpose were in force at the date at which this volume states the law.
5 Foreign Marriage Act 1892 s 4(4). As to the office of Registrar General for England and Wales see REGISTRATION CONCERNING THE INDIVIDUAL vol 39(2) (Reissue) PARA 605 et seq.
6 See the Foreign Marriage Act 1892 s 4(6). He must write the word 'forbidden' against the entry of the intended marriage in the book of notices and add his name and address and a statement of the capacity by virtue of which his consent is required: s 4(6)(a), (b).
7 Foreign Marriage Act 1892 s 4(6).

122. Refusal of solemnisation of marriage. Before a marriage is solemnised in a foreign country under the Foreign Marriage Act 1892[1], the marriage officer[2] must be satisfied that:

(1) at least one of the parties is a United Kingdom national[3];

(2) the authorities of the foreign country will not object to the solemnisation of the marriage[4];

(3) insufficient facilities exist for the marriage of the parties under the law of that country[5]; and

(4) the parties will be regarded as validly married by the law of the country in which each party is domiciled[6].

The marriage officer is not required to solemnise a marriage, or to allow it to be solemnised in his presence, if in his opinion its solemnisation would be inconsistent with international law or the comity of nations[7].

If the marriage officer refuses to solemnise the marriage of any person requiring it to be solemnised, or to allow it to be solemnised in his presence, by reason of any of the provisions described above, that person has a right of appeal to a Secretary of State, who must give the marriage officer his decision on the appeal[8]. The marriage officer must forthwith inform the parties of, and conform to, the Secretary of State's decision[9].

1 See PARA 119.
2 As to the meaning of 'marriage officer' see PARA 119 note 2.
3 Foreign Marriage Order 1970, SI 1970/1539, art 3(1)(a) (amended by SI 1990/598). As to the meaning of 'United Kingdom national' see PARA 119 note 3.
4 Foreign Marriage Order 1970, SI 1970/1539, art 3(1)(b).
5 Foreign Marriage Order 1970, SI 1970/1539, art 3(1)(c).
6 Foreign Marriage Order 1970, SI 1970/1539, art 3(1)(d) (amended by SI 1990/598).
7 Foreign Marriage Act 1892 s 19.
8 Foreign Marriage Act 1892 ss 5(3), 19 proviso; Foreign Marriage Order 1970, SI 1970/1539, art 3(2).
9 Foreign Marriage Act 1892 s 5(4) (amended by the Foreign Marriage (Amendment) Act 1988 s 3(2)).

123.   Objections.   On payment of the proper fee[1] any person may enter with the marriage officer[2] a caveat, signed by him or on his behalf and stating his residence and the ground of his objection against the solemnisation of the marriage of any named person, and thereupon the marriage cannot be solemnised until either the marriage officer has examined the matter and is satisfied that the caveat ought not to obstruct solemnisation of the marriage, or the caveat has been withdrawn by the person entering it[3]. In a case of doubt the marriage officer may transmit a copy of the caveat with such statement respecting it as he thinks fit to the Secretary of State, who must refer it to the Registrar General for whichever part of the United Kingdom he considers appropriate[4]; and the Registrar General must give his decision in writing to the Secretary of State, who must communicate it to the marriage officer[5]. The marriage officer must forthwith inform the parties of, and conform to, the decision of the Registrar General[6].

1   As to the proper fee see PARA 120 note 5.
2   As to the meaning of 'marriage officer' see PARA 119 note 2.
3   Foreign Marriage Act 1892 s 5(1).
4   Ie to the Registrar General for England and Wales, the Registrar General of Births, Deaths and Marriages for Scotland or the Registrar General in Northern Ireland: Foreign Marriage Act 1892 s 5(2) (amended by the Foreign Marriage (Amendment) Act 1988 s 3(1)). As to the office of Registrar General for England and Wales see REGISTRATION CONCERNING THE INDIVIDUAL vol 39(2) (Reissue) PARA 605 et seq.
5   Foreign Marriage Act 1892 s 5(2).
6   Foreign Marriage Act 1892 s 5(4) (amended by the Foreign Marriage (Amendment) Act 1988 s 3(2)).

124.   Oath before marriage.   Before a marriage is solemnised under the Foreign Marriage Act 1892[1], each of the parties must appear before the marriage officer[2] and make and subscribe an oath in a book kept by the officer for the purpose[3]:

(1)   that he or she believes that there is no impediment to the marriage by reason of kindred or alliance or otherwise[4];

(2)   that they have both for the immediately preceding three weeks had their usual residence within the marriage officer's district[5]; and

(3)   where either party is under the age of 18 and domiciled in a country other than Scotland:

(a)   that any necessary consent has been obtained[6]; or

(b)   that the necessity of obtaining consent has been dispensed with[7]; or

(c)   if the party is domiciled in England or a country outside the United Kingdom, either that he or she is a widow or widower or that there is no person having authority to give such consent[8].

1   See PARA 119.
2   As to the meaning of 'marriage officer' see PARA 119 note 2.
3   Foreign Marriage Act 1892 s 7.
4   Foreign Marriage Act 1892 s 7(a).
5   Foreign Marriage Act 1892 s 7(b). This part of the oath must be omitted in cases where, under the Foreign Marriage Order 1970, SI 1970/1539, art 4(1), the Secretary of State has authorised the marriage officer to dispense with the requirements of the Foreign Marriage Act 1892 as to residence and notice (see PARA 120 text and note 10): Foreign Marriage Order 1970, SI 1970/1539, art 4(2).
6   Foreign Marriage Act 1892 s 7(c)(i) (s 7(c) substituted by the Foreign Marriage (Amendment) Act 1988 s 2(2)). For a form of oath see the Foreign Marriage Order 1970, SI 1970/1539, Schedule Form 2. As to consents see PARA 121.

7   Foreign Marriage Act 1892 s 7(c)(ii) (as substituted: see note 6).
8   Foreign Marriage Act 1892 s 7(c)(iii) (as substituted: see note 6).

125.   Solemnisation of marriage.   After the expiration of 14 days after notice
of an intended marriage has been entered[1], if no lawful impediment to the
marriage is shown to the satisfaction of the marriage officer[2] and the marriage
has not been forbidden[3], it may be solemnised under the Foreign Marriage
Act 1892[4]. It must be solemnised at the official house of the marriage officer[5],
with open doors, between the hours of 8 am and 6 pm in the presence of two or
more witnesses, either by the marriage officer or, if the parties so desire, by some
other person in his presence, according to such form and ceremony as the parties
see fit to adopt[6]. If a corresponding declaration is not otherwise included in the
form adopted by the parties, each party must, in some part of the ceremony and
in the presence of the marriage officer, declare that he or she knows of no lawful
impediment to the marriage[7] and that he or she takes the other as lawful wedded
wife or husband[8].

1   See PARA 120.
2   See PARA 124. As to the meaning of 'marriage officer' see PARA 119 note 2.
3   See PARA 121.
4   Foreign Marriage Act 1892 s 8(1). The marriage officer is entitled to a proper fee: s 9(1). As to
    the proper fee see also PARA 120 note 5.
5   'Official house of the marriage officer' means the office at which the officer's business is
    transacted, and the official house of residence of that officer, and, in the case of any officer who
    is an officer for solemnising marriages in the official house of an ambassador, the ambassador's
    official house: Foreign Marriage Act 1892 s 24. Every place within the curtilage or precincts of
    the building which is for the time being used for the purpose of the marriage officer's office is
    part of his official house, and every place to which the public have ordinary access in that
    official house is deemed to be part of the office: Foreign Marriage Order 1970, SI 1970/1539,
    art 5. The certificate of a Secretary of State as to any house, office, chapel, or other place being,
    or being part of, the official house of a British ambassador or consul is conclusive: Foreign
    Marriage Act 1892 s 16(2).
6   Foreign Marriage Act 1892 s 8(2) (substituted by the Foreign Marriage (Amendment) Act 1988
    s 4).
7   See the Foreign Marriage Act 1892 s 8(3) (substituted by the Foreign Marriage (Amendment)
    Act 1988 s 4).
8   See the Foreign Marriage Act 1892 s 8(4) (added by the Foreign Marriage (Amendment)
    Act 1988 s 4).

126.   Registration and proof of marriage.   The marriage officer[1] must
forthwith register in duplicate a marriage solemnised under the Foreign Marriage
Act 1892[2] in two marriage register books[3], according to the form provided by
law for the registration of marriages in England, or as near to that form as the
difference of circumstances permits[4]. In January of each year the marriage officer
must forward to a Secretary of State, for transmission to the Registrar General
for England and Wales, a certified copy of all the entries of marriage made in the
register book during the preceding year, or if there has been no entry during that
year, a certificate of that fact[5].

The marriage is proved by production of the official certificate of marriage[6].
After a marriage has been solemnised it is not necessary, in support of the
marriage, to give any proof of the requisite residence of either of the parties prior
to the marriage, or of the consent of any person whose consent was required by
law, and evidence to the contrary may not be given in any legal proceeding
touching the validity of the marriage[7]. Where a marriage purports to have been
solemnised and registered under the Act in the official house of a British
ambassador or consul[8], it is not necessary in support of the marriage to give any

proof of the authority of the marriage officer by or before whom the marriage was solemnised and registered, and evidence of his want of authority[9] may not be given in any such proceeding[10].

1	As to the meaning of 'marriage officer' see PARA 119 note 2.

2	See PARA 119.

3	The register books must be furnished to him from time to time by the Registrar General for England and Wales, through the Secretary of State: Foreign Marriage Act 1892 s 9(2) (amended by the Foreign Marriage (Amendment) Act 1988 s 5(1)). As to the office of Registrar General for England and Wales see REGISTRATION CONCERNING THE INDIVIDUAL vol 39(2) (Reissue) PARA 605 et seq.

4	Foreign Marriage Act 1892 s 9(2). Every entry must be signed by the marriage officer (or by the person solemnising the marriage if other than that officer), by both parties and by two witnesses: s 9(3). Entries must be in regular order from the beginning to the end of the book, and the number of the entry in each duplicate must be the same: s 9(4). The marriage officer may ask the parties for the required particulars: s 9(5).

5	Foreign Marriage Act 1892 s 10(1) (amended by the Foreign Marriage (Amendment) Act 1988 s 5(1)). Every copy must be certified, and certificate given, under the marriage officer's hand and official seal: Foreign Marriage Act 1892 s 10(1). For a form of certificate see the Foreign Marriage Order 1970, SI 1970/1539, art 8, Schedule, Form 3. If either party is shown in a copy of a certificate received by the Registrar General for England and Wales to be from Scotland or Northern Ireland, that Registrar General must send a copy entry to the appropriate Registrar General in Scotland or Northern Ireland: art 6(1) (so numbered by SI 1990/598). The marriage officer must keep the duplicate books until they are filled, and then send one to the Secretary of State for transmission to the Registrar General for England and Wales: Foreign Marriage Act 1892 s 10(2) (amended by the Foreign Marriage (Amendment) Act 1988 s 5(1)).

	Where a marriage officer has no seal of office, reference to the official seal must be construed as reference to any seal ordinarily used by him, if authenticated by his signature with his official name and description: Foreign Marriage Act 1892 s 11(5).

6	The provisions and penalties of the Marriage Registration Acts relating to any registrar or register of marriages, or certified copies, extend to marriage officers and their registers and certified copies, so far as applicable: Foreign Marriage Act 1892 s 17. 'Marriage Registration Acts' means enactments for the time being in force in England relating to the registration of marriages: s 17 (definition added by the Foreign Marriage (Amendment) Act 1988 s 5(2)). Any books, notices or documents directed to be kept by a marriage officer are documents of such a public nature as to be admissible in evidence on mere production from his custody: Foreign Marriage Act 1892 s 16(1). See further REGISTRATION CONCERNING THE INDIVIDUAL.

7	Foreign Marriage Act 1892 s 13(1). As to the requirements of residence see PARAS 120, 124. As to the necessary consents see PARA 121.

8	For these purposes, 'ambassador' includes a minister and a chargé d'affaires; and 'consul' means a consul-general, consul, vice-consul, pro-consul, or consular agent: Foreign Marriage Act 1892 s 24.

9	Ie whether by reason of his not being duly authorised, or of any prohibitions or restrictions under the marriage regulations or otherwise: Foreign Marriage Act 1892 s 13(2).

10	Foreign Marriage Act 1892 s 13(2) (amended by the Foreign Marriage Act 1947 s 4). Cf *Watts (otherwise Carey) v Watts* (1922) 38 TLR 430.

**127.	Effect of non-compliance with the statutory requirements.**	The requirements of the Foreign Marriage Act 1892 as to notices[1], consents[2], the oath before marriage[3] and registration of the marriage[4] are directory only and not mandatory, so that a marriage solemnised under the Act may be valid even if these requirements have not been complied with[5]. On the other hand, the requirements of the Act as to the solemnisation of the marriage[6] are crucial, and they must be complied with in order for the marriage to be valid[7].

1	See PARA 120.

2	See PARA 121.

3	See PARA 124.

4	See PARA 126.

5	*Collett v Collett* [1968] P 482, [1967] 2 All ER 426.

6   See PARA 125.
7   *Collett v Collett* [1968] P 482, [1967] 2 All ER 426.

128.   Certificate of no impediment to marriage. A holder of British nationality[1] who desires to be married in a foreign country to a foreigner according to the law of that country may, if it is desired for the purpose of complying with the law of the foreign country to obtain a certificate that after proper notices have been given no legal impediment to the marriage has been shown to exist, give notice of the marriage:

(1)   if he is resident in any part of the United Kingdom other than Scotland, to a superintendent registrar of marriages[2]; or

(2)   if he is resident abroad, to the marriage officer[3],

and apply to the registrar or marriage officer for such certificate[4]. After certain conditions[5] have been complied with, the registrar or marriage officer must give the certificate unless it is forbidden[6] or a caveat is in operation[7], or some legal impediment to the marriage is shown to exist[8].

Where arrangements have been made to the satisfaction of Her Majesty with any foreign country for the issue by the proper officers of that country, in the case of persons subject to the marriage law of that country proposing to marry holders of British nationality in any part of the United Kingdom except Scotland, of certificates that, after proper notices have been given, no legal impediment has been shown to exist to the marriage, regulations may be made by Order in Council:

(a)   requiring such a person to give notice of the fact that he is subject to the marriage law of that country to the person by whom or in whose presence the marriage is to be solemnised; and

(b)   forbidding any person to whom such notice is given to solemnise the marriage or to allow it to be solemnised until such a certificate is produced to him[9].

Her Majesty may by Order in Council make general regulations prescribing forms to be used for these purposes and making such other provisions as seem necessary or expedient, and may by Order in Council revoke, alter or add to any previous such Order in Council[10].

1   The Marriage with Foreigners Act 1906 refers to 'British subjects' but by virtue of the British Nationality Act 1981 s 51(1) such references should now be taken to be references to 'Commonwealth citizens': see BRITISH NATIONALITY, IMMIGRATION AND ASYLUM vol 4(2) (2002 Reissue) PARAS 9, 11, 66.
2   Marriage with Foreigners Act 1906 s 1(1) (amended by the Marriage (Scotland) Act 1977 ss 28(1), 29(3), Sch 2). See also the Marriage with Foreigners Act 1906 s 4.
3   Marriage with Foreigners Act 1906 s 1(1) (as amended: see note 2). A 'marriage officer' for these purposes is a marriage officer for the time being under the Foreign Marriage Act 1892, including a person empowered under s 18 to register a foreign marriage celebrated under local law: Marriage with Foreigners Act 1906 s 4. See also CONFLICT OF LAWS vol 8(3) (Reissue) PARAS 215, 224.
4   Marriage with Foreigners Act 1906 s 1(1) (as amended: see note 2). Fees may be charged as fixed under the Consular Fees Act 1980: Marriage with Foreigners Act 1906 s 1(4) (amended by the Consular Fees Act 1980 s 1(5)). As to the levying, application and remission of, and accounting for, fees see the Consular Fees Act 1980 s 1(3); the Consular Fees Regulations 1981, SI 1981/476; the Consular Fees Order 2008, SI 2008/676; and FOREIGN RELATIONS LAW vol 18(2) (Reissue) PARA 610.
5   The conditions are as follows:
    (1)   the applicant must sign a notice stating the name, surname, profession, condition, nationality and residence of each of the parties to the marriage, and whether each party is or is not a minor (Marriage with Foreigners Act 1906 Schedule para 1);

(2)　the applicant must at the time of giving the notice make and subscribe, in a book to be kept by the registrar or marriage officer for the purpose, an oath:

(a)　that he believes there to be no impediment to the marriage by reason of kindred or alliance or otherwise (Schedule para 2(a));

(b)　that he has for three weeks immediately preceding had his usual residence within the district of the registrar or officer (Schedule para 2(b)); and

(c)　if the applicant (not being a widow or widower) is under 18, that the consent of persons whose consent is required by law has been obtained (see note 8), or that there is no person having authority to give such consent, as the case may be (Schedule para 2(c));

(3)　the registrar or officer must file every such notice and keep it with the archives of his office, and must forthwith enter in a book of notices kept for the purpose, and post up in some conspicuous place in his office, a copy of every such notice, and must keep it so posted for at least 21 days (Schedule para 3); and

(4)　the book in which the notice is so entered, and the copy which is so posted, must be open at all reasonable times without fee to the inspection of any person (Schedule para 4).

6　Any person whose consent is required by law to marriages solemnised in England may forbid the certificate by writing the word 'forbidden' opposite the entry of the application in the book of notices, and by subscribing his name and residence and the character by reason of which he is authorised to forbid the certificate: Marriage with Foreigners Act 1906 Schedule para 5.

7　Any person may enter with the registrar or officer a caveat against the granting of the certificate, signed by him or on his behalf, and stating his residence and the grounds of his objection: Marriage with Foreigners Act 1906 Schedule para 6(a). The registrar or officer must examine into the matter of the caveat and decide whether it ought to obstruct the giving of the certificate or not, but he may if he thinks fit refer the matter to the Registrar General; if he decides the question himself, and decides that the caveat ought to obstruct the giving of the certificate, the applicant for the certificate may appeal to the Registrar General in manner provided by regulations: Schedule para 6(b). The caveat ceases to operate if it is withdrawn by the persons entering it or if it is decided by the registrar, the marriage officer or the Registrar General that it ought not to obstruct the giving of the certificate: Schedule para 6(c). As to the office of Registrar General for England and Wales see REGISTRATION CONCERNING THE INDIVIDUAL vol 39(2) (Reissue) PARA 605 et seq.

　　If a person enters a caveat on grounds which the registrar, the marriage officer or the Registrar General on appeal declares to be frivolous, that person is liable to pay as a debt to the applicant such sum as the registrar, the officer or the Registrar General considers to be proper compensation for the damage caused to the applicant by the entering of the caveat: s 1(3).

8　Marriage with Foreigners Act 1906 s 1(1) (as amended: see note 2).

9　Marriage with Foreigners Act 1906 s 2(1) (amended by the Marriage (Scotland) Act 1977 ss 28(1), 29(3), Sch 2). At the date at which this volume states the law, no Order in Council making such regulations had been made. If a person knowingly acts in contravention of, or fails to comply with, any such regulations, he is guilty of an offence and liable on conviction on indictment to a fine or imprisonment for up to one year: Marriage with Foreigners Act 1906 s 2(2) (amended by virtue of the Criminal Law Act 1977 s 32(1)); Courts Act 1971 s 1(2), (3).

　　Nothing in the Marriage with Foreigners Act 1906 s 2 relates to a marriage between two persons professing the Jewish religion solemnised according to Jewish usage in the presence of the secretary of a synagogue authorised by what is now the Marriage Act 1949 s 53(c) or the Marriages (Ireland) Act 1844 to register such a marriage, or a deputy appointed in writing under the hand of the secretary, and approved by the president for the time being of the London committee of deputies of the British Jews by writing under his hand: Marriage with Foreigners Act 1906 s 2(3).

10　Marriage with Foreigners Act 1906 s 3. At the date at which this volume states the law, no such Order in Council had been made.

(5)　NAVAL, MILITARY AND AIR FORCE MARRIAGES

129.　Licensing of chapels for banns and marriages. The use of any chapel which is certified by the Admiralty to be a naval chapel or a chapel which is certified by a Secretary of State to be a military or air force chapel for the publication therein of banns of any marriage between parties of whom one at least is a qualified person[1], and for the solemnisation therein, whether according to the rites of the Church of England[2] or otherwise, of such a marriage may be authorised in accordance with the relevant statutory provisions[3]. Any such chapel may be licensed for marriage according to the rites of the Church of England[4].

With respect to marriages otherwise than according to the rites of the Church of England, the Registrar General[5] must, on the application of the Admiralty, in the case of a naval chapel, or of the Secretary of State, in the case of any other chapel, register any such chapel for the solemnisation therein of marriages between parties of whom one at least is a qualified person; and, while any chapel is so registered:

(1)   any such marriages which could lawfully be solemnised in a registered building[6] situated in the same registration district[7] as the chapel may be solemnised in the chapel[8]; and

(2)   the provisions of the Marriage Act 1949 relating to marriages otherwise than according to the rites of the Church of England and to the registration of such marriages apply[9] in relation to the chapel, and in relation to marriages solemnised or intended to be solemnised therein otherwise than according to those rites, as if the chapel were a registered building[10].

The Registrar General must, on the application of the Admiralty or a Secretary of State, as the case may be, cancel the registration of any chapel so registered by him[11].

Immediately after so registering, or so cancelling the registration of, any chapel, the Registrar General must cause notice of that fact to be published in the London Gazette and in some other newspaper circulating in the registration district in which the chapel is situated and to be given to the superintendent registrar[12] of that district, who must record the registration or cancellation in such manner as may be prescribed by the Registrar General[13].

Whilst any such licence in respect of the chapel is in force, any such banns or marriages which could lawfully be published[14] or solemnised[15] in the parish church of the parish[16] in which the chapel is situated may be published or solemnised in the chapel[17]; and the statutory provisions[18] relating to marriages according to the rites of the Church of England apply, with certain exceptions[19] and subject to certain modifications[20], in relation to the chapel and the publication of banns there and marriages solemnised or intended to be solemnised there according to those rites, as if the chapel were a parish church[21].

Where a licence has been issued in respect of a chapel the diocesan bishop may at any time revoke the licence, and must do so if the Admiralty or, as the case may be, a Secretary of State applies for its revocation[22].

1   For these purposes, 'qualified person' means a person who, at the relevant date: (1) is serving in any of the regular armed forces of the Crown; (2) has served in any force included in head (1) otherwise than with a commission granted or under an engagement entered into only for the purpose of a war or other national emergency; (3) is, as a member of a reserve of officers, a reserve force, the Territorial Army or the Auxiliary Air Force, called out on actual or permanent service or embodied; or (4) is a daughter, son, step-daughter or step-son of a person qualified under any of heads (1)–(3): Marriage Act 1949 s 68(2)(a)–(c), (e) (amended by the Armed Forces Act 1981 ss 20(1), 28(2), Sch 3 para 8, Sch 5 Pt I; and the Armed Forces Act 2001 Sch 6, Pt 6 para 31(a)). The reference to 'a person serving in any of the regular armed forces of the Crown' includes a reference to a member of a visiting force or a military member of a headquarters: Visiting Forces and International Headquarters (Application of Law) Order 1999, SI 1999/1736, art 12(2), Sch 6.

      'Relevant date' means: (a) in a case where notice is given under the Marriage Act 1949 s 8 (see PARA 68) before the publication of banns, the date of the notice; (b) in a case where banns are published without such notice, the date of the first publication of banns; (c) in a case where an oath is taken under s 16 (see PARA 77) for the purpose of obtaining a common licence, the date of taking the oath; and (d) in any other case, the date when notice of marriage is given to the superintendent registrar under s 27 (see PARA 87); and the expression 'daughter' does not include a stepdaughter: s 68(3) (amended by the Children Act 1975 s 108(1)(b), Sch 4 Pt I). As to banns see PARAS 58, 68; and as to common licences see PARAS 58, 76 et seq. The Marriage Act 1949 s 68(3) is further amended from such day as the Secretary of State may by order appoint by the deletion of the words 'and the expression "daughter" docs not include a stepdaughter': scc the Armed Forces Act 2001 ss 35(1), 38, 39(2), (4)–(6), Sch 7. At the date at which this volume states the law no such order had been made.

By virtue of the Civil Partnership Act 2004 s 246(1):

a person's stepchild includes the child of that person's civil partner;

a person's step-parent includes the civil partner of that person's parent;

a person's stepdaughter includes the daughter of that person's civil partner;

a person's stepson includes the son of that person's civil partner;

a person's stepfather includes the civil partner of that person's father;

a person's stepmother includes the civil partner of that person's mother;

a person's stepbrother includes the son of the civil partner of that person's parent; and

a person's stepsister includes a person who is the daughter of the civil partner of A's parent.

By virtue of s 246(2):

'brother-in-law' includes civil partner's brother;

'daughter-in-law' includes daughter's civil partner;

'father-in-law' includes father's civil partner;

'mother-in-law' includes mother's civil partner;

'parent-in-law' includes civil partner's parent;

'sister-in-law' includes civil partner's sister; and

'son-in-law' includes son's civil partner.

Such references apply in relation to (i) the Workmen's Compensation Act 1925 s 4(3) (member of a family); (ii) the Marriage Act 1949 s 68(2)(e) (solemnisation of marriages of stepchildren of servicemen in naval, military and air force chapels etc); (iii) the Leasehold Reform Act 1967 s 7(7) (rights of members of family succeeding to tenancy on death: member of another's family) (see LANDLORD AND TENANT vol 27(3) (2006 Reissue) PARA 1441), s 18(3) (residential rights and exclusion of enfranchisement or extension: adult member of another's family) (see LANDLORD AND TENANT vol 27(3) (2006 Reissue) PARA 1488; (iv) the Employers' Liability (Compulsory Insurance) Act 1969 s 2(2) (employees to be covered) (see EMPLOYMENT vol 16(1A) (Reissue) PARA 42); (v) the Parliamentary and other Pensions Act 1972 s 27(5) (pensions for dependants of Prime Minister or Speaker) (see PARLIAMENT vol 34 (Reissue) PARA 628); (vi) the Consumer Credit Act 1974 s 184(5) (associates) (see CONSUMER CREDIT vol 9(1) (Reissue) PARA 92); (vii) the Fatal Accidents Act 1976 s 1(5) (right of action for wrongful act causing death) (see DAMAGES vol 12(1) (Reissue) PARA 932); (viii) the Credit Unions Act 1979 s 31(1) (interpretation, etc); (ix) the Estate Agents Act 1979 s 32(3) ('associate': meaning of relative) (see AGENCY vol 1 (2008) PARA 242); (x) the Pneumoconiosis etc (Workers' Compensation) Act 1979 s 3(4) ('child' and 'relative': establishment of relationship) (see SOCIAL SECURITY AND PENSIONS vol 44(2) (Reissue) PARA 169); (xi) the Administration of Justice Act 1982 s 13(1) (deduction of relationships); (xii) the Mental Health Act 1983 s 12(5) (general provisions as to medical recommendations: persons who may not give recommendations) (see MENTAL HEALTH vol 30(2) (Reissue) PARA 483), s 25C(10) (supervision applications: meaning of 'close relative') (see MENTAL HEALTH vol 30(2) (Reissue) PARA 529); (xiii) the Mobile Homes Act 1983 s 5(3) (interpretation: member of another's family) (see LANDLORD AND TENANT vol 27(2) (2006 Reissue) PARA 1273); (xiv) the Inheritance Tax Act 1984 s 11(6) (dispositions for maintenance of family) (see INHERITANCE TAXATION vol 24 (Reissue) PARA 425), s 22(2) (gifts in consideration of marriage) (see INHERITANCE TAXATION vol 24 (Reissue) PARA 519), s 71(8) (accumulation and maintenance trusts) (see INHERITANCE TAXATION vol 24 (Reissue) PARA 608); (xv) the Companies Act 1985 s 153(4) (transactions not prohibited by s 151) (see COMPANIES vol 7(1) (2004 Reissue) PARA 663), s 203(1) (notification of family and corporate interests: person interested in shares) (see COMPANIES vol 7(1) (2004 Reissue) PARA 732), s 327(2) (extension of s 323 to spouses and children) (see COMPANIES vol 7(1) (2004 Reissue) PARA 732), s 328(8) (extension of s 324 to spouses and children) (see COMPANIES vol 7(2) (2004 Reissue) PARA 1057), S 346(2) ('connected persons') (see FINANCIAL SERVICES AND INSTITUTIONS vol 50 (2008) PARA 2433), s 430E(8) (associates) (see COMPANIES vol 7(2) (2004 Reissue) PARA 1466), s 742A(6) (meaning of 'offer to the public') (see COMPANIES vol 7(1) (2004 Reissue) PARA 297), s 743(b) ('employees' share scheme') (see COMPANIES vol 7(1) (2004 Reissue) PARA 326); (xvi) the Housing Act 1985 s 113(2) (members of a person's family) (LANDLORD AND TENANT vol 27(2) (2006 Reissue) PARA 1319), s 186(2) (members of a person's family) (see LANDLORD AND TENANT vol 27(3) (2006 Reissue) PARA 1827); (xvii) the Airports Act 1986 s 20(6) (powers of investment and disposal in relation to public airport companies) (see AVIATION vol 2(3) (Reissue) PARA 458); (xviii) the Insolvency Act 1986 s 435(8) (meaning of 'associate') (see BANKRUPTCY AND INDIVIDUAL INSOLVENCY vol 3(2) (2002 Reissue) PARA 5; (xix) the Building Societies Act 1986 s 70(2)(a), (c), (3)(a), (4) (interpretation) (see FINANCIAL SERVICES AND INSTITUTIONS vol 50 (2008) PARA 1961); (xx) the Landlord and Tenant Act 1987 s 4(6) (relevant disposals) (see LANDLORD AND TENANT vol 27(3) (2006 Reissue) PARA 1750); (xxi) the Income and Corporation Taxes Act 1988 Sch 14 para 2(5) (life assurance premiums payable to friendly societies and industrial assurance companies) (see INCOME TAXATION vol 23(2) (Reissue) PARA 1021); (xxii) the Companies Act 1989 s 52(2)(a) (meaning of 'associate') (see COMPANIES vol 7(2) (2004 Reissue) PARA 1332); (xxiii) the Children Act 1989 s 105(1) (interpretation) (see CHILDREN vol 5(3) (2008 Reissue) PARA 3); (xxiv) the Broadcasting Act 1990 Sch 2 para 1(2) (restrictions on the holding of licences) (see TELECOMMUNICATIONS AND BROADCASTING vol 45(1) PARA 345); (xxv) the Taxation of Chargeable Gains Act 1992 Sch 5 paras 2(7), 2A(10), 9(11) (attribution of gains to settlors with interest in non-resident or dual resident settlement) (see CAPITAL GAINS TAXATION vol 5(1) (2004 reissue) PARAS 143, 145); (xxvi) the Friendly Societies Act 1992 s 77(3)(c) (information on appointed actuary to be annexed to balance sheet) (see FINANCIAL SERVICES AND INSTITUTIONS vol 50 (2008) PARA 2347), s 119A(2) (meaning of 'associate'); (xxvii) the Charities Act 1993 Sch 5 para 2(1) (meaning of 'connected person' for purposes of s 36(2)) (see CHARITIES vol 5(2) (2001 Reissue) PARA 343); (xxviii) the Leasehold Reform, Housing and Urban Development Act 1993 s 10(5) (premises with a resident landlord: adult member of another's family) (see LANDLORD AND TENANT vol 27(3) PARA 1454); (xxix) the Employment Rights Act 1996 s 16(1) (domestic servants); (xxx) the Family Law Act 1996 s 63(1) (interpretation of Pt 4) (see EMPLOYMENT vol 16(1A) (Reissue) PARA 233); (xxxi) the Housing Act 1996 s 62(2) (members of a person's family: Pt 1) (see HOUSING vol 22 (2006 Reissue) PARA 113), s 140(2) (members of a person's family: Chapter 1) (see LANDLORD AND TENANT vol 27(2) (2006 Reissue) PARA 1290), s 143P(3) (members of a person's family: Chapter 1A) (see LANDLORD AND TENANT vol 27(2) (2006 Reissue) PARA 1378), s 178(3) (meaning of 'associated person') (see HOUSING vol 22 (2006 Reissue) PARA 278); (xxxii) the Financial Services and Markets Act 2000 s 422(4)(b) (controller) (see FINANCIAL SERVICES AND INSTITUTIONS vol 49 (2008) PARA 591), Sch 11 (offers of securities) (see FINANCIAL SERVICES AND INSTITUTIONS vol 49 (2008) PARA 694); (xxxiii) the Care Standards Act 2000 s 80(4A) (basic definitions); (xxxiv) the Commonhold and Leasehold Reform Act 2002 Sch 6 para 3(8) (premises excluded from right to manage) (see LANDLORD AND TENANT vol 27(1) PARA 369); (xxxv) the Enterprise Act 2002 s 127(6) (associated persons) (see TRADE, INDUSTRY AND INDUSTRIAL RELATIONS); (xxxvi) the Income Tax (Earnings and Pensions) Act 2003 s 242(2) (works transport services) (see INCOME TAXATION), s 270A(3)(a) (limited exemption for qualifying childcare vouchers) (see INCOME TAXATION), s 318(3) (childcare: exemption for employer-provided care) (see INCOME TAXATION), s 318A(3) (childcare: limited exemption for other care) (see income taxation), s 318C(8) (childcare: meaning of 'qualifying child care') (see INCOME TAXATION), s 371(7) (travel costs and expenses where duties performed abroad: visiting spouse's or child's travel) (see INCOME TAXATION), s 374(9) (non-domiciled employee's spouse's or child's travel costs and expenses where duties performed in United Kingdom) (see INCOME TAXATION); and (xxxvii) the Sexual Offences Act 2003 s 27(3)(a)–(c) (family relationships) (see CRIMINAL LAW, EVIDENCE AND PROCEDURE vol 11(1) (2006 Reissue) PARA 192), s 54(9) (general interpretation) (see CRIMINAL LAW, EVIDENCE AND PROCEDURE vol 11(1) (2006 Reissue) PARA 217): Civil Partnership Act 2004 Sch 21.

    For the purposes of any such provisions: (A) 'brother' includes civil partner's brother; (B) 'daughter-in-law' includes daughter's civil partner; (C) 'father-in-law' includes civil partner's father; (D) 'mother-in-law' includes civil partner's mother; (E) 'parent-in-law' includes civil partner's parent; (F) 'sister-in-law' includes civil partner's sister; and (G) 'son-in-law' includes son's civil partner: Civil Partnership Act 2004 s 246(2).

2   As to the meaning of references to the Church of England see PARA 53 note 6.

3   Marriage Act 1949 s 68(1), (2). The relevant statutory provisions are those contained in Pt V (ss 68–71: see PARA 23): s 68(1). Nothing in Pt V is to be taken to confer on any person a right to be married in a chapel to which Pt V applies: s 68(6). As to proof of marriages in naval, military and air force chapels see PARA 23.

4   See the Marriage Act 1949 s 69; and PARA 130. As to the provisions of the Marriage Act 1949 which are excluded or modified in relation to marriages in naval, military and air force chapels according to the rites of the Church of England see s 69(1), Sch 4 Pts I, II. On the issue or revocation of such a licence the register of the diocese must register that fact and give notice thereof in writing to the Admiralty or a Secretary of State, as the case may be, who will cause a

copy of the notice to be published in the London Gazette and in some newspaper circulating in the diocese and to be sent to the Registrar General: s 69(3).

5   As to the meaning of 'Registrar General' see PARA 46 note 5.
6   As to the meaning of 'registered building' see PARA 54 note 3.
7   As to the meaning of 'registration district' see PARA 87 note 4.
8   Marriage Act 1949 s 70(1)(a).
9   Ie excluding the provisions specified in the Marriage Act 1949 s 70(1)(b), Sch 4 Pt III. The provisions so excluded are s 17 proviso (see PARA 54), s 41 (see PARA 187), s 42 (see PARA 188), s 43(1) proviso (see PARA 107), s 44(1) proviso (see PARA 104): Sch 4 Pt III (amended by the Marriage Acts Amendment Act 1958 s 1(2); the Immigration and Asylum Act 1949 Sch 14 paras 3, 32, Sch 16).
10 Marriage Act 1949 s 70(1)(b). The provisions of the Marriage Act 1949 specified in Sch 4 Pt IV, ie s 27(3) (see PARA 87 note 9) and ss 43, 44, 54 (see PARAS 107–108) apply subject to the modifications therein specified: s 70(1) proviso.
11 Marriage Act 1949 s 70(2).
12 As to the meaning of 'superintendent registrar' see PARA 22 note 1.
13 Marriage Act 1949 s 70(3). At the date at which this volume states the law no such manner had been prescribed.
14 As to the place of publication of banns see Marriage Act 1949 s 6; and PARA 59 et seq. For the exclusion or modification of certain provisions of s 6 in relation to naval, military and air force chapels, see notes 9, 10; PARA 65 note 3; and PARA 66 note 4.
15 For the places in which marriages can be solemnised, see Marriage Act 1949 s 12 (after publication of banns), s 15 (by common licence), and s 17 (under superintendent registrar's certificate); and see PARAS 59, 76, 80.
16 As to the meanings of 'parish church' and 'parish' see PARA 59 note 8.
17 Marriage Act 1949 s 69(1)(a).
18 See PARA 59 et seq.
19 The provisions excluded are set out in the Marriage Act 1949 Sch 4 Pt I. They are s 6(4) (see PARA 66), s 15(1)(b) (see PARA 59), s 17 proviso (see PARA 54), s 18 (see PARA 61), s 20 (see PARA 62), s 35(3) (see PARA 80), s 44(1) proviso (see PARA 104), and ss 53–57, 59, 60, so far as they relate to the registration of marriages by clergymen and to the duties of incumbents in relation to marriage register books (see PARAS 84–86).
20 The provisions modified are set out in Marriage Act 1949 Sch 4 Pt II. They are s 6(1) (see PARA 65), s 7(3) (see PARA 75), s 8 (see PARA 68), s 15(1)(a) (see PARA 59), s 16(1) (see PARA 77), s 27(3), which relates to notices of marriage to the superintendent registrar, and s 50 (see PARA 98).
21 Marriage Act 1949 s 69(1)(b).
22 Marriage Act 1949 s 69(2). See also note 3.

130. Marriages in chapels. The Admiralty or any person authorised by it, in the case of a naval chapel, and the Secretary of State or any person authorised by him, in the case of any other licensed chapel[1], must appoint one or more clergymen for the purpose of registering marriages solemnised in the chapel according to the rites of the Church of England[2]. No marriage may be solemnised in the chapel according to those rites except in the presence of a clergyman so appointed[3].

The provisions of the Marriage Act 1949 and of any regulations made under it[4] relating to the registration of marriages by authorised persons apply in relation to marriages solemnised according to the rites of the Church of England in such a chapel as they apply in relation to marriages solemnised in a registered building without the presence of a registrar[5].

1   As to the licensing of chapels see PARA 129.
2   Marriage Act 1949 s 69(4).
3   Marriage Act 1949 s 69(4). It is not necessary in support of such a marriage to prove that it was solemnised in the presence of a clergyman duly appointed under s 69(4), and no evidence may be given to prove the contrary in any proceedings touching the validity of any such marriage: s 71 (see PARA 23).
4   Ie regulations made under Marriage Act 1949 s 74: see REGISTRATION CONCERNING THE INDIVIDUAL vol 8(3) (Reissue) PARA 606.

5   Marriage Act 1949 s 69(5). However, for any reference in those provisions to an authorised person there must be substituted a reference to a clergyman appointed under s 69(4), and for any reference in them to the trustees or governing body of a registered building there must be substituted a reference to the Admiralty or any person authorised by it in the case of a naval chapel or a Secretary of State or any person authorised by him in the case of any other chapel: s 69(5).

131. Issue of certificates on board Her Majesty's ships. Where a marriage is intended to be solemnised in England on the authority of certificates of a superintendent registrar[1] between parties of whom one is residing in England and the other is an officer, seaman or marine borne on the books of one of Her Majesty's ships at sea, the officer, seaman or marine may give notice of his intention to the captain or other officer commanding the ship, together with the name and address of the other party to the marriage and such other information as may be necessary to enable the officer commanding to fill up a certificate[2]. At the time of giving the notice, the officer, seaman or marine must make and sign such a declaration as is required to accompany notice of marriage given to a superintendent registrar[3], and the captain or other officer may attest the declaration and thereupon issue a certificate[4].

The certificate must be in such form as may be prescribed by the Admiralty, and has the like force and effect as a superintendent registrar's certificate[5]. All provisions of the Marriage Act 1949[6], including penal provisions, relating to notices and declarations for obtaining certificates from superintendent registrars, and to such certificates, apply in the case of certificates issued on board Her Majesty's ships, subject to such adaptations as may be made by Her Majesty by Order in Council[7]. Where a naval officer's certificate has been issued, the superintendent registrar of the district in England in which the other party resides may accept notice of marriage given by that party as if both parties were residing in different registration districts[8] in England[9].

1   As to the meaning of 'superintendent registrar' see PARA 22 note 1.
2   Marriage Act 1949 s 39(1) (amended by the Immigration and Asylum Act 1999 Sch 14 paras 3, 21).
3   As to declarations to accompany notice of marriage see PARA 90.
4   Marriage Act 1949 s 39(1).
5   Marriage Act 1949 s 39(2) (amended by the Marriage Act 1983 Sch 1 paras 1, 10(a); the Marriage (Prohibited Degrees of Relationship) Act 1986 s 1(4), Sch 1 para 6(a)).
6   Ie other than the Marriage Act 1949 s 27A (see PARA 172) and s 27B (see PARA 93).
7   Marriage Act 1949 s 39(2). At the date at which this volume states the law no Orders in Council had been so made but, by virtue of the Marriage Act 1949 s 79(2), the Order in Council dated 21 December 1908, SR & O 1908/1316, has effect as if so made.
8   As to the meaning of 'registration district' see PARA 87 note 4.
9   Marriage Act 1949 s 39(3) (amended by the Marriage Act 1983 Sch 1 paras 1, 10(b); the Marriage (Prohibited Degrees of Relationship) Act 1986 Sch 1 para 6(b)). The statutory provisions relating to notices of marriage and the issue of certificates (see PARA 87 et seq) apply: Marriage Act 1949 s 39(3).

(6) CIVIL PARTNERSHIPS

(i) In general

132. The standard and special procedure. Provision is made for two types of civil partnership[1] registration: the standard procedure[2] and the special procedure[3], which provides for a civil partnership registration to take place quickly and applies where one of the proposed civil partners is seriously ill and not expected to recover.

1   As to the meaning of 'civil partnership' see PARA 2 note 1.
2   As to the standard procedure see PARA 133 et seq.
3   As to the special procedure see PARA 140 et seq.

(ii) The Standard Procedure

133.   Notice of proposed civil partnership and declaration. For two people to register as civil partners[1] of each other under the standard procedure, a notice of proposed civil partnership must be given:

(1)   where the proposed civil partners have resided in the area of the same registration authority[2] for the period of seven days immediately before the giving of the notice, by each of them to that registration authority[3]; or

(2)   where the proposed civil partners have not resided in the area of the same registration authority for that period, by each of them to the registration authority in whose area he or she has resided for that period[4].

The notice must include the necessary declaration[5], made and signed by the person giving the notice at the time when the notice is given and in the presence of an authorised person[6], and the authorised person must attest the declaration by adding his name, description and place of residence[7].

The registration authority must ensure that the fact that the notice has been given, the information in it, and the fact that the authorised person has attested the declaration are recorded in the register[8] as soon as possible[9]. A notice of proposed civil partnership is recorded once this has been done[10].

Special provision is made in connection with civil partnerships involving persons subject to immigration control[11].

1   As to the meaning of 'civil partner' see PARA 2 note 1.
2   'Registration authority' means a county council, the council of any district comprised in an area for which there is no county council, a London borough council, the Common Council of the City of London or the Council of the Isles of Scilly: Civil Partnership Act 2004 s 28(a). As to local government areas and authorities in England and Wales see LOCAL GOVERNMENT vol 29(1) (Reissue) PARA 23 et seq. As to the London boroughs and their councils see LONDON GOVERNMENT vol 29(2) (Reissue) PARAS 30, 35–39, 59 et seq. As to the Common Council of the City of London see LONDON GOVERNMENT vol 29(2) (Reissue) PARAS 51–55.
3   Civil Partnership Act 2004 s 8(1)(a) (s 8(1) substituted by SI 2005/2000). A notice of proposed civil partnership must contain such information as may be prescribed by regulations: s 8(3) (see the Civil Partnership (Registration Provisions) Regulations 2005, SI 2005/3176). As to the information to be contained in, and the forms of, notice of proposed civil partnerships see the Civil Partnership (Registration Provisions) Regulations 2005, SI 2005/3176, reg 3, Forms 1, 1(w), 2, 2(w), 3, 3(w), 4, 4(w), 5, 5(w).
4   Civil Partnership Act 2004 s 8(1)(b) (as substituted: see note 3).
5   'Necessary declaration' means a solemn declaration in writing:
     (1)   that the proposed civil partner believes that there is no impediment of kindred or affinity or other lawful hindrance to the formation of the civil partnership (Civil Partnership Act 2004 s 8(4)(a)); and
     (2)   that the proposed civil partners have for the period of seven days immediately before the giving of the notice had their usual places of residence in the area of the registration authority, or in the areas of the registration authorities, to which notice is given or, in relation to proposed civil partnerships involving a person who is subject to immigration control, that the notice of proposed civil partnership is give in compliance with the Civil Partnership Act 2004 Sch 23 para 4(1) (see PARA 179): Civil Partnership Act 2004 s 8(4)(b), Sch 23 para 7(2)(a) (amended by SI 2005/2000).
     If one of the proposed civil partners is a child and is not a surviving civil partner, the necessary declaration must also:
     (a)   state in relation to each appropriate person that that person's consent has been

obtained, that the need to obtain that person's consent has been dispensed with (see PARAS 46, 47), or that the court has given consent (see PARA 47) (Civil Partnership Act 2004 Sch 2 para 5); or

(b)　　state that no person exists whose consent is required to a civil partnership between the child and another person (Sch 2 para 5).

The fee for the attestation by an authorised person of the necessary declaration is £30 to be paid to the registration authority to which the notice is given: Registration of Civil Partnerships (Fees) Order 2005, SI 2005/1996, Schedule.

6　'Authorised person' means an employee or officer or other person provided by a registration authority who is authorised by that authority to attest notices of proposed civil partnership: Civil Partnership Act 2004 s 8(6).

7　Civil Partnership Act 2004 s 8(3).

8　'Register' means the system the Registrar General must provide for keeping any records that relate to civil partnerships and are required by the Civil Partnership Act 2004 Chapter 1 (ss 1–36) to be made: see s 30(2), (4). The system may, in particular, enable those records to be kept together with other records kept by the Registrar General: s 30(3).

9　Civil Partnership Act 2004 s 8(5).

10　Civil Partnership Act 2004 s 8(7).

11　See the Civil Partnership Act 2004 Sch 23 para 7(1); and PARAS 178, 179.

134. Registration authority's power to require evidence. A registration authority[1] to which a notice of proposed civil partnership is given[2] may require the person giving the notice to provide it with specified evidence[3]:

(1)　relating to that person[4]; or

(2)　if the registration authority considers that the circumstances are exceptional, relating not only to that person but also to that person's proposed civil partner[5].

Such a requirement may be imposed at any time before the registration authority issues the civil partnership schedule[6].

1　As to the meaning of 'registration authority' see PARA 133 note 2.

2　Ie under the Civil Partnership Act 2004 s 8(1): see PARA 133.

3　'Specified evidence' means, in relation to a person, such evidence as may be specified in guidance issued by the Registrar General:

(1)　of the person's name and surname (Civil Partnership Act 2004 s 9(3)(a));

(2)　of the person's age (s 9(3)(b));

(3)　as to whether the person has previously formed a civil partnership or a marriage and, if so, as to the ending of the civil partnership or marriage (s 9(3)(c) (amended by SI 2005/2000)); and

(4)　of the person's nationality (s 9(3)(d)).

4　Civil Partnership Act 2004 s 9(1)(a).

5　Civil Partnership Act 2004 s 9(1)(b).

6　Civil Partnership Act 2004 s 9(2). The text refers to the issue of a civil partnership schedule under s 14: see PARA 138.

135. Civil partnership within the qualified prohibition. Where two people in certain circumstances are prohibited from entering into a civil partnership[1] but intend to register as civil partners[2] of each other by signing a civil partnership schedule[3] the fact that a notice of proposed civil partnership[4] has been given must not be recorded in the register[5] unless the registration authority[6]:

(1)　is satisfied by the production of evidence that both the proposed civil partners have reached 21[7]; and

(2)　has received a declaration made by each of the proposed civil partners specifying their affinal relationship, and declaring that the younger of them has not at any time before reaching 18 been a child of the family in relation to the other[8].

Either of the proposed civil partners may apply to the High Court for a declaration that, given that both of them have reached 21, and the younger of those persons has not at any time before reaching 18 been a child of the family[9] in relation to the other, there is no impediment of affinity to the formation of the civil partnership[10].

If a registration authority receives from a person who is not one of the proposed civil partners a written statement signed by that person which alleges that a declaration[11] is false in a material particular, and the register shows that such a statement has been received[12], the registration authority in whose area it is proposed that the registration take place must not issue a civil partnership schedule unless a High Court declaration is obtained[13].

1　As to conditionally prohibited civil partnerships see PARA 39.
2　As to the meaning of 'civil partners' see PARA 2 note 1.
3　As to the meaning of 'civil partnership schedule' see PARA 138.
4　As to notices of proposed civil partnership see PARA 133.
5　As to the meaning of 'register' see PARA 133 note 7.
6　As to the meaning of 'registration authority' see PARA 133 note 2.
7　Civil Partnership Act 2004 Sch 1 para 5(1)(a). This does not apply if a declaration is obtained under Sch 1 para 7 (see the text and note 10): Sch 1 para 5(2).
8　Civil Partnership Act 2004 Sch 1 para 5(1)(b). This does not apply if a declaration is obtained under Sch 1 para 7 (see the text and note 10): Sch 1 para 5(2). A declaration under Sch 1 para 5(1)(b) must contain such information and must be signed and attested in such manner as prescribed under the Civil Partnership (Registration Provisions) Regulations 2005, SI 2005/3176: see the Civil Partnership Act 2004 Sch 1 para 5(3). The fact that a declaration has been received must be recorded in the register: Sch 1 para 5(4). A declaration must be filed and kept by the registration authority: Sch 1 para 5(5).
9　As to the meaning of 'child of the family' see PARA 39 note 2.
10　Civil Partnership Act 2004 Sch 1 para 7(1). Such an application may be made whether or not any statement has been received by the registration authority under Sch 1 para 6 (see the text and notes 12–13): Sch 1 para 7(2).
11　Ie a declaration under the Civil Partnership Act 2004 Sch 1 para 5 (see the text and note 8).
12　Civil Partnership Act 2004 Sch 1 para 6(1).
13　Civil Partnership Act 2004 Sch 1 para 6(2). The text refers to obtaining a declaration under Sch 1 para 7 (see the text and note 10).

136.　Publication of notice. Where a notice of proposed civil partnership[1] has been given to a registration authority[2], it must keep the relevant information[3] on public display during the waiting period[4]. All information that a registration authority is required for the time being to keep on public display must be kept on display by it at one register office provided for a district within its area[5].

For these purposes, 'waiting period', in relation to a notice of proposed civil partnership, means the period beginning the day after the notice is recorded and ending at the end of the period of 15 days beginning with that day[6].

If, on an application being made to the Registrar General[7], he is satisfied that there are compelling reasons for shortening the period of 15 days because of the exceptional circumstances of the case, he may shorten it to such period as he considers appropriate[8]. The applicant must complete the prescribed form[9] and pass it to the registration authority in whose area notice of proposed civil partnership has been given[10]. The registration authority must immediately forward the completed application and the prescribed fee[11] to the Registrar General[12]. If the Registrar General requires further information, he may request that the registration authority obtain the information required from the applicant and forward it to the Registrar General, or request the information from the applicant directly[13]. After the Registrar General has considered the application he must as soon as practicable notify the applicant and the registration authority which forwarded the completed application form of his decision[14].

1   As to notices of proposed civil partnership see PARA 133.
2   As to the meaning of 'registration authority' see PARA 133 note 2.
3   'Relevant information' means:
    (1)   the name of the person giving the notice (Civil Partnership Act 2004 s 10(2)(a));
    (2)   the name of that person's proposed civil partner (s 10(2)(b)); and
    (3)   such other information included in the notice of proposed civil partnership as may be prescribed (s 10(2)(c) (amended by SI 2005/2000)). At the date at which this volume states the law no regulations prescribing any such information had been made.
4   Civil Partnership Act 2004 s 10(1) (amended by SI 2005/2000).
5   Civil Partnership Act 2004 s 10(3) (added by SI 2005/2000).
6   Civil Partnership Act 2004 s 11.
7   As to the Registrar General see PARA 46 note 5.
8   Civil Partnership Act 2004 s 12(1). Regulations may make provision with respect to the making, and granting, of applications under s 12(1), and may provide for: (1) the power conferred to be exercised by a registration authority on behalf of the Registrar General in such classes of case as are prescribed by the regulations; and (2) the making of an appeal to the Registrar General against a decision taken by a registration authority in accordance with such regulations: s 12(2), (3). A registration authority may shorten the waiting period on behalf of the Registrar General if there has been an unavoidable delay in recording the notice of proposed civil partnership in accordance with s 8(5) (see PARA 133) and, in consequence of that delay, the proposed civil partners will be unable to form a civil partnership on the date which had been agreed with the authorised person when the notice of proposed civil partnership was attested: Civil Partnership (Registration Provisions) Regulations 2005, SI 2005/3176, reg 8. As to the meaning of 'authorised person' see PARA 133 note 6.
9   As to the prescribed forms see the Civil Partnership (Registration Provisions) Regulations 2005, SI 2005/3176, reg 7(2).
10 Civil Partnership (Registration Provisions) Regulations 2005, SI 2005/3176, reg 7(1), (3).
11 The prescribed fee is £28: Registration of Civil Partnerships (Fees) Order 2005, SI 2005/1996, reg 2, Schedule.
12 Civil Partnership (Registration Provisions) Regulations 2005, SI 2005/3176, reg 7(1), (4).
13 Civil Partnership (Registration Provisions) Regulations 2005, SI 2005/3176, reg 7(1), (5).
14 Civil Partnership (Registration Provisions) Regulations 2005, SI 2005/3176, reg 7(1), (6).

137.   Forbidding the issue of a civil partnership schedule.   Where it has been recorded in the register[1] that a notice of proposed civil partnership[2] between a child[3] and another person has been given, any person whose consent is required to a child and another person registering as civil partners[4] of each other[5] may forbid the issue of a civil partnership schedule[6] by giving any registration authority[7] written notice that he forbids it[8]. On receiving the notice, the registration authority must as soon as is practicable record in the register the fact that the issue of a civil partnership schedule has been forbidden[9]. If the issue of a civil partnership schedule has been forbidden under these provisions, the notice of proposed civil partnership and all proceedings on it are void[10]. However this is not the case where the court has given its consent[11] to the civil partnership[12].

1   As to the meaning of 'register' see PARA 133 note 7.
2   As to notices of proposed civil partnership see PARA 133.
3   As to the meaning of 'child' see PARA 38 note 1.
4   As to the meaning of 'civil partner' see PARA 2 note 1.
5   As to such consent see PARA 46.
6   As to civil partnership schedules see PARA 138.
7   As to the meaning of 'registration authority' see PARA 133 note 2.
8   Civil Partnership Act 2004 Sch 2 para 6(1), (2). Such a notice must specify:
    (1)   the name of the person giving it (Sch 2 para 6(3)(a));
    (2)   his place of residence (Sch 2 para 6(3)(b)); and
    (3)   the capacity, in relation to either of the proposed civil partners, in which he forbids the issue of the civil partnership schedule (Sch 2 para 6(3)(c)).
9   Civil Partnership Act 2004 Sch 2 para 6(4).
10 Civil Partnership Act 2004 Sch 2 para 6(5).

11 Ie by virtue of the Civil Partnership Act 2004 Sch 2 para 3 (see PARA 47).
12 Civil Partnership Act 2004 Sch 2 para 6(6).

138.   Issue of a civil partnership schedule. As soon as the waiting period[1] in relation to each notice of proposed civil partnership[2] has expired, the registration authority[3] in whose area it is proposed that the registration take place is under a duty, at the request of one or both of the proposed civil partners, to issue a document to be known as a 'civil partnership schedule'[4], unless the registration authority is not satisfied that there is no lawful impediment to the formation of the civil partnership[5].

Any person may object to the issue of a civil partnership schedule by giving any registration authority notice of his objection[6]. If such an objection is given:

(1) the registration authority must ensure that the fact that it has been given and the information in it are recorded in the register[7] as soon as possible[8]; and

(2) no civil partnership schedule is to be issued until either the relevant registration authority[9] has investigated the objection and is satisfied that the objection ought not to obstruct the issue of the civil partnership schedule or the objection has been withdrawn by the person who made it[10].

If the registration authority refuses to issue a civil partnership schedule because an objection to its issue has been made or the registration authority is not satisfied that there is no lawful impediment to the formation of the civil partnership, either of the proposed civil partners may appeal to the Registrar General[11] who must either confirm the refusal or direct that a civil partnership schedule be issued[12]. If the Registrar General declares that the grounds on which the objection is made are frivolous and ought not to obstruct the issue of the civil partnership schedule[13], the person who made the objection is liable for the costs of the proceedings before the Registrar General and damages recoverable by the proposed civil partner to whom the objection relates[14]. This also applies if the registration authority refuses to issue a civil partnership schedule as a result of a representation made to it, and, on an appeal against the refusal, the Registrar General declares that the representation is frivolous and ought not to obstruct the issue of the civil partnership schedule[15].

1 As to the waiting period see PARA 136.
2 As to notices of proposed civil partnership see PARA 133.
3 As to the meaning of 'registration authority' see PARA 133 note 2.
4 Civil Partnership Act 2004 s 14(1). As to the information contained in such a schedule see the Civil Partnership (Registration Provisions) Regulations 2005, SI 2005/3176, Forms 9, 9(w).
5 Civil Partnership Act 2004 s 14(3). The duty does not apply if the issue of a civil partnership schedule has been forbidden under Sch 2 para 6 (see PARA 137): Sch 2 para 8. If a proposed civil partnership is between a child and another person, the civil partnership schedule must contain a statement that the issue of the civil partnership schedule has not been forbidden under Sch 2 para 6 (see PARA 137): Sch 2 para 9. If, for the purpose of obtaining a civil partnership schedule, a person declares that the consent of any person or persons whose consent is required under s 4 (see PARA 47) has been given, the registration authority may refuse to issue the civil partnership schedule unless satisfied by the production of written evidence that the consent of that person or those persons has in fact been given: Sch 2 para 7.
6 Civil Partnership Act 2004 s 13(1). Such a notice of objection must:
    (1)   state the objector's place of residence and the ground of objection (s 13(2)(a)); and
    (2)   be signed by or on behalf of the objector (s 13(2)(b)).
    Section 13 does not apply in relation to a civil partnership where two people are conditionally prohibited from entering into a civil partnership, except so far as an objection to the issue of a civil partnership schedule is made on a ground other than the affinity between the proposed civil partners: Sch 1 para 8.

7   As to the meaning of 'register' see PARA 133 note 7.
8   Civil Partnership Act 2004 s 13(3).
9   For these purposes 'relevant registration authority' means the authority which first records that a notice of proposed civil partnership has been given by one of the proposed civil partners: Civil Partnership Act 2004 s 14(5).
10 Civil Partnership Act 2004 s 14(4).
11 Civil Partnership Act 2004 s 15(1). As to the meaning of 'Registrar General' see PARA 46 note 5.
12 Civil Partnership Act 2004 s 15(2).
13 See the Civil Partnership Act 2004 s 16(1); and PARA 138.
14 See the Civil Partnership Act 2004 s 16(3); and PARA 138. For the purpose of enabling any person to recover any such costs and damages, a copy of a declaration of the Registrar General purporting to be sealed with the seal of the General Register Office is evidence that the Registrar General has made the declaration: s 16(4).
15 See the Civil Partnership Act 2004 s 16(2); and PARA 138.

139.   Time for civil partnership registration. The proposed civil partners may not register as civil partners[1] of each other on the production of the civil partnership schedule[2] until the waiting period[3] in relation to each notice of proposed civil partnership[4] has expired[5]. They may then register as civil partners by signing the civil partnership schedule on any day in the applicable period[6] between 8 am and 6 pm[7]. If they do not register as civil partners by signing the civil partnership schedule before the end of the applicable period the notices of proposed civil partnership and the civil partnership schedule are void, and no civil partnership registrar[8] may officiate at the signing of the civil partnership schedule by them[9].

1   As to the meaning of 'civil partner' see PARA 2 note 1.
2   As to civil partnership schedules see PARA 138.
3   As to the waiting period see PARA 136.
4   As to notices of proposed civil partnership see PARA 133.
5   Civil Partnership Act 2004 s 17(1).
6   'Applicable period' means, in relation to two people registering as civil partners of each other, the period of 12 months beginning with:
    (1)   the day on which the notices of proposed civil partnership are recorded (Civil Partnership Act 2004 s 17(4)(a)); or
    (2)   if the notices are not recorded on the same day, the earlier of those days (s 17(4)(b)).
7   Civil Partnership Act 2004 s 17(2).
8   'Civil partnership registrar' means an individual who is designated by a registration authority as a civil partnership registrar for its area: Civil Partnership Act 2004 s 29(1). As to the meaning of 'registration authority' see PARA 133 note 2. It is the duty of each registration authority to ensure that there is a sufficient number of civil partnership registrars for its area to carry out in that area the functions of civil partnership registrars: s 29(2). Each registration authority must inform the Registrar General as soon as is practicable of any designation it has made of a person as a civil partnership registrar, and of the ending of any such designation: s 29(3). As to the meaning of 'Registrar General' see PARA 46 note 5.
9   Civil Partnership Act 2004 s 17(3).

(iii)   Special Procedure for Civil Partnerships of Seriously Ill Persons

140.   Notice of proposed civil partnership and declaration. For two people to register as civil partners[1] of each other under the special procedure, one of them must give a notice of proposed civil partnership to the registration authority[2] for the area in which it is proposed that the registration take place and comply with any requirements made to produce evidence[3].

The notice must include the necessary declaration[4], made and signed by the person giving the notice at the time when the notice is given and in the presence of an authorised person[5], and the authorised person must attest the declaration by adding his name, description and place of residence[6].

The registration authority must ensure that the fact that the notice has been given, the information in it, and the fact that the authorised person has attested the declaration are recorded in the register[7] as soon as possible[8]. A notice of proposed civil partnership is recorded once this has been done[9].

On receiving a notice of proposed civil partnership and any evidence[10], the registration authority must inform the Registrar General, and comply with any directions the Registrar General may give for verifying the evidence given[11].

1   As to the meaning of 'civil partner' see PARA 2 note 1.
2   As to the meaning of 'registration authority' see PARA 133 note 2.
3   Civil Partnership Act 2004 s 21(1). The text refers to any requirements made under s 22 (see PARA 141). If a child and another person intend to register as civil partners of each other under the special procedure and the consent of any person to the child registering as the civil partner of that person is required, the person giving the notice of proposed civil partnership to the registration authority must produce to the authority such evidence as the Registrar General may require to satisfy him that the consent has in fact been given: Sch 2 para 13(1), (2). This is in addition to the power to require evidence under s 22 (see PARA 141): Sch 2 para 13(3).
4   As to the necessary declaration see PARA 133 note 4. If one of the proposed civil partners is a child and is not a surviving civil partner, the necessary declaration must also (1) state in relation to each appropriate person (a) that that person's consent has been obtained; (b) that the need to obtain that person's consent has been dispensed with (see PARA 47); or (c) that the court has given consent (see PARA 47); or (2) state that no person exists whose consent is required to a civil partnership between the child and another person: Civil Partnership Act 2004 Sch 2 para 11. The fee for the attestation by an authorised person of the necessary declaration to be paid to the registration authority to which the notice is given is £30: Registration of Civil Partnerships (Fees) Order 2005, SI 2005/1996, Schedule.
5   As to the meaning of 'authorised person' see PARA 133 note 6.
6   Civil Partnership Act 2004 ss 8(3), 21(3).
7   As to the meaning of 'register' see PARA 133 note 7.
8   Civil Partnership Act 2004 s 8(5).
9   Civil Partnership Act 2004 s 8(7).
10 Ie given under the Civil Partnership Act 2004 s 22 (see PARA 141).
11 Civil Partnership Act 2004 s 23.

141.   Registrar General's power to require evidence.   The person giving a notice of proposed civil partnership[1] to a registration authority[2] under the special procedure must produce such evidence as the Registrar General[3] may require to satisfy him:

(1)   that there is no lawful impediment to the formation of the civil partnership[4];

(2)   that one of the proposed civil partners[5]:

    (a)   is seriously ill and not expected to recover[6];

    (b)   cannot be moved to a place where they could be registered as civil partners of each other under the standard procedure[7]; and

    (c)   understands the nature and purport of signing a Registrar General's licence[8]; and

(3)   that there is sufficient reason why a licence should be granted[9].

1   As to notices of proposed civil partnership see PARA 140.
2   As to the meaning of 'registration authority' see PARA 133 note 2.
3   As to the meaning of 'Registrar General' see PARA 46 note 5.
4   Civil Partnership Act 2004 s 22(1)(a).
5   Civil Partnership Act 2004 s 22(1)(b). The certificate of a registered medical practitioner is sufficient evidence of any or all of such matters: s 22(3).
6   Civil Partnership Act 2004 s 22(2)(a) (s 22(2) substituted by SI 2005/2000).
7   Civil Partnership Act 2004 s 22(2)(b) (as substituted see note 6).
8   Civil Partnership Act 2004 s 22(2)(c) (as substituted see note 6).
9   Civil Partnership Act 2004 s 22(1)(c).

142. Forbidding the issue of a Registrar General's licence. Where it has been recorded in the register[1] that a notice of proposed civil partnership[2] between a child[3] and another person has been given, any person whose consent is required to a child and another person registering as civil partners[4] of each other[5] may forbid the Registrar General[6] to give authority for the issue of his licence[7], by giving any registration authority[8] written notice that he forbids it[9]. On receiving the notice, the registration authority must as soon as is practicable record in the register the fact that such authorisation has been forbidden[10]. If authorisation has been forbidden under these provisions, the notice of proposed civil partnership and all proceedings on it are void[11]. However, this is not the case where the court has given its consent[12] to the civil partnership[13].

1   As to the meaning of 'register' see PARA 133 note 7.
2   As to notices of proposed civil partnership see PARA 140.
3   As to the meaning of 'child' see PARA 38 note 1.
4   As to the meaning of 'civil partner' see PARA 2 note 1.
5   As to such consent see PARA 46.
6   As to the meaning of 'Registrar General' see PARA 46 note 5.
7   As to such licences see PARA 143.
8   As to the meaning of 'registration authority' see PARA 133 note 2.
9   Civil Partnership Act 2004 Sch 2 paras 6(1), (2), 12(a). Such a notice must specify:
    (1)   the name of the person giving it (Sch 2 para 6(3)(a));
    (2)   his place of residence (Sch 2 para 6(3)(b)); and
    (3)   the capacity, in relation to either of the proposed civil partners, in which he forbids the
            issue of the civil partnership schedule (Sch 2 para 6(3)(c)).
10   Civil Partnership Act 2004 Sch 2 paras 6(4), 12(a).
11   Civil Partnership Act 2004 Sch 2 paras 6(5), 12(a).
12   Ie by virtue of the Civil Partnership Act 2004 Sch 2 para 10 (see PARA 47).
13   Civil Partnership Act 2004 Sch 2 paras 6(6), 12(b).

143. Issue of a Registrar General's licence. Where a notice of proposed civil partnership[1] is given to a registration authority[2], it may issue a Registrar General's[3] licence if, and only if, given authority to do so by the Registrar General[4]. Such a licence must state that it is issued on the Registrar General's authority[5]. The Registrar General may not give his authority unless he is satisfied that one of the proposed civil partners is seriously ill and not expected to recover[6]; but, if so satisfied, he must give his authority unless a lawful impediment to the issue of his licence has been shown to his satisfaction to exist[7].

Any person may object to the Registrar General giving authority for the issue of his licence by giving the Registrar General or any registration authority notice of his objection[8]. If a notice of objection is given to a registration authority, it must ensure that the fact that it has been given and the information in it are recorded in the register[9] as soon as possible[10]. Where an objection has been made to the Registrar General giving authority for the issue of his licence, he is not to give that authority until:

(1)   he has investigated the objection and decided whether it ought to obstruct the issue of his licence[11]; or

(2)   the objection has been withdrawn by the person who made it[12].

If the Registrar General declares that the grounds on which the objection is made are frivolous and ought not to obstruct the issue of his licence, the person who made the objection is liable for the costs of the proceedings before the Registrar General, and damages recoverable by the proposed civil partner to whom the objection relates[13]. For the purpose of enabling any person to recover any such costs and damages, a copy of a declaration of the Registrar General purporting to be sealed with the seal of the General Register Office is evidence that the Registrar General has made the declaration[14].

1 As to notices of proposed civil partnership see PARA 140.
2 Ie under the Civil Partnership Act 2004 s 21 (see PARA 140): s 25(1). As to the meaning of 'registration authority' see PARA 133 note 2.
3 As to the meaning of 'Registrar General' see PARA 46 note 5.
4 Civil Partnership Act 2004 s 25(2).
5 Civil Partnership Act 2004 s 25(4). As to the contents of such a licence see the Civil Partnership (Registration Provisions) Regulations 2005, SI 2005/3176.
6 Civil Partnership Act 2004 s 25(3)(a).
7 Civil Partnership Act 2004 s 25(3)(b). The duty of the Registrar General to give authority for the issue of his licence does not apply if he has been forbidden to do so under Sch 2 para 12 (see PARA 142): Sch 2 para 14.
8 Civil Partnership Act 2004 s 24(1). A notice of objection must: (1) state the objector's place of residence and the ground of objection; and (2) be signed by or on behalf of the objector: s 24(2).
9 As to the meaning of 'register' see PARA 133 note 7.
10 Civil Partnership Act 2004 s 24(3).
11 Civil Partnership Act 2004 s 25(6)(a). Any such decision is final: s 25(7).
12 Civil Partnership Act 2004 s 25(6)(b).
13 Civil Partnership Act 2004 s 26(1), (2).
14 Civil Partnership Act 2004 s 26(3).

144. Time for civil partnership registration. Where a Registrar General's licence[1] has been issued, the proposed civil partners[2] may register as civil partners by signing it at any time within one month from the day on which the notice of proposed civil partnership was given[3]. If they do not register as civil partners by signing the licence within the one month period the notice of proposed civil partnership and the licence are void, and no civil partnership registrar[4] may officiate at the signing of the licence by them[5].

1 As to a Registrar General's licence see PARA 22. As to the meaning of 'Registrar General' see PARA 46 note 5.
2 As to proposed civil partners see PARA 133. As to the meaning of 'civil partner' see PARA 2 note 1.
3 Civil Partnership Act 2004 s 27(1). As to notices of proposed civil partnership see PARA 133 et seq.
4 As to the meaning of 'civil partnership registrar' see PARA 139 note 8.
5 Civil Partnership Act 2004 s 27(2).

(iv) Registration of Civil Partnerships Abroad

A. REGISTRATION GENERALLY

145. Registration of civil partnerships abroad. Her Majesty may, by Order in Council, make provision for two people to register as civil partners[1] of each other in prescribed countries or territories outside the United Kingdom, and in the presence of a prescribed officer of Her Majesty's diplomatic service in cases where the officer is satisfied that:

(1) at least one of the proposed civil partners is a United Kingdom national[2];

(2) the proposed civil partners would have been eligible to register as civil partners of each other in such part of the United Kingdom as is determined in accordance with the order[3];

(3) the authorities of the country or territory in which it is proposed that they register as civil partners will not object to the registration[4]; and

(4)   insufficient facilities exist for them to enter into an overseas
        relationship[5] under the law of that country or territory[6].

An officer is not required to allow two people to register as civil partners of
each other if in his opinion the formation of a civil partnership between them
would be inconsistent with international law or the comity of nations[7].

1   As to the meaning of 'civil partners' see PARA 2 note 1.
2   Civil Partnership Act 2004 s 210(1), (2)(a). Such an Order may make provision for appeals
     against a refusal to allow two people to register as civil partners of each other: s 210(4). 'United
     Kingdom National' means a person who is: (1) a British citizen, a British overseas territories
     citizen, a British Overseas citizen or a British National (Overseas); (2) a British subject under the
     British Nationality Act 1981; or (3) a British protected person, within the meaning of the British
     Nationality Act 1981: Civil Partnership Act 2004 s 245(1). As to British citizens see BRITISH
     NATIONALITY, IMMIGRATION AND ASYLUM vol 4(2) (2002 Reissue) PARAS 8, 23–43. As to
     British overseas territories citizens and citizenship (formerly known as British dependent
     territories citizens and citizenship) see BRITISH NATIONALITY, IMMIGRATION AND ASYLUM
     vol 4(2) (2002 Reissue) PARAS 8, 44–57. As to British national (overseas) status see BRITISH
     NATIONALITY, IMMIGRATION AND ASYLUM vol 4(2) (2002 Reissue) PARAS 8, 63–65. As to
     British overseas citizens see BRITISH NATIONALITY, IMMIGRATION AND ASYLUM vol 4(2) (2002
     Reissue) PARAS 8, 58–62. As to British subjects see BRITISH NATIONALITY, IMMIGRATION AND
     ASYLUM vol 4(2) (2002 Reissue) PARAS 9, 66–71. As to British protected persons see BRITISH
     NATIONALITY, IMMIGRATION AND ASYLUM vol 4(2) (2002 Reissue) PARAS 10, 72–76.
3   Civil Partnership Act 2004 s 210(2)(b).
4   Civil Partnership Act 2004 s 210(2)(c).
5   As to the meaning of 'overseas relationship' see PARA 2 note 4.
6   Civil Partnership Act 2004 s 210(2)(d).
7   Civil Partnership Act 2004 s 210(3).

146.   Notice of proposed civil partnership.   A person may give signed notice to
a civil partnership officer[1] of his and another person's intention to register as
civil partners[2] of each other if both persons have been resident within the
consular district of the civil partnership officer for a period of seven days
immediately preceding the giving of the notice[3]. Two people may not register as
civil partners of each other unless one of them has given signed notice to the civil
partnership officer at least 14 days previously[4].

The signed notice must contain the following information for both people
who intend to register the civil partnership:
    (1)   name[5];
    (2)   surname[6];
    (3)   nationality[7];
    (4)   age[8];
    (5)   residence[9]; and
    (6)   the part of the United Kingdom which[10] the proposed civil partners
            have jointly elected will be the relevant part for the civil partnership
            registration[11].

A notice of proposed civil partnership must also include a solemn declaration,
made and signed by the person giving the notice at the time when the notice is
given, and in the presence of a civil partnership officer, and the civil partnership
officer must attest the declaration by signature[12].

The civil partnership officer may demand evidence of any of the information
contained in the signed notice before posting that notice[13].

1   As to the meaning of 'civil partnership officer' see PARA 18 note 1.
2   As to the meaning of 'civil partner' see PARA 2 note 1.
3   Civil Partnership (Registration Abroad and Certificates) Order 2005, SI 2005/2761, art 5(1).
     The civil partnership officer may demand evidence of any of the information contained in the
     signed notice before posting that notice: art 5(6). A civil partnership will not be formed if notice

has not been given within the preceding three months: art 9(1). Where an investigation has been made into an objection under art 8(2) (see PARA 148), the notice will be valid until three months after the person concerned was informed that the civil partnership could be registered, after which period the civil partnership must not be formed: art 9(2).

4 Civil Partnership (Registration Abroad and Certificates) Order 2005, SI 2005/2761, art 5(2).
5 Civil Partnership (Registration Abroad and Certificates) Order 2005, SI 2005/2761, art 5(3)(a).
6 Civil Partnership (Registration Abroad and Certificates) Order 2005, SI 2005/2761, art 5(3)(b).
7 Civil Partnership (Registration Abroad and Certificates) Order 2005, SI 2005/2761, art 5(3)(c).
8 Civil Partnership (Registration Abroad and Certificates) Order 2005, SI 2005/2761, art 5(3)(d).
9 Civil Partnership (Registration Abroad and Certificates) Order 2005, SI 2005/2761, art 5(3)(e).
10 Ie for the purposes of the Civil Partnership (Registration Abroad and Certificates) Order 2005, SI 2005/2761, art 7(1) (see PARA 149).
11 Civil Partnership (Registration Abroad and Certificates) Order 2005, SI 2005/2761, art 5(3)(f).
12 Civil Partnership (Registration Abroad and Certificates) Order 2005, SI 2005/2761, art 5(4). The solemn declaration must include the following information: (1) whether he has throughout the past seven days been resident within the district of the civil partnership officer; and (2) whether there is any impediment of kindred or affinity, or other lawful hindrance to the formation of the civil partnership: art 5(5).
13 Civil Partnership (Registration Abroad and Certificates) Order 2005, SI 2005/2761, art 5(6).

147. Publication of notice. The civil partnership officer[1] must display the relevant information[2] from a notice of proposed civil partnership[3] in a conspicuous place within his office and continue to display it for a period of 14 consecutive days before the civil partnership to which it refers may be formed[4].

The civil partnership officer must file every notice of proposed civil partnership received and keep it within the archives of his office[5].

1 As to the meaning of 'civil partnership officer' see PARA 18 note 1.
2 'Relevant information' means: (1) the name of the person giving the notice (Civil Partnership (Registration Abroad and Certificates) Order 2005, SI 2005/2761, art 6(3)(a)); (2) the name of that person's proposed civil partner (art 6(3)(b)); (3) the nationality of those persons (art 6(3)(c)); (4) the age of those persons (art 6(3)(d)); and (5) the date on which notice was given (art 6(3)(e)).
3 As to a notice of proposed civil partnership see PARA 146.
4 Civil Partnership (Registration Abroad and Certificates) Order 2005, SI 2005/2761, art 6(2).
5 Civil Partnership (Registration Abroad and Certificates) Order 2005, SI 2005/2761, art 6(1).

148. Objection. Any person may enter an objection with the civil partnership officer[1], signed by the person or on his behalf, stating his name, residence and the ground of objection against the registration of a civil partnership[2] by the person named therein[3]. Where such an objection has been lodged, the person named therein may not form a civil partnership until either the objection has been withdrawn by the person who entered it, or the civil partnership officer is satisfied that the objection ought not to obstruct the person named from forming a civil partnership[4].

1 As to the meaning of 'civil partnership officer' see PARA 18 note 1.
2 As to the registration of a civil partnership see PARA 56.
3 Civil Partnership (Registration Abroad and Certificates) Order 2005, SI 2005/2761, art 8(1).
4 Civil Partnership (Registration Abroad and Certificates) Order 2005, SI 2005/2761, art 8(2).

149. Consent. Where either proposed civil partner[1] is under the age of 18, and the proposed civil partners have elected[2] that the part of the United Kingdom which will be the relevant part for the civil partnership registration[3] is England and Wales, then, save in the case of an election in respect of England and Wales where the proposed civil partner under the age of 18 is a surviving civil partner or a widow or widower, the written consent of the appropriate persons[4] is required to be given to the civil partnership officer[5] before a person under the age of 18 and another person may register as civil partners of each other[6].

Where the consent of appropriate persons is required, the necessary declaration[7] must also state in relation to each appropriate person that that person's consent has been obtained or state that no person exists whose consent is required to a civil partnership between the proposed civil partner under 18 and another person[8].

The Secretary of State may dispense with the requirement to obtain consent if he is satisfied that it cannot be obtained because of the absence, inaccessibility or disability of the person whose consent is so required[9].

On request by personal attendance of any person whose consent is required, the civil partnership officer must produce the notice and such person may forbid the formation of the civil partnership referred to in the notice at any time before the proposed civil partners have registered as civil partners of each other by writing the word 'forbidden' on the notice, together with his name and address and a statement of his capacity so to forbid[10].

These provisions do not affect any need to obtain the consent of the High Court before a ward of court[11] and another person may register as civil partners of each other[12].

1 As to the meaning of 'proposed civil partner' see PARA 146.
2 Ie under the Civil Partnership (Registration Abroad and Certificates) Order 2005, SI 2005/2761, art 5(3)(f) (see PARA 146).
3 As to civil partnership registration see PARA 56.
4 As to the appropriate persons see, by virtue of Civil Partnership (Registration Abroad and Certificates) Order 2005, SI 2005/2761, art 7(1); the Civil Partnership Act 2004 s 4, Sch 2; and PARA 149.
5 As to the meaning of 'civil partnership officer' see PARA 18 note 1.
6 Civil Partnership (Registration Abroad and Certificates) Order 2005, SI 2005/2761, art 7(1).
7 As to the necessary declaration see PARA 146.
8 Civil Partnership (Registration Abroad and Certificates) Order 2005, SI 2005/2761, art 7(2).
9 Civil Partnership (Registration Abroad and Certificates) Order 2005, SI 2005/2761, art 7(3).
10 Civil Partnership (Registration Abroad and Certificates) Order 2005, SI 2005/2761, art 7(4). If forbidden, the notice and all proceedings on it are void: art 7(4).
11 As to wards of the court see PARA 46.
12 Civil Partnership (Registration Abroad and Certificates) Order 2005, SI 2005/2761, art 7(5).

150. Time for civil partnership. Two people may register as civil partners[1] of each other once the 14 day period[2] has elapsed and while the notice which they have given has not expired[3]. They may then register as civil partners in the presence of the civil partnership officer[4] at his official house[5] in the presence of two witnesses, at a time to be set by the civil partnership officer between the hours of 8 am and 6 pm, local time[6].

The civil partnership document must be signed by the two persons registering as civil partners of each other, the two witnesses and the civil partnership officer[7]. The civil partnership document must contain the following information:

(1) date and place of registration[8];
(2) for each of the two persons registering as civil partners of each other:
    (a) name[9];
    (b) nationality[10];
    (c) residence[11];
    (d) date of birth[12]; and
    (e) place of birth[13];
(3) for each of the two witnesses:

      (i)   name[14]; and

      (ii)   residence[15]; and

  (4)   for the civil partnership officer: name[16].

1   As to the meaning of 'civil partner' see PARA 2 note 1.
2   As to the 14 day period see PARA 146.
3   Civil Partnership (Registration Abroad and Certificates) Order 2005, SI 2005/2761, art 10(1).
    As to the expiry of a notice see PARA 146 note 3.
4   As to the meaning of 'civil partnership officer' see PARA 18 note 1.
5   Every place within the curtilage or precincts of the building which is for the time being used as
    the office of the civil partnership officer will be part of his official house and every place to
    which the public have ordinary access in such official house will be deemed to be part of the
    office of the civil partnership officer: Civil Partnership (Registration Abroad and Certificates)
    Order 2005, SI 2005/2761, art 10(5). A certificate of the Secretary of State as to any house or
    other place being, or being part of, the official house of a civil partnership officer will be
    conclusive: art 10(6).
6   Civil Partnership (Registration Abroad and Certificates) Order 2005, SI 2005/2761, art 10(2).
7   Civil Partnership (Registration Abroad and Certificates) Order 2005, SI 2005/2761, art 10(3).
8   Civil Partnership (Registration Abroad and Certificates) Order 2005, SI 2005/2761,
    art 10(4)(a).
9   Civil Partnership (Registration Abroad and Certificates) Order 2005, SI 2005/2761,
    art 10(4)(b)(i).
10 Civil Partnership (Registration Abroad and Certificates) Order 2005, SI 2005/2761,
    art 10(4)(b)(ii).
11 Civil Partnership (Registration Abroad and Certificates) Order 2005, SI 2005/2761,
    art 10(4)(b)(iii).
12 Civil Partnership (Registration Abroad and Certificates) Order 2005, SI 2005/2761,
    art 10(4)(b)(iv).
13 Civil Partnership (Registration Abroad and Certificates) Order 2005, SI 2005/2761,
    art 10(4)(b)(v).
14 Civil Partnership (Registration Abroad and Certificates) Order 2005, SI 2005/2761,
    art 10(4)(c)(i).
15 Civil Partnership (Registration Abroad and Certificates) Order 2005, SI 2005/2761,
    art 10(4)(c)(ii).
16 Civil Partnership (Registration Abroad and Certificates) Order 2005, SI 2005/2761,
    art 10(4)(d)(i).

151. Proof of civil partnership. After two people have registered as civil partners[1] of each other it will not be necessary to prove:

  (1)   that the civil partners fulfilled any requirement of residence[2] that may have been on them[3];

  (2)   that any necessary consent[4] was obtained[5];

  (3)   that the civil partnership officer[6] had authority to register the civil partners[7]; or

  (4)   that registration took place within the official house[8] of the civil partnership officer[9],

and no evidence to prove the contrary will be given in any legal proceeding touching the validity of the civil partnership[10].

1   As to the meaning of 'civil partner' see PARA 2 note 1.
2   As to the requirement of residence see PARA 145.
3   Civil Partnership (Registration Abroad and Certificates) Order 2005, SI 2005/2761, art 12(a).
4   As to consent see PARA 41 et seq.
5   Civil Partnership (Registration Abroad and Certificates) Order 2005, SI 2005/2761, art 12(b).
6   As to the meaning of 'civil partnership officer' see PARA 18 note 1.
7   Civil Partnership (Registration Abroad and Certificates) Order 2005, SI 2005/2761, art 12(c).
8   As to the official house of the civil partnership officer see PARA 150 note 5.
9   Civil Partnership (Registration Abroad and Certificates) Order 2005, SI 2005/2761, art 12(d).
10 Civil Partnership (Registration Abroad and Certificates) Order 2005, SI 2005/2761, art 12.

152.   Certificate of no impediment to civil partnership. A United Kingdom national[1] who wishes to register an overseas relationship[2] with a person who is not a United Kingdom national or a Commonwealth citizen[3], may apply to the registration authority[4], or to the civil partnership officer[5] responsible for the area in which he resides, or to the civil partnership officer responsible for the consular district in which the overseas relationship is to be registered, for a certificate that no impediment to the civil partnership being registered has been shown to the Registrar General[6] or civil partnership officer to exist[7].

Where the person making the application is resident within the United Kingdom, he must, before the certificate may be issued, first give notice to the registration authority, together with payment of the appropriate fee[8], stating that he has been resident in the United Kingdom throughout the previous 21 days, following which giving of notice the certificate may be issued after a further period of 21 days has elapsed[9].

Where the person making the application is resident outside the United Kingdom, he must, before the certificate may be issued, first give notice to the appropriate civil partnership officer stating that he has been resident in the area where he resides throughout the previous 21 days, following which giving of notice the certificate may be issued after a further period of 21 days has elapsed[10].

The registration authority or civil partnership officer must not issue the certificate if he is aware of any reason why such a certificate should not be issued[11] and may request from the applicant any information which he considers relevant to the decision whether or not to issue the certificate[12].

1   As to the meaning of 'United Kingdom national' see PARA 145 note 2.
2   As to the meaning of 'overseas relationship' see PARA 19 note 1.
3   Ie a citizen of a country listed in the British Nationality Act 1981 Sch 3 (see BRITISH NATIONALITY, IMMIGRATION AND ASYLUM vol 4(2) (2002 Reissue) PARA 11): Civil Partnership (Registration Abroad and Certificates) Order 2005, SI 2005/2761, art 17(1). Article 17 is made pursuant to the Civil Partnership Act 2004 s 240, which provides that Her Majesty may by Order in Council make provision for the issue of certificates of no impediment to:
   (1)   United Kingdom nationals (s 240(1)(a)); and
   (2)   such other persons if under any enactment for the time being in force in any country mentioned in the British Nationality Act 1981 Sch 3 (see BRITISH NATIONALITY, IMMIGRATION AND ASYLUM vol 4(2) (2002 Reissue) PARA 11) that person is a citizen of that country, as may be prescribed (Civil Partnership Act 2004 s 240(1)(b), (2)),
   who wish to enter into overseas relationships in prescribed countries or territories outside the United Kingdom with persons who are not United Kingdom nationals and who do not fall under head (2): s 240(1), (2). A certificate of no impediment is a certificate that, after proper notices have been given, no legal impediment to the recipient entering into the overseas relationship has been shown to the person issuing the certificate to exist: s 240(3).
4   As to the meaning of 'registration authority' see PARA 133 note 2.
5   As to the meaning of 'civil partnership officer' see PARA 18 note 1.
6   As to the meaning of 'Registrar General' see PARA 46 note 5.
7   Civil Partnership (Registration Abroad and Certificates) Order 2005, SI 2005/2761, art 17(1).
8   The appropriate fee is £30.00: Registration of Civil Partnerships (Fees) (No 2) Order 2005, SI 2005/3167, Schedule.
9   Civil Partnership (Registration Abroad and Certificates) Order 2005, SI 2005/2761, art 17(2).
10 Civil Partnership (Registration Abroad and Certificates) Order 2005, SI 2005/2761, art 17(3).
11 Civil Partnership (Registration Abroad and Certificates) Order 2005, SI 2005/2761, art 17(4).
12 Civil Partnership (Registration Abroad and Certificates) Order 2005, SI 2005/2761, art 17(5).

B. REGISTRATION BY ARMED FORCES PERSONNEL

153.   Registration by armed forces personnel. Her Majesty may by Order in Council[1] make provision for two people to register as civil partners[2] of each other in prescribed countries or territories outside the United Kingdom[3], and in the presence of an officer[4] in cases where the officer is satisfied that:

(1)   at least one of the proposed civil partners:

    (a)   is a member of a part of Her Majesty's forces serving in the country or territory[5];

    (b)   is employed in the country or territory in such other capacity as may be prescribed[6]; or

    (c)   is a child[7] of a person falling under head (a) or (b) and has his home with that person in that country or territory[8];

(2)   the proposed civil partners would have been eligible to register as civil partners of each other in such part of the United Kingdom as is determined in accordance with the order[9]; and

(3)   such other requirements as may be prescribed are complied with[10].

1   See the Civil Partnership (Armed Forces) Order 2005, SI 2005/3188; and PARA 154 et seq.

2   As to the meaning of 'civil partner' see PARA 2 note 1.

3   'Prescribed countries or territories' means Australia, Canada, Falkland Islands, Germany, Gibraltar, Nepal, the United States of America and the Sovereign Base Areas of Akrotiri and Dhekelia: Civil Partnership (Armed Forces) Order 2005, SI 2005/3188, art 2. 'Country or territory outside the United Kingdom' includes references to ships which are for the time being in the waters of a country or territory outside the United Kingdom, to forces serving in any such ship and to persons employed in any such ship: Civil Partnership Act 2004 s 211(5)(a). If it appears to Her Majesty that any law in force in Canada, the Commonwealth of Australia or New Zealand, or in a territory of either of the former two countries, makes, in relation to forces raised there, provision similar to that made by s 211, Her Majesty may by Order in Council make provision for securing that the law in question has effect as part of the law of the United Kingdom: s 242.

4   As to the registering officer see PARA 154 note 3.

5   Civil Partnership Act 2004 s 211(1), (2)(a)(i). Reference to forces serving in a country or territory include references to ships which are for the time being in the waters of a country or territory outside the United Kingdom, to forces serving in any such ship and to persons employed in any such ship: s 211(5)(b).

6   Civil Partnership Act 2004 s 211(2)(a)(ii). References to persons employed in a country or territory include references to ships which are for the time being in the waters of a country or territory outside the United Kingdom, to forces serving in any such ship and to persons employed in any such ship: s 211(5)(c). The employment and capacities arise when: (1) a person is serving Her Majesty or is otherwise employed being a person to whom either the provisions of the Naval Discipline Act 1957 are applied by s 118(2) (see ARMED FORCES vol 2(2) (Reissue) PARA 311), to whom the provisions of the Army Act 1955 Pt 2 (ss 24–143) are applied by s 209(2) (see ARMED FORCES vol 2(2) (Reissue) PARA 311) or to whom the provision of the Air Force Act 1955 Pt 2 (ss 24–143) are applied by s 209(2) (see ARMED FORCES vol 2(2) (Reissue) PARA 311); and (2) that person is involved in the performance of any of the following functions, namely, administrative, executive, judicial, clerical, typing, duplicating, machine operating, paper keeping, managerial, professional, instructional, scientific, experimental, technical, industrial or labouring functions: Civil Partnership (Armed Forces) Order 2005, SI 2005/3188, arts 3, 4.

7   In determining for this purpose whether one person is the child of another, a person who is or was treated by another as a child of the family in relation to a marriage to which the other is or was a party, or a civil partnership in which the other is or was a civil partner, is to be regarded as the other's child: Civil Partnership Act 2004 s 211(3).

8   Civil Partnership Act 2004 s 211(2)(a)(iii).

9   Civil Partnership Act 2004 s 211(2)(b). In relation to two people proposing to become civil partners, the part of the United Kingdom will be such part as the proposed civil partners jointly elect in accordance with the Civil Partnership (Armed Forces) Order 2005, SI 2005/3188, art 6(2)(g) (see PARA 154 text and note 11) will apply to the civil partnership registration: art 5.

10   Civil Partnership Act 2004 s 211(2)(c). For these purposes, it is a requirement that where either civil partner is under the age of 18, and the proposed civil partners have elected that for the purposes of the Civil Partnership (Armed Forces) Order 2005, SI 2005/3188, arts 5, 6(2)(g), the part of the United Kingdom which is to be the relevant part for the civil partnership registration is either England and Wales or Northern Ireland then, save in the case of an election in respect

of England and Wales where the proposed civil partner under the age of 18 is a surviving civil partner or widow or widower, the written consent of appropriate persons is required: art 7(1). The written consent must be given to the registering officer before a person under the age of 18 and another person may register as civil partners of each other, and determination of appropriate persons must be decided in accordance with the Civil Partnership Act 2004 s 4, Sch 2 (see PARA 46): Civil Partnership (Armed Forces) Order 2005, SI 2005/3188, art 7(1). Where the consent of appropriate persons is required under this article, the necessary declaration under art 6(3) (see PARA 154) must also state in relation to each appropriate person that that person's consent has been obtained or state that no person exists whose consent is required to a civil partnership between the proposed civil partner under 18 and another person: art 7(2). On request by personal attendance of any person whose consent is required, the registering officer must produce the notice given under art 6(1) (see PARA 154) and such person may forbid the formation of the civil partnership referred to in the notice at any time before the proposed civil partners have registered as civil partners by writing 'forbidden' on the notice, together with his name and address and a statement of his capacity to so forbid: art 7(3). If forbidden, the notice and all proceedings are void: art 7(3).

154. Notice and declaration of proposed civil partnership. Two people who wish to register as civil partners[1] where one of the parties is a member of the armed forces[2] must give a notice of proposed civil partnership to a registering officer[3]. The notice of proposed civil partnership must contain the following information for both persons who intend to register the civil partnership:

(1)   name[4];
(2)   surname[5];
(3)   occupation[6];
(4)   age[7];
(5)   address[8];
(6)   whether he or she is or has been a civil partner or married[9]; and
(7)   the part of the United Kingdom which the proposed civil partners have jointly elected[10] will be the relevant part of the United Kingdom for the civil partnership registration[11].

A notice of proposed civil partnership must also include the necessary declaration, made and signed by the person giving the notice at the time when the notice is given, and in the presence of a registering officer and the registering officer must attest the declaration by adding his name, description and place of residence[12].

Where a notice of proposed civil partnership is given to a registering officer he must ensure that the following information is recorded as soon as possible:

(a)   the fact that the notice has been given and the information in it[13]; and
(b)   the fact that the registering officer has attested the declaration[14].

1   As to the meaning of 'civil partners' see PARA 2 note 1.
2   See PARA 153.
3   Civil Partnership (Armed Forces) Order 2005, SI 2005/3188, art 6(1). 'Registering officer' means an officer appointed by virtue of the Registration of Births, Deaths and Marriages (Special Provisions) Act 1957: Civil Partnership Act 2004 s 211(1)(b); Civil Partnership (Registration Abroad and Certificates) Order 2005, SI 2005/2761, art 1(2).
4   Civil Partnership (Armed Forces) Order 2005, SI 2005/3188, art 6(2)(a).
5   Civil Partnership (Armed Forces) Order 2005, SI 2005/3188, art 6(2)(b).
6   Civil Partnership (Armed Forces) Order 2005, SI 2005/3188, art 6(2)(c).
7   Civil Partnership (Armed Forces) Order 2005, SI 2005/3188, art 6(2)(d).
8   Civil Partnership (Armed Forces) Order 2005, SI 2005/3188, art 6(2)(e).
9   Civil Partnership (Armed Forces) Order 2005, SI 2005/3188, art 6(2)(f).
10   Ie for the purposes of the Civil Partnership Act 2004 s 211(2)(b) (see PARA 153).
11   Civil Partnership (Armed Forces) Order 2005, SI 2005/3188, art 6(2)(g).
12   Civil Partnership (Armed Forces) Order 2005, SI 2005/3188, art 6(3). The 'necessary declaration' is a solemn declaration in writing that the proposed civil partner believes that the proposed civil partners are eligible to form a civil partnership with each other in such part of the

United Kingdom as they have jointly elected will be the relevant part for the civil partnership registration and that he knows of no other lawful impediment to the formation of the civil partnership: art 6(4).

13 Civil Partnership (Armed Forces) Order 2005, SI 2005/3188, art 6(5)(a).
14 Civil Partnership (Armed Forces) Order 2005, SI 2005/3188, art 6(5)(b).

155.   Evidence. The registering officer[1] to whom a notice of proposed civil partnership[2] is given may require the person giving the notice to provide him with evidence[3] relating to that person, or if the registering officer considers that the circumstances are exceptional, relating not only to that person but also to that person's proposed civil partner[4].

1   As to the meaning of 'registering officer' see PARA 154 note 3.
2   As to a notice of proposed civil partnership see PARA 154.
3   'Evidence', in relation to a person, means evidence:
    (1)   of the person's name and surname (Civil Partnership (Armed Forces) Order 2005, SI 2005/3188, art 8(2)(a));
    (2)   of the person's age (art 8(2)(b)); and
    (3)   as to whether the person has previously formed a civil partnership or a marriage and, if so, as to the ending of the civil partnership or marriage (art 8(2)(c)).
4   Civil Partnership (Armed Forces) Order 2005, SI 2005/3188, art 8(1).

156.   Objection to an intended registration of a proposed civil partnership. Any person may object to an intended registration of a proposed civil partnership[1] giving any registering officer[2] notice of his objection[3]. A notice of objection must:
    (1)   state the objector's place of residence and the ground of objection[4]; and
    (2)   be signed by or on behalf of the objector[5].
If a notice is given to a registering officer, he must ensure that the fact that it has been given and the information in it are recorded as soon as possible[6]. Where an objection has been lodged, the person named therein may not form a civil partnership until either the objection has been withdrawn by the person who entered it, or the registering officer is satisfied that the objection ought not to obstruct the person named from forming a civil partnership[7].

1   As to a proposed civil partnership see PARA 154.
2   As to the meaning of 'registering officer' see PARA 154 note 3.
3   Civil Partnership (Armed Forces) Order 2005, SI 2005/3188, art 10(1).
4   Civil Partnership (Armed Forces) Order 2005, SI 2005/3188, art 10(2)(a).
5   Civil Partnership (Armed Forces) Order 2005, SI 2005/3188, art 10(2)(b).
6   Civil Partnership (Armed Forces) Order 2005, SI 2005/3188, art 10(3).
7   Civil Partnership (Armed Forces) Order 2005, SI 2005/3188, art 10(4).

157.   Publicising of proposed civil partnership. Where a notice of proposed civil partnership[1] has been given to a registering officer[2], he must keep the relevant information[3] on public display within a conspicuous place in his office during the waiting period[4].

1   As to a proposed civil partnership see PARA 154.
2   As to the meaning of 'registering officer' see PARA 154 note 3.
3   For these purposes 'relevant information' means:
    (1)   the name of the person giving the notice (Civil Partnership (Armed Forces) Order 2005, SI 2005/3188, art 9(2)(a)); and
    (2)   the name of that person's proposed civil partner (art 9(2)(b)).
4   Civil Partnership (Armed Forces) Order 2005, SI 2005/3188, art 9(1). For these purposes, 'waiting period' means the period beginning the day after the notice is recorded and ending at the end of the period of 15 days beginning with that day: art 9(3).

158.   Formation of civil partnership by registration. Two people are to be regarded as having registered as civil partners[1] of each other once each of them has signed the civil partnership register[2]:

(1)   at the invitation of, and in the presence of, a registering officer[3]; and

(2)   in the presence of each other and two witnesses[4].

After the civil partnership register has been signed it must also be signed in the presence of the civil partners and each other, by each of the two witnesses, and the registering officer[5].

No religious service is to be used while the registering officer is officiating at the signing of a civil partnership register[6].

1   As to the meaning of civil partner see PARA 2 note 1.
2   Civil Partnership (Armed Forces) Order 2005, SI 2005/3188, art 12(1). This applies regardless of whether art 12(3) (see the text and note 5) has been complied with: art 12(2). 'Civil partnership register' means a register supplied to the registering officer by the Registrar General for England and Wales: art 1(2). As to the meaning of 'register' see PARA 133 note 7. As to the meaning of 'registering officer' see PARA 154 note 3. As to the meaning of 'Registrar General' see PARA 46 note 5.
3   Civil Partnership (Armed Forces) Order 2005, SI 2005/3188, art 12(1)(a).
4   Civil Partnership (Armed Forces) Order 2005, SI 2005/3188, art 12(1)(b).
5   Civil Partnership (Armed Forces) Order 2005, SI 2005/3188, art 12(3).
6   Civil Partnership (Armed Forces) Order 2005, SI 2005/3188, art 12(4).

159.   Time for civil partnership. The proposed civil partners[1] may not register as civil partners of each other until the waiting period[2] in relation to each notice of proposed civil partnership[3] has expired[4]. They may register as civil partners of each other by signing the civil partnership register[5] before a registering officer[6] at his office on any day in the applicable period[7] at a time to be set by him[8]. If they do not register as civil partners before the end of the applicable period the notices of proposed civil partnership are void, and no registering officer may officiate at the signing of the civil partnership register by them[9].

1   As to the meaning of 'civil partners' see PARA 2 note 1.
2   As to the meaning of 'waiting period' see PARA 157 note 4.
3   As to notices of proposed civil partnership see PARA 154.
4   Civil Partnership (Armed Forces) Order 2005, SI 2005/3188, art 11(1).
5   As to the meaning of 'civil partnership register' see PARA 158 note 2.
6   As to the meaning of 'registering officer' see PARA 154 note 3.
7   'Applicable period' means in relation to two people registering as civil partners of each other, the period of 12 months beginning with the day on which the notices of proposed civil partnerships are recorded or, if the notices are not recorded on the same day, the earlier of those days: Civil Partnership (Armed Forces) Order 2005, SI 2005/3188, art 11(4).
8   Civil Partnership (Armed Forces) Order 2005, SI 2005/3188, art 11(2).
9   Civil Partnership (Armed Forces) Order 2005, SI 2005/3188, art 11(3).

160.   Commanding officer's certificate of no impediment to civil partnership. Where two people wish to register as civil partners[1] of each other in England and Wales and one of them, the applicant, is an officer, seaman or marine borne on the books of one of Her Majesty's ships at sea and the other is resident in England and Wales, the applicant must give signed notice of his intention to form the civil partnership with the other person in England and Wales to the officer[2] containing the following information[3]:

(1)   name[4];

(2)   surname[5];

(3)   whether he or she is or has been a civil partner or married[6]; and

(4)   the name and surname of the proposed civil partner[7].

The notice must include a declaration signed by the applicant in the presence of the officer declaring that he believes that there is no impediment of kindred or affinity[8] or other lawful hindrance to the formation of the civil partnership and the officer must attest the declaration by adding his name, description and place of residence[9]. The officer having been given the notice and having attested the declaration may issue a certificate that no legal impediment to the formation of the civil partnership has been shown to the officer to exist[10].

The officer may demand evidence of any of the information contained in the signed notice[11] and must file every such notice given within the archives of his ship[12].

1   As to the meaning of 'civil partners' see PARA 2 note 1.
2   'Officer' means the captain or other officer in command of the ship: Civil Partnership (Armed Forces) Order 2005, SI 2005/3188, art 14(2). Article 14 is made pursuant to the Civil Partnership Act 2004 s 239 (amended by SI 2005/2000), which provides that Her Majesty may by Order in Council make provision in relation to cases where two people wish to register as civil partners of each other in England and Wales under the Civil Partnership Act 2004 Pt 2 Chapter 1 (ss 2–35), and one of them is an officer, seaman or marine borne on the books of one of Her Majesty's ships at sea and the other is resident in England and Wales for the issue to the officer by the captain or other officer in command of the ship, of a certificate of no impediment (s 239(1) (amended by SI 2005/2000)). The Order may provide for the issue of the certificate to be subject to the giving of such notice and the making of such declarations as may be prescribed: Civil Partnership Act 2004 s 239(2). A certificate of no impediment is a certificate that no legal impediment to the formation of the civil partnership has been shown to the officer issuing the certificate to exist: s 239(3) (amended by SI 2005/2000).
3   Civil Partnership (Armed Forces) Order 2005, SI 2005/3188, art 14(1), (2).
4   Civil Partnership (Armed Forces) Order 2005, SI 2005/3188, art 14(2)(a).
5   Civil Partnership (Armed Forces) Order 2005, SI 2005/3188, art 14(2)(b).
6   Civil Partnership (Armed Forces) Order 2005, SI 2005/3188, art 14(2)(c).
7   Civil Partnership (Armed Forces) Order 2005, SI 2005/3188, art 14(2)(d).
8   As to degrees of affinity see PARA 37.
9   Civil Partnership Armed Forces) Order 2005, SI 2005/3188, art 14(3).
10 Civil Partnership Armed Forces) Order 2005, SI 2005/3188, art 14(6).
11 Civil Partnership Armed Forces) Order 2005, SI 2005/3188, art 14(4).
12 Civil Partnership Armed Forces) Order 2005, SI 2005/3188, art 14(5).

(7) MARRIAGE OF SERIOUSLY ILL PERSONS BY REGISTRAR GENERAL'S LICENCE

161. Marriages of seriously ill persons. The Registrar General[1] may issue a licence for the solemnisation of marriage if he is satisfied that one of the persons to be married is seriously ill, is not expected to recover and cannot be moved to a place at which the marriage could[2] be solemnised[3].

Any marriage which may be solemnised on the authority of certificates of a superintendent registrar[4] may be solemnised on the authority of the Registrar General's licence[5] elsewhere than at a registered building[6], the office of a superintendent registrar or approved premises[7]; but any such marriage must not be solemnised according to the rites of the Church of England or the Church in Wales[8].

1   As to the meaning of 'Registrar General' see PARA 46 note 5.
2   Ie under the provisions of the Marriage Act 1949: see PARA 54.
3   Marriage (Registrar General's Licence) Act 1970 s 1(2) (amended by the Marriage Act 1983 s 2(3)). For these purposes, the provisions of the Marriage Act 1949 relating to marriages in pursuance of s 26(1)(dd) (see PARA 54) are to be disregarded: Marriage (Registrar General's Licence) Act 1970 s 1(2).
4   As to the meaning of 'superintendent registrar' see PARA 22 note 1. As to the marriages which may be so solemnised see PARA 54; and as to the grant of certificates see PARA 95 et seq.

5   As to the grant of such a licence see PARA 165.
6   As to the meaning of 'registered building' see PARA 54 note 3.
7   Marriage (Registrar General's Licence) Act 1970 s 1(1) (amended by the Marriage Act 1994 Schedule para 9; the Immigration and Asylum Act 1999 Sch 14 paras 38, 39). As to the meaning of 'approved premises' see PARA 54 note 6.
8   Marriage (Registrar General's Licence) Act 1970 s 1(1) proviso. Nothing in the Marriage (Registrar General's Licence) Act 1970 affects the right of the Archbishop of Canterbury or of any other person by virtue of the Ecclesiastical Licences Act 1533 (see PARA 76) to grant special licences to marry at any convenient time or place, or affects the validity of any marriage solemnised on the authority of such a licence: Marriage (Registrar General's Licence) Act 1970 s 19. As to special licences see PARAS 58, 76.

162.   Notice of marriage.   Where a marriage is intended to be solemnised on the authority of the Registrar General's[1] licence[2], notice must be given in the prescribed form[3], by either of the persons to be married, to the superintendent registrar[4] of the registration district[5] in which it is intended that the marriage is to be solemnised; and the notice must state by or before whom it is intended that the marriage is to be solemnised[6].

1   As to the meaning of 'Registrar General' see PARA 46 note 5.
2   As to the grant of such a licence see PARA 165.
3   As to the prescribed form of notice see the Registration of Marriage Regulations 1986, SI 1986/1442, Sch 1, Form 3 (amended by SI 2000/3164; SI 2005/3177). The Registrar General, with the approval of the Secretary of State, may by statutory instrument make regulations prescribing anything which is required in the Marriage (Registrar General's Licence) Act 1970 to be prescribed: s 18(1) (amended by SI 1996/273; SI 2008/678). Any power to make regulations includes power to vary or revoke those regulations: Marriage (Registrar General's Licence) Act 1970 s 18(2). In exercise of the power so conferred the Registrar General made the Registration of Marriage Regulations 1986, SI 1986/1442 (amended by SI 1987/2088; SI 1995/744; SI 1997/2204; SI 2000/3164; SI 2005/155; SI 2005/3177; SI 2007/2164).
4   As to the meaning of 'superintendent registrar' see PARA 22 note 1.
5   As to the meaning of 'registration district' see PARA 87 note 4.
6   Marriage (Registrar General's Licence) Act 1970 s 2(1). The provisions of the Marriage Act 1949 s 27(4) (entries in the marriage notice book: see PARA 92) apply to notices of marriage on the authority of the Registrar General's licence: Marriage (Registrar General's Licence) Act 1970 ss 1(2), 2(2). The provisions of the Marriage Act 1949 s 28 (declaration to accompany notice of marriage: see PARA 90) apply to the giving of notice under the Marriage (Registrar General's Licence) Act 1970 with the exception of the Marriage Act 1949 s 28(1)(b) and with the modification that in s 28(2) references to the registrar of births and deaths or of marriages and deputy registrar are to be omitted: Marriage (Registrar General's Licence) Act 1970 ss 1(2), 2(3). A fee of £3 is payable by the Registrar General to the superintendent registrar for the entry of the notice of marriage: s 17(2).

163.   Evidence of capacity, consent etc to be produced.   The person giving notice of marriage by Registrar General's licence[1] must produce to the superintendent registrar[2] such evidence as the Registrar General may require to satisfy him:

(1)   that there is no lawful impediment to the marriage[3];
(2)   that the consent of any person whose consent to the marriage is required[4] has been duly given[5];
(3)   that there is sufficient reason why a licence should be granted[6]; and
(4)   that one of the persons to be married is seriously ill, is not expected to recover and cannot be moved to a place at which the marriage could normally be solemnised[7], and that the sick person is able to, and does, understand the nature and purport of the marriage ceremony[8].

On receipt of the notice of marriage and the evidence so required, the superintendent registrar must inform the Registrar General and must comply with any directions he may give for verifying the evidence given[9].

1 Ie under the Marriage (Registrar General's Licence) Act 1970 s 2: see PARA 162. As to the meaning of 'Registrar General' see PARA 46 note 5.

2 As to the meaning of 'superintendent registrar' see PARA 22 note 1.

3 Marriage (Registrar General's Licence) Act 1970 s 3(a). If a person gives false information by way of evidence, he is guilty of an offence: see PARA 183.

4 Ie under the Marriage Act 1949 s 3: see PARAS 46–48. The provisions of s 3 apply for the purposes of the Marriage (Registrar General's Licence) Act 1970 to a marriage intended to be solemnised by Registrar General's licence as they apply to a marriage intended to be solemnised on the authority of certificates of a superintendent registrar under the Marriage Act 1949 Pt III (ss 26–52) (see PARA 54 et seq) with the modification that, if the consent of any person whose consent is required cannot be obtained by reason of absence or inaccessibility or by reason of his being under any disability, the superintendent registrar is not required to dispense with the necessity for that person's consent and the Registrar General may dispense with the necessity of obtaining that person's consent, whether or not there is any other person whose consent is also required: Marriage (Registrar General's Licence) Act 1970 ss 1(2), 6 (amended by the Immigration and Asylum Act 1999 Sch 14 paras 38, 41).

5 Marriage (Registrar General's Licence) Act 1970 ss 1(2), 3(b) (amended by the Children Act 1989 Sch 15). See also note 3. Proof of such a matter is not necessary to the validity of the marriage, once solemnised: see the Marriage Act 1949 s 48(1)(b) (applied by the Marriage (Registrar General's Licence) Act 1970 s 12); and PARA 22.

6 Marriage (Registrar General's Licence) Act 1970 s 3(c). See also note 3.

7 Ie the conditions contained in the Marriage (Registrar General's Licence) Act 1970 s 1(2) must be satisfied: see PARA 161.

8 Marriage (Registrar General's Licence) Act 1970 s 3(d). See also note 3. The certificate of a registered medical practitioner is sufficient evidence of any or all of the matters referred to in s 3(d): s 3 proviso. 'Registered medical practitioner' means a fully registered person within the meaning of the Medical Act 1983 (see MEDICAL PROFESSIONS vol 30(1) (Reissue) PARAS 3–4): Interpretation Act 1978 Sch 1 (amended by the Medical Act 1983 Sch 5 para 18).

9 Marriage (Registrar General's Licence) Act 1970 s 4.

164.   Caveat.   A caveat may be entered against the issue of the Registrar General's[1] licence in the same way as a caveat against the issue of a superintendent registrar's[2] certificate[3]; but a caveat in respect of the Registrar General's licence may be entered with either the superintendent registrar or the Registrar General, and in either case it is for the Registrar General to examine into the matter of the caveat and to decide whether or not the licence should be granted, and his decision is final[4].

1 As to the meaning of 'Registrar General' see PARA 46 note 5.

2 As to the meaning of 'superintendent registrar' see PARA 22 note 1.

3 Ie the provisions of the Marriage Act 1949 s 29 (see PARA 96) apply with modifications: see the text and note 4.

4 Marriage (Registrar General's Licence) Act 1970 ss 1(2), 5 (amended by the Immigration and Asylum Act 1999 Sch 14 paras 30, 40, Sch 16). The references to the superintendent registrar in the Marriage Act 1949 s 29 are to be taken to refer to the superintendent registrar of the registration district in which the marriage is intended to be solemnised: Marriage (Registrar General's Licence) Act 1970 s 5. As to the meaning of 'registration district' see PARA 87 note 4.

165.   Issue of licence by Registrar General; period of validity.   Where the marriage is intended to be solemnised on the authority of the Registrar General[1] and he is satisfied that sufficient grounds exist why a licence should be granted, he must issue a licence in the prescribed form[2] unless any lawful impediment to the issue of the licence has been shown to his satisfaction to exist or the issue of the licence has[3] been forbidden[4].

A marriage may be solemnised on the authority of the Registrar General's licence at any time within one month from the day on which the notice of marriage was entered in the marriage notice book[5]. If the marriage is not solemnised within that period, the notice of marriage and the licence are void, and no person may solemnise the marriage on the authority of them[6].

1   As to the meaning of 'Registrar General' see PARA 46 note 5.
2   For the prescribed form of notice see the Registration of Marriage Regulations 1986, SI 1986/1442, Sch 1, Form 11 (amended by SI 2000/3164; SI 2005/3177). A fee of £15 is payable to the Registrar General in respect of the issue of his licence; and he has power to remit the fee, in whole or in part, in any case where it appears to him that the payment of that fee would cause hardship to the parties to the intended marriage: Marriage (Registrar General's Licence) Act 1970 s 17(1).
3   Ie under the Marriage Act 1949 s 30: see PARA 95.
4   Marriage (Registrar General's Licence) Act 1970 s 7.
5   Marriage (Registrar General's Licence) Act 1970 s 8(1). For these purposes, 'marriage notice book' has the same meaning as in the Marriage Act 1949 s 78(1) (see PARA 92): Marriage (Registrar General's Licence) Act 1970 s 20(2).
6   Marriage (Registrar General's Licence) Act 1970 s 8(2). If any person does so solemnise the marriage, he is guilty of an offence: see PARA 183.

166.   Place and manner of solemnisation.   A marriage on the authority of the Registrar General's[1] licence must be solemnised in the place stated in the notice of marriage[2].

Such a marriage must be solemnised at the wish of the persons to be married either:

(1)   according to such form or ceremony, not being the rites or ceremonies of the Church of England or the Church in Wales, as the persons to be married see fit to adopt[3]; or

(2)   by civil ceremony[4].

Except where the marriage is solemnised according to the usages of the Society of Friends[5] or is a marriage between two persons professing the Jewish religion according to the usages of the Jews[6]:

(a)   it must be solemnised in the presence of a registrar[7], save that, where the marriage is to be by civil ceremony, it must be solemnised in the presence of the superintendent registrar[8] as well as the registrar[9]; and

(b)   the persons to be married must in some part of the ceremony in the presence of two or more witnesses and the registrar, and, where appropriate, the superintendent registrar, make the prescribed declaration and say to one another the prescribed[10] words[11].

If a marriage is solemnised in the presence of a registrar of marriages and before, during or immediately after solemnisation of the marriage the registrar has reasonable grounds for suspecting that the marriage will be, or is, a sham marriage[12], he must report his suspicion to the Secretary of State without delay and in such form and manner as may be prescribed by regulations[13].

1   As to the meaning of 'Registrar General' see PARA 46 note 5.
2   Marriage (Registrar General's Licence) Act 1970 s 9. As to where such marriage cannot be solemnised see PARA 161.
3   Marriage (Registrar General's Licence) Act 1970 s 10(1)(a). No person who is a clergyman within the meaning of the Marriage Act 1949 s 78(1) (see PARA 23 note 5) may solemnise any marriage which is solemnised on the authority of the Registrar General: Marriage (Registrar General's Licence) Act 1970 s 10(4).
4   Marriage (Registrar General's Licence) Act 1970 s 10(1)(b).
5   As to marriage according to the usages of the Society of Friends see PARA 116.
6   As to marriage between persons professing the Jewish religion according to the usages of the Jews see PARA 118.
7   For these purposes, 'registrar' has the same meaning as in the Marriage Act 1949 s 78(1) (see PARA 88 note 1): Marriage (Registrar General's Licence) Act 1970 s 20(2).
8   As to the meaning of 'superintendent registrar' see PARA 22 note 1.
9   Marriage (Registrar General's Licence) Act 1970 s 10(2). A fee of £2 is payable by the Registrar General to a superintendent registrar, and also to a registrar, for attending a marriage by

Registrar General's licence and these fees are to be retained by those officers: s 17(2). It is an offence to solemnise the marriage without the presence of a registrar, except in the case of a Quaker or Jewish marriage: see PARA 183.

10 Ie the declaration and words prescribed by the Marriage Act 1949 s 44(3) or s 44(3A): see PARA 105.

11 Marriage (Registrar General's Licence) Act 1970 s 10(3) (amended by the Marriage Ceremony (Prescribed Words) Act 1996 s 1(2)(b)).

12 As to sham marriages see PARA 11.

13 Immigration and Asylum Act 1999 s 24(2), (3). As to the prescribed form and manner see PARA 11 note 7.

167. Civil marriage followed by religious ceremony. If the parties to a marriage solemnised on the authority of the Registrar General's[1] licence before a superintendent registrar[2] desire to add the religious ceremony ordained or used by the church or persuasion of which they are members and have given notice of their desire to do so, a clergyman[3] or minister of that church or persuasion may, if he sees fit, on the production of a certificate of their marriage before the superintendent registrar and on payment of the customary fees, if any, read or celebrate in the presence of the parties to the marriage the marriage service of the church or persuasion to which he belongs or nominate some other minister to do so[4].

1 As to the meaning of 'Registrar General' see PARA 46 note 5.

2 As to the meaning of 'superintendent registrar' see PARA 22 note 1.

3 For these purposes 'clergyman' has the same meaning as in the Marriage Act 1949 s 78(1) (see PARA 23 note 5): Marriage (Registrar General's Licence) Act 1970 s 20(2).

4 Marriage (Registrar General's Licence) Act 1970 s 11(1). The provisions of the Marriage Act 1949 s 46(2), (3) (see PARA 57) apply to such a reading or celebration as they apply to the reading or celebration of a marriage service following a marriage solemnised in the office of a superintendent registrar: Marriage (Registrar General's Licence) Act 1970 ss 1(2), 11(2).

168. Documentary authority for marriage. Where a marriage is to be solemnised on the authority of the Registrar General's[1] licence, a document issued by the superintendent registrar[2] stating that the Registrar General's licence has been granted and that authority for the marriage to be solemnised has been given must be delivered before the marriage:

(1)   if the marriage is to be solemnised according to the usages of the Society of Friends[3], to the registering officer of that Society for the place where the marriage is to be solemnised[4];

(2)   if the marriage is to be solemnised according to the usages of persons professing the Jewish religion[5], to the officer of the synagogue by whom the marriage is required to be registered[6]; and

(3)   in any other case, to the registrar[7] in whose presence the marriage is[8] to be solemnised[9].

Such a marriage must be registered in accordance with the statutory provisions[10] which apply to the registration of marriages solemnised in the presence of a registrar or according to the usages of the Society of Friends or of persons professing the Jewish religion[11].

1 As to the meaning of 'Registrar General' see PARA 46 note 5.

2 As to the meaning of 'superintendent registrar' see PARA 22 note 1.

3 As to marriage according to the usages of the Society of Friends see PARA 116.

4 Marriage (Registrar General's Licence) Act 1970 s 14(a).

5 As to marriage according to the usages of persons professing the Jewish religion see PARA 118.

6 Marriage (Registrar General's Licence) Act 1970 s 14(b).

7 As to the meaning of 'registrar' see PARA 88 note 1.

8   Ie under the Marriage Act 1949 Pt IV (ss 53–67): see REGISTRATION CONCERNING THE INDIVIDUAL.
9   Marriage (Registrar General's Licence) Act 1970 s 14(c).
10   Ie the provisions of the Marriage Act 1949: see PARAS 115–118. As to offences in relation to the registration of marriages and a Registrar General's licence see PARAS 181, 183.
11   Marriage (Registrar General's Licence) Act 1970 ss 1(2), 15.

(8) HOUSEBOUND OR DETAINED PERSONS

169. Housebound persons. A person is 'housebound' if in relation to him a statement is made by a registered medical practitioner[1] that:

(1)   because of illness or disability he ought not to move or be moved from the place where he is at the time when the statement is made[2]; and

(2)   it is likely to be the case for at least the following three months that because of the illness or disability that person ought not to move or be moved from that place[3],

and he is not a detained person[4]. In order for a person to qualify as 'housebound' for these purposes each notice of his or her marriage[5] or proposed civil partnership[6] must be accompanied by a statement to the above effect[7].

1   As to registered medical practitoners see MEDICAL PRACTITIONERS vol 30(1) (Reissue) PARA 4.
2   Marriage Act 1949 ss 27A(7), 78(3) (ss 27A, 78(3) added by the Marriage Act 1983 Sch 1 paras 6, 21); Marriage Act 1983 s 1(2)(a)(i); Civil Partnership Act 2004 s 18(2)(a).
3   Marriage Act 1949 s 27A(7) (as added: see note 2); Marriage Act 1983 s 1(2)(a)(ii); Civil Partnership Act 2004 s 18(2)(b).
4   Marriage Act 1949 s 78(3)(b) (as added: see note 2); Marriage Act 1983 s 1(2)(b); Civil Partnership Act 2004 s 18(5). As to detained persons see PARA 170.
5   Ie in accordance with the Marriage Act 1949 s 27 (see PARA 87).
6   As to giving notice of a proposed civil partnership see PARA 133.
7   See the Marriage Act 1949 ss 27A(3), 78(3); the Marriage Act 1983 s 1(2); the Civil Partnership Act 2004 s 18(3); and PARA 174.

170. Detained persons. A person is a 'detained person' if he or she is for the time being detained:

(1)   as a patient in a hospital[1] otherwise than by virtue of a short-term detention[2] under the Mental Health Act 1983[3];

(2)   in a prison or other place to which the Prison Act 1952 applies[4].

1   'Patient' and 'hospital' have the same meanings as in the Mental Health Act 1983 Pt II (ss 2–34) (see MENTAL HEALTH vol 30(2) (Reissue) PARAS 435, 415 respectively): Marriage Act 1949 s 78(4) (added by the Marriage Act 1983 Sch 1 para 21); Marriage Act 1983 s 1(4); Civil Partnership Act 2004 s 19(7).
2   Ie a detention under the Mental Health Act 1983 s 2, 4, 5, 35, 36 or 136 (see MENTAL HEALTH).
3   Marriage Act 1949 s 78(4)(a) (as added: see note 1); Marriage Act 1983 s 1(4)(a); Civil Partnership Act 2004 s 19(2)(a).
4   Marriage Act 1949 s 78(4)(b) (as added: see note 1); Marriage Act 1983 s 1(4)(b); Civil Partnership Act 2004 s 19(2)(b).

171. Marriages of housebound and detained persons. The marriage of a person who is housebound[1] or is a detained person[2] may be solemnised in England and Wales, on the authority of certificates of a superintendent registrar[3], at the place where that person usually resides[4].

Nothing in these provisions is to be taken to relate or have any reference to any marriage according to the uses of the Society of Friends[5] or any marriage between two persons professing the Jewish religion[6] according to the usages of the Jews[7].

1   As to the meaning of 'housebound' see PARA 169.
2   As to the meaning of 'detained' see PARA 170.
3   Ie a certificate issued under the Marriage Act 1949 Pt III (ss 26–52): see PARA 54 et seq. As to the meaning of 'superintendent registrar' see PARA 22 note 1.
4   Marriage Act 1949 s 26(1)(dd) (added by the Marriage Act 1983 Sch 1 para 4); Marriage Act 1983 s 1(1) (amended by the Immigration and Asylum Act 1999 Sch 14 para 77(a)). For these purposes, a person who is housebound or is a detained person is to be taken, if he or she would not otherwise be, to be usually resident at the place where he or she is for the time being: Marriage Act 1949 s 78(5) (added by the Marriage Act 1983 Sch 1 para 21); Marriage Act 1983 s 1(5).
5   As to marriages according to the uses of the Society of Friends see PARA 116.
6   As to marriages between two persons professing the Jewish religion according to the usages of the Jews see PARA 118.
7   Marriage Act 1983 s 1(6).

172. Notice of marriage of housebound and detained persons to be solemnised at a person's residence or place of detention. The following provisions apply in relation to any marriage[1] intended to be solemnised, otherwise than according to the usages of the Society of Friends or between persons professing the Jewish religion according to the usages of the Jews, at the residence of a person who is housebound[2] or is a detained person[3] (the 'relevant person')[4].

Where the relevant person is not a detained person, each notice of marriage[5] must be accompanied by a medical statement[6] relating to that person made not more than 14 days before the date on which the notice is given[7].

Where the relevant person is a detained person, each notice of marriage[8] must be accompanied by a statement made in the prescribed form[9] by the responsible authority[10] not more than 21 days before the date on which notice of the marriage is given:

(1)   identifying the establishment where the person is detained[11]; and
(2)   stating that the responsible authority has no objection to that establishment being specified in the notice of marriage as the place where that marriage is to be solemnised[12].

Each person who gives notice of the marriage to the superintendent registrar must give the superintendent registrar the prescribed particulars, in the prescribed form[13], of the person by or before whom the marriage is intended to be solemnised[14].

The superintendent registrar must not enter the particulars given in the marriage notice book[15] until he has received the required[16] statement and particulars[17].

The fact that a superintendent registrar has received a statement[18] must be entered in the marriage notice book together with the particulars given in the notice of marriage; and any such statement together with the form received by the superintendent registrar[19] must be filed and kept with the records of the office of the superintendent registrar or, where notice of marriage is required to be given to two superintendent registrars, of each of them[20].

1   Ie any marriage intended to be solemnised at a person's residence in pursuance of the Marriage Act 1949 s 26(1)(dd) (see PARA 171).
2   As to the meaning of 'housebound' see PARA 169.
3   As to the meaning of 'detained person' see PARA 170.
4   Marriage Act 1949 s 27A(1) (added by the Marriage Act 1983 Sch 1 para 6). The superintendent registrar is entitled to receive from any person intending to be married in pursuance of the Marriage Act 1949 s 26(1)(dd) on whom he attends at a place other than his office in order to be given notice of marriage the sum of £47: s 27(7) (added by the Marriage Act 1983, Sch 1 paras 1, 5; amended by SI 2002/3076; SI 2005/1997). As to the meaning of 'superintendent registrar' see PARA 22 note 1.

5 Ie the notice required by the Marriage Act 1949 s 27: see PARA 87.

6 'Medical statement' means a statement in the form prescribed by the Registration of Marriages Regulation 1986, SI 1986/1442, reg 5(a), Sch 1 Form 5 (amended by SI 2000/3164) by a registered medical practitioner that in his opinion at the time the statement is made the person in question is 'housebound' as described in PARA 169: Marriage Act 1949 s 27A(2) (added by the Marriage Act 1983 Sch 1 para 6).

7 Marriage Act 1949 s 27A(2) (added by the Marriage Act 1983 Sch 1 para 6; amended by the Immigration and Asylum Act 1999 Sch 14 paras 3, 9(a)); Marriage Act 1983 s 1(2)(a) (amended by the Immigration and Asylum Act 1999 Sch 14 para 77).

8 See note 5.

9 For the prescribed form of statement see the Registration of Marriages Regulations 1986, SI 1986/1442, Sch 1, Form 6 (amended by SI 2000/3164).

10 For these purposes, 'responsible authority' means: (1) if the person is detained in a hospital, within the meaning of the Mental Health Act 1983 Pt II (ss 2–34: see MENTAL HEALTH vol 30(2) (Reissue) PARA 417), the managers of that hospital, within the meaning of s 145(1) (see MENTAL HEALTH vol 30(2) (Reissue) PARA 439); or (2) if the person is detained in a prison or other place to which the Prison Act 1952 applies (see PRISONS), the governor or other officer for the time being in charge of that prison or other place: Marriage Act 1949 s 27A(7) (added by the Marriage Act 1983 Sch 1 para 6)).

11 Marriage Act 1949 s 27A(3)(a) (added by the Marriage Act 1983 Sch 1 para 6; amended by the Immigration and Asylum Act 1999 Sch 14 paras 3, 9).

12 Marriage Act 1949 s 27A(3)(b) (added by the Marriage Act 1983 Sch 1 para 6; amended by the Immigration and Asylum Act 1999 Sch 14 paras 3, 9(a)). Such an objection can relate only to the convenience and availability of the establishment in which the marriage can be performed and not to a consideration of public policy matters: *R (on the application of the Crown Prosecution Service) v Registrar for Births, Deaths and Marriages* [2002] EWCA Civ 1661, [2002] QB 1222, [2003] 1 All ER 540.

13 For the prescribed form of particulars see the Registration of Marriages Regulations 1986, SI 1986/1442 Sch 1, Form 7 (amended by SI 2000/3164); and for the corresponding form in Welsh see the Registration of Marriages (Welsh Language) Regulations 1999, SI 1999/1621, Sch 1, Form 4 (amended by SI 2000/3164).

14 Marriage Act 1949 s 27A(4) (added by the Marriage Act 1983 Sch 1 para 6; amended by the Immigration and Asylum Act 1999 Sch 14 paras 3, 9(b)).

15 As to the meaning of 'marriage notice book' see PARA 92.

16 Ie the statement and particulars required by the Marriage Act 1949 s 27A(2), (3) or (4) (see the text and notes 1–14).

17 Marriage Act 1949 s 27A(5) (added by the Marriage Act 1983 Sch 1 para 6).

18 Ie under the Marriage Act 1949 s 27A(2) or, as the case may be, s 27A(3).

19 Ie the form received under Marriage Act 1949 s 27A(4).

20 Marriage Act 1949 s 27A(6) (added by the Marriage Act 1983 Sch 1 para 6; amended by the Immigration and Asylum Act 1999 Sch 14 paras 3, 9(c)).

173. Solemnisation of marriage at place of residence. The marriage of a person who is housebound[1] or is a detained person[2] at the place where he or she usually resides[3] may be solemnised according to the rites of the Church of England[4].

The marriage, otherwise than according to the rites of the Church of England, the usages of the Society of Friends or between two persons professing the Jewish religion according to the usages of the Jews, may be solemnised according to a relevant form, rite or ceremony[5] in the presence of a registrar[6] of the registration district[7] in which the place where the marriage is solemnised is situated and of two witnesses; and each of the persons contracting the marriage must make the prescribed declaration and use the prescribed form of words[8] as are required in the case of marriages in registered buildings[9].

Where such a marriage is not so solemnised, it must be solemnised in the presence of the superintendent registrar[10] and a registrar of the registration district in which the place where the marriage is solemnised is situated and in the presence of two witnesses; and the persons to be married must make the prescribed declaration[11] and use the prescribed form of words[12] as are required in the case of marriages in registered buildings[13]. No religious service may, however, be used at any marriage solemnised in the presence of a superintendent registrar[14].

If a marriage is solemnised in the presence of a registrar of marriages and before, during or immediately after solemnisation of the marriage the registrar has reasonable grounds for suspecting that the marriage will be, or is, a sham marriage[15], he must report his suspicion to the Secretary of State without delay and in such form and manner as may be prescribed by regulations[16].

A marriage solemnised at a person's residence in the presence of a registrar must be registered by that registrar[17].

1   As to the meaning of 'housebound' see PARA 169.
2   As to the meaning of 'detained person' see PARA 170.
3   Ie a marriage solemnised in pursuance of the Marriage Act 1949 s 26(1)(dd): see PARA 161.
4   See the Marriage Act 1949 s 17; and PARA 54.
5   For these purposes, 'relevant form, rite or ceremony' means a form, rite or ceremony of a body of persons who meet for religious worship in any registered building, being a form, rite or ceremony in accordance with which members of that body are married in any such registered building: Marriage Act 1949 s 45A(5) (added by the Marriage Act 1983 s 1(7), Sch 1 paras 1, 11). As to the meaning of 'registered building' see PARA 54 note 3.
6   As to the meaning of 'registrar' see PARA 88 note 1.
7   As to the meaning of 'registration district' see PARA 87 note 4.
8   Ie the declaration and form of words set out in the Marriage Act 1949 s 44(3) or s 44(3A): see PARA 105.
9   Marriage Act 1949 s 45A(1), (2) (added by the Marriage Act 1983 Sch 1 paras 1, 11; amended by the Marriage Ceremony (Prescribed Words) Act 1996 s 1(2)).
10 As to the meaning of 'superintendent registrar' see PARA 22 note 1.
11 See note 8.
12 See note 8.
13 Marriage Act 1949 s 45A(3) (added by the Marriage Act 1983 Sch 1 paras 1, 11; amended by the Marriage Ceremony (Prescribed Words) Act 1996 s 1(2)).
14 Marriage Act 1949 s 45A(4) (added by the Marriage Act 1983 Sch 1 paras 1, 11). A religious ceremony may, however, follow a marriage in the presence of a superintendent registrar (see the Marriage Act 1949 s 46; and PARA 57); but the religious ceremony may not be entered as a marriage in any marriage register book kept under the Marriage Act 1949 (see s 46(2); and PARA 57).
15 As to the meaning of 'sham marriage' see PARA 11.
16 Immigration and Asylum Act 1999 s 24(2), (3). As to the prescribed form and manner see PARA 11 note 7.
17 See the Marriage Act 1949 s 53(d) (amended by the Marriage Act 1983 Sch 1 paras 1, 16); and REGISTRATION CONCERNING THE INDIVIDUAL vol 39(2) (Reissue) PARA 558.

174.   Civil partnerships of housebound persons. Where two people wish to register as civil partners[1] of each other at the place where one of them is housebound[2], the procedure under which they may register as civil partners of each other is the same as the standard procedure[3] except that:

(1)   each notice of proposed civil partnership[4] must be accompanied by a medical statement[5] which must have been made not more than 14 days before the day on which the notice is recorded[6];

(2)   the fact that the registration authority[7] to whom the notice is given has received the medical statement must be recorded in the register[8]; and

(3)   the applicable period[9] is the period of three months beginning with:
   (a)   the day on which the notices of proposed civil partnership are recorded[10]; or
   (b)   if the notices are not recorded on the same day, the earlier of those days[11].

1   As to the meaning of 'civil partner' see PARA 2 note 1.

2   As to the meaning of 'housebound' see PARA 169.

3   As to the standard procedure see PARA 133 et seq.

4   As to notice of proposed civil partnership see PARA 133.

5   Ie a statement under the Civil Partnership Act 2004 s 18(2): see PARA 169 note 2. A medical statement must contain such information and must be made in such manner as may be prescribed by regulations: s 18(4). As to such information see the Civil Partnership (Registration Provisions) Regulations 2005, SI 2005/3176, Forms 6, 6(w). A medical statement may not be made in relation to a person who is detained: Civil Partnership Act 2004 s 18(5).

6   Civil Partnership Act 2004 s 18(1), (3)(a).

7   As to the meaning of 'registration authority' see PARA 133 note 2.

8   Civil Partnership Act 2004 s 18(3)(b). As to the meaning of 'register' see PARA 133 note 7.

9   Ie for the purposes of the Civil Partnership Act 2004 s 17 (see PARA 139).

10 Civil Partnership Act 2004 s 18(3)(c)(i).

11 Civil Partnership Act 2004 s 18(3)(c)(ii).

175.   Civil partnerships of detained persons. Where two people wish to register as civil partners[1] of each other at the place where one of them is detained[2], the procedure under which they may register as civil partners of each other is the same as the standard procedure[3] except that:

(1)   each notice of proposed civil partnership[4] must be accompanied by a supporting statement[5], which must have been made not more than 21 days before the day on which the notice is recorded[6];

(2)   the fact that the registration authority to whom the notice is given has received the supporting statement must be recorded in the register[7]; and

(3)   the applicable period[8] is the period of three months beginning with:

   (a)   the day on which the notices of proposed civil partnership are recorded[9]; or

   (b)   if the notices are not recorded on the same day, the earlier of those days[10].

1   As to the meaning of 'civil partner' see PARA 2 note 1.

2   As to the meaning of 'detained' see PARA 170.

3   As to the standard procedure see PARA 133 et seq.

4   As to notice of proposed civil partnership see PARA 133.

5   'Supporting statement' means, in relation to a detained person, a statement made by the responsible authority which:

   (1)   identifies the establishment where the person is detained (Civil Partnership Act 2004 s 19(4)(a)); and

   (2)   states that the responsible authority has no objection to that establishment being specified in a notice of proposed civil partnership as the place at which the person is to register as a civil partner (s 19(4)(b)).

   A supporting statement must contain such information and must be made in such manner as may be prescribed by regulations: s 19(5). As to such prescribed information see the Civil Partnership (Registration Provisions) Regulations 2005, SI 2005/3175, Forms 7, 7(w).

   'Responsible authority' means:

   (a)   if the person is detained in a hospital, the hospital's managers (Civil Partnership Act 2004 s 19(6)(a));

   (b)   if the person is detained in a prison or other place to which the Prison Act 1952 (see PRISONS) applies, the governor or other officer for the time being in charge of that prison or other place (Civil Partnership Act 2004 s 19(6)(b)).

6   Civil Partnership Act 2004 s 19(1), (3)(a).

7   Civil Partnership Act 2004 s 19(3)(b). As to the meaning of 'register' see PARA 133 note 7.

8   Ie for the purposes of the Civil Partnership Act 2004 s 17 (see PARA 139).

9   Civil Partnership Act 2004 s 19(3)(c)(i).

10 Civil Partnership Act 2004 s 19(3)(c)(ii).

(9) PERSONS SUBJECT TO IMMIGRATION CONTROL

176. Marriage where a party is subject to immigration control. Where a marriage is to be solemnised on the authority of certificates issued by a superintendent registrar[1] and a party to the marriage is subject to immigration control[2], the superintendent registrar must not enter in the marriage notice book[3] notice of a marriage unless satisfied, by the provision of specified evidence[4], that the party subject to immigration control:

(1) has an entry clearance[5] granted expressly for the purpose of enabling him to marry in the United Kingdom[6];

(2) has the written permission of the Secretary of State to marry in the United Kingdom[7]; or

(3) falls within a class specified by the Secretary of State[8].

1 Ie under the Marriage Act 1949 Pt III (ss 26–52) (see PARA 87 et seq).
2 Asylum and Immigration (Treatment of Claimants, etc) Act 2004 s 19(1). 'Person subject to immigration control' means a person who is not an EEA national and requires leave to enter or remain in the United Kingdom, whether or not that leave has been given: s 19(4)(a). 'EEA national' means a national of a State which is a contracting party to the Agreement on the European Economic Area (Oporto, 2 May 1992 (Cm 2073; OJ L1, 3.1.94, p 3)): s 19(4)(b).
3 As to the meaning of 'marriage notice book' see PARA 92.
4 'Specified evidence' means such evidence as may be specified in guidance issued by the Registrar General: Asylum and Immigration (Treatment of Claimants, etc) Act 2004 s 19(4)(d).
5 'Entry clearance' has the same meaning as given by the Immigration Act 1971 s 33(1) (see BRITISH NATIONALITY, IMMIGRATION AND ASYLUM vol 4(2) (2002 Reissue) PARA 96): Asylum and Immigration (Treatment of Claimants, etc) Act 2004 s 19(4)(c).
6 Asylum and Immigration (Treatment of Claimants, etc) Act 2004 s 19(3)(a).
7 Asylum and Immigration (Treatment of Claimants, etc) Act 2004 s 19(3)(b). As to permissions see the Immigration (Procedure for Marriage) Regulations 2005, SI 2005/15, regs 7, 8, Sch 2.
8 Asylum and Immigration (Treatment of Claimants, etc) Act 2004 s 19(3)(c). As to the specified classes of persons see the Immigration (Procedure for Marriage) Regulations 2005, SI 2005/15, reg 6.

177. Special provision for the giving of notices. Where a marriage is to be solemnised on the authority of certificates issued by a superintendent registrar[1] and a party to the marriage is subject to immigration control[2], the notices required to be given[3]:

(1) must be given to the superintendent registrar of a registration district specified for these purposes[4];

(2) must be delivered to the superintendent registrar in person by the two parties to the marriage[5];

(3) may be given only if each party to the marriage has been resident in a registration district for the period of seven days immediately before the giving of his or her notice (although the district need not be that in which the notice is given and the parties need not have resided in the same district)[6]; and

(4) must state, in relation to each party, the registration district by reference to which the above provision is satisfied[7].

1 Ie under the Marriage Act 1949 Pt III (ss 26–52) (see PARA 87 et seq).
2 As to the meaning of 'person subject to immigration control' see PARA 176 note 2.
3 Ie under the Marriage Act 1949 s 27: see PARA 87 et seq.
4 Asylum and Immigration (Treatment of Claimants, etc) Act 2004 s 19(1), (2)(a). As to the specified registration districts see the Immigration (Procedure for Marriage) Regulations 2005, SI 2005/15, reg 3, Sch 1.
5 Asylum and Immigration (Treatment of Claimants, etc) Act 2004 s 19(2)(b).

6   Asylum and Immigration (Treatment of Claimants, etc) Act 2004 s 19(2)(c).
7   Asylum and Immigration (Treatment of Claimants, etc) Act 2004 s 19(2)(d).

178.   Civil partnership where a party is subject to immigration control. Where a civil partnership[1] is to be formed in England and Wales by two persons of whom one is subject to immigration control[2], by signing a civil partnership schedule[3]:

(1)   the necessary declaration[4] must include a statement that the person subject to immigration control fulfils the qualifying condition[5], and the reason why[6]; and

(2)   the fact that a notice of proposed civil partnership[7] has been given must not be recorded in the register[8] unless the registration authority[9] is satisfied by the production of specified evidence[10] that the person fulfils the qualifying condition[11].

1   As to the meaning of 'civil partnership' see PARA 2 note 1.
2   See the Civil Partnership Act 2004 s 249. For these purposes, a person is subject to immigration control if: (1) he is not an EEA national; and (2) under the Immigration Act 1971 (see BRITISH NATIONALITY, IMMIGRATION AND ASYLUM) he requires leave to enter or remain in the United Kingdom, whether or not leave has been given: Civil Partnership Act 2004 Sch 23 para 1(2). 'EEA national' means a national of a State which is a contracting party to the Agreement on the European Economic Area (Oporto, 2 May 1992 (Cm 2073; OJ L1, 3.1.94, p 3)), as it has effect from time to time: Civil Partnership Act 2004 Sch 23 para 1(3).
3   As to the meaning of 'civil partnership schedule' see PARA 138.
4   Ic the necessary declaration under the Civil Partnership Act 2004 s 8 (see PARA 133).
5   'Qualifying condition' means that the party subject to immigration control:
     (1)   has an entry clearance granted expressly for the purpose of enabling him to form a civil partnership in the United Kingdom (Civil Partnership Act 2004 Sch 23 para 2(1)(a));
     (2)   has the written permission of the Secretary of State to form a civil partnership in the United Kingdom (Sch 23 para 2(1)(b)); or
     (3)   falls within a class specified by the Secretary of State (Sch 23 para 2(1)(c)).
     As to permissions see the Immigration (Procedure for Formation of Civil Partnerships) Regulation 2005, SI 2005/2917, reg 3, Sch 1; as to the specified classes see reg 4. 'Entry clearance' has the meaning given by the Immigration Act 1971 s 33(1) (see BRITISH NATIONALITY, IMMIGRATION AND ASYLUM vol 4(2) (2002 Reissue) PARA 96): Civil Partnership Act 2004 Sch 23 para 2(2).
6   Civil Partnership Act 2004 Sch 23 para 5.
7   As to the meaning of 'proposed civil partnership' see PARA 133.
8   As to the meaning of 'register' see PARA 133 note 7.
9   As to the meaning of 'registration authority' see PARA 133 note 2.
10   'Specified evidence' means such evidence as may be specified by guidance issued by the Registrar General: Civil Partnership Act 2004 Sch 23 para 6(2).
11   Civil Partnership Act 2004 Sch 23 para 6(1).

179.   Special provision for the giving of notices. Where a civil partnership[1] is to be formed in England and Wales by two persons one of whom is subject to immigration control[2] by signing a civil partnership schedule[3], each notice of proposed civil partnership[4]:

(1)   must be given to a registration authority specified for these purposes[5];

(2)   must be delivered to the relevant individual[6] in person by the two proposed civil partners[7];

(3)   may be given only if each of the proposed civil partners has been resident in the area of a registration authority for the period of seven days immediately before the giving of his or her notice (although the area need not be that in which the notice is given and the proposed civil partners need not have resided in the area of the same registration authority)[8]; and

(4)   must state, in relation to each of the proposed civil partners, the
        registration authority by reference to which the above provision is
        satisfied[9].

1   Ie under the Marriage Act 1949 Pt III (ss 26–52) (see PARA 87 et seq).
2   As to the meaning of 'person subject to immigration control' see PARA 178 note 2.
3   As to the meaning of 'civil partnership schedule' see PARA 138.
4   Ie under the Civil Partnership Act 2004 Pt 2 Chapter 1 (ss 2–36): see PARA 133 et seq.
5   Civil Partnership Act 2004 Sch 23 paras 3, 4(1)(a). As to the specified registration authorities
    see the Immigration (Procedure for Marriage) Regulations 2005, SI 2005/15, reg 5(1), Sch 2.
6   'Relevant individual' means such employee or officer or other person provided by the specified
    registration authority as is determined in accordance with regulations made by the Secretary of
    State (Civil Partnership Act 2004 Sch 23 para 4(2)); see the Immigration (Procedure for
    Formation of Civil Partnerships) Regulations 2005, SI 2005/2917, reg 5(2).
7   Civil Partnership Act 2004 Sch 23 para 4(1)(b).
8   Civil Partnership Act 2004 Sch 23 para 4(1)(c) (Sch 23 para 4(1)(c), (d) added by SI 2005/2000).
9   Civil Partnership Act 2004 Sch 23 para 4(1)(d) (as added: see note 8).

(10) OFFENCES

180. Offences relating to solemnisation of marriages. If a person knowingly
and wilfully:
(1)   solemnises a marriage at any other time than between the hours of 8 am
        and 6 pm[1], not being a marriage by special licence[2], a marriage
        according to the usages of the Society of Friends[3] or a marriage between
        two persons professing the Jewish religion[4] according to the usages of
        the Jews[5];
(2)   solemnises a marriage according to the rites of the Church of England
        without banns of matrimony having been duly published[6], not being a
        marriage solemnised on the authority of a special licence, a common
        licence[7] or certificates of a superintendent registrar[8];
(3)   solemnises a marriage according to such rites, not being a marriage by
        special licence or a marriage of a person who is housebound or a
        detained person[9], in any place other than a church or other building in
        which banns may be published[10];
(4)   solemnises a marriage according to such rites falsely pretending to be in
        holy orders[11],
he is guilty of an offence and liable on conviction to imprisonment for a term not
exceeding 14 years[12].
    If a person knowingly and wilfully:
(a)   solemnises a marriage, not being a marriage by special licence, a
        marriage according to the usages of the Society of Friends or a marriage
        between two persons professing the Jewish religion according to the
        usages of the Jews, in any place other than a church or other building in
        which marriages may be solemnised according to the rites of the Church
        of England or the registered building[13], office, approved premises[14] or
        person's residence specified as the place where the marriage was to be
        solemnised in the required[15] notices of marriage and certificates[16];
(b)   solemnises a marriage[17] on premises which purport to be approved
        premises but are not approved premises[18];
(c)   solemnises a marriage in any such registered building, not being a
        marriage in the presence of an authorised person[19], in the absence of a
        registrar[20] of the district[21] in which the registered building is situated[22];
(d)   solemnises a marriage of a person who is housebound or a detained

person[23], otherwise than according to the rites of the Church of England, in the absence of a registrar of the registration district in which the place where the marriage is solemnised is situated[24];

(e)   solemnises a marriage in the office of a superintendent registrar[25] in the absence of a registrar of the district in which the office is situated[26];

(f)   solemnises a marriage on approved premises[27] in the absence of a registrar of the district in which the premises are situated[28];

(g)   solemnises a marriage on the authority of certificates of a superintendent registrar before the expiry of the waiting period[29] in relation to each notice of marriage[30]; or

(h)   solemnises a marriage on the authority of certificates of a superintendent registrar after the expiration of the period which is[31], in relation to the marriage, the applicable period[32],

he is guilty of an offence and liable on conviction to imprisonment for a term not exceeding five years[33].

If a superintendent registrar knowingly and wilfully:

(i)   issues any certificate for marriage before the expiry of 15 days from the day on which the notice of marriage was entered in the marriage notice book[34];

(ii)   issues any certificate for marriage after the expiration of the period which is[35], in relation to that marriage, the applicable period[36];

(iii) issues any certificate the issue of which has been forbidden[37] by any person entitled to forbid the issue of such a certificate[38]; or

(iv)   solemnises or permits to be solemnised in his office or, in the case of a marriage on approved premises[39] or in a person's residence[40], in any other place any marriage which is[41] void[42],

he is guilty of an offence and liable on conviction to imprisonment for a term not exceeding five years[43].

No prosecution under the above provisions is to be commenced after the expiration of three years from the commission of the offence[44].

1   As to the hours between which a marriage must in general be solemnised see PARA 82.
2   As to special licences see PARAS 58, 76.
3   As to marriages according to the usages of the Society of Friends see PARA 116.
4   As to marriages between two persons professing the Jewish religion according to the usages of the Jews see PARA 118.
5   Marriage Act 1949 s 75(1)(a).
6   As to the publication of banns of matrimony see PARAS 58, 65 et seq.
7   As to common licences see PARAS 58, 76.
8   Marriage Act 1949 s 75(1)(b) (amended by the Immigration and Asylum Act 1999 Sch 14 paras 3, 30(1), (2)). As to the meaning of 'superintendent registrar' see PARA 22 note 1.
9   Ie a marriage in pursuance of the Marriage Act 1949 s 26(1)(dd) (see PARA 171 et seq).
10 Marriage Act 1949 s 75(1)(c) (amended by the Marriage Act 1983 Sch 1 paras 1, 20).
11 Marriage Act 1949 s 75(1)(d).
12 Marriage Act 1949 s 75(1).
13 For these purposes, any reference to a registered building is to be construed as including a reference to any chapel registered under the Marriage Act 1949 s 70 (see PARA 129): s 75(5). As to the meaning of 'registered building' generally see PARA 54 note 3; as to the registration of buildings for marriages see PARAS 186–189.
14 As to the meaning of 'approved premises' see PARA 54 note 6.
15 Ie required by the Marriage Act 1949 Pt III (ss 26–52): see PARA 87 et seq.
16 Marriage Act 1949 s 75(2)(a) (amended by the Marriage Act 1983 Sch 1 paras 1, 20; the Marriage Act 1994 Schedule paras 1, 7; the Immigration and Asylum Act 1999 Sch 14 paras 3, 30(1), (3)(a)).
17 Ie a marriage purporting to be in pursuance of the Marriage Act 1949 s 26(1)(bb) (see PARA 54).

18　Marriage Act 1949 s 75(2)(aa) (added by the Marriage Act 1994 Schedule paras 1, 7). As to the approval of premises for marriage see PARAS 190–202.
19　As to the meaning of 'authorised person' see PARA 107.
20　As to the meaning of 'registrar' see PARA 88 note 1.
21　As to the meaning of 'registration district' see PARA 87 note 4.
22　Marriage Act 1949 s 75(2)(b).
23　See note 9.
24　Marriage Act 1949 s 75(2)(bb) (added by the Marriage Act 1983 Sch 1 para 20).
25　As to the meaning of 'superintendent registrar' see PARA 22 note 1.
26　Marriage Act 1949 s 75(2)(c).
27　Ie in pursuance of the Marriage Act 1949 s 26(1)(bb) (see PARA 54).
28　Marriage Act 1949 s 75(2)(cc) (added by the Marriage Act 1994 Schedule paras 1, 7).
29　For these purposes, 'waiting period' has the same meaning as in the Marriage Act 1949 s 31(4A) (see PARA 94): s 75(2A) (added by the Immigration and Asylum Act 1999 Sch 14 paras 3, 30(1), (4)).
30　Marriage Act 1949 s 75(2)(d) (amended by the Immigration and Asylum Act 1999 Sch 14 paras 3, 30(1), (3)(b)).
31　Ie for the purposes of the Marriage Act 1949 s 33 (see PARA 101).
32　Marriage Act 1949 s 75(2)(e) (amended by SI 1997/986; the Immigration and Asylum Act 1999 Sch 14 paras 3, 30(1), (3)(c)).
33　Marriage Act 1949 s 75(2).
34　Marriage Act 1949 s 75(3)(a) (substituted by the Immigration and Asylum Act 1999 Sch 14 paras 3, 30(1), (5)). As to the meaning of 'marriage notice book' see PARA 92.
35　See note 31.
36　Marriage Act 1949 s 75(3)(b) (amended by SI 1997/986; the Immigration and Asylum Act 1999 Sch 14 paras 3, 30(1), (6), Sch 16).
37　Ie under the Marriage Act 1949 s 30 (see PARA 95).
38　Marriage Act 1949 s 75(3)(c).
39　See note 27.
40　See note 9.
41　Ie by virtue of any of the provisions of the Marriage Act 1949 Pt III (ss 26–52).
42　Marriage Act 1949 s 75(3)(d) (amended by the Marriage Act 1983 Sch 1 para 20; the Marriage Act 1994 Schedule paras 1, 7).
43　Marriage Act 1949 s 75(3).
44　Marriage Act 1949 s 75(4).

181.　Offences relating to registration of marriages. Any person who refuses or without reasonable cause omits to register any marriage which he is required by the Marriage Act 1949 to register, and any person having custody of a marriage register book or a certified copy of a marriage register book or part thereof who carelessly loses or injures such book or copy or carelessly allows such book or copy to be injured while in his keeping is guilty of an offence and liable on summary conviction to a fine not exceeding level 3 on the standard scale[1].

Where any person who is required[2] to make and deliver to a superintendent registrar a certified copy of entries in the marriage register book kept by him, or a certificate that no entries have been made therein since the date of the last certified copy, refuses to deliver any such copy or certificate, or fails to deliver any such copy or certificate during any month in which he is required to do so, he is guilty of an offence and liable on summary conviction to a fine not exceeding level 1 on the standard scale[3].

Any registrar[4] who knowingly and wilfully registers any marriage which is void[5] is guilty of an offence and liable to imprisonment for a term not exceeding five years[6]; but no prosecution for such an offence may be commenced after the expiration of three years from the commission of the offence[7].

1　Marriage Act 1949 s 76(1) (amended by the Criminal Justice Act 1982 ss 38, 46). As to the meaning of 'standard scale' see PARA 84 note 3. The balance of any sum paid or recovered on account of a fine imposed under the Marriage Act 1949 s 76(1) or s 76(2) must be paid: (1) in the case of a fine imposed under s 76(1), into the Exchequer; and (2) in the case of a fine imposed under s 76(2), to the Registrar General or such other person as may be appointed by the Treasury, for the use of Her Majesty: s 76(4). Subject as may be prescribed, a superintendent registrar may prosecute any person guilty of an offence under s 76(1) or (2) committed within his district; and any costs incurred by the superintendent registrar in prosecuting any such person, being costs which are not otherwise provided for, must be defrayed out of moneys provided by Parliament: s 76(5). As to the meaning of 'Registrar General' see PARA 46 note 5; and as to the meaning of 'superintendent registrar' see PARA 22 note 1.

2   Ie under the Marriage Act 1949 Pt IV (ss 53–67) (see REGISTRATION CONCERNING THE INDIVIDUAL).
3   Marriage Act 1949 s 76(2) (amended by the Criminal Justice Act 1982 ss 38, 46). See also note 1.
4   As to the meaning of 'registrar' see PARA 88 note 1.
5   Ie by virtue of any of the provisions of the Marriage Act 1949 Pt III (ss 26–52) (see PARA 87). As to void marriages see PARA 326.
6   Marriage Act 1949 s 76(3).
7   Marriage Act 1949 s 76(6).

182. Offences by authorised persons. Any authorised person[1] who refuses or fails to comply with the provisions of the Marriage Act 1949 or of any regulations made under it[2] is guilty of an offence and, unless the offence is one for which a specific penalty is provided under the provisions of that Act[3], is liable on conviction on indictment to imprisonment for a term not exceeding two years or a fine or on summary conviction to a fine not exceeding the prescribed sum, and on conviction ceases to be an authorised person[4].

1   As to the meaning of 'authorised person' see PARA 107.
2   Ie under the Marriage Act 1949 s 74 (see PARAS 87 note 2, 107 note 6).
3   Ie under Marriage Act 1949 ss 72–76. See eg s 76(1), (2); PARA 181; and REGISTRATION CONCERNING THE INDIVIDUAL vol 39(2) (Reissue) PARAS 527–530.
4   Marriage Act 1949 s 77 (amended by the Criminal Law Act 1977 s 32(1); the Magistrates' Courts Act 1980 s 32(2)). As to the meaning of 'prescribed sum' see PARA 77 note 16.

183. Offences in relation to a Registrar General's licence. It is an offence knowingly and wilfully:

(1)   to solemnise a marriage by Registrar General's[1] licence in any place other than the place specified in the licence[2];

(2)   to solemnise a marriage by Registrar General's licence without the presence of a registrar[3], except in the case of a marriage according to the usages of the Society of Friends[4] or a marriage between two persons professing the Jewish religion[5] according to the usages of the Jews[6];

(3)   to solemnise a marriage by Registrar General's licence after the expiration of one month from the date of entry of the notice of marriage in the marriage notice book[7];

(4)   to give false information by way of evidence required[8] by the Registrar General[9];

(5)   to give a false medical certificate[10];

and any person guilty of any of the above offences is liable on conviction on indictment to imprisonment for a term not exceeding three years or a fine, or to both, or on summary conviction to a fine not exceeding the prescribed sum[11].

    A superintendent registrar who knowingly and wilfully solemnises or permits to be solemnised in his presence, or a registrar who knowingly and wilfully registers a marriage by Registrar General's licence which is void[12], is guilty of an offence and liable on conviction on indictment to imprisonment for a term not exceeding three years or a fine, or to both, or on summary conviction to a fine not exceeding the prescribed sum[13].

No prosecution under the above provisions is to be commenced after the expiration of three years from the commission of the offence[14].

1   As to the meaning of 'Registrar General' see PARA 46 note 5.
2   Marriage (Registrar General's Licence) Act 1970 s 16(1)(a).
3   As to the meaning of 'registrar' see PARA 88 note 1.
4   As to marriage according to the usages of the Society of Friends see PARA 116.
5   As to marriage between two persons professing the Jewish religion according to the usages of the Jews see PARA 118.
6   Marriage (Registrar General's Licence) Act 1970 s 16(1)(b).
7   Marriage (Registrar General's Licence) Act 1970 s 16(1)(c). As to the meaning of 'marriage notice book' see PARA 92.
8   Ie as required by the Marriage (Registrar General's Licence) Act 1970 s 3 (see PARA 163).
9   Marriage (Registrar General's Licence) Act 1970 s 16(1)(d).
10 Marriage (Registrar General's Licence) Act 1970 s 16(1)(e). As to the giving of a medical certificate see s 3(d); and PARA 163.
11 Marriage (Registrar General's Licence) Act 1970 s 16(1) (amended by the Criminal Law Act 1977 s 32(1); the Magistrates' Courts Act 1980 s 32(2)). As to the meaning of 'prescribed sum' see PARA 77 note 16. The provisions of the Marriage Act 1949 s 75(1)(a), (2)(a) (offence of knowingly and wilfully solemnising a marriage out of hours or in an unauthorised place: see PARA 180) do not apply to a marriage solemnised on the authority of the Registrar General's licence: Marriage (Registrar General's Licence) Act 1970 s 16(4).
12 Ie by virtue of the Marriage Act 1949 Pt III (ss 26–52) (see PARA 87 et seq). As to void marriages see PARA 326.
13 Marriage (Registrar General's Licence) Act 1970 ss 1(2), 16(2) (amended by the Criminal Law Act 1977 s 32(1); the Magistrates' Courts Act 1980 s 32(2)).
14 Marriage (Registrar General's Licence) Act 1970 s 16(3).

184. Making false statements etc with reference to marriage.   If any person:
   (1)   for the purpose of procuring a marriage, or a certificate or licence for marriage, knowingly and wilfully makes a false oath, or makes or signs a false declaration, notice or certificate required under any Act of Parliament for the time being in force relating to marriage[1];
   (2)   knowingly and wilfully makes, or knowingly and wilfully causes to be made, for the purpose of being inserted in any register of marriage, a false statement as to any particular required by law to be known and registered relating to marriage[2];
   (3)   forbids the issue of any certificate or licence for marriage by falsely representing himself to be a person whose consent to the marriage is required by law, knowing such representation to be false[3]; or
   (4)   with respect to a declaration relating to a marriage within the prohibited degrees of affinity[4], enters a caveat[5] or makes a declaration[6] which he knows to be false in a material particular[7],

he is guilty of an offence and liable on conviction on indictment to imprisonment for a term not exceeding seven years or a fine, or to both, or on summary conviction to a fine not exceeding the prescribed sum[8].

No prosecution for knowingly and wilfully making a false declaration for the purpose of procuring a marriage out of the district in which the parties, or one of them, dwell may take place after the expiration of 18 months from the solemnisation of the marriage to which the declaration refers[9].

1   Perjury Act 1911 s 3(1)(a).
2   Perjury Act 1911 s 3(1)(b). If a new surname has been acquired by repute, the use of such reputed name in a notice of marriage will not support an indictment: *R v Smith* (1865) 4 F & F 1099.
3   Perjury Act 1911 s 3(1)(c).
4   Ie a declaration made under the Marriage Act 1949 s 16(1A) (see PARA 77) or s 27B(2) (see PARA 93).

5   Ie under the Marriage Act 1949 s 16(2) (see PARA 78).
6   Ie mentioned in the Marriage Act 1949 s 27B(4) (see PARA 93).
7   Perjury Act 1911 s 3(1)(d) (added by the Marriage (Prohibited Degrees of Relationship) Act 1986 s 4).
8   Perjury Act 1911 s 3(1) (amended by the Criminal Justice Act 1925 s 28(1); the Criminal Justice Act 1967 s 92(1), Sch 3, Pt I). As to the meaning of 'prescribed sum' see PARA 77 note 16. If it appears to a registrar that an offence under the Perjury Act 1911 has been committed, he must report the matter to the Registrar General: see the Registration of Marriages Regulations 1986, SI 1986/1442, reg 20(1); and REGISTRATION CONCERNING THE INDIVIDUAL vol 39(2) (Reissue) PARA 527.
9   Perjury Act 1911 s 3(2).

185. Making false statements etc with reference to civil partnerships.   A person commits an offence if:

(1)   for the purpose of procuring the formation of a civil partnership[1], or certain documents relating to the formation of civil partnerships[2], he makes or signs a declaration[3] or gives a notice or certificate so required knowing that the declaration, notice or certificate is false[4];

(2)   for the purpose of a record being made in any register relating to civil partnerships, he makes a statement as to any information which is required to be registered[5], or causes such a statement to be made knowing that the statement is false[6];

(3)   he forbids the issue of a document mentioned in head (1) or head (2) by representing himself to be a person whose consent to a civil partnership between a child and another person is required[7] knowing the representation to be false[8]; or

(4)   with respect to a declaration[9] he makes a statement[10] which he knows to be false in a material particular[11].

A person guilty of such an offence is liable:

(a)   on conviction on indictment, to imprisonment for a term not exceeding seven years or to a fine or both[12]; or

(b)   on summary conviction, to a fine not exceeding the statutory maximum[13].

1   As to the meaning of 'civil partnership' see PARA 2 note 1.
2   Ie: (1) a civil partnership schedule (see PARA 138) or a Registrar General's licence (see PARA 143); (2) a document required by an Order in Council under the Civil Partnership Act 2004 s 210 (see PARA 145) or s 211 (see PARA 153) as an authority for two people to register as civil partners of each other; or (3) a certificate of no impediment under s 240 (see PARA 152): s 80(2).
3   Ie a declaration required under the Civil Partnership Act 2004 Pt 2 (ss 2–80) or Pt 5 (ss 210–245): s 80(1)(a).
4   Civil Partnership Act 2004 s 80(1)(a). The Perjury Act 1911 (see CRIMINAL LAW, EVIDENCE AND PROCEDURE vol 11(2) (2006 Reissue) PARA 712 et seq) has effect as if the Civil Partnership Act 2004 s 80 were contained in it: s 80(4).
5   Ie under the Civil Partnership Act 2004 Pt 2 or Pt 5.
6   Civil Partnership Act 2004 s 80(1)(b).
7   Ie under the Civil Partnership Act 2004 Pt 2 or Pt 5.
8   Civil Partnership Act 2004 s 80(1)(c).
9   Ie under the Civil Partnership Act 2004 Sch 1 para 5(1) (see PARA 135).
10 Ie under the Civil Partnership Act 2004 Sch 1 para 6 (see PARAS 135, 137).
11 Civil Partnership Act 2004 s 80(1)(d).
12 Civil Partnership Act 2004 s 80(3)(a).
13 Civil Partnership Act 2004 s 80(3)(b). 'Statutory maximum', with reference to a fine or penalty on summary conviction for an offence, is the prescribed sum within the meaning of the Magistrates' Courts Act 1980 s 32: see the Interpretation Act 1978 s 5, Sch 1 (definition added by the Criminal Justice Act 1988 s 170(1), Sch 15 para 58); and CRIMINAL LAW, EVIDENCE AND PROCEDURE vol 11(4) (2006 Reissue) PARA 1674; MAGISTRATES vol 29(2) (Reissue) PARA 804. 'Prescribed sum' means £5,000 or such sum as is for the time being substituted in this definition

by order under the Magistrates' Courts Act 1980 s 143(1): see s 32(9) (amended by the Criminal Justice Act 1991 s 17(2)); and CRIMINAL LAW, EVIDENCE AND PROCEDURE vol 11(4) (2006 Reissue) PARA 1675; MAGISTRATES vol 29(2) (Reissue) PARA 804.

3. REGISTRATION AND APPROVAL OF PREMISES

(1) REGISTRATION OF BUILDINGS FOR MARRIAGES

186. Application for registration of building. Any proprietor or trustee of a building which has been certified as required by law as a place of religious worship[1] may apply to the superintendent registrar[2] of the registration district[3] in which the building is situated for the building to be registered for the solemnisation of marriages[4]. A building may be so registered for the solemnisation of marriages whether it is a separate building or forms part of another building[5].

Any person making such an application must deliver to the superintendent registrar a certificate, signed in duplicate by at least 20 householders and dated not earlier than one month before the making of the application, stating that the building is being used by them as their usual place of public religious worship, and that they desire that it should be registered; and both certificates must be countersigned by the proprietor or trustee by whom they are delivered[6].

1 Places of religious worship may be certified, under the Places of Worship Registration Act 1855 s 2, to the Registrar General through the superintendent registrar of the district, but certification is not compulsory unless the place is to be used for marriages: see ECCLESIASTICAL LAW vol 14 PARA 1410 et seq. A list of certified places of religious worship is kept by the Registrar General and is open to public inspection: see ECCLESIASTICAL LAW vol 14 PARA 1410. Certification effected before 1 January 1950 continues in force by virtue of the Marriage Act 1949 s 79(2). Proof of certification of a building is not necessary to the validity of a marriage solemnised in it: see PARA 22.
2 As to the meaning of 'superintendent registrar' see PARA 22 note 1.
3 As to the meaning of 'registration district' see PARA 87 note 4.
4 Marriage Act 1949 s 41(1) (amended by the Marriage (Registration of Buildings) Act 1990 s 1(1)). The provisions of the Marriage Act 1949 relating to the registration of buildings apply in relation to the registration of a shared church building, with certain modifications: see the Sharing of Church Buildings Act 1969 s 6(1), Sch 1; and ECCLESIASTICAL LAW vol 14 PARA 1412.
5 Marriage Act 1949 s 41(7) (substituted by the Marriage (Registration of Buildings) Act 1990 s 1(1)).
6 Marriage Act 1949 s 41(2) (substituted by the Marriage Acts Amendment Act 1958 s 1(1)(a)).

187. Registration of building. On receipt of the certificates accompanying an application to register a building[1], the superintendent registrar[2] must send them both to the Registrar General[3], who must register the building accordingly in a book kept for the purpose at the General Register Office[4], and, having indorsed the date of registration on both certificates, must keep one with the records of the General Register Office, and return the other to the superintendent registrar to be kept with the records of his office[5].

On the return of the certificate, the superintendent registrar must:

(1) enter the date of registration in a book provided for that purpose by the Registrar General[6];

(2) give a certificate of registration signed by him, on durable materials, to the proprietor or trustee by whom the certificates accompanying the application were countersigned[7]; and

(3) give public notice of the registration of the building by advertisement in a newspaper circulating in the county in which the building is situated, and in the London Gazette[8].

For every such entry, certificate and notice the superintendent registrar is entitled to receive a fee of £120 at the time of the delivery to him of the certificates in duplicate[9].

1   As to these certificates see PARA 86.
2   As to the meaning of 'superintendent registrar' see PARA 22 note 1.
3   As to the meaning of 'Registrar General' see PARA 46 note 5.
4   See the Marriage Act 1949 s 41(3). As to the General Register Office see REGISTRATION CONCERNING THE INDIVIDUAL vol 39(2) (Reissue) PARA 605.
5   Marriage Act 1949 s 41(4).
6   Marriage Act 1949 s 41(5)(a).
7   Marriage Act 1949 s 41(5)(b).
8   Marriage Act 1949 s 41(5)(c).
9   Marriage Act 1949 s 41(6) (amended by SI 2002/3076).

188. Cancellation of registration. Where, on an application made by or through the superintendent registrar[1] of the registration district[2] in which the building is situated, it is shown to the satisfaction of the Registrar General[3] that a registered building[4] is no longer used for the purpose of public religious worship by the congregation on whose behalf it was registered, he must cause the registration to be cancelled[5].

Where the Registrar General so cancels the registration of any building, he must inform the superintendent registrar, who must enter that fact and the date in the books provided for the registration of buildings, and must certify and publish the cancellation in the same manner as in the case of the registration of a building[6].

Where the registration of any building has been so cancelled, it is not lawful to solemnise any marriage in the disused building, unless the building has been registered[7] again[8].

1   As to the meaning of 'superintendent registrar' see PARA 22 note 1.
2   As to the meaning of 'registration district' see PARA 87 note 4.
3   As to the meaning of 'Registrar General' see PARA 46 note 5.
4   As to the registration of buildings see PARAS 186–187.
5   Marriage Act 1949 s 42(1) (amended by the Marriage Acts Amendment Act 1958 s 1(1)). In such a case the certification under the Places of Worship Registration Act 1855 will be cancelled: see s 8; and ECCLESIASTICAL LAW vol 14 PARA 1410.
6   Marriage Act 1949 s 42(3) (amended by the Marriage Acts Amendment Act 1958 s 1(1)). As to the certifying and publishing of notice of registration see PARA 187.
7   Ie in accordance with the Marriage Act 1949 Pt III (ss 26–52): see PARAS 186, 187.
8   Marriage Act 1949 s 42(5) (amended by the Marriage Acts Amendment Act 1958 s 1(1)). The solemnisation of marriage in an unauthorised place is an offence: see PARA 180.

189. List of registered buildings. The Registrar General[1] must in every year make out and cause to be printed a list of all chapels[2] and registered buildings[3], stating in that list the county and registration district[4] in which each chapel or building is situated, and the names and places of residence of the superintendent registrars[5], registrars[6], and deputy registrars of each district[7]; and a copy of every such list made by the Registrar General must be sent to each registrar and superintendent registrar[8].

1   As to the meaning of 'Registrar General' see PARA 46 note 5.
2   The Registrar General compiles the list of chapels from returns made to him annually by registrars of dioceses: see the Marriage Act 1949 s 73(1); and PARA 64.
3   As to the meaning of 'registered building' see PARA 54 note 3.
4   As to the meaning of 'registration district' see PARA 87 note 4.
5   As to the meaning of 'superintendent registrar' see PARA 22 note 1.
6   As to the meaning of 'registrar' see PARA 88 note 1.

7   Marriage Act 1949 s 73(2).
8   Marriage Act 1949 s 73(3).

(2) APPROVALS OR PREMISES FOR MARRIAGES AND CIVIL PARTNERSHIPS

190.   Powers of the Secretary of State. The Secretary of State may by regulations make provision for and in connection with the approval by local authorities[1] of premises for the solemnisation of marriages[2] or the approval by registration authorities[3] of premises for the registration of civil partnerships[4] on approved premises[5].

The matters dealt with by the regulations may include:

(1)   the kinds of premises in respect of which approvals may be granted[6];

(2)   the procedure to be followed in relation to applications for approval[7];

(3)   the considerations to be taken into account by a local authority in determining whether to approve any premises[8];

(4)   the duration and renewal of approvals[9];

(5)   the conditions that must or may be imposed by a local authority or registration authority on granting or renewing an approval[10];

(6)   the determination and charging by local authorities or registration authorities of fees in respect of applications for the approval of premises and in respect of the renewal of approvals[11];

(7)   the circumstances in which a local authority or registration authority must or may revoke an approval[12];

(8)   the review of any decision to refuse an approval or the renewal of an approval, to impose conditions on granting or renewing an approval or to revoke an approval[13];

(9)   the notification to the Registrar General[14] of all approvals granted, renewed or revoked[15];

(10)   the keeping by local authorities or registration authorities of registers of approved premises[16];

(11)   the issue by the Registrar General of guidance supplementing the provisions made by the regulations[17].

1   For these purposes, 'local authority' means a county council, metropolitan district council, London borough council or the Common Council of the City of London: Marriage Act 1949 s 46A(3) (added by the Marriage Act 1994 s 1(2); and amended by the City of London (Approved Premises for Marriage) Act 1996 s 3(2)).
2   Ie in pursuance of the Marriage Act 1949 s 26(1)(bb): see PARA 54.
3   As to the meaning of 'registration authority' see PARA 133 note 2.
4   Ie for the purposes of the Civil Partnership Act 2004 s 6(3A)(a): see PARA 56.
5   Marriage Act 1949 s 46A(1) (added by the Marriage Act 1994 s 1(2); amended by SI 2008/678); Civil Partnership Act 2004 s 6A(1) (s 6A added by SI 2005/2000; amended by SI 2008/678). In exercise of the power so conferred the Marriages and Civil Partnerships (Approved Premises) Regulations 2005, SI 2005/3168, were made: see PARA 191 et seq. As to the meaning of 'approved premises' see PARA 54 note 6. As to the solemnisation of marriages on approved premises see PARA 111. As to the registration of civil partnerships on approved premises see PARA 133 et seq.
6   Marriage Act 1949 s 46A(2)(a) (as added: see note 5); Civil Partnership Act 2004 s 6A(2)(a) (as added: see note 5).
7   Marriage Act 1949 s 46A(2)(b) (as added: see note 5); Civil Partnership Act 2004 s 6A(2)(b) (as added: see note 5).
8   Marriage Act 1949 s 46A(2)(c) (as added: see note 5); Civil Partnership Act 2004 s 6A(2)(c) (as added: see note 5).
9   Marriage Act 1949 s 46A(2)(d) (as added: see note 5); Civil Partnership Act 2004 s 6A(2)(d) (as added: see note 5).

10 Marriage Act 1949 s 46A(2)(e) (as added: see note 5); Civil Partnership Act 2004 s 6A(2)(e) (as added: see note 5).

11 Marriage Act 1949 s 46A(2)(f) (as added: see note 5); Civil Partnership Act 2004 s 6A(2)(f) (as added: see note 5).

12 Marriage Act 1949 s 46A(2)(g) (as added: see note 5); Civil Partnership Act 2004 s 6A(2)(g) (as added: see note 5).

13 Marriage Act 1949 s 46A(2)(h) (as added: see note 5); Civil Partnership Act 2004 s 6A(2)(h) (as added: see note 5).

14 As to the meaning of 'Registrar General' see PARA 46 note 5.

15 Marriage Act 1949 s 46A(2)(i) (as added: see note 5); Civil Partnership Act 2004 s 6A(2)(i) (as added: see note 5).

16 Marriage Act 1949 s 46A(2)(j) (as added: see note 5); Civil Partnership Act 2004 s 6A(2)(j) (as added: see note 5).

17 Marriage Act 1949 s 46A(2)(k) (as added: see note 5); Civil Partnership Act 2004 s 6A(2)(k) (as added: see note 5). Without prejudice to the width of the Marriage Act 1949 s 46A(2)(e) or the Civil Partnership Act 2004 s 6A(2)(e) (see text head (5)), the Secretary of State must exercise his power to provide for the imposition of conditions as there mentioned so as to secure that members of the public are permitted to attend any marriage solemnised on approved premises in pursuance of s 26(1)(bb) (see PARA 54) or when two people sign the civil partnership schedule on approved premises in accordance with s 6(3A)(a) (see PARA 56): s 46B(2) (added by the Marriage Act 1994 s 1(2); amended by SI 2008/678); Civil Partnership Act 2004 s 6A(3) (as so added; amended by SI 2008/678).

191. Application for approval of premises. Application for approval[1] may be made by a proprietor or a trustee of premises[2].

The applicant[3] must deliver to the proper officer[4] of the authority[5]:

(1)   an application in writing, including the name and address of the applicant and such other information concerning the prescribed requirements[6] as the authority may reasonably have required[7];

(2)   a plan of the premises which clearly identifies the room or rooms in which the proceedings will take place if approval is granted[8]; and

(3)   if the authority so requires, a fee[9], or an amount on account of that fee[10].

The applicant must provide the authority with such additional information as it may reasonably require in order to determine the application[11].

As soon as practicable after receiving an application the authority must:

(a)   arrange for the premises to be inspected[12]; and

(b)   if the functions of the authority[13] have not been delegated to the proper officer, seek and have regard to his recommendation in relation to the application[14].

1 For these purposes, unless the context otherwise requires, 'approval' means approval of premises for the solemnisation of marriages in pursuance of the Marriage Act 1949 s 26(1)(bb) and as a place at which two people may register as civil partners of each other in pursuance of the Civil Partnership Act 2004 s 6(3A)(a) (see PARA 56 note 11); and 'approved premises' is to be construed accordingly: Marriages and Civil Partnerships (Approved Premises) Regulations 2005, SI 2005/3168, reg 2(1).

2 Marriages and Civil Partnerships (Approved Premises) Regulations 2005, SI 2005/3168, reg 3(1). For these purposes, unless the context otherwise requires, 'premises' means a permanently immovable structure comprising at least a room, or any boat or other vessel which is permanently moored: reg 2(1).

3 For these purposes, unless the context otherwise requires, 'applicant' means an applicant for approval; and 'application' is to be construed accordingly: Marriages and Civil Partnerships (Approved Premises) Regulations 2005, SI 2005/3168, reg 2(1).

4 For these purposes, unless the context otherwise requires, 'proper officer' means the proper officer referred to in the Registration Service Act 1953 s 13(2)(h) (see REGISTRATION CONCERNING THE INDIVIDUAL vol 39(2) (Reissue) PARA 625): Marriages and Civil Partnerships (Approved Premises) Regulations 2005, SI 2005/3168, reg 2(1).

5   For these purposes, unless the context otherwise requires, 'authority', in relation to any
    premises, means the body which is the local authority for the area in which those premises are
    situated, being one of the bodies specified as such by the Marriage Act 1949 s 46A(3) (see PARA
    190 note 1) or the Civil Partnership Act 2004 s 28 (see PARA 47 note 1): Marriages and Civil
    Partnerships (Approved Premises) Regulations 2005, SI 2005/3168, reg 2(1).
6   Ie the requirements set out in the Marriages and Civil Partnerships (Approved Premises)
    Regulations 2005, SI 2005/3168, Sch 1: see PARA 193.
7   Marriages and Civil Partnerships (Approved Premises) Regulations 2005, SI 2005/3168,
    reg 3(2)(a).
8   Marriages and Civil Partnerships (Approved Premises) Regulations 2005, SI 2005/3168,
    reg 3(2)(b). 'Proceedings' means the solemnisation of marriages or the formation of civil
    partnerships: reg 2(1).
9   Such fee is to be determined in accordance with the Marriages and Civil Partnerships (Approved
    Premises) Regulations 2005, SI 2005/3168, reg 12 (see PARA 200): reg 3(2)(c).
10 Marriages and Civil Partnerships (Approved Premises) Regulations 2005, SI 2005/3168,
    reg 3(2)(c).
11 Marriages and Civil Partnerships (Approved Premises) Regulations 2005, SI 2005/3168,
    reg 3(3).
12 Marriages and Civil Partnerships (Approved Premises) Regulations 2005, SI 2005/3168,
    reg 3(4)(a).
13 Ie under the Marriages and Civil Partnerships (Approved Premises) Regulations 2005,
    SI 2005/3168: see PARA 192 et seq.
14 Marriages and Civil Partnerships (Approved Premises) Regulations 2005, SI 2005/3168,
    reg 3(4)(b).

192.   Public consultation. As soon as practicable after receiving an
application[1] the authority[2] must:

(1)   make the application and the plan accompanying it available to
      members of the public for inspection at all reasonable hours during the
      working day until such time as the application has been finally
      determined or withdrawn[3]; and

(2)   ensure that public notice of the application is given by advertisement in
      a newspaper, which may be a newspaper distributed free of charge,
      which is in general circulation at intervals of not more than one week in
      the area in which the premises[4] are situated[5].

The notice referred to in head (2) above must:

(a)   identify the premises and the applicant[6];

(b)   indicate the address at which the application and the plan
      accompanying it may be inspected in accordance with head (1) above[7];

(c)   state that any person may give notice in writing of an objection to the
      grant of approval, with reasons for the objection, within 21 days from
      the date on which the newspaper in which the advertisement appears is
      published[8]; and

(d)   state the address of the offices of the authority to which such notice of
      objection should be given[9].

Before reaching a decision on the application, the authority must consider any
notice of objection given as mentioned in head (c) above[10].

1   As to the meaning of 'application' see PARA 191 note 3.
2   As to the meaning of 'authority' see PARA 191 note 5.
3   Marriages and Civil Partnerships (Approved Premises) Regulations 2005, SI 2005/3168,
    reg 4(1)(a).
4   As to the meaning of 'premises' see PARA 191 note 2.
5   Marriages and Civil Partnerships (Approved Premises) Regulations 2005, SI 2005/3168,
    reg 4(1)(b).
6   Marriages and Civil Partnerships (Approved Premises) Regulations 2005, SI 2005/3168,
    reg 4(2)(a). As to the meaning of 'applicant' see PARA 191 note 3.

7   Marriages and Civil Partnerships (Approved Premises) Regulations 2005, SI 2005/3168,
    reg 4(2)(b).

8   Marriages and Civil Partnerships (Approved Premises) Regulations 2005, SI 2005/3168,
    reg 4(2)(c).

9   Marriages and Civil Partnerships (Approved Premises) Regulations 2005, SI 2005/3168,
    reg 4(2)(d).

10 Marriages and Civil Partnerships (Approved Premises) Regulations 2005, SI 2005/3168,
    reg 4(3).

193.   Grant or refusal of approval. The authority[1] may grant approval[2] only if
it is satisfied:

(1)   that the application[3] has been duly made[4];

(2)   that the premises[5] fulfil the prescribed requirements, that is to say:

(a)   having regard to their primary use, situation, construction and
state of repair, the premises are, in the opinion of the authority, a
seemly and dignified venue for the proceedings[6];

(b)   the premises are regularly available to the public for use for the
solemnisation of marriages or the formation of civil partnerships[7];

(c)   the premises have the benefit of such fire precautions as may
reasonably be required by the authority, having consulted with the
fire and rescue authority (in England) or the fire authority (in
Wales), and such other reasonable provision for the health and
safety of persons employed in or visiting the premises as the
authority considers appropriate[8];

(d)   the premises must not be religious premises[9] or a register office[10];

(e)   the room or rooms in which the proceedings are to take place, if
approval is granted, are identifiable by description as a distinct
part of the premises[11]; and

(3)   that the premises fulfil any other reasonable requirements which the
authority considers appropriate to ensure that the facilities provided at
the premises are suitable[12].

The authority may refuse to grant approval if, notwithstanding that it is
satisfied as to the matters set out in heads (1) to (3) above, it considers, having
regard to the number of other approved premises[13] in its area, that the
superintendent registrar and a registrar or a civil partnership registrar as the case
may be, are unlikely to be available regularly to attend proceedings on the
premises[14].

The authority must as soon as practicable notify the applicant[15] and any
person who has given notice of objection[16] in writing of its decision, including
any conditions imposed[17] by the authority[18].

If approval is refused, or conditions other than the standard conditions[19] are
attached to the approval, or approval is granted after a person has given notice
of objection[20], the authority must set out in any notification given by it[21] its
reasons for reaching that decision[22].

If approval is refused or conditions other than the standard conditions[23] are
attached to the approval, the authority must notify the applicant of the right to
seek a review[24] of its decision[25].

1   As to the meaning of 'authority' see PARA 191 note 5.
2   As to the meaning of 'approval' see PARA 191 note 1.
3   As to the meaning of 'application' see PARA 191 note 3.

4   Marriages and Civil Partnerships (Approved Premises) Regulations 2005, SI 2005/3168, reg 5(1)(a). The application must be duly made in accordance with the Marriages and Civil Partnerships (Approved Premises) Regulations 2005, SI 2005/3168: see PARAS 191–192; and PARA 194 et seq.

5   As to the meaning of 'premises' see PARA 191 note 2.

6   Marriages and Civil Partnerships (Approved Premises) Regulations 2005, SI 2005/3168, Sch 1 para 1. As to the meaning of 'proceedings' see PARA 191 note 8.

7   Marriages and Civil Partnerships (Approved Premises) Regulations 2005, SI 2005/3168, Sch 1 para 2.

8   Marriages and Civil Partnerships (Approved Premises) Regulations 2005, SI 2005/3168, Sch 1 para 3.

9   As to the meaning of 'religious premises' see the Civil Partnership Act 2004 s 6(2); and PARA 56 note 10.

10   Marriages and Civil Partnerships (Approved Premises) Regulations 2005, SI 2005/3168, Sch 1 para 4. However Sch 1 para 4 does not apply to premises in which a register officer is situated, provided that the room which is subject to approval is not the same room as the room which is the register office: Sch 1 para 4.

11   Marriages and Civil Partnerships (Approved Premises) Regulations 2005, SI 2005/3168, Sch 1 para 5.

12   Marriages and Civil Partnerships (Approved Premises) Regulations 2005, SI 2005/3168, reg 5(1)(c).

13   As to the meaning of 'approved premises' see PARA 191 note 1.

14   Marriages and Civil Partnerships (Approved Premises) Regulations 2005, SI 2005/3168, reg 5(2).

15   As to the meaning of 'applicant' see PARA 191 note 3.

16   Ie in accordance with the Marriages and Civil Partnerships (Approved Premises) Regulations 2005, SI 2005/3168, reg 4(2)(c): see PARA 192 head (c).

17   Ie under Marriages and Civil Partnerships (Approved Premises) Regulations 2005, SI 2005/3168, reg 6: see PARA 194.

18   Marriages and Civil Partnerships (Approved Premises) Regulations 2005, SI 2005/3168, reg 5(3). As to the giving of notice see PARA 201.

19   Ie other than the conditions specified in Marriages and Civil Partnerships (Approved Premises) Regulations 2005, SI 2005/3168, reg 6(1)(a), Sch 2: see PARA 194 heads (1)–(14).

20   Ie in accordance with the Marriages and Civil Partnerships (Approved Premises) Regulations 2005, SI 2005/3168, reg 4(2)(c): see PARA 192 head (c).

21   Ie under the Marriages and Civil Partnerships (Approved Premises) Regulations 2005, SI 2005/3168, reg 5(3) (see text and note 18).

22   Marriages and Civil Partnerships (Approved Premises) Regulations 2005, SI 2005/3168, reg 5(4).

23   Ie other than the conditions specified in Marriages and Civil Partnerships (Approved Premises) Regulations 2005, SI 2005/3168, reg 6(1)(a), Sch 2: see PARA 194 heads (1)–(14).

24   Ie under the Marriages and Civil Partnerships (Approved Premises) Regulations 2005, SI 2005/3168, reg 9: see PARA 197.

25   Marriages and Civil Partnerships (Approved Premises) Regulations 2005, SI 2005/3168, reg 5(5).

194.   Conditions attached to the approval.   On grant of an approval[1], the authority[2] must attach to the approval the following conditions (the 'standard conditions')[3]:

(1)   the holder of the approval[4] must ensure that there is at all times an individual with responsibility for ensuring compliance with these conditions (the 'responsible person') and that the responsible person's occupation, seniority, position of responsibility in relation to the premises, or other factors (his 'qualification'), indicate that he is in a position to ensure compliance with these conditions[5];

(2)   the responsible person or, in his absence, an appropriately qualified deputy appointed by him, must be available on the premises[6] for a minimum of one hour prior to and throughout each of the proceedings[7];

(3)   the holder must notify the authority of his name and address

immediately on his becoming the holder of an approval[8] and of the name, address and qualification of the responsible person immediately on the appointment of a new responsible person[9];

(4)   the holder must notify the authority immediately of any change to any of the following:

    (a)   the layout of the premises, as shown in the plan submitted with the approved application, or in the use of the premises[10];

    (b)   the name or full postal address of the approved premises[11];

    (c)   the description of the room or rooms in which proceedings are to take place[12];

    (d)   the name or address of the holder of the approval[13]; and

    (e)   the name, address or qualification of the responsible person[14];

(5)   the approved premises must be made available at all reasonable times for inspection by the authority[15];

(6)   a suitable notice stating that the premises have been duly approved for the proceedings and identifying and giving directions to the room in which the proceedings are to take place must be displayed at each public entrance to the premises for one hour prior to the ceremony and throughout the ceremony[16];

(7)   no food or drink may be sold or consumed in the room in which the proceedings take place for one hour prior to that ceremony or during those proceedings[17];

(8)   all proceedings must take place in a room which was identified as one to be used for that purpose on the plan submitted with the approved application[18];

(9)   the room in which the proceedings are conducted must be separate from any other activity on the premises at the time of the proceedings[19];

(10)   the arrangements for, and content of, the proceedings must meet with the prior approval of the superintendent registrar[20] of the district[21] in which the approved premises are situated[22];

(11)   any proceedings conducted on approved premises must not be religious in nature[23];

(12)   public access to any proceedings in approved premises must be permitted without charge[24];

(13)   any reference to the approval of premises on any sign or notice, or on any stationery or publication, or within any advertisement may state that the premises have been approved by the authority as a venue for marriage[25] and the formation of civil partnerships[26] but must not state or imply any recommendation of the premises or its facilities by the authority, the Registrar General[27] or any of the officers or employees of either of them[28];

(14)   if a change of name to the premises occurs after the issue of the certificate for marriage or the civil partnership document but before the proceedings, the former name of the approved premises as recorded in the certificate for marriage or the civil partnership document must remain valid for its duration for the purpose of the proceedings[29].

In addition, on grant of an approval, the authority may attach to the approval such further conditions as it considers reasonable in order to ensure that the facilities provided at the premises are suitable and that the proceedings on the premises do not give rise to a nuisance of any kind[30].

Immediately after the grant of an approval the holder of that approval must notify to the proper officer[31] the name, address and qualification of the responsible person[32].

1 As to the meaning of 'approval' see PARA 191 note 1.
2 As to the meaning of 'authority' see PARA 191 note 5.
3 Marriages and Civil Partnerships (Approved Premises) Regulations 2005, SI 2005/3168, reg 6(1)(a).
4 For these purposes, unless the context otherwise requires, 'holder of an approval' means the person on whose application the approval was granted or a person who is deemed to be the holder of an approval under the Marriages and Civil Partnerships (Approved Premises) Regulations 2005, SI 2005/3168, reg 7(2) (see PARA 195): reg 2(1).
5 Marriages and Civil Partnerships (Approved Premises) Regulations 2005, SI 2005/3168, Sch 2 para 1. As to the meaning of 'application' see PARA 191 note 3.
6 As to the meaning of 'premises' see PARA 191 note 2.
7 Marriages and Civil Partnerships (Approved Premises) Regulations 2005, SI 2005/3168, Sch 2 para 2. As to the meaning of 'proceedings' see PARA 191 note 8.
8 Ie under Marriages and Civil Partnerships (Approved Premises) Regulations 2005, SI 2005/3168, reg 7(2).
9 Marriages and Civil Partnerships (Approved Premises) Regulations 2005, SI 2005/3168, Sch 2 para 3.
10 Marriages and Civil Partnerships (Approved Premises) Regulations 2005, SI 2005/3168, Sch 2 para 4(a).
11 Marriages and Civil Partnerships (Approved Premises) Regulations 2005, SI 2005/3168, Sch 2 para 4(b). As to the meaning of 'approved premises' see PARA 191 note 1.
12 Marriages and Civil Partnerships (Approved Premises) Regulations 2005, SI 2005/3168, Sch 2 para 4(c).
13 Marriages and Civil Partnerships (Approved Premises) Regulations 2005, SI 2005/3168, Sch 2 para 4(d).
14 Marriages and Civil Partnerships (Approved Premises) Regulations 2005, SI 2005/3168, Sch 2 para 4(e).
15 Marriages and Civil Partnerships (Approved Premises) Regulations 2005, SI 2005/3168, Sch 2 para 5.
16 Marriages and Civil Partnerships (Approved Premises) Regulations 2005, SI 2005/3168, Sch 2 para 6.
17 Marriages and Civil Partnerships (Approved Premises) Regulations 2005, SI 2005/3168, Sch 2 para 7.
18 Marriages and Civil Partnerships (Approved Premises) Regulations 2005, SI 2005/3168, Sch 2 para 8.
19 Marriages and Civil Partnerships (Approved Premises) Regulations 2005, SI 2005/3168, Sch 2 para 9.
20 As to the meaning of 'superintendent registrar' see PARA 46 note 2.
21 As to the meaning of 'registration district' see PARA 87 note 4.
22 Marriages and Civil Partnerships (Approved Premises) Regulations 2005, SI 2005/3168, Sch 2 para 10.
23 Marriages and Civil Partnerships (Approved Premises) Regulations 2005, SI 2005/3168, Sch 2 para 11(1). In particular the proceedings must not:
    (1) include extracts from an authorised religious marriage service or from sacred religious texts (Sch 2 para 11(2)(a));
    (2) be led by a minister of religion or other religious leader (Sch 2 para 11(2)(b));
    (3) involve a religious ritual or series of rituals (Sch 2 para 11(2)(c));
    (4) include hymns or other religious chants (Sch 2 para 11(2)(d)); or
    (5) include any form of worship (Sch 2 para 11(2)(e)).
    But the proceedings may include readings, songs or music that contains an incidental reference to a god or deity in an essentially non-religious context: Sch 2 para 11(3). For this purpose any material used by way of introduction to, in any interval between parts of, or by way of conclusion to the proceedings is treated as forming part of the proceedings: Sch 2 para 11(4).
24 Marriages and Civil Partnerships (Approved Premises) Regulations 2005, SI 2005/3168, Sch 2 para 12.
25 Ie in pursuance of the Marriage Act 1949 s 26(1)(bb): see PARA 54.
26 Ic under the Civil Partnership Act 2004 s 6(3A)(a): see PARA 56.

27 As to the meaning of 'Registrar General' see PARA 46 note 5.

28 Marriages and Civil Partnerships (Approved Premises) Regulations 2005, SI 2005/3168, Sch 2 para 13.

29 Marriages and Civil Partnerships (Approved Premises) Regulations 2005, SI 2005/3168, Sch 2 para 14.

30 Marriages and Civil Partnerships (Approved Premises) Regulations 2005, SI 2005/3168, reg 6(1)(b).

31 As to the meaning of 'proper officer' see PARA 191 note 4.

32 Marriages and Civil Partnerships (Approved Premises) Regulations 2005, SI 2005/3168, reg 6(2).

195. Expiry and renewal of approval. An approval[1] is valid[2] for a period of three years[3]; and it remains in force[4] notwithstanding that the holder[5] ceases to have a proprietary interest in the premises[6] and the person to whom his interest is transferred is deemed to be the holder in his place[7].

An application for renewal of an approval may be made by the holder of that approval not more than 12 months before it is due to expire[8]. If an application for renewal has been so made and that application has not been finally determined or withdrawn before the date on which the approval would otherwise expire, the approval continues in effect until such time as the application is finally determined or withdrawn[9].

Where the holder fails to apply for the renewal of approval and the approval expires in consequence of this failure, an application for renewal may be made[10] and within one month of the expiry must reinstate the approval and an approval so reinstated must continue in effect until such time as the application is finally determined or withdrawn[11].

1 As to the meaning of 'approval' see PARA 191 note 1.

2 Ie subject to the Marriages and Civil Partnerships (Approved Premises) Regulations 2005, SI 2005/3168, reg 7(5), (6) and reg 8 (see PARA 196).

3 Marriages and Civil Partnerships (Approved Premises) Regulations 2005, SI 2005/3168, reg 7(1).

4 Ie without prejudice to the provisions of the Marriages and Civil Partnerships (Approved Premises) Regulations 2005, SI 2005/3168, as to the duration of approval or revocation of approval (see PARA 196), or any condition as to notification of change of ownership (see PARA 194).

5 As to the meaning of 'holder of an approval' see PARA 194 note 4.

6 As to the meaning of 'premises' see PARA 191 note 2.

7 Marriages and Civil Partnerships (Approved Premises) Regulations 2005, SI 2005/3168, reg 7(2).

8 Marriages and Civil Partnerships (Approved Premises) Regulations 2005, SI 2005/3168, reg 7(3). Regulation 3(2)–(4) (see PARA 191), reg 4 (see PARA 192), reg 5 (see PARA 193) and reg 6 (see PARA 194) apply to an application to renew an approval as they apply to an application for approval and as though any reference in them to an applicant were to an application for renewal and to a grant of approval were to a renewal of approval: reg 7(4).

9 Marriages and Civil Partnerships (Approved Premises) Regulations 2005, SI 2005/3168, reg 7(5).

10 Ie in accordance with the Marriages and Civil Partnerships (Approved Premises) Regulations 2005, SI 2005/3168, reg 7(4) (see note 8).

11 Marriages and Civil Partnerships (Approved Premises) Regulations 2005, SI 2005/3168, reg 7(6).

196. Revocation of approval. An authority[1] which has granted an approval[2] may revoke it if it is satisfied that:

(1) the holder[3] has failed to comply with one or more of the conditions attached to the approval[4]; or

(2) the use or structure of the premises[5] has changed so that, having regard

to the requirements for the grant of an approval[6] and any requirements set by the authority[7], the premises are no longer suitable for any proceedings[8].

Before so revoking an approval, the authority must deliver to the holder of that approval a notice in writing specifying the ground or grounds on which it proposes to revoke the approval and inviting the holder to make written representations as to the proposed revocation within such period, being not less than 14 days, as is specified in the notice[9]. The authority must deliver a copy of such a notice to the superintendent registrar[10] for the district[11] in which the premises are situated[12] and to the civil partnership registrars[13] and person authorised[14] for the area in which the premises are situated[15].

Before reaching a final decision on the proposed revocation, the authority must take into account any representations made to it within the specified period[16] by or on behalf of the holder of the approval[17].

If the authority decides to revoke the approval, it must deliver a further notice in writing to the holder, stating the date on which the approval is to cease to have effect and the procedure whereby such decision may[18] be subject to review[19].

The Registrar General[20] may direct the authority to revoke any approval if, in his opinion, there have been breaches of the law relating to marriage on the approved premises[21]. Before directing any such revocation, the Registrar General must notify the holder of the grounds on which she proposes to direct that the approval be revoked and deliver a notice in writing to the holder inviting him to make representations in writing as to the proposed revocation within such period, being not less than 14 days, as she specifies[22].

Before reaching a final decision on the proposed direction, the Registrar General must take into account any representations made to him within the specified period[23] by or on behalf of the holder of the approval[24].

The authority must forthwith revoke any approval with immediate effect if directed to do so in writing by the Registrar General[25] and deliver a notice of revocation in writing to the holder[26].

The authority must revoke any approval with immediate effect as soon as practicable after being requested to do so by the holder of that approval and deliver a notice of revocation in writing to the holder[27].

On receipt of notice of revocation under the above provisions[28], the holder of an approval must forthwith give notice of revocation to all parties who have made arrangements for any proceedings to take place in the premises which were approved but whose proceedings have not yet taken place there[29].

1   As to the meaning of 'authority' see PARA 191 note 5.
2   As to the meaning of 'approval' see PARA 191 note 1.
3   As to the meaning of 'holder of an approval' see PARA 194 note 4.
4   Marriages and Civil Partnerships (Approved Premises) Regulations 2005, SI 2005/3168, reg 8(1)(a). The conditions attached to the approval mentioned in the text refer to conditions attached under reg 6(1): see PARA 194.
5   As to the meaning of 'premises' see PARA 191 note 2.
6   Ie the requirements set out in the Marriages and Civil Partnerships (Approved Premises) Regulations 2005, SI 2005/3168, Sch 1: see PARA 193.
7   Ie in accordance with the Marriages and Civil Partnerships (Approved Premises) Regulations 2005, SI 2005/3168, reg 5(1)(c): see PARA 193 head (3).
8   Marriages and Civil Partnerships (Approved Premises) Regulations 2005, SI 2005/3168, reg 8(1)(b). As to the meaning of 'proceedings' see PARA 191 note 8.
9   Marriages and Civil Partnerships (Approved Premises) Regulations 2005, SI 2005/3168, reg 8(2). As to the giving of notice see PARA 201.
10 As to the meaning of 'superintendent registrar' see PARA 46 note 2.
11 As to the meaning of 'registration district' see PARA 87 note 4.

12 Marriages and Civil Partnerships (Approved Premises) Regulations 2005, SI 2005/3168, reg 8(3)(a).
13 As to the meaning of 'civil partnership registrar' see PARA 133 note 7.
14 Ie a person authorised under the Civil Partnership Act 2004 s 8(6): see PARA 866.
15 Marriages and Civil Partnerships (Approved Premises) Regulations 2005, SI 2005/3168, reg 8(3)(b).
16 Ie the period referred to in Marriages and Civil Partnerships (Approved Premises) Regulations 2005, SI 2005/3168, reg 8(2).
17 Marriages and Civil Partnerships (Approved Premises) Regulations 2005, SI 2005/3168, reg 8(4).
18 Ie under the Marriages and Civil Partnerships (Approved Premises) Regulations 2005, SI 2005/3168, reg 9: see PARA 197.
19 Marriages and Civil Partnerships (Approved Premises) Regulations 2005, SI 2005/3168, reg 8(5).
20 As to the meaning of 'Registrar General' see PARA 46 note 5.
21 Marriages and Civil Partnerships (Approved Premises) Regulations 2005, SI 2005/3168, reg 8(6). As to the meaning of 'approved premises' see PARA 191 note 1.
22 Marriages and Civil Partnerships (Approved Premises) Regulations 2005, SI 2005/3168, reg 8(7).
23 Ie the period referred to in the Marriages and Civil Partnerships (Approved Premises) Regulations 2005, SI 2005/3168, reg 8(7).
24 Marriages and Civil Partnerships (Approved Premises) Regulations 2005, SI 2005/3168, reg 8(8).
25 Ie under the Marriages and Civil Partnerships (Approved Premises) Regulations 2005, SI 2005/3168, reg 8(6).
26 Marriages and Civil Partnerships (Approved Premises) Regulations 2005, SI 2005/3168, reg 8(9).
27 Marriages and Civil Partnerships (Approved Premises) Regulations 2005, SI 2005/3168, reg 8(10).
28 Ie under the Marriages and Civil Partnerships (Approved Premises) Regulations 2005, SI 2005/3168, reg 8(5), (9) or (10).
29 Marriages and Civil Partnerships (Approved Premises) Regulations 2005, SI 2005/3168, reg 8(11).

197. Reviews. An applicant[1] who is aggrieved in relation to a decision to refuse an approval[2] or to attach to an approval conditions other than the standard conditions[3] may request a review of that decision[4].

A holder of an approval[5] who is aggrieved in relation to a decision:

(1)   to refuse to renew that approval[6]; or

(2)   to attach to the renewal of that approval conditions other than the standard conditions[7]; or

(3)   to revoke that approval save in the specified circumstances[8],

may request a review of that decision[9].

A person requesting such a review[10] must deliver his request to the proper officer[11] of the authority[12], accompanied if the authority so requires, except in the case of a request to review a decision to revoke an approval, by a fee[13], or an amount on account of that fee[14].

The proper officer must immediately arrange for review of the decision by the authority and neither an officer nor any member of a committee or sub-committee of the authority which made the decision on behalf of the authority is to take part in the decision on the review[15].

On a review of a decision, the authority may[16]:

(a)   confirm the original decision[17];

(b)   vary an original decision to grant or renew approval, in particular by removing conditions attached by the authority[18] or by attaching new or different conditions[19]; or

(c)   substitute a different decision, which may, where the original decision was to revoke an approval, be a decision that the approval should not be revoked but should be subject to new or different conditions than those which were previously attached to it[20].

The authority must give notice in writing to the applicant or holder of its decision on review, stating its reasons for that decision and, except where the original decision is confirmed, the date from which it takes effect[21].

1 As to the meaning of 'applicant' see PARA 191 note 3.
2 As to the meaning of 'approval' see PARA 191 note 1.
3 As to the meaning of 'standard conditions' see PARA 194.
4 Marriages and Civil Partnerships (Approved Premises) Regulations 2005, SI 2005/3168, reg 9(1).
5 As to the meaning of 'holder of an approval' see PARA 194 note 4.
6 Marriages and Civil Partnerships (Approved Premises) Regulations 2005, SI 2005/3168, reg 9(2)(a).
7 Marriages and Civil Partnerships (Approved Premises) Regulations 2005, SI 2005/3168, reg 9(2)(b).
8 Marriages and Civil Partnerships (Approved Premises) Regulations 2005, SI 2005/3168, reg 9(2)(c). The specified circumstances mentioned in the text refer to the Marriages and Civil Partnerships (Approved Premises) Regulations 2005, SI 2005/3168, reg 8(9) or (10): see PARA 196.
9 Marriages and Civil Partnerships (Approved Premises) Regulations 2005, SI 2005/3168, reg 9(2).
10 Ie under the Marriages and Civil Partnerships (Approved Premises) Regulations 2005, SI 2005/3168, reg 9(1) or (2).
11 As to the meaning of 'proper officer' see PARA 191 note 4.
12 As to the meaning of 'authority' see PARA 191 note 5.
13 Such fee is to be determined in accordance with the Marriages and Civil Partnerships (Approved Premises) Regulations 2005, SI 2005/3168, reg 12 (see PARA 200): reg 9(3).
14 Marriages and Civil Partnerships (Approved Premises) Regulations 2005, SI 2005/3168, reg 9(3).
15 Marriages and Civil Partnerships (Approved Premises) Regulations 2005, SI 2005/3168, reg 9(4).
16 Ie acting in accordance with the Marriages and Civil Partnerships (Approved Premises) Regulations 2005, SI 2005/3168, reg 5(1), (2): see PARA 193.
17 Marriages and Civil Partnerships (Approved Premises) Regulations 2005, SI 2005/3168, reg 9(5)(a).
18 Ie under the Marriages and Civil Partnerships (Approved Premises) Regulations 2005, SI 2005/3168, reg 6(1)(b): see PARA 194.
19 Marriages and Civil Partnerships (Approved Premises) Regulations 2005, SI 2005/3168, reg 9(5)(b).
20 Marriages and Civil Partnerships (Approved Premises) Regulations 2005, SI 2005/3168, reg 9(5)(c).
21 Marriages and Civil Partnerships (Approved Premises) Regulations 2005, SI 2005/3168, reg 9(6). As to the giving of notices see PARA 201.

198. Registers of approved premises. Each authority[1] must keep a register of all premises[2] which are approved by the authority, containing:

(1)   the name and full postal address of the approved premises[3];

(2)   the description of the room or rooms in which proceedings are to take place[4];

(3)   the name and address of the holder of the approval[5];

(4)   the date of grant of the approval[6];

(5)   the due date of expiry of that approval[7];

(6)   if the approval is renewed, the date of renewal[8];

(7)   if the approval is revoked, the date on which the revocation takes effect[9]; and

(8)   the name, address and qualification[10] of the responsible person[11].

The proper officer[12] must make the appropriate entries in the register immediately after the grant of an approval and must amend the register immediately after receiving notification that any of the details listed in heads (1) to (8) above have changed, or on renewal or revocation of an approval[13].

Immediately after making or amending any entry in the register, the proper officer must deliver a copy of the entry or amendment to the Registrar General[14] and to the superintendent registrar[15] for the district[16] in which the premises in question are situated[17] and to the civil partnership registrars and persons authorised[18] for the area in which the premises are situated[19].

The register must be open to public inspection during normal working hours[20]; and it must be kept in permanent form which may include its maintenance on a computer[21].

1   As to the meaning of 'authority' see PARA 191 note 5.
2   As to the meaning of 'premises' see PARA 191 note 2.
3   Marriages and Civil Partnerships (Approved Premises) Regulations 2005, SI 2005/3168, reg 10(1)(a). As to the meaning of 'approved premises' see PARA 191 note 1.
4   Marriages and Civil Partnerships (Approved Premises) Regulations 2005, SI 2005/3168, reg 10(1)(b). As to the meaning of 'proceedings' see PARA 191 note 8.
5   Marriages and Civil Partnerships (Approved Premises) Regulations 2005, SI 2005/3168, reg 10(1)(c). As to the meaning of 'holder of an approval' see PARA 194 note 4.
6   Marriages and Civil Partnerships (Approved Premises) Regulations 2005, SI 2005/3168, reg 10(1)(d).
7   Marriages and Civil Partnerships (Approved Premises) Regulations 2005, SI 2005/3168, reg 10(1)(e).
8   Marriages and Civil Partnerships (Approved Premises) Regulations 2005, SI 2005/3168, reg 10(1)(f).
9   Marriages and Civil Partnerships (Approved Premises) Regulations 2005, SI 2005/3168, reg 10(1)(g).
10 As to the meaning of 'qualification' see PARA 194.
11 Marriages and Civil Partnerships (Approved Premises) Regulations 2005, SI 2005/3168, reg 10(1). As to the meaning of 'responsible person' see PARA 194.
12 As to the meaning of 'proper officer' see PARA 191 note 4.
13 Marriages and Civil Partnerships (Approved Premises) Regulations 2005, SI 2005/3168, reg 10(2).
14 Marriages and Civil Partnerships (Approved Premises) Regulations 2005, SI 2005/3168, reg 10(3)(a). As to the meaning of 'Registrar General' see PARA 46 note 5.
15 As to the meaning of 'superintendent registrar' see PARA 46 note 2.
16 As to the meaning of 'registration district' see PARA 87 note 4.
17 Marriages and Civil Partnerships (Approved Premises) Regulations 2005, SI 2005/3168, reg 10(3)(b).
18 Ie authorised under the Civil Partnership Act 2004 s 8(6): see PARA 133 note 6.
19 Marriages and Civil Partnerships (Approved Premises) Regulations 2005, SI 2005/3168, reg 10(3)(c).
20 Marriages and Civil Partnerships (Approved Premises) Regulations 2005, SI 2005/3168, reg 10(4).
21 Marriages and Civil Partnerships (Approved Premises) Regulations 2005, SI 2005/3168, reg 10(5).

199. Guidance concerning grants of approval and approved premises. The Registrar General[1] may issue guidance supplementing the statutory provisions[2] relating to the approval of premises[3].

1   As to the meaning of 'Registrar General' see PARA 46 note 5.
2   Ie the Marriages and Civil Partnerships (Approved Premises) Regulations 2005, SI 2005/3168: see PARA 191 et seq and PARAS 200, 201.
3   Marriages and Civil Partnerships (Approved Premises) Regulations 2005, SI 2005/3168, reg 11.

200. Fees. An authority[1] may[2] determine a fee in respect of an application[3] or the renewal of an approval, and may determine that fee either for that particular application or renewal or for applications or renewals generally or of any particular class[4].

A fee determined for a particular application or renewal must not exceed the amount which reasonably represents the costs incurred or to be incurred by the authority in respect of that application or renewal[5].

A fee determined for applications or renewals generally or of a particular class must not exceed the amount which reasonably represents the average costs incurred or likely to be incurred by the authority in respect of an application or renewal, or, as the case may be, in respect of an application or renewal of that class[6].

A fee determined in respect of an application or renewal may not include an amount representing costs incurred in respect of any review or possible review[7] unless and until such a review is requested in relation to that application or renewal; but, where such a review is requested, an authority may determine an additional fee in respect of that application or renewal[8], taking into account only the additional costs arising from review[9].

An authority may charge a fee in respect of an application or renewal, or an amount on account of such fee, even though it may not yet have incurred any cost in respect of that application or renewal[10].

The superintendent registrar[11] in whose presence persons are married on approved premises[12] is entitled to receive from them a fee of an amount determined by the authority as reasonably representing all the costs to it of providing a registrar[13] and superintendent registrar to attend at a solemnisation[14]; and the authority may set different fees for different cases or circumstances[15].

Where a civil partnership registrar[16] for any area attends when two people sign the civil partnership schedule on approved premises, the authority for the area must be entitled to receive from them a fee of an amount determined by it as reasonably representing all the costs to it of providing the civil partnership registrar to attend at the formation[17]; and the authority may set different fees for different cases or circumstances[18].

1 As to the meaning of 'authority' see PARA 191 note 5.
2 Ie in accordance with the Marriages and Civil Partnerships (Approved Premises) Regulations 2005, SI 2005/3168, reg 12(2)–(4).
3 As to the meaning of 'application' see PARA 191 note 3.
4 Marriages and Civil Partnerships (Approved Premises) Regulations 2005, SI 2005/3168, reg 12(1).
5 Marriages and Civil Partnerships (Approved Premises) Regulations 2005, SI 2005/3168, reg 12(2).
6 Marriages and Civil Partnerships (Approved Premises) Regulations 2005, SI 2005/3168, reg 12(3).
7 Ie under the Marriages and Civil Partnerships (Approved Premises) Regulations 2005, SI 2005/3168, reg 9: see PARA 197.
8 Ie in accordance with the Marriages and Civil Partnerships (Approved Premises) Regulations 2005, SI 2005/3168, reg 12(2) or (3).
9 Marriages and Civil Partnerships (Approved Premises) Regulations 2005, SI 2005/3168, reg 12(4).
10 Marriages and Civil Partnerships (Approved Premises) Regulations 2005, SI 2005/3168, reg 12(5).
11 As to the meaning of 'superintendent registrar' see PARA 46 note 2.
12 As to the meaning of 'approved premises' see PARA 191 note 1.
13 As to the meaning of 'registrar' see PARA 88 note 1.

14 Marriages and Civil Partnerships (Approved Premises) Regulations 2005, SI 2005/3168, reg 12(6).
15 Marriages and Civil Partnerships (Approved Premises) Regulations 2005, SI 2005/3168, reg 12(8).
16 As to the meaning of 'civil partnership registrar' see PARA 139 note 8.
17 Marriages and Civil Partnerships (Approved Premises) Regulations 2005, SI 2005/3168, reg 12(7).
18 Marriages and Civil Partnerships (Approved Premises) Regulations 2005, SI 2005/3168, reg 12(8).

201.   Notices.   If there is more than one holder of an approval[1], any notice which is required[2] to be delivered to the holder is validly delivered if it is delivered[3] to any one of the holders of the approval at the address entered in the register[4] in respect of that holder[5].

1   As to the meaning of 'holder of an approval' see PARA 194 note 4.
2   Ie under the Marriages and Civil Partnerships (Approved Premises) Regulations 2005, SI 2005/3168: see PARA 191 et seq.
3   Ie in accordance with the other provisions of the Marriages and Civil Partnerships (Approved Premises) Regulations 2005, SI 2005/3168: see PARA 191 et seq.
4   Ie under the Marriages and Civil Partnerships (Approved Premises) Regulations 2005, SI 2005/3168, reg 10(1)(c): see PARA 198 head (3).
5   Marriages and Civil Partnerships (Approved Premises) Regulations 2005, SI 2005/3168, reg 13.

202.   Change of name of approved premises.   If a change of name of the approved premises[1] occurs after the issue of the certificate for marriage or the civil partnership but before the proceedings, that change does not affect the validity of the certificate for marriage or the civil partnership document[2].

1   As to the meaning of 'approved premises' see PARA 191 note 1.
2   Marriages and Civil Partnerships (Approved Premises) Regulations 2005, SI 2005/3168, reg 15.

4. LEGAL INCIDENTS OF MARRIAGE AND CIVIL PARTNERSHIP

(1) STATUS OF MARRIED PERSONS AND CIVIL PARTNERS

203.   Contractual basis and effect of marriage. The best known description of marriage as a legal concept is that it is the fulfilment of a contract satisfied by the solemnisation of the marriage, but marriage, directly it exists, creates by law a relation between the parties and what is called a status of each[1]. The status of an individual, used as a legal term, means the legal position of the individual in or with regard to the rest of a community[2]. That relation between the parties, and that status of each of them with regard to the community, which are constituted on marriage are not imposed or defined by contract or agreement but by law[3].

1   *Niboyet v Niboyet* (1878) 4 PD 1 at 11, CA per Brett LJ. As to the domicile of married women see PARA 214; and CONFLICT OF LAWS vol 8(3) (Reissue) PARA 54.

2   See note 1.

3   See note 1.

204.   Position of married women in civil law. The following provisions derive from enactments specifically referring to 'marriage' and 'married women' and for which no corresponding civil partnership provision has been made: however, it is submitted that these provisions must now also apply, to the extent that they have any continuing relevance, to the contractual rights of either party to a marriage and, presumably, to civil partners.

A married woman is capable of acquiring, holding and disposing of any property in all respects as if she were a feme sole[1]. No restriction on anticipation or alienation attached, or purported to be attached, to the enjoyment of property by a woman is of any effect if it could not have been attached to the enjoyment of that property by a man[2].

A married woman may render herself liable in respect of any tort[3] and is liable for all her debts and obligations howsoever incurred[4]: she may be sued in tort in all respects as if she were a feme sole[5] and is subject to the law relating to bankruptcy and to the enforcement of judgments and orders in the same way[6]. A woman's husband is not, by reason only of his being her husband, liable in respect of any tort committed by her whether before or after the marriage, or in respect of any contract entered into, or debt or obligation incurred, by her before the marriage or in respect of any contract entered into, or debt or obligation incurred, by her after the marriage in respect of which he would not otherwise[7] have been liable[8]. He is not liable to be sued or to be made a party to any legal proceedings brought in respect of any such tort, contract, debt or obligation[9]. A married couple is not, however, prevented from rendering themselves, or being rendered, jointly liable in respect of any tort, and of suing or being sued in tort as if they were not married[10]; moreover, where a tort is committed by a wife with her husband's express authority, or where she is in the position of his agent and the tort is committed in the ordinary course of the agency, the husband and the wife are liable jointly and severally and both or either of them may be sued as in any other case of principal and agent[11].

The execution by will of a general power of appointment makes the property appointed liable for the appointor's debts and obligations[12]; a married woman cannot be compelled to exercise such a power in favour of creditors[13], but, under the bankruptcy laws, the property of a bankrupt includes the capacity to exercise all such powers in respect of property as might have been exercised by the bankrupt for his or her own benefit[14].

1   Law Reform (Married Women and Tortfeasors) Act 1935 s 1(a). 'Feme sole' means an unmarried woman, including a widowed or divorced woman. All property which immediately before 22 August 1935 (ie the date on which the Law Reform (Married Women and Tortfeasors) Act 1935 received the Royal Assent) was the separate property of a married woman or was then held for her separate use in equity, and all property belonging, at the time of her marriage, to a woman married on or after that date, or acquired by or devolving on a married woman on or after that date, belongs to her in all respects as if she were a feme sole and may be disposed of accordingly: s 2(1). Nothing in Pt I (ss 1–5) prevents a husband and wife from acquiring, holding and disposing of any property jointly or as tenants in common: s 4(2)(c). As to the general right of a married woman to bring civil proceedings for the protection and security of her property see PARA 210; as to her right to bring criminal proceedings see PARA 208; as to the removal of the limitations on her right to sue her husband in tort see PARA 211; as to the summary decision of questions as to property between husband and wife see PARA 224 et seq; and as to the restraining or avoidance of transactions made with a view to defeating a spouse's claim for financial relief in matrimonial proceedings see PARAS 586–588.

2   Married Women (Restraint upon Anticipation) Act 1949 s 1(1). This provision has effect whatever is the date of the passing, execution or coming into operation of the Act or instrument containing the provision by virtue of which the restriction was attached or purported to be attached: s 1(2). The power to impose a restraint on anticipation by an instrument executed on or after 1 January 1936 had already been abolished by the Law Reform (Married Women and Tortfeasors) Act 1935 s 2(2) (repealed), subject to certain special provisions as to when particular instruments were to be deemed to have been executed: s 2(3) (repealed).

3   Law Reform (Married Women and Tortfeasors) Act 1935 s 1(b).

4   Law Reform (Married Women and Tortfeasors) Act 1935 ss 1(b), (c), 2(1). As to the capacity of spouses to make independent contracts see PARA 205; as to contracts between spouses see PARA 206.

5   Law Reform (Married Women and Tortfeasors) Act 1935 s 1(c).

6   Law Reform (Married Women and Tortfeasors) Act 1935 s 1(d). As to the enforcement of judgments and orders see PARAS 210, 623 et seq.

7   Ie if the Law Reform (Married Women and Tortfeasors) Act 1935 had not been passed.

8   Law Reform (Married Women and Tortfeasors) Act 1935 ss 3(a), 4(2)(a); and see *Barber v Pidgen* [1937] 1 KB 664, [1937] 1 All ER 115, CA. Conversely, the husband is not exempt from liability in respect of any contract entered into, or debt or obligation (not being a debt or obligation arising out of the commission of a tort) incurred, by the wife after the marriage in respect of which he would have been liable if the Law Reform (Married Women and Tortfeasors) Act 1935 had not been passed: s 4(2)(b). As to liability to pay non-domestic rates see RATING AND COUNCIL TAX vol 39(1B) (Reissue) PARA 3 et seq; and as to liability to pay council tax see RATING AND COUNCIL TAX vol 39(1B) (Reissue) PARA 240.

9   Law Reform (Married Women and Tortfeasors) Act 1935 s 3(b). Where a man domiciled in England is married there to a woman who has contracted obligations abroad, the extent of his liability when sued in the English courts in respect of such obligations is governed by English law, and not by the law of the place where the obligations were contracted: *De Greuchy v Wills* (1879) 4 CPD 362.

10   Law Reform (Married Women and Tortfeasors) Act 1935 s 4(2)(c). A husband and wife may be jointly liable for the tort of conspiracy, even though they are the only parties to the conspiracy: *Midland Bank Trust Co Ltd v Green (No 3)* [1982] Ch 529, [1981] 3 All ER 744, CA (there is no place in the modern law for the mediaeval fiction of unity between husband and wife and, except in so far as the doctrine of unity is retained by statute or judicial decision, a husband and wife are to be treated as separate and equal parties). A husband cannot, however, conspire with his wife alone to commit a criminal act: see PARA 208.

11   *Taylor v Green* (1837) 8 C & P 316 (fraudulent misrepresentations by wife to intending purchaser of business managed by her on behalf of husband; husband liable); *Miell v English* (1866) 15 LT 249 (husband liable for injuries to servant sustained while carrying out wife's directions); *Burdett v Horne* (1911) 28 TLR 83, CA (misrepresentations by wife with husband's knowledge, authority and acquiescence; husband and wife joint tortfeasors). As to the liability of one spouse who permits the other spouse to use his or her car see *Morgans v Launchbury* [1973] AC 127, [1972] 2 All ER 606, HL; and AGENCY vol 1 (2008) PARAS 14, 151. As to the statutory right of contribution between joint tortfeasors see the Civil Liability (Contribution)

Act 1978 ss 1, 2; DAMAGES vol 12(1) (Reissue) PARA 837 et seq; and TORT vol 45(2) (Reissue) PARA 349 et seq. If either husband or wife is sued alone in respect of a tort jointly committed and judgment is obtained, the judgment recovered is no bar to an action against the other spouse: see ss 3, 6(1); DAMAGES vol 12(1) (Reissue) PARAS 348, 349; and TORT vol 45(2) (Reissue) PARAS 838, 840.

12 See the Administration of Estates Act 1925 s 32(1) (which applies generally to the exercise of general powers of appointment by deceased persons); and EXECUTORS AND ADMINISTRATORS vol 17(2) (Reissue) PARAS 387, 416. As to the exercise of powers of appointment by married women generally see PARA 232. As to the effect of marriage and civil partnership on wills and intestacy see PARA 209.

13 *Hulme v Tenant* (1778) 1 Bro CC 16.

14 See the Insolvency Act 1986 s 283(4); and BANKRUPTCY AND INDIVIDUAL INSOLVENCY vol 3(2) (2002 Reissue) PARA 216.

205. Spouses' and civil partners' contracts. The principle by which a person who executes a deed in his own name is personally liable on it, even though he is in fact an agent for another[1], and the principle by which a person who signs a bill of exchange, cheque or promissory note is personally liable unless he adds words indicating that he signs for or on behalf of a principal[2], apply in relation to spouses and civil partners.

In the case of a contract in writing other than a deed, a bill of exchange, a cheque or a promissory note the question whether a spouse or civil partner is to be taken to have contracted on his or her own behalf or as agent of his or her spouse or civil partner or a third party must, it seems, be determined in accordance with the general principle which applies in determining whether a person has contracted as principal or agent[3], namely by reference to the intention of the parties ascertained from the terms of the written agreement when construed as a whole with reference to the surrounding circumstances, the construction of the contract being a matter of law[4]. If, on the construction of a written contract by an agent, the agent undertakes personal liability, extrinsic evidence of intention is not admissible to exonerate the agent from liability, although by way of equitable defence the agent may set up an express agreement with the other contracting party to that effect[5].

Spouses and civil partners may contract jointly or jointly and severally with their spouses or civil partner or a third person[6].

A spouse or civil partner living apart from their spouse or civil partner will be presumed to contract on their own behalf unless a contrary intention appears[7].

1 See AGENCY vol 1 (2008) PARA 157.

2 See the Bills of Exchange Act 1882 s 26(1); AGENCY vol 1 (2008) PARA 157; FINANCIAL SERVICES AND INSTITUTIONS vol 49 (2008) PARAS 1473–1477.

3 See *Bowes v Shand* (1877) 2 App Cas 455, HL; *Young v Schuler* (1883) 11 QBD 651, CA; *Southwell v Bowditch* (1876) 1 CPD 374, CA. As to the construction of written instruments generally see DEEDS AND OTHER INSTRUMENTS vol 13 (2007 Reissue) PARA 164 et seq.

4 See generally AGENCY vol 1 (2008) PARA 1. As to contracts between spouses and civil partners see PARA 206. It has been held that where a contract entered into by a married woman is not reduced to writing, the question whether she is to be deemed to have contracted on her own behalf or as agent for her husband is one of fact, and depends on the circumstances of the particular case: see *Bentley v Griffin* (1814) 5 Taunt 356; *Metcalfe v Shaw* (1811) 3 Camp 22. Although the mere fact that goods are invoiced in the name of the wife does not necessarily indicate that the tradesman intended to give credit to her as a principal (see *Jewsbury v Newbold* (1857) 26 LJ Ex 247; *Paquin Ltd v Beauclerk* [1906] AC 148, HL. Cf *Fick and Fick Ltd v Assimakis* [1958] 3 All ER 182, [1958] 1 WLR 1006, CA), that fact coupled with the circumstance that she herself paid for a portion of the goods, or has previously paid for goods of a similar kind, becomes almost conclusive evidence of such an intention (see *Bentley v Griffin* (1814) 5 Taunt 356; *Freestone v Butcher* (1840) 9 C & P 643; and see *Lea Bridge District Gas Co v Malvern* [1917] 1 KB 803, DC (contract made by widow before remarriage for supply

of gas; presumption of continuance on remarriage)). A married woman who contracts on her own behalf is solely liable: see the Law Reform (Married Women and Tortfeasors) Act 1935 s 1; and PARA 204.

5 See AGENCY vol 1 (2008) PARA 157; DEEDS AND OTHER INSTRUMENTS vol 13 (2007 Reissue) PARA 186. As to the admission of extrinsic evidence to vary or add to a written agreement generally see DEEDS AND OTHER INSTRUMENTS vol 13 (2007 Reissue) PARA 185 et seq.

6 See *French v Howie* [1906] 2 KB 674, CA. The power of a husband and wife to contract jointly is not affected by the Law Reform (Married Women and Tortfeasors) Act 1935 Pt I (ss 1–5): see s 4(2)(c); and PARA 204. Where husband and wife are jointly liable under a contract, judgment recovered against one of them in respect of damage suffered through breach of the contract is no longer a bar to an action against the other in respect of the same damage: see the Civil Liability (Contribution) Act 1978 ss 3, 6(1); and CONTRACT vol 9(1) (Reissue) PARA 1087. As to the right of one joint contractor, if sued alone, to insist on his co-contractor being joined see CONTRACT vol 9(1) (Reissue) PARA 1080.

7 *Hodgson v Williamson* (1880) 15 ChD 87. See also PARA 267.

206. Contracts between spouses and civil partners. It is provided by statute that a married woman[1] may contract with her husband as with a third person, and that they may sue one another on any contract made during the marriage[2] in the same manner and with the same effect as if the contract had been entered into by the wife as a principal with a third person[3]: independently of statute, it has been held that a wife may sue her husband for the repayment of money lent[4] and that a husband may sue his wife for money lent or money paid by him at her request after marriage[5] and may become a purchaser for value of her property[6].

1 Although these provisions derive from an enactments specifically referring to 'marriage' and 'married women' and from common law decisions pre-dating the concept of civil partnerships, it is submitted that these provisions must now also apply, to the extent that they have any continuing relevance, to the contractual rights of either party to a marriage and, presumably, to civil partners.

2 See the Law Reform (Married Women and Tortfeasors) Act 1935 ss 1(b), (c), 4(2)(c); and PARA 204. Mere mutual promises made in the ordinary domestic relationship of husband and wife do not, however, necessarily constitute a contract enforceable at law: *Balfour v Balfour* [1919] 2 KB 571, CA (agreement by husband to give wife an allowance for expenses). In *Pettitt v Pettitt* [1970] AC 777 at 816, [1969] 2 All ER 385 at 408, HL, Lord Upjohn said: 'That case (*Balfour v Balfour*) illustrates the well-known doctrine that in their ordinary day to day life spouses do not intend to contract in a legally binding sense with one another, though I am bound to confess that in my opinion the facts of that case stretched that doctrine to its limits'; and see *Pettitt v Pettitt* at 806 and at 400 per Lord Hodson, and at 821, 822 and at 413 per Lord Diplock. See also *Gould v Gould* [1970] 1 QB 275, [1969] 3 All ER 728, CA; *Merritt v Merritt* [1970] 2 All ER 760, [1970] 1 WLR 1211, CA (agreement after the parties had separated held intended to create legal relations); *Jones v Padavatton* [1969] 2 All ER 616 at 618, [1969] 1 WLR 328 at 330, CA per Danckwerts LJ; *Spellman v Spellman* [1961] 2 All ER 498, [1961] 1 WLR 921, CA (husband promised to buy wife car; husband acquired car on hire purchase; not intended to create legal relations); *Fribance v Fribance* [1957] 1 All ER 357, [1957] 1 WLR 384, CA; *Hoddinott v Hoddinott* [1949] 2 KB 406, CA.

In general, time runs both in favour of and against a wife in respect of any cause of action founded on any contract made with her husband (see *Re Lady Hastings, Hallett v Hastings* (1887) 35 ChD 94, CA (loan by husband to wife on an oral promise by her to repay the amount out of her separate estate; debt held barred after six years); and see *Lowe v Fox* (1885) 15 QBD 667, CA); but the application of the general provision relating to limitation of actions may be subject to special principles applicable to transactions between husband and wife (see eg *Re Dixon, Heynes v Dixon* [1900] 2 Ch 561, CA (loan by wife to husband at interest; time does not run so long as they live together in amity, because a gift of the interest is presumed)) and to the particular provisions relating to actions in respect of trust property, as, for example, where the husband has received money as a trustee for his wife (see eg *Re Eyre-Williams, Williams v Williams* [1923] 2 Ch 533). Actions in respect of trust property are governed by the Limitation Act 1980 s 21: see LIMITATION PERIODS vol 68 (2008) PARA 1140.

Where a wife seeks to avoid a contract with her husband on the ground of undue influence or duress, the burden of proof is on her: see *Gillman v Gillman* (1946) 174 LT 272 (wife signed agreement to separate, but later said she had no knowledge of its contents; no misrepresentation by husband; wife held bound by contents and no duty on husband to prove absence of undue influence).

3   *Boston v Boston* [1904] 1 KB 124, CA; *Re Shaw, Shaw v Jones* (1906) 94 LT 93; and see *Hunt v Hunt* (1908) 25 TLR 132.

4   See *Woodward v Woodward* (1863) 3 De GJ & Sm 672; *Horrell v Horrell* (1882) 46 JP 295. A loan to a husband of money belonging to the wife, though not her separate property nor held for her separate use, was valuable consideration for a settlement on the wife of the money so lent: *Re Home, ex p Home* (1885) 54 LT 301.

5   *Butler v Butler* (1885) 16 QBD 374, CA. The husband could sue his wife in equity, independently of statute, on a contract with him by which she intended to bind property held to her separate use: *Butler v Butler*.

6   *Hewison v Negus* (1853) 16 Beav 594.

207.   Bankruptcy of spouse or civil partner.   A spouse or civil partner may prove as a creditor in their spouse or civil partner's bankruptcy and is entitled to be paid pari passu with the other creditors in respect of any contract with that spouse or civil partner, not being a loan for the purpose of a trade or business carried on by him or her[1]. Where a loan is made by a spouse or civil partner to the other spouse or civil partner for the purpose of a trade or business carried on by him or her, the loan forms part of his or her assets in case of his or her bankruptcy, and the spouse or civil partner who made the loan is not entitled to claim any dividend as a creditor until all claims of the other creditors for valuable consideration in money or money's worth have been satisfied[2].

Where a loan is made by a spouse or civil partner to the other spouse or civil partner for purposes unconnected with the trade or business of the borrower, the lender may prove in the borrower's bankruptcy in competition with his or her other creditors, and is entitled to receive a dividend pari passu with them[3]. Where the loan is to a partnership firm of which the borrower is a member, the lender may prove against the joint estate of the partners, and is entitled to receive a dividend pari passu with the other creditors of the firm[4].

1   See BANKRUPTCY AND INDIVIDUAL INSOLVENCY vol 3(2) (2002 Reissue) PARA 490 et seq.

2   See BANKRUPTCY AND INDIVIDUAL INSOLVENCY vol 3(2) (2002 Reissue) PARA 575.

3   *Re Clark, ex p Schulze* [1898] 2 QB 330, CA; *Re Tidswell, ex p Tidswell* (1887) 56 LJQB 548; *Mackintosh v Pogose* [1895] 1 Ch 505 (all involving loans from a wife to her husband, but applicable mutatis mutandis to any loans between spouses or civil partners).

4   *Re Tuff, ex p Nottingham* (1887) 19 QBD 88 (loans from a wife to her husband, but applicable mutatis mutandis to any loans between spouses or civil partners). It has been held that if a wife is a partner with her husband, she will be postponed to other creditors: *Re Childs, ex p New* (1874) 9 Ch App 508.

208.   Criminal liability of spouse or civil partner for acts of other spouse or civil partner.   A spouse or civil partner will not be liable for the criminal acts of his or her spouse or civil partner unless he or she is in the position of an agent and an offence is committed in the course of the agency[1]. In the case of the offences, mainly statutory, where mens rea is not essential, a spouse or civil partner may be criminally liable for the act of his or her spouse or civil partner as agent, even where the offence is committed without his or her authority or connivance[2].

A person cannot conspire with his or her spouse or civil partner alone[3], but may in the ordinary way participate in, or aid, abet, counsel or procure, the commission of an offence by him or her[4]. Provision is made in connection with the institution of proceedings against spouses and civil partners[5].

1   See CRIMINAL LAW, EVIDENCE AND PROCEDURE vol 11(1) (2006 Reissue) PARA 59 et seq. The presumption of law that an offence committed by a wife in the presence of her husband was

committed under the coercion of the husband was abolished by the Criminal Justice Act 1925 s 47, but that provision also provided that on a charge against a wife for any offence other than treason or murder it is a good defence to prove that the offence was committed in the presence of, and under the coercion of, the husband. As to marital coercion generally see CRIMINAL LAW, EVIDENCE AND PROCEDURE vol 11(1) (2006 Reissue) PARA 24.

2   As to strict liability for offences generally see CRIMINAL LAW, EVIDENCE AND PROCEDURE vol 11(1) (2006 Reissue) PARA 15.

3   See the Criminal Law Act 1977 s 2(2)(a); and CRIMINAL LAW, EVIDENCE AND PROCEDURE vol 11(1) (2006 Reissue) PARA 67. This rule does not apply to the tort of conspiracy: see PARA 204.

4   See CRIMINAL LAW, EVIDENCE AND PROCEDURE vol 11(1) (2006 Reissue) PARA 49. It is an offence for any person, knowing or believing that another has committed an offence, to do without lawful authority or reasonable excuse any act with intent to impede that other person's apprehension or prosecution (see the Criminal Law Act 1967 s 4(1); and CRIMINAL LAW, EVIDENCE AND PROCEDURE vol 11(1) (2006 Reissue) PARA 58), and this applies to a wife who harbours her husband unless coercion by the husband can be proved (see the Criminal Justice Act 1925 s 47; *R v Holley* [1963] 1 All ER 106, [1963] 1 WLR 199, CCA; and CRIMINAL LAW, EVIDENCE AND PROCEDURE vol 11(1) (2006 Reissue) PARA 24).

5   See the Theft Act 1968 s 30(2); and CRIMINAL LAW, EVIDENCE AND PROCEDURE vol 11(1) (2006 Reissue) PARA 291. Subject to certain exceptions, proceedings may not be instituted against a person for any offence of stealing or doing unlawful damage to property which at the time of the offence belonged to that person's spouse or civil partner or for any attempt, incitement or conspiracy to commit such an offence, unless proceedings are instituted by or with the consent of the Director of Public Prosecutions: see s 30(4); and CRIMINAL LAW, EVIDENCE AND PROCEDURE vol 11(1) (2006 Reissue) PARA 291. As to the competency of a defendant's spouse or civil partner to give evidence for the prosecution see PARA 212.

209.   Effect of marriage and civil partnership on wills and intestacy. A will is, in general, revoked by the testator's marriage or by the formation of a civil partnership between the testator and another person[1], even if the marriage or civil partnership is voidable and whether or not it is in fact avoided[2]. Where it appears from a will that at the time it was made the testator was expecting to be married to, or to enter into a civil partnership with, a particular person, and that he intended that the will or a disposition in it should not be revoked by the marriage or civil partnership, the will or disposition is not revoked by the marriage or civil partnership[3].

Where, after a testator has made a will, his or her marriage or civil partnership is dissolved or annulled, then the provisions of that will appointing executors or trustees or conferring a power of appointment, if they appoint or confer the power on the former spouse or civil partner, take effect as if the former spouse or civil partner had died on the date on which the marriage or civil partnership is dissolved or annulled, and any property which, or an interest in which, is devised or bequeathed to the former spouse or civil partner passes as if the former spouse or civil partner had died on that date[4].

If, while a decree of judicial separation or a separation order is in force and the separation is continuing, either of the parties to the marriage or civil partnership dies intestate as respects all or any of his or her real or personal property, that property devolves as if the other party had then been dead[5].

1   See the Wills Act 1837 ss 18(1), 18B(1); and WILLS vol 50 (2005 Reissue) PARAS 379, 382. As to pre-1983 wills see WILLS vol 50 (2005 Reissue) PARA 380.

2   See *Re Roberts, Roberts v Roberts* [1978] 3 All ER 225, [1978] 1 WLR 653, CA. As to void and voidable marriages and civil partnerships see PARA 326 et seq.

3   See the Wills Act 1837 ss 18(3), (4), 18B(3)–(6); and WILLS vol 50 (2005 Reissue) PARAS 381, 383.

4   See the Wills Act 1837 ss 18A, 18C; and WILLS vol 50 (2005 Reissue) PARAS 468–470. This does not prejudice any right of the former spouse or civil partner to apply for financial provision

under the Inheritance (Provision for Family and Dependants) Act 1975: see the Wills Act 1837 ss 18A(2), 18C(3); PARAS 538–541; and EXECUTORS AND ADMINISTRATORS vol 17(2) (Reissue) PARA 665 et seq.

5   Matrimonial Causes Act 1973 s 18(2); Civil Partnership Act 2004 s 57.

210.   Proceedings by and against married women.   A married woman may sue or be sued in contract[1] or in tort[2] or otherwise in all respects as if she were a feme sole[3], but this does not prevent a husband and wife from rendering themselves, or being rendered, jointly liable in respect of any tort, contract, debt or obligation, and of suing and being sued either in tort or in contract or otherwise, in like manner as if they were not married[4]. A married woman is subject to the enforcement of judgments and orders in all respects as if she were a feme sole[5]. Note that these provisions derive from enactments specifically referring to 'marriage' and 'married women' and for which no corresponding civil partnership provision has been made, and their continuing significance should be considered in the light of this.

It has been held that if a married woman obtains an injunction subject to an undertaking as to damages[6], her sole undertaking is sufficient[7].

1   As to the liability of a married woman on contracts entered into before her marriage, and as to the statutory exemption of her husband from liability as such on her ante-nuptial contracts, see PARA 204; as to the respective liability of a husband and wife on the contracts of the wife during the marriage see PARA 256 et seq; and as to the right of a husband or wife to sue one another on contracts entered into during the marriage see PARA 206.
2   See PARAS 204, 211.
3   See the Law Reform (Married Women and Tortfeasors) Act 1935 s 1(c); and PARA 204.
4   Law Reform (Married Women and Tortfeasors) Act 1935 s 4(2)(c). See also PARA 204. As to joint contracts by a married woman and a third person see PARA 205; and as to joint liability of a husband and wife in tort see PARA 204.
5   Law Reform (Married Women and Tortfeasors) Act 1935 s 1(d). The court may order that a married woman be examined as to her means in the same way as any other judgment debtor: *Countess of Aylesford v Great Western Rly Co* [1892] 2 QB 626, DC. As to a married woman's liability to be made bankrupt see PARA 204.
6   As to the giving of an undertaking as to damages on application for an injunction see INJUNCTIONS vol 24 (Reissue) PARA 982 et seq.
7   *Re Prynne* (1885) 53 LT 465; *Pike v Cave* (1893) 62 LJ Ch 937.

211.   Proceedings between spouses or civil partners.   Where an action in tort is brought by one of the parties to a marriage or a civil partnership against the other[1] during the subsistence of the relationship, the court may stay proceedings if it appears:

(1)   that no substantial benefit would accrue to either party from the continuation of the proceedings[2]; or

(2)   that the question or questions in issue could more conveniently be disposed of on an application[3] to the court[4];

and the court may[5], in such an action, either exercise any power which could be exercised on such an application, or give such directions as it thinks fit for the disposal[6] of any question arising in the proceedings[7].

Spouses and civil partners are entitled to apply for maintenance from the other spouse or civil partner[8] and for financial relief following or pending divorce, dissolution or separation[9]. They can also apply for financial provision from the estate of a deceased spouse or civil partner or former spouse or civil partner[10]. A spouse or civil partner who has no beneficial estate or interest in the family home may have home rights[11]; and a spouse or civil partner may in certain circumstances apply to the court for an occupation order[12] or a non-molestation order[13]. Spouses and civil partners may sue each other in conversion or for wrongful interference with goods[14], and may be restrained from interfering with the other's separate trade or business[15].

1   The Law Reform (Husband and Wife) Act 1962 s 1(1) provides that 'each of the parties to a marriage shall have the like right to bring proceedings against the other in respect of a wrongful or negligent act or omission, or for the prevention of a wrongful act, as if they were not married': to the extent that such provision is not now obsolete, it may be inferred from the related provisions described in the text and notes 2–15 that civil partners also have the like right to bring proceedings against the other in tort. The Law Reform (Husband and Wife) Act 1962 s 3(3) provides that a reference for this purpose to the parties to a marriage includes references to the persons who were parties to a marriage which has been dissolved: it may be inferred that this also extends to civil partners and civil partnerships which have been dissolved. As to the rights of spouses to sue one another in contract see PARA 205. A husband has no right enforceable at law or in equity to stop his wife having, or a registered medical practitioner performing, a legal abortion: *Paton v Trustees of British Pregnancy Advisory Service* [1979] QB 276, [1978] 2 All ER 987, followed in *C v S* [1988] QB 135, [1987] 1 All ER 1230, CA (boyfriend).

2   Law Reform (Husband and Wife) Act 1962 s 1(2)(a); Civil Partnership Act 2004 s 69(1), (2)(a). The question whether consortium has come to an end and whether the claimant's proper remedy would not be found in a magistrates' court are matters to be taken into consideration in deciding whether proceedings should be allowed to continue: *McLeod v McLeod* [1963] CLY 1676.

3   Ie an application under the Married Women's Property Act 1882 s 17 or the Civil Partnership Act 2004 s 66: see PARA 224.

4   Law Reform (Husband and Wife) Act 1962 s 1(2)(b); Civil Partnership Act 2004 s 69(2)(b).

5   Ie without prejudice to the Law Reform (Husband and Wife) Act 1962 s 1(2)(b) or the Civil Partnership Act 2004 s 69(2)(b) (see the text and notes 3–4).

6   Ie under the Married Women's Property Act 1882 s 17 or the Civil Partnership Act 2004 s 66: see PARA 224.

7   Law Reform (Husband and Wife) Act 1962 s 1(2); Civil Partnership Act 2004 s 69(3). See *Church v Church* (1983) 13 Fam Law 254 (wife's claim for damages against her husband for personal injuries caused by his violence towards her transferred to the Family Division so that the question of quantum could be dealt with in conjunction with the wife's claim for ancillary relief following a divorce).

8   See PARA 542 et seq.

9   See PARA 450 et seq.

10   See the Inheritance (Provision for Family and Dependants) Act 1975; PARAS 538–541; and EXECUTORS AND ADMINISTRATORS vol 17(2) (Reissue) PARA 665 et seq.

11   See PARA 285 et seq.

12   See PARA 289 et seq.

13   See PARA 716 et seq.

14   As to such proceedings see TORT vol 45(2) (Reissue) PARA 542 et seq.

15   *Wood v Wood* (1871) 19 WR 1049 (hotel settled on the wife to be managed by her for the benefit of herself and her children); *Gaynor v Gaynor* [1901] IR 217 (public house belonging to the wife); *Donnelly v Donnelly* (1886) 31 Sol Jo 45; *Green v Green* (1840) 5 Hare 400n.

212.   Compellability of spouses and civil partners as witnesses. Any enactment or rule of law relating to the giving of evidence[1] by a spouse applies in relation to a civil partner[2] as it applies in relation to the spouse[3].

No special rules govern the competence of the spouse or civil partner of a defendant to give evidence in criminal proceedings[4]. However, the spouse or civil partner of the defendant is compellable to give evidence on behalf of the defendant[5], and is compellable to give evidence for the prosecution or on behalf of any person jointly charged with the defendant, unless they are themselves charged in the proceedings, if:

(1)   the offence charged involves an assault on, or injury or a threat of injury to, the spouse or civil partner of the accused or a person who was at the material time under the age of 16[6];

(2)   the offence charged is a sexual offence alleged to have been committed in respect of a person who was at the material time under that age[7]; or

(3)   the offence charged consists of attempting or conspiring to commit, or of aiding, abetting, counselling, procuring or inciting the commission of, an offence falling within head (1) or head (2) above[8].

In any proceedings a person who has been but is no longer married to the accused or has been but is no longer a civil partner of the accused is compellable to give evidence as if that person and the accused had never been married or had never been civil partners of each other[9].

Spouses and civil partners of parties are competent witnesses in civil proceedings[10]. In any legal proceedings other than criminal proceedings, a person may refuse to answer any question or produce any document or thing if to do so would tend to expose the spouse or civil partner of that person to proceedings for a criminal offence or for the recovery of a penalty[11].

1   References to 'giving evidence' are to giving evidence in any way (whether by supplying information, making discovery, producing documents or otherwise): Civil Partnership Act 2004 s 84(4).
2   This does not include a former civil partner: Civil Partnership Act 2004 s 84(3).
3   Civil Partnership Act 2004 s 84(1). This is subject to any specific amendment made by or under the Civil Partnership Act 2004 which relates to the giving of evidence by a civil partner: s 84(4).
4   As to the general competency requirements for witnesses see CRIMINAL LAW, EVIDENCE AND PROCEDURE vol 11(3) (2006 Reissue) PARA 1401.
5   See the Police and Criminal Evidence Act 1984 s 80(2); and CRIMINAL LAW, EVIDENCE AND PROCEDURE vol 11(3) (2006 Reissue) PARA 1405. The failure of the spouse or civil partner of the accused to give evidence is not to be made the subject of any comment by the prosecution: see s 80A; and CRIMINAL LAW, EVIDENCE AND PROCEDURE vol 11(3) (2006 Reissue) PARA 1405.
6   See the Police and Criminal Evidence Act 1984 s 80(2A), (3)(a), (4), (4A); and CRIMINAL LAW, EVIDENCE AND PROCEDURE vol 11(3) (2006 Reissue) PARA 1405.
7   See the Police and Criminal Evidence Act 1984 s 80(3)(b); and CRIMINAL LAW, EVIDENCE AND PROCEDURE vol 11(3) (2006 Reissue) PARA 1405.
8   See the Police and Criminal Evidence Act 1984 s 80(3)(c); and CRIMINAL LAW, EVIDENCE AND PROCEDURE vol 11(3) (2006 Reissue) PARA 1405.
9   See the Police and Criminal Evidence Act 1984 s 80(5), (5A); and CRIMINAL LAW, EVIDENCE AND PROCEDURE vol 11(3) (2006 Reissue) PARA 1405.
10   See EVIDENCE vol 17(1) (Reissue) PARA 951 (noting in particular, in connection with husbands and wives, the Evidence Amendment Act 1853 s 1).
11   See the Civil Evidence Act 1968 s 14(1); and EVIDENCE vol 17(1) (Reissue) PARA 959. As to evidence of spouses in proceedings instituted in consequence of adultery see s 16(5); and PARA 828.

213.   Corroboration. Magistrates' courts should not, in general, act upon the uncorroborated testimony of either of the parties to a marriage or civil partnership[1], particularly where their evidence is in direct conflict[2]. It is dangerous to act on a complainant's evidence alone[3] especially in a case where the complainant charges the defendant with conduct which from its nature must have happened in private and prima facie with the complainant's assent, such as abnormal sexual practices, though even in such a case there is no absolute rule of law that corroboration is necessary[4]. It has been said that the practice of the court is to look for corroboration and, if on the face of the complainant's own evidence it is available, to require corroboration before finding an offence proved[5]. In spite of these rules of practice it is open to a court to act on the uncorroborated evidence of a spouse or civil partner if it is in no doubt where the truth lies[6].

1   *Forster v Forster* (1910) 54 Sol Jo 403.
2   *Joseph v Joseph* [1915] P 122.
3   *Williams v Williams* (1932) 96 JP 267, DC; cf *Williams v Williams* (1928) 93 JP 32, DC; *Marjoram v Marjoram* [1955] 2 All ER 1, [1955] 1 WLR 520, DC (wife's evidence corroborated by husband's evidence).

4	*DB v WB* [1935] P 80, DC; and see *Davidson v Davidson* [1953] 1 All ER 611, [1953] 1 WLR 387, DC (retrial ordered as apparently magistrates' court had failed to direct itself as to desirability, though not necessity, of corroboration, and to consider question of acquiescence by wife); *Lawson v Lawson* [1955] 1 All ER 341, [1955] 1 WLR 200, CA (wife not consenting party; no rule as to corroboration applicable); *Alli v Alli* [1965] 3 All ER 480, DC.
5	*Alli v Alli* [1965] 3 All ER 480.
6	*Alli v Alli* [1965] 3 All ER 480 at 484, DC per Sir Jocelyn Simon P.

**214.	Domicile of married women.** The domicile of a married woman is, instead of being the same as her husband's by virtue only of marriage[1], to be ascertained by reference to the same factors as in the case of any other individual capable of having an independent domicile[2].

1	For a judicial statement of the former rule see *Indyka v Indyka* [1969] 1 AC 33 at 81, [1967] 2 All ER 689 at 711, HL per Lord Pearce ('it is a principle of English law that the wife acquires the husband's domicile and that she cannot ... acquire a domicile of her own choice'). See also *A-G for Alberta v Cook* [1926] AC 444 at 458–462, PC per Lord Merrivale (where the earliest authorities for the former rule are cited).
2	Domicile and Matrimonial Proceedings Act 1973 s 1(1). As to domicile generally see CONFLICT OF LAWS vol 8(3) (Reissue) PARA 35 et seq. Where immediately before 1 January 1974 (ie the date on which s 1 came into force by virtue of s 17(5)) a woman was married and then had her husband's domicile by dependence, she is to be treated as retaining that domicile (as a domicile of choice, if it is not also her domicile of origin) unless and until it is changed by acquisition or revival of another domicile either on or after 1 January 1974: s 1(2).

**215.	Wife's assumption of husband's name.** When a woman on her marriage assumes her husband's surname in substitution for her father's surname, it may be said that she acquires a new name by repute. The change of name is in fact, rather than in law, a consequence of the marriage. Having assumed her husband's name, she is entitled to retain it notwithstanding the dissolution or annulment of the marriage or her own remarriage unless she then chooses to resume her maiden name or acquires another name by reputation, provided that no one thereby suffers any injury of which the law can take notice[1].

The court has no power to enjoin a peeress who obtains a decree of divorce against her husband from afterwards continuing to call herself by the title of which she had the use whilst married to her first husband, even if she remarries with a commoner[2].

1	See *Earl Cowley v Countess Cowley* [1900] P 118 (on appeal [1900] P 305, CA; affd [1901] AC 450, HL); *Fendall (otherwise Goldsmid) v Goldsmid* (1877) 2 PD 263; *Du Boulay v Du Boulay* (1869) LR 2 PC 430.
2	*Earl Cowley v Countess Cowley* [1900] P 118; on appeal [1900] P 305, CA; affd [1901] AC 450, HL.

(2) MAINTENANCE AND COHABITATION

**216.	Husband's duty at common law.** The common law imposed a range of duties on a husband concerning the support and maintenance of his wife which, having been largely superseded by statute[1], are now of doubtful practical application. They are as follows:

(1)	a husband has a duty to maintain his wife according to his means of supporting her[2];
(2)	a husband may be liable for certain debts contracted by his wife[3];
(3)	if a wife leaves her husband without his consent and in circumstances which do not justify her in living apart, his obligation to maintain her is suspended for so long as she wilfully absents herself[4];

(4)   if a wife commits adultery, his obligation to maintain her ceases altogether[5];

(5)   where only husband and wife are concerned, a husband separated from his wife by agreement is under no liability to maintain her unless the agreement to separate is subject to an express or implied term that the husband is to provide maintenance for the wife[6]; and

(6)   the parties may agree to arrangements whereby the husband is released from his duty to maintain the wife[7].

1   See the various statutory provisions giving spouses and civil partners the right to claim maintenance, eg the Matrimonial Causes Act 1973 s 27; the Domestic Proceedings and Magistrates' Courts Act 1978 s 1; the Civil Partnership Act 2004 Sch 5 Pt 9 (paras 39–45), Sch 6; and PARAS 542 et seq, 553 et seq.

2   *Read v Legard* (1851) 6 Exch 636; *Johnston v Sumner* (1858) 3 H & N 261; *Millichamp v Millichamp* (1931) 146 LT 96 (where the first duty of a husband was held to be towards his wife rather than his mother). There is no presumption of law that a wife is dependent on the earnings of her husband merely because of his legal obligation to maintain her: *New Monckton Collieries Ltd v Keeling* [1911] AC 648, HL. The common law right of the wife is a right to support, but not a right to an allowance: *Lilley v Lilley* [1960] P 158 at 178, [1959] 3 All ER 283 at 288, CA; *Northrop v Northrop* [1968] P 74 at 108, [1967] 2 All ER 961 at 973, CA. The fact that the husband becomes bankrupt does not affect his common law obligations to maintain his wife: *Hounslow London Borough v Peake* [1974] 1 All ER 688 at 691, [1974] 1 WLR 26 at 30, DC.

3   As to this presumption of authority see PARA 263 et seq. A wife left without means is not entitled as an agent of necessity to pledge her husband's credit for necessaries: see PARA 267.

4   *Jones v Newtown and Llanidloes Guardians* [1920] 3 KB 381 (where it was held that a husband's liability to an order under the Poor Law Amendment Act 1850 s 5 (repealed), that he make payments towards his wife's maintenance, existed only where he was under a common law duty to support her, and that a common law duty which had ceased as a result of her wilful desertion had revived on her subsequently becoming of unsound mind and so incapable of voluntary conduct); *Stopher v National Assistance Board* [1955] 1 QB 486 at 494, [1955] 1 All ER 700 at 704, DC per Lord Goddard CJ. See also *National Assistance Board v Wilkinson* [1952] 2 QB 648, [1952] 2 All ER 255, DC (where a husband's liability to an order under the National Assistance Act 1948 was held to be similarly dependent on the existence of a common law duty of support, and so not to exist in respect of a wife wilfully in desertion); *National Assistance Board v Parkes* [1955] 2 QB 506, [1955] 3 All ER 1, CA (common law principle affirmed; decision in *National Assistance Board v Wilkinson* [1952] 2 QB 648, [1952] 2 All ER 255, DC approved as correct, but explained on other grounds (see PARA 217)); and see *Treharne v Treharne* (1966) 111 Sol Jo 34, DC; *Topley v Topley* (1967) 111 Sol Jo 497, DC; *Gray v Gray* [1976] Fam 324, [1976] 3 All ER 225; *Newmarch v Newmarch* [1978] Fam 79, [1978] 1 All ER 1.

5   *R v Flintan* (1830) 1 B & Ad 227 (wife's desertion and adultery; husband not liable under the Vagrancy Act 1824 s 3 (repealed so far as relevant), to penalty for neglecting and refusing to maintain her); *Culley v Charman* (1881) 7 QBD 89 (decided under the Poor Law Amendment Act 1868 s 33 (repealed)); *Mitchell v Torrington Union* (1897) 76 LT 724 (husband not heard of for 27 years; wife married again; husband returned; husband not liable to guardians of the poor in respect of her maintenance). At common law a husband was under no duty to support an adulterous wife notwithstanding that he may himself have been guilty of cruelty or other misconduct (*Govier v Hancock* (1796) 6 Term Rep 603), unless he connived at or condoned her offence or he continues to hold her out as still having the ordinary authority of a wife (see PARA 272; and as to holding out generally see PARA 269 et seq).

6   *Northrop v Northrop* [1968] P 74 at 96, [1967] 2 All ER 961 at 965, CA per Willmer LJ, and at 116 and at 978 per Winn LJ; *National Assistance Board v Parkes* [1955] 2 QB 506 at 516, [1955] 3 All ER 1 at 3, CA per Denning LJ and at 525 and at 9 per Romer LJ.

7   *Sutocki v Sutocka* (1963) 107 Sol Jo 373, CA.

217. Statutory duty of spouses and civil partners. For the purposes of social fund awards and income support, spouses and civil partners are liable to maintain one another[1]. The statutory duty to maintain is absolute and is not ousted by unjustifiable desertion or by adultery, but desertion and adultery are circumstances to which the court is entitled to have regard in deciding whether or not an order should be made[2]. Circumstances which would relieve spouses and civil partners of their duty at common law will not, however, be regarded as constituting an answer to the application for payment towards the cost of welfare benefits provided; consequently, where spouses or civil partners have separated by consent, an order may be made requiring them to contribute to the cost of one another's benefits not only if the separation agreement contained no provision at all as to maintenance[3] but even if one party agreed under it to accept a specified allowance which does not at the relevant date amount to reasonable maintenance[4], or even if a party has agreed to be responsible for maintaining himself[5].

1   See SOCIAL SECURITY AND PENSIONS vol 44(2) (Reissue) PARAS 236, 397, 398.
2   *National Assistance Board v Parkes* [1955] 2 QB 506, [1955] 3 All ER 1, CA, explaining *National Assistance Board v Wilkinson* [1952] 2 QB 648, [1952] 2 All ER 255, DC. See also *Lilley v Lilley* [1960] P 158 at 169, [1959] 3 All ER 283, CA; *Northrop v Northrop* [1968] P 74, [1967] 2 All ER 961, CA.
3   *Stopher v National Assistance Board* [1955] 1 QB 486, [1955] 1 All ER 700, DC.
4   *National Assistance Board v Prisk* [1954] 1 All ER 400, [1954] 1 WLR 443, DC.
5   *National Assistance Board v Parkes* [1955] 2 QB 506, [1955] 3 All ER 1, CA.

218.   Failure to provide reasonable maintenance.   If a person persistently refuses or neglects to maintain his spouse or civil partner, and in consequence of that refusal or neglect specified benefits are paid to or in respect of him or her, that person is guilty of an offence[1]. The court's statutory powers to order payments by a party to a marriage or civil partnership who has failed to provide reasonable maintenance for the other party[2], and to vary or insert financial arrangements in maintenance agreements[3], are considered elsewhere, as are the special statutory provisions as to the maintenance liabilities of members of Her Majesty's forces[4].

1   See SOCIAL SECURITY AND PENSIONS vol 44(2) (Reissue) PARA 397.
2   See the Matrimonial Causes Act 1973 s 27; the Domestic Proceedings and Magistrates' Courts Act 1978 s 1; the Civil Partnership Act 2004 Sch 5 Pt 9 (paras 39–45), Sch 6; and PARAS 542 et seq, 553 et seq.
3   See the Matrimonial Causes Act 1973 s 35; the Civil Partnership Act 2004 Sch 5 para 69; and PARA 700 et seq.
4   See PARAS 693–695; and ARMED FORCES vol 2(2) (Reissue) PARAS 74–77.

219.   Duty to cohabit.   There is no enforceable duty to cohabit[1]. At common law, where a wife was living apart by her own desire, the court would not grant a writ of habeas corpus to the husband to restore her to his custody[2], and where a wife refused to live with him, a husband was not entitled to restrain her by force or to keep her in confinement, even if she was acting unreasonably[3]; indeed, it is an offence at common law for a man to take and carry away his wife against her will, whether she is cohabiting with him or not at the time[4].

1   The remedy of restitution of conjugal rights was abolished by the Matrimonial Proceedings and Property Act 1970 s 20 (repealed). As to enticement and harbouring see PARA 221. A prolonged refusal to cohabit may constitute desertion for which there are statutory forms of relief: see PARA 363 et seq. In general, the sexual relationship in marriage cannot be enforced or restrained by court order: see *Paton v Trustees of British Pregnancy Advisory Service* [1978] 2 All ER 987 at 990, [1978] 3 WLR 687 at 690. As to the duty to cohabit under common law (to the extent that it continues to exist) see *Wilkinson v Wilkinson* (1871) LR 12 Eq 604 (condition in gift by will that donee was to cease to reside with husband held void); *Re Moore, Trafford v Maconochie* (1888) 39 ChD 116, CA. Cf *Davies v Elmslie* [1938] 1 KB 337, [1937] 4 All ER 471, CA (agreement consistent with ultimate intention of spouses to rejoin each other not contrary to

public policy). Where the court grants a decree of judicial separation, it is no longer obligatory for the petitioner to cohabit with the respondent: Matrimonial Causes Act 1973 s 18(1); and see *R v Clarke* [1949] 2 All ER 448. As to agreements for future separation see PARA 424.

2   *R v Leggatt* (1852) 18 QB 781.
3   *R v Jackson* [1891] 1 QB 671, CA (wife, kept in confinement by husband, discharged on habeas corpus), overruling *Re Cochrane* (1840) 8 Dowl 630.
4   *R v Reid* [1973] QB 299, [1972] 2 All ER 1350, CA.

220.   Marital rape.   The rule that a husband could not be criminally liable for raping his wife if he had sexual intercourse with her without her consent no longer forms part of the law of England since a husband and wife are now to be regarded as equal partners in marriage and it is unacceptable that by marriage the wife submits herself irrevocably to sexual intercourse in all circumstances or that it is an incident of modern marriage that the wife consents to intercourse in all circumstances, including sexual intercourse obtained only by force[1].

1   See *R v R (rape: marital exemption)* [1992] 1 AC 599, [1991] 4 All ER 481, HL.

221.   Enticement, harbouring and loss of consortium.   No person is liable in tort under the law of England and Wales:
   (1)   to any other person on the ground only of his having induced the wife or husband of that other person to leave or remain apart from the other spouse[1];
   (2)   to any other person for harbouring the wife of that other person[2];
   (3)   to a husband on the ground only of his having deprived him of the services or society of his wife[3].
A husband may, however, maintain an action in respect of impairment, as distinct from total loss, of consortium[4].

1   Law Reform (Miscellaneous Provisions) Act 1970 s 5(a).
2   Law Reform (Miscellaneous Provisions) Act 1970 s 5(c).
3   Administration of Justice Act 1982 s 2(a).
4   *Hodgson v Trapp* [1988] 1 FLR 69, [1988] Fam Law 60 (wife sustained serious injuries in an accident; the wife's consortium as an alert, capable and adult partner to the husband had been gross and had left him with a vegetative, inert and childlike charge).

222.   Gifts and legacies inducing separation.   A gift of income to a married person living with his or her spouse, or presumably to a civil partner living with his or her civil partner, to be paid only during such time as the parties should live apart, is void, as it is contrary to the policy of the law that spouses (or civil partners) should be separated without their consent and a gift in these terms would tend to bring about such a separation[1]. If a condition having the same tendency is attached to a legacy or gift to a married person or a civil partner, the condition is void as encouraging that person to commit a breach of duty, and the legacy or gift will be treated as unconditional[2]. Where, however, the married person or civil partner is not living with his or her spouse or civil partner at the date of the gift, and the object of the gift is to maintain the married person or civil partner during the separation rather than to induce that person to continue to live apart from his or her spouse or civil partner, the gift is valid[3].

1   *Re Moore, Trafford v Maconochie* (1888) 39 ChD 116, CA (gift by will of a sum to be paid weekly during such time as the legatee should live apart from her husband, for her maintenance while so living apart; the legatee was living with her husband at the time of the testator's death, but separated from him some time afterwards; legacy held to be void), distinguishing *Wren v Bradley* (1848) 2 De G & Sm 49 (gift when parties were separated, with a condition defeating it if wife returned to cohabitation, held valid). See also GIFTS vol 20(1) (Reissue) PARA 57.

2 *Wilkinson v Wilkinson* (1871) LR 12 Eq 604 (gift by will of residue to married woman with a conditional gift over if she did not cease to reside in the place where her husband carried on business within 18 months of the testator's death; held that she took free from the condition).

3 *Re Charleton, Bracey v Sherwin* (1911) 55 Sol Jo 330; *Re Lovell, Sparks v Southall* [1920] 1 Ch 122; *Mather v Rhodes* (1934) 78 Sol Jo 414.

223. Confidences. Confidences will be protected even after divorce or dissolution[1] unless both parties have assented to making their private lives public[2]. It has been held that the implied obligation of confidence is a concomitant of marriage (and, presumably, of civil partnership) and remains enforceable, even where the party seeking to restrain publication has published limited details and does not come with clean hands, provided that the 'balance of perfidy' is in that party's favour in that the claimant's publication was less pernicious than that proposed or published by the defendant[3]. A party's infidelity does not negate entitlement to protection for past confidences[4]. In view of the number of persons likely to be interested in disclosures, the extent of an injunction may differ from that used to protect other forms of confidence[5].

Where spouses or civil partners have regarded their relationship as being in the public domain rather than their own private business, it may be that the court would refuse to grant an injunction to restrain publication of confidences[6].

1 *Duchess of Argyll v Duke of Argyll* [1967] Ch 302, [1965] 1 All ER 611.
2 *Lennon v News Group Newspapers Ltd and Twist* [1978] FSR 573, CA.
3 *Duchess of Argyll v Duke of Argyll* [1967] Ch 302 at 330, [1965] 1 All ER 611 at 625 per Ungoed-Thomas J.
4 *Duchess of Argyll v Duke of Argyll* [1967] Ch 302 at 331, [1965] 1 All ER 611 at 626.
5 *A-G v Observer Ltd, A-G v Times Newspapers Ltd* [1990] 1 AC 109 at 255, 256, sub nom *A-G v Guardian Newspapers (No 2)* [1988] 3 All ER 545 at 643, HL.
6 See *Lennon v News Group Newspapers Ltd and Twist* [1978] FSR 573, CA.

(3) OWNERSHIP OF PROPERTY

(i) Resolution of Disputes

224. Resolution of disputes involving property. Where any question arises between spouses or civil partners[1] as to the title to or possession of property[2], either party may apply to the court[3] for its determination and the court may make such order with respect to the property as it thinks fit[4]. Such an application may be made by either of the parties notwithstanding that their marriage or civil partnership has been dissolved or annulled so long as the application is made within the period of three years beginning with the date of dissolution or annulment[5].

This procedure was devised as a means of resolving a question as to title and is not a means of giving a title not previously existing[6]: wider powers of adjustment of property rights also exist[7]. It is also applicable in relation to the property of engaged couples and persons who have entered into a civil partnership agreement[8].

1 Cohabitants may have rights in property which is vested in the other cohabitant where it was acquired for their joint benefit; these rights do not arise by statute but under the principles of constructive or resulting trusts: see *Cooke v Head* [1972] 2 All ER 38, [1972] 1 WLR 518, CA; *Richards v Dove* [1974] 1 All ER 888; and PARA 284. In *Shaw v Fitzgerald* [1992] 1 FCR 162, [1992] 1 FLR 357, it was held that the court has jurisdiction to hear an application by a man claiming a beneficial interest in a woman's property on the basis that there had been an agreement to marry, even though, when the alleged agreement was made, the man was married and could not have given immediate effect to the alleged agreement.

2   The Married Women's Property Act 1882 s 24 provides that 'property' includes a thing in action; no corresponding provision is made by the Civil Partnership Act 2004. As to the property to which the court's powers extend see PARA 227.

3   Ie may apply to the High Court or such county court as may be prescribed by rules of court, which may for these purposes confer jurisdiction on county courts whatever the situation or value of the property in dispute: Married Women's Property Act 1882 s 17 (amended by the Matrimonial and Family Proceedings Act 1984 s 43); Civil Partnership Act 2004 s 66(1), (3). For the applicable rules see the Family Proceedings Rules 1991, SI 1991/1247, rr 3.6, 3.7; and PARA 955 et seq. The Limitation Act 1980 s 23 (actions for an account to be brought within six years: see LIMITATION PERIODS vol 68 (2008) PARA 1008) does not apply to an application under these provisions: *Spoor v Spoor* [1966] 3 All ER 120. Proceedings may be commenced, or, if already commenced, continued, by a deceased party's personal representatives: see *Re Cummins, Cummins v Thompson* [1972] Ch 62, [1971] 3 All ER 782, CA.

4   Married Women's Property Act 1882 s 17 (as amended: see note 3); Civil Partnership Act 2004 s 66(2).

5   Matrimonial Proceedings and Property Act 1970 s 39; Civil Partnership Act 2004 s 68. References in these provisions to a spouse or civil partner are to be construed accordingly: Matrimonial Proceedings and Property Act 1970 s 39; Civil Partnership Act 2004 s 68(2). As to applications where an agreement to enter into a marriage or civil partnership is terminated see PARA 230.

6   See *Pettitt v Pettitt* [1970] AC 777 at 798, [1969] 2 All ER 385 at 392, HL per Lord Morris of Borth-y-Gest; and PARA 225.

7   See PARA 499 et seq. Save in exceptional cases, it is undesirable for parties to divorce or dissolution proceedings to make an application under the Married Women's Property Act 1882 s 17 or the Civil Partnership Act 2004 s 66 for the determination of property rights as between them; the proper course is to make appropriate applications for financial provision and property adjustment orders (see PARA 450 et seq): see *Fielding v Fielding* [1978] 1 All ER 267, [1967] 1 WLR 1146n, CA; and PARA 278. However, in order to take advantage of such applications it is essential for the parties to take care to initiate proceedings before remarrying or entering into a subsequent civil partnership: *Fielding v Fielding*.

8   See the Law Reform (Miscellaneous Provisions) Act 1970 s 2(2); the Civil Partnership Act 2004 s 74(3); and PARA 230. As to the meaning of 'civil partnership agreement' see PARA 16.

225.   General extent of court's powers. In exercising its jurisdiction over property disputes between spouses or civil partners[1], the court has power to ascertain the respective rights of the parties to the disputed property, and may make such order as may be appropriate for its return or for restitution[2]. The court has no power to vary established or agreed rights merely because in the light of subsequent events it thinks that the original agreement was unfair[3], but it does seem that the court has power to vary orders made under the dispute resolution provisions[4] where there has been a change in the value of the property before the order for its sale has been carried into effect[5].

The statutory provision is a procedural provision only and the question for the court is 'Whose is this?', and not 'To whom shall this be given?'[6]. Although the court has no power under this provision to vary established property rights, it may, in its discretion[7], prevent one of the parties from enforcing those rights if the result would be unjust to the other party[8]. In general, however, the rights of the parties must be judged on the general principles applicable in any court of law when considering questions of title to property, while making full allowances in view of the parties' relationship, and where the original conveyance or lease of the land declares not merely in whom the legal title is to vest but in whom the beneficial title is to vest, that necessarily concludes the question of title as between the parties for all time, and in the absence of fraud or mistake at the time of the transaction the parties cannot go behind it at any subsequent time even on death or dissolution[9].

1 Ie under the Married Women's Property Act 1882 s 17 or the Civil Partnership Act 2004 s 66:
   see PARA 224. As to the principles to be applied in determining property rights see PARAS
   278–284.

2 See PARA 224.

3 *Cobb v Cobb* [1955] 2 All ER 696 at 700, [1955] 1 WLR 731 at 737, CA per Romer LJ,
   approved in *Pettit v Pettit* [1970] AC 777, [1969] 2 All ER 385, HL. See also *Fribance v
   Fribance* [1957] 1 All ER 357, [1957] 1 WLR 384, CA; *Tasker v Tasker* [1895] P 1 (jewels given
   to wife were her property). In *Short v Short* [1960] 3 All ER 6 at 18, [1960] 1 WLR 833 at
   849, CA, Devlin LJ stated that the powers of the court under the Married Women's Property
   Act 1882 s 17 were substantially the same as in any other proceeding where the ownership or
   possession of property was in question; and that the court's discretion was no wider and no
   narrower than the ordinary discretion of the court in such cases. This statement was approved
   by Lord Upjohn in *National Provincial Bank Ltd v Ainsworth* [1965] AC 1175 at 1235, [1965]
   2 All ER 472 at 486, HL, who added that the Married Women's Property Act 1882 s 17 was a
   purely procedural one, providing a very useful summary method of determining between
   husband and wife questions of title and the right to possession of property, but did not confer
   any new substantive rights on either of the spouses. Cf the comments of Lord Denning MR in
   Jansen v Jansen [1965] P 478 at 488, [1965] 3 All ER 363 at 366, CA, and note that provision
   for civil partnerships corresponding to that made by the Married Women's Property Act 1882
   s 17 is made by the Civil Partnership Act 2004 s 66 (see PARA 224). See also PARAS 278–284.

4 Ie under the Married Women's Property Act 1882 s 17 or the Civil Partnership Act 2004 s 66:
   see PARA 224.

5 *Gee v Gee* (1972) 116 Sol Jo 219, CA.

6 *Pettitt v Pettitt* [1970] AC 777 at 798, [1969] 2 All ER 385 at 393, HL per Lord Morris of
   Borth-y-Gest. See also *Pettitt v Pettitt* at 792 and at 388 per Lord Reid, at 807 and at 401 per
   Lord Hodson, at 812 and at 404, 405 per Lord Upjohn, and at 819 and at 410 per
   Lord Diplock; *Taylor v Taylor* [1968] 1 All ER 843 at 847, [1968] 1 WLR 378 at 383, 384, CA
   per Danckwerts LJ (where the wife issued a summons under the Married Women's Property
   Act 1882 s 17, seeking a declaration that she and her husband were the joint beneficial owners
   of the matrimonial home and registered a lis pendens under the Land Charges Act 1925 in
   respect of those proceedings; it was held, on appeal, that her interest was at the most a share in
   the proceeds of sale and not an interest in land and accordingly the entry in the register was not
   a proper one and should be vacated under the court's inherent jurisdiction to remove improper
   entries from the register; the Married Women's Property Act 1882 s 17 was a purely procedural
   provision and not intended to alter the rights of parties in the property in question). See also
   Burke v Burke [1974] 2 All ER 944 at 947, [1974] 1 WLR 1063 at 1066, CA per Buckley LJ.

7 See note 1.

8 See *Bedson v Bedson* [1965] 2 QB 666, [1965] 3 All ER 307, CA (where the court refused to
   allow a wife to force a sale of the property at that time as such a sale would defeat the husband's
   right to apply to the court for a property adjustment order under what is now the Matrimonial
   Causes Act 1973 s 24(1)(c) (see PARA 510)). Cf *Rawlings v Rawlings* [1964] P 398, [1964]
   2 All ER 804, CA (home sold), followed in *Re Solomon (a bankrupt), ex p Trustee of Property
   of Bankrupt v Solomon* [1967] Ch 573, sub nom *Re Debtor, ex p Trustee v Solomon* [1966]
   3 All ER 255 (property sold because it was equitable to make such an order in all the
   circumstances); cf also *Burke v Burke* [1974] 2 All ER 944, [1974] 1 WLR 1063, CA (home
   sold; in exercising its discretion whether or not the husband as trustee should continue to
   postpone the execution of the trust for sale, the court had to have regard to all the relevant
   circumstances of the case and to the situation of the beneficial owners; the children's interests
   were to be taken into consideration only in so far as they affected the equities as between the
   husband and wife; dictum of Salmon LJ in *Rawlings v Rawlings* at 419 and at 814
   disapproved).

9 *Pettitt v Pettitt* [1970] AC 777 at 813, [1969] 2 All ER 385 at 405, HL per Lord Upjohn. See
   also *Wilson v Wilson* [1963] 2 All ER 447, [1963] 1 WLR 601, CA; *Re John's Assignment
   Trusts, Niven v Niven* [1970] 2 All ER 210n, [1970] 1 WLR 955 (where husband and wife
   purchased a leasehold house and shop chiefly out of the proceeds of sale of the former
   matrimonial home, the assignment containing an express declaration of trust for the husband
   and wife as beneficial joint tenants; the husband then claimed to be the sole beneficial owner,
   and it was held that no sufficient ground was shown entitling him to go behind the express trust
   in the assignment which, as drawn, accorded with the probable intentions of the parties at the
   time, and that accordingly the house and shop were held for them both in equal shares).

226. Power to order sale. The court's power to make orders concerning disputes relating to matrimonial or civil partnership property[1] includes power to order a sale of the property[2]. The rights of occupation of a spouse or civil partner who has no proprietary, contractual or statutory interest in the family home are protected by statute[3], whereas a spouse or civil partner who has a proprietary or contractual right to remain in occupation may enforce that right at common law[4]. A right of occupation is, therefore, not a right which falls to be determined by a court dealing only with proceedings relating to property disputes[5], although the court may take such matters into account in determining whether to order a sale of the property in question or to make any other order which would necessarily exclude a spouse or civil partner from occupation[6]. It has been held that where parties were joint owners of a property, the court would not make an order for delivery up of it to one party only (in this case, the wife)[7]. Where the parties are co-owners, and the wife was an innocent party, it could be wrong to order a sale because the husband could have been under a duty to provide her with a roof over her head[8]: however, such a matter can best be considered by the court when dealing with financial provision and property adjustment[9], when the amount payable to one party might be less by reason that that party continues to occupy the family home[10]. There is no authority that the provisions for dealing with property disputes[11] give the court jurisdiction to turn one party out of occupation of the family home where both parties have equal rights of ownership[12]. After decree absolute or the making of a final order for dissolution, if one party desires to remain in the property which was the property of the other the parties must set up some kind of contract unless a claim for relief can be established by way of transfer of property[13].

1 Ie the power conferred by the Married Women's Property Act 1882 s 17 and the Civil Partnership Act 2004 s 66: see PARA 224. As to the principles to be applied in determining property rights see PARAS 278–284.
2 Matrimonial Causes (Property and Maintenance) Act 1958 s 7(7); Civil Partnership Act 2004 s 66(2).
3 See the Family Law Act 1996 s 30 et seq; and PARA 285 et seq.
4 *Gurasz v Gurasz* [1970] P 11, [1969] 3 All ER 822, CA; and see *Tarr v Tarr* [1973] AC 254, [1972] 2 All ER 295, HL.
5 Ie under the Married Women's Property Act 1882 s 17 or the Civil Partnership Act 2004 s 66: see PARA 224.
6 See eg *Cobb v Cobb* [1955] 2 All ER 696, [1955] 1 WLR 731, CA; *Bedson v Bedson* [1965] 2 QB 666, [1965] 3 All ER 307, CA; *Burke v Burke* [1974] 2 All ER 944, [1974] 1 WLR 1063, CA.
7 *Richman v Richman* [1950] WN 233; *Bedson v Bedson* [1965] 2 QB 666, [1965] 3 All ER 307, CA (wife and husband joint owners of home; sale refused); cf *Cobb v Cobb* [1955] 2 All ER 696, [1955] 1 WLR 731, CA (cited in note 8).
8 *Cobb v Cobb* [1955] 2 All ER 696, [1955] 1 WLR 731, CA (house conveyed to spouses as joint tenants; both assumed responsibility for repayments, although in fact they were deducted from the husband's wages because the money had been advanced by his employer; this was compensated for by a joint arrangement as to housekeeping expenses; the marriage then broke down; held that he could not be given an order for sale with vacant possession); applied in *McDowell v McDowell* (1957) 169 Estates Gazette 264, CA, distinguishing *Lee v Lee* [1952] 2 QB 489n, [1952] 1 All ER 1299, CA. Cf *Jackson v Jackson* [1970] 3 All ER 854, [1971] 1 WLR 59 (where the court exercised discretion, having regard to the conduct of the parties and the circumstances of the case, to order sale under the Law of Property Act 1925 s 30 (repealed), where the cost of allowing the wife to remain in the matrimonial home was in excess of anything the husband would be ordered to pay in matrimonial proceedings); affd [1971] 3 All ER 774, [1971] 1 WLR 1539, CA (where it was emphasised that the house was larger than was reasonably required by the wife: see at 778, 780, 782 and at 1543, 1544, 1547); *Re Hardy's Trust, Sutherst v Sutherst* (1970) 114 Sol Jo 864; *Farquharson v Farquharson* (1971) 115 Sol Jo 444, CA (question whether the matrimonial home should be sold was linked with the question of maintenance); *Burke v Burke* [1974] 2 All ER 944, [1974] 1 WLR 1063, CA.

9 See PARA 450 et seq.
10 See *Cobb v Cobb* [1955] 2 All ER 696 at 699, [1955] 1 WLR 731 at 734, CA per Denning LJ.
11 Ie the Married Women's Property Act 1882 s 17 and the Civil Partnership Act 2004 s 66: see
   PARA 224.
12 *McDowell v McDowell* (1957) 169 Estates Gazette 264, CA.
13 *Vaughan v Vaughan* [1953] 1 QB 762, [1953] 1 All ER 209, CA. As to transfers of property see
   PARA 499 et seq. In *Vaughan v Vaughan* it was held that if the wife had a contract giving her the
   right to remain in the house for the rest of her life, it would be a post-nuptial settlement which
   the divorce court could vary: see *Vaughan v Vaughan* at 768 and at 212 per Denning LJ; and see
   PARA 511. In proceedings by the husband under the Married Women's Property Act 1882 for
   possession of the matrimonial home of which he was tenant, the adjournment of the proceedings
   until either the husband had provided the wife with suitable alternative accommodation, or until
   the pending divorce proceedings had been heard, was held, on appeal, to be a judicial exercise of
   the discretion conferred by the 1882 Act: *Short v Short* [1960] 3 All ER 6, [1960] 1 WLR
   833, CA.

227. Property to which court's powers extend. The most common dispute
between spouses and civil partners is that relating to a house, particularly the
family home where both parties claim to have contributed to the cost in varying
degrees[1], or the contents thereof[2]. A dowry given on a Jewish marriage has been
the subject of an application under the provisions[3] concerning property
disputes[4]; and so too have been title deeds to property[5], jewellery[6], wedding
presents[7], gifts[8], and the benefit of a hire-purchase agreement[9]. A loan by one
party to the other is not, however, a matter which may be dealt with by the court
in such proceedings[10].

It is no longer necessary that the property should still be in the possession of
the other party or that there should be an identifiable fund in existence[11]. It has
been held that the jurisdiction of the English court is not limited to property in
England and Wales but can extend to property abroad, and a party cannot oust
the court's jurisdiction by removing property from England and Wales[12],
although the court may have no power to exercise jurisdiction where the
property in question is already the subject matter of proceedings in a foreign
court[13]. Where the property in dispute is land which is held by the parties as
joint tenants, a notice of severance may prevent proceedings being taken under
the dispute resolution provisions[14]. It has been held that a summons and
supporting affidavit under the dispute resolution provisions[15] may operate as the
severance of a joint tenancy[16].

1 See eg *Hutchinson v Hutchinson* [1947] 2 All ER 792; *Stewart v Stewart* [1948] 1 KB 507,
   [1947] 2 All ER 813, CA; *Re Rogers' Question* [1948] 1 All ER 328, CA. As to the meaning of
   an undertaking by a husband to a wife to make a house available 'for her use' see *Morss v Morss*
   [1972] Fam 264, [1972] 1 All ER 1121, CA.
2 See eg *W v W* [1951] 2 TLR 1135.
3 Ie under the Married Women's Property Act 1882 s 17, for which the corresponding civil
   partnership provision is the Civil Partnership Act 2004 s 66: see PARA 224.
4 *Joseph (otherwise King) v Joseph* [1909] P 217; *Kelner v Kelner* [1939] P 411, [1939] 3 All ER
   957.
5 *Re Knight's Question* [1959] Ch 381, [1958] 1 All ER 812.
6 *Tasker v Tasker* [1895] P 1.
7 *Samson v Samson* [1960] 1 All ER 653, [1960] 1 WLR 190, CA; and see PARA 247.
8 *Glaister-Carlisle v Glaister-Carlisle* (1968) 112 Sol Jo 215, CA (alleged gift of a dog).
9 *Spellman v Spellman* [1961] 2 All ER 498, [1961] 1 WLR 921, CA.
10 *Crystall v Crystall* [1963] 2 All ER 330, [1963] 1 WLR 574, CA.
11 See the Matrimonial Causes (Property and Maintenance) Act 1958 s 7; the Civil Partnership
   Act 2004 s 67; and PARA 228.
12 See *Razelos v Razelos* [1969] 3 All ER 929, [1970] 1 WLR 392 (where a wife instituted
   proceedings in respect of shares held by the husband in the United States of America and in
   respect of realty in Greece, all of which she alleged had been purchased with her money; and it

was held that the court had jurisdiction in respect of the shares as they had at one time been in the husband's possession and under his control in England and the fact that he had put them out of his possession in the United States did not oust that jurisdiction, and that the court's jurisdiction in respect of the realty in Greece stemmed from the husband's presence in England at the time that the summons was issued, and there was no evidence that an order in respect of that realty would be ineffectual in Greece). The court will not exercise its jurisdiction where an order would be ineffective: see *Hamlin v Hamlin* [1986] Fam 11, [1985] 2 All ER 1037, CA, applying *Razelos v Razelos*.

13 See *Re Granz's Question, Granz v Granz* (1968) 112 Sol Jo 439 (where, the parties being domiciled in Switzerland by the law of which the husband had management and control of the property belonging to both parties during the subsistence of the marriage, the wife commenced proceedings under the Married Women's Property Act 1882 s 17 in England in respect of property which the husband had brought to England but in respect of which the Swiss court had already refused to make an order in favour of the wife; it was held that until an order was made by the Swiss court to the contrary the husband's right to the possession of that property was unqualified and the right to its management unfettered, and the English court had no power to exercise jurisdiction which was vested in the Swiss court).

14 *Radziej (otherwise Sierkowska) v Radziej* [1967] 1 All ER 944, [1967] 1 WLR 659; affd [1968] 3 All ER 624, [1968] 1 WLR 1928, CA.

15 See note 3.

16 See *Re Draper's Conveyance, Nihan v Porter* [1969] 1 Ch 486, [1967] 3 All ER 853 (where the summons, coupled with the supporting affidavit, clearly showed an intention on the wife's part that she wished the property to be sold and the proceeds distributed, one-half to her and one-half to the husband).

228.   Property no longer in possession of spouse or civil partner.   Any right of a spouse or civil partner to apply to the court for the resolution of a property dispute[1] includes the right to make such an application where that person claims that the other party has had in his possession or under his control:

(1)   money to which, or to a share of which, the first person was beneficially entitled[2]; or

(2)   property, other than money, to which, or to an interest in which, that person was beneficially entitled[3],

and that either that money or other property has ceased to be in the possession or under the control of the other party or that the first person does not know whether it is still in the possession or under the control of the other party[4].

Where, on such an application, the court is satisfied:

(a)   that the other party has had in his possession or under his control that money or other property[5]; and

(b)   that he has not made to the applicant in respect of it such payment or disposition[6] as would have been appropriate in the circumstances[7],

it may order that party to pay to the applicant:

(i)   in a case falling within head (1) above, such sum in respect of the money to which the application relates, or the applicant's share thereof[8]; or

(ii)   in a case falling within head (2) above, such sum in respect of the value of the property to which the application relates, or the applicant's interest therein[9].

Where it appears to the court that there is any property which represents the whole or part of the money or property in question and is property in respect of which an order for the resolution of a property dispute[10] could have been made had an application been made for one in a question as to the title to or possession of that property, the court may, either in substitution for or in addition to making an order for payment referred to above, make such order as it could have made had there been an application as to the title to or possession of that property[11].

These provisions also apply in relation to the property of engaged couples and persons who have entered into a civil partnership agreement[12].

1   Ie under the Married Women's Property Act 1882 s 17 or the Civil Partnership Act 2004 s 66: see PARA 224. Such an application may be made by either of the parties notwithstanding that their marriage or civil partnership has been dissolved or annulled so long as the application is made within the period of three years beginning with the date of dissolution or annulment; Matrimonial Proceedings and Property Act 1970 s 39; Civil Partnership Act 2004 s 68. References in these provisions to a spouse or civil partner are to be construed accordingly: Matrimonial Proceedings and Property Act 1970 s 39; Civil Partnership Act 2004 s 68(2).

2   Matrimonial Causes (Property and Maintenance) Act 1958 s 7(1)(a), (5); Civil Partnership Act 2004 s 67(1)(a). For these purposes it does not matter whether the first person is beneficially entitled to the money or share because it represents the proceeds of property to which, or to an interest in which, he was beneficially entitled, or for any other reason: Matrimonial Causes (Property and Maintenance) Act 1958 s 7(1)(a); Civil Partnership Act 2004 s 67(2). The Matrimonial Causes (Property and Maintenance) Act 1958 s 8(1) provides that for these purposes 'property' means any real or personal property, any estate or interest in real or personal property, any money, any negotiable instrument, debt or other chose in action and any other right or interest whether in possession or not. No corresponding provision is made by the Civil Partnership Act 2004.

3   Matrimonial Causes (Property and Maintenance) Act 1958 s 7(1)(b); Civil Partnership Act 2004 s 67(1)(b).

4   Matrimonial Causes (Property and Maintenance) Act 1958 s 7(1); Civil Partnership Act 2004 s 67(1).

5   Matrimonial Causes (Property and Maintenance) Act 1958 s 7(2)(a); Civil Partnership Act 2004 s 67(3)(a).

6   The Matrimonial Causes (Property and Maintenance) Act 1958 s 8(1) provides that for these purposes 'disposition' does not include any provision contained in a will or codicil, but includes any conveyance, assurance or gift of property of any description, whether made by an instrument or otherwise. No corresponding provision is made by the Civil Partnership Act 2004.

7   Matrimonial Causes (Property and Maintenance) Act 1958 s 7(2)(b); Civil Partnership Act 2004 s 67(3)(b).

8   Matrimonial Causes (Property and Maintenance) Act 1958 s 7(3)(a); Civil Partnership Act 2004 s 67(4)(a). The Matrimonial Causes (Property and Maintenance) Act 1958 s 7(3) provides that the payment to be made is 'such sum in respect of the money to which the application relates, or the applicant's share thereof, as the case may be', while the Civil Partnership Act 2004 s 69(4) provides that it is to be 'such sum in respect of the money to which the application relates, or [the applicant's] share of it, as the court considers appropriate': quaere whether there is any meaningful distinction between these wordings. Any power of a judge which is exercisable under the Married Women's Property Act 1882 s 17 and the Civil Partnership Act 2004 s 66 (see PARA 224) is exercisable in relation to an application made under these provisions: Matrimonial Causes (Property and Maintenance) Act 1958 s 7(6) (substituted by the Matrimonial and Family Proceedings Act 1984 Sch 1 para 3); Civil Partnership Act 2004 s 67(6).

9   Matrimonial Causes (Property and Maintenance) Act 1958 s 7(3)(b); Civil Partnership Act 2004 s 67(4)(b). These provisions contain similar drafting discrepancies to those described in note 8. As to the powers of a judge see note 8.

10 Ie an order under the Married Women's Property Act 1882 s 17 or the Civil Partnership Act 2004 s 66: see PARA 224.

11 Matrimonial Causes (Property and Maintenance) Act 1958 s 7(4); Civil Partnership Act 2004 s 67(5). The court may also make an order in respect of property which, although once in the relevant party's possession, is at the time of the hearing out of his possession and abroad: see *Razelos v Razelos* [1969] 3 All ER 929, [1970] 1 WLR 390; and PARA 227 note 12.

12 See the Law Reform (Miscellaneous Provisions) Act 1970 s 2(2); the Civil Partnership Act 2004 s 74(3); and PARA 230. As to the meaning of 'civil partnership agreement' see PARA 16.

229.   Property of former spouses or civil partners.   Where a marriage or civil partnership has been dissolved, and there is a dispute between the former spouses or civil partners as to property pooled by them during the marriage or civil partnership[1], the principles to be applied in determining the ownership of those resources are the same as if the proceedings had been brought during the currency of the marriage or civil partnership[2]. The breakdown of the marriage or civil partnership is irrelevant in the determination of a question as to where ownership lay before breakdown[3]. It is also possible that, after dissolution, the transaction may be regarded as an ante-nuptial settlement (or civil partnership equivalent) and may be variable as such[4].

1   As to the right of either of the parties to a marriage or civil partnership which has been dissolved or annulled to apply to the court under the Married Women's Property Act 1882 s 17 or the Civil Partnership Act 2004 s 66 see PARA 224.
2   See *Pettitt v Pettitt* [1970] AC 777 at 793, [1969] 2 All ER 385 at 389, HL per Lord Reid; and PARA 278 et seq. Cf *Jones v Challenger* [1961] 1 QB 176, [1960] 1 All ER 785, CA; *Jackson v Jackson* [1971] 3 All ER 774, [1971] 1 WLR 1539, CA.
3   See *Pettitt v Pettitt* [1970] AC 777 at 803, [1969] 2 All ER 385 at 397, HL per Lord Morris of Borth-y-Gest.
4   See PARA 510 et seq.

230.   Rights over property where engagement or civil partnership agreement terminated.   Where an agreement to marry or a civil partnership agreement[1] is terminated, the statutory provisions conferring a share or an enlarged share of property on persons who have contributed to improvements to that property[2] apply in relation to any property in which either or both of the parties to the agreement had a beneficial interest while the agreement was in force as they apply in relation to property in which a spouse or civil partner has a beneficial interest[3], and the statutory provisions relating to the resolution of property disputes between spouses or civil partners[4] apply to any dispute between, or claim by one of, the parties in relation to property in which either or both had a beneficial interest while the agreement was in force, as if the parties were married or were civil partners of each other[5].

1   As to the meaning of 'civil partnership agreement' see PARA 16.
2   Ie the Matrimonial Proceedings and Property Act 1970 s 37 and the Civil Partnership Act 2004 s 65 (see PARA 283).
3   Law Reform (Miscellaneous Provisions) Act 1970 s 2(1); Civil Partnership Act 2004 s 74(1), (2).
4   Ie the Married Women's Property Act 1882 s 17, the Matrimonial Causes (Property and Maintenance) Act 1958 s 7, and the Civil Partnership Act 2004 ss 66, 67 (see PARAS 224, 228).
5   Law Reform (Miscellaneous Provisions) Act 1970 s 2(2); Civil Partnership Act 2004 s 74(3). An application made by virtue of this provision must be made within three years of the termination of the agreement: Law Reform (Miscellaneous Provisions) Act 1970 s 2(2); Civil Partnership Act 2004 s 74(4). As to undue influence being exercised by one party to an engagement over the other see *Zamet v Hyman* [1961] 3 All ER 933, [1961] 1 WLR 1442, CA.
    It is also provided, in relation to agreements to marry, that any rule of law relating to the rights of husbands and wives in relation to property in which either or both has or have a beneficial interest applies, in relation to any property in which either or both of the parties to the agreement had a beneficial interest while the agreement was in force, as it applies in relation to property in which a husband or wife has a beneficial interest: see the Law Reform (Miscellaneous Provisions) Act 1970 s 2(1); and see also *Mossop v Mossop* [1989] Fam 77, [1988] 2 All ER 202, CA (court has no jurisdiction to make a property transfer order under the Matrimonial Causes Act 1973 s 24(1) (see PARA 499 et seq) in relation to an unmarried couple who have called off their engagement (or, presumably, to make a property transfer order under the Civil Partnership Act 2004 Sch 5 Pt 2 (paras 6–9) (see PARA 499 et seq) in relation to persons who have terminated a civil partnership agreement).

(ii) Property Rights in the Family Home

231.   Property rights in the event of separation.   The court has wide discretionary powers in proceedings for divorce, dissolution, nullity or judicial or legal separation to distribute matrimonial and civil partnership property as it sees fit without having to ascertain the shares of the parties in the property[1]. If property is purchased in joint names without any declaration of trust there is a prime facie case that both the legal and beneficial interests in the property are joint and equal[2], although the respective parties' shares in the property will vary according to the share of the purchase money each provided and the contributions each has made to, for example, mortgage repayments[3]. The position is further complicated where the house is taken in only one of the two names[4]. A person may acquire a share or an enlarged share in joint property by making or contributing to improvements to that property[5].

Spouses' and civil partners' rights of occupation are also protected by statute[6], under which it is provided that where one spouse or civil partner is entitled to occupy a dwelling house and the other spouse or civil partner is not so entitled, the spouse or civil partner not so entitled has a right not to be evicted or excluded from the dwelling house or any part of it by the other spouse or civil partner except with the leave of the court and, if not in occupation of the dwelling house, has a right with the leave of the court so given to enter into and occupy it[7]. These rights are known as 'home rights'.

1   See *Fielding v Fielding* [1978] 1 All ER 267, [1977] 1 WLR 1146n; and PARA 278.
2   See *Stack v Dowden* [2007] UKHL 17, [2007] 2 AC 432, [2007] 2 All ER 929; and PARA 279. The intention to share the beneficial interest may be inferred by the court from the actions of the parties (see PARA 281), and provision is made as to their exact quantification (see PARA 282).
3   See PARA 279.
4   See PARA 280.
5   See PARA 283.
6   Ie the Family Law Act 1996 s 30 et seq (see PARA 285 et seq).
7   See the Family Law Act 1996 s 30(1), (2); and PARA 285.

(iii) Powers of Appointment

232.   Married woman's right to exercise power. A married woman[1] has always been able to execute a power of appointment limited or reserved to her, over either real or personal estate, whether the power is to be executed inter vivos or by will[2], the form of instrument required depending on the terms of the power. A power to appoint by deed only cannot be exercised by will[3], nor can a power to appoint by will only be exercised by deed[4]. A will executed and attested as required by law in ordinary cases is, however, a sufficient execution by a married woman of a power to appoint by will, even where the formalities required by the instrument creating the power have not been complied with[5]. There is nothing to prevent the exercise of a joint power given to husband and wife[6].

1   The provisions described in this paragraph derive from common law decisions (and, in one case, an enactment) specifically dealing only with 'marriage' and 'married women' and pre-dating the concept of civil partnerships, and their continuing significance should be considered in the light of this.
2   *Peacock v Monk* (1751) 2 Ves Sen 190; *Downes v Timperon* (1828) 4 Russ 334; *Doe d Blomfield v Eyre* (1848) 5 CB 713, Ex Ch; *Pride v Bubb* (1871) 7 Ch App 64; *Guise v Small* (1793) 1 Anst 277.
3   *Earl of Darlington v Pulteney* (1775) 1 Cowp 260; *Bushell v Bushell* (1803) 1 Sch & Lef 90.
4   *Reid v Shergold* (1805) 10 Ves 370; *Sockett v Wray* (1794) 4 Bro CC 483; *Anderson v Dawson* (1808) 15 Ves 532.
5   In this respect the Wills Act 1837 s 27 (see POWERS vol 36(2) (Reissue) PARA 310), applied to the wills of married woman made during marriage, even though that Act did not alter the capacity of a married woman to make a will: *Bernard v Minshull* (1859) John 276.
6   Law Reform (Married Women and Tortfeasors) Act 1935 s 4(2)(d).

233.   Power not suspended by marriage. Marriage[1] does not operate to suspend a power of appointment given to a single woman[2]; and, where a general power is given to a single woman under a settlement of her property, with trusts in default of appointment for herself and any future husband, the power may be exercised by her during the marriage[3]. A power in a marriage settlement to appoint at any time during and notwithstanding the marriage cannot, however, be exercised during widowhood or a second marriage[4].

1   The provisions described in this paragraph derive from common law decisions specifically dealing only with 'marriage' and 'married women' and pre-dating the concept of civil partnerships, and their continuing significance should be considered in the light of this.
2   *Burnet v Mann* (1748) 1 Ves Sen 156.
3   *Wood v Wood* (1870) LR 10 Eq 220.
4   *Horseman v Abbey* (1819) 1 Jac & W 381; *Morris v Howes* (1845) 4 Hare 599; on appeal 16 LJ Ch 121. The making of a will during marriage has, however, been held a good exercise of a power to appoint by will during marriage, even though the wife survived the husband: *Re Safford's Settlement, Davies v Burgess* [1915] 2 Ch 211.

234.   Minority. The minority of a married woman[1] does not affect her capacity to exercise a power of appointment with regard to personal estate by deed or will if it appears to have been the donor's intention that the power should be exercisable during minority[2]. A minor married woman cannot, however, exercise a power of appointment over real estate if it is coupled with an interest, that is to say if the exercise of the power will affect her own freehold interest[3].

A will made by a married woman in exercise of a power of appointment does not require her husband's assent[4].

1   The provisions described in this paragraph derive from common law decisions specifically dealing only with 'marriage' and 'married women' and pre-dating the concept of civil partnerships, and their continuing significance should be considered in the light of this. The age of majority for all persons is now reached on attaining the age of 18: see the Family Law Reform Act 1969 s 1(1); and CHILDREN AND YOUNG PERSONS vol 5(3) (2008 Reissue) PARA 1.
2   *Re D'Angibau, Andrews v Andrews* (1880) 15 ChD 228, CA; *Re Cardross's Settlement* (1878) 7 ChD 728; *Re Sutton, Boscawen v Wyndham* [1921] 1 Ch 257.
3   *Hearle v Greenbank* (1749) 3 Atk 695.
4   *Re Anstis, Chetwynd v Morgan, Morgan v Chetwynd* (1886) 31 ChD 596, CA; and see *Re James, Hole v Bethune* [1910] 1 Ch 157.

235.   Effect of appointment by will. If a married woman[1] who has a general power of appointment by will[2] expresses an intention by her will that it is to operate[3] on all property over which she has a power of appointment, she thereby makes the property her own and prevents it from going as in default of appointment, even though the will may fail effectively to dispose of the property by reason of the death of the residuary devisee or legatee in her lifetime[4].

1   The provisions described in this paragraph derive from common law decisions specifically dealing only with 'marriage' and 'married women' and pre-dating the concept of civil partnerships, and their continuing significance should be considered in the light of this.
2   See the Wills Act 1837 s 27; *Re Powell's Trusts* (1869) 39 LJ Ch 188; and POWERS vol 36(2) (Reissue) PARA 310.
3   For the purpose of the rule against perpetuities, time runs from the death of the married woman: *Rous v Jackson* (1885) 29 ChD 521; cf *Re Powell's Trusts* (1869) 39 LJ Ch 188; and PERPETUITIES AND ACCUMULATIONS vol 35 (Reissue) PARA 1062.
4   *Willoughby Osborne v Holyoake* (1882) 22 ChD 238; *Re Pinede's Settlement* (1879) 12 ChD 667.

236.   Power to appoint in favour of husband or herself. A married woman[1] may exercise a general power of appointment in favour of herself[2], her husband[3] or herself and her husband jointly[4]; and, if any appointment to the husband is impeached on the ground of his undue influence, the burden of proving its invalidity lies on the party impeaching it[5].

1　The provisions described in this paragraph derive from common law decisions specifically dealing only with 'marriage' and 'married women' and pre-dating the concept of civil partnerships, and their continuing significance should be considered in the light of this.

2　*Bower v Smith* (1871) LR 11 Eq 279; and see *Fussell v Dowding* (1872) LR 14 Eq 421; *Bond v Taylor* (1861) 2 John & H 473.

3　*Wood v Wood* (1870) LR 10 Eq 220; *Re D'Angibau, Andrews v Andrews* (1880) 15 ChD 228, CA; *Bernard v Minshull* (1859) John 276; *Allen v Papworth* (1731) 1 Ves Sen 163 (bill by husband and wife submitting that the property subject to the power should be applied in payment of his debts, held equivalent to an appointment by her, and decreed accordingly).

4　*Wood v Wood* (1870) LR 10 Eq 220. See also the Law Reform (Married Women and Tortfeasors) Act 1935 s 4(2)(d) (there is nothing to prevent the exercise of a joint power given to husband and wife); and PARA 232.

5　*Nedby v Nedby* (1852) 5 De G & Sm 377 (income given to wife for life for her separate use, with power to appoint the remainder by deed or will; it was sought to set aside an appointment by deed in favour of the husband on the ground of ignorance and want of professional advice, the deed having been prepared by the husband's solicitor; appointment upheld).

237.　Contracts as to exercise of power.　A married woman[1] may by deed release or contract not to exercise any power, whether coupled with an interest or not, and it is not necessary that the husband should concur[2].

Where a married woman has a general power of appointment by will, a contract by her to exercise it in favour of a particular person will not be specifically enforced, but the breach of such a contract gives rise to a claim for damages against her estate, and, if the power of appointment is exercised, the appointed property forms part of her assets[3].

1　The provisions described in this paragraph derive from common law decisions specifically dealing only with 'marriage' and 'married women' and pre-dating the concept of civil partnerships, and their continuing significance should be considered in the light of this.

2　Power to release or to contract not to exercise a power of appointment is conferred generally by the Law of Property Act 1925 s 155: see POWERS vol 36(2) (Reissue) PARA 376. As to the principle that a married woman may act without her husband's concurrence see *Re Chisholm's Settlement, Re Hemphill's Settlement, Hemphill v Hemphill* [1901] 2 Ch 82, CA (life interest in personalty subject to restraint on anticipation, with power of appointment; the power could be released by deed without acknowledgment); *Re Onslow, Plowden v Gayford* (1888) 39 ChD 622; *Re Davenport, Turner v King* [1895] 1 Ch 361.

3　*Re Parkin, Hill v Schwarz* [1892] 3 Ch 510 (covenant by wife in favour of the trustees of her marriage settlement to exercise any power of appointment which might become vested in her; she became the donee of a general testamentary power and exercised it in favour of others; the trustees of the settlement were not entitled to specific performance, but they had a claim for damages against her executors to the extent of her assets, the measure of the damages being the value of the appointed property, which formed part of her assets).

238.　Defective execution.　A defective execution of a power in favour of creditors or purchasers for valuable consideration will be remedied in equity[1], provided that there was an attempt to exercise it in their favour[2].

1　*Hughes v Wells* (1852) 9 Hare 749; *Sergison v Sealey* (1742) 2 Atk 412 at 415; *Tollet v Tollet* (1728) 2 P Wms 489; *Cotter v Layer* (1731) 2 P Wms 623; and see POWERS vol 36(2) (Reissue) PARA 359 et seq.

2　*Bull v Vardy* (1791) 1 Ves 270. As to a defective appointment in favour of a husband see PARA 236.

(iv) Equity of Exoneration

239.　Right of indemnity where one party's property charged for other's benefit.　If the property of a spouse or a civil partner[1] is mortgaged or charged in order to raise money for the payment of the other spouse or civil partner's debts, or otherwise for the other spouse or civil partner's benefit, it is presumed, in the absence of evidence showing an intention to the contrary, that the first spouse or civil partner meant to charge the property merely by way of security, and in such case that spouse or a civil partner is in the position of surety[2] and is entitled to be indemnified by the other spouse or civil partner, and to throw the debt primarily on that person's estate to the exoneration of his own[3].

The right to exoneration is, however, a presumptive right only; it depends on the intention of the parties to be ascertained from all the circumstances of each particular case[4]. It may be rebutted by evidence showing that the first spouse or civil partner intended to make a gift of the property to the other[5]; and it has been held to be rebutted where the money was raised to pay debts which, though legally one party's, had been contracted by reason of the extravagant mode of living of both[6].

No presumption of a right to exoneration arises where the money is raised to discharge the debts or obligations of the party whose property is being mortgaged or charged, or otherwise for that person's benefit[7]; and, where the mortgage of one spouse or civil partner's estate is contemporaneous with a settlement of it, the whole will be presumed to be one transaction so as to exclude that person's claim to indemnity, especially if the money is raised for the purpose of discharging any of their debts or charges on the estate, even though more money has been raised than is necessary for that purpose[8].

The court may order an inquiry as to which sums forming part of the money raised under the charge went solely to the benefit of the other spouse or civil partner, whether in their business or on their personal account, and which went for the benefit of the spouse or civil partner whose property has been mortgaged or charged, either solely or jointly with their spouse or civil partner or children; and, in respect of the latter sums, the spouse or civil partner whose property has been mortgaged or charged has no right of exoneration[9].

Equity of exoneration is waived and barred if the right is disclaimed and the executors of the disclaimer's spouse or civil partner pay legacies on the faith of the disclaimer[10].

1   Although the provisions described in this paragraph and PARAS 240–244 derive from common law decisions pre-dating the concept of civil partnerships, and are concerned with protecting the property of a wife against her husband's creditors, it is submitted that they must now apply equally to the property of either party to a marriage and also to the property of civil partners.

2   See *Stamford, Spalding and Boston Banking Co v Ball* (1862) 4 De GF & J 310 (where a wife's reversionary interest in personalty, held for her separate use, was assigned to trustees for a bank on trust to receive the same and retain and pay certain money due from her husband, there being no proviso for redemption or power of sale, it was held that the bank was not entitled to foreclosure but only to retain the money due from the husband when the wife's interest fell into possession).

3   *Earl of Huntingdon v Countess Dowager Huntingdon* (1702) 2 Bro Parl Cas 1, HL (wife joined with husband in mortgage of her freeholds of inheritance; husband paid off the mortgage, and took an assignment of it in trust for himself; it was held that the wife's heir was entitled to the property as against the devisee of the husband); *Pocock v Lee* (1707) 2 Vern 604 (wife joined husband in mortgage, the equity of redemption being reserved to husband and wife and their heirs; the husband having died, it was held that the mortgage must be discharged out of his estate in exoneration of that of the wife); *Hudson v Carmichael* (1854) Kay 613; *Parteriche v Powlet* (1742) 2 Atk 383; *Aguilar v Aguilar Lousada* (1820) 5 Madd 414 (contest between wife and husband's assignee in bankruptcy); *Gee v Smart* (1857) 8 E & B 313; *Tate v Austin* (1714) 1 P Wms 264; cf *Grant v Callaghan* (1956) 107 L Jo 105.

See also *Lancaster v Evors* (1847) 10 Beav 266 (after her death the wife's creditors are entitled to claim the benefit of her right, but, as a general rule, interest will not be allowed on the sum which she is entitled to be repaid); and as to jurisdiction see *Drummond v Drummond* (1868) 37 LJ Ch 811 (action by plaintiff domiciled in England against defendant resident in

Scotland to have plaintiff's Scottish real estate exonerated; the defendant having appeared, the court accepted jurisdiction). As to a guarantor's rights to exoneration generally see FINANCIAL SERVICES AND INSTITUTIONS vol 49 (2008) PARA 1151 et seq.

4   *Paget v Paget* [1898] 1 Ch 470, CA. See also *Noyes v Pollock* (1886) 32 ChD 53, CA; *Skottowe v Williams, Williams v Skottowe* (1861) 3 De GF & J 535.
5   *Clinton v Hooper* (1791) 3 Bro CC 201.
6   *Paget v Paget* [1898] 1 Ch 470, CA.
7   *Earl Kinnoul v Money* (1767) 3 Swan 202; *Gray v Dowman* (1858) 27 LJ Ch 702; *Bagot v Oughton* (1717) 1 P Wms 347; *Re Pittortou, ex p Trustee of Property of Bankrupt v Bankrupt* [1985] 1 All ER 285, [1985] 1 WLR 58 (money used for general household and family living expenses will be treated as used for the joint benefit of the wife and the husband).
8   *Lewis v Nangle* (1752) 1 Cox Eq Cas 240.
9   *Re Pittortou, ex p Trustee of Property of Bankrupt v Bankrupt* [1985] 1 All ER 285, [1985] 1 WLR 58.
10 *Clinton v Hooper* (1791) 3 Bro CC 201.

240.   Position where other spouse or civil partner is party to a mortgage. Where a spouse or civil partner[1] joins in the mortgage of his spouse or civil partner's property and covenants for repayment, or where it appears on the face of the mortgage deed that the money was paid to him, there is a presumption that the money was raised for his benefit and that his spouse or civil partner is a surety for it[2], although extrinsic evidence is admissible to show the contrary[3].

1   See PARA 239 note 1.
2   *Hudson v Carmichael* (1854) Kay 613; *Hall v Hall* [1911] 1 Ch 487; and see *Lewis v Nangle* (1752) 1 Cox Eq Cas 240 per Lord Thurlow. Spouses and civil partners may sue jointly for money received in respect of an advance to them both on the security of the property of one of them: *Jones v Cuthbertson* (1873) LR 8 QB 504.
3   *Hudson v Carmichael* (1854) Kay 613; *Gray v Dowman* (1858) 27 LJ Ch 702; *Hall v Hall* [1911] 1 Ch 487.

241.   Property charged partly for benefit of other spouse or civil partner. If the property of a spouse or civil partner[1] is charged partly for their spouse or civil partner's benefit and partly for the discharge of their own debts and obligations, the first spouse or civil partner is presumptively entitled to exoneration to the extent of the other's interest[2].

1   See PARA 239 note 1.
2   *Gee v Smart* (1857) 8 E & B 313 at 319.

242.   Estates of both spouses or civil partners charged for one party's benefit. Where the estates of both spouses or civil partners[1] are mortgaged or charged for the benefit of one of them, the other is prima facie entitled to place the mortgage debt primarily on the property of the first[2].

1   See PARA 239 note 1.
2   *Bagot v Oughton* (1717) 1 P Wms 347; *Gray v Dowman* (1858) 27 LJ Ch 702; and see *Pitt v Pitt* (1823) Turn & R 180.

243.   Charge of property over which one party has general power. The presumptive right to exoneration[1] extends to cases where one spouse or civil partner[2] mortgages for the benefit of the other spouse or civil partner property over which the first spouse or civil partner has a general power of appointment[3], and even to cases of property over which they have a joint power, if the property is limited to the first spouse or civil partner in default of appointment[4].

1   See PARA 239.
2   See PARA 239 note 1.
3   *Thomas v Thomas* (1855) 25 LJ Ch 159.

4   *Re Trueman, ex p Trueman* (1872) 42 LJ Bcy 1; cf *Scholefield v Lockwood* (1863) 4 De GJ & Sm 22.

244.   Effect of bankruptcy.   Where the property of a spouse or civil partner[1] is mortgaged or charged for the benefit of their spouse or civil partner and the second spouse or civil partner becomes bankrupt, the first spouse or civil partner will be able, if the equity of exoneration is applied, to throw the burden of any charge or mortgage on to the bankrupt's beneficial interest in any jointly held property[2].

1   See PARA 239 note 1.
2   *Re Pittortou, ex p Trustee of Property of Bankrupt v Bankrupt* [1985] 1 All ER 285, [1985] 1 WLR 58; and see *Re a Debtor (No 24 of 1971), ex p Marley v Trustee of Property of Debtor* [1976] 2 All ER 1010, [1976] 1 WLR 952, DC.

(v) Minor Financial Matters

245.   Joint banking account.   Where spouses or civil partners[1] have a common purse and a pool of their resources, whether in a joint banking account or otherwise, the remuneration of one party is usually regarded as being earned on behalf of both and to be joint property, and amounts paid in and withdrawn by each party are irrelevant[2]. This will not be the case, however, where one party provides all the money in the joint account and it is simply used as a matter of convenience of administration[3].

1   Although the provisions described in this paragraph derive from common law decisions pre-dating the concept of civil partnerships, it is submitted that they must now apply equally to the property of either party to a marriage and also to the property of civil partners.
2   See *Jones v Maynard* [1951] Ch 572, [1951] 1 All ER 802 (where a husband authorised his wife to draw on his bank account which was then operated as a joint account into which both paid their income and earnings, his payments being much the larger, and from time to time he withdrew money to pay for investments which he purchased in his own name, and it was held that the principle of equality ought to be applied and the wife was entitled to half the final balance in the joint account and to half the value of the investments existing at the date when the account was closed). Cf *Re Bishop, National Provincial Bank Ltd v Bishop* [1965] Ch 450, [1965] 1 All ER 249 (where a joint account was opened for a husband and wife on the terms that either could draw on it; then, in the absence of evidence to the contrary, each spouse could draw on it not only for the benefit of them both but also for his, or her, individual benefit). See also the Married Women's Property Act 1964 s 1 (if any question arises as to the right of a husband or wife to money derived from any allowance made by the husband for the expenses of the matrimonial home or for similar purposes, or to any property acquired out of such money, the money or property is, in the absence of any agreement between them to the contrary, to be treated as belonging to the husband and the wife in equal shares).
3   *Heseltine v Heseltine* [1971] 1 All ER 952 at 956, [1971] 1 WLR 342 at 347, CA per Lord Denning MR.

246.   Paraphernalia.   The term 'paraphernalia' comprises jewels and ornaments, exclusive of old family jewels[1], which belong to the husband but which the wife is permitted to wear[2]. It is extremely doubtful whether the doctrine of paraphernalia is applicable at the present day[3], but it cannot be treated as definitely obsolete[4], and the relevant law would appear to be as follows.

Jewels and trinkets given to the wife by relatives or friends are generally considered her property, and not paraphernalia[5]. In case of gifts by the husband, there is a presumption that they are intended as absolute gifts, and not as gifts of paraphernalia, if they are given to the wife at Christmas, or on her birthday, or in order to settle differences[6]. During the lifetime of the husband, paraphernalia cannot be disposed of by the wife[7]; but they may be sold, pledged or given away by him[8]. On the death of the husband, paraphernalia belong to the wife, subject to liability for the husband's debts on failure of other assets[9], and the husband cannot, therefore, dispose of them by will[10]; they are not liable to satisfy his legacies[11]; and, if he has pledged them during his life, his widow is entitled to have them redeemed out of his personalty, to the prejudice of legatees[12].

1　*Jervoise v Jervoise* (1853) 23 LJ Ch 703; and see *Laing v Walker* (1891) 64 LT 527; *Lord Hastings v Douglas* (1634) Cro Car 343.
2　*Viscountess Bindon's Case* (1586) Moore KB 213; *Burton v Pierpoint* (1722) 2 P Wms 78; *Graham v Londonderry* (1746) 3 Atk 393.
3　The doctrine was discussed at length in *Masson, Templier & Co v De Fries* [1909] 2 KB 831, CA (where Farwell LJ stated his opinion that after the Married Women's Property Act 1882 it had ceased to exist). Cf *Tasker v Tasker* [1895] P 1 at 4 per Sir Francis Jeune P (the Married Women's Property Act 1882 had not abolished the general law as to gifts of paraphernalia, although 'the law of paraphernalia and the practice of constituting paraphernalia are unfamiliar, if not antiquated').
4　See *Masson, Templier & Co v De Fries* [1909] 2 KB 831 at 840, CA per Kennedy LJ ('the only occasion on which an issue as to paraphernalia might perhaps still be raised is a dispute as to the possession of property in the nature of ornaments and the like articles between a wife and the representative of her deceased husband'); but see note 3.
5　*Graham v Londonderry* (1746) 3 Atk 393; *Lucas v Lucas* (1738) 1 Atk 270; but see *Jervoise v Jervoise* (1853) 17 Beav 566.
6　*Tasker v Tasker* [1895] P 1; cf *Masson, Templier & Co v De Fries* [1909] 2 KB 831, CA.
7　*Masson, Templier & Co v De Fries* [1909] 2 KB 831, CA.
8　*Graham v Londonderry* (1746) 3 Atk 393 at 394.
9　*Ridout v Earl of Plymouth* (1740) 2 Atk 104; *Burton v Pierpoint* (1722) 2 P Wms 78; *Lord Townshend v Windham* (1750) 2 Ves Sen 1 at 7; *Parker v Harvey* (1726) 4 Bro Parl Cas 604 at 609.
10　*Seymour v Tresilian* (1737) 3 Atk 358 at 359.
11　*Graham v Londonderry* (1746) 3 Atk 393 at 395. The right of the widow to paraphernalia may, however, be barred by a provision in the marriage settlement (*Cholmely v Cholmely* (1688) 2 Vern 82), or by agreement between her and her husband, or by her election or acquiescence, as e g where he bequeaths them to her for life, by her taking under the will instead of claiming them absolutely (*Clarges v Duchess of Albemarle* (1691) 2 Vern 245).
12　See note 11.

247.　Wedding presents and gifts on formation of civil partnership. If there is no evidence of the donor's intention, the court may infer that wedding presents from the husband's family were meant for him, and those from the wife's family for her[1]. It is likely that a similar inference could be made in relation to civil partnerships.

1　*Samson v Samson* [1960] 1 All ER 653, [1960] 1 WLR 190, CA. As to the property of formerly engaged couples see PARAS 230, 253.

(vi)　Gifts between Parties

248.　Rules concerning gifts and transfers. It is provided by statute that husband and wife are empowered to convey to each other freeholds and choses in action[1] and that they may also make gifts to each other of leaseholds and chattels[2]: these provisions are almost certainly obsolete, and have not been amended so as also to apply to civil partners. The statutory provisions concerning the exemption from inheritance tax of transfers between spouses and the treatment of disposals between spouses for the purposes of capital gains tax have, however, been extended to include civil partners[3].

1　See the Law of Property Act 1925 s 72(2); and GIFTS vol 20(1) (Reissue) PARA 5. As to property rights in the family home see PARA 278 et seq.

2   See the Law of Property Act 1925 s 37; and GIFTS vol 20(1) (Reissue) PARA 5. A gift from
husband to wife or from wife to husband must, in general, be established in the same way as a
gift between strangers: see GIFTS vol 20(1) (Reissue) PARA 5.

3   See the Inheritance Tax Act 1984 s 18; INHERITANCE TAXATION vol 24 (Reissue) PARA 515; the
Taxation of Chargeable Gains Act 1992 s 58; and CAPITAL GAINS TAXATION vol 5(1) (2004
Reissue) PARAS 101, 102.

249.   Undue influence.   It has been held that a gift from a wife to her
husband[1], in order to be valid, had to be made by her freely and voluntarily, with
a full knowledge and understanding of the nature of the transaction, and without
any pressure or the exercise of undue influence on the husband's part[2]. The
burden of proving undue influence is on the wife[3], but, although no presumption
of undue influence exists[4], husband and wife are not treated in this respect as
strangers, and, especially where the gift is of a large amount or of considerable
value, the husband may without much difficulty be required to show that the
transaction was fair and proper[5].

1   The provisions described in this paragraph derive from common law decisions specifically
dealing with gifts between husbands and wives and pre-dating the concept of civil partnerships,
and their continuing significance should be considered in the light of this.

2   *Willis v Barron* [1902] AC 271, HL (deeds by which the wife surrendered her rights under a
post-nuptial settlement without consideration set aside, the solicitor who prepared them being
one of the trustees, and having failed to explain to her the real nature of the transaction or to see
that she had advice independent of her husband); *Turnbull & Co v Duval* [1902] AC 429,
PC (deed executed by wife as security for husband's debt set aside on the grounds of pressure,
want of independent advice, and concealment of material facts), applied in *Kingsnorth Trust Ltd
v Bell* [1986] 1 All ER 423, [1986] 1 WLR 119, CA; *Chaplin & Co Ltd v Brammall* [1908]
1 KB 233, CA (guarantee for husband's debts obtained by him from wife without sufficiently
explaining the nature of the transaction); *Hughes v Wells* (1852) 9 Hare 749; *Milnes v Busk*
(1794) 2 Ves 488; *Essex v Atkins* (1808) 14 Ves 542; *Beck v Beck* (1916) 50 ILT 135
(assignment by wife without independent advice set aside though made for an illegal purpose).
Where, however, on a disposition by deed acknowledged the wife consented to payment of the
purchase money being made to the husband, it was held that she could not dispute the validity
of the gift: *Tennent v Welch* (1888) 37 ChD 622. As to the impeachment on the grounds of
undue influence of transactions between husband and wife see also MISREPRESENTATION AND
FRAUD vol 31 (2003 Reissue) PARA 850.

3   *Bank of Montreal v Stuart* [1911] AC 120, HL; *Re Lloyds Bank Ltd, Bomze and Lederman v
Bomze* [1931] 1 Ch 289 at 301, 302; and see MISREPRESENTATION AND FRAUD vol 31 (2003
Reissue) PARA 850.

4   As to presumed undue influence see EQUITY vol 16(2) (Reissue) PARA 667; and see
MISREPRESENTATION AND FRAUD vol 31 (2003 Reissue) PARA 850.

5   *Re Lloyds Bank Ltd, Bomze and Lederman v Bomze* [1931] 1 Ch 289 at 302 per Maugham J.

250.   Fraudulent dispositions.   Dispositions between spouses or civil partners
may be voidable under the provisions relating to transactions defrauding
creditors[1], transactions at an undervalue and preferences[2], or voluntary
dispositions of land made with intent to defraud subsequent purchasers[3].

Where a gift of chattels takes the form of a deed of gift and the deed is not
duly registered as a bill of sale and the chattels remain in the possession or
apparent possession of the grantor, the deed is void as against the grantor's
creditors[4]. This is, however, subject to the principle that, where two persons are
together in the enjoyment of chattels, the law refers possession to the one who
has the legal title; and, if one spouse gives or sells to the other chattels in the
matrimonial home, the chattels are, in general, deemed to pass into the
possession of the donee or purchaser and not to remain in the possession or
apparent possession of the settlor or vendor[5].

1   See the Insolvency Act 1986 Pt XVI (ss 423–425); and BANKRUPTCY AND INDIVIDUAL
INSOLVENCY vol 3(2) (2002 Reissue) PARAS 663–667.

2   See the Insolvency Act 1986 ss 339–342; and BANKRUPTCY AND INDIVIDUAL INSOLVENCY
     vol 3(2) (2002 Reissue) PARAS 653–662.
3   See the Law of Property Act 1925 s 173; and MISREPRESENTATION AND FRAUD vol 31 (2003
     Reissue) PARA 868 et seq.
4   See FINANCIAL SERVICES AND INSTITUTIONS vol 50 (2008) PARAS 1849–1850.
5   See FINANCIAL SERVICES AND INSTITUTIONS vol 50 (2008) PARA 1852.

251.   Receipt of one party's property by the other. Where a spouse or civil
partner receives property or money belonging to his spouse or civil partner, and
the circumstances are not such as to establish a gift[1] or loan[2], the receiving
spouse or civil partner is accountable as a trustee for the other party[3] and, so
long as the receiving spouse or civil partner retains the property or money, or if
he converts it to his own use, he is not entitled to the benefit of any statute of
limitation[4].

If a spouse or civil partner is liable to pay interest to his spouse or civil
partner, or to that spouse or civil partner's trustees, in respect of a capital sum
due from the first spouse or civil partner, and the first spouse or civil partner is
permitted to retain this interest in circumstances such that a gift of it is presumed
in his favour[5], the period of limitation in respect of his capital liability does not
run in his favour during the time the presumption continues[6].

1   See PARA 248.
2   See *Woodward v Woodward* (1863) 3 De GJ & Sm 672; and PARA 206.
3   *Parker v Brooke* (1804) 9 Ves 583; *Dixon v Dixon* (1878) 9 ChD 587 (a trustee of stock for the
     separate use of a married woman transferred it into the joint names of himself and her husband,
     and the husband, after receiving the dividends for six years, sold the stock and applied the
     proceeds to his own use; it was held that the wife was entitled to have the stock replaced by the
     husband, and to an account against him of the arrears of income from the time of the wrongful
     sale). Where a husband executed a voluntary settlement in favour of his wife which contained an
     assignment of leasehold property to the trustees of the settlement, and the husband subsequently
     obtained a renewal of the lease in his own name, he was held, in taking the new lease, to have
     acted for the benefit of his wife and as agent for her and the trustees of the settlement, and the
     new lease was held to be subject to the trusts of the settlement: *Re Lulham, Brinton v Lulham*
     (1885) 53 LT 9, CA. A third person who, with notice of a wife's claim to goods or chattels, deals
     with them on the husband's instructions in a manner inconsistent with her title is liable to her:
     Davis v Artingstall (1880) 49 LJ Ch 609 (auctioneer entrusted by husband with goods for sale).
     See also *Heseltine v Heseltine* [1971] 1 All ER 952, [1971] 1 WLR 342, CA (where the wife
     transferred considerable properties and assets to husband but had no independent legal advice as
     she trusted her husband; it was held that the transfers were not intended as absolute gifts but as
     transfers for family purposes, that it would be inequitable to permit the husband to retain the
     assets for himself beneficially, and that he held them as trustee for the wife alone, although he
     was to be given credit for payments made by him for family purposes out of the capital and
     interest).
4   *Wassell v Leggatt* [1896] 1 Ch 554 (husband took possession by force in 1876 of a legacy to
     which his wife was entitled and died in 1894 without having repaid any portion of it, although
     she had from time to time demanded repayment; he was held to be a trustee, and his executors
     were, therefore, accountable). As to the limitation of actions in respect of trust property see the
     Limitation Act 1980 s 21; and LIMITATION PERIODS vol 68 (2008) PARA 1140.
5   As to gifts see PARA 248.
6   *Re Hawes, Re Burchell, Burchell v Hawes* (1892) 62 LJ Ch 463 (wife's trustees lent her money
     to the husband on mortgage; she and her husband lived together, and he paid no interest under
     the mortgage; it was held that, so long as they were living together, a gift of the interest to him
     was presumed, and time did not run in his favour as regards his liability to repay the sum
     borrowed). See also *Re Dixon, Haynes v Dixon* [1900] 2 Ch 561, CA.

252.   Discharge of incumbrances. Where a spouse or civil partner pays off
incumbrances on his spouse or civil partner's estate he is entitled, in the absence
of proof of an intention to the contrary, to a charge on the property for the sums
so paid[1].

1   *Outram v Hyde* (1875) 24 WR 268; *Pitt v Pitt* (1823) Turn & R 180; *Gooch v Gooch* (1851) 15 Jur 1166. As to the equitable rights of a person other than the mortgagor who pays off a mortgage debt see eg *Chetwynd v Allen* [1899] 1 Ch 353.

253. Gifts between engaged couples and persons who have entered into a civil partnership agreement. A party to an agreement to marry or a civil partnership agreement[1] who makes a gift of property to the other party to the agreement on the condition, express or implied, that it is to be returned if the agreement is terminated is not prevented from recovering the property by reason only of having terminated the agreement[2]. The gift of an engagement ring, however, is presumed to be an absolute gift, although this presumption may be rebutted by proving that the ring was given on the condition, express or implied, that it was to be returned if the marriage did not take place for any reason[3].

1   As to the meaning of 'civil partnership agreement' see PARA 16.
2   Law Reform (Miscellaneous Provisions) Act 1970 s 3(1); Civil Partnership Act 2004 s 74(5).
3   Law Reform (Miscellaneous Provisions) Act 1970 s 3(2), reversing the presumption that engagement rings are conditional gifts (see *Jacobs v Davis* [1917] 2 KB 532).

(vii) Property Rights after Spouse or Civil Partner's Death

254. Rights of surviving spouse or civil partner in deceased's estate. Where a person dies domiciled in England and Wales and is survived by his or her spouse or civil partner, that spouse or civil partner may apply to the court for an order on the ground that the disposition of the deceased's estate effected by his or her will or the law relating to intestacy, or the combination of the will and that law, is not such as to make reasonable financial provision for the applicant[1]. Among the orders which the court has power to make on such an application are orders for the transfer to the applicant, or for the settlement for the benefit of the applicant, of such property comprised in the deceased's estate as may be specified in the order[2].

Where at the time of an intestate's death the surviving spouse or civil partner of the intestate is resident in a dwelling house an interest in which forms part of the intestate's residuary estate, the surviving spouse or civil partner may require the personal representative of the intestate to appropriate the intestate's interest in the house in or towards satisfaction of any absolute interest of the surviving spouse or civil partner in the residuary estate[3].

1   See the Inheritance (Provision for Family and Dependants) Act 1975 s 1(1); PARA 539; and EXECUTORS AND ADMINISTRATORS vol 17(2) (Reissue) PARAS 666–667. Application may also be made by a person, other than the spouse or civil partner or former spouse or civil partner of the deceased who was living in the same household as the deceased as the spouse or civil partner of the deceased during the whole of the period of two years ending immediately before the date when the deceased died: see s 1(1A); and EXECUTORS AND ADMINISTRATORS vol 17(2) (Reissue) PARA 667.
2   See the Inheritance (Provision for Family and Dependants) Act 1975 s 2(1)(c), (d); PARA 539; and EXECUTORS AND ADMINISTRATORS vol 17(2) (Reissue) PARA 691. As to the matters to be considered by the court and the mode of procedure see generally EXECUTORS AND ADMINISTRATORS vol 17(2) (Reissue) PARA 671 et seq.
3   See the Intestates' Estates Act 1952 Sch 2; and EXECUTORS AND ADMINISTRATORS vol 17(2) (Reissue) PARAS 593–594.

255. Statutory tenant by succession. On the death of a protected or statutory tenant there may be a transmission to a surviving spouse or civil partner who becomes a statutory or assured tenant by succession[1].

1   See LANDLORD AND TENANT vol 27(2) (2006 Reissue) PARA 844 et seq.

(4) AUTHORITY TO MAKE CONTRACTS

(i) Authority and Liability

256.   Authority to contract.   It has been held that a wife[1] has no authority, by virtue of the marriage alone, to contract on behalf of her husband without his authority[2], and that in order that the husband may be bound he must expressly or impliedly authorise the contract[3], or must have so conducted himself as to be estopped from denying the authority[4], or must have ratified the contract[5]. It has also been held that a wife has neither presumed nor implied authority in any case to contract on behalf of her husband and herself jointly[6], unless they carry on a business in partnership[7].

On the general principles applicable to the law of agency, a spouse or civil partner who contracts professedly on behalf of his spouse or civil partner but who has no authority to do so may be liable to be sued for breach of warranty of authority, even though he has so contracted in good faith[8].

It has been held that where a contract made by a wife on her husband's behalf was expressly authorised by him he was liable, and entitled to sue, on it as in the case of a contract made by any other agent[9].

1   Although the provisions described in this paragraph and PARAS 257–273 derive from common law decisions concerning the authority of a wife to contract on behalf of her husband or on behalf of them both, it is submitted that they must now apply, to the extent that they have any continuing relevance, to the contractual rights of either party to a marriage and, presumably, to civil partners.

2   *Debenham v Mellon* (1880) 6 App Cas 24, HL.

3   *Debenham v Mellon* (1880) 6 App Cas 24, HL.

4   As to agency by estoppel see PARA 269.

5   As to ratification see PARA 269 et seq.

6   *Morel Bros & Co Ltd v Earl of Westmoreland* [1904] AC 11, HL.

7   As to the power of a partner to bind the firm see the Partnership Act 1890 s 5; and PARTNERSHIP vol 79 (2008) PARA 45.

8   As to the general principles on which an agent may be liable for breach of warranty of authority see AGENCY vol 1 (2008) PARA 160. The decision in *Smout v Ilbery* (1842) 10 M & W 1 (where it was held that a wife was not liable where, unknown to her, her authority had at the date of contract been determined by her husband's death) must be considered as overruled in so far as it was based on the view that an agent innocently continuing to act without knowledge of revocation of his authority is not liable to a third party, and is no longer law in so far as it was based on the former inability of a married woman to render herself personally liable on a contract: see *Yonge v Toynbee* [1910] 1 KB 215, CA; and AGENCY vol 1 (2008) PARA 160. As to the effect of a party's death on the right to pledge his credit see PARAS 262, 271.

9   *Stevenson v Hardie* (1773) 2 Wm Bl 872 (loan to wife at husband's request).

257.   Bills, notes and cheques.   It is essential to liability on a bill of exchange, promissory note or cheque[1] that the signature of the person to be liable should be written on the instrument as that of the contracting party[2]; and the only person who can be liable as the acceptor of a bill of exchange, except when it is accepted for honour, is the drawee[3].

It has been held that if a bill of exchange is drawn on a husband[4], and is accepted by his wife with his authority, express or implied[5], he is liable as acceptor; and this is so, it seems, even where the acceptance is in the wife's name[6]. If the husband is not named as the drawee, he is not liable as acceptor, even if the acceptance is in his name or is expressed to be on his behalf and it is proved that he expressly authorised it[7]. Where a bill of exchange, promissory note or cheque is signed by a wife as drawee, indorser or maker, with her husband's authority, express or implied[8], he is liable on it if the signature is in his name or is expressed to be written on his behalf[9], but not otherwise[10].

1   As to the liability of the parties to bills of exchange, promissory notes and cheques generally see FINANCIAL SERVICES AND INSTITUTIONS vol 49 (2008) PARA 1574 et seq.
2   See the Bills of Exchange Act 1882 s 23; and FINANCIAL SERVICES AND INSTITUTIONS vol 49 (2008) PARAS 1467–1468. As to the application of s 23 to cheques and promissory notes see ss 73, 89; and FINANCIAL SERVICES AND INSTITUTIONS vol 49 (2008) PARA 1405.
3   *Polhill v Walter* (1832) 3 B & Ad 114; *Davis v Clarke* (1844) 6 QB 16. See generally FINANCIAL SERVICES AND INSTITUTIONS vol 49 (2008) PARA 1451 et seq.
4   See PARA 256 note 1.
5   Where a wife had the general management of her husband's business, and was in the habit of drawing and indorsing bills and notes for the purposes of the business, it was held that the question whether the indorsement of a note in his name was within the scope of her authority was one of fact, and that the jury was justified in finding that it was: *Lord v Hall* (1849) 8 CB 627. Where, however, in an action on a bill of exchange accepted in the name of the husband, there was no evidence as to who had written the acceptance, it was held that evidence of the fact of the wife having discounted the bill and applied the proceeds in discharge of the husband's debts was not sufficient proof of his having authorised the acceptance: *Goldstone v Tovey* (1839) 6 Bing NC 98. In *Lindus v Bradwell* (1848) 5 CB 583, a promise by a husband to pay a bill drawn on him and accepted by his wife in her own name was held sufficient evidence of his having either authorised or ratified the acceptance.
6   *Lindus v Bradwell* (1848) 5 CB 583; and see AGENCY vol 1 (2008) PARAS 47, 128; FINANCIAL SERVICES AND INSTITUTIONS vol 49 (2008) PARA 1452.
7   *Polhill v Walter* (1832) 3 B & Ad 114.
8   See note 5.
9   *Aggs v Nicholson* (1856) 1 H & N 165.
10 See the Bills of Exchange Act 1882 s 23; *Ducarrey v Gill* (1830) Mood & M 450; and FINANCIAL SERVICES AND INSTITUTIONS vol 49 (2008) PARAS 1467–1468.

258.   Undisclosed principal.   It has been held that, except in the case of bills of exchange, promissory notes and cheques, a husband[1] is liable, and entitled to sue, on a contract which is in fact made by his wife on his behalf and with his express or implied authority, even though it was made by the wife in her own name and without disclosing that she was a married woman[2].

Where it is not inconsistent with the terms of a written contract, extrinsic evidence may be given in order to show that the contract was made on one party's behalf so as to render him liable or to entitle him to sue on it[3].

1   See PARA 256 note 1.
2   *Paquin Ltd v Beauclerk* [1906] AC 148, HL. However, although the mere fact that goods are invoiced in the name of the wife does not necessarily indicate that the tradesman intended to give credit to her as a principal (see *Jewsbury v Newbold* (1857) 26 LJ Ex 247; *Paquin Ltd v Beauclerk*. Cf *Fick and Fick Ltd v Assimakis* [1958] 3 All ER 182, [1958] 1 WLR 1006, CA), that fact coupled with the circumstance that she herself paid for a portion of the goods, or has previously paid for goods of a similar kind, becomes almost conclusive evidence of such an intention (see *Bentley v Griffin* (1814) 5 Taunt 356; *Freestone v Butcher* (1840) 9 C & P 643; and see *Lea Bridge District Gas Co v Malvern* [1917] 1 KB 803, DC (contract made by widow before remarriage for supply of gas; presumption of continuance on remarriage)). See also the Law Reform (Married Women and Tortfeasors) Act 1935 s 1(b); and PARA 204. As to the rights and liabilities of undisclosed principals generally see AGENCY vol 1 (2008) PARA 125 et seq; and as to the effect of exclusive credit being given see PARA 259.
3   See DEEDS AND OTHER INSTRUMENTS vol 13 (2007 Reissue) PARA 186.

259.   Exclusive credit.   It has been held that a husband[1] is not liable on a contract made by his wife exclusively on her own behalf[2], or made on the credit of a third person[3], or in any case where the other contracting party elects, with a knowledge of the circumstances, to give exclusive credit to the wife[4]. If the contract is such that the husband and wife can only be liable on it alternatively (and not jointly or jointly and severally[5]) and the other contracting party sues the wife to judgment on the contract, he will be conclusively taken to have elected to give exclusive credit to her[6], but, in any case other than where he has obtained judgment, the question whether he has made such an election is one of fact depending on the particular circumstances[7]. If, however, leave to sign judgment against the wife is obtained but judgment is never signed, proceedings may be taken against the husband if the circumstances of the case do not show that a conclusive election had been made to charge the wife to the exclusion of the husband[8].

1   See PARA 256 note 1.
2   *Jewsbury v Newbold* (1857) 26 LJ Ex 247; *Freestone v Butcher* (1840) 9 C & P 643; *Taylor v Brittan* (1823) 1 C & P 16n; *Bentley v Griffin* (1814) 5 Taunt 356. Where a wife ordered clothes in excessive quantities unsuited to the husband's style of living, and credit was given to her, it was held that the supplier was not entitled to recover against the husband for such portion of the goods as the jury considered necessaries: *Metcalfe v Shaw* (1811) 3 Camp 22.
3   *Harvey v Norton* (1840) 4 Jur 42 (a married woman living with her uncle apart from her husband ordered necessaries from a tradesman on the credit of the uncle, who had previously paid for necessaries supplied to her by the same tradesman; the husband was not liable, even though he did not make the wife any allowance).
4   *Callot v Nash* (1923) 39 TLR 292; *French v Howie* [1906] 2 KB 674, CA; *Addison v Gandassequi* (1812) 4 Taunt 574; *Bentley v Griffin* (1814) 5 Taunt 356; *Metcalfe v Shaw* (1811) 3 Camp 22; and see AGENCY vol 1 (2008) PARA 132.
5   As to joint and several liability see PARA 205.
6   *Morel Bros & Co Ltd v Earl of Westmoreland* [1904] AC 11, HL. The rule stated in the text applies even though the judgment against the wife is for only a portion of the amount claimed, unless it appears that there were in effect two contracts by her, one on her own behalf in respect of the items for which judgment has been entered against her, and the other as agent for her husband in respect of the residue of the amount claimed: *French v Howie* [1906] 2 KB 674, CA; *Debenham's Ltd v Perkins* (1925) 133 LT 252.
7   *Calder v Dobell* (1871) LR 6 CP 486, Ex Ch; *Curtis v Williamson* (1874) LR 10 QB 57. As to goods invoiced in the name of the wife generally see PARA 205.
8   *Christopher (Hove) Ltd v Williams* [1936] 3 All ER 68, CA. As to the common law doctrine of election, and as to the effect of judgment against one of two persons alternatively liable, see further ESTOPPEL vol 16(2) (Reissue) PARA 962.

260.   Separate business.   It has been held that in the absence of proof of express authority or holding out[1], a husband[2] is not liable on any contracts made by his wife for the purposes of a trade or business carried on by her separately from him[3].

1   As to holding out see PARA 269 et seq.
2   See PARA 256 note 1.
3   *Re Shepherd, ex p Shepherd* (1879) 10 ChD 573, CA.

261.   Acknowledgment of debt.   Where a debt has been contracted by a wife[1] with the authority, express or implied, of her husband, she has implied authority to acknowledge it on her husband's behalf[2]; but, in order to interrupt the operation of the period of limitation, the acknowledgment must be in writing and signed by her as his agent[3].

1   See PARA 256 note 1.
2   *Gregory v Parker* (1808) 1 Camp 394 (necessaries ordered by wife); *Anderson v Sanderson* (1817) 2 Stark 204; *Palethorp v Furnish* (1783) 2 Esp 511n; *Emerson v Blonden* (1794) 1 Esp 141 (acknowledgment by wife carrying on husband's business).
3   See the Limitation Act 1980 s 30; and LIMITATION PERIODS vol 68 (2008) PARA 1185. Where an unsigned letter acknowledging a debt was written by the wife at the husband's dictation, and was enclosed in the same envelope with another letter signed by her and containing a reference to the unsigned acknowledgment, it was held that there was no sufficient signature by her as her husband's agent: *Ingram v Little* (1883) Cab & El 186.

262.   Termination of authority.   A wife's authority to pledge her husband's credit[1] is revoked by his death, and a contract made by her after his death in the exercise of her presumed authority to pledge his credit does not bind his estate, even if the contract was made by both parties in ignorance of his death[2], although his executors or administrators may ratify the contract if they choose to do so[3]. A wife's authority to pledge her husband's credit is terminated by his bankruptcy[4]. A wife judicially separated has in general no authority to pledge her husband's credit[5]. An act of adultery on the part of the wife may revoke any authority to pledge her husband's credit[6].

1   See PARA 256 note 1.
2   *Blades v Free* (1829) 9 B & C 167; and see AGENCY vol 1 (2008) PARA 188. Where, however, the husband has expressly held out the wife as his agent, it seems that notice to the other party of revocation of her authority by death may be required in order to free his estate from liability: see PARA 271. As to a wife's liability for breach of warranty of authority to contract on behalf of her husband see PARA 256.
3   *Foster v Bates* (1843) 12 M & W 226.
4   See *Drew v Nunn* (1879) 4 QBD 661 at 665, CA; and see AGENCY vol 1 (2008) PARA 190.
5   See PARA 268.
6   See e g *Atkyns v Pearce* (1857) 2 CBNS 763. As to the position where the wife's misconduct is condoned by the husband see PARA 272.

(ii) Contract for Necessaries

263.   Presumption of authority from cohabitation.   It has been held that where a husband and wife[1] are living together, the wife is presumed to have her husband's authority to pledge his credit for necessaries suitable to their style of living[2]. This presumption, which is founded on the mere fact of cohabitation as husband and wife, also arises and is of equal force where a man lives with a woman to whom he is not married and allows her to pass as his wife; and, if in such a case necessaries are ordered on his credit by the woman with whom he lives, he is liable, even if the supplier is aware that they are not married[3].

1   See PARA 256 note 1.
2   *Jolly v Rees* (1864) 15 CBNS 628; *Harrison v Grady* (1865) 13 LT 369; *Miss Gray Ltd v Earl Cathcart* (1922) 38 TLR 562. See also PARA 205. If a wife orders necessaries with her husband's authority, and nothing is said by her and no inquiries are made by the tradesman as to whether she is contracting on her husband's behalf or her own, she will be taken to have contracted as the agent of her husband, and the tradesman as having given credit to him, unless from the circumstances of the case it is plain that the tradesman has treated her as the debtor: *Paquin Ltd v Beauclerk* [1906] AC 148, HL; *Freestone v Butcher* (1840) 9 C & P 643. See also *Fick and Fick Ltd v Assimakis* [1958] 3 All ER 182, [1958] 1 WLR 1006, CA (where the tradesman had plainly treated the wife as his debtor). It is not necessary, in order to exclude liability, that she should profess to contract as an agent: it is sufficient if she does so in fact: *Paquin Ltd v Beauclerk*.
    This authority to pledge the husband's credit for necessaries is distinct from the former agency of necessity of a wife left without means: see PARAS 216, 267. The presumption of authority to pledge the husband's credit for necessaries does not necessarily extend to the borrowing of money to pay for them: see *Knox v Bushell* (1857) 3 CBNS 334; but c f *Re Cook, ex p Vernall* (1892) 10 Morr 8 at 10 per Vaughan Williams J.
3   *Ryan v Sams* (1848) 12 QB 460; *Watson v Threlkeld* (1798) 2 Esp 637; *Robinson v Nahon* (1808) 1 Camp 245; *Blades v Free* (1829) 9 B & C 167. No presumption of authority arises from the mere circumstance that a man allows a woman to whom he is not married to assume his name, where he does not live with her; it is the fact of cohabitation as man and wife that raises the presumption: *Gomme v Franklin* (1859) 1 F & F 465. The presumption of authority does not continue after the parties have separated (*Munro v De Chemant* (1815) 4 Camp 215; *Swan and Edgar Ltd v Mathieson* (1910) 27 TLR 153), although liability may be incurred subsequently to the separation by estoppel (*Ryan v Sams* (1848) 12 QB 460: see PARA 269).

264. Necessaries suitable to style of living. The presumed authority for the wife to pledge her husband's credit[1] is confined to necessaries[2] suitable to his style of living[3] or that permitted by him to be assumed by the wife[4] and belonging to a department of the household usually entrusted to the wife[5], but, if she has the management of his household, it extends to household provisions and all other things incidental to the ordinary course of such management[6]. The presumption does not extend to articles of luxury[7], nor will any authority be presumed where the orders given are extravagant in their nature or are for excessive quantities of goods[8].

The question whether things ordered by a wife are suitable necessaries does not depend on the actual means of the husband but on the style of living assumed by him, or permitted by him to be assumed by the wife[9]. A husband has the right to determine in what style he will live and to fix his standard of expenditure[10]. On the one hand, he may choose to assume, or permit his wife to assume, an appearance far beyond his means[11]; and, on the other hand, although a wealthy man, he may prefer to live on a very small sum[12].

The burden of proving that articles supplied are suitable necessaries lies, as a general rule, on the person seeking to charge the husband[13]; but such things as articles of dress delivered at the joint residence will be presumed to be necessaries unless and until it is shown that they are either unsuitable or extravagant[14].

1 See PARA 256 note 1.
2 For examples of goods and services which constitute necessaries see *Hunt v De Blaquiere* (1829) 5 Bing 550 at 559 (food, clothes and medicine); *Morgan v Chetwynd* (1865) 4 F & F 451 (articles of dress); *Harrison v Grady* (1865) 13 LT 369 and *Forristall v Lawson, Connelly v Lawson* (1876) 34 LT 903 (medical attendance); *Shoolbred v Baker* (1867) 16 LT 359; *Phillipson v Hayter* (1870) LR 6 CP 38 (ordinary or necessary clothing for the children); *Jenkinson v Bullock* (1891) 8 TLR 61 (millinery).
3 *Montague v Benedict* (1825) 3 B & C 631; 2 Smith LC (13th Edn) 447; *Atkins v Curwood* (1837) 7 C & P 756; *Hunt v De Blaquiere* (1829) 5 Bing 550; *Morgan v Chetwynd* (1865) 4 F & F 451; *Debenham v Mellon* (1880) 6 App Cas 24, HL; *Canham v Howard* (1887) 3 TLR 458.
4 See the text and notes 9–12.
5 *Phillipson v Hayter* (1870) LR 6 CP 38.
6 *Ruddock v Marsh* (1857) 1 H & N 601; *Emmett v Norton* (1838) 8 C & P 506; *Debenham v Mellon* (1880) 6 App Cas 24, HL; *Phillipson v Hayter* (1870) LR 6 CP 38.
7 *Phillipson v Hayter* (1870) LR 6 CP 38.
8 *Metcalfe v Shaw* (1811) 3 Camp 22; *Debenham v Mellon* (1880) 6 App Cas 24, HL; *Lane v Ironmonger* (1844) 13 M & W 368; *Freestone v Butcher* (1840) 9 C & P 643; *Walter v Aldridge* (1884) 1 TLR 138. In an action against husband and wife for goods supplied to the wife which were held not to be necessaries, judgment was given against the wife with costs and for the husband with costs, the husband's remedy to be against the wife: *Knight v Gordon* (1931) 76 Sol Jo 68.
9 *Harrison v Grady* (1865) 13 LT 369; *Phillipson v Hayter* (1870) LR 6 CP 38; *Morgan v Chetwynd* (1865) 4 F & F 451; and see *Miss Gray Ltd v Earl Cathcart* (1922) 38 TLR 562 at 566 per McCardie J; and *Callot v Nash* (1923) 39 TLR 292 at 293 per McCardie J. Subject to the principle stated in the text, the question whether things supplied are necessaries is one of fact: *Dennys v Sargeant* (1834) 5 C & P 419; *Phillipson v Hayter* (1870) LR 6 CP 38.
10 See note 9.
11 *Waithman v Wakefield* (1807) 1 Camp 120.
12 He must, however, in such a case limit his expenditure in clear and definite terms: see PARA 265.
13 *Phillipson v Hayter* (1870) LR 6 CP 38.
14 *Jewsbury v Newbold* (1857) 26 LJ Ex 247; *Clifford v Laton* (1827) 3 C & P 15.

265. Rebuttal of presumption of authority. The presumption of authority from spouses'[1] cohabitation is only one of fact[2] and may be rebutted by proof that the husband had prohibited his wife from pledging his credit or expressly revoked her authority to do so[3]. It is not necessary for the husband, in order to escape liability, to show that he gave any notice of the prohibition or revocation[4], except where his conduct has been such as to create an estoppel between him and the person supplying the necessaries[5]. If, however, the husband did give actual notice to that person not to supply goods to his wife, the supplier is precluded from relying on any presumption of authority, even though the wife may not herself have been forbidden to pledge her husband's credit[6].

Where a husband intends to prohibit his wife from pledging his credit, in order that the prohibition may be effectual, he must forbid her to do so in plain and definite terms; merely protesting against her rate of expenditure is not sufficient to deprive her of her presumed authority[7].

1   See PARA 256 note 1.
2   *Lane v Ironmonger* (1844) 13 M & W 368; *Freestone v Butcher* (1840) 9 C & P 643; *Reid v Teakle* (1853) 13 CB 627.
3   *Jolly v Rees* (1864) 15 CBNS 628; *Debenham v Mellon* (1880) 6 App Cas 24, HL; *Sabine v Legge* (1921) 152 LT Jo 364; *Miss Gray Ltd v Earl Cathcart* (1922) 38 TLR 562. As to the revocation of an agent's authority generally see AGENCY vol 1 (2008) PARA 177 et seq.
4   See note 3.
5   See PARA 269.
6   *Etherington v Parrot* (1703) 1 Salk 118.
7   *Shoolbred v Baker* (1867) 16 LT 359; *Morgan v Chetwynd* (1865) 4 F & F 451.

266.   Adequate or agreed allowance for necessaries.   The presumption of authority may also be rebutted by proof that the wife[1] was sufficiently provided with necessaries[2], or with an adequate allowance for the purpose of purchasing them[3]. If, by arrangement with her husband, the wife is allowed a definite sum for household and other expenses, the presumption of authority is rebutted whether the allowance is adequate or not, because in such case they must be taken to have agreed that she should not pledge his credit beyond the amount of the allowance, even if he did not in definite terms prohibit her from doing so[4]; but this will not be the case where the wife manages her husband's household and is held out as having the usual authority of a housekeeper[5]. The mere fact that the wife has adequate separate means is not sufficient to rebut the presumption that she has authority to pledge her husband's credit for necessaries[6].

1   See PARA 256 note 1.
2   *Seaton v Benedict* (1828) 5 Bing 28; *Debenham v Mellon* (1880) 6 App Cas 24, HL; *Re Cook, ex p Vernall* (1892) 10 Morr 8; *Miss Gray Ltd v Earl Cathcart* (1922) 38 TLR 562.
3   *Reneaux v Teakle* (1853) 8 Exch 680; *Holt v Brien* (1821) 4 B & Ald 252; *Morgan v Chetwynd* (1865) 4 F & F 451; *Slater v Parker* (1908) 24 TLR 621; *Miss Gray Ltd v Earl Cathcart* (1922) 38 TLR 562. It will not be rebutted by proof of an allowance found to be inadequate, unless fixed by arrangement between the husband and wife: see note 4.
4   *Remmington v Broadwood* (1902) 18 TLR 270, CA (definite allowance for personal expenditure and clothing); *Morel Bros & Co Ltd v Earl of Westmoreland* [1904] AC 11, HL (agreed allowance for household expenses); but the principle stated in the text does not apply unless the amount of the allowance is fixed and definite. Where a portion of the husband's income and the whole of the wife's were paid to a separate account kept for mutual convenience, on which the wife drew for household expenses, and the amounts paid in by the husband varied, it was held that the arrangement did not amount to a prohibition from pledging his credit, and that he was liable on the wife's orders for necessaries: *Goodyear v Part* (1897) 13 TLR 395.
5   See PARA 270.
6   *Re Wood's Estate, Davidson v Wood* (1863) 32 LJ Ch 400; *Seymour v Kingscote* (1922) 38 TLR 586; *Callot v Nash* (1923) 39 TLR 292 at 292, 293 per McCardie J. The fact that the wife has separate means must, however, be taken into consideration in determining whether credit was given to the husband or the wife: *Freestone v Butcher* (1840) 9 C & P 643.

267.   Proof of authority.   In the absence of evidence to the contrary[1], a wife[2] living apart[3] from her husband does not have authority to pledge his credit, and in an action against the husband on a contract entered into by her the claimant has the burden of proving either that the circumstances of the separation are such as to justify her in pledging her husband's credit, or that she was expressly authorised to do so or was held out as having authority so as to create an estoppel against the husband[4]. In the absence of any such holding out, it is immaterial whether the claimant knew that the wife was separated from her husband or not[5].

1   Eg separation due to the husband's profession or calling: *Travers v Sen* (1917) 33 TLR 202; cf *R v Creamer* [1919] 1 KB 564, CCA.
2   See PARA 256 note 1.
3   As to when a husband and wife can be said to be living apart generally see *Santos v Santos* [1972] Fam 247, [1972] 2 All ER 246, CA.
4   *Johnston v Summer* (1858) 3 H & N 261; *Wilson v Glossop* (1888) 20 QBD 354, CA; *Edwards v Towels* (1843) 5 Man & G 624; *Bird v Jones* (1828) 3 Man & Ry KB 121; *Mainwaring v Leslie* (1826) 2 C & P 507; *Reed v Moore* (1832) 5 C & P 200; *Clifford v Laton* (1827) 3 C & P 15. As to holding out see PARA 269.
5   *Wallis v Biddick* (1873) 22 WR 76; *Willson v Smyth* (1831) 1 B & Ad 801.

268.   Judicial separation.   A wife judicially separated from her husband[1] has no authority to pledge his credit[2]. The husband's liability on any contract entered into by the wife before the date of the decree of judicial separation is not, however, affected by the decree, even though the contract may be a continuing one in respect of which liabilities are incurred subsequently to the date of the decree[3].

1   See PARA 256 note 1.
2   See *Re Wingfield and Blew* [1904] 2 Ch 665 at 678, 680, 684, CA.
3   See *Re Wingfield and Blew* [1904] 2 Ch 665, CA (where the wife, under the husband's implied authority, retained a solicitor to defend divorce proceedings brought by the husband and to conduct an action of detinue against him, and the husband was held liable to pay her costs). A decree of judicial separation did not affect the court's power to order the husband to give security for the costs of the wife's defence in divorce proceedings: *Sheppard v Sheppard* [1905] P 185.

(iii) Ratification and Holding Out

269.   Agency by estoppel.   Where by his conduct a husband holds out his wife[1] as having authority to pledge his credit, he will not be permitted to deny that she has that authority with respect to any person contracting with her on the faith of the holding out[2]. Failure to disclose that the wife had no authority to act on the husband's behalf may amount to a representation that she had that authority[3].

If a husband pays for goods ordered by his wife on his credit, he is deemed to hold her out to the supplier as having authority to give subsequent orders for goods of a similar kind[4]. The principle is not confined to necessaries but, by paying for necessaries bought on his credit, a husband does not hold his wife out as having authority to order things which are not suitable to his style of living or that permitted by him to be assumed by the wife[5]. Dealing with a tradesman for ready money is not a holding out that the wife has any authority to deal on credit[6].

1   See PARA 256 note 1.
2   *Filmer v Lynn* (1835) 4 Nev & MKB 559; *Jetley v Hill* (1884) Cab & El 239; *M'George v Egan* (1839) 5 Bing NC 196.

3   See *Spiro v Lintern* [1973] 3 All ER 319, [1973] 1 WLR 1002, CA; and ESTOPPEL vol 16(2)
    (Reissue) PARA 1059.
4   *Wallis v Biddick* (1873) 22 WR 76; *Hinton v Hudson* (1677) Freem KB 248; *Filmer v Lynn*
    (1835) 4 Nev & MKB 559; but see *Durrant v Holdsworth* (1886) 2 TLR 763.
5   *Atkins v Curwood* (1837) 7 C & P 756.
6   *Wallis v Biddick* (1873) 22 WR 76.

270. Person managing household.   It has been held that where a wife manages
her husband's household[1] she is deemed to be held out by him as having the
usual authority of a housekeeper, and, therefore, as having authority to order on
his credit such provisions as are generally bought on credit[2]. Although the
husband may have made her a sufficient allowance for housekeeping expenses,
he will be liable on any such orders if the tradesman in question had no notice of
the allowance[3].

1   See PARA 256 note 1.
2   Thus, if the wife manages her husband's business, she is deemed to be held out as having the
    ordinary authority of such a manager: *Meredith v Footner* (1843) 11 M & W 202; *Anderson v
    Sanderson* (1817) 2 Stark 204; *Smallpiece v Dawes* (1835) 7 C & P 40. See also *Petty v
    Anderson* (1825) 3 Bing 170 (where a wife had carried on her husband's business while he was
    in prison, and he was held liable for goods supplied with his knowledge after his return,
    although the invoices were made out in her name).
3   *Ruddock v Marsh* (1857) 1 H & N 601; *Debenham v Mellon* (1880) 6 App Cas 24, HL. This
    principle is limited to goods which are usually bought on credit: see *Morel Bros & Co Ltd v Earl
    of Westmoreland* [1904] AC 11, HL. Where the tradesman has notice of the allowance, the
    husband is not liable: *Holt v Brien* (1821) 4 B & Ald 252. Cf the cases cited in PARA 266 notes
    3, 4.

271. Revocation of authority.   If a wife is held out as having authority to
contract on her husband's behalf[1], the person to whom she is so held out is
entitled to assume that her authority continues until he has notice to the
contrary[2]. A husband is, therefore, liable for the price of goods supplied to his
wife after a separation if he held her out to the supplier as having authority to
pledge his credit while they were living together and the supplier has had no
notice of the separation[3].

A general notice by advertisement in a newspaper of the revocation of a wife's
authority to pledge her husband's credit does not affect his liability to persons to
whom he has held her out as having authority unless he can show that the
advertisement came to their actual knowledge[4].

Where, after the husband's death, goods are supplied to the wife in ignorance
of her husband's death on the basis of her presumed authority to pledge his
credit, his estate is not liable[5]. Where, however, the husband has expressly held
out his wife to the other contracting party as his agent, it seems that notice of
revocation of her authority by death may be required if the husband's estate is to
escape liability[6].

1   See PARA 256 note 1.
2   *Drew v Nunn* (1879) 4 QBD 661, CA.
3   *Wallis v Biddick* (1873) 22 WR 76; *Hinton v Hudson* (1677) Freem KB 248; *Filmer v Lynn*
    (1835) 4 Nev & MKB 559. The principle applies where a man and woman who are not married
    live together as husband and wife (*Ryan v Sams* (1848) 12 QB 460), but merely cohabiting with
    a woman and allowing her to pass as a wife is not sufficient to render the person living with her
    liable on her contracts after a separation if he did not, by paying for goods ordered on his credit
    while they were living together, or otherwise, hold her out as having authority to pledge his
    credit (*Munro v De Chemant* (1815) 4 Camp 215).
4   *Hunt v De Blaquiere* (1829) 5 Bing 550 at 560; cf *Swan and Edgar Ltd v Mathieson* (1910) 27
    TLR 153. See also *Vickers v Vickers* 1966 SLT (Notes) 69 (husband and wife living apart;

husband not entitled to publish advertisement where he had no grounds for believing wife had incurred or was going to incur debts for which tradesmen would seek to make him liable).
5   See PARA 262.
6   See *Drew v Nunn* (1879) 4 QBD 661 at 668, CA.

272.   Husband's liability after wife's misconduct. If a husband[1], knowing that his wife is guilty of misconduct of such a kind as to justify his bringing proceedings for divorce[2], permits her to continue to reside in his house with the children or otherwise holds her out as still having the ordinary authority of a wife, he will be liable for necessaries supplied to her by persons ignorant of the relevant facts to the same extent as if the misconduct had not occurred[3].

1   See PARA 256 note 1.
2   As to the conduct and circumstances which may constitute a ground for divorce see PARA 346 et seq.
3   *Norton v Fazan* (1798) 1 Bos & P 226 (adultery).

273.   Ratification. Where a contract is made by a wife on behalf of her husband[1] but without his authority, he may, by ratifying the contract, render it as binding, both with respect to himself and the other contracting party[2], as if it had been entered into with his previous express authority[3]. This rule applies to a contract of any kind[4], provided that it is in fact made on the husband's behalf and credit is given to him, but it does not apply to a contract entered into by the wife on her own behalf[5], or professedly on behalf of some third person[6]. A ratification by a husband of a contract made on his behalf discharges the wife from liability for breach of warranty of authority[7].

An express promise to pay a debt incurred by the wife without authority is a sufficient ratification to render the husband liable[8], and the fact that he sees his wife wearing things which are not suitable to his style of living but were ordered on his credit, and that he does not express disapproval, is some evidence of a ratification[9]. It is only necessary that the husband's conduct should be such as to show an intention to recognise the transaction as binding on him[10]; but a ratification may be conditional, and will then bind the husband only if the condition is fulfilled[11].

1   See PARA 256 note 1.
2   *Millard v Harvey* (1864) 34 Beav 237 (wife bought land without her husband's knowledge; ratification by the husband rendered the contract binding on the seller).
3   *Montague v Benedict* (1825) 3 B & C 631; *Lane v Ironmonger* (1844) 13 M & W 368; *Waithman v Wakefield* (1807) 1 Camp 120. See generally AGENCY vol 1 (2008) PARA 58 et seq.
4   *Stevenson v Hardie* (1773) 2 Wm Bl 872 (loan to the wife); *Lindus v Bradwell* (1848) 5 CB 583 and see the cases cited in notes 2, 3.
5   *Saunderson v Griffiths* (1826) 5 B & C 909; *Keighley, Maxsted & Co v Durant* [1901] AC 240, HL; *Bentley v Griffin* (1814) 5 Taunt 356.
6   *Heath v Chilton* (1844) 12 M & W 632; cf *Wilson v Barker* (1833) 4 B & Ad 614.
7   *Spittle v Lavender* (1821) 5 Moore CP 270; *Risbourg v Bruckner* (1858) 3 CBNS 812. As to the liability of the wife for breach of warranty of authority see PARA 256.
8   *Harrison v Hall* (1832) 1 Mood & R 185; *Lindus v Bradwell* (1848) 5 CB 583; *Hornbuckle v Hornbury* (1817) 2 Stark 177.
9   *Montague v Benedict* (1825) 3 B & C 631; cf *Atkins v Curwood* (1837) 7 C & P 756.
10   *Jenner v Hill* (1858) 1 F & F 269; *West v Wheeler* (1849) 2 Car & Kir 714. In *Waithman v Wakefield* (1807) 1 Camp 120, the husband's failure to return goods ordered by the wife was deemed to be ratification. As to the wife's agency by estoppel see PARA 269.
11   *Holt v Brien* (1821) 4 B & Ald 252 (where the husband promised to pay, provided that he was not arrested for the debt).

(5) LIFE ASSURANCE POLICIES

274. Policies effected by spouses or civil partners for one another's benefit. In general, where a person takes out an insurance policy on his life expressed to be for the benefit of a third party, the policy money belongs to his estate unless he has constituted himself a trustee for the third party[1]. However, a policy effected by a spouse or a civil partner on his or her own life and expressed to be for the benefit of his or her spouse, civil partner or children[2] or spouse or civil partner and children, or any of them, creates a trust in favour of the objects[3] named, and the money payable under the policy does not, so long as any object of the trust remains unperformed, form part of the estate of the insured, and is not subject to his or her debts[4]. If, however, it is proved that the policy was effected and premiums paid with intent to defeat the creditors of the insured, they are entitled to receive out of the money payable under the policy a sum equal to the premiums so paid[5].

1   See *Re Engelbach's Estate, Tibbetts v Engelbach* [1924] 2 Ch 348; GIFTS vol 20(1) (Reissue) PARA 47; INSURANCE vol 25 (2003 Reissue) PARAS 557, 559; cf CONTRACT vol 9(1) (Reissue) PARA 749. For the principle that, where a father effects an insurance on his life in the name of his child, it constitutes a gift to the child see *Re Richardson, Weston v Richardson* (1882) 47 LT 514; and TRUSTS vol 48 (2007 Reissue) PARA 715.

2   For these purposes, 'children' includes illegitimate children (Family Law Reform Act 1969 s 19(1)), although this does not affect policies effected before 1 January 1970 (s 19(3)). A child adopted before 30 December 2005 is treated in law, where the adopters are a married couple, as if he had been born as a child of the marriage, whether or not he was in fact born after the marriage was solemnised, and a child adopted after that date is treated in law, from the date of the adoption (but subject to any contrary intention) as if born as the legitimate child of the adopters or adopter: see the Adoption Act 1976 s 39(1)(a); the Adoption and Children Act 2002 s 67(1), (2); and CHILDREN AND YOUNG PERSONS vol 5(3) (2008 Reissue) PARAS 376, 377.

3   'Object' in this context means purpose: see *Cousins v Sun Life Assurance Society* [1933] Ch 126, CA, distinguishing and doubting *Robb v Watson* [1910] 1 IR 243 (where the word 'object' as used in the expression 'so long as any object of the trust remains' in the Married Women's Property Act 1870 s 11 was construed as meaning beneficiary).

4   Married Women's Property Act 1882 s 11; Civil Partnership Act 2004 s 70. An endowment policy effected by a husband, payable at the end of 20 years and expressed to be for his wife's benefit if he should die before that date but otherwise for the benefit of himself or his estate, was a policy effected on his own life and expressed to be for the benefit of his wife within the meaning of the Married Women's Property Act 1882 s 11: *Re Ioakimidis' Policy Trusts, Ioakimidis v Hartcup* [1925] Ch 403. See also *Re Gladitz, Guaranty Executor and Trustee Co Ltd v Gladitz* [1937] Ch 588, [1937] 3 All ER 173; *Griffiths v Fleming* [1909] 1 KB 805, CA; *Re Policy of Equitable Life Assurance Society of the United States and Mitchell* (1911) 27 TLR 213; *Re Fleetwood's Policy* [1926] Ch 48.

      The Married Women's Property Act 1882 s 11 (amended by the Law Reform (Married Women and Tortfeasors) Act 1935 Sch 1) specifically provides that a married woman may effect a policy of insurance on her own life, or on the life of her husband, for her own benefit, and that the benefit of such policy enures accordingly: no corresponding provision is made in respect of civil partners and this provision may now be considered obsolete.

5   See note 4.

275. Effect of policy for benefit of spouse, civil partner or children. Where a policy effected[1] by a spouse or civil partner on his life is expressed to be for the benefit of a spouse or civil partner named in the policy and that benefit is not expressed to be conditional on the second spouse or civil partner surviving the insured[2], the beneficiary spouse or civil partner takes an immediate vested interest which on his death in the insured's lifetime passes to the beneficiary's personal representatives[3] and is not affected by the insured's subsequent marriage or remarriage or subsequent entering into a civil partnership[4]. Similar principles apply in the case of a policy in favour of named children of the insured[5]. If in the case of a policy in favour of a named spouse or civil partner the insured continues to pay the premiums after the death of the named spouse or civil partner in order to keep the policy alive, he or his estate is entitled to a lien on the policy money for the amount of the premiums so paid as being money expended by him as a trustee for the preservation of the trust property[6]. Such a policy constitutes a post-nuptial settlement (or civil partnership equivalent) which the court has power to vary in the event of a decree or order of divorce, dissolution or nullity being pronounced during the life of the spouses or civil partners[7].

If a spouse or civil partner effects a policy in favour of his spouse or civil partner but no named spouse or civil partner is mentioned in the policy, and if the spouse or civil partner living at the date of the policy dies in the lifetime of the insured and the insured does not marry, remarry or enter into a subsequent civil partnership, it seems that, even if benefit to the deceased spouse or civil partner is not made expressly conditional on him surviving the insured, the policy money forms part of the insured's estate[8]. If the insured party remarries or enters into a subsequent civil partnership, the subsequent spouse or civil partner (if he survives the insured) is, it seems, entitled to the benefit of the policy[9] in the absence of any indication to the contrary[10]. Similarly, if the policy is in favour of the widow or widower or surviving civil partner of the insured, the subsequent spouse or civil partner is entitled to the benefit[11]. Where the policy is in favour of the spouse or civil partner and children, or the children only, of the insured, children of the first and second marriages or civil partnerships will be entitled to participate alike[12].

Where a policy is expressed to be for the benefit of the spouse or civil partner and children of the insured, they take concurrently as joint tenants, unless a contrary intention appears[13].

If a policy is effected for the benefit of the spouse or civil partner or the children of the insured if that spouse or civil partner or those children survive the insured, and by the terms of the policy an option is conferred on the insured, if living at the expiration of a particular period, to receive the cash value of the policy or to convert it into a paid-up policy, the option must be exercised for the benefit of the persons contingently entitled to the benefit of the policy[14].

Where the purposes of the trust created by any such policy fail, and there is no indication to the contrary in the policy, the insurance money forms part of the estate of the insured and may be recovered by his personal representatives[15].

1 Ie pursuant to the Married Women's Property Act 1882 s 11 and the Civil Partnership Act 2004 s 70: see PARA 274.

2 For examples of a policy for the benefit of a named wife if surviving see eg *Re Policy of Equitable Life Assurance Society of the United States and Mitchell* (1911) 27 TLR 213; *Re Fleetwood's Policy* [1926] Ch 48.

3 *Cousins v Sun Life Assurance Society* [1933] Ch 126, CA, approving and following *Prescott v Prescott* [1906] 1 IR 155, and not following *Robb v Watson* [1910] 1 IR 243, or views expressed in *Re Collier* [1930] 2 Ch 37 at 42, 43 (a decision as to a policy in which the wife was not named: see note 8).

4 See *Prescott v Prescott* [1906] 1 IR 155; *Re Smith's Estate, Bilham v Smith* [1937] Ch 636, [1937] 3 All ER 472.

5 See *Cousins v Sun Life Assurance Society* [1933] Ch 126 at 140, CA per Romer LJ.

6 *Re Smith's Estate, Bilham v Smith* [1937] Ch 636, [1937] 3 All ER 472.

7 See *Gunner v Gunner and Stirling* [1949] P 77, [1948] 2 All ER 771; and PARA 511.

8 *Re Collier* [1930] 2 Ch 37 (husband became bankrupt in lifetime of wife; policy money belonged to the husband's trustee in bankruptcy); but see *Cousins v Sun Life Assurance Society*

[1933] Ch 126 at 137, CA (where the grounds stated for the decision in *Re Collier* were criticised as erroneous by Lawrence LJ). As to the effect of the failure of the objects of the trusts of the policy see further the text and note 15.

9   *Re Browne's Policy, Browne v Browne* [1903] 1 Ch 188 (policy for benefit of wife or children; widow and child by second marriage entitled to benefit jointly with children of first marriage); *Cousins v Sun Life Assurance Society* [1933] Ch 126 at 135, CA.

10 See *Re Griffith's Policy* [1903] 1 Ch 739 (policy for benefit of wife or, if she was dead, children; widow by second marriage not entitled to participate but children of first and second marriages entitled to participate in equal shares).

11 *Re Parker's Policies* [1906] 1 Ch 526 (policies in favour of assured's widow or widow and children or some or one of them as he should by deed or will appoint; appointment by deed to second wife who survived assured).

12 *Re Browne's Policy, Browne v Browne* [1903] 1 Ch 188 (cited in note 10); *Re Griffith's Policy* [1903] 1 Ch 739 (cited in note 10); *Re Parker's Policies* [1906] 1 Ch 526 at 529.

13 *Re Seyton, Seyton v Satterthwaite* (1887) 34 ChD 511; *Re Davies' Policy Trusts* [1892] 1 Ch 90 (not following dicta in *Re Adam's Policy Trusts* (1883) 23 ChD 525, to the effect that the wife took a life interest with remainder to the children); *Re Browne's Policy, Browne v Browne* [1903] 1 Ch 188.

14 *Re Policy of Equitable Life Assurance Society of the United States and Mitchell* (1911) 27 TLR 213; *Re Fleetwood's Policy* [1926] Ch 48.

15 *Cleaver v Mutual Reserve Fund Life Association* [1892] 1 QB 147, CA (policy by husband for benefit of wife; wife murdered husband; the trust in her favour having failed by her criminal act on the ground of public policy, the husband's representatives were entitled to recover the policy money); and see *Re Collier* [1930] 2 Ch 37; *Robb v Watson* [1910] 1 IR 243; but, as to the criticism of the decision in these cases that the trusts created by the policies had failed, see notes 3, 8 and PARA 274 note 3.

276.   Appointment of trustees. In the case of a policy effected by a spouse or a civil partner on his own life and expressed to be for the benefit of his spouse, civil partner or children[1], the insured may, by the policy or by any memorandum under his hand, appoint a trustee or trustees of the money payable under the policy, and from time to time appoint a new trustee or new trustees of it, and may make provision for the appointment of new trustees and for the investment of the money payable under the policy[2]. In default of any such appointment, the policy immediately on its being effected vests in the insured and his legal representatives in trust for the objects named in the policy[3]. The receipt of a trustee or trustees duly appointed, or, in default of any such appointment or of notice thereof to the insurance office, the receipt of the legal personal representatives of the insured, is a good discharge to the office for the sum secured by the policy, or for the value thereof, in whole or in part[4].

1   Ie a policy effected pursuant to the Married Women's Property Act 1882 s 11 and the Civil Partnership Act 2004 s 70: see PARA 274.

2   Married Women's Property Act 1882 s 11; Civil Partnership Act 2004 s 70.

3   Married Women's Property Act 1882 s 11; Civil Partnership Act 2004 s 70. As to 'objects' see PARA 274 note 3.

4   Married Women's Property Act 1882 s 11; Civil Partnership Act 2004 s 70.

277.   Lien for payment of premiums. If a spouse or civil partner pays the premiums on a policy effected by his spouse or civil partner on their own life and for their own benefit[1] the payer is not, nor are his representatives after his death, entitled to any lien on the policy for the premiums so paid in the absence of a contract between himself and his spouse or civil partner giving him such a lien[2].

1   Ie a policy effected pursuant to the Married Women's Property Act 1882 s 11 and the Civil Partnership Act 2004 s 70: see PARA 274.

2   *Re Leslie, Leslie v French* (1883) 23 ChD 552. Similarly, it has been held that if a wife voluntarily pays the premiums on a policy on her husband's life which is subject to their marriage settlement, and on which he has covenanted to pay the premiums, she is not entitled to

a lien on the policy for what she has paid: *Re Jones' Settlement, Stunt v Jones* [1915] 1 Ch 373; but see *Re McKerrell, McKerrell v Gowans* [1912] 2 Ch 648 (joint policy).

5. PROPERTY RIGHTS IN THE FAMILY HOME

(1) APPLICABLE PRINCIPLES IN DETERMINATION OF PROPERTY RIGHTS

278. Resolution of disputes. Disputes between spouses and civil partners rarely require resolution of their strict property rights under trust law as the court has wide discretionary powers in proceedings for divorce, dissolution, nullity or judicial or legal separation to distribute the property as it sees fit without having to ascertain the shares of the parties in the property[1]. In the rare cases where it is necessary to do so[2], it is clearly established that the proper approach is through the law of trusts[3]. What is less clearly established is exactly which trust principles apply; in particular, the cases commonly fail to distinguish between resulting[4], implied and constructive[5] trusts. A further complication is the uncertain relationship with the doctrine of proprietary estoppel[6]. When they uphold a claim, the courts are often content to say that it is on the ground of constructive trust or proprietary estoppel without attempting to distinguish between them[7]. If, however, there is an express declaration of trust, it will be conclusive in the absence of fraud or mistake[8].

1   See *Fielding v Fielding* [1978] 1 All ER 267, [1977] 1 WLR 1146n; PARAS 458 et seq, 499 et seq, 520–522.
2   See eg *Re Cummins, Cummins v Thompson* [1972] Ch 62, [1971] 3 All ER 782, CA; *Lloyds Bank plc v Rosset* [1991] 1 AC 107, [1990] 1 All ER 1111, HL.
3   *Pettitt v Pettitt* [1970] AC 777, [1969] 2 All ER 385, HL; *Gissing v Gissing* [1971] AC 886, [1970] 2 All ER 780, HL; *Lloyds Bank plc v Rosset* [1991] 1 AC 107, [1990] 1 All ER 1111, HL.
4   As to resulting trusts see TRUSTS vol 48 (2007 Reissue) PARA 705 et seq.
5   As to constructive trusts see TRUSTS vol 48 (2007 Reissue) PARA 687 et seq.
6   In *Grant v Edwards* [1986] Ch 638 at 656, [1986] 2 All ER 426 at 439, CA, Browne-Wilkinson V-C said that the common intention constructive trust and proprietary estoppel rest on the same foundation; but in *Stokes v Anderson* [1991] FCR 539 at 543, [1991] 1 FLR 391 at 399, CA, Nourse LJ observed that they were not yet assimilated. In *Re Basham* [1987] 1 All ER 405, [1986] 1 WLR 1498, the equity which arises in cases of proprietary estoppel was said to be in the nature of a constructive trust. See also *Taylor v Dickens* [1998] 3 FCR 455, [1998] 1 FLR 806; *Gillett v Holt* [2001] Ch 210, [2000] 2 All ER 289, CA. See also ESTOPPEL vol 16(2) (Reissue) PARA 1089 et seq.
7   *Lloyds Bank plc v Rosset* [1991] 1 AC 107, [1990] 1 All ER 1111, HL; *Hammond v Mitchell* [1992] 2 All ER 109, [1991] 1 WLR 127.
8   *Pettitt v Pettitt* [1970] AC 777, [1969] 2 All ER 385, HL; *Pink v Lawrence* (1977) 36 P & CR 98, CA; *Brykiert v Jones* (1981) 125 Sol Jo 323, CA; *Bernard v Josephs* [1982] Ch 391, [1982] 3 All ER 162, CA; *Goodman v Gallant* [1986] Fam 106, [1986] 1 All ER 311, CA; *Turton v Turton* [1988] Ch 542, [1987] 2 All ER 641, CA; *Re Gorman (a bankrupt), ex p trustee of bankrupt v bankrupt* [1990] 1 All ER 717, [1990] 1 WLR 616.

279. Property purchased in joint names. Where a domestic property is conveyed into the joint names of cohabitants without any declaration of trust there is a prime facie case that both the legal and beneficial interests in the property are joint and equal[1]. If the purchase money was provided out of jointly pooled resources, an equitable joint tenancy exists[2]; but, if the purchase money was provided in unequal shares, each party has an equitable tenancy in common under a resulting trust with shares proportionate to his or her respective contributions to the purchase price[3]. Provision of the purchase price may arise from payment of mortgage instalments or of the deposit or of legal fees[4]. It may arise indirectly, as where one party's salary is used for household expenses and holidays so that the other party's salary which would otherwise have to bear such expenses may be used to pay the mortgage instalments[5]. Where property is bought with the aid of a mortgage, the court has to assess each of the parties' respective contributions in a broad sense; but the court is entitled to look only at the financial contributions, or their real or substantial equivalent, to the acquisition of the property[6]. Prima facie, if the purchase is financed in whole or in part on mortgage, the person who assumed liability for the mortgage payments, as between the joint owners, is to be treated as having contributed the mortgage money[7].

1　See *Stack v Dowden* [2007] UKHL 17, [2007] 2 AC 432, [2007] 2 All ER 929. An express declaration as to the parties' beneficial interests would be conclusive in the absence of fraud or mistake: *Pettitt v Pettitt* [1970] AC 777 at 813, [1969] 2 All ER 385 at 405, HL; *Leak (formerly Bruzzi) v Bruzzi* [1974] 2 All ER 1196, [1974] 1 WLR 1528, CA; *Pink v Lawrence* (1977) 36 P & CR 98, CA; *Bernard v Josephs* [1982] Ch 391, [1982] 3 All ER 162, CA; *Re Gorman (a bankrupt), ex p trustee of bankrupt v bankrupt* [1990] 1 All ER 717, [1990] 1 WLR 616.

2　Clear evidence is required that the parties did in fact pool their assets in one jointly owned fund, as English law knows no doctrine of 'family assets' or 'family property': *Pettitt v Pettitt* [1970] AC 777, [1969] 2 All ER 385, HL; *Gissing v Gissing* [1971] AC 886, [1970] 2 All ER 780, HL; *Cowcher v Cowcher* [1972] 1 All ER 943, [1972] 1 WLR 425.

3　*Bernard v Josephs* [1982] Ch 391, [1982] 3 All ER 162, CA (where the principles applicable to spouses were applied to an unmarried couple); *Oxley v Hiscock* [2004] EWCA Civ 546, [2005] Fam 211, [2004] 3 All ER 703, [2004] 2 FCR 295 (same); see also *Brassford v Patel* [2007] BPIR 1049, [2007] All ER (D) 256 (Feb) (the fact that the property was held in joint names could be treated as evidence that it was to be held in equal shares notwithstanding unequal contributions, but each case depends upon its own facts). *Young v Young* [1984] FLR 375, [1984] Fam Law 271, CA is an unusual case where the house was in joint names but the man had made no contribution and was held to have no beneficial interest.

4　*Gissing v Gissing* [1971] AC 886, [1970] 2 All ER 780, HL; *Re Densham (a bankrupt), ex p trustee of bankrupt v Densham* [1975] 3 All ER 726, [1975] 1 WLR 1519. The contribution must be to capital expenditure and not to income expenditure, eg rent: *Savage v Dunningham* [1974] Ch 181, [1973] 3 All ER 429.

5　It seems essential that there should be some common intention or agreement that the party's relieving payments are to entitle him or her to a corresponding interest in the house: see *Pettitt v Pettitt* [1970] AC 777, [1969] 2 All ER 385, HL; *Gissing v Gissing* [1971] AC 886, [1970] 2 All ER 780, HL; *Cowcher v Cowcher* [1972] 1 All ER 943, [1972] 1 WLR 425; *McFarlane v McFarlane* [1972] NI 59, NI CA; *Eves v Eves* [1975] 3 All ER 768, [1975] 1 WLR 1338, CA; *Re Densham (a bankrupt), ex p trustee of bankrupt v Densham* [1975] 3 All ER 726, [1975] 1 WLR 1519; *Allen v Snyder* [1977] 2 NSWLR 685, NSW CA; *Burns v Burns* [1984] Ch 317, [1984] 1 All ER 244, CA. Lord Denning MR has indicated otherwise (see *Hargrave v Newton* [1971] 3 All ER 866, [1971] 1 WLR 1611, CA; *Hazell v Hazell* [1972] 1 All ER 923, [1972] 1 WLR 301, CA), but these decisions have been criticised (see (1972) LQR 333; (1971) 115 Sol Jo 615).

6　*Burns v Burns* [1984] Ch 317 at 344, [1984] 1 All ER 244 at 264, CA; *Bernard v Josephs* [1982] Ch 391, [1982] 3 All ER 162, CA.

7　*Re Gorman (a bankrupt), ex p trustee of bankrupt v bankrupt* [1990] 1 All ER 717, [1990] 1 WLR 616; *Huntingford v Hobbs* [1993] 1 FCR 45, [1993] 1 FLR 736, CA.

280. Property purchased in one name only. Where the house is taken in only one of the two names, the position is more complicated. Subject to any express declaration of trust[1], where property is purchased in one party's name but both parties contribute to the purchase price, the other party acquires an interest under a resulting trust proportionate to his or her contribution to the purchase price[2], or alternatively may make a claim under a constructive trust. On such a claim the first and fundamental question which must always be resolved is whether, independently of any inference to be drawn from the conduct of the parties in the course of sharing the house as their home and managing their joint affairs, there has at any time prior to acquisition, or exceptionally at some later date, been any agreement, arrangement or understanding reached between them that the property is to be shared beneficially[3]. This common intention, which has been said to mean a shared intention communicated between them[4] and which must relate to the beneficial ownership of the property[5] can only be based on evidence of express discussions between the parties, however imperfectly remembered and however imprecise their terms may have been[6]. Once a finding to this effect is made, it will only be necessary for the party asserting a claim to a beneficial interest against the party entitled to the legal estate to show that he or she has acted to his or her detriment or significantly altered his or her position in reliance on the agreement in order to give rise to a constructive trust or proprietary estoppel[7].

1   See PARA 278 text and note 8. See also *McHardy & Sons (a firm) v Warren* [1994] 2 FLR 338, [1994] Fam Law 567, CA (where it was held that it could be inferred, where a parent had made a deposit on his child's first matrimonial home, that the bride and groom had equal interests in the home, it being irrelevant that the title was registered in the name of only one of the spouses). Similarly, in *Halifax Building Society v Brown* [1995] 3 FCR 110, [1996] 1 FLR 103, CA, it was held that a loan to a married couple from one of their parents to finance a deposit on a house was capable of founding an inference of a common intention to share the property beneficially, even if the house was conveyed into the husband's name alone.

2   *Pettitt v Pettitt* [1970] AC 777, [1969] 2 All ER 385, HL; *Gissing v Gissing* [1971] AC 886, [1970] 2 All ER 780, HL; *Cowcher v Cowcher* [1972] 1 All ER 943, [1972] 1 WLR 425; *Re Densham (a bankrupt), ex p trustee of bankrupt v Densham* [1975] 3 All ER 726, [1975] 1 WLR 1519.

3   *Lloyds Bank plc v Rosset* [1991] 1 AC 107, [1990] 1 All ER 1111, HL, citing the leading cases of *Pettitt v Pettitt* [1970] AC 777, [1969] 2 All ER 385, HL; *Gissing v Gissing* [1971] AC 886, [1970] 2 All ER 780, HL. As to improvements to the property see PARA 283.

4   *Springette v Defoe* [1992] 2 FCR 561 at 567, [1992] 2 FLR 388 at 393, CA per Dillon LJ. A common intention by laymen to own their home jointly will be taken to mean an intention to own it equally: *Savill v Goodall* [1994] 1 FCR 325, [1993] 1 FLR 755, CA.

5   In *Lloyds Bank plc v Rosset* [1991] 1 AC 107 at 130, [1990] 1 All ER 1111 at 1117, HL, Lord Bridge of Harwich observed that neither a common intention that the house is to be renovated as a joint venture nor a common intention that the house is to be shared by parents and children as the family home throws any light on their intentions with respect to its beneficial ownership. See also *Winkworth v Edward Baron Development Co Ltd* [1987] 1 All ER 114, [1986] 1 WLR 1512, HL.

6   See *Grant v Edwards* [1986] Ch 638, [1986] 2 All ER 426, CA; *Hammond v Mitchell* [1992] 2 All ER 109, [1991] 1 WLR 1127. See also *Ungurian v Lesnoff* [1990] Ch 206, [1989] 3 WLR 840.

7   *Lloyds Bank plc v Rosset* [1991] 1 AC 107, [1990] 1 All ER 1111, HL, distinguished in *Lloyds Bank plc v Carrick* [1996] 4 All ER 630, [1996] 2 FCR 771, CA; *Hammond v Mitchell* [1992] 2 All ER 109, [1991] 1 WLR 1127.

281.   No evidence of agreement or arrangement to share beneficial interest.   It may be that there is no evidence to support a finding of an agreement or arrangement to share the beneficial interest, however reasonable it might have been for the parties to make such an agreement if they had applied their minds to the question. Here the court, relying entirely on the conduct of the parties, may first infer from it a common intention to share the property beneficially. If the inference can properly be drawn, the same conduct may be relied on to show that the party has acted to his or her detriment or has significantly altered his or her position in reliance on the inferred agreement. While direct contributions to the purchase price by a party who is not the legal owner, whether initially or by payment of mortgage instalments, would readily justify the court in drawing the inference of a common intention, it has been said to be very doubtful whether anything less would do[1]. If the conduct does not justify the court in drawing the necessary inference, the court cannot impute to the parties a common intention which they did not have by forming its own opinion as to what reasonable persons in the position of parties would have intended.

Even if a common intention is established, a claimant will not succeed unless he establishes that he has acted to his detriment on the basis of that common intention[2]. The fact that one partner gratuitously cooks and cleans and looks after any children does not alone entitle him to any share in the house[3].

1   *Lloyds Bank plc v Rosset* [1991] 1 AC 107 at 133, [1990] 1 All ER 1111 at 1119, HL per Lord Bridge of Harwich. However, in *Burns v Burns* [1984] Ch 317, [1984] 1 All ER 244, CA and *Grant v Edwards* [1986] Ch 638, [1986] 2 All ER 426, CA it seems to have been thought that indirect contributions would suffice, provided that they are referable to the acquisition of the property. The need for referability was repeated in *Windeler v Whitehall* [1990] FCR 268, [1990] 2 FLR 505. See also *Layton v Martin* [1986] 2 FLR 227, [1986] Fam Law 212; *R v Robson* (1990) 92 Cr App Rep 1, CA.

2   *Midland Bank plc v Dobson and Dobson* [1986] 1 FLR 171, [1986] Fam Law 55, 75, CA; *Grant v Edwards* [1986] Ch 638, [1986] 2 All ER 426, CA.

3   *Kowalczuk v Kowalczuk* [1973] 2 All ER 1042, [1973] 1 WLR 930, CA; *Burns v Burns* [1984] Ch 317, [1984] 1 All ER 244, CA; *Thomas v Fuller-Brown* [1988] 1 FLR 237, [1988] Fam Law 53, CA; *Howard v Jones* [1989] Fam Law 231, CA.

282.   Quantification of beneficial interests. So far as quantification of the claimant's beneficial interest is concerned, which also depends on the common intention of the parties, either express or, more usually, to be inferred from all the circumstances[1], the court can take into account both direct and indirect contributions[2]. The court may infer an agreement as to the proportion of the parties' beneficial interests notwithstanding positive evidence that they neither discussed nor intended any such agreement[3]. As a last resort the court can fall back on the maxim 'equality is equity' where each has clearly made a substantial contribution but it is virtually impossible to quantify contribution precisely[4]. The value of the respective shares will be determined when the property is sold or where one party buys out the other[5].

1   *Stokes v Anderson* [1991] FCR 539 at 543, [1991] 1 FLR 391 at 399, CA.

2   See *Marsh v von Sternberg* [1986] 1 FLR 526, [1986] Fam Law 160 (discount to sitting tenant); *Risch v McFee* (1990) 61 P & CR 42, [1991] FCR 168, CA (interest-free loan); *Springett v Defoe* [1992] 2 FCR 561, [1992] 2 FLR 388, CA (discount under the right to buy); *Drake v Whipp* [1996] 2 FCR 296, [1996] 1 FLR 826, CA (where a constructive trust exists, a 'broad brush' approach can be adopted by a court in order to determine the parties' respective beneficial interests in a house); *Brassford v Patel* [2007] BPIR 1049, [2007] All ER (D) 256 (Feb) (quantification of beneficial interests reflecting wife's provision of initial deposit). The shares should normally be ascertained as at the date of separation: *Bernard v Josephs* [1982] Ch 391, [1982] 3 All ER 162, CA per Denning MR and Kerr LJ (but see the different views of Griffiths LJ). All the members of the court agreed, however, that acts and events up to at least the date of separation were circumstances from which the common intention could be inferred. See also *Gissing v Gissing* [1971] AC 886 at 909, [1970] 2 All ER 780 at 793, HL per Lord Diplock, cited by Fox LJ in *Burns v Burns* [1984] Ch 317 at 327, [1984] 1 All ER 244 at 251, CA and by Nourse LJ in *Stokes v Anderson* [1991] FCR 539 at 542, 543, [1991] 1 FLR 391 at 399, CA; *Passee v Passee* [1988] 1 FLR 263, [1988] Fam Law 132, CA.

3   *Midland Bank plc v Cooke* [1995] 4 All ER 562, [1996] 1 FCR 442, CA.

4   *Pettit v Pettit* [1970] AC 777 at 813, 814, [1969] 2 All ER 385 at 406, HL per Lord Upjohn, cited by Griffith LJ in *Bernard v Josephs* [1982] Ch 391 at 402, [1982] 3 All ER 162 at 169, CA; *Gissing v Gissing* [1971] AC 886 at 903, [1970] 2 All ER 780 at 788, HL per Lord Pearson, cited by May LJ in *Burns v Burns* [1984] Ch 317 at 337, [1984] 1 All ER 244 at 259, CA.

5   *Bernard v Josephs* [1982] Ch 391, [1982] 3 All ER 162, CA; *Gordon v Douce* [1983] 2 All ER 228, [1983] 1 WLR 563, CA; *Walker v Hall* [1984] FLR 126, [1984] Fam Law 21, CA; *Turton v Turton* [1988] Ch 542, [1987] 2 All ER 641, CA, disapproving *Hall v Hall* (1981) 3 FLR 379, CA. As to the equitable accounting that must take place before the money is distributed see *Shinh v Shinh* [1977] 1 All ER 97, 6 Fam Law 245; *Suttill v Graham* [1977] 3 All ER 1117, [1977] 1 WLR 819, CA; *Bernard v Josephs*; *Re Gorman (a bankrupt), ex p trustee of bankrupt v bankrupt* [1990] 1 All ER 717, [1990] 1 WLR 616; *Re Pavlou (a bankrupt)* [1993] 3 All ER

955, [1993] 1 WLR 1046; *Wilcox v Tait* [2006] EWCA Civ 1867, [2007] 3 FCR 611, [2007] 2 FLR 871; *Young v Laurentani* [2007] EWHC 1244 (Ch), [2008] 1 FCR 669, [2007] 2 FLR 1211.

283. Improvements to property. Where a spouse or civil partner contributes in money or money's worth to the improvement of real or personal property in which, or in the proceeds of sale of which, either or both of the spouses or civil partners has or have a beneficial interest, then, if the contribution is of a substantial nature[1], and subject to any agreement between them to the contrary express or implied, the spouse or civil partner so contributing is to be treated as having then acquired by virtue of his or her contribution a share or an enlarged share, as the case may be, in that beneficial interest of such an extent as may have then been agreed or, in default of such agreement, as may seem in all the circumstance just to any court before which the question of the existence or extent of the beneficial interest of that spouse or civil partner arises, whether in proceedings between them or in any other proceedings[2].

These provisions are also applicable in relation to the property of engaged couples and persons who have entered into a civil partnership agreement[3].

1 As to the meaning of 'substantial nature' see *Button v Button* [1968] 1 All ER 1064, [1968] 1 WLR 457, CA (cleaning, decorating and gardening insufficient); *Pettitt v Pettitt* [1970] AC 777, [1969] 2 All ER 385, HL (usual 'do-it-yourself' jobs by husband insufficient); *Harnett v Harnett* [1973] Fam 156, [1973] 2 All ER 593; affd [1974] 1 All ER 764, [1974] 1 WLR 219, CA (the contribution must not only be substantial but identifiable with the relevant improvement; general contributions are not sufficient).

2 Matrimonial Proceedings and Property Act 1970 s 37; Civil Partnership Act 2004 s 65. The Matrimonial Proceedings and Property Act 1970 s 37 restored the decision in *Appleton v Appleton* [1965] 1 All ER 44, [1965] 1 WLR 25, CA, which had been overruled by *Pettitt v Pettitt* [1970] AC 777, [1969] 2 All ER 385, HL. As to the circumstances in which the court will declare a beneficial interest see *Davis v Vale* [1971] 2 All ER 1021, [1971] 1 WLR 1022, CA (wife provided wholly or partly money to connect up the electricity supply; she paid for a water heater, a sink unit, a wall and an iron gate, and three fireplaces; beneficial interest declared). As to the calculation of the share in the beneficial interest see *Griffiths v Griffiths* [1973] 3 All ER 1155, [1973] 1 WLR 1454; on appeal [1974] 1 All ER 932, [1974] 1 WLR 1350, CA; *Re Nicholson, Nicholson v Perks* [1974] 2 All ER 386, [1974] 1 WLR 476. For older cases as to reimbursement of expenditure by the husband on improvements to his wife's property see *Campion v Cotton* (1810) 17 Ves 263; *Neesom v Clarkson* (1845) 4 Hare 97; *Wiles v Cooper* (1846) 9 Beav 294; *Hamer v Tilsley* (1859) John 486. In connection with contributions made by a party to a recognised overseas relationship see the Civil Partnership (Treatment of Overseas Relationships) Order 2005, SI 2005/3042, art 3(2).

3 See the Law Reform (Miscellaneous Provisions) Act 1970 s 2(1); the Civil Partnership Act 2004 s 74(1), (2); and PARA 230. As to the meaning of 'civil partnership agreement' see PARA 16.

284. Property rights of cohabitants. The principles which apply to property rights of spouses (and, presumably, civil partners)[1] also govern the property rights of cohabitants[2] in the absence of a valid, express declaration of trust[3]. It has been held that the absence of the commitment of marriage may, however, mean that the court will not make the same assumptions and draw the same inferences from the behaviour of an unmarried couple as in the case of a married couple[4], and that only if the court is satisfied that the relationship was intended to involve the same degree of commitment as marriage is it legitimate to regard the couple as no different from a married couple, for example, if they have children by each other and intend to marry when free to do so[5]. In the case of engaged couples where the agreement to marry is terminated, any rule of law relating to property in which either or both has or have a beneficial interest applies[6].

Where a cohabiting couple have made no clear agreement as to the ownership of property, it will inevitably be difficult for a claimant without a legal interest to show that he or she has an equitable interest. Accordingly the following practice should be followed:

(1)　it is essential that all issues, including that of maintenance, should be raised at the earliest stage so that an informed judgment can be made as to the forum and the procedure which will provide the quickest and most effective way of dealing with them;

(2)　if issues of disputed ownership of household chattels need to be decided, the proper way is by way of a claim for a declaration or inquiry as to the beneficial interest, supported by affidavit evidence[7];

(3)　disclosure should be made early in the proceedings and enforced strictly;

(4)　when formulating a claim to a beneficial interest in substantial assets such as property and investments, the express discussions between the parties should be pleaded in the greatest detail, both as to language and circumstance;

particularity will have the advantage to both sides of enabling the strength of the claim to be assessed at an early stage, with sufficient definition to provide for a reasonable compromise[8].

1　See PARA 278 et seq.

2　*Cooke v Head* [1972] 2 All ER 38, [1972] 1 WLR 518, CA; *Richards v Dove* [1974] 1 All ER 888; *Eves v Eves* [1975] 3 All ER 768, [1975] 1 WLR 1338, CA; *Bernard v Josephs* [1982] Ch 391, [1982] 3 All ER 162, CA; *Burns v Burns* [1984] Ch 317, [1984] 1 All ER 244, CA. See also *Bristol and West Building Society v Henning* [1985] 2 All ER 606, [1985] 1 WLR 778, CA; *Equity and Law Home Loans Ltd v Prestidge* [1992] 1 All ER 909, [1992] 1 WLR 137, CA; *Oxley v Hiscock* [2004] EWCA Civ 546, [2005] Fam 211, [2004] 3 All ER 703, [2004] 2 FCR 295; *Stack v Dowden* [2007] UKHL 17, [2007] 2 AC 432, [2007] 2 All ER 929. Cf *Fitzpatrick v Sterling Housing Association Ltd* [2001] 1 AC 27, [1999] 4 All ER 705, HL.

3　An express declaration is conclusive in the absence of fraud or mistake: *Bernard v Josephs* [1982] Ch 391, [1982] 3 All ER 162, CA; *Re Gorman (a bankrupt), ex p trustee of bankrupt v bankrupt* [1990] 1 All ER 717, [1990] 1 WLR 616. See also the cases cited in PARA 278 note 8.

4　*Bernard v Josephs* [1982] Ch 391, [1982] 3 All ER 162, CA.

5　*Eves v Eves* [1975] 3 All ER 768, [1975] 1 WLR 1338, CA.

6　See the Law Reform (Miscellaneous Provisions) Act 1970 s 2; and PARA 230. Reliance on this provision appears to be of little assistance as no special rules of trust law, except the presumption of advancement which itself is of little significance where evidence of intention is available, apply to husband and wife unless, perhaps, the provision empowers the court to use all the powers of the Matrimonial Causes Act 1973 to adjust the rights of property of engaged couples. This point was left open in *Bernard v Josephs* [1982] Ch 391, [1982] 3 All ER 162, CA. See also *Mossop v Mossop* [1989] Fam 77, [1988] 2 All ER 202, CA; *Shaw v Fitzgerald* [1992] 1 FCR 162, [1992] 1 FLR 357.

7　Ie on lines similar to the procedure for resolving disputes under the Married Women's Property Act 1882 s 17 and the Civil Partnership Act 2004 s 66: see PARA 224 et seq.

8　*Hammond v Mitchell* [1992] 2 All ER 109, sub nom *H v M (property dispute)* [1991] FCR 938, sub nom *H v M (property: beneficial interests)* [1992] 1 FLR 229 (unmarried couple living together; property purchased in man's sole name; couple lived in, and carried on trading activities in, property; woman held, on the basis of an express agreement, to be entitled to a beneficial interest in the property).

(2) HOME RIGHTS

285.　Rights where one spouse or civil partner has no estate.　If:

(1)　one spouse or civil partner[1] is entitled to occupy a dwelling house[2] by virtue of a beneficial estate or interest or contract or any enactment giving that spouse or civil partner the right to remain in occupation[3]; and

(2)   the other spouse or civil partner is not so entitled[4],

the spouse or civil partner not so entitled has[5] the following rights ('home rights'):

(a)   if in occupation, a right not to be evicted or excluded from the dwelling house or any part of it by the other spouse or civil partner except with the leave[6] of the court[7];

(b)   if not in occupation, a right with the leave of the court so given to enter into and occupy the dwelling house[8].

If by virtue of his or her home rights a spouse or civil partner is so entitled to occupy a dwelling house or any part of a dwelling house, any payment or tender made or other thing done by that spouse or civil partner in or towards satisfaction of any liability of the other spouse or civil partner in respect of rent, mortgage payments[9] or other outgoings affecting the dwelling house is, whether or not it is made or done in pursuance of an order of the court[10], as good as if made or done by the other spouse or civil partner[11].

A spouse or civil partner's home rights continue only so long as the marriage or civil partnership subsists, except to the extent that an order of the court[12] otherwise provides and only so long as the other spouse or civil partner is entitled[13] to occupy the dwelling house, except where provision is made[14] for those rights to be a charge on an estate or interest in the dwelling house[15].

1   As to the meaning of 'civil partner' see PARA 2 note 1.

2   For these purposes 'dwelling house' includes any building or part of a building which is occupied as a dwelling, any caravan, house-boat or structure which is occupied as a dwelling, and any yard, garden, garage or outhouse belonging to it and occupied with it: Family Law Act 1996 s 63(1). However, the inclusion in this definition of caravans, house-boats or structures which are occupied as a dwelling is disapplied for the purposes of s 31 (see PARA 286; and LAND CHARGES vol 26 (2004 Reissue) PARA 638), s 32 (see LAND CHARGES vol 26 (2004 Reissue) PARA 638), s 53 (see PARA 310 et seq) and s 54 (see note 3) and such other provisions of Pt IV (ss 30–63), if any, as may be prescribed: s 63(4).

     Section 30 does not apply to a dwelling house which has at no time been, and which was at no time intended by the spouses or civil partners to be, a family home of theirs: Family Law Act 1996 s 30(7) (ss 30(1)–(9), 54 amended by the Civil Partnership Act 2004 Sch 9 paras 1, 12); and see *Collins v Collins* (1973) 4 Fam Law 133, CA; *Syed v Syed* (1980) 1 FLR 129; *Barnett v Hassett* [1982] 1 All ER 80, [1981] 1 WLR 1385. The test whether a house is a matrimonial home (or, presumably, a civil partnership home) is an objective one: *Hall v King* [1988] 1 FLR 376, CA; and see *Moore v Moore* [2004] EWCA Civ 1243, [2004] 3 FCR 461, [2005] 1 FLR 666. Whether the whole of a hotel was matrimonial home was a matter of fact and degree: *Kinzler v Kinzler* [1985] Fam Law 26, CA. As to claims by mortgagees see PARA 287.

3   Family Law Act 1996 s 30(1)(a) (as amended: see note 2). In determining for these purposes whether a person is entitled to occupy a dwelling house by virtue of an estate or interest, any right to possession of the dwelling house conferred on a mortgagee of the dwelling house under or by virtue of his mortgage is to be disregarded, whether or not the mortgagee is in possession: s 54(1), (2). Where a person is entitled to occupy a dwelling house by virtue of an estate or interest, a connected person does not, by virtue of any home rights or any rights conferred by an occupation order (ie an order under s 35 (see PARAS 297, 298) or s 36 (see PARAS 301, 302)), have any larger right against the mortgagee to occupy the dwelling house than the entitled person has by virtue of his estate or interest and of any contract with the mortgagee (s 54(3) (as so amended)), although this does not apply, in the case of home rights, if under s 31 (see PARA 286; and LAND CHARGES vol 26 (2004 Reissue) PARA 638) those rights are a charge, affecting the mortgagee, on the estate or interest mortgaged (s 54(4) (as so amended)). For these purposes, 'connected person', in relation to any person, means that person's spouse, former spouse, civil partner, former civil partner, cohabitant or former cohabitant: ss 54(5), 55(1) (s 54(5) as so amended). As to the meaning of 'cohabitants' and 'former cohabitants' see PARA 292 note 5. 'Mortgage', 'mortgagor' and 'mortgagee' have the same meaning as in the Law of Property Act 1925 (see MORTGAGE vol 32 (2005 Reissue) PARA 301): Family Law Act 1996 s 63(1).

4   Family Law Act 1996 s 30(1)(b) (as amended: see note 2).

5   Ie subject to the provisions of the Family Law Act 1996 Pt IV (ss 30–63). On an application for
    home rights the court has no jurisdiction to grant an injunction against third parties with a right
    of occupation, and the Court of Appeal cannot amend the grounds of appeal to reflect an
    entirely new cause of action so that the matter must be remitted to the court of first instance for
    separate, new proceedings against the third parties to be consolidated with the application under
    s 30: *Kalsi v Kalsi* [1992] 2 FCR 1, [1992] 1 FLR 511, CA.
6   Ie given by an order under the Family Law Act 1996 s 33: see PARA 292. As to the meaning of
    'court' see PARA 958.
7   Family Law Act 1996 s 30(2)(a) (as amended: see note 2). A spouse or civil partner's occupation
    by virtue of his or her home rights:
    (1)   is to be treated, for the purposes of the Rent (Agriculture) Act 1976 and the Rent
          Act 1977 (other than the Rent Act 1977 Pt V (ss 77–85) (see LANDLORD AND TENANT
          vol 27(2) (2006 Reissue) PARA 989 et seq) and ss 103–106 (see LANDLORD AND
          TENANT vol 27(2) (2006 Reissue) PARA 1002 et seq)) as occupation by the other spouse
          as the other spouse's residence (Family Law Act 1996 s 30(4)(a) (as amended: see note
          2)); and
    (2)   if by virtue of his or her home rights the spouse or civil partner occupies the dwelling
          house as his or her only or principal home, is to be treated, for the purposes of the
          Housing Act 1985 (see LANDLORD AND TENANT vol 27(2) (2006 Reissue) PARA 1300 et
          seq), the Housing Act 1988 Pt I (ss 1–45) (see LANDLORD AND TENANT vol 27(2) (2006
          Reissue) PARA 1011 et seq) and the Housing Act 1996 Pt V Chapter I (ss 124–143) (see
          LANDLORD AND TENANT vol 27(2) (2006 Reissue) PARA 1286 et seq), as occupation by
          the other spouse or civil partner as that spouse or civil partner's only or principal home
          (Family Law Act 1996 s 30(4)(b) (as so amended; also amended by SI 1997/74)).
    A person who has an equitable interest in a dwelling house or in its proceeds of sale, but is
    not a person in whom there is vested, whether solely or as joint tenant, a legal estate in fee
    simple or a legal term of years absolute in the dwelling house, is to be treated, only for the
    purpose of determining whether he or she has home rights, as not being entitled to occupy the
    dwelling house by virtue of that interest: Family Law Act 1996 s 30(9) (as amended: see note 2).
8   Family Law Act 1996 s 30(2)(b) (as amended: see note 2). As to the nature of an occupation by
    virtue of home rights see note 7.
9   For these purposes 'mortgage payments' includes any payments which, under the terms of the
    mortgage, the mortgagor is required to make to any person: Family Law Act 1996 s 63(1).
10 Ie under the Family Law Act 1996 s 40: see PARA 294.
11 Family Law Act 1996 s 30(3) (as amended: see note 2); and see *Penn v Dunn* [1970] 2 QB 686,
    [1970] 2 All ER 858, CA; *Hastings and Thanet Building Society v Goddard* [1970] 3 All ER
    954, [1970] 1 WLR 1544, CA. If a spouse or civil partner is entitled under the Family Law
    Act 1996 s 30 to occupy a dwelling house or any part of a dwelling house and makes any
    payment in or towards satisfaction of any liability of the other spouse or civil partner in respect
    of mortgage payments affecting the dwelling house, the person to whom the payment is made
    may treat it as having been made by the second spouse or civil partner, but the fact that that
    person has treated any such payment as having been so made does not affect any claim of the
    first spouse or civil partner against the second spouse or civil partner to an interest in the
    dwelling house by virtue of the payment: s 30(5) (as so amended). If a spouse or civil partner is
    entitled under s 30 to occupy a dwelling house or part of a dwelling house by reason of an
    interest of the other spouse or civil partner under a trust, the provisions of s 30(3)–(5) apply in
    relation to the trustees as they apply in relation to the other spouse or civil partner: s 30(6) (as
    so amended).
12 Ie under the Family Law Act 1996 s 33(5): see PARA 297.
13 Ie as mentioned in the Family Law Act 1996 s 30(1).
14 Ie by the Family Law Act 1996 s 31: see PARA 286.
15 Family Law Act 1996 s 30(8) (as amended: see note 2). See *Moore v Moore* [2004] EWCA Civ
    1243, [2004] 3 FCR 461, [2005] 1 FLR 666.

286.   Effect of home rights as charge on dwelling house. If, at any time during
a marriage or civil partnership[1], one spouse or civil partner is entitled to occupy
a dwelling house[2] by virtue of a beneficial estate or interest[3], the other spouse or
civil partner's home rights[4] are a charge on the estate or interest[5].

If a spouse or civil partner's home rights are a charge on an estate or interest
in the dwelling house and that estate or interest is surrendered to merge in some
other estate or interest expectant on it in such circumstances that, but for the

merger, the person taking the estate or interest would be bound by the charge, the surrender has effect subject to the charge and the persons thereafter entitled to the other estate or interest are, for so long as the estate or interest surrendered would have endured if not so surrendered, to be treated[6] as deriving title to the other estate or interest under the other spouse or civil partner or, as the case may be, under the trustees for the other spouse or civil partner, by virtue of the surrender[7]. If the title to the legal estate by virtue of which a spouse or civil partner is entitled to occupy a dwelling house, including any legal estate held by trustees for that spouse or civil partner, is registered[8], registration of a land charge affecting the dwelling house[9] is to be effected by registering[10] a notice[11].

1   As to the meanings of 'civil partnership' and 'civil partner' see PARA 2 note 1.
2   As to the meaning of 'dwelling house' see PARA 285 note 2.
3   Family Law Act 1996 s 31(1) (s 31(1), (2), (9), (10) amended by the Civil Partnership Act 2004 Sch 9 para 2). In determining whether a person is entitled to occupy a dwelling house by virtue of an estate or interest, any right to possession of the dwelling house conferred on a mortgagee of the dwelling house under or by virtue of his mortgage is to be disregarded, whether or not the mortgagee is in possession: see PARA 285 note 3.
4   As to the meaning of 'home rights' see PARA 285.
5   Family Law Act 1996 s 31(2) (as amended: see note 3). Any such charge is a Class F land charge: see the Land Charges Act 1972 s 2(7); the Family Law Act 1996 s 31(3)–(8), (12), (13); and LAND CHARGES vol 26 (2004 Reissue) PARA 638.
6   Ie for all purposes of the Family Law Act 1996 Pt IV (ss 30–63).
7   Family Law Act 1996 s 31(9) (as amended: see note 3).
8   Ie under the Land Registration Act 2002 or any enactment replaced by that Act: Family Law Act 1996 s 31(10) (amended by the Land Registration Act 2002 Sch 11 para 34; Family Law Act 1996 s 31(10) as amended: see note 3). As to registration under the Land Registration Act 2002 see LAND REGISTRATION vol 26 (2004 Reissue) PARA 801 et seq.
9   Ie by virtue of the Family Law Act 1996 Pt IV (ss 30–63).
10   Ie under the Land Registration Act 2002: see note 8.
11   Family Law Act 1996 s 31(10)(a) (as amended: see note 8). In such circumstances a spouse or civil partner's home rights are not capable of falling within the Land Registration Act 2002 Sch 1 para 2 or Sch 3 para 2 (as to which see LAND REGISTRATION vol 26 (2004 Reissue) PARAS 866, 962): Family Law Act 1996 s 31(10)(b) (substituted by the Land Registration Act 2002 Sch 11 para 34; Family Law Act 1996 s 31(10)(b) as amended: see notes 3, 8). As to the restriction on registration where a spouse or civil partner is entitled to more than one charge, contracts for sale of a house affected by a registered charge required to include a term requiring the cancellation of registration before completion, and the cancellation of registration after divorce, dissolution etc see LAND CHARGES vol 26 (2004 Reissue) PARA 638.

287. Claims by mortgagees. If a mortgagee[1] of land which consists of or includes a dwelling house[2] brings a claim in any court for the enforcement of his security, a connected person[3] who is not already a party to the claim is entitled to be made a party[4] if:

(1)   the connected person is enabled[5] to meet the mortgagor's[6] liabilities under the mortgage[7];

(2)   he has applied to the court[8] before the claim is finally disposed of in that court[9]; and

(3)   the court sees no special reason against his being made a party to the claim and is satisfied:

    (a)   that he may be expected to make such payments or do such other things in or towards satisfaction of the mortgagor's liabilities or obligations as might affect the outcome of the proceedings[10]; or

    (b)   that the expectation of it should be[11] considered[12].

If a mortgagee of land which consists, or substantially consists, of a dwelling house brings a claim for the enforcement of his security, and at the relevant time[13] there is:

(i) in the case of unregistered land, a land charge of Class F registered against the person who is the estate owner at the relevant time or any person who, where the estate owner is a trustee, preceded him as trustee during the subsistence of the mortgage[14]; or

(ii) in the case of registered land, a subsisting registration of a notice[15] or, as the case may be, a notice or caution[16],

then, if the person on whose behalf the land charge is registered or the notice or caution is entered, is not a party to the claim, the mortgagee must serve notice of the claim on him[17].

1 As to the meaning of 'mortgagee' see PARA 285 note 3.
2 As to the meaning of 'dwelling house' see PARA 285 note 2.
3 As to the meaning of 'connected person' see PARA 285 note 3.
4 Family Law Act 1996 s 55(1), (2).
5 Ie by the Family Law Act 1996 s 30(3) or (6) (see PARA 285), or by s 30(3) or (6) as applied by s 35(13) (see PARA 297 note 2) or s 36(13) (see PARA 301).
6 As to the meaning of 'mortgagor' see PARA 285 note 3.
7 Family Law Act 1996 s 55(3)(a). As to the meaning of 'mortgage' see PARA 285 note 3.
8 As to the meaning of 'court' see PARA 958.
9 Family Law Act 1996 s 55(3)(b).
10 Family Law Act 1996 s 55(3)(c)(i).
11 Ie under the Administration of Justice Act 1970 s 36: see MORTGAGE vol 32 (2005 Reissue) PARA 755.
12 Family Law Act 1996 s 55(3)(c)(ii).
13 If: (1) an official search has been made on behalf of the mortgagee which would disclose any land charge of Class F, notice or caution within the Family Law Act 1996 s 56(1)(a) or (b) (see the text and notes 14–16); (2) a certificate of the result of the search has been issued; and (3) the claim is commenced within the priority period, the relevant time is the date of the certificate: s 56(3). In any other case, the relevant time is the time when the claim is commenced: s 56(4). The priority period is, for both registered and unregistered land, the period for which, in accordance with the Land Charges Act 1972 s 11(5), (6) (see LAND CHARGES vol 26 (2004 Reissue) PARAS 614, 701), a certificate on an official search operates in favour of a purchaser: Family Law Act 1996 s 56(5). As to Class F land charges see LAND CHARGES vol 26 (2004 Reissue) PARA 638.
14 Family Law Act 1996 s 56(1)(a).
15 Ie under the Family Law Act 1996 s 31(10) (see PARA 286) or the Matrimonial Homes Act 1983 s 2(8) (repealed).
16 Family Law Act 1996 s 56(1)(b). The 'notice or caution' referred to in the text is a notice or caution under the Matrimonial Homes Act 1967 s 2(7) (repealed).
17 Family Law Act 1996 s 56(2).

288. Rights of bankrupts. Nothing in the initial period of bankruptcy, that is to say the period beginning with the day of the presentation of the petition for the bankruptcy order and ending with the vesting of the bankrupt's estate in a trustee, is to be taken as having given rise to any home rights in relation to a dwelling house comprised in the bankrupt's estate[1]. Where a spouse or civil partner's home rights are a charge on the estate or interest of the other spouse or civil partner, or of trustees for the other spouse or civil partner, and the other spouse or civil partner is adjudged bankrupt, the charge continues to subsist notwithstanding the bankruptcy and binds the trustee of the bankrupt's estate and persons deriving title under that trustee[2].

Where a person who is entitled to occupy a dwelling house by virtue of a beneficial interest is adjudged bankrupt and any persons under the age of 18 with whom that person had at some time occupied that dwelling house had their home with that person at the time when the bankruptcy petition was presented and at the commencement of the bankruptcy, then, whether or not the bankrupt's spouse or civil partner, if any, has home rights, the bankrupt has the following rights as against the trustee of his estate:

(1)   if in occupation, a right not to be evicted or excluded from the dwelling house or any part of it, except with the leave of the court[3];

(2)   if not in occupation, a right with the leave of the court to enter into and occupy the dwelling house[4].

1   See the Insolvency Act 1986 s 336(1); and BANKRUPTCY AND INDIVIDUAL INSOLVENCY vol 3(2) (2002 Reissue) PARA 648. As to home rights see PARA 285 et seq.
2   See the Insolvency Act 1986 s 336(2)(a); and BANKRUPTCY AND INDIVIDUAL INSOLVENCY vol 3(2) (2002 Reissue) PARA 648.
3   See the Insolvency Act 1986 s 337(1), (2)(a)(i); and BANKRUPTCY AND INDIVIDUAL INSOLVENCY vol 3(2) (2002 Reissue) PARA 650.
4   See the Insolvency Act 1986 s 337(2)(a)(ii); and BANKRUPTCY AND INDIVIDUAL INSOLVENCY vol 3(2) (2002 Reissue) PARA 650.

(3) OCCUPATION ORDERS

(i) Applications and Orders

289.   Applications to the court.   An application may be made to the court[1] for an order (an 'occupation order')[2] by:

(1)   a person who has an estate or interest or has home rights[3];

(2)   a former spouse or civil partner with no existing right to occupy[4];

(3)   a cohabitant or former cohabitant with no existing right to occupy[5];

(4)   a person who is a former spouse or civil partner with no existing right to occupy[6]; or

(5)   a person who is a cohabitant or former cohabitant with no existing right to occupy[7].

An application for an occupation order may be made in other family proceedings[8] or without any other family proceedings being instituted[9].

If an application for an occupation order is made[10] and the court considers that it has no power to make the order under the relevant statutory provision, but that it has power to make an order under one of the other relevant statutory provisions, the court may make an order under that other statutory provision[11].

The fact that a person has applied for an occupation order[12], or that an occupation order has been made, does not affect the right of any person to claim a legal or equitable interest in any property in any subsequent proceedings[13].

A child under the age of 16 may not apply for an occupation order except with the leave of the court[14]; and the court may grant such leave only if it is satisfied that the child has sufficient understanding to make the proposed application for the occupation order[15].

It has been held that an occupation order, which overrides proprietary rights, is of such a Draconian nature that it should be restricted to exceptional cases and used as a last resort[16].

1   As to the meaning of 'court' see PARA 958.
2   Family Law Act 1996 ss 39(1), 63(1). The fee payable on applying for an occupation order, or on applying simultaneously for both a non-molestation order (see PARA 716 et seq) and an occupation order is £60: Family Proceedings Fees Order 2008, SI 2008/1054, Sch 1, Fee 1.3.
3   Ie under the Family Law Act 1996 s 33: see PARAS 292–293, 295. As to home rights see PARA 285 et seq.
4   Ie under the Family Law Act 1996 s 35: see PARAS 292–293, 295.
5   Ie under the Family Law Act 1996 s 36: see PARAS 301–302, 304.
6   Ie under the Family Law Act 1996 s 37: see PARAS 305–307.

7   Ie under the Family Law Act 1996 s 38: see PARAS 305–307.
8   By virtue of the Family Law Act 1996 s 63(1), (2) (amended by the Adoption and Children
    Act 2002 Sch 3 paras 85, 88; the Civil Partnership Act 2004 Sch 9 para 14; the Forced Marriage
    (Civil Protection) Act 2007 Sch 2 para 3), 'family proceedings' means any proceedings under:
    (1)   the inherent jurisdiction of the High Court in relation to children (see CHILDREN AND
          YOUNG PERSONS vol 5(3) (2008 Reissue) PARA 200);
    (2)   the Family Law Act 1996 Pt IV (ss 30–63) (see PARAS 285 et seq, 292 et seq);
    (3)   the Matrimonial Causes Act 1973 (see PARA 317 et seq);
    (4)   the Adoption Act 1976 (see CHILDREN AND YOUNG PERSONS vol 5(3) (2008 Reissue)
          PARA 375 et seq);
    (5)   the Domestic Proceedings and Magistrates' Courts Act 1978 (see PARA 553 et seq);
    (6)   the Matrimonial and Family Proceedings Act 1984 Pt III (ss 12–27) (see PARAS 530 et
          seq, 938 et seq);
    (7)   the Children Act 1989 Pt I (ss 1–7), Pt III (ss 17–30) and Pt IV (ss 31–42) (see
          CHILDREN AND YOUNG PERSONS vol 5(3) (2008 Reissue) PARAS 125, 133 et seq, 270 et
          seq, CHILDREN AND YOUNG PERSONS vol 5(4) (2008 Reissue) PARA 851 et seq);
    (8)   the Human Fertilisation and Embryology Act 1990 s 30 (see CHILDREN AND YOUNG
          PERSONS vol 5(3) (2008 Reissue) PARA 106);
    (9)   the Adoption and Children Act 2002 (see CHILDREN AND YOUNG PERSONS vol 5(3)
          (2008 Reissue) PARA 331 et seq);
    (10) the Civil Partnership Act 2004 Schs 5–7 (see PARA 458 et seq); and
    (11) the Family Law Act 1996 Pt IVA (ss 63A–63S) (see PARA 723 et seq).
9   Family Law Act 1996 s 39(2).
10 Ie under the Family Law Act 1996 s 33, 35, 36, 37 or 38 (see PARA 292 et seq).
11 Family Law Act 1996 s 39(3). As to the relevant statutory provisions see note 10.
12 Ie under the Family Law Act 1996 ss 35–38.
13 Family Law Act 1996 s 39(4). For these purposes, 'subsequent proceedings' includes subsequent
    proceedings under Pt IV (ss 30–63): s 39(4).
14 Family Law Act 1996 s 43(1).
15 Family Law Act 1996 s 43(2).
16 *Chalmers v John* [1999] 2 FCR 110, [1999] 1 FLR 392, CA (a court should be cautious about
    making a definitive occupation order at an interlocutory stage where a final hearing is
    imminent); *G v G (occupation order)* [2000] 3 FCR 53, [2000] 2 FLR 36, CA; *Re Y (children)
    (occupation order)* [2000] 2 FCR 470, CA. Each case will turn on its own particular facts: *B v B
    (occupation order)* [1999] 2 FCR 251, [1999] 1 FLR 715, CA (spouses lived in council
    accommodation; husband had treated wife with serious domestic violence and in consequence
    wife left matrimonial home with young daughter; wife and daughter rehoused in bed and
    breakfast accommodation; husband stayed in matrimonial home with his minor son; wife
    applied for occupation order; court had to balance harm to each of the two children; it was held
    that the son would suffer greater harm if occupation order made).

290.   Orders without notice.   The court[1] may, in any case where it considers
that it is just and convenient to do so, make an occupation order[2] even though
the respondent has not been given such notice of the proceedings as would
otherwise be required by rules of court[3]. In determining whether to exercise these
powers, the court must have regard to all the circumstances including:
    (1)   any risk of significant harm[4] to the applicant or a relevant child[5],
          attributable to conduct of the respondent, if the order is not made
          immediately[6];
    (2)   whether it is likely that the applicant will be deterred or prevented from
          pursuing the application if an order is not made immediately[7]; and
    (3)   whether there is reason to believe that the respondent is aware of the
          proceedings but is deliberately evading service and that the applicant or
          a relevant child will be seriously prejudiced by the delay involved where
          the court is a magistrates' court, in effecting service of proceedings or in
          any other case, in effecting substituted service[8].
If the court makes an order without notice it must afford the respondent an
opportunity to make representations relating to the order as soon as just and
convenient at a full hearing[9].

If, at a full hearing, the court makes an occupation order (the 'full order'), then:

(a) for the purposes of calculating the maximum period for which the full order may be made to have effect, the relevant statutory provision[10] is to apply as if the period for which the full order will have effect began on the date on which the initial order[11] first had effect; and

(b) the provisions relating to the extension of orders[12] are to apply as if the full order and the initial order were a single order[13].

1 As to the meaning of 'court' see PARA 958.
2 As to the meaning of 'occupation order' see PARA 289.
3 Family Law Act 1996 s 45(1). As to the attachment of a power of arrest to an order made by virtue of s 45(1) see s 47(3); and PARA 988. Where an order has been made under s 45(1) and a power of arrest has been attached by virtue of s 47(3), the court may vary or discharge the order under s 49(1), in so far as that order confers a power of arrest: see s 49(4); and PARA 722. As to enforcement and arrest generally see PARA 988 et seq. As to an appeal against the making of any order by a magistrates' court or any refusal to make such an order see s 61; and PARA 308.
   If an order is made without notice, it must be strictly limited in time and operate only until the earliest day on which a hearing with notice can be arranged: *Ansah v Ansah* [1977] Fam 138, [1977] 2 All ER 638, CA; *Masich v Masich* (1977) 7 Fam Law 245, CA; *Practice Note* [1978] 2 All ER 919, sub nom *Practice Direction* [1978] 1 WLR 925; *Loseby v Newman* [1996] 1 FCR 647, [1995] 2 FLR 754, CA. While an ouster order is made without notice, it must be strictly limited in time, and any application to discharge it should be treated as urgent business; if there are listing difficulties, the matter should always be referred to a judicial officer, preferably a judge: *G v G (exclusion order)* [1990] FCR 572, [1990] 1 FLR 395, CA.
4 For these purposes 'harm' means: (1) in relation to a person who has reached the age of 18 years, ill-treatment or the impairment of health; and (2) in relation to a child (ie a person under the age of 18), ill-treatment or the impairment of health or development: Family Law Act 1996 s 63(1). 'Ill-treatment' includes forms of ill-treatment which are not physical and, in relation to a child, includes sexual abuse; 'health' includes physical or mental health; and 'development' means physical, intellectual, emotional, social or behavioural development: s 63(1). Where the question of whether harm suffered by a child is 'significant' turns on the child's health or development, his health or development is to be compared with that which could reasonably be expected of a similar child: s 63(3). See *Banks v Banks* [1999] 1 FLR 726 (wife suffering from dementia; it was held that presence of wife in matrimonial home would cause additional strain but would not cause husband significant harm).
5 'Relevant child', in relation to any proceedings under the Family Law Act 1996 Pt IV (ss 30–63) means: (1) any child who is living with or might reasonably be expected to live with either party to the proceedings; (2) any child in relation to whom an order under the Adoption Act 1976, the Adoption and Children Act 2002 or the Children Act 1989 is in question in the proceedings; and (3) any other child whose interests the court considers relevant: Family Law Act 1996 ss 62(2), 63(1) (s 62(2) amended by the Adoption and Children Act 2002 Sch 3 paras 85, 86).
6 Family Law Act 1996 s 45(2)(a).
7 Family Law Act 1996 s 45(2)(b).
8 Family Law Act 1996 s 45(2)(c).
9 Family Law Act 1996 s 45(3). For these purposes, 'full hearing' means a hearing of which notice has been given to all the parties in accordance with rules of court: s 45(5).
10 For these purposes, 'relevant statutory provision' means the Family Law Act 1996 s 33(10) (see PARA 292), s 35(10) (see PARA 297), s 36(10) (see PARA 301), s 37(5) (see PARA 305) or s 38(6) (see PARA 305): s 45(5).
11 For these purposes, 'initial order' means an occupation order made by virtue of the Family Law Act 1996 s 45(1): s 45(5).
12 Ie the Family Law Act 1996 s 36(10) (see PARA 301) or, as the case may be, s 38(6) (see PARA 305).
13 Family Law Act 1996 s 45(4).

291. Undertakings. In any case where the court[1] has power to make an occupation order[2] it may accept an undertaking from any party to the proceedings[3]; but no power of arrest may be attached to any undertaking so given[4]. The court must not accept such an undertaking in any case where a power of arrest would otherwise be attached to the order[5]. An undertaking so given to a court is enforceable as if the court had made an occupation order in terms corresponding to those of the undertaking[6].

These provisions have effect without prejudice to the powers of the High Court and the county court apart from those provisions[7].

1   As to the meaning of 'court' see PARA 958.
2   As to the meaning of 'occupation order' see PARA 289.
3   Family Law Act 1996 s 46(1). An undertaking can be enforced on breach by applying for a committal but there can be no appeal from an undertaking: *McConnell v McConnell* (1980) 10 Fam Law 214, CA.
4   Family Law Act 1996 s 46(2). As to the enforcement of undertakings see PARA 997.
5   Family Law Act 1996 s 46(3) (s 46(3), (4) amended by the Domestic Violence, Crime and Victims Act 2004 Sch 10 para 37).
6   Family Law Act 1996 s 46(4) (as amended: see note 5).
7   Family Law Act 1996 s 46(5).

(ii) Circumstances and Conditions for Orders

A. APPLICANT HAVING ESTATE OR INTEREST OR HOME RIGHTS

292. Right to apply for an occupation order. If:
(1)   a person (the 'person entitled'):
    (a)   is entitled to occupy a dwelling house[1] by virtue of a beneficial estate or interest or contract or by virtue of any enactment giving him or her the right to remain in occupation[2]; or
    (b)   has home rights[3] in relation to a dwelling house[4]; and
(2)   the dwelling house:
    (a)   is or at any time has been the home of the person entitled and of another person with whom he or she is associated[5]; or
    (b)   was at any time intended by the person entitled and any such other person to be their home[6],
the person entitled may apply to the court[7] for an occupation order[8] containing any of the provisions which may be specified[9] in such an order[10].

An occupation order may not be made under these provisions after the death of either of the parties[11], and, except in the case of an order made by virtue of the death of the other spouse or civil partner[12], ceases to have effect on the death of either party[13]; and such an order may, in so far as it has continuing effect, be made for a specified period, until the occurrence of a specified event or until further order[14].

1   As to the meaning of 'dwelling house' see PARA 285 note 2.
2   Family Law Act 1996 s 33(1)(a)(i). For a case where there was insufficient evidence to satisfy the court that a father was entitled to occupy the property by virtue of a beneficial interest in it, permitting him to apply for an order under s 33 see *S v F (occupation order)* [2000] 3 FCR 365, [2000] 1 FLR 255; in connection with the contractual rights of a wife see *Moore v Moore* [2004] EWCA Civ 1243, [2004] 3 FCR 461, [2005] 1 FLR 666. As to appeals against the making of any such order by a magistrates' court or any refusal to make such an order see the Family Law Act 1996 s 61; and PARA 308. As to variation and discharge see PARA 309. As to enforcement and arrest see PARA 988 et seq.
3   As to the meaning of 'home rights' see PARA 285.
4   Family Law Act 1996 s 33(1)(a)(ii) (s 33(1)(a)(ii) amended, ss 33(2A), 44(3), (4), 62(3)(aa), (eza) added, s 62(1) amended, by the Civil Partnership Act 2004 Sch 9 paras 4, 10, 13; Family Law Act 1996 s 62(1) amended, s 62(3)(ea) added, by the Domestic Violence, Crime and Victims Act 2004 s 4, Sch 10 paras 40, 41).
5   Family Law Act 1996 s 33(1)(b)(i). A person is 'associated' with another person for the purposes of the Family Law Act 1996 Pt IV (ss 30–63) if:

(1)   they are or have been married to each other (s 62(3)(a));
(2)   they are or have been civil partners of each other (s 62(3)(aa) (as added: see note 4));
(3)   they are cohabitants or former cohabitants (s 62(3)(b));
(4)   they live or have lived in the same household, otherwise than merely by reason of one of them being the other's employee, tenant, lodger or boarder (s 62(3)(c));
(5)   they are relatives (s 62(3)(d));
(6)   they have agreed to marry one another, whether or not that agreement has been terminated (s 62(3)(e));
(7)   they have entered into a civil partnership agreement (as defined by the Civil Partnership Act 2004 s 73 (see PARA 16)) (whether or not that agreement has been terminated) (s 62(3)(eza) (as so added));
(8)   they have or have had an intimate personal relationship with each other which is or was of significant duration (s 62(3)(ea));
(9)   in relation to any child, they are both persons who are parents of the child or they have or have had parental responsibility for the child (s 62(3)(f), (4)); or
(10)   they are parties to the same family proceedings (other than proceedings under Pt IV (s 62(3)(g)).

A body corporate and another person are not, by virtue of head (9) or (10), to be regarded for these purposes as associated with each other: s 62(6).

If:

(a)   a child has been adopted (s 62(5));
(b)   an adoption agency within the meaning of the Adoption and Children Act 2002 s 2 (see CHILDREN AND YOUNG PERSONS vol 5(3) (2008 Reissue) PARAS 331, 394–395) has power to place him for adoption under s 19 (placing children with parental consent: see CHILDREN AND YOUNG PERSONS vol 5(3) (2008 Reissue) PARAS 332–333) or he has become the subject of an order under s 21 (placement orders: see CHILDREN AND YOUNG PERSONS vol 5(3) (2008 Reissue) PARAS 335–337) (Family Law Act 1996 s 62(5), (7)(a) (s 62(5) amended, s 62(7) added, by the Adoption and Children Act 2002 Sch 3 paras 85–87)); or
(c)   a child is freed for adoption by virtue of an order made under the Adoption Act 1976 s 18 (repealed) or a corresponding Scottish or Northern Irish provision (Family Law Act 1996 62(7)(b) (as so added)),

two persons are also associated with each other if one is a natural parent of the child or a parent of such a natural parent and the other is the child or any person who has become a parent of the child by virtue of an adoption order or has applied for an adoption order or with whom the child has at any time been placed for adoption (s 62(5) (as so amended)).

For these purposes 'cohabitants' are two persons who are neither married to each other nor civil partners of each other but are living together as husband and wife or as if they were civil partners; and 'cohabit and 'former cohabitants' are to be read accordingly (although 'former cohabitants' does not include cohabitants who have subsequently married each other or become civil partners of each other): ss 62(1), 63(1) (as amended: see note 4). 'Relative', in relation to a person, means: (1) the father, mother, stepfather, stepmother, son, daughter, stepson, stepdaughter, grandmother, grandfather, grandson or granddaughter of that person or of that person's spouse, former spouse, civil partner or former civil partner; or (2) the brother, sister, uncle, aunt, niece, nephew or first cousin (whether of the full blood or of the half blood or by marriage or civil partnership) of that person or of that person's spouse, former spouse, civil partner or former civil partner, and includes, in relation to a person who is cohabiting or has cohabited with another person, any person who would fall within head (1) or (2) if the parties were married to each other or were civil partners of each other: s 63(1) (as so amended).

As to the interpretation of these provisions (in the context of a non-molestation order) see also PARA 717 note 5. As to the meaning of 'child' see PARA 290 note 4. As to the meaning of 'parental responsibility' see the Children Act 1989 s 3; and CHILDREN AND YOUNG PERSONS vol 5(3) (2008 Reissue) PARA 134 (definition applied by the Family Law Act 1996 s 63(1)). As to the meaning of 'family proceedings' see PARA 289 note 8.

6   Family Law Act 1996 s 33(1)(b)(ii).
7   As to the meaning of 'court' see PARA 958.
8   As to the meaning of 'occupation order' see PARA 289. As to the provisions that may be included in an order see PARAS 293–294; as to the matters to which the court must have regard see PARA 295. As to the effect of an order where the home rights are a charge on the dwelling house see PARA 296.
9   Ie any of the provisions specified in the Family Law Act 1996 s 33(3)–(5): see PARA 293.
10   Family Law Act 1996 s 33(1). If an agreement to marry or a civil partnership agreement (as defined by the Civil Partnership Act 2004 s 73: see PARA 16) is terminated, no application under

s 33 may be made by virtue of s 62(3)(e) or s 62(3)(eza) (see note 5) by reference to that agreement after the end of the period of three years beginning with the day on which it is terminated: s 33(2), (2A) (s 33(2A) as added: see note 4). The court must not make an order under s 33 by virtue of s 62(3)(e) or s 62(3)(eza) unless there is produced to it evidence in writing of the existence of the agreement to marry or the civil partnership agreement (s 44(1), (3) (s 44(3) as so added)), although this does not apply if the court is satisfied that the agreement to marry or the civil partnership agreement was evidenced by the gift of an engagement ring by one party to the agreement to the other in contemplation of their marriage, or a gift by one party to the agreement to the other as a token of the agreement, or a ceremony entered into by the parties in the presence of one or more other persons assembled for the purpose of witnessing the ceremony (s 44(2), (4) (s 44(4) as so added)).

11 Ie either of the parties mentioned in the Family Law Act 1996 s 33(1).
12 Ie except in the case of an order made by virtue of the Family Law Act 1996 s 33(5)(a): see PARA 293.
13 Family Law Act 1996 s 33(9).
14 Family Law Act 1996 s 33(10).

293. **Provisions that may be included in an order.** An occupation order[1] may:

(1)   enforce the applicant's entitlement to remain in occupation as against the other person (the 'respondent')[2];

(2)   require the respondent to permit the applicant to enter and remain in the dwelling house[3] or part of the dwelling house[4];

(3)   regulate the occupation of the dwelling house by either or both parties[5];

(4)   if the respondent is entitled to occupy a dwelling house by virtue of a beneficial estate or interest or contract or by virtue of any enactment giving the respondent the right to remain in occupation[6], prohibit, suspend or restrict the exercise by the respondent of the right to occupy the dwelling house[7];

(5)   if the respondent has home rights[8] in relation to the dwelling house and the applicant is the other spouse or civil partner, restrict or terminate those rights[9];

(6)   require the respondent to leave the dwelling house or part of the dwelling house[10]; or

(7)   exclude the respondent from a defined area in which the dwelling house is included[11].

An order may also declare that the applicant is entitled to occupy a dwelling house by virtue of a beneficial estate or interest or contract or by virtue of any enactment giving the applicant the right to remain in occupation[12], or declare that the applicant has home rights[13].

If the applicant has home rights and the respondent is the other spouse or civil partner, such an order made during the marriage or civil partnership may provide that those rights are not brought to an end by the death of the other spouse or civil partner or the termination, otherwise than by death, of the marriage or civil partnership[14].

1   As to the meaning of 'occupation order' see PARA 289; as to the making of an order see PARA 292. As to the matters to which the court must have regard see PARA 295. As to the effect of an occupation order where the home rights are a charge on the dwelling house see PARA 296.
2   Family Law Act 1996 s 33(3)(a).
3   As to the meaning of 'dwelling house' see PARA 285 note 2.
4   Family Law Act 1996 s 33(3)(b).
5   Family Law Act 1996 s 33(3)(c).
6   Ie if the respondent is entitled as mentioned in the Family Law Act 1996 s 33(1)(a)(i): see PARA 292.
7   Family Law Act 1996 s 33(3)(d).
8   As to the meaning of 'home rights' see PARA 285.

9 Family Law Act 1996 s 33(3)(e) (s 33(3)(e), (4), (5) amended by the Civil Partnership Act 2004 Sch 9 para 4).
10 Family Law Act 1996 s 33(3)(f).
11 Family Law Act 1996 s 33(3)(g).
12 Ie that the applicant is entitled as mentioned in the Family Law Act 1996 s 33(1)(a)(i) (see PARA 292).
13 Family Law Act 1996 s 33(4) (as amended: see note 9).
14 Family Law Act 1996 s 33(5) (as amended: see note 9). The court may exercise its powers under s 33(5) in any case where it considers that in all the circumstances it is just and reasonable to do so: s 33(8).

294.   Additional obligations etc which may be imposed.   On, or at any time after, making an occupation order[1] where the applicant has an estate or interest or has home rights[2] the court[3] may:

(1)   impose on either party obligations as to the repair and maintenance of the dwelling house[4] or the discharge of rent, mortgage payments[5] or other outgoings affecting the dwelling house[6];

(2)   order a party occupying the dwelling house or any part of it, including a party who is entitled to do so by virtue of a beneficial estate or interest or contract or by virtue of any enactment giving that party the right to remain in occupation, to make periodical payments to the other party in respect of the accommodation, if the other party would, but for the order, be entitled to occupy the dwelling house by virtue of a beneficial estate or interest or contract or by virtue of any such enactment[7];

(3)   grant either party possession or use of furniture or other contents of the dwelling house[8];

(4)   order either party to take reasonable care of any furniture or other contents of the dwelling house[9];

(5)   order either party to take reasonable steps to keep the dwelling house and any furniture or other contents secure[10].

Such an order ceases to have effect when the occupation order to which it relates ceases to have effect[11].

1   As to the meaning of 'occupation order' see PARA 289. As to the provisions that may be included in an order see PARA 293; as to the matters to which the court must have regard see PARA 295.
2   Ie an occupation order under the Family Law Act 1996 s 33: see PARAS 292–293.
3   As to the meaning of 'court' see PARA 958.
4   As to the meaning of 'dwelling house' see PARA 285 note 2.
5   As to the meaning of 'mortgage payments' see PARA 285 note 9.
6   Family Law Act 1996 s 40(1)(a). Section 40 confers no power on a court to commit a defaulter to prison for non-payment: *Nwogbe v Nwogbe* [2000] 3 FCR 345, [2000] 2 FLR 744, CA.
7   Family Law Act 1996 s 40(1)(b).
8   Family Law Act 1996 s 40(1)(c).
9   Family Law Act 1996 s 40(1)(d).
10 Family Law Act 1996 s 40(1)(e).
11 Family Law Act 1996 s 40(3).

295.   Matters to which the court must have regard.   In deciding whether so to exercise its powers with regard to the making of an occupation order[1] and, if so, in what manner, the court[2] must have regard to all the circumstances including:

(1)   the housing needs and housing resources of each of the parties and of any relevant child[3];

(2)   the financial resources of each of the parties[4];

(3)   the likely effect of any order, or of any decision by the court not to exercise such powers, on the health[5], safety or well-being of the parties and of any relevant child[6]; and

(4)   the conduct of the parties in relation to each other and otherwise[7].

If it appears to the court that the applicant or any relevant child is likely to suffer significant harm[8] attributable to conduct of the respondent[9] if such an order containing one or more of the applicable provisions[10] is not made, the court must make the order unless it appears to it that:

(a)   the respondent or any relevant child is likely to suffer significant harm if the order is made[11]; and

(b)   the harm likely to be suffered by the respondent or child in that event is as great as, or greater than, the harm attributable to conduct of the respondent which is likely to be suffered by the applicant or child if the order is not made[12].

In deciding whether and, if so, how to exercise its additional powers[13], the court must have regard to all the circumstances of the case including:

(i)   the financial needs and financial resources of the parties[14]; and

(ii)   the financial obligations which they have, or are likely to have in the foreseeable future, including financial obligations to each other and to any relevant child[15].

A court considering whether to make an occupation order must also consider whether to make a non-molestation order[16].

1   Ie the powers conferred by the Family Law Act 1996 s 33(3) (see PARA 293). As to the meaning of 'occupation order' see PARA 289; as to the making of an order see PARA 292. As to the effect of an order where the home rights are a charge on the dwelling house see PARA 296.

2   As to the meaning of 'court' see PARA 958.

3   Family Law Act 1996 s 33(6)(a). As to the meaning of 'relevant child' see PARA 290 note 5; as to the meaning of 'child' see PARA 290 note 4.

4   Family Law Act 1996 s 33(6)(b).

5   As to the meaning of 'health' see PARA 290 note 4.

6   Family Law Act 1996 s 33(6)(c).

7   Family Law Act 1996 s 33(6)(d).

8   As to the meanings of 'harm' and 'significant harm' see PARA 290 note 4.

9   The correct approach to the test laid down in the Family Law Act 1996 s 33(7) (see the text and notes 11–12) is to assess the effect of the conduct on the applicant or any relevant child rather than to concentrate on the intention of the respondent: *G v G (occupation order)* [2000] 3 FCR 53, [2000] 2 FLR 36, CA.

10   Ie the provisions included in the Family Law Act 1996 s 33(3) (see PARA 293).

11   Family Law Act 1996 s 33(7)(a).

12   Family Law Act 1996 s 33(7)(b).

13   As to these see PARA 294.

14   Family Law Act 1996 s 40(2)(a).

15   Family Law Act 1996 s 40(2)(b).

16   Ie must also consider whether to exercise the power conferred by the Family Law Act 1996 s 42(2)(b) (see PARA 717): s 42(4A) (added by the Domestic Violence, Crime and Victims Act 2004 Sch 10 para 36).

296.   Effect of order where rights are charge on dwelling house.   If a spouse or civil partner's home rights[1] are a charge on the estate or interest of the other spouse or civil partner or of trustees for the other spouse or civil partner, an occupation order[2] against the other spouse or civil partner has, except so far as a contrary intention appears, the same effect against persons deriving title under the other spouse or civil partner or under the trustees and affected by the charge[3].

1   As to the meaning of 'home rights' see PARA 285.

2   Ie an order under the Family Law Act 1996 s 33: see PARAS 292–295. As to the meaning of 'occupation order' see PARA 289.

3   Family Law Act 1996 s 34(1)(a) (s 34(1) amended by the Civil Partnership Act 2004 Sch 9
     para 5). Sections 30(3)–(6), 33(1), (3), (4), (10) (see PARAS 285, 292–293) apply in relation to
     any person deriving title under the other spouse or civil partner or under the trustees and
     affected by the charge as they apply in relation to the other spouse or civil partner: s 34(1)(b) (as
     so amended). The court may make an order under s 33 by virtue of s 34(1)(b) if it considers that
     in all the circumstances it is just and reasonable to do so: s 34(2).

B.   ONE FORMER SPOUSE OR CIVIL PARTNER WITH NO EXISTING RIGHT TO OCCUPY

297.   Right to apply for an occupation order. If:

(1)   one former spouse or civil partner is entitled to occupy a dwelling
       house[1] by virtue of a beneficial estate or interest or contract, or by
       virtue of any enactment giving him or her the right to remain in
       occupation[2];

(2)   the other former spouse or civil partner is not so entitled[3]; and

(3)   the dwelling house was at any time their family home[4] or was at any
       time intended by them to be their family home[5],

the former spouse or civil partner not so entitled may apply to the court[6] for an
occupation order[7] against the other former spouse or civil partner (the
'respondent')[8].

An order may not be so made after the death of either of the former spouses
or civil partners and ceases to have effect on the death of either of them[9]; and it
must be limited so as to have effect for a specified period not exceeding six
months, but may be extended on one or more occasions for a further specified
period not exceeding six months[10].

1   As to the meaning of 'dwelling house' see PARA 285 note 2.
2   Family Law Act 1996 s 35(1)(a) (s 35(1)(a), (b), (2), (9), (11), (12) amended, s 35(1)(c), (13)(a),
     (b) substituted, by the Civil Partnership Act 2004 Sch 9 para 6). A former spouse or civil partner
     who has an equitable interest in the dwelling house or in the proceeds of sale of the dwelling
     house but in whom there is not vested, whether solely or as joint tenant, a legal estate in fee
     simple or a legal term of years absolute in the dwelling house is to be treated (but only for the
     purpose of determining whether he or she is eligible to apply under s 35) as not being entitled to
     occupy the dwelling house by virtue of that interest: s 35(11) (as so amended). This does not
     prejudice any right of such a former spouse or civil partner to apply for an order under s 33 (see
     PARA 292): s 35(12) (as so amended).
3   Family Law Act 1996 s 35(1)(b) (as amended: see note 2).
4   As to the test for whether a property is a family home see PARA 285 note 2.
5   Family Law Act 1996 s 35(1)(c) (as substituted: see note 2).
6   As to the meaning of 'court' see PARA 958.
7   As to the meaning of 'occupation order' see PARA 289. As to the provisions that may be included
     in an order see PARAS 298, 299; as to the matters to which the court must have regard see PARA
     300.
8   Family Law Act 1996 s 35(2) (as amended: see note 2). As to appeals against the making of any
     such order by a magistrates' court or any refusal to make such an order see s 61; and PARA 308.
     As to variation and discharge see PARA 309. As to enforcement and arrest see PARA 998 et seq.
     So long as an order under s 35 remains in force, s 30(3)–(6) (see PARA 285) applies in relation to
     the applicant as if he or she were the person entitled to occupy the dwelling house by virtue of
     s 30 and as if the respondent were the person entitled as mentioned in s 30(1)(a) (see PARA 285):
     s 35(13)(a), (b) (as so substituted).
9   Family Law Act 1996 s 35(9) (as amended: see note 2). As to the provisions that must or may be
     included in such an order see PARA 293; and as to the additional provisions that may be included
     in such an order see PARA 294.
10   Family Law Act 1996 s 35(10).

298.   Provisions that must or may be included in an order. If the applicant for
an occupation order[1] is in occupation, the order must contain provision giving
the applicant the right not to be evicted or excluded from the dwelling house[2] or

any part of it by the respondent[3] for the period specified in the order and prohibiting the respondent from evicting or excluding the applicant during that period[4]. If the applicant is not in occupation, an order must contain provision giving the applicant the right to enter into and occupy the dwelling house for the period specified in the order and requiring the respondent to permit the exercise of that right[5]. An order may also:

(1)   regulate the occupation of the dwelling house by either or both of the parties[6];

(2)   prohibit, suspend or restrict the exercise by the respondent of the right to occupy the dwelling house[7];

(3)   require the respondent to leave the dwelling house or part of the dwelling house[8]; or

(4)   exclude the respondent from a defined area in which the dwelling house is included[9].

1   Ie an order under the Family Law Act 1996 s 35: see PARA 297. As to the meaning of 'occupation order' see PARA 289. As to the matters to which the court must have regard see PARA 300.
2   As to the meaning of 'dwelling house' see PARA 285 note 2.
3   As to the meaning of 'respondent' see PARA 297.
4   Family Law Act 1996 s 35(3). As to the additional provisions that may be included in such an order see PARA 294.
5   Family Law Act 1996 s 35(4).
6   Family Law Act 1996 s 35(5)(a).
7   Family Law Act 1996 s 35(5)(b).
8   Family Law Act 1996 s 35(5)(c).
9   Family Law Act 1996 s 35(5)(d).

299. Additional obligations etc which may be imposed. On, or at any time after, making an occupation order[1] where the applicant is a former spouse or civil partner with no existing right to occupy[2] the court[3] may:

(1)   impose on either party obligations as to the repair and maintenance of the dwelling house[4] or the discharge of rent, mortgage payments[5] or other outgoings affecting the dwelling house[6];

(2)   order a party occupying the dwelling house or any part of it, including a party who is entitled to do so by virtue of a beneficial estate or interest or contract or by virtue of any enactment giving that party the right to remain in occupation, to make periodical payments to the other party in respect of the accommodation, if the other party would, but for the order, be entitled to occupy the dwelling house by virtue of a beneficial estate or interest or contract or by virtue of any such enactment[7];

(3)   grant either party possession or use of furniture or other contents of the dwelling house[8];

(4)   order either party to take reasonable care of any furniture or other contents of the dwelling house[9];

(5)   order either party to take reasonable steps to keep the dwelling house and any furniture or other contents secure[10].

Such an order ceases to have effect when the occupation order to which it relates ceases to have effect[11].

1   As to the meaning of 'occupation order' see PARA 289. As to the provisions that may be included in an order see PARA 298; as to the matters to which the court must have regard see PARA 300.
2   Ie an occupation order under the Family Law Act 1996 s 35: see PARAS 297–298.
3   As to the meaning of 'court' see PARA 958.
4   As to the meaning of 'dwelling house' see PARA 285 note 2.

5   As to the meaning of 'mortgage payments' see PARA 285 note 9.
6   Family Law Act 1996 s 40(1)(a). Section 40 confers no power on a court to commit a defaulter to prison for non-payment: *Nwogbe v Nwogbe* [2000] 3 FCR 345, [2000] 2 FLR 744, CA.
7   Family Law Act 1996 s 40(1)(b).
8   Family Law Act 1996 s 40(1)(c).
9   Family Law Act 1996 s 40(1)(d).
10 Family Law Act 1996 s 40(1)(e).
11 Family Law Act 1996 s 40(3).

300.   Matters to which the court must have regard.   In deciding whether to make an occupation order[1] and, if so, in what manner, the court[2] must have regard to all the circumstances including:

(1)   the housing needs and housing resources of each of the parties and of any relevant child[3];

(2)   the financial resources of each of the parties[4];

(3)   the likely effect of any order, or of any decision by the court not to exercise its powers[5], on the health[6], safety or well-being of the parties and of any relevant child[7];

(4)   the conduct of the parties in relation to each other and otherwise[8];

(5)   the length of time that has elapsed since the parties ceased to live together[9];

(6)   the length of time that has elapsed since the marriage or civil partnership was dissolved or annulled[10]; and

(7)   the existence of any pending proceedings between the parties for a property adjustment order[11], an order for financial relief against parents[12] or relating to the legal or beneficial ownership of the dwelling house[13].

In deciding whether to exercise its power to regulate the occupation of the dwelling house, to prohibit, suspend or restrict the exercise of a right to occupy, to require the vacation of the dwelling house or a part thereof[14] and, if so, in what manner, the court must have regard to all the circumstances including the matters mentioned in heads (1) to (5) above[15].

If the court decides to make an occupation order[16] and it appears to it that, if the order does not include a relevant provision, the applicant or any relevant child is likely to suffer significant harm[17] attributable to conduct of the respondent[18], the court must include the relevant provision in the order unless it appears to the court that:

(a)   the respondent or any relevant child is likely to suffer significant harm if the provision is included in the order[19]; and

(b)   the harm likely to be suffered by the respondent or child in that event is as great as or greater than the harm attributable to conduct of the respondent which is likely to be suffered by the applicant or child if the provision is not included[20].

In deciding whether and, if so, how to exercise its additional powers[21], the court must have regard to all the circumstances of the case including:

(i)   the financial needs and financial resources of the parties[22]; and

(ii)   the financial obligations which they have, or are likely to have in the foreseeable future, including financial obligations to each other and to any relevant child[23].

1   Ie an order under the Family Law Act 1996 s 35 (see PARA 297) containing provision of the kind referred to in s 35(3) or (4) (see PARA 298). As to the meaning of 'occupation order' see PARA 289; as to the making of an order see PARA 297.
2   As to the meaning of 'court' see PARA 958.

3   Family Law Act 1996 s 35(6)(a). As to the meaning of 'relevant child' see PARA 290 note 5; as to
     the meaning of 'child' see PARA 290 note 4. As to the circumstances set out in s 35(6) see *S v F
     (occupation order)* [2000] 3 FCR 365, [2000] 1 FLR 255.
4   Family Law Act 1996 s 35(6)(b).
5   Ie under the Family Law Act 1996 s 35(3) or (4) (see PARA 298).
6   As to the meaning of 'health' see PARA 290 note 4.
7   Family Law Act 1996 s 35(6)(c).
8   Family Law Act 1996 s 35(6)(d).
9   Family Law Act 1996 s 35(6)(e).
10   Family Law Act 1996 s 35(6)(f) (s 35(6)(f), (g) amended by the Civil Partnership Act 2004 Sch 9
     para 6).
11   Ie an order under the Matrimonial Causes Act 1973 s 24 or the Civil Partnership Act 2004 Sch 5
     Pt 2 (see PARA 499 et seq).
12   Ie an order under the Children Act 1989 Sch 1 para 1(2)(d) or (e) (see CHILDREN AND YOUNG
     PERSONS vol 5(3) (2008 Reissue) PARA 539.
13   Family Law Act 1996 s 35(6)(g) (as amended: see note 10).
14   Ie in deciding whether to exercise the court's power to include one or more of the provisions
     referred to in the Family Law Act 1996 s 35(5) (see PARA 298).
15   Family Law Act 1996 s 35(7).
16   See note 1.
17   As to the meanings of 'harm' and 'significant harm' see PARA 290 note 4.
18   Cf PARA 295 note 9.
19   Family Law Act 1996 s 35(8)(a).
20   Family Law Act 1996 s 35(8)(b).
21   As to these see PARA 299.
22   Family Law Act 1996 s 40(2)(a).
23   Family Law Act 1996 s 40(2)(b).

C. ONE COHABITANT OR FORMER COHABITANT WITH NO EXISTING RIGHT TO OCCUPY

301.   Right to apply for an occupation order.   If:

(1)   one cohabitant[1] or former cohabitant[2] is entitled to occupy a dwelling
       house[3] by virtue of a beneficial estate or interest or contract or by virtue
       of any enactment giving that cohabitant the right to remain in
       occupation[4];

(2)   the other cohabitant or former cohabitant is not so entitled[5]; and

(3)   that dwelling house is the home in which they cohabit or a home in
       which they at any time cohabited or intended so to cohabit[6],

the cohabitant or former cohabitant not so entitled may apply to the court[7] for
an occupation order[8] against the other cohabitant or former cohabitant (the
'respondent')[9].

Such an order may not be made after the death of either of the parties and
ceases to have effect on the death of either of them[10]; and it must be limited so as
to have effect for a specified period not exceeding six months, but may be
extended on one occasion for a further specified period not exceeding six
months[11].

1   As to the meanings of 'cohabitants' and 'cohabit' see PARA 292 note 5.
2   As to the meaning of 'former cohabitants' see PARA 292 note 5.
3   As to the meaning of 'dwelling house' see PARA 285 note 2.
4   Family Law Act 1996 s 36(1)(a). A person who has an equitable interest in the dwelling house
     or in the proceeds of sale of the dwelling house but in whom there is not vested, whether solely
     or as joint tenant, a legal estate in fee simple or a legal term of years absolute in the dwelling
     house is to be treated (but only for the purpose of determining whether that person is eligible to
     apply under s 36) as not being entitled to occupy the dwelling house by virtue of that interest
     (s 36(11)), although this does not prejudice any right of such a person to apply for an order
     under s 33 (see PARA 292) (s 36(12)).
5   Family Law Act 1996 s 36(1)(b).

6   Family Law Act 1996 s 36(1)(c) (amended by the Domestic Violence, Crime and Victims Act 2004 Sch 10 para 34).
7   As to the meaning of 'court' see PARA 958.
8   As to the meaning of 'occupation order' see PARA 289. As to the provisions that may be included in an order see PARAS 302, 303; as to the matters to which the court must have regard see PARA 304.
9   Family Law Act 1996 s 36(2). As to appeals against the making of any such order by a magistrates' court or any refusal to make such an order see PARA 308. As to variation and discharge see PARA 309. As to enforcement and arrest see PARA 988 et seq. Although an order under s 36 is not intended to determine property rights, it is not improper for an applicant to seek such an order for the purpose of obtaining an order for the transfer of a tenancy, provided that the conditions of s 36 are satisfied: *Gay v Sheeran* [1999] 3 All ER 795 at 807, 808, [2000] 1 WLR 673 at 686, CA per Peter Gibson LJ.
10   Family Law Act 1996 s 36(9). So long as an order under s 36 remains in force, the provisions of s 30(3)–(6) (see PARA 285) apply in relation to the applicant as if he were the person entitled to occupy the dwelling house by virtue of s 30 and as if the respondent were the person entitled as mentioned in s 30(1)(a) (see PARA 285): s 36(13) (amended by the Civil Partnership Act 2004 Sch 9 para 7).
11   Family Law Act 1996 s 36(10).

302. Provisions that must or may be included in an order. If the applicant is in occupation, an occupation order[1] must contain provision giving the applicant the right not to be evicted or excluded from the dwelling house[2] or any part of it by the respondent[3] for the period specified in the order and prohibiting the respondent from evicting or excluding the applicant during that period[4]. If the applicant is not in occupation, an order must contain provision giving the applicant the right to enter into and occupy the dwelling house for the period specified in the order and requiring the respondent to permit the exercise of that right[5].

An order may also:

(1)   regulate the occupation of the dwelling house by either or both of the parties[6];

(2)   prohibit, suspend or restrict the exercise by the respondent of the right to occupy the dwelling house[7];

(3)   require the respondent to leave the dwelling house or part of the dwelling house[8]; or

(4)   exclude the respondent from a defined area in which the dwelling house is included[9].

1   Ie an order under the Family Law Act 1996 s 36: see PARA 301. As to the meaning of 'occupation order' see PARA 289. As to the matters to which the court must have regard see PARA 304.
2   As to the meaning of 'dwelling house' see PARA 285 note 2.
3   As to the meaning of 'respondent' see PARA 301.
4   Family Law Act 1996 s 36(3). As to the additional provisions that may be included in such an order see PARA 303.
5   Family Law Act 1996 s 36(4).
6   Family Law Act 1996 s 36(5)(a).
7   Family Law Act 1996 s 36(5)(b).
8   Family Law Act 1996 s 36(5)(c).
9   Family Law Act 1996 s 36(5)(d).

303. Additional obligations etc which may be imposed. On, or at any time after, making an occupation order[1] where the applicant is a cohabitant or former cohabitant with no existing right to occupy[2], the court[3] may:

(1)   impose on either party obligations as to the repair and maintenance of

the dwelling house[4] or the discharge of rent, mortgage payments[5] or other outgoings affecting the dwelling house[6];

(2)　order a party occupying the dwelling house or any part of it, including a party who is entitled to do so by virtue of a beneficial estate or interest or contract or by virtue of any enactment giving that party the right to remain in occupation, to make periodical payments to the other party in respect of the accommodation, if the other party would, but for the order, be entitled to occupy the dwelling house by virtue of a beneficial estate or interest or contract or by virtue of any such enactment[7];

(3)　grant either party possession or use of furniture or other contents of the dwelling house[8];

(4)　order either party to take reasonable care of any furniture or other contents of the dwelling house[9];

(5)　order either party to take reasonable steps to keep the dwelling house and any furniture or other contents secure[10].

Such an order ceases to have effect when the occupation order to which it relates ceases to have effect[11].

1　As to the meaning of 'occupation order' see PARA 289. As to the provisions that may be included in an order see PARA 302; as to the matters to which the court must have regard see PARA 304.
2　Ie an occupation order under the Family Law Act 1996 s 36: see PARAS 301–302.
3　As to the meaning of 'court' see PARA 958.
4　As to the meaning of 'dwelling house' see PARA 285 note 2.
5　As to the meaning of 'mortgage payments' see PARA 285 note 9.
6　Family Law Act 1996 s 40(1)(a). Section 40 confers no power on a court to commit a defaulter to prison for non-payment: *Nwogbe v Nwogbe* [2000] 3 FCR 345, [2000] 2 FLR 744, CA.
7　Family Law Act 1996 s 40(1)(b).
8　Family Law Act 1996 s 40(1)(c).
9　Family Law Act 1996 s 40(1)(d).
10　Family Law Act 1996 s 40(1)(e).
11　Family Law Act 1996 s 40(3).

304.　Matters to which the court is to have regard. In deciding whether to make an occupation order[1] and, if so, in what manner, the court[2] must have regard to all the circumstances including:

(1)　the housing needs and housing resources of each of the parties and of any relevant child[3];

(2)　the financial resources of each of the parties[4];

(3)　the likely effect of any order, or of any decision by the court not to exercise its powers[5], on the health[6], safety or well-being of the parties and of any relevant child[7];

(4)　the conduct of the parties in relation to each other and otherwise[8];

(5)　the nature of the parties' relationship and in particular the level of commitment involved in it[9];

(6)　the length of time during which they have cohabited[10];

(7)　whether there are or have been any children who are children of both parties or for whom both parties have or have had parental responsibility[11];

(8)　the length of time that has elapsed since the parties ceased to live together[12]; and

(9)　the existence of any pending proceedings between the parties for an order for financial relief against parents[13] or relating to the legal or beneficial ownership of the dwelling house[14].

In deciding whether to exercise its power to regulate the occupation of the dwelling house, to prohibit, suspend or restrict the exercise of a right to occupy, to require the vacation of the dwelling house or a part thereof[15] and, if so, in what manner, the court must have regard to all the circumstances including the matters mentioned in heads (1) to (4) above[16] and to the questions of whether the applicant or any relevant child is likely to suffer significant harm[17] attributable to conduct of the respondent[18] if the relevant provision is not included in the order and whether the harm likely to be suffered by the respondent or child if the provision is included is as great as or greater than the harm attributable to conduct of the respondent which is likely to be suffered by the applicant or child if the provision is not included[19].

In deciding whether and, if so, how to exercise its additional powers[20], the court must have regard to all the circumstances of the case including:

(a) the financial needs and financial resources of the parties[21]; and

(b) the financial obligations which they have, or are likely to have in the foreseeable future, including financial obligations to each other and to any relevant child[22].

1 Ie an order under the Family Law Act 1996 s 36 (see PARA 301) containing provision of the kind referred to in s 36(3) or (4) (see PARA 302). As to the meaning of 'occupation order' see PARA 289; as to the making of an order see PARA 301.
2 As to the meaning of 'court' see PARA 958.
3 Family Law Act 1996 s 36(6)(a). As to the meaning of 'relevant child' see PARA 290 note 5; as to the meaning of 'child' see PARA 290 note 4. As to the circumstances set out in s 36(6) see *S v F (occupation order)* [2000] 3 FCR 365, [2000] 1 FLR 255.
4 Family Law Act 1996 s 36(6)(b).
5 Ie under the Family Law Act 1996 s 36(3) or (4) (see PARA 302).
6 As to the meaning of 'health' see PARA 290 note 4.
7 Family Law Act 1996 s 36(6)(c).
8 Family Law Act 1996 s 36(6)(d).
9 Family Law Act 1996 s 36(6)(e) (s 36(6)(e), (f) amended by the Domestic Violence, Crime and Victims Act 2004 s 2(2), Sch 10 para 34).
10 Family Law Act 1996 s 36(6)(f) (as amended: see note 9). As to the meaning of 'cohabited' see PARA 292 note 5.
11 Family Law Act 1996 s 36(6)(g).
12 Family Law Act 1996 s 36(6)(h).
13 Ie an order under the Children Act 1989 Sch 1 para 1(2)(d) or (e) (see CHILDREN AND YOUNG PERSONS vol 5(3) (2008 Reissue) PARA 539.
14 Family Law Act 1996 s 36(6)(i).
15 Ie in deciding whether to exercise the court's power to include one or more of the provisions referred to in the Family Law Act 1996 s 36(5) (see PARA 302).
16 Family Law Act 1996 s 36(7).
17 As to the meanings of 'harm' and 'significant harm' see PARA 290 note 4.
18 Cf PARA 295 note 9.
19 Family Law Act 1996 s 36(8).
20 As to these see PARA 303.
21 Family Law Act 1996 s 40(2)(a).
22 Family Law Act 1996 s 40(2)(b).

D. NEITHER SPOUSE, CIVIL PARTNER, COHABITANT OR FORMER COHABITANT ENTITLED TO OCCUPY

305. Right to apply for an occupation order. If:

(1) one spouse, former spouse, civil partner, former civil partner, cohabitant[1] or former cohabitant and the other spouse, former spouse, civil partner, former civil partner, cohabitant or former cohabitant

occupy a dwelling house[2] which is or was the family home[3] or, in the case of cohabitants and former cohabitants, is the home in which they cohabit[4]; but

(2)   neither of them is entitled to remain in occupation by virtue of a beneficial estate or interest or contract or by virtue of any enactment giving them the right to remain in occupation[5],

either of the parties may apply to the court[6] for an occupation order[7] against the other[8].

Such an order must be limited so as to have effect for a specified period not exceeding six months, but may be extended on one or more occasions for a further specified period not exceeding six months[9].

1   As to the meanings of 'cohabitant' and 'cohabit' see PARA 292 note 5.
2   As to the meaning of 'dwelling house' see PARA 285 note 2.
3   As to the test for whether a property is a family home see PARA 285 note 2.
4   Family Law Act 1996 ss 37(1)(a), (1A)(a), 38(1)(a) (s 37(1A) added by the Civil Partnership Act 2004 Sch 9 para 8; Family Law Act 1996 s 38(1)(a) amended by the Domestic Violence, Crime and Victims Act 2004 Sch 10 para 35).
5   Family Law Act 1996 ss 37(1)(b), (1A)(b), 38(1)(b).
6   As to the meaning of 'court' see PARA 958.
7   As to the meaning of 'occupation order' see PARA 289. As to the provisions that may be included in an order see PARA 306; as to the matters to which the court must have regard see PARA 307.
8   Family Law Act 1996 ss 37(2), 38(2). As to appeals against the making of any such order by a magistrates' court or any refusal to make such an order see PARA 308. As to variation and discharge see PARA 309. As to enforcement and arrest see PARA 988 et seq.
9   Family Law Act 1996 ss 37(5), 38(6).

306.   Provisions that may be included in an order.   An occupation order[1] may:

(1)   require the respondent to permit the applicant to enter and remain in the dwelling house[2] or part of the dwelling house[3];

(2)   regulate the occupation of the dwelling house by either or both of the parties[4];

(3)   require the respondent to leave the dwelling house or part of the dwelling house[5]; or

(4)   exclude the respondent from a defined area in which the dwelling house is included[6].

1   Ie an order under the Family Law Act 1996 s 37 or s 38: see PARA 305. As to the meaning of 'occupation order' see PARA 289. As to the matters to which the court must have regard see PARA 307.
2   As to the meaning of 'dwelling house' see PARA 285 note 2.
3   Family Law Act 1996 ss 37(3)(a), 38(3)(a).
4   Family Law Act 1996 ss 37(3)(b), 38(3)(b) (s 37(3)(b) amended by the Civil Partnership Act 2004 Sch 9 para 8).
5   Family Law Act 1996 ss 37(3)(c), 38(3)(c).
6   Family Law Act 1996 ss 37(3)(d), 38(3)(d).

307.   Matters to which the court must have regard.   In deciding whether to exercise its powers with regard to the making of an occupation order where neither spouse, civil partner or cohabitant, or former spouse, civil partner or cohabitant, is entitled to occupy the dwelling house[1] and, if so, in what manner, the court[2] must have regard to all the circumstances including:

(1)   the housing needs and housing resources of each of the parties and of any relevant child[3];

(2)   the financial resources of each of the parties[4];

(3)   the likely effect of any order, or of any decision by the court not to exercise such powers, on the health[5], safety or well-being of the parties and of any relevant child[6];

(4)   the conduct of the parties in relation to each other and otherwise[7]; and

(5)   in the case of cohabitants or former cohabitants, the questions of whether the applicant or any relevant child is likely to suffer significant harm[8] attributable to conduct of the respondent if the relevant provision is not included in the order and whether the harm likely to be suffered by the respondent or child if the provision is included is as great as or greater than the harm attributable to conduct of the respondent which is likely to be suffered by the applicant or child if the provision is not included[9].

In deciding whether to exercise its powers with regard to the making of an occupation order relating to spouses or civil partners or former spouses or civil partners[10], if it appears to the court that the applicant or any relevant child is likely to suffer significant harm attributable to conduct of the respondent[11] if such an order containing one or more of the applicable provisions[12] is not made, the court must make the order unless it appears to it that:

(a)   the respondent or any relevant child is likely to suffer significant harm if the order is made[13]; and

(b)   the harm likely to be suffered by the respondent or child in that event is as great as, or greater than, the harm attributable to conduct of the respondent which is likely to be suffered by the applicant or child if the order is not made[14].

1   Ie the powers conferred by the Family Law Act 1996 ss 37(3), 38(3) (see PARA 306). As to the meaning of 'occupation order' see PARA 289; as to the making of an order see PARA 305.

2   As to the meaning of 'court' see PARA 958.

3   Family Law Act 1996 ss 33(6)(a), 37(4), 38(4)(a). As to the meaning of 'relevant child' see PARA 290 note 5; as to the meaning of 'child' see PARA 290 note 4.

4   Family Law Act 1996 ss 33(6)(b), 38(4)(b).

5   As to the meaning of 'health' see PARA 290 note 4.

6   Family Law Act 1996 ss 33(6)(c), 38(4)(c).

7   Family Law Act 1996 ss 33(6)(d), 38(4)(d).

8   As to the meanings of 'harm' and 'significant harm' see PARA 290 note 4.

9   Family Law Act 1996 s 38(4)(e), (5).

10   See note 1.

11   The correct approach to the test laid down in the Family Law Act 1996 s 33(7) (see the text and notes 13–14) is to assess the effect of the conduct on the applicant or any relevant child rather than to concentrate on the intention of the respondent: *G v G (occupation order)* [2000] 3 FCR 53, [2000] 2 FLR 36, CA.

12   Ie the provisions included in the Family Law Act 1996 s 37(3) (see PARA 306).

13   Family Law Act 1996 s 33(7)(a).

14   Family Law Act 1996 s 33(7)(b).

(iii) Appeals

308. Appeals. An appeal lies to the High Court against the making by a magistrates' court of an occupation order[1] or any refusal by a magistrates' court to make such an order, but no appeal lies against any exercise by a magistrates' court of the power to decline jurisdiction[2] if it considers that the case can more conveniently be dealt with by another court[3]. On such an appeal the High Court may make such orders as may be necessary to give effect to its determination of the appeal[4]; and, where an order is so made, the High Court may also make such incidental or consequential orders as appear to it to be just[5]. Any order of the

High Court made on such an appeal, other than one directing that an application be reheard by a magistrates' court, is to be treated, for the purposes of the enforcement of the order and of any power to vary, revive or discharge orders[6], as if it were an order of the magistrates' court from which the appeal was brought and not an order of the High Court[7].

1   As to the meaning of 'occupation order' see PARA 289. As to the jurisdiction of courts for these purposes see PARA 958.
2   Ie under the Family Law Act 1996 s 59(2): see PARA 960.
3   Family Law Act 1996 s 61(1). See further PARA 986.
4   Family Law Act 1996 s 61(2).
5   Family Law Act 1996 s 61(3).
6   As to variation and discharge see PARA 309.
7   Family Law Act 1996 s 61(4).

(iv) Variation and Discharge

309. Power to vary or discharge. An occupation order[1] may be varied or discharged by the court[2] on an application by the respondent or the person on whose application the order was made[3]. If a person's home rights[4] are[5] a charge on the estate or interest of another person or of trustees for the other person, an occupation order in favour of a person who has an estate or interest or home rights[6] against the other person may also be varied or discharged by the court on an application by any person deriving title under the other person or under the trustees and affected by the charge[7].

Proceedings to extend, vary or discharge an occupation order, or proceedings the determination of which may have the effect of varying or discharging such an order, must be made to the court which made the order[8]; but a court may[9] transfer proceedings so made to any other court[10].

1   As to the meaning of 'occupation order' see PARA 289.
2   As to the meaning of 'court' see PARA 958.
3   Family Law Act 1996 s 49(1). An application to vary, extend or discharge an order must be made in accordance with the Family Proceedings Rules 1991, SI 1991/1247, Appendix 1, Form FL403 (added by SI 1997/1893); and the Family Proceedings Rules 1991, SI 1991/1247, r 3.9 (see PARA 975) applies to the hearing of such an application: r 3.9(8) (substituted by SI 1997/1893).

    Where an order is made varying or discharging the relevant provisions of an occupation order the proper officer or the designated officer for the court must immediately inform the officer who received a copy of the form under the Family Proceedings Rules 1991, SI 1991/1247, r 3.9A(1A) (see PARA 975) or the Family Proceedings Courts (Matrimonial Proceedings etc) Rules 1991, SI 1991/1991, r 20(1A) (see PARA 978) and, if the applicant's address has changed, the officer for the time being in charge of the police station for the new address, and deliver a copy of the order to any officer so informed: Family Proceedings Rules 1991, SI 1991/1247, r 3.9A(2) (added by SI 1997/1893; amended by SI 2007/1622); Family Proceedings Courts (Matrimonial Proceedings etc) Rules 1991, SI 1991/1991, r 20(2) (r 20 substituted by SI 1997/1894; Family Proceedings Courts (Matrimonial Proceedings etc) Rules 1991, SI 1991/1991, r 20(2) amended by SI 2005/617; SI 2007/1628). As to the meaning of 'proper officer' see PARA 461 note 5.
4   As to the meaning of 'home rights' see PARA 285.
5   Ie under the Family Law Act 1996 s 31 (see PARA 286; and LAND CHARGES vol 26 (2004 Reissue) PARA 638).
6   Ie under the Family Law Act 1996 s 33 (see PARA 292 et seq).
7   Family Law Act 1996 s 49(3) (amended by the Civil Partnership Act 2004 Sch 9 para 11).
8   Family Law Act 1996 (Part IV) (Allocation of Proceedings) Order 1997, SI 1997/1896, art 5(1).
9   Ie in accordance with the Family Law Act 1996 (Part IV) (Allocation of Proceedings) Order 1997, SI 1997/1896, arts 6–14: see PARA 964 et seq.
10 Family Law Act 1996 (Part IV) (Allocation of Proceedings) Order 1997, SI 1997/1896, art 5(2).

(4) TRANSFER OF TENANCY ORDERS

310. Cases in which the court may make an order. If one spouse or civil partner is entitled, either in his or her own right or jointly with the other spouse or civil partner, to occupy a dwelling house[1] by virtue of a relevant tenancy[2], the court[3] may make a transfer of tenancy order[4] either:

(1) on granting a decree of divorce, a decree of nullity of marriage or a decree of judicial separation or at any time thereafter (whether, in the case of a decree of divorce or nullity of marriage, before or after the decree is made absolute)[5]; or

(2) at any time when it has power to make a property adjustment order[6] with respect to the civil partnership[7];

however, if either spouse or civil partner remarries or forms a subsequent civil partnership[8] he or she will not be entitled to apply[9] for a transfer of tenancy order[10].

The court may also make a transfer of tenancy order if one cohabitant[11] is entitled, either in his own right or jointly with the other cohabitant, to occupy a dwelling house by virtue of a relevant tenancy and the cohabitants cease to cohabit[12]; the court must not, however, make the order unless the dwelling house is or was the family home[13] or, in the case of cohabitants, a home in which they cohabited[14].

If:

(a) a spouse or civil partner is entitled to occupy a dwelling house by virtue of a tenancy, the power to make a transfer of tenancy order does not affect the operation of the statutory provisions relating to the right to occupy the family home[15] in relation to the other spouse or civil partner's home rights[16];

(b) a spouse, civil partner or cohabitant is entitled to occupy a dwelling house by virtue of a tenancy, the court's powers to make a transfer of tenancy order are additional to the power[17] to make an occupation order[18].

The court may also make a transfer of tenancy order pursuant to an overseas divorce, dissolution, annulment or legal separation[19], on an application by one of the parties to the marriage or civil partnership, if one of the parties is entitled, either in his or her own right or jointly with the other party, to occupy a dwelling house[20] situated in England or Wales by virtue of a tenancy which is a relevant tenancy[21] for these purposes[22].

1   As to the meaning of 'dwelling house' see PARA 285 note 2.
2   Family Law Act 1996 Sch 7 para 2(1) (Sch 7 paras 2(1), 15 amended, Sch 7 paras 2(2), 13 substituted, Sch 7 para 4(aa) added, by the Civil Partnership Act 2004 Sch 9 para 16). For these purposes, by virtue of the Family Law Act 1996 Sch 7 para 1 (amended by SI 1997/74), 'relevant tenancy' means:
   (1)   a protected tenancy or statutory tenancy within the meaning of the Rent Act 1977 (see LANDLORD AND TENANT vol 27(2) (2006 Reissue) PARA 818 et seq);
   (2)   a statutory tenancy within the meaning of the Rent (Agriculture) Act 1976 (see LANDLORD AND TENANT vol 27(2) (2006 Reissue) PARA 1134 et seq);
   (3)   a secure tenancy within the meaning of the Housing Act 1985 s 79 (see LANDLORD AND TENANT vol 27(2) (2006 Reissue) PARA 1300);
   (4)   an assured tenancy or assured agricultural occupancy within the meaning of the Housing Act 1988 Pt I (ss 1–45) (see LANDLORD AND TENANT vol 27(2) (2006 Reissue) PARAS 1018, 1183 et seq); or
   (5)   an introductory tenancy within the meaning of the Housing Act 1996 Pt V Chapter I (ss 124–143) (see LANDLORD AND TENANT vol 27(2) (2006 Reissue) PARA 1286 et seq).
   'Tenancy' includes a subtenancy: Family Law Act 1996 Sch 7 para 1.

3   As to the meaning of 'court' see PARA 958. For these purposes, 'court' does not include a
     magistrates' court: Family Law Act 1996 Sch 7 para 1.
4   Ie an order under the Family Law Act 1996 Sch 7 Pt II (paras 6–9) (see PARA 312 et seq).
5   Family Law Act 1996 Sch 7 para 2(2)(a) (as substituted: see note 2). Rules of court may provide
     that an application for a transfer of tenancy order by reference to an order or decree may not,
     without the leave of the court by which that order was made or decree was granted, be made
     after the expiration of such period from the order or grant as may be prescribed by the rules:
     Sch 7 para 14(2).
6   Ie under the Civil Partnership Act 2004 Sch 5 Pt 2 (paras 6–9) (see PARA 499 et seq).
7   Family Law Act 1996 Sch 7 para 2(2)(b) (as substituted: see note 2). See note 5.
8   Ie after the grant of a decree dissolving or annulling a marriage or after the making of a nullity
     order: Family Law Act 1996 Sch 7 para 13(1), (2) (as substituted: see note 2). References to
     remarrying, marrying and forming a civil partnership include references to cases where the
     marriage or civil partnership is by law void or voidable: Sch 7 para 13(3) (as so substituted). As
     to void and voidable marriages and civil partnerships see PARA 326 et seq.
9   Ie by reference to the grant of the relevant decree or the making of the relevant order: Family
     Law Act 1996 Sch 7 para 13(1), (2) (as substituted: see note 2).
10   Family Law Act 1996 Sch 7 para 13(1), (2) (as substituted: see note 2).
11   As to the meanings of 'cohabitant' and 'cohabit' see PARA 292 note 5.
12   Family Law Act 1996 Sch 7 para 3 (Sch 7 paras 3, 4(b) amended by the Domestic Violence,
     Crime and Victims Act 2004 Sch 10 para 42); and see *Gay v Sheeran* [1999] 3 All ER 795,
     [2000] 1 WLR 673, CA.
13   Family Law Act 1996 Sch 7 para 4(a), (aa) (Sch 7 para 4(aa) as added: see note 2).
14   Family Law Act 1996 Sch 7 para 4(b) (as amended: see note 12).
15   Ie the Family Law Act 1996 s 30 (see PARA 285) and s 31 (see PARA 286; and LAND CHARGES
     vol 26 (2004 Reissue) PARA 638).
16   Family Law Act 1996 Sch 7 para 15(1) (as amended: see note 2).
17   Ie under the Family Law Act 1996 ss 33, 35, 36 (see PARAS 292–304).
18   Family Law Act 1996 Sch 7 para 15(2) (as amended: see note 2).
19   As to financial relief following an overseas divorce, dissolution, annulment or legal separation
     see PARA 530 et seq.
20   As to a 'dwelling house' for these purposes see PARA 285 note 2.
21   See note 2.
22   Matrimonial and Family Proceedings Act 1984 s 22(1), (2) (s 22 substituted by the Family Law
     Act 1996 Sch 8 para 52); Civil Partnership Act 2004 Sch 7 para 13. The provisions of the
     Family Law Act 1996 Sch 7 para 10 (see PARA 314), Sch 7 para 11 (see PARA 315) and Sch 7
     para 14(1) (see PARA 311) apply in relation to any order under the Matrimonial and Family
     Proceedings Act 1984 s 22 or the Civil Partnership Act 2004 Sch 7 para 13 as they apply to an
     order under the Family Law Act 1996 Sch 7 Pt II (paras 6–9): Matrimonial and Family
     Proceedings Act 1984 s 22(3) (as so substituted); Civil Partnership Act 2004 Sch 7 para 13.

311.   Matters to which the court must have regard.   In determining whether to
exercise its powers to make a transfer of tenancy order[1] and, if so, in what
manner, the court[2] must have regard to all the circumstances of the case
including (but not limited to[3]):
   (1)   the circumstances in which the tenancy[4] was granted to either or both of
          the spouses[5], civil partners[6] or cohabitants[7] or, as the case requires, the
          circumstances in which either or both of them became tenant under the
          tenancy[8];
   (2)   the housing needs and housing resources of each of the parties and of
          any relevant child[9];
   (3)   the financial resources of each of the parties[10];
   (4)   the likely effect of any order, or of any decision by the court not to
          exercise its powers, on the health[11], safety or well-being of the parties
          and of any relevant child[12]; and
   (5)   the suitability of the parties as tenants[13].
   Where the parties are cohabitants and only one of them is entitled to occupy
the dwelling house[14] by virtue of the relevant tenancy[15], the court must also have
regard to:

(a)   the nature of the parties' relationship and in particular the level of commitment involved in it[16];

(b)   the length of time during which they have cohabited[17];

(c)   whether there are or have been any children who are children of both parties or for whom both parties have or have had parental responsibility[18];

(d)   the length of time that has elapsed since the parties ceased to live together[19].

Provision is also made for giving the landlord of the dwelling house to which a transfer of tenancy order will relate an opportunity of being heard[20].

1   Ie under the Family Law Act 1996 Sch 7 Pt II (paras 6–9): see PARA 312 et seq.
2   As to the 'court' see PARA 310 note 3.
3   The matters to which the court may have regard are not limited to those specified by the Family Law Act 1996 Sch 7 para 5 (see the text and notes 4–19), since the court should look at the case in the round and have regard to all relevant circumstances: see *Lake v Lake* [2006] EWCA Civ 1250, [2007] 1 FLR 427, [2006] All ER (D) 297 (Jul).
4   As to the meaning of 'tenancy' see PARA 310 note 2.
5   For these purposes 'spouse' includes, where the context requires, a former spouse: Family Law Act 1996 Sch 7 para 1.
6   For these purposes 'civil partner' includes, where the context requires, a former civil partner: Family Law Act 1996 Sch 7 para 1 (definition 'civil partner' added, Sch 7 para 5(a) amended, by the Civil Partnership Act 2004 Sch 9 para 16).
7   As to the meanings of 'cohabitant' and 'cohabit' see PARA 292 note 5. For these purposes, 'cohabitant' includes, where the context requires, former cohabitant: Family Law Act 1996 Sch 7 para 1.
8   Family Law Act 1996 Sch 7 para 5(a) (as amended: see note 6).
9   Family Law Act 1996 s 33(6)(a), Sch 7 para 5(b). As to the meaning of 'relevant child' see PARA 290 note 5; as to the meaning of 'child' see PARA 290 note 4.
10   Family Law Act 1996 s 33(6)(b).
11   As to the meaning of 'health' see PARA 290 note 4.
12   Family Law Act 1996 s 33(6)(c).
13   Family Law Act 1996 Sch 7 para 5(c).
14   As to the meaning of 'dwelling house' see PARA 285 note 2.
15   As to the meaning of 'relevant tenancy' see PARA 310 note 2.
16   Family Law Act 1996 s 36(6)(e), Sch 7 para 5(b) (s 36(6)(e), (f) amended by the Domestic Violence, Crime and Victims Act 2004 s 2(2), Sch 10 para 34).
17   Family Law Act 1996 s 36(6)(f) (as amended: see note 16).
18   Family Law Act 1996 s 36(6)(g).
19   Family Law Act 1996 s 36(6)(h).
20   See the Family Law Act 1996 Sch 7 para 14(1); the Family Proceedings Act 1991, SI 1991/1247, r 3.8(12), (13); and PARA 974. For these purposes 'landlord' includes: (1) any person from time to time deriving title under the original landlord; and (2) in relation to any dwelling house, any person other than the tenant who is, or (but for the Rent Act 1977 Pt VII (ss 98–107) (see LANDLORD AND TENANT vol 27(2) (2006 Reissue) PARAS 942 et seq, 1002 et seq) or the Rent (Agriculture) Act 1976 Pt II (ss 6–19) (see LANDLORD AND TENANT vol 27(2) (2006 Reissue) PARA 1156 et seq)) would be, entitled to possession of the dwelling house: Family Law Act 1996 Sch 7 para 1.

312.   Protected, secure or assured tenancies or assured agricultural tenancies.
If a spouse[1], civil partner[2] or cohabitant[3] is entitled to occupy the dwelling house[4] by virtue of a protected tenancy[5], a secure tenancy[6], an assured tenancy or assured agricultural occupancy[7] or an introductory tenancy[8], the court[9] may by order direct that, as from such date as may be specified in the order, there is, by virtue of the order and without further assurance, to be transferred to, and vested in, the other spouse, civil partner or cohabitant:

(1)   the estate or interest which the spouse, civil partner or cohabitant so entitled had in the dwelling house immediately before that date by

virtue of the lease or agreement creating the tenancy[10] and any assignment of that lease or agreement, with all rights, privileges and appurtenances attaching to that estate or interest but subject to all covenants, obligations, liabilities and incumbrances to which it is subject[11]; and

(2)   where the spouse, civil partner or cohabitant so entitled is an assignee of such lease or agreement, the liability of that spouse, civil partner or cohabitant under any covenant of indemnity by the assignee express or implied in the assignment of the lease or agreement to that spouse, civil partner or cohabitant[12].

If an order is so made, any liability or obligation to which the spouse, civil partner or cohabitant so entitled is subject under any covenant having reference to the dwelling house in the lease or agreement, being a liability or obligation falling due to be discharged or performed on or after the date so specified, is not enforceable against that spouse, civil partner or cohabitant[13].

If the spouse, civil partner or cohabitant so entitled is a successor[14], his former spouse or civil partner or former cohabitant (or, in the case of judicial separation or a separation order, his spouse or civil partner) is deemed also to be[15] a successor[16].

1   As to the meaning of 'spouse' see PARA 311 note 5.
2   As to the meaning of 'civil partner' see PARA 311 note 6.
3   As to the meaning of 'cohabitant' see PARA 311 note 7.
4   As to the meaning of 'dwelling house' see PARA 285 note 2. For these purposes, references to a spouse, civil partner or a cohabitant being entitled to occupy a dwelling house by virtue of a relevant tenancy apply whether that entitlement is in that person's own right or jointly with the other spouse or cohabitant: Family Law Act 1996 Sch 7 para 6 (Sch 7 para 7(1) amended, Sch 7 para 7(3), (3A) added, by SI 1997/74; Family Law Act 1996 Sch 7 paras 6, 7(1)–(3), (5) amended, Sch 7 para 7(3), (3A), (4) substituted, by the Civil Partnership Act 2004 Sch 9 para 16). As to the meaning of 'relevant tenancy' see PARA 310 note 2.
        The court cannot make a transfer order under these provisions unless all the requirements of a relevant tenancy are satisfied at the relevant time. Thus, where an applicant relies on the cohabitant's entitlement to occupy a dwelling house by virtue of a secure tenancy, it is not sufficient that the cohabitant's tenancy would be a secure tenancy if he or she were to exercise his or her entitlement to occupy. Such a conclusion would give effect to the ordinary and natural meaning of Sch 7 para 3(1) (see PARA 310) whose language is of present entitlement. Moreover, the time when cohabitation ceases is not the relevant time for the purposes of Sch 7 paras 3(1), 7(1), and Sch 7 para 3(2) (see PARA 310) merely states a precondition for making the order. In any event the court cannot make an order under these provisions if the estate or interest to be transferred is that of a cohabitant who is a joint tenant with a person other than the intended transferee. Such a conclusion flows from the words 'in his own right or jointly with the other cohabitant' in Sch 7 para 3(1) which are words of limitation and must be construed as meaning a sole entitlement or a joint entitlement with the other cohabitant: *Gay v Sheeran* [1999] 3 All ER 795, [2000] 1 WLR 673, CA.
5   Ie within the meaning of the Rent Act 1977: see LANDLORD AND TENANT vol 27(2) (2006 Reissue) PARA 818 et seq.
6   Ie within the meaning of the Housing Act 1985: see LANDLORD AND TENANT vol 27(2) (2006 Reissue) PARA 1300.
7   Ie within the meaning of the Housing Act 1988 Pt I (ss 1–45): see LANDLORD AND TENANT vol 27(2) (2006 Reissue) PARAS 1018, 1183 et seq. If the transfer under these provisions is of an assured agricultural occupancy, then, for the purposes of the Housing Act 1988 Pt I Ch III (ss 24, 25) (see LANDLORD AND TENANT vol 27(2) (2006 Reissue) PARA 1183 et seq): (1) the agricultural worker condition is fulfilled with respect to the dwelling house while the spouse, civil partner or cohabitant to whom the assured agricultural occupancy is transferred continues to be the occupier under that occupancy; and (2) that condition is to be treated as so fulfilled by virtue of the same provision of Sch 3 (see LANDLORD AND TENANT vol 27(2) (2006 Reissue) PARA 1184) as was applicable before the transfer: Family Law Act 1996 Sch 7 para 7(5) (as amended: see note 4).

8 Ie within the meaning of the Housing Act 1988 Pt V Chapter I (ss 124–143): see LANDLORD AND TENANT vol 27(2) (2006 Reissue) PARA 1286 et seq.
9 As to the 'court' see PARA 310 note 3.
10 As to the meaning of 'tenancy' see PARA 310 note 2.
11 Family Law Act 1996 Sch 7 para 7(1)(a) (as amended: see note 4; also amended by SI 1997/74).
12 Family Law Act 1996 Sch 7 para 7(1)(b) (as amended: see note 4).
13 Family Law Act 1996 Sch 7 para 7(2) (as amended: see note 4).
14 Ie within the meaning of the Housing Act 1985 Pt IV (ss 79–117) (see LANDLORD AND TENANT vol 27(2) (2006 Reissue) PARA 1300 et seq), the Housing Act 1996 s 132 (see LANDLORD AND TENANT vol 27(2) (2006 Reissue) PARA 1290) or for the purposes of the Housing Act 1988 s 17 (see LANDLORD AND TENANT vol 27(2) (2006 Reissue) PARA 1084): Family Law Act 1996 Sch 7 para 7(3), (3A), (4) (as amended, added and substituted: see note 4).
15 Ie within the meaning of the provisions listed in note 14, as applicable.
16 Family Law Act 1996 Sch 7 para 7(3), (3A), (4) (as amended, added and substituted: see note 4).

313. Statutory tenancies. If the spouse[1], civil partner[2] or cohabitant[3] is entitled to occupy the dwelling house[4] by virtue of a statutory tenancy[5], the court[6] may by order direct that, as from the date specified in the order:

(1) that spouse, civil partner or cohabitant is to cease to be entitled to occupy the dwelling house[7]; and

(2) the other spouse, civil partner or cohabitant is to be deemed to be the tenant or, as the case may be, the sole tenant under that statutory tenancy[8].

1 As to the meaning of 'spouse' see PARA 311 note 5.
2 As to the meaning of 'civil partner' see PARA 311 note 6.
3 As to the meaning of 'cohabitant' see PARA 311 note 7.
4 As to the meaning of 'dwelling house' see PARA 285 note 2.
5 Ie within the meaning of the Rent Act 1977 or the Rent (Agriculture) Act 1976 (see LANDLORD AND TENANT vol 27(2) (2006 Reissue) PARAS 818 et seq, 1134 et seq).
6 As to the 'court' see PARA 310 note 3.
7 Family Law Act 1996 Sch 7 paras 8(1), (2)(a), 9(1), (2)(a) (Sch 7 paras 8, 9 amended by the Civil Partnership Act 2004 Sch 9 para 16).
8 Family Law Act 1996 Sch 7 paras 8(2)(b), 9(2)(b) (as amended: see note 7). The question whether the statutory provisions of the Rent Act 1977 as to the succession by the surviving spouse or civil partner of a deceased tenant, or by a member of the deceased tenant's family, to the right to retain possession (ie Sch 1 paras 1–3 or, as the case may be, Sch 1 paras 5–7 (see LANDLORD AND TENANT vol 27(2) (2006 Reissue) PARAS 843–844)) are capable of having effect in the event of the death of the person deemed by an order under these provisions to be the tenant or sole tenant under the statutory tenancy is to be determined according as those provisions have or have not already had effect in relation to the statutory tenancy: Family Law Act 1996 Sch 7 para 8(3) (as amended: see note 7). A spouse, civil partner or cohabitant who pursuant to these provisions is deemed to be the tenant under a statutory tenancy under the Rent (Agriculture) Act 1976 is a statutory tenant in his or her own right, or a statutory tenant by succession, according as the other spouse, civil partner or cohabitant was a statutory tenant in his or her own right or a statutory tenant by succession: Sch 7 para 9(3) (as so amended).

314. Compensation. If the court[1] makes a transfer of tenancy order[2] it may by the order direct the making of a payment by the spouse[3], civil partner[4] or cohabitant[5] to whom the tenancy[6] is transferred (the 'transferee') to the other spouse, civil partner or cohabitant (the 'transferor')[7]. On making an order for the payment of such a sum, the court may[8]:

(1) direct that payment of that sum or any part of it is to be deferred until a specified date or until the occurrence of a specified event[9]; or

(2) direct that that sum or any part of it is to be paid by instalments[10],

but the court must not give any such direction unless it appears to it that immediate payment of the sum required by the order would cause the transferee financial hardship which is greater than any financial hardship that would be caused to the transferor if the direction were given[11].

Where an order has been so made[12], the court may, on the application of the transferee or the transferor exercise its powers under heads (1) and (2) above, or vary any direction previously given under heads (1) and (2) above, at any time before the sum whose payment is required by the order is paid in full[13].

In deciding whether to exercise its powers under these provisions and, if so, in what manner, the court must have regard to all the circumstances including:

(a)   the financial loss that would otherwise be suffered by the transferor as a result of the order[14];

(b)   the financial needs and financial resources of the parties[15]; and

(c)   the financial obligations which the parties have, or are likely to have in the foreseeable future, including financial obligations to each other and to any relevant child[16].

1   As to the 'court' see PARA 310 note 3.
2   As to the cases in which a court may make a transfer of tenancy order see PARA 310.
3   As to the meaning of 'spouse' see PARA 311 note 5.
4   As to the meaning of 'civil partner' see PARA 311 note 6.
5   As to the meaning of 'cohabitant' see PARA 311 note 7.
6   As to the meaning of 'tenancy' see PARA 310 note 2.
7   Family Law Act 1996 Sch 7 para 10(1) (amended by the Civil Partnership Act 2004 Sch 9 para 16).
8   Ie without prejudice to the Family Law Act 1996 Sch 7 para 10(1): see the text and notes 1–7.
9   Family Law Act 1996 Sch 7 para 10(2)(a).
10 Family Law Act 1996 Sch 7 para 10(2)(b).
11 Family Law Act 1996 Sch 7 para 10(5).
12 Ie by virtue of the Family Law Act 1996 Sch 7 para 10(1): see the text and notes 1–7.
13 Family Law Act 1996 Sch 7 para 10(3).
14 Family Law Act 1996 Sch 7 para 10(4)(a).
15 Family Law Act 1996 Sch 7 para 10(4)(b).
16 Family Law Act 1996 Sch 7 para 10(4)(c). As to the meaning of 'relevant child' see PARA 290 note 5; as to the meaning of 'child' see PARA 290 note 4.

315.   Liabilities and obligations in respect of the dwelling house.   If the court[1] makes a transfer of tenancy order[2], it may by the order direct that both of the spouses[3], civil partners[4] or cohabitants[5] are to be jointly and severally liable to discharge or perform any or all of the liabilities and obligations in respect of the dwelling house[6], whether arising under the tenancy[7] or otherwise, which:

(1)   have at the date of the order fallen due to be discharged or performed by one only of them[8]; or

(2)   but for the direction, would before the date specified as the date on which the order is to take effect[9] fall due to be discharged or performed by one only of them[10].

If the court gives such a direction, it may further direct that either spouse, civil partner or cohabitant is to be liable to indemnify the other in whole or in part against any payment made or expenses incurred by the other in discharging or performing any such liability or obligation[11].

1   As to the 'court' see PARA 310 note 3.
2   As to the cases in which a court may make a transfer of tenancy order see PARA 310.
3   As to the meaning of 'spouse' see PARA 311 note 5.
4   As to the meaning of 'civil partner' see PARA 311 note 6.
5   As to the meaning of 'cohabitant' see PARA 311 note 7.
6   As to the meaning of 'dwelling house' see PARA 285 note 2.
7   As to the meaning of 'tenancy' see PARA 310 note 2.

8   Family Law Act 1996 Sch 7 para 11(1)(a) (Sch 7 para 11(1), (2) amended, Sch 7 para 12 substituted, by the Civil Partnership Act 2004 Sch 9 para 16).

9   In the case of a marriage in respect of which a decree of divorce or nullity has been granted, the date specified in a transfer of tenancy order as the date on which the order is to take effect must not be earlier than the date on which the decree is made absolute, and in the case of a civil partnership in respect of which a dissolution or nullity order has been made, the date specified in a transfer of tenancy order as the date on which the order is to take effect must not be earlier than the date on which the order is made final: Family Law Act 1996 Sch 7 para 12 (as substituted: see note 8).

10 Family Law Act 1996 Sch 7 para 11(1)(b) (as amended: see note 8).

11 Family Law Act 1996 Sch 7 para 11(2) (as amended: see note 8).

(5) MESHER AND MARTIN ORDERS

316.   Making and terms of orders.   Mesher[1] and Martin[2] orders are orders made originally in respect of matrimonial proceedings, but which are presumably also applicable in respect of civil partnership proceedings, which take effect as trusts under which the sale of a property is deferred until certain events occur or by way of charges over the property, where the realisation of the charge is postponed until the happening of those events. Under the terms of a Mesher order the sale is postponed, or realisation of the charge is deferred, until the death or remarriage of the party in occupation, the youngest child of the family attaining a certain age or ceasing full-time secondary or tertiary education, whichever is the later, or further order of the court[3]; and under the terms of a Martin order the sale is postponed, or realisation of the charge is deferred, until the death or remarriage of the party in occupation, such earlier date as he or she ceases to live at the property, or further order of the court[4].

There are a number of possible variations to such orders, such as:

(1)   the insertion of a provision whereby the property is sold, or the charge is realised, on the party in occupation cohabiting[5];

(2)   the insertion of a provision whereby the party in occupation is permitted to sell the former home and transfer the relevant trust or charge to a substitute property[6];

(3)   orders whereby the parties' respective interests in the property are varied from their existing equitable interests[7];

(4)   the insertion of provision for the sale of the property to occur when the children attain a later age than that stated above[8];

(5)   the insertion of provision for the adjournment of the determination of the parties' shares in the property at the end of the period of deferment[9]; and

(6)   the insertion of provision for the party in occupation to pay an occupational rent to the other party[10].

It was recognised that Mesher orders had distinct disadvantages[11] and that the effect of a Mesher order may be simply to avoid facing the facts as they exist[12]. In particular, a Mesher order may render the party in occupation unable to rehouse himself or herself at the end of the period of deferment[13]. Further, it has been recognised that children do not simply cease to be dependent on attaining the age of majority or when ceasing education[14]. A party in occupation cannot apply for an extension of the period of deferment provided by a Mesher or Martin order[15]. The provision in a Mesher or Martin order that the sale or charge is deferred on various conditions including until 'further order' does not permit the court on a subsequent application to make an order extending the term or varying the provisions of the order, save to the extent that the subsequent order is consistent with the clear intention of the original order[16].

1   Ie so called after the decision in *Mesher v Mesher and Hall* (1973) [1980] 1 All ER 126n, CA.
2   Ie so called after the decision in *Martin v Martin* [1978] Fam 12, [1977] 3 All ER 762, CA.
3   *Mesher v Mesher and Hall* (1973) [1980] 1 All ER 126n, CA. See eg *Alonso v Alonso* (1974) 4 Fam Law 164, 118 Sol Jo 660, CA; *Browne (formerly Pritchard) v Pritchard* [1975] 3 All ER 721, [1975] 1 WLR 1366, CA; *Drinkwater v Drinkwater* [1984] FLR 627, [1984] Fam Law 245, CA.
4   *Martin v Martin* [1978] Fam 12, [1977] 3 All ER 762, CA.
5   *Chadwick v Chadwick* [1985] FLR 606, [1985] Fam Law 96, CA.
6   *T v T (financial provision)* [1990] FCR 169, sub nom *Re T (divorce: interim maintenance: discovery)* [1990] 1 FLR 1.
7   *Chamberlain v Chamberlain* [1974] 1 All ER 33, [1973] 1 WLR 1557, CA (wife's interest increased to two-thirds).
8   *Harnett v Harnett* [1973] Fam 156, [1973] 2 All ER 593; affd [1974] 1 All ER 764, [1974] 1 WLR 219, CA.
9   *Sakkas v Sakkas* [1987] Fam Law 414.
10 *Harvey v Harvey* [1982] Fam 83, [1983] 1 All ER 693, CA.
11 See *Martin v Martin* [1978] Fam 12 at 21, [1977] 3 All ER 762 at 769, CA per Ormrod LJ.
12 *Harvey v Harvey* [1982] Fam 83, [1983] 1 All ER 693, CA.
13 *Clutton v Clutton* [1991] 1 All ER 340, [1991] 1 WLR 359, CA.
14 *Harvey v Harvey* [1982] Fam 83, [1983] 1 All ER 693, CA; *Harnett v Harnett* [1973] Fam 156, [1973] 2 All ER 593; affd [1974] 1 All ER 764, [1974] 1 WLR 219, CA.
15 *Omielan v Omielan* [1996] 3 FCR 329, [1996] 2 FLR 306; *Thompson v Thompson* [1986] Fam 38, [1985] 2 All ER 243, CA; *Knibb v Knibb* [1987] 2 FLR 396, [1987] Fam Law 346, CA.
16 *Thompson v Thompson* [1986] Fam 38, [1985] 2 All ER 243, CA.

6. MATRIMONIAL AND CIVIL PARTNERSHIP CAUSES

(1) THE CAUSES

317.   Matrimonial and civil partnership causes. A 'matrimonial cause' is an action for divorce[1], nullity of marriage[2], or judicial separation[3]; and a 'civil partnership cause' is an action for the dissolution[4] or annulment[5] of a civil partnership or for the legal separation of civil partners[6]. Proceedings may be brought for:

(1)   the annulment of a marriage or civil partnership which is void or voidable[7];

(2)   divorce, or the dissolution of a civil partnership, where a marriage or civil partnership has broken down irretrievably[8];

(3)   an order which provides for the separation of spouses or civil partners where any fact which may prove irretrievable breakdown exists[9]; and

(4)   a decree or order of presumption of death pertaining to a spouse or civil partner[10].

There are also a number of related and subsidiary causes which may be brought[11].

1   As to actions for divorce see PARAS 346–414.
2   As to actions for nullity see PARAS 319–345.
3   As to judicial separation see PARAS 346–414.
4   As to the dissolution of a civil partnership see PARAS 346–414.
5   As to the annulment of a civil partnership see PARAS 319–345.

6   Matrimonial and Family Proceedings Act 1984 s 32 (amended by the Civil Partnership Act 2004 Sch 27 para 91). As to the meaning of 'civil partner' see PARA 2 note 1. As to the legal separation of civil partners see PARAS 346–414.

7   See PARAS 319–345.
8   See PARAS 346–449.
9   See PARAS 346–449.
10 See PARAS 415–417.
11 See PARA 318.

318.   Related and subsidiary causes. In addition to the matrimonial and civil partnership causes which may be brought[1], a petition may be brought by a party to a marriage or a civil partnership for a declaration of marital or civil partnership status[2], reasonable maintenance[3] and financial provision and relief[4]. These causes are not matrimonial or civil partnership causes for the purposes of the provisions relating to the distribution and transfer of family business[5], but are often brought in connection with such causes.

1   As to the matrimonial and civil partnership causes which may be brought see PARA 317.
2   As to declarations of marital or civil partnership status see PARAS 421–422.
3   As to applications for maintenance see PARA 542 et seq.
4   As to financial provision and relief see PARA 419 et seq.

5   Ie for the purposes of the Matrimonial and Family Proceedings Act 1984 Pt V (ss 32–42). As to the meanings of 'matrimonial cause' and 'civil partnership cause' for those purposes see PARA 317.

(2) NULLITY

(i) Powers of Annulment

319. The applicable law. Provision is made by statute for the annulment of marriages and civil partnerships[1]. The provisions for each are broadly the same, requiring the establishment of one or more grounds the nature of which will determine whether the marriage or civil partnership is void[2] or is voidable[3]. A void marriage or civil partnership is regarded as never having taken place at all, while a voidable marriage or civil partnership may be annulled only as respects any time after the decree or order of nullity has been made absolute or final[4].

1   See the Matrimonial Causes Act 1973 ss 11–16; the Civil Partnership Act 2004 ss 49–54; and PARA 320 et seq.
2   As to void marriages and civil partnerships see PARAS 326–330.
3   As to voidable marriages and civil partnerships see PARAS 331–343.
4   See PARA 320.

320. Nature and effect of annulment. A void marriage or civil partnership is void ipso jure, the decree or order being merely declaratory[1]. Where a marriage or civil partnership is void in law, the purpose of a nullity suit is to place the fact on record by a judgment equivalent to a judgment in rem[2], but there is no need for such a decree or order[3].

A voidable marriage or civil partnership is regarded as valid and subsisting until a decree of nullity or a nullity order has been obtained[4] during the lifetime of the parties[5]. A decree of nullity granted in respect of a voidable marriage, or a nullity order made where a civil partnership is voidable, operates to annul the marriage or civil partnership only as respects any time after the decree has been made absolute or the order has been made final, the marriage or civil partnership being treated (despite the decree or order) as if it had existed up to that time[6].

1   Where a marriage or civil partnership is void, the courts regard the marriage or civil partnership as never having taken place and no matrimonial or civil partnership status as ever having been conferred: see *R v Algar* [1954] 1 QB 279 at 287, [1953] 2 All ER 1381 at 1383, CCA. As to the grounds on which marriages and civil partnerships are considered void see PARAS 326–330. Void marriages (and, presumably, civil partnerships) may be impeached after the deaths of the parties to the marriage or civil partnership: see PARA 322.
2   See *Salvesen (or von Lorang) v Administrator of Austrian Property* [1927] AC 641, HL.
3   *De Reneville v De Reneville* [1948] P 100 at 110, 111, [1948] 1 All ER 56 at 59, 60, CA. Nothing in the provisions of the Matrimonial Causes Act 1973 restating additional grounds for a decree of nullity in respect of voidable marriages celebrated before 1 August 1971 (as to which see PARA 345) is to be construed as validating any marriage which is by law void but with respect to which a decree of nullity has not been granted: Sch 1 para 11(4).
4   As to who may institute proceedings for a decree of nullity see PARAS 322, 323. A 'nullity order' is an order of the court which annuls a civil partnership which is void or voidable: Civil Partnership Act 2004 s 37(1)(b).
5   See *R v Algar* [1954] 1 QB 279, [1953] 2 All ER 1381, CCA (former wife's evidence inadmissible in criminal proceedings against husband for a crime committed during coverture but prosecuted after decree of nullity on ground of impotence); *Wiggens v Wiggens (otherwise Brooks) and Ingram* [1958] 2 All ER 555, [1958] 1 WLR 1013.
6   Matrimonial Causes Act 1973 s 16; Civil Partnership Act 2004 s 37(3); and see *Re Roberts, Roberts v Roberts* [1978] 3 All ER 225, [1978] 1 WLR 653, CA; *Ward v Secretary of State for Social Services* [1990] FCR 361, sub nom *R v Secretary of State for Social Services, ex p Ward* [1990] 1 FLR 119, DC; *P v P (ouster: decree nisi of nullity)* [1995] 1 FCR 47, [1994] 2 FLR 400, CA. Different provisions apply in respect of marriages celebrated before 1 August 1971: see PARAS 344–345.

321. Bars to relief. The court must not grant a decree of nullity on the ground that a marriage is voidable, or a nullity order on the ground that a civil partnership is voidable, if the respondent satisfies the court:

(1)   that the petitioner[1], with knowledge that it was open to him to have the marriage avoided or obtain the nullity order, so conducted himself in relation to the respondent as to lead the respondent reasonably to believe that he would not seek to do so[2]; and

(2)   that it would be unjust to the respondent to grant the decree or make the order[3].

Without prejudice to these provisions, the court must not grant a decree or order of nullity where want of consent, mental disorder, pregnancy or, in the case of a marriage, venereal disease is alleged, or where the respondent is a person whose gender at the time of the marriage or civil partnership had become[4] an acquired gender[5], unless:

(a)   it is satisfied that proceedings were instituted within three years from the date of the marriage or the formation of the civil partnership[6]; or

(b)   leave for the institution of proceedings after the expiration of that period has been granted[7];

and the court may not grant such a decree or order on the grounds that an interim gender recognition certificate[8] has, after the time of the marriage or civil partnership, been issued to either party to the marriage or civil partnership[9] unless it is satisfied that proceedings were instituted within the period of six months from the date of issue of the certificate[10].

Without prejudice to any of these provisions, the court must not grant a decree or order of nullity in cases where pregnancy or (in the case of a marriage) venereal disease is alleged, or on the grounds that the respondent is a person whose gender at the time of the marriage had become[11] an acquired gender[12], unless it is satisfied that the petitioner was at the time of the marriage ignorant of the facts alleged[13].

In cases of void marriages (or, presumably, civil partnerships) a plea of conduct or of unjustness does not constitute a bar[14] for there can be no estoppel in the case of a void marriage[15].

1   Every cause must be begun by petition: see the Family Proceedings Rules 1991, SI 1991/1247, r 2.2(1); and PARA 755 et seq. 'Cause' means a matrimonial or civil partnership cause (see PARA 317) or proceedings for presumption of death and dissolution under the Matrimonial Causes Act 1973 s 19 or the Civil Partnership Act 2004 s 55 (see PARAS 415–416): Family Proceedings Rules 1991, SI 1991/1247, r 1.2(1) (definition substituted by SI 2005/2922). Although the Civil Partnership Act 2004 uses the expressions 'application' and 'applicant', the corresponding provisions of the Matrimonial Causes Act 1973 and the Family Proceedings Rules 1991, SI 1991/1247, refer to 'petition' and 'petitioners', and that terminology has generally been adopted throughout this title where the context is of initiating a cause.

2   Matrimonial Causes Act 1973 s 13(1)(a); Civil Partnership Act 2004 s 51(1)(a). As to the circumstances in which the period for bringing proceedings may be extended see PARA 323. As to the meaning of 'nullity order' see PARA 320 note 4.

References to the old cases of insincerity, collateral motives and delay may be of some assistance: see *Anon* (1857) Dea & Sw 295 at 299 per Dr Lushington; *H (falsely called C) v C* (1859) 1 Sw & Tr 605 (husband's impotence not proved; financial reasons and long delay by wife, dismissal of petition); affd on appeal in *Castleden v Castleden* (1861) 9 HL Cas 186; *E– v T– (falsely called E–)* (1863) 3 Sw & Tr 312 (11 years' delay; man's forbearance); *M– (falsely called B–) v B–* (1864) 3 Sw & Tr 550 (long delay, though apparently no finding as to husband's capacity or incapacity); *T (falsely called D) v D* (1866) LR 1 P & D 127 (wife left after eight years because of cruelty, husband's impotence not proved; petition dismissed); *Mansfield (falsely called Cuno) v Cuno* (1873) 42 LJP & M 65, HL (objection of delay may be overcome when proof of impotence complete, but not otherwise; delay indicates want of sense of injury); *B–n v B–n* (1854) 1 Ecc & Ad 248, PC (distinguishing such a suit from one on account of adultery);

but see dictum of Sir W Scott in *Guest v Shipley (falsely called Guest)* (1820) 2 Hag Con 321 at 323; *W (falsely called R) v R* (1876) 1 PD 405 at 408 (suit brought after 16 years' separation; collateral motive; the maxim that the law helps those who are watchful and not those who sleep directly applicable); *G v M* (1885) 10 App Cas 171, HL; *M (otherwise D) v D* (1885) 10 PD 75; *L (otherwise B) v B* [1895] P 274 (seven years' delay by wife); *Moss v Moss* [1897] P 263 (wife pregnant by another man at time of marriage); *S v B (falsely called S)* (1905) 21 TLR 219 (17 years' delay by clergyman owing to the nature of his office); *M v M (otherwise H)* (1906) 22 TLR 719 (deed executed in ignorance of remedy); *T v T (otherwise J)* (1931) 47 TLR 629 (14 years' delay by husband petitioner); *Nash (otherwise Lister) v Nash* [1940] P 60, [1940] 1 All ER 206 (insincerity not concerned with petitioner's character or conduct before marriage); *Clarke (otherwise Talbott) v Clarke* [1943] 2 All ER 540 (15 years' delay; decree granted); *Dredge v Dredge (otherwise Harrison)* [1947] 1 All ER 29 (17 years' delay; reasons for delay; decree granted); *Clifford v Clifford* [1948] P 187, [1948] 1 All ER 394, CA (27 years' delay; decree granted); *REL (otherwise R) v EL* [1949] P 211, sub nom *L v L* [1949] 1 All ER 141 (artificial insemination with husband's seed); *W v W* [1952] P 152 at 157, [1952] 1 All ER 858 at 860, CA (a desire, by itself, to get rid of a financial responsibility is not insincerity); *Tindall v Tindall* [1953] P 63, [1953] 1 All ER 139, CA (wife, without knowledge of facts and law, applied for relief in magistrates' court; marriage approbated); *Slater v Slater* [1953] P 235, [1953] 1 All ER 246, CA (adoption; petitioner unaware of legal position; no other act of approbation); *L v L* [1954] NZLR 386, distinguishing on the facts *Slater v Slater* [1953] P 235, [1953] 1 All ER 246, CA; *Allardyce v Allardyce* 1954 SC 419 (24 years' delay; decree granted); *Scott v Scott (otherwise Fone)* [1959] P 103n, [1959] 1 All ER 531; *Copham (otherwise Dobbin) v Copham* (1959) Times, 15 January (eight years' delay; misinformation by Roman Catholic priest that marriage had been consummated); *Dicker v Dicker (otherwise Parris)* (1959) Times, 10 November (23 years' delay); *Notley v Notley (otherwise Roberts)* (1960) Times, 4 November (33 years' delay; ignorance of the law of nullity); *Bullock v Bullock* [1960] 2 All ER 307, [1960] 1 WLR 975, DC (bigamous marriage approbated); *Q v V* (1960) Times, 12 May (AID; no approbation); *G v G (otherwise H)* [1961] P 87, [1960] 3 All ER 56 (bigamous marriage); *Hayward v Hayward (otherwise Prestwood)* [1961] P 152, [1961] 1 All ER 236; *D v D (nullity: statutory bar)* [1979] Fam 70, sub nom *D v D (nullity)* [1979] 3 All ER 337.

3   Matrimonial Causes Act 1973 s 13(1)(b); Civil Partnership Act 2004 s 51(1)(b). See the cases cited in note 2.

4   Ie under the Gender Recognition Act 2004: see CONSTITUTIONAL LAW AND HUMAN RIGHTS.

5   Ie where proceedings are brought by virtue of the Matrimonial Causes Act 1973 s 12(c), (d), (e), (f) or (h) or the Civil Partnership Act 2004 s 50(1)(a), (b), (c), or (e) (see PARAS 331, 332, 333, 334, 343).

6   Matrimonial Causes Act 1973 s 13(2)(a) (s 13(2) substituted by the Matrimonial and Family Proceedings Act 1984 s 2(1), (2); Matrimonial Causes Act 1973 s 13(2)–(4) amended, s 13(2A) added, by the Gender Recognition Act 2004 Sch 4 paras 4, 6); Civil Partnership Act 2004 s 51(2)(a).

7   Matrimonial Causes Act 1973 s 13(2)(b); Civil Partnership Act 2004 s 51(2)(b). As to the granting of leave after the expiration of the specified period see PARA 323.

8   Ie under the Gender Recognition Act 2004: see CONSTITUTIONAL LAW AND HUMAN RIGHTS.

9   Ie where proceedings are brought by virtue of the Matrimonial Causes Act 1973 s 12(g) or the Civil Partnership Act 2004 s 50(1)(d) (see PARA 334).

10 Matrimonial Causes Act 1973 s 13(2A) (as added: see note 6); Civil Partnership Act 2004 s 51(5).

11 See note 4.

12 Ie where proceedings are brought by virtue of the Matrimonial Causes Act 1973 s 12(e), (f) or (h) or the Civil Partnership Act 2004 s 50(1)(c), or (e) (see PARAS 333, 334, 343).

13 Matrimonial Causes Act 1973 s 13(3) (as amended: see note 6); Civil Partnership Act 2004 s 51(6).

14 *Grant (falsely called Giannetti) v Giannetti* [1913] P 137; *Andrews (falsely called Ross) v Ross* (1888) 14 PD 15; *Wilkins v Wilkins* [1896] P 108, CA; *Miles v Chilton (falsely called Miles)* (1849) 1 Rob Eccl 684. See also *Hayward v Hayward (otherwise Prestwood)* [1961] P 152, [1961] 1 All ER 236, not following *Woodland v Woodland (otherwise Belin or Barton)* [1928] P 169; *Guest v Shipley (falsely called Guest)* (1820) 2 Hag Con 321 (absence of estoppel where marriage not denied in previous suit); *Corbett v Corbett (otherwise Ashley)* [1971] P 83 at 108, 109, [1970] 2 All ER 33 at 50, 51.

15 *Hayward v Hayward (otherwise Prestwood)* [1961] P 152, [1961] 1 All ER 236; *Vervaeke v Smith (Messina and A-G intervening)* [1983] 1 AC 145, [1982] 2 All ER 144, HL.

322.   Who may institute proceedings.   Suits for annulling void, as distinct from voidable, marriages[1] may be instituted not only by the parties but also by persons having a financial interest in the matter[2] and even after both parties are dead[3]. A marriage voidable[4] for impotence or for any other cause may only be put in issue by a party to it and during the lifetime of both parties[5]. A party may petition on the ground of his own impotence[6].

1   As to the distinction between void and voidable marriages and civil partnerships see PARA 319 et seq.

2   *Faremouth v Watson* (1811) 1 Phillim 355 (brought by sisters of man who married deceased wife's sister, who were interested in the question of his leaving lawful issue; such marriages were then only voidable); *Wells v Cottam (falsely called Wells)* (1863) 3 Sw & Tr 364; *Ray v Sherwood and Ray* (1836) 1 Curt 193; affd sub nom *Sherwood v Ray* (1837) 1 Moo PCC 353 (father's petition on grounds of affinity); *Bevan v McMahon and Bevan (falsely called McMahon)* (1859) 2 Sw & Tr 58 (mother's petition; no jurisdiction); *Choppy v Bibi (otherwise Choppy)* [1967] AC 158, [1966] 1 All ER 203, PC. A 'slight interest' is sufficient: see *Faremouth v Watson* per Sir John Nicholl. Anyone whose title to property would be affected, or on whom a legal liability would be cast, though contingently, by the natural result of a marriage, ie the birth of issue, should have a right to contest its validity: *Sherwood v Ray* at 399 per Parke B.

3   *Elliott v Gurr* (1812) 2 Phillim 16 at 19; *Ray v Sherwood and Ray* (1836) 1 Curt 193 at 199 (affd sub nom *Sherwood v Ray* (1837) 1 Moo PCC 353); *A v B* (1868) LR 1 P & D 559; *Fowke v Fowke* [1938] Ch 774 at 781, 782, [1938] 2 All ER 638 at 646, 647; *De Reneville v De Reneville* [1948] P 100 at 110, [1948] 1 All ER 56 at 59, CA per Lord Greene MR; *Harthan v Harthan* [1949] P 115 at 131, 132, [1948] 2 All ER 639 at 645, CA per Lord Merriman P.

4   A voidable marriage remains a marriage until one of the spouses seeks to get rid of the tie: *Inverclyde (otherwise Tripp) v Inverclyde* [1931] P 29 at 41. Whether, as between the parties to them, marriages duly solemnised but unconsummated may or may not be treated as absolutely null and void, it is certainly not open to a third person to make an objection on the ground of impotence, when neither of the parties concerned has done any act to raise the question or to signify an election to treat the contract as void: see *Cavell v Prince* (1866) LR 1 Exch 246.

5   *A v B* (1868) LR 1 P & D 559 (suit by next of kin of deceased wife).

6   *Harthan v Harthan* [1949] P 115, [1948] 2 All ER 639, CA; but see PARA 341.

323.   Persons suffering mental disorder.   In the case of proceedings for the grant of a decree or order of nullity where the grounds are want of consent, mental disorder, pregnancy or, in the case of a marriage, venereal disease, or where the respondent is a person whose gender at the time of the marriage had become[1] an acquired gender[2], a judge may, on an application made to him, grant leave for the institution of proceedings after the expiration of the period of three years from the date of the marriage or civil partnership if:

(1)   he is satisfied that the applicant has at some time during that period suffered from mental disorder[3]; and

(2)   he considers that in all the circumstances of the case it would be just to grant leave for the institution of proceedings[4].

Such an application for leave may be made after the expiration of the period of three years from the date of the marriage[5].

1   Ie under the Gender Recognition Act 2004: see CONSTITUTIONAL LAW AND HUMAN RIGHTS.

2   Ie where proceedings are brought by virtue of the Matrimonial Causes Act 1973 s 12(c), (d), (e), (f) or (h) or the Civil Partnership Act 2004 s 50(1)(a), (b), (c), or (e) (see PARAS 331, 332, 333, 334, 343).

3   Matrimonial Causes Act 1973 s 13(4)(a) (s 13(4), (5) added by the Matrimonial and Family Proceedings Act 1984 s 2; Matrimonial Causes Act 1973 s 13(4) amended by the Gender Recognition Act 2004 Sch 4 paras 4, 6); Civil Partnership Act 2004 s 51(3)(a).

4   Matrimonial Causes Act 1973 s 13(4)(b) (as amended: see note 3); Civil Partnership Act 2004 s 51(3)(b).

5   Matrimonial Causes Act 1973 s 13(5) (as added: see note 3); Civil Partnership Act 2004 s 51(4).

324.   Marriages and civil partnerships governed by foreign law or celebrated abroad under English law.   Where, apart from the Matrimonial Causes Act 1973[1], any matter affecting the validity of a marriage would fall to be determined, in accordance with the rules of private international law, by reference to the law of a country outside England and Wales, nothing in the provisions of that Act setting out the grounds on which a marriage is void[2] or voidable[3] or setting out the bars to relief[4] precludes the determination of the matter as aforesaid or requires the application to the marriage of the grounds or bar there mentioned, except so far as applicable in accordance with those rules[5]. However, no marriage is to be treated as valid by virtue of these provisions if, at the time when it purports to have been celebrated, either party was already a civil partner[6].

In the case of a marriage which purports to have been celebrated under the Foreign Marriage Acts 1892 to 1947[7], or has taken place outside England and Wales and purports to be marriage under common law, the provisions of the Matrimonial Causes Act 1973 setting out the grounds on which a marriage is void[8] are without prejudice to any ground on which the marriage may be void under those Acts or, as the case may be, by virtue of the rules governing the celebration of marriages outside England and Wales under common law[9].

Where two people register as civil partners in Scotland or Northern Ireland the civil partnership will be void if it would be void under the applicable Scottish or Northern Irish provisions and will be voidable if it would be voidable under applicable England and Wales provisions[10]. Where two people register as civil partners overseas[11] the civil partnership is void if neither is a United Kingdom national or part of Her Majesty's forces, if they would be ineligible to register as civil partners in the United Kingdom[12], or if a requirement prescribed for these purposes by an Order in Council under the relevant provision is not complied with[13] and is voidable if it would be voidable under the applicable provision[14]. Where two people have registered an apparent or alleged overseas relationship[15] the civil partnership is void if the relationship is not an overseas relationship or even though the relationship is an overseas relationship the parties are not treated[16] as having formed a civil partnership[17] and is voidable if the overseas relationship is voidable under the relevant domestic or overseas law[18].

1   Cf the Domicile and Matrimonial Proceedings Act 1973 s 5(3); and PARA 750.
2   See PARAS 326–330.
3   See PARAS 331–343.
4   See PARA 321.
5   Matrimonial Causes Act 1973 s 14(1) (s 14(1) amended, s 14(3) added, by the Civil Partnership Act 2004 Sch 27 para 41).
6   Matrimonial Causes Act 1973 s 14(3) (as added: see note 5). As to the meaning of 'civil partner' see PARA 2 note 1.
7   See PARAS 119–128.
8   See PARAS 326–330.
9   Matrimonial Causes Act 1973 s 14(2).
10 Civil Partnership Act 2004 s 54(1), (2). The applicable provisions are s 123 (void in Scotland), s 173 (void in Northern Ireland) and s 50(1) (see PARAS 331–334) (Scottish and Northern Irish civil partnerships will be voidable in these circumstances, although in the case of a Scottish civil partnership only in the circumstances described in s 50(1)(d)): s 54(1), (2). Section 51 (bars to relief where civil partnership is voidable: see PARAS 321, 323) applies for these purposes: s 54(9)(a), (11).
11 Ie under an Order in Council under the Civil Partnership Act 2004 s 210 (registration at British consulates etc) (see PARA 145) or s 211 (registration by armed forces personnel) (see PARA 153).
12 Ie if the condition in the Civil Partnership Act 2004 s 210(2)(a) or (b) (see PARA 145) or s 211(2)(a) or (b) (see PARA 153) is not met.
13 Civil Partnership Act 2004 s 54(3), (4)(a).

14   Civil Partnership Act 2004 s 54(4)(b)(i), (5). The applicable provision for the purposes of England and Wales is s 50(1) (see PARAS 331–334): s 54(4)(b)(i). Section 51 (bars to relief where civil partnership is voidable: see PARAS 321, 323) applies for these purposes: s 54(9)(a), (11).

15   As to the meaning of 'overseas relationship' see PARA 2 note 4.

16   Ie under the Civil Partnership Act 2004 Pt 5 Chapter 2 (ss 212–218) (see PARA 19).

17   Civil Partnership Act 2004 s 54(6), (7).

18   Civil Partnership Act 2004 s 54(8). The civil partnership is voidable under the relevant domestic law if the circumstances fall within s 50(1)(d) or, where either of the parties was domiciled in England and Wales or Northern Ireland at the time when the overseas relationship was registered, the circumstances fall within s 50(1)(a), (b), (c) or (e), and the relevant overseas law is the law of the country or territory where the overseas relationship was registered (including its rules of private international law): s 54(8)(b), (c), (10). Section 51 (bars to relief where civil partnership is voidable: see PARAS 321, 323) applies for these purposes: s 54(9)(b), (c), (11).

325. Legitimacy of children of voidable marriages. Since a decree of nullity operates to annul a marriage only as respects any time after the decree has been made absolute, and the marriage is treated as if it had existed up to that time, it is to be inferred that children of the marriage will remain legitimate[1].

1   See the Matrimonial Causes Act 1973 s 16; and PARA 320. Where a decree of nullity was granted on or before 31 July 1971 (ie the day before the day on which the Nullity of Marriage Act 1971 came into force) in respect of a voidable marriage, any child who would have been the legitimate child of the parties to the marriage if at the date of the decree it has been dissolved, instead of being annulled, is deemed to be their legitimate child: Matrimonial Causes Act 1973 Sch 1 para 12. As to voidable marriages before 1 August 1971 see PARA 345.

(ii) Void Marriages and Civil Partnerships

326. Grounds on which marriage is void. A marriage celebrated after 31 July 1971[1] is void[2] if:

(1)   the parties are within the prohibited degrees of relationship[3];

(2)   either party is under the age of 16[4];

(3)   the parties have intermarried in disregard of certain requirements as to the formation of marriage[5];

(4)   at the time of the marriage either party was already lawfully married or a civil partner[6];

(5)   the parties are not respectively male and female[7]; or

(6)   in the case of a polygamous marriage[8] entered into outside England and Wales, either party was at the time of the marriage domiciled[9] in England and Wales[10].

These are the only grounds on which a marriage celebrated after 31 July 1971 is void[11].

1   Ie the day before the day on which the Nullity of Marriage Act 1971 came into force. As to void marriages before 1 August 1971 see PARA 344.

2   As to the nature and effect of void marriages see PARA 320.

3   Matrimonial Causes Act 1973 s 11(a)(i) (s 11(a) amended by the Marriage Act 1983 s 2(4); and the Marriage (Prohibited Degrees of Relationship) Act 1986 s 6(4)). As to the prohibited degrees of relationship see PARAS 35–40. The grounds specified in the Matrimonial Causes Act 1973 s 11(a) (see the text and notes 4–5) render a marriage void on the ground that it is not a valid marriage under the provisions of the Marriage Acts 1949 to 1986: s 11(a) (as so amended).

4   Matrimonial Causes Act 1973 s 11(a)(ii) (as amended: see note 3). As to the minimum age for marriage see PARAS 32, 41.

5   Matrimonial Causes Act 1973 s 11(a)(ii) (as amended: see note 3). See *A-M v A-M (divorce: jurisdiction: validity of marriage)* [2001] 2 FLR 6. As to such requirements see PARAS 328–330.

6   Matrimonial Causes Act 1973 s 11(b) (amended by the Civil Partnership Act 2004 Sch 27 para 40). As to the meaning of 'civil partner' see PARA 2 note 1. As to the standard of proof where an issue arises as to the authenticity and effect of a document purporting to dissolve an earlier marriage see *Wicken v Wicken* [1999] Fam 224, [1999] 2 WLR 1166.

7   Matrimonial Causes Act 1973 s 11(c). The criteria are biological: see the cases cited in PARA 1
     note 2. A person whose sex had been correctly classified as birth cannot later become, or come
     to be regarded as, a person of the opposite sex for the purposes of s 11(c): see *Bellinger v
     Bellinger* [2003] UKHL 21, [2003] 2 AC 467, [2003] 2 All ER 593 (in which the House of
     Lords declared that the non-recognition of gender reassignment for the purposes of marriage
     was not compatible with the Convention for the Protection of Human Rights and Fundamental
     Freedoms (Rome, 4 November 1950; TS 71 (1953); Cmd 8969) arts 8, 12 (right to respect for
     private and family life; right to marry and found a family: see CONSTITUTIONAL LAW AND
     HUMAN RIGHTS vol 8(2) (Reissue) PARAS 150 et seq, 162), a situation which has been
     subsequently addressed by legislation (see the Matrimonial Causes Act 1973 s 12(g), (h); and
     PARA 334)).
8   For these purposes, a marriage is not polygamous if at its inception neither party has any spouse
     additional to the other: Matrimonial Causes Act 1973 s 11 (amended by the Private
     International Law (Miscellaneous Provisions) Act 1995 Schedule para 2(1), (2)). A potentially
     polygamous marriage is not void: see the Private International Law (Miscellaneous Provisions)
     Act 1995 s 5(1); and CONFLICT OF LAWS vol 8(3) (Reissue) PARA 240.
9   As to domicile see CONFLICT OF LAWS vol 8(3) (Reissue) PARA 35 et seq.
10   Matrimonial Causes Act 1973 s 11(d), rectifying the anomaly created by *Hussain v Hussain*
     [1983] Fam 26, [1982] 3 All ER 369, CA. As to polygamous marriages generally see PARA 9.
11   Matrimonial Causes Act 1973 s 11.

327.   Grounds on which civil partnership is void.   Where two people register
as civil partners[1] of each other in England and Wales the civil partnership is void[2]
if:

(1)   at the time when they do so, they are not eligible[3] to register as civil
       partners of each other[4];
(2)   at the time when they do so they both know:
       (a)   that due notice of proposed civil partnership has not been given[5];
       (b)   that the civil partnership document[6] has not been duly issued[7];
       (c)   that the civil partnership document is void[8] owing to failure to
              register within the specified period[9];
       (d)   that the place of registration is a place other than that specified in
              the notices (or notice) of proposed civil partnership and the civil
              partnership document[10];
       (e)   that a civil partnership registrar[11] is not present[12]; or
       (f)   that the place of registration is on premises that are not approved
              premises[13] although the registration is purportedly in accordance
              with the provisions[14] governing the place of registration[15]; or
(3)   the civil partnership document is void[16] because the civil partnership is
       between a child and another person in circumstances where any person
       whose consent is required before the child can register has given written
       notice to the registration authority that he forbids the registration of the
       civil partnership[17].

1   As to the meaning of 'civil partner' see PARA 2 note 1. As to registration see PARA 132 et seq.
2   As to the requisites of a civil partnership see PARAS 2, 4.
3   Ie under the Civil Partnership Act 2004 s 3 (see PARAS 2, 4).
4   Civil Partnership Act 2004 s 49(a).
5   Civil Partnership Act 2004 s 49(b)(i). As to the giving of notice see PARA 133.
6   As to the meaning of 'civil partnership document' see PARA 56 note 7.
7   Civil Partnership Act 2004 s 49(b)(ii). As to the issuing of the civil partnership document see
     PARA 150.
8   Ie under the Civil Partnership Act 2004 s 17(3) (see PARA 139) or s 27(2) (see PARA 144).
9   Civil Partnership Act 2004 s 49(b)(iii).
10   Civil Partnership Act 2004 s 49(b)(iv).
11   As to the meaning of 'civil partnership registrar' see PARA 139 note 8.
12   Civil Partnership Act 2004 s 49(b)(v).
13   As to the approval of premises see PARA 190 et seq.

14 Ie the Civil Partnership Act 2004 s 6(3A)(a) (see PARA 56).
15 Civil Partnership Act 2004 s 49(b)(vi) (added by SI 2005/2000).
16 Ie under the Civil Partnership Act 2004 Sch 2 para 6(2), (5) (see PARA 137).
17 Civil Partnership Act 2004 s 49(c).

328. Marriages according to rites of the Church of England. If any persons knowingly and wilfully intermarry according to the rites of the Church of England[1], otherwise than by special licence[2]:

(1) except in the case of a marriage of a person who is housebound or a detained person[3], in any place other than a church or other building in which banns may be published[4];

(2) without banns having been duly published[5], a common licence having been obtained[6], or certificates having been duly issued[7] by a superintendent registrar[8] to whom due notice of marriage has been given[9];

(3) on the authority of a publication of banns which is void[10], a common licence which is void[11] or certificates of a superintendent registrar which are[12] void[13]; or

(4) in the case of a marriage on the authority of a superintendent registrar's certificates, in any place other than the church building or other place specified in the notices of marriage and certificates as the place where the marriage is to be solemnised[14],

or if they knowingly and wilfully consent to or acquiesce in the solemnisation of the marriage by any person who is not in Holy Orders[15], the marriage is void[16].

Guilty knowledge and wilfulness on the part of one of the parties will not invalidate the marriage unless the other participates in it[17]. If a party is described by a false name and the banns are, in consequence, incorrectly published, the marriage is valid if the wrong name has been given by mistake or where the name given has been assumed and is generally accredited[18], or where there was no intention of concealing identity[19] and, even if the false name has been given fraudulently, the marriage is nevertheless valid if one party marries without knowledge of the falsity[20]. If, however, both parties are cognisant of the fraud or intend concealment by the use of the false name, there is no due publication, and the marriage is void[21].

1 As to references to the Church of England see PARA 53 note 6.
2 As to marriage by special licence see PARA 58.
3 Ie except in the case of a marriage in pursuance of the Marriage Act 1949 s 26(1)(dd) (see PARA 54).
4 Marriage Act 1949 s 25(a) (amended by the Marriage Act 1983 Sch 1 para 3). As to the buildings in which banns may be published see PARA 65 et seq.
5 As to the publication of banns see PARA 65 et seq. As to parties 'knowingly and wilfully' marrying without due publication of banns see *Hooper (otherwise Harrison) v Hooper* [1959] 2 All ER 575, [1959] 1 WLR 1021.
6 As to the granting of a common licence see PARA 76 et seq.
7 Ie under the Marriage Act 1949 Pt III (ss 26–52) (see PARA 54 et seq).
8 As to the meaning of 'superintendent registrar' see PARA 22 note 1.
9 Marriage Act 1949 s 25(b) (s 25(b)–(d) amended by the Immigration and Asylum Act 1999 Sch 14 paras 3, 7).
10 Ie void by virtue of the Marriage Act 1949 s 3(3) (declaration of dissent from marriage of minor: see PARA 52) or s 12(2) (marriage not solemnised within three months of publication of banns: see PARA 71).
11 Ie void by virtue of the Marriage Act 1949 s 16(3) (marriage not solemnised within three months after grant of licence: see PARA 79).
12 Ie by virtue of the Marriage Act 1949 s 33(2) (marriage not solemnised within the applicable period: see PARA 101).

13 Marriage Act 1949 s 25(c) (as amended: see note 9).
14 Marriage Act 1949 s 25(d) (as amended: see note 9).
15 As to who may solemnise a marriage according to the rites of the Church of England see PARA 80.
16 Marriage Act 1949 s 25. As to the effect of a void marriage see PARA 320. As to criminal liability for solemnising a marriage according to the rites of the Church of England without due publication of banns or at an unauthorised place or under false pretence of Holy Orders see PARAS 59, 65, 80.
17 *R v Wroxton Inhabitants* (1833) 4 B & Ad 640 at 646; *Wright v Elwood* (1835) 1 Curt 49; *Wright v Elwood* (1837) 1 Curt 662; *Dormer (falsely called Williams) v Williams* (1838) 1 Curt 870; *Holmes v Simmons (falsely called Holmes)* (1868) LR 1 P & D 523; *Templeton v Tyree* (1872) LR 2 P & D 420; *Greaves v Greaves* (1872) LR 2 P & D 423; *R v Rea* (1872) LR 1 CCR 365. The marriage of a minor actually solemnised without the necessary parental consent is valid: *R v Birmingham Inhabitants* (1828) 8 B & C 29.
18 *Dancer v Dancer* [1949] P 147, [1948] 2 All ER 731. See further PARA 69.
19 *Chipchase v Chipchase* [1939] P 391, [1939] 3 All ER 895; for subsequent proceedings see *Chipchase v Chipchase (otherwise Leetch, otherwise Matthews)* [1942] P 37, [1941] 1 All ER 560.
20 *R v Wroxton Inhabitants* (1833) 4 B & Ad 640; *Wright v Elwood* (1835) 1 Curt 49; *Wright v Elwood* (1837) 1 Curt 662; *Gompertz v Kensit* (1872) LR 13 Eq 369; *Templeton v Tyree* (1872) LR 2 P & D 420.
21 See the Marriage Act 1949 s 25(b) (as amended: see note 9); and the test stated in *Dancer v Dancer* [1949] P 147 at 150, [1948] 2 All ER 731 at 734, citing *Chipchase v Chipchase* [1939] P 391 at 397, [1939] 3 All ER 895 at 899, 900. See also *Midgeley (falsely called Wood) v Wood* (1859) 30 LJPM & A 57; *Wormald v Neale and Wormald (falsely called Neale)* (1868) 19 LT 93; *Small v Small and Furber* (1923) 67 Sol Jo 277; and see PARA 69.

329. Marriages under Registrar General's licence. If any persons knowingly and wilfully intermarry under the authority of a Registrar General's licence[1]:

(1) without having given due notice of marriage to the superintendent registrar[2];

(2) without a Registrar General's licence[3];

(3) on the authority of a licence which is[4] void[5];

(4) in any place other than the place specified in the notice of marriage and the Registrar General's licence[6];

(5) in the absence of a registrar[7], or, where the marriage is by civil ceremony, of a superintendent registrar[8], except where the marriage is solemnised according to the usages of the Society of Friends or is a marriage between two persons professing the Jewish religion according to the usages of the Jews[9],

the marriage is void[10].

1 As to a Registrar General's licence see PARA 161 et seq. As to the meaning of 'Registrar General' see PARA 46 note 5.
2 Marriage Act 1949 s 49(a); Marriage (Registrar General's Licence) Act 1970 s 13. As to the giving of notice of marriage see PARA 87 et seq.
3 Marriage Act 1949 s 49(b) (amended by the Immigration and Asylum Act 1999 Sch 14 para 27); Marriage (Registrar General's Licence) Act 1970 s 13(a) (amended by the Immigration and Asylum Act 1999 Sch 14 paras 38, 42).
4 Ie by virtue of the Marriage (Registrar General's Licence) Act 1970 s 8(2) (see PARA 165).
5 Marriage Act 1949 s 49(d); Marriage (Registrar General's Licence) Act 1970 s 13(c).
6 Marriage Act 1949 s 49(e); Marriage (Registrar General's Licence) Act 1970 s 13(d).
7 As to the meaning of 'registrar' see PARA 88 note 1.
8 As to the meaning of 'superintendent registrar' see PARA 22 note 1.
9 Marriage Act 1949 s 49(f), (g); Marriage (Registrar General's Licence) Act 1970 s 13(e).
10 Marriage Act 1949 s 49; Marriage (Registrar General's Licence) Act 1970 s 13. As to the criminal liability for improper solemnisation of such a marriage see PARA 180.

330. Marriages under superintendent registrar's certificates. If any persons knowingly and wilfully intermarry under the provisions relating to marriage under superintendent registrar's certificates[1]:

(1) without having given due notice of marriage to the superintendent registrar[2];

(2) without a certificate for marriage having been duly issued, in respect of each of the persons to be married, by the superintendent registrar to whom notice of marriage was given[3];

(3) on the authority of certificates which are[4] void[5];

(4) in any place other than the church, chapel, registered building[6], office or other place specified in the notices of marriage and certificates of the superintendent registrar[7];

(5) in the case of a marriage purporting to be a marriage on approved premises[8], on any premises that at the time the marriage is solemnised are not approved premises[9];

(6) in the case of a marriage in a registered building, not being a marriage in the presence of an authorised person[10], in the absence of a registrar[11] of the registration district[12] in which the registered building is situated[13];

(7) in the case of a marriage in the office of a superintendent registrar, in the absence of the superintendent registrar or of a registrar of the registration district of that superintendent registrar[14];

(8) in the case of a marriage on approved premises, in the absence of the superintendent registrar of the registration district in which the premises are situated or in the absence of a registrar of that district[15]; or

(9) in the case of a marriage solemnised, otherwise than according to the rites of the Church of England, at the place where a person usually resides[16], in the absence of any superintendent registrar or registrar whose presence at that marriage is[17] required[18],

the marriage is void[19].

1   Ie under the Marriage Act 1949 Pt III (ss 26–52) (see PARA 54 et seq).
2   Marriage Act 1949 s 49(a). As to the meaning of 'superintendent registrar' see PARA 22 note 1. As to notice of marriage generally see PARA 87 et seq. As to the giving of notice of marriage by an officer, seaman or marine on one of Her Majesty's ships at sea see PARA 131.
3   Marriage Act 1949 s 49(b) (s 49(b), (c), (d), (e) amended by the Immigration and Asylum Act 1999 Sch 14 paras 3, 27). As to the issue of certificates of marriage generally see PARA 54; and as to the issue of certificates on board Her Majesty's ships see PARA 131.
4   Ie by virtue of the Marriage Act 1949 s 33(2) (marriage not solemnised within the applicable period: see PARA 101).
5   Marriage Act 1949 s 49(d) (as amended: see note 3).
6   As to the meaning of 'registered building' see PARA 54 note 3.
7   Marriage Act 1949 s 49(e) (as amended: see note 3).
8   Ie in the case of a marriage purporting to be in pursuance of the Marriage Act 1949 s 26(1)(bb) (see PARA 54). As to the meaning of 'approved premises' see PARA 54 note 6.
9   Marriage Act 1949 s 49(ee) (s 49(ee), (gg) added, s 49(f) amended, by the Marriage Act 1994 Schedule paras 1, 3).
10   As to the meaning of 'authorised person' see PARA 107.
11   As to the meaning of 'registrar' see PARA 88 note 1.
12   As to the meaning of 'registration district' see PARA 87 note 4.
13   Marriage Act 1949 s 49(f) (as amended: see note 9). As to the persons required to be present see PARA 106.
14   Marriage Act 1949 s 49(g). As to the persons required to be present see PARA 102.
15   Marriage Act 1949 s 49(gg) (as added: see note 9).
16   Ie in the case of a marriage to which the Marriage Act 1949 s 45A applies (see PARA 173).
17   Ie as required by the Marriage Act 1949 s 45A.
18   Marriage Act 1949 s 49(h) (added by the Marriage Act 1983 Sch 1 para 13).

19 Marriage Act 1949 s 49. As to the nature and effect of void marriages see PARA 320; and as to
the criminal liability for solemnising a marriage at an unauthorised place, or out of time or in
the absence of a registrar, see PARA 180 et seq.

(iii) Voidable Marriages and Civil Partnerships

A. CONSENT, MENTAL DISORDER, PREGNANCY AND GENDER REASSIGNMENT

331.   Failure to give valid consent. A marriage[1] or civil partnership is voidable
on the ground that either party did not validly consent to it, whether in
consequence of duress[2], mistake[3], unsoundness of mind[4] or otherwise[5].

1   Ie a marriage celebrated after 31 July 1971 (the day before the date on which the Nullity of
Marriage Act 1971 (repealed) came into force). As to voidable marriages before 1 August 1971
see PARA 345.
2   As to duress see PARA 43.
3   As to mistake see PARA 44.
4   As to unsoundness of mind see PARAS 45, 332.
5   Matrimonial Causes Act 1973 s 12(c); Civil Partnership Act 2004 s 50(1)(a). See *Re Roberts,
Roberts v Roberts* [1978] 3 All ER 225, [1978] 1 WLR 653, CA. The grounds specified in the
Matrimonial Causes Act 1973 s 12 are the only grounds on which a marriage celebrated after
31 July 1971 is voidable (s 12); no corresponding restriction is explicitly imposed in respect of
civil partnerships, but it may be inferred in relation to the grounds specified in the Civil
Partnership Act 2004 s 50.

332.   Mental disorder. A marriage[1] or civil partnership is voidable on the
ground that at the time of the marriage or civil partnership either party, though
capable of giving a valid consent, was suffering, whether continuously or
intermittently, from mental disorder[2] of such a kind or to such an extent as to be
unfitted for marriage or civil partnership[3]. A party may maintain his own past
mental incapacity as a ground for annulment[4].

1   Ie a marriage celebrated after 31 July 1971 (the day before the date on which the Nullity of
Marriage Act 1971 (repealed) came into force). As to voidable marriages before 1 August 1971
see PARA 345.
2   Ie within the meaning of the Mental Health Act 1983: see MENTAL HEALTH vol 30(2) (Reissue)
PARA 402.
3   Matrimonial Causes Act 1973 s 12(d); Civil Partnership Act 2004 s 50(1)(b), (2). As to the
exclusivity of these grounds see PARA 331 note 5. As to the burden of proving the existence of
mental disorder see PARA 45. See also *Bennett v Bennett* [1969] 1 All ER 539, [1969] 1 WLR
430 (where it was held that in order to succeed a petitioner had to establish mental disorder
within the meaning of Mental Health Act 1959 s 4 (repealed), and had to go on to show that, as
a result thereof, the respondent was incapable of living in a married state and of carrying out the
ordinary duties and obligations of marriage); c f *Re Roberts, Roberts v Roberts* [1978] 3 All ER
225, [1978] 1 WLR 653, CA.
4   *Turner v Meyers* (1808) 1 Hag Con 414. See also *Parnell v Parnell* (1814) 2 Hag Con 169;
Morison v Morison (1745) cited 2 Hag Con 169 at 170; *Fust v Bowerman* (1790) cited 2 Hag
Con 171, 2 Add 402; *Baldwin v Baldwin* (1919) Times, 30 and 31 July (marriage during escape
from asylum); *Paspati v Paspati* [1914] P 110.

333.   Pregnancy by some other person. A marriage[1] or civil partnership is
voidable on the ground that at the time of the marriage or civil partnership the
respondent was pregnant by some person other than the petitioner[2].

1   Ie a marriage celebrated after 31 July 1971 (the day before the date on which the Nullity of
Marriage Act 1971 (repealed) came into force). As to voidable marriages before 1 August 1971
see PARA 345.
2   Matrimonial Causes Act 1973 s 12(f); Civil Partnership Act 2004 s 50(1)(c). As to the
exclusivity of these grounds see PARA 331 note 5. See *Jackson v Jackson (otherwise Prudom)*

[1939] P 172, [1939] 1 All ER 471; *Smith v Smith* [1948] P 77, [1947] 2 All ER 741, CA; *W v W* (1965) 109 Sol Jo 920 (could not be proved husband was not the father; petition dismissed).

334. Gender reassignment. A marriage[1] or civil partnership is voidable on the ground that an interim gender recognition certificate[2] has, after the time of the marriage or the formation of the civil partnership, been issued to either party to the marriage or civil partnership[3], or on the ground that the respondent is a person whose gender at the time of the marriage or civil partnership had become[4] the acquired gender[5] and the court is satisfied that the applicant was at the time of the marriage or civil partnership ignorant of this[6].

1   Ie a marriage celebrated after 31 July 1971 (the day before the date on which the Nullity of Marriage Act 1971 (repealed) came into force). As to voidable marriages before 1 August 1971 see PARA 345.
2   Ie under the Gender Recognition Act 2004: see CONSTITUTIONAL LAW AND HUMAN RIGHTS. All documents in family proceedings brought under these provisions must, while they are in the custody of the court, be kept in a place of special security: Family Proceedings Rules 1991, SI 1991/1247, r 10.21B (added by SI 2005/559; amended by SI 2005/2922). As to the annulment of marriages and civil partnerships on gender reassignment grounds see further the Gender Recognition Act 2004 ss 5, 5A, 6; the Family Proceedings Rules 1991, SI 1991/1247, r 2.51C.
3   Matrimonial Causes Act 1973 s 12(g) (s 12(g), (h) added, s 13(3) amended, by the Gender Recognition Act 2004 Sch 2 paras 1, 2, Sch 4 paras 4–6); Civil Partnership Act 2004 s 50(1)(d). As to the exclusivity of these grounds see PARA 331 note 5.
4   See note 2.
5   Matrimonial Causes Act 1973 s 12(h) (as added: see note 3); Civil Partnership Act 2004 s 50(1)(e).
6   Matrimonial Causes Act 1973 s 13(3) (as amended: see note 3); Civil Partnership Act 2004 s 51(6).

B. FAILURE TO CONSUMMATE MARRIAGE

335. Test of consummation. The test of consummation is penetration[1], but penetration for a brief period without emission inside or outside the wife might in particular circumstances not amount to ordinary and complete intercourse[2]. The possibility of incipient or imperfect coitus is not enough to establish consummation[3], but, once coitus is established[4], it is not affected by the use of contraceptives[5], nor, it would appear, is the coitus affected by its being coitus interruptus[6].

The cause of non-consummation may be wilful refusal, even where the spouse at fault is incapable[7], but, where both incapacity and wilful refusal are alleged, the court must still ascertain the cause of the non-consummation[8].

1   See *R v R (otherwise F)* [1952] 1 All ER 1194; and note 4. See also *Baxter v Baxter* [1948] AC 274 at 290, [1947] 2 All ER 886 at 892, HL per Lord Jowitt LC ('In [the Matrimonial Causes Act 1973 s 12] Parliament used the word 'consummate' as that word is understood in common parlance and in the light of social conditions known to exist').
2   *W (otherwise K) v W* [1967] 3 All ER 178n, [1967] 1 WLR 1554.
3   *D–e v A–g* (1845) 1 Rob Eccl 279 at 299 per Dr Lushington; *B v B* [1955] P 42, sub nom *D v D* [1954] 2 All ER 598. For cases on fecundatio ab extra and artificial insemination see PARA 340 notes 1, 2.
4   As to what constitutes coitus see *R v R (otherwise F)* [1952] 1 All ER 1194 (where it was held that a marriage can be consummated by erectio and intromissio without emissio).
5   *Baxter v Baxter* [1948] AC 274, [1947] 2 All ER 886, HL, overruling *Cowen v Cowen* [1946] P 36, [1945] 2 All ER 197, CA, and disapproving *J (otherwise S) v J* [1947] P 158, [1947] 2 All ER 43, CA.
6   See *White (otherwise Berry) v White* [1948] P 330, [1948] 2 All ER 151, followed in *Cackett (otherwise Trice) v Cackett* [1950] P 253, [1950] 1 All ER 677; and not following *Grimes*

(otherwise Edwards) v Grimes [1948] P 323, [1948] 2 All ER 147 (where it was held that coitus interruptus did not amount to consummation). Cf *R v R (otherwise F)* [1952] 1 All ER 1194 (cited in note 4).

7 *S v S (otherwise C)* [1956] P 1 at 10, [1954] 3 All ER 736 at 740, not following obiter dictum in *Morgan v Morgan* [1949] WN 250, CA.

8 See PARA 863.

336.   Incapacity to consummate marriage.   A marriage[1] is voidable on the ground that the marriage has not been consummated[2] owing to the incapacity of either party to consummate it[3]. A party is incapable of consummating a marriage if his or her mental health or physical condition makes consummation of the marriage a practical impossibility[4]. The condition must be one which existed at the time of the marriage[5].

1 Ie a marriage celebrated after 31 July 1971 (the day before the date on which the Nullity of Marriage Act 1971 (repealed) came into force). As to voidable marriages before 1 August 1971 see PARA 345.

2 As to the test for consummation see PARA 335.

3 Matrimonial Causes Act 1973 s 12(a). As to the exclusivity of these grounds see PARA 331 note 5.

4 *G– v G–* (1871) LR 2 P & D 287; *S v S (otherwise C)* [1956] P 1, [1954] 3 All ER 736. See also *M v M (otherwise B)* [1957] P 139, [1956] 3 All ER 769 (wife took no steps to have operation to cure incapacity); *B (otherwise S) v B* [1958] 2 All ER 76, [1958] 1 WLR 619; *S v S (otherwise W)* [1963] P 162, [1962] 2 All ER 816, CA; *Corbett v Corbett (otherwise Ashley)* [1971] P 83, [1970] 2 All ER 33. In any proceedings for nullity of marriage, evidence on the question of sexual capacity must be heard in camera unless in any case the judge is satisfied that in the interests of justice any such evidence ought to be heard in open court: Matrimonial Causes Act 1973 s 48(2).

5 A defect arising subsequently is not a ground for annulment: *Brown v Brown* (1828) 1 Hag Ecc 523. As to the practice of the ecclesiastical courts on this point see *Napier v Napier (otherwise Goodban)* [1915] P 184 at 190, CA per Pickford LJ.

337.   Opportunity of cure.   If there is some physical defect which can be cured without danger to the party suffering from it, the court is entitled to require that opportunity for cure is to be given to that party before proceeding to a decree[1]. A spouse is to be regarded as incurable, and consummation, therefore, a practical impossibility, if the condition could only be remedied by an operation attended by danger[2] or if the spouse is at fault by refusing to submit to an operation[3]. In deciding whether a state of impotence at the date of the marriage and continuing to the date of the action is remediable, the court must take into consideration further medical or surgical treatment which might remove the cause of the disability[4].

1 *Brown v Brown* (1828) 1 Hag Ecc 523; and see *Welde (alias Aston) v Welde* (1731) 2 Lee 580 at 586; *S– (falsely called E–) v E–* (1863) 3 Sw & Tr 240. Cf *L v L (falsely called W)* (1882) 7 PD 16 (operation involving no great risk to life; decree granted). The former practice of the court of adjourning a suit for further attempts when it deemed fit is obsolete: see *T v M (falsely called T)* (1865) LR 1 P & D 31; *M– (falsely called H–) v H–* (1864) 3 Sw & Tr 517 at 523.

2 In *W– v H– (falsely called W–)* (1861) 2 Sw & Tr 240 at 244, 245, it was said that, where a congenital malformation could be removed only at considerable risk to life, it would not be proper for a petitioner to propose that the respondent's life be placed in danger.

3 *S v S (otherwise C)* [1956] P 1, [1954] 3 All ER 736, applying observations of Lord Penzance in *G– v G–* (1871) LR 2 P & D 287 at 291, and citing *H v H* (31 March 1954, unreported), CA.

4 *WY v AY* 1946 SC 27, applied in *S v S (otherwise C)* [1956] P 1, [1954] 3 All ER 736 (where the husband was held to have failed to prove that his marriage was unconsummated through his wife's incapacity, for, though at the date of the presentation of the petition the wife was incapable, at the date of hearing she was willing to undergo, and during an adjournment (not for that purpose: see note 1) did undergo, an operation which removed the impediment); *S v S (otherwise W)* [1963] P 162, [1962] 3 All ER 816, CA; *Corbett v Corbett (otherwise Ashley)* [1971] P 83, [1970] 2 All ER 33.

338.   Refusal of medical examination or treatment. A refusal by a respondent in a suit for nullity on the ground of impotence to undergo examination or treatment raises an inference[1] of incapacity on which the court may grant a decree, on affirmative evidence by or on behalf of the petitioner[2].

1   In *W v S (otherwise W)* [1905] P 231, Sir Gorell Barnes P expressly refrained from inferring impotence from the wife's refusal to submit to medical examination, although he conceded that there were some cases where such an inference should be made.

2   *Sparrow (falsely called Harrison) v Harrison* (1841) 3 Curt 16 (affd sub nom *Harrison v Harrison* (1848) 4 Moo PCC 96), PC; *W– v H– (falsely called W–)* (1861) 2 Sw & Tr 240; *E v F. (otherwise T)* (1902) 50 WR 607; *B (otherwise H) v B* [1901] P 39; *S v B (falsely called S)* (1905) 21 TLR 219 (decree granted; inference drawn notwithstanding delay of 17 years); *W v S (otherwise W)* [1905] P 231; *G v G (falsely called K)* (1908) 25 TLR 328, CA (wife petitioner's refusal to undergo minor operation); *W v W (otherwise L)* [1912] P 78; *Re L (an infant)* [1968] P 119, [1967] 2 All ER 1110 (affd [1968] P 119 at 144, [1968] 1 All ER 20, CA). Cf, however, *Intract v Intract (otherwise Jacobs)* [1933] P 190 (woman respondent of unsound mind; order for inspection); and see *T v M (falsely called T)* (1865) LR 1 P & D 31. As to procedure on medical inspection see PARA 803 et seq.

339.   Sterility and contraception. Proof that a wife is incapable of becoming a mother is not a sufficient ground for a decree of nullity, if she is capable of having sexual intercourse[1]. The sterility of a husband, whether natural or artificial, as by the use of contraceptives, is also no ground for annulment[2].

1   *B–n v B–n* (1854) 1 Ecc & Ad 248, PC; *Baxter v Baxter* [1948] AC 274, [1947] 2 All ER 886, HL; cf *D–e v A–g (falsely calling herself D–e)* (1845) 1 Rob Eccl 279 (where there were further defects); *L– v L– (otherwise D–)* (1922) 38 TLR 697.

2   *Baxter v Baxter* [1948] AC 274, [1947] 2 All ER 886, HL, disapproving *J (otherwise S) v J* [1947] P 158, [1947] 2 All ER 43, CA; *R v R (otherwise F)* [1952] 1 All ER 1194 (penetration, but no ejaculation).

340.   Malformation etc. It is open to a husband[1] or wife[2] to petition the court as soon as he or she discovers that the other, from malformation or other defect, is incapable of sexual intercourse.

1   Decrees were granted to husbands in *D–e v A–g (falsely calling herself D–e)* (1845) 1 Rob Eccl 279 (wife with no uterus and a vagina forming a cul-de-sac; complete coitus impossible); *W– v H– (falsely called W–)* (1861) 2 Sw & Tr 240 (congenital malformation of wife, rendering consummation impossible, only removable at considerable risk to her); *B v B* [1955] P 42, sub nom *D v D* [1954] 2 All ER 598 (wife with no vagina, artificial vagina created but defect not curable and proper intercourse impossible); *G– v G–* (1871) LR 2 P & D 287 (a middle-aged wife successfully resisted intercourse for nearly three years; no malformation; refusal to submit to remedies, because dangerous); *P v L (falsely called P)* (1873) 3 PD 73n (wife, aged 18, hysterical, struck husband when he attempted intercourse; threats to drown herself; refused remedies; said no sexual desire); *H v P (falsley called H)* (1873) LR 3 P & D 126 (three years' cohabitation; husband's attempts excited hysteria and flight; wife, aged 25, refused examination; cf the remarks of Hannen P in *S v A (otherwise S)* (1878) 3 PD 72 as to incapacity being inferred from persistent refusal); *L v L (falsely called W)* (1882) 7 PD 16 (wife aged 23; vaginismus; slept with husband occasionally for three years; refused slightly dangerous operation); *F v P (falsely called F)* (1896) 75 LT 192 (widow, no children, not a virgin, slept with second husband for five months; no defect in either; she admitted non-consummation; decree granted on ground of latent incapacity arising from hysteria); *E v E (otherwise T)* (1902) 50 WR 607 (wife resisted full intercourse for six months; declined to have children; refused inspection); *P v P (otherwise G)* (1909) 25 TLR 638 (respondent's declaration of incapacity); *C v C (otherwise H)* (1911) 27 TLR 421 (invincible repugnance; no cohabitation); *F v P (otherwise F)* (1911) 27 TLR 429 (one day's cohabitation, resistance and hysteria); *W v W (otherwise L)* [1912] P 78 (no cohabitation; respondent wrote, 'I can never be a wife to you'); *Vickery v Vickery (otherwise Cox)* (1920) 37 TLR 332 (prolonged resistance and hysteria over seven years); *G v G* [1924] AC 349, HL (invincible repugnance; incapacity inferred); *Clarke (otherwise Talbott) v Clarke* [1943] 2 All ER 540 (wife refused intercourse for 14 years, though she conceived a child by the husband through fecundatio ab extra, i e she had conceived without

penetration actually occurring); cf *Snowman v Snowman* [1934] P 186 (two miscarriages through fecundatio ab extra); *M v M (otherwise B)* [1957] P 139, [1956] 3 All ER 769 (vaginismus; wife had not bothered to have an operation); *G v G (otherwise H)* [1961] P 87, [1960] 3 All ER 56 (wife's offer to undergo operation not genuine); *Corbett v Corbett (otherwise Ashley)* [1971] P 83, [1970] 2 All ER 33.

Decrees were refused in *Briggs v Morgan* (1820) 3 Phillim 325 (second marriage of wife of advanced age); *Brown v Brown* (1828) 1 Hag Ecc 523 (man 60, woman 52; court not satisfied impediment in wife had not been removed, but observed that he ought to take her tanquam soror, ie live with her as if she were his sister); *S v A (otherwise S)* (1878) 3 PD 72 (parties lived together nine years; court not satisfied as to husband's attempts); *Napier v Napier (otherwise Goodban)* [1915] P 65; affd [1915] P 184, CA (wife's refusal; incapacity not inferred); *Finegan v Finegan (otherwise McHardy)* (1917) 33 TLR 173 (wife's stipulation before marriage for no intercourse; incapacity not inferred); *Hudston v Hudston (otherwise Newbigging)* (1922) 39 TLR 108 (persistent refusal: see PARA 342); *T v T (otherwise J)* (1931) 47 TLR 629 (husband's allegation of non-consummation not accepted); *SY v SY (otherwise W)* [1963] P 37, sub nom *S v S (otherwise W) (No 2)* [1962] 3 All ER 55, CA (incapacity curable by operation).

2   Decrees were granted to wives in *Pollard (falsely called Wybourn) v Wybourn* (1828) 1 Hag Ecc 725 (husband 41, wife 17; 11 years later she was virgo intacta; he, having confessed his impotence, left the country); *N–r (falsely called M–e) v M–e* (1853) 2 Rob Eccl 625 (husband 45, wife 30; slept together for nearly two years; wife virgo intacta; husband impotent quoad hanc; per curiam, if both appear capable, the impotence must be attributed to the husband, unless the woman resists; but see PARA 863); *G–s (falsely called T–e) v T–e* (1854) 1 Ecc & Ad 389 (separation at end of three months; no perfect signs of virginity or of connection; husband, although no visible defect, believed to be incurably impotent); *Lewis (falsely called Hayward) v Hayward* (1866) 35 LJP & M 105, HL (virgo intacta after 14 years; onus on husband); *B (otherwise H) v B* [1901] P 39 (separate beds, eight months after marriage, against wife's wish; afterwards same bed and attempts; deed of separation unwillingly executed by wife; husband refused examination); *R (otherwise K) v R* (1907) 24 TLR 65 (wife seduced by another before marriage; husband admitted impotence); *J (otherwise K) v J* (1908) 24 TLR 622 (man's masturbation); *C (otherwise H) v C* [1921] P 399 (petitioner's evidence of man's impotence accepted, medical evidence inconclusive); *Kay v Kay* (1934) 152 LT 264 (wife virgin after three years; husband's incapacity inferred); *REL (otherwise R) v EL* [1949] P 211, sub nom *L v L* [1949] 1 All ER 141 (wife had child by artificial insemination using husband's seed).

Decrees were refused in *U (falsely called J) v J* (1867) LR 1 P & D 460 (doctor's evidence uncertain and husband denied; wife's assertion not accepted), commented on in *C (otherwise H) v C* [1921] P 399; *S– (falsely called E–) v E–* (1863) 3 Sw & Tr 240 (court refused to assume permanent incapacity where, during a cohabitation of under three months, two attempts were made, unsuccessful owing to the husband's habit of masturbation (possibly curable), and the wife's health was affected); but cf *J (otherwise K) v J*.

341.   **Petitioner's own incapacity.**   A nullity suit is maintainable on the ground of the petitioner's own incapacity[1], provided that he or she was not aware of the incapacity at the time of the marriage, unless it is unjust in all the circumstances[2]. The spouse whose defect or misfortune is the cause of the non-consummation is not entitled as of right in all circumstances to insist on a decree, regardless of the wishes, rights and interests of the spouse against whom no defect can be alleged[3].

An averment of impotency quoad hunc or quoad hanc[4] is sufficient to support a decree of nullity[5].

1   *Harthan v Harthan* [1949] P 115, [1948] 2 All ER 639, CA. See also *Hodgkins v Hodgkins* [1950] P 183, [1950] 1 All ER 619, CA; *A v A (sued as B)* (1887) 19 LR Ir 403, CA; *G v G (falsely called K)* (1908) 25 TLR 328, CA (where the wife petitioner could have been cured by a slight operation; Cozens-Hardy MR at 329 said that it was a matter for the court's discretion, which it would exercise sparingly). Cf *Norton v Seton (falsely called Norton)* (1819) 3 Phillim 147; *Halfen (otherwise Boddington) v Boddington* (1881) 6 PD 13.

2   *Harthan v Harthan* [1949] P 115, [1948] 2 All ER 639, CA.

3   *Pettit v Pettit* [1963] P 177 at 186, 190, [1962] 3 All ER 37 at 40, 41, 44, CA; *Morgan v Morgan (otherwise Ransom)* [1959] P 92, [1959] 1 All ER 539; *Mogridge v Mogridge* (1965) 109 Sol Jo 814, CA.

4   Ie impotency in respect of that particular man or woman.

5   *C (otherwise H) v C* [1921] P 399; and see *G v G (falsely called K)* (1908) 25 TLR 328, CA; *G v G* [1912] P 173; *N–r (falsely called M–e) v M–e* (1853) 2 Rob Eccl 625. See *The Countess of Essex's Case* (1613) 2 State Tr 785 at 858 (where the doctrine was first accepted).

342.   Wilful refusal to consummate.   A marriage[1] is voidable on the ground that the marriage has not been consummated[2] owing to the wilful refusal of the respondent to consummate it[3]. 'Wilful refusal' means a settled and definite decision come to without just excuse; but in order to determine whether there has been a refusal regard must be had to the whole history of the marriage[4]. The number of refused proposals for consummation required to establish wilful refusal will, therefore, vary with the circumstances of each case[5]. In some cases parties marry on the understanding that there will be no sexual intercourse[6]. The manner in which the proposals were made is to be considered, in particular whether they were made with the necessary tact, persuasion and encouragement which an ordinary spouse would use in the circumstances[7]. Wilful refusal must have persisted up to the date of the presentation of the petition[8]. The burden of proving affirmatively that the marriage has not been consummated is on the petitioner[9].

1   Ie a marriage celebrated after 31 July 1971 (the day before the date on which the Nullity of Marriage Act 1971 (repealed) came into force). As to voidable marriages before 1 August 1971 see PARA 345.
2   As to the test for consummation see PARA 335.
3   Matrimonial Causes Act 1973 s 12(b). As to the exclusivity of these grounds see PARA 331 note 5.
4   *Horton v Horton* [1947] 2 All ER 871, HL; *S v S (otherwise C)* [1956] P 1, [1954] 3 All ER 736 (mere neglect to comply with a request is not necessarily the same as a refusal (see at 16 and at 744); whether refusal to have treatment amounts to wilful refusal depends on the history of the marriage as a whole (see at 15, 16 and at 743, 744)); *Jodla v Jodla (otherwise Czarnomska)* [1960] 1 All ER 625, [1960] 1 WLR 236 (Roman Catholics were married in a register office, it being agreed that a church ceremony should follow; failure by the husband to arrange for that ceremony, in spite of repeated requests by the wife for him to do so; amounted to wilful refusal on his part), followed in *Kaur v Singh* [1972] 1 All ER 292, [1972] 1 WLR 105, CA (failure to arrange Sikh religious ceremony). In a Canadian case it was held that refusal to consummate may be inferred where one spouse refuses to live with the other: see *G v G* [1974] 1 WWR 79, Man SC. See also *A v J (nullity proceedings)* [1989] 1 FLR 110, [1989] Fam Law 63.
5   See *Morgan v Morgan* [1949] WN 250, CA (parties lived together four days in all) (for comment on observations in that case see *S v S (otherwise C)* [1956] P 1 at 10, [1954] 3 All ER 736 at 740); *Way v Way* [1950] P 71, [1949] 2 All ER 959 ('Russian marriage' case; consummation proposed on two nights only); *Brown (otherwise Nuttall) v Brown* (1955) Times, 15 February (two nights; wife glad to get rid of husband who was incapable in respect of former marriage; it was held that there was no wilful refusal and no incapacity in respect of present marriage).
6   As to the effect of companionship agreements see *Scott v Scott (otherwise Fone)* [1959] P 103n, [1959] 1 All ER 531; *Morgan v Morgan (otherwise Ransom)* [1959] P 92, [1959] 1 All ER 539.
7   *Baxter v Baxter* [1947] 1 All ER 387 at 388, CA; on appeal [1948] AC 274, [1947] 2 All ER 886, HL; *Tudzinski v Tudzinska (otherwise Rusin)* (1960) Times, 9 November.
8   *S v S (otherwise C)* [1956] P 1 at 15, [1954] 3 All ER 736 at 743; *W v W (child of the family)* [1984] FLR 796 at 799, CA.
9   *Harthan v Harthan* as reported in [1948] 2 All ER 639 at 642, CA; *Potter v Potter* (1975) 5 Fam Law 161, CA; *A v J (nullity proceedings)* [1989] 1 FLR 110, [1989] Fam Law 63.

C. VENEREAL DISEASE

343.   Venereal disease.   A marriage[1] is voidable on the ground that at the time of the marriage the respondent was suffering from venereal disease[2] in a communicable[3] form[4].

1 Ie a marriage celebrated after 31 July 1971 (the day before the date on which the Nullity of Marriage Act 1971 (repealed) came into force). As to voidable marriages before 1 August 1971 see PARA 345.

2 Ie presumably whether innocently contracted or not: cf *Butler v Butler* [1917] P 244.

3 See *Lawrence v Lawrence* (2 June 1954, unreported) ('communicable' meant 'communicable to any person', so that, where the wife's syphilis was communicable to a child of the marriage but not to the husband, the husband was entitled to a decree).

4 Matrimonial Causes Act 1973 s 12(e); and see *C v C* (1962) 106 Sol Jo 959 (syphilis; decree granted). As to the exclusivity of these grounds see PARA 331 note 5.

(iv) Marriages Celebrated before 1 August 1971

344. Void marriages. A marriage celebrated before 1 August 1971[1] is void:

(1) where the marriage is bigamous[2];

(2) where there is a mistake as to identity of the person with whom the contract of marriage is made or as to the nature, but not the effect of, the ceremony[3];

(3) where the parties to the marriage are within the prohibited degrees of consanguinity and affinity[4];

(4) where the due forms and ceremonies are not observed in the marriage[5];

(5) where either party is not of age[6];

(6) where the marriage is a sham[7];

(7) where the parties are not respectively male and female[8].

1 Ie the date on which the Nullity of Marriage Act 1971 came into force. As to void marriages celebrated after that date see PARA 326 et seq.

2 Ie where at the time of the ceremony of marriage one spouse was already married and the other party to the previous marriage was still alive and the marriage still subsisting: see PARA 10; *Dalrymple v Dalrymple* (1811) 2 Hag Con 54 (on appeal (1814) 2 Hag Con 137n); *Hayes (falsely called Watts) v Watts* (1819) 3 Phillim 43. A decree of nullity follows as of right: *Miles v Chilton (falsely called Miles)* (1849) 1 Rob Eccl 684; *Andrews (falsely called Ross) v Ross* (1888) 14 PD 15; cf *Turner v Meyers* (1808) 1 Hag Con 414 at 418. The presumption of law that a person, who has not been seen or heard of for not less than seven years, is dead is rebuttable, and the onus of proving death at any particular date is on the person to whose title that fact is essential: see *Lal Chand Marwari v Mahant Ramrup Gir* (1925) 42 TLR 159, PC; *Ivett v Ivett* (1930) 94 JP 237; *Spurgeon v Spurgeon* (1940) 46 TLR 396 (husband's disappearance 22 years previously); *Parkinson v Parkinson* [1939] P 346, [1939] 3 All ER 108 (separation deed; absence of over seven years; facts disclosed left matter of wife's death one of pure speculation; husband held to be entitled to decree); *Tweney v Tweney* [1946] P 180, [1946] 1 All ER 564 (husband disappeared; after ten years, the wife who had made all reasonable attempts to trace him, without success, remarried; she was held to be entitled to pray for a decree dissolving her second marriage, for the second marriage had been properly celebrated, and no evidence had been given to lead the court to doubt that fact); *Chard v Chard (otherwise Northcott)* [1956] P 259, [1955] 3 All ER 721; *Bradshaw v Bradshaw* [1956] P 274n, DC; *Bullock v Bullock* [1960] 2 All ER 307, [1960] 1 WLR 975, DC; *Bennett v Bennett* (1961) 105 Sol Jo 885, CA; cf *Re Peete, Peete v Crompton* [1952] 2 All ER 599; and *Re Watkins, Watkins v Watkins* [1953] 2 All ER 1113, [1953] 1 WLR 1323 (cases under the Inheritance (Family Provision) Act 1938 s 1 as to who could be described as a widow). See also *Bowzer v Ricketts (falsely calling herself Bowzer)* (1795) 1 Hag Con 213; *Bruce v Burke* (1825) 2 Add 471; *Miles v Chilton (falsely called Miles)* (1849) 1 Rob Eccl 684 (misconduct no bar); *Chichester v Mure (falsely called Chichester)* (1863) 3 Sw & Tr 223; *Rogers (otherwise Briscoe, falsely called Halmshaw) v Halmshaw* (1864) 3 Sw & Tr 509; *Noble v Noble and Godman* (1869) LR 1 P & D 691 (marriage between decree nisi and decree absolute bigamous); *Wickham v Wickham* (1880) 6 PD 11; *Bateman v Bateman (otherwise Harrison)* (1898) 78 LT 472; *Trew v Trew (otherwise Lineham)* (1953) Times, 13 February (wife's first marriage in 1922; newspaper report of husband's death 1936; remarriage 1938, but husband in fact living); *Kassim (otherwise Widmann) v Kassim (otherwise Hassim)* [1962] P 224, [1962] 3 All ER 426.

3 See eg *Mehta (otherwise Kohn) v Mehta* [1945] 2 All ER 690 (Hindu ceremony of marriage mistaken for betrothal ceremony). The law in respect of marriage celebrated after 31 July 1971 is different: see PARA 326 et seq.

4   See PARAS 35–37.
5   See PARA 53 et seq.
6   See PARA 41.
7   Eg a mock marriage in a masquerade: see *Moss v Moss* [1897] P 263 at 269. See also *Dunn v Dunn's Trustees* 1930 SC 131 at 135, 141, 146; but cf *Dalrymple v Dalrymple* (1811) 2 Hag Con 54 at 105 (on appeal (1814) 2 Hag Con 137n); *M'Adam v Walker* (1813) 1 Dow 148 at 190; *Bell v Graham* (1859) 13 Moo PCC 242; *Dysart Peerage Case* (1881) 6 App Cas 489 at 537, HL; *H v H* [1954] P 258 at 267, [1953] 2 All ER 1229 at 1233.
8   *Corbett v Corbett (otherwise Ashley)* [1971] P 83, [1970] 2 All ER 33 (the test is a biological one); *Talbot (otherwise Poyntz) v Talbot (otherwise Talbot)* (1967) 111 Sol Jo 213.

345.   Voidable marriages.   A marriage celebrated before 1 August 1971[1] is voidable where either party is impotent[2], where the marriage has been induced by threats, fear or duress[3], or where one spouse was intoxicated at the time of the ceremony[4].

Without prejudice to any other grounds on which a marriage celebrated before 1 August 1971 is by law void[5] or voidable, a marriage celebrated before that date is voidable on the ground:

(1)   that the marriage has not been consummated owing to the wilful refusal of the respondent spouse to consummate it[6];
(2)   that, at the time of the marriage either party to the marriage:
    (a)   was of unsound mind[7];
    (b)   was suffering from mental disorder[8] of such a kind or to such an extent as to be unfitted for marriage and the procreation of children[9]; or
    (c)   was subject to recurrent attacks[10] of insanity or epilepsy[11];
(3)   that at the time of the marriage the respondent was suffering from venereal disease[12] in a communicable form[13];
(4)   that at the time of the marriage the respondent was pregnant by some person other than the petitioner[14]; or
(5)   that an interim gender recognition certificate[15] has been issued to either party to the marriage[16].

In cases falling under heads (2)–(4) above the court[17] must not grant a decree unless it is satisfied that:

(i)   the petitioner was, at the time of the marriage, ignorant of the facts alleged[18];
(ii)   proceedings were instituted within a year from the date of the marriage[19]; and
(iii)   marital intercourse with the consent of the petitioner has not taken place since the petitioner discovered[20] the existence of the grounds for a decree[21],

and in a case falling within head (5) above the court must not grant a decree of nullity unless it is satisfied that proceedings were instituted within six months from the date of issue of the interim gender recognition certificate[22].

1   Ie the date on which the Nullity of Marriage Act 1971 came into force. As to voidable marriages celebrated after that date see PARA 331 et seq.
2   Ie where there is practical impossibility, subsisting at the time of the marriage, of consummating the marriage: see *Greenstreet (falsely called Cumyns) v Cumyns* (1612) 2 Hag Con 332; *Brown v Brown* (1828) 1 Hag Ecc 523 (impotency must subsist at the time of marriage); *A v B* (1868) LR 1 P & D 559 (marriage rendered voidable); *G– v G–* (1871) LR 2 P & D 287 (practical impossibility of consummation); *Turner v Thompson* (1888) 13 PD 37; *S v S (otherwise C)* [1956] P 1 at 14, [1954] 3 All ER 736 at 741, applying *G– v G–* and *H v H* (31 March 1954, unreported), CA. See generally PARA 336.
3   See *H v H* [1954] P 258 at 266, [1953] 2 All ER 1229 at 1232 (consent to marriage negatived by fear of remaining in a particular country; marriage to obtain a foreign passport; no valid

marriage in absence of consent); *Silver (otherwise Kraft) v Silver* [1955] 2 All ER 614, [1955] 1 WLR 728 (ceremony of marriage to enable parties to represent themselves as man and wife; valid marriage where no element of duress); *Parojcic (otherwise Ivetic) v Parojcic* [1959] 1 All ER 1 at 3, 4, [1958] 1 WLR 1280 at 1283; *Buckland v Buckland (otherwise Camilleri)* [1968] P 296, [1967] 2 All ER 300; *Singh v Singh* [1971] P 226, [1971] 2 All ER 828, CA; *Szechter (otherwise Karsov) v Szechter* [1971] P 286, [1970] 3 All ER 905; and PARAS 42, 43.

4   *Sullivan v Sullivan (falsely called Oldacre)* (1818) 2 Hag Con 238 at 246; affd sub nom *Sullivan v Oldacre (falsely called Sullivan)* (1819) 3 Phillim 45; cf *Johnston v Brown* 1823 2 Sh (Ct of Sess) 495 at 495, 496 (in both these cases such a marriage appears to have been considered void). See contra *Roblin v Roblin* (1881) 28 Gr 439; and see *Reid v Aull* (1914) 32 OLR 68, Ont HC.

5   See also PARA 320.

6   Matrimonial Causes Act 1973 Sch 1 para 11(1)(a).

7   Matrimonial Causes Act 1973 Sch 1 para 11(1)(b)(i).

8   Ie within the meaning of the Mental Health Act 1959 (repealed): see now the Mental Health Act 1983 s 1(2); and MENTAL HEALTH vol 30(2) (Reissue) PARA 402. In relation to a marriage celebrated before 1 November 1960, the marriage is voidable if, at the time of the marriage, either party was a mental defective within the meaning of the Mental Deficiency Acts 1913 to 1938 (repealed): Matrimonial Causes Act 1973 Sch 1 para 11(2).

9   Matrimonial Causes Act 1973 Sch 1 para 11(1)(b)(ii).

10 In relation to a marriage celebrated before 1 November 1960, the word 'fits' is to be substituted for the word 'attacks': Matrimonial Causes Act 1973 Sch 1 para 11(2). See also *Robinson v Robinson (by his guardian)* [1965] P 192, [1964] 3 All ER 232; *Woolley v Woolley (by her guardian)* [1968] P 29, [1968] 3 All ER 855.

11 Matrimonial Causes Act 1973 Sch 1 para 11(1)(b)(iii). See *Bennett v Bennett* [1969] 1 All ER 539, [1969] 1 WLR 430; *Speller (otherwise Spearman) v Speller* (1952) Times, 25 November (wife petitioner appearing in person successfully pleaded her own insanity at the time of the marriage). Where the court is satisfied on this ground, it will not investigate a charge of wilful refusal to consummate the marriage: *Iddenden (otherwise Brians) v Iddenden* [1958] 3 All ER 241, [1958] 1 WLR 1041.

12 See *C v C* (1962) 106 Sol Jo 959.

13 Matrimonial Causes Act 1973 Sch 1 para 11(1)(c).

14 Matrimonial Causes Act 1973 Sch 1 para 11(1)(d). See *Jackson v Jackson (otherwise Prudom)* [1939] P 172, [1939] 1 All ER 471; *Smith v Smith* [1948] P 77, [1947] 2 All ER 741, CA. In *Liff v Liff (otherwise Rigby)* [1948] WN 128, evidence as to blood groups of the spouses and the child was admitted.

15 Ie under the Gender Recognition Act 2004: see CONSTITUTIONAL LAW AND HUMAN RIGHTS.

16 Matrimonial Causes Act 1973 Sch 1 para 11(1)(e) (Sch 1 para 11(1)(e), (3A) added by the Gender Recognition Act 2004 Sch 2 paras 1, 4).

17 As to the meaning of 'court' see PARA 346 note 2.

18 Matrimonial Causes Act 1973 Sch 111 para 11(3)(a). See *W v W* (1965) 109 Sol Jo 920.

19 Matrimonial Causes Act 1973 Sch 111 para 11(3)(b). See *Chaplin v Chaplin* [1949] P 72, [1948] 2 All ER 408, CA (time limitation absolute; not affected by equitable principle of granting relief for fraudulent concealment, in this case of pregnancy per alium).

20 See *Smith v Smith* [1948] P 77, [1947] 2 All ER 741, CA (pregnancy per alium; marital intercourse with knowledge of facts on which a reasonable person would have drawn such a conclusion, although petitioner did not).

21 Matrimonial Causes Act 1973 Sch 111 para 11(3)(c). Where the proceedings in respect of the marriage are instituted after 31 July 1971, the application of s 13(1) (see PARA 321) in relation to the marriage is without prejudice to Sch 1 para 11(1)–(3)(a)–(c): Sch 1 para 11(3). See also *Watts v Watts* (1968) 112 Sol Jo 964.

22 Matrimonial Causes Act 1973 Sch 1 para 11(3A) (as added: see note 16).

(3) DIVORCE, DISSOLUTION AND JUDICIAL AND LEGAL SEPARATION

(i) Grounds

346. Irretrievable breakdown sole ground for divorce, dissolution or separation. The sole ground on which a petition for divorce or an application for a dissolution order[1] may be presented or made to the court[2] by either party to a marriage or civil partnership is that the marriage or civil partnership has broken down irretrievably[3].

A petition for judicial separation or a separation order[4] may be presented or made to the court by either party to a marriage or civil partnership on the ground that any such fact as may prove irretrievable breakdown[5] exists[6].

1 A dissolution order is an order of the court which dissolves a civil partnership on the ground that it has broken down irretrievably: Civil Partnership Act 2004 s 37(1)(a).

2 For the purposes of matrimonial and civil partnership proceedings generally 'court', except where the context otherwise requires, means the High Court or, where a county court has jurisdiction by virtue of the Matrimonial and Family Proceedings Act 1984 Pt V (ss 32–44) (see PARA 731 et seq), a county court: Matrimonial Causes Act 1973 s 52(1) (amended by the Matrimonial and Family Proceedings Act 1984 Sch 1 para 16); Matrimonial and Family Proceedings Act 1984 s 27; Civil Partnership Act 2004 s 37(4), Sch 5 para 80(3), Sch 7 para 19. For the purposes of relevant provisions of the Family Law Act 1986 'court' means the High Court or a county court: s 63.

A petition for divorce or an application for the dissolution of a civil partnership is a civil and not a criminal proceeding: see *Galler v Galler* [1954] P 252 at 257, [1954] 1 All ER 536 at 540, CA (following the speech of Lord MacDermott in *Preston-Jones v Preston-Jones* [1951] AC 391 at 417, [1951] 1 All ER 124 at 138, HL); *Mordaunt v Moncreiffe* (1874) LR 2 Sc & Div 374, HL; *Branford v Branford* (1879) 4 PD 72; *Davis v Davis* [1950] P 125 at 128, [1950] 1 All ER 40 at 42, CA; *Gower v Gower* [1950] 1 All ER 804 at 806, CA; *Bater v Bater* [1951] P 35 at 38, [1950] 2 All ER 458 at 460, CA; *Hornal v Neuberger Products Ltd* [1957] 1 QB 247, [1956] 3 All ER 970, CA. It has been held that marriage, whether solemnised in a church or a register office, whether contracted between Christians or between those who have no religious belief, must in each case have the same legal consequences, and that the solution to the questions which arise for determination in divorce cases must be found on the true construction of the relevant Acts of Parliament, not from a consideration of the Christian doctrine of marriage as laid down in the Book of Common Prayer: *Weatherley v Weatherley* [1947] AC 628 at 633, [1947] 1 All ER 563 at 565, HL per Lord Jowitt LC; and see *Baxter v Baxter* [1948] AC 274 at 286, [1947] 2 All ER 886 at 890, HL per Lord Jowitt LC. The law of the land cannot be co-extensive with the law of morals; nor can the civil consequences of marriage be identical with the religious consequences: *Weatherley v Weatherley*; see also *Buchler v Buchler* [1947] P 25 at 41–42, [1947] 1 All ER 319 at 324, CA per Lord Greene MR.

3 Matrimonial Causes Act 1973 s 1(1); Civil Partnership Act 2004 s 44(1). As to the bar on petitions and applications in first year of a marriage or civil partnership see PARA 757; as to proof of breakdown see PARA 347; and as to the duty of the court on a petition or application see PARA 348.

These requirements are to be read disjunctively, the two separate requirements being, first, that the marriage or civil partnership has irretrievably broken down and, secondly, that the court is satisfied of one or more of the facts proving such irretrievable breakdown (see PARA 347): *Buffery v Buffery* [1988] FCR 465, [1988] 2 FLR 365, CA, approving *Livingstone-Stallard v Livingstone-Stallard* [1974] Fam 47 at 54, [1974] 2 All ER 766 at 771 per Dunn J and *O'Neill v O'Neill* [1975] 3 All ER 289 at 292, [1975] 1 WLR 1118 at 1121, CA per Cairns LJ.

4 A separation order is an order of the court which provides for the separation of the civil partners: Civil Partnership Act 2004 s 37(1)(b). As to the meaning of 'civil partner' see PARA 2 note 1.

5 Ie any such fact as is mentioned in the Matrimonial Causes Act 1973 s 1(2) or the Civil Partnership Act 2004 s 44(5) (see PARA 347).

6 Matrimonial Causes Act 1973 s 17(1); Civil Partnership Act 2004 s 56(1). The provisions of the Matrimonial Causes Act 1973 s 2 and the Civil Partnership Act 2004 s 45 apply for the

purposes of a petition for judicial separation or a separation order as they apply in relation to a petition for divorce or dissolution: Matrimonial Causes Act 1973 s 17(1); Civil Partnership Act 2004 s 56(4).

A decree or order for separation does not in general constitute a bar to a suit for divorce, dissolution or separation: see *Yeatman v Yeatman and Rummell* (1870) 21 LT 733; *Brown v Brown and Shelton* (1874) LR 3 P & D 202; but see *Besant v Wood* (1879) 12 ChD 605; *Gandy v Gandy* (1882) 7 PD 168, CA. See also *Kunski v Kunski and Josephs* (1907) 23 TLR 615; *Matthews v Matthews* (1860) 3 Sw & Tr 161 (dismissal of petition brought six years after alleged cruelty and desertion on ground of a collateral purpose); *Flower v Flower* (1873) LR 3 P & D 132 (judicial separation). As to the need to plead any objections see also *Williams v Williams* (1866) LR 1 P & D 178. Cf *Stone v Stone and Osborne* [1917] P 125 (husband granted divorce despite his statutory desertion). As to the extent to which agreements for separation may be a bar to petitions founded on desertion see PARA 371 et seq.

347.   Proof of irretrievable breakdown. The court[1] must not hold that a marriage or civil partnership has broken down irretrievably[2] unless the petitioner[3] satisfies[4] the court of one or more of the following facts[5], that is to say:

(1)   that the respondent has behaved in such a way that the petitioner cannot reasonably be expected to live with the respondent[6];

(2)   that the respondent has deserted the petitioner for a continuous period of at least two years immediately preceding the presentation of the petition or the making of the application[7];

(3)   that the parties have lived apart[8] for a continuous period of at least two years immediately preceding the presentation of the petition or the making of the application ('two years' separation') and the respondent consents to a decree being granted or a dissolution order being made[9];

(4)   that the parties have lived apart for a continuous period of at least five years immediately preceding the presentation of the petition or the making of the application ('five years' separation')[10]; and

(5)   in the case of marriages only, that the respondent has committed adultery and the petitioner finds it intolerable to live with the respondent[11].

If in any proceedings for divorce or dissolution the respondent alleges and proves any of these facts, treating the respondent as the petitioner and the petitioner as the respondent for that purpose, the court may give to the respondent the relief to which he would have been entitled if he had presented a petition seeking that relief[12].

1   As to the meaning of 'court' see PARA 346 note 2.
2   See PARA 346. The date at which the breakdown must be proved to be irretrievable is the date of the hearing of the suit: *Pheasant v Pheasant* [1972] Fam 202, [1972] 1 All ER 587.
3   As to petitions and applications see PARA 321 note 1.
4   As to the standard of proof required see PARAS 352, 369, 393. A simple assertion by one party of irretrievable breakdown is not sufficient on its own to satisfy the court: *Ash v Ash* [1972] Fam 135, [1972] 1 All ER 582.
5   Matrimonial Causes Act 1973 s 1(2); Civil Partnership Act 2004 s 44(3); and see *Buffery v Buffery* [1988] FCR 465, [1988] 2 FLR 365, CA (cited in PARA 346 note 3). See also *Morley v Morley* (1972) 117 Sol Jo 69 (wife alleged two facts, one of which the husband admitted; he was not seeking to rely on conduct in any proceedings by the wife for financial provision; the court declined to investigate the unadmitted fact and granted a decree on the admitted one); cf *Mustafa v Mustafa* [1975] 3 All ER 355, [1975] 1 WLR 1277 (husband alleged adultery which wife denied but cross-prayed on the grounds that the marriage had irretrievably broken down and also alleged adultery by husband which he admitted; it was held that, in order to understand the underlying matters which would affect the ancillary issues, all the allegations must be investigated). Where there are facts sufficient to enable a court to grant a decree of dissolution, it is in general wrong to permit a party to have other allegations investigated: *Grenfell v Grenfell* [1978] Fam 128, [1978] 1 All ER 561, CA.

6   Matrimonial Causes Act 1973 s 1(2)(b); Civil Partnership Act 2004 s 44(5)(a). See PARA 359.
7   Matrimonial Causes Act 1973 s 1(2)(c); Civil Partnership Act 2004 s 44(5)(d). See PARA 363.
     The court may treat a period of desertion as having continued at a time when the deserting party
     was incapable of continuing the necessary intention if the evidence before the court is such that,
     had that party not been so incapable, the court would have inferred that the desertion continued
     at that time: Matrimonial Causes Act 1973 s 2(4); Civil Partnership Act 2004 s 45(5).
8   For the purposes of the Matrimonial Causes Act 1973 ss 1(2)(d), (e), 2 and the Civil Partnership
     Act 2004 ss 44(5)(b), (c), 45 a husband and wife or civil partners are to be treated as living apart
     unless they are living with each other in the same household, and references in these provisions
     to the parties to a marriage or civil partnership living with each other are construed as references
     to their living with each other in the same household: Matrimonial Causes Act 1973 s 2(6); Civil
     Partnership Act 2004 s 45(8). See *Mouncer v Mouncer* [1972] 1 All ER 289, [1972] 1 WLR 321
     (parties living in the same household and not living apart); *Santos v Santos* [1972] Fam 247,
     [1972] 2 All ER 246, CA ('living apart' does not mean the same as 'has deserted', nor does
     'living apart' impute any fault). The legislation does not use the word 'house', which relates to
     something physical, but 'household', which has an abstract meaning, and the word 'household'
     essentially refers to people held together by a particular kind of tie, even if temporarily
     separated: see *Santos v Santos* (preferring *Smith v Smith* [1940] P 49, [1939] 4 All ER 533 to
     Evans v Evans [1948] 1 KB 175, [1947] 2 All ER 656, DC); *Fuller (otherwise Penfold) v Fuller*
     [1973] 2 All ER 650, [1973] 1 WLR 730, CA (parties living in the same household but
     nevertheless living apart); and PARA 368.
9   Matrimonial Causes Act 1973 s 1(2)(d); Civil Partnership Act 2004 s 44(5)(b). See PARA 407. As
     to the meaning of 'dissolution order' see PARA 346 note 1.
10   Matrimonial Causes Act 1973 s 1(2)(e); Civil Partnership Act 2004 s 44(5)(c). See PARA 410 et
     seq.
11   Matrimonial Causes Act 1973 s 1(2)(a). See PARA 350 et seq. The absence of adultery from the
     list of 'facts' which may establish the irretrievable breakdown of a civil partnership under the
     Civil Partnership Act 2004 s 44(5) is the only difference between that list and the list of 'facts'
     which may establish the irretrievable breakdown of a marriage under the Matrimonial Causes
     Act 1973 s 1(2); however, since adultery as a fact leading to divorce additionally requires that
     the petitioner finds it intolerable to live with the respondent, a situation which is already
     covered by the Matrimonial Causes Act 1973 s 1(2)(b) and the Civil Partnership Act 2004
     s 44(5)(a) (see the text and note 6), it may be argued that the inclusion of adultery as a 'fact' for
     the purposes of the Matrimonial Causes Act 1973 is otiose and that for this reason adultery has
     been deliberately omitted from the Civil Partnership Act 2004.
12   Matrimonial Causes Act 1973 s 20; Civil Partnership Act 2004 s 62.

348.   Inquiry into facts and making of order or decree. On a petition for
divorce or judicial separation or an application for a dissolution or separation
order[1] it is the duty of the court[2] to inquire, so far as it reasonably can, into the
facts[3] alleged by the petitioner or applicant and into any facts alleged by the
respondent[4]. If the court is satisfied on the evidence of any such fact, then (unless
the proceedings are for divorce or dissolution and it is satisfied on all the
evidence that the marriage or civil partnership has not broken down
irretrievably), it must grant the decree or order sought[5].

1   As to the meanings of 'dissolution order' and 'separation order' see PARA 346 notes 1, 4.
2   As to the meaning of 'court' see PARA 346 note 2.
3   As to the facts which are proof of irretrievable breakdown see PARA 347.
4   Matrimonial Causes Act 1973 ss 1(3), 17(2); Civil Partnership Act 2004 ss 44(2), 56(2). As to
     the position in undefended causes see PARAS 814, 816. Once the judge has certified that the
     petitioner or applicant has proved the contents of the petition or application and is entitled to
     the decree or order sought, the court is bound to grant the decree or order: see *Day v Day*
     [1980] Fam 29, [1979] 2 All ER 187, CA.
5   Matrimonial Causes Act 1973 ss 1(4), 17(2) (s 1(4) amended by the Matrimonial and Family
     Proceedings Act 1984 Sch 1 para 10); Civil Partnership Act 2004 ss 44(4), 56(3). This is subject
     to the Matrimonial Causes Act 1973 s 5 and the Civil Partnership Act 2004 s 47 (refusal of
     divorce or dissolution in five-year separation cases on grounds of grave hardship: see PARA 411)
     and to the Matrimonial Causes Act 1973 s 41 or, as the case may be, the Civil Partnership
     Act 2004 s 63 (restriction on making orders affecting children: see PARA 884). The provisions of
     the Matrimonial Causes Act 1973 ss 6, 7 (see PARAS 414, 859) also apply for the purpose of

encouraging the reconciliation of parties to separation proceedings and of enabling the parties to a marriage to refer to the court for its opinion an agreement or arrangement relevant to actual or contemplated separation proceedings as they apply in relation to a petition for divorce: Matrimonial Causes Act 1973 s 17(3).

Where a respondent seeks to rely on the Matrimonial Causes Act 1973 s 1(4) (or, presumably, the Civil Partnership Act 2004 s 44(4)) it is desirable that the submission (that the marriage or civil partnership has not broken down irretrievably) together with particulars of the positive case in support of that submission should be pleaded in the answer: *Kisala v Kisala* (1973) 117 Sol Jo 664.

(ii) Adultery

349. Meaning of 'adultery'. For the purposes of a petition for divorce[1], 'adultery' means voluntary[2] sexual intercourse[3] between a married person and a person of the opposite sex[4], who is not the other spouse[5], during the subsistence[6] of the marriage[7]. In the case of a polygamous marriage permitted by the appropriate personal law or laws[8], it would appear that one wife is not entitled to rely on her husband's sexual intercourse with the other wife (or with a concubine whose status is legally recognised[9]) as adultery[10].

It is immaterial that the marriage has not been consummated[11], unless, perhaps, the offender seeks, in answer, to avoid the marriage on that ground[12]. One act of adultery may be sufficient[13]. When sexual intercourse[14] is proved to have taken place between the respondent and someone other than the petitioner, that intercourse is deemed to have been voluntary, and it is for the respondent to show that it was not so[15]. The motive for the respondent's adultery is irrelevant[16].

1 Adultery is a 'fact' for the purposes of divorce but not for the purposes of the dissolution of a civil partnership: see the Matrimonial Causes Act 1973 s 1(2); the Civil Partnership Act 2004 s 44(5); and PARA 347.

2 If a wife is raped by another man, it is not adultery by her: *Redpath v Redpath and Milligan* [1950] 1 All ER 600, CA; *Clarkson v Clarkson* (1930) 46 TLR 623; *Coffey v Coffey* [1898] P 169. Thus, where intercourse was not voluntary, it was held that the wife had not committed adultery, but that the co-respondent had (*Long v Long and Johnson* (1890) 15 PD 218; *Clark v Clark* (1954) Times, 3 June, CA (rape not proved by wife; inference of adultery properly drawn)). It is not adultery if the spouse is unable to understand the nature of the sexual act (*Yarrow v Yarrow* [1892] P 92). Adultery is not a criminal offence (*Blunt v Park Lane Hotel Ltd* [1942] 2 KB 253, [1942] 2 All ER 187, CA; *Tilley v Tilley* [1949] P 240 at 258, [1948] 2 All ER 1113 at 1122, CA); it has been described as a 'quasi-criminal offence' (*Ginesi v Ginesi* [1948] P 179 at 181, [1948] 1 All ER 373 at 374, CA; *Fairman v Fairman* [1949] P 341 at 344, [1949] 1 All ER 938 at 940, DC), but this description was condemned in *Gower v Gower* [1950] 1 All ER 804 at 805, 806, CA; and in *Bater v Bater* [1951] P 35, [1950] 2 All ER 458, CA; and see *Branford v Branford* (1879) 4 PD 72 at 73; *Lewis v Lewis* [1958] P 193, [1958] 1 All ER 859, CA.

3 To constitute adultery as a ground of divorce, some penetration of the woman by the man must be found to have taken place, but it is not necessary that such penetration should constitute a complete act of intercourse; cf the meaning of 'consummation' in nullity cases (see PARA 335). The act of sexual intercourse need not be complete, but an attempt without penetration is insufficient: *Dennis v Dennis (Spillett cited)* [1955] P 153, [1955] 2 All ER 51, CA. See also *Sapsford v Sapsford and Furtado* [1954] P 394, [1954] 2 All ER 373 (masturbation of the co-respondent by the respondent does not amount to adultery), following the dicta in *Rutherford v Richardson* [1923] AC 1 at 11, HL, and in *Thompson (otherwise Hulton) v Thompson* [1938] P 162 at 173, [1938] 2 All ER 727 at 732; affd [1939] P 1, [1938] 4 All ER 1, CA. Hence artificial insemination of a wife by a donor who is not the husband will not constitute adultery, since there is no penetration of the woman by the man: see *MacLennan v MacLennan* 1958 SC 105. As to the evidence from which adultery may be inferred see PARA 353 et seq.

4 As to the principles to be applied in the determination of the sexual condition of an individual see PARA 1 note 2.

5   Sexual intercourse between two unmarried persons is not adultery (*Chorlton v Chorlton* [1952] P 169, [1952] 1 All ER 611, DC (proceedings for discharge of maintenance order on ground of adultery by divorced wife); cf *Abson v Abson* [1952] P 55, [1952] 1 All ER 370 (application for discharge of maintenance order on ground of adultery; intercourse between divorced wife and married man; held by Karminski J that wife had committed adultery, Lord Merriman P leaving the question undecided whether wife's conduct amounted to adultery for the particular purpose of the application in question; but it was held that order should be discharged as wife's right to maintenance should be dealt with by High Court)). See also *Dennis v Dennis (Spillett cited)* [1955] P 153, [1955] 2 All ER 51, CA; *Styles v Styles and Jackson* (1890) 62 LT 613; *Mawford v Mawford* (1866) 14 WR 516; *Weatherley v Weatherley* (1854) 1 Ecc & Ad 193 as criticised in *Fitzgerald v Fitzgerald* (1862) 32 LJPM & A 12; *Graves v Graves* (1842) 3 Curt 235; *Dillon v Dillon* (1842) 3 Curt 86; *Perrin v Perrin* (1822) 1 Add 1; *Reeves v Reeves* (1813) 2 Phillim 125; and cf *Best v Best* (1823) 1 Add 411.

6   The adultery alleged must take place prior to the presentation of the petition, but evidence of adultery after the date is admissible to assist the court in determining the nature of former acts of familiarity: see *Wales v Wales* [1900] P 63; *Boddy v Boddy and Grover* (1860) 30 LJPM & A 23; cf *Duke of Norfolk's Case* (1692) 12 State Tr 927 at 945. Evidence of ante-nuptial intercourse is usually inadmissible, but it is otherwise where the adultery is charged with a person with whom there had been ante-nuptial intercourse: see *Goode v Goode and Hamson* (1861) 2 Sw & Tr 253 at 258; *Weatherley v Weatherley* (1854) 1 Ecc & Ad 193; *Graves v Graves* (1842) 3 Curt 235; *Dillon v Dillon* (1842) 3 Curt 86; *Sullivan v Sullivan* (1824) 2 Add 299 at 306; *Perrin v Perrin* (1822) 1 Add 1; *Ewing v Wheatley* (1814) 2 Hag Con 175 at 183; cf *Fitzgerald v Fitzgerald* (1862) 32 LJPM & A 12.

7   The marriage must be proved: see *Evans v Evans and Robinson* (1859) 1 Sw & Tr 328; *Guest v Shipley (falsely called Guest)* (1820) 2 Hag Con 321 at 322. Both parties to the marriage must be alive: see *Stanhope v Stanhope* (1886) 11 PD 103; *Grant v Grant and Bowles and Pattison* (1862) 2 Sw & Tr 522.

8   See PARA 9; and CONFLICT OF LAWS vol 8(3) (Reissue) PARAS 234–240.

9   Cf *Lee v Lau* [1967] P 14, [1964] 2 All ER 248.

10   See PARA 9; and CONFLICT OF LAWS vol 8(3) (Reissue) PARAS 234–240; Law Com No 42 (Family Law Report on Polygamous Marriages) para 50; *Onobrauche v Onobrauche* (1978) 8 Fam Law 107.

11   *Waters v Waters and Gentel* (1875) 33 LT 579; *Ousey v Ousey and Atkinson* (1874) LR 3 P & D 223; *Graves v Graves* (1864) 3 Sw & Tr 350; *Patrick v Patrick* (1810) 3 Phillim 496.

12   See PARA 331 et seq. In such a case the question of annulment must be tried first: *S (otherwise P) v S* [1970] P 208, [1970] 2 All ER 251.

13   *Douglas v Douglas* [1951] P 85 at 96, [1950] 2 All ER 748 at 753, CA; *Churchman v Churchman* [1945] P 44 at 50, [1945] 2 All ER 190 at 194, CA; *Conradi v Conradi, Worrall and Way* (1868) LR 1 P & D 514 at 522; *Gipps v Gipps and Hume* (1864) 11 HL Cas 1 at 28. See, however, PARA 350.

14   Ie coitus is established: see PARA 335 note 4. As to proof see PARA 352 et seq.

15   *Redpath v Redpath and Milligan* [1950] 1 All ER 600, CA. As to the effect of drink or drugs see *Goshawk v Goshawk* (1965) 109 Sol Jo 290 (wife had committed adultery, although her memory of what had occurred was destroyed by drink); *Benton v Benton* [1958] P 12, [1957] 3 All ER 544, CA (tranquillising drug did not affect husband's reasoning powers; intercourse was voluntary and adulterous); *Prior v Prior and Strong* (1929) 73 Sol Jo 441. As to insanity see *N v N (C (by her guardian) intervening)* (1963) 107 Sol Jo 1025; *S v S (O otherwise P (by her guardian) intervening)* [1962] P 133, [1961] 3 All ER 133; *Hanbury v Hanbury* [1892] P 222; affd 8 TLR 559. Cf *Morton v Morton, Daly and McNaught* [1937] P 151, [1937] 2 All ER 470 (no defence for co-respondent to prove that he was seduced by respondent). As to inferring adultery from proof of inclination, association or opportunity see PARA 353.

16   *Woolf v Woolf* [1931] P 134 at 145, CA.

350.   Adultery as proof of irretrievable breakdown.

The mere fact that the respondent has committed adultery is not enough to satisfy the test of irretrievable breakdown of marriage; the petitioner must also find it intolerable to live with the respondent[1].

1   See the Matrimonial Causes Act 1973 s 1(2)(a); and PARA 347. As to the requirement of intolerability see *Cleary v Cleary* [1974] 1 All ER 498, [1974] 1 WLR 73, CA, followed with some misgivings in *Carr v Carr* [1974] 1 All ER 1193, [1974] 1 WLR 1534, CA; *Pheasant v Pheasant* [1972] Fam 202 at 207, [1972] 1 All ER 587 at 589. The test is an objective one:

Goodrich v Goodrich [1971] 2 All ER 1340, [1971] 1 WLR 1142. As to the effect of living together after adultery see PARA 351. See also *Anderson v Anderson* (1972) 117 Sol Jo 33 (it is necessary only to prove the adultery and that the petitioner finds it intolerable to live with the respondent; the allegation that adultery did not cause the irretrievable breakdown is irrelevant, since it is not a matter in issue between the parties).

351.   Living with each other after knowledge of adultery.   The petitioner is not entitled to rely on the respondent's adultery if, after it has become known to the petitioner, the parties have lived with each other¹ for a period exceeding, or periods together exceeding, six months². Where the parties to a marriage have lived with each other for a lesser period than that stated above after it became known to one party that the other had committed adultery, then, in any proceedings for divorce in which the petitioner relies on that adultery, the fact that the parties have lived with each other after that time is to be disregarded in determining whether the petitioner finds it intolerable to live with the respondent³.

1   As to living together see PARA 347 note 7.
2   Matrimonial Causes Act 1973 s 2(1); and see *Biggs v Biggs and Wheatley* [1977] Fam 1, [1977] 1 All ER 20 (parties lived with each other for a period exceeding six months after grant of decree nisi and before decree absolute; decree nisi rescinded).
3   Matrimonial Causes Act 1973 s 2(2).

352.   Burden and standard of proof.   The burden of proof of adultery is throughout¹ on the person who alleges it², for there is a presumption of innocence³. Adultery must be proved to the satisfaction⁴ of the court⁵, that is on a preponderance of probability⁶; but the degree of probability depends on the subject matter, and, in proportion as the offence is grave, so ought the proof to be clear⁷. Divorce is a civil proceeding and the analogies of criminal law are not apt⁸.

1   *Marczuk v Marczuk* [1956] P 217 at 226, [1955] 3 All ER 758 at 761; revsd on another point [1956] P 217 at 238, [1956] 1 All ER 657, CA.
2   *Gliksten v Gliksten and Deane* (1917) 116 LT 543; and see *Fairman v Fairman* [1949] P 341 at 344, [1949] 1 All ER 938 at 940, DC, approved in *Galler v Galler* [1954] P 252, [1954] 1 All ER 536, CA; cf *Davis v Davis* [1950] P 125 at 128, 129, [1950] 1 All ER 40 at 42, 43, CA.
3   *Owen v Owen* (1831) 4 Hag Ecc 261; *Redpath v Redpath and Milligan* [1950] 1 All ER 600, CA; and see *Storey v Storey and Laycock* (1954) Times, 3 March, CA.
4   See the Matrimonial Causes Act 1973 s 1(4); and PARA 348. See also *Allen v Allen* (1 February 1951, unreported), CA per Sir Raymond Evershed MR, as referred to in *Davis v Davis* [1950] P 125, [1950] 1 All ER 40, CA.
5   Ie of the trial judge, who is sole arbiter of the facts, unless he misdirects himself: see *Watt (or Thomas) v Thomas* [1947] AC 484, [1947] 1 All ER 582, HL, applied in *Ginesi v Ginesi* [1948] P 179, [1948] 1 All ER 373, CA; *Fairman v Fairman* [1949] P 341, [1949] 1 All ER 938, DC; *Simpson v Simpson* [1951] P 320, [1951] 1 All ER 955, DC. As to the practice see PARA 776.
6   *Blyth v Blyth* [1966] AC 643, [1966] 1 All ER 524, HL. See also *F v F* [1968] P 506, [1968] 1 All ER 242; *Bastable v Bastable and Sanders* [1968] 3 All ER 701, [1968] 1 WLR 1684, CA; *Galler v Galler* [1954] P 252, [1954] 1 All ER 536, CA; *England v England* [1953] P 16 at 22, [1952] 2 All ER 784 at 787, DC; *Preston-Jones v Preston-Jones* [1951] AC 391 at 400, 401, [1951] 1 All ER 124 at 127, HL (a case where a child could be illegitimate by a finding of adultery; proof beyond reasonable doubt demanded); *Gower v Gower* [1950] 1 All ER 804 at 805, 806, CA; *Ginesi v Ginesi* [1948] P 179, [1948] 1 All ER 373, CA; *Churchman v Churchman* [1945] P 44 at 51, [1945] 2 All ER 190 at 195, CA; cf *Davis v Davis* [1950] P 125 at 126, [1950] 1 All ER 40 at 42, CA (cruelty); *Bater v Bater* [1951] P 35 at 38, [1950] 2 All ER 458 at 460, CA (cruelty).
7   *Blyth v Blyth* [1966] AC 643 at 669, [1966] 1 All ER 524 at 536, HL per Lord Denning; and see *Miller v Minister of Pensions* [1947] 2 All ER 372; *Preston-Jones v Preston-Jones* [1951] AC 391 at 400, 401, [1951] 1 All ER 124 at 127, HL per Lord Simonds; *Judd v Minister of*

Pensions and National Insurance [1966] 2 QB 580, [1965] 3 All ER 642; cf *Serio v Serio* (1983) 4 FLR 756, 765, CA (presumption of legitimacy); *H v H (minor) (child abuse: evidence)* [1990] Fam 86, sub nom *H v H and C (Kent County Council intervening) (child abuse: evidence)* [1989] 3 All ER 740, CA (allegation of sexual abuse).

8 See PARA 346 note 2.

353. Direct and circumstantial evidence. In nearly every case the fact of adultery[1] is proved by confessions[2] or is inferred from circumstances which by fair inference lead to that necessary conclusion[3]. There must be proof of disposition or inclination and opportunity for committing adultery[4], but the conjunction of strong inclination with evidence of opportunity does not lead to an irrebuttable presumption that adultery has been committed[5], nor is the court bound to infer adultery from evidence of opportunity alone[6].

Unless the court is suspicious that a true case is not being disclosed to it, in which case it would closely scrutinise the facts, the evidence of a single witness or of paid detectives will be accepted[7].

1 Direct evidence of adultery is rare. It may, indeed, be disbelieved because it purports to be direct evidence (see *Sopwith v Sopwith* (1859) 4 Sw & Tr 243; *Alexander v Alexander and Amos* (1860) 2 Sw & Tr 95), but it is otherwise where, suspicions having been aroused, the innocent party watches for proof of adultery (*Douglas v Douglas* [1951] P 85, [1950] 2 All ER 748, CA; *Mudge v Mudge and Honeysett* [1950] P 173, [1950] 1 All ER 607; cf *Manning v Manning* [1950] 1 All ER 602, CA. See also *Woodward v Woodward and Curd* [1959] 1 All ER 641, [1959] 1 WLR 493).

2 See PARA 354. As to the practice see PARA 776.

3 See *Allen v Allen and Bell* [1894] P 248 at 251, 252, CA, approving *Loveden v Loveden* (1810) 2 Hag Con 1 at 2 per Sir William Scott. See also *Davidson v Davidson* (1856) Dea & Sw 132; *Grant v Grant* (1839) 2 Curt 16 (affd by Judicial Committee of the Privy Council); *Chambers v Chambers* (1810) 1 Hag Con 439; *Alexander v Alexander and Amos* (1860) 2 Sw & Tr 95 (where the court refused to believe a wife guilty of a flagrant act when she had behaved with propriety for 20 years); *Blum v Blum* (1963) 107 Sol Jo 512, CA (husband booked double room at hotel, went there with woman not his wife; husband's explanation not accepted; adultery proved); *Gould v Gould* (1963) 107 Sol Jo 831, DC. See also note 6.

4 *Farnham v Farnham* (1925) 133 LT 320 at 321; and see *Raspin v Raspin* [1953] P 230, [1953] 2 All ER 349n; *Storey v Storey and Laycock* (1954) Times, 3 March, CA (opportunity but inclination not proved); *Corke v Corke and Cook* [1958] P 93, [1958] 1 All ER 224, CA; *Cox v Cox* [1958] 1 All ER 569, [1958] 1 WLR 340, DC (inclination but no opportunity); *Greville-Bell v Greville-Bell and Primo De Rivera* (1958) Times, 21 November (daily association, kissing, diary entries, oral confession by wife, inclination and opportunity; adultery found).

   Although evidence as to certain acts of familiarity may be insufficient in itself to prove charges of adultery made in a petition, the court will pay regard to evidence that the man and woman charged have lived together as husband and wife: see *Wales v Wales* [1900] P 63; *Boddy v Boddy and Grover* (1860) 30 LJPM & A 23.

5 *England v England* [1953] P 16 at 19, 20, [1952] 2 All ER 784 at 786, DC, distinguishing *Woolf v Woolf* [1931] P 134; *Raspin v Raspin* [1953] P 230, [1953] 2 All ER 349n; cf *Sapsford v Sapsford and Furtado* [1954] P 394, [1954] 2 All ER 373.

6 See *Farnham v Farnham* (1925) 133 LT 320. 'From opportunities alone no inference of misconduct can fairly be drawn unless the conduct of the parties prior, contemporaneous or subsequent justifies the inference that such feelings existed between the parties that opportunities if given would be used for misconduct': *Ross v Ellison (or Ross)* [1930] AC 1 at 21, HL per Lord Atkin, applied in *Tyndale v Tyndale* (1958) unreported. Indecencies and familiarities short of adultery constitute, however, a strong presumption of the complete offence: see *Elwes v Elwes* (1794) 1 Hag Con 269 at 276; *Chettle v Chettle* (1821) 3 Phillim 507; *Hamerton v Hamerton* (1828) 2 Hag Ecc 8 at 14 (on appeal (1829) 2 Hag Ecc 618); *Robinson v Robinson and Lane* (1859) 1 Sw & Tr 362 at 276 per Cockburn CJ. See also *Thompson (otherwise Hulton) v Thompson* [1939] P 1, [1938] 4 All ER 1, CA; *Chalmers v Chalmers* [1930] P 154 at 156, 46 TLR 269 at 270; *Hallam v Hallam* (1930) 47 TLR 207 (virginity throwing doubt on petitioner's story); *Russell v Russell and Mayer* (1923) 39 TLR 287 (on appeal [1924] P 1, CA; [1924] AC 687, HL); *Rutherford v Richardson* [1923] AC 1 at 11, HL; *Russell v Russell* (1922) Times, 22 July; *Harry v Harry* (1919) Times, 4, 5 April; *Jolly v Jolly*

and Fryer (1919) 63 Sol Jo 777 (wife virgo intacta; adultery proved); *Hunt v Hunt* (1856) Dea & Sw 121. As to the requirement of penetration see PARA 349 note 3.
7   As to corroboration see PARA 354.

354.   Corroboration and confessions.   The evidence of the petitioner alone was seldom accepted without corroboration, either by a witness, or at least strong surrounding circumstances, but the modern practice is generally to accept such evidence, unless the facts arouse the suspicion of the court that a true case is not being disclosed in the sense that adultery may not in fact have been committed[1]. It is permissible to administer requests for information as to whether or not a party has committed adultery in order to obtain an admission or a denial[2]. Until the enactment of the Civil Evidence Act 1968 an unsworn admission out of court was evidence against the person making it, but not against the other person implicated by it[3]. The result was that the court, accepting that admission, could hold that the respondent wife had committed adultery with the co-respondent, but that the case against the co-respondent had not been proved[4]. In such a case a decree nisi was pronounced against the respondent but the co-respondent or other accused party was, on application, dismissed from the suit[5]. Such a result may well still occur, but in certain circumstances out-of-court statements are admissible as evidence whether made orally or in a document[6]. In undefended proceedings for divorce in which it is alleged that the respondent has committed adultery, the respondent's signature on a statement in writing admitting the adultery can be identified by the petitioner[7]. Although a confession of adultery by a respondent spouse with a named person may[8] be admissible evidence against that person, the trial judge has to decide what weight is to be attached to it[9]. The evidence of a respondent wife or husband on oath in the proceedings was always and still is evidence against the other man or woman[10]. In cases where one party admits to adultery and the other contests it, corroboration is desirable, since such evidence is the evidence of an accomplice[11]. In the case of all supposed confessions, one must look at the words used and their context[12]. Although adultery can be proved by admissions tending to show that it had been committed, it cannot be disproved by statements tending to show it was not committed, made afterwards to third parties by the person charged[13]. Admissions by a minor, made before proceedings, that he or she had committed adultery, are admissible as evidence in matrimonial proceedings[14]. Absence of a prior caution does not render inadmissible a confession of adultery[15].

1   It used to be said that strong supporting evidence was required: see *White v White and Jerome* (1890) 62 LT 663; *Curtis v Curtis* (1905) 21 TLR 676; *Getty v Getty* [1907] P 334; cf *Warwick v Warwick and Giovanni* (1907) Times, 25 July (cruelty); *Riches v Riches and Clinch* (1918) 35 TLR 141 (petitioner's evidence only). As to what is corroboration see *Senat v Senat* [1965] P 172, [1965] 2 All ER 505.
2   *Nast v Nast and Walker* [1972] Fam 142, [1972] 1 All ER 1171, CA; *C v C* [1973] 3 All ER 770, [1973] 1 WLR 568.
3   *Robinson v Robinson and Lane* (1859) 1 Sw & Tr 362 at 365; *Rutherford v Richardson* [1923] AC 1 at 6, HL; and see the cases cited in note 11.
4   *Crawford v Crawford and Dilke* (1886) 11 PD 150, CA (wife found guilty on her own confession and co-respondent dismissed from suit because no evidence against him).
5   *Rutherford v Richardson* [1923] AC 1, HL.
6   See the Civil Evidence Act 1995 s 1; and EVIDENCE vol 17(1) (Reissue) PARA 653.
7   See the Civil Evidence Act 1995 s 7(2); and EVIDENCE vol 17(1) (Reissue) PARAS 665–667.
8   Ie under the Civil Evidence Act 1995 s 1; see EVIDENCE vol 17(1) (Reissue) PARA 653.
9   See the Civil Evidence Act 1995 s 4; and EVIDENCE vol 17(1) (Reissue) PARA 660.
10   *Spring v Spring and Jiggins* [1947] 1 All ER 886 at 888, criticised on the question of corroboration in *Fairman v Fairman* [1949] P 341, [1949] 1 All ER 938, which was approved in *Galler v Galler* [1954] P 252, [1954] 1 All ER 536, CA.

11　*Best v Best* (1823) 1 Add 411; *Fairman v Fairman* [1949] P 341 at 346, [1949] 1 All ER 938, approved in *Galler v Galler* [1954] P 252, [1954] 1 All ER 536, CA. See also *Ciocci v Ciocci* (1854) 1 Ecc & Ad 121 at 133; *R v Rudd* (1948) 64 TLR 240; *Lawson v Lawson* [1955] 1 All ER 341, [1955] 1 WLR 200, CA; *Senat v Senat* [1965] P 172, [1965] 2 All ER 505 (corroboration of evidence of woman named desirable); cf *Davis v Davis* [1950] P 125 at 126, [1950] 1 All ER 40 at 43, CA.

12　*Smith v Smith* [1957] 2 All ER 397 at 399, DC.

13　*Corke v Corke and Cook* [1958] P 93, [1958] 1 All ER 224, CA.

14　*Alderman v Alderman and Dunn* [1958] 1 All ER 391, [1958] 1 WLR 177.

15　*Hathaway v Hathaway* [1970] 2 All ER 701, [1970] 1 WLR 1156n, DC.

355.　Birth of a child as evidence of adultery. The evidence of a husband or wife is admissible in any proceedings to prove that marital intercourse did or did not take place between them during any period[1]. If it is proved by admissible evidence[2] that a wife has given birth to a child of whom the husband cannot have been the father, that is proof of the wife's adultery[3]. The presumption of legitimacy need not be rebutted by proof beyond reasonable doubt[4]. Where the alleged period of gestation diverges largely from the normal, the burden of proof is a light one and is easily discharged[5].

1　Matrimonial Causes Act 1973 s 48(1). The evidence need not be in oral form: *Re Jenion, Jenion v Wynne* [1952] Ch 454, [1952] 1 All ER 1228, CA.

2　As to blood and other scientific tests see CHILDREN AND YOUNG PERSONS vol 5(3) (2008 Reissue) PARA 113 et seq.

3　A child born in wedlock is presumed to be the issue of the married couple, but the presumption can be rebutted if the court is satisfied that, in the nature of things, the wife could not have conceived the child through the agency of her husband: see CHILDREN AND YOUNG PERSONS vol 5(3) (2008 Reissue) PARA 94.

4　See the Family Law Reform Act 1969 s 26; CHILDREN AND YOUNG PERSONS vol 5(3) (2008 Reissue) PARA 95; *Preston-Jones v Preston-Jones* [1951] AC 391 at 401, [1951] 1 All ER 124 at 128, HL per Lord Simonds LC, at 414 and at 136 per Lord Morton, at 417 and at 138 per Lord MacDermott. Cf *S v S, W v Official Solicitor* [1972] AC 24, [1970] 3 All ER 107, HL. Sexual intercourse with contraceptives will not satisfy the burden of proving adultery: *Watson v Watson* [1954] P 48, sub nom *W v W* [1953] 2 All ER 1013 (evidence of abstention from intercourse at the time of conception is required).

5　*Preston-Jones v Preston-Jones* [1951] AC 391 at 403, [1951] 1 All ER 124 at 128, HL per Lord Simonds LC (360 days' period of gestation not impossible, but child normal at birth; decree on grounds of adultery).

356.　Previous decree or order. Where either party to a divorce has at any time on the same or substantially the same facts as those in the petition or answer been granted a decree of judicial separation or an order made, or having effect as if made, under, the Matrimonial Proceedings (Magistrates' Courts) Act 1960 or the Domestic Proceedings and Magistrates' Courts Act 1978 or any corresponding enactments in force in Northern Ireland, the Isle of Man or any of the Channel Islands, the court may treat the decree or order as sufficient proof of any adultery or other fact by reference to which it was granted; but it must not grant a decree of divorce without receiving evidence from the petitioner[1].

1　See the Matrimonial Causes Act 1973 s 4(1), (2); and PARA 830.

357.　Decree nisi as evidence of adultery. Where adultery is proved against a respondent and the court is satisfied that the petitioner finds it intolerable to live with the respondent[1] with the consequence that a decree nisi of divorce is pronounced against the respondent, the decree is conclusive evidence of that adultery, and the respondent cannot be heard to deny that finding in subsequent proceedings between the same parties[2]. A finding of adultery as a fact on which a decree nisi has proceeded is not res judicata, however, so as to bar the intervention of the Queen's Proctor on the ground that the decree was obtained contrary to the justice of the case[3]. Where a co-respondent has been found to have committed adultery on a husband's petition for divorce, the co-respondent is not estopped in a subsequent divorce suit between him and his own wife from denying the adultery so found in the previous suit, although the decree in the former suit is admissible against him[4].

1   See PARA 349 et seq.
2   *Conradi v Conradi, Worrall and Way* (1868) LR 1 P & D 514 at 518. See also *Evans v Evans and Robinson* (1858) 1 Sw & Tr 173; *Palmer v Palmer* (1859) 1 Sw & Tr 551 (effect of foreign decree); *Sopwith v Sopwith* (1861) 2 Sw & Tr 160; *Harriman v Harriman* [1909] P 123 at 142, CA per Fletcher Moulton LJ; cf *Hall v Hall and Richardson* (1879) 48 LJP 57; *Hartley v Hartley and Fleming* (1919) 35 TLR 298.
3   *Chalmers v Chalmers* [1930] P 154 (intervener alleged to be a virgin). See PARA 877.
4   See the Civil Evidence Act 1968 s 12; PARA 358; and EVIDENCE vol 17(1) (Reissue) PARA 596. As to the effect of convictions see s 11; and EVIDENCE vol 17(1) (Reissue) PARA 593.

358.   Findings in other proceedings.   A transcript of the official shorthand writer's note is evidence for certain purposes, for example to prove an admission[1]. Where the adultery of a party to a matrimonial suit has been declared and adjudged to have been proved in a decree pronounced in a previous suit between the same parties, such decree is conclusive evidence of adultery, and the party implicated cannot be heard to deny his guilt[2]. The case is, however, different where the previous proceedings were not between the same parties; thus, if a co-respondent has been found guilty of adultery in a suit instituted against him by a husband, he is not estopped in subsequent proceedings between himself and his wife from denying adultery[3].

Subsisting convictions by or before any court in the United Kingdom or by a court-martial there or elsewhere[4], and subsisting findings of adultery and paternity in civil proceedings[5], are admissible in any civil proceedings.

1   Cf *Brinkley v Brinkley* [1965] P 75, [1963] 1 All ER 493, DC. See also *Nottingham Guardians v Tomkinson* (1879) 4 CPD 343; *Taylor v Taylor* [1970] 2 All ER 609, [1970] 1 WLR 1148, CA; *Stupple v Royal Insurance Co* [1971] 1 QB 50, [1970] 3 All ER 230, CA; *Practice Direction* [1969] 2 All ER 873, [1969] 1 WLR 1192. The observations of a judge at a criminal trial are not evidence against a respondent to whom they are addressed: *Coffey v Coffey* [1898] P 169; cf *Whybrow v Whybrow* (1953) Times, 16 June (cruelty petition; evidence of husband's conviction for attempted murder of wife not admitted); *Ingram v Ingram* [1956] P 390, [1956] 1 All ER 785. As to cases on the judge's notes see *Conradi v Conradi, Worrall and Way (Queen's Proctor intervening)* (1868) LR 1 P & D 514; and see *Ling v Ling and Croker* (1858) 1 Sw & Tr 180; cf *Stoate v Stoate* (1861) 2 Sw & Tr 223.
2   *Conradi v Conradi, Worrall and Way (Queens Proctor intervening)* (1868) LR 1 P & D 514 (petitioner's adultery had been established against him in a suit brought by him against his wife, whom he charged with adultery with a co-respondent; afterwards he presented a fresh petition, alleging subsequent adultery with other co-respondents; on the Queen's Proctor's intervention, alleging the petitioner's adultery, the jury found the petitioner not guilty, but the court held that the decree in the former suit was conclusive as to adultery having been committed). In applying this decision to a case where a petitioner claims relief on the ground of the respondent's adultery established in previous proceedings between the same parties, it must be borne in mind that, by what is now the Matrimonial Causes Act 1973 s 1(2)(a) (see PARAS 347, 350), relief is dependent on the court being satisfied on the evidence that the case for the petitioner is proved; hence no estoppels binding the parties were necessarily sufficient to entitle a party to such relief, and the court was not bound to be satisfied of the necessary facts because the one party is estopped as against the other from denying them: *Harriman v Harriman* [1909] P 123 at 142, CA; and see PARA 734. See also *Hartley v Hartley and Fleming* (1919) 35 TLR 298 (where it was held that the confession by a wife of her adultery, in criminal proceedings against her husband, bound her); *Sopwith v Sopwith* (1861) 2 Sw & Tr 160; cf *Evans v Evans and Robinson* (1858) 1 Sw & Tr 173 (petition for judicial separation on ground of adultery failed; it

was held that a petition for divorce on ground of same adultery was not estopped by previous proceedings); *Palmer v Palmer* (1859) 1 Sw & Tr 551 (decree of competent foreign court).

3   *Partington v Partington and Atkinson* [1925] P 34, affd on this point, but revsd on another point, by *Hollington v F Hewthorn & Co* [1943] KB 587, [1943] 2 All ER 35, CA.

4   See the Civil Evidence Act 1968 s 11; and EVIDENCE vol 17(1) (Reissue) PARA 593. As to the information to be included in a petition where a previous conviction is pleaded see PARA 763.

5   See the Civil Evidence Act 1968 s 12; and EVIDENCE vol 17(1) (Reissue) PARA 596. If such a finding is relied on to prove adultery in later matrimonial proceedings in the High Court or a divorce county court, a transcript of the judgment, or an appropriate extract, recording the finding will be required by the court at the hearing. Any party to the original proceedings may order the transcript from the official shorthand writer; and any other person requiring such a transcript may make application to a district judge for permission for the official shorthand writer to supply a copy: *Practice Direction* [1969] 2 All ER 873, [1969] 1 WLR 1192.

(iii) Behaviour

359.   Behaviour as proof of irretrievable breakdown.   The court[1] may find that a marriage or civil partnership has broken down irretrievably where the petitioner or applicant[2] satisfies the court that the respondent has behaved[3] in a such a way that he cannot reasonably be expected to live with the respondent[4].

1   As to the meaning of 'court' see PARA 346 note 2.
2   As to petitioners and applicants see PARA 321 note 1.
3   See PARA 360 note 1.
4   See the Matrimonial Causes Act 1973 s 1(2)(b); the Civil Partnership Act 2004 s 44(5)(a); and PARA 347. As to the duty of the court to inquire into the facts see PARA 348. As to the effect of parties living with each other after the final incident of behaviour relied on by the petitioner see PARA 361.

360.   Consideration of whether petitioner or applicant can reasonably be expected to live with the respondent.   The court must consider the effect of the respondent's behaviour[1], whether such behaviour is voluntary or involuntary[2], on the particular petitioner[3]. This involves a consideration not only of the behaviour of the respondent but of the character, personality, disposition and behaviour of the petitioner[4]. A party's disinclination and boredom with the relationship does not entitle the court to dissolve it[5]. Conduct of sufficient gravity to justify a party leaving may be relied on but not simple desertion by the respondent[6]. Association, not resulting in actual sexual intercourse, with another person might constitute behaviour of a kind to justify a finding of irretrievable breakdown[7]. The fact that one party is living with the other party at the time of the hearing does not of itself establish that the first party should reasonably be expected to live with that other party[8].

The matter has been approached by considering whether any right-thinking person would come to the conclusion that the party in question had behaved in such a way that the other party could not reasonably be expected to live with him or her, taking into account the whole of the circumstances and the characters and personalities of the parties and their shared history[9].

1   The behaviour of the respondent must be looked at in the light of all the surrounding circumstances, including the degree of provocation: *Welfare v Welfare* (1977) 8 Fam Law 55. The test of behaviour is a subjective test: *Birch v Birch* [1992] 2 FCR 545, [1992] 1 FLR 564, CA. There is no rule that the respondent is required to plead more than a simple denial: see *Haque v Haque* [1977] 3 All ER 667, [1977] 1 WLR 888 (cited in PARA 782 note 1). As to the effect of parties living with each other after the final incident of behaviour relied on by the petitioner see PARA 361.

2   See *Thurlow v Thurlow* [1976] Fam 32, [1975] 2 All ER 979 (where Rees J considered that negative behaviour by the respondent, ie involuntary behaviour stemming from mental or physical illness, could be such that it would be unreasonable to expect the petitioner to endure it

even after taking full account of all the obligations of the married state; the court would consider the capacity of the petitioner to withstand the stresses imposed by the behaviour, the steps taken to cope with it, the length of time during which the petitioner had been called on to bear it and the actual or potential effect on the petitioner's health; Rees J specifically disagreed with the decision in *Smith v Smith* (1973) Times, 15 December (where it was held that the actions of a spouse suffering from mental illness and which were involuntary did not constitute 'behaviour' within the similar provisions of the Divorce Reform Act 1969 s 2(1)(b) (repealed)); *O'Neill v O'Neill* [1975] 3 All ER 289, [1975] 1 WLR 1118, CA (husband made home disagreeable and cast doubts on the paternity of the children; decree granted).

3 *Katz v Katz* [1972] 3 All ER 219, [1972] 1 WLR 955; *Pheasant v Pheasant* [1972] Fam 202, [1972] 1 All ER 587. It is the state of the relationship between the parties which is being examined, not whether conduct is good or bad: *Carew-Hunt v Carew-Hunt* (1972) Times, 28 June. Continued financial irresponsibility may in certain circumstances constitute unreasonable behaviour: *Carter-Fea v Carter-Fea* [1987] Fam Law 131, CA. For a case where a husband's dogmatic and male chauvinistic attitude towards his sensitive wife was held to constitute behaviour with which a wife could not reasonably be expected to live see *Birch v Birch* [1992] 2 FCR 545, [1992] 1 FLR 564, CA. Where refusal of sexual intercourse is the main ground alleged in support of a petition based on unreasonable behaviour, the court must consider very carefully the allegations by, and the reasons of, both parties, since many different factors need to be taken into account: *Mason v Mason* (1980) 11 Fam Law 143, CA. The allegations must be sufficiently pleaded: *Butterworth v Butterworth* [1998] 1 FCR 159, [1997] 2 FLR 336, CA; cf *Cotterell v Cotterell* [1998] 3 FCR 199, CA (petition of wife on ground of unreasonable behaviour; decree nisi granted to wife on ground of unreasonable behaviour but rescinded when parties reconciled; on second petition decree nisi granted on ground of unreasonable behaviour; details of unreasonable behaviour after reconciliation not set out in judgment; decree properly granted). As to petitioners and applicants see PARA 321 note 1.

4 *Ash v Ash* [1972] Fam 135, [1972] 1 All ER 582; *Richards v Richards* [1972] 3 All ER 695, [1972] 1 WLR 1073 (mental illness; no unreasonable behaviour; but see note 1); *Shears v Shears* (1972) 117 Sol Jo 33 (wife's behaviour in obtaining ex parte injunctions ordering husband to leave matrimonial home on grounds which afterwards proved baseless, and in her persistent refusal to allow husband access to his child constituted behaviour in such a way that he could not reasonably be expected to live with her). It is not appropriate to consider whether the conduct was grave and weighty; the test to be applied is whether a right-thinking person, looking at the particular husband and wife, would conclude that one could not reasonably be expected to live with the other, taking into account all the circumstances of the case and the respective characters and personalities of the two parties concerned: *Buffery v Buffery* [1988] FCR 465, [1988] 2 FLR 365, CA.

5 *Kisala v Kisala* (1973) 3 Fam Law 90. It was also said in that case that, when a respondent desires to plead that the relationship has not broken down irretrievably, the common form denial of the petition does not achieve sufficient clarity. See also *Andrews v Andrews* [1974] 3 All ER 643.

6 *Morgan v Morgan* (1973) 117 Sol Jo 223. Simple desertion comes within the provisions of the Matrimonial Causes Act 1973 s 1(2)(c): see *Morgan v Morgan*; and PARA 363. It is not sufficient to prove conduct amounting to no more than desertion or behaviour leading up to desertion: *Stringfellow v Stringfellow* [1976] 2 All ER 539, [1976] 1 WLR 645, CA (facts established by wife showed nothing more than a matrimonial relationship which had broken down and desertion by husband; wife had failed to show that husband had behaved in such a way that she could not reasonably be expected to live with him).

7 *Wachtel v Wachtel* [1973] Fam 72, [1973] 1 All ER 113.

8 *Bradley v Bradley* [1973] 3 All ER 750, [1973] 1 WLR 1291, CA. It may not be reasonable to expect one of the parties to live there but, albeit unreasonable, he or she may have no option but to be there: see *Bradley v Bradley* at 752 and at 1294 per Lord Denning MR.

9 *Livingstone-Stallard v Livingstone-Stallard* [1974] Fam 47 at 54, [1974] 2 All ER 766 at 771; applied in *Bergin v Bergin* [1983] 1 All ER 905, [1983] 1 WLR 279, DC (cited in PARA 553 note 5). See *Stevens v Stevens* [1979] 1 WLR 885 (a wife may be granted a decree based on her husband's behaviour, even though she was the cause of the breakdown of the marriage); *Welfare v Welfare* (1977) 8 Fam Law 55 (where a wife failed to satisfy the court that she could not reasonably be expected to live with her husband; the reason she could not live with him was not because of his behaviour but because of her passion for another man); *Buffery v Buffery* [1988] FCR 465, [1988] 2 FLR 365, CA (no unreasonable behaviour; husband and wife had simply grown apart).

361.   Living together after final incident of behaviour allegation. Where in any proceeding for divorce, dissolution or judicial or legal separation the petitioner[1] alleges that the respondent has behaved in such a way that he cannot reasonably be expected to live with the respondent[2], but the parties have lived with each other[3] for a period or periods after the date of the occurrence of the final incident relied on by the petitioner and held by the court[4] to support his allegation, that fact is to be disregarded in determining for the purposes of satisfying the court whether the petitioner cannot reasonably be expected to live with the respondent if the length of that period or of those periods together was six months or less[5]. This does not mean that, if the parties are together for more than six months after the final occurrence, it is necessarily a bar[6].

1   As to petitions and applications see PARA 321 note 1.
2   See the Matrimonial Causes Act 1973 s 1(2)(b); the Civil Partnership Act 2004 s 44(5)(a); and PARAS 347, 359, 360.
3   As to references to the parties living with each other see PARA 347 note 7.
4   As to the meaning of 'court' see PARA 346 note 2.
5   Matrimonial Causes Act 1973 ss 2(3), 17(1); Civil Partnership Act 2004 ss 45(1), (2), 56(4). A petitioner who relies on the respondent's behaviour may be required to give information relating to the parties' living arrangements: see the Family Proceedings Rules 1991, SI 1991/1247, r 2.24(3), (3A), Appendix 1, Form M7 paras (a)–(e) (r 2.24(3) substituted, r 2.24(3A) added, by SI 2005/2922; Family Proceedings Rules 1991, SI 1991/1247, Appendix 1, Form M7 paras (a)–(e) substituted by SI 2003/2839).
6   *Bradley v Bradley* [1973] 3 All ER 750, [1973] 1 WLR 1291, CA (wife stayed in same house as husband because she had nowhere else to go; not there of her own free will; divorce refused; case remitted for rehearing).

(iv) Desertion

A. FUNDAMENTAL PRINCIPLES

362.   Meaning of 'desertion'. In its essence desertion[1] means the intentional, permanent forsaking and abandonment[2] of one party by the other[3] without that other's consent[4], and without reasonable cause[5]. It is a total repudiation of one party's obligations[6]. In view of the large variety of circumstances and of modes of life involved, the court has discouraged attempts at defining desertion, there being no general principle applicable to all cases[7].

Desertion is not the withdrawal from a place but from a state of things[8], for what the law seeks to enforce is the recognition and discharge of the common obligations of the parties' joint state[9]; the state of things may usually be termed, for short, 'the home'[10]. There can be desertion without previous cohabitation by the parties, or (in the case of a marriage) without there having been consummation[11].

The person who actually withdraws from cohabitation is not necessarily the deserting party[12]. The fact that a husband makes an allowance to a wife whom he has abandoned is no answer to a charge of desertion[13].

Consensual divorce or dissolution is available in certain circumstances[14] but consent to separation is not the same as consent to divorce or dissolution and, if there is consent to separation, there is no desertion.

1   As to desertion as a fact proving irretrievable breakdown see PARA 347; and see *Perry v Perry* [1952] P 203 at 210, 211, [1952] 1 All ER 1076 at 1079, CA.
2   *Hopes v Hopes* [1949] P 227 at 235, [1948] 2 All ER 920 at 925, CA per Denning LJ; *Jackson v Jackson* [1924] P 19 at 23 (approved in *Weatherley v Weatherley* [1947] AC 628 at 632, [1947] 1 All ER 563 at 565, HL, and in *Herod v Herod* [1939] P 11 at 21, 22, [1938] 3 All ER 722 at 730); *Perry v Perry* [1952] P 203 at 205, [1952] 1 All ER 1076 at 1082, CA per

Sir Raymond Evershed MR; *Beeken v Beeken* [1948] P 302 at 311, CA; *Buchler v Buchler* [1947] P 25 at 29, 48, [1947] 1 All ER 319 at 320, 327, CA; *Williams v Williams* [1943] 2 All ER 746 at 752, CA per du Parcq LJ (a total repudiation of the obligations of marriage); *Thomas v Thomas* (1923) 39 TLR 520 at 521 (affd [1924] P 194, CA); *Tulk v Tulk* [1907] VLR 64 at 65; *R v Leresche* [1891] 2 QB 418 at 420, CA; *Townsend v Townsend* (1873) LR 3 P & D 129 at 131; *Fitzgerald v Fitzgerald* (1869) LR 1 P & D 694 at 697, as explained in *Pulford v Pulford* [1923] P 18; *Williams v Williams* (1864) 3 Sw & Tr 547; *Haswell v Haswell and Sanderson* (1859) 1 Sw & Tr 502 at 505.

3   As to mutual desertion see PARA 367.
4   *Ward v Ward* (1858) 1 Sw & Tr 185; *Thompson v Thompson* (1858) 1 Sw & Tr 231; *Smith v Smith* (1859) 1 Sw & Tr 359 at 361; *Haviland v Haviland* (1863) 32 LJPM & A 65; *Buckmaster v Buckmaster* (1869) LR 1 P & D 713; *Charter v Charter* (1901) 84 LT 272; *Harriman v Harriman* [1909] P 123 at 148, CA; *Fengl v Fengl* [1914] P 274; *Walter v Walter* [1921] P 302; *Pardy v Pardy* [1939] P 288 at 305, [1939] 3 All ER 779 at 784, CA; *Spence v Spence* [1939] 1 All ER 52 at 56, 57; *Edwards v Edwards* [1948] P 268 at 269, [1948] 1 All ER 157 at 158, DC; *Pearson v Pearson* [1948] WN 225, CA; *Kinnane v Kinnane* [1954] P 41, [1953] 2 All ER 1144; *Clark v Clark (by her guardian)* [1956] 1 All ER 823, [1956] 1 WLR 345; *Ingram v Ingram* [1956] P 390 at 411, [1956] 1 All ER 785 at 797; *Pinnick v Pinnick* [1957] 1 All ER 873 at 875, [1957] 1 WLR 644 at 647; *Bosley v Bosley* [1958] 2 All ER 167, [1958] 1 WLR 645, CA; *Parkinson v Parkinson* (1959) Times, 14 April, DC; *Gallagher v Gallagher* [1965] 2 All ER 967, [1965] 1 WLR 1110, CA; *Nutley v Nutley* [1970] 1 All ER 410, [1970] 1 WLR 217, CA.
5   Ie without the consent or fault of the person asking for relief: see *Lane v Lane* [1951] P 284 at 286; affd [1952] P 34, [1952] 1 All ER 223n, CA; *Day v Day* [1957] P 202 at 210, 211, [1957] 1 All ER 848 at 853. As to 'just cause' see PARA 380 et seq.
6   *Williams v Williams* [1943] 2 All ER 746 at 752, CA per du Parcq LJ; *Perry v Perry* [1952] P 203 at 215, [1952] 1 All ER 1076 at 1082, CA per Sir Raymond Evershed MR; cf *Williams v Williams* (1864) 3 Sw & Tr 547 at 548 (to neglect opportunities of consorting with a wife is not necessarily to desert her). See also *Thomas v Thomas* (1923) 39 TLR 520 at 521 ('wilful breaking off of conjugal relations'); affd [1924] P 194, CA.
7   *Weatherley v Weatherley* [1947] AC 628 at 631, [1947] 1 All ER 563 at 564, HL per Lord Jowitt LC; *Perry v Perry* [1952] P 203 at 215, [1952] 1 All ER 1076 at 1082, CA; *Lane v Lane* [1951] P 284 at 286 (affd [1952] P 34, [1952] 1 All ER 223n, CA); *Cohen v Cohen* [1940] AC 631 at 645, 646, [1940] 2 All ER 331 at 339, HL; *Herod v Herod* [1939] P 11 at 21, [1938] 3 All ER 722 at 730; *Jackson v Jackson* [1924] P 19 at 23; *Pulford v Pulford* [1923] P 18 at 22 (definitions are dangerous); *Frowd v Frowd* [1904] P 177 at 179; *Williams v Williams* (1864) 3 Sw & Tr 547; *Graves v Graves* (1864) 3 Sw & Tr 350 at 353; *Thompson v Thompson* (1858) 1 Sw & Tr 231 at 233.
8   *Pulford v Pulford* [1923] P 18 at 21 per Lord Merrivale P (no cohabitation after marriage; there was nevertheless desertion); *Pardy v Pardy* [1939] P 288 at 302, [1939] 3 All ER 779 at 782, CA per Sir Wilfred Greene MR; *Lane v Lane* [1951] P 284 at 286; affd [1952] P 34, [1952] 1 All ER 223n, CA.
9   *Pulford v Pulford* [1923] P 18 at 22.
10 *Lane v Lane* [1951] P 284 at 286 per Lord Merriman P; affd [1952] P 34, [1952] 1 All ER 223n, CA.
11 *Timoney v Timoney* [1926] NI 75 at 79; *De Laubenque v De Laubenque* [1899] P 42; *Lee Shires v Lee Shires* (1910) 54 Sol Jo 874; *Shaw v Shaw* [1939] P 269, [1939] 2 All ER 381; and see *Bradshaw v Bradshaw* [1897] P 24 at 26, 27; *Buckmaster v Buckmaster* (1869) LR 1 P & D 713; *Fassbender v Fassbender* [1938] 3 All ER 389 (restitution of conjugal rights).
12 *Sickert v Sickert* [1899] P 278 at 284; *Buchler v Buchler* [1947] P 25 at 45, [1947] 1 All ER 319 at 326, CA. As to constructive desertion see PARA 391 et seq.
13 *MacDonald v MacDonald* (1859) 4 Sw & Tr 242.
14 See PARA 407.

363. Desertion as proof of irretrievable breakdown.

The court[1] may find that a marriage or civil partnership has broken down irretrievably if the petitioner[2] satisfies[3] the court that the respondent has deserted him for a continuous period[4] of at least two years immediately preceding the presentation of the petition[5].

1   As to the meaning of 'court' see PARA 346 note 2.
2   As to petitioners and applicants see PARA 321 note 1.
3   As to the burden and standard of proof see PARA 369.

4   As to 'desertion' see PARA 362. As to the requirement for a continuous period see PARA 364.

5   See the Matrimonial Causes Act 1973 s 1(2)(c); the Civil Partnership Act 2004 s 44(5)(d); and PARA 347. As to the duty of the court to inquire into the facts see PARA 348. As to constructive desertion see PARA 391 et seq.

364. Duration of desertion. Desertion is a course of conduct[1] which exists independently of its duration[2]; but, as a fact on which a petition for divorce or application for the dissolution of a civil partnership[3] may be founded, it must exist for a continuous[4] period of at least two years immediately preceding the presentation of the petition or the making of the application[5] or, where the offence appears as a cross-charge, of the answer[6]. Desertion differs from other facts[7] constituting irretrievable breakdown in that the cause of action of desertion is not complete, but is inchoate, until the suit is constituted[8]. Desertion is a continuing matter[9].

1   *Thomas v Thomas* [1924] P 194 at 199, CA; *W v W (No 2)* [1954] P 486 at 502, [1954] 2 All ER 829 at 832, CA.

2   *Jordan v Jordan* [1939] P 239 at 251, [1939] 2 All ER 29 at 36; *Beeken v Beeken* [1948] P 302 at 308, CA; cf *Thomas v Thomas* [1924] P 194 at 199, CA.

3   As to petitions and applications see PARA 321 note 1.

4   See note 5.

5   See the Matrimonial Causes Act 1973 s 1(2)(c); the Civil Partnership Act 2004 s 44(5)(d); and PARAS 347, 362. The period must be 'a continuous period' and cannot be satisfied by aggregating with a period of less than two years an earlier, but detached, period of whatever duration: see *Jordan v Jordan* [1939] P 239 at 248, 249, [1939] 2 All ER 29 at 33, 34, citing a decision of Hodson J in *Cohen v Cohen* [1939] 2 All ER 39n; revsd without affecting this point [1940] AC 631, [1940] 2 All ER 331, HL; *Perry v Perry* [1952] P 203 at 211, 212, [1952] 1 All ER 1076 at 1079, CA per Sir Raymond Evershed MR; *W v W (No 2)* [1954] P 486 at 502, [1954] 2 All ER 829 at 832, 833, CA per Sir Raymond Evershed MR. See, however, *Green v Green* [1946] P 112, [1946] 1 All ER 308 (where, on a consideration of the wording of the Matrimonial Causes Act 1937 s 6(3) (repealed), a period of desertion of less than three years, i e the relevant period of desertion in the Matrimonial Causes Act 1937 (repealed), before the making of a non-cohabitation clause (inadvertently inserted in a maintenance order made by justices) was aggregated with a period of desertion of less than three years after the deletion of the non-cohabitation clause so as to provide a period of three years' desertion immediately preceding the presentation of the petition); and see PARAS 365–366. See also *Bush v Bush* [1939] P 142, [1938] 4 All ER 598; *Lett v Lett* (1907) 23 TLR 569; *Churner v Churner* (1912) 106 LT 769. As to the periods of cohabitation of which no account is to be taken see PARA 365; and as to living apart see PARA 407 et seq.

    In computing the two-year period, the day of separation is to be excluded from the computation: cf *Warr v Warr* [1975] Fam 25, [1975] 1 All ER 85.

6   *Faulkner v Faulkner* [1941] 2 All ER 748.

7   See PARA 347.

8   *Perry v Perry* [1952] P 203 at 211, [1952] 1 All ER 1076 at 1079, CA per Sir Raymond Evershed MR; and see at 213, 228, 232 and at 1081, 1089, 1092.

9   See *Hartnell v Hartnell* [1951] WN 555 at 556, DC; *Teall v Teall* [1938] P 250 at 256, [1938] 3 All ER 349 at 352.

365. No account of periods of living together. In considering whether the period for which the respondent has deserted the petitioner[1] has been continuous[2], no account is to be taken of any one period, not exceeding six months, or of any two or more periods, not exceeding six months in all, during which the parties resumed living with each other[3]; but no period during which the parties lived with each other is to count as part of the period of desertion[4].

1   As to petitioners and applicants see PARA 321 note 1.

2   Ie for the purposes the Matrimonial Causes Act 1973 s 1(2)(c) or the Civil Partnership Act 2004 s 44(5)(d): see PARAS 347, 362, 364.

3   As to references to the parties living with each other see PARA 347 note 7.

4   Matrimonial Causes Act 1973 s 2(5); Civil Partnership Act 2004 s 45(6), (7); and see *Morgan v Morgan* (1973) 117 Sol Jo 223; cf *Santos v Santos* [1972] Fam 247, [1972] 2 All ER 246, CA.

366.   Presumed time of desertion following prior decree or order of judicial or legal separation.   Where a petition for divorce or an application for a dissolution order[1] follows a decree of judicial separation or a separation order[2] containing a provision exempting one party to the marriage or civil partnership from the obligation to cohabit with the other or requiring civil partners to live apart, then, for the purpose of that petition or application, a period of desertion immediately preceding the institution of proceedings for the decree or order is deemed, if the parties have not resumed cohabitation and the decree or order has been continuously in force since it was granted or made, immediately to precede the presentation of the petition or application[3].

For the purposes of establishing the fact of desertion[4], the court[5] may treat as a period during which the respondent has deserted the petitioner any period during which there is in force:

(1)   an injunction granted by the High Court or a county court excluding the respondent from the family home[6]; or

(2)   an order made[7] by the High Court or a county court which prohibits the exercise by the respondent of the right to occupy a dwelling house in which the petitioner and the respondent have or at any time have had a family home[8].

A petitioner may rely on a period of desertion prior to a foreign decree of separation[9].

1   Ie in such a case as is mentioned in the Matrimonial Causes Act 1973 s 4(1) or the Civil Partnership Act 2004 s 46(1), (2): see PARA 758. As to the meaning of 'dissolution order' see PARA 346 note 1. As to petitions and applications see PARA 321 note 1.
2   As to the meaning of 'separation order' see PARA 346 note 4.
3   Matrimonial Causes Act 1973 s 4(3) (s 4(3) amended, s 4(5) added, by the Domestic Proceedings and Magistrates' Courts Act 1978 s 62); Civil Partnership Act 2004 s 46(4). See *Green v Green* [1946] P 112, [1946] 1 All ER 308 (cited in PARA 364 note 5). In the case of a marriage, this is subject to the Matrimonial Causes Act 1973 s 4(5) (as so added), which contains transitional provisions relating to certain orders made before 1981: s 4(3) (as so amended). As to corroboration see PARA 370.
4   Ie under the Matrimonial Causes Act 1973 s 1(2)(c) or the Civil Partnership Act 2004 s 44(5)(d): see PARAS 347, 363, 364.
5   As to the meaning of 'court' see PARA 346 note 2.
6   Matrimonial Causes Act 1973 s 4(4)(a) (s 4(4) added by the Domestic Proceedings and Magistrates' Courts Act 1978 s 62(b); amended by the Matrimonial Homes Act 1983 Sch 2); Civil Partnership Act 2004 s 46(5)(a).
7   Ie under the Family Law Act 1996 s 33 or s 37 (see PARAS 292–293, 305).
8   Matrimonial Causes Act 1973 s 4(4)(b) (as added and amended: see note 6); Civil Partnership Act 2004 s 46(5)(b).
9   *Tursi v Tursi* [1958] P 54, [1957] 2 All ER 828, following *Ainslie v Ainslie* (1927) 39 CLR 381; cf *Pandiani v Pandiani* (1963) 107 Sol Jo 832.

367.   Mutual desertion.   Whilst it has been said that it is possible in law for a husband and wife to have deserted each other[1], the view that two parties in respect of the same parting may each be guilty of desertion at the same time has been doubted[2] and disapproved[3].

1   *Hosegood v Hosegood* (1950) 66 (pt 1) TLR 735 at 740, CA per Denning LJ, criticising *Walter v Walter* (1949) 65 TLR 680; *Beigan v Beigan* [1956] P 313 at 320, [1956] 2 All ER 630 at 632, CA per Denning LJ; *Wevill v Wevill* (1962) 106 Sol Jo 155; *Price v Price* [1968] 3 All ER 543, [1968] 1 WLR 1735 (overruled but not on this point which was specifically not discussed: see [1970] 2 All ER 497, [1970] 1 WLR 993, CA).

2   *Simpson v Simpson* [1951] P 320 at 330, [1951] 1 All ER 955 at 960, DC; and see *Spence v Spence* [1939] 1 All ER 52 at 58.

3   *Lang v Lang* (1953) Times, 7 July, CA; and see *Price v Price* [1970] 2 All ER 497 at 498, [1970] 1 WLR 993 at 994, CA per Davies LJ, and at 501 and at 997 per Sachs LJ.

368.   Elements of desertion; factum and animus.   For desertion to exist there must be both the factum, or physical separation, and the animus deserendi[1], or the intention to desert in the sense of bringing cohabitation to an end. The necessary ingredients of desertion must, however, continue throughout the statutory period[2]. For the purpose of establishing irretrievable breakdown founded on the fact of desertion for a continuous period of two years[3], the court[4] may treat desertion as having continued at a time when the deserting party was incapable of continuing the necessary intention if the evidence before the court is such that, had the party not been so incapable, the court would have inferred that his desertion continued at that time[5].

A de facto separation may take place without there being an animus deserendi[6], as where there is a separation by mutual consent[6], or a compulsory separation[7]; but, if that animus supervenes, desertion will begin from that moment, whether or not that change of mind is communicated[8], unless there is consent to the separation by the other party[9]. There may, however, be animus deserendi without separation[10], as where the parties live not as two households under the same roof[11] but as one household[12]. The animus may be evidenced by the fact of presentation of a petition[13].

Where the factum and animus both exist, an offer in good faith to resume cohabitation[14] may be made by the deserting party, for desertion is a continuing offence[15], and refusal of such an offer may turn the tables and convert the hitherto deserted party into a deserter[16]. Where one party indicates to the other that, if he or she leaves, there will be no question of having him or her back, and that other party subsequently leaves, the leaving amounts to desertion if he or she has the necessary animus[17]. It follows that the mere fact that one party is glad to see the other go makes no difference to the quality of the act of leaving[18]. Once a party has left, it has been held that a prompt and decisive determination evinced by the other party that he or she should not return may put the former in the same position in law as if he or she had rejected an offer of reconciliation of the other party[19], but this proposition has been doubted[20].

1   *Sickert v Sickert* [1899] P 278 at 282; *Pardy v Pardy* [1939] P 288 at 302, [1939] 3 All ER 779 at 782, CA per Sir Wilfred Greene MR; *Earnshaw v Earnshaw* [1939] 2 All ER 698 at 699, CA; *Spence v Spence* [1939] 1 All ER 52 at 58; *Buchler v Buchler* [1947] P 25 at 29, [1947] 1 All ER 319 at 320, CA; *Edwards v Edwards* [1948] P 268 at 269, [1948] 1 All ER 157 at 158; *Hopes v Hopes* [1949] P 227, [1948] 2 All ER 920, CA; *Perry v Perry* [1952] P 203 at 212, [1952] 1 All ER 1076 at 1080, CA; *Lang v Lang* [1955] AC 402 at 417, [1954] 3 All ER 571 at 573, PC; *Price v Price* [1970] 2 All ER 497, [1970] 1 WLR 993, CA (animus but no factum). See also *French-Brewster v French-Brewster* (1889) 62 LT 609 (question of animus left to the jury); *Davis v Davis* (1920) 124 LT 795 (soldier's visits on leave to wife; adultery with another woman resumed immediately after last leave; desertion as from resumption). It has been said that desertion is a question of fact (*R v Davidson etc, Durham Justices* (1889) 5 TLR 199 at 200, DC (where it was also stated that formal declaration of an intention to desert is not necessary); *Re Duckworth* (1889) 5 TLR 608 at 609; *R v Leresche* [1891] 2 QB 418 at 420, CA; *Balcombe v Balcombe* [1908] P 176 at 180); and so is the continuance of desertion (*Pratt v Pratt* [1939] AC 417 at 427, [1939] 3 All ER 437 at 442, HL).

2   *Crowther v Crowther* [1951] AC 723 at 735, [1951] 1 All ER 1131 at 1132, HL.

3   Ie under the Matrimonial Causes Act 1973 s 1(2)(c) or the Civil Partnership Act 2004 s 44(5)(d): see PARAS 347, 362, 364.

4   As to the meaning of 'court' see PARA 346 note 2.

5   Matrimonial Causes Act 1973 s 2(4); Civil Partnership Act 2004 s 45(5).

6   See the cases in PARA 362 note 4.

7   *Beeken v Beeken* [1948] P 302, CA.

8   *Nutley v Nutley* [1970] 1 All ER 410, [1970] 1 WLR 217, CA.

9   *Pardy v Pardy* [1939] P 288 at 302, [1939] 3 All ER 779 at 782, CA; *Williams v Williams* [1939] P 365 at 368, [1939] 3 All ER 825 at 827, CA (overruled on another point in *Crowther v Crowther* [1951] AC 723, [1951] 1 All ER 1131, HL); *Gatehouse v Gatehouse* (1867) LR 1 P & D 331; *Stickland v Stickland* (1876) 35 LT 767; *Mahoney v M'Carthy* [1892] P 21 at 25, 26 (it is a matter of evidence); *Davis v Davis* (1920) 124 LT 795; *Beeken v Beeken* [1948] P 302, CA; *Gallagher v Gallagher* [1965] 2 All ER 967, [1965] 1 WLR 1110, CA (withdrawal of consent to separation must be genuine); *Nutley v Nutley* [1970] 1 All ER 410, [1970] 1 WLR 217, CA. As to consent fraudulently obtained, and consequently of no effect, see *Harrison v Harrison* (1910) 54 Sol Jo 619; *Crabb v Crabb* (1868) LR 1 P & D 601 at 604; *Lepre v Lepre* [1963] 2 All ER 49 at 58.

10 *Hopes v Hopes* [1949] P 227 at 231, 235, 238, [1948] 2 All ER 920 at 922, 924, 926, CA; *Le Brocq v Le Brocq* [1964] 3 All ER 464, [1964] 1 WLR 1085, CA.

11 *Powell v Powell* [1922] P 278; *Diver v Diver* (unreported), referred to in *Jackson v Jackson* [1924] P 19 at 28, *Smith v Smith* [1940] P 49 at 53, 54, *Wilkes v Wilkes* [1943] P 41 at 42, *Hopes v Hopes* [1949] P 227 at 232; *Smith v Smith* [1940] P 49, [1939] 4 All ER 533; *Wilkes v Wilkes* [1943] P 41, [1943] 1 All ER 433; *Shilston v Shilston* (1945) 174 LT 105; *Wanbon v Wanbon* [1946] 2 All ER 366 (desertion found even where there was 'only one household'); *Angel v Angel* [1946] 2 All ER 635 (principles discussed); *Hopes v Hopes* [1949] P 227, [1948] 2 All ER 920, CA (where *Wanbon v Wanbon* was doubted, and *Evans v Evans* [1948] 1 KB 175, [1947] 2 All ER 656, DC (a decision on the meaning of 'resides with' in the Summary Jurisdiction (Separation and Maintenance) Act 1925 s 1(4) (repealed)) was disapproved by Denning LJ; and see *Naylor v Naylor* [1962] P 253, [1961] 2 All ER 129, DC). *Evans v Evans* was, however, followed in *Wheatley v Wheatley* [1950] 1 KB 39, [1949] 2 All ER 428, DC; in *Curtin v Curtin* [1952] 2 QB 552, [1952] 1 All ER 1348, DC; and in *Hewitt v Hewitt* [1952] 2 QB 627, [1952] 2 All ER 250, DC; but in *Santos v Santos* [1972] Fam 247 at 262, [1972] 2 All ER 246 at 255, CA, it was said that the Divorce Reform Act 1969 s 2(5) (repealed: see now the Matrimonial Causes Act 1973 s 2(6); the Civil Partnership Act 2004 s 45(8); and PARA 347) 'conclusively' resolved the conflict against *Evans v Evans*, and in favour of the view taken in *Smith v Smith* and *Hopes v Hopes*; and see *Mouncer v Mouncer* [1972] 1 All ER 289, [1972] 1 WLR 321. See also *Hanson v Hanson* (1954) Times, 10 March, CA (two households, but no desertion on facts); c f *Fishburn v Fishburn* as reported in [1955] 1 All ER 230 at 233, following *Hopes v Hopes*. See also *Walker v Walker* [1952] 2 All ER 138, CA; *Thomas v Thomas* [1948] 2 KB 294, [1948] 2 All ER 98, DC; *Baker v Baker* [1952] 2 All ER 248, CA; c f *Wily v Wily* [1918] P 1 at 3 (mere unwillingness to live under the same roof not a defence to a petition for restitution of conjugal rights (a remedy abolished by the Matrimonial Proceedings and Property Act 1970 s 20 (repealed)); *Weatherley v Weatherley* [1947] AC 628, [1947] 1 All ER 563, HL (refusal of sexual intercourse by itself not desertion); and *Jones v Jones* [1952] 2 TLR 225 at 226, CA.

12 *Jackson v Jackson* [1924] P 19 at 25, 26; *Stevens v Stevens* (1929) 93 JP 120; *Littlewood v Littlewood* [1943] P 11, [1942] 2 All ER 515; *Wanbon v Wanbon* [1946] 2 All ER 366 (desertion nevertheless found), doubted in *Hopes v Hopes* [1949] P 227, [1948] 1 All ER 920, CA; *Angel v Angel* [1946] 2 All ER 635; *Everitt v Everitt* [1949] P 374, [1949] 1 All ER 908, CA; *Bull v Bull* [1953] P 224, [1953] 2 All ER 601, CA (one roof, despite two short periods of actual desertion); and see *Weatherley v Weatherley* [1947] AC 628, [1947] 1 All ER 563, HL; and *Powell v Powell* [1922] P 278 at 279 (neglect or contempt insufficient).

13 *Gerrard v Gerrard* (1958) Times, 18 November; *Pursey v Pursey* (1959) Times, 9 April; and see PARA 369. As to petitions and applications see PARA 321 note 1.

14 See PARA 397.

15 See PARA 364.

16 See *Thomas v Thomas* [1946] 1 All ER 170.

17 *Beigan v Beigan* [1956] P 313, [1956] 2 All ER 630, CA.

18 *Pizey v Pizey and Stephenson* [1961] P 101 at 108, [1961] 2 All ER 658 at 662, CA per Willmer J.

19 See *Fishburn v Fishburn* [1955] P 29 at 41, [1955] 1 All ER 230 at 236 per Willmer J; *Barnett v Barnett* [1955] P 21, [1954] 3 All ER 689. The result in such a case is that the party who shows the determination to have nothing further to do with the other cannot show desertion, and thus, if the deserted party will not have the deserter back, a stalemate may be reached.

20 *Beigan v Beigan* [1956] P 313, [1956] 2 All ER 630, CA.

369. Burden and standard of proof. The burden is on the petitioner to show that desertion without cause subsisted throughout the statutory period[1]. The deserting party must be shown to have persisted in the intention to desert throughout the whole of the two-year period[2], save where he was incapable of continuing the necessary intention[3]. It has been said that a petitioner should be able honestly to say that he or she was all along willing to fulfil his or her duties, and that the desertion was against his or her will, and continued throughout the statutory period without his or her consent[4]; but in practice it is accepted that once desertion has been started by the fault of the deserting party, it is no longer necessary for the deserted party to show that during the two years preceding the presentation of the petition he or she actually wanted the other to come back[5], for the intention to desert is presumed to continue[6]. That presumption may, however, be rebutted[7]. Where one of the parties has deserted the other, the desertion is not necessarily brought to an end by the commencement or conclusion of proceedings, but it is a question of fact in each case whether the desertion has been terminated[8]. If on the facts it appears that a petitioner has made it plain to the deserting party that he or she will not be received back, or has repelled all the advances made in such regard, the petitioner cannot complain that there has been persistence without cause in the desertion[9].

The mere act of one party leaving will in general make it easy to infer that the departing party intended to bring the relationship to an end[10].

The court must be satisfied on the evidence that desertion is proved[11]. This appears to mean that desertion like other facts constituting irretrievable breakdown must be proved by a preponderance of probability, the degree of probability depending on the subject matter[12].

1   *Pratt v Pratt* [1939] AC 417 at 420, [1939] 3 All ER 437 at 438, HL per Lord Macmillan; *Dunn v Dunn* [1949] P 98 at 103, [1948] 2 All ER 822 at 823, CA per Denning LJ; *Arding v Arding* [1954] 2 All ER 671n, [1954] 1 WLR 944; *Perry v Perry* [1963] 3 All ER 766, [1964] 1 WLR 91. See also *Yeatman v Yeatman* (1868) LR 1 P & D 489 at 491, 494; *Oldroyd v Oldroyd* [1896] P 175 at 182; *Beer v Beer* (1906) 22 TLR 338 at 340; *Greene v Greene* [1916] P 188 at 190; *Williams v Williams* [1943] 2 All ER 746 at 751, 752, CA; *Glenister v Glenister* [1945] P 30 at 37, [1945] 1 All ER 513 at 518; *Emanuel v Emanuel* [1946] P 115 at 188, [1945] 2 All ER 494 at 496; *Beer v Beer (Neilson cited)* [1948] P 10 at 14, [1947] 2 All ER 711 at 713; *Kafton v Kafton* [1948] 1 All ER 435 at 438, CA; *Arding v Arding* [1954] 2 All ER 671n, [1954] 1 WLR 944. As to the statutory period see PARA 364.

2   *Pratt v Pratt* [1939] AC 417 at 420, [1939] 3 All ER 437 at 438, HL.

3   See PARA 368.

4   *Pratt v Pratt* [1939] AC 417 at 421, 422, [1939] 3 All ER 437 at 438, 439, HL per Lord Macmillan (citing with approval *Macaskill v Macaskill* 1939 SC 187 at 193); *Herod v Herod* [1939] P 11 at 19, 20, 32, 33, [1938] 3 All ER 722 at 728, 729, 737, 738; and see *Mackenzie v Mackenzie* [1895] AC 384 at 389, HL per Lord Herschell LC; *Cohen v Cohen* [1940] AC 631 at 638, [1940] 2 All ER 331 at 334, 335, HL per Lord Romer; *Crowther v Crowther* [1951] AC 723 at 731, 734, 735, [1951] 1 All ER 1131 at 1133, 1135, 1136, HL; *Perry v Perry* [1952] P 203 at 211, 213, 228, 232, [1952] 1 All ER 1076 at 1079, 1081, 1089, 1092, CA; cf *Harriman v Harriman* [1909] P 123 at 148, CA per Buckley LJ (one party may be thankful that the other party has gone, but that other party may nevertheless be in desertion), and the comment on that case in *Spence v Spence* [1939] 1 All ER 52 at 57, 58, and *Kinnane v Kinnane* [1954] P 41 at 46, [1953] 2 All ER 1144 at 1147; *French-Brewster v French-Brewster* (1889) 62 LT 609. See also *Wallace v Wallace* 1952 SC 197 at 169, but note the warning at 170 (English conceptions of desertion are different from Scottish; and see *Crowther v Crowther* [1951] AC 723 at 734, [1951] 1 All ER 1131 at 1135, HL); *Cairns v Cairns* [1940] NI 183 (petitioner must be prepared to take respondent back, but need have no emotional desire to do so).

5   *Beigan v Beigan* [1956] P 313 at 319, [1956] 2 All ER 630 at 632, CA; *Bevan v Bevan* [1955] 3 All ER 332 at 335, [1955] 1 WLR 1142 at 1147; *Church v Church* [1952] P 313, [1952] 2 All ER 441 (where Willmer J followed *Sifton v Sifton* [1939] P 221 at 226, [1939] 1 All ER

109 at 113). See also *Crowther v Crowther* [1951] AC 723 at 731, 734, 735, [1951] 1 All ER 1131 at 1133, 1135, 1136, HL; *Pratt v Pratt* [1939] AC 417 at 421, [1939] 3 All ER 437 at 438, 439, HL (in some cases it would be a mockery for the innocent party to pretend that there was a desire for resumption); *Lane v Lane* [1951] P 284 at 288, DC; affd [1952] P 34, [1952] 1 All ER 223n, CA (constructive desertion; expelled wife had to prove husband meant, and continued at all material times to mean, what he said; otherwise she failed); cf *Dunn v Dunn* [1949] P 98 at 103, [1948] 2 All ER 822 at 823, CA; *Warburton v Warburton* (1965) 109 Sol Jo 290, CA. As to the position where the deserted party decides from the outset not to have the deserting party back see PARA 368.

6   *Bowron v Bowron* [1925] P 187 at 195, CA; *Sifton v Sifton* [1939] P 221 at 226, [1939] 1 All ER 109 at 111; *Williams v Williams* [1939] P 365 at 369, [1939] 3 All ER 825 at 828, CA (overruled on another point in *Crowther v Crowther* [1951] AC 723, [1951] 1 All ER 1131, HL).

7   See PARA 394.

8   *W v W (No 2)* [1954] P 486, [1954] 2 All ER 829, CA, applying observations of Lord Romer in *Cohen v Cohen* [1940] AC 631 at 635, [1940] 2 All ER 331 at 332, 333, HL (overruling *Stevenson v Stevenson* [1911] P 191, CA), where the question is posed; but see also *Cohen v Cohen* [1940] AC 631 at 645, [1940] 2 All ER 331 at 339, HL (where Lord Romer points out that there may be cases where the petition contains gross charges against the respondent so reckless and so unfounded that the respondent cannot reasonably be expected to make any attempt to bring his desertion to an end). See also PARA 368.

9   See *Pratt v Pratt* [1939] AC 417 at 420, [1939] 3 All ER 437 at 438, HL; *Cohen v Cohen* [1940] AC 631 at 638, 639, [1940] 2 All ER 331 at 335, HL; and the cases cited in note 4; but see also the cases in note 5, and the practice indicated in the text thereto.

10 *Buchler v Buchler* [1947] P 25 at 30, [1947] 1 All ER 319 at 320, CA per Lord Greene MR.

11 See the Matrimonial Causes Act 1973 s 1(4); the Civil Partnership Act 2004 s 44(4); and PARA 348.

12 *Blyth v Blyth* [1966] AC 643 at 669, 673, 674, [1966] 1 All ER 524 at 536, 539, HL.

370. Corroboration. Corroboration is not required as an absolute rule of law; there is no rule which prevents a tribunal from finding desertion proved in the absence of corroboration[1]. If the court requires corroboration in an undefended suit, it will usually relate to the circumstances and terms of the separation and not to the duration of the desertion[2].

1   *Marjoram v Marjoram* [1955] 2 All ER 1 at 7, [1955] 1 WLR 520 at 524, DC; *Stone v Stone* [1949] P 165 at 168, CA; *Tilley v Tilley* [1949] P 240 at 252, 261, [1948] 2 All ER 1113 at 1117, 1124, CA (no one can corroborate himself); *DB v WB* [1935] P 80 at 82, 85; *Joseph v Joseph* [1915] P 122 at 124; *Judd v Judd* [1907] P 241 at 243; cf *Robinson v Robinson and Lane* (1859) 1 Sw & Tr 362 at 392; *Williams v Williams* (1932) 147 LT 219 at 220, 221; *Alli v Alli* [1965] 3 All ER 480, DC; *Forster v Forster* (1910) 54 Sol Jo 403 goes too far in saying there must be corroboration: *Lawson v Lawson* [1955] 1 All ER 341, [1955] 1 WLR 200, CA.

2   *Barron v Barron* [1963] 1 All ER 215, [1963] 1 WLR 57; *Forte v Forte* (1966) 110 Sol Jo 52.

B. DESERTION AND CONSENSUAL SEPARATION

371. Time and method of consent. There is no desertion if there is agreement to separate[1], or to the continuance of a separation[2]. Consent to separation is a question of fact[3]; the fact that one party leaves the other does not in itself mean that there is agreement to separate, even if neither party wishes to live with the other[4]. The consent may be oral or in writing[5], or may be implied[6]. The court is slow to infer a term that the separation is to be forever with no opportunity for any unilateral change of mind[7]; but, where there is no such term in the agreement to separate, it is open to either party to terminate the consensual separation by making the appropriate offer to return[8].

It follows that desertion may be terminated by a subsequent deed consenting to the separation[9], or by any other agreement or arrangement between the parties to that effect[10].

1   See the cases cited in PARA 362 note 4. It has been held that there may be a consensual separation on the implied undertaking by both parties that one party's liability to support the other is to continue: see *Kinnane v Kinnane* [1954] P 41 at 48, [1953] 2 All ER 1144 at 1148 per Pearce J (desertion found); and see *Macdonald v Macdonald* (1859) 4 Sw & Tr 242 (allowance by husband; no consent); *Nott v Nott* (1866) LR 1 P & D 251 (allowance by wife; no consent). Separation agreements entered into before 1 January 1938 may in some circumstances be disregarded in establishing desertion: see the Matrimonial Causes Act 1973 Sch 1 para 8; *O'Brien v O'Brien* (1959) Times, 16 July; *Pearce v Pearce* [1960] 3 All ER 21 at 24, 25, [1960] 1 WLR 855 at 859, 860, CA.

2   *Pardy v Pardy* [1939] P 288 at 305, [1939] 3 All ER 779 at 785, CA; *Spence v Spence* [1939] 1 All ER 52 at 58 (consent to separation forbidden; otherwise there could be consensual divorce (not permitted at that date: see now PARA 407). This does not mean that one party may not be thankful that the other has gone, but that there must not be consent: *Harriman v Harriman* [1909] P 123 at 148, CA; *Spence v Spence* at 57, 58; *Pizey v Pizey and Stephenson* [1961] P 101 at 108, [1961] 2 All ER 658 at 662, CA; *Phair v Phair* (1963) 107 Sol Jo 554, CA; *Warburton v Warburton* (1965) 109 Sol Jo 290, CA.

3   See *Graeff v Graeff* (1928) 93 JP 48 (tacit consent to separation; no evidence of desertion); *Pardy v Pardy* [1939] P 288 at 305, 307, [1939] 3 All ER 779 at 785, 786, CA.

4   *Phair v Phair* (1963) 107 Sol Jo 554, CA (wife told husband to go; he wanted to leave anyway; as he was given no option in the matter, he was not in desertion, she was); and see *Ingram v Ingram* [1956] P 390, [1956] 1 All ER 785.

5   *Fengl v Fengl* [1914] P 274, DC; cf *Walter v Walter* [1921] P 302 (oral agreement to separate).

6   *Spence v Spence* [1939] 1 All ER 52; *Graeff v Graeff* (1928) 93 JP 48; *Barnett v Barnett* [1955] P 21 at 28, [1954] 3 All ER 689 at 694.

7   *Bosley v Bosley* [1958] 2 All ER 167 at 173, [1958] 1 WLR 645 at 653, CA (maintenance agreement was at most agreement to separate for an indefinite period; husband was in desertion prior to the agreement and on the facts remained so after it).

8   *Fraser v Fraser* [1969] 3 All ER 654, [1969] 1 WLR 1787.

9   *Lord Long of Wraxall v Lady Long of Wraxall* [1940] 4 All ER 230, CA; cf *Crabtree v Crabtree* [1953] 2 All ER 56, [1953] 1 WLR 708, CA.

10   *Harvey v Harvey* [1956] P 102, [1952] 3 All ER 772, CA; *Pizey v Pizey and Stephenson* [1961] P 101, [1961] 2 All ER 658, CA. See also PARA 372.

372. Desertion without resumption of cohabitation. A separation which begins by being consensual[1] may be changed into desertion without a previous resumption of cohabitation. It has been said that the separation must lose its consensual element on both sides[2], but this proposition is confined to deeds where the parties have covenanted to live apart for joint lives or for some other definite period and does not apply to agreements to live separately for an indefinite period, these latter agreements being terminable on the will of either party either immediately or perhaps on reasonable notice if the other terms of a particular agreement are such as to lead to the inference that such a term should be implied[3]. The withdrawal of consent to separation must be genuine[4].

1   See *Adamson v Adamson* (1907) 23 TLR 434 (wife not consenting to a deed); cf *Piper v Piper* [1902] P 198 at 200, 201; *Holroyd v Holroyd* (1920) 36 TLR 479 (wife not consenting party).

2   *Pardy v Pardy* [1939] P 288 at 302, 303, 306, 307, [1939] 3 All ER 779 at 785, 786, CA. See also *Clark v Clark (No 2)* [1939] P 257 at 260, [1939] 2 All ER 392 at 394; *Basing v Basing* (1864) 3 Sw & Tr 516 (temporary separation agreed; wife to follow husband to Australia; he never sent money, and formed adulterous association there); *Mahoney v M'Carthy* [1892] P 21 at 25, 26 (temporary separation agreed; husband went to America for work; agreement as to resumption of cohabitation not clear; away ten years, communicated with wife on one occasion at most; animus not inferred); *Keech v Keech* (1868) LR 1 P & D 641 (wife left Jamaica for England because of ill-health; husband wanted her back; wife did not return or offer to return when she recovered; husband not in desertion); *Thompson v Thompson* (1858) 1 Sw & Tr 231 (husband left Leeds for London to seek work; wife did not answer his letters; husband not in desertion); *Gatehouse v Gatehouse* (1867) LR 1 P & D 331 (husband turned out of house by mother-in-law; wife stayed, husband saw wife as often as he could, corresponded with her; husband then formed adulterous association; wife heard and ceased to write to him, and he at same time broke off all association with wife; desertion as from time husband abandoned wife for other woman); *Farmer v Farmer* (1884) 9 PD 245 (desertion commenced from time wife

discovered adultery of husband although he had corresponded with and visited wife while living with another woman); *Sotherden v Sotherden* [1940] P 73 at 79, 80, [1940] 1 All ER 252 at 256, CA (applying *Gatehouse v Gatehouse* and *Pulford v Pulford* [1923] P 18). Cf *Huxtable v Huxtable* (1899) 68 LJP 83; *Chudley v Chudley* (1893) 69 LT 617; *Henty v Henty* (1875) 33 LT 263; *Stickland v Stickland* (1876) 35 LT 767; and *Smith v Smith* (1888) 58 LT 639, in all of which cases temporary separations only were agreed to, and desertion supervened.

3   *Hall v Hall* [1960] 1 All ER 91, [1960] 1 WLR 52; *Gallagher v Gallagher* [1965] 2 All ER 967, [1965] 1 WLR 1110, CA.
4   *Fraser v Fraser* [1969] 3 All ER 654, [1969] 1 WLR 1787.

373. Agreement to pay maintenance. An agreement to pay maintenance while the parties live apart is not necessarily an agreement that one party agrees to the other living apart. The question is one of construction of the particular deed; and, if it is found to be simply a deed defining quantum and duration of payment, and not a bargain to live apart, desertion may run[1]. Indeed, the desertion may have commenced before the maintenance agreement and continue to run after the agreement has been reached[2]. An agreement to pay maintenance may be oral or in writing[3]; and the same considerations apply as with a deed[4].

1   *Crabtree v Crabtree* [1953] 2 All ER 56, [1953] 1 WLR 708, CA, applying *Lord Long of Wraxall v Lady Long of Wraxall* [1940] 4 All ER 230 at 233, CA. See also *Macdonald v Macdonald* (1859) 4 Sw & Tr 242; *Nott v Nott* (1866) LR 1 P & D 251 (where allowances not under a deed did not constitute consent to separation).
2   *Bosley v Bosley* [1958] 2 All ER 167, [1958] 1 WLR 645, CA.
3   See PARAS 371, 427.
4   See *Peters' Executors v IRC* [1941] 2 All ER 620, CA (effect of a binding oral separation agreement in relation to income tax).

374. Repudiation and affirmation of separation deed. It has been held that if a husband who has left his wife under the terms of a separation deed subsequently repudiates the deed, but continues to live apart from his wife, it is easy to infer that his intention to live apart, which was originally based on the consent of both parties, has become an intention to desert; if, however, the party alleging desertion has during the relevant period affirmed the continuing validity of a separation deed, as by suing for maintenance under it, there cannot be desertion, since the necessary repudiation of consent on his or her part cannot be shown[1]. Further, if one party has repudiated the deed and the other can show that during the relevant period he or she had no intention of relying on the deed and was always ready and willing in spite of it to resume cohabitation, that other party cannot be said to have consented to the separation, for the separation is no longer due to the consensus of the parties[2], and the agreement is a dead letter which no longer regulates their relations[3]. Breach of a particular covenant in a separation deed may not amount to repudiation; but the breach may be so fundamental or so persistent or may have such a significance when regarded in the light of all the circumstances of the case as to justify the inference that repudiation is intended[4].

Whether a person remains party to a separation after a separation deed has been repudiated is a question of fact in each case, the answer to which depends on the true inference to be drawn from the words and conduct of the parties[5]. The burden of proving continued acceptance of a separation after repudiation of a deed lies on the party who repudiates[6].

1   *Clark v Clark* (No 2) [1939] P 257 at 259, [1939] 2 All ER 392 at 394.
2   *Pardy v Pardy* [1939] P 288 at 303, 305, 306, [1939] 3 All ER 779 at 783, 784, CA. For a former view on this proposition see *Crabb v Crabb* (1868) LR 1 P & D 601 (separation in first instance consensual; that aspect was not affected by husband's virtual repudiation of deed; no relation back).

3   *Pardy v Pardy* [1939] P 288 at 307, [1939] 3 All ER 779 at 786, CA. See also *Looker v Looker*
    [1918] P 132; *Walsh v Walsh* (1919) 122 LT 463; *Roe v Roe* [1916] P 163; *Smith v Smith*
    [1915] P 288; *Hussey v Hussey* (1913) 109 LT 192; *Balcombe v Balcombe* [1908] P 176.
4   *Pardy v Pardy* [1939] P 288 at 304, [1939] 3 All ER 779 at 784, CA.
5   *Pardy v Pardy* [1939] P 288 at 305, 307, [1939] 3 All ER 779 at 784, 786, CA.
6   *Clark v Clark* (No 2) [1939] P 257 at 260, [1939] 2 All ER 392 at 394, explaining *Norman v
    Norman* (1939) unreported.

375.   Effect of an invalid or illegal separation deed.   An agreement by the
parties to a marriage (or, presumably, a civil partnership), entered into before
that marriage, to live afterwards apart has been held to be void as being against
public policy, even if the agreement is afterwards confirmed[1]. Where parties
entered into an illegal separation agreement after a marriage, it was open to one
of them to reassert his or her rights to cohabitation, and refusal of consortium
after such reassertion put the refusing party in desertion[2].

1   *Scott v Scott (otherwise Fone)* [1959] P 103n at 106, [1959] 1 All ER 531 at 533, 534 (nullity
    case); *Re Allan, Allan v Midland Bank Executor and Trustee Co Ltd* [1954] Ch 295, [1954]
    1 All ER 646, CA; *Re Williams' Settlement, Greenwell v Humphries* [1929] 2 Ch 361, CA;
    Brodie v Brodie [1917] P 271; *Lily, Duchess of Marlborough v Duke of Marlborough* [1901]
    1 Ch 165 at 171, CA; *Marshall v Marshall* (1879) 5 PD 19 at 23; *Cocksedge v Cocksedge*
    (1844) 14 Sim 244.
2   *Papadopoulos v Papadopoulos* [1936] P 108; and see *Joseph v Joseph* [1953] 2 All ER 710 at
    712, 713, [1953] 1 WLR 1182, CA; c f *Rosenberg v Rosenberg* (1954) Times, 16 July (deed after
    marriage did not, on facts of it, contemplate future separation; evidence not admissible to
    contradict clear terms of deed).

376.   Effect of Jewish divorce.   A get or Jewish bill of divorcement obtained in
England has no legal validity in English law in that it does not effect a divorce,
and it does not in itself constitute an agreement to separate under English law;
but, if in a particular case it does not amount to repudiation by one spouse of the
other but involves an agreement between the spouses that thereafter they should
live apart, it may thereby terminate any existing desertion and prevent any future
separation from amounting to desertion[1]. The court must have regard to all the
surrounding circumstances in which the get comes into existence, including the
facts following it, to see whether the desertion is terminated by the get[2].

1   *Joseph v Joseph* [1953] 2 All ER 710, [1953] 1 WLR 1182, CA, distinguishing *Papadopoulos v
    Papadopoulos* [1936] P 108; and see *Leeser (otherwise May) v Leeser (otherwise Bohrer)* (1955)
    Times, 5 February (husband's consent to divorce wife by Jewish religious law, followed by her
    remarriage in a country where that divorce was an effective dissolution, which it was not in
    England, did not, on facts, amount to connivance at the subsequent adultery); *Tursi v Tursi*
    [1958] P 54, [1957] 2 All ER 828; *Gillon v Gillon* (1961) Times, 4 July; *Silver v Silver* (1962)
    106 Sol Jo 1012. As to the recognition of extra-judicial divorces obtained by means of
    proceedings, including gets, see *Berkovits v Grinberg (A-G intervening)* [1995] Fam 142, [1995]
    2 All ER 681; and CONFLICT OF LAWS vol 8(3) (Reissue) PARAS 255, 256.
2   *Corbett v Corbett* [1957] 1 All ER 621, [1957] 1 WLR 486 (the get did not terminate desertion).
    See also *Garrow v Garrow* (1966) 110 Sol Jo 850. As to Jewish religious provisions see 'Jewish
    Divorces' (1973) 123 NLJ 829.

C.   DESERTION WITHOUT SEPARATION

377.   Where parties live under same roof.   While there is no desertion if there
is no separation[1], there may be an animus deserendi without a separation, as
where the parties, although at arm's length, live as one household[2] under the
same roof. There would, however, be the factum of separation if in fact the
parties lived as two households[3] under the same roof, even where, because of
compulsion, they live in the same bedroom[4]. The onus of proving separation in

these as in other desertion cases is on the person alleging desertion[5]; but it must be borne in mind that no account may be taken of certain periods during which the parties have resumed living with each other in the same household[6].

1 See PARA 368.
2 See the cases cited in PARA 368 note 11.
3 See the cases cited in PARA 368 note 10.
4 *Beeken v Beeken* [1948] P 302 at 311, CA per Lord Merriman P (parties interned by Japanese); c f *Kaye (formerly Kazlowski) v Kazlowska* (1953) Times, 1 April (impossible for wife to leave Cracow; impossible for husband to go to Cracow; wife not in desertion); and *Szajna v Szajna* (1954) Times, 19 June (wife could have left Poland; husband could not go there; wife in desertion).
5 *Everitt v Everitt* [1949] P 374 at 390, [1949] 1 All ER 908 at 920, CA.
6 See PARA 365.

378. Matters not amounting to separation. To neglect opportunities of consorting with a partner is not necessarily desertion; indifference, want of proper solicitude, illiberality, denial of reasonable means, are not desertion, so long as there is maintained such degree of manner of intercourse as might naturally be expected from the calling and means of the parties[1]. Regard must, therefore, be had to the opportunities for cohabitation available to the parties in question, for these opportunities may be restricted[2]; and there may be a cohabitation and a separation therefrom even when the parties have not lived together physically under the same roof[3].

A temporary separation for mutual convenience does not put an end to cohabitation[4].

1 *Williams v Williams* (1864) 3 Sw & Tr 547 at 548 (husband and wife domestic servants in different employments).
2 *Williams v Williams* (1864) 3 Sw & Tr 547 (matrimony is made for all; and matrimonial intercourse must accommodate itself to the weightier considerations of material life); *Huxtable v Huxtable* (1899) 68 LJP 83.
3 *Bradshaw v Bradshaw* [1897] P 24 at 26 (wife a domestic servant); and see the cases cited in PARA 362 note 11. See also *Abercrombie v Abercrombie* [1943] 2 All ER 465 (there may be a resumption of cohabitation after separation without the parties coming together in a matrimonial home); and as to that case see *Perry v Perry* [1952] P 203 at 217, [1952] 1 All ER 1076 at 1083, CA.
4 *Chudley v Chudley* (1893) 69 LT 617, CA; *Thomas v Thomas* [1924] P 194 at 199, CA (a mere temporary parting is equivocal, unless and until its purpose and object are made plain). Cf *Wynne v Wynne* [1898] P 18 (fraudulent misrepresentation as to parting for limited period); and *Harrison v Harrison* (1910) 54 Sol Jo 619 (separation deed for six months; a few days after deed husband left for New Zealand with another woman); followed in *Lepre v Lepre* [1963] 2 All ER 49 at 58; and see the cases cited in PARA 372 note 2 and PARAS 380, 382.

379. Refusal of sexual intercourse. When the parties are living together, persistent refusal of sexual intercourse by one of them, without any other disruptive conduct on the part of either, has been held not to constitute desertion[1], for it does not produce either separation or living apart[2]; but persistent refusal without explanation over a long period of time may justify the other party in leaving[3], and this is so in all cases where the circumstances are such that the refusing party must be taken to realise that the refusal will probably bring the relationship to an end[4]. Refusal of sexual intercourse may be evidence from which, with other evidence, an intention to bring about a separation may be inferred[5]. Where there is refusal as a condition of resumption of cohabitation between parties who have already separated, that refusal amounts to desertion where the party stipulating that there should be no sexual intercourse in the future knows that such a proposal is unacceptable to the other party, and there are no circumstances such as physical causes or an absolute psychological barrier equivalent to a structural incapacity justifying the refusal[6].

1   *Weatherley v Weatherley* [1947] AC 628, [1947] 1 All ER 563, HL, approving *Jackson v Jackson* [1924] P 19. Cf *Beevor v Beevor* [1945] 2 All ER 200 (wife's invincible repugnance); *Perry v Perry* [1952] P 203 at 215, 216, [1952] 1 All ER 1076 at 1082, CA.
2   *Jackson v Jackson* [1924] P 19 at 23, 24, following *Orme v Orme* (1824) 2 Add 382.
3   *Sheldon v Sheldon* [1966] P 62, [1966] 2 All ER 257, CA.
4   *Slon v Slon* [1969] P 122, [1969] 1 All ER 759, CA. See also *Sheldon v Sheldon* [1966] P 62, [1966] 2 All ER 257, CA; *Hughes v Hughes* (1966) 110 Sol Jo 349, CA. Cf *Mason v Mason* (1980) 11 Fam Law 143, CA (cited in PARA 360 note 3).
5   *Scotcher v Scotcher* [1947] P 1; *Fletcher v Fletcher* [1945] 1 All ER 582 (withdrawal to religious community and refusal of sexual intercourse; desertion); *Lawrance v Lawrance* [1950] P 84, DC; *Cann v Cann* (1967) 111 Sol Jo 810 (unreasonable refusal by wife, together with insults, lack of consideration and refusal to perform household duties; she thereby manifested an intention to desert).
6   *Hutchinson v Hutchinson* [1963] 1 All ER 1, [1963] 1 WLR 280, DC.

D. SEPARATION WITH JUST CAUSE

380.   Effect of separation with cause.   Desertion must be without cause if it is to constitute one of the facts on which a claim of irretrievable breakdown may be founded[1]. It follows that a separation with cause does not constitute desertion.

1   See PARA 363; and *Day v Day* [1957] P 202 at 210, [1957] 1 All ER 848 at 853; *G v G* [1964] P 133, [1964] 1 All ER 129, DC; *Quoraishi v Quoraishi* [1985] FLR 780, [1985] Fam Law 308, CA (polygamous marriage).

381.   Conduct amounting to just cause.   It seems that any fact constituting irretrievable breakdown[1] would justify the other party in withdrawing from cohabitation[2]. Further, conduct which falls short of a fact constituting irretrievable breakdown may provide just cause for separation[3].

1   See PARA 347.
2   Before the passing of the Divorce Reform Act 1969 (repealed), any matrimonial offence, if proved, was a ground for the other spouse withdrawing from cohabitation: see *Glenister v Glenister* [1945] P 30 at 40, 41, [1945] 1 All ER 513 at 519; *Sickert v Sickert* [1899] P 278 at 283.
3   *Williams v Williams* [1943] 2 All ER 746 at 752, CA per du Parcq LJ; *Young v Young* [1964] P 152, [1962] 3 All ER 120, DC; *Clark v Clark (by her guardian)* [1956] 1 All ER 823, [1956] 1 WLR 345; *Edwards v Edwards* [1950] P 8 at 11, 14, [1949] 2 All ER 145 at 147, 148, CA per Bucknill LJ; *Glenister v Glenister* [1945] P 30 at 37, 41, [1945] 1 All ER 513 at 518, 519 (referring to *Russell v Russell* [1895] P 315, CA; on appeal [1897] AC 395, HL); *Herod v Herod* [1939] P 11 at 25, [1938] 3 All ER 722 at 732 (any other misconduct or neglect); *Thomas v Thomas* [1924] P 194 at 201, CA; *Synge v Synge* [1900] P 180 at 180, 193, 197 (affd [1901] P 317, CA); *Yeatman v Yeatman* (1868) LR 1 P & D 489 at 491, 492, 494; *Haswell v Haswell and Sanderson* (1859) 1 Sw & Tr 502 (explained in *Cox v Cox* [1958] 1 All ER 569 at 573, [1958] 1 WLR 340 at 345, 346, DC). See also PARA 385.

382.   Enforced separations.   The court will not find desertion merely because one party spends a holiday away from the other[1]. It has been held that if a woman marries a man whose work compels him to live out of England, she impliedly agrees that he should not be compelled to live with her in England[2], and that if a woman whose husband is compelled by reason of his work to live out of England makes it impossible through her conduct for her to stay with him abroad, she cannot complain of separation without just cause if the husband offers to maintain her elsewhere, and refuses to give up his employment abroad and join her[3].

Where a separation is enforced, it is impossible to infer from the mere fact of withdrawal from cohabitation any intention to bring cohabitation permanently to an end, but such an intention may be shown independently; in that case, the extraneous circumstances which necessitate the separation are no longer a cause of separation but are a mere excuse for it[4].

1   See *G v G* [1930] P 72 at 75.
2   *G v G* [1930] P 72 at 76 (a husband is bound to maintain his wife and children, and, therefore, to earn a living, and it is for him to choose how and where he earns that living, provided that his choice is genuine and not merely a cloak to avoid living with his wife); as to the duty to maintain see also *Lilley v Lilley* [1960] P 158 at 180, [1959] 3 All ER 283 at 289, CA per Hodson LJ (obligation to maintain not affected by enforced separation).
3   *G v G* [1930] P 72 at 75 (wife's persistent extravagance; also she incensed husband's partners against her); cf *Powell v Powell* (1957) Times, 22 February, CA (wife returned to father's home in Greece; husband would not give up home and job in England; decree granted to husband).
4   *G v G* [1964] P 133 at 136, [1964] 1 All ER 129 at 131, DC.

383.   Limited separation; duty to offer to return.   When a party is living apart from the other by agreement for a limited purpose, it is the duty of that other party to offer to return to the other when that purpose has been accomplished[1].

1   *Keech v Keech* (1868) LR 1 P & D 641 (wife's illness caused her to leave Jamaica where husband lived and was employed but she made no effort to return); and see *Powell v Powell* (1957) Times, 22 February, CA (wife went to visit father in Greece because she was homesick, but refused to return).

384.   Choice of home.   There is no absolute rule whereby either party is entitled to dictate to the other where their home shall be; the matter is to be settled by agreement between the parties, by a process of give and take, and by reasonable accommodation[1]. It is not against public policy for parties to enter into a prior agreement on what is to be their home, and, unless the reasons on which the agreement was based cease to exist, or if some changed circumstances give good reason for change in the home, the agreement stands[2]. Neither party, it has been said, has a casting vote[3]; it has further been suggested that, if the parties are both unreasonable, each might be entitled on the ground of the other's desertion[4], but this proposition has been doubted and disapproved[5]. The parties should so arrange their affairs that they spend their time together and not apart[6], and, where there is a difference of view, reason must prevail[7].

It has been held that a wife does not succeed in establishing that a husband has not provided her with a reasonable home by showing that, having left him unreasonably, she has, by her independent action, found accommodation somewhere else which he is unwilling to accept[8].

1   *Jackson v Jackson* (1932) 146 LT 406 at 407 (husband's taking house next door to his mother was not an abuse of the husband's marital duties, despite irritation it was likely to cause, as he did not put wife under mother's domination); *Walter v Walter* (1949) 65 TLR 680; *Dunn v Dunn* [1949] P 98 at 103, [1948] 2 All ER 822 at 823, CA per Denning LJ; *Murray v Murray* (1961) Times, 22 November. See also *Fletcher v Fletcher* [1945] 1 All ER 582 (offer of home in religious community held to be unreasonable); *Kenward v Kenward* [1951] P 124 at 136, [1950] 2 All ER 297 at 304, CA per Sir Raymond Evershed MR (considering the effect on the validity of a marriage by Russian law on place of spouses' matrimonial home). It has been held that it is a husband's duty to provide his wife with a home according to his circumstances: see *Millichamp v Millichamp* (1931) 146 LT 96 at 97 (his first duty).
2   *King v King* [1942] P 1, [1941] 2 All ER 103. See also *Hosegood v Hosegood* (1950) 66 (pt 1) TLR 735, CA; *Walter v Walter* (1949) 65 TLR 680; *Dunn v Dunn* [1949] P 98, [1948] 2 All ER 822, CA (location of a husband's work is a most important consideration to be borne in mind in selecting the situation of the matrimonial home, although in some cases the wife's business and livelihood may be a predominant consideration); and *Mansey v Mansey* [1940] P 139 at 140,

[1940] 2 All ER 424 at 426 per Henn Collins J (if the husband says he wants to live in such and such a place, then, assuming always that he is not doing it to spite his wife, and that the accommodation is of a kind expected to be occupied by a man in his position, the wife is under the necessity of sharing that home with him, or being in desertion).

3 See *Dunn v Dunn* [1949] P 98 at 103, [1948] 2 All ER 822 at 824, CA per Denning LJ. In *McGowan v McGowan* [1948] 2 All ER 1032 at 1035, it was said that the proposition that neither party has a casting vote is but another way of stating that neither has, as a matter of law, the right to choose the home.

4 *Hosegood v Hosegood* (1950) 66 (pt 1) TLR 735 at 740, CA per Denning LJ, criticising *Walter v Walter* (1949) 65 TLR 680 (where Willmer J held that, where each was obstinate, neither proved that the other was in desertion, nor that the separation was brought about by the fault of the other).

5 See PARA 367.

6 *Dunn v Dunn* [1949] P 98 at 103, 104, [1948] 2 All ER 822 at 823, CA.

7 *McGowan v McGowan* [1948] 2 All ER 1032 at 1035 per Pilcher J. See also *Butland v Butland* (1913) 29 TLR 729 (wife drank to excess); *Fisk v Fisk* (1920) 122 LT 803 (husband's daughters by a previous marriage; husband had no just cause to refuse to have wife back).

8 *McGowan v McGowan* [1948] 2 All ER 1032 at 1035.

385. Illness. It is difficult to establish that a separation caused by the illness, physical or mental, of one party, necessitating that party remaining in hospital or otherwise being separated from the other for the relevant continuous period[1], amounts to desertion without just cause[2]; but the absent party must retain the intention to return to cohabitation when reasonably able to do so[3].

1 See PARA 364.

2 *Keeley v Keeley* [1952] 2 TLR 756 at 761, CA per Singleton LJ (such an allegation should be pleaded); *Pulford v Pulford* [1923] P 18 at 23 (cohabitation only suspended while wife in asylum); *Beevor v Beevor* [1945] 2 All ER 200; *G v G* [1964] P 133, [1964] 1 All ER 129, DC; *Perry v Perry* [1963] 3 All ER 766, [1964] 1 WLR 91; cf *Hanbury v Hanbury* [1892] P 222 (affd 8 TLR 559, CA). An insane wife may have an animus deserendi: *Crowther v Crowther* [1951] AC 723, [1951] 1 All ER 1131, HL; and see PARA 389. The illness of one party does not justify the other party in renouncing his obligations: see PARA 390.

3 *Lilley v Lilley* [1960] P 158 at 169, [1959] 3 All ER 283, CA; *Tickle v Tickle* [1968] 2 All ER 154, [1968] 1 WLR 937, DC; *G v G* [1964] P 133, [1964] 1 All ER 129, DC.

E. ABSENCE OF INTENTION TO DESERT

386. Position of deserting party. Once desertion has begun in a manner consistent with a continuing intention to desert, the desertion will continue in law notwithstanding the fact that subsequently physical inability to end the desertion, such as imprisonment, prevents the deserting party from returning[1]. It is the character of the leaving that is material[2], provided that the intention to desert is shown to continue, whether by positive evidence or by the absence of anything to negative the presumption that the desertion, once established, continues to run[3].

1 *Lilley v Lilley* [1960] P 158 at 169, [1959] 3 All ER 283, CA (neurotic wife who said that she would never return to her husband was guilty of desertion); *Drew v Drew* (1888) 13 PD 97 at 99 (desertion, later imprisonment; desertion continued); *Astrope v Astrope* (1859) 29 LJP & M 27 (same); *Williams v Williams* [1938] 4 All ER 445 (same); and see *Crowther v Crowther* [1951] AC 723, [1951] 1 All ER 1131, HL; and PARA 389.

2 *Drew v Drew* (1888) 13 PD 97 at 98; *Wynne v Wynne* [1898] P 18 at 20.

3 *Beeken v Beeken* [1948] P 302 at 308, CA (compulsory de facto separation with supervening animus deserendi); *Ingram v Ingram* [1956] P 390 at 410, [1956] 1 All ER 785 at 797; *Czepek v Czepek* [1962] 3 All ER 990; but see *Kaye (formerly Kazlowski) v Kazlowska* (1953) Times, 1 April (parties kept apart because of international difficulties), and cf *Szajna v Szajna* (1954) Times, 19 June (wife could have left Poland but refused to; husband could not return there because of political situation). Cf *Williamson v Williamson* (1882) 7 PD 76; *Townsend v Townsend* (1873) LR 3 P & D 129 at 131; and *Lawrence v Lawrence* (1862) 2 Sw & Tr 575.

387.　Absence of animus deserendi.　To constitute actual desertion there must be not only a separation but also the animus deserendi[1]; in constructive desertion the deserting party must have intended to bring the consortium to an end[2], or to have acted with the knowledge that that was what would probably happen[3].

1　See PARA 368; *Buchler v Buchler* [1947] P 25 at 29, [1947] 1 All ER 319 at 320, CA (as to which see *Hall v Hall* [1962] 3 All ER 518, [1962] 1 WLR 1246, CA); *Crowther v Crowther* [1951] AC 723 at 734, 735, [1951] 1 All ER 1131 at 1135, 1136, HL.
2　*Buchler v Buchler* [1947] P 25 at 29, 30, [1947] 1 All ER 319 at 320, CA per Lord Greene MR; but see *Burton v Burton* (1969) 113 Sol Jo 852, DC.
3　*Gollins v Gollins* [1964] AC 644 at 666, [1963] 2 All ER 966 at 973, HL; *Lang v Lang* [1955] AC 402, [1954] 3 All ER 571, PC.

388.　Proof of intention.　In a simple case of constructive desertion, the intention to desert may be inferred if the circumstances are such as to justify the inference. In the case of simple desertion the mere act of one party leaving will in general make the inference an easy one[1], but there may be just cause[2]. In the case of constructive desertion, if one party without just cause or excuse persists in doing what he or she knows the other will not and should not tolerate, and that other party in consequence leaves, the party who is left is the deserter whatever his or her intention may have been; one must look at the facts, and while intention may aggravate the facts, the absence of intention will not defeat the charge of constructive desertion[3].

Where desertion is once established, but the separation is enforced through other circumstances, the intention to continue the desertion must be proved by positive evidence or by negative inference[4].

1　*Buchler v Buchler* [1947] P 25 at 30, [1947] 1 All ER 319 at 320, CA (as to which see *Hall v Hall* [1962] 3 All ER 518, [1962] 1 WLR 1246, CA).
2　As to just cause see PARA 380 et seq.
3　*Gollins v Gollins* [1964] AC 644 at 666, [1963] 2 All ER 966 at 974, HL.
4　See PARA 386.

389.　Effect of insanity on desertion.　There is no reason for imputing an irrebuttable inability on the part of a person who suffers from a mental disorder to form an intention to desert or, once desertion has begun and is followed by mental disorder, to keep such an intention[1]. For the purpose of proving irretrievable breakdown by reason of desertion[2], the court may treat a period of desertion as having continued at a time when the deserting party was incapable of continuing the necessary intention if the evidence before the court is such that, had that party not been so incapable, the court would have inferred that his desertion continued at that time[3]. An allegation that a party is mentally ill, so as to be incapable of forming an intention to desert, should be pleaded[4]. Illness, whether mental or physical, may amount to just cause for separation[5]; but, where a sick person is medically advised that there should be a temporary separation, albeit that the situation at the end of that period cannot be envisaged, and takes advantage of that temporary situation to manifest an indication to disrupt cohabitation permanently, that person is in desertion from the time of such indication[6].

Where one party leaves the other, acting on a genuinely held but delusional belief that he or she has just cause for doing so, the rights of a party in relation to a charge of desertion are to be judged as if that belief were true[7].

1　*Crowther v Crowther* [1951] AC 723 at 732, [1951] 1 All ER 1131 at 1134, HL (overruling *Williams v Williams* [1939] P 365, [1939] 3 All ER 825, CA; distinguishing *Jones v Newtown and Llanidloes Guardians* [1920] 3 KB 381, DC; and approving *Bennett v Bennett* [1939] P 274 at 278, [1939] 2 All ER 387 at 390, 391). In *Wickens v Wickens* [1952] 2 All ER 98, CA, the principle of *Crowther v Crowther* was applied (the case is reported mainly on the question when a guardian ad litem of a person of unsound mind should be appointed: see now CHILDREN AND YOUNG PERSONS vol 5(3) (2008) PARA 225); and see *Keeley v Keeley* [1952] 2 TLR 756, CA, applied in *Lilley v Lilley* [1960] P 158 at 181, [1959] 3 All ER 283 at 289, CA; *Clark v Clark (by her guardian)* [1956] 1 All ER 823, [1956] 1 WLR 345; *Kaczmarz v Kaczmarz (by her guardian)* [1967] 1 All ER 416 at 423, [1967] 1 WLR 317 at 327; *G v G* [1964] P 133, [1964] 1 All ER 129, DC (wife left husband because of danger to health and safety of the children; she was not in desertion).

2 See PARA 363.

3 See the Matrimonial Causes Act 1973 s 2(4); the Civil Partnership Act 2004 s 45(5); and PARA 347. For the previous law see *Crowther v Crowther* [1951] AC 723 at 733, [1951] 1 All ER 1131 at 1134, HL, in so far as continuance of desertion is concerned. See also *Osborne v Osborne (by her guardian)* (1961) 105 Sol Jo 650. See also *Keeley v Keeley* [1952] 2 TLR 756, CA (there is a natural reluctance in any court to find that a patient in a mental hospital has deserted his or her spouse); *Lilley v Lilley* [1960] P 158 at 181, [1959] 3 All ER 283 at 289, CA; *Perry v Perry* [1963] 3 All ER 766, [1964] 1 WLR 91; cf *Smith v Smith* (1973) 118 Sol Jo 184; *Santos v Santos* [1972] Fam 247, [1972] 2 All ER 246, CA; *Thurlow v Thurlow* [1976] Fam 32, [1975] 2 All ER 979. As to the circumstances in which the court may find that the effect of the behaviour of a mentally ill respondent makes it impossible for the petitioner to live with him see PARA 360 note 2.

4 *Keeley v Keeley* [1952] 2 TLR 756 at 761, CA.

5 *Perry v Perry* [1963] 3 All ER 766, [1964] 1 WLR 91.

6 *Tickle v Tickle* [1968] 2 All ER 154, [1968] 1 WLR 937, DC.

7 *Perry v Perry* [1963] 3 All ER 766 at 769, [1964] 1 WLR 91 at 96; *Santos v Santos* [1972] Fam 247, [1972] 2 All ER 246, CA; *Thurlow v Thurlow* [1976] Fam 32, [1975] 2 All ER 979.

390. Petitioner mentally or otherwise ill. The fact that the petitioner[1] is in a mental hospital, or is otherwise ill in hospital, does not excuse the respondent who has renounced his or her obligations to that person; and, if during the period of the illness the respondent disappears and does not return when the applicant's recovery is effected, desertion begins as from the date of the respondent's renunciation of his or her obligations[2].

1 As to petitioners and applicants see PARA 321 note 1.

2 *Sotherden v Sotherden* [1940] P 73, [1940] 1 All ER 252, CA, applying *Pulford v Pulford* [1923] P 18, and *Gatehouse v Gatehouse* (1867) LR 1 P & D 331; *Perry v Perry* [1963] 3 All ER 766, [1964] 1 WLR 91. See also *Leng v Leng* [1946] 2 All ER 590 (husband's neurotic condition, and no more, not just cause for wife's separation); *Hayward v Hayward* (1858) 1 Sw & Tr 81 at 84 (husband not entitled to turn lunatic wife out of doors); cf *Santos v Santos* [1972] Fam 247, [1972] 2 All ER 246, CA; *Thurlow v Thurlow* [1976] Fam 32, [1975] 2 All ER 979 (cited in PARA 360 note 2).

F. CONSTRUCTIVE DESERTION

391. Doctrine of constructive desertion. Desertion is not to be tested merely by ascertaining which party left first[1]. If one party is forced by the conduct[2] of the other to leave, it may be that the party responsible for the driving out is guilty of desertion[3]; so, for example, if a husband without just cause or excuse persists in doing things which he knows his wife will probably not tolerate, and which no ordinary woman would tolerate, and then she leaves, the husband will have deserted her whatever his desire or intention may have been[4]. There is no substantial difference between the case of a man who intends to cease cohabitation and leaves his wife and the case of a man who, with the same intention, compels his wife by his conduct to leave him[5]. This is the doctrine of constructive desertion[6]. It is to be observed that conduct by the respondent amounting to constructive desertion will, in the nature of things, constitute behaviour which is such that the petitioner cannot reasonably be expected to live with the respondent[7]; and, if such an allegation is made, it obviates the need to wait for the period of two years necessary in the case of desertion[8].

1   *Sickert v Sickert* [1899] P 278 at 284; *Bowron v Bowron* [1925] P 187, CA; *Spence v Spence* [1939] 1 All ER 52 at 57; *Buchler v Buchler* [1947] P 25, [1947] 1 All ER 319, CA; *Simpson v Simpson* [1951] P 320 at 331, [1951] 1 All ER 955 at 960, 961; *Lang v Lang* [1955] AC 402 at 417, [1954] 3 All ER 571 at 573, PC.

2   *Sullivan v Sullivan* [1970] 2 All ER 168, [1970] 1 WLR 1008, CA (pregnancy by another man at time of marriage did not amount to expulsive conduct).

3   *Graves v Graves* (1864) 3 Sw & Tr 350; *Koch v Koch* [1899] P 221 (husband refused to discharge servant with whom he had committed adultery; wife left); *Pulford v Pulford* [1923] P 18 at 21; *Jones v Jones* [1952] 2 TLR 225, CA (wife instigated justices into ordering husband to leave matrimonial home; wife in desertion from that time); *Pratt v Pratt* (1962) 106 Sol Jo 876, CA (married life made impossible).

4   *Gollins v Gollins* [1964] AC 644 at 666, [1963] 2 All ER 966 at 974, HL per Lord Reid; *Rothery v Rothery* (1966) Times, 30 March, DC.

5   *Sickert v Sickert* [1899] P 278 at 282; *Charter v Charter* (1901) 84 LT 272 at 273; *Harriman v Harriman* [1909] P 123 at 135, CA; *Thomas v Thomas* [1924] P 194 at 199, 203, CA; *Pike v Pike* [1954] P 81n at 86, [1953] 1 All ER 232 at 233, CA.

6   *Pike v Pike* [1954] P 81n at 86, 88, [1953] 1 All ER 232 at 233, 235, CA; *Kashich v Kashich* (1951) 116 JP 6, DC; *Simpson v Simpson* [1951] P 320 at 326, [1951] 1 All ER 955 at 957; *Lawrance v Lawrance* [1950] P 84 at 86, DC; *Hosegood v Hosegood* (1950) 66 (pt 1) TLR 735 at 736–738, CA; *Winnan v Winnan* [1949] P 174 at 179, 181, [1948] 2 All ER 862 at 864, 865, CA; *Buchler v Buchler* [1947] P 25 at 29, 48, [1947] 1 All ER 319 at 320, 327, CA; *Spence v Spence* [1939] 1 All ER 52 at 58; *Herod v Herod* [1939] P 11 at 21, 23, [1938] 3 All ER 722 at 729, 731; *Teall v Teall* [1938] P 250 at 256, [1938] 3 All ER 349 at 352; *Bowron v Bowron* [1925] P 187 at 191, CA. It has been said in the House of Lords that the House may have to consider, should the point come before it, whether there is sufficient warrant for the doctrine: see *Weatherley v Weatherley* [1947] AC 628 at 632, [1947] 1 All ER 563 at 564, 565, HL per Lord Jowitt LC.

7   See PARA 360. As to petitioners and applicants see PARA 321 note 1.

8   See PARA 364.

392.   Animus and factum.   It is as necessary in cases of constructive desertion to prove both the factum and the animus on the part of the party charged with the desertion as it is in cases of actual desertion[1]. The practical difference between the two cases lies in the circumstances which will constitute such proof, for, while the intention to bring the consortium to an end exists[2] in both cases, in actual desertion there is an abandonment, whereas in constructive desertion there is expulsion by words or by other conduct[3].

1   See PARA 368.

2   See, however, *Gollins v Gollins* [1964] AC 644 at 666, [1963] 2 All ER 966 at 974, HL per Lord Reid ('He did not act with the intention of driving her out, but he acted with the knowledge that that was what would probably happen').

3   *Buchler v Buchler* [1947] P 25 at 29, 30, 45, [1947] 1 All ER 319 at 325, 326, CA. See also the 'simple case' of constructive desertion referred to in *Pike v Pike* [1954] P 81n at 87, [1953] 1 All ER 232 at 235, CA per Hodson LJ, and see at 86 and at 235, 236 per Denning LJ.

393.   Onus and standard of proof.   In a case of constructive desertion, the onus of proving that the intention to desert continues may be much lighter than in a case of mere withdrawal from cohabitation[1]. A mere wish or intention that the other party should leave is insufficient by itself to constitute constructive desertion[2]. The wish or intention must be accompanied by conduct which is of such grave and weighty character as to make cohabitation virtually impossible[3], and which the court can properly regard as equivalent to expulsion in fact[4].

It is also said, however, that, when the fact of separation is proved, the intent to bring the home to an end can be inferred, amongst other things, from words so plain, that the party using them may be taken to mean what he says[5]; if there is no background of ill-treatment, it may well be more difficult to prove that mere words of expulsion were intended to be final, conclusive and effective than if there is such a background[6].

Conduct short of a fact[7] in itself constituting irretrievable breakdown might be sufficient to justify the other party in leaving[8]; but it is essential to examine the actual facts in order to see whether the conduct of the party who is to blame can fairly and clearly be said to have crossed the borderline which divides blameworthy conduct causing unhappiness to the other party from conduct equivalent to expulsion[9]. The ordinary wear and tear, or mere inconsiderate conduct which is one of the risks, of conjugal life does not in itself suffice[10]; however where a husband induced by his conduct, not by mere hearsay, a belief in his wife that he was conducting an improper affair with another woman, and the wife acting on that belief left the husband or turned him out, she is not in desertion[11]. Likewise, in a marriage there may be conduct in relation to a third person which is neither adulterous nor giving rise to a reasonable belief in adultery but which nevertheless is so inconsistent with the married relationship as to amount to expulsive conduct[12].

Once constructive desertion has ensued owing to a party's conduct, that desertion continues until appropriate steps are taken to terminate it[13].

1　*Herod v Herod* [1939] P 11 at 22, [1938] 3 All ER 722 at 730.
2　*Buchler v Buchler* [1947] P 25 at 45, [1947] 1 All ER 319 at 325, CA per Lord Greene MR; *Charter v Charter* (1901) 84 LT 272 ('Go where you like. Do what you like'; wife left and refused to return; husband not in desertion); *Lane v Lane* [1952] P 34 at 39, [1952] 1 All ER 223n, CA per Jenkins LJ dissenting; *Partridge v Partridge* (1957) Times, 13 December (wife knew husband who was unpleasant with drink did not want her to go, although he told her to).
3　*Rothery v Rothery* (1966) Times, 30 March, DC (wife pregnant by another man agreed with husband to give up child on its birth so that marriage might continue; she failed to do so and, therefore, had constructively deserted); *Saunders v Saunders* [1965] P 499 at 507, [1965] 1 All ER 838 at 843, DC; *Edwards v Edwards (Moore intervening)* (1965) 109 Sol Jo 175; *Hall v Hall* [1962] 3 All ER 518, [1962] 1 WLR 1246, CA; *Pratt v Pratt* (1962) 106 Sol Jo 876, CA; *Kemp v Kemp* [1961] 2 All ER 764, [1961] 1 WLR 1030, DC; *Pizey v Pizey and Stephenson* [1961] P 101, [1961] 2 All ER 658, CA; *McMillan v McMillan* 1961 SLT 429; *Cox v Cox* [1958] 1 All ER 569 at 572, 573, [1958] 1 WLR 340 at 344–346; *Patching v Patching* (1958) Times, 25 April, DC; *Roe v Roe* [1956] 3 All ER 478 at 483, [1956] 1 WLR 1380 at 1385, 1386, DC; *Pike v Pike* [1954] P 81n at 82, [1953] 1 All ER 232 at 233, CA; *Timmins v Timmins* [1953] 2 All ER 187 at 191, [1953] 1 WLR 757 at 761, 762, CA per Denning LJ; *Lane v Lane* [1952] P 34, [1952] 1 All ER 223n, CA; *Chilton v Chilton* [1952] P 196, [1952] 1 All ER 1322, DC; *Jones v Jones* [1952] 2 TLR 225, CA; *Price v Price* [1951] 1 All ER 877 (affd [1951] P 413, [1951] 2 All ER 580n, CA); *Allen v Allen* [1951] 1 All ER 724, CA; *Hosegood v Hosegood* (1950) 66 (pt 1) TLR 735, CA; *Lawrance v Lawrance* [1950] P 84, DC (husband's refusal of sexual intercourse); *Edwards v Edwards* [1950] P 8, [1949] 2 All ER 145, CA; *Winnan v Winnan* [1949] P 174, [1948] 2 All ER 862, CA (wife preferred cats to husband; husband left; wife in desertion) (but see comment on this case in *Bartholomew v Bartholomew* [1952] 2 All ER 1035, CA (dirty wife; no evidence that she wished to bring consortium to an end; husband left; wife not in desertion); cf *Kaslefsky v Kaslefsky* [1951] P 38, [1950] 2 All ER 398, CA (cruelty)); *Holborn v Holborn* [1947] 1 All ER 32 at 33 (unreasonable and inconsiderate sexual demands); *Buchler v Buchler* [1947] P 25 at 30, 41, 42, 45, [1947] 1 All ER 319 at 320, 323, 324, 325, CA (occasional angry remarks that wife could clear out and live with her mother if she did not like the very close friendship of husband with his bailiff, not sufficiently grave and weighty, for, even if the animus existed, there was no factum of expulsion); *Leng v Leng* [1946] 2 All ER 590 (neurotic condition of husband, nothing else; wife left; no desertion by husband); *Fletcher v Fletcher* [1945] 1 All ER 582 (husband's membership of religious community, and refusal of sexual intercourse; wife refused to live with him in the community; husband in desertion); *Glenister v Glenister* [1945] P 30, [1945] 1 All ER 513; *Teall v Teall* [1938] P 250 at 256, [1938] 3 All ER 349 at 352 (mere discovery of past adultery insufficient); *Pizzala v Pizzala* (1896) 12 TLR 451 (husband adhered to mistress; wife left; husband in desertion); cf *Haviland v Haviland* (1863) 3 Sw & Tr 114 ('Go to your mistress if you like and when you are tired of her come back to me'; not necessarily consent); *Dickinson v*

Dickinson (1889) 62 LT 330 (husband brought mistress into matrimonial home; wife left; husband in desertion); *Yeatman v Yeatman* (1868) LR 1 P & D 489 at 493, 494 (mere frailty of temper insufficient).

4 *Buchler v Buchler* [1947] P 25 at 34, 43, 45, [1947] 1 All ER 319 at 322, 324, 325, CA; *Kaslefsky v Kaslefsky* [1951] P 38 at 41, [1950] 2 All ER 398 at 399, CA per Buckley LJ; *Young v Young* [1964] P 152, [1962] 3 All ER 120, DC.

5 *Lane v Lane* [1951] P 284 at 286, 287, DC; affd [1952] P 34, [1952] 1 All ER 223n, CA.

6 *Lane v Lane* [1951] P 284 at 287, DC; and see on appeal [1952] P 34 at 38, [1952] 1 All ER 223n at 224, CA per Somervell LJ; *Young v Young* [1964] P 152, [1962] 3 All ER 120, DC.

7 As to such facts see PARA 347.

8 *Buchler v Buchler* [1947] P 25 at 30, 45, [1947] 1 All ER 319 at 320, 326, CA.

9 *Buchler v Buchler* [1947] P 25 at 35, [1947] 1 All ER 319 at 322, CA; and see *Pew v Pew* (1951) unreported, CA, referred to in *Simpson v Simpson* [1951] P 320 at 335–339, [1951] 1 All ER 955 at 963–965, DC; *Hall v Hall* [1962] 3 All ER 518, [1962] 1 WLR 1246, CA (drunkenness). See also *Hanson v Hanson* (1954) Times, 10 March, CA (inadequacy of housekeeping allowance). It has been suggested that, where the faults are equal on each side, the act of a party leaving with the intention not to return constitutes desertion: *Spence v Spence* [1939] 1 All ER 52 at 58.

10 *Buchler v Buchler* [1947] P 25 at 35m 45, 47, [1947] 1 All ER 319 at 322, 326, CA; *Squire v Squire* [1949] P 51 at 72, [1948] 2 All ER 51 at 60, CA; *Edwards v Edwards* [1950] P 8 at 13, [1949] 2 All ER 145 at 148, CA; *Simpson v Simpson* [1951] P 320 at 342, [1951] 1 All ER 955 at 967; *Rothery v Rothery* (1966) Times, 30 March, DC. See also *Bartholomew v Bartholomew* [1952] 2 All ER 1035, CA; *Marjoram v Marjoram* [1955] 2 All ER 1 at 8, [1955] 1 WLR 520 at 527 (sluttishness alone did not constitute a ground sufficient to establish constructive desertion).

11 *Hunter v Hunter* (1961) 105 Sol Jo 990, DC; see also *Baker v Baker* [1954] P 33 at 35, [1953] 2 All ER 1199 at 1200, DC (husband deliberately induced wife to believe that he had committed adultery).

12 *Hind v Hind* [1969] 1 All ER 1083 at 1086, [1969] 1 WLR 480 at 484, DC.

13 *Burton v Burton* (1969) 113 Sol Jo 852, DC.

394. Presumptions. Where conduct of the required nature is established, the necessary intention is readily inferred[1], for prima facie a person is presumed to intend the natural and probable consequences of his acts[2], and it is not necessary to show in a case of constructive desertion some definite evidence of a clear intention on the part of one party to drive the other away. The maxim does not express an irrebuttable presumption of law, and it is only to be applied in connection with conduct which can fairly be described as expulsive[3].

This presumption is not necessarily rebutted by evidence that the party guilty of expulsive conduct in fact had no desire to cause the other party to leave or even desired him or her not to leave[4].

1 *Buchler v Buchler* [1947] P 25 at 30, [1947] 1 All ER 319 at 321, CA.

2 *Pizzala v Pizzala* (1896) 12 TLR 451; *Sickert v Sickert* [1899] P 278 at 284; *Edwards v Edwards* [1948] P 268 at 269–273, [1948] 1 All ER 157 at 158–160, DC; *Squire v Squire* [1949] P 51 at 56, 57, [1948] 2 All ER 51 at 53, CA (cruelty), approving *Edwards v Edwards*; *Hosegood v Hosegood* (1950) 66 (pt 1) TLR 735 at 738, 739, CA; *Simpson v Simpson* [1951] P 320 at 326, 332, [1951] 1 All ER 955 at 957, 960, 961 (cruelty); *Kaslefsky v Kaslefsky* [1951] P 38 at 46, [1950] 2 All ER 398 at 403, CA (cruelty); *Jamieson v Jamieson* [1952] AC 525 at 540, [1952] 1 All ER 875 at 881, HL; *Lane v Lane* [1952] P 34 at 38, [1952] 1 All ER 223n at 224, CA; cf *Spence v Spence* [1939] 1 All ER 52 at 58 (intention to desert must be implied); *Herod v Herod* [1939] P 11 at 22, [1938] 3 All ER 722 at 730; *R v Steane* [1947] KB 997 at 1003, [1947] 1 All ER 813 at 815, CCA; *Lane v Lane* [1952] P 34 at 38, [1952] 1 All ER 223n at 224, CA (if the words of expulsion are used and the other party leaves, the natural conclusion is that the words had their intended effect, unless there is some reason to take a different view); *Rothery v Rothery* (1966) Times, 30 March, DC.

3 *Simpson v Simpson* [1951] P 320 at 334, [1951] 1 All ER 955 at 962; *Jamieson v Jamieson* [1952] AC 525 at 540, [1952] 1 All ER 875 at 881, HL; *Lang v Lang* [1955] AC 402 at 427, [1954] 3 All ER 571 at 579, PC; *Waters v Waters* [1956] P 344 at 360, [1956] 1 All ER 432 at 440, DC.

4   See *Lang v Lang* [1955] AC 402 at 423–425, [1954] 3 All ER 571 at 577, 578, PC, citing the
     summary by Denning LJ in *Hosegood v Hosegood* (1950) 66 (pt 1) TLR 735 at 738, CA, of the
     two schools of thought on constructive desertion. That summary explained that one school of
     thought held that a person was not guilty of constructive desertion, however bad his conduct,
     unless he had in fact an intention to bring married life to an end (thus applying a subjective test,
     admitting that there are cases where the intention can be presumed, but asserting that, if in truth
     the facts negative any intention to disrupt married life, the courts should not attribute that
     intention to the spouse), while the other school, which was that followed in *Lang v Lang*, took
     the view that, even if a spouse had no wish in fact to disrupt married life, he or she was
     presumed to intend the natural consequences of his or her acts; so that, if one spouse's conduct
     is so bad that the other spouse is forced to leave, the former is guilty of constructive desertion,
     however much he or she may have desired the other to remain. The subjective test approved by
     the first school of thought is supported by the decision in *Boyd v Boyd* [1938] 4 All ER 181, by
     Denning LJ in *Hosegood v Hosegood* at 738 (but see *W v W (No 2)* [1962] P 49, [1961]
     2 All ER 626, DC), and again by Denning LJ in *Bartholomew v Bartholomew* [1952] 2 All ER
     1035 at 1037, CA. The second school of thought is supported by the decision in *Edwards v
     Edwards* [1948] P 268, [1948] 1 All ER 157, DC, and by *Simpson v Simpson* [1951] P 320 at
     333, 334, [1951] 1 All ER 955 at 961, 962. It was pointed out in *Lang v Lang* at 427 and at
     579, that both schools of thought accept the position that the animus deserendi may be inferred
     from acts alone. The Judicial Committee, in that case, considered what the legal result was
     where an intention to bring about a particular result (inferred from conduct) co-existed with a
     wish that the result would not ensue, concluding that conduct which a reasonable man must
     know would lead in all probability to the departure of his wife and would disrupt the home led
     to the inference that he intended that consequence, whether or not he in fact wished it, though
     the inference was open to be rebutted by evidence: *Lang v Lang* at 429 and at 580. In *Marjoram
     v Marjoram* [1955] 2 All ER 1 at 8, [1955] 1 WLR 520 at 526, 527, Lord Merriman P, while
     not himself entering into a full consideration of the authorities, said that, in *Lang v Lang* the
     subjective test was decisively rejected by the Judicial Committee; so, too, *Waters v Waters* [1956]
     P 344 at 360, [1956] 1 All ER 432 at 440, DC; *Ingram v Ingram* [1956] P 390, [1956] 1 All ER
     785 at 798; *W v W (No 2)*; *Burton v Burton* (1969) 113 Sol Jo 852, DC. See also *Fishburn v
     Fishburn* [1955] P 29 at 36, [1955] 1 All ER 230 at 233 (intention, not desire, the material
     consideration).

395.   Conduct with third parties and past history. The conduct relied on may
be conduct of the offending party with or relating to a third person[1]. Conduct
can always be looked at in the light of past history which throws light on it; and
acts of minor significance in themselves may in the light of past history be of
serious import[2], as, for example, where there has been a previous finding of
constructive desertion against one of the parties[3].

1   *Edwards v Edwards* [1948] P 268 at 270, 271, [1948] 1 All ER 157 at 159, DC; and see *Buchler
     v Buchler* [1947] P 25, [1947] 1 All ER 319, CA; *Lewis v Lewis* [1956] P 205n, [1955] 3 All ER
     598, DC (husband guilty of isolated indecent assault on woman in cinema; no ground for wife
     alleging constructive desertion thereby, for, in view of the then existing statutory provisions as to
     divorce for unnatural sexual practices, this would be creating a new ground of divorce; further,
     since the assault was without consent, adultery could be negatived, and the wife had no ground
     for refusing to be reconciled with husband); *Harvey v Harvey* [1956] P 102, [1955] 3 All ER
     772, CA (wife left home because husband refused to turn out wastrel son); *Chadwick v
     Chadwick* (1964) Times, 24 October, DC (whether husband must put wife before the child of a
     previous marriage is a question of what is reasonable in the circumstances); *Rothery v Rothery*
     (1966) Times, 30 March, DC (wife refused to have her child by adulterous union adopted;
     husband entitled to leave).
2   *Lane v Lane* [1951] P 284; affd [1952] P 34 at 45, CA.
3   *Lane v Lane* [1952] P 34, [1952] 1 All ER 223n, CA; cf *Dixon v Dixon* [1953] P 103, [1953]
     1 All ER 910.

G. TERMINATION OF DESERTION

396.   Ways of terminating desertion. Desertion continues until it is
terminated. Termination may take place by the fact of return; or by a
supervening intention to return coupled with an approach to the deserted party,

made in good faith, with a view to resumption of life together; or by a supervening consensus, for example under a separation agreement made in good faith[1]. A mere intention to return, unaccompanied by some notification to the deserted party, will not terminate desertion[2]. Whilst the court has never discouraged attempts at reconciliation by a deserting party[3], there is now statutory provision enabling the parties to resume living with each other for one period of six months or for two or more periods not exceeding six months in all[4].

It is a question of fact in each case whether the commencement or conclusion of dissolution or nullity proceedings terminates the desertion[5], although a decree of judicial separation terminates the desertion during the continuance of the decree[6].

1   *Williams v Williams* [1939] P 365 at 368, 369, [1939] 3 All ER 825 at 827, CA per Sir Wilfred Greene MR (overruled on another point in *Crowther v Crowther* [1951] AC 723, [1951] 1 All ER 1131, HL); *Pratt v Pratt* [1939] AC 417, [1939] 3 All ER 437, HL; *Harvey v Harvey* [1956] P 102, [1955] 3 All ER 772, CA; *Pizey v Pizey and Stephenson* [1961] P 101, [1961] 2 All ER 658, CA.

2   *Williams v Williams* [1939] P 365 at 369, [1939] 3 All ER 825 at 828, CA per Sir Wilfred Greene MR; cf *Bevan v Bevan* [1955] 3 All ER 332 at 335, [1955] 1 WLR 1142 at 1146, DC.

3   *Cohen v Cohen* [1940] AC 631 at 645, [1940] 2 All ER 331 at 339, HL per Lord Romer. See also the Matrimonial Causes Act 1973 s 6; the Civil Partnership Act 2004 s 42; and PARA 414.

4   See the Matrimonial Causes Act 1973 s 2(5); the Civil Partnership Act 2004 s 45(6); and PARA 365. As to the effect of sexual intercourse on continuance of desertion see PARA 404.

5   *W v W (No 2)* [1954] P 486, [1954] 2 All ER 829, CA; *Williams v Williams* [1939] P 365, [1939] 3 All ER 825, CA; *Gerrard v Gerrard* (1958) Times, 18 November; *Pursey v Pursey* (1959) Times, 9 April.

6   See PARA 406. As to the effect of such a decree on the statutory period required in charges of desertion see PARA 366.

397.   Offer to return.   If the deserting party genuinely desires to return, his or her partner cannot in law refuse reinstatement[1], although there may be cases where a mere offer to return without an assurance of a change of habits may not be enough[2]; further, the consequences of a party's conduct may be permanent[3] so that the deserting party has no right to be taken back[4]. The matter must be looked at objectively from the point of view of a reasonable person to whom the offer is made[5]. The offer must be genuine, that is to say it must be made in good faith in the sense that it is an offer to return permanently which, if accepted, will be implemented, and is an offer containing an assurance to terminate the conduct, if any[6], that caused the separation[7]. An offer must likewise be made in good faith where the parties separated consensually[8]. In rejecting such an offer, it is not sufficient simply to assert that it is not genuine; some real ground for rejection must be proved[9]. It is often prudent to test an offer by acceptance[10], particularly if there is no indication as to the lack of genuineness of the offer[11].

1   *Perry v Perry* [1952] P 203 at 211, [1952] 1 All ER 1076 at 1080, CA; *Leng v Leng* [1946] 2 All ER 590 (husband neurotic; no reason on that account for wife to refuse to have him back); *Fleming v Fleming* [1942] 2 All ER 337, DC; *Joseph v Joseph* [1939] P 385 (wife's bona fide offer turned down); cf *Tickler v Tickler* [1943] 1 All ER 57 at 60, CA (deserted party may so act as to make it clear that reconciliation is impossible, and may thus provide good cause for the continuing separation); and see *Lang v Lang* (1953) Times, 7 July, CA (wife's insistence on home at place of her employment as housekeeper unreasonable, and she became deserting party in consequence; not possible to hold both parties in desertion at the same time; and see PARA 367 text and notes 2, 3).

2   *W v W (No 2)* [1954] P 486, [1954] 2 All ER 829, CA; *Price v Price* [1951] P 413 at 416, CA; *Holborn v Holborn* [1947] 1 All ER 32 (husband had made excessive sexual demands; wife entitled to leave him, but position not permanent, and, if husband learnt his lesson, wife would not be entitled to stay away from him).

3 *Thomas v Thomas* [1924] P 194 at 202, CA per Scrutton LJ; and in the court of first instance (1923) 39 TLR 520 at 521 per Sir Henry Duke P (there may be no place for repentance).
4 *Everitt v Everitt* [1949] P 374 at 385, [1949] 1 All ER 908 at 916, CA, applying *Edwards v Edwards* [1948] P 268 at 272, [1948] 1 All ER 157 at 160; *Leng v Leng* [1946] 2 All ER 590 at 591; *Basing v Basing* (1864) 3 Sw & Tr 516 at 517; *R v Davidson etc, Durham Justices* (1889) 5 TLR 199, DC; *Edwards v Edwards* (1893) 62 LJP 33 (husband living with another woman; wife entitled to refuse his offer to return); *Graves v Graves* (1864) 3 Sw & Tr 350; cf *Garcia v Garcia* (1888) 13 PD 216 (husband insisted on keeping marriage secret; wife suspected adultery and withdrew from cohabitation; husband in desertion).
5 *Weddell v Weddell* (1961) 105 Sol Jo 153, CA.
6 *Irvin v Irvin* [1968] 1 All ER 271, [1968] 1 WLR 464, DC.
7 *Gaskell v Gaskell* (1963) 108 Sol Jo 37, DC; *Trevor v Trevor* (1965) 109 Sol Jo 574, CA; and see *Ogden v Ogden* [1969] 3 All ER 1055, [1969] 1 WLR 1425 at 1436, CA (wife not entitled to reject genuine offer not containing assurances as to future conduct since she had not sought such assurances).
8 *Fraser v Fraser* [1969] 3 All ER 654, [1969] 1 WLR 1787.
9 *Parkinson v Parkinson* (1959) Times, 14 April, DC.
10 *Dunn v Dunn* [1967] P 217 at 227–229, [1965] 1 All ER 1043 at 1049, DC.
11 *Storey v Storey* [1965] 1 All ER 1052n at 1053, CA; but see *Dunn v Dunn* [1967] P 217, [1965] 1 All ER 1043, DC.

398. Effect of refusal of offer made in good faith. A refusal of an offer to return made in good faith where there is no right to refuse it[1] converts the deserted party into the deserting party[2]. A refusal which has no effect on the mind of the deserting party does not necessarily end the desertion[3].

1 *Perry v Perry* [1952] P 203 at 232, [1952] 1 All ER 1076 at 1092, CA; *Harvey v Harvey* [1956] P 102 at 108, [1955] 3 All ER 772 at 774, CA; *Weddell v Weddell* (1961) 105 Sol Jo 153, CA.
2 *Thomas v Thomas* [1946] 1 All ER 170; cf *Joseph v Joseph* [1939] P 385.
3 *Brewer v Brewer* [1962] P 69, [1961] 3 All ER 957, CA.

399. Declaration against having other party back. Where the deserted party, suffering from a deep sense of grievance, says to the deserting party, who is showing no contrition for and almost no recognition of what he has done: 'I do not want to see you any more', or words to that effect, those words do not exonerate the deserter from doing something to bring an end to the state of desertion which he started; if and when the deserter makes further efforts at reconciliation, those efforts must be tested against the background in which they are made, to judge whether they amount to genuine efforts for reconciliation[1]. Where, however, a deserted party evinces a firm and decisive determination in advance that the deserting party should not return, the deserted party has put it out of the power of the deserting party, if so minded, to express repentance and terminate the desertion, so that the deserted party is in the same position as he or she would have been if an approach had been made in good faith and rejected[2]; but the proper test is to ascertain whether the deserted party's conduct has had any actual effect in preventing the deserter from seeking a reconciliation[3]. A declaration by the deserted party that he or she will have nothing more to do with the alleged deserter may, in the circumstances, tend strongly against the existence of desertion, especially if the declaration is communicated to the alleged deserter[4]. A deserted party cannot complain if what he or she has said or done has in fact caused the deserting party to desist from making any attempt at reconciliation which the deserting party would otherwise have made[5]; but, if a deserted party develops an aversion to the other party or forms an attachment for someone else, such aversion or other attachment does not bar relief unless it has the effect of preventing a reconciliation and driving away a party who is, or might otherwise become, willing to return[6].

1   *Bevan v Bevan* [1955] 3 All ER 332 at 336, [1955] 1 WLR 1142 at 1147, DC.

2   *Fishburn v Fishburn* [1955] P 29 at 41, [1955] 1 All ER 230 at 234–236 (wife locked door
    against husband; no desertion by him), following *Barnett v Barnett* [1955] P 21, [1954]
    3 All ER 689. These cases were doubted obiter in *Beigan v Beigan* [1956] P 313, [1956]
    2 All ER 630, CA, the real objection being to the words 'if so minded'; Denning LJ at 319 and
    at 632 said that, if a wife locks the door against her husband, it does not automatically
    terminate his desertion any more than her own adultery would do. See also *Gibson v Gibson*
    (1956) Times, 18 July, CA. As to the effect of an offer made in good faith see PARA 398.

3   *Beigan v Beigan* [1956] P 313, [1956] 2 All ER 630, CA. See also note 2.

4   *Brewer v Brewer* [1962] P 69 at 89, [1961] 3 All ER 957 at 967, CA.

5   *Brewer v Brewer* [1962] P 69 at 82, [1961] 3 All ER 957 at 964, CA.

6   *Brewer v Brewer* [1962] P 69 at 90, [1961] 3 All ER 957 at 968, CA.

400.   Genuineness of offer to return.   The intention to desert is presumed to
continue, unless the deserting party proves genuine repentance and sincere and
reasonable attempts to reconcile[1]; for desertion is not a single act complete in
itself and revocable by a single act of repentance[2]. A deserting party cannot
obliterate his or her misconduct by subsequent offers, as to the genuineness of
which the deserted party may, on reasonable grounds, entertain doubts[3]. If the
deserted party has ample grounds for refusing any offer to resume cohabitation
made by the other party, the question of genuineness of the offer does not
arise[4]. It would follow that, if there has been unreasonable conduct, that should
also be considered[5].

The quality of an attempt at reconciliation is to be judged by the conduct
generally of the deserting party[6].

1   *Bowron v Bowron* [1925] P 187 at 195, 196, CA (constructive desertion; no 'efforts to recover'
    wife); *Charter v Charter* (1901) 84 LT 272 (husband told wife to go, but construed as mutual
    separation; husband's request to wife to return refused; husband not in desertion); *Thomas v
    Thomas* [1924] P 194 at 201, CA; *Pratt v Pratt* [1939] AC 417 at 422, 427, [1939] 3 All ER
    437 at 438, 442, HL; *Ware v Ware* [1942] P 49, [1942] 1 All ER 50 (offer not genuine);
    Abercrombie v Abercrombie [1943] 2 All ER 465 at 468; *Price v Price* [1951] P 413 at 416, CA;
    Casey v Casey [1952] 1 All ER 453; *W v W (No 2)* [1954] P 486, [1954] 2 All ER 829, CA;
    Gaskell v Gaskell (1963) 108 Sol Jo 37, DC, approved in *Trevor v Trevor* (1965) 109 Sol Jo
    574, CA. As to the phrase 'lack of sincerity' in these cases see *Wells v Wells* [1954] 3 All ER 491
    at 492, 493, [1954] 1 WLR 1390 at 1393, 1394, CA.

2   *Thomas v Thomas* [1924] P 194 at 199, CA.

3   *Thomas v Thomas* [1924] P 194 at 199, 201, CA; *R v Davidson etc, Durham Justices* (1889) 5
    TLR 199, DC (offer not bona fide; no effort to terminate desertion, and no offer until brought
    before magistrates); *Re Duckworth* (1889) 5 TLR 608; *Martin v Martin* (1898) 78 LT 568; *W v
    W (No 2)* [1954] P 486, [1954] 2 All ER 829, CA.

4   *Volp v Volp* (14 October 1940, unreported), but noted on this point in *Everitt v Everitt* [1949]
    P 374 at 384, [1949] 1 All ER 908 at 915, CA. Where in a marriage the deserting spouse has
    committed adultery and has deserted, an offer to return to cohabitation may be refused by the
    deserted spouse, because he or she is under no obligation to condone the adultery: *Cargill v
    Cargill* (1858) 1 Sw & Tr 235; *Basing v Basing* (1864) 3 Sw & Tr 516; *Knapp v Knapp* (1880)
    6 PD 10 at 11; *Farmer v Farmer* (1884) 9 PD 245; *Everitt v Everitt* [1949] P 374, [1949]
    1 All ER 908, CA (wife justified in believing adultery committed; desertion not terminated by
    offer, nor retrospectively terminated by finding that the belief could not be made out), overruling
    Lodge v Lodge (1890) 15 PD 159. Where the conduct relied on is adultery, the deserted spouse
    should consider bringing the petition on that fact (see the Matrimonial Causes Act 1973
    s 1(2)(a); PARAS 347, 350; and *Barker v Barker* [1950] 1 All ER 812 at 816, CA per Bucknill LJ
    (adultery is the solid basis of the decree; constructive desertion in such a case is somewhat of a
    legal fiction)).

5   See PARAS 359, 360.

6   *Thomas v Thomas* [1924] P 194 at 199, 203, CA; *Dunn v Dunn* [1967] P 217, [1965] 1 All ER
    1043, DC; *Trevor v Trevor* (1965) 109 Sol Jo 574, CA; *Barnard v Barnard* [1965] 1 All ER
    1050n, [1965] 2 WLR 56n, CA; *Turpin v Turpin* [1965] 1 All ER 1051n, [1965] 2 WLR 956n;
    Storey v Storey [1965] 1 All ER 1052n, CA; *Nowell v Nowell* (1953) Times, 25 February, CA

(vague offer of house in United States). An offer or proposal to provide a home must be definite or distinct: *Cudlipp v Cudlipp* (1858) 1 Sw & Tr 229 at 230.

401. When the offer is a stratagem. The offer to return must not be a stratagem to interrupt the continuous period of desertion[1]. Where he or she has made life together intolerable[2], the deserting party must be really contrite and anxious for a resumption[3]. The fact that an offer of resumption is spontaneous and not made on the advice or at the instigation of legal advisers, or that the offer is not made for the purpose of being used in legal proceedings, adds to its weight and sincerity[4].

1 See PARAS 364–365.
2 See *Price v Price* [1951] 1 All ER 877 at 880, 881; affd [1951] P 413, [1951] 2 All ER 580n, CA.
3 See *Ware v Ware* [1942] P 49, [1942] 1 All ER 50 (deserting spouse not ready to behave properly as wife); *Pratt v Pratt* [1939] AC 417 at 422, [1939] 3 All ER 437 at 438, HL. Such repentance is not necessary where the hostility of the deserting party against the deserted party has been confined to hostile statements and litigation: *Price v Price* [1951] P 413, [1951] 2 All ER 580n, CA; cf *Wily v Wily* [1918] P 1.
4 *Pratt v Pratt* [1939] AC 417 at 427, [1939] 3 All ER 437 at 442, HL per Lord Romer; *Re Duckworth* (1889) 5 TLR 608 at 609 (offer sent in lawyer's letter not in good faith); *Martin v Martin* (1898) 78 LT 568 (offer in solicitor's letter not genuine); *Price v Price* [1951] P 413, [1951] 2 All ER 580n, CA (offer through solicitors held to be in good faith); and see PARA 400 note 1.

402. Offer subject to conditions. The deserting party is not entitled to put unreasonable conditions in an offer to return[1].

1 *Hutchinson v Hutchinson* [1963] 1 All ER 1, [1963] 1 WLR 280, DC (husband's condition of no intercourse); *Barrett v Barrett* [1948] P 277, CA (husband asked wife to return to him without their daughters; unreasonable); *McGowan v McGowan* [1948] 2 All ER 1032 (cited in PARA 384 note 7); *Slawson v Slawson* [1942] 2 All ER 527 (wife offered to return only as housekeeper; no question of health, age or danger of childbirth, or the like; offer did not terminate her desertion); *Lacey v Lacey* (1931) 146 LT 48 (wife's offer to return to husband merely for sake of children); *Millichamp v Millichamp* (1931) 146 LT 96 (offer of unreasonable home); cf *Jackson v Jackson* (1932) 146 LT 406; and see *Synge v Synge* [1901] P 317, CA (wife's condition of no intercourse); *French-Brewster v French-Brewster* (1889) 62 LT 609 at 611; *Dallas v Dallas* (1874) 43 LJP & M 87 (husband's offer to return if wife would write letter amounting to confession of insanity, and exonerating certain woman from suspicion; unreasonable). See also *Gibson v Gibson* (1859) 29 LJP & M 25 (apparently a mutual separation; wife offered to have husband back if he gave up gambling and drinking; court doubted whether that conditional offer would have started desertion running if other evidence of husband's intention to desert not available).

403. Resumption of cohabitation. Desertion can be ended by resumption of cohabitation[1]. There can be no completely exhaustive definition of 'cohabitation'[2], and each case must be decided on its own facts and merits[3], but desertion does not cease to run until a true reconciliation has been effected[4].

The resumption of cohabitation depends on the intention of both parties[5], and there can be a resumption of cohabitation without the parties necessarily living with each other in the same house[6].

If there is a resumption of cohabitation, the nature of the resumption and the consequent termination of the desertion cannot be altered by a condition subsequent[7]; but, if the parties resume cohabitation for a period or periods not exceeding six months in all, no account is to be taken of that period or those periods[8].

1 *Thomas v Thomas* [1924] P 194 at 199, CA. See also the Domestic Proceedings and Magistrates' Courts Act 1978 s 25; the Civil Partnership Act 2004 Sch 6 para 29; and PARA 658.

2   *Mummery v Mummery* [1942] P 107 at 109, [1942] 1 All ER 553 at 555; *Abercrombie v
     Abercrombie* [1943] 2 All ER 465 at 469; *Lowry v Lowry* [1952] P 252 at 256, 257, [1952]
     2 All ER 61 at 62, 63 (residing together as man and wife).

3   *Abercrombie v Abercrombie* [1943] 2 All ER 465 at 470; *Casey v Casey* [1952] 1 All ER 453 at
     454 (wife asked back only to look after children; not genuine offer); *Perry v Perry* [1952] P 203
     at 215, [1952] 1 All ER 1076 at 1082, CA per Sir Raymond Evershed MR.

4   In considering whether a period of desertion has been continuous, the court does not take
     account of certain periods during which the parties resume living together: see the Matrimonial
     Causes Act 1973 s 2(5); the Civil Partnership Act 2004 s 45(6); and PARA 365. As to the effect
     of sexual intercourse see PARA 404.

5   *Abercrombie v Abercrombie* [1943] 2 All ER 465 at 469; *Rowell v Rowell* [1900] 1 QB 9 at
     13, CA; *Mummery v Mummery* [1942] P 107 at 109, 110, [1942] 1 All ER 553 at 555; *Bartram
     v Bartram* [1950] P 1 at 5, 6, [1949] 2 All ER 270 at 271, CA (wife returned as lodger because
     nowhere else to go); *Lowry v Lowry* [1952] P 252 at 257, [1952] 2 All ER 61 at 63; *Perry v
     Perry* [1952] P 203 at 214, 215, 225, 226, 232, [1952] 1 All ER 1076 at 1082, 1088, 1092, CA,
     disapproving dicta in *Viney v Viney* [1951] P 457, [1951] 2 All ER 204, DC.

6   *Abercrombie v Abercrombie* [1943] 2 All ER 465 at 469, 470 (husband, doctor, had no settled
     abode); *Germany v Germany* [1938] P 202 at 207, [1938] 3 All ER 64 at 71 (doctor living for
     convenience in another doctor's house); cf *Thurston v Thurston* (1910) 26 TLR 388
     (intermittent visits to wife during statutory period by husband, without intention of remaining
     or of resuming marital intercourse, did not constitute a return to cohabitation). See, however,
     the Matrimonial Causes Act 1973 s 2(6); the Civil Partnership Act 2004 s 45(8) (parties to a
     marriage or civil partnership to be treated as living apart unless they are living with each other
     in the same household); and PARA 347. Cf PARA 412.

7   *Abercrombie v Abercrombie* [1943] 2 All ER 465 at 468, 470, 471 (no trial, probationary or
     tentative period possible); *Perry v Perry* [1952] P 203, [1952] 1 All ER 1076, CA.

8   See the Matrimonial Causes Act 1973 s 2(5); the Civil Partnership Act 2004 s 45(6); and PARA
     365.

404.   Effect of sexual intercourse.   The mere fact that sexual intercourse has
taken place between the parties is not decisive on the issue of resumption of
cohabitation, though it is of great weight[1]; in any event, the statutory provision
in cases of divorce, dissolution and judicial and legal separation as to living
together for not more than six months must be considered[2]. Sexual intercourse is
of more consequence when it takes place in a home where the parties have earlier
lived together than when it takes place at some other address[3], and the age of the
parties is also relevant for consideration in determining the significance of the
intercourse[4]. The birth of a child from an isolated act of intercourse is irrelevant
as respect the question whether cohabitation has been resumed[5].

   In view of the mutual intention required to resume cohabitation[6], no
distinction is made as to which party is in desertion, when considering the effect
of sexual intercourse by itself[7].

   The legal effect of sexual intercourse may well be substantially different where
the case is one of constructive desertion as opposed to simple desertion[8].

1   *Abercrombie v Abercrombie* [1943] 2 All ER 465 at 469; *Rowell v Rowell* [1900] 1 QB 9 at
     14, CA; *Mummery v Mummery* [1942] P 107, [1942] 1 All ER 553 (single act of sexual
     intercourse; no resumption); *Perry v Perry* [1952] P 203, [1952] 1 All ER 1076, CA; *Marczuk v
     Marczuk* [1956] P 217, [1955] 3 All ER 758 (acts incidental to visits to obtain money; no
     resumption); revsd on another point [1956] P 217 at 238, [1956] 1 All ER 657, CA; *Pizey v
     Pizey and Stephenson* [1961] P 101 at 108, [1961] 2 All ER 658 at 662, CA; *Ives v Ives* [1968]
     P 375, [1967] 3 All ER 79; *France v France* [1969] P 46, [1969] 2 All ER 870, CA.

2   See PARA 365.

3   *Lowry v Lowry* [1952] P 252 at 258, [1952] 2 All ER 61 at 64.

4   *Perry v Perry* [1952] P 203 at 215, [1952] 1 All ER 1076 at 1082, CA per Sir Raymond
     Evershed MR; *Casey v Casey* [1952] 1 All ER 453 at 454.

5   *Perry v Perry* [1952] P 203 at 218, [1952] 1 All ER 1076 at 1084, CA per Sir Raymond
     Evershed MR and at 226 and at 1087 per Jenkins LJ.

6   See PARA 403.

7   *Perry v Perry* [1952] P 203 at 232, [1952] 1 All ER 1076 at 1092, CA per Hodson LJ. In this case certain dicta in *Viney v Viney* [1951] P 457, [1951] 2 All ER 204 were disapproved, but it was pointed out that, as evidence of resumption, acts of sexual intercourse may weigh somewhat more heavily against a husband than a wife: see *Perry v Perry* at 217 and at 1082 per Sir Raymond Evershed MR.

8   *Howard v Howard* [1965] P 65, [1962] 2 All ER 539, DC, distinguishing *Perry v Perry* [1952] P 203, [1952] 1 All ER 1076, CA.

405. 'Living separate' and resuming cohabitation. The issue whether parties are 'living separate' within the meaning of a deed of separation, and the issue whether they have resumed cohabitation so as to end a period of desertion, involve the same considerations[1]; but, for the purposes of divorce, dissolution and judicial and legal separation, the expressions 'living apart' and 'living with each other' each have a statutory meaning[2].

1   *Abercrombie v Abercrombie* [1943] 2 All ER 465 at 469; *Rowell v Rowell* [1900] 1 QB 9, CA; *Perry v Perry* [1952] P 203 at 230, [1952] 1 All ER 1076 at 1091, CA per Hodson LJ.

2   See the Matrimonial Causes Act 1973 s 2(6); the Civil Partnership Act 2004 s 45(8); and PARA 347 note 8.

406. Effect of decree of judicial separation or separation order. A decree of judicial separation (or, presumably, a separation order[1]) terminates desertion so long as it remains in force[2]. The party against whom the decree or order is made no longer has the right to cohabit with the other party[3]; and, for this reason, the fact that a deserting party stays away because of his intention to desert and not because of obedience to the decree does not affect the termination of the desertion[4].

1   As to the meaning of 'separation order' see PARA 346 note 4.

2   *Harriman v Harriman* [1909] P 123 at 135, 137, CA (approving *Dodd v Dodd* [1906] P 189, and overruling *Smith v Smith* [1905] P 249, and *Failes v Failes* [1906] P 326). In *Dodd v Dodd*, *Levy v Levy* (1904) 21 TLR 157 was also disapproved. The decision in *Harriman v Harriman* was approved in *Cohen v Cohen* [1940] AC 631 at 644, [1940] 2 All ER 331 at 338, HL. As to the recognition of foreign decrees of judicial separation see *Tursi v Tursi* [1958] P 54, [1957] 2 All ER 828; and PARA 20.

3   *Harriman v Harriman* [1909] P 123 at 137, 146, 154, CA; *Robinson v Robinson* [1919] P 352 at 354, 355; *Taylor v Taylor* (1907) 23 TLR 566 at 567.

4   *Robinson v Robinson* [1919] P 352, not following the dictum of Buckley LJ in *Harriman v Harriman* [1909] P 123 at 148, CA.

(v) Separation

A. TWO YEARS' LIVING APART AND CONSENT TO DIVORCE OR DISSOLUTION

407. Evidence of irretrievable breakdown. The court[1] may find that a marriage or civil partnership has broken down irretrievably where the petitioner[2] satisfies the court that the parties have lived apart[3] for a continuous period of at least two years immediately preceding the presentation of the petition or the making of the application and the respondent consents[4] to a decree being granted or a dissolution order being made[5]. It is undesirable that there should be cross-decrees or orders where each party alleges that they have lived apart for two years and the other consents to a decree[6].

1   As to the meaning of 'court' see PARA 346 note 2. As to the duty of the court to make inquiries see PARA 348.

2   As to petitioners and applicants see PARA 321 note 1.

3   As to the meaning of 'living apart' see PARA 347 note 8.

4   As to consent see PARA 408; and as to the position where the respondent may have been misled
    into giving consent see PARA 409.
5   See the Matrimonial Causes Act 1973 s 1(2)(d); the Civil Partnership Act 2004 s 44(5)(b); and
    PARA 347. As to the meaning of 'dissolution order' see PARA 346 note 1. As to continuity see
    PARA 412; and as to the periods of living together which are not to be taken into account see
    PARA 413. The day on which the separation took place is to be excluded when computing the
    two-year period: *Warr v Warr* [1975] Fam 25, [1975] 1 All ER 85 (wife failed to prove the
    statutory period had expired when she presented her petition; petition dismissed).
6   *Darvill v Darvill* (1973) 117 Sol Jo 223.

408.   What constitutes consent.   A positive act of consent is required[1]; and an
indication that a party does not object to a decree or order being granted will not
amount to a consent[2]. Rules of court make provision for the purpose of ensuring
that, where the parties have lived apart for a continuous period of two years[3]
and the petitioner[4] alleges that the respondent consents to a decree being granted
or a dissolution order[5] being made, the respondent has been given such
information as will enable him to understand the consequences to him of his
consenting to a decree being granted or an order being made and the steps which
he must take to indicate that he consents to the grant of a decree or the making
of an order[6]. Where consent in writing has been given, it may be that this
requirement as to giving information may in exceptional cases be waived by the
court[7]. The consent must be a valid, continuing and subsisting consent when the
case is heard, remaining operative as the expression of the respondent's state of
mind up to the conclusion of proceedings[8]. Consent means voluntary consent,
not so-called consent obtained by submission to force or threats or the like[9].

1   *McG (formerly R) v R* [1972] 1 All ER 362, sub nom *McGill v Robson* [1972] 1 WLR 237;
    Matcham v Matcham (1976) 6 Fam Law 212.
2   *McG (formerly R) v R* [1972] 1 All ER 362 at 363, 364, sub nom *McGill v Robson* [1972]
    1 WLR 237 at 238, 239. As to the giving of consent by persons of unsound mind see *Mason v
    Mason* [1972] Fam 302 at 306, [1972] 3 All ER 315 at 317, 318; and PARAS 42, 45.
3   See PARAS 407, 412.
4   As to petitioners and applicants see PARA 321 note 1.
5   As to the meaning of 'dissolution order' see PARA 346 note 1.
6   See the Matrimonial Causes Act 1973 s 2(7); the Civil Partnership Act 2004 s 45(3), (4); and the
    Family Proceedings Rules 1991, SI 1991/1247, r 2.9(5), Appendix 1, Forms M6, M6A
    (amended by SI 2005/2922). See also PARA 786.
7   *McG (formerly R) v R* [1972] 1 All ER 362 at 364, [1972] 1 WLR 237 at 239.
8   *Beales v Beales* [1972] Fam 210 at 221, 222, sub nom *McGill v Robson* [1972] 2 All ER 667 at
    674. Whether a person who has given consent, whereupon the other party has acted to his or
    her detriment, can ever be estopped from withdrawing the consent has not yet been decided: see
    Beales v Beales at 222 and at 674.
9   See *Lawson v Lawson* [1955] 1 All ER 341, [1955] 1 WLR 200, CA.

409.   Respondent misled into giving consent.   Where the court[1] has granted a
decree of divorce or a dissolution order[2] on the basis of a finding that the
petitioner[3] was entitled to rely on the fact of two years' separation[4] coupled with
the respondent's consent to a decree being granted or a dissolution order being
made and has made no such finding as to any other fact which might be evidence
of irretrievable breakdown[5], the court may, on an application made by the
respondent[6], rescind the decree or the conditional dissolution order if it is
satisfied that the petitioner misled the respondent, whether intentionally or
unintentionally, about any matter which the respondent took into account[7] in
deciding to give his consent[8].

1   As to the meaning of 'court' see PARA 346 note 2.
2   As to the meaning of 'dissolution order' see PARA 346 note 1.
3   As to petitioners and applicants see PARA 321 note 1.

4   See PARA 407.

5   Ie any other fact mentioned in the Matrimonial Causes Act 1973 s 1(2) or the Civil Partnership Act 2004 s 44(5) (see PARA 347).

6   In the case of a divorce decree such application may be made at any time before the decree is made absolute: Matrimonial Causes Act 1973 s 10(1). Corresponding provision is not made by the Civil Partnership Act 2004 s 48(1), but may be inferred from the reference in the text to the rescission of the conditional dissolution order.

7   As to information to be given to the respondent see PARA 408.

8   Matrimonial Causes Act 1973 s 10(1); Civil Partnership Act 2004 s 48(1). Thus, where a divorce case is proceeding on the basis of two years' separation, the Matrimonial Causes Act 1973 s 10 will have effect if a Jewish wife gives her consent to a divorce on the basis that the husband will obtain a get, and he fails to do so, and the refusal to initiate the procedure for a get might result in grave financial or other hardship under s 5 (see PARA 411): *N v N (divorce: ante-nuptial agreement)* [1999] 2 FCR 583, sub nom *N v N (jurisdiction: pre-nuptial agreement)* [1999] 2 FLR 745. As to the making absolute of a decree nisi and the making final of a conditional dissolution order see PARA 864 et seq.

B.   FIVE YEARS' LIVING APART: NO CONSENT TO DIVORCE OR DISSOLUTION REQUIRED

410.   Evidence of irretrievable breakdown.   The court[1] may find that a marriage or civil partnership has broken down irretrievably where the petitioner satisfies the court that the parties have lived apart[2] for a continuous period of at least five years immediately preceding the presentation of the petition[3]. The petition should contain no allegation of fault against the respondent[4]. There is no need for any consent by the respondent, and indeed the respondent cannot ask for the petition to be rejected but must limit his request to those matters which he denies[5]. There are, however, statutory restrictions[6].

1   As to the meaning of 'court' see PARA 346 note 2. As to the duty of the court to make inquiries see PARA 348.

2   As to the meaning of 'living apart' see PARA 347 note 8.

3   See the Matrimonial Causes Act 1973 s 1(2)(e); the Civil Partnership Act 2004 s 44(5)(c); and PARA 347. As to petitions and applications see PARA 321 note 1. As to continuity see PARA 412; and as to the periods of living together which are not to be taken into account see PARA 413. The day on which the separation took place is to be excluded when computing the five-year period: *Warr v Warr* [1975] Fam 25, [1975] 1 All ER 85 (wife failed to prove the statutory period had expired when she presented her petition; petition dismissed). Where both parties petition for a divorce or dissolution on different facts, one of which is that contained in the Matrimonial Causes Act 1973 s 1(2)(e) or the Civil Partnership Act 2004 s 44(5)(c), the court must decide whether five years' separation has been established and, if so, grant a divorce or dissolution without hearing evidence of the other petition: *Grenfell v Grenfell* [1978] Fam 128, [1978] 1 All ER 561, CA.

4   *Chapman v Chapman* [1972] 3 All ER 1089, [1972] 1 WLR 1544, CA (in the ordinary way there should be no order for costs in these cases).

5   See *Parsons v Parsons* [1975] 3 All ER 344, [1975] 1 WLR 1272 (it is mandatory for the court to grant a decree to the petitioner in a suit based on the Matrimonial Causes Act 1973 s 1(2)(e); there is no basis on which to grant a decree nisi to the respondent).

6   See PARA 411.

411.   Refusal of divorce or dissolution after five years' living apart.   The respondent to a petition for divorce or an application for a dissolution order[1] alleging five years' separation[2] may oppose the grant of a decree or the making of an order on the ground that the dissolution of the marriage or civil partnership will result in grave financial or other hardship[3] to the respondent and that it would be wrong in all the circumstances to dissolve the marriage or civil partnership[4].

Where the grant of a decree or the making of an order is so opposed, then:

(1)   if the court[5] finds that the petitioner is entitled to rely in support of his

petition on the fact of five years' separation and makes no such finding
as to any other fact[6] constituting irretrievable breakdown[7]; and

(2)	if the court would otherwise[8] grant a decree or make an order[9],
the court must consider all the circumstances, including the conduct[10] of the
parties and the interests of those parties and of any children or other persons
concerned[11]; and, if the court is of opinion that the dissolution will result in
grave financial or other hardship[12] to the respondent and that it would in all the
circumstances be wrong to dissolve the marriage or civil partnership, it must
dismiss the petition[13].

1	As to the meaning of 'dissolution order' see PARA 346 note 1. As to petitions and applications
	see PARA 321 note 1.
2	As to 'five years' separation' see PARA 410.
3	For these purposes 'grave financial hardship' means exactly what the words say and has to be
	considered subjectively in relation to the particular relationship and the circumstances in which
	the parties lived while it subsisted: *Talbot v Talbot* (1971) 115 Sol Jo 870; and see *Parkes v
	Parkes* [1971] 3 All ER 870, [1971] 1 WLR 1481, CA; *Julian v Julian* (1972) 116 Sol Jo 763
	(potential loss of pension rights; petition dismissed); *Mathias v Mathias* [1972] Fam 287, [1972]
	3 All ER 1, CA (army and state pensions; no grave financial or other hardship); *Parker v Parker*
	[1972] Fam 116, [1972] 1 All ER 410 (loss of police widow's pension could be made up by
	deferred annuity or by policy producing specified sum on maturity); *Brickell v Brickell* [1974]
	Fam 31, [1973] 3 All ER 508, CA; *Burvill v Burvill* (1974) 118 Sol Jo 205; *Reiterbund v
	Reiterbund* [1975] Fam 99, [1975] 1 All ER 280, CA (social security benefits would not be less
	than those receivable as widow's pension; no hardship); *Le Marchant v Le Marchant* [1977]
	3 All ER 610, [1977] 1 WLR 559, CA (loss of index-linked pension; grave financial hardship);
	Jackson v Jackson [1994] 2 FCR 393, [1993] 2 FLR 848, CA (loss of widow's pension; no
	hardship since loss offset by entitlement to income support); *K v K (financial provision)* [1996]
	3 FCR 158, sub nom *K v K (financial relief: widow's pension)* [1997] 1 FLR 35 (loss of widow's
	pension; grave financial hardship); *Archer v Archer* [1999] 2 FCR 158, [1999] 1 FLR 327, CA
	(loss of widow's pension where wife had substantial capital assets did not constitute financial
	hardship). 'Other hardship' must mean something other than 'financial': *Banik v Banik* [1973]
	3 All ER 45 at 48, [1973] 1 WLR 860 at 864, CA (putting forward a case that a divorce would
	result in the respondent becoming a social outcast in her own community might amount to a
	defence of grave hardship; see also *Banik v Banik (No 2)* (1973) 117 Sol Jo 874; *Parghi v Parghi*
	(1973) 117 Sol Jo 582 (Hindus, well educated; the approach to divorce of educated persons in
	India is similar to that of the western world; grant of decree would not add to hardship already
	suffered by separation; but divorce might cause hardship to Hindu wife in different
	circumstances); *Rukat v Rukat* [1975] Fam 63, [1975] 1 All ER 343, CA). 'Grave' applies not
	only to financial but also to other hardship: *Rukat v Rukat* [1975] Fam 63, [1975] 1 All ER
	343, CA. See also note 12. Whilst in one sense the test to be applied is subjective, in so far as the
	court is concerned, looking at the matter through the respondent's eyes, with whether the
	particular respondent is going to suffer hardship, nevertheless the court must then apply an
	objective test to all the relevant facts: see *Rukat v Rukat* at 75 and at 352, 353 per Ormrod LJ;
	Balraj v Balraj (1980) 11 Fam Law 110 at 111, 112, CA per Cumming-Bruce LJ.
4	Matrimonial Causes Act 1973 s 5(1); Civil Partnership Act 2004 s 47(1); and see *Grenfell v
	Grenfell* [1978] Fam 128, [1978] 1 All ER 561, CA. Where a prima facie case of grave financial
	hardship is set up, the proper approach is that the petition should be dismissed unless the
	petitioner meets the answer by putting forward reasonable proposals, acceptable to the court,
	which are sufficient to remove the financial hardship: *Le Marchant v Le Marchant* [1977]
	3 All ER 610, [1977] 1 WLR 559, CA; and see *Lee v Lee* (1973) 117 Sol Jo 616 (married son
	seriously ill; husband, petitioner, made reasonable financial proposals which involved sale of
	house in which wife lived; if the house were sold, wife would find it almost impossible to get
	other accommodation enabling her to assist son; hardship; petition dismissed). See also *Patel v
	Patel* (1977) 8 Fam Law 215 (where husband seeks divorce from wife who is overseas, she
	should be properly represented and made aware of her rights, especially under the Matrimonial
	Causes Act 1973 s 5).
5	As to the meaning of 'court' see PARA 346 note 2.
6	Ie any other fact mentioned in the Matrimonial Causes Act 1973 s 1(2) or the Civil Partnership
	Act 2004 s 44(5) (see PARA 347).
7	Matrimonial Causes Act 1973 s 5(2)(a); Civil Partnership Act 2004 s 47(2)(a), (b).
8	Ie apart from the Matrimonial Causes Act 1973 s 5 or the Civil Partnership Act 2004 s 47.

9   Matrimonial Causes Act 1973 s 5(2)(b); Civil Partnership Act 2004 s 47(2)(c).
10 For these purposes 'conduct' is not confined to misconduct in the old sense of a matrimonial offence but must clearly include it: *Brickell v Brickell* [1974] Fam 31 at 38, [1973] 3 All ER 508 at 512, CA per Davies LJ (wife might suffer grave financial hardship by the loss of a widow's pension, but not right in circumstances to rescind decree nisi that had been pronounced), overruling *Dorrell v Dorrell* [1972] 3 All ER 343 at 347, [1972] 1 WLR 1087 at 1092.
11 Matrimonial Causes Act 1973 s 5(2); Civil Partnership Act 2004 s 47(3)(a).
12 For these purposes 'hardship' includes the loss of the chance of acquiring any benefit which the respondent might acquire if the marriage or civil partnership were not dissolved: Matrimonial Causes Act 1973 s 5(3); Civil Partnership Act 2004 s 47(4); and see *Johnson v Johnson* (1981) 12 Fam Law 116 (index-linked pension).
13 Matrimonial Causes Act 1973 s 5(2); Civil Partnership Act 2004 s 47(3)(b).

C. GENERAL PRINCIPLES

412. Establishing continuity. The period of living apart[1] whether for two[2] or five[3] years must be continuous[4]. In most cases, the parties will not be considered to have been living apart whilst both recognise the relationship as continuing, even though they are separated[5]. Thus, the relationship does not end by reason of a separation brought about by the pressure of external circumstances such as absence on professional or business pursuits, or in search of health, or, it may be, even of pleasure; sexual intercourse, dwelling under the same roof, society and protection, support, recognition in public and in private, correspondence during separation, may be regarded separately as different elements, the presence or absence of which go to show more or less conclusively that the relationship does or does not exist, the weight of each of these elements varying with the health, position in life, and all the circumstances of the parties[6]. The court must look for a definite termination of the consortium before the physical fact of being apart can be said to constitute separation[7]. Cohabitation does not necessarily imply living together physically under the same roof[8]. Where the parties are separated but not living apart, it is open to one of the parties to decide henceforth to live apart and such decision need not be communicated by word or conduct to the other party; an uncommunicated ending of recognition that a relationship is subsisting can mark the moment at which the parties begin to live apart[9].

1   As to 'living apart' see PARA 347 note 8.
2   See PARA 407.
3   See PARA 410.
4   See PARAS 407, 413.
5   See *Santos v Santos* [1972] Fam 247 at 263, [1972] 2 All ER 246 at 255, CA per Sachs LJ.
6   *Tulk v Tulk* [1907] VLR 64 at 65, applied in *Main v Main* (1949) 78 CLR 636 at 642; and *Santos v Santos* [1972] Fam 247, [1972] 2 All ER 246, CA; and see *Collins v Collins* (1961) 3 FLR 17; *R v Creamer* [1919] 1 KB 564, CCA; *Eadie v IRC* [1924] 2 KB 198.
7   *Collins v Collins* (1961) 3 FLR 17 at 22, applied in *Santos v Santos* [1972] Fam 247, [1972] 2 All ER 246, CA; and see *Mouncer v Mouncer* [1972] 1 All ER 289, [1972] 1 WLR 321 (living together); *Hollens v Hollens* (1971) 115 Sol Jo 327 (living apart).
8   *Bradshaw v Bradshaw* [1897] P 24 at 26, applied in *Santos v Santos* [1972] Fam 247, [1972] 2 All ER 246, CA; and see *Nugent-Head v Jacob* [1948] AC 321, [1948] 1 All ER 414, HL. See also PARA 403 note 6.
9   *Santos v Santos* [1972] Fam 247 at 259–262, [1972] 2 All ER 246 at 253–255, CA per Sachs LJ.

413. No account of periods of living together. In considering whether the period for which the parties to a marriage or civil partnership have lived apart[1] has been a continuous[2] period of at least two years[3] or, as the case may be, five years[4], no account is to be taken of any one period, not exceeding six months, or of any two or more periods, not exceeding six months, in all during which the parties resumed living with each other; but no period during which the parties lived with each other is to count as part of the period for which they lived apart[5].

1 As to 'living apart' see PARA 347 note 8.
2 As to continuity see PARA 412.
3 See PARA 407.
4 See PARA 410.
5 Matrimonial Causes Act 1973 s 2(5); Civil Partnership Act 2004 s 44(6), (7). Thus where two years' living apart is claimed, the parties can spend up to 20% of the relevant time together, ie six months in two years six months, without interrupting the continuity of the separation, and where five years' living apart is claimed, the parties can spend about 9% of the time together, ie six months in five years and six months: see *Santos v Santos* [1972] Fam 247 at 261, [1972] 2 All ER 246 at 254, 255, CA per Sachs LJ.

(vi) Reconciliation

414. Duty to consider reconciliation. In divorce, dissolution or judicial or legal separation proceedings the petitioner's solicitor[1] is required to certify whether he has discussed with the petitioner the possibility of a reconciliation and given the petitioner the names and address of persons qualified to help effect a reconciliation between parties to a marriage or civil partnership who have become estranged[2]. If at any stage of the proceedings it appears to the court[3] that there is a reasonable possibility of a reconciliation between the parties the court may adjourn the proceedings for such period as it thinks fit to enable attempts to be made to effect such a reconciliation[4].

1 As from a day to be appointed this duty is expressed to fall on a person's 'legal representative' rather than their solicitor: Matrimonial Causes Act 1973 s 6(1) (prospectively amended by the Legal Services Act 2007 Sch 21 para 29); Civil Partnership Act 2004 s 42(2) (prospectively amended by the Legal Services Act 2007 Sch 21 para 150). At the date at which this volume states the law no such day had been appointed. As to petitioners and applicants see PARA 321 note 1.
2 Matrimonial Causes Act 1973 ss 6(1), 17(3) (s 6(1) prospectively amended: see note 1); Civil Partnership Act 2004 s 42(1), (2) (prospectively amended: see note 1); Family Proceedings Rules 1991, SI 1991/1247, r 2.6(3), Appendix 1, Form M3 (amended by SI 2005/2922).
    The Secretary of State may, with the approval of the Treasury, make grants, subject to such conditions as he considers appropriate, in connection with the provision of marriage support services, research into the causes of marital breakdown, and research into ways of preventing marital breakdown: Family Law Act 1996 s 22(1), (3) (s 22 amended by SI 2003/3191). In exercising this power the Secretary of State is to have regard, in particular, to the desirability of services of that kind being available when they are first needed: Family Law Act 1996 s 22(2) (as so amended).
3 As to the meaning of 'court' see PARA 346 note 2.
4 Matrimonial Causes Act 1973 s 6(2); Civil Partnership Act 2004 s 42(3). This power is additional to any other power of the court to adjourn proceedings: Matrimonial Causes Act 1973 s 6(2); Civil Partnership Act 2004 s 42(3).

(4) PRESUMPTION OF DEATH

415. Application and grounds for presumption. Any married person or civil partner[1] who alleges that reasonable grounds exist for supposing that the other party to the marriage or civil partnership is dead may present a petition to the court[2] to have it presumed that the other party is dead and to have the marriage or civil partnership dissolved[3]. If satisfied that such reasonable grounds exist, the court may[4] grant a decree of presumption of death and dissolution of the marriage[5] or a presumption of death order which dissolves a civil partnership[6].

1 As to the meaning of 'civil partner' see PARA 2 note 1.

2   As to petitions and applications see PARA 321 note 1. As to the meaning of 'court' see PARA 346 note 2.

3   Matrimonial Causes Act 1973 s 19(1) (amended by the Domicile and Matrimonial Proceedings Act 1973 Sch 6); Civil Partnership Act 2004 s 55(1). As to procedure see PARA 750 et seq. Neither collusion nor any other conduct on the part of the petitioner which has at any time been a bar to relief in matrimonial proceedings constitutes a bar to the grant of presumption of death and dissolution of marriage: Matrimonial Causes Act 1973 s 19(6). Collusion as a bar to relief in divorce and nullity was abolished by the Divorce Reform Act 1969 Sch 2 (repealed) and the Nullity of Marriage Act 1971 s 6 (repealed).

4   The relief is discretionary: *Thompson v Thompson* [1956] P 414 at 425, [1956] 1 All ER 603 at 608.

5   Matrimonial Causes Act 1973 s 19(1) (as amended: see note 3). The decree is a decree dissolving the marriage: *Deacock v Deacock* [1958] P 230, [1958] 2 All ER 633, CA. It follows that there is a right to remarry thereafter, although the Matrimonial Causes Act 1965 s 8(1), which specifically stated this right, has been repealed and not replaced.

6   Civil Partnership Act 2004 s 55(1). A 'presumption of death order' is an order made by the court which dissolves a civil partnership on the ground that one of the civil partners is presumed to be dead: s 37(1)(c).

416. Presumption from absence of seven years or more. In any proceedings for a decree of presumption of death and dissolution of marriage or a presumption of death order and dissolution of a civil partnership[1] the fact that for a period of seven years or more the other party to the marriage or civil partnership has been continually absent from the petitioner[2], and the petitioner has no reason to believe that the other party has been living within that time, is evidence that the other party is dead until the contrary is proved[3].

The petitioner must give evidence that he has no reason to believe that the other party has been living within the period, and then, where the facts leave the matter as one of speculation, the court may grant the decree or order[4]. Failure to make appropriate inquiries may prove fatal to the petition[5]. Each case must be determined on its own facts; there is no other presumption of law as to continuance of life or death[6]. Absence under a separation agreement does not bar the petition, though continual absence from the petitioner where the parties have bound themselves to live apart proves very little[7].

1   See PARA 415.

2   As to petitioners and applicants see PARA 321 note 1.

3   Matrimonial Causes Act 1973 s 19(3); Civil Partnership Act 2004 s 55(2).

4   *Thompson v Thompson* [1956] P 414 at 425, [1956] 1 All ER 603 at 608; *Parkinson v Parkinson* [1939] P 346, [1939] 3 All ER 108 (decree made); *Tweney v Tweney* [1946] P 180, [1946] 1 All ER 564 (husband disappeared; exhaustive inquiries fruitless; after ten years wife remarried informing registrar and second husband of all circumstances; second marriage presumed valid until evidence to contrary adduced; no such evidence adduced; wife granted decree nisi against second husband); *Spurgeon v Spurgeon* (1930) 46 TLR 396; *Re Watkins, Watkins v Watkins* [1953] 2 All ER 1113, [1953] 1 WLR 1323; *Re Peete, Peete v Crompton* [1952] 2 All ER 599 at 602 (evidence of husband's death not accepted); *Chipchase v Chipchase* [1939] P 391, [1939] 3 All ER 895; *Anon (validity of marriage)* (1953) Times, 17 October; cf *Chard v Chard (otherwise Northcott)* [1956] P 259, [1955] 3 All ER 721 (nullity case on ground of bigamy).

5   *Bradshaw v Bradshaw* [1956] P 274n at 282n; *Ward v Ward* (1956) Times, 10 February, CA; *Bullock v Bullock* [1960] 2 All ER 307, [1960] 1 WLR 975, DC (inquiries made by police; death presumed); *Bennett v Bennett* (1961) 105 Sol Jo 885, CA.

6   *MacDarmaid v A-G* [1950] P 218 at 221, [1950] 1 All ER 497 at 499; cf *Chard v Chard (otherwise Northcott)* [1956] P 259 at 270, [1955] 3 All ER 721 at 727 (any presumption of continuance of life being one of fact, due weight can be given in each case to the different circumstances of any given individual, eg whether a friendless orphan or a gregarious man in public life, whether in good or bad health, and whether following a quiet or a dangerous occupation).

7   *Parkinson v Parkinson* [1939] P 346 at 351, [1939] 3 All ER 108 at 110.

417. Respondent found alive. If a petition for a decree of presumption of death has been made in relation to a party to a marriage, and after decree nisi, but before decree absolute, that party is found to be alive, the court will rescind the decree and dismiss the petition[1]; and where a party obtains a decree absolute and the other party is later found to be alive, that other party is entitled to seek financial provision from the petitioner[2]. These provisions are presumably also applicable, mutatis mutandis, in respect of an application for a presumption of death order in relation to a civil partner.

1 *Manser v Manser* [1940] P 224, [1940] 4 All ER 238, applying *Fender v St John-Mildmay* [1938] AC 1 at 28, [1937] 3 All ER 402 at 419, HL; and see *Stanhope v Stanhope* (1886) 11 PD 103 at 109, CA; *Maxted v Maxted* (1961) Times, 26 January (decree nisi rescinded); *Gallacher v Gallacher (Queen's Proctor showing cause)* (1964) 108 Sol Jo 523.
2 *Deacock v Deacock* [1958] P 230, [1958] 2 All ER 633, CA.

(5) RELATED AND SUBSIDIARY CAUSES

(i) Division of Property

418. Property rights in the family home. By virtue of their status as spouses or civil partners, the parties to a marriage or a civil partnership have a number of statutory rights relating to the occupation or ownership of the family home which are enforceable by registering a charge on the property[1] or by order of the court[2]; provision is also made for the transfer of tenancies[3]. Rights in a family home also arise under the common law[4].

1 See the Family Law Act 1996 Pt IV (ss 30–63); and PARA 285 et seq.
2 See the Married Women's Property Act 1882; the Civil Partnership Act 2004 ss 65–69; and PARA 224 et seq. As to Mesher and Martin orders see PARA 316.
3 See the Family Law Act 1996 Sch 7; and PARA 310 et seq.
4 See PARA 278 et seq.

(ii) Financial Relief and Provision of Reasonable Maintenance

419. Applications for financial provision and relief. On a petition for divorce, dissolution, annulment, judicial or legal separation or presumption of death application may be made to the court for various kinds of relief[1]. Although the statutory provisions do not state explicitly what is to be the aim of the court in exercising its powers to grant relief it is implicit that the purpose of those powers is to enable the court to make fair financial arrangements in the absence of agreement between the former spouses or civil partners, and the court's powers must always be exercised with that objective in view[2].

Financial relief is also available in England and Wales where a marriage or civil partnership has been dissolved or annulled, or the parties have been legally separated, by means of judicial or other proceedings in an overseas country and the divorce, dissolution, annulment or legal separation is entitled to be recognised as valid in England and Wales[3].

1 See PARA 450 et seq. As to petitions and applications see PARA 321 note 1.
2 See *White v White* [2001] 1 AC 596 at 604, 605, [2001] 1 All ER 1 at 8, HL per Lord Nicholls of Birkenhead; applied in *Cowan v Cowan* [2001] EWCA Civ 679, [2002] Fam 97, [2001] 2 FCR 331.
3 See PARA 530 et seq.

420. Financial provision in case of failure to provide reasonable maintenance. The court may make provision by means of financial provision orders in the case of failure by one party to a marriage or civil partnership to provide reasonable maintenance for the other party or a child of the family, whether or not a petition for divorce, dissolution, annulment or judicial or legal separation has been made[1]; and it may also at any stage of the proceedings make an order for maintenance pending the outcome of proceedings[2].

1 See PARA 542 et seq. As to petitions and applications see PARA 321 note 1.
2 See PARA 456.

(iii) Declarations of Marital or Civil Partnership Status

421. Right to apply for declaration. Any person may apply to the High Court or a county court for one or more of the following declarations in relation to a marriage or civil partnership specified in the application[1]:

(1) a declaration that the marriage or civil partnership was at its inception a valid marriage or civil partnership[2];

(2) a declaration that the marriage or civil partnership subsisted on a date specified in the application[3];

(3) a declaration that the marriage or civil partnership did not subsist on a date so specified[4];

(4) a declaration that the validity of a divorce, dissolution, annulment or legal separation obtained in any country outside England and Wales in respect of the marriage or civil partnership is entitled to recognition in England and Wales[5]; and

(5) a declaration that the validity of a divorce, dissolution, annulment or legal separation so obtained in respect of the marriage or civil partnership is not entitled to recognition in England and Wales[6].

1 Family Law Act 1986 s 55(1) (amended by the Child Support, Pensions and Social Security Act 2000 Sch 8 paras 3, 4(a)); Civil Partnership Act 2004 s 58(1). As to procedure on such an application see PARA 1001 et seq.
2 Family Law Act 1986 s 55(1)(a); Civil Partnership Act 2004 s 58(1)(a). As to valid marriages and civil partnerships see PARAS 3, 4; as to void marriages and civil partnerships see PARA 326 et seq. The court has no power to declare that a marriage or civil partnership was at its inception void: see the Family Law Act 1986 s 58(5)(a); the Civil Partnership Act 2004 s 59(5); and PARA 1004.
3 Family Law Act 1986 s 55(1)(b); Civil Partnership Act 2004 s 58(1)(b).
4 Family Law Act 1986 s 55(1)(c); Civil Partnership Act 2004 s 58(1)(c).
5 Family Law Act 1986 s 55(1)(d); Civil Partnership Act 2004 s 58(1)(d).
6 Family Law Act 1986 s 55(1)(e); Civil Partnership Act 2004 s 58(1)(e).

422. Applications by third parties. Where an application for a declaration of marital or civil partnership status[1] is made to a court by any person other than a party to the marriage or civil partnership to which the application relates, the court must refuse to hear the application if it considers that the applicant does not have a sufficient interest in the determination of that application[2].

1 See PARAS 421, 1001 et seq.
2 Family Law Act 1986 s 55(3) (amended by the Child Support, Pensions and Social Security Act 2000 Sch 8 paras 3, 4(b)); Civil Partnership Act 2004 s 58(2).

(iv) Separation Agreements

A. FORM AND VALIDITY

423. Valid agreements. An agreement between a husband and wife (or, presumably, between civil partners) to live apart, whether with or without cause, is not contrary to public policy[1] and is in general[2] valid and enforceable, provided that it is made in contemplation of, and is followed by, an immediate separation[3].

A separation agreement is not abrogated where, on the outbreak of war, one party is living in enemy territory and the other is in the United Kingdom[4]. Parties who are already living apart, whether by agreement or otherwise, may enter into an agreement for the maintenance of one by the other[5].

1   This was not so formerly, voluntary separations being regarded as encroaching on the jurisdiction of the ecclesiastical courts in matrimonial causes, and it was only gradually that the courts of equity, in particular, ceased to regard such agreements as invalid: see *Besant v Wood* (1879) 12 ChD 605 at 620, per Jessel MR; *Wilson v Wilson* (1848) 1 HL Cas 538; *Wilson v Wilson* (1854) 5 HL Cas 40; *Hunt v Hunt* (1862) 4 De GF & J 221.
2   There are qualifications to the comprehensive effectiveness of separation agreements: e g they do not prevent subsequent recovery of contribution to the cost of certain social security benefits (see PARA 217), provisions as to parental responsibility for children are not enforceable unless they are for the children's benefit (see PARA 441), and the parties cannot by contract oust the court's jurisdiction to order maintenance (see PARA 697).
3   *Re Meyrick's Settlement* [1921] 1 Ch 311 at 319; *Hunt v Hunt* (1862) 4 De GF & J 221; *Vansittart v Vansittart* (1858) 2 De G & J 249; and see *Courtney v Courtney* [1923] 2 IR 31. As to agreements for future separation see PARA 424. The execution by the husband of a separation deed at the request of a third person was a legal consideration for a promise by the third person to pay a sum of money towards the husband's debts: *Jones v Waite* (1842) 9 Cl & Fin 101, HL. As to mutual promises that are not contracts see PARA 206.
4   *Bevan v Bevan* [1955] 2 QB 227, [1955] 2 All ER 206. If statute so requires, the payments should throughout the war be made to the custodian of enemy property: *Bevan v Bevan*.
5   As to the consideration for an agreement to maintain see PARA 431; as to the court's statutory power to vary written maintenance agreements see PARA 700 et seq; and as to the validity of a provision in a written maintenance agreement restricting any right to apply to the court for maintenance see PARA 697.

424.   Void agreements; public policy.   Any agreement or settlement during cohabitation providing for the event of a future, as distinguished from an immediate, separation is void as being contrary to public policy[1]; so also is an agreement, entered into before marriage (or, presumably, the registration of a civil partnership), that the parties will afterwards live separate and apart, even if the agreement is afterwards confirmed[2]. A provision contemplating future separation contained in a deed executed by parties living apart with the object and result of bringing them together again is, however, not contrary to public policy[3].

1   See CONTRACT vol 9(1) (Reissue) PARA 864.
2   *Brodie v Brodie* [1917] P 271.
3   *Re Meyrick's Settlement* [1921] 1 Ch 311; *Lurie v Lurie* [1938] 3 All ER 156; *Ewart v Ewart* [1959] P 23 at 31, [1958] 3 All ER 561 at 564. As to gifts made with the intention of inducing married couples to live apart see PARA 222.

425.   Agreement not to sue in respect of past matters.   A clause in a separation deed by which the parties agree not to take proceedings against each other in respect of any behaviour which had taken place before the execution of the deed, or providing that in case of any proceedings in respect of any subsequent behaviour no previous misconduct is to be pleaded or alleged or to be admissible in evidence, is not, if the agreement is honestly entered into, void as being against public policy or as tending to pervert the course of justice[1].

1   *L v L* [1931] P 63. This clause is conveniently known as a 'Rose v Rose clause': see *Rose v Rose* (1883) 8 PD 98, CA. See also *Rowley v Rowley* (1864) 3 Sw & Tr 338 (affd (1866) LR 1 Sc & Div 63); *Norman v Norman* [1908] P 6; *Harris v Harris and Woodden* (1872) 21 WR 80;

Gooch v Gooch [1893] P 99; *Ehlers v Ehlers* (1915) 113 LT 1215; *Crocker v Crocker* [1921] P 25, CA; *Rosenberg v Rosenberg* (1954) Times, 16 July (deed of reconciliation held valid though parties afterwards separated). As to the effect of such a clause in the event of a subsequent petition for divorce or dissolution see PARA 438.

426.   Compromise of certain criminal proceedings.   A contract for separation is not invalid merely because it is entered into by way of compromise of criminal proceedings between the parties for an assault by one of them on the other or for any other crime which would formerly have been a misdemeanour[1].

1   *McGregor v McGregor* (1888) 21 QBD 424, CA (cross-summonses for assault withdrawn on oral agreement to live apart, the husband paying the wife a weekly sum for herself and the children, she agreeing to indemnify him against any debts contracted by her; wife entitled to sue for arrears). See also *Elworthy v Bird* (1825) 2 Sim & St 372. As to the enforceability of agreements to conceal more serious offences see CONTRACT vol 9(1) (Reissue) PARA 848.

427.   Formalities and presumption of legality.   No particular formality is necessary for the validity of a contract for separation[1]. It may be made by deed, but a mere oral agreement is binding[1]. A deed of separation may be varied by a subsequent written agreement not by deed[2]. An agreement for separation is presumed to be legal until the contrary is proved, the burden of proving illegality lying on the person alleging it[3].

1   *McGregor v McGregor* (1888) 21 QBD 424, CA; *Aldridge v Aldridge (otherwise Morton)* (1888) 13 PD 210; *Sweet v Sweet* [1895] 1 QB 12; *Lacey v Lacey* (1931) 146 LT 48 (memorandum of agreement to live separate and apart); and see *Courtney v Courtney* [1923] 2 IR 31. The intervention of a trustee for the wife was formerly necessary owing to her inability to contract with her husband (see *Walrond v Walrond* (1858) John 18), and also in some cases because spouses could not convey property directly to one another. As to the removal of these disabilities see PARA 204. A written agreement for separation is not admissible in evidence unless stamped: *Fengl v Fengl* [1914] P 274. An oral agreement was inferred, although the husband had refused to sign a written agreement, in *Peters' Executors v IRC* [1941] 2 All ER 620, CA.
2   *Berry v Berry* [1929] 2 KB 316.
3   *Jones v Waite* (1842) 9 Cl & Fin 101, HL; *Clough v Lambert* (1839) 10 Sim 174.

428.   Separation articles.   An executory contract for separation, formerly called separation articles, may be specifically enforced[1]. There is, however, an important difference, as regards illegal provisions, between separation articles and a separation deed. If any portion of an executory contract is contrary to public policy or otherwise illegal, specific performance will not be granted of any part of it[2], whereas, if some of the clauses in a separation deed are legal and others illegal, those which are legal may be enforceable by the courts[3].

1   *Wilson v Wilson* (1848) 1 HL Cas 538 at 572; *Vansittart v Vansittart* (1858) 2 De G & J 249, considered in *Cahill v Cahill* (1883) 8 App Cas 420 at 430 et seq, HL.
2   *Vansittart v Vansittart* (1858) 2 De G & J 249; *Walrond v Walrond* (1858) John 18.
3   *Hamilton v Hector* (1872) LR 13 Eq 511; and see *Bennett v Bennett* [1952] 1 KB 249, [1952] 1 All ER 413, CA.

429.   Fraud and misrepresentation.   If one of the parties to a contract for separation is induced to enter into it by a fraudulent misrepresentation with reference to material facts, such as the previous misconduct of the other party, or in ignorance of material facts fraudulently concealed, the contract is voidable at the instance of the party deceived[1] and the deed may be ordered to be rescinded[2]. This rule applies even where it is agreed that all past causes of complaint are to be condoned, if the contract is made in reliance on a positive assertion of innocence[3]. Where the misrepresentation was not fraudulent, the party deceived may nevertheless be entitled to rescind if the misrepresentation has become a term of the contract[4]. A fraudulent misrepresentation which is not believed is no ground for setting the contract aside[5].

1 *Evans v Carrington* (1860) 2 De GF & J 481 (deed executed by husband in ignorance of wife's previous adultery, fraudulently concealed); *Evans v Edmonds* (1853) 13 CB 777 (wife's trustee represented that she was virtuous and moral, whereas he had committed adultery with her; contract voidable, although it was not shown that the wife was privy to the misrepresentation); *Crabb v Crabb* (1868) LR 1 P & D 601 (wife not bound by separation agreement as husband never had any intention of fulfilling it). Cf *Wales v Wadham* [1977] 2 All ER 125, [1977] 1 WLR 199 (where after his wife's remarriage a husband claimed that he had been induced to enter into a separation agreement by her false representation that she would not remarry, and it was held that in the circumstances there were no grounds for setting the agreement aside as the wife was under no contractual duty to disclose to her husband her intention to remarry, the agreement not being a contract uberrimae fidei).

2 *Hulton v Hulton* [1917] 1 KB 813, CA (false representations and concealment by husband as to means). See also *J-PC v J-AF* [1955] P 215, sub nom *J v J* [1955] 2 All ER 617, CA; *Payne v Payne* [1968] 1 All ER 1113, [1968] 1 WLR 390, CA; *Wilkins v Wilkins* [1969] 2 All ER 463, [1969] 1 WLR 922; *Wales v Wadham* [1977] 2 All ER 125, [1977] 1 WLR 199 (cited in note 1).

3 *Brown v Brown* (1868) LR 7 Eq 185 (covenant by husband to condone all past causes of complaint and take no proceedings in reference to them, wife positively asserting her innocence).

4 See the Misrepresentation Act 1967 s 1; and CONTRACT vol 9(1) (Reissue) PARA 987.

5 *Wasteneys v Wasteneys* [1900] AC 446, PC.

430. Duress and mistake. A person will not be bound by a separation agreement to which she is induced to consent by threats of violence[1] or other undue pressure[2] on the part of the other party. Threats of proceedings for dissolution, nullity or judicial or legal separation are not, however, such duress as will entitle either party to resist performance of an agreement for separation, even in the case of a threat by the wife of a nullity suit on the ground of the husband's impotence[3]. A contract for separation entered into under a mutual mistake of fact which is material to the existence of the agreement, such as a mistake as to the validity of the marriage or civil partnership, is void[4].

1 *Lambert v Lambert* (1767) 2 Bro Parl Cas 18, HL.

2 *Adamson v Adamson* (1907) 23 TLR 434 (husband and his solicitor told wife that the only way to get any money was to sign the agreement, otherwise the husband would leave her, and she would get nothing; she had no independent advice; she was not bound by the agreement); *Holroyd v Holroyd* (1920) 36 TLR 479 (similar case); and see *Crabb v Crabb* (1868) LR 1 P & D 601; and cf *Biffin v Bignell* (1862) 7 H & N 877; *de Pret-Roose v de Pret-Roose* (1934) 78 Sol Jo 914 (threat by husband to remove children not amounting to duress). As to duress generally see CONTRACT vol 9(1) (Reissue) PARAS 710, 711; and as to undue influence see CONTRACT vol 9(1) (Reissue) PARA 712 et seq; MISREPRESENTATION AND FRAUD vol 31 (2003 Reissue) PARA 839 et seq. The burden of proving undue influence is on the party who alleges it: *Gillman v Gillman* (1946) 174 LT 272. The court will not look with favour on assignments of proprietary interests in the matrimonial home made without legal advice: see *Backhouse v Backhouse* [1978] 1 All ER 1158 at 1166, [1978] 1 WLR 243 at 252.

3 *Wilson v Wilson* (1848) 1 HL Cas 538 at 572.

4 *Galloway v Galloway* (1914) 30 TLR 531; *Law v Harragin* (1917) 33 TLR 381; and see *Butcher v Vale* (1891) 8 TLR 93; *Wilkins v Wilkins* [1969] 2 All ER 463, [1969] 1 WLR 922; *B (GC) v B (BA)* [1970] 1 All ER 913, sub nom *Brister v Brister* [1970] 1 WLR 664. As to mistake of fact generally see CONTRACT vol 9(1) (Reissue) PARA 703 et seq.

431. Valuable consideration. In a separation deed or agreement, the mere agreement to live apart is sufficient valuable consideration[1], whether for the purpose of enforcing specific performance of separation articles[2] no part of which is contrary to public policy[3], or for supporting a separation deed or agreement against creditors or subsequent purchasers[4].

Where a husband and wife who were already living apart entered into an agreement for the maintenance of the wife by the husband, consideration on the wife's part for the husband's covenant to maintain was afforded by a covenant by the wife to support herself out of the maintenance payments[5].

1   A separation agreement was formerly regarded as voluntary, unless there was some valuable consideration on both sides beyond the mere covenants to live apart. This principle was partly founded on the former incapacity of a husband and wife to contract with one another (see *Walrond v Walrond* (1858) John 18) and partly on the view formerly held that separations by agreement were contrary to public policy (see PARA 423 note 1). For examples of valuable consideration see *Stephens v Olive* (1786) 2 Bro CC 90; *Hobbs v Hull* (1788) 1 Cox Eq Cas 445; *Worrall v Jacob* (1817) 3 Mer 256; *Jee v Thurlow* (1824) 2 B & C 547; *Logan v Birkett* (1833) 1 My & K 220; *Wellesley v Wellesley* (1839) 10 Sim 256; *Jodrell v Jodrell* (1845) 9 Beav 45; *Wilson v Wilson* (1848) 1 HL Cas 538; *Walrond v Walrond*; *Vansittart v Vansittart* (1858) 2 De G & J 249; *Gibbs v Harding* (1870) 5 Ch App 336; *Marshall v Marshall* (1879) 5 PD 19; *Hart v Hart* (1881) 18 ChD 670; *Aldridge v Aldridge (otherwise Morton)* (1888) 13 PD 210; *McGregor v McGregor* (1888) 21 QBD 424, CA; *Re Pope, ex p Dicksee* [1908] 2 KB 169, CA; *Hulse v Hulse* (1910) 103 LT 804. *Horton v Horton (No 2)* [1961] 1 QB 215, [1960] 3 All ER 649, CA (consideration for supplemental agreement was the compromise of a possible claim for rectification of the original agreement).
2   As to separation articles see PARA 428.
3   As to agreements and covenants contrary to public policy see PARAS 424, 698; and CONTRACT vol 9(1) (Reissue) PARA 841.
4   See *Re Weston, Davies v Tagart* [1900] 2 Ch 164 (wife living apart in pursuance of her covenant: held valuable consideration and sufficient to support an assignment of property to trustees for her benefit against the husband's trustee in bankruptcy); *Aldridge v Aldridge (otherwise Morton)* (1888) 13 PD 210 (mutual agreements to live apart and not to sue one another for nullity of the marriage; the agreement of each was sufficient valuable consideration to support the agreement by the other not to sue); and see *McGregor v McGregor* (1888) 21 QBD 424, CA; *Courtney v Courtney* [1923] 2 IR 31.
5   See *Williams v Williams* [1957] 1 All ER 305, [1957] 1 WLR 148, CA. As to the court's statutory power to vary written maintenance agreements see PARA 700 et seq.

B. CONSTRUCTION AND OPERATION

432.   Usual clauses.   In an agreement entered into for the execution of a separation deed 'with the usual covenants and clauses', 'usual' is to be construed with reference to the surrounding circumstances and to the conveyancing practice and custom in such cases[1]. The 'usual clauses' have included a covenant by the husband to permit the wife to live separate and apart without molestation or interference by him and a covenant by the wife to indemnify the husband against debts contracted by her during the separation[2].

A condition that the wife would remain chaste (a 'dum casta' clause) was not a 'usual clause' and would not be implied, whether in a separation agreed to as part of a compromise of a divorce suit[3] or otherwise[4].

1   *Hart v Hart* (1881) 18 ChD 670 at 687.
2   See *Wilson v Wilson* (1854) 5 HL Cas 40; *Hart v Hart* (1881) 18 ChD 670 at 684; *Gibbs v Harding* (1870) 5 Ch App 336; and PARAS 434 (non-molestation), 435 (indemnity). The wife may also indemnify the husband against debts incurred before the deed, but this is not usual: *Brailey v Brailey* [1922] P 15, CA.
3   *Hart v Hart* (1881) 18 ChD 670.
4   *Fearon v Earl of Aylesford* (1884) 14 QBD 792, CA. See also PARA 438.

433.   Estoppel where deed acted on.   Where a wife acted on a deed of separation and accepted benefits under it, she was estopped from denying that she had contracted; and a recital in a deed to which she was a party of an agreement to live apart was sufficient evidence of a contract by her to that effect[1].

1   *Clark v Clark* (1885) 10 PD 188, CA; *Re Weston, Davies v Tagart* [1900] 2 Ch 164.

434.   Covenant not to molest.   To amount to molestation something must be done by one party, or on his or her authority, with the intention of annoying the other, and it must be an annoyance in fact[1]. Where a spouse's intention in petitioning for divorce was primarily to annoy the other spouse, that act has been held to amount to molestation, but there would be no breach of the covenant if the intention is primarily to bring the marriage to an end[2].

1   *Fearon v Earl of Aylesford* (1884) 14 QBD 792, CA (adultery by wife, even though followed by birth of an illegitimate child, held not to be a breach of a covenant not to molest the husband; but to put the child forward as legitimate would be such a breach); and see *Besant v Wood* (1879) 12 ChD 605; *Sweet v Sweet* [1895] 1 QB 12.
2   *Hunt v Hunt* [1897] 2 QB 547, CA (divorce proceedings by husband abroad; held not a molestation in absence of intention to annoy). The same applies to petitions for judicial or legal separation: *Thomas v Everard* (1861) 6 H & N 448. It would now be difficult to establish such molestation.

435.   Covenant to indemnify against debts.   A covenant in general terms to indemnify the husband against the wife's debts was held to extend to costs incurred by the husband in defending actions on her contracts for necessaries[1]; and a covenant of indemnity against debts which the wife had then contracted, or should thereafter contract during the separation, was held to include debts for necessaries contracted by the wife as agent for the husband while they were living together[2]. The indemnity is, however, confined to debts contracted during the separation unless the contrary is expressed[3].

1   *Duffield v Scott* (1789) 3 Term Rep 374.
2   *Summers v Ball* (1841) 8 M & W 596; *Brailey v Brailey* [1922] P 15, CA.
3   See note 2.

436.   How far provisions construed as permanent.   The extent to which the provisions of a separation deed are to be regarded as permanent, and how far they are to be construed as limited to the period during which the separation continues, depends on the intention of the parties, to be ascertained from the terms of the deed as a whole and the circumstances of the particular case[1]. An agreement to pay maintenance while the parties live apart is not necessarily an agreement that one party agrees to the other living apart; the question is one of construction of the particular agreement[2].

Provisions relating to the settlement of property will be construed as permanent unless a contrary intention plainly appears[3]. A covenant by one party for payment of an annuity to the other will be construed as permanent, or as limited to the time during which they remain separated, according to the expressed or presumed intention of the parties[4]. The fact that the first party covenants to pay the annuity during the other's life is some indication of an intention that it should be permanent, but is not conclusive[5]. Where a covenant for the payment of an annuity is regarded as a permanent provision, it is enforceable against the payer's executors or administrators after his death[6].

An annuity for maintenance and support payable under a separation deed, unless made payable in advance[7], accrues from day to day, and is apportionable in the event of the recipient's death between the dates fixed for the payment of instalments[8], but such an annuity is not assignable by the recipient[9].

1   *Randle v Gould* (1857) 8 E & B 457; *Rowell v Rowell* [1900] 1 QB 9, CA; *Wilson v Mushett* (1832) 3 B & Ad 743; and see PARA 447.
2   See *Crabtree v Crabtree* [1953] 2 All ER 56, [1953] 1 WLR 708, CA; *Lord Long of Wraxall v Lady Long of Wraxall* [1940] 4 All ER 230, 233, CA; *Bosley v Bosley* [1958] 2 All ER 167, [1958] 1 WLR 645, CA; *Parkinson v Parkinson* (1959) Times, 14 April, DC; and PARA 373.
3   *Ruffles v Alston* (1875) LR 19 Eq 539 (wife entitled to money secured by her brother's promissory note; on a separation the brother covenanted to hold the money in trust for the wife and husband successively for their lives, and then for the children; it was held that there was a permanent settlement); *Negus v Forster* (1882) 46 LT 675, CA; *Re Spark's Trusts, Spark v Massey* [1904] 1 Ch 451; compromised [1904] 2 Ch 121, CA (funds vested in trustee in trust for wife and children; it was held that there was a permanent settlement). Cf *O'Malley v Blease* (1869) 20 LT 899.
4   See *Kirk v Eustace* [1937] AC 491, [1937] 2 All ER 715, HL (covenant by husband to pay weekly sum to wife 'during her life'; death of husband; husband's estate remained liable to pay weekly sum to widow); cf *Langstone v Hayes* [1946] KB 109, [1946] 1 All ER 114, CA (covenant by husband to pay annuity to wife, until annuity determined as thereafter provided; annuity to be determined on resumption of cohabitation; terms of deed assumed husband to be still alive; husband's estate not liable). See also *Goslin v Clark* (1862) 12 CBNS 681 (covenant to pay annuity during life of wife held permanent); *Clough v Lambert* (1839) 10 Sim 174; *Randle v Gould* (1857) 8 E & B 457; *Rowell v Rowell* [1900] 1 QB 9, CA; *Nicol v Nicol* (1886) 31 ChD 524, CA; *Negus v Forster* (1882) 46 LT 675, CA; *Chapman v Guest* (1887) 3 TLR 438; *Crouch v Waller* (1859) 4 De G & J 302; *Re Gilling, Procter v Watkins* (1905) 74 LJ Ch 335.
5   See note 4.
6   *Kirk v Eustace* [1937] AC 491, [1937] 2 All ER 715, HL; *Clough v Lambert* (1839) 10 Sim 174; *Atkinson v Littlewood* (1874) LR 18 Eq 595; cf *Re Gilling, Procter v Watkins* (1905) 74 LJ Ch 335; *Macnaghten v Paterson* [1907] AC 483, PC (provision for payment of annuity with power to reduce the amount). Where provision is made for payments to be reduced on a diminution of income, executors are not bound to sell non-income bearing assets of the estate to prevent a reduction in payments: see *Re Korda* (1957) Times, 23 November; affd (1958) Times, 19 July, CA. As to the alteration by the court of an agreement after the death of one of the parties see PARA 700 et seq.
7   *Trevalion v Anderton* (1897) 66 LJQB 489, CA.
8   See the Apportionment Act 1870 ss 2, 3; *Howell v Hanforth* (1775) 2 Wm Bl 1016; and RENTCHARGES AND ANNUITIES vol 39(2) (Reissue) PARA 839 et seq.
9   *Hyde v Price* (1797) 3 Ves 437.

437. Trust for benefit of children. A trust in a separation deed for the benefit of children is construed, prima facie, as including only children born or conceived prior to the separation, and not those who may be born after a reconciliation and resumption of cohabitation[1].

1   *Hulme v Chitty* (1846) 9 Beav 437; and see *Re Spark's Trusts, Spark v Massey* [1904] 1 Ch 451; compromised [1904] 2 Ch 121, CA.

438. Subsequent misconduct. A covenant or agreement by either party not to take proceedings for divorce or dissolution or judicial or legal separation on the basis of any existing fact from which irretrievable breakdown may be inferred is not a bar to proceedings in the event, and on the basis, of subsequent conduct from which such a breakdown may be inferred[1]. Where there has been express condonation by deed of all behaviour before the date of the deed one party cannot rely, as between himself and the other party, on that other party's conduct before the date of the deed for the purpose of a petition for divorce or dissolution[2].

It has been held that there is no implied condition in a contract for separation that the wife will remain chaste[3]; and, in the absence of a dum casta clause, the wife's subsequent adultery is no defence, either at law or in equity, to an action against the husband on his covenant to pay her an annuity[4].

1   *Kunski v Kunski* (1907) 23 TLR 615; and see *Dowling v Dowling* [1898] P 228; *Bourne v Bourne* [1913] P 164; *Ehlers v Ehlers* (1915) 113 LT 1215; *Thompson v Thompson* [1916] P

165; *Lister v Lister* [1922] P 227. As to the facts from which irretrievable breakdown may be inferred see PARA 347; and as to the validity of such an agreement see PARA 425.

2   *Rowley v Rowley* (1864) 3 Sw & Tr 338; *Rose v Rose* (1883) 8 PD 98, CA; and see PARA 347. As to petitions and applications see PARA 321 note 1.

3   *Fearon v Earl of Aylesford* (1884) 14 QBD 792, CA; and see PARA 432.

4   *Wasteneys v Wasteneys* [1900] AC 446, PC; *Sweet v Sweet* [1895] 1 QB 12; *Hart v Hart* (1881) 18 ChD 670; *Fearon v Earl of Aylesford* (1884) 14 QBD 792, CA; *Jee v Thurlow* (1824) 2 B & C 547; *Baynon v Batley* (1832) 8 Bing 256. An unconditional covenant to pay an annuity in a separation deed will be restricted by a recital of an agreement to pay dum casta: *Crouch v Crouch* [1912] 1 KB 378. As to the effect of divorce see PARA 442.

439.   Effect of breach.   A breach of the provisions of a contract for separation does not preclude the party committing the breach from setting up and enforcing the contract, unless the breach is of such a deliberate and substantial nature as to amount to a repudiation of the contract[1]. Covenants for the payment of an annuity, covenants for the maintenance of children and non-molestation covenants will be construed as independent covenants in the absence of an express provision making one dependent on the other[2].

1   *Durand v Durand* (1789) 2 Cox Eq Cas 207; *Besant v Wood* (1879) 12 ChD 605 at 627; *Kunski v Kunski* (1898) 68 LJP 18 (default by husband in payment of weekly allowance not sufficient to prevent his setting up the contract); *Kennedy v Kennedy* [1907] P 49 (husband ceased to pay allowance, and expressed his intention to make no further payments; held to be a repudiation by husband); *Balcombe v Balcombe* [1908] P 176; and see *Smith v Smith* [1915] P 288; *Roe v Roe* [1916] P 163.

2   *Fearon v Earl of Aylesford* (1884) 14 QBD 792, CA (where molestation by the wife was held no defence to an action for recovery of the annuity); *Crouch v Waller* (1859) 4 De G & J 302 (where the wife was held unfit to have the custody of the children).

440.   Satisfaction of annuity by legacy.   Whether a bequest by will of one party operates as a satisfaction of an annuity which he has contracted to pay to the other party by a separation deed depends on the ordinary rules as to the satisfaction of debts by legacies[1].

1   *Atkinson v Littlewood* (1874) LR 18 Eq 595 (bequest of annuity of same amount as under separation deed; the widow was put to her election); *Horlock v Wiggins, Wiggins v Horlock* (1888) 39 ChD 142, CA (separation deed and will contemporaneous; legacy held not a satisfaction); *Coates v Coates* [1898] 1 IR 258 (covenant to pay 15 shillings a week for life; bequest of 12 shillings a week for life and the use of a house and furniture was not a satisfaction); *Re Manners, Public Trustee v Manners* [1949] Ch 613, [1949] 2 All ER 201, CA (separation deed providing for annuity of £250 for life; bequest of sum for purchase of annuity of £250 was, on construction, no satisfaction).

441.   Provisions as to parental responsibility and contact.   Provisions in a separation agreement as to parental responsibility for and contact with children will not be enforced by the court as, in proceedings where the parental responsibility for or upbringing of a minor is in question, its duty is to regard the minor's welfare as the first and paramount consideration[1], although as part of the exercise of this duty it may have regard to the agreement reached by the parties. Although the court will not enforce the parental responsibility and contact provisions, the other provisions of the agreement are not thereby rendered unenforceable[2].

Where one party undertakes to support children for whom he or she has parental responsibility and the other party covenants to pay an annuity, that other party's liability on the covenant is not necessarily affected by the fact that the children are removed from his or her parental responsibility on the ground of his or her unfitness[3].

In relation to a covenant for their maintenance in a separation deed, the children are not in the position of beneficiaries and have no right of action on that covenant[4].

1   See the Children Act 1989 s 1; and CHILDREN AND YOUNG PERSONS vol 5(3) (2008 Reissue) PARA 300 et seq.
2   See *Jump v Jump* (1883) 8 PD 159.
3   *Crouch v Waller* (1859) 4 De G & J 302; and see *Rowell v Rowell* (1903) 89 LT 288, CA (where the husband covenanted to pay an additional weekly sum to the wife for the maintenance and education of a son as long as he was under 21, and it was held that the husband was not relieved of his liability to pay the additional sum merely because the son was maintained and educated at little expense to the wife).
4   *Gandy v Gandy* (1885) 30 ChD 57, CA; and see *Crouch v Waller* (1859) 4 De G & J 302.

442. Effect of divorce, dissolution, annulment and judicial or legal separation. A dissolution or annulment of the marriage (or, presumably, the civil partnership) does not of itself affect those provisions of a separation agreement which constitute a permanent settlement of property, nor a party's liability on a covenant to pay an annuity to the other by way of a permanent provision[1]; but such provisions may be varied by the court in pursuance of its jurisdiction with regard to the variation of settlements[2], or its general power to alter financial arrangements contained in separation deeds[3].

The provisions of a separation agreement are not affected by a decree of judicial or legal separation as such, but the court has jurisdiction to make orders as to financial provision and property adjustment[4] and may alter financial arrangements in the agreement in certain circumstances[5].

1   *Charlesworth v Holt* (1873) LR 9 Exch 38 (covenant to pay an annuity during the spouses' joint lives so long as they should live separate and apart; it was held that the obligation was not limited to the duration of the marriage and that a dissolution of the marriage on the ground of the wife's adultery did not affect the husband's liability on the covenant); *May v May* [1929] 2 KB 386, CA. For a different result on the construction of a particular agreement see *Covell v Sweetland* [1968] 2 All ER 1016, [1968] 1 WLR 1466 (agreement ceased on decree absolute). See also *Rowley v Rowley* (1866) LR 1 Sc & Div 63, HL; *Grant v Budd* (1874) 30 LT 319; *Goslin v Clark* (1862) 12 CBNS 681; c f *Re Gilling, Procter v Watkins* (1905) 74 LJ Ch 335. See also *Adams v Adams* [1941] 1 KB 536, [1941] 1 All ER 334, CA (deed not affected by decree of nullity on ground of physical incapacity); *Fowke v Fowke* [1938] Ch 774, [1938] 2 All ER 638; and PARA 436 note 4.
2   *Worsley v Worsley and Wignall* (1869) LR 1 P & D 648 (covenant by husband to pay annuity for joint lives); *Benyon v Benyon and O'Callaghan* (1876) 1 PD 447 (husband, having received an allowance from the wife under a separation deed, held entitled, in a suit for dissolution of the marriage on the ground of her subsequent adultery, to apply to the court for an increased provision out of her income); and see *Cooper v Cooper and Ford* [1932] P 75; *Tomkins v Tomkins* [1948] P 170, [1948] 1 All ER 237, CA (husband's covenant to pay weekly sum during joint lives discharged). As to the variation of settlements generally see PARA 510 et seq.
3   As to this power see PARA 700 et seq.
4   See PARA 419 et seq.
5   See PARA 700 et seq.

C. REMEDIES FOR BREACH

443. Specific performance. The remedy for a refusal by either party to carry out the terms of an executory agreement for separation is an action for specific performance[1]. In order to maintain such an action it is not necessary that there should be any valuable consideration other than the mutual promises to separate and live apart[2].

In an action for specific performance of separation articles, the court will not inquire into the cause of the separation[3].

1   *Besant v Wood* (1879) 12 ChD 605; *Wilson v Wilson* (1848) 1 HL Cas 538 (agreement for separation in consideration of abandonment by wife of proceedings for nullity of marriage); *Hart v Hart* (1881) 18 ChD 670 (agreement for separation by way of compromise of proceedings for divorce); *Seeling v Crawley* (1700) 2 Vern 386; *Guth v Guth* (1792) 3 Bro CC 614 (offer by husband to resume cohabitation no answer to action for specific performance); *Fletcher v Fletcher* (1788) 2 Cox Eq Cas 99; and see *R v Mead* (1758) 1 Burr 542; *Lord Vane's Case* (1744) 13 East 171n at 173n; and *R v Winton* (1792) 5 Term Rep 89 (where a writ of habeas corpus was applied for to discharge a wife who was detained by the husband notwithstanding an agreement of separation). A wife may sue her husband for breach of a separation deed entered into when both parties were domiciled in England, notwithstanding that at the date of the issue of the writ the husband is domiciled abroad: *Drexel v Drexel* [1916] 1 Ch 251. As to the principle that a breach of a contract for separation does not necessarily preclude the party committing the breach from enforcing the contract see PARA 439.
2   See PARA 431.
3   *Wilson v Wilson* (1848) 1 HL Cas 538 at 574. As to separation articles see PARA 428.

444.   Injunction.   An injunction may be granted restraining either party to a contract for separation from molesting the other party[1] or from otherwise committing a breach of an enforceable provision of the contract[2]. Proceedings which have actually been begun in breach of the contract cannot be restrained by injunction[3], the remedy in such case being to plead the contract by way of defence in the proceedings[4].

1   *Sanders v Rodway* (1852) 16 Beav 207 at 211. As to non-molestation orders generally see PARA 716 et seq.
2   *Besant v Wood* (1879) 12 ChD 605. As to void agreements and provisions see PARAS 424, 697.
3   *Marshall v Marshall* (1879) 5 PD 19; *Clark v Clark* (1885) 10 PD 188, CA. See also the Supreme Court Act 1981 s 49(3); and INJUNCTIONS vol 24 (Reissue) PARA 945.
4   *Marshall v Marshall* (1879) 5 PD 19; *Clark v Clark* (1885) 10 PD 188, CA; *Gandy v Gandy* (1882) 7 PD 168, CA; *Aldridge v Aldridge (otherwise Morton)* (1888) 13 PD 210 (nullity suit); cf *Bishop v Bishop, Judkins v Judkins* [1897] P 138, CA. A separation agreement may be a bar to proceedings for divorce, dissolution or judicial or legal separation founded on desertion: see PARA 371.

445.   Breach of covenant.   A wife may sue her husband on his covenants with her in a separation agreement[1]; presumably the same is true of civil partners. To entitle a third person, not a party to the agreement, to sue either of the contracting parties, the third person must possess an actual beneficial right which places him in the position of a beneficiary[2]. A volunteer who is a party to a separation deed and a direct covenantee under it is entitled to damages for breach of a covenant contained in the deed[3].

1   As to the right of a husband and wife to sue one another in contract see PARA 206. Formerly, where a trustee was joined for the wife, she could sue her husband on his covenants with her trustee if the trustee refused to do so: *Gandy v Gandy* (1885) 30 ChD 57, CA; and see *Archard v Coulsting* (1843) 6 Man & G 75 (where the wife sued in the names of her trustee's executors on giving them security for costs).
2   *Gandy v Gandy* (1885) 30 ChD 57, CA. See generally CONTRACT vol 9(1) (Reissue) PARA 762; EQUITY vol 16(2) (Reissue) PARA 609. As to trusts for the benefit of children see PARA 437.
3   *Cannon v Hartley* [1949] Ch 213, [1949] 1 All ER 50 (action by a daughter who was a party to a deed of separation between her parents for breach by her father of a covenant to settle after-acquired property).

446.   Proof for annuity in bankruptcy.   An annuity covenanted to be paid in a separation deed is a debt provable in the payer's bankruptcy, and no claim in respect of the annuity can afterwards be maintained by the recipient[1]. The estimated value of such an annuity may be proved for, even if it is determinable on the happening of specified events[2].

1   *Victor v Victor* [1912] 1 KB 247, CA; *McQuiban v McQuiban* [1913] P 208; *Dewe v Dewe, Snowdon v Snowdon* [1928] P 113.
2   *Re Batey, ex p Neal* (1880) 14 ChD 579, CA; and see BANKRUPTCY AND INDIVIDUAL INSOLVENCY vol 3(2) (2002 Reissue) PARA 503. Where the recipient or their trustee proves for the ascertained value of such an annuity and receives a dividend, there is no obligation to refund any portion of the dividend merely because, by reason of the recipient's death, the amount of the dividend may happen to exceed the sum which would have been payable by the payer if he had remained solvent: *Re Pannell, ex p Bates* (1879) 11 ChD 914, CA.

D. EFFECT OF RECONCILIATION

447. Whether agreement determined. A separation agreement sometimes contains an express provision that, in the event of a reconciliation and the resumption of cohabitation, the provisions of the agreement are to cease; but it may be expressly provided that certain trusts are to continue notwithstanding an agreement by the parties to live together again[1]. In the absence of express provision, the question to what extent a contract for separation is affected by a reconciliation depends on the intention of the parties to be ascertained from the terms of the contract as a whole and the circumstances of the particular case[2].

Where a covenant for payment of an annuity is to be construed as limited to the period of separation[3], a subsequent agreement that if the recipient will return to cohabitation the payer will continue the payment is valid, and will have the effect of making the annuity permanent[4].

1   *Wilson v Mushett* (1832) 3 B & Ad 743.
2   See PARA 436; and see *Marquis of Westmeath v Marchioness of Westmeath* (1831) 1 Dow & Cl 519; *Bateman v Countess of Ross* (1813) 1 Dow 235, HL; *Angier v Angier* (1718) Gilb Ch 152; *O'Malley v Blease* (1869) 20 LT 899. In the case of a separation deed between unmarried parties who had cohabited, it was held that an annuity granted by the deed did not cease on a resumption of cohabitation: *Re Abdy, Rabbeth v Donaldson* [1895] 1 Ch 455, CA.
3   See PARA 436.
4   *Webster v Webster* (1853) 4 De GM & G 437.

448. Arrears of annuity. The fact that the parties are reconciled and resume cohabitation does not of itself operate as an accord and satisfaction of arrears, accrued during the separation, of an agreed allowance, even if the allowance was payable only during the continuance of the separation[1].

1   *Macan v Macan* (1900) 70 LJQB 90.

449. Resumption of cohabitation necessary. The mere circumstance that the parties cease to be separated, in the sense that they reside together in a state of hostility, is not sufficient to terminate the provisions of a separation agreement[1], nor is a reconciliation, as evidenced by friendly correspondence, without a resumption of cohabitation[2]. Casual acts of sexual intercourse are not alone conclusive evidence that the parties have ceased to live apart within the meaning of a separation deed[3].

1   *Bateman v Countess of Ross* (1813) 1 Dow 235, HL.
2   *Frampton v Frampton* (1841) 4 Beav 287.
3   *Rowell v Rowell* [1900] 1 QB 9, CA. As to resumption of cohabitation generally see PARAS 403–405.

7. FINANCIAL RELIEF

(1) FINANCIAL RELIEF ON DIVORCE, DISSOLUTION, NULLITY, SEPARATION AND PRESUMPTION OF DEATH

(i) Financial Provision Orders

A. SCOPE AND EFFECT OF ORDERS

450. Meaning of 'financial provision order'. A financial provision order is an order for periodical payments or lump sum provision available[1] for the purpose of adjusting the financial position of the parties to a marriage or a civil partnership, and children, in connection with proceedings for divorce, dissolution, nullity or judicial or legal separation, that is to say:

(1)　　any order for periodical payments in favour of a party to a marriage or civil partnership or in favour of a child of the family[2];

(2)　　any order for secured periodical payments in favour of a party to a marriage or civil partnership or in favour of a child of the family[3]; and

(3)　　any order for lump sum provision in favour of a party to a marriage or civil partnership or in favour of a child of the family[4].

Any order for the attachment of pension income[5] is a financial provision order rather than any new or distinct species of order[6].

Either party to a marriage or civil partnership may apply for a financial provision order[7]; and one party may institute proceedings seeking financial relief in favour of the other party against himself or herself[8].

1　Ie under the Matrimonial Causes Act 1973 and the Civil Partnership Act 2004 see PARA 458 et seq. 'Financial provision order' is defined, in the terms set out in the text, by the Family Proceedings Rules 1991, SI 1991/1247, r 1.2 (definition substituted by SI 2005/2922), citing the orders mentioned in the Matrimonial Causes Act 1973 s 21(1) and the Civil Partnership 2004 Sch 5 paras 2(1), 80(1).

2　See PARAS 458 et seq, 492 et seq.

3　See PARAS 467 et seq, 492 et seq.

4　See PARAS 476 et seq, 492 et seq.

5　Ie under the Matrimonial Causes Act 1973 s 25B or the Civil Partnership Act 2004 Sch 5 para 24: see PARA 485 et seq.

6　*T v T (financial relief: pensions)* [1998] 2 FCR 364, [1998] 1 FLR 1072.

7　See the Matrimonial Causes Act 1973 s 23; the Civil Partnership Act 2004 Sch 5 paras 1, 2; and PARA 458 et seq. For applications by husbands against their wives see *Griffiths v Griffiths* [1974] 1 All ER 932, [1974] 1 WLR 1350, CA; *Calderbank v Calderbank* [1976] Fam 93, [1975] 3 All ER 333, CA; *P v P (financial provision: lump sum)* [1978] 3 All ER 70, [1978] 1 WLR 483, CA; *B v B (financial provision)* (1982) 3 FLR 298, sub nom *B v B* 12 Fam Law 92, CA. In seeking to achieve a fair outcome, there is no place for discrimination between the parties: *White v White* [2001] 1 AC 596, [2001] 1 All ER 1, HL; applied in *Dharamshi v Dharamshi* [2001] 1 FCR 492, [2001] 1 FLR 736, CA; *Cowan v Cowan* [2001] EWCA Civ 679, [2002] Fam 97, [2001] 2 FCR 331.

8　*Simister v Simister* [1987] 1 All ER 233, [1986] 1 WLR 1463; *Peacock v Peacock* [1984] 1 All ER 1069, [1984] 1 WLR 532; *Sherdley v Sherdley* [1988] AC 213, [1987] 2 All ER 54, HL; *Dart v Dart* [1997] 1 FCR 21, [1996] 2 FLR 286, CA.

451. Relationship of financial provision and property adjustment orders. Financial provision orders[1] and property adjustment orders[2] are inter-related, particularly in relation to the family home and lump sum payments, and the court ought not ordinarily to look at the various reliefs in isolation from one another[3]. Nor is it usually necessary to decide the exact property rights of the parties as against one another. Where, however, assets are owned jointly with third parties, precise ascertainment of the beneficial interests of the parties may be necessary[4]. The court is particularly concerned with preserving homes for the parties and their children[5].

The court should state what new trusts or dispositions are to be effected in consequence of its orders[6].

1 See PARA 450.
2 See PARA 498 et seq.
3 *Button v Button* [1968] 1 All ER 1064 at 1067, [1968] 1 WLR 457 at 462, CA per Lord Denning MR; *Baynham v Baynham* [1969] 1 All ER 305 at 307, [1968] 1 WLR 1890 at 1894, CA per Lord Denning MR. The court should be free to make either a property adjustment order or a lump sum order whichever turns out to be the more convenient in the circumstances: *Doherty v Doherty* [1976] Fam 71 at 79, [1975] 2 All ER 635 at 640, CA per Ormrod LJ.
4 See eg *Harwood v Harwood* [1992] 1 FCR 1, [1991] 2 FLR 274, CA; and PARAS 280, 601. A spouse or civil partner must identify by reference to an established principle some proper basis for seeking to extend a financial claim to assets which appear to be held by a third party: see *A v A* [2007] EWHC 99 (Fam), [2007] 2 FLR 467.
5 *Browne (formerly Pritchard) v Pritchard* [1975] 3 All ER 721, [1975] 1 WLR 1366, CA.
6 *Jones v Jones* [1972] 3 All ER 289, [1972] 1 WLR 1269.

452. Effect of subsequent marriage or civil partnership. If after the grant of a decree dissolving or annulling a marriage or the making of a dissolution or nullity order in relation to a civil partnership either party to that marriage or civil partnership forms a subsequent marriage or civil partnership[1], that party is not entitled to apply, by reference to the grant of that decree or to that dissolution or nullity order, for a financial provision order[2] or a property adjustment order[3] in his or her favour against the other party to that marriage or civil partnership[4].

Any application for financial relief must, therefore, be made in the correct form prior to any subsequent marriage or remarriage or the formation of a subsequent civil partnership by the intended applicant. It has been held that a party who has remarried cannot rely on the fact that the other party has made an application in order to confer jurisdiction on the court to make an order in his or her favour; if he or she seeks an order, he or she must apply for it and, if he or she has remarried before making an application, he or she is deprived of the right to apply[5].

1 References in the Matrimonial Causes Act 1973 to remarriage and to the formation of a civil partnership by a person, and references in the Civil Partnership Act 2004 Sch 5 to a subsequent marriage or a subsequent civil partnership, include references to a marriage or civil partnership which is by law void or voidable: Matrimonial Causes Act 1973 s 52(3), (3A) (s 52(3A) added by the Civil Partnership Act 2004 Sch 27 para 46); Civil Partnership Act 2004 Sch 5 para 80(4), (5). As to void and voidable marriages and civil partnerships see PARA 326 et seq.
2 As to the meaning of 'financial provision order' see PARA 450.
3 As to the property adjustment orders see PARA 498 et seq.
4 Matrimonial Causes Act 1973 s 28(3) (amended by the Matrimonial and Family Proceedings Act 1984 s 5(3); and by the Civil Partnership Act 2004 Sch 27 para 43(1), (4)); Civil Partnership Act 2004 Sch 5 para 48.
5 See *Robin v Robin* (1983) 4 FLR 632, 13 Fam Law 147, CA. In *Jackson v Jackson* [1973] Fam 99, [1973] 2 All ER 395 it was held that an application in the petition was sufficient; in *Wilson v Wilson* [1976] Fam 142, [1976] 3 All ER 464, CA it was held that an application for periodical payments in the petition did not permit a claim for a lump sum to be brought after remarriage; in *Doherty v Doherty* [1976] Fam 71, [1975] 2 All ER 635, CA it was held that an application before the remarriage for a transfer of property order carried with it the right to apply for a lump sum; in *Hargood (formerly Jenkins) v Jenkins* [1978] Fam 148, sub nom *Jenkins v Hargood (formerly Jenkins)* [1978] 3 All ER 1001 it was held that an indication in the acknowledgment of service of the petition of an intention to claim ancillary relief was

insufficient; and in *Nixon v Fox (formerly Nixon)* [1978] Fam 173, [1978] 3 All ER 995 it was held that the wife's application before her remarriage for a periodical payments order in favour of her child did not permit an application for a lump sum after her remarriage.

453.   Financial relief in nullity proceedings. The court has power to make financial and property orders on the application of either party to a marriage or civil partnership, including both parties in nullity proceedings[1]. This is so even though the marriage is void ipso jure, for example on the ground that the respondent 'wife' has a husband living at the time of her second 'marriage'[2] or in a case where the parties to the marriage ceremony are not respectively male and female[3]. Further, an order for periodical payments has been made in favour of a wife respondent against whom a decree of nullity on the ground of her wilful refusal to consummate the marriage had been made[4].

The situation now is that the court has a statutory duty to have regard to all the circumstances of the case, and the old cases, while no doubt of some assistance in some instances, must be viewed in the light of the statutory duty as interpreted by the courts[5].

1   See PARA 458 et seq. Marriages and civil partnerships which are void ipso jure (see PARA 326 et seq) are included: *Ramsay v Ramsay (otherwise Beer)* (1913) 108 LT 382. As to the principles on which such periodical provision was allotted in cases of nullity see *Gardiner (otherwise Phillips) v Gardiner* (1920) 36 TLR 294. It has been said that there is no fixed proportion, the amount depending on the particular facts of the case, and to be decided on the sense of propriety and moral justice of the court: see *Dunbar (otherwise White) v Dunbar* [1909] P 90; *Gullan v Gullan (otherwise Goodwin)* [1913] P 160; *Sharpe (otherwise Morgan) v Sharpe* [1909] P 20 (cases of impotence where there had been a marriage settlement); *Clifton (otherwise Packe) v Clifton* [1936] P 182, [1936] 2 All ER 886 (short cohabitation, the petitioner having means); and *Dailey v Dailey (otherwise Smith)* [1947] 1 All ER 847; on appeal [1947] 2 All ER 269n, CA. See also *K v K (otherwise R)* [1910] P 140 (nullity on the ground of respondent's insanity; order by consent made at the time of the decree nisi); *Gullan v Gullan (otherwise Goodwin)* [1913] P 160 (respondent's impotence); *Edwards v Edwards (otherwise Cowtan)* [1934] P 84.

2   As to the exercise of this jurisdiction see *Whiston v Whiston* [1995] Fam 198, [1998] 1 All ER 423, CA (bigamous marriage constituting criminal act); *Rampal v Rampal (No 2)* [2001] EWCA Civ 989, [2002] Fam 85, [2001] 2 FCR 552 (the authorities do not establish a rule that no bigamist is entitled to apply for financial relief; the operation of public policy on statutory claims in fields other than financial provision after divorce leads to the conclusion that the general rule is that the principle of ex turpi causa non oritur actio is not to be applied absolutely, but in the exercise of a proportionate judgment after careful scrutiny of the nature of the crime and the relevant surrounding circumstances; wife knew at the time that the marriage was bigamous and alleged bigamy after 22 years only when the husband filed proceedings for ancillary relief; husband thus not precluded from making application for ancillary relief on the grounds of public policy). See also *Ramsay v Ramsay (otherwise Beer)* (1913) 108 LT 382; but see *Bateman v Bateman (otherwise Harrison)* (1898) 78 LT 472; explaining *Wilkins v Wilkins* [1896] P 108, CA.

3   *Corbett v Corbett (otherwise Ashley)* [1971] P 83, [1970] 2 All ER 33 (operated male transsexual); and see *S-T (formerly J) v J* [1998] Fam 103, [1998] 1 All ER 431, CA (transsexual male, born female, committed perjury when making false declaration that there was no legal hindrance to marriage with a woman; subsequent application for ancillary relief by transsexual not barred in limine but refused on the facts).

4   *Dailey v Dailey (otherwise Smith)* [1947] 1 All ER 847; on appeal [1947] 2 All ER 269n, CA (where a decree of nullity on the ground of wilful refusal to consummate the marriage was made against the wife, and it was held that the fact that the husband had continued to live with his wife for 21 years was a matter to be considered under the heading 'conduct of parties'; it was also held that the court had power to order part of the maintenance to be secured for her life in the special circumstances of the case).

5   See PARA 589 et seq.

454. Financial relief in proceedings for presumption of death and dissolution of marriage or civil partnership. An order for periodical payments has been held to be available after a decree of presumption of death and dissolution[1], if the presumed deceased is in fact still alive[2]. All the financial reliefs are available in such circumstances.

1   As to presumption of death and dissolution of marriages and civil partnerships see PARA 415 et seq.

2   *Deacock v Deacock* [1958] P 230, [1958] 2 All ER 633, CA (wife respondent alive; obtained order 13 years after decree), overruling *Wall v Wall* [1950] P 112, [1949] 2 All ER 927 on this point; cf *Purse v Purse* [1981] Fam 143, [1981] 2 All ER 465, CA.

455. Order against or in favour of person suffering from mental disorder. The fact that one party is incapable through mental disorder of managing his affairs and that a receiver of his estate has been appointed does not debar the other party from claiming and obtaining orders for financial provision, including maintenance pending suit or the outcome of proceedings[1], and property adjustment[2].

Where the court[3] makes an order[4] requiring payments, including a lump sum payment, to be made, or property to be transferred, to a spouse or a civil partner, and the court is satisfied that the person in whose favour the order is made lacks capacity[5], then, subject to any order, direction or authority made or given in relation to that person[6], the court may order the payments to be made, or as the case may be, the property to be transferred, to such persons having charge of that person as the court may direct[7].

1   As to maintenance pending suit or the outcome of proceedings see PARA 456.

2   *CL v CFW* [1928] P 223 (the primary duty of those concerned with the case of a person suffering from mental disorder is to apply his estate for his maintenance). The Family Division will not usurp the jurisdiction of the Court of Protection: *Swettenham v Swettenham* [1939] 3 All ER 989, CA.

3   As to the meaning of 'court' see PARA 346 note 2.

4   Ie under the Matrimonial Causes Act 1973 Pt II (ss 21–40A) or the Civil Partnership Act 2004 Sch 5 (see PARA 458 et seq).

5   Ie within the meaning of the Mental Capacity Act 2005: see s 2; and MENTAL HEALTH vol 30(2) (Reissue) PARA 641 et seq.

6   Ie under the Mental Capacity Act 2005: see MENTAL HEALTH vol 30(2) (Reissue) PARA 641 et seq.

7   Matrimonial Causes Act 1973 s 40 (amended by the Mental Capacity Act 2005 Sch 6 para 19); Civil Partnership Act 2004 Sch 5 para 78. Note that Sch 5 para 78 has not been amended by the Mental Capacity Act 2005 so as to correspond to the amended provisions of the Matrimonial Causes Act 1973 s 40; thus the Civil Partnership Act 2004 Sch 5 para 78 continues to refer to a person being 'incapable, by reason of mental disorder within the meaning of the Mental Health Act 1983, of managing and administering his or her property and affairs' rather than to that person 'lacking capacity', and refers to being subject to any order, direction or authority made or given in relation to the relevant person under the Mental Health Act 1983 Pt VII (ss 93–113) rather than to an order, direction or authority made or given under the Mental Capacity Act 2005. However, it is submitted that the correct reading of these provisions for both marriages and civil partnerships is that set out in the text.

    As to the application of the Matrimonial Causes Act 1973 s 40 and the Civil Partnership Act 2004 Sch 5 para 78 to interim orders for maintenance under the Matrimonial and Family Proceedings Act 1984 s 1 and the Civil Partnership Act 2004 Sch 7 para 5 (see PARA 536) and to orders for financial provision and property adjustment under the Matrimonial and Family Proceedings Act 1984 s 17 and the Civil Partnership Act 2004 Sch 7 para 9 (see PARA 531), as those provisions apply to like orders under the Matrimonial Causes Act 1973 Pt II (ss 21–40A) and the Civil Partnership Act 2004 Sch 5, see the Matrimonial and Family Proceedings Act 1984 s 21; the Civil Partnership Act 2004 Sch 7 para 14; and PARA 537. As to the procedure where one party is a child or a protected party see PARA 1019 et seq.

456.   Maintenance pending suit or the outcome of proceedings.   On a petition[1] for divorce, dissolution, nullity or judicial or legal separation the court[2] may make an order requiring either spouse or civil partner to make to the other such periodical payments for his or her maintenance and for such term, being a term beginning not earlier than the date of the date on which the petition was presented and ending with the date on which proceedings are determined, as the court thinks reasonable[3]. Such maintenance is not assignable[4]. Either party may apply at any stage of the proceedings for an order under these provisions[5]; and the ability of the court to make an order commences with the presentation of the petition[6] and survives until decree absolute or dissolution order or the death of either party[7].

Although the court is not directed to consider the factors to which it is otherwise to have regard in deciding whether to exercise its powers in granting financial relief[8], those factors may nevertheless provide guidance in applications for maintenance pending suit or the outcome of proceedings. In seeking to make such orders as it thinks reasonable, the court will make a broad assessment of the parties' financial circumstances and will seek to ensure that the parties' interim needs are met pending the more extensive inquiry that will take place at the substantive hearing[9]. The order should take into account the standard of living of the parties during the marriage or civil partnership[10] and in an appropriate case the duration thereof[11], and may include an element towards the payee's costs[12].

The court will rarely embark on an inquiry about conduct at the stage at which it is adjudicating on maintenance pending suit or the outcome of proceedings[13], although in an appropriate case it may do so[14].

An order for maintenance pending suit or the outcome of proceedings may be varied, discharged, suspended in whole or in part and revived in the same manner as substantive orders for periodical payments[15]; and repayment may be ordered in certain circumstances[16].

1   As to petitions and applications see PARA 321 note 1.
2   As to the meaning of 'court' see PARA 346 note 2.
3   Matrimonial Causes Act 1973 ss 22, 52(2)(b); Civil Partnership Act 2004 Sch 5 para 38. As to the procedure on an application for such maintenance see PARA 902 et seq.
4   *Taylor (formerly Kraupl) v National Assistance Board* [1956] P 470, [1956] 2 All ER 455; on appeal on other grounds [1957] P 101, [1957] 1 All ER 183, CA; [1958] AC 532, [1957] 3 All ER 703, HL; and see *Re Robinson* (1884) 27 ChD 160, CA; *Watkins v Watkins* [1896] P 222 at 226, 227, CA per Lindley LJ; *Paquine v Snary* [1909] 1 KB 688, CA; *Campbell v Campbell* [1922] P 187 at 192; *Smith v Smith* [1923] P 191 at 204, CA per Scrutton LJ.
5   See the Family Proceedings Rules 1991, SI 1991/1247, r 2.69F; PARA 923; and *Dart v Dart* [1997] 1 FCR 21 at 28, [1996] 2 FLR 286 at 293, CA.
6   *M v M* [1928] P 123.
7   *Stanhope v Stanhope* (1886)11 PD 103, CA.
8   Ie principally under the Matrimonial Causes Act 1973 s 25 and the Civil Partnership Act 2004 Sch 5 paras 20, 21: see PARA 589 et seq.
9   See e g *Peacock v Peacock* [1984] 1 All ER 1069, [1984] 1 WLR 532; *F v F (maintenance pending suit)* (1983) 4 FLR 382, 13 Fam Law 16.
10   *T v T (financial provision)* [1990] FCR 169, sub nom *Re T (divorce: interim maintenance: discovery)* [1990] 1 FLR 1.
11   *F v F (maintenance pending suit)* (1983) 4 FLR 382, 13 Fam Law 16.
12   *A v A (maintenance pending suit: payment of legal fees)* [2001] 1 WLR 605, sub nom *A v A (maintenance pending suit: provision for legal costs)* [2001] 1 FCR 226 (wife had acute need for good representation; husband could afford to pay the sum ordered and it was reasonable to require him to do so); *G v G (maintenance pending suit: legal costs)* [2002] EWHC 306 (Fam), [2002] 3 FCR 339, [2003] 2 FLR 71.
13   *Offord v Offord* (1981) 3 FLR 309, 11 Fam Law 208.

14 *F v F (maintenance pending suit)* (1983) 4 FLR 382, 13 Fam Law 16.

15 See the Matrimonial Causes Act 1973 s 31(1), (2)(a); the Civil Partnership Act 2004 Sch 5 para 50(1)(c); and PARA 567.

16 See the Matrimonial Causes Act 1973 s 33(1), (2)(a); the Civil Partnership Act 2004 Sch 5 para 64(1), (2)(a): and PARA 573.

457. Orders under former legislation. The provisions of the Matrimonial Causes Act 1965 dealing with financial provisions[1] were repealed by the Matrimonial Proceedings and Property Act 1970; and in turn the financial provisions[2] of the 1970 Act were repealed by the Matrimonial Causes Act 1973[3]. The Matrimonial Proceedings and Property Act 1970 enacted transitional provisions and savings in respect of existing orders and applications[4], and like transitional provisions and savings appear in the Matrimonial Causes Act 1973[5].

The Matrimonial Causes Act 1965 provided for the court, on granting a decree of divorce or nullity or at any time thereafter, to make one or more of the following orders:

(1) an order requiring the husband to secure to the wife, to the satisfaction of the court, a lump or annual sum for any term not exceeding her life;

(2) an order requiring the husband to pay to the wife a monthly or weekly sum for her maintenance during their joint lives; and

(3) an order requiring the husband to pay to the wife a lump sum, provided that, where the wife petitioned for divorce on the ground of her husband's insanity, the position of the spouses was reversed and the court's power was confined to making equivalent orders against the wife and in favour of the husband[6].

The Act further provided for the court, on the grant of a decree of judicial separation or at any time thereafter, to order the payment of alimony or a lump sum or both to the wife except in a case where the wife's petition was presented on the ground of the husband's insanity, in which circumstances the court was empowered to order equivalent relief in favour of the husband[7].

All such orders, other than orders for the payment of a lump sum, may now be varied, discharged, suspended or revived as if they were orders for the making of periodical payments or secured periodical payments under the Matrimonial Causes Act 1973[8], except that an order for secured provision made before 16 December 1949 may only be varied in certain circumstances[9].

1 Ie the Matrimonial Causes Act 1965 ss 15–22 (repealed).

2 Ie the Matrimonial Proceedings and Property Act 1970 ss 1–8 (repealed).

3 Matrimonial Causes Act 1973 s 54(1), Sch 3.

4 Matrimonial Proceedings and Property Act 1970 s 28, Sch 1 (repealed). Orders made under the Matrimonial Causes Acts 1950 to 1963 were deemed to have been made under the corresponding provisions of the Matrimonial Causes Act 1965: Sch 1 para 1 (repealed).

5 Matrimonial Causes Act 1973 s 53, Sch 1 Pt III.

6 Matrimonial Causes Act 1965 ss 16(1), (3), 19 (repealed).

7 Matrimonial Causes Act 1965 s 20(1) (repealed).

8 Matrimonial Causes Act 1973 Sch 1 para 17(1), (2), applying s 31 as modified by Sch 1 para 17(3). As to the variation of orders under s 31 generally see PARAS 567, 568. Provision is also made for the variation, discharge or suspension of surviving orders for maintenance under suits for restitution of conjugal rights, abolished as a remedy by the Matrimonial Proceedings and Property Act 1970 s 20: see the Matrimonial Causes Act 1973 Sch 1 para 18.

9 Matrimonial Causes Act 1973 Sch 1 para 17(4) (which provides that such an order for secured provision may only be varied where the court is satisfied that the case is one of exceptional hardship which cannot be met by discharge, variation or suspension of any other maintenance order made or deemed to have been made under the Matrimonial Causes Act 1965 s 16(1)(b) (repealed)).

B. PERIODICAL PAYMENTS

458. Power to make order. Where the court[1]:

(1)　grants a decree of divorce, a decree of nullity of marriage or a decree of judicial separation[2]; or

(2)　makes a dissolution, nullity or separation order in respect of a civil partnership[3],

it may[4] make an order that either party to the marriage or civil partnership is to make to the other such periodical payments, for such term, as may be specified in the order (a 'periodical payments order')[5]. The court may order periodical payments to be made in a currency other than sterling but it should allow the parties to make representations about the currency in which the order will be made[6].

1　As to the meaning of 'court' see PARA 346 note 2.
2　Matrimonial Causes Act 1973 s 23(1).
3　Civil Partnership Act 2004 Sch 5 para 1(1)(a).
4　Ie on granting the decree or making the order or at any time thereafter (whether, in the case of a decree of divorce or of nullity of marriage, before or after the decree is made absolute): Matrimonial Causes Act 1973 s 23(1); Civil Partnership Act 2004 Sch 5 para 1(1).
5　Matrimonial Causes Act 1973 ss 21(1)(a), 23(1)(a); Civil Partnership Act 2004 Sch 5 paras 2(1)(a), (2), 80(1)(a). Where on or after the grant of a decree of divorce or nullity of marriage or an order for dissolution or nullity of a civil partnership an application is made by a party to the marriage or civil partnership for a periodical payments order in his or her favour, then, if the court considers that no continuing obligation should be imposed on either party to make periodical payments in favour of the other (see PARA 592), the court may dismiss the application with a direction that the applicant is not entitled to make any future application under the Matrimonial Causes Act 1973 s 23(1)(a) or the Civil Partnership Act 2004 Sch 5 para 2(1)(a) in relation to that marriage or civil partnership for a financial provision order: Matrimonial Causes Act 1973 s 25A(3) (added by the Matrimonial and Family Proceedings Act 1984 s 3); Civil Partnership Act 2004 Sch 5 para 23(4).
　　As to the date when the order takes effect see PARA 459; and as to pension attachments see PARA 485 et seq. The court's power exists by virtue of the statutory provisions; and it cannot order periodical payments to be made otherwise than within these terms (see *Milne v Milne* (1981) 2 FLR 286, CA; *Sabbagh v Sabbagh* [1985] FLR 29, [1985] Fam Law 187); in particular, it is implicit in the concept of periodical payments that where there has been a capital adjustment between the parties, the function of periodical payments should not be seen as furthering the payee's ability to mine the payer's income for further capital (see *J v J (ancillary relief: periodical payments)* [2004] EWHC 53 (Fam), [2004] 1 FCR 709, [2004] All ER (D) 141 (Mar)).
　　Orders whereby the court might express periodical payments in favour of a spouse or civil partner to continue dum sola are obsolete: remarriage, or the formation of a civil partnership, by a person in whose favour the order has been made automatically determines the order: see the Matrimonial Causes Act 1973 s 28; the Civil Partnership Act 2004 Sch 5 paras 47, 48; and PARAS 452, 460. As to the issues of conduct to which the court is to have regard when considering matters of financial provision see the Matrimonial Causes Act 1973 s 25; the Civil Partnership Act 2004 Sch 5 paras 20, 21; and PARA 589 et seq.
　　The court may also make a periodical payments order in case of failure by one party to the marriage to provide reasonable maintenance for the other: see the Matrimonial Causes Act 1973 s 27(6)(a); the Civil Partnership Act 2004 Sch 5 para 41(1)(a); and PARA 543. Periodical payments may also be made pending suit or the outcome of proceedings: see PARA 456.
6　*R v Cambridge County Court, ex p Ireland* [1985] FLR 102, [1985] Fam Law 23.

459. Date order takes effect. Where a periodical payments order[1] is made on or after granting a decree of divorce or nullity of marriage or making a dissolution or nullity order in respect of a civil partnership[2], neither the order nor any settlement made in pursuance of it is to take effect[3] unless the decree has been made absolute or, as the case may be, the dissolution or nullity order has been made final[4].

1   As to the meaning of 'periodical payments order' see PARA 458.

2   Ie under the Matrimonial Causes Act 1973 s 23(1)(a) or the Civil Partnership Act 2004 Sch 5 paras 1(1), 2(1)(a): see PARA 458.

3   Ie without prejudice to the power to give a direction under the Matrimonial Causes Act 1973 s 30 or the Civil Partnership Act 2004 Sch 5 para 76 for the settlement of an instrument by conveyancing counsel: see PARA 473.

4   Matrimonial Causes Act 1973 s 23(5); Civil Partnership Act 2004 Sch 5 para 4. In respect of a marriage, it has been held that the court has no jurisdiction, even with consent, to make a substantive order before a decree nisi is pronounced, and that an order made before a decree nisi is pronounced cannot be rectified under the court's inherent jurisdiction or under the slip rule: see *Board (Board intervening) v Checkland* [1987] 2 FLR 257, CA, following *Munks v Munks* [1985] FLR 576, [1985] Fam Law 131, CA. However, a court may approve a draft consent order in advance of a decree nisi and direct that it should take effect at a future date: *Pounds v Pounds* [1994] 4 All ER 777, [1994] 1 WLR 1535, CA. Presumably the same situation would obtain in respect of a dissolution or nullity order relating to a civil partnership.

460.   Duration of continuing periodical payments orders.   The term to be specified in a periodical payments order[1] in favour of a party to a marriage or civil partnership is to be[2] such term as the court[3] thinks fit, except that the term must not begin before the date of the making of an application for the order and must be so defined as not to extend beyond the death of either of the parties or, where the order is made on or after the grant of a decree of divorce or nullity of marriage or the making of a dissolution or nullity order relating to a civil partnership, the remarriage, or the formation of a subsequent civil partnership or marriage, by the party in whose favour the order is made[4].

Where a periodical payments order in favour of a party to a marriage or civil partnership is made on or after the grant of a decree of divorce or nullity of marriage or the making of a dissolution or nullity order relating to a civil partnership, the court may direct that that party is not to be entitled to apply[5] for the extension of the term specified in the order[6].

1   As to the meaning of 'periodical payments order', and as to the making of a periodical payments order, see PARA 458.

2   Ie subject, in the case of an order made on or after the grant of a decree of divorce or nullity of marriage, to the provisions of the Matrimonial Causes Act 1973 s 25A(2) (see PARA 592) and s 31(7) (see PARA 568), or, in the case of an order made on or after the making of a dissolution or nullity order relating to a civil partnership, to the provisions of the Civil Partnership Act 2004 Sch 5 para 23(3) (see PARA 592) and Sch 5 para 59(4) (see PARA 568).

3   As to the meaning of 'court' see PARA 346 note 2.

4   Matrimonial Causes Act 1973 s 28(1)(a) (s 28(1) amended by the Matrimonial and Family Proceedings Act 1984 s 5(1); and by the Civil Partnership Act 2004 Sch 27 para 43(1), (2)); Civil Partnership Act 2004 Sch 5 para 47(1), (2), (4). As to references to remarriage, to a subsequent marriage and to the formation of a subsequent civil partnership see PARA 452 note 1. As to the application of these provisions to interim orders for maintenance under the Matrimonial and Family Proceedings Act 1984 s 14 or the Civil Partnership Act 2004 Sch 7 para 5 (see PARA 536) and to orders for financial provision and property adjustment under the Matrimonial and Family Proceedings Act 1984 s 17 or the Civil Partnership Act 2004 Sch 7 para 9 (see PARA 531), as they apply to like orders under the Matrimonial Causes Act 1973 Pt II (ss 21–40A) and the Civil Partnership Act 2004 Sch 5, see the Matrimonial and Family Proceedings Act 1984 s 21; the Civil Partnership Act 2004 Sch 7 para 14; and PARA 537.

Where a periodical payments order in favour of a party to a marriage or civil partnership is made otherwise than on or after the grant of a decree of divorce or nullity of marriage or the making of a dissolution or nullity order relating to a civil partnership (see PARA 542 et seq), and the marriage or civil partnership in question is subsequently dissolved or annulled but the order continues in force, the order ceases to have effect, notwithstanding anything in it, on the remarriage, or the formation of a subsequent civil partnership or marriage, by that party, except in relation to any arrears due under it on the date of the remarriage, marriage or formation of the civil partnership: Matrimonial Causes Act 1973 s 28(2) (amended by the Civil Partnership Act 2004 Sch 27 para 43(3)); Civil Partnership Act 2004 Sch 5 para 47(6).

5	Ie under the Matrimonial Causes Act 1973 s 31 or the Civil Partnership Act 2004 Sch 5 para 51:
	see PARA 567.
6	Matrimonial Causes Act 1973 s 28(1A) (added by the Matrimonial and Family Proceedings
	Act 1984 s 5(2)); Civil Partnership Act 2004 Sch 5 para 47(5).

461. Request for periodical payments order at same rate as order for maintenance pending suit or the outcome of proceedings. Where at or after the date of a decree nisi of divorce or nullity of marriage or a conditional order of dissolution or nullity of civil partnership an order for maintenance pending suit or outcome of proceedings, as the case may be[1], is in force, the party in whose favour the order was made may, if he has made an application for a periodical payments order[2] for himself in his petition or answer, as the case may be, request the district judge[3] in writing to make such an order (a 'corresponding order') providing for payments at the same rate as those provided for by the order for maintenance pending suit or outcome of proceedings[4].

Where such a request is made, the proper officer[5] must serve on the other spouse or civil partner a notice of request in the prescribed form[6] requiring him, if he objects to the making of a corresponding order, to give notice to that effect to the court and to the applicant within 14 days after service of the notice in the prescribed form[7]. If the other spouse or civil partner does not give notice of objection within the time so specified, the district judge may make a corresponding order without further notice to that spouse or civil partner and without requiring the attendance of the applicant or his solicitor, and must in that case serve a copy of the order on the applicant as well as on the other spouse or civil partner[8].

1	As to orders for maintenance pending suit or the outcome of proceedings see PARA 456.
2	As to the meaning of 'periodical payments order', and as to the making of a periodical payments
	order, see PARA 458.
3	As to the meaning of 'district judge' see PARA 737 note 3.
4	Family Proceedings Rules 1991, SI 1991/1247, r 2.67(1) (amended by SI 2005/2922).
5	'Proper officer' means the family proceedings department manager (in relation to the principal
	registry), the court manager (in relation to any other court or registry), or other officer of the
	court or registry acting on his behalf in accordance with directions given by the
	Lord Chancellor: Family Proceedings Rules 1991, SI 1991/1247, r 1.2(1) (amended by
	SI 1997/1056).
6	For the prescribed form of notice of request see the Family Proceedings Rules 1991,
	SI 1991/1247, Appendix 1A, Form I (added by SI 1999/3491; substituted by SI 2000/2267).
7	Family Proceedings Rules 1991, SI 1991/1247, r 2.67(2) (amended by SI 1999/3491;
	SI 2005/2922).
8	Family Proceedings Rules 1991, SI 1991/1247, r 2.67(3) (amended by SI 2005/2922).

462. Interim orders. A party may apply at any stage of the proceedings for an order for interim periodical payments[1]; and, pending the final determination of the application, the district judge[2] may[3] make an interim order on such terms as he thinks just[4]. Such orders are usually made where further investigations or inquiry are required, or where an application is adjourned part heard and interim provision is considered necessary. Interim orders may be varied, discharged, suspended in whole or in part and revived in the same manner as substantive orders for periodical payments[5].

1	See the Family Proceedings Rules 1991, SI 1991/1247, r 2.69F; and PARA 923.
2	As to the meaning of 'district judge' see PARA 737 note 3.
3	Ie subject to the Family Proceedings Rules 1991, SI 1991/1247, r 2.69F.
4	See the Family Proceedings Rules 1991, SI 1991/1247, r 2.64(2): and PARA 933.
5	See the Matrimonial Causes Act 1973 s 31(1), (2)(a); the Civil Partnership Act 2004 Sch 5
	para 50(1)(c); and PARA 567.

463. Matters to which the court is to have regard. In deciding whether to exercise its power to make a periodical payments order[1] and, if so, in what manner, the court[2] is to have regard to certain matters[3]. The court must also consider whether it would be appropriate so to exercise its powers that the financial obligations of each party towards the other will be terminated as soon after the grant of the decree of divorce or nullity of marriage or the making of the dissolution or nullity order as the court considers just and reasonable[4].

In applying its discretion, the court will take into account the cohabitation of a party claiming periodical payments as one of the circumstances of the case[5]; but the court will not force a person to become dependent on their new partner[6].

Although there is no statutory period of limitation that applies to proceedings for financial relief, delay may be one of the factors to which the court will have regard when considering all the circumstances of the case[7].

1 As to the meaning of 'periodical payments order', and as to the making of a periodical payments order, see PARA 458.
2 As to the meaning of 'court' see PARA 346 note 2.
3 See the Matrimonial Causes Act 1973 s 25(1), (2); the Civil Partnership Act 2004 Sch 5 paras 20, 21; and PARA 589 et seq. As to this requirement see generally *Rye v Rye* [2002] EWHC 956 (Fam), [2002] 2 FLR 981, [2002] All ER (D) 249 (May).
4 See the Matrimonial Causes Act 1973 s 25A; the Civil Partnership Act 2004 Sch 5 para 23; and PARA 592.
5 See e g *Suter v Suter and Jones* [1987] Fam 111, [1987] 2 All ER 336, CA; *Atkinson v Atkinson* [1988] Fam 93, [1987] 3 All ER 849, CA.
6 *Hepburn v Hepburn* [1989] FCR 618, [1989] 1 FLR 373, CA. Subsequent marriages and civil partnerships bring about a termination of the right to periodical payments: see PARA 452.
7 See PARA 595.

464. Unfair pressure on payer. The making of an order for an amount or amounts larger than the circumstances of the parties warrant, so as to bring pressure on the payer to do something he not unreasonably refuses to do, is wrong in principle[1]; it has been held that where the trustees of a settlement had a discretion to make payments to a husband from trust funds and, in the exercise of that discretion, did not make such payments, the court could not order the husband to pay maintenance to the wife amounting to most of his income in order to bring pressure to bear on the trustees to exercise their discretion in a way they did not wish to exercise it[2]. The court may, however, make orders that encourage trustees to enhance the means of the maintaining party, so long as no improper pressure is brought to bear on the trustees[3].

1 *Wakeford v Wakeford* [1953] 2 All ER 827, [1953] 1 WLR 1222, DC.
2 *Howard v Howard* [1945] P 1, [1945] 1 All ER 91, CA; *B v B (financial provision)* (1982) 3 FLR 298, 12 Fam Law 92, CA. See also *Browne v Browne* [1989] 1 FLR 291, [1989] Fam Law 147, CA (court wrong to exert pressure on a discretionary trustee; court must look at reality of situation).
3 *Thomas v Thomas* [1996] 2 FCR 544, [1995] 2 FLR 668, CA.

465. Orders of other courts. Before taking proceedings for divorce, dissolution, judicial or legal separation or nullity, a spouse or civil partner may have obtained an order in a magistrates' court[1], including an order that the other spouse or civil partner should make such periodical payments as the magistrates' court considers reasonable[2]. The existence of this order must be taken into account on an application for periodical payments; and, since it is undesirable that there should be more than one financial order current at the same time from two courts, the proper course may well be to discharge the magistrates' court's order. The High Court and county courts have power to discharge the magistrates' court's order without it being necessary to make a separate application for this purpose in the magistrates' court[3].

Orders of foreign courts will be taken into account, although the court's attitude to such orders may depend on their enforceability in England and Wales[4]. Previous orders for financial provision in proceedings for judicial separation between the parties will also be taken into account where a periodical payments application is made within the framework of a divorce suit.

1 Ie under the Domestic Proceedings and Magistrates' Courts Act 1978 s 2(1)(a) or the Civil Partnership Act 2004 Sch 6 para 2(1)(a): see PARA 553.

2 See PARA 553.

3 See the Domestic Proceedings and Magistrates' Courts Act 1978 s 28; the Civil Partnership Act 2004 Sch 6 para 46(a); and PARA 566.

4 *Harrop v Harrop* [1920] 3 KB 386; *Re Macartney, Macfarlane v Macartney* [1921] 1 Ch 522; *Beatty v Beatty* [1924] 1 KB 807, CA; *Simons v Simons* [1939] 1 KB 490, [1938] 4 All ER 436. See also CONFLICT OF LAWS vol 8(3) (Reissue) PARAS 158, 292.

466.   Alienation and bankruptcy.   Periodical payments, unlike secured periodical payments[1], under an order of the court in matrimonial or civil partnership proceedings cannot be assigned nor can they be released or taken in execution[2]. Even though the right to arrears of periodical payments may be assignable[3], the court is unlikely to enforce arrears in favour of an assignee[4]. Neither arrears of such periodical payments nor future payments constitute a debt or liability for purposes of insolvency[5], and a debt provable in the bankruptcy is, therefore, not created[6]. A spouse or civil partner remains liable under a periodical payments order[7] notwithstanding his or her bankruptcy and subsequent discharge[8].

1 See PARA 467 et seq.

2 *Re Robinson* (1884) 27 ChD 160, CA; *Watkins v Watkins* [1896] P 222, CA; *Campbell v Campbell* [1922] P 187. Cf the Matrimonial Causes Act 1973 s 39; the Civil Partnership Act 2004 Sch 5 para 77; and PARAS 505, 509.
   For an agreement between a wife and her solicitors assigning to the latter her rights in any financial provision and property adjustment orders which she might obtain in the proceedings, excluding periodical payments, in order to meet the solicitor's bill see *Sears Tooth (a firm) v Payne Hicks Beach (a firm)* [1998] 1 FCR 231, [1997] 2 FLR 116 (cited in PARA 484 note 1).

3 *Watkins v Watkins* [1896] P 222 at 228, CA per Lindley LJ.

4 *Re Robinson* (1844) 27 ChD 160, CA.

5 Ie within the meaning of the Insolvency Rules 1986, SI 1986/1925, r 12.3(2): see BANKRUPTCY AND INDIVIDUAL INSOLVENCY vol 3(2) (2002 Reissue) PARA 491.

6 *Re Rice, ex p Rice* (1864) 10 LT 103; cf *Victor v Victor* [1912] 1 KB 247, CA; *McQuiban v McQuiban* [1913] P 208 (payments under separation deeds provable).

7 As to the meaning of 'periodical payments order', and as to the making of a periodical payments order, see PARA 458.

8 *Linton v Linton* (1885) 15 QBD 239, CA; *Re Hawkins, ex p Hawkins* [1894] 1 QB 25; *Kerr v Kerr* [1897] 2 QB 439; *James v James* [1964] P 303, [1963] 2 All ER 465, DC. As to arrears under a separation deed see, however, *Victor v Victor* [1912] 1 KB 247, CA; *McQuiban v McQuiban* [1913] P 208.
   As to the respective rights of a bankrupt and her trustee in bankruptcy, where maintenance is payable under a deed, see *Re Tennant's Application* [1956] 2 All ER 753, [1956] 1 WLR 874, CA; as to the respective rights of sequestrators and a trustee in bankruptcy, where it is sought to enforce arrears of maintenance under an order see *Coles v Coles* [1957] P 68, [1956] 3 All ER 542; and as to the effect of a husband's undertakings in an order regarding the matrimonial home when a bankruptcy order was made against him see *Re Solomon (a bankrupt), ex p Trustee of Property of Bankrupt v Solomon* [1967] Ch 573; *Re A Debtor, ex p Trustee v Solomon* [1966] 3 All ER 255.

467.   Power to make order. Where the court[1]:

(1)   grants a decree of divorce, a decree of nullity of marriage or a decree of judicial separation[2]; or

(2)   makes a dissolution, nullity or separation order in respect of a civil partnership[3],

it may[4] make an order that either party to the marriage or civil partnership is to secure to the other, to the satisfaction of the court, such periodical payments, for such term, as may be specified in the order (a 'secured periodical payments order')[5]. The court may order periodical payments to be made in a currency other than sterling but it should allow the parties to make representations about the currency in which the order will be made[6].

An order to secure periodical payments is intended to impose an obligation on the payer to establish a capital asset from which the recipient will be maintained. The payer is not under an obligation to pay a specific amount of maintenance; rather the obligation is to create the security from which the maintenance will be paid[7]. Consequently such orders are rare; in most instances available capital will be distributed between the parties and any maintenance obligation will be imposed by means of a regular order for periodical payments.

1   As to the meaning of 'court' see PARA 346 note 2.

2   Matrimonial Causes Act 1973 s 23(1).

3   Civil Partnership Act 2004 Sch 5 para 1(1)(a).

4   Ie on granting the decree or making the order or at any time thereafter (whether, in the case of a decree of divorce or of nullity of marriage, before or after the decree is made absolute): Matrimonial Causes Act 1973 s 23(1); Civil Partnership Act 2004 Sch 5 para 1(1).

5   Matrimonial Causes Act 1973 ss 21(1)(b), 23(1)(b); Civil Partnership Act 2004 Sch 5 paras 2(1)(b), (2), 80(1)(b). Where on or after the grant of a decree of divorce or nullity of marriage or an order for dissolution or nullity of a civil partnership an application is made by a party to the marriage or civil partnership for a secured periodical payments order in his or her favour, then, if the court considers that no continuing obligation should be imposed on either party to secure periodical payments in favour of the other (see PARA 592), the court may dismiss the application with a direction that the applicant is not entitled to make any future application under the Matrimonial Causes Act 1973 s 23(1)(b) or the Civil Partnership Act 2004 Sch 5 para 2(1)(b) in relation to that marriage or civil partnership for a financial provision order: Matrimonial Causes Act 1973 s 25A(3) (added by the Matrimonial and Family Proceedings Act 1984 s 3); Civil Partnership Act 2004 Sch 5 para 23(4).

As to the date when the order takes effect see PARA 468; and as to pension attachments see PARA 485 et seq. As to the court's power to make periodical payments generally cf the cases cited in PARA 458 note 5. Orders whereby the court might express secured periodical payments in favour of a spouse or civil partner to continue dum sola are obsolete: remarriage, or the formation of a civil partnership, by a person in whose favour the order has been made automatically determines the order: see the Matrimonial Causes Act 1973 s 28; the Civil Partnership Act 2004 Sch 5 paras 47, 48; and PARAS 460, 452. As to the issues of conduct to which the court is to have regard when considering matters of financial provision see the Matrimonial Causes Act 1973 s 25; the Civil Partnership Act 2004 Sch 5 paras 20, 21; and PARA 589 et seq.

The court may also make a secured periodical payments order in case of failure by one party to the marriage to provide reasonable maintenance for the other: see the Matrimonial Causes Act 1973 s 27(6)(b); the Civil Partnership Act 2004 Sch 5 para 41(1)(b); and PARA 543.

6   *R v Cambridge County Court, ex p Ireland* [1985] FLR 102, [1985] Fam Law 23.

7   See *Shearn v Shearn* [1931] P 1.

468.   Date order takes effect. Where a secured periodical payments order is made[1] on or after granting a decree of divorce or nullity of marriage or making a dissolution or nullity order in respect of a civil partnership[2], neither the order nor any settlement made in pursuance of it is to take effect[3] unless the decree has been made absolute or, as the case may be, the dissolution or nullity order has been made final[4].

1　As to the meaning of 'secured periodical payments order', and as to the making of a secured periodical payments order, see PARA 467.
2　Ie under the Matrimonial Causes Act 1973 s 23(1)(b) or the Civil Partnership Act 2004 Sch 5 paras 1(1), 2(1)(b): see PARA 467.
3　Ie without prejudice to the power to give a direction under the Matrimonial Causes Act 1973 s 30 or the Civil Partnership Act 2004 Sch 5 para 76 for the settlement of an instrument by conveyancing counsel: see PARA 473.
4　Matrimonial Causes Act 1973 s 23(5); Civil Partnership Act 2004 Sch 5 para 4. In respect of a marriage, it has been held that the court has no jurisdiction, even with consent, to make a substantive order before a decree nisi is pronounced, and that an order made before a decree nisi is pronounced cannot be rectified under the court's inherent jurisdiction or under the slip rule: see *Board (Board intervening) v Checkland* [1987] 2 FLR 257, CA, following *Munks v Munks* [1985] FLR 576, [1985] Fam Law 131, CA. However, a court may approve a draft consent order in advance of a decree nisi and direct that it should take effect at a future date: *Pounds v Pounds* [1994] 4 All ER 777, [1994] 1 WLR 1535, CA. Presumably the same situation would obtain in respect of a dissolution or nullity order relating to a civil partnership.

469. Duration of continuing secured periodical payments orders. The term to be specified in a secured periodical payments order[1] in favour of a party to a marriage or civil partnership is to be[2] such term as the court[3] thinks fit, except that the term must not begin before the date of the making of an application for the order and must be so defined as not to extend beyond the death of the party in whose favour the order is made or, where the order is made on or after the grant of a decree of divorce or nullity of marriage or the making of a dissolution or nullity order relating to a civil partnership, the remarriage, or the formation of a subsequent civil partnership or marriage, by the party in whose favour the order is made[4].

Where a secured periodical payments order in favour of a party to a marriage or civil partnership is made on or after the grant of a decree of divorce or nullity of marriage or the making of a dissolution or nullity order relating to a civil partnership, the court may direct that that party is not to be entitled to apply[5] for the extension of the term specified in the order[6].

1　As to the meaning of 'secured periodical payments order', and as to the making of a secured periodical payments order, see PARA 467.
2　Ie subject, in the case of an order made on or after the grant of a decree of divorce or nullity of marriage, to the provisions of the Matrimonial Causes Act 1973 s 25A(2) (see PARA 592) and s 31(7) (see PARA 568), or, in the case of an order made on or after the making of a dissolution or nullity order relating to a civil partnership, to the provisions of the Civil Partnership Act 2004 Sch 5 para 23(3) (see PARA 592) and Sch 5 para 59(4) (see PARA 568).
3　As to the meaning of 'court' see PARA 346 note 2.
4　Matrimonial Causes Act 1973 s 28(1)(b) (s 28(1) amended by the Matrimonial and Family Proceedings Act 1984 s 5(1); and by the Civil Partnership Act 2004 Sch 27 para 43(1), (2)); Civil Partnership Act 2004 Sch 5 para 47(1), (3), (4). As to references to remarriage, to a subsequent marriage and to the formation of a subsequent civil partnership see PARA 452 note 1. As to the application of these provisions to interim orders for maintenance under the Matrimonial and Family Proceedings Act 1984 s 14 or the Civil Partnership Act 2004 Sch 7 para 5 (see PARA 536) and to orders for financial provision and property adjustment under the Matrimonial and Family Proceedings Act 1984 s 17 or the Civil Partnership Act 2004 Sch 7 para 9 (see PARA 531), as they apply to like orders under the Matrimonial Causes Act 1973 Pt II (ss 21–40A) and the Civil Partnership Act 2004 Sch 5, see the Matrimonial and Family Proceedings Act 1984 s 21; the Civil Partnership Act 2004 Sch 7 para 14; and PARA 537.
　　Where a secured periodical payments order in favour of a party to a marriage or civil partnership is made otherwise than on or after the grant of a decree of divorce or nullity of marriage or the making of a dissolution or nullity order relating to a civil partnership (see PARA

542 et seq), and the marriage or civil partnership in question is subsequently dissolved or annulled but the order continues in force, the order ceases to have effect, notwithstanding anything in it, on the remarriage, or the formation of a subsequent civil partnership or marriage, by that party, except in relation to any arrears due under it on the date of the remarriage, marriage or formation of the civil partnership: Matrimonial Causes Act 1973 s 28(2) (amended by the Civil Partnership Act 2004 Sch 27 para 43(3)); Civil Partnership Act 2004 Sch 5 para 47(6).

5   Ie under the Matrimonial Causes Act 1973 s 31 or the Civil Partnership Act 2004 Sch 5 para 51: see PARA 567.

6   Matrimonial Causes Act 1973 s 28(1A) (added by the Matrimonial and Family Proceedings Act 1984 s 5(2)); Civil Partnership Act 2004 Sch 5 para 47(5).

470.   Interim orders.   A party may apply at any stage of the proceedings for an order for interim secured periodical payments[1]; and, pending the final determination of the application, the district judge[2] may[3] make an interim order on such terms as he thinks just[4]. Such orders are usually made where further investigations or inquiry are required, or where an application is adjourned part heard and interim provision is considered necessary. Interim orders may be varied, discharged, suspended in whole or in part and revived in the same manner as substantive orders for secured periodical payments[5].

1   See the Family Proceedings Rules 1991, SI 1991/1247, r 2.69F; and PARA 923. As to the making of a secured periodical payments order see PARA 467.
2   As to the meaning of 'district judge' see PARA 737 note 3.
3   Ie subject to the Family Proceedings Rules 1991, SI 1991/1247, r 2.69F.
4   See the Family Proceedings Rules 1991, SI 1991/1247, r 2.64(2): and PARA 933.
5   See the Matrimonial Causes Act 1973 s 31(1), (2)(a); the Civil Partnership Act 2004 Sch 5 para 50(1)(c); and PARA 567.

471.   Matters to which the court is to have regard.   In deciding whether to exercise its power to make a secured periodical payments order[1] and, if so, in what manner, the court[2] is to have regard to certain matters[3]. The court must also consider whether it would be appropriate so to exercise its powers that the financial obligations of each party towards the other will be terminated as soon after the grant of the decree of divorce or nullity of marriage or the making of the dissolution or nullity order as the court considers just and reasonable[4].

The court will take into account the effect on the payer of tying up the asset that provides the security[5] and also the need to have security for the payment of maintenance[6]; and the court has an unfettered discretion in deciding whether to make such an order and, if so, on what terms[7].

Although there is no statutory period of limitation that applies to proceedings for financial relief, delay may be one of the factors to which the court will have regard when considering all the circumstances of the case[8].

1   As to the meaning of 'secured periodical payments order', and as to the making of a secured periodical payments order, see PARA 467.
2   As to the meaning of 'court' see PARA 346 note 2.
3   See the Matrimonial Causes Act 1973 s 25(1), (2); the Civil Partnership Act 2004 Sch 5 paras 20, 21; and PARA 589 et seq. As to this requirement see generally *Rye v Rye* [2002] EWHC 956 (Fam), [2002] 2 FLR 981, [2002] All ER (D) 249 (May).
4   See the Matrimonial Causes Act 1973 s 25A; the Civil Partnership Act 2004 Sch 5 para 23; and PARA 592.
5   *Shearn v Shearn* [1931] P 1.
6   Eg because the payer may leave the jurisdiction or prove to be unreliable in the payment of normal maintenance: see *Barker v Barker* [1952] P 184, [1952] 1 All ER 1128, CA; *Chichester v Chichester* [1936] P 129, [1936] 1 All ER 271.
7   *Shearn v Shearn* [1931] P 1.
8   See PARA 595.

472. Property that may be the subject of a secured periodical payments order.
When the court intends to make a secured periodical payments order[1] it will
usually indicate that intention to the parties and invite them to agree on the asset
which is to provide the security. The appropriate security will usually be stocks,
shares or real property. It will usually be unduly onerous to order that the whole
of one party's capital assets should provide the security[2]. If the parties cannot
agree which property is to provide the security, the court will do so. It is,
however, wrong to delegate that task to conveyancing counsel[3], although, once
the intentions of the court are determined, it may direct that conveyancing
counsel draft any necessary documents in order to put that intention into effect[4].
The court will rarely require reversionary interests to provide the necessary
security[5].

1   As to the meaning of 'secured periodical payments order', and as to the making of a secured
    periodical payments order, see PARA 467.
2   *Barker v Barker* [1952] P 184, [1952] 1 All ER 1128, CA.
3   *Barker v Barker* [1952] P 184, [1952] 1 All ER 1128, CA.
4   See PARA 473.
5   *Allison v Allison* [1927] P 308.

473. Deed to secure payments. Where the court[1] decides to make a financial
provision order requiring any payments to be secured[2], it may direct that the
matter be referred to one of the conveyancing counsel of the court for him to
settle a proper instrument to be executed by all necessary parties[3]. Where the
order is to be made in proceedings for divorce, dissolution, nullity of marriage or
civil partnership or judicial or legal separation, the court may, if it thinks fit,
defer the grant of the decree or the making of the order in question until the
instrument has been duly executed[4].

The court may order the lodgment of documents for the purpose of settling
the deed[5]. Where a person refuses or neglects to execute a deed securing
payments as ordered by the court, the court may order that execution be effected
by such person as it nominates for that purpose, and a deed so executed operates
as if executed by the party originally directed to execute it[6]. The court has power
to order the rectification of a deed[7] and to vary it[8].

1   As to the meaning of 'court' see PARA 346 note 2.
2   See PARA 467 et seq.
3   Matrimonial Causes Act 1973 s 30(a); Civil Partnership Act 2004 Sch 5 para 76(1)(a), (2).
4   Matrimonial Causes Act 1973 s 30(b); Civil Partnership Act 2004 Sch 5 para 76(3).
5   *Bartlett v Bartlett* (1918) 34 TLR 518.
6   See the Supreme Court Act 1981 s 39; the County Courts Act 1984 s 38; and PARA 641. See also
    Howarth v Howarth (1886) 11 PD 68 at 95, CA; cf *De Ricci v De Ricci* [1891] P 378
    (application arising out of a compromise, which had become a rule of court).
7   *Burroughes v Abbott* [1922] 1 Ch 86; cf *Philipson v Philipson* (1933) 148 LT 455. Except for
    fraud, such a deed is irrevocable: *Bradley v Bradley* (1882) 7 PD 237.
8   See the Matrimonial Causes Act 1973 s 31(3); the Civil Partnership Act 2004 Sch 5 para 45(3);
    and PARA 567.

474. Effect of death of spouse or civil partner. Where a secured periodical
payments order is made[1], the party in favour of whom the order is made has an
enforceable claim which is maintainable after the death of the other party against
that party's estate, whether or not the effect of the order is to create a charge on
property of that other party, and the order may be enforced against his or her
personal representatives; the court may order the personal representatives to
execute the necessary deed[2].

The right to apply for an order for secured periodical payments is, however, not a cause of action which survives[3] against a person's estate[4]. It has been held that an application by a personal representative of the party against whom an order was made to extinguish or diminish periodical payments payable under the order could not be maintained[5].

Where the person liable to make payments under a secured periodical payments order has died, an application relating to that order and to any order[6] for the sale of property which requires the proceeds of sale of property to be used for securing those payments, to vary or discharge the order or to suspend any provision temporarily or to revive a suspended provision[7] may be made by the person entitled to payments under the order or by the personal representatives of the deceased person, but, except with the permission of the court, no such application may be made after the end of the period of six months from the date on which representation in regard to the estate of that person is first taken out[8].

The personal representatives of a deceased person against whom a secured periodical payments order was made are not liable for having distributed any part of the estate of the deceased after the expiration of the period of six months on the ground that they ought to have taken into account the possibility that the court might permit such an application to be made after that period by the person entitled to payments under the order; but any power to recover any part of the estate so distributed arising by virtue of the making of an order to vary, discharge, suspend or revive is not thereby prejudiced[9].

1   As to the meaning of 'secured periodical payments order', and as to the making of a secured periodical payments order, see PARA 467.
2   *Hyde v Hyde* [1948] P 198, [1948] 1 All ER 362; *Mosey v Mosey and Barker* [1956] P 26, [1955] 2 All ER 391.
3   As to the survival of causes of action after death generally see the Law Reform (Miscellaneous Provisions) Act 1934 s 1; PARAS 684–686; and EXECUTORS AND ADMINISTRATORS vol 17(2) (Reissue) PARA 814.
4   *Dipple v Dipple* [1942] P 65, [1942] 1 All ER 234.
5   *Mosey v Mosey and Barker* [1956] P 26, [1955] 2 All ER 391.
6   Ie an order made under the Matrimonial Causes Act 1973 s 24A(1) or the Civil Partnership Act 2004 Sch 5 paras 10, 11: see PARA 520.
7   Ie under the Matrimonial Causes Act 1973 s 31(1), (2)(c) or the Civil Partnership Act 2004 Sch 5 para 50(1)(b): see PARA 567.
8   Matrimonial Causes Act 1973 s 31(6) (amended by the Matrimonial Homes and Property Act 1981 s 8(2)(b)); Civil Partnership Act 2004 Sch 5 para 60(1)–(3). As to the matters to which the court is to have regard in exercising its powers see the Matrimonial Causes Act 1973 s 31(7); the Civil Partnership Act 2004 Sch 5 para 59; and PARA 568. In considering for these purposes the question when representation was first taken out, a grant limited to settled land or to trust property must be left out of account, and a grant limited to real estate or to personal estate must be left out of account, unless a grant limited to the remainder of the estate has previously been made or is made at the same time: Matrimonial Causes Act 1973 s 31(9); Civil Partnership Act 2004 Sch 5 para 60(6).
        Where a person against whom a secured periodical payments order was so made has died and an application is made under the Matrimonial Causes Act 1973 s 31(6) or the Civil Partnership Act 2004 Sch 5 para 60 for the variation or discharge of that order or for the revival of the operation of any provision thereof which has been suspended, the court has power to direct that the application made under either of those provisions is to be deemed to have been accompanied by an application for an order under the Inheritance (Provision for Family and Dependants) Act 1975 s 2 (see EXECUTORS AND ADMINISTRATORS vol 17(2) (Reissue) PARAS 691–692): ss 18(1)(a), 18A(1)(a) (s 18A added by the Civil Partnership Act 2004 Sch 4 para 25). Where the court gives such a direction, it has power, in the proceedings on the application under the Matrimonial Causes Act 1973 s 31(6) or the Civil Partnership Act 2004 Sch 5 para 60 to make any order which the court would have had power to make under the provisions of the Inheritance (Provision for Family and Dependants) Act 1975 if the application made under the Matrimonial Causes Act 1973 s 31(6) or the Civil Partnership Act 2004 Sch 5 para 60 had been

made jointly with an application for an order under the Inheritance (Provision for Family and Dependants) Act 1975 s 2; and the court has power to give such consequential directions as may be necessary for enabling the court to exercise any of the powers available to the court under the Inheritance (Provision for Family and Dependants) Act 1975 in the case of an application under s 2: ss 18(2), 18A(2) (s 18A(2) as so added). Where an order made under s 15(1) or s 15ZA(1) (see PARA 882) is in force with respect to a party to a marriage or civil partnership, the court may not give a direction under s 18(1) or s 18A(1) with respect to any application under the Matrimonial Causes Act 1973 s 31(6) or the Civil Partnership Act 2004 Sch 5 para 60 by that party on the death of the other party: Inheritance (Provision for Family and Dependants) Act 1975 ss 18(3), 18A(3) (s 18A(3) as so added).

Where an application for an order under s 2 is made to the court by any person who was at the time of the death of the deceased entitled to payments from the deceased under a secured periodical payments order, then, in the proceedings on that application, the court has power, if an application is duly made by that person or by the personal representative of the deceased, to vary or discharge that order or to revive the operation of any provision thereof which has been suspended: see s 16; and EXECUTORS AND ADMINISTRATORS vol 17(2) (Reissue) PARA 695.

9   Matrimonial Causes Act 1973 s 31(8); Civil Partnership Act 2004 Sch 5 para 60(4), (5).

475.   Alienation. Secured periodical payments are alienable and chargeable, unless the deed securing them provides against alienation[1].

1   *Harrison v Harrison* (1888) 13 PD 180, CA; *Maclurcan v Maclurcan* (1897) 77 LT 474, CA (wife, after accepting sum for releasing husband, applied to court to set aside the deed of arrangement); *Hyde v Hyde* [1948] P 198, [1948] 1 All ER 362; *Mosey v Mosey and Barker* [1956] P 26 at 41, [1955] 2 All ER 391 at 394.

D.   LUMP SUM PAYMENTS

476.   Power to make order. Where the court[1]:

(1)   grants a decree of divorce, a decree of nullity of marriage or a decree of judicial separation[2]; or

(2)   makes a dissolution, nullity or separation order in respect of a civil partnership[3],

it may[4] make an order that either party to the marriage or civil partnership is to pay to the other such lump sum or sums as may be so specified (an 'order for the payment of a lump sum')[5]. Only a single order may be made which may, where appropriate, include provision for the payment of more than one lump sum as, for example, where one sum is to be paid immediately and a further sum contingently on the happening of a future event such as the falling in of a reversionary interest in an estate to which one of the parties is entitled[6]. An order for the payment of a lump sum may[7] provide for the payment of that sum by instalments of such amount as may be specified in the order and may require the payment of the instalments to be secured to the satisfaction of the court[8].

The court has no jurisdiction to make an interim order for the payment of a lump sum[9]; and nor may the court make an administrative order of appropriation to allocate a particular asset to meet the interim needs of either party prior to the final hearing[10]. There is also no power to make a lump sum order on the variation of other financial provision orders[11].

1   As to the meaning of 'court' see PARA 346 note 2.
2   Matrimonial Causes Act 1973 s 23(1).
3   Civil Partnership Act 2004 Sch 5 para 1(1)(a).
4   Ie on granting the decree or making the order or at any time thereafter (whether, in the case of a decree of divorce or of nullity of marriage, before or after the decree is made absolute): Matrimonial Causes Act 1973 s 23(1); Civil Partnership Act 2004 Sch 5 para 1(1).
5   Matrimonial Causes Act 1973 ss 21(1)(c), 23(1)(c); Civil Partnership Act 2004 Sch 5 paras 2(1)(c), (2), 80(1)(c). As to the date when the order takes effect see PARA 481; and as to pension attachments see PARA 485 et seq. As to the court's power to make periodical payments

generally c f the cases cited in PARA 458 note 5. The court has no power to order payment to third parties (see eg *Milne v Milne* (1981) 2 FLR 286, CA); nor can the court dealing with an application for financial relief exercise a quasi bankruptcy jurisdiction and order one party to the marriage or civil partnership to make direct payments of debts to a third party (*Mullard v Mullard* (1981) 3 FLR 330, 12 Fam Law 63, CA; *Burton v Burton* [1986] 2 FLR 419, [1986] Fam Law 330). As to the issues of conduct to which the court is to have regard when considering matters of financial provision see the Matrimonial Causes Act 1973 s 25; the Civil Partnership Act 2004 Sch 5 paras 20, 21; and PARA 589 et seq.

There is nothing to prevent a person who has received a lump sum in divorce or dissolution proceedings from applying subsequently for a lump sum under the Inheritance (Provision for Family and Dependants) Act 1975 (see *Re Farrow* [1987] 1 FLR 205, [1987] Fam Law 14 (wife awarded lump sum after decree of divorce subsequently awarded further lump sum under the Inheritance (Provision for Family and Dependants) Act 1975)) unless he or she is no longer entitled to make a claim by virtue of s 15: see PARA 882; and EXECUTORS AND ADMINISTRATORS vol 17(2) (Reissue) PARA 667.

6 *de Lasala v de Lasala* [1980] AC 546 at 559, 560, [1979] 2 All ER 1146 at 1154, PC; and see *Coleman v Coleman* [1973] Fam 10, [1972] 3 All ER 886; *Carson v Carson* [1983] 1 All ER 478, [1983] 1 WLR 285, CA; *Norman v Norman* [1983] 1 All ER 486, [1983] 1 WLR 295; *Dinch v Dinch* [1987] 1 All ER 818, [1987] 1 WLR 252, HL.

7 Ie without prejudice to the generality of the Matrimonial Causes Act 1973 s 23(1)(c) or the Civil Partnership Act 2004 Sch 5 para 2(1)(c) (see the text and notes 1–5).

8 Matrimonial Causes Act 1973 s 23(3)(c); Civil Partnership Act 2004 Sch 5 para 3(3), (4). Such an instalment order may be varied: see the Matrimonial Causes Act 1973 s 31(2)(d); the Civil Partnership Act 2004 Sch 5 para 50(1)(e); and PARA 567. Although it has been held that the court will not permit a second lump sum to be achieved by some other proceedings since that would be inequitable (see *Minton v Minton* [1979] AC 593, [1979] 1 All ER 79, HL; *Banyard v Banyard* [1984] FLR 643, CA; *Nurcombe v Nurcombe* [1985] 1 All ER 65, [1985] 1 WLR 370, CA), the court may now make an order for the payment of a further lump sum where a periodical payments order (see PARA 458 et seq) or secured periodical payments order (see PARA 467 et seq) is discharged or such an order is varied so that payments under the order are required to be made or secured only for such further period as is determined by the court (see the Matrimonial Causes Act 1973 s 31(7B); the Civil Partnership Act 2004 Sch 5 para 53(2), (3); and PARA 569).

As to the application of the Matrimonial Causes Act 1973 s 23(3) and the Civil Partnership Act 2004 Sch 5 para 3 to interim orders for maintenance under the Matrimonial and Family Proceedings Act 1984 s 14 or the Civil Partnership Act 2004 Sch 7 para 5 (see PARA 536) and to orders for financial provision and property adjustment under the Matrimonial and Family Proceedings Act 1984 s 17 or the Civil Partnership Act 2004 Sch 7 para 9 (see PARA 531), as they apply to like orders under the Matrimonial Causes Act 1973 Pt II (ss 21–40A) and the Civil Partnership Act 2004 Sch 5, see the Matrimonial and Family Proceedings Act 1984 s 21; the Civil Partnership Act 2004 Sch 7 para 14; and PARA 537.

9 *Bolsom v Bolsom* (1982) 4 FLR 21, [1982] Fam Law 143, CA; *Wicks v Wicks* [1999] Fam 65, [1998] 1 All ER 977, CA.

10 *Wicks v Wicks* [1999] Fam 65, [1998] 1 All ER 977, CA.

11 See PARA 569.

477. Lump sum provision for liabilities and expenses.

An order that a party to a marriage or civil partnership is to pay a lump sum[1] to the other party may[2] be made for the purpose of enabling that other party to meet any liabilities or expenses reasonably incurred by him or her in maintaining himself or herself or any child of the family[3] before making an application for an order in his or her favour[4].

1 As to the meaning of 'order for the payment of a lump sum', and as to the making of such orders, see PARA 476.

2 Ie without prejudice to the generality of the Matrimonial Causes Act 1973 s 23(1)(c) or the Civil Partnership Act 2004 Sch 5 para 2(1)(c): see PARA 476.

3 'Child of the family', in relation to the parties to a marriage or in relation to two people who are civil partners of each other, means a child of both of those parties and any other child, not being a child placed with those parties as foster parents by a local authority or voluntary organisation, who has been treated by both of those parties as a child of their family: Matrimonial Causes Act 1973 s 52(1) (amended by the Children Act 1989 Sch 12 para 33); Matrimonial and Family

Proceedings Act 1984 s 27; Civil Partnership Act 2004 Sch 5 para 80(2), Sch 7 para 1(4). 'Child' is defined for the purposes of the Matrimonial Causes Act 1973, in relation to one or both of the parties to a marriage, as including an illegitimate child of that party or, as the case may be, of both parties: s 52(1) (as so amended). In deciding for these purposes whether a child is a child of the family, grandparents are not in any special position: *Re A (a minor) (child of the family)* [1998] 1 FCR 458, sub nom *Re A (child of the family)* [1998] 1 FLR 347, CA.

4   Matrimonial Causes Act 1973 s 23(3)(a); Civil Partnership Act 2004 Sch 5 para 3(1), (4). As to lump sum provision specifically for the benefit of a child see the Matrimonial Causes Act 1973 s 23(1)(f); the Civil Partnership Act 2004 Sch 5 para 3(2)(f); and PARA 492. As to the application of the Matrimonial Causes Act 1973 s 23(3) and the Civil Partnership Act 2004 Sch 5 para 3 to interim orders for maintenance under the Matrimonial and Family Proceedings Act 1984 s 14 or the Civil Partnership Act 2004 Sch 7 para 5 (see PARA 536) and to orders for financial provision and property adjustment under the Matrimonial and Family Proceedings Act 1984 s 17 or the Civil Partnership Act 2004 Sch 7 para 9 (see PARA 531), as they apply to like orders under the Matrimonial Causes Act 1973 Pt II (ss 21–40A) and the Civil Partnership Act 2004 Sch 5, see the Matrimonial and Family Proceedings Act 1984 s 21; the Civil Partnership Act 2004 Sch 7 para 14; and PARA 537.

478. Adjournments.   Although the court has an unfettered discretion to adjourn proceedings[1], the court will generally be reluctant to adjourn an application for the payment of a lump sum unless there is a real possibility of capital from a specific source and an adjournment is the only way to do justice between the parties[2].

1   See eg *Gibson or Scoullar or Archibald v Archibald* [1989] 1 All ER 257, [1989] 1 WLR 123, HL.

2   See *MT v MT (financial provision: lump sum)* [1991] FCR 649, [1992] 1 FLR 362; *D v D (financial provision: lump sum order)* [2001] 1 FCR 561, sub nom *D v D (lump sum: adjournment of application)* [2001] 1 FLR 633. For examples of cases where the court has agreed to an application to adjourn see *Morris v Morris* (1977) 7 Fam Law 244, CA (application relating to husband's army gratuity); *Hardy v Hardy* (1981) 2 FLR 321, 11 Fam Law 153, CA (application adjourned due to husband's inheritance expectations from father); *Davies v Davies* [1986] 1 FLR 497, [1986] Fam Law 138 (adjournment due to real possibility of future assets from partnership dissolution); *MT v MT (financial provision: lump sum)* (husband expected to inherit substantial capital from estate of his father). For examples of cases where an application for adjournment has been refused see *Rodewald v Rodewald* [1977] Fam 192, [1977] 2 All ER 609, CA (wife's application for adjournment to assist her with council house transfer); *Smith v Smith* (1982) 4 FLR 154 (wife's application for adjournment so as to await improvement in company's performance); *Scheeres v Scheeres* [1999] 2 FCR 476, [1999] 1 FLR 241 (same).

479. Circumstances in which interest is payable.   Where the court[1] makes an order for the payment of a lump sum[2] and directs that payment of that sum or any part of it is to be deferred or that that sum or any part of it is to be paid by instalments, the court may order that the amount deferred or the instalments is or are to carry interest at such rate as may be specified by the order from such date, not earlier than the date of the order[3], as may be so specified, until the date when payment of it is due[4].

1   As to the meaning of 'court' see PARA 346 note 2.

2   As to the meaning of 'order for the payment of a lump sum', and as to the making of such orders, see PARA 476.

3   For these purposes, the expression 'the date of the order' refers to the date on which the court orders payment of a lump sum and not to any subsequent date: *L v L (lump sum: interest)* [1995] 1 FCR 60, [1994] 2 FLR 324.

4   Matrimonial Causes Act 1973 s 23(6) (added by the Administration of Justice Act 1982 s 16); Civil Partnership Act 2004 Sch 5 para 3(5)–(7). It is not appropriate for interest to be payable where the recipient is receiving benefits worth more than the interest which would be payable: see *H v H (lump sum: interest payable)* [2005] EWHC 1513 (Fam), [2006] 1 FLR 327.

480.   Time at which application should be made. Although, in general, it may not be right for the court to entertain an original application for a lump sum order many years after the granting of a decree or order, it may be justified by the circumstances of the case[1]. Where, however, the application is in substance an application to vary a periodical payments or secured periodical payments order[2], the court has refused to grant a lump sum payment[3].

1   *Jones v Jones* [1971] 3 All ER 1201, CA. See also *Re W* (1975) 119 Sol Jo 439 (wife, aged 75, divorced 29 years previously, entitled to lump sum from husband's estate).
2   As to making of periodical payments orders and secured periodical payments orders see PARAS 458 et seq, 467 et seq.
3   *Powys v Powys* [1971] P 340 at 355, [1971] 3 All ER 116 at 127, 128. See also PARA 569.

481.   Date order takes effect. Where an order for payment of a lump sum or sums is made[1] on or after granting a decree of divorce or nullity of marriage or making a dissolution or nullity order in respect of a civil partnership[2], neither the order nor any settlement made in pursuance of it is to take effect[3] unless the decree has been made absolute or, as the case may be, the dissolution or nullity order has been made final[4].

1   As to the meaning of 'order for the payment of a lump sum', and as to the making of such orders, see PARA 476.
2   Ie under the Matrimonial Causes Act 1973 s 23(1)(c) or the Civil Partnership Act 2004 Sch 5 paras 1(1), 2(1)(c): see PARA 476.
3   Ie without prejudice to the power to give a direction under the Matrimonial Causes Act 1973 s 30 or the Civil Partnership Act 2004 Sch 5 para 76 for the settlement of an instrument by conveyancing counsel: see PARA 473.
4   Matrimonial Causes Act 1973 s 23(5); Civil Partnership Act 2004 Sch 5 para 4. In respect of a marriage, it has been held that the court has no jurisdiction, even with consent, to make a substantive order before a decree nisi is pronounced, and that an order made before a decree nisi is pronounced cannot be rectified under the court's inherent jurisdiction or under the slip rule: see *Board (Board intervening) v Checkland* [1987] 2 FLR 257, CA, following *Munks v Munks* [1985] FLR 576, [1985] Fam Law 131, CA. However, a court may approve a draft consent order in advance of a decree nisi and direct that it should take effect at a future date: *Pounds v Pounds* [1994] 4 All ER 777, [1994] 1 WLR 1535, CA. Presumably the same situation would obtain in respect of a dissolution or nullity order relating to a civil partnership.

482.   Matters to which the court is to have regard. In deciding whether to exercise its power to make an order for payment of a lump sum or sums[1] and, if so, in what manner, the court[2] is to have regard to certain matters[3]. The court must also consider whether it would be appropriate so to exercise its powers that the financial obligations of each party towards the other will be terminated as soon after the grant of the decree of divorce or nullity of marriage or the making of the dissolution or nullity order as the court considers just and reasonable[4].

Although there is no statutory period of limitation that applies to proceedings for financial relief, delay may be one of the factors to which the court will have regard when considering all the circumstances of the case[5].

1   As to the meaning of 'order for the payment of a lump sum', and as to the making of such orders, see PARA 476.
2   As to the meaning of 'court' see PARA 346 note 2.
3   See the Matrimonial Causes Act 1973 s 25(1), (2); the Civil Partnership Act 2004 Sch 5 paras 20, 21; and PARA 589 et seq. As to this requirement see generally *Rye v Rye* [2002] EWHC 956 (Fam), [2002] 2 FLR 981, [2002] All ER (D) 249 (May).
4   See the Matrimonial Causes Act 1973 s 25A; the Civil Partnership Act 2004 Sch 5 para 23; and PARA 592.
5   See PARA 595.

483.   Duxbury calculations.   A Duxbury calculation[1] is intended as a method of determining the lump sum that would capitalise an entitlement to maintenance. The calculation was conceived to address the Court of Appeal's observations[2] that the recipient of a lump sum was expected to expend it, or so much of it as was intended to meet future income needs, by drawing both on its capital as well as relying on the income it could produce and that the practice had grown up for accountants to devise a computer program which could calculate the lump sum which, if invested on various assumptions, would produce enough to meet the recipient's needs for life[3].

Caution must, however, be shown when adopting a Duxbury calculation[4]. A Duxbury calculation is useful as a guide in assessing the amount of money required to provide for a person's financial needs. It is a means of capitalising an income requirement but that is all. Financial needs are only one of the factors to be taken into account in arriving at the amount of an award. The amount of capital required to provide for an older person's financial needs may well be less than the amount required to provide for a younger person's financial needs. It by no means follows that, in a case where resources exceed the parties' financial needs, the older person's award will be less than those of the younger person. Indeed the older person's award may be substantially larger[5].

1   Ie so named after *Duxbury v Duxbury* (1985) [1992] Fam 62n, [1990] 2 All ER 77, CA.
2   Ie in *Preston v Preston* [1982] Fam 17, [1982] 1 All ER 41, CA.
3   See *B v B* [1990] FCR 105 at 110, [1990] 1 FLR 20 at 24 per Ward J.
4   See e g *Gojkovic v Gojkovic* [1992] Fam 40, [1990] 2 All ER 84, CA; *Vicary v Vicary* [1993] 1 FCR 533, [1992] 2 FLR 271, CA; *F v F (ancillary relief: substantial assets)* [1996] 2 FCR 397, [1995] 2 FLR 45; *Fournier v Fournier* [1999] 2 FCR 20, [1998] 2 FLR 990, CA; *A v A (financial provision)* [1998] 3 FCR 421, [1998] 2 FLR 180. In particular, Duxbury calculations may well be inappropriate in relation to younger partners where the marriage or civil partnership was of short duration (see *F v F (ancillary relief: substantial assets)*; *White v White* [2001] 1 AC 596, [2001] 1 All ER 1, HL; and PARA 604) and also in relation to older partners (see *White v White*; and PARA 604). It has been said that a person's budget may be expected to diminish in later years: see *F v F (ancillary relief: substantial assets)*; *A v A (financial provision)*.
5   See *White v White* [2001] 1 AC 596 at 609, [2001] 1 All ER 1 at 12, HL per Lord Nicholls of Birkenhead.

484.   Alienation and bankruptcy.   A deed of assignment of rights under a lump sum order is valid as a contract for valuable consideration to assign a future chose in action, the essence of a lump sum order being that it carries all the incidents of outright ownership[1]. A lump sum order is a debt provable in the bankruptcy of the person against whom the order has been made[2].

1   *Sears Tooth (a firm) v Payne Hicks Beach (a firm)* [1998] 1 FCR 231, [1997] 2 FLR 116 (rights assigned in favour of solicitors in consideration of the provision of legal services; agreement not champertous or otherwise contrary to public policy).
2   *Curtis v Curtis* [1969] 2 All ER 207, [1969] 1 WLR 422, CA.

E. PENSION ATTACHMENTS

485.   Power to make order.   Where, having regard to any benefits under a pension arrangement[1], the court[2] determines to make[3] a financial provision order[4], that order may, to the extent to which it is made having regard to any benefits under a pension arrangement, require the person responsible for the pension arrangement[5] in question, if at any time any payment in respect of any benefits under the arrangement becomes due to the party with pension rights[6], to make a payment for the benefit of the other party[7]. The order must express the amount of any payment required to be so made as a percentage of the payment which becomes due to the party with pension rights[8].

Any such payment by the person responsible for the arrangement:

(1) discharges so much of his liability to the party with pension rights as corresponds to the amount of the payment[9]; and

(2) is to be treated for all purposes as a payment made by the party with pension rights in or towards the discharge of his liability under the order[10].

Where the party with pension rights has a right of commutation under the arrangement, the order may require him to exercise it to any extent[11]; but the power so conferred may not be exercised for the purpose of commuting a benefit payable to the party with pension rights to a benefit payable to the other party[12].

The powers conferred by these provisions[13] may not be exercised in relation to a pension arrangement which is the subject of a pension sharing order[14] in relation to the marriage or civil partnership or has been the subject of pension sharing between the parties to the marriage or the civil partnership[15]. These provisions are also modified in connection with pension payments for which responsibility has been assumed by the Board of the Pension Protection Fund[16].

1   As to the duty of the court to have regard to benefits under pension arrangements see PARA 590. 'Benefits under a pension arrangement', or 'pension benefits', include benefits by way of pension, whether under a pension arrangement or not: Matrimonial Causes Act 1973 s 25B(7C) (ss 25B, 25D added by the Pensions Act 1995 s 166(1); Matrimonial Causes Act 1973 s 25B(3), (4), (6)(a), (7) amended, s 25B(7A)–(7C) added, ss 25B(5), 25D(3), (4) substituted, by the Welfare Reform and Pensions Act 1999 Sch 4 paras 1(1), (4)–(9), 3(1), (5)); Civil Partnership Act 2004 Sch 5 para 24(3). 'Pension arrangement' for these purposes means: (1) an occupational pension scheme; (2) a personal pension scheme; (3) a retirement annuity contract; (4) an annuity or insurance policy purchased, or transferred, for the purpose of giving effect to rights under an occupational pension scheme or a personal pension scheme; and (5) an annuity purchased, or entered into, for the purpose of discharging liability in respect of a pension credit under the Welfare Reform and Pensions Act 1999 s 29(1)(b) (see SOCIAL SECURITY AND PENSIONS) or under corresponding Northern Ireland legislation: Matrimonial Causes Act 1973 s 25D(3) (as so added and substituted); Civil Partnership Act 2004 Sch 5 paras 16(4), 29(2). As to the meanings of 'occupational pension scheme' and 'personal pension scheme' see the Pension Schemes Act 1993 s 1; and SOCIAL SECURITY AND PENSIONS vol 44(2) (Reissue) PARAS 701, 741 (definitions applied by the Matrimonial Causes Act 1973 s 25D(3) (as so added and substituted) and the Civil Partnership Act 2004 Sch 5 paras 16(5)). 'Retirement annuity contract' means a contract or scheme approved under the Income and Corporation Taxes Act 1988 Pt XIV Chapter III (ss 618–629 (see SOCIAL SECURITY AND PENSIONS vol 44(2) (Reissue) PARA 677 et seq)): Matrimonial Causes Act 1973 s 25D(3) (as so added and substituted); Civil Partnership Act 2004 Sch 5 paras 16(5).

2   As to the meaning of 'court' see PARA 346 note 2.

3   Ie under the Matrimonial Causes Act 1973 s 23 or the Civil Partnership Act 2004 Sch 5 paras 1–5 (see PARA 450 et seq).

4   Matrimonial Causes Act 1973 s 25B(3) (as added and amended: see note 1); Civil Partnership Act 2004 Sch 5 para 25(1). As to the application of the Matrimonial Causes Act 1973 s 25B(3)–(7B) and the Civil Partnership Act 2004 Sch 5 para 25(1)–(8) (see the text and notes 4–16) to interim orders for maintenance under the Matrimonial and Family Proceedings Act 1984 s 14 or the Civil Partnership Act 2004 Sch 7 para 5 (see PARA 536) and to orders for financial provision and property adjustment under the Matrimonial and Family Proceedings Act 1984 s 17 or the Civil Partnership Act 2004 Sch 7 para 9 (see PARA 531), as they apply to like orders under the Matrimonial Causes Act 1973 Pt II (ss 21–40A) and the Civil Partnership Act 2004 Sch 5, see the Matrimonial and Family Proceedings Act 1984 s 21; the Civil Partnership Act 2004 Sch 7 para 14; and PARA 537.

5   For these purposes references to the person responsible for a pension arrangement are: (1) in the case of an occupational pension scheme or a personal pension scheme, to the trustees or managers of the scheme; (2) in the case of a retirement annuity contract or an annuity falling within note 1 head (4) or (5) above, the provider of the annuity; and (3) in the case of an insurance policy falling within note 1 head (4) above, the insurer: Matrimonial Causes Act 1973

s 25D(4) (as added and substituted: see note 1); Welfare Reform and Pensions Act 1999 s 26(2); Civil Partnership Act 2004 Sch 5 para 29(3). 'Trustees or managers', in relation to an occupational pension scheme or a personal pension scheme, means: (a) in the case of a scheme established under a trust, the trustees of the scheme; and (b) in any other case, the managers of the scheme: Matrimonial Causes Act 1973 s 25D(3) (as so added and substituted); Welfare Reform and Pensions Act 1999 s 26(1); Civil Partnership Act 2004 Sch 5 para 29(3).

6   For these purposes the 'party with pension rights' means the party to the marriage or civil partnership who has or is likely to have benefits under a pension arrangement: Matrimonial Causes Act 1973 s 25D(3) (as added and substituted: see note 1); Civil Partnership Act 2004 Sch 5 para 29(1).

7   Matrimonial Causes Act 1973 s 25B(4) (as added and amended: see note 1); Civil Partnership Act 2004 Sch 5 para 25(2). See also note 5.

8   Matrimonial Causes Act 1973 s 25B(5) (added and substituted: see note 1); Civil Partnership Act 2004 Sch 5 para 25(3). See also note 5.

9   Matrimonial Causes Act 1973 s 25B(6)(a) (as added and amended: see note 1); Civil Partnership Act 2004 Sch 5 para 25(4)(a). See also note 5.

10 Matrimonial Causes Act 1973 s 25B(6)(b) (as added: see note 1); Civil Partnership Act 2004 Sch 5 para 25(4)(b). See also note 5.

11 Matrimonial Causes Act 1973 s 25B(7) (as added and amended: see note 1); Civil Partnership Act 2004 Sch 5 para 25(5). See also note 5. The Matrimonial Causes Act 1973 s 25B and the Civil Partnership Act 2004 Sch 5 para 25 (see the text and notes 1–4, 8–16) apply to any payment due in consequence of commutation in pursuance of the order as it applies to other payments in respect of benefits under the arrangement: s 25B(7) (as so added and amended); Civil Partnership Act 2004 Sch 5 para 25(6).

12 Matrimonial Causes Act 1973 s 25B(7A) (as added: see note 1); Civil Partnership Act 2004 Sch 5 para 25(7). See also note 5.

13 Ie by the Matrimonial Causes Act 1973 s 25B(4), (7) and the Civil Partnership Act 2004 Sch 5 para 25(2), (5) (see the text and notes 1–4, 7).

14 As to pension sharing orders see PARA 523 et seq.

15 Matrimonial Causes Act 1973 s 25B(7B) (as added: see note 1); Civil Partnership Act 2004 Sch 5 para 25(8). See also note 5.

16 See the Matrimonial Causes Act 1973 s 25E(2)–(10) (added by the Pensions Act 2004 Sch 12 para 3; prospectively amended by the Pensions Act 2008 Sch 5 paras 1, 6); the Civil Partnership Act 2004 Sch 5 paras 31–37; the Divorce etc (Pension Protection Fund) Regulations 2006, SI 2006/1932; the Dissolution etc (Pension Protection Fund) Regulations 2006, SI 2006/1934.

486.   Lump sums.   If the benefits which a party to a marriage or a civil partnership with pension rights[1] has or is likely to have under a pension arrangement[2] include any lump sum payable in respect of his death, the power of the court[3] to order that party to pay a lump sum to the other party[4] includes power by order:

(1)   to require the person responsible for the pension arrangement[5], if he has power to determine the person to whom the sum, or any part of it, is to be paid, to pay the whole or part of that sum, when it becomes due, to the other party[6];

(2)   to require the party with pension rights, if he has power to nominate the person to whom the sum, or any part of it, is to be paid, to nominate the other party in respect of the whole or part of that sum[7]; and

(3)   in any other case, to require the person responsible for the pension arrangement in question to pay the whole or part of that sum, when it becomes due, for the benefit of the other party instead of to the person to whom, apart from the order, it would be paid[8].

Any payment by the person responsible for the arrangement under an order made under a financial provision order[9] by virtue of these provisions discharges so much of his liability in respect of the party with pension rights as corresponds to the amount of the payment[10]. The powers conferred by these provisions may not be exercised in relation to a pension arrangement which is the subject of a pension sharing order[11] in relation to the marriage or civil partnership or has been the subject of pension sharing between the parties to the marriage or civil partnership[12]. These provisions may also be modified in connection with pension payments for which responsibility has been assumed by the Board of the Pension Protection Fund[13].

1 As to the party with pension rights see PARA 485 note 6.
2 As to the meaning of 'pension arrangement' see PARA 485 note 1.
3 Ie under the Matrimonial Causes Act 1973 s 23 or the Civil Partnership Act 2004 Sch 5 paras 1–5 (see PARA 450 et seq). As to the meaning of 'court' see PARA 346 note 2.
4 As to making of orders for the payment of a lump sum see PARA 476.
5 As to the person responsible for a pension arrangement see PARA 485 note 5.
6 Matrimonial Causes Act 1973 s 25C(1), (2)(a) (s 25C added by the Pensions Act 1995 s 166(1); Matrimonial Causes Act 1973 s 25C(1)–(3) amended, s 25C(4) added, by the Welfare Reform and Pensions Act 1999 Sch 4 para 2); Civil Partnership Act 2004 Sch 5 para 26(1)–(3). As to the application of the Matrimonial Causes Act 1973 s 25C and the Civil Partnership Act 2004 Sch 5 para 26 to interim orders for maintenance under the Matrimonial and Family Proceedings Act 1984 s 14 or the Civil Partnership Act 2004 Sch 7 para 5 (see PARA 536) and to orders for financial provision and property adjustment under the Matrimonial and Family Proceedings Act 1984 s 17 or the Civil Partnership Act 2004 Sch 7 para 9 (see PARA 531), as they apply to like orders under the Matrimonial Causes Act 1973 Pt II (ss 21–40A) and the Civil Partnership Act 2004 Sch 5, see the Matrimonial and Family Proceedings Act 1984 s 21; the Civil Partnership Act 2004 Sch 7 para 14; and PARA 537.
7 Matrimonial Causes Act 1973 s 25C(2)(b) (as added: see note 6); Civil Partnership Act 2004 Sch 5 para 26(4).
8 Matrimonial Causes Act 1973 s 25C(2)(c) (as added and amended: see note 6); Civil Partnership Act 2004 Sch 5 para 26(5).
9 Ie an order made under the Matrimonial Causes Act 1973 s 23 or the Civil Partnership Act 2004 Sch 5 paras 1–5 (see PARA 450 et seq).
10 Matrimonial Causes Act 1973 s 25C(3) (as added and amended: see note 6); Civil Partnership Act 2004 Sch 5 para 26(6).
11 As to pension sharing orders see PARA 523 et seq.
12 Matrimonial Causes Act 1973 s 25C(4) (as added: see note 6); Civil Partnership Act 2004 Sch 5 para 26(7).
13 See the Matrimonial Causes Act 1973 s 25E(6) (added by the Pensions Act 2004 Sch 12 para 3); the Civil Partnership Act 2004 Sch 5 para 33. At the date at which this volume states the law the regulations made under those provisions containing modifications relating to pension payments for which responsibility has been assumed by the Board of the Pension Protection Fund (ie the Divorce etc (Pension Protection Fund) Regulations 2006, SI 2006/1932, and the Dissolution etc (Pension Protection Fund) Regulations 2006, SI 2006/1934) made no modifications to any of the provisions of the Matrimonial Causes Act 1973 s 25C(4) or the Civil Partnership Act 2004 Sch 5 para 26.

487. Acquisition of rights under new pension arrangement. Where:

(1) a financial provision order[1] to which are attached[2] benefits under a pension arrangement[3] imposes any requirement on the person responsible for a pension arrangement[4] (the 'first arrangement') and the party with pension rights[5] acquires rights under another pension arrangement (the 'new arrangement') which are derived, directly or indirectly, from the whole of his rights under the first arrangement[6]; and

(2) the person responsible for the new arrangement has been given notice in accordance with regulations made by the Lord Chancellor[7],

the order has effect as if it had been made instead in respect of the person responsible for the new arrangement[8].

1 Ie an order made under the Matrimonial Causes Act 1973 s 23 or the Civil Partnership Act 2004 Sch 5 paras 1–5 (see PARA 450 et seq).
2 Ie by virtue of the Matrimonial Causes Act 1973 s 25B or s 25C or the Civil Partnership Act 2004 Sch 5 para 25 or Sch 5 para 26 (see PARAS 485, 486).
3 As to the meaning of 'pension arrangement' see PARA 485 note 1.
4 As to the person responsible for a pension arrangement see PARA 485 note 5.

5   As to the party with pension rights see PARA 485 note 6.
6   Matrimonial Causes Act 1973 s 25D(1)(a) (s 25D added by the Pensions Act 1995 s 166(1);
    Matrimonial Causes Act 1973 s 25D(1), (3) substituted, s 25D(2) amended, s 25D(2A) added,
    by the Welfare Reform and Pensions Act 1999 Sch 4 para 3, Sch 13); Civil Partnership Act 2004
    Sch 5 para 27(a), (b).
7   Matrimonial Causes Act 1973 s 25D(1)(b) (as added: see note 6); Civil Partnership Act 2004
    Sch 5 para 27(c). The person responsible for the first arrangement must give notice to the person
    responsible for the new arrangement and to the other party to the marriage or civil partnership:
    Divorce etc (Pensions) Regulations 2000, SI 2000/1123, reg 4(1), (2); Dissolution etc (Pensions)
    Regulations 2005, SI 2005/2920, reg 4(1), (2). Both notices must be given within the period
    provided by the Pension Schemes Act 1993 s 99 (see SOCIAL SECURITY AND PENSIONS vol 44(2)
    (Reissue) PARA 958) for the person responsible for the first arrangement to carry out what the
    member requires and before the expiry of 21 days after the person responsible for the first
    arrangement has made all required payments to the person responsible for the new arrangement:
    Divorce etc (Pensions) Regulations 2000, SI 2000/1123, reg 4(5); Dissolution etc (Pensions)
    Regulations 2005, SI 2005/2920, reg 4(5). The notice may be sent by fax or by ordinary
    first-class post to the last known address of the intended recipient and is deemed to have been
    received on the seventh day after the day on which it was sent: Divorce etc (Pensions)
    Regulations 2000, SI 2000/1123, reg 8; Dissolution etc (Pensions) Regulations 2005,
    SI 2005/2920, reg 8.
        By virtue of the Divorce etc (Pensions) Regulations 2000, SI 2000/1123, reg 4(3) and the
    Dissolution etc (Pensions) Regulations 2005, SI 2005/2920, reg 4(3), the notice to the person
    responsible for the new arrangement must include copies of:
    (1)   every financial provision order made under the Matrimonial Causes Act 1973 s 23 or
          the Civil Partnership Act 2004 Sch 5 paras 1–5 (as the case may be) imposing any
          requirement on the person responsible for the first arrangement in relation to the rights
          transferred;
    (2)   any order varying such an order (Divorce etc (Pensions) Regulations 2000,
          SI 2000/1123, reg 4(3)(b); Dissolution etc (Pensions) Regulations 2005, SI 2005/2920,
          reg 4(3)(b));
    (3)   all information or particulars which the other party has been required to supply under
          any provision of the Family Proceedings Rules 1991, SI 1991/1247, r 2.70 (see PARA
          926 et seq) for the purpose of enabling the person responsible for the first arrangement
          to provide information, documents or representations to the court to enable it to decide
          what, if any, requirement should be imposed on that person or to comply with any
          order imposing such a requirement;
    (4)   any notice given by the other party to the person responsible for the first arrangement
          under the Divorce etc (Pensions) Regulations 2000, SI 2000/1123, reg 6 or the
          Dissolution etc (Pensions) Regulations 2005, SI 2005/2920, reg 6 (see PARA 491); and
    (5)   where the pension rights under the first arrangement were derived wholly or partly
          from rights held under a previous pension arrangement, any notice given to the person
          responsible for the previous arrangement under the Divorce etc (Pensions)
          Regulations 2000, SI 2000/1123, reg 4(2) or the Dissolution etc (Pensions)
          Regulations 2005, SI 2005/2920, reg 4(2) on the occasion of that acquisition of rights.
        By virtue of the Divorce etc (Pensions) Regulations 2000, SI 2000/1123, reg 4(4) and the
    Dissolution etc (Pensions) Regulations 2005, SI 2005/2920, reg 4(4), the notice to the other
    party must contain:
    (a)   the fact that the pension rights have been transferred;
    (b)   the date on which the transfer takes effect;
    (c)   the name and address of the person responsible for the new arrangement; and
    (d)   the fact that the financial provision order is to have effect as if it had been made in
          respect of the person responsible for the new arrangement.
        The Divorce etc (Pensions) Regulations 2000, SI 2000/1123, and the Dissolution etc
    (Pensions) Regulations 2005, SI 2005/2920, are made pursuant to the powers conferred on the
    Lord Chancellor by the Matrimonial Causes Act 1973 s 25D(2), (2A) (as added and amended:
    see note 6) and the Civil Partnership Act 2004 Sch 5 para 28 to make regulations:
    (i)   in relation to any provision of the Matrimonial Causes Act 1973 s 25B or s 25C or the
          Civil Partnership Act 2004 Sch 5 para 25 or Sch 5 para 26 which authorises the court
          making an order under the Matrimonial Causes Act 1973 s 23 or the Civil Partnership
          Act 2004 Sch 5 paras 1–5 to require the person responsible for a pension arrangement
          to make a payment for the benefit of the other party, making provision as to the person
          to whom, and the terms on which, the payment is to be made;
    (ii) in relation to payment under a mistaken belief as to the continuation in force of a

provision included in an order under the Matrimonial Causes Act 1973 s 23 or the Civil Partnership Act 2004 Sch 5 paras 1–5 by virtue of the Matrimonial Causes Act 1973 s 25B or s 25C or the Civil Partnership Act 2004 Sch 5 para 25 or Sch 5 para 26 making provision about the rights or liabilities of the payer, the payee or the person to whom the payment was due;

(iii) requiring notices to be given in respect of changes of circumstances relevant to such orders which include provision made by virtue of the Matrimonial Causes Act 1973 s 25B or s 25C or the Civil Partnership Act 2004 Sch 5 para 25 or Sch 5 para 26;

(iv) making provision for the person responsible for a pension arrangement to be discharged in circumstances prescribed by regulations from a requirement imposed by virtue of the Matrimonial Causes Act 1973 s 25B or s 25C or the Civil Partnership Act 2004 Sch 5 para 25 or Sch 5 para 26; and

(v) making provision about calculation and verification in relation to the valuation of benefits under a pension arrangement or shareable state scheme rights, for the purposes of the court's functions in connection with the exercise of any of its powers under the Matrimonial Causes Act 1973 Pt II (ss 21–40A) or the Civil Partnership Act 2004 Sch 5 (such regulations may include provision for calculation or verification in accordance with guidance from time to time prepared by a prescribed person and provision by reference to regulations under the Welfare Reform and Pensions Act 1999 s 30 or s 49(4) (see SOCIAL SECURITY AND PENSIONS)).

As to the meaning of 'court' see PARA 346 note 2. As to 'shareable state scheme rights' see, by virtue of the Matrimonial Causes Act 1973 s 25D(3) and the Civil Partnership Act 2004 Sch 5 para 28(1)(a), the Matrimonial Causes Act 1973 s 21A(1) and the Civil Partnership Act 2004 Sch 5 para 16(3); and PARA 523.

8   Matrimonial Causes Act 1973 s 25D(1) (as added and substituted: see note 6); Civil Partnership Act 2004 Sch 5 para 27.

488. Valuation of pension benefits. For the purposes of the court's functions in connection with the exercise of any of its powers relating to financial relief[1], benefits under a pension arrangement[2] are to be calculated and verified in the manner set out for the purposes of pensions legislation[3], and:

(1) the benefits are to be valued as at a date to be specified by the court, being not earlier than one year before the date of the petition[4] and not later than the date on which the court is exercising its power[5]; and

(2) in determining that value, the court may have regard to information furnished[6] by the person responsible for the pension arrangement[7].

1   Ie under the Matrimonial Causes Act 1973 Pt II (ss 21–40A) or the Civil Partnership Act 2004 Sch 5: see PARA 450 et seq.

2   As to the meaning of 'pension arrangement' see PARA 485 note 1 (definition applied by the Divorce etc (Pensions) Regulations 2000, SI 2000/1123, reg 2(d) and the Dissolution etc (Pensions) Regulations 2005, SI 2005/2920, reg 2(d)).

3   Ie set out in the Pensions on Divorce etc (Provision of Information) Regulations 2000, SI 2000/1048, reg 3 (see SOCIAL SECURITY AND PENSIONS).

4   As to petitions and applications see PARA 321 note 1.

5   Divorce etc (Pensions) Regulations 2000, SI 2000/1123, reg 3(1)(a); Dissolution etc (Pensions) Regulations 2005, SI 2005/2920, reg 3(1)(a). In specifying a date for this purpose the court may have regard to the date specified in any information furnished as mentioned in head (2) in the text: Divorce etc (Pensions) Regulations 2000, SI 2000/1123, reg 3(1)(c); Dissolution etc (Pensions) Regulations 2005, SI 2005/2920, reg 3(1)(c).

6   Ie pursuant to the Pensions on Divorce etc (Provision of Information) Regulations 2000, SI 2000/1048 (see SOCIAL SECURITY AND PENSIONS), the Occupational Pension Schemes (Disclosure of Information) Regulations 1996, SI 1996/1655, reg 5, Sch 2 (see SOCIAL SECURITY AND PENSIONS vol 44(2) (Reissue) PARA 800), the Occupational Pension Schemes (Transfer Values) Regulations 1996, SI 1996/1847, reg 11, Sch 1 (see SOCIAL SECURITY AND PENSIONS vol 44(2) (Reissue) PARA 960), the Pension Schemes Act 1993 s 93A (see SOCIAL SECURITY AND PENSIONS vol 44(2) (Reissue) PARA 952) or s 94(1)(a) or (aa) (see SOCIAL SECURITY AND PENSIONS vol 44(2) (Reissue) PARA 953), the Pension Schemes Act 1993 s 94(1)(b) or the Personal Pension Schemes (Disclosure of Information) Regulations 1987, SI 1987/1110, reg 5(1), Sch 2 para 2(a) or, where applicable, Sch 2 para 2(b) (see SOCIAL SECURITY AND

PENSIONS vol 44(2) (Reissue) PARA 963): Divorce etc (Pensions) Regulations 2000, SI 2000/1123, reg 3(2); Dissolution etc (Pensions) Regulations 2005, SI 2005/2920, reg 3(2).

7 Divorce etc (Pensions) Regulations 2000, SI 2000/1123, reg 3(1)(b); Dissolution etc (Pensions) Regulations 2005, SI 2005/2920, reg 3(1)(b). As to the person responsible for a pension arrangement see PARA 485 note 5 (definition applied by the Divorce etc (Pensions) Regulations 2000, SI 2000/1123, reg 2(d) and the Dissolution etc (Pensions) Regulations 2005, SI 2005/2920, reg 2(d)).

489.   Reduction in benefits.   Where:

(1)   a financial provision order to which are attached benefits under a pension arrangement has been made[1] imposing any requirement on the person responsible for the pension arrangement[2]; and

(2)   an event has occurred[3] which is likely to result in a significant reduction in the benefits payable under the arrangement[4],

the person responsible for the arrangement must, within 14 days of the occurrence of such event, give notice to the other party of that event and the likely extent of the reduction in the benefits payable under the arrangement[5]. Where the event consists of a transfer of some but not all of the rights of the party with pension rights from the arrangement, the person responsible for the first arrangement must, within 14 days of the transfer, give notice to the other party of the name and address of the person responsible for any pension arrangement under which the party with pension rights has acquired rights as a result of that event[6].

1   Ie where an order under the Matrimonial Causes Act 1973 s 23 or the Civil Partnership Act 2004 Sch 5 paras 1–5 (see PARA 450 et seq), or the Matrimonial and Family Proceedings Act 1984 s 17 or the Civil Partnership Act 2004 Sch 7 para 9 (see PARA 531), has been made by virtue of the Matrimonial Causes Act 1973 s 25B or s 25C or the Civil Partnership Act 2004 Sch 5 para 25 or Sch 5 para 26 (see PARAS 485, 486). As to the meaning of 'pension arrangement' see PARA 485 note 1 (definition applied by the Divorce etc (Pensions) Regulations 2000, SI 2000/1123, reg 2(d) and the Dissolution etc (Pensions) Regulations 2005, SI 2005/2920, reg 2(d)).

2   Divorce etc (Pensions) Regulations 2000, SI 2000/1123, reg 5(1)(a); Dissolution etc (Pensions) Regulations 2005, SI 2005/2920, reg 5(1)(a). As to the person responsible for a pension arrangement see PARA 485 note 5 (definition applied by the Divorce etc (Pensions) Regulations 2000, SI 2000/1123, reg 2(d) and the Dissolution etc (Pensions) Regulations 2005, SI 2005/2920, reg 2(d)).

3   Ie an event other than the transfer from the arrangement of all the rights of the party with pension rights in the circumstances set out in the Matrimonial Causes Act 1973 s 25D(1)(a) or the Civil Partnership Act 2004 Sch 5 para 27 (see PARA 487) or a reduction in the value of assets held for the purposes of the arrangement by reason of a change in interest rates or other market conditions: Divorce etc (Pensions) Regulations 2000, SI 2000/1123, reg 5(1)(b)(i), (ii); Dissolution etc (Pensions) Regulations 2005, SI 2005/2920, reg 5(1)(b)(i), (ii). As to the party with pension rights see PARA 485 note 6 (definition applied by the Divorce etc (Pensions) Regulations 2000, SI 2000/1123, reg 2(d) and the Dissolution etc (Pensions) Regulations 2005, SI 2005/2920, reg 2(d)).

4   Divorce etc (Pensions) Regulations 2000, SI 2000/1123, reg 5(1)(b); Dissolution etc (Pensions) Regulations 2005, SI 2005/2920, reg 5(1)(b).

5   Divorce etc (Pensions) Regulations 2000, SI 2000/1123, reg 5(2); Dissolution etc (Pensions) Regulations 2005, SI 2005/2920, reg 5(2). The notice may be sent by fax or by ordinary first-class post to the last known address of the intended recipient and is deemed to have been received on the seventh day after the day on which it was sent: Divorce etc (Pensions) Regulations 2000, SI 2000/1123, reg 8; Dissolution etc (Pensions) Regulations 2005, SI 2005/2920, reg 8.

6   Divorce etc (Pensions) Regulations 2000, SI 2000/1123, reg 5(3); Dissolution etc (Pensions) Regulations 2005, SI 2005/2920, reg 5(3).

490.   Change of circumstances.   Where:

(1)   a financial provision order to which are attached benefits under a

pension arrangement has been made[1] imposing any requirement on the person responsible for the pension arrangement[2]; and

(2)   either any of the particulars supplied by the other party[3] for any specified purpose[4] has ceased to be accurate[5] or the order has ceased to have effect by reason of the remarriage or the formation of a subsequent civil partnership or subsequent marriage by the other party or otherwise[6],

the other party must, within 14 days of the event, give notice of it to the person responsible for the arrangement[7].

Where, because of the inaccuracy of the particulars supplied by the other party[8] or because the other party has failed to give notice of their having ceased to be accurate, it is not reasonably practicable for the person responsible for the pension arrangement to make a payment to the other party as required by the order, it may instead make that payment to the party with pension rights[9] and it is then discharged of liability to the other party to the extent of that payment[10]. Where an applicable event[11] has occurred and, because the other party has failed to give such notice[12], the person responsible for the pension arrangement makes a payment to the other party as required by the order, its liability to the party with pension rights is discharged to the extent of that payment and the other party must, within 14 days of the payment being made, make a payment to the party with pension rights to the extent of that payment[13].

1   Ie where an order under the Matrimonial Causes Act 1973 s 23 or the Civil Partnership Act 2004 Sch 5 paras 1–5 (see PARA 450 et seq), or the Matrimonial and Family Proceedings Act 1984 s 17 or the Civil Partnership Act 2004 Sch 7 para 9 (see PARA 531), has been made by virtue of the Matrimonial Causes Act 1973 s 25B or s 25C or the Civil Partnership Act 2004 Sch 5 para 25 or Sch 5 para 26 (see PARAS 485, 486). As to the meaning of 'pension arrangement' see PARA 485 note 1 (definition applied by the Divorce etc (Pensions) Regulations 2000, SI 2000/1123, reg 2(d) and the Dissolution etc (Pensions) Regulations 2005, SI 2005/2920, reg 2(d)).

2   Divorce etc (Pensions) Regulations 2000, SI 2000/1123, reg 6(1)(a); Dissolution etc (Pensions) Regulations 2005, SI 2005/2920, reg 6(1)(a). As to the person responsible for a pension arrangement see PARA 485 note 5 (definition applied by the Divorce etc (Pensions) Regulations 2000, SI 2000/1123, reg 2(d) and the Dissolution etc (Pensions) Regulations 2005, SI 2005/2920, reg 2(d)).

3   Ie under the Family Proceedings Rules 1991, SI 1991/1247, r 2.70: see PARA 927 et seq.

4   Ie any purpose mentioned in the Divorce etc (Pensions) Regulations 2000, SI 2000/1123, reg 4(3)(c) or, as the case may be, the Dissolution etc (Pensions) Regulations 2005, SI 2005/2920, reg 4(3)(c): see PARA 487.

5   Divorce etc (Pensions) Regulations 2000, SI 2000/1123, reg 6(1)(b), (2)(a); Dissolution etc (Pensions) Regulations 2005, SI 2005/2920, reg 6(1)(b), (2)(a).

6   Divorce etc (Pensions) Regulations 2000, SI 2000/1123, reg 6(1)(b), (2)(b) (amended by SI 2005/2114); Dissolution etc (Pensions) Regulations 2005, SI 2005/2920, reg 6(1)(b), (2)(b). As to references to remarriage, to a subsequent marriage and to the formation of a subsequent civil partnership see PARA 452 note 1.

7   Divorce etc (Pensions) Regulations 2000, SI 2000/1123, reg 6(3); Dissolution etc (Pensions) Regulations 2005, SI 2005/2920, reg 6(3). The notice may be sent by fax or by ordinary first-class post to the last known address of the intended recipient and is deemed to have been received on the seventh day after the day on which it was sent: Divorce etc (Pensions) Regulations 2000, SI 2000/1123, reg 8; Dissolution etc (Pensions) Regulations 2005, SI 2005/2920, reg 8.

8   See note 3.

9   As to the party with pension rights see PARA 485 note 6 (definition applied by the Divorce etc (Pensions) Regulations 2000, SI 2000/1123, reg 2(d) and the Dissolution etc (Pensions) Regulations 2005, SI 2005/2920, reg 2(d)).

10   Divorce etc (Pensions) Regulations 2000, SI 2000/1123, reg 6(4); Dissolution etc (Pensions) Regulations 2005, SI 2005/2920, reg 6(4).

11 Ie an event described in the Divorce etc (Pensions) Regulations 2000, SI 2000/1123, reg 6(2)(b) or the Dissolution etc (Pensions) Regulations 2005, SI 2005/2920, reg 6(2)(b) (see the text and note 6).
12 Ie in accordance with the Divorce etc (Pensions) Regulations 2000, SI 2000/1123, reg 6(3) or the Dissolution etc (Pensions) Regulations 2005, SI 2005/2920, reg 6(3) (see the text and notes 1–7).
13 Divorce etc (Pensions) Regulations 2000, SI 2000/1123, reg 6(5); Dissolution etc (Pensions) Regulations 2005, SI 2005/2920, reg 6(5).

491. Transfer of rights. Where:

(1) a transfer of rights has[1] taken place[2];

(2) notice has been duly[3] given[4];

(3) any of the specified events[5] has occurred[6];

(4) the other party has not, before receiving notice[7], given notice of that event[8] to the person responsible for the first arrangement[9],

the other party must, within 14 days of the event, give notice of it to the person responsible for the new arrangement[10].

Where, because of the inaccuracy of the particulars supplied by the other party[11] for any specified purpose[12] or because the other party has failed to give notice of their having become inaccurate, it is not reasonably practicable for the person responsible for the new arrangement to make a payment to the other party as required by the order, it may instead make that payment to the party with pension rights[13] and it is then discharged of liability to the other party to the extent of that payment[14]. Where the other party, within one year from the transfer, gives to the person responsible for the first arrangement notice of the specified event[15] in purported compliance with these provisions[16], the person responsible for the first arrangement must send that notice to the person responsible for the new arrangement and give the other party a second notice[17]; and the other party is deemed to have given notice under these provisions[18] to the person responsible for the new arrangement[19].

1 Ie in the circumstances set out in the Matrimonial Causes Act 1973 s 25D(1)(a) or the Civil Partnership Act 2004 Sch 5 para 27: see PARA 487.
2 Divorce etc (Pensions) Regulations 2000, SI 2000/1123, reg 7(1)(a); Dissolution etc (Pensions) Regulations 2005, SI 2005/2920, reg 7(1)(a).
3 Ie in accordance with the Divorce etc (Pensions) Regulations 2000, SI 2000/1123, reg 4(2)(a), (b) or the Dissolution etc (Pensions) Regulations 2005, SI 2005/2920, reg 4(2)(a), (b): see PARA 487.
4 Divorce etc (Pensions) Regulations 2000, SI 2000/1123, reg 7(1)(b); Dissolution etc (Pensions) Regulations 2005, SI 2005/2920, reg 7(1)(b).
5 Ie any of the events specified in the Divorce etc (Pensions) Regulations 2000, SI 2000/1123, reg 6(2) or the Dissolution etc (Pensions) Regulations 2005, SI 2005/2920, reg 6(2): see PARA 490.
6 Divorce etc (Pensions) Regulations 2000, SI 2000/1123, reg 7(1)(c); Dissolution etc (Pensions) Regulations 2005, SI 2005/2920, reg 7(1)(c).
7 Ie under the Divorce etc (Pensions) Regulations 2000, SI 2000/1123, reg 4(2)(b) or the Dissolution etc (Pensions) Regulations 2005, SI 2005/2920, reg 4(2)(b): see PARA 487.
8 Ie under the Divorce etc (Pensions) Regulations 2000, SI 2000/1123, reg 6(3) or the Dissolution etc (Pensions) Regulations 2005, SI 2005/2920, reg 6(3): see PARA 490.
9 Divorce etc (Pensions) Regulations 2000, SI 2000/1123, reg 7(1)(d); Dissolution etc (Pensions) Regulations 2005, SI 2005/2920, reg 7(1)(d). As to the person responsible for a pension arrangement see PARA 485 note 5 (definition applied by the Divorce etc (Pensions) Regulations 2000, SI 2000/1123, reg 2(d) and the Dissolution etc (Pensions) Regulations 2005, SI 2005/2920, reg 2(d)).
10 Divorce etc (Pensions) Regulations 2000, SI 2000/1123, reg 7(2); Dissolution etc (Pensions) Regulations 2005, SI 2005/2920, reg 7(2). The notice may be sent by fax or by ordinary first-class post to the last known address of the intended recipient and is deemed to have been

received on the seventh day after the day on which it was sent: Divorce etc (Pensions) Regulations 2000, SI 2000/1123, reg 8; Dissolution etc (Pensions) Regulations 2005, SI 2005/2920, reg 8.

11 Ie under the Family Proceedings Rules 1991, SI 1991/1247, r 2.70: see PARA 927 et seq.

12 Ie any purpose mentioned in the Divorce etc (Pensions) Regulations 2000, SI 2000/1123, reg 4(3)(c) or, as the case may be, the Dissolution etc (Pensions) Regulations 2005, SI 2005/2920, reg 4(3)(c): see PARA 487.

13 As to the party with pension rights see PARA 485 note 6 (definition applied by the Divorce etc (Pensions) Regulations 2000, SI 2000/1123, reg 2(d) and the Dissolution etc (Pensions) Regulations 2005, SI 2005/2920, reg 2(d)).

14 Divorce etc (Pensions) Regulations 2000, SI 2000/1123, reg 7(3); Dissolution etc (Pensions) Regulations 2005, SI 2005/2920, reg 7(3).

15 Ie any of the events specified in the Divorce etc (Pensions) Regulations 2000, SI 2000/1123, reg 6(2) or the Dissolution etc (Pensions) Regulations 2005, SI 2005/2920, reg 6(2): see PARA 490.

16 Ie in purported compliance with the Divorce etc (Pensions) Regulations 2000, SI 2000/1123, reg 7(2) or the Dissolution etc (Pensions) Regulations 2005, SI 2005/2920, reg 7(2) (see the text and notes 1–10).

17 Ie under the Divorce etc (Pensions) Regulations 2000, SI 2000/1123, reg 4(2)(b) or the Dissolution etc (Pensions) Regulations 2005, SI 2005/2920, reg 4(2)(b): see PARA 487.

18 Ie under the Divorce etc (Pensions) Regulations 2000, SI 2000/1123, reg 7(2) or the Dissolution etc (Pensions) Regulations 2005, SI 2005/2920, reg 7(2) (see the text and notes 1–10).

19 Divorce etc (Pensions) Regulations 2000, SI 2000/1123, reg 7(4); Dissolution etc (Pensions) Regulations 2005, SI 2005/2920, reg 7(4). On complying with this requirement, the person responsible for the first arrangement is, however, discharged from any further obligation under the Divorce etc (Pensions) Regulations 2000, SI 2000/1123, reg 4 or the Dissolution etc (Pensions) Regulations 2005, SI 2005/2920, reg 4, whether in relation to the event in question or any further event specified in the Divorce etc (Pensions) Regulations 2000, SI 2000/1123, reg 6(2) or the Dissolution etc (Pensions) Regulations 2005, SI 2005/2920, reg 6(2), which may be notified to it by the other party: Divorce etc (Pensions) Regulations 2000, SI 2000/1123, reg 7(5); Dissolution etc (Pensions) Regulations 2005, SI 2005/2920, reg 7(5).

F. ORDERS FOR THE BENEFIT OF CHILDREN

492. Power to make financial provision orders for the benefit of children. Where the court[1]:

(1) grants a decree of divorce, a decree of nullity of marriage or a decree of judicial separation[2]; or

(2) makes a dissolution, nullity or separation order in respect of a civil partnership[3],

it may[4] make an order:

(a) that a party to the marriage or civil partnership is to make to such person as may be specified in the order for the benefit of a child of the family[5], or to such a child, such periodical payments, for such term, as may be so specified (a 'periodical payments order')[6];

(b) that a party to the marriage or civil partnership is to secure to such person as may be so specified for the benefit of a child of the family, or to such a child, to the satisfaction of the court, such periodical payments, for such term, as may be so specified (a 'secured periodical payments order')[7]; or

(c) that a party to the marriage or civil partnership is to pay to such person as may be so specified for the benefit of a child of the family, or to such a child, such lump sum as may be so specified (an 'order for the payment of a lump sum')[8].

The court may also make any one or more of the orders mentioned in heads (a) to (c) above:

(i)   in any proceedings for divorce, dissolution, nullity of marriage or civil partnership or judicial or legal separation, before granting a decree or making the order[9]; and

(ii)   where any such proceedings are dismissed after the beginning of the trial, either forthwith or within a reasonable period after the dismissal[10].

No such order may be made in favour of a child who has attained the age of 18[11] unless he is in full time education[12] or there are special circumstances which justify the making of an order[13]. The court will not make a clean break order terminating a parent's responsibility to maintain children[14].

1   As to the meaning of 'court' see PARA 346 note 2.

2   Matrimonial Causes Act 1973 s 23(1).

3   Civil Partnership Act 2004 Sch 5 para 1(1)(a).

4   Ie on granting the decree or making the order or at any time thereafter (whether, in the case of a decree of divorce or of nullity of marriage, before or after the decree is made absolute): Matrimonial Causes Act 1973 s 23(1); Civil Partnership Act 2004 Sch 5 para 1(1). The power of the court to make an order in favour of a child of the family is exercisable from time to time: Matrimonial Causes Act 1973 s 23(4); Civil Partnership Act 2004 Sch 5 para 1(3). As to the matters to which the court is to have regard in deciding how to exercise its powers to make orders for the benefit of children see PARAS 597, 598; and as to the duration of orders in favour of children see PARA 495. In deciding the amount of an order for or to a child, the court may consider the rate of foster care allowance that would be applicable to the child (see eg *Cresswell v Eaton* [1991] 1 All ER 484, [1991] 1 WLR 1113) or the child support rate for the child (see eg *E v C (calculation of child maintenance)* [1996] 1 FCR 612, sub nom *E v C (child maintenance)* [1996] 1 FLR 472). However, none of those approaches is necessarily determinative and the court retains a broad discretion in relation to the quantification of maintenance for a child. Where, however, the court does have jurisdiction, it will regard the parents' obligation to maintain children as a primary responsibility: see *R v R (financial provision)* [1988] FCR 307 at 315, sub nom *R v R* [1988] 1 FLR 89 at 97, CA per Slade LJ; *Freeman v Swatridge* [1984] FLR 762, [1984] Fam Law 215, CA.

5   As to the meanings of 'child of the family' and (for the purposes of the Matrimonial Causes Act 1973) 'child' see PARA 477 note 3.

6   Matrimonial Causes Act 1973 ss 21(1)(a), 23(1)(d); Civil Partnership Act 2004 Sch 5 paras 2(1)(d), (2), 80(1)(a). As to periodical payments orders see PARA 458 et seq. Orders for periodical payments may be reduced by sums payable as child support maintenance pursuant to the Child Support Act 1991: see PARA 497.

7   Matrimonial Causes Act 1973 ss 21(1)(b), 23(1)(e); Civil Partnership Act 2004 Sch 5 paras 2(1)(e), (2), 80(1)(b). As to secured periodical payments orders see PARA 467 et seq. Where the court has made an order for a secured periodical payments order or an order for the payment of a lump sum (see the text and note 8), it may, on making the order or at any time thereafter, make a further order for the sale of such property as may be specified in the order: see the Matrimonial Causes Act 1973 s 24A; the Civil Partnership Act 2004 Sch 5 para 10; and PARA 520.

8   Matrimonial Causes Act 1973 ss 21(1)(c), 23(1)(f); Civil Partnership Act 2004 Sch 5 paras 2(1)(f), (2), 80(1)(c). As to orders for the payment of a lump sum see PARA 476 et seq. An order for the payment of a lump sum to or for the benefit of a child of the family may be made for the purposes of enabling any liabilities or expenses reasonably incurred by or for the benefit of that child before the making of an application for a financial provision order in his favour to be met: Matrimonial Causes Act 1973 s 23(3)(b); Civil Partnership Act 2004 Sch 5 para 3(2). An order for the payment of a lump sum may provide for the payment of that sum by instalments of such amount as may be specified in the order and may require the payment of the instalments to be secured to the satisfaction of the court: Matrimonial Causes Act 1973 s 23(3)(c); Civil Partnership Act 2004 Sch 5 para 3(3). As to the application of the Matrimonial Causes Act 1973 ss 23(3), 29 and the Civil Partnership Act 2004 Sch 5 paras 3, 5, 49 to interim orders for maintenance under the Matrimonial and Family Proceedings Act 1984 s 14 or the Civil Partnership Act 2004 Sch 7 para 5 (see PARA 536) and to orders for financial provision and property adjustment under the Matrimonial and Family Proceedings Act 1984 s 17 or the Civil Partnership Act 2004 Sch 7 para 9 (see PARA 531), as they apply to like orders under the Matrimonial Causes Act 1973 Pt II (ss 21–40A) and the Civil Partnership Act 2004 Sch 5, see the Matrimonial and Family Proceedings Act 1984 s 21; the Civil Partnership Act 2004 Sch 7 para 14; and PARA 537. As to the court's power to adjourn proceedings see PARA 478.

Where the court makes an order for the payment of a lump sum and directs that payment of that sum or any part of it is to be deferred or that that sum or any part of it is to be paid by instalments, the court may order that the amount deferred or the instalments is or are to carry interest at such rate as may be specified by the order from such date, not earlier than the date of the order, as may be so specified, until the date when payment of it is due: Matrimonial Causes Act 1973 s 23(6) (added by the Administration of Justice Act 1982 s 16); Civil Partnership Act 2004 Sch 5 para 3(5)–(7). For these purposes, the expression 'the date of the order' refers to the date on which the court orders payment of a lump sum and not to any subsequent date: *L v L (lump sum: interest)* [1995] 1 FCR 60, [1994] 2 FLR 324. It is not appropriate for interest to be payable where the recipient is receiving benefits worth more than the interest which would be payable: see *H v H (lump sum: interest payable)* [2005] EWHC 1513 (Fam), [2006] 1 FLR 327.

It is rare for the court to make an order for the payment of a lump sum in favour of a child: see e g *Chamberlain v Chamberlain* [1974] 1 All ER 33, [1973] 1 WLR 1557, CA; *Griffiths v Griffiths* [1984] Fam 70, [1984] 2 All ER 626, CA; *Kiely v Kiely* [1988] 1 FLR 248, [1988] Fam Law 51, CA. It is wrong to make an order for the payment of a lump sum in favour of a child so as to avoid the statutory charge which arises under what is now the Access to Justice Act 1999 s 10(7) (see LEGAL AID VOL 65 (2008) PARA 97): *Draskovic v Draskovic* (1980) 11 Fam Law 87. Further, the court cannot remedy any perceived absurdities that arise under the Child Support Act 1991 by making capital provision for children: *Phillips v Pearce* [1996] 2 FCR 237, sub nom *Phillips v Peace* [1996] 2 FLR 230.

9　　Matrimonial Causes Act 1973 s 23(2)(a); Civil Partnership Act 2004 Sch 5 para 1(2)(a). See also *P (LE) v P (JM)* [1971] P 318, [1971] 2 All ER 728.

10　Matrimonial Causes Act 1973 s 23(2)(b); Civil Partnership Act 2004 Sch 5 para 1(2)(b). Where the court makes an order in favour of a child under this provision it may from time to time, subject to the restrictions imposed on the making of financial provision orders in favour of children who have attained the age of 18 (see the text and notes 11–13), make a further order in his favour of any of the kinds mentioned in the text and notes 4–8: Matrimonial Causes Act 1973 s 23(4); Civil Partnership Act 2004 Sch 5 para 1(4).

11　Matrimonial Causes Act 1973 s 29(1); Civil Partnership Act 2004 Sch 5 paras 5, 49(1)(a).

12　Ie unless it appears to the court that the child is, or will be, or if an order were made without complying with the Matrimonial Causes Act 1973 s 29(1) or the Civil Partnership Act 2004 Sch 5 para 49(1)(a) (see the text and note 11) would be, receiving instruction at an educational establishment or undergoing training for a trade, profession or vocation, whether or not he is also, or will also be, in gainful employment: Matrimonial Causes Act 1973 s 29(3)(a); Civil Partnership Act 2004 Sch 5 para 49(5)(a). As to 'trade, profession or vocation' see *Richardson v Richardson* [1993] 4 All ER 673, [1994] 1 WLR 186; *Downing v Downing (Downing intervening)* [1976] Fam 288, [1976] 3 All ER 474.

13　Matrimonial Causes Act 1973 s 29(3)(b); Civil Partnership Act 2004 Sch 5 para 49(5)(b). Physical or other disability may amount to such special circumstances: *C v F (disabled child: maintenance orders)* [1999] 1 FCR 39, [1998] 2 FLR 1, CA; *T v S (financial provision for children)* [1994] 1 FCR 743, [1994] 2 FLR 883.

14　See *Crozier v Crozier* [1994] Fam 114, [1996] 2 All ER 362.

493.　Application by parent, guardian etc for financial relief in respect of children. Any of the following persons, namely:

(1)　a parent or guardian of any child of the family[1];

(2)　any person in whose favour a residence order[2] has been made with respect to a child of the family, and any applicant for such an order[3];

(3)　any other person who is entitled to apply for a residence order with respect to a child[4];

(4)　a local authority, where an order has been made[5] placing a child in the care of a local authority[6];

(5)　the Official Solicitor, if appointed[7] the litigation friend of a child of the family[8]; and

(6)　a child of the family who has been given leave to intervene in the cause for the purpose of applying for relief[9],

may apply for an order for relief as respects that child by notice in the prescribed form[10].

1   Family Proceedings Rules 1991, SI 1991/1247, r 2.54(1)(a). As to the meanings of 'child of the family' and (for the purposes of the Matrimonial Causes Act 1973) 'child' see PARA 477 note 3.
2   As to the meaning of 'residence order' see the Children Act 1989 s 8(1); and CHILDREN AND YOUNG PERSONS vol 5(3) (2008 Reissue) PARA 262 (definition applied by the Family Proceedings Rules 1991, SI 1991/1247, r 2.54(2)).
3   Family Proceedings Rules 1991, SI 1991/1247, r 2.54(1)(b).
4   Family Proceedings Rules 1991, SI 1991/1247, r 2.54(1)(c).
5   Ie under the Children Act 1989 s 31(1)(a) (see CHILDREN AND YOUNG PERSONS vol 5(3) (2008 Reissue) PARA 271).
6   Family Proceedings Rules 1991, SI 1991/1247, r 2.54(1)(d) (amended by SI 2005/2922).
7   Ie under the Family Proceedings Rules 1991, SI 1991/1247, r 9.5 (see CHILDREN AND YOUNG PERSONS vol 5(3) (2008 Reissue) PARA 231).
8   Family Proceedings Rules 1991, SI 1991/1247, r 2.54(1)(e).
9   Family Proceedings Rules 1991, SI 1991/1247, r 2.54(1)(f).
10 Family Proceedings Rules 1991, SI 1991/1247, r 2.54(1) (amended by SI 1999/3491). For the prescribed form of notice see the Family Proceedings Rules 1991, SI 1991/1247, Appendix 1A, Form A (added by SI 1999/3491; substituted by SI 2000/2267). As to procedure see PARA 902. Only rarely will a child be involved as a party to proceedings for financial relief. Applications are, however, sometimes made by children in order to secure the payment of educational expenses: see eg *Downing v Downing (Downing intervening)* [1976] Fam 288, [1976] 3 All ER 474 (daughter obtained leave to intervene in order to seek a maintenance order in her own favour to meet her educational expenses); *B v B (financial provision for child)* [1998] 1 FCR 49, sub nom *B v B (adult student: liability to support)* [1998] 1 FLR 373, CA (father's argument that maintenance for his daughter should end when she became a grant-aided student rejected).

494.   Matters to which the court is to have regard.   In deciding whether to exercise its power to make a periodical payments order[1], a secured periodical payments order[2] or an order for the payment of a lump sum[3] in respect of a child[4] and, if so, in what manner, the court[5] is to have regard to certain matters[6]. In the case of secured periodical payments, the court will take into account the effect on the payer of tying up the asset that provides the security[7] and also the need to have security for the payment of maintenance[8]; and the court has an unfettered discretion in deciding whether to make such an order and, if so, on what terms[9].

Although there is no statutory period of limitation that applies to proceedings for financial relief, delay may be one of the factors to which the court will have regard when considering all the circumstances of the case[10].

1   As to the meaning of 'periodical payments order', and as to the making of a periodical payments order, see PARA 458.
2   As to the meaning of 'secured periodical payments order', and as to the making of a secured periodical payments order, see PARA 467.
3   As to the meaning of 'order for the payment of a lump sum', and as to the making of such orders, see PARA 476.
4   As to the making of financial orders in favour of children see PARA 492 et seq. As to the meaning (for the purposes of the Matrimonial Causes Act 1973) of 'child' see PARA 477 note 3.
5   As to the meaning of 'court' see PARA 346 note 2.
6   See the Matrimonial Causes Act 1973 s 25(1)–(3); the Civil Partnership Act 2004 Sch 5 paras 20–22; and PARA 589 et seq. As to this requirement see generally *Rye v Rye* [2002] EWHC 956 (Fam), [2002] 2 FLR 981, [2002] All ER (D) 249 (May).
7   *Shearn v Shearn* [1931] P 1.
8   Eg because the payer may leave the jurisdiction or prove to be unreliable in the payment of normal maintenance: see *Barker v Barker* [1952] P 184, [1952] 1 All ER 1128, CA; *Chichester v Chichester* [1936] P 129, [1936] 1 All ER 271.
9   *Shearn v Shearn* [1931] P 1.
10 See PARA 595.

495.   Duration of orders.   The term to be specified in a periodical payments[1] or secured periodical payments[2] order in favour of a child[3] must not extend beyond the date of the child's eighteenth birthday[4], unless he is in full time education[5] or there are special circumstances which justify the making of an order[6]. The term may begin with the date of the making of an application for the order in question or any later date[7], subject to the proviso that a term beginning on such date must not extend beyond the date of the birthday of the child next following his attaining the upper limit of the compulsory school age[8] unless the court considers that in the circumstances of the case the welfare of the child requires that it should extend to a later date[9]. Alternatively, where a maintenance calculation[10] (the 'current calculation') is in force with respect to a child[11] and an application is made[12] for a periodical payments or secured periodical payments order in favour of that child[13] before the end of the period of six months beginning with the making of the current calculation[14], the term to be specified in any such order made on that application may be expressed to begin on, or at any time after, whichever is the later of the date six months before the application is made[15] and the date on which the current calculation took effect or, where successive maintenance calculations have been continuously in force with respect to a child, on which the first of those calculations took effect[16]. If a maintenance calculation ceases to have effect[17] and an application is made, before the end of the period of six months beginning with the date on which the calculation so ceased[18], for a periodical payments or secured periodical payments order in favour of a child with respect to whom that maintenance calculation was in force immediately before it ceased to have effect, the term to be specified in any such order made on that application may begin with the date on which that maintenance calculation ceased to have effect or any later date[19].

1   As to the meaning of 'periodical payments order', and as to the making of a periodical payments order, see PARA 458.
2   As to the meaning of 'secured periodical payments order', and as to the making of a secured periodical payments order, see PARA 467.
3   As to the making of financial orders in favour of children see PARA 492 et seq. As to the meaning (for the purposes of the Matrimonial Causes Act 1973) of 'child' see PARA 477 note 2.
4   Matrimonial Causes Act 1973 s 29(2)(b); Civil Partnership Act 2004 Sch 5 para 49(3)(b).
5   Ie unless it appears to the court that the child is, or will be, or if an order were made without complying with the Matrimonial Causes Act 1973 s 29(2)(b) or the Civil Partnership Act 2004 Sch 5 para 49(3)(b) (see the text and note 15) would be, receiving instruction at an educational establishment or undergoing training for a trade, profession or vocation, whether or not he is also, or will also be, in gainful employment: Matrimonial Causes Act 1973 s 29(3)(a); Civil Partnership Act 2004 Sch 5 para 49(5)(a). As to 'trade, profession or vocation' see *Richardson v Richardson* [1993] 4 All ER 673, [1994] 1 WLR 186; *Downing v Downing (Downing intervening)* [1976] Fam 288, [1976] 3 All ER 474.
6   Matrimonial Causes Act 1973 s 29(3)(b); Civil Partnership Act 2004 Sch 5 para 49(5)(b). Physical or other disability may amount to such special circumstances: *C v F (disabled child: maintenance orders)* [1999] 1 FCR 39, [1998] 2 FLR 1, CA; *T v S (financial provision for children)* [1994] 1 FCR 743, [1994] 2 FLR 883.
7   Matrimonial Causes Act 1973 s 29(2); Civil Partnership Act 2004 Sch 5 para 49(2)(a).
8   As to compulsory school age see the Education Act 1996 s 8; and EDUCATION vol 15(1) (2006 Reissue) PARA 15.
9   Matrimonial Causes Act 1973 s 29(2)(a) (amended by the Matrimonial and Family Proceedings Act 1984 s 5(4); and the Education Act 1996 Sch 37 para 136); Civil Partnership Act 2004 Sch 5 para 49(3)(a), (4).
10 For these purposes 'maintenance calculation' has the same meaning as it has in the Child Support Act 1991 by virtue of s 54 as read with any regulations in force thereunder (see CHILDREN AND YOUNG PERSONS vol 5(3) (2008 Reissue) PARA 554): Matrimonial Causes Act 1973 s 52(1) (definition added by SI 1993/623; and amended by the Child Support, Pensions and Social Security Act 2000 Sch 3 para 3); Civil Partnership Act 2004 Sch 5 para 49(11).

11 Matrimonial Causes Act 1973 s 29(5)(a) (s 29(5)–(8) added by SI 1993/623; amended by the Child Support, Pensions and Social Security Act 2000 Sch 3 para 3); Civil Partnership Act 2004 Sch 5 para 49(7)(a).

12 Ie under the Matrimonial Causes Act 1973 Pt II (ss 25–40A) or the Civil Partnership Act 2004 Sch 5 (see PARA 467 et seq).

13 Ie in accordance with the Child Support Act 1991 s 8 (see CHILDREN AND YOUNG PERSONS vol 5(3) (2008 Reissue) PARAS 556, 560).

14 Matrimonial Causes Act 1973 s 29(5)(b) (as added and amended: see note 11); Civil Partnership Act 2004 Sch 5 para 49(7)(b).

15 Matrimonial Causes Act 1973 s 29(2), (6)(a) (as added and amended: see note 11); Civil Partnership Act 2004 Sch 5 para 49(2)(b), (8)(a).

16 Matrimonial Causes Act 1973 s 29(6)(b) (as added and amended: see note 11); Civil Partnership Act 2004 Sch 5 para 49(8)(b).

17 Ie by or under any provision of the Child Support Act 1991.

18 Matrimonial Causes Act 1973 s 29(8) (as added and amended: see note 11); Civil Partnership Act 2004 Sch 5 para 49(10).

19 Matrimonial Causes Act 1973 s 29(7) (as added and amended: see note 11); Civil Partnership Act 2004 Sch 5 para 49(9).

496. Death of person paying. Any periodical payments order in favour of a child[1] ceases to have effect, notwithstanding anything in the order, on the death of the person liable to make payments under the order, except in relation to any arrears due under the order on the date of the death[2].

1 As to the meaning of 'periodical payments order', and as to the making of a periodical payments order, see PARA 458. As to the making of financial orders in favour of children see PARA 492 et seq. As to the meaning (for the purposes of the Matrimonial Causes Act 1973) of 'child' see PARA 477 note 2.

2 Matrimonial Causes Act 1973 s 29(4); Civil Partnership Act 2004 Sch 5 para 49(6).

497. Child support. Where a child has an absent or non-resident parent, each of those parents is responsible for maintaining him and is to be taken to have met this by making periodical payments of maintenance with respect to the child of such amount, and at such intervals, as may be determined in accordance with the provisions of the Child Support Act 1991[1].

Where a maintenance calculation requires the making of periodical payments[2], it is the duty of the non-resident parent with respect to whom the calculation was made to make those payments[3]. The court may make an order under which one party is to make periodical payments to the other, such payments to be reduced pro tanto by any sums payable as child support maintenance pursuant to the Child Support Act 1991 (a 'Segal order'); however, in order to preserve the legitimacy of such an order it is crucial that the order contains a substantial ingredient of spousal support[4].

1 See the Child Support Act 1991 ss 1(1), (2), 3(1); and CHILDREN AND YOUNG PERSONS vol 5(3) (2008 Reissue) PARA 555.

2 As to periodical payments orders see PARA 458 et seq. As to secured periodical payments orders see PARA 467 et seq.

3 See the Child Support Act 1991 s 1(3); and CHILDREN AND YOUNG PERSONS vol 5(3) (2008 Reissue) PARA 555.

4 *Dorney-Kingdom v Dorney-Kingdom* [2000] 3 FCR 20, [2000] 2 FLR 855, CA.

(ii) Property Adjustment Orders

A. SCOPE AND EFFECT OF ORDERS

498. Meaning of 'property adjustment order'. A 'property adjustment order' is an order dealing with property rights available[1] for the purpose of adjusting the financial position of the parties to a marriage or civil partnership and any children of the family[2] on or after the grant of a decree of divorce, nullity of marriage or judicial separation or the making of an order of dissolution, nullity of civil partnership or legal separation, that is to say:

(1)   any order for a transfer of property[3];

(2)   any for a settlement of property[4]; and

(3)   any order for a variation of settlement[5].

Either party to a marriage or civil partnership may apply for a property adjustment order[6].

1   Ie subject to the provisions of the Matrimonial Causes Act 1973 and the Civil Partnership Act 2004: see the Matrimonial Causes Act 1973 s 21(2) and the Civil Partnership Act 2004 Sch 5 para 7. As to the relationship between property adjustment orders and financial provision orders see PARA 451. As to the making of property orders for the benefit of children see PARAS 518–519. As to the effect of a subsequent marriage or civil partnership on a property adjustment order see PARA 452. As to the making of property orders in nullity proceedings see PARA 453. As to the making of property adjustment orders against or in favour of persons suffering from mental disorder see PARA 455. As to orders under former legislation see PARA 457. Provision for adjusting the financial position of the parties to a marriage or civil partnership may also be made by way of a Mesher or Martin order: see PARA 316. As to the implementation of property orders and orders for sale in ancillary proceedings where one of the parties is under mental incapacity see *Practice Note (ancillary relief orders: conveyancing for mentally incapacitated adults)* [2006] 1 FLR 480.

2   As to the meanings of 'child of the family' and (for the purposes of the Matrimonial Causes Act 1973) 'child' see PARA 477 note 3.

3   Ie any order under the Matrimonial Causes Act 1973 s 24(1)(a) or the Civil Partnership Act 2004 Sch 5 para 7(1)(a): see PARAS 499, 518.

4   Ie any order under the Matrimonial Causes Act 1973 s 24(1)(b) or the Civil Partnership Act 2004 Sch 5 para 7(1)(b): see PARAS 506, 518.

5   Ie any order under the Matrimonial Causes Act 1973 s 24(1)(c) or the Civil Partnership Act 2004 Sch 5 para 7(1)(c): see PARAS 510, 518.

6   See the Matrimonial Causes Act 1973 s 24; the Civil Partnership Act 2004 Sch 5 paras 6, 7; and PARA 499 et seq. For applications by husbands against their wives see *Griffiths v Griffiths* [1974] 1 All ER 932, [1974] 1 WLR 1350, CA; *Calderbank v Calderbank* [1976] Fam 93, [1975] 3 All ER 333, CA; *P v P (financial provision: lump sum)* [1978] 3 All ER 70, [1978] 1 WLR 483, CA; *B v B (financial provision)* (1982) 3 FLR 298, sub nom *B v B* 12 Fam Law 92, CA. In seeking to achieve a fair outcome, there is no place for discrimination between the parties: *White v White* [2001] 1 AC 596, [2001] 1 All ER 1, HL; applied in *Dharamshi v Dharamshi* [2001] 1 FCR 492, [2001] 1 FLR 736, CA; *Cowan v Cowan* [2001] EWCA Civ 679, [2002] Fam 97, [2001] 2 FCR 331.

B.   TRANSFERS OF PROPERTY

499.   Power to order transfer of property.   Where the court[1]:

(1)   grants a decree of divorce, a decree of nullity of marriage or a decree of judicial separation[2]; or

(2)   makes a dissolution, nullity or separation order in respect of a civil partnership[3],

it may[4] make an order that a party to the marriage or civil partnership is to transfer to the other party, to any child of the family[5] or to such person as may be specified in the order for the benefit of such a child such property[6] as may be so specified[7]. This is subject to the restrictions imposed[8] on the making of orders for a transfer of property in favour of children who have attained the age of 18[9].

1   As to the meaning of 'court' see PARA 346 note 2.

2   Matrimonial Causes Act 1973 s 24(1).

3   Civil Partnership Act 2004 Sch 5 para 6(1)(a).

4   Ie on granting the decree or making the order or at any time thereafter (whether, in the case of
     a decree of divorce or of nullity of marriage, before or after the decree is made absolute):
     Matrimonial Causes Act 1973 s 24(1); Civil Partnership Act 2004 Sch 5 para 6(1).
5   As to the meaning of 'child of the family' see PARA 477 note 3.
6   Ie property to which the first-mentioned party is entitled, either in possession or reversion:
     Matrimonial Causes Act 1973 s 24(1)(a); Civil Partnership Act 2004 Sch 5 para 7(1)(a), (3). As
     to the property that may be the subject of a property adjustment order see PARA 500. From the
     moment it takes effect, a transfer of property order confers an equitable interest in the property
     on the person to whom it is ordered to be transferred, and such an interest is a 'right' to which
     the other party's estate is subject for the purposes of the Insolvency Act 1986 s 283(5) (see
     BANKRUPTCY AND INDIVIDUAL INSOLVENCY vol 3(2) (2002 Reissue) PARA 216): see *Mountney v
     Treharne* [2002] EWCA Civ 1174, [2003] Ch 135, [2002] 3 WLR 1760 (husband made
     bankrupt one day after making of property adjustment order; trustee in bankruptcy took
     property subject to wife's equitable interest under order and she was therefore entitled to enforce
     order against trustee).
7   Matrimonial Causes Act 1973 s 24(1)(a); Civil Partnership Act 2004 Sch 5 para 7(1)(a). As to
     the date when the order takes effect see PARA 502; as to the care needed in drafting orders see
     PARA 933; as to the effect of a subsequent marriage or civil partnership see PARA 452; and as to
     the evidence required on an application for a property transfer order where the application
     relates to land see PARA 918. In considering the assets of the parties, the court will usually have
     regard to their net values: see *White v White* [2001] 1 AC 596 at 612, [2001] 1 All ER 1 at
     15, HL per Lord Nicholls of Birkenhead; *O'D v O'D* [1976] Fam 83, sub nom *O'Donnell v
     O'Donnell* [1975] 2 All ER 993, CA.
         If it is intended that an order should deal finally and conclusively with all applications for
     capital relief, including property adjustment, it should specifically say so (*Dinch v Dinch* [1987]
     1 All ER 818, [1987] 1 WLR 252, HL); and, if an order is expressed to deal conclusively with all
     forms of property adjustment, a subsequent application for a property adjustment order cannot
     be made (*Carson v Carson* [1983] 1 All ER 478, [1983] 1 WLR 285, CA; *Norman v Norman*
     [1983] 1 All ER 486, [1983] 1 WLR 295; *Sandford v Sandford* [1986] 1 FLR 412, [1986] Fam
     Law 104, CA; *Dinch v Dinch*). Where an order is made under the Matrimonial Causes Act 1973
     s 24(1)(a), (b), (c) or (d) or, presumably, the Civil Partnership Act 2004 Sch 5 para 7(1)(a), (b),
     (c) or (d), this does not, in the absence of express provision in the order, prevent a later claim for
     an order under another of those provisions from being made: *Carson v Carson* [1983] 1 All ER
     478, [1983] 1 WLR 285, CA.
8   Ie by the Matrimonial Causes Act 1973 s 29(1), (3) and the Civil Partnership Act 2004 Sch 5
     para 49(1), (5): see PARA 518.
9   Matrimonial Causes Act 1973 s 24(1)(a); Civil Partnership Act 2004 Sch 5 para 9.

500.   Property that may be the subject of a property adjustment order. No
limitation is imposed as to the nature of the property in respect of which the
jurisdiction to make a property adjustment order[1] may be exercised; and,
provided that the property is sufficiently identifiable to be susceptible of
specification in the order, it may be made the subject of a property adjustment
order[2]. A share or interest in property is itself property for these purposes. Thus,
a periodic tenancy may be the subject of a transfer of property order[3], as will
property acquired after the end of the marriage or civil partnership[4].

Where property is situated abroad, the court has jurisdiction in personam
between the parties but it will not have jurisdiction in rem[5]. Even though the
court may have jurisdiction in relation to property abroad, it may, in its
discretion, decline to exercise that jurisdiction where any order would be
unenforceable[6].

The court cannot exercise its power of transfer in derogation of the rights of
third parties; it can only deal with property to the extent that one of the parties
is entitled to it, whether in possession or in reversion. Third parties who may be
affected by a property adjustment order made in proceedings for financial relief
should be given notice of the proceedings and be afforded the right to make
representations before they suffer any prejudice[7]. Where a third party does
intervene, the court may determine the extent of that party's interest in any

property under dispute as part of the proceedings for relief[8]. The court does not, however, lose its power to make a property adjustment order in respect of property which is also the subject of an application to enforce a confiscation or similar order under criminal proceedings[9].

1 As to the meaning of 'property adjustment order' see PARA 498.
2 See the Matrimonial Causes Act 1973 s 24(1)(a); the Civil Partnership Act 2004 Sch 5 para 7(1)(a); and PARA 499.
3 See *Jones v Jones* [1997] Fam 59, [1997] 2 WLR 373, CA; *Newlon Housing Trust v Alsulamein* [1999] 1 AC 313, [1998] 4 All ER 1, HL. As to the transfer of tenancies generally see PARA 310 et seq.
4 See e g *Schuller v Schuller* [1990] FCR 626, [1990] 2 FLR 193. Whilst assets acquired prior to the marriage or civil partnership may be the subject of a property adjustment order, the origin of the property may be relevant when the court decides how to exercise its statutory jurisdiction under the Matrimonial Causes Act 1973 s 25(2) or the Civil Partnership Act 2004 Sch 5 para 20 (see PARA 589): see *White v White* [2001] 1 AC 596 at 610, [2001] 1 All ER 1 at 13, 14, HL per Lord Nicholls of Birkenhead.
5 See *Hamlin v Hamlin* [1986] Fam 11, [1985] 2 All ER 1037, CA.
6 *Hamlin v Hamlin* [1986] Fam 11, [1985] 2 All ER 1037, CA; and see *Nunnely v Nunnely and Marrian* (1880) 15 PD 186; *Forsyth v Forsyth* [1891] P 363; *Tallack v Tallack and Broekema* [1927] P 211; *Goff v Goff* [1934] P 107; *Whyler v Lyons* [1963] P 274, [1963] 1 All ER 821; *Razelos v Razelos* [1969] 3 All ER 929, sub nom *Razelos v Razelos (No 2)* [1970] 1 WLR 392.
7 See the Family Proceedings Rules 1991, SI 1991/1247, r 2.59; and PARA 918.
8 *Tebbutt v Haynes* [1981] 2 All ER 238, CA; *Harwood v Harwood* [1992] 1 FCR 1, [1991] 2 FLR 274, CA.
9 See *Customs and Excise Comrs v A* [2002] EWCA Civ 1039, [2003] Fam 55 [2003] 2 All ER 736. There is, however, a strong public policy argument against distributing the proceeds of crime via a property adjustment order, particularly if the party applying for the order knew of the criminal activity: see *Richards v Richards* [2006] EWCA Civ 849, [2006] 2 FCR 452, [2006] 2 FLR 1220.

501. No power to make an interim property adjustment order. The court has no jurisdiction to make an interim property adjustment order[1]. Further, the court does not have an administrative power of appropriation to allocate a particular asset to meet the interim needs of either party before the final hearing[2].

1 See *Bolsom v Bolsom* (1982) 4 FLR 21, 12 Fam Law 143, CA; *Wicks v Wicks* [1999] Fam 65, [1998] 1 All ER 977, CA (the Family Proceedings Rules 1991, SI 1991/1247, rr 2.64(2), 2.69F (see PARAS 923, 933) both permit applications for maintenance pending suit or the outcome of proceedings, interim periodical payments and interim variation orders only). As to the meaning of 'property adjustment order' see PARA 498.
2 *Wicks v Wicks* [1999] Fam 65, [1998] 1 All ER 977, CA.

502. Date order takes effect. Where a transfer of property order is made on or after granting a decree of divorce or nullity of marriage or making a dissolution or nullity order in respect of a civil partnership[1], neither the order nor any settlement made in pursuance of it is to take effect[2] unless the decree has been made absolute or, as the case may be, the dissolution or nullity order has been made final[3].

1 Ie under the Matrimonial Causes Act 1973 s 24(1)(a) or the Civil Partnership Act 2004 Sch 5 para 7(1)(a): see PARA 499.
2 Ie without prejudice to the power to give a direction under the Matrimonial Causes Act 1973 s 30 or the Civil Partnership Act 2004 Sch 5 para 76 for the settlement of an instrument by conveyancing counsel: see PARA 473.
3 Matrimonial Causes Act 1973 s 24(3); Civil Partnership Act 2004 Sch 5 para 8. In respect of a marriage, it has been held that the court has no jurisdiction, even with consent, to make a substantive order before a decree nisi is pronounced, and that an order made before a decree nisi is pronounced cannot be rectified under the court's inherent jurisdiction or under the slip rule: see *Board (Board intervening) v Checkland* [1987] 2 FLR 257, CA, following *Munks v Munks*

[1985] FLR 576, [1985] Fam Law 131, CA. However, a court may approve a draft consent order in advance of a decree nisi and direct that it should take effect at a future date: *Pounds v Pounds* [1994] 4 All ER 777, [1994] 1 WLR 1535, CA. Presumably the same situation would obtain in respect of a dissolution or nullity order relating to a civil partnership.

503.   Matters to which the court is to have regard.   In deciding whether to exercise its power to make a transfer of property order and, if so, in what manner, the court[1] is to have regard to certain matters[2]. The court must also consider whether it would be appropriate so to exercise its powers that the financial obligations of each party towards the other will be terminated as soon after the grant of the decree of divorce or nullity of marriage or the making of the dissolution or nullity order as the court considers just and reasonable[3].

Although there is no statutory period of limitation that applies to proceedings for financial relief, delay may be one of the factors to which the court will have regard when considering all the circumstances of the case[4].

1   As to the meaning of 'court' see PARA 346 note 2.
2   See the Matrimonial Causes Act 1973 s 25(1), (2); the Civil Partnership Act 2004 Sch 5 paras 20, 21; and PARA 589. As to the matters to which the court is to have regard in the case of children of the family see PARAS 597–598.
3   See the Matrimonial Causes Act 1973 s 25A; the Civil Partnership Act 2004 Sch 5 para 23; and PARA 592.
4   See PARA 595.

504.   Deed of transfer.   Where the court[1] decides to make a property adjustment order[2] requiring any payments to be secured, it may direct that the matter be referred to one of the conveyancing counsel for him to settle a proper instrument to be executed by all necessary parties[3]. Where the order is to be made in proceedings for divorce, dissolution, nullity of marriage civil partnership or judicial or legal separation, the court may, if it thinks fit, defer the grant of the decree or the making of the order in question until the instrument has been duly executed[4].

The court may order the lodgment of documents for the purpose of settling the deed[5]. Where a person refuses or neglects to execute a deed securing payments as ordered by the court, the court may order that execution be effected by such person as it nominates for that purpose, and a deed so executed operates as if executed by the party originally directed to execute it[6].

1   As to the meaning of 'court' see PARA 346 note 2.
2   As to the meaning of 'property adjustment order' see PARA 498.
3   Matrimonial Causes Act 1973 s 30(a); Civil Partnership Act 2004 Sch 5 para 76(1)(a), (2).
4   Matrimonial Causes Act 1973 s 30(b); Civil Partnership Act 2004 Sch 5 para 76(3). There is only one decree in suits for judicial separation (see *M v M* [1928] P 123 at 126, 127) and no transfer of property order may be made in judicial separation proceedings before the decree has been granted (see the Matrimonial Causes Act 1973 s 24(1)).
5   *Bartlett v Bartlett* (1918) 34 TLR 518.
6   See the Supreme Court Act 1981 s 39; the County Courts Act 1984 s 38; and PARA 641. See also *Howarth v Howarth* (1886) 11 PD 68 at 95, CA; cf *De Ricci v De Ricci* [1891] P 378 (application arising out of a compromise, which had become a rule of court).

505.   Bankruptcy of transferor.   From the moment it takes effect, a transfer of property order[1] confers an equitable interest in the property on the person to whom it is ordered to be transferred, and such an interest is a 'right' to which the other party's estate is subject[2] for the purposes of establishing what constitutes his estate[3]. The fact that a transfer of property had to be made in order to comply with a property adjustment order[4] does not prevent that settlement or transfer from being a transaction in respect of which an order may be made under the statutory provisions relating to transfers at an undervalue and preferences[5].

1   See PARA 499 et seq.
2   Ie pursuant to the Insolvency Act 1986 s 283(5) (see BANKRUPTCY AND INDIVIDUAL INSOLVENCY vol 3(2) (2002 Reissue) PARA 216).
3   See *Mountney v Treharne* [2002] EWCA Civ 1174, [2003] Ch 135, [2002] 3 WLR 1760 (husband made bankrupt one day after making of property adjustment order; trustee in bankruptcy took property subject to wife's equitable interest under order and she was therefore entitled to enforce order against trustee).
4   As to the meaning of 'property adjustment order' see PARA 498.
5   Matrimonial Causes Act 1973 s 39 (amended by the Insolvency Act 1985 Sch 8 para 23 and the Insolvency Act 1986 Sch 14); Civil Partnership Act 2004 Sch 5 para 77. As to the statutory provisions relating to transfers at an undervalue and preferences see the Insolvency Act 1986 ss 339, 340; and BANKRUPTCY AND INDIVIDUAL INSOLVENCY vol 3(2) (2002 Reissue) PARA 653 et seq. As to the application of these provisions to interim orders for maintenance under the Matrimonial and Family Proceedings Act 1984 s 14 or the Civil Partnership Act 2004 Sch 7 para 5 (see PARA 536) and to orders for financial provision and property adjustment under the Matrimonial and Family Proceedings Act 1984 s 17 or the Civil Partnership Act 2004 Sch 7 para 9 (see PARA 531), as they apply to like orders under the Matrimonial Causes Act 1973 Pt II (ss 21–40A) and the Civil Partnership Act 2004 Sch 5, see the Matrimonial and Family Proceedings Act 1984 s 21; the Civil Partnership Act 2004 Sch 7 para 14; and PARA 537.

C.   SETTLEMENTS OF PROPERTY

506.   Power to settle property.   Where the court[1]:
(1)   grants a decree of divorce, a decree of nullity of marriage or a decree of judicial separation[2]; or
(2)   makes a dissolution, nullity or separation order in respect of a civil partnership[3],
it may[4] make an order that a settlement of such property[5] as may be so specified be made to the satisfaction of the court for the benefit of the other party to the marriage or civil partnership and of the children of the family[6] or either or any of them[7].

1   As to the meaning of 'court' see PARA 346 note 2.
2   Matrimonial Causes Act 1973 s 24(1).
3   Civil Partnership Act 2004 Sch 5 para 6(1)(a).
4   Ie on granting the decree or making the order or at any time thereafter (whether, in the case of a decree of divorce or of nullity of marriage, before or after the decree is made absolute): Matrimonial Causes Act 1973 s 24(1); Civil Partnership Act 2004 Sch 5 para 6(1).
5   Ie property to which the first-mentioned party is entitled, either in possession or reversion: Matrimonial Causes Act 1973 s 24(1)(b); Civil Partnership Act 2004 Sch 5 para 7(1)(b).
6   As to the meaning of 'child of the family' see PARA 477 note 3.
7   Matrimonial Causes Act 1973 s 24(1)(b); Civil Partnership Act 2004 Sch 5 para 7(1)(b). As to when a settlement of property order takes effect see PARA 507. As to the care needed in drafting orders see PARA 933.

507.   Date order takes effect.   Where an order is made for a settlement of property[1] on or after granting a decree of divorce or nullity of marriage or making a dissolution or nullity order in respect of a civil partnership[2], neither the order nor any settlement made in pursuance of it is to take effect[3] unless the decree has been made absolute or, as the case may be, the dissolution or nullity order has been made final[4].

1   Ie under the Matrimonial Causes Act 1973 s 24(1)(b): see PARA 506.
2   Ie under the Civil Partnership Act 2004 Sch 5 para 7(1)(b): see PARA 506.

3   Ie without prejudice to the power to give a direction under the Matrimonial Causes Act 1973
     s 30 or the Civil Partnership Act 2004 Sch 5 para 76 for the settlement of an instrument by
     conveyancing counsel: see PARA 473.
4   Matrimonial Causes Act 1973 s 24(3); Civil Partnership Act 2004 Sch 5 para 8. In respect of a
     marriage, it has been held that the court has no jurisdiction, even with consent, to make a
     substantive order before a decree nisi is pronounced, and that an order made before a decree nisi
     is pronounced cannot be rectified under the court's inherent jurisdiction or under the slip rule:
     see *Board (Board intervening) v Checkland* [1987] 2 FLR 257, CA, following *Munks v Munks*
     [1985] FLR 576, [1985] Fam Law 131, CA. However, a court may approve a draft consent
     order in advance of a decree nisi and direct that it should take effect at a future date: *Pounds v
     Pounds* [1994] 4 All ER 777, [1994] 1 WLR 1535, CA. Presumably the same situation would
     obtain in respect of a dissolution or nullity order relating to a civil partnership.

508.   Matters to which the court is to have regard.   In deciding whether to
exercise its power to make a property order and, if so, in what manner, the
court[1] is to have regard to certain matters[2]. The court must also consider
whether it would be appropriate so to exercise its powers that the financial
obligations of each party towards the other will be terminated as soon after the
grant of the decree of divorce or nullity of marriage or the making of the
dissolution or nullity order as the court considers just and reasonable[3].

   Although there is no statutory period of limitation that applies to proceedings
for financial relief, delay may be one of the factors to which the court will have
regard when considering all the circumstances of the case[4].

1   As to the meaning of 'court' see PARA 346 note 2.
2   See the Matrimonial Causes Act 1973 s 25(1), (2); the Civil Partnership Act 2004 Sch 5
     paras 20, 21; and PARA 589. As to the matters to which the court is to have regard in the case of
     children of the family see PARAS 597–598.
3   See the Matrimonial Causes Act 1973 s 25A; the Civil Partnership Act 2004 Sch 5 para 23; and
     PARA 592.
4   See PARA 595.

509.   Bankruptcy of settlor.   The fact that a settlement of property had to be
made in order to comply with a property adjustment order[1] does not prevent
that settlement or transfer from being a transaction in respect of which an order
may be made under the statutory provisions relating to transfers at an
undervalue and preferences[2].

1   As to the meaning of 'property adjustment order' see PARA 498.
2   Matrimonial Causes Act 1973 s 39 (amended by the Insolvency Act 1985 Sch 8 para 23 and the
     Insolvency Act 1986 Sch 14); Civil Partnership Act 2004 Sch 5 para 77. As to the statutory
     provisions relating to transfers at an undervalue and preferences see the Insolvency Act 1986
     ss 339, 340; and BANKRUPTCY AND INDIVIDUAL INSOLVENCY vol 3(2) (2002 Reissue) PARA 653
     et seq. As to the application of these provisions to interim orders for maintenance under the
     Matrimonial and Family Proceedings Act 1984 s 14 or the Civil Partnership Act 2004 Sch 7
     para 5 (see PARA 536) and to orders for financial provision and property adjustment under the
     Matrimonial and Family Proceedings Act 1984 s 17 or the Civil Partnership Act 2004 Sch 7
     para 9 (see PARA 531), as they apply to like orders under the Matrimonial Causes Act 1973 Pt II
     (ss 21–40A) and the Civil Partnership Act 2004 Sch 5, see the Matrimonial and Family
     Proceedings Act 1984 s 21; the Civil Partnership Act 2004 Sch 7 para 14; and PARA 537.

D.   VARIATION OF SETTLEMENTS

(A)   Powers of the Court

510.   Order for variation of settlement.   Where the court[1]:
   (1)   grants a decree of divorce, a decree of nullity of marriage or a decree of
          judicial separation[2]; or

(2)   makes a dissolution, nullity or separation order in respect of a civil
       partnership[3],

it may[4] make an order:

(a)   varying for the benefit of the parties to the marriage or civil partnership
       and of the children of the family[5] or either or any of them any relevant
       settlement[6];

(b)   extinguishing or reducing the interest of either of the parties to the
       marriage or civil partnership under such a settlement[7].

A settlement, in so far as it is not varied by an order of the court, remains
unaffected by a decree or order of dissolution[8].

1   As to the meaning of 'court' see PARA 346 note 2.
2   Matrimonial Causes Act 1973 s 24(1).
3   Civil Partnership Act 2004 Sch 5 para 6(1)(a).
4   Ie on granting the decree or making the order or at any time thereafter (whether, in the case of
    a decree of divorce or of nullity of marriage, before or after the decree is made absolute):
    Matrimonial Causes Act 1973 s 24(1); Civil Partnership Act 2004 Sch 5 para 6(1). As to the
    effect of this see *Charalambous v Charalambous* [2004] EWCA Civ 1030, [2004] 2 FCR 721,
    [2004] 2 FLR 1093. As to the effect of a subsequent marriage or civil partnership on the courts'
    power to make or vary financial or property orders see PARA 452.
5   As to the meaning of 'child of the family' see PARA 477 note 3. The court may make an order
    under head (a) in the text notwithstanding that there are no children of the family: Matrimonial
    Causes Act 1973 s 24(2); Civil Partnership Act 2004 Sch 5 para 7(2).
        Where an application is made to the High Court or a designated county court for an order
    for a variation of settlement, the court must, unless it is satisfied that the proposed variation
    does not adversely affect the rights or interests of any children concerned, direct that the
    children be separately represented on the application, either by a solicitor or by a solicitor and
    counsel, and may appoint the Official Solicitor or other fit person to be the litigation friend of
    the children for the purpose of the application: Family Proceedings Rules 1991, SI 1991/1247,
    r 2.57(1) (amended by SI 2005/2922). On any other application for ancillary relief the court
    may give such a direction or make such appointment as it is empowered to give or make by this
    provision: Family Proceedings Rules 1991, SI 1991/1247, r 2.57(2). Before a person other than
    the Official Solicitor is so appointed litigation friend, there must be filed a certificate by the
    solicitor acting for the children that the person proposed as guardian has no interest in the
    matter adverse to that of the children and that he is a proper person to be such guardian:
    r 2.57(3). As to the meaning of 'designated county court' see PARA 737 note 3.
6   Matrimonial Causes Act 1973 s 24(1)(c) (s 24(1)(c), (d) amended by the Welfare Reform and
    Pensions Act 1999 Sch 3 paras 1, 3); Civil Partnership Act 2004 Sch 5 para 7(1)(c). The relevant
    settlements for these purposes are ante-nuptial and post-nuptial settlements and, in relation to
    civil partnerships, settlements made on the civil partners during the subsistence of a civil
    partnership or in anticipation of its formation; settlements made by will or codicil are included,
    but not settlements in the form of a pension arrangement (within the meaning of either the
    Matrimonial Causes Act 1973 s 25D or the Civil Partnership Act 2004 Sch 5 para 16(4), as the
    case may be (see PARA 487)): Matrimonial Causes Act 1973 s 24(1)(c) (as so amended); Civil
    Partnership Act 2004 Sch 5 para 7(3) (although see *Brooks v Brooks* [1996] AC 375, [1995] 3
    ALL ER 257, HL, where a pension scheme was held to be a post-nuptial settlement for the
    purposes of the Matrimonial Causes Act 1973 s 24(1)(c)). In order to determine what is an
    ante-nuptial or a post-nuptial settlement, the court is entitled to take into consideration the
    relevant facts to ascertain what was the substance of the transaction (*Parrington v Parrington*
    [1951] 2 All ER 916), and the motive in entering into a settlement is irrelevant (*Prescott
    (formerly Fellowes) v Fellowes* [1958] P 260 at 268, [1958] 3 All ER 55, CA, revsg [1958] P
    260, [1958] 1 All ER 824; and see PARA 511 note 2). As to the settlements with which the court
    can deal under these provisions see further PARA 511. As to when a variation of settlement order
    takes effect see PARA 516. As to the court's power to make orders attaching pension benefits see
    PARA 485 et seq; and as to the court's power to make pension-sharing orders see PARA 523 et
    seq.
7   Matrimonial Causes Act 1973 s 24(1)(d) (as amended: see note 6); Civil Partnership Act 2004
    Sch 5 para 7(1)(d). As to the relevant settlements for these purposes see note 6. See further PARA
    513.
8   *Fitzgerald v Chapman* (1875) 1 ChD 563.

511. Settlements with which the court can deal. The power conferred on the court to vary a settlement[1] is a power enabling it to make orders with reference to the application of property settled not by any instrument under which the parties take a beneficial interest but by settlements and settlements only, made either in contemplation of, or during, the marriage or civil partnership of the parties whose marriage or civil partnership is in question[2]. In deciding whether to vary a settlement as an ante-nuptial or post-nuptial settlement, the court should give a broad interpretation to the meaning of those terms[3]. The court has no power to vary a settlement which is made by either party in general terms and not after, in contemplation of or identifiable with the marriage or civil partnership before the court, but which merely gives the settlor power to appoint an interest to any future party[4]; nor may it vary an annuity purchased by one party for another[5].

'Property' for these purposes includes not only income[6] but capital with which the court may also deal[7], and settled property is to be taken to mean the property of which, under the settlement, the parties, or their children, are the beneficiaries[8]. Certain types of annuity may be included[9], as may moneys payable under a policy of life assurance in which the petitioner has a contingent interest[10], property taken under a settlement in a representative capacity[11], and an expectancy which has been settled[12]. A life policy taken out by a husband after marriage so as to benefit his wife has been held to be a post-nuptial settlement which the court can vary, even though not expressly issued under the Married Women's Property Act 1882[13], with the result that the husband did not become the trustee for the wife under the policy[14]. Where third persons enter into covenants to pay an annuity to the parties to the marriage or civil partnership, that annuity is settled property for the purposes of the statutory provisions[15]. A settled estate, contrasted with an estate in fee simple, must be understood to be one in which the usual powers of alienation, of devising, and transmitting are restrained by the limitations of the settlement[16]. Heirlooms may be dealt with[17]. Absolute gifts which involve no periodical payments cannot be varied under the statutory provisions[18], but, if there are periodical payments still to be made at the time when the court has to inquire into the existence of the settlement, then, provided that the nuptial (or corresponding civil partnership) element is present, there can be a settlement[19].

Covenants in a settlement by persons who are not the parties to the marriage or civil partnership are subject to variation by the court[20]. The court inquires into settlements as they were at the date of the divorce or dissolution[21], but varies them in the light of circumstances as they exist at the time of the application to vary[22]; in making the inquiry, the court must ascertain what is the actual (not the gross) income of the trust fund[23]. A conveyance by which the wife gave to the husband a half share in a house of which she owned the freehold was held to be a settlement which the court could vary[24]; but this decision has been criticised by the Court of Appeal as going beyond the latitude which the authorities have conferred on the interpretation of the words 'settled property' under the provisions applicable to the variation of settlements[25]. In any event, one must now have regard to the powers of the court to order transfers and settlements of property[26], and all the cases must be considered in the light of these powers. Where land and a house on it were conveyed to the husband and wife as purchasers in fee simple on trust for sale, the net rents and profits until sale and the proceeds of sale to be held on trust for themselves as joint tenants, both parties having contributed, the Court of Appeal held that there was power to vary the conveyance as it was a settlement made by the parties on themselves, the legal interests and beneficial interests being such as to give it the attributes of a settlement[27]. Further, where the wife contributed to the purchase price of the matrimonial home, which was conveyed into the name of the husband only, there was a resulting trust in favour of the wife to the extent she had contributed and, as there was a nuptial element present, it was held that the transaction constituted a post-nuptial settlement which the court had power to vary[28]. Where the conveyance of property originally constituted a nuptial settlement, the nuptial element was not lost by one party giving to the other notice of severance after decree nisi[29]. A deed transferring a house to the wife in consideration for a certain sum, part of which was paid, and a bond by the wife to pay the balance to the husband by instalments, were together held to constitute a settlement which could be varied[30].

1 See PARA 510.
2 *Loraine v Loraine and Murphy* [1912] P 222, CA. However, in *Worsley v Worsley and Wignall* (1869) LR 1 P & D 648 at 651, Lord Penzance said: 'The court would have a great difficulty in saying that any deed which is a settlement of property, made after marriage, and on the parties to the marriage, is not a post-nuptial settlement ... the substantial feature to bring the case within the clause of the statute is that a sum of money is paid to a woman in her character as wife, or is settled upon her in that character and whilst she continues a wife'; cf *Prinsep v Prinsep* [1929] P 225 at 232 per Hill J. See also *Young v Young* [1962] P 27, [1961] 3 All ER 695, CA (deed executed after decree nisi and before decree absolute by which husband covenanted to pay maintenance for wife and children; not a post-nuptial settlement within the contemplation of the statute, as on a true construction of the deed the nuptial element was lacking, the deed being executed on the footing that the marriage was to be dissolved); although cf *Charalambous v Charalambous* [2004] EWCA Civ 1030, [2004] 2 FCR 721, [2004] 2 FLR 1093 (the court may vary a post-nuptial settlement even if the features which had made it 'nuptial' have been removed). In order to be variable, a settlement must be one in relation to the marriage or civil partnership which is the subject of the decree or order: *Burnett v Burnett* [1936] P 1; and see *Joss v Joss* [1943] P 18, [1943] 2 All ER 102. The expression 'post-nuptial settlement' has been very widely interpreted, and it has been held that the mere wording of the instrument is immaterial: *Bosworthick v Bosworthick* [1927] P 64, CA (bond securing an annuity to husband); *Gulbenkian v Gulbenkian* [1927] P 237 (life policy effected after marriage with a contingent interest of the other party in the policy moneys); *Janion v Janion* (1926) [1929] P 237n (settlement by husband with trusts in favour of himself and any wife or issue as the Public Trustee in his discretion should think fit; cf *Hargreaves v Hargreaves* [1926] P 42); *Melvill v Melvill and Woodward* [1930] P 99; revsd [1930] P 159, CA (settlement by a wife on herself and her children after her husband had filed a petition for divorce). It is clear that the property need not have been settled by the parties, if it was settled on them: *Paul v Paul and Farquhar* (1870) LR 2 P & D 93 (property settled by the father of the respondent); *Nepean (otherwise Lee Warner) v Nepean* [1925] P 97 (covenants by petitioner's parents); *Prinsep v Prinsep* [1929] P 225; on appeal [1930] P 35, CA (settlements made by husband's mother in favour of husband and his issue); *Gunner v Gunner and Stirling* [1949] P 77, [1948] 2 All ER 771; *Bown v Bown and Weston* [1949] P 91, [1948] 2 All ER 778 (life insurance policy taken out by husband after marriage for benefit of wife held to be a settlement which may be dealt with); *Brown v Brown* [1959] P 86 [1959] 2 All ER 266, CA (house conveyed to spouses as purchasers in fee simple on trust for sale, net rents and profits before sale and proceeds of sale 'upon trust for themselves as joint tenants'; conveyance held to be a settlement). An absolute assignment of property, however, is not a settlement, and the court has no jurisdiction to vary its provisions: *Hubbard (otherwise Rogers) v Hubbard* [1901] P 157, CA, applied in *Prescott (formerly Fellowes) v Fellowes* [1958] P 260 at 268, [1958] 3 All ER 55, CA; revsg [1958] P 260, [1958] 1 All ER 824 (cited in note 19); *Chalmers v Chalmers* (1892) 68 LT 28. As to the need for a periodical payment see *Hindley v Hindley* [1957] 2 All ER 653, [1957] 1 WLR 898; *Prescott (formerly Fellowes) v Fellowes*; *Young v Young* (1973) 117 Sol Jo 204 (indivisible deed as to use of house owned by husband and his brother and as to periodical payments from husband to wife; no jurisdiction to vary under the Matrimonial Causes Act 1973 s 24, nor was the deed a maintenance agreement within ss 34, 35).
3 *Brooks v Brooks* [1996] AC 375, [1995] 3 All ER 257, HL.
4 *Hargreaves v Hargreaves* [1926] P 42.

5 *Brown v Brown* [1937] P 7, [1936] 2 All ER 1616; *Prescott (formerly Fellowes) v Fellowes*
   [1958] P 260 at 268, [1958] 3 All ER 55, CA (an absolute gift is not a settlement which can be
   varied); but c f the cases referred to in note 2.
6 Income received in the United Kingdom from land owned abroad is 'property': *Style v Style and
   Keiller* [1954] P 209 at 212, [1953] 2 All ER 836 at 838; overruled on other grounds [1954] P
   209 at 215, [1954] 1 All ER 442, CA; c f *Hunter v Hunter and Waddington* [1962] P 1, [1961]
   2 All ER 121.
7 *Ponsonby v Ponsonby* (1884) 9 PD 58; affd 9 PD 122, CA.
8 *Dormer (otherwise Ward) v Ward* [1900] P 130; on appeal [1901] P 20, CA. An appointment in
   exercise of a power to appoint a life interest in property for the benefit of any party who might
   survive the appointor becomes ineffectual on a dissolution: *Re Williams' Settlement, Greenwell
   v Humphries* [1929] 2 Ch 361, CA.
9 *Jump v Jump* (1883) 8 PD 159; *Bosworthick v Bosworthick* [1927] P 64, CA (bond securing
   husband an immediate annuity); but c f *Brown v Brown* [1937] P 7, [1936] 2 All ER 1616
   (absolute gift of annuity); and see the cases referred to in note 2.
10 *Gulbenkian v Gulbenkian* [1927] P 237.
11 *Blood v Blood* [1902] P 190, CA.
12 *E v E (otherwise T)* (1902) 18 TLR 643.
13 Ie under the Married Women's Property Act 1882 s 11: see PARA 277 et seq. Note that s 11 has
   been expressly extended to include policies of assurance effected by civil partners (see the Civil
   Partnership Act 2004 s 70; and PARA 277 et seq).
14 *Bown v Bown and Weston* [1949] P 91, [1948] 2 All ER 778, distinguishing *Gunner v Gunner
   and Stirling* [1949] P 77, [1948] 2 All ER 771. See also *Lort-Williams v Lort-Williams* [1951] P
   395, [1951] 2 All ER 241, CA (where it was held that a life policy did not cease to be variable
   merely because the provision is contingent rather than absolute, nor yet because it might, by its
   terms, be applicable for the benefit of a wife by a subsequent marriage, the words used in the
   policy being 'for the benefit of the widow or children or any of them'); and note 13.
15 *Nepean (otherwise Lee Warner) v Nepean* [1925] P 97.
16 *Micklethwait v Micklethwait* (1859) 4 CBNS 790. See also *MacLean v MacLean* [1951]
   1 All ER 967, CA (reversionary interest).
17 *Beauchamp v Beauchamp and Watt* (1904) 20 TLR 273, CA.
18 Ie under the Matrimonial Causes Act 1973 s 24(1)(c) or the Civil Partnership Act 2004 Sch 5
   para 7(1)(c): see PARA 510.
19 *Prescott (formerly Fellowes) v Fellowes* [1958] P 260 at 268, [1958] 3 All ER 55, CA
   (ante-nuptial deed; wife agreed 'in consideration of' intended marriage to transfer to husband
   'as an absolute gift unaffected by anything hereinafter contained' £15,000 securities; securities
   transferred shortly after marriage, which was subsequently dissolved; it was held that the
   material date was the decree absolute; the transfer of securities was then a completed transaction
   and no periodical payments were involved; the securities were, therefore, not settled property),
   applying *Hubbard (otherwise Rogers) v Hubbard* [1901] P 157, CA and doubting *Smith v Smith*
   [1945] 1 All ER 584 and *Halpern v Halpern* [1951] P 204, [1951] 1 All ER 315.
20 *Nepean (otherwise Lee Warner) v Nepean* [1925] P 97; *Prinsep v Prinsep* [1929] P 225; on
   appeal [1930] P 35, CA.
21 *Jacobs v Jacobs* [1943] P 7, [1942] 2 All ER 471, CA; c f *Prescott (formerly Fellowes) v Fellowes*
   [1958] P 260 at 268, [1958] 3 All ER 55, CA.
22 *Johnson v Johnson* [1950] P 23, [1949] 2 All ER 247, CA.
23 *Savary v Savary* (1898) 79 LT 607, CA.
24 *Halpern v Halpern* [1951] P 204, [1951] 1 All ER 315, criticised in *Prescott (formerly Fellowes)
   v Fellowes* [1958] P 260 at 268, [1958] 3 All ER 55, CA; *Smith v Smith* [1945] 1 All ER 584.
   See also *Bacon v Bacon* [1947] P 151, [1947] 2 All ER 327. Cf *Sievwright v Sievwright* [1956]
   3 All ER 616, [1956] 1 WLR 1452 (where the house was sold after decree absolute, the proceeds
   to be held in trust by solicitors pending determination of outstanding questions; the wife then
   authorised part payment of the proceeds of sale to the husband; four years later, she applied out
   of time to vary the settlement and sought to have included as part of the settlement funds the
   amount paid over to the husband; it was held that it could not be so included as it was no longer
   traceable, and the husband had not received it in a fiduciary capacity; remaining proceeds of sale
   did form part of settlement funds).
25 *Prescott (formerly Fellowes) v Fellowes* [1958] P 260 at 280, [1958] 3 All ER 55 at 61, CA per
   Hodson LJ.
26 See PARAS 499 et seq, 506 et seq.
27 *Brown v Brown* [1959] P 86, [1959] 2 All ER 266, CA (the wife was making substantial
   contributions in respect of mortgage repayments etc, but this fact itself did not give the

conveyance the attributes of settlement, since none of the payments had to be made by virtue of the conveyance). See also *Bedson v Bedson* [1965] 2 QB 666, [1965] 3 All ER 307, CA.

28 *Cook v Cook* [1962] P 181, [1962] 2 All ER 262; affd [1962] P 235, [1962] 2 All ER 811, CA.

29 See *Radziej (otherwise Sierkowska) v Radziej* [1967] 1 All ER 944, [1967] 1 WLR 659; affd [1968] 3 All ER 624, [1968] 1 WLR 1928, CA; *Bedson v Bedson* [1965] 2 QB 666, [1965] 3 All ER 307, CA. Cf *Young v Young* (1973) 117 Sol Jo 204 (cited in note 2).

30 *Parrington v Parrington* [1951] 2 All ER 916.

512. Legitimacy not decided in variation of settlement proceedings. In proceedings for variation of a marriage settlement[1] the court will not decide a question of legitimacy[2], but it may direct the Official Solicitor to petition, on behalf of the child, for a declaration of parentage, legitimacy or legitimation[3], if it is for the child's benefit[4] (the variation proceedings meanwhile standing over), or that the issue be tried separately, with the applicant as claimant and the trustees, the Official Solicitor (as litigation friend) and the respondent as defendants[5]. Usually, however, any question of paternity or status of a child will now be considered by the judge at or before the hearing of the divorce or nullity suit[6], and certainly, where it is reasonably possible, before a variation of settlement is considered.

1 See PARA 510.
2 *Pryor v Pryor and Shelford* (1887) 12 PD 165.
3 Ie under the Family Law Act 1986 s 56: see CHILDREN AND YOUNG PERSONS vol 5(3) (2008 Reissue) PARA 122. See also *Douglas v Douglas and Trevor* (1897) 78 LT 88.
4 *Re Chaplin's Petition* (1867) LR 1 P & D 328.
5 *Evans v Evans and Blyth* [1904] P 274, [1904] P 378.
6 *Practice Direction* [1965] 1 All ER 905, [1965] 1 WLR 600.

513. Extinguishing or reducing a party's interests and powers. Under the statutory power of the court to make an order extinguishing or reducing the interest of either of the parties to a marriage or civil partnership under a settlement[1], a party's rights, powers and interests, including derivative interests[2], in the fund brought into settlement by the other party, may be extinguished as if that party were dead[3]. The effect of the inclusion in the order of the words 'as if he were now dead' (or such corresponding wording as may apply in the case of a civil partnership) is not only to extinguish that party's interests; it involves by necessary implication the proposition that the applicant is to be treated as the survivor of the parties, notwithstanding that both are living[4]. As regards the funds brought into settlement by the respondent, the whole, or part[5], of the respondent's income may be diverted to the children[6], or to the applicant and the children[7], and, in exceptional circumstances, the respondent's interests, even in his or her own fund, may be extinguished[8]. Similarly a respondent's powers of appointment over his or her own fund may, though not in every case[9], be extinguished on the ground that the opportunity of judging the children's requirements no longer exists[10]; or an applicant's powers may be postponed[11]; but extinguishing the power of appointing new trustees is on a different footing, and, if the respondent has still an interest in the fund, the court usually[12] refuses to do so[13]. The court may take into account the future maintenance of a wife or civil partner and children of the family when dealing with the variation of settlement[14]. A life interest of a wife, after the husband's life interest, 'until she shall marry again' meant her remarriage after the death of the husband not her remarriage after divorcing him[15].

1 See the Matrimonial Causes Act 1973 s 24(1)(d); the Civil Partnership Act 2004 Sch 5 para 7(1)(d); and PARA 510.

2 *Blood v Blood* [1902] P 78; affd [1902] P 190, CA.
3 *Pearce v Pearce and French* (1861) 30 LJPM & A 182; *Pryor v Pryor and Shelford* (1887) 12 PD 165; *Whitton v Whitton* [1901] P 348; and *Blood v Blood* [1902] P 78; affd [1902] P 190, CA. Where a respondent's power to appoint is extinguished, it is desirable to include in the order a clause conferring on the petitioner 'such power of appointment as she would have had if the respondent were dead and she had survived him'. See also *Wadham v Wadham* [1938] 1 All ER 206. Cf *Re Allsopp's Marriage Settlement Trusts, Public Trustee v Cherry* [1959] Ch 81, [1958] 2 All ER 393 (effect of extinguishing respondent's interest on discretionary trust connected therewith); *Re Poole's Settlements' Trusts, Poole v Poole* [1959] 2 All ER 340, [1959] 1 WLR 651 (see note 4); *Spizewski v Spizewski and Krywanski* [1970] 1 All ER 794n, [1970] 1 WLR 522, CA (wife's interest extinguished subject to her receiving just compensation); *Jones v Jones* [1972] 3 All ER 289, [1972] 1 WLR 1269 (the practice whereby a settlement was ordered to be varied by extinguishing the rights of one party thereunder as if he were 'now dead' and the other party had survived him was not appropriate where the interests of the beneficiaries were those of tenants in common; the order should be that the property 'shall as from the date of this order be held on trust for the (wife) absolutely').
4 *Re Poole's Settlements' Trusts, Poole v Poole* [1959] 2 All ER 340, [1959] 1 WLR 651 (usual order extinguishing respondent's rights, powers and interests 'as if she were now dead'; husband's subsequent exercise of power of appointment as the survivor under the principal settlement held to be valid, though the order did not state that the settlement was to have effect as if she had died); and see *Smith v Smith* [1970] 1 All ER 244, [1970] 1 WLR 155, CA.
5 *Tupper v Tupper and Terrell* (1890) 62 LT 665.
6 *Webster v Webster and Mitford* (1862) 3 Sw & Tr 106.
7 *Noel v Noel* (1885) 10 PD 179.
8 *Kaye v Kaye* (1902) 86 LT 638, CA (where there was one child, and an income of only £45 per annum); cf *Ponsonby v Ponsonby* (1884) 9 PD 58.
9 *Davies v Davies and M'Carthy* (1868) 37 LJ P & M 17; *Maudslay v Maudslay* (1877) 2 PD 256; *Nevill v Nevill* (1893) 69 LT 463.
10 *Noel v Noel* (1885) 10 PD 179 (wife's power of appointment not to take effect until after husband's death since she did not have care and control of the children and did not have the opportunity of exercising a judgment as to the propriety of making dispositions of her property among them); *Pryor v Pryor and Shelford* (1887) 12 PD 165; *Bosvile v Bosvile and Craven* (1888) 13 PD 76.
11 *Evered v Evered and Graham* (1874) 31 LT 101 (in favour of the child of the marriage).
12 Ie but not in *Oppenheim v Oppenheim and Ricotti* (1884) 9 PD 60, which does not conflict with *Davies v Davies and M'Carthy* (1868) 37 LJP & M 17; in *Maudslay v Maudslay* (1877) 2 PD 256, the power was extinguished by consent.
13 *Hope v Hope and Erdody* (1874) LR 3 P & D 226; *Pryor v Pryor and Shelford* (1887) 12 PD 165; *Bosvile v Bosvile and Craven* (1888) 13 PD 76; *Tupper v Tupper and Terrell* (1890) 62 LT 665.
14 *Smith v Smith* [1970] 1 All ER 244, [1970] 1 WLR 155, CA (husband's interest in house extinguished but wife to make no further application for maintenance or financial provision).
15 *Re Monro's Settlement, Monro v Hill* [1933] Ch 82.

514. Effect of decree or order of nullity on settled property. A decree or order of nullity granted or made in respect of a voidable marriage or civil partnership[1] operates to annul the marriage or civil partnership only as respects any time after the decree has been made absolute or the order has been made final, and the marriage or civil partnership is to be treated, notwithstanding the decree or order, as if it had existed up to that time[2]. The court has power[3] to make orders with reference to the application of the property settled by a relevant settlement[4] in existence at the time of the decree or order, and for these purposes the court may deal with the provisions of the settlement as if they were extended and varied so as to make the words 'parties to the marriage' (or, presumably, 'parties to the civil partnership') connote parties whose marriage or civil partnership was no marriage or civil partnership, and the words 'children' and 'respective parents' construed accordingly[5]. Moreover, the court has power to order that covenants to pay an annuity by the 'husband' or 'wife' or other persons who were parties to the settlement remain in force, either wholly or in part, for the benefit of the parties to the avoided 'marriage' (or civil partnership), or of their children[6]; and the court may direct that the settled property be conveyed to the respective settlors, freed from the trusts of the settlement[7].

A decree absolute annulling a voidable marriage on the ground of incapacity did not render void a separation agreement containing a maintenance clause[8].

1   As to voidable marriages and civil partnerships see PARA 331 et seq.
2   See the Matrimonial Causes Act 1973 s 16; the Civil Partnership Act 2004 s 37(3); and PARA 320.
3   Ie by virtue of the Matrimonial Causes Act 1973 s 24(1)(c), (d) and the Civil Partnership Act 2004 Sch 5 para 7(1)(c), (d); see PARA 510.
4   See PARA 510 note 6; and as to the settlements with which the court can deal see PARA 511.
5   *Dormer (otherwise Ward) v Ward* [1901] P 20 at 33, CA per Vaughan Williams LJ (but in this case the husband was the settlor: see *Re Ames' Settlement, Dinwiddy v Ames* [1946] Ch 217 at 221, [1946] 1 All ER 689 at 692); and see *Attwood (otherwise Pomeroy) v Attwood* [1903] P 7; *Sharpe (otherwise Morgan) v Sharpe* [1909] P 20. It was formerly specifically enacted that children of the parties to a voidable marriage, if they would have been legitimate had the marriage been dissolved, are deemed to be legitimate notwithstanding the annulment: see the Matrimonial Causes Act 1965 s 11, now repealed as no longer necessary in view of what is now the Matrimonial Causes Act 1973 s 16 (see PARA 320).
6   *Dormer (otherwise Ward) v Ward* [1901] P 20, CA; *Nepean (otherwise Lee Warner) v Nepean* [1925] P 97.
7   *Leeds v Leeds* (1886) 57 LT 373; *A v M* (1884) 10 PD 178; *Attwood (otherwise Pomeroy) v Attwood* [1903] P 7.
8   *Adams v Adams* [1941] 1 KB 536, [1941] 1 All ER 334, CA.

(B) Duration and Effect

515.   When the court will revise its order. The court can, in a proper case, revise its own order but in respect only of matters arising before making it[1], as where a mistake was made, common to all parties, in drawing up the order[2], even though the applicant is appealing[3] against the order as made; or by reason of facts existing at the date of its order but not brought to its notice at the time[4]. Where, however, the mistake is not one of expression but of substance, and has been acquiesced in by the parties, the court will not make an order for further variation of the settlement[5].

The court must not exercise its power to vary or discharge an order for settlement of property[6] or temporarily to suspend or, where suspended, revive any provision of such an order except on an application made in proceedings for the rescission of the decree of judicial separation or the separation order by reference to which the order was made or for the dissolution of the marriage or civil partnership in question[7]. The restricted powers of variation, discharge, suspension and revival applicable to an order for settlement apply also in relation to any instrument executed in pursuance of the order[8].

1   *Gladstone v Gladstone* (1876) 1 PD 442; *Benyon v Benyon and O'Callaghan* (1890) 15 PD 29; on appeal 15 PD 54, CA.
2   *Arkwright v Arkwright* (1895) 73 LT 287; and see *Garratt v Garratt and Garratt* [1922] P 230.
3   *E v E (otherwise T)* [1903] P 88.
4   *Newte v Newte and Keen* [1933] P 117.
5   *Taylor v Taylor* (1926) 161 LT Jo 236 (court rejected motion to vary an order made 34 years previously, by which no provision was made for the petitioning wife after the respondent's death, though the settlement contained a provision to that effect).
6   Ie an order under the Matrimonial Causes Act 1973 s 24(1)(b)–(d) or the Civil Partnership Act 2004 Sch 5 para 7(1)(b)–(d) (see PARAS 506, 510, 518).
7   Matrimonial Causes Act 1973 s 31(1), (2)(e), (4); Civil Partnership Act 2004 Sch 5 para 56. As to the matters to which the court is to have regard in considering such an application see PARA 568.
8   Matrimonial Causes Act 1973 s 31(3); Civil Partnership Act 2004 Sch 5 para 50(3).

516. When order takes effect. Up to the operative date[1] of an order for variation of a settlement, dividends due and payable pass under the original settlement[2], but the order should not be made retrospective if this involves the trustees in refund of sums paid since the decree absolute or final order. Regard must be had for the rights of persons who were in the position of mortgagees[3] before the application[4], though thereafter it is in the nature of a pending suit, and it has been held that nothing done after the application has been filed, but before it has been heard, diminishes the power of the court over the settlement[5].

1　In proceedings for divorce, dissolution or nullity, this must be after the decree is made absolute or the order is made final: see PARA 507.
2　*Paul v Paul and Farquhar* (1870) LR 2 P & D 93.
3　*Nevill v Nevill* (1893) 69 LT 463 (trustee in bankruptcy); *Smith v Smith* [1945] 1 All ER 584 (mortgagee).
4　*Wigney v Wigney* (1882) 7 PD 228; and see *Chalmers v Chalmers* (1892) 68 LT 28.
5　*Constantinidi v Constantinidi and Lance* [1904] P 306, CA; *Clarke v Clarke and Lindsay* [1911] P 186 at 189, CA; but see *Morgan v Morgan and Kirby* [1923] P 1.

517. Injunctions. Even before there was statutory power to do so, injunctions were granted in suitable cases restraining the respondent from disposing of the funds of a settlement prior to the application for variation, but the court had to be satisfied that prima facie there was a settlement[1]. Where the court is satisfied that there is about to be or has been a disposition intended to prevent or reduce the court's power to vary a settlement, it has statutory power to make a restraining or protecting or setting aside order[2].

1　*Hindley v Hindley* [1957] 2 All ER 653, [1957] 1 WLR 898, distinguishing *Scott v Scott* [1951] P 193, [1950] 2 All ER 1154, CA, on the ground that if there was a settlement, the funds were not property out of which the respondent might have to satisfy an order; it was held, on the facts, that there was no prima facie settlement, there being no 'element of periodicity'. See also *Bosworthick v Bosworthick* [1927] P 64 at 72, CA; *Parrington v Parrington* [1951] 2 All ER 916 at 920.
2　See the Matrimonial Causes Act 1973 s 37; the Civil Partnership Act 2004 Sch 5 paras 74, 75; and PARA 586.

E. ORDERS FOR THE BENEFIT OF CHILDREN

518. Power to make property adjustment orders for the benefit of children. Where the court[1]:

(1)　grants a decree of divorce, a decree of nullity of marriage or a decree of judicial separation[2]; or

(2)　makes a dissolution, nullity or separation order in respect of a civil partnership[3],

it may[4] make an order:

(a)　that a party to the marriage or civil partnership is to transfer to any child of the family[5] or to such person as may be specified in the order for the benefit of such a child such property[6] as may be so specified[7];

(b)　that a settlement of such property[8] as may be so specified be made to the satisfaction of the court for the benefit of the children of the family or either or any of them[9]; or

(c)　varying for the benefit of the children of the family[10] or either or any of them any relevant settlement[11].

No transfer of property order[12] may be made in favour of a child who has attained the age of 18[13] unless he is in full time education[14] or there are special circumstances which justify the making of an order[15].

Only rarely will the court settle property on children[16]; and there is no presumption in favour of a settlement on children merely because one party has the means to make such a settlement[17]. The court will not make a clean break order terminating a parent's responsibility to maintain children[18].

1   As to the meaning of 'court' see PARA 346 note 2.
2   Matrimonial Causes Act 1973 s 24(1).
3   Civil Partnership Act 2004 Sch 5 para 6(1)(a).
4   Ie on granting the decree or making the order or at any time thereafter (whether, in the case of a decree of divorce or of nullity of marriage, before or after the decree is made absolute): Matrimonial Causes Act 1973 s 24(1); Civil Partnership Act 2004 Sch 5 para 6(1). See also *Charalambous v Charalambous* [2004] EWCA Civ 1030, [2004] 2 FCR 721, [2004] 2 FLR 1093. As to the matters to which the court is to have regard in deciding how to exercise its powers to make orders for the benefit of children see PARAS 597–598; and as to the duration of orders in favour of children see PARA 495. As to the effect of a subsequent marriage or civil partnership on the courts' power to make or vary financial or property orders see PARA 452.
5   As to the meaning of 'child of the family' see PARA 477 note 3.
6   Ie property to which the first-mentioned party is entitled, either in possession or reversion: Matrimonial Causes Act 1973 s 24(1)(a); Civil Partnership Act 2004 Sch 5 para 7(1)(a), (3). As to the property that may be the subject of a property adjustment order under these provisions see PARAS 499 note 6, 500.
7   Matrimonial Causes Act 1973 s 24(1)(a); Civil Partnership Act 2004 Sch 5 para 7(1)(a). See further PARA 499 note 7.
8   Ie property to which the first-mentioned party is entitled, either in possession or reversion: Matrimonial Causes Act 1973 s 24(1)(b); Civil Partnership Act 2004 Sch 5 para 7(1)(b).
9   Matrimonial Causes Act 1973 s 24(1)(b); Civil Partnership Act 2004 Sch 5 para 7(1)(b). As to when a settlement of property order takes effect see PARA 507. As to the care needed in drafting orders see PARA 933.
10 The court may make an order under head (c) in the text notwithstanding that there are no children of the family: Matrimonial Causes Act 1973 s 24(2); Civil Partnership Act 2004 Sch 5 para 7(2). See also the Family Proceedings Rules 1991, SI 1991/1247, r 2.57; and PARA 510 note 5.
11 Matrimonial Causes Act 1973 s 24(1)(c) (s 24(1)(c), (d) amended by the Welfare Reform and Pensions Act 1999 Sch 3 paras 1, 3); Civil Partnership Act 2004 Sch 5 para 7(1)(c). As to the relevant settlements for these purposes see PARA 510 note 6. As to the settlements with which the court can deal under these provisions see further PARA 511. As to when a variation of settlement order takes effect see PARA 516. As to the court's power to make orders attaching pension benefits see PARA 485 et seq; and as to the court's power to make pension-sharing orders see PARA 523 et seq.
12 Ie no order under the Matrimonial Causes Act 1973 s 24(1)(a) or the Civil Partnership Act 2004 Sch 5 para 7(1)(a) (see the text and notes 4–7).
13 Matrimonial Causes Act 1973 s 29(1); Civil Partnership Act 2004 Sch 5 paras 9, 49(1)(b).
14 Ie unless it appears to the court that the child is, or will be, or if an order were made without complying with the Matrimonial Causes Act 1973 s 29(1) or the Civil Partnership Act 2004 Sch 5 para 49(1)(b) (see the text and note 13) would be, receiving instruction at an educational establishment or undergoing training for a trade, profession or vocation, whether or not he is also, or will also be, in gainful employment: Matrimonial Causes Act 1973 s 29(3)(a); Civil Partnership Act 2004 Sch 5 para 49(5)(a). As to 'trade, profession or vocation' see *Richardson v Richardson* [1993] 4 All ER 673, [1994] 1 WLR 186; *Downing v Downing (Downing intervening)* [1976] Fam 288, [1976] 3 All ER 474.
15 Matrimonial Causes Act 1973 s 29(3)(b); Civil Partnership Act 2004 Sch 5 para 49(5)(b). Physical or other disability may amount to such special circumstances: *C v F (disabled child: maintenance orders)* [1999] 1 FCR 39, [1998] 2 FLR 1, CA; *T v S (financial provision for children)* [1994] 1 FCR 743, [1994] 2 FLR 883.
16 *Chamberlain v Chamberlain* [1974] 1 All ER 33, [1973] 1 WLR 1557, CA; *Kiely v Kiely* [1988] 1 FLR 248, [1988] Fam Law 51, CA; *Lord Lilford v Glynn* [1979] 1 All ER 441, [1979] 1 WLR 78, CA.
17 *Lord Lilford v Glynn* [1979] 1 All ER 441, [1979] 1 WLR 78, CA.
18 See *Crozier v Crozier* [1994] Fam 114, [1996] 2 All ER 362.

519.   Matters to which the court is to have regard. In deciding whether to exercise its power to make a property adjustment order[1] in respect of a child and, if so, in what manner, the court[2] is to have regard to certain matters[3]. The court must also consider whether it would be appropriate so to exercise its powers that the financial obligations of each party towards the other will be terminated as soon after the grant of the decree of divorce or nullity of marriage or the making of the dissolution or nullity order as the court considers just and reasonable[4].

Although there is no statutory period of limitation that applies to proceedings for financial relief, delay may be one of the factors to which the court will have regard when considering all the circumstances of the case[5].

1   As to the meaning of 'property adjustment order' see PARA 498.
2   As to the meaning of 'court' see PARA 346 note 2.
3   See PARAS 597–598; and as to the matters to which the court is to have regard generally see PARA 589.
4   See the Matrimonial Causes Act 1973 s 25A; the Civil Partnership Act 2004 Sch 5 para 23; and PARA 592.
5   See PARA 595.

(iii) Orders for Sale of Property

520.   Power to make orders.   Where the court[1] makes[2] a secured periodical payments order[3], an order for the payment of a lump sum[4] or a property adjustment order[5] it may[6] make a further order for the sale of such property[7] as may be specified in the order (a 'sale of property order')[8]. Any such order may contain such consequential or supplementary provisions as the court thinks fit and, without prejudice to the generality thereof, may include:

(1)   provision requiring the making of a payment out of the proceeds of sale of the property to which the order relates[9]; and

(2)   provision requiring any such property to be offered for sale to a person, or class of persons, specified in the order[10].

Where a party to a marriage or civil partnership has a beneficial interest in any property, or in the proceeds of sale thereof, and some other person who is not a party to the marriage or civil partnership also has a beneficial interest in that property or in the proceeds of sale thereof[11], then, before deciding whether to make a sale of property order in relation to that property, it is the duty of the court to give that other person an opportunity to make representations with respect to the order[12].

1   As to the meaning of 'court' see PARA 346 note 2.
2   Ie under the Matrimonial Causes Act 1973 s 23 or s 24 or the Civil Partnership Act 2004 Sch 5 paras 1–9 (see PARAS 467 et seq, 476 et seq, 498 et seq).
3   As to the meaning of 'secured periodical payments order', and as to the making of a secured periodical payments order, see PARA 467.
4   As to the meaning of 'order for the payment of a lump sum', and as to the making of such orders, see PARA 476.
5   As to the meaning of 'property adjustment order' see PARA 498.
6   Ie on making the order in question or at any time thereafter: Matrimonial Causes Act 1973 s 24A(1) (s 24A added by the Matrimonial Homes and Property Act 1981 s 7); Civil Partnership Act 2004 Sch 5 para 10(1).
7   Ie property in which or in the proceeds of sale of which either or both of the parties to the marriage or civil partnership has or have a beneficial interest, either in possession or reversion: Matrimonial Causes Act 1973 s 24A(1) (as added: see note 6); Civil Partnership Act 2004 Sch 5 para 11(1). For these purposes, property may include the shares in a company, but not its assets: see *Crittenden v Crittenden* [1991] FCR 70, [1990] 2 FLR 361, CA. The rights of the parties pursuant to an order for the sale of the family home and redistribution of the net proceeds are those existing at the time when the order takes effect (see PARA 521) and not at the time when the property is subsequently sold and the proceeds of sale divided: *Re Harper (a bankrupt),*

Harper v O'Reilly [1998] 3 FCR 475, sub nom *Harper v O'Reilly and Harper* [1997] 2 FLR 816. There is no 'beneficial interest' in assets held by a trustee in bankruptcy: see *Ram v Ram (No 2)* [2004] EWCA Civ 1684, [2004] 3 FCR 673, [2005] 2 FLR 75.

8   Matrimonial Causes Act 1973 s 24A(1) (as added: see note 6); Civil Partnership Act 2004 Sch 5 paras 10(1), (2), 11(1), (4). As to the time when a sale of property order takes effect see PARA 521; as to the matters to which the court is to have regard see PARA 522. As to the variation of sale of property orders see PARA 500. Quaere whether the court has jurisdiction to make an order for sale in the absence of any of the types of order specified in the Matrimonial Causes Act 1973 s 24A(1) or the Civil Partnership Act 2004 Sch 5 para 10(1) (see the text and notes 1–5): see *R v Rushmoor Borough Council, ex p Barrett* [1989] QB 60, [1989] 2 All ER 268, CA. Orders for sale may also be made under the Married Women's Property 1882 s 17 and the Civil Partnership Act 2004 s 66 (see PARA 224 et seq) and the Trusts of Land and Appointment of Trustees Act 1996 s 14 (see TRUSTS vol 48 (2007 Reissue) PARA 1038).

9   Matrimonial Causes Act 1973 s 24A(2)(a) (as added: see note 6); Civil Partnership Act 2004 Sch 5 para 11(2), (3)(a). The court may not order the payment of unsecured debts from the net proceeds of sale of a property: *Burton v Burton* [1986] 2 FLR 419, [1986] Fam Law 330. Where a sale of property order contains a provision requiring the proceeds of the sale of the property to which the order relates to be used to secure periodical payments to a party to the marriage or civil partnership, the order ceases to have effect on the death or remarriage of, or on the formation of a subsequent marriage or civil partnership by, that person: Matrimonial Causes Act 1973 s 24A(5) (as added (see note 6); amended by the Civil Partnership Act 2004 Sch 27 para 42); Civil Partnership Act 2004 Sch 5 para 13. As to references to remarriage, to a subsequent marriage and to the formation of a subsequent civil partnership see PARA 452 note 1.

As to the application of the Matrimonial Causes Act 1973 s 24A(2), (5), (6) and the Civil Partnership Act 2004 Sch 5 paras 11, 13, 14 to interim orders for maintenance under the Matrimonial and Family Proceedings Act 1984 s 14 or the Civil Partnership Act 2004 Sch 7 para 5 (see PARA 536) and to orders for financial provision and property adjustment under s 17 or the Civil Partnership Act 2004 Sch 7 para 9 (see PARA 531), as they apply to like orders under the Matrimonial Causes Act 1973 Pt II (ss 21–40A) and the Civil Partnership Act 2004 Sch 5, see the Matrimonial and Family Proceedings Act 1984 s 21; the Civil Partnership Act 2004 Sch 7 para 14; and PARA 537.

10   Matrimonial Causes Act 1973 s 24A(2)(b) (as added: see note 6); Civil Partnership Act 2004 Sch 5 para 11(3)(b). See note 9.

11   A trustee in bankruptcy may be such a person: see *Ram v Ram (No 2)* [2004] EWCA Civ 1684, [2004] 3 FCR 673, [2005] 2 FLR 75.

12   Matrimonial Causes Act 1973 s 24A(6) (as added (see note 6); further added by the Matrimonial and Family Proceedings Act 1984 Sch 1 para 11); Civil Partnership Act 2004 Sch 5 para 14(1), (2). Any representations made by such other person are to be included among the circumstances to which the court is required to have regard (ie under the Matrimonial Causes Act 1973 s 25(1) or the Civil Partnership Act 2004 Sch 5 para 20: see PARA 589) in deciding how to exercise its powers: Matrimonial Causes Act 1973 s 24A(6) (as so added); Civil Partnership Act 2004 Sch 5 para 14(3). See note 9.

521.   Date order takes effect.   A sale of property order[1] made on or after the grant of a decree of divorce or nullity of marriage or on or after the making of a dissolution or nullity order in relation to a civil partnership does not take effect unless the decree has been made absolute or the order has been made final, as the case may be[2]. The court[3] may also direct that a sale of property order, whenever made, or such provision thereof as the court may specify, is not to take effect until the occurrence of an event specified by the court or the expiration of a period so specified[4].

1   As to the making of sale of property orders see PARA 520.
2   Matrimonial Causes Act 1973 s 24A(3) (s 24A added by the Matrimonial Homes and Property Act 1981 s 7); Civil Partnership Act 2004 Sch 5 para 12(1).
3   As to the meaning of 'court' see PARA 346 note 2.
4   Matrimonial Causes Act 1973 s 24A(4) (as added: see note 2); Civil Partnership Act 2004 Sch 5 para 12(2). As to the application of the Matrimonial Causes Act 1973 s 24A(4) and the Civil Partnership Act 2004 Sch 5 para 12 to interim orders for maintenance under the Matrimonial and Family Proceedings Act 1984 s 14 or the Civil Partnership Act 2004 Sch 7 para 5 (see PARA 536) and to orders for financial provision and property adjustment under s 17 or the Civil

Partnership Act 2004 Sch 7 para 9 (see PARA 531), as they apply to like orders under the Matrimonial Causes Act 1973 Pt II (ss 21–40A) and the Civil Partnership Act 2004 Sch 5, see the Matrimonial and Family Proceedings Act 1984 s 21; the Civil Partnership Act 2004 Sch 7 para 14; and PARA 537.

522. Matters to which the court is to have regard. In deciding whether to exercise its power to make an order for the sale of property[1] and, if so, in what manner, the court[2] is to have regard to certain matters[3]. The court must also consider whether it would be appropriate so to exercise its powers that the financial obligations of each party towards the other will be terminated as soon after the grant of the decree of divorce or nullity of marriage or the making of the dissolution or nullity order as the court considers just and reasonable[4].

Although there is no statutory period of limitation that applies to proceedings for financial relief, delay may be one of the factors to which the court will have regard when considering all the circumstances of the case[5].

1   As to the making of sale of property orders see PARA 520.
2   As to the meaning of 'court' see PARA 346 note 2.
3   See the Matrimonial Causes Act 1973 s 25(1), (2); the Civil Partnership Act 2004 Sch 5 paras 20, 21; and PARA 589 et seq. As to this requirement see generally *Rye v Rye* [2002] EWHC 956 (Fam), [2002] 2 FLR 981, [2002] All ER (D) 249 (May).
4   See the Matrimonial Causes Act 1973 s 25A; the Civil Partnership Act 2004 Sch 5 para 23; and PARA 592.
5   See PARA 595.

(iv) Pension Sharing Orders and Pension Compensation Sharing Orders

523. Meanings of 'pension sharing order' and 'pension compensation sharing order'. A 'pension sharing order' is an order which:

(1)   provides that the shareable rights under a specified pension arrangement[1] of a party to a marriage or a civil partnership, or the shareable state scheme rights[2] of a party to a marriage or a civil partnership, are to be subject to pension sharing for the benefit of the other party to the marriage or a civil partnership[3]; and

(2)   specifies the percentage value to be transferred[4].

As from a day to be appointed[5] it is provided that a 'pension compensation sharing order' is an order which:

(a)   provides that the shareable rights to PPF compensation[6] of a party to a marriage or a civil partnership that derive from rights under a specified[7] pension scheme are to be subject to pension compensation sharing for the benefit of the other party[8]; and

(b)   specifies the percentage value to be transferred[9].

1   For these purposes, the reference to 'shareable rights under a pension arrangement' is to rights in relation to which pension sharing is available under the Welfare Reform and Pensions Act 1999 Pt IV Chapter I (ss 27–46) (see SOCIAL SECURITY AND PENSIONS) or under corresponding Northern Ireland legislation: Matrimonial Causes Act 1973 s 21A(2)(a) (s 21A added by the Welfare Reform and Pensions Act 1999 Sch 3 paras 1, 2); Civil Partnership Act 2004 Sch 5 para 16(2). As to the meaning of 'pension arrangement' see PARA 485 note 1.
2   For these purposes, the reference to 'shareable state scheme rights' is to rights in relation to which pension sharing is available under the Welfare Reform and Pensions Act 1999 Pt IV Chapter II (ss 47–51) (see SOCIAL SECURITY AND PENSIONS) or under corresponding Northern Ireland legislation: Matrimonial Causes Act 1973 s 21A(2)(b) (as added: see note 1); Civil Partnership Act 2004 Sch 5 para 16(3).
3   Matrimonial Causes Act 1973 s 21A(1)(a) (as added: see note 1); Civil Partnership Act 2004 Sch 5 paras 15(2), 16(1)(a).

4　Matrimonial Causes Act 1973 s 21A(1)(b) (as added: see note 1); Civil Partnership Act 2004
　　Sch 5 para 16(1)(b).
5　The Matrimonial Causes Act 1973 ss 21B, 21C and the Civil Partnership Act 2004 Sch 5
　　paras 19A, 19B, 19F are added, as from a day to be appointed, by the Pensions Act 2008 s 120,
　　Sch 6 paras 1, 2, 14, 15. At the date at which this volume states the law no day had been
　　appointed for the coming into force of these provisions.
6　The reference to 'shareable rights to PPF compensation' is a reference to rights in relation to
　　which pension compensation sharing is available under the Pensions Act 2008 Pt 3 Chapter 1
　　(ss 107–120: pension compensation on divorce etc) or under corresponding Northern Ireland
　　legislation: Matrimonial Causes Act 1973 s 21B(2)(a) (prospectively added: see note 5); Civil
　　Partnership Act 2004 Sch 5 para 19B(2) (as so prospectively added). 'PPF compensation' means
　　compensation payable under the pension compensation provisions; and 'pension compensation
　　provisions' means the Pensions Act 2004 Pt 2 Chapter 3 (ss 126–181) (pension protection: see
　　SOCIAL SECURITY AND PENSIONS) and any regulations or order made under it, the Pensions
　　Act 2008 Pt 3 Chapter 1 and any regulations or order made under it, and any provision
　　corresponding to those provisions in force in Northern Ireland: Matrimonial Causes Act 1973
　　s 21C (as so prospectively added); Civil Partnership Act 2004 Sch 5 para 19F (as so
　　prospectively added).
7　'Specified' means specified in the order: Matrimonial Causes Act 1973 s 21B(2)(c) (prospectively
　　added: see note 5); Civil Partnership Act 2004 Sch 5 para 19B(3) (as so prospectively added).
8　Matrimonial Causes Act 1973 ss 21B(1)(a), (2)(b) (prospectively added: see note 5); Civil
　　Partnership Act 2004 Sch 5 paras 19A(2), 19B(1)(a) (as so prospectively added).
9　Matrimonial Causes Act 1973 s 21B(1)(b) (prospectively added: see note 5); Civil Partnership
　　Act 2004 Sch 5 para 19B(1)(b) (as so prospectively added).

524.　Making of pension sharing orders and pension compensation sharing orders. The court[1] may make one or more pension sharing orders[2] on granting a decree of divorce or a decree of nullity of marriage, whether before or after the decree is made absolute, on making a dissolution or nullity order relating to a civil partnership, or at any time thereafter[3]. An order may not, however, be made in relation to:

(1)　a pension arrangement[4] which is the subject of a pension sharing order in relation to the marriage or civil partnership or has been the subject of pension sharing between the parties to the marriage or civil partnership[5];

(2)　shareable state scheme rights[6] if such rights are the subject of a pension sharing order in relation to the marriage or civil partnership or such rights have been the subject of pension sharing between the parties to the marriage or civil partnership[7]; or

(3)　the rights of a person under a pension arrangement if there is in force a pension requirement[8] which relates to benefits or future benefits to which he is entitled under the pension arrangement[9].

As from a day to be appointed[10] the court may also, on application, make a pension compensation sharing order[11] on granting a decree of divorce or a decree of nullity of marriage, whether before or after the decree is made absolute, on making a dissolution or nullity order relating to a civil partnership, or at any time thereafter[12]. A pension compensation sharing order may not, however, be made in relation to rights to PPF compensation[13] that:

(a)　are the subject of pension attachment[14];

(b)　derive from rights under a pension scheme that were the subject of pension sharing between the parties to the marriage or civil partnership[15];

(c)　are the subject of pension compensation attachment[16]; or

(d)　are or have been the subject of pension compensation sharing between the parties to the marriage or civil partnership[17].

In deciding whether to exercise its power to make a pension sharing order or a pension compensation sharing order and, if so, in what manner, the court[18] is to have regard to certain matters[19]. The court must also consider whether it would be appropriate so to exercise its powers that the financial obligations of each party towards the other will be terminated as soon after the grant of the decree of divorce or nullity of marriage or the making of the dissolution or nullity order as the court considers just and reasonable[20].

Although there is no statutory period of limitation that applies to proceedings for financial relief, delay may be one of the factors to which the court will have regard when considering all the circumstances of the case[21].

1   As to the meaning of 'court' see PARA 346 note 2.
2   As to the meaning of 'pension sharing order' see PARA 523. No pension sharing order may be made if the proceedings in which the decree is granted were begun before 1 December 2000: see the Welfare Reform and Pensions Act 1999 s 85(3)(a); the Welfare Reform and Pensions Act 1999 (Commencement No 5) Order 2000, SI 2000/1116, art 2(e); and *S v S (rescission of decree nisi: pension sharing provision)* [2002] 1 FCR 193, [2002] 1 FLR 457; *H v H (rescission of decree nisi: pension sharing provision)* [2002] EWHC 767 (Fam), [2002] 2 FLR 116, [2002] All ER (D) 285 (May); *Rye v Rye* [2002] EWHC 956 (Fam), [2002] 2 FLR 981, [2002] All ER (D) 249 (May).
3   Matrimonial Causes Act 1973 s 24B(1) (s 24B added by the Welfare Reform and Pensions Act 1999 Sch 3 paras 1, 4); Civil Partnership Act 2004 Sch 5 para 15(1). Thus, pension sharing orders are not available in proceedings for judicial or legal separation. As to the date on which a pension sharing order takes effect see PARA 525; as to the matters to which the court is to have regard see PARA 524. As to the procedure on an application for a pension sharing order see PARA 576 et seq; as to the court's duty to stay pension sharing orders see PARA 525; and as to the variation of pension sharing orders see PARA 529.
4   As to the meaning of 'pension arrangement' see PARA 485 note 1.
5   Matrimonial Causes Act 1973 s 24B(3) (as added: see note 3); Civil Partnership Act 2004 Sch 5 para 18(1). As to the application of the Matrimonial Causes Act 1973 s 24B(3)–(5) and the Civil Partnership Act 2004 Sch 5 para 18 to interim orders for maintenance under the Matrimonial and Family Proceedings Act 1984 s 14 or the Civil Partnership Act 2004 Sch 7 para 5 (see PARA 536) and to orders for financial provision and property adjustment under s 17 or the Civil Partnership Act 2004 Sch 7 para 9 (see PARA 531), as they apply to like orders under the Matrimonial Causes Act 1973 Pt II (ss 21–40A) and the Civil Partnership Act 2004 Sch 5, see the Matrimonial and Family Proceedings Act 1984 s 21; the Civil Partnership Act 2004 Sch 7 para 14; and PARA 537.
6   As to the meaning of 'shareable state scheme rights' see PARA 523 note 2.
7   Matrimonial Causes Act 1973 s 24B(4) (as added: see note 3); Civil Partnership Act 2004 Sch 5 para 18(2). See note 5.
8   Ie a requirement imposed by the Matrimonial Causes Act 1973 s 25B or s 25C or the Civil Partnership Act 2004 Sch 5 paras 24–29 (see PARA 485 et seq).
9   Matrimonial Causes Act 1973 s 24B(5) (as added: see note 3); Civil Partnership Act 2004 Sch 5 para 18(3). See note 5.
10 The Matrimonial Causes Act 1973 s 24E and the Civil Partnership Act 2004 Sch 5 paras 19A, 19D are added, as from a day to be appointed, by the Pensions Act 2008 s 120, Sch 6 paras 1, 3, 14, 15. At the date at which this volume states the law no day had been appointed for the coming into force of these provisions.
11 As to the meaning of 'pension compensation sharing order' see PARA 523.
12 Matrimonial Causes Act 1973 s 24E(1) (prospectively added: see note 10); Civil Partnership Act 2004 Sch 5 para 19A(1) (as so prospectively added).
13 As to the meaning of 'PPF compensation' see PARA 523 note 6.
14 Matrimonial Causes Act 1973 s 24E(3)(a) (prospectively added: see note 10); Civil Partnership Act 2004 Sch 5 para 19D(1)(a) (as so prospectively added). For these purposes rights to PPF compensation 'are the subject of pension attachment' if any of the following three conditions is met:
    (1)   that the rights derive from rights under a pension scheme in relation to which an order was made under the Matrimonial Causes Act 1973 s 23 or the Civil Partnership Act 2004 Sch 5 Pt 1 imposing a requirement by virtue of the Matrimonial Causes Act 1973 s 25B(4) or the Civil Partnership Act 2004 Sch 5 para 25(2) (see PARA 485) and that order, as modified under the Matrimonial Causes Act 1973 s 25E(3) or the

Civil Partnership Act 2004 Sch 5 para 31 (see PARA 485), remains in force (Matrimonial Causes Act 1973 s 24E(4), (5) (as so prospectively added); Civil Partnership Act 2004 Sch 5 para 19D(2), (3) (as so prospectively added));

(2) that the rights derive from rights under a pension scheme in relation to which an order was made under the Matrimonial Causes Act 1973 s 23 or the Civil Partnership Act 2004 Sch 5 Pt 1 imposing a requirement by virtue of the Matrimonial Causes Act 1973 s 25B(7) or the Civil Partnership Act 2004 Sch 5 para 25(5) (see PARA 485), and that order either has been complied with or has not been complied with and, as modified under the Matrimonial Causes Act 1973 s 25E(3) or the Civil Partnership Act 2004 Sch 5 para 32 (see PARA 485), remains in force (Matrimonial Causes Act 1973 s 24E(6) (as so prospectively added); Civil Partnership Act 2004 Sch 5 para 19D(4) (as so prospectively added)); or

(3) that the rights derive from rights under a pension scheme in relation to which an order was made under the Matrimonial Causes Act 1973 s 23 or the Civil Partnership Act 2004 Sch 5 Pt 1 imposing a requirement by virtue of the Matrimonial Causes Act 1973 s 25C or the Civil Partnership Act 2004 Sch 5 para 26 (see PARA 486), and remains in force (Matrimonial Causes Act 1973 s 24E(7) (as so prospectively added); Civil Partnership Act 2004 Sch 5 para 19D(5) (as so prospectively added)).

15 Matrimonial Causes Act 1973 s 24E(3)(b) (prospectively added: see note 10); Civil Partnership Act 2004 Sch 5 para 19D(1)(b) (as so prospectively added). For this purpose rights under a pension scheme 'were the subject of pension sharing between the parties to the marriage or civil partnership' if the rights were at any time the subject of a pension sharing order in relation to the marriage or civil partnership or a previous marriage or civil partnership between the same parties: Matrimonial Causes Act 1973 s 24E(8) (as so prospectively added); Civil Partnership Act 2004 Sch 5 para 19D(6) (as so prospectively added).

16 Matrimonial Causes Act 1973 s 24E(3)(c) (prospectively added: see note 10); Civil Partnership Act 2004 Sch 5 para 19D(1)(c) (as so prospectively added). For this purpose rights to PPF compensation 'are the subject of pension compensation attachment' if there is in force a requirement imposed by virtue of the Matrimonial Causes Act 1973 s 25F or the Civil Partnership Act 2004 Sch 5 para 34A (see PARA 526) relating to them: Matrimonial Causes Act 1973 s 24E(9) (as so prospectively added); Civil Partnership Act 2004 Sch 5 para 19D(7) (as so prospectively added).

17 Matrimonial Causes Act 1973 s 24E(3)(d) (prospectively added: see note 10); Civil Partnership Act 2004 Sch 5 para 19D(1)(d) (as so prospectively added). For this purpose rights to PPF compensation 'are or have been the subject of pension compensation sharing between the parties to the marriage or civil partnership' if they are or have ever been the subject of a pension compensation sharing order in relation to the marriage or civil partnership or a previous marriage or civil partnership between the same parties: Matrimonial Causes Act 1973 s 24E(10) (as so prospectively added); Civil Partnership Act 2004 Sch 5 para 19D(8) (as so prospectively added).

18 As to the meaning of 'court' see PARA 346 note 2.

19 See the Matrimonial Causes Act 1973 s 25(1), (2); the Civil Partnership Act 2004 Sch 5 paras 20, 21; and PARA 589 et seq. As to this requirement see generally *Rye v Rye* [2002] EWHC 956 (Fam), [2002] 2 FLR 981, [2002] All ER (D) 249 (May).

20 See the Matrimonial Causes Act 1973 s 25A; the Civil Partnership Act 2004 Sch 5 para 23; and PARA 592.

21 See PARA 595.

525. Date orders take effect. A pension sharing order[1] takes effect not earlier than seven days after the end of the period for filing notice of appeal against the order[2]; at the date at which this volume states the law no provision has been made for the taking effect of a pension compensation sharing order[3]. It is also provided that a pension sharing order and (as from a day to be appointed) a pension compensation sharing order is not to take effect unless the decree or order on or after which it is made[4] has been made absolute or, as the case may be, final[5].

1 As to the meaning of 'pension sharing order' see PARA 523; as to the making of pension sharing orders see PARA 524.

2 Divorce etc (Pensions) Regulations 2000, SI 2000/1123, reg 9(1); Dissolution etc (Pensions) Regulations 2005, SI 2005/2920, reg 9(1). The filing of a notice of appeal within the time

allowed for doing so prevents the order taking effect before the appeal has been dealt with: Divorce etc (Pensions) Regulations 2000, SI 2000/1123, reg 9(2); Dissolution etc (Pensions) Regulations 2005, SI 2005/2920, reg 9(3). These provisions are made pursuant to the Matrimonial Causes Act 1973 s 24C (ss 24B, 24C added by the Welfare Reform and Pensions Act 1999 Sch 3 paras 1, 4) and the Civil Partnership Act 2004 Sch 5 para 19(2), (3).

3   As to pension compensation sharing orders see PARAs 523, 524. As from a day to be appointed it is provided that no pension compensation sharing order may be made so as to take effect before the end of such period after the making of the order as may be prescribed by regulations made by the Lord Chancellor: Matrimonial Causes Act 1973 s 24F (ss 24E, 24F prospectively added by the Pensions Act 2008 Sch 6 paras 1, 3); Civil Partnership Act 2004 Sch 5 para 19E(2), (3) (Sch 5 para 19E prospectively added by the Pensions Act 2008 Sch 6 paras 14, 15). At the date at which this volume states the law no such day had been appointed and no such regulations had been made.

4   As to the decrees and orders on and after which pension sharing orders and pension compensation sharing orders may be made see PARA 524.

5   Matrimonial Causes Act 1973 ss 24B(2), 24E(2) (s 24B(2) as added (see note 2); s 24E(2) prospectively added (see note 3)); Civil Partnership Act 2004 Sch 5 paras 19(1), 19E(1) (Sch 5 para 19E prospectively added: see note 3).

526.   Attachment of pension compensation. As from a day to be appointed[1] it is provided that where, having regard to any PPF compensation[2] to which a party to a marriage or civil partnership is or is likely to be entitled, the court determines to make an order[3] for financial provision on divorce, dissolution, nullity or separation[4], then:

(1)   to the extent to which the order is made having regard to such compensation, it may require the Board of the Pension Protection Fund, if at any time any payment in respect of PPF compensation becomes due to the party with compensation rights[5], to make a payment for the benefit of the other party[6]; and

(2)   where the party with compensation rights has a right to commute any PPF compensation, the order may require that party to exercise it to any extent[7].

These powers[8] may not be exercised in relation to rights to PPF compensation that:

(a)   derive from rights under a pension scheme that were at any time the subject of a pension sharing order[9] in relation to the marriage or civil partnership or a previous marriage or civil partnership between the same parties[10]; or

(b)   are or have ever been the subject of a pension compensation sharing order[11] in relation to the marriage or civil partnership or a previous marriage or civil partnership between the same parties[12].

1   The Matrimonial Causes Act 1973 ss 25F, 25G and the Civil Partnership Act 2004 Sch 5 paras 34A, 34B are added, and s 37(1) is amended, as from a day to be appointed, by the Pensions Act 2008 s 120, Sch 6 paras 1, 7, 14, 17(1), (3)–(5). At the date at which this volume states the law no day had been appointed for the coming into force of these provisions.

2   As to the meaning of 'PPF compensation' see PARA 523 note 6.

3   Ie an order under the Matrimonial Causes Act 1973 s 23 or the Civil Partnership Act 2004 Sch 5 Pt 1 (paras 1–5) (see PARA 458 et seq).

4   Matrimonial Causes Act 1973 s 25F(1) (prospectively added: see note 1); Civil Partnership Act 2004 Sch 5 para 34A(1) (as so prospectively added).

5   'Party with compensation rights' means the party to the marriage or civil partnership who is or is likely to be entitled to PPF compensation; and 'other party' (which is only defined in relation to marriage) means the other party to the marriage: Matrimonial Causes Act 1973 s 25G(5) (prospectively added: see note 1); Civil Partnership Act 2004 Sch 5 para 37(1) (definition as so prospectively added).

6   Matrimonial Causes Act 1973 s 25F(2) (prospectively added: see note 1); Civil Partnership Act 2004 Sch 5 para 34A(2) (as so prospectively added). The order must express the amount of

any payment required to be made by virtue of this requirement as a percentage of the payment which becomes due to the party with compensation rights: Matrimonial Causes Act 1973 s 25F(3) (as so prospectively added); Civil Partnership Act 2004 Sch 5 para 34A(3) (as so prospectively added). Any such payment by the Board of the Pension Protection Fund discharges so much of its liability to the party with compensation rights as corresponds to the amount of the payment and is treated for all purposes as a payment made by the party with compensation rights in or towards the discharge of that party's liability under the order: Matrimonial Causes Act 1973 s 25F(4) (as so prospectively added); Civil Partnership Act 2004 Sch 5 para 34A(4) (as so prospectively added).

As from a day to be appointed (see note 1) the Lord Chancellor may by regulations:

(1)   make provision, in relation to any provision of the Matrimonial Causes Act 1973 s 25F or the Civil Partnership Act 2004 Sch 5 para 34A which authorises the court making an order under the Matrimonial Causes Act 1973 s 23 or the Civil Partnership Act 2004 Sch 5 Pt 1 to require the Board of the Pension Protection Fund to make a payment for the benefit of the other party, as to the person to whom, and the terms on which, the payment is to be made (Matrimonial Causes Act 1973 s 25G(1)(a) (as so prospectively added); Civil Partnership Act 2004 Sch 5 para 34B(1)(a) (as so prospectively added));

(2)   make provision, in relation to payment under a mistaken belief as to the continuation in force of a provision included by virtue of the Matrimonial Causes Act 1973 s 25F or the Civil Partnership Act 2004 Sch 5 para 34A in an order under the Matrimonial Causes Act 1973 s 23 or the Civil Partnership Act 2004 Sch 5 Pt 1, about the rights or liabilities of the payer, the payee or the person to whom the payment was due (Matrimonial Causes Act 1973 s 25G(1)(b) (as so prospectively added); Civil Partnership Act 2004 Sch 5 para 34B(1)(b) (as so prospectively added));

(3)   require notices to be given in respect of changes of circumstances relevant to orders under the Matrimonial Causes Act 1973 s 23 or the Civil Partnership Act 2004 Sch 5 Pt 1 which include provision made by virtue of the Matrimonial Causes Act 1973 s 25F or the Civil Partnership Act 2004 Sch 5 para 34A (Matrimonial Causes Act 1973 s 25G(1)(c) (as so prospectively added); Civil Partnership Act 2004 Sch 5 para 34B(1)(c) (as so prospectively added));

(4)   make provision for the Board of the Pension Protection Fund to be discharged in prescribed circumstances from a requirement imposed by virtue of the Matrimonial Causes Act 1973 s 25F or the Civil Partnership Act 2004 Sch 5 para 34A (Matrimonial Causes Act 1973 s 25G(1)(d) (as so prospectively added); Civil Partnership Act 2004 Sch 5 para 34B(1)(d) (as so prospectively added)); and

(5)   make provision (which may include provision for calculation or verification in accordance with guidance from time to time prepared by a prescribed person and provision by reference to regulations under the Pensions Act 2008 s 112) about calculation and verification in relation to the valuation of PPF compensation for the purposes of the court's functions in connection with the exercise of any of its powers under these provisions (Matrimonial Causes Act 1973 s 25G(1)(e), (2) (as so prospectively added); Civil Partnership Act 2004 Sch 5 para 34B(1)(e), (2) (as so prospectively added)).

At the date at which this volume states the law no such orders had been made.

7   Matrimonial Causes Act 1973 s 25F(5) (prospectively added: see note 1); Civil Partnership Act 2004 Sch 5 para 34A(5) (as so prospectively added). These provisions apply to any payment due in consequence of commutation in pursuance of the order as they apply to other payments in respect of PPF compensation (Matrimonial Causes Act 1973 s 25F(5) (as so prospectively added); Civil Partnership Act 2004 Sch 5 para 34A(6) (as so prospectively added)), but the power conferred by the Matrimonial Causes Act 1973 s 25F(5) and the Civil Partnership Act 2004 Sch 5 para 34A(5) may not be exercised for the purpose of commuting compensation payable to the party with compensation rights to compensation payable to the other party (Matrimonial Causes Act 1973 s 25F(6) (as so prospectively added); Civil Partnership Act 2004 Sch 5 para 34A(7) (as so prospectively added)).

8   Ie the powers conferred by the Matrimonial Causes Act 1973 s 25F(2), (5) and the Civil Partnership Act 2004 Sch 5 para 34A(2), (5) (see the text and notes 1–7).

9   As to the meaning of 'pension sharing order' see PARA 523; as to the making of pension sharing orders see PARA 524.

10   Matrimonial Causes Act 1973 s 25F(7)(a) (prospectively added: see note 1); Civil Partnership Act 2004 Sch 5 para 34A(8)(a) (as so prospectively added).

11   As to the meaning of 'pension compensation sharing order' see PARA 523; as to the making of pension compensation sharing orders see PARA 524.

12 Matrimonial Causes Act 1973 s 25F(7)(b) (prospectively added: see note 1); Civil Partnership
    Act 2004 Sch 5 para 34A(8)(b) (as so prospectively added).

527.   Apportionment of charges. If a pension sharing order[1] relates to rights
under a pension arrangement[2], or (as from a day to be appointed[3]) if a pension
compensation sharing order is made[4], the court[5] may include in the order
provision about the apportionment between the parties of any charge[6] in respect
of pension sharing costs[7].

1   As to the meaning of 'pension sharing order' see PARA 523; as to the making of pension sharing
    orders see PARA 524.
2   As to the meaning of 'pension arrangement' see PARA 485 note 1.
3   The Matrimonial Causes Act 1973 s 24G and the Civil Partnership Act 2004 Sch 5 para 19C are
    added, as from a day to be appointed, by the Pensions Act 2008 s 120, Sch 6 paras 1, 3, 14, 15.
    At the date at which this volume states the law no day had been appointed for the coming into
    force of these provisions.
4   As to the meaning of 'pension compensation sharing order' see PARA 523; as to the making of
    pension compensation sharing orders see PARA 524.
5   As to the meaning of 'court' see PARA 346 note 2.
6   Ie in relation to a pension sharing order relating to rights under a pension arrangement, any
    charge under the Welfare Reform and Pensions Act 1999 s 41 (see SOCIAL SECURITY AND
    PENSIONS) or under corresponding Northern Ireland legislation (Matrimonial Causes Act 1973
    s 24D (added by the Welfare Reform and Pensions Act 1999 Sch 3 paras 1, 4); Civil Partnership
    Act 2004 Sch 5 para 17); and in relation to a pension compensation sharing order, any charge
    under the Pensions Act 2008 s 117 or under corresponding Northern Ireland legislation
    (Matrimonial Causes Act 1973 s 24G (prospectively added: see note 3); Civil Partnership
    Act 2004 Sch 5 para 19C (as so prospectively added).
7   Matrimonial Causes Act 1973 ss 24D, 24G (as added and prospectively added: see notes 3, 6);
    Civil Partnership Act 2004 Sch 5 paras 17, 19C (Sch 5 para 19C prospectively added: see note
    3). As to the application of the Matrimonial Causes Act 1973 ss 24D, 24G and the Civil
    Partnership Act 2004 Sch 5 paras 17, 19C to interim orders for maintenance under the
    Matrimonial and Family Proceedings Act 1984 s 14 or the Civil Partnership Act 2004 Sch 7
    para 5 (see PARA 536) and to orders for financial provision and property adjustment under the
    Matrimonial and Family Proceedings Act 1984 s 17 or the Civil Partnership Act 2004 Sch 7
    para 9 (see PARA 531), as they apply to like orders under the Matrimonial Causes Act 1973 Pt II
    (ss 21–40A) and the Civil Partnership Act 2004 Sch 5, see the Matrimonial and Family
    Proceedings Act 1984 s 21; the Civil Partnership Act 2004 Sch 7 para 14; and PARA 537.

**528.   Appeals relating to pension sharing orders and pension compensation
sharing orders which have taken effect.** Where an appeal against a pension
sharing order[1] is begun on or after the day on which the order takes effect:
   (1)   if the pension sharing order relates to a person's rights under a pension
         arrangement[2], the appeal court may not set aside or vary the order if the
         person responsible for the pension arrangement[3] has acted to his
         detriment in reliance on the taking effect of the order[4];
   (2)   if the pension sharing order relates to a person's shareable state scheme
         rights[5], the appeal court may not set aside or vary the order if the
         Secretary of State has acted to his detriment in reliance on the taking
         effect of the order[6].
In determining for these purposes whether a person has acted to his detriment
in reliance on the taking effect of the order, the appeal court may disregard any
detriment which in its opinion is insignificant[7].
   Where these provisions apply, the appeal court may make such further orders,
including one or more pension sharing orders, as it thinks fit for the purpose of
putting the parties in the position it considers appropriate[8].
   As from a day to be appointed[9] if, where an appeal against a pension
compensation sharing order[10] is begun on or after the day on which the order

takes effect, the Board of the Pension Protection Fund has acted to its detriment in reliance on the taking effect of the order[11], the appeal court may not set aside or vary the order but may make such further orders (including a pension compensation sharing order) as it thinks fit for the purpose of putting the parties in the position it considers appropriate[12].

1   As to the meaning of 'pension sharing order' see PARA 523; as to the making of pension sharing orders see PARA 524.
2   As to the meaning of 'pension arrangement' see PARA 485 note 1.
3   As to the person responsible for the pension arrangement see the Matrimonial Causes Act 1973 s 25D(4); the Civil Partnership Act 2004 Sch 5 para 29(3); and PARA 485 note 6 (definition applied by the Matrimonial Causes Act 1973 s 40A(7) (s 40A added by the Welfare Reform and Pensions Act 1999 Sch 3 paras 1, 10)) and the Civil Partnership Act 2004 Sch 5 para 79(7)).
4   Matrimonial Causes Act 1973 s 40A(1), (2) (as added: see note 3); Civil Partnership Act 2004 Sch 5 para 79(1), (2). The Matrimonial Causes Act 1973 s 24C and the Civil Partnership Act 2004 Sch 5 para 19 (when pension sharing orders take effect: see PARA 525) only apply to a pension sharing order under the Matrimonial Causes Act 1973 s 40A or the Civil Partnership Act 2004 Sch 5 para 79 (ie pursuant to the provisions described in this paragraph) if the decision of the appeal court can itself be the subject of an appeal: Matrimonial Causes Act 1973 s 40A(6) (as so added); Civil Partnership Act 2004 Sch 5 para 79(6).
5   As to the meaning of 'shareable state scheme rights' see PARA 523 note 2.
6   Matrimonial Causes Act 1973 s 40A(3) (as added: see note 3); Civil Partnership Act 2004 Sch 5 para 79(3).
7   Matrimonial Causes Act 1973 s 40A(4) (as added: see note 3); Civil Partnership Act 2004 Sch 5 para 79(4).
8   Matrimonial Causes Act 1973 s 40A(5) (as added: see note 3); Civil Partnership Act 2004 Sch 5 para 79(5).
9   The Matrimonial Causes Act 1973 s 40B and the Civil Partnership Act 2004 Sch 5 para 79A are added, as from a day to be appointed, by the Pensions Act 2008 s 120, Sch 6 paras 1, 9, 14, 19. At the date at which this volume states the law no day had been appointed for the coming into force of these provisions.
10 As to the meaning of 'pension compensation sharing order' see PARA 523; as to the making of pension compensation sharing orders see PARA 524.
11 In determining for these purposes whether the Board has acted to its detriment the appeal court may disregard any detriment which in the court's opinion is insignificant: Matrimonial Causes Act 1973 s 40B(3) (prospectively added: see note 9); Civil Partnership Act 2004 Sch 5 para 79A(3) (as so prospectively added).
12 Matrimonial Causes Act 1973 s 40B(1), (2) (prospectively added: see note 9); Civil Partnership Act 2004 Sch 5 para 79A(1), (2) (as so prospectively added). The Matrimonial Causes Act 1973 s 24F and the Civil Partnership Act 2004 Sch 5 para 19E (when pension sharing orders take effect: see PARA 525) only apply to a pension compensation sharing order under the Matrimonial Causes Act 1973 s 40B or the Civil Partnership Act 2004 Sch 5 para 79A (ie pursuant to the provisions described in the text and notes 9–11) if the decision of the appeal court can itself be the subject of an appeal: Matrimonial Causes Act 1973 s 40B(4) (as so prospectively added); Civil Partnership Act 2004 Sch 5 para 79A(4) (as so prospectively added).

529. Variation of pension sharing orders and pension compensation sharing orders. In relation to a pension sharing order or (as from a day to be appointed[1]) a pension compensation sharing order, which is made at a time before a decree of divorce or nullity has been made absolute or an order for dissolution or nullity has been made final (the 'relevant order')[2], the general power to vary or discharge orders[3] may be exercised:

(1)   only on an application made before the relevant order has or, but for head (2) below, would have taken effect[4]; and

(2)   only if, at the time when the application is made, the decree has not been made absolute or the order has not been made final[5].

No pension sharing order may be made on an application for the variation of a periodical payments order[6] or secured periodical payments order[7] made following divorce, dissolution etc[8].

1   The Civil Partnership Act 2004 Sch 5 para 50(1)(a) is amended, as from a day to be appointed, by the Pensions Act 2008 s 120, Sch 6 paras 14, 18(1), (7), (a)–(c). At the date at which this volume states the law no day had been appointed for the coming into force of these provisions. Owing to the different drafting of the corresponding provisions of the Matrimonial Causes Act 1973 (ie s 31(4A)), no corresponding prospective amendments have been made to that Act.

2   As to the meanings of 'pension sharing order' and 'pension compensation sharing order' see PARA 523; and as to the variation of orders in the specific circumstances referred to in the text see the Matrimonial Causes Act 1973 s 31(2)(g); the Civil Partnership Act 2004 Sch 5 para 50(1)(i); and PARA 567.

3   Ie the powers conferred by the Matrimonial Causes Act 1973 s 31 and the Civil Partnership Act 2004 Sch 5 Pt 11 (paras 50–62): see PARAS 567–568.

4   Matrimonial Causes Act 1973 s 31(4A)(a)(i) (s 31(4A)–(4C) added by the Welfare Reform and Pensions Act 1999 Sch 3 para 7(3)); Civil Partnership Act 2004 Sch 5 para 57(1)(a)(i) (prospectively amended: see note 1). An application made in accordance with this provision prevents the relevant order from taking effect before the application has been dealt with: Matrimonial Causes Act 1973 s 31(4A)(b) (as so added); Civil Partnership Act 2004 Sch 5 para 57(1)(b) (as so prospectively amended).

5   Matrimonial Causes Act 1973 s 31(4A)(a)(ii) (as added: see note 4); Civil Partnership Act 2004 Sch 5 para 57(1)(a)(ii).

6   As to the meaning of 'periodical payments order', and as to the making of a periodical payments order, see PARA 458.

7   As to the meaning of 'secured periodical payments order', and as to the making of a secured periodical payments order, see PARA 467.

8   See the Matrimonial Causes Act 1973 s 31(5); Civil Partnership Act 2004 Sch 5 para 58(2); and PARA 569.

(v) Financial Relief and Property Adjustment following Overseas Divorce, Dissolution, Separation or Annulment

530. Applications for financial relief after overseas divorce etc. Where:

(1)   a marriage or civil partnership has been dissolved or annulled, or the parties to a marriage or civil partnership have been legally separated, by means of judicial or other proceedings in an overseas country[1]; and

(2)   the divorce, dissolution, annulment or legal separation is entitled to be recognised in England and Wales[2],

either party may apply to the court[3] for an order for financial relief[4]. Applications may be made retrospectively[5], but a person is not entitled to make an application in relation to a marriage or civil partnership which has been dissolved or annulled in an overseas country if he or she has formed a subsequent marriage or civil partnership[6].

Where a person applies for an order for financial relief under these provisions he or she may also apply[7] for a transfer of tenancy order[8], and the court may make such an order if the applicant is properly entitled[9].

1   Matrimonial and Family Proceedings Act 1984 s 12(1)(a); Civil Partnership Act 2004 Sch 7 para 1(1)(a). For these purposes 'overseas country' means a country or territory outside the British Islands: Matrimonial and Family Proceedings Act 1984 s 27; Civil Partnership Act 2004 Sch 7 para 1(3). As to the meaning of 'British Islands' see STATUTES vol 44(1) (Reissue) PARA 1383.

2   Matrimonial and Family Proceedings Act 1984 s 12(1)(b); Civil Partnership Act 2004 Sch 7 para 1(1)(b). Thus these provisions do not apply to transnational divorces which do not fall within either the Matrimonial and Family Proceedings Act 1984 s 12 or the Civil Partnership Act 2004 Sch 7 para 1 and are not entitled to recognition in English law: see *Re Fatima* [1986] AC 527, sub nom *Fatima v Secretary of State for the Home Department* [1986] 2 All ER 32, HL; *Berkovits v Grinberg (A-G intervening)* [1995] Fam 142 at 157, 158, [1995] 2 All ER 681 at 694, 695. As to the recognition of foreign divorces, dissolutions, annulments etc see PARA 20; and CONFLICT OF LAWS vol 8(3) (Reissue) PARAS 242–260.

3   Ie in the manner prescribed by rules of court: Matrimonial and Family Proceedings Act 1984 s 12(1); Civil Partnership Act 2004 Sch 7 para 2(3). As to the meaning of 'court' see PARA 346

note 2. As to the applicable rules of court see PARA 941. The leave of the court is required for such an application: see PARA 938. If either party wishes an order to be made in his or her favour, that party must make an application of his or her own and cannot simply rely on the other party's application: see *Robin v Robin* (1983) 4 FLR 632, 13 Fam Law 147, CA.

4   Matrimonial and Family Proceedings Act 1984 s 12(1); Civil Partnership Act 2004 Sch 7 para 2(1). Specified provisions of the Matrimonial Causes Act 1973 Pt II and the Civil Partnership Act 2004 Sch 5 relating to financial relief and property adjustment in the event of divorce, dissolution, nullity etc are applied in relation to orders for financial provision and property adjustment under these provisions: see PARA 537. For these purposes an 'order for financial relief' is an order under the Matrimonial and Family Proceedings Act 1984 s 17 or the Civil Partnership Act 2004 Sch 7 para 9 (orders for financial provision, property adjustment and pension sharing: see PARA 531) or an order under the Matrimonial and Family Proceedings Act 1984 s 22 or the Civil Partnership Act 2004 Sch 7 para 13 (orders for transfers of tenancies of dwelling houses: see PARA 310): Matrimonial and Family Proceedings Act 1984 s 12(4); Civil Partnership Act 2004 Sch 7 para 2(2) (note that this definition is specifically disapplied by the Matrimonial and Family Proceedings Act 1984 s 12(4) for the purposes of s 19 (see PARA 535), s 23 (see PARA 586–587) and s 24 (see PARA 588); differences in the style of drafting of the Civil Partnership Act 2004 means that no similar disapplication is required in respect of the corresponding provisions of that Act (ie Sch 7 paras 12, 15–18)). In connection with the principles underpinning these provisions see *Hewitson v Hewitson* [1995] Fam 100, [1995] 1 All ER 472, CA (wife who had been granted a clean break final order by a court of competent jurisdiction in California not thereafter given leave to apply for relief, notwithstanding a temporary resumption of cohabitation with her former husband in England after the divorce); *N v N (overseas divorce: financial relief)* [1997] 1 FCR 573, sub nom *N v N (foreign divorce: financial relief)* [1997] 1 FLR 900 (husband had not made out a substantial ground).

   On an application for financial relief under these provisions the court may direct that the children be separately represented on the application, either by a solicitor or by a solicitor and counsel, and may appoint the Official Solicitor or other fit person to be guardian ad litem of the children for the purpose of the application: Family Proceedings Rules 1991, SI 1991/1247, Appendix 4 para 2(2), (3) (Appendix 4 added by SI 2005/2922). Before a person other than the Official Solicitor is appointed guardian ad litem under this rule the solicitor acting for the children must file a certificate that the person proposed as guardian has no interest in the matter adverse to that of the children and that he is a proper person to be such guardian: Family Proceedings Rules 1991, SI 1991/1247, Appendix 4 para 2(4) (as so added).

5   See the Civil Partnership Act 2004 Sch 7 para 1(2), which provides that Sch 7 paras 1–16 apply even if the date of the dissolution, annulment or legal separation is earlier than 5 December 2005 (ie the date on which those provisions were brought substantively into force by the Civil Partnership Act 2004 (Commencement No 2) Order 2005, SI 2005/3175), and *Chebaro v Chebaro* [1987] Fam 127, [1987] 1 All ER 999, CA, in which it was held that on its true construction the Matrimonial and Family Proceedings Act 1984 s 12(1) has retrospective effect so that the court has power to grant relief notwithstanding the fact that an overseas divorce was obtained before 16 September 1985 (ie the date on which s 12 was brought into force by the Matrimonial and Family Proceedings Act 1984 (Commencement No 2) Order 1985, SI 1985/1316).

6   Matrimonial and Family Proceedings Act 1984 s 12(2) (s 12(2) amended, s 12(3) substituted, by the Civil Partnership Act 2004 Sch 27 para 90); Civil Partnership Act 2004 Sch 7 paras 2(2)(a), 3(1). References to the forming of a subsequent marriage or civil partnership include a reference to the forming of a marriage or civil partnership which is by law void or voidable: Matrimonial and Family Proceedings Act 1984 s 12(3) (as so substituted); Civil Partnership Act 2004 Sch 7 para 3(2).

7   Ie if he is entitled, either in his own right or jointly with the party, to occupy a dwelling-house in England or Wales by virtue of a tenancy which is a relevant tenancy within the meaning of the Family Law Act 1996 Sch 7 (transfer of certain tenancies on divorce, dissolution etc or on separation of cohabitants: see PARA 310 et seq). Applications must be made in the manner prescribed by rules of court: Matrimonial and Family Proceedings Act 1984 s 12(1); Civil Partnership Act 2004 Sch 7 para 2(3). As to the applicable rules of court see PARA 941. The leave of the court is required for such an application: see PARA 938. A person is not entitled to make an application in relation to a marriage or civil partnership which has been dissolved or annulled in an overseas country if he has formed a subsequent marriage or civil partnership: Matrimonial and Family Proceedings Act 1984 s 12(2) (as amended: see note 6); Civil Partnership Act 2004 Sch 7 para 3(1).

8   Ie any order which the court may make under the Family Law Act 1996 Sch 7 Pt 2 (order transferring tenancy or switching statutory tenants: see PARA 310 et seq).

9   Matrimonial and Family Proceedings Act 1984 s 22(1), (2) (s 22 substituted by the Family Law
     Act 1996 Sch 8 para 52); Civil Partnership Act 2004 Sch 7 paras 2(1), 13(1), (2). The applicant
     is properly entitled if: (1) in respect of a marriage, a divorce order, separation order or decree of
     nullity had been made or granted in England and Wales; or (2) in respect of a civil partnership,
     it had power to make a property adjustment order under the Civil Partnership Act 2004 Sch 5
     Pt 2 (paras 6–9): Matrimonial and Family Proceedings Act 1984 s 22(2) (as so substituted); Civil
     Partnership Act 2004 Sch 7 para 13(2). The provisions of the Family Law Act 1996 Sch 7
     para 10 (see PARA 314), Sch 7 para 11 (see PARA 315) and Sch 7 para 14(1) (see PARA 310–311)
     apply in relation to any order under the Matrimonial and Family Proceedings Act 1984 s 22 or
     the Civil Partnership Act 2004 Sch 7 para 13 as they apply to an order under the Family Law
     Act 1996 Sch 7 Pt II (paras 6–9): Matrimonial and Family Proceedings Act 1984 s 22(3) (as so
     substituted); Civil Partnership Act 2004 Sch 7 para 13(3).

531.   Orders for financial provision and property adjustment.   If an
application for an order for financial relief[1] is made in relation to a recognised
overseas divorce, dissolution, separation or annulment[2], the court[3] may[4] make a
financial provision order, a property adjustment order, a pension sharing order
or (as from a day to be appointed[5]) a pension compensation sharing order[6]. If
pursuant to these powers the court makes a secured periodical payments order[7],
an order for the payment of a lump sum[8] or a property adjustment order[9], then,
on making that order or at any time thereafter, the court may[10] make an order
for the sale of property[11] which the court would otherwise[12] have power to
make[13].

1   As to the meaning of 'order for financial relief' see PARA 530 note 4.
2   As to the making of such applications see PARA 530.
3   As to the meaning of 'court' see PARA 346 note 2.
4   Ie subject to the Matrimonial and Family Proceedings Act 1984 s 20 or, as the case may be, the
     Civil Partnership Act 2004 Sch 7 para 11 (restriction on court's powers where jurisdiction
     depends on family home in England and Wales: see PARA 533).
5   The Matrimonial and Family Proceedings Act 1984 s 17(1)(c) is added, and the Civil
     Partnership Act 2004 Sch 7 para 9(2) is amended, as from a day to be appointed, by the
     Pensions Act 2008 s 120, Sch 6 paras 10, 11, 20(1), (2). At the date at which this volume states
     the law no day had been appointed for the coming into force of these provisions.
6   Matrimonial and Family Proceedings Act 1984 s 17(1) (substituted by the Welfare Reform and
     Pensions Act 1999 Sch 12 paras 2, 3; prospectively amended (see note 5)); Civil Partnership
     Act 2004 Sch 7 para 9(1), (5). Thus:
     (1)   the court may make any one or more of the orders which it could make under the
            Matrimonial Causes Act 1973 Pt II (ss 21–40A) (see PARA 450 et seq) if a decree of
            divorce, a decree of nullity of marriage or a decree of judicial separation in respect of
            the marriage had been granted in England and Wales, that is to say any order such as is
            mentioned in s 23(1) (see PARA 458 et seq) or any order such as is mentioned in s 24(1)
            (see PARA 499 et seq) (Matrimonial and Family Proceedings Act 1984 s 17(1)(a) (as so
            substituted));
     (2)   if a marriage has been dissolved or annulled, the court may make one or more orders
            each of which would be a pension sharing order (within the meaning of the
            Matrimonial Causes Act 1973 Pt II: see PARA 523) in relation to the marriage
            (Matrimonial and Family Proceedings Act 1984 s 17(1)(b) (as so substituted));
     (3)   as from a day to be appointed (see note 5), if the marriage has been dissolved or
            annulled, the court may make an order which would be a pension compensation
            sharing order (within the meaning of the Matrimonial Causes Act 1973 Pt II: see PARA
            523) in relation to the marriage (Matrimonial and Family Proceedings Act 1984
            s 17(1)(c) (as so prospectively added));
     (4)   if a civil partnership has been dissolved or annulled, the court may make any one or
            more of the orders which it could make under the Civil Partnership Act 2004 Sch 5 Pt 1
            (paras 1–5), Pt 2 (paras 6–9), Pt 4 (paras 15–19) or (as from a day to be appointed (see
            note 5)) Pt 4A (paras 19A–19F) (financial provision, property adjustment, pension
            sharing and pension compensation sharing: see PARAS 458 et seq, 499 et seq, 523 et seq)
            if a dissolution order or nullity order had been made in respect of the civil partnership
            under of Pt 2 Chapter 2 (Sch 7 para 9(2) (as so prospectively amended)); and
     (5)   if civil partners have been legally separated, the court may make any one or more of the

orders which it could make under Sch 5 Pt 1 or Pt 2 (financial provision and property adjustment: see PARAS 458 et seq, 499 et seq) if a separation order had been made in respect of the civil partners under Pt 2 Chapter 2 (Sch 7 para 9(3)).

As to the matters to which the court is to have regard in exercising its powers to make orders for financial provision and property adjustment see PARA 532. Specified provisions of the Matrimonial Causes Act 1973 Pt II and the Civil Partnership Act 2004 Sch 5 relating to financial relief and property adjustment in the event of divorce, dissolution, nullity etc are applied in relation to orders for financial provision and property adjustment under these provisions: see PARA 537.

7　As to the meaning of 'secured periodical payments order', and as to the making of a secured periodical payments order, see PARA 467. The Matrimonial and Family Proceedings Act 1984 defines 'secured periodical payments order' for these purposes as meaning such an order as is specified in the Matrimonial Causes Act 1973 s 23(1)(b) or (e) (see PARAS 467, 492): Matrimonial and Family Proceedings Act 1984 s 27. The Civil Partnership Act 2004 refers to a 'secured periodical payments order' as being any order which would be such an order if made under Sch 5: Sch 7 para 9(4)(a).

8　As to the meaning of 'order for the payment of a lump sum', and as to the making of such orders, see PARA 476.

9　As to the meaning of 'property adjustment order' see PARA 498. The Matrimonial and Family Proceedings Act 1984 defines 'property adjustment order' for these purposes as meaning such an order as is specified in the Matrimonial Causes Act 1973 s 24(1)(a), (b), (c) or (d) (see PARAS 499, 506, 510, 518): Matrimonial and Family Proceedings Act 1984 s 27. The Civil Partnership Act 2004 refers to a 'property adjustment order' as being any order which would be such an order if made under Sch 5: Sch 7 para 9(4)(c).

10　See note 4.

11　Ie any order mentioned in the Matrimonial Causes Act 1973 s 24A(1) or the Civil Partnership Act 2004 Sch 5 Pt 3 (paras 10–14) (see PARA 520).

12　Ie if the order under the Matrimonial and Family Proceedings Act 1984 s 17(1) or the Civil Partnership Act 2004 Sch 7 para 9(2) or (3) (see the text and notes 1–6) had been made under the Matrimonial Causes Act 1973 Pt II (ss 21–40A) or the Civil Partnership Act 2004 Sch 7.

13　Matrimonial and Family Proceedings Act 1984 s 17(2); Civil Partnership Act 2004 Sch 7 para 9(4).

532. Matters to which the court is to have regard. In deciding whether to make an order for financial provision or property adjustment in relation to a recognised overseas divorce, dissolution, separation or annulment[1] and, if so, in what manner, the court[2] must have regard to all the circumstances of the case, first consideration being given to the welfare of any child of the family[3] who has not attained the age of 18[4]. As regards the exercise of those powers in relation to one of the parties to a marriage or civil partnership, the court must, in particular, have regard to the matters which it is required to take into account[5] when making financial provision, property adjustment or pension sharing orders generally[6]; additional matters must be taken into account[7] where the exercise of the court's powers involves a child of the family[8]. The court is also under a duty to consider the termination of financial obligations[9].

When an order has been made by a court outside England and Wales for the making of payments or the transfer of property by a party to the marriage or civil partnership, the court, in considering in accordance with these provisions the financial resources of the other party to the marriage or civil partnership or a child of the family, must have regard to the extent to which that order has been complied with or is likely to be complied with[10].

1　Ie in deciding whether to exercise its powers under the Matrimonial and Family Proceedings Act 1984 s 17 or the Civil Partnership Act 2004 Sch 7 para 9: see PARA 531. As to the making of applications in this regard see PARA 530.
2　As to the meaning of 'court' see PARA 346 note 2.
3　As to the meaning of 'child of the family' see PARA 477 note 3.

4   Matrimonial and Family Proceedings Act 1984 s 18(1), (2); Civil Partnership Act 2004 Sch 7 para 10(1), (2). The welfare of child is the first but not the paramount consideration: cf *Suter v Suter and Jones* [1987] Fam 111, [1987] 2 All ER 336, CA (cited in PARA 589).

5   Ie under the Matrimonial Causes Act 1973 s 25(2)(a)–(h) and the Civil Partnership Act 2004 Sch 5 para 21(2) (see PARA 590). These matters include, where applicable:

    (1)   so far as relating to the matters to which the court is required to have regard under the Matrimonial Causes Act 1973 s 25(2)(a) and the Civil Partnership Act 2004 Sch 5 para 21(2)(a) (regard to be had to financial resources generally), any benefits under a pension arrangement which either party to the marriage or civil partnership has or is likely to have and any PPF compensation to which either party is or is likely to be entitled, whether or not in the foreseeable future (Matrimonial and Family Proceedings Act 1984 s 18(3A)(a) (s 18(3A), (7) added by the Welfare Reform and Pensions Act 1999 s 22 and amended by the Pensions Act 2004 Sch 12 para 4); Civil Partnership Act 2004 Sch 7 para 10(4)); and

    (2)   so far as relating to the matters to which the court is required to have regard under the Matrimonial Causes Act 1973 s 25(2)(h) and the Civil Partnership Act 2004 Sch 5 para 21(2)(h) (regard to be had to benefits that cease to be acquirable), any benefits under a pension arrangement which, by reason of the dissolution or annulment of the marriage or civil partnership, a party to the marriage or civil partnership will lose the chance of acquiring, and any PPF compensation which, by reason of the dissolution or annulment, a party to the marriage or civil partnership will lose the chance of acquiring entitlement to (Matrimonial and Family Proceedings Act 1984 s 18(3A)(b) (as so added and amended); Civil Partnership Act 2004 Sch 7 para 10(5)).

    As to the meaning of 'pension arrangement' see PARA 485 note 1 (definition applied by the Matrimonial and Family Proceedings Act 1984 s 18(7)(a) and the Civil Partnership Act 2004 Sch 7 para 10(9)(a)). Until a day to be appointed 'PPF compensation' means compensation payable under the Pensions Act 2004 Pt 2 Chapter 3 (ss 126–181) (pension protection: see SOCIAL SECURITY AND PENSIONS) or corresponding Northern Ireland legislation; as from that day it means compensation payable under the Pensions Act 2004 Pt 2 Chapter 3 and any regulations or order made under it, the Pensions Act 2008 Pt 3 Chapter 1 and any regulations or order made under it, and any provision corresponding to those provisions in force in Northern Ireland: Matrimonial and Family Proceedings Act 1984 s 18(7)(c) (as so added and amended; prospectively substituted by the Pensions Act 2008 s 120, Sch 6 paras 10, 12); Civil Partnership Act 2004 Sch 5 para 30(3), Sch 7 para 10(9)(c) (Sch 5 para 30(3) prospectively repealed, Sch 7 para 10(9)(c) prospectively amended, by the Pensions Act 2008 Sch 6 paras 14, 17, 20(3), Sch 11 Pt 4). At the date at which this volume states the law no day had been appointed for the coming into force of these amendments. References to 'benefits under a pension arrangement' include any benefits by way of pension, whether under a pension arrangement or not: Matrimonial and Family Proceedings Act 1984 s 18(7) (as so added); Civil Partnership Act 2004 Sch 7 para 10(9)(b).

6   Matrimonial and Family Proceedings Act 1984 s 18(3); Civil Partnership Act 2004 Sch 7 para 10(3)(a).

7   Ie the matters referred to in the Matrimonial Causes Act 1973 s 25(3)(a)–(e) and the Civil Partnership Act 2004 Sch 5 para 22(2) (see PARA 597) or, where the court's powers are being exercised against a party to the marriage or civil partnership in favour of a child of the family who is not the child of that party, the matters referred to in the Matrimonial Causes Act 1973 s 25(4)(a)–(c) and the Civil Partnership Act 2004 Sch 5 para 22(3) (see PARA 598).

8   Matrimonial and Family Proceedings Act 1984 s 18(4), (5); Civil Partnership Act 2004 Sch 7 para 10(6), (7).

9   Ie, the court is under duties corresponding with those imposed by the Matrimonial Causes Act 1973 s 25A(1), (2) and the Civil Partnership Act 2004 Sch 5 para 23(2), (3) (see PARA 592) where it decides to exercise under the Matrimonial Causes Act 1973 s 17 or the Civil Partnership Act 2004 Sch 7 para 9 (see PARA 531) any powers corresponding to those referred to in the Matrimonial Causes Act 1973 s 25A(1), (2) or the Civil Partnership Act 2004 Sch 5 para 23(2), (3): Matrimonial and Family Proceedings Act 1984 s 18(3); Civil Partnership Act 2004 Sch 7 para 10(3)(b).

10   Matrimonial and Family Proceedings Act 1984 s 18(6); Civil Partnership Act 2004 Sch 7 para 10(8).

533.   Restriction of powers of court where jurisdiction depends on family home in England and Wales. Where the court[1] has jurisdiction to entertain an application for an order[2] for financial provision or property adjustment in relation to a recognised overseas divorce, dissolution, separation or annulment[3] by reason only of the situation in England or Wales of a dwelling house[4] which was a family home of the parties, the court may[5] make any one or more of the following orders, but no other:

(1) an order that either party to the marriage or civil partnership is to pay to the other such lump sum as may be specified in the order[6];

(2) an order that a party to the marriage or civil partnership is to pay to such person as may be so specified for the benefit of a child of the family[7], or to such a child, such lump sum as may be so specified[8];

(3) an order that a party to the marriage or civil partnership is to transfer to the other party, to any child of the family or to such person as may be so specified for the benefit of such a child, the interest of the first-mentioned party in the dwelling house, or such part of that interest as may be so specified[9];

(4) an order that a settlement of the interest of a party to the marriage or civil partnership in the dwelling house, or such part of that interest as may be so specified, be made to the satisfaction of the court for the benefit of the other party to the marriage or civil partnership and of the children of the family or either or any of them[10];

(5) an order varying for the benefit of the parties to the marriage or civil partnership and of the children of the family or either or any of them any relevant settlement[11] made on the parties to the marriage or the civil partnership, so far as that settlement relates to an interest in the dwelling house[12];

(6) an order extinguishing or reducing the interest of either of the parties to the marriage or the civil partnership under a relevant settlement, so far as that interest is an interest in the dwelling house[13]; and

(7) an order for the sale of the interest of a party to the marriage or civil partnership[14] in the dwelling house[15].

Where, in the circumstances mentioned above, the court makes an order for the payment of a lump sum by a party to the marriage or civil partnership, the amount of the lump sum must not exceed, or where more than one such order is made the total amount of the lump sums must not exceed in aggregate, the following amount:

(a) if the interest of that party in the dwelling house is sold in pursuance of an order under head (7) above, the amount of the proceeds of sale of that interest[16] after deducting therefrom any costs incurred in the sale thereof[17]; or

(b) if the interest of that party is not so sold, the amount which in the opinion of the court represents the value of that interest[18].

1 As to the meaning of 'court' see PARA 346 note 2.

2 Ie an order under the Matrimonial and Family Proceedings Act 1984 s 17 or the Civil Partnership Act 2004 Sch 7 para 9: see PARA 531. As to the making of applications in this regard see PARA 530. Specified provisions of the Matrimonial Causes Act 1973 Pt II and the Civil Partnership Act 2004 Sch 5 relating to financial relief and property adjustment in the event of divorce, dissolution, nullity etc are applied in relation to orders for financial provision and property adjustment under these provisions: see PARA 537.

3 As to the jurisdiction of the court in these matters see PARAS 939–940.

4 'Dwelling-house' includes any building or part thereof which is occupied as a dwelling, and any yard, garden, garage or outhouse belonging to the dwelling-house and occupied therewith: Matrimonial and Family Proceedings Act 1984 s 27; Civil Partnership Act 2004 Sch 7 para 19.

5 Ie under the Matrimonial and Family Proceedings Act 1984 s 17 or the Civil Partnership Act 2004 Sch 7 para 9.

6   Matrimonial and Family Proceedings Act 1984 s 20(1)(a); Civil Partnership Act 2004 Sch 7 para 11(1), (2)(a).
7   As to the meaning of 'child of the family' see PARA 477 note 3.
8   Matrimonial and Family Proceedings Act 1984 s 20(1)(b); Civil Partnership Act 2004 Sch 7 para 11(2)(b).
9   Matrimonial and Family Proceedings Act 1984 s 20(1)(c); Civil Partnership Act 2004 Sch 7 para 11(2)(c).
10 Matrimonial and Family Proceedings Act 1984 s 20(1)(d); Civil Partnership Act 2004 Sch 7 para 11(2)(d).
    Where, on an application for financial relief under the Matrimonial and Family Proceedings Act 1984 Pt III (ss 12–27) or the Civil Partnership Act 2004 Sch 7 (see PARA 530 et seq) an application is made for an order for a variation of settlement the court must, unless it is satisfied that the proposed variation does not adversely affect the rights or interests of any children concerned, direct that the children be separately represented on the application, either by a solicitor or by a solicitor and counsel, and may appoint the Official Solicitor or other fit person to be guardian ad litem of the children for the purpose of the application: Family Proceedings Rules 1991, SI 1991/1247, Appendix 4 para 2(1), (2) (Appendix 4 added by SI 2005/2922). Before a person other than the Official Solicitor is appointed guardian ad litem under this rule the solicitor acting for the children must file a certificate that the person proposed as guardian has no interest in the matter adverse to that of the children and that he is a proper person to be such guardian: Family Proceedings Rules 1991, SI 1991/1247, Appendix 4 para 2(4) (as so added).
11 Ie any ante-nuptial or post-nuptial settlement, or any settlement made during the subsistence of the civil partnership or in anticipation of its formation, including such a settlement made by will or codicil: Matrimonial and Family Proceedings Act 1984 s 20(1)(e); Civil Partnership Act 2004 Sch 7 para 11(7).
12 Matrimonial and Family Proceedings Act 1984 s 20(1)(e); Civil Partnership Act 2004 Sch 7 para 11(2)(e).
13 Matrimonial and Family Proceedings Act 1984 s 20(1)(f); Civil Partnership Act 2004 Sch 7 para 11(2)(f).
14 For these purposes, where the interest of a party to the marriage or civil partnership in the dwelling house is held jointly or in common with any other person or persons, the reference to the interest of a party to the marriage or civil partnership is to be construed as including a reference to the interest of that other person, or the interest of those other persons, in the dwelling house: Matrimonial and Family Proceedings Act 1984 s 20(3)(a); Civil Partnership Act 2004 Sch 7 para 11(6)(a).
15 Matrimonial and Family Proceedings Act 1984 s 20(1)(g); Civil Partnership Act 2004 Sch 7 para 11(2)(g).
16 For these purposes, where the interest of a party to the marriage or civil partnership in the dwelling house is held jointly or in common with any other person or persons, the reference to the amount of the proceeds of a sale order under the Matrimonial and Family Proceedings Act 1984 s 20(1)(g) or Civil Partnership Act 2004 Sch 7 para 11(2)(g) is to be construed as a reference to that part of those proceeds which is attributable to the interest of that party to the marriage in the dwelling house: Matrimonial and Family Proceedings Act 1984 s 20(3)(b); Civil Partnership Act 2004 Sch 7 para 11(6)(b).
17 Matrimonial and Family Proceedings Act 1984 s 20(2)(a); Civil Partnership Act 2004 Sch 7 para 11(3), (4), (5)(a).
18 Matrimonial and Family Proceedings Act 1984 s 20(2)(b); Civil Partnership Act 2004 Sch 7 para 11(5)(b).

534.   Restriction on applications for financial relief from estate of deceased former spouse or civil partner.   On making an order for financial provision or property adjustment in relation to a recognised overseas divorce, dissolution, separation or annulment[1] the court[2] may[3] order that the other party to the marriage or civil partnership[4] will not on the death of the applicant be entitled to apply for an order for financial provision from the deceased's estate[5]. Where such an order[6] has been made with respect to a party to a marriage or civil partnership which has been dissolved or annulled or a marriage or civil partnership the parties to which have been legally separated, then, on the death of the other party to that marriage or civil partnership (in the case of a marriage or civil partnership the parties to which have been legally separated, while the legal separation is in force), the court may not entertain an application[7] for an order for financial provision from the deceased's estate made by the surviving party[8].

1   Ie an order under the Matrimonial and Family Proceedings Act 1984 s 17 or the Civil Partnership Act 2004 Sch 7 para 9: see PARA 531. As to the making of applications in this regard see PARA 530. Specified provisions of the Matrimonial Causes Act 1973 Pt II and the Civil Partnership Act 2004 Sch 5 relating to financial relief and property adjustment in the event of divorce, dissolution, nullity etc are applied in relation to orders for financial provision and property adjustment under these provisions: see PARA 537.

2   For the purposes of the Inheritance (Provision for Family and Dependants) Act 1975 ss 15A(1), 15B(1) 'court' means the High Court or, where a county court has jurisdiction by virtue of the Matrimonial and Family Proceedings Act 1984 Pt V (ss 32–44) (see PARA 732 et seq), a county court: Inheritance (Provision for Family and Dependants) Act 1975 ss 15A(1), 15B(2) (s 15A added by the Matrimonial and Family Proceedings Act 1984 s 25; Inheritance (Provision for Family and Dependants) Act 1975 s 15B added by the Civil Partnership Act 2004 Sch 4 para 22). This corresponds to the definition of 'court' for the purposes of matrimonial and civil partnership proceedings generally set out in PARA 346 note 2.

3   Ie if the court considers it just to do so, and on the application of either of the parties to the marriage or civil partnership: Inheritance (Provision for Family and Dependants) Act 1975 ss 15A(1), 15B(1) (as added: see note 2).

4   Ie the spouse or civil partner. For the purposes of the Inheritance (Provision for Family and Dependants) Act 1975, any reference to a spouse, wife, husband or civil partner is to be treated as including a reference to a person who in good faith entered into a void marriage or civil partnership with the deceased unless either the marriage or civil partnership of or between the deceased and that person was dissolved or annulled during the lifetime of the deceased and the dissolution or annulment is recognised by the law of England and Wales, or that person has during the lifetime of the deceased formed a subsequent marriage or civil partnership: s 25(4), (4A) (s 25(4) amended, s 25(4A), (5A) added, s 25(5) substituted, by the Civil Partnership Act 2004 Sch 4 para 27). Any reference to the formation of, or to a person who has formed, a subsequent marriage or civil partnership includes (as the case may be) a reference to the formation of, or to a person who has formed, a marriage or civil partnership which is by law void or voidable: Inheritance (Provision for Family and Dependants) Act 1975 s 25(5) (as so substituted). The formation of a marriage or civil partnership is treated for these purposes as the formation of a subsequent marriage or civil partnership, in relation to either of the spouses or civil partners, notwithstanding that the previous marriage or civil partnership of that spouse or civil partner was void or voidable: s 25(5A) (as so added). As to void and voidable marriages and civil partnerships see PARA 326 et seq.

5   Inheritance (Provision for Family and Dependants) Act 1975 ss 15A(1), 15B(1) (as added: see note 2). The 'order for financial provision from the deceased's estate' referred to in the text is an order under the Inheritance (Provision for Family and Dependants) Act 1975 s 2; as to which see EXECUTORS AND ADMINISTRATORS vol 17(2) (Reissue) PARAS 691–692.

6   Ie an order under the Inheritance (Provision for Family and Dependants) Act 1975 s 15A(1) or s 15B(1) (see the text and notes 1–5).

7   Ie an application under the Inheritance (Provision for Family and Dependants) Act 1975 s 2 (see EXECUTORS AND ADMINISTRATORS vol 17(2) (Reissue) PARAS 691–692).

8   Inheritance (Provision for Family and Dependants) Act 1975 ss 15A(2), (3), 15B(3), (4) (as added: see note 2).

535. Consent orders for financial provision or property adjustment. On an application for a consent order[1] for financial provision or property adjustment in relation to a recognised overseas divorce, dissolution, separation or annulment[2], including an application for a consent order varying or discharging such an order, the court[3] may[4], unless it has reason to think that there are other circumstances into which it ought to inquire, make an order in the terms agreed on the basis only of the prescribed[5] information furnished with the application[6].

1   For these purposes, 'consent order', in relation to an application for an order, means an order in the terms applied for to which the respondent agrees: Matrimonial and Family Proceedings Act 1984 s 19(3); Civil Partnership Act 2004 Sch 7 para 12(5).

2   Ie an order under the Matrimonial and Family Proceedings Act 1984 s 17 or the Civil
     Partnership Act 2004 Sch 7 para 9: see PARA 531. As to the making of applications in this regard
     see PARA 530.
         Where an application is made for a consent order there must be lodged with every
     application two copies of a draft of the order in the terms sought, one of which must be
     indorsed with a statement signed by the respondent to the application signifying his agreement,
     and a statement of information (which may be made in more than one document) which must
     include:
     (1)   the duration of the marriage or civil partnership, as the case may be, the age of each
            party and of any minor or dependent child of the family (Family Proceedings
            Rules 1991, SI 1991/1247, Appendix 4 para 5(1)(b), (2)(a) (Appendix 4 added by
            SI 2005/2922));
     (2)   an estimate in summary form of the approximate amount or value of the capital
            resources and net income of each party and of any minor child of the family (Family
            Proceedings Rules 1991, SI 1991/1247, Appendix 4 para 5(2)(b) (as so added));
     (3)   what arrangements are intended for the accommodation of each of the parties and any
            minor child of the family (Appendix 4 para 5(2)(c) (as so added));
     (4)   whether either party has subsequently married or formed a civil partnership or has any
            present intention to do so or to cohabit with another person (Appendix 4 para 5(2)(d)
            (as so added));
     (5)   where the order includes provision to be made under the Matrimonial and Family
            Proceedings Act 1984 s 17(1)(a) of a kind which could be made by an order under the
            Matrimonial Causes Act 1973 s 25B or s 25C, under the Matrimonial and Family
            Proceedings Act 1984 s 17(1)(b), or under the Civil Partnership Act 2004 Sch 7
            para 9(2) of a kind which could be made by an order under Sch 5 para 15, 25 or 26
            (orders relating to pension sharing: see PARA 523 et seq), a statement confirming that
            the person responsible for the pension arrangement in question has been served with the
            documents required by the Family Proceedings Rules 1991, SI 1991/1247, r 2.70(11)
            (see PARA 927) and that no objection to such an order has been made by that person
            within 21 days from such service (Appendix 4 para 5(2)(e) (as so added));
     (6)   where the terms of the order provide for a transfer of property, a statement confirming
            that any mortgagee of that property has been served with notice of the application and
            that no objection to such a transfer has been made by the mortgagee within 14 days
            from such service (Appendix 4 para 5(2)(f) (as so added)); and
     (7)   any other especially significant matters (Appendix 4 para 5(2)(g) (as so added)).
         Where an application is made for a consent order for interim periodical payments pending
     the determination of the application or for an order varying an order for periodical payments,
     the statement of information required by these provisions need include only the information in
     respect of net income mentioned in head (2) above: Appendix 4 para 5(3) (as so added). Where
     all or any of the parties attend the hearing of an application for financial relief the court may
     dispense with the lodging of a statement of information in accordance with heads (1)–(7) above
     and give directions for the information which would otherwise be required to be given in such a
     statement to be given in such a manner as it sees fit: Appendix 4 para 5(4) (as so added).
         Specified provisions of the Matrimonial Causes Act 1973 Pt II and the Civil Partnership
     Act 2004 Sch 5 relating to financial relief and property adjustment in the event of divorce,
     dissolution, nullity etc are applied in relation to orders for financial provision and property
     adjustment under these provisions: see PARA 537.
3   As to the meaning of 'court' see PARA 346 note 2.
4   Ie notwithstanding the Matrimonial and Family Proceedings Act 1984 s 18 or the Civil
     Partnership Act 2004 Sch 7 para 10 (see PARA 532).
5   For these purposes 'prescribed' means prescribed by rules of court: Matrimonial and Family
     Proceedings Act 1984 s 19(3); Civil Partnership Act 2004 Sch 7 para 12(5). The information so
     prescribed is that set out in the Family Proceedings Rules 1991, SI 1991/1247, r 2.61(1) (see
     PARA 714): r 3.18(3) (substituted by SI 2005/2922).
6   Matrimonial and Family Proceedings Act 1984 s 19(1), (2); Civil Partnership Act 2004 Sch 7
     para 12(1)–(3). Cf the Matrimonial Causes Act 1973 s 33A (as added and amended); and PARA
     713.

536.   Interim orders.   Where leave is granted[1] for the making of an application
for an order for financial provision or property adjustment in relation to a
recognised overseas divorce, dissolution, separation or annulment[2] and it
appears to the court[3] that the applicant or any child of the family[4] is in

immediate need of financial assistance, the court may make an interim order for maintenance[5]. An interim order may be made subject to such conditions as the court thinks fit[6], but the court must not make an interim order if it appears to the court that it has jurisdiction to entertain the application for financial relief by reason only[7] that either or both of the parties to the marriage or civil partnership had at the date of the application for leave a beneficial interest in possession in a dwelling house[8] situated in England and Wales which was at some time during the marriage or civil partnership the family home of the parties[9].

1 Ie under the Matrimonial and Family Proceedings Act 1984 s 13 or the Civil Partnership Act 2004 Sch 7 para 4: see PARA 938.
2 Ie an order under the Matrimonial and Family Proceedings Act 1984 s 17 or the Civil Partnership Act 2004 Sch 7 para 9: see PARA 531. As to the making of applications in this regard see PARA 530. Specified provisions of the Matrimonial Causes Act 1973 Pt II and the Civil Partnership Act 2004 Sch 5 relating to financial relief and property adjustment in the event of divorce, dissolution, nullity etc are applied in relation to orders for financial provision and property adjustment under these provisions: see PARA 537.
3 As to the meaning of 'court' see PARA 346 note 2.
4 As to the meaning of 'child of the family' see PARA 477 note 3.
5 Matrimonial and Family Proceedings Act 1984 s 14(1); Civil Partnership Act 2004 Sch 7 para 5(2). An 'interim order for maintenance' is an order requiring the other party to the marriage or civil partnership to make to the applicant or to the child such periodical payments, and for such term, being a term beginning not earlier than the date of the grant of leave and ending with the date of the determination of the application for an order for financial relief, as the court thinks reasonable: Matrimonial and Family Proceedings Act 1984 s 14(1); Civil Partnership Act 2004 Sch 7 para 5(2), (3). As to the mode of application see PARA 941.
6 Matrimonial and Family Proceedings Act 1984 s 14(3); Civil Partnership Act 2004 Sch 7 para 5(5).
7 Ie by reason only of the Matrimonial and Family Proceedings Act 1984 s 15(1)(c) or the Civil Partnership Act 2004 Sch 7 para 7(4) (see PARA 939).
8 As to the meaning of 'dwelling house' see PARA 533 note 4.
9 Matrimonial and Family Proceedings Act 1984 s 14(2); Civil Partnership Act 2004 Sch 7 para 5(4).

537. Supplementary provisions. Where an order for financial provision or property adjustment in relation to a recognised overseas divorce, dissolution, separation or annulment[1], or an interim order for maintenance in anticipation of the making of such an order[2], is made, provision as to the following matters is also made[3]:

(1) provision as to lump sums[4];
(2) provision as to orders for sale[5];
(3) provisions about pension sharing and (as from a day to be appointed[6]) pension compensation sharing[7];
(4) the power, by a financial provision order, to attach payments under a pension arrangement or (as from a day to be appointed[8]) pension compensation payments, or to require the exercise of a right of commutation under a pension arrangement or (as from a day to be appointed) of pension compensation, and the extension of lump sum powers in relation to death benefits under a pension arrangement[9];
(5) orders relating to pensions where the Board of the Pension Protection Fund has assumed responsibility[10];
(6) the duration of continuing financial provision orders in favour of a party to the marriage or civil partnership or in favour of children, and the age limit on making certain orders in favour of children[11];
(7) directions for the settlement of an instrument for securing payments or effecting property adjustment[12];

(8)   the variation, discharge etc of certain orders for financial relief[13];

(9)   arrears and repayments[14];

(10)   settlements etc made in compliance with a property adjustment order voidable on the bankruptcy of the settlor[15];

(11)   payments etc under an order made in favour of a person suffering from mental disorder[16]; and

(12)   appeals relating to pension sharing orders or (as from a day to be appointed[17]) pension compensation sharing orders which have taken effect[18].

Supplementary provision may also be made by regulations[19].

1   Ie an order under the Matrimonial and Family Proceedings Act 1984 s 17 or the Civil Partnership Act 2004 Sch 7 para 9: see PARA 531. As to the making of applications in this regard see PARA 530.

2   Ie an order under the Matrimonial and Family Proceedings Act 1984 s 14 or the Civil Partnership Act 2004 Sch 7 para 5: see PARA 536.

3   Ie the provisions of the Matrimonial Causes Act 1973 Pt II and the Civil Partnership Act 2004 Sch 5 described in the text and notes 4–18 apply in relation to an order made under the Matrimonial and Family Proceedings Act 1984 s 14 or s 17 or the Civil Partnership Act 2004 Sch 7 para 5 or 9 as they apply in relation to a like order made under the Matrimonial Causes Act 1973 Pt II or the Civil Partnership Act 2004 Sch 5: Matrimonial and Family Proceedings Act 1984 s 21(1) (s 21(1) renumbered and amended, s 21(2)–(5) added, by the Welfare Reform and Pensions Act 1999 s 22(1), (4), (5), Sch 12 paras 2, 4(a)–(c), Sch 13 Pt II; Matrimonial and Family Proceedings Act 1984 s 21(1) amended by the Pensions Act 2004 Sch 12 para 4); Civil Partnership Act 2004 Sch 7 para 14(1). The provisions of the Matrimonial and Family Proceedings Act 1984 s 21(1), (2), (4) are further amended, and the Civil Partnership Act 2004 Sch 7 para 14(1), (2), (4) are amended, as from a day to be appointed, by the Pensions Act 2008 s 120, Sch 6 paras 10, 13, 14, 20. At the date at which this volume states the law no day had been appointed for the coming into force of those amendments.

4   See the Matrimonial Causes Act 1973 s 23(3); the Civil Partnership Act 2004 Sch 5 para 3(1)–(3), (7); and PARAS 476, 477, 492.

5   See the Matrimonial Causes Act 1973 s 24A(2), (4)–(6); the Civil Partnership Act 2004 Sch 5 paras 11(2)–(4), 12(2), 13, 14; and PARAS 520, 521.

6   See note 3.

7   See the Matrimonial Causes Act 1973 ss 24B(3)–(5), 24C, 24D, 24E(3)–(10), 24F, 24G; the Civil Partnership Act 2004 Sch 5 paras 17, 18, 19(2), (3), 19C, 19D, 19E(2), (3); and PARAS 523–525, 527.

8   See note 3.

9   See the Matrimonial Causes Act 1973 ss 25B(3)–(7B), 25C, 25F; the Civil Partnership Act 2004 Sch 5 paras 25, 26, 34A; and PARAS 485, 486. The specified provisions do not apply (ie as described in note 3) where the court has jurisdiction to entertain an application for an order for financial relief by reason only of the situation in England or Wales of a dwelling house which was a family home of the parties: Matrimonial and Family Proceedings Act 1984 s 21(2) (as added and prospectively amended: see note 3); Civil Partnership Act 2004 Sch 7 para 14(2) (as so prospectively amended). The Matrimonial Causes Act 1973 s 25D(1) and the Civil Partnership Act 2004 Sch 5 para 27 (see PARA 487) apply in relation to an order made under the Matrimonial and Family Proceedings Act 1984 s 17 or the Civil Partnership Act 2004 Sch 7 para 9 by virtue of these provisions as they apply in relation to an order made under the Matrimonial Causes Act 1973 s 23 or the Civil Partnership Act 2004 Sch 5 Pt 1 (paras 1–5) (see PARA 458 et seq) by virtue of the Matrimonial Causes Act 1973 s 25B or s 25C or the Civil Partnership Act 2004 Sch 5 para 25 or 26: Matrimonial and Family Proceedings Act 1984 s 21(3) (as so added); Civil Partnership Act 2004 Sch 7 para 14(3).

10   See the Matrimonial Causes Act 1973 s 25E(2)–(10); the Civil Partnership Act 2004 Sch 5 paras 31–37; and PARA 485.

11   See the Matrimonial Causes Act 1973 ss 28(1), (2), 29; the Civil Partnership Act 2004 Sch 5 paras 47(1)–(4), (6), 49; and PARAS 460, 469, 495.

12   See the Matrimonial Causes Act 1973 s 30 (except s 30(b)); the Civil Partnership Act 2004 Sch 5 para 76; and PARAS 473, 504.

13   See the Matrimonial Causes Act 1973 s 31 (except s 31(2)(e), (4)); the Civil Partnership Act 2004 Sch 5 paras 50–54, 57–62 (except para 50(1)(g)); and PARAS 474, 515, 567–570.

14 See the Matrimonial Causes Act 1973 ss 32, 33, 38; the Civil Partnership Act 2004 Sch 5 paras 63–65; and PARAS 573–575, 679.

15 See the Matrimonial Causes Act 1973 s 39; the Civil Partnership Act 2004 Sch 5 para 77; and PARAS 505, 509.

16 See the Matrimonial Causes Act 1973 s 40; the Civil Partnership Act 2004 Sch 5 para 78; and PARA 455.

17 See note 3.

18 See the Matrimonial Causes Act 1973 ss 40A, 40B; the Civil Partnership Act 2004 Sch 5 paras 79, 79A; and PARA 528.

19 See the Matrimonial and Family Proceedings Act 1984 s 21(4), (5) (as added and prospectively amended: see note 3) and the Civil Partnership Act 2004 Sch 7 para 14(4), (5) (as so prospectively amended), which provide that the Lord Chancellor may by regulations make for the purposes of the Matrimonial and Family Proceedings Act 1984 Pt III (ss 12–27) and the Civil Partnership Act 2004 Sch 7 provision corresponding to any provision which may be made by him under the Matrimonial Causes Act 1973 s 25D(2)–(2B) or the Civil Partnership Act 2004 Sch 5 para 28(1)–(3) (see PARA 487) or (as from a day to be appointed) under the Matrimonial Causes Act 1973 s 25G(1)–(3) or the Civil Partnership Act 2004 Sch 5 paras 34B–36 (see PARAS 485, 526, 567). In exercise of the power so conferred the Secretary of State made the Divorce etc (Pensions) Regulations 2000, SI 2000/1123, and the Dissolution etc (Pensions) Regulations 2005, SI 2005/2920: see PARA 487 et seq.

(vi) Financial Relief following Death of Former Spouse or Civil Partner

538. Effect of death of parties. The right to apply for secured periodical payments after a decree absolute or dissolution order is not a cause of action which survives[1] against a deceased respondent's estate[2]. Further, the survival of both parties to a marriage (or, presumably, a civil partnership) is a prerequisite to the commencement of proceedings for the variation of a settlement[3]; but an order for secured periodical payments made for a wife, civil partner or child in proceedings for divorce, dissolution, nullity or judicial or legal separation, or for maintenance on proof of failure to provide reasonable maintenance, may be varied, after the death of the person liable to make payments, where application is made within six months from the date when representation is first taken out, either at the instance of that person's personal representatives or against them[4]. If the amount received by the person entitled to payments since the death exceeds that which is reasonable, in the changed circumstances resulting from the death, for him or her to have received, an order for the repayment of the excess may be made[5]. In the absence of an order directing security for periodical payments, the court has no jurisdiction to order a person's personal representatives to make payments for his children after his death[6].

1 Ie the provisions of the Law Reform (Miscellaneous Provisions) Act 1934 s 1(1) (see EXECUTORS AND ADMINISTRATORS vol 17(2) (Reissue) PARA 814) do not apply: see the cases cited in notes 2, 3.

2 *Dipple v Dipple* [1942] P 65, [1942] 1 All ER 234; *Sugden v Sugden* [1957] P 120, [1957] 1 All ER 300, CA (order for maintenance of children payable 'until further order'; wife claimed from husband's executrix arrears accrued after death of husband and sought declaration that executrix was liable to continue payment; it was held that, on a true construction of the order, the obligation ended on the death of the husband). Unless the death is strictly proved, the decree will be made absolute (or, presumably, in the case of a civil partnership the order will be made final): *Dering v Dering and Blakely* (1868) LR 1 P & D 531.

3 *D'Este v D'Este* [1973] Fam 55 at 61, sub nom *D(J) v D(S)* [1973] 1 All ER 349 at 354.

4 See the Matrimonial Causes Act 1973 s 31(6)–(9); the Civil Partnership Act 2004 Sch 5 paras 53, 54, 59–62; and PARAS 474, 550, 567–569.

5 See the Matrimonial Causes Act 1973 s 33; the Civil Partnership Act 2004 Sch 5 para 64; and PARA 573.

6 *Sugden v Sugden* [1957] P 120 at 135, [1957] 1 All ER 300 at 302, CA per Denning LJ and at 137, 304 per Hodson LJ; *Hinde v Hinde* [1953] 1 All ER 171, [1953] 1 WLR 175, CA.

539.   Making payments from deceased's estate.   If the court is satisfied that the disposition of a deceased's estate effected by his will, or by the law relating to intestacy, or the combination of the two, is not such as to make reasonable financial provision for that person's spouse or civil partner, or former spouse or civil partner, or for a child of the family, it may, on the application of or on behalf of the affected party, make one or more of a number of orders for the purpose of making good the insufficiency[1]. Such orders may require the making of periodical or lump sum payments out of the deceased's estate[2], the transfer or settlement of property comprised in the estate[3], or the variation of settlements entered into by the deceased in anticipation or during the subsistence of the marriage or civil partnership[4]. Financial relief may be granted pursuant to these provisions where a party to a marriage or civil partnership dies while proceedings for financial relief following divorce, dissolution, nullity or judicial or legal separation are pending[5], and may also be granted as part of an application for the variation of a secured periodical payments order or a maintenance agreement[6].

1   See the Inheritance (Provision for Family and Dependants) Act 1975 ss 1, 2; and EXECUTORS AND ADMINISTRATORS vol 17(2) (Reissue) PARAS 691–692.
2   See the Inheritance (Provision for Family and Dependants) Act 1975 s 2(1)(a), (b); and EXECUTORS AND ADMINISTRATORS vol 17(2) (Reissue) PARA 691.
3   See the Inheritance (Provision for Family and Dependants) Act 1975 s 2(1)(c)–(e); and EXECUTORS AND ADMINISTRATORS vol 17(2) (Reissue) PARA 691.
4   See the Inheritance (Provision for Family and Dependants) Act 1975 s 2(1)(f), (g); and EXECUTORS AND ADMINISTRATORS vol 17(2) (Reissue) PARA 691.
5   See the Inheritance (Provision for Family and Dependants) Act 1975 ss 14, 14A; and PARA 540. The right to apply for relief in these circumstances may, however, be restricted: see ss 15, 15ZA; and PARA 882.
6   See the Inheritance (Provision for Family and Dependants) Act 1975 ss 18, 18A; and PARA 541.

540.   Application for financial provision or property adjustment order where financial relief not previously granted.   Where:

(1)   a decree of divorce or nullity of marriage has been made absolute or a decree of judicial separation has been granted, or a dissolution order, nullity order, separation order or presumption of death order has been made in relation to a civil partnership[1];

(2)   one of the parties to the marriage or civil partnership[2] dies within 12 months from the date on which the order was made[3]; and

(3)   either an application for a financial provision order[4] or a property adjustment order[5] has not been made by the other party or such an application has been made but the proceedings on the application have not been determined at the time of the death of the deceased[6],

then if an application for an order making good an inadequacy in the financial provision made for the surviving party following the death of the deceased[7] is made by the surviving party, the court[8] has power[9], if it thinks it just to do so, to treat the surviving party as if the decree of divorce or nullity of marriage had not been made absolute, the decree of judicial separation had not been granted, or the dissolution, nullity, separation or presumption of death order had not been made, as the case may be[10].

1   Inheritance (Provision for Family and Dependants) Act 1975 ss 14(1), 14A(1)(a) (s 14A added by the Civil Partnership Act 2004 Sch 4 para 20). Note that these provisions do not apply in relation to a decree of judicial separation or a separation order unless at the date of the death of the deceased the decree or order was in force and the separation was continuing: Inheritance (Provision for Family and Dependants) Act 1975 ss 14(2), 14A(3) (as so added).

2   As to the parties to a marriage or civil partnership for these purposes see PARA 534 note 4.
3   Inheritance (Provision for Family and Dependants) Act 1975 ss 14(1), 14A(1)(b) (as added: see
    note 1).
4   Ie under the Matrimonial Causes Act 1973 s 23 or the Civil Partnership Act 2004 Sch 5 Pt 1
    (paras 1–5) (see PARA 458 et seq).
5   Ie under the Matrimonial Causes Act 1973 s 24 or the Civil Partnership Act 2004 Sch 5 Pt 2
    (paras 6–9) (see PARA 499 et seq).
6   Inheritance (Provision for Family and Dependants) Act 1975 ss 14(1), 14A(1)(c) (as added: see
    note 1).
7   Ie an order under the Inheritance (Provision for Family and Dependants) Act 1975 s 2: see PARA
    539; and EXECUTORS AND ADMINISTRATORS vol 17(2) (Reissue) PARAS 691–692. For the power
    of the court to order that the surviving party is not to be entitled to apply for an order under s 2
    see ss 15, 15ZA; and PARA 882. As to overseas divorces, dissolutions etc see ss 15A, 15B; and
    PARA 534.
8   As to the meaning of 'court' see PARA 534 note 2.
9   Ie notwithstanding anything in the Inheritance (Provision for Family and Dependants) Act 1975
    s 1 or s 3 (see EXECUTORS AND ADMINISTRATORS vol 17(2) (Reissue) PARAS 665 et seq, 671 et
    seq).
10 Inheritance (Provision for Family and Dependants) Act 1975 ss 14(1), 14A(2) (as added: see
    note 1).

541. Application for variation to be accompanied by order for financial provision. Where:

(1)   a person against whom a secured periodical payments order was made[1] has died and an application is made[2] for the variation or discharge of that order or for the revival of the operation of any suspended provision of the order[3]; or

(2)   a party to a maintenance agreement[4] has died and an application is made[5] for the alteration[6] of the agreement[7],

the court[8] has power[9] to direct that the application[10] be deemed to have been accompanied by an application for an order[11] making good an inadequacy in the financial provision made for the surviving party following the death of the deceased[12].

1   Ie under the Matrimonial Causes Act 1973 s 23 or the Civil Partnership Act 2004 Sch 5 (see
    PARA 467 et seq).
2   Ie under the Matrimonial Causes Act 1973 s 31(6) or the Civil Partnership Act 2004 Sch 5
    para 60 (see PARA 474).
3   Inheritance (Provision for Family and Dependants) Act 1975 ss 18(1)(a), 18A(1)(a) (s 18A
    added by the Civil Partnership Act 2004 Sch 4 para 25).
4   Ie a maintenance agreement (within the meaning of the Matrimonial Causes Act 1973 s 34 or
    the Civil Partnership Act 2004 Sch 5 Pt 13 (paras 66–73) (see PARA 697)) which provides for the
    continuation of payments under the agreement after the death of one of the parties: Inheritance
    (Provision for Family and Dependants) Act 1975 ss 18(1)(b), 18A(1)(b) (as added: see note 3).
5   Ie under the Matrimonial Causes Act 1973 s 36(1) or the Civil Partnership Act 2004 Sch 5
    para 73 (see PARA 701).
6   Ie under the Matrimonial Causes Act 1973 s 35 or the Civil Partnership Act 2004 Sch 5 para 69
    (see PARA 700 et seq).
7   Inheritance (Provision for Family and Dependants) Act 1975 ss 18(1)(b), 18A(1)(b) (as added:
    see note 3).
8   As to the meaning of 'court' see PARA 534 note 2.
9   Ie unless an order made under the Inheritance (Provision for Family and Dependants) Act 1975
    s 15(1) or s 15ZA(1) (see PARA 882) is in force with respect to a spouse or civil partner, in which
    case the court may not give the direction referred to in the text with respect to any application
    made under the Matrimonial Causes Act 1973 s 31(6) or s 36(1) or the Civil Partnership
    Act 2004 Sch 5 para 60 or Sch 5 para 73 (see PARAS 474, 701) by that spouse or civil partner on
    the death of the other spouse or civil partner: Inheritance (Provision for Family and Dependants)
    Act 1975 ss 18(3), 18A(3) (as added: see note 3).
10 Ie the application under the Matrimonial Causes Act 1973 s 31(6) or s 36(1) or under the Civil
    Partnership Act 2004 Sch 5 para 60 or Sch 5 para 73.

11 Ie an order under the Inheritance (Provision for Family and Dependants) Act 1975 s 2: see PARA
    539; and EXECUTORS AND ADMINISTRATORS vol 17(2) (Reissue) PARAS 691–692. For the power
    of the court to order that the surviving party is not to be entitled to apply for an order under s 2
    see ss 15, 15ZA; and PARA 882. As to overseas divorces, dissolutions etc see ss 15A, 15B; and
    PARA 534.
12 Inheritance (Provision for Family and Dependants) Act 1975 ss 18(1), 18A(1) (as added: see
    note 3). Where the court gives such a direction it also has power, in the proceedings on the
    application under the Matrimonial Causes Act 1973 s 31(6) or s 36(1) or the Civil Partnership
    Act 2004 Sch 5 para 60 or Sch 5 para 73, to make any order which the court would have had
    power to make under the provisions of the Inheritance (Provision for Family and Dependants)
    Act 1975 if the application under the Matrimonial Causes Act 1973 s 31(6) or s 36(1) or the
    Civil Partnership Act 2004 Sch 5 para 60 or Sch 5 para 73 had been made jointly with an
    application for an order under the Inheritance (Provision for Family and Dependants) Act 1975
    s 2: ss 18(2), 18A(2) (as so added). The court also has power to give such consequential
    directions as may be necessary for enabling the court to exercise any of the powers available to
    the court under the Inheritance (Provision for Family and Dependants) Act 1975 in the case of
    an application for an order under s 2: ss 18(2), 18A(2) (as so added).

INDEX

Matrimonial and Civil Partnership Law

ADULTERY
  meaning, 349
  before presentation of petition, 349n[6]
  burden and standard of proof, 352
  co-respondent—
    amendment of petition to add, 772
    counter-charges, adding to petition, 773
    death, enforcement of costs after, 1040
    defence, 785
    naming, 761
  confession, proof by, 353, 354
  dismissal of alleged adulterer from suit, 852
  divorced person, not committed by, 349n[5]
  evidence of—
    birth of child as, 355
    corroboration, 354
    decree nisi as, 357
    direct and circumstantial, 353
    generally, 829
    other proceedings, findings in, 358
    previous decree or order, 356
  irretrievable breakdown, as proof of, 350
  living together after, 351
  non-consummation, irrelevance of, 349
  particulars of charge, 790
  penetration, requirement of, 349n[3]
  proceedings, co-respondent as party to, 760

AGENCY
  estoppel, by, 269

AIR FORCE CHAPEL
  banns, licensing for, 129
  marriage in—
    clergymen, appointment of, 130
    legality and validity of, 23
    licensing, 129
    solemnisation, 55, 130

ANCILLARY RELIEF
  meaning, 902
  active case management, 903
  application for—
    answer, service of statement in, 919
    avoidance of disposition order, evidence on application for, 918, 931
    delay in, 917
    form, 916
    intention to proceed with, 924
    interim orders, for, 923
    judge, reference to, 936
    leave to apply, 917
    mitigating issues, failure to pursue, 922
    open proposals, 921
    petitioner or respondent, by, 916
    property adjustment order, evidence on application for, 918
    right to be heard, 920
  costs, 1037
  district judge, investigation by, 931
  expert evidence, rules for, 932
  hearing—
    arrangements for, 937
    district judge, investigation by, 931
  inspection appointment, 931
  interlocutory procedure—
    disclosure of documents, 925
    financial dispute resolution appointment—
      adjournment, 930
      procedure at, 930
      purpose of, 929
    financial statements, 925
    first appointment—
      conduct of, 928
      objective, 928
      procedure before, 925
    intention to proceed with application, 924
    pension attachments, 927

ANCILLARY RELIEF—*continued*
  interlocutory procedure—*continued*
    pension sharing, special provision
      for, 926
  orders, 933
  overriding objective, 903
  pension attachment order, contents of,
    934, 935
  pension sharing order, content of, 934
  pre-application protocol—
    aim of proceedings, 915
    correspondence, 913
    disclosure requirements, 910
    expert evidence, 914
    first letter, 908
    general principles, 907
    issues, identification of, 911
    negotiation and settlement,
      application not issued on
      prospect of, 909
    proportionality, principle of, 907
    purpose of, 905
    scope of, 906
    steps outlines in, 905
    voluntary disclosure, 912
  rules for, 902–904
ANNULMENT
  outside England and Wales, recognition
    of, 20
ARMED FORCES
  arms and equipment, execution
    against, 694
  pay—
    assignment, prohibition, 693
    deductions of maintenance payments
      from, 695
ASSURED AGRICULTURAL
    OCCUPANCY
  tenancy order, transfer of, 312
ASSURED TENANCY
  tenancy order, transfer of, 312
ATTACHMENT OF EARNINGS ORDER
  alternative remedies, interrelation with,
    631
  application for, 627
  bankruptcy order, effect of, 689
  cessation of, 635
  deduction, rate of—
    normal, 632
    protected earnings rate, 632
    reduction of, 633
  discharge, 634
  earnings: meaning, 630
  effect of, 629
  financial orders, enforcement of, 943
  lapse, 634

ATTACHMENT OF EARNINGS
    ORDER—*continued*
  magistrates' court, by, 656
  making of, 627
  particulars in, 629
  payment of sums under, 629
  persons applying for, 628
  power of courts, 628
  variation, 634
BANKRUPTCY
  annuity under separation agreement,
    proof for, 446
  enforcement of orders after—
    attachment of earnings order, 689
    bankrupt judgment creditor, by, 690
    discharge from, 687
    financial provision orders, 689
    individual voluntary arrangements,
      691
    proceedings, 687
    process issued before commencement
      of bankruptcy, 688
    restrictions on proceedings, 688
  equity of exoneration, effect on, 244
  financial relief during subsistence of
    marriage or civil partnership, effect
    on, 552
  home rights of bankrupt, 288
  lump sum order, effect on, 484
  means of enforcement, as, 692
  periodical payments order, effect on,
    466
  settlor under settlement of property
    order, of, 509
  spouse or civil partner, of, 207
  transferor under transfer of property
    order, of, 505
BANNS OF MARRIAGE
  certificate of—
    banns outside England and Wales,
      of, 73
    production of, 72
    signature, 72
  chapel, licensing, 62
  church being repaired or rebuilt,
    where, 61
  Church of England marriage after
    publication of, 58
  extra-parochial places, in church of, 63
  legality and validity of marriage under,
    21
  marriage of child, declaration of
    dissent, 52
  naval, military and air force chapels,
    licensing, 129
  notice of, 68

References are to paragraph numbers; superior figures refer to notes

BANNS OF MARRIAGE—*continued*
  pastoral reorganisation, effect of, 60
  place for marriage after, 59
  publication—
    audible manner, in, 69
    clergyman, by, 70
    completion in other church, 67
    extra-parochial places, person residing in, 65
    Her Majesty's ships, on, 74
    layman, by, 70
    mode of, 69
    outside England and Wales, 73
    parish of residence, in, 65
    place of, 59
    register book, from, 75
    three months, void after, 71
    true name for purpose of, 69
    usual place of worship, in, 66
    wrong name, use of, 69
BIGAMY
  offence of, 10
BILL OF EXCHANGE
  spouse or civil partner, liability of, 257
CAPACITY
  marriage or civil partnership, to enter into—
    disabilities, effect of, 33
    domicile, governed by law of, 31
    foreign domicile, disabilities imposed by, 33
    invalid, 31
    legal, generally, 31
    minimum age, 32
    new partnership, entry into, 34
CHARGING ORDER
  financial orders, enforcement of, 944
  making of, 636
  principles applied, 638
  property subject to charge, 637
  sale, enforcement by, 639
CHEQUE
  spouse or civil partner, liability of, 257
CHILD
  county court jurisdiction, 733
  decrees and orders affecting, restriction on, 884
  family proceedings, orders in, 885
  orders for benefit of. *See* FINANCIAL PROVISION ORDER
  property adjustment order for benefit of. *See* PROPERTY ADJUSTMENT ORDER
  separate representation, 743
  separation agreement, provisions in. *See* SEPARATION AGREEMENT

CHILD—*continued*
  voidable marriage, of, legitimacy, 325
CHILD SUPPORT
  financial relief, and, 497, 551
CHURCH OF ENGLAND MARRIAGE
  authorising, methods of, 58
  chapel, licensing, 62
  chapels, list of, 64
  church being repaired or rebuilt, where, 61
  common licence—
    affidavit leading to grant of, 77
    authority of, 58
    caveat against grant, 78
    grant of, 76
    responsibility for, 77
    solemnisation, places of, 59
    validity, period of, 79
  entitlement—
    church service, conditions for, 57
    extra-parochial places, in church of, 63
    parish: meaning, 59n[8]
    parish church, in, 59
    pastoral reorganisation, effect of, 60
  register books—
    keeping, 86
    provision of, 75
    superintendent general, copies for, 86
  registration—
    duty of, 85
    house-bound person, marriage of, 85n[3]
    requirement, 85
  solemnisation—
    church, conduct of ceremony in, 83
    common licence, on, 59
    duty of minister, 81
    offences, 180
    person conducting, 80
    places of, 59
    time of, 82
  special licence, grant of, 58, 76
  superintendent registrar's certificate, on authority of, 54
  void, grounds of, 328
CIVIL PARTNERS
  acts of other civil partner, criminal liability for, 208
  agreement, having entered into—
    gifts between, ownership of, 253
    property no longer in possession, disputes relating to, 228
  bankruptcy of, 207
  bills, notes and cheques, liability on, 257

References are to paragraph numbers; superior figures refer to notes

CIVIL PARTNERS—*continued*
cohabitation, duty of, 219
confidences, protection of, 223
contracts between, 206
contracts by, 205
contracts on behalf of the other, 256
corroboration of evidence of, 213
joint banking account, 245
liability to maintain each other, 217
life assurance policy. *See* LIFE
　ASSURANCE POLICY
maintenance—
　application for, 211
　liability for, 217
　reasonable, failure to provide, 218
proceedings between, 211
property, ownership of—
　disputes, resolution of—
　　application to court, 224
　　former civil partner, property of,
　　　229
　　powers of court, 225
　　property to which powers extend,
　　　227
　　sale, power to order, 226
　　termination of civil partnership
　　　agreement, on, 230
　equity of exoneration—
　　bankruptcy, effect of, 244
　　estates of both civil partners
　　　charged for one party's
　　　benefit, 242
　　indemnity, right of, 239
　　other civil partner party to
　　　mortgage, where, 240
　　presumptive right, 239
　　property charged for other's benefit,
　　　right of indemnity, 239
　　property charged partly to other's
　　　benefit, 241
　　property over which one party has
　　　general power, charge of, 243
　　waiver, 239
　gifts between parties—
　　fraudulent dispositions, 250
　　rules for, 248
　　undue influence as to, 249
　gifts on formation of partnership,
　　247
　incumbrances, discharge of, 252
　joint banking account, 245
　receipt as trustee, 251
separation agreement. *See* SEPARATION
　AGREEMENT
separation, gifts and legacies inducing,
　222

CIVIL PARTNERS—*continued*
statutory tenant by succession, as, 255
surviving civil partner, rights in
　deceased's estate, 254
witness, compellability as, 212

CIVIL PARTNERSHIP
meaning, 2
agreement for, unenforceable, 16
annulment—
　applicable law, 319
　bars to relief, 321
　civil partnership celebrated abroad,
　　324
　financial relief in proceedings, 453
　foreign law, civil partnership governed
　　by, 324
　institution of proceedings, 322
　nature and effect of, 320
　person suffering mental disorder,
　　proceedings by person suffering,
　　323
　settled property, effect on, 514
approval of buildings for—
　application for, 191
　conditions, 194
　expiry and renewal of, 195
　fees, 200
　grant or refusal of, 193
　guidance as to, 199
　name, change of, 202
　notices, 201
　public consultation, 192
　registers, 198
　regulations, 190
　review of decision, 197
　revocation, 196
　Secretary of State, powers of, 190
capacity to enter into—
　disabilities, effect of, 33
　domicile, governed by law of, 31
　foreign domicile, disabilities imposed
　　by, 33
　invalid, 31
　legal, generally, 31
　minimum age, 32
　new partnership, entry into, 34
causes. *See* MATRIMONIAL AND CIVIL
　PARTNERSHIP CAUSES
celebrated outside England and Wales,
　proof of, 27
conditions for, 2
consent to. *See* CONSENT TO MARRIAGE
　OR CIVIL PARTNERSHIP
detained persons, of, 170, 175
dissolution. *See* DISSOLUTION OF CIVIL
　PARTNERSHIP

CIVIL PARTNERSHIP—*continued*
  document, 56
  false statement, making, 185
  housebound persons, of, 169, 174
  minimum age for, 32
  notice—
    abroad—
      armed forces personnel, by, 154
      giving of, 146
      publication, 147
    publication of, 136
    requirement of, 133
    special procedure, 140
  nullity, decree of, 34
  offences, relief from liability, 5
  outside England and Wales, 18
  overseas, proof of, 835
  overseas relationships treated as, 19
  person subject to immigration control,
    involving, 26
  persons subject to immigration control,
    of—
    notice, giving of, 179
    requirements for, 178
  pre-registration agreement,
    unenforceability, 712
  prohibited degrees of relationship—
    absolute prohibition, 38
    adoptive relationships, 38
    child of the family: meaning, $39n^2$
    civil partnership within, effect of, 35
    conditional prohibition, 39
    English law, application of, 35
    law of domicile, application of, 35
  proof of, 26
  property. *See* CIVIL PARTNERSHIP
    PROPERTY
  qualified prohibition, within, 135
  registered abroad, proof of, 29
  registration—
    abroad—
      armed forces personnel, by. *See*
        armed forces personnel, by
        below
      consent to, 149
      no impediment, certificate of, 152
      objection to, 148
      proof of, 151
      proposed partnership, nature of,
        146
      provision for, 145
      publication of notice, 147
      time for, 150
    armed forces personnel, by—
      declaration, 154

CIVIL PARTNERSHIP—*continued*
  registration—*continued*
    armed forces personnel,
      by—*continued*
      evidence, registering officer
        requiring, 155
      formation of, 158
      no impediment, certificate of, 160
      notice of, 154
      objection to, 156
      provision for, 153
      publicising, 157
      time for, 159
    detained persons, by, 56
    formation by, 56
    house-bound persons, by, 56
    time for—
      abroad, 150
      armed forces personnel, by, 159
      special procedure, 144
      standard procedure, 139
  requisites of, 4
  schedule—
    meaning, 138
    forbidding issue of, 137
    issue of, 138
  separation order—
    financial relief. *See* FINANCIAL RELIEF
    irretrievable breakdown—
      behaviour as proof of, 359–361
      desertion. *See* DESERTION
      facts, inquiry into, 348
      reconciliation, duty to consider,
        414
      separation. *See* SEPARATION
      sole ground, as, 346, 347
    reconciliation, duty to consider, 414
  sham, 11
  special procedure—
    declaration, 140
    evidence, power of Registrar General
      to require, 141
    notice of, 140
    provision for, 132
    Registrar General's licence—
      forbidding issue of, 142
      issue of, 143
    registration, time for, 144
    seriously ill persons, of, 140
  standard procedure—
    declaration, 133
    notice—
      publication of, 136
      requirement of, 133
    proposed partnership, nature of, 133
    provision for, 132

References are to paragraph numbers; superior figures refer to notes

CIVIL PARTNERSHIP—*continued*
  standard procedure—*continued*
    qualified prohibition, partnership
      within, 135
    registration authority—
      meaning, 133n[2]
      evidence, power to require, 134
    registration, time for, 139
    schedule—
      meaning, 138
      forbidding issue of, 137
      issue of, 138
  status, declaration of—
    Attorney General, intervention by,
      1002
    domicile and residence of parties,
      1000
    jurisdiction, 1000
    making of, 1004
    petition—
      answer to, 1003
      contents of, 1001
      procedure on, 1003
  validation, 5
  void—
    grounds of, 327
    ipso jure, 320
  voidable—
    gender reassignment certificate,
      ignorance of, 334
    mental disorder, party suffering
      from, 332
    pregnancy by some other person, 333
    valid and subsisting until decree,
      being, 320
    valid consent, failure to give, 331
  wills and intestacy, effect on, 209
CIVIL PARTNERSHIP PROPERTY
  disputes—
    applications during lives of parties,
      reference to judge, 957
    applications, procedure on, 955
    hearing, 956
    order, making, 956
    title or possession, relating to, 955
  occupation order. *See* OCCUPATION
    ORDER
CIVIL PARTNERSHIP SETTLEMENT
  meaning, 710
  form of, 710
  subsistence of partnership, during, 711
  voluntary, 711
COHABITATION
  after ceremony, presumption of marriage
    from, 7
  ceremony, without, 6

COLONIAL REGISTER
  proof of facts in, 30
CONSENT TO MARRIAGE OR CIVIL
  PARTNERSHIP
  parental—
    absence, effect of, 51
    court, granted by—
      application for, 48
      effect of, 47
    dispensing with need for, 47
    evidence of, 49
    false declaration of, 49
    marriage of child, declaration of
      dissent, 52
    person under 18, for, 46
    refusal of, 47
    unobtainable, 47
    ward of court, for, 46, 47
    withdrawal of, 50
  parties, of—
    absence, reasons for, 42
    duress, effect of, 43
    failure, effect of, 331
    fraudulent misrepresentation, effect
      of, 43
    intoxication, effect of, 43
    minimum age of, 41
    mistake, effect of, 44
    prima facie presumption, 42
    unsoundness of mind, want founded
      on, 45
    valid, giving, 42
CONTRACT
  authority of spouse to make—
    authorisation of, 256
    bills, notes and cheques, liability on,
      257
    undisclosed principal, spouse as, 258
  civil partner, by, on behalf of the other,
    256
  exercise of power of appointment, as
    to, 237
  judicial separation, effect of, 268
  made exclusively by wife, no liability of
    husband on, 259
  necessaries, for—
    adequate or agreed allowance for,
      266
    cohabitation, presumption of
      authority from, 263
    judicial separation, effect of, 268
    presumption of authority, rebuttal,
      265
    proof of authority, 267
    style of living, suitable to, 264
  ratification by spouse, 273

References are to paragraph numbers; superior figures refer to notes

CONTRACT—*continued*
　separate business, no liability of spouse
　　for, 260
　spouse or civil partner, between, 206
　spouse or civil partner, by, 205
COUNTY COURT
　allocation of family proceedings, 749
　appeals to, 737
　children, protection of, 733
　divorce and civil partnership
　　proceedings, 732
　divorce, 811
　fees, 1036
　financial relief jurisdiction, 733
　High Court, transfer of business from,
　　745
　High Court, transfer of business to, 746
　maintenance, application for. *See*
　　MAINTENANCE
　matrimonial and civil partnership
　　causes, jurisdiction. *See*
　　MATRIMONIAL AND CIVIL
　　PARTNERSHIP CAUSES
　non-molestation order. *See*
　　NON-MOLESTATION ORDER
　occupation order. *See* OCCUPATION
　　ORDER
COURT OF APPEAL
　application for new trial, hearing, 738
DEATH, PRESUMPTION OF
　absence of seven years or more, from,
　　416
　application for, 415
　decrees. *See* DECREE ABSOLUTE; DECREE
　　NISI
　financial relief, application for, 419
　grounds of, 415
　petition for decree, additional
　　requirements, 762
　respondent found alive, effect of, 417
DECREE ABSOLUTE
　application for—
　　judge, to, 867
　　spouse against whom made, by, 868
　　stay of, 872
　central index of, 878
　certificate, 878
　death of party after, jurisdiction of
　　court, 881
　final effect of, 879
　financial hardship and protection,
　　application for consideration, 873
　indorsement, 878
　no impeachment of, 880
　notice, lodging, 866
　nullity, decree of, 34

DECREE ABSOLUTE—*continued*
　right to apply for, 865
　unimpeachable, being, 864
DECREE NISI
　absolute, made, 864
　appeals, 883
　child of the family, consideration of
　　interests of, 884
　grant of, 863
　material facts not before court, where,
　　877
　nullity, decree of, 34
　Queen's Proctor, intervention by, 875
　religious usages, declaration of
　　compliance with, 874
　rescission of—
　　consent, by, 869
　　effect of, 871
　　party misled into giving consent,
　　　where, 870
　stay of application to make final, 872
　third party, intervention by, 876
DESERTION
　meaning, 362
　bare denial, insufficiency in answer, 782
　burden and standard of proof, 369
　compulsory, 368
　consensual separation, and—
　　maintenance, agreement to pay, 373
　　resumption of cohabitation, absence
　　　of, 372
　　time and method of consent, 371
　consent to, 362
　constructive—
　　burden and standard of proof, 393
　　doctrine of, 391
　　factum and animus of, 392
　　intention, and, 387
　　past history, 395
　　presumptions, 394
　　third parties, conduct with, 395
　corroboration, 370
　duration, 364
　elements of, 368
　factum and animus of, 368
　intention, 368
　intention, absence of—
　　constructive desertion, 387
　　deserting party, position of, 386
　　insanity, effect of, 389
　　petitioner, mental or other illness of,
　　　390
　　proof, 388
　irretrievable breakdown, proof of, 363
　Jewish divorce, effect of, 376

DESERTION—*continued*
  just cause, request for particulars of,
    788
  just cause, separation with—
    conduct amounting to, 381
    effect of, 380
    enforced separation, 382
    home, choice of, 384
    illness, causes by, 385
    offer to return, duty of, 383
  mutual, 367
  periods of living together, no account
    of, 365
  physical, 368
  prior decree of judicial or legal
    separation, presumed time
    following, 366
  separation deed—
    invalid or illegal, effect of, 375
    repudiation or affirmation of, 374
  separation, without—
    matters not amounting to separation,
      378
    same roof, parties living under, 377
    sexual intercourse, refusal of, 379
  state of things, withdrawal from, 362
  termination—
    cohabitation, resumption of—
      intention of parties, 403
      living separately, while, 405
      nature of, 403
    declaration against having other
      back, 399
    judicial separation, effect of decree
      of, 406
    means of, 396
    offer to return—
      conditions, subject to, 402
      genuine, to be, 397, 400
      good faith, in, 397
      refusal, effect of, 398
      stratagem, as, 401
    separation order, effect of, 406
    sexual intercourse, effect of, 404
  time of answer, up to, 781

DETAINED PERSONS
  meaning, 170
  civil partnership of, 175
  marriage of—
    notice of, 172
    place of residence, solemnisation at,
      171, 173

DISCOVERY
  defended cases, in—
    documents, of, 799
    interrogatories, by, 800

DISCOVERY—*continued*
  defended cases, in—*continued*
    exemptions from, 801

DISSOLUTION OF CIVIL
  PARTNERSHIP
  conditional order—
    appeals, 883
    child of the family, consideration of
      interests of, 884
    grant of, 863
    material facts not before court,
      where, 877
    Queen's Proctor, intervention by, 875
    rescission of—
      consent, by, 869
      effect of, 871
      party misled into giving consent,
        where, 870
    stay of application to make final, 872
    third party, intervention by, 876
  costs, 1038
  final order—
    application for—
      civil partner against whom made,
        by, 868
      judge, to, 867
    central index of, 878
    certificate, 878
    death of party after, jurisdiction of
      court, 881
    final effect of, 879
    financial hardship and protection,
      application for consideration,
      873
    grant of, 864
    indorsement, 878
    no impeachment of, 880
    notice, lodging, 866
    right to apply for, 865
    stay of, 872
  financial relief. *See* FINANCIAL RELIEF
  irretrievable breakdown—
    behaviour as proof of—
      applicant reasonably expected to
        live with respondent, 360
      final incident, living together after,
        361
      generally, 359
    desertion. *See* DESERTION
    facts, inquiry into, 348
    proof of, 347
    reconciliation, duty to consider, 414
    separation. *See* SEPARATION
    sole ground, as, 346
  petition. *See* PETITION

DISSOLUTION OF CIVIL
    PARTNERSHIP—*continued*
previous proceedings, not precluded
    by, 758
reconciliation, duty to consider, 414
DIVORCE
adultery. *See* ADULTERY
costs, 1038
decrees. *See* DECREE ABSOLUTE; DECREE
    NISI
financial relief. *See* FINANCIAL RELIEF
irretrievable breakdown—
    adultery. *See* ADULTERY
    behaviour as proof of—
        final incident, living together after,
            361
        generally, 359
        petitioner reasonably expected to
            live with respondent, 360
    desertion. *See* DESERTION
    facts, inquiry into, 348
    proof of, 347
    reconciliation, duty to consider, 414
    separation. *See* SEPARATION
    sole ground, as, 346
Jewish, effect on desertion, 376
outside England and Wales, recognition
    of, 20
petition. *See* PETITION
previous proceedings, not precluded
    by, 758
reconciliation, duty to consider, 414
DOCUMENTS
discovery. *See* DISCOVERY
notice to produce or admit, 802
DOMICILE
married woman, of, 214
parties to marriage, of, 8
DURESS
consent to marriage, effect on, 43
separation agreement, effect on, 430
ENGAGED COUPLES
gifts between, ownership of, 253
property ownership, resolution of
    disputes—
    no longer in possession, relating to,
        228
    termination of engagement, on, 230
ESTOPPEL
agency by, 269
principle, application of, 734
separation agreement, acting on, 433
EVIDENCE
affidavit, by, 837
identity, of, 836

EVIDENCE—*continued*
matrimonial and civil partnership
    proceedings, in—
    adultery alleged, where, 829
    affidavit, by, 837
    competence and compellability of
        parties, 828
    conflicting testimony, 832
    convictions as, 830
    cross-examination, 831
    expert, 827
    generally, 825
    identity, of, 836
    marriage or overseas relationship
        celebrated outside England and
        Wales, of, 835
    other proceedings, evidential effect
        of, 830
    privilege, claiming, 833
    refusal to admit, 825
    sexual capacity, of, 834
    subpoena, issue of, 826
    witness summons, issue of, 826
witness. *See* WITNESS
EXECUTION AGAINST GOODS
enforceable orders, 651
goods exempt from seizure, 652
writ or warrant of delivery, obtaining,
    653
FAMILY BUSINESS
children—
    protection of, 733
    separate representation, 743
distribution and transfer, directions for,
    744
judicial review, 741
jurisdiction—
    appeals, 737
    county court—
        allocation of proceedings, 749
        appeals, 737
        children, protection of, 733
        divorce and civil partnership
            proceedings, 732
        financial relief, 733
        estoppel, principle of, 734
        foreign co-respondents, over, 742
        High Court Family Division, of, 731
        magistrates' court, scope of, 735
        res judicata, 734
new trial, application for, 738
rehearing—
    application for, 739
    magistrates, by, 740
transfer—
    directions for, 744

FAMILY BUSINESS—*continued*
 transfer—*continued*
 from county court to High Court,
 746
 from High Court to county court,
 745
 order for, 747
 procedure, 748

FAMILY HOME
 home rights—
 bankrupts, of, 288
 continuation during subsistence of
 marriage or civil partnership,
 285
 dwelling house—
 meaning, 285n[2]
 charge on, 286
 entitlement to occupy, 285
 mortgagees, claims by, 287
 no estate, one spouse or civil partner
 having, 285
 Martin order, 316
 Mesher order, 316
 occupation order. *See* OCCUPATION
 ORDER
 property rights in—
 agreement or arrangement to share
 beneficial interest, no
 evidence of, 281
 beneficial interest, quantification of,
 282
 charge, registration of, 418
 cohabitants, of, 284
 common intention to share
 beneficially, establishment of,
 281
 discretionary powers of court, 231
 disputes, resolution of, 278
 home rights. *See* home rights *above*
 joint names, property purchased in,
 279
 occupation, 231
 occupation order. *See* OCCUPATION
 ORDER
 one name, property purchased in,
 280
 property improvements, contribution
 to, 283
 registration, 676
 separation, in event of, 231
 statutory, 418
 tenancy order, transfer of. *See*
 TRANSFER OF TENANCY ORDER
 rights, registration, 676
 transfer of tenancy. *See* TRANSFER OF
 TENANCY ORDER

FAMILY PROCEEDINGS
 children, orders relating to, 885
 costs—
 death of co-respondent, enforcement
 after, 1040
 divorce and dissolution proceedings,
 in, 1038
 financial relief proceedings, in, 1039
 generally, 1037
 magistrates' court proceedings, in,
 1041
 public funding, 1042
 fees, 1036

FINANCIAL PROVISION ORDER
 meaning, 450
 ancillary relief. *See* ANCILLARY RELIEF
 assessment, principles of. *See* FINANCIAL
 RELIEF (assessment, principles of)
 attempt to defeat claims, prevention
 of—
 avoidance of transactions, 587
 prevention of transactions, 588
 protected claims, 586
 children, for benefit of—
 age of child, 492
 child support, effect on, 497
 duration, 495
 matters to which court has regard,
 494
 parent or guardian, application by,
 493
 person paying, death of, 496
 power to make, 492
 types of, 492
 death of former spouse or civil partner,
 following—
 effect of death, 538
 no previous grant, where, 540
 payments from estate, 539
 variation, application for, 541
 dissolution of marriage or civil
 partnership proceedings, in, 454
 enforcement. *See* FINANCIAL RELIEF
 (enforcement)
 former legislation, orders under, 457
 lump sum order—
 meaning, 476
 adjournment of proceedings, 478
 alienation of, 484
 application, time for, 480
 bankruptcy, effect of, 484
 date when taking effect, 481
 Duxbury calculations, 483
 instalments, payment by, 476
 interest, circumstances for, 479
 interim, no power for, 476

FINANCIAL PROVISION
    ORDER—*continued*
  lump sum order—*continued*
    liabilities and expenses, provision
      for, 477
    matters to which court has regard,
      482
    power to make, 476
  sale of property, order for—
    date when taking effect, 521
    matters to which court has regard,
      522
    power to make, 520
    variation, discharge and suspension.
      See variation, discharge and
      suspension *below*
  maintenance pending suit or outcome of
    proceedings, 456
  party applying for, 450
  pension attachment—
    ancillary relief order, 934
    ancillary relief, application for, 927
    benefits—
      meaning, 485n[1]
      reduction in, 489
      valuation, 488
    change of circumstances, notice of,
      490
    lump sums, for, 486
    new arrangement, acquisition of
      rights under, 487
    person responsible for, documents
      supplied to, 935
    power to make, 485
    transfer of rights, 491
  periodical payments order—
    meaning, 458
    alienation of, 466
    bankruptcy, effect of, 466
    continuing, duration of, 460
    date when taking effect, 459
    delay, effect of, 463
    interim, 462
    maintenance pending suit or outcome
      of proceedings, at same rate as,
      461
    matters to which court has regard,
      463
    other courts, effect of orders of, 465
    payer, unfair pressure on, 464
    power to make, 458
    variation, discharge and suspension.
      See variation, discharge and
      suspension *below*
  person suffering from mental disorder,
    against or in favour of, 455

FINANCIAL PROVISION
    ORDER—*continued*
  presumption of death proceedings, in,
    454
  property adjustment order, relationship
    with, 451
  secured periodical payments order—
    meaning, 467
    alienation of, 475
    continuing, duration of, 469
    date when taking effect, 468
    death of former spouse or civil
      partner, application after, 538
    death of spouse or civil partner, effect
      of, 474
    deed to secure payments, 473
    interim, 470
    matters to which court has regard,
      471
    power to make, 467
    property subject to, 472
    sale of property, order for—
      date when taking effect, 521
      matters to which court has regard,
        522
      power to make, 520
    variation, discharge and suspension.
      See variation, discharge and
      suspension *below*
  subsequent marriage or civil
    partnership, effect of, 452
  subsistence of marriage or civil
    partnership, during. *See*
    MAINTENANCE
  variation, discharge and suspension—
    High Court orders—
      cessation of order owing to
        subsequent marriage or civil
        partnership—
        collection of sums due, 575
        repayment, order for, 574
      matters to which court has regard,
        568
      orders subject to, 567
      periodical payments orders—
        powers of court, 569
        revival in respect of child, 571
        variation in respect of child, 570
      repayment, order for—
        changed circumstances, in, 573
        subsequent marriage or civil
          partnership, after, 574
      secured periodical payments
        orders—
        powers of court, 569
        variation in respect of child, 570

FINANCIAL PROVISION
ORDER—*continued*
variation, discharge and
suspension—*continued*
High Court orders—*continued*
secured periodical payments
orders—*continued*
variation or discharge following
death of former spouse, 572
magistrates' court orders—
cessation of order owing to
subsequent marriage or civil
partnership—
collection of sums due, 585
repayment, order for, 584
instalments, payment of lump sum
by, 582
lump sum, power to order on
variation, 577
matters to which court has regard,
579
means of payment, power to
impose, 580
periodical payments order, revival
of, 583
person outside England and Wales,
proceedings by or against, 581
powers, 576
repayment, order for after
subsequent marriage or civil
partnership, 584
taking effect, power to specify time
of, 578

FINANCIAL RELIEF
ancillary relief. *See* ANCILLARY RELIEF
application for, 419
arrears, application for leave to
enforce, 949
assessment, principles of—
adult children, provision for, 605
age of parties, relevance of, 615
agreement, reaching, 596
all circumstances of case, duty to
consider, 589
businesses, interests in, 609
children, welfare of—
party against whom order sought,
not child of, 598
party against whom order sought,
of, 597
conduct of parties, consideration of,
621
consent orders, 596
contributions—
financial, 619
inherited money and property, 620

FINANCIAL RELIEF—*continued*
assessment, principles of—*continued*
contributions—*continued*
parties', consideration of, 618
court's powers, overall purpose of,
591
delay, effect of, 595
disability of party, consideration of,
617
duration of marriage or civil
partnership, 616
Duxbury calculations, 604
earning capacity, 600
equity of division, no presumption
of, 607
income taken into account, 599
loss of benefits, consideration of
value, 622
needs, obligations and
responsibilities—
consideration of, 610
debts, 613
lists of expenditure, 613
long-term housing, 612
matters to which court has regard,
611
particular matters taken into
account, 590
property and financial resources, 601
reasonable requirements of parties,
603
reconciliation, possibility of, 594
remarriage and cohabitation,
disclosure of, 593
standard of living, consideration of,
614
state benefits, 602
substantial assets, in case of, 608
unforeseen contingencies, payments
for, 606
consent order—
application for—
information to be supplied, 714
powers of court, 713
procedure on, 715
drawing up, duty on, 715
making of, 713
costs in proceedings, estimates and
statement of, 1039
county court jurisdiction, 733
death of former spouse or civil partner,
following—
effect of death, 538
no previous grant, where, 540
payments from estate, 539

FINANCIAL RELIEF—*continued*
  deceased former spouse or civil partner,
    application from estate of, 882
  dissolution of marriage or civil
    partnership proceedings, in, 454
  divorce, dissolution, nullity, separation
    and presumption of death, on—
    ancillary relief. *See* ANCILLARY RELIEF
    procedural code, 902–904
    proceedings, 902
    substantive and financial matters,
      desirability of considering
      together, 904
  enforcement—
    agreements in financial orders, of,
      625
    armed forces personnel—
      arms and equipment, execution
        against, 694
      assignment of pay, prohibition, 693
      pay, deductions of maintenance
        payments from, 695
    arrears—
      application for leave to enforce,
        949
      more than 12 months old, 679
    attachment of earnings. *See*
      ATTACHMENT OF EARNINGS
      ORDER
    bankruptcy of party, after—
      bankrupt judgment creditor, by,
        690
      discharge from, 687
      enforcement proceedings, 687
      financial provision orders, 689
      individual voluntary arrangements,
        691
      means of enforcement, as, 692
      process issued before
        commencement of
        bankruptcy, 688
      restrictions on proceedings, 688
    charging order. *See* CHARGING ORDER
    civil judgments, of, 623
    county court orders in High Court
      following transfer, 952
    death of party, after—
      arrears, 686
      consent orders, 686
      contract, rights under, 686
      costs orders, 686
      enforceability, 685
      lapse of claims, applications and
        orders on, 684
      lump sum orders, 686

FINANCIAL RELIEF—*continued*
  enforcement—*continued*
    death of party, after—*continued*
      periodical payments, arrears of,
        686
    execution against goods—
      enforceable orders, 651
      goods exempt from seizure, 652
      writ or warrant of delivery,
        obtaining, 653
    execution of documents, order for,
      641
    High Court orders in county court,
      951
    High Court procedure, 623, 954
    injunctions—
      Anton Piller order, 662
      assets, to preserve, 660
      consideration whether to grant,
        659
      Mareva, 661
      search order, 662
      types of, 659
    interest on judgments and orders,
      of—
      effect of proceedings, 681
      High Court and county court,
        between, 682
      limitation, 683
      means of, 680
    interest payments, in county court,
      950
    interests in land, registration of, 676
    judgment summons—
      meaning, 642
      application for, 945
      committal on, 643
      examination of means, order for,
        642
      generally, 945
      law as to, 643
      means and ability to pay, inquiry
        into, 643
    limitation of actions, 678
    magistrates' court order, registration
      in High Court, 948
    magistrates' courts, in—
      attachment of earnings, 656
      committal, by, 656
      distress, warrant of, 656
      enforceable orders, 655
      maintenance orders, 655
      means of, 655
      methods of, 656
      parties living together, effect of,
        658

FINANCIAL RELIEF—*continued*
 enforcement—*continued*
  magistrates' courts, in—*continued*
   payment of money, order for, 657
  maintenance agreements, of, 626
  maintenance orders, registration of.
   See MAINTENANCE
  means of payment orders—
   meaning, 646
   methods of payment, 646
   periodical maintenance payments,
    as to, 644
   powers of court, 645
  possession of land—
   orders for, 654
   writ or warrant of, 947
  receiver by way of equitable
   execution—
   appointment of, 647
   estate or interest in land, in relation
    to, 648
   function of, 647
   scope of receivership, 648
  reciprocal, 677
  sequestration, by—
   meaning, 649
   generally, 946
   property capable being seized, 650
  third party debt order, power to
   make, 640
  transfer of proceedings, following,
   953
  undertakings, of, 624
  writ ne exeat regno, 663
 financial provision orders. *See*
  FINANCIAL PROVISION ORDER
 interest payments, enforcement in
  county court, 950
 nullity proceedings, in, 453
 overseas divorce, dissolution, separation
  or annulment, on—
  application for, 530, 938
  appropriate venue for application,
   duty of court to consider, 940
  avoidance of transaction order,
   application for, 941
  consent order, 535
  deceased former spouse or civil
   partner, restrictions on
   applications from estate of, 534
  domicile and residence of parties, 939
  family home in England and Wales,
   restriction of powers where
   jurisdiction depends on, 533
  hearing, 942
  interim order, 536

FINANCIAL RELIEF—*continued*
 overseas divorce, dissolution, separation
  or annulment, on—*continued*
  leave of court for, 938
  matters to which court has regard,
   532
  mode of application, 941
  order for, 531, 942
  originating summons, 941
  property, transfer or settlement of,
   938n[7]
  supplementary provisions, 537
 pension compensation sharing. *See*
  PENSION COMPENSATION SHARING
  ORDER
 pension sharing. *See* PENSION SHARING
  ORDER
 presumption of death proceedings, in,
  454
 property adjustment order. *See*
  PROPERTY ADJUSTMENT ORDER
 subsistence of marriage or civil
  partnership, during—
  High Court, powers of—
   alienation, 552
   available orders, 543
   bankruptcy, effect of, 552
   child support, effect on, 551
   continuing periodical payments
    order, duration of, 546
   death of person paying, effect of,
    550
   failure to provide reasonable
    maintenance, on, 542
   interim orders, 545
   matters to which court has regard,
    544
   payer, unfair pressure on, 549
   secured periodical payments
    order—
    continuing, duration of, 546
    deed to secure payments, 548
    property subject to, 547
  magistrates' courts, powers of—
   agreed orders, 554
   application to, 553
   available orders, 553
   case more suitable for High Court,
    refusal of, 565
   children, orders for benefit of—
    age limit, 558
    duration of, 561
    person paying, death of, 562
    types of, 557
   divorce or dissolution, effect of,
    566

FINANCIAL RELIEF—*continued*
  subsistence of marriage or civil
      partnership, during—*continued*
    magistrates' courts, powers
        of—*continued*
      interim orders—
        duration, 564
        power to make, 563
      matters to which court has regard,
          559
      parties living apart by agreement,
          periodical payments orders,
          556
      periodical payments orders—
        duration of, 560
        parties living part by agreement,
            556
      sufficiency of agreed payments, 555
FORCED MARRIAGE
  meaning, 723
  validity, 12
FORCED MARRIAGE PROTECTION
    ORDER
  appeal against, 987
  application for—
    form of, 980
    generally, 724
    hearing, 984
    notice, service of, 980
  arrested person, application for bail,
      995
  commencement of proceedings, 973
  content of, 728
  duration, 728
  final order for, 980
  inspection or disclosure of document,
      claim to withhold, 982
  making without prior application, 725
  matters to which court has regard, 726
  medical examination and report,
      remand of person for, 994
  non-party, order for disclosure against,
      983
  parties to proceedings, 981
  power of arrest, attachment of—
    arrest under, 990
    arrest without, 991
    generally, 989
  power to make, 723
  powers of court—
    arrest, following, 992
    contempt proceedings, 961
    jurisdiction, 958
  remand of person failing to comply
      with, 993
  transfer of proceedings, 973

FORCED MARRIAGE PROTECTION
    ORDER—*continued*
  undertakings instead of, 729
  variation or discharge, power of, 730
  variation, extension or discharge,
      application for, 985
  without-notice, 727
FOREIGN MARRIAGE
  marriage officer, conduct by—
    meaning, 119n[3]
    validity of, 119
  United Kingdom national, involving—
    consent to, 121
    intended, notice of, 120
    no impediment, certificate of, 128
    non-compliance with statutory
        requirements, effect of, 127
    oath before, 124
    objections to, 123
    official certificate, 126
    proof of, 126
    registration, 126
    solemnisation—
      conditions for, 125
      refusal of, 122
    validity of, 119
  proof of facts in, 30
  validity of, 119
FRAUD
  separation agreement, effect on, 429
FRAUDULENT MISREPRESENTATION
  consent to marriage, effect on, 43
HER MAJESTY'S FORCES
  chaplain, marriage by, 17
HER MAJESTY'S SHIP
  banns of marriage, publication of, 74
  marriage certificate, issue on board, 131
HIGH COURT
  applications, mode of making, 1006
  court bundles, 1016
  decrees and orders, drawing up, 1011
  disclosure of addresses, restrictions on,
      1009
  documents, filing, 1012
  documents retained in court, inspection
      of, 1013
  Family Division—
    business assigned to, 731
    county court, transfer of business
        from, 746
    county court, transfer of business to,
        745
    distribution and transfer of business,
        directions for, 744
    matrimonial and civil partnership
        causes jurisdiction, 750

HIGH COURT—*continued*
family proceedings, rules of court, 1005
fees, 1036
human rights applications—
appeals, 1027
declaration of incompatibility sought,
notification of Crown, 1025
information required, 1024
Minister or other parties, joining,
1026
maintenance, application for. *See*
MAINTENANCE
newspaper reports, restrictions on, 1015
notice, mode of giving, 1008
official shorthand notes, 1014
polygamous marriages, proceedings
relating to, 1010
service—
documents, of—
bailiff, by, in proceedings in
Principal Registry, 1020
child, on, 1019
officer of court, by, proof of, 1021
out of England and Wales, 1022
parties acting in person, on, 1018
protected party, on, 1019
solicitors, on, 1017
orders, of, 1023
time, computation of, 1007
HOUSEBOUND PERSONS
meaning, 169
civil partnership of, 174
marriage of—
notice of, 172
place of residence, solemnisation at,
171, 173
HUMAN RIGHTS
appeals, 1027
applications—
declaration of incompatibility sought,
notification of Crown, 1025
information required, 1024
Minister or other parties, joining,
1026
IMMIGRATION CONTROL
persons subject to—
meaning, 176n2
civil partnership of—
notice, giving of, 179
requirements for, 178
marriage of—
notice, giving of, 177
requirements for, 176
INJUNCTION
financial relief orders, enforcement of—
Anton Piller order, 662

INJUNCTION—*continued*
financial relief orders, enforcement
of—*continued*
assets, to preserve, 660
consideration whether to grant, 659
Mareva, 661
search order, 662
types of, 659
non-molestation order. *See*
NON-MOLESTATION ORDER
INTESTACY
marriage and civil partnership, effect
of, 209
INTOXICATION
consent to marriage, effect on, 43
INTRODUCTORY TENANCY
tenancy order, transfer of, 312
JEWISH MARRIAGE
foreign jurisdiction, in, 24
legality and validity, proof of, 24
notification, 117
parties to, domicile, 8
prohibited degrees of relationship, 35n6
returns of, 24n1
solemnisation, 118
JUDGMENT SUMMONS
meaning, 642
committal on, 643
examination of means, order for, 642
financial orders, enforcement of, 945
law as to, 643
means and ability to pay, inquiry into,
643
JUDGMENTS
civil, enforcement of, 623
JUDICIAL REVIEW
application for, 741
JUDICIAL SEPARATION
adultery. *See* ADULTERY
credit, loss of authority to pledge, 268
financial relief. *See* FINANCIAL RELIEF
irretrievable breakdown—
adultery. *See* ADULTERY
behaviour as proof of—
final incident, living together after,
361
generally, 359
petitioner reasonably expected to
live with respondent, 360
desertion. *See* DESERTION
proof of, 347, 348
reconciliation, duty to consider, 414
separation. *See* SEPARATION
sole ground, as, 346
outside England and Wales, recognition
of, 20

JUDICIAL SEPARATION—*continued*
reconciliation, duty to consider, 414
LEGITIMACY
variation of marriage settlement, not
decided on, 512
LIFE ASSURANCE POLICY
lien for payment of premiums, 277
spouse or civil partner, effected by for
one another's benefit, 274
spouse, civil partner or children, for,
275
trustees, appointment of, 276
MAGISTRATES' COURT
costs, 1041
documentary evidence in, 1028
documents—
amendment, 1032
confidentiality, 1033
service—
effecting, 1029
proper, rehearing absent, 1030
family proceedings, rules of court, 1005
jurisdiction, scope of, 735
justices' clerk, delegation by, 1035
maintenance, application for. *See*
MAINTENANCE
non-molestation order. *See*
NON-MOLESTATION ORDER
occupation order. *See* OCCUPATION
ORDER
oral evidence, note of, 1034
proceedings, timing, 1031
rehearing by, 740
res judicata in, 736
MAINTENANCE
agreements. *See* MAINTENANCE
AGREEMENTS
application by spouse or civil partner
for, 211
application for, 211
enforcement. *See* FINANCIAL RELIEF
(enforcement)
financial provision, 420
husband's common law duty as to, 216
magistrates' court orders, 655
outcome of proceedings, pending, 456
pending suit, 456
provision during subsistence of marriage
or civil partnership—
High Court and county courts,
application to—
affidavit accompanying originating
application, 887
hearing, 891
inspection appointment, fixing, 889
judge, reference to, 892

MAINTENANCE—*continued*
provision during subsistence of marriage
or civil partnership—*continued*
High Court and county courts,
application to—*continued*
mode of service, 888
order, making, 891
originating application, 886
respondent's affidavit in answer and
reply, 890
variation, discharge or suspension
of order, application for, 893
magistrates' court, application to—
appeals, 900
conduct of proceedings, directions
for, 895
constitution of court after
adjournment, 898
decision of court, 899
directions appointments and
hearings, procedure at, 896
making, 894
orders on appeal, 901
principles, 897
reasonable, failure to provide, 218, 420,
542
registration of orders—
cancellation, 675
enforcement by, 664
High Court, magistrates' court orders
in—
application for, 671
effect of, 672
interest on sums recoverable, 673
orders subject to, 671
variation, 674
magistrates' court, High Court and
county court orders in—
application for, 667
effect of, 668
orders subject to, 666
rate of payments, variation of, 669,
670
registered order, enforcement, 665
separation, agreement to pay on, 373
services personnel, deduction from pay
of, 695
spouses and civil partners, statutory
duty of, 217
MAINTENANCE AGREEMENTS
meaning, 696
alteration of—
change in circumstances, on, 702
court, by—
death of one party, after, 701
lives of parties, during, 700

MAINTENANCE
    AGREEMENTS—*continued*
  alteration of—*continued*
    duration of, 704
    grounds for, 702
    magistrates' court, power of, 703
    scope of, 703
    subsequent proceedings, 705
  covenants in—
    consideration, for, 698
    ineffective, 699
    public policy, 698
  deceased person, in relation to, 701n[7]
  financial arrangement: meaning, 696n[3]
  restriction of rights, purported, 697
  validity of, 697
  variation, application for—
    death of party, after, 707
    hearing, 708
    lifetime of parties, in, 706, 709
    order, making, 708

MARITAL STATUS
  declaration of—
    Attorney General, intervention by,
      1002
    domicile and residence of parties,
      1000
    jurisdiction, 1000
    making of, 1004
    petition—
      answer to, 1003
      contents of, 1001
      procedure on, 1003
    right to apply for, 421
    third party, application by, 422

MARRIAGE
  agreement for, unenforceable, 16
  ante-nuptial agreements,
    unenforceability, 712
  arranged, validity, 12
  bigamous, 10
  buildings for—
    approval of—
      application for, 191
      conditions, 194
      expiry and renewal of, 195
      fees, 200
      grant or refusal of, 193
      guidance as to, 199
      name, change of, 202
      notices, 201
      public consultation, 192
      registers, 198
      regulations, 190
      review of decision, 197
      revocation, 196

MARRIAGE—*continued*
  buildings for—*continued*
    approval of—*continued*
      Secretary of State, powers of, 190
    registered, list of, 189
    registration—
      application for, 186
      cancellation, 188
      certificate of, 187
      superintendent registrar, by, 187
  capacity to enter into—
    disabilities, effect of, 33
    domicile, governed by law of, 31
    foreign domicile, disabilities imposed
      by, 33
    invalid, 31
    legal, generally, 31
    minimum age, 32
    remarriage, for, 34
  chaplain in HM Force, by, 17
  Church of England. *See* CHURCH OF
    ENGLAND MARRIAGE
  Church of England doctrine, under, 1
  consent to. *See* CONSENT TO MARRIAGE
    OR CIVIL PARTNERSHIP
  contractual basis of, 203
  detained persons, of—
    meaning, 170
    notice of, 172
    place of residence, solemnisation at,
      171, 173
  effect of, 203
  English law, recognised by, 1
  false statement, making, 184
  forced. *See* FORCED MARRIAGE
  foreign. *See* FOREIGN MARRIAGE
  housebound persons, of—
    meaning, 169
    notice of, 172
    place of residence, solemnisation at,
      171, 173
  invalid, confirmation of—
    order, by, 15
    statute, by, 14
  Jewish. *See* JEWISH MARRIAGE
  lawful, methods of, 53
  legality and validity, proof of—
    banns, after, 21
    celebrated outside England and
      Wales, 27
    certificates as evidence, 25
    common licence, authority of, 21
    Foreign Marriages Act, under, 28
    Jewish marriage, 24
    naval, military and air force chapels,
      in, 23

References are to paragraph numbers; superior figures refer to notes

MARRIAGE—*continued*
  legality and validity, proof
      of—*continued*
    registers as evidence, 25
    Registrar General's licence, under, 22
    superintendent registrar's licence,
        under, 22
  matrimonial property. *See*
      MATRIMONIAL PROPERTY
  merchant ships, in, 17
  minimum age for, 32
  naval, military and air force chapels,
      in—
    clergymen, appointment of, 130
    legality and validity of, 23
    licensing, 129
    solemnisation, 55, 130
  nullity. *See* NULLITY OF MARRIAGE
  offences—
    authorised person, by, 182
    false statement, making, 184
    Registrar General's licence, relating
        to, 183
    registration, relating to, 181
    solemnisation, relating to, 180
  outside England and Wales, 17
  overseas, proof of, 835
  parties to, domicile, 8
  place of, 53
  polygamous. *See* POLYGAMOUS
      MARRIAGE
  presumption of—
    cohabitation after ceremony, from, 7
    cohabitation without ceremony,
        from, 6
  presumption of validity, 3
  prohibited degrees of relationship—
    absolute prohibition, 36
    adoptive relationships, 36
    child of the family: meaning, 37n[3]
    conditional prohibition, 37
    dignities and rights, saving of, 40
    English law, application of, 35
    law of domicile, application of, 35
    legalised, 40n[1]
    marriage within, effect of, 35
    notification of marriage within, 93
  Quaker. *See* QUAKER MARRIAGE
  Registrar General's certificate, by—
    place of, 53
    registration, offences, 181
    requisites of, 3
  royal family, members of, 13
  separation agreement. *See* SEPARATION
      AGREEMENT

MARRIAGE—*continued*
  seriously ill persons, of—
    Registrar General's licence, by—
      caveat, entry of, 164
      civil, followed by religious
          ceremony, 167
      documentary authority for, 168
      evidence required, 163
      issue of, 161
      manner of solemnisation, 166
      notice of, 162
      period of validity, 165
      place of solemnisation, 161, 166
  sham, 11
  solemnisation, 1
  temporary, 1
  trial, 1
  valid, requisites of, 3
  void. *See* VOID MARRIAGE
  voidable. *See* VOIDABLE MARRIAGE
  wills and intestacy, effect on, 209
MARRIAGE SETTLEMENT
  meaning, 710
  form of, 710
  post-nuptial, 711
  voluntary, 711
MARRIED PERSONS. *See also* SPOUSE
  status, 203
MARRIED WOMEN
  civil law, position in, 204
  domicile, 214
  husband's name, assumption of, 215
  powers of appointment—
    contract as to exercise of, 237
    defect in execution, 236, 238
    exercise of, 232
    husband or herself, power to appoint
        in favour of, 236
    marriage, effect of, 233
    minority, effect of, 234
    will, appointment by, 235
  proceedings by and against, 210
MATRIMONIAL AND CIVIL
    PARTNERSHIP CAUSES
  meaning, 317
  admissibility, examination of, 754
  co-respondent as party to proceedings,
      760
  compromise—
    agreement or arrangement for opinion
        of court, 860
    disclosure, 861
    reaching agreement, 861
  death of party to proceedings, 862
  declaration of status. *See* MARITAL
      STATUS

MATRIMONIAL AND CIVIL PARTNERSHIP CAUSES—*continued*

decrees. *See* DECREE ABSOLUTE; DECREE NISI

defended: meaning, 812

designated courts, 811

directions for trial—
  affidavit, 813
  concurrent proceedings in another jurisdiction, where, 817
  conditions for, 814
  place of trial, as to—
    determination of, 818
    varying, 819
  request, contents of, 816

discovery. *See* DISCOVERY; DOCUMENTS

dismissal for want of prosecution—
  application for, 856, 858
  notice to respondent, 857
  withdrawal, 859

evidence. *See* EVIDENCE; WITNESS

failure to appear, 863

financial relief. *See* FINANCIAL RELIEF

jurisdiction—
  counterclaim, to examine, 753
  county court, 750
  decrees granted outside England and Wales, 752
  district judge, of, 813
  England and Wales, courts in, 751
  examination as to, 754
  High Court, of, 750

medical inspections. *See* VOIDABLE MARRIAGE

nullity. *See* NULLITY OF MARRIAGE

particulars—
  application for, 787
  explanatory affidavit, 792
  just cause to desertion, of, 788
  names of witnesses, disclosure of, 791
  striking out, 790
  voluntary, 789

petition. *See* PETITION

related and subsidiary, 318

separation agreement. *See* SEPARATION AGREEMENT

special procedure list—
  meaning, 814
  administrative process, as, 825
  disposal of causes in, 815

stay of proceedings—
  inherent jurisdiction, under, 846
  mental illness of respondent, effect of, 846

MATRIMONIAL AND CIVIL PARTNERSHIP CAUSES—*continued*

stay of proceedings—*continued*
  pending actions in other jurisdictions—
    application for order, 839
    consequences of, 844
    court, own motion of, 839
    discharge of order, 843
    discretionary, 842
    obligatory, 841
    particulars, furnishing, 840
  procedural purposes, for—
    failure to comply with order, 845
    inherent jurisdiction, under, 846
    irregularity, 845
    mental illness of respondent, effect of, 846
    refusal of, 847

trial—
  adjournments, 851
  dismissal of alleged adulterer from suit, 852
  further evidence, 852
  hearing, notice of, 822
  judge without jury, by, 823
  judgment, 855
  methods of, 848
  mode of, 823, 824
  no case to answer, submission of, 852
  order of speeches, 850
  order of witnesses, 849
  place of—
    determination of, 818
    directions, varying, 819
    petition, causes commenced by, 821
  previous judgment, findings of fact in, 849
  Queen's Proctor, intervention by, 853, 854
  right to begin, 849
  separate, of issues, 824
  time of, 820

undefended: meaning, 812

witness. *See* WITNESS

MATRIMONIAL PROPERTY

disputes—
  applications during lives of parties, reference to judge, 957
  applications, procedure on, 955
  hearing, 956
  order, making, 956
  title or possession, relating to, 955

occupation order. *See* OCCUPATION ORDER

MATRIMONIAL RELIEF
  meaning, 9n[3]
MATRIMONY
  solemnisation, 1
MENTALLY DISORDERED PERSON
  financial provision order against or in
    favour of, 455
  intention to desert spouse, absence of,
    389
MERCHANT SHIP
  marriage in, 17
MILITARY CHAPEL
  banns, licensing for, 129
  marriage in—
    clergymen, appointment of, 130
    legality and validity of, 23
    licensing, 129
    solemnisation, 55, 130
MISREPRESENTATION
  separation agreement, effect on, 429
MISTAKE
  consent to marriage, effect on, 44
  separation agreement, effect on, 430
NAVAL CHAPEL
  banns, licensing for, 129
  marriage in—
    clergymen, appointment of, 130
    legality and validity of, 23
    licensing, 129
    solemnisation, 55, 130
NON-MOLESTATION ORDER
  meaning, 716
  appeal against, 721, 986
  application for, 717
  arrested person, application for bail,
    995
  child under 16, application by, 717
  commencement of proceedings, 962
  enforcement—
    committal, by—
      order, 996
      suspension of order, powers of
        magistrates' court, 998
      undertakings, of, 997
    guardianship order, power to make,
      999
    hospital admission, power to order,
      999
  family proceedings, in, 717
  High Court and county court
      procedure—
    application, form of, 974
    hearing, 975
    service of application, 974
  magistrates' court procedure—
    application, form of, 977

NON-MOLESTATION
    ORDER—*continued*
  magistrates' court procedure—*continued*
    information as to orders made,
      provision of, 978
    service of application, 977
    variation, extension or discharge,
      application for, 979
  making of, 717
  matters to which court has regard, 718
  medical examination and report,
      remand of person for, 994
  powers of court—
    arrest, following, 992
    contempt proceedings, 961
    county court, 959
    jurisdiction, 716, 958
    magistrates' court, 960
  remand of person failing to comply
    with, 993
  terms of, 716
  transfer of proceedings—
    county court to family proceedings
      court, 969
    county court to High Court, 970
    county courts, between, 968
    family proceedings court to county
      court, 966
    family proceedings court to High
      Court, 967
    family proceedings courts, between,
      965
    High Court and county court,
      between, 964
    High Court to county court, 972
    High Court to family proceedings
      court, 971
  undertakings, party giving, 720
  variation or discharge, power of, 722
  victim of domestic violence, third party
    acting for, 963
  without-notice, 719

NULLITY OF MARRIAGE. *See also* VOID
    MARRIAGE; VOIDABLE MARRIAGE
  applicable law, 319
  bars to relief, 321
  bigamous, 10
  decree of. *See* DECREE ABSOLUTE;
    DECREE NISI
  financial relief in proceedings, 453
  foreign law, marriage governed by, 324
  institution of proceedings, 322
  marriage celebrated abroad, 324
  nature and effect of, 320
  offence, charge in petition, 795

NULLITY OF MARRIAGE—*continued*
person suffering mental disorder,
    proceedings by person suffering,
    323
petition, additional requirements for.
    See PETITION
same sex, parties being, 1
settled property, effect on, 514
sexual capacity, evidence of, 834

OCCUPATION ORDER
meaning, 289
appeals, 308, 986
application for, 289
arrested person, application for bail,
    995
commencement of proceedings, 962
discharge, power of, 309
enforcement—
    committal, by—
        order, 996
        suspension of order, powers of
            magistrates' court, 998
        undertakings, of, 997
        guardianship order, power to make,
            999
        hospital admission, power to order,
            999
estate, interest or home rights, applicant
    having—
    additional obligations, 294
    charge on dwelling house, effect as,
        296
    death of either party, effect of, 292
    matters to which court has regard,
        295
    provisions in order, 293
    right to apply, 292
High Court and county court
    procedure—
    application, form of, 974
    hearing, 975
    investigative matters, 976
    service of application, 974
last resort, used in, 289
magistrates' court procedure—
    application, form of, 977
    information as to orders made,
        provision of, 978
    service of application, 977
    variation, extension or discharge,
        application for, 979
medical examination and report,
    remand of person for, 994

OCCUPATION ORDER—*continued*
neither spouse, civil partner, cohabitant
    or former cohabitant entitled to
    occupy—
    matters to which court has regard,
        307
    provisions in order, 306
    right to apply, 305
notice, without, 290
one cohabitant or former cohabitant
    with no existing right to occupy—
    additional obligations, 303
    matters to which court has regard,
        304
    provisions in order, 302
    right to apply, 301
one former spouse or civil partner with
    no existing right to occupy—
    additional obligations, 299
    matters to which court has regard,
        300
    provisions in order, 298
    right to apply, 297
power of arrest, attachment of—
    arrest under, 990
    arrest without, 991
    generally, 988
powers of court—
    arrest, following, 992
    contempt proceedings, 961
    county court, 959
    jurisdiction, 958
    magistrates' court, 960
remand of person failing to comply
    with, 993
transfer of proceedings—
    county court to family proceedings
        court, 969
    county court to High Court, 970
    county courts, between, 968
    family proceedings court to county
        court, 966
    family proceedings court to High
        Court, 967
    family proceedings courts, between,
        965
    High Court and county court,
        between, 964
    High Court to county court, 972
    High Court to family proceedings
        court, 971
undertakings, 291
variation, power of, 309
victim of domestic violence, third party
    acting for, 963

References are to paragraph numbers; superior figures refer to notes

OVERSEAS DIVORCE OR
   DISSOLUTION
   recognition of, 20

PENSION
   attachment. *See* FINANCIAL PROVISION
      ORDER
   compensation sharing. *See* PENSION
      COMPENSATION SHARING ORDER
   sharing. *See* PENSION SHARING ORDER

PENSION COMPENSATION SHARING
   ORDER
   meaning, 523
   appeals, 528
   charges, apportionment of, 527
   date when taking effect, 525
   making, 524
   matters to which court has regard, 524
   shareable rights to PPF compensation:
      meaning, 523n[6]
   variation, 529

PENSION SHARING ORDER
   meaning, 523
   ancillary relief—
      interlocutory procedure, 926
      order, 934
   appeals, 528
   assessment, principles of. *See* FINANCIAL
      RELIEF (assessment, principles of)
   charges, apportionment of, 527
   date when taking effect, 525
   making, 524
   matters to which court has regard, 524
   shareable rights under pension
      arrangement: meaning, 523n[1]
   shareable state scheme rights: meaning,
      523n[2]
   variation, 529

PETITION
   amendment—
      application for leave, 769, 770
      co-respondent, to add, 772
      counter-charges, adding to petition,
         773
      leave for, 770
      other documents, of, 774
      relief prayed for, changing, 771
      service of, 770
   answer to—
      bare denials, 782
      consent to grant of decree or order,
         786
      contents of, 780
      counter-charges in, 793
      cross-prayer in, 793, 796
      desertion up to time of, 781

PETITION—*continued*
   answer to—*continued*
      desertion, insufficiency of bare
         denial, 782
      filing, 779
      prayer for relief in, 780
      reply—
         contents of, 780
         filing, 797
         service of, 798
         subsequent proceedings, filing, 797
      service of, 798
      subsequent pleadings, contents of,
         780
      supplementary, 774
      third persons, allegations against, 783
      time for, 779
   civil partnership proceedings county
      court, in, 755
   commencement by, 755
   contents of, 756
   death of party to proceedings, 862
   defence—
      co-respondent, by, 785
      party cited, by, 785
      scope of, 784
   directions for trial, filing and
      amendment of pleadings after, 775
   dismissal for want of prosecution—
      application for, 856, 858
      notice to respondent, 857
      withdrawal, 859
   divorce county court, in, 755
   documents accompanying, 767
   evidence of conviction, petitioner relying
      on, 763
   failure to appear, 863
   filing, 768
   first year of marriage or civil
      partnership, bar in, 757
   marital or civil partnership status, for
      declaration of—
      answer to, 1003
      contents of, 1001
      procedure on, 1003
   not proceeded with, notice of, 796
   notice of discontinuance, 755
   nullity, for—
      additional requirements, 759
      offence, separate petition for, 795
   omission of information from, 756n[1]
   pleadings, service of, 798
   prayer—
      contents of, 764
      cross-prayer, 793, 796
      indorsement after, 765

References are to paragraph numbers; superior figures refer to notes

PETITION—*continued*
  prayer—*continued*
    judicial separation, for, 794
    separation order, for, 794
  presumption of death, for decree of,
    762
  previous proceedings, not precluded
    by, 758
  service of—
    acknowledgement of, 776
    dispensing with, 778
    means of, 776
    officer of court, on, 776
    party, on, 776
    substituted, 777
  signature, 766
  supplementary—
    answer, 774
    filing, 769, 770
    requirement, 769
    service of, 770
  third persons, allegations against, 783
  withdrawal, 859

POLYGAMOUS MARRIAGE
  adultery: meaning, 349
  High Court proceedings, 1010
  validity, 9

POWER OF APPOINTMENT
  married woman, of—
    contract as to exercise of, 237
    defect in execution, 236, 238
    exercise of, 232
    husband or herself, power to appoint
      in favour of, 236
    marriage, effect of, 233
    minority, effect of, 234
    will, appointment by, 235

PROMISSORY NOTE
  spouse or civil partner, liability of, 257

PROPERTY ADJUSTMENT ORDER
  meaning, 498
  ancillary relief. *See* ANCILLARY RELIEF
  assessment, principles of. *See* FINANCIAL
    RELIEF (assessment, principles of)
  attempt to defeat claims, prevention
    of—
    avoidance of transactions, 587
    prevention of transactions, 588
    protected claims, 586
  children, for benefit of—
    matters to which court has regard,
      519
    power to make, 518
    settlement of property, 518
    transfer of property, 518

PROPERTY ADJUSTMENT
  ORDER—*continued*
  death of former spouse or civil partner,
    following—
    effect of death, 538
    no previous grant, where, 540
    payments from estate, 539
    variation, application for, 541
  enforcement. *See* FINANCIAL RELIEF
    (enforcement)
  financial provision order, relationship
    with, 451
  overseas divorce, dissolution, etc,
    after—
    application for, 530
    consent order, 535
    deceased former spouse or civil
      partner, restrictions on
      applications from estate of, 534
    family home in England and Wales,
      restriction of powers where
      jurisdiction depends on, 533
    interim order, 536
    matters to which court has regard,
      532
    order for, 531
    supplementary provisions, 537
  party applying for, 498
  property subject to, 500
  sale of property, order for—
    date when taking effect, 521
    matters to which court has regard,
      522
    power to make, 520
  settlement of property—
    bankruptcy of settlor, effect of, 509
    child, for benefit of, 518
    date when taking effect, 507
    matters to which court has regard,
      508
    power to order, 506
  transfer of property, for—
    abroad, property situated, 500
    bankruptcy of transferor, effect of,
      505
    child, for benefit of, 518
    date when taking effect, 502
    deed of transfer, 504
    equitable interest, conferring, 505
    interim, no power to make, 501
    matters to which court has regard,
      503
    power to order, 499
    property subject to, 500
    third parties, rights of, 500

PROPERTY ADJUSTMENT
  ORDER—*continued*
  variation of settlement—
    applicable settlements, 511
    date when taking effect, 516
    injunction restraining disposal of
      funds, 517
    legitimacy, not deciding, 512
    party's interests and powers,
      extinguishing or reducing, 513
    power to order, 510
    property subject to, 511
    revision of, 515
    third party, covenants by, 511
  variation, discharge and suspension—
    matters to which court has regard,
      568
    orders subject to, 567
PROTECTED TENANCY
  succession to, 255
  tenancy order, transfer of, 312
QUAKER MARRIAGE
  notification, 115
  solemnisation, 116
QUEEN'S PROCTOR
  intervention by—
    conditional dissolution made final,
      showing cause against, 875
    decree nisi made absolute, showing
      cause against, 875
    trial, in, 853, 854
RAPE
  marital, 220
RECEIVER
  equitable execution, by way of—
    appointment of, 647
    estate or interest in land, in relation
      to, 648
    function of, 647
    scope of receivership, 648
REGISTER OF MARRIAGE
  evidence of marriage, as, 25
REGISTRAR GENERAL
  licence—
    legality and validity of marriage
      under, 22
    offences, 183
    place of, 53
    seriously ill persons, marriage of—
      caveat, entry of, 164
      civil, followed by religious
        ceremony, 167
      documentary authority for, 168
      evidence required, 163
      issue of, 161
      manner of solemnisation, 166

REGISTRAR GENERAL—*continued*
  licence—*continued*
    seriously ill persons, marriage
      of—*continued*
      notice of, 162
      period of validity, 165
      place of solemnisation, 161, 166
    void marriage, grounds of, 329
    parental consent to marriage, dispensing
      with, 47
RES JUDICATA
  magistrates' court, in, 736
  principle, application of, 734
ROYAL FAMILY
  marriage of members of, 13
SEPARATION
  agreement. *See* SEPARATION AGREEMENT
  continuity, establishing, 412
  five years' living apart and no consent
    to divorce or dissolution—
    financial hardship and protection,
      application for consideration,
      873
    financial or other hardship, objection
      on grounds of, 411
    irretrievable breakdown, evidence of,
      410
    opposition to divorce or dissolution,,
      411
  periods of living together, no account
    of, 413
  two years' living apart and consent to
    divorce or dissolution—
    consent to grant of decree or order—
      generally, 786
      positive act of, 408
      respondent misled into giving, 409
      voluntary, 408
    irretrievable breakdown, evidence of,
      407
SEPARATION AGREEMENT
  annuity under—
    bankruptcy, proof in, 446
    legacy, satisfaction by, 440
    permanent, construed as, 436
    reconciliation, arrears on, 448
  breach—
    covenant, of, 445
    effect of, 439
    injunction against, 444
    specific performance, action for, 443
  children—
    parental responsibility and contact,
      provisions as to, 441
    trust for benefit of, 437

References are to paragraph numbers; superior figures refer to notes

SEPARATION AGREEMENT—*continued*
covenants—
breach of, 445
debts, indemnification against, 435
non-molestation, 434
not to take divorce etc proceedings, 438
criminal proceedings, compromise of, 426
divorce, etc, effect of, 442
duress, effect of, 430
enemy territory, one party in, 423
estoppel where acted on, 433
formalities, 427
fraud, effect of, 429
legality, presumption of, 427
mere agreement to live apart, 431
misrepresentation, effect of, 429
mistake, effect of, 430
parental responsibility and contact, provisions as to, 441
past matters, agreement not to sue for, 425
permanent, provisions construed as, 436
public policy, void for, 424
reconciliation, effect of—
arrears of annuity, as to, 448
cohabitation, requirement to resume, 449
determination on, 447
separation articles, 428
settlement of property, provisions for, 436
specific enforcement, 428
specific performance, action for, 443
subsequent misconduct, effect of, 438
usual clauses, 432
valid, 423
valuable consideration for, 431
void, 424
SEQUESTRATION
meaning, 649
enforcement of orders by, 649
financial orders, enforcement of, 946
property capable being seized, 650
SETTLED PROPERTY
decree or order of nullity, effect of, 514
SETTLEMENT
civil partnership. *See* CIVIL PARTNERSHIP SETTLEMENT
marriage. *See* MARRIAGE SETTLEMENT
property adjustment order—
bankruptcy of settlor, effect of, 509
child, for benefit of, 518
date when taking effect, 507

SETTLEMENT—*continued*
property adjustment order—*continued*
matters to which court has regard, 508
power to make, 506
variation, order on divorce, etc—
applicable settlements, 511
date when taking effect, 516
injunction restraining disposal of funds, 517
legitimacy, not deciding, 512
party's interests and powers, extinguishing or reducing, 513
power to make, 510
property subject to, 511
revision of, 515
third party, covenants by, 511
SPOUSE
acts of other spouse, criminal liability for, 208
authority to make contracts—
authorisation of, 256
undisclosed principal, as, 258
bankruptcy of, 207
bills, notes and cheques, liability on, 257
cohabitation, duty of, 219
confidences, protection of, 223
contract for necessaries—
adequate or agreed allowance for, 266
cohabitation, presumption of authority from, 263
judicial separation, effect of, 268
presumption of authority, rebuttal, 265
proof of authority, 267
style of living, suitable to, 264
contracts between, 206
contracts by, 205
corroboration of evidence of, 213
debt, acknowledgement of, 261
enticement to leave, 221
exclusive credit, contract for, 259
harbouring, 221
joint banking account, 245
liability to maintain each other, 217
life assurance policy. *See* LIFE ASSURANCE POLICY
loss or impairment of consortium, 221
maintenance—
application for, 211
husband's common law duty as to, 216
liability for, 217
reasonable, failure to provide, 218

SPOUSE—*continued*
  marital rape, 220
  proceedings between, 211
  property, ownership of—
    disputes, resolution of—
      application to court, 224
      former spouse, property of, 229
      no longer in possession, relating
        to, 228
      powers of court, 225
      property to which powers extend,
        227
      sale, power to order, 226
    equity of exoneration—
      bankruptcy, effect of, 244
      estates of both spouses charged for
        one party's benefit, 242
      indemnity, right of, 239
      other spouse party to mortgage,
        where, 240
      presumptive right, 239
      property charged for other's benefit,
        right of indemnity, 239
      property charged partly to other's
        benefit, 241
      property over which one party has
        general power, charge of, 243
      waiver, 239
  family home. *See* FAMILY HOME
  gifts between parties—
    fraudulent dispositions, 250
    rules for, 248
    undue influence as to, 249
  incumbrances, discharge of, 252
  joint banking account, 245
  paraphernalia, 246
  receipt as trustee, 251
  wedding presents, 247
  ratification of contract by, 273
  separate business, no liability for, 260
  separation agreement. *See* SEPARATION
    AGREEMENT
  separation, gifts and legacies inducing,
    222
  statutory tenant by succession, as, 255
  surviving, rights in deceased's estate,
    254
  wife's authority to pledge husband's
    credit—
    agency by estoppel, 269
    household, management of, 270
    revocation of, 271
    termination of, 262
    wife's misconduct, liability of husband
      after, 272
  witness, compellability as, 212

STATUTORY TENANCY
  succession to, 255
  tenancy order, transfer of, 313

SUPERINTENDENT REGISTRAR
  meaning, 22n[1]
  certificate, marriage on authority of—
    caveat, entry of, 96
    Church of England, in, 58
    delivery of certificate, 98
    district registrar, delivery of certificate
      to, 103
    evidence, power to require, 91
    forbidding, 95
    forms of, 54
    Her Majesty's Dominions, one party
      resident in, 114
    issue of, 80n[4], 97
    Jewish marriage—
      notification, 117
      solemnisation, 118
    marriage notice book, entry in, 92
    Northern Ireland, one party resident
      in, 113
    notice—
      content of, 87
      declaration accompanying, 90
      giving of, 87
      misdescription, effect of, 89
      presence of registrar, requiring
        presence of, 88
      publication, 94
      want of, effect, 89
    presence of registrar, without, 99
    prohibited degrees, notification where
      within, 93
    Quaker marriage—
      notification, 115
      solemnisation, 116
    registered building, solemnisation in—
      meaning, 54n[3]
      authorised person—
        appointment, 107
        presence of, 106
        registration by, 108
      declaration, 105
      form and ceremony, 104, 105
      marriage register books—
        custody of, 109
        errors in, 108
        registration in, 108
        searches in, 110
      requirements, 106
      time for, 104
    registration district in which neither
      party resides, in, 100
    Scotland, one party resident in, 112

References are to paragraph numbers; superior figures refer to notes

SUPERINTENDENT
  REGISTRAR—*continued*
  certificate, marriage on authority
    of—*continued*
    solemnisation—
      approved premises, in, 111
      Jewish marriage, 118
      Quaker marriage, of, 116
      registered building, in, 104–110
      superintendent registrar's office,
        in, 102, 103
      time of, 101
    superintendent registrar's office, in,
      102
    void marriage, grounds of, 330
  copies of register for, 86
  evidence, power to require, 91
THIRD PARTY DEBT ORDER
  power to make, 640
TRANSFER OF TENANCY ORDER
  assured agricultural occupancy, 312
  assured tenancy, 312
  cases in which order made, 310
  cohabitant, in favour of, 310
  compensation for, 314
  introductory tenancy, 312
  landlord, hearing, 311
  liabilities and obligations, order relating
    to, 315
  matters to which court has regard, 311
  overseas divorce etc, pursuant to, 310
  overseas divorce, dissolution, etc,
    application after, 530
  protected tenancy, 312
  statutory tenancy, 313
UNSOUNDNESS OF MIND
  consent to marriage or civil partnership,
    effect on, 45
VOID MARRIAGE
  celebrated before 1 August 1971,
    grounds, 344
  Church of England, according to rites
    of, 328
  grounds of, 326
  ipso jure, 320
  party instituting annulment
    proceedings, 322
  Registrar General's licence, under, 329
  requisites of valid marriage, absence of,
    3
  Superintendent Registrar's certificate,
    under, 330
VOIDABLE MARRIAGE
  celebrated before 1 August 1971,
    grounds, 345
  children, legitimacy of, 325

VOIDABLE MARRIAGE—*continued*
  failure to consummate—
    cause of, 335
    cure, opportunity of, 337
    incapacity, 336
    malformation, due to, 340
    medical examination or treatment,
      refusal of, 338
    medical inspections—
      application for, 803
      appointment of inspectors, 803
      attendance of inspectors at trial,
        808
      dispensing with, 810
      incapacity, in case of, 803
      notice of, 805
      parties, identification of, 807
      place of, 805, 806
      refusal of, 810
      reports, 807
      respondent outside jurisdiction,
        where, 809
      trial, notice of, 805
      wilful refusal, in case of, 804
    petitioner, incapacity of, 341
    sterility, irrelevance of, 339
    test of consummation, 335
    use of contraceptives, irrelevance of,
      339
    wilful refusal, 342, 804
  grounds of—
    celebrated before 1 August 1971, 345
    gender reassignment certificate,
      ignorance of, 334
    mental disorder, party suffering
      from, 332
    pregnancy by some other person, 333
    valid consent, failure to give, 331
    venereal disease, party suffering
      from, 343
  requisites of valid marriage, absence of,
    3
  sexual capacity, evidence of, 834
  valid and subsisting until decree, being,
    320
WILL
  marriage and civil partnership, effect
    of, 209
  power of appointment, exercise by
    married woman, 235
WITNESS
  adultery, evidence of, 829
  cross-examination, 831
  examination out of court, 838
  matrimonial and civil partnership
    causes, disclosure of name in, 791

References are to paragraph numbers; superior figures refer to notes

WITNESS—*continued*
  parties, competence and compellability,
    828
  privilege, claiming, 833
  spouse or civil partner, compellability
    of, 212

WITNESS—*continued*
  subpoena, issue of, 826
  summons, issue of, 826

Words and Phrases

Words in parentheses indicate the context in which the word or phrase is used

applicant—
  (Family Proceedings Rules 1991,
    SI 1991/1247), 918n[5]
  (Registration of Marriages
    Regulations 1986, SI 1986/1442),
    94n[11]
approved premises, 54n[6]
attachment of earnings order, 629
authorised chapel, 57n[9]
authorised person (solemnisation of
  marriage), 107
avoidance of disposition order, 902n[6]
brother, 36n[1]
cause (Family Proceedings Rules 1991,
  SI 1991/1247), 321n[1]
charging order, 636
child—
  (Civil Partnership Act 2004), 46n[1]
  (Family Proceedings Rules 1991,
    SI 1991/1247), 765n[1]
  (Marriage Act 1949), 37n[3]
  (Matrimonial Causes Act 1973), 477n[3]
child of the family—
  (Family Proceedings Rules 1991,
    SI 1991/1247), 707n[9]
  (Marriage Act 1949), 37n[3]
  (Matrimonial Causes Act 1973), 477n[3]
civil partner, 2n[1]
civil partnership, 2n[1]
civil partnership agreement, 16
civil partnership cause, 317
civil partnership document, 56n[7]
civil partnership officer, 18n[1]
civil partnership proceedings, 732n[2]
civil partnership proceedings county
  court, 732
civil partnership register, 158n[2]
civil partnership registrar, 139n[7]
civil partnership schedule, 138
clergyman, 23n[5]
cohabit, 292n[5]
cohabitants, 292n[5]
consanguinity, 35n[1]
county court maintenance order, 628n[3]
court of trial, 821n[4]
defeat (claim for financial relief), 586
defended cause, 812
detained person, 170
development (occupation orders), 290n[4]
directions appointment, 894n[6]
dissolution order, 346n[1]

dissolution town, 813n[2]
district judge, 737n[3]
district registry, 737n[3]
divorce county court, 732
divorce town, 813n[2]
dwelling house, 285n[2], 533n[4]
ecclesiastical district, 21n[3]
family business, 737n[2]
family proceedings, 737n[2]
FDR appointment, 925n[22]
file, 894n[2]
financial arrangements, 696n[3]
financial provision order, 450
five years' separation, 347
force (forced marriages), 723
forced marriage protection order, 724n[2]
former cohabitants, 292n[5]
harm (occupation order), 290n[4]
health (occupation order), 290n[4]
High Court maintenance order, 628n[2]
High Court order, 666n[1]
home rights, 285
housebound persons, 169
ill-treatment (occupation order), 290n[4]
incumbent, 85n[1]
inspection appointment, 889
judge, 737n[3]
judgment summons, 945n[7]
lump sum order, 844n[4]
maintenance agreement, 696, 701n[7]
maintenance order, 628n[1], 642n[5]
maintenance payments, 627n[2]
marriage notice book, 92
marriage officer, 119n[3]
Martin order, 316
matrimonial cause, 317
matrimonial proceedings, 732n[2]
matrimonial relief, 9n[3]
means of payment order, 646
Mesher order, 316
necessary declaration, 133n[5]
non-molestation order, 716
notice of intention to defend, 779n[1]
nullity order, 320n[4]
occupation order, 289
officer of the service, 831n[4]
official house, 150n[5]
official house of the marriage officer,
  125n[5]
order for financial relief, 530n[4]

References are to paragraph numbers; superior figures refer to notes

order for maintenance pending suit, 902n[7]

order for maintenance pending the outcome of proceedings, 902n[7]

order for the payment of a lump sum—
(during subsistence of marriage or civil partnership), 543
(for the benefit of children), 492
(generally), 476

overseas relationship, 19n[1]

patient, 170n[1]

pension arrangement, 485n[1]

pension attachment order, 926

pension sharing compensation order, 523

pension sharing order, 523

periodical maintenance order, 644n[2]

periodical payments order—
(during subsistence of marriage or civil partnership), 543
(for the benefit of children), 492
(generally), 458

person responsible for a pension arrangement, 485n[6]

PPF compensation, 523n[6]

presumption of death order, 415n[6]

principal registry, 737n[3]

proper officer, 461n[4]

property adjustment order, 498

protected party, 765n[1]

register, 133n[8], 667n[12]

registered building, 54n[3]

registering officer, 154n[3]

registrar, 88n[1]

Registrar General, 46n[5]

registration authority, 133n[2]

registration district, 87n[4]

relative, 292n[5]

retirement annuity contract, 485n[1]

secured periodical payments order—
(during subsistence of marriage or civil partnership), 543
(for the benefit of children), 492
(generally), 467

separation order, 346n[4]

sham marriage, 11

shareable rights to PPF compensation, 523n[6]

shareable rights under a pension arrangement, 523n[1]

shareable state scheme rights, 523n[2]

significant harm (occupation order), 290n[4]

sister, 36n[1]

specified relationship (civil partnership), 19n[1]

subject to immigration control, 87n[2]

superintendent registrar, 22n[1]

supporting statement, 175n[5]

trustees or governing body, 107n[3]

two years' separation, 347

undefended cause, 812

usual place of worship, 66

waiting period (Civil Partnership Act 2004), 136

Welsh family proceedings officer, 831n[4]

wilful refusal (to consummate marriage), 342